THE COLLINS
POCKET REFERENCE
GERMAN
DICTIONARY

GERMAN·ENGLISH ENGLISH·GERMAN

COLLINS
London and Glasgow

First published 1989

© William Collins Sons & Co. Ltd. 1989

First reprint 1990

ISBN 0 00 433258 X

Printed in Great Britain
Collins Clear-Type Press

INTRODUCTION

This dictionary of German and English is designed to provide the user with wide-ranging and up-to-date coverage of the two languages, and is ideal for both school and reference use.

A special feature of Collins dictionaries is the comprehensive 'sign-posting' of meanings on both sides of the dictionary, guiding the user to the most appropriate translation for a given context. We hope you will find this dictionary easy and pleasant to consult for all your study and reference needs.

Abbreviations used in the dictionary	iv
Regular German noun endings	vii
Phonetic symbols	viii
GERMAN-ENGLISH	1-211
ENGLISH-GERMAN	1-218
German verb forms	219
English verb forms	223
Numbers	225
Time	227

ABKÜRZUNGEN

ABBREVIATIONS

Adjektiv	a	adjective
Abkürzung	abk, abbr	abbreviation
Akkusativ	acc	accusative
Adverb	ad	adverb
Landwirtschaft	AGR	agriculture
Akkusativ	akk	accusative
Anatomie	ANAT	anatomy
Architektur	ARCHIT	architecture
Artikel	art	article
Astrologie	ASTROL	astrology
Astronomie	ASTRON	astronomy
attributiv	attr	attributive
Kraftfahrzeuge	AUT	automobiles
Hilfsverb	aux	auxiliary
Luftfahrt	AVIAT	aviation
besonders	bes	especially
Biologie	BIOL	biology
Botanik	BOT	botany
britisch	Brit	British
Chemie	CHEM	chemistry
Film	CINE	cinema
Konjunktion	cj	conjunction
umgangssprachlich (! vulgär)	col(!)	colloquial (! particularly offensive)
Handel	COMM	commerce
Komparativ	comp	comparative
Computer	COMPUT	computing
Kochen und Backen	COOK	cooking
zusammengesetztes Wort	cpd	compound
Dativ	dat	dative
kirchlich	ECCL	ecclesiastical
Eisenbahn	EISENB	railways
Elektrizität	ELEK, ELEC	electricity
besonders	esp	especially
und so weiter	etc	et cetera
etwas	etw	something
Euphemismus, Hüllwort	euph	euphemism
Femininum	f	feminine
übertragen	fig	figurative
Finanzwesen	FIN	finance
Genitiv	gen	genitive
Geographie	GEOG	geography
Geologie	GEOL	geology
Grammatik	GRAM	grammar
Geschichte	HIST	history
unpersönlich	impers	impersonal
unbestimmt	indef	indefinite
nicht getrennt gebraucht	insep	inseparable
Interjektion, Ausruf	interj	interjection
interrogativ, fragend	interrog	interrogative

ABKÜRZUNGEN

ABBREVIATIONS

unveränderlich	inv	invariable
unregelmäßig	irreg	irregular
jemand	jd	somebody
jemandem	jdm	(to) somebody
jemanden	jdn	somebody
jemandes	jds	somebody's
Rechtswesen	JUR	law
Konjunktion	kj	conjunction
Kochen und Backen	KOCH	cooking
Komparativ	komp	comparative
Sprachwissenschaft	LING	linguistics
wörtlich	lit	literal
literarisch	liter	literary
Literatur	LITER	of literature
Maskulinum	m	masculine
Mathematik	MATH	mathematics
Medizin	MED	medicine
Meteorologie	MET	meteorology
militärisch	MIL	military
Bergbau	MIN	mining
Musik	MUS	music
Substantiv, Hauptwort	n	noun
nautisch, Seefahrt	NAUT	nautical, naval
Nominativ	nom	nominative
Neutrum	nt	neuter
Zahlwort	num	numeral
Objekt	obj	object
oder	od	or
sich	o.s.	oneself
Parlament	PARL	parliament
abschätzig	pej	pejorative
Photographie	PHOT	photography
Physik	PHYS	physics
Plural	pl	plural
Politik	POL	politics
besitzanzeigend	poss	possessive
Partizip Perfekt	pp	past participle
Präfix, Vorsilbe	präf, pref	prefix
Präposition	präp, prep	preposition
Typographie	PRINT	printing
Pronomen, Fürwort	pron	pronoun
Psychologie	PSYCH	psychology
1. Vergangenheit, Imperfekt	pt	past tense
Radio	RAD	radio
Eisenbahn	RAIL	railways
Relativ-	rel	relative
Religion	REL	religion
jemand(-en, -em)	sb	someone, somebody
Schulwesen	SCH	school

ABKÜRZUNGEN

ABBREVIATIONS

Naturwissenschaft	**SCI**	science
schottisch	**Scot**	Scottish
Singular, Einzahl	**sing**	singular
etwas	**sth**	something
Suffix, Nachsilbe	**suff**	suffix
Superlativ	**superl**	superlative
Technik	**TECH**	technology
Nachrichtentechnik	**TEL**	telecommunications
Theater	**THEAT**	theatre
Fernsehen	**TV**	television
Typographie	**TYP**	printing
umgangssprachlich (! vulgär)	**umg(!)**	colloquial (! particularly offensive)
Hochschulwesen	**UNIV**	university
unpersönlich	**unpers**	impersonal
unregelmäßig	**unreg**	irregular
(nord)amerikanisch	**US**	(North) America
gewöhnlich	**usu**	usually
Verb	**v**	verb
intransitives Verb	**vi**	intransitive verb
reflexives Verb	**vr**	reflexive verb
transitives Verb	**vt**	transitive verb
Zoologie	**ZOOL**	zoology
zusammengesetztes Wort	**zW**	compound
zwischen zwei Sprechern	**—**	change of speaker
ungefähre Entsprechung	**≃**	cultural equivalent
eingetragenes Warenzeichen	**®**	registered trademark

REGULAR GERMAN NOUN ENDINGS

nom		gen	pl
-ant	*m*	-anten	-anten
-anz	*f*	-anz	-anzen
-ar	*m*	-ar(e)s	-are
-chen	*nt*	-chens	-chen
-ei	*f*	-ei	-eien
-elle	*f*	-elle	-ellen
-ent	*m*	-enten	-enten
-enz	*f*	-enz	-enzen
-ette	*f*	-ette	-etten
-eur	*m*	-eurs	-eure
-euse	*f*	-euse	-eusen
-heit	*f*	-heit	-heiten
-ie	*f*	-ie	-ien
-ik	*f*	-ik	-iken
-in	*f*	-in	-innen
-ine	*f*	-ine	-inen
-ion	*f*	-ion	-ionen
-ist	*m*	-isten	-isten
-ium	*nt*	-iums	-ien
-ius	*m*	-ius	-iusse
-ive	*f*	-ive	-iven
-keit	*f*	-keit	-keiten
-lein	*nt*	-leins	-lein
-ling	*m*	-lings	-linge
-ment	*nt*	-ments	-mente
-mus	*m*	-mus	-men
-schaft	*f*	-schaft	-schaften
-tät	*f*	-tät	-täten
-tor	*m*	-tors	-toren
-ung	*f*	-ung	-ungen
-ur	*f*	-ur	-uren

PHONETIC SYMBOLS / LAUTSCHRIFT

[:] length mark   Längezeichen ['] stress mark   Betonung
['] glottal stop   Knacklaut

all vowel sounds are approximate only
alle Vokallaute sind nur ungefähre Entsprechungen

lie	[aɪ]	weit	day	[eɪ]
now	[aʊ]	Haut	girl	[ɜ:]
above	[ə]	bitte	board	[ɔ:]
green	[i:]	viel	root	[u:]	Hut
pity	[ɪ]	Bischof	come	[ʌ]	Butler
rot	[ɒ,ɔ]	Post	salon	[ɔ̃]	Champignon
full	[ʊ]	Pult	avant (garde)	[ɑ̃]	Ensemble
			fair	[ɛə]	mehr
bet	[b]	Ball	beer	[ɪə]	Bier
dim	[d]	dann	toy	[ɔɪ]	Heu
face	[f]	Faß	pure	[ʊə]	
go	[g]	Gast	wine	[w]	
hit	[h]	Herr	thin	[θ]	
you	[j]	ja	this	[ð]	
cat	[k]	kalt			
lick	[l]	Last	Hast	[a]	mash
must	[m]	Mast	Ensemble	[ã]	avant (garde)
nut	[n]	Nuß	Metall	[e]	meths
bang	[ŋ]	lang	häßlich	[ɛ]	
pepper	[p]	Pakt	Cousin	[ɛ̃]	
sit	[s]	Rasse	vital	[i]	
shame	[ʃ]	Schal	Moral	[o]	
tell	[t]	Tal	Champignon	[õ]	salon
vine	[v]	was	ökonomisch	[ø]	
loch	[x]	Bach	gönnen	[œ]	
zero	[z]	Hase	Heu	[ɔy]	toy
leisure	[ʒ]	Genie	kulant	[u]	
			physisch	[y]	
bat	[æ]		Müll	[ʏ]	
farm	[ɑ:]	Bahn	ich	[ç]	
set	[e]	Kette			

[*]   r can be pronounced before a vowel; Bindungs-R

DEUTSCH - ENGLISCH
GERMAN - ENGLISH

A

A, a [aː] *nt* A, a.

à [a] *präp* at.

Aal [aːl] *m* -(e)s, -e eel.

Aas [aːs] *nt* -es, -e *od* **Äser** carrion; **~geier** *m* vulture.

ab [ap] ◆*präp* +*dat* from; **Kinder ~ 12 Jahren** children from the age of 12; **~ morgen** from tomorrow; **~ sofort** as of now ◆*ad* **1** off; **links ~** to the left; **der Knopf ist ~** the button has come off; **~ nach Hause!** off you go home **2** (*zeitlich*): **von da ~** from then on; **von heute ~** from today, as of today **3** (*auf Fahrplänen*): **München ~ 12.20** leaving Munich 12.20 **4 ~ und zu** *od* **an** now and then *od* again.

Abänderung [ˈapˈɛndərʊŋ] *f* alteration.

Abart [ˈapˈaːrt] *f* (*BIOL*) variety; **a~ig** *a* abnormal.

Abbau [ˈapbaʊ] *m* -(e)s dismantling; (*Verminderung*) reduction (*gen* in); (*Verfall*) decline (*gen* in); (*MIN*) mining; quarrying; (*CHEM*) decomposition; **a~en** *vt* dismantle; (*MIN*) mine; quarry; (*verringern*) reduce; (*CHEM*) break down.

abbeißen [ˈapbaɪsən] *vt unreg* bite off.

Abberufung [ˈapbəruːfʊŋ] *f* recall.

abbestellen [ˈapbəʃtɛlən] *vt* cancel.

abbezahlen [ˈapbətsaːlən] *vt* pay off.

abbiegen [ˈapbiːgən] *unreg vi* turn off; (*Straße*) bend // *vt* bend; (*verhindern*) ward off.

Abbild [ˈapbɪlt] *nt* portrayal; (*einer Person*) image, likeness; **a~en** [ˈapbɪldən] *vt* portray; **~ung** *f* illustration.

Abbitte [ˈapbɪtə] *f*: **~ leisten** *od* **tun** make one's apologies (*bei* to).

abblenden [ˈapblɛndən] *vti* (*AUT*) dip (*Brit*), dim (*US*).

Abblendlicht *nt* dipped (*Brit*) *od* dimmed (*US*) headlights *pl*.

abbrechen [ˈapbrɛçən] *vti unreg* break off; (*Gebäude*) pull down; (*Zelt*) take down; (*aufhören*) stop; (*COMPUT*) abort.

abbrennen [ˈapbrɛnən] *unreg vt* burn off; (*Feuerwerk*) let off // *vi* (*aux sein*) burn down.

abbringen [ˈapbrɪŋən] *vt unreg*: **jdn von etw ~** dissuade sb from sth; **jdn vom Weg ~** divert sb.

abbröckeln [ˈapbrœkəln] *vti* crumble off *od* away.

Abbruch [ˈapbrux] *m* (*von Verhandlungen etc*) breaking off; (*von Haus*) demolition; **jdm/etw ~ tun** harm sb/sth; **a~reif** *a* only fit for demolition.

abbrühen [ˈapbryːən] *vt* scald; **abgebrüht** (*umg*) hard-boiled.

abbuchen [ˈapbuːxən] *vt* debit.

abbürsten [ˈapbyrstən] *vt* brush off.

abdanken [ˈapdaŋkən] *vi* resign; (*König*) abdicate.

Abdankung *f* resignation; abdication.

abdecken [ˈapdɛkən] *vt* uncover; (*Tisch*) clear; (*Loch*) cover.

abdichten [ˈapdɪçtən] *vt* seal; (*NAUT*) caulk.

abdrehen [ˈapdreːən] *vt* (*Gas*) turn off; (*Licht*) switch off; (*Film*) shoot // *vi* (*Schiff*) change course.

Abdruck [ˈapdrʊk] *m* (*Nachdrucken*) reprinting; (*Gedrucktes*) reprint; (*Gips~*, *Wachs~*) impression; (*Finger~*) print; **a~en** *vt* print, publish.

abdrücken [ˈapdrʏkən] *vt* make an impression of; (*Waffe*) fire; (*Person*) hug, squeeze.

Abend [ˈaːbənt] *m* -s, -e evening; **guten ~** good evening; **zu ~ essen** have dinner *od* supper; **a~** *ad* evening; **~brot** *nt*, **~essen** *nt* supper; **~kasse** *f* box office; **~kurs** *m* evening classes *pl*; **~land** *nt* West; **a~lich** *a* evening; **~mahl** *nt* Holy Communion; **~rot** *nt* sunset; **abends** *ad* in the evening.

Abenteuer [ˈaːbəntɔyər] *nt* -s, - adventure; **a~lich** *a* adventurous.

Abenteurer *m* -s, - adventurer; **~in** *f* adventuress.

aber [ˈaːbər] *kj* but; (*jedoch*) however; **das ist ~ schön** that's really nice; **nun ist ~ Schluß!** now that's enough!; **vielen Dank — bitte!** thanks a lot — you're welcome // *ad*: **tausend und ~ tausend** thousands upon thousands; **A~glaube** *m* superstition; **~gläubisch** *a* superstitious.

aberkennen [ˈapˈɛrkɛnən] *vt unreg*: **jdm etw ~** deprive sb of sth, take sth (away) from sb.

Aberkennung *f* taking away.

abermals [ˈaːbərmaːls] *ad* once again.

Abf. *abk* (= *Abfahrt*) dep.

abfahren ['apfa:rən] *unreg vi* leave, depart // *vt* take *od* cart away; *(Strecke)* drive; *(Reifen)* wear; *(Fahrkarte)* use.

Abfahrt ['apfa:rt] *f* departure; *(SKI)* descent; *(Piste)* run; **Abfahrtslauf** *m* *(SKI)* descent, run down; **Abfahrtszeit** *f* departure time.

Abfall ['apfal] *m* waste; *(von Speisen etc)* rubbish *(Brit)*, garbage *(US)*; *(Neigung)* slope; *(Verschlechterung)* decline; **~eimer** *m* rubbish bin *(Brit)*, garbage can *(US)*; **a~en** *vi unreg (lit, fig)* fall *od* drop off; *(POL, vom Glauben)* break away; *(sich neigen)* fall *od* drop away.

abfällig ['apfɛlɪç] *a* disparaging, deprecatory.

abfangen ['apfaŋən] *vt unreg* intercept; *(Person)* catch; *(unter Kontrolle bringen)* check.

abfärben ['apfɛrbən] *vi (lit)* lose its colour; *(Wäsche)* run; *(fig)* rub off.

abfassen ['apfasən] *vt* write, draft.

abfertigen ['apfɛrtɪgən] *vt* prepare for dispatch, process; *(an der Grenze)* clear; *(Kundschaft)* attend to.

Abfertigung *f* preparing for dispatch, processing; clearance.

abfeuern ['apfɔyərn] *vt* fire.

abfinden ['apfɪndən] *unreg vt* pay off // *vr* come to terms; **sich mit jdm ~/ nicht ~** put up with/not get on with sb.

Abfindung *f (von Gläubigern)* payment; *(Geld)* sum in settlement.

abflauen ['apflauən] *vi (Wind, Erregung)* die away, subside; *(Nachfrage, Geschäft)* fall *od* drop off.

abfliegen ['apfli:gən] *unreg vi (Flugzeug)* take off; *(Passagier auch)* fly // *vt (Gebiet)* fly over.

abfließen ['apfli:sən] *vi unreg* drain away.

Abflug ['apflu:k] *m* departure; *(Start)* take-off; **~zeit** *f* departure time.

Abfluß ['apflʊs] *m* draining away; *(Öffnung)* outlet.

Abfuhr ['apfu:r] *f* -, **-en** removal; *(fig)* snub, rebuff.

abführen ['apfy:rən] *vt* lead away; *(Gelder, Steuern)* pay // *vi (MED)* have a laxative effect.

Abführmittel ['apfy:rmɪtəl] *nt* laxative, purgative.

abfüllen ['apfʏlən] *vt* draw off; *(in Flaschen)* bottle.

Abgabe ['apga:bə] *f* handing in; *(von Ball)* pass; *(Steuer)* tax; *(eines Amtes)* giving up; *(einer Erklärung)* giving.

Abgang ['apgaŋ] *m (von Schule)* leaving; *(THEAT)* exit; *(Ausscheiden)* passing; *(Fehlgeburt)* miscarriage; *(Abfahrt)* departure; *(der Post, von Waren)* dispatch.

Abgas ['apga:s] *nt* waste gas; *(AUT)* exhaust.

abgeben ['apge:bən] *unreg vt (Gegenstand)* hand *od* give in; *(Ball)* pass; *(Wärme)* give off; *(Amt)* hand over; *(Schuß)* fire; *(Erklärung, Urteil)* give; *(darstellen, sein)* make; **jdm etw ~** *(überlassen)* let sb have sth // *vr:* **sich mit jdm/etw ~** associate with sb/bother with sth.

abgehen ['apge:ən] *unreg vi* go away, leave; *(THEAT)* exit; *(Baby)* die; *(Knopf etc)* come off; *(abgezogen werden)* be taken off; *(Straße)* branch off; **etw geht jdm ab** *(fehlt)* sb lacks sth // *vt (Strecke)* go *od* walk along.

abgelegen ['apgəle:gən] *a* remote.

abgemacht ['apgəmaxt] *a* fixed; **~!** done.

abgeneigt ['apgənaɪkt] *a* averse to, disinclined.

Abgeordnete(r) ['apgə'ɔrdnətə(r)] *mf* member of parliament; elected representative.

abgeschmackt ['apgəʃmakt] *a* tasteless.

abgesehen ['apgəze:ən] *a:* **es auf jdn/ etw ~ haben** be after sb/sth; **~ von ... apart from ...**

abgespannt ['apgəʃpant] *a* tired out.

abgestanden ['apgəʃtandən] *a* stale; *(Bier auch)* flat.

abgestorben ['apgəʃtɔrbən] *a* numb; *(BIOL, MED)* dead.

abgetragen ['apgətra:gən] *a* shabby, worn out.

abgewinnen ['apgəvɪnən] *vt unreg:* **einer Sache etw/Geschmack ~** get sth/pleasure from sth.

abgewöhnen ['apgəvø:nən] *vt:* **jdm/ sich etw ~** cure sb of sth/give sth up.

abgleiten ['apglaɪtən] *vi unreg* slip, slide.

Abgott ['apgɔt] *m* idol.

abgöttisch ['apgœtɪʃ] *a:* **~ lieben** idolize.

abgrenzen ['apgrɛntsən] *vt (lit, fig)* mark off; fence off.

Abgrund ['apgrʊnt] *m (lit, fig)* abyss.

abhacken ['aphakən] *vt* chop off.

abhalten ['aphaltən] *vt unreg (Versammlung)* hold; **jdn von etw ~** *(fernhalten)* keep sb away from sth; *(hindern)* keep sb from sth.

abhanden [ap'handən] *a:* **~ kommen** get lost.

Abhandlung ['aphandlʊŋ] *f* treatise, discourse.

Abhang ['aphaŋ] *m* slope.

abhängen ['aphɛŋən] *vt (Bild)* take down; *(Verfolger)* shake off // *vi unreg (Fleisch)* hang; **von jdm/etw ~** depend on sb/

sth.

abhängig ['aphɛnɪç] a dependent (von on); **A~keit** f dependence (von on).

abhärten ['aphɛrtən] vtr toughen (o.s.) up; **sich gegen etw ~** inure o.s. to sth.

abhauen ['aphauən] unreg vt cut off; (Baum) cut down // vi (umg) clear off od out.

abheben ['aphɛːbən] unreg vt lift (up); (Karten) cut; (Masche) slip; (Geld) withdraw, take out // vi (Flugzeug) take off; (Rakete) lift off; (KARTEN) cut // vr stand out (von from), contrast (von with).

abhelfen ['aphɛlfən] vi unreg (+dat) remedy.

abhetzen ['aphɛtsən] vr wear od tire o.s. out.

Abhilfe ['aphɪlfə] f remedy; **~ schaffen** put things right.

abholen ['aphoːlən] vt (Gegenstand) fetch, collect; (Person) call for; (am Bahnhof etc) pick up, meet.

abhören ['aphøːrən] vt (Vokabeln) test; (Telefongespräch) tap; (Tonband etc) listen to.

Abhörgerät nt bug.

Abitur [abi'tuːr] nt -s, -e German school leaving examination; **Abituri'ent(in** f) m candidate for school leaving certificate.

Abk. abk (= Abkürzung) abbr.

abkanzeln ['apkantsəln] vt (umg) bawl out.

abkapseln ['apkapsəln] vr shut od cut o.s. off.

abkaufen ['apkaufən] vt: **jdm etw ~** buy sth from sb.

abkehren ['apkeːrən] vt (Blick) avert, turn away // vr turn away.

abklingen ['apklɪŋən] vi unreg die away; (Radio) fade out.

abknöpfen ['apknœpfən] vt unbutton; **jdm etw ~** (umg) get sth off sb.

abkochen ['apkɔxən] vt boil.

abkommen ['apkɔmən] vi unreg get away; **von der Straße/von einem Plan ~** leave the road/give up a plan; **A~** nt -s, - agreement.

abkömmlich ['apkœmlɪç] a available, free.

abkratzen ['apkratsən] vt scrape off // vi (umg) kick the bucket.

abkühlen ['apkyːlən] vt cool down // vr (Mensch) cool down od off; (Wetter) get cool; (Zuneigung) cool.

abkürzen ['apkʏrtsən] vt shorten; (Wort auch) abbreviate; **den Weg ~** take a short cut.

Abkürzung f (Wort) abbreviation; (Weg) short cut.

abladen ['aplaːdən] vt unreg unload.

Ablage ['aplaːgə] f (für Akten) tray; (für Kleider) cloakroom.

ablassen ['aplasən] unreg vt (Wasser, Dampf) let off; (vom Preis) knock off // vi: **von etw ~** give sth up, abandon sth.

Ablauf ['aplauf] m (Abfluß) drain; (von Ereignissen) course; (einer Frist, Zeit) expiry (Brit), expiration (US); **a~en** unreg vi (abfließen) drain away; (Ereignisse) happen; (Frist, Zeit, Paß) expire // vt (Sohlen) wear (down od out).

ablegen ['apleːgən] vt put od lay down; (Kleider) take off; (Gewohnheit) get rid of; (Prüfung) take, sit; (Zeugnis) give.

Ableger m -s, - layer; (fig) branch, offshoot.

ablehnen ['apleːnən] vt reject; (Einladung) decline, refuse // vi decline, refuse.

Ablehnung f rejection; refusal.

ableiten ['aplaɪtən] vt (Wasser) divert; (deduzieren) deduce; (Wort) derive.

Ableitung f diversion; deduction; derivation; (Wort) derivative.

ablenken ['aplɛŋkən] vt turn away, deflect; (zerstreuen) distract // vi change the subject.

Ablenkung f distraction.

ablesen ['apleːzən] vt unreg read out; (Meßgeräte) read.

abliefern ['apliːfərn] vt deliver; **etw bei jdm/einer Dienststelle ~** hand sth over to sb/in at an office.

Ablieferung f delivery.

abliegen ['apliːgən] vi unreg be some distance away; (fig) be far removed.

ablösen ['apløːzən] vt (abtrennen) take off, remove; (in Amt) take over from; (Wache) relieve.

Ablösung f removal; relieving.

abmachen ['apmaxən] vt take off; (vereinbaren) agree.

Abmachung f agreement.

abmagern ['apmaːgərn] vi get thinner.

Abmagerungskur f diet; **eine ~ machen** go on a diet.

Abmarsch ['apmarʃ] m departure.

abmelden ['apmɛldən] vt (Zeitungen) cancel; (Auto) take off the road; **jdn bei der Polizei ~** register sb's departure with the police // vr give notice of one's departure; (im Hotel) check out.

abmessen ['apmɛsən] vt unreg measure.

Abmessung f measurement.

abmontieren ['apmɔntiːrən] vt take off.

abmühen ['apmyːən] vr wear o.s. out.

Abnahme ['apnaːmə] f -, -n removal; (COMM) buying; (Verringerung) decrease (gen in).

abnehmen ['apneːmən] unreg vt take

off, remove; (*Führerschein*) take away; (*Geld*) get (*jdm* out of sb); (*kaufen, umg: glauben*) buy (*jdm* from sb); (*Prüfung*) hold; (*Maschen*) decrease; jdm Arbeit ~ take work off sb's shoulders // vi decrease; (*schlanker werden*) lose weight.

Abnehmer m -s, - purchaser, customer.

Abneigung ['apnaigun] f aversion, dislike.

abnorm [ap'nɔrm] a abnormal.

abnutzen ['apnutsən] vt wear out.

Abnutzung f wear (and tear).

Abonnement [abɔn(ə)'mãː] nt -s, -s subscription.

Abonnent(in f) [abɔ'nɛnt(in)] m subscriber.

abonnieren [abɔ'niːrən] vt subscribe to.

Abordnung [ap'ɔrdnun] f delegation.

Abort [a'bɔrt] m -(e)s, -e lavatory.

abpacken ['appakən] vt pack.

abpassen ['appasən] vt (*Person, Gelegenheit*) wait for; (*in Größe: Stoff etc*) adjust.

abpfeifen ['appfaifən] vti unreg (SPORT): (**das Spiel**) ~ blow the whistle (for the end of the game).

Abpfiff ['appfif] m final whistle.

abplagen ['applaːgən] vr wear o.s. out.

Abprall ['appral] m rebound; (*von Kugel*) ricochet; **a~en** vi bounce off; ricochet.

abputzen ['apputsən] vt clean.

abraten ['apraːtən] vi unreg advise, warn (*jdm von etw* sb against sth).

abräumen ['aprɔymən] vt clear up od away.

abreagieren ['apreagiːrən] vt (*Zorn*) work off (*an +dat* on) // vr calm down.

abrechnen ['aprɛçnən] vt deduct, take off // vi (*lit*) settle up; (*fig*) get even.

Abrechnung f settlement; (*Rechnung*) bill.

Abrede ['apreːdə] f: etw in ~ stellen deny od dispute sth.

abregen ['apreːgən] vr (*umg*) calm od cool down.

Abreise ['apraizə] nf departure; **a~n** vi leave, set off.

abreißen ['apraisən] vt unreg (*Haus*) tear down; (*Blatt*) tear off.

abrichten ['apriçtən] vt train.

abriegeln ['apriːgəln] vt (*Tür*) bolt; (*Straße, Gebiet*) seal off.

Abriß ['apris] m -sses, -sse (*Übersicht*) outline.

Abruf ['apruːf] m: **auf** ~ on call; **a~en** vt unreg (*Mensch*) call away; (COMM: *Ware*) request delivery of.

abrunden ['aprundən] vt round off.

abrüsten ['aprystən] vi disarm.

Abrüstung f disarmament.

abrutschen ['aprutʃən] vi slip; (AVIAT) sideslip.

Abs. abk (= *Absender*) sender, from.

Absage ['apzaːgə] f -, -n refusal; **a~n** vt cancel, call off; (*Einladung*) turn down // vi cry off; (*ablehnen*) decline.

absägen ['apzɛːgən] vt saw off.

Absatz ['apzats] m (COMM) sales pl; (*Bodensatz*) deposit; (*neuer Abschnitt*) paragraph; (*Treppen~*) landing; (*Schuh~*) heel; **~gebiet** nt (COMM) market.

abschaben ['apʃaːbən] vt scrape off; (*Möhren*) scrape.

abschaffen ['apʃafən] vt abolish, do away with.

Abschaffung f abolition.

abschalten ['apʃaltən] vti (*lit, umg*) switch off.

abschätzen ['apʃɛtsən] vt estimate; (*Lage*) assess; (*Person*) size up.

abschätzig ['apʃɛtsiç] a disparaging, derogatory.

Abschaum ['apʃaum] m -(e)s scum.

Abscheu ['apʃɔy] m -(e)s loathing, repugnance; **a~erregend** a repulsive, loathsome; **a~lich** [ap'ʃɔyliç] a abominable.

abschicken ['apʃikən] vt send off.

abschieben ['apʃiːbən] vt unreg push away; (*Person*) pack off.

Abschied ['apʃiːt] m -(e)s, -e parting; (*von Armee*) discharge; ~ nehmen say good-bye (*von jdm* to sb), take one's leave (*von jdm* of sb); **seinen** ~ **nehmen** (MIL) apply for discharge; **Abschiedsbrief** m farewell letter.

abschießen ['apʃiːsən] vt unreg (*Flugzeug*) shoot down; (*Geschoß*) fire; (*umg: Minister*) get rid of.

abschirmen ['apʃirmən] vt screen.

abschlagen ['apʃlaːgən] vt unreg (*abhacken, COMM*) knock off; (*ablehnen*) refuse; (MIL) repel.

abschlägig ['apʃlɛːgiç] a negative.

Abschlagszahlung f interim payment.

abschleifen ['apʃlaifən] unreg vt grind down; (*Rost*) polish off // vr wear off.

Abschlepp- ['apʃlɛp] zW: **~dienst** m (AUT) breakdown service (*Brit*), towing company (*US*); **a~en** vt (take in) tow; **~seil** nt towrope.

abschließen ['apʃliːsən] unreg vt (*Tür*) lock; (*beenden*) conclude, finish; (*Vertrag, Handel*) conclude // vr (*sich isolieren*) cut o.s. off.

Abschluß ['apʃlus] m (*Beendigung*) close, conclusion; (COMM: *Bilanz*) balancing; (*von Vertrag, Handel*) conclusion; **zum** ~ in conclusion; **~prüfung** f final exam.

abschmieren ['apʃmiːrən] vt (AUT) grease, lubricate.

abschneiden ['apʃnaidən] unreg vt cut

off // vi do, come off.

Abschnitt ['apʃnɪt] m section; (MIL) sector; (Kontroll~) counterfoil; (MATH) segment; (Zeit~) period.

abschnüren ['apʃnyːrən] vt constrict.

abschöpfen ['apʃœpfən] vt skim off.

abschrauben ['apʃraubən] vt unscrew.

abschrecken ['apʃrɛkən] vt deter, put off; (mit kaltem Wasser) plunge in cold water; ~d a deterrent; ~des Beispiel warning.

abschreiben ['apʃraibən] vt unreg copy; (verlorengeben) write off; (COMM) deduct.

Abschrift ['apʃrɪft] f copy.

Abschuß ['apʃus] m (eines Geschützes) firing; (Herunterschießen) shooting down; (Tötung) shooting.

abschüssig ['apʃʏsɪç] a steep.

abschütteln ['apʃʏtəln] vt shake off.

abschwächen ['apʃvɛçən] vt lessen; (Behauptung, Kritik) tone down // vr lessen.

abschweifen ['apʃvaifən] vi wander.

Abschweifung f digression.

abschwellen ['apʃvɛlən] vi unreg (Geschwulst) go down; (Lärm) die down.

abschwören ['apʃvøːrən] vi unreg (+dat) renounce.

abseh- ['apzeː] zW: ~bar a foreseeable; in ~barer Zeit in the foreseeable future; das Ende ist ~bar the end is in sight; ~en unreg vt (Ende, Folgen) foresee // vi: von etw ~en refrain from sth; (nicht berücksichtigen) leave sth out of consideration.

abseits ['apzaits] ad out of the way // präp +gen away from; A~ nt (SPORT) offside.

Absend- ['apzɛnd] zW: a~en vt unreg send off, dispatch; ~er m -s, - sender; ~ung f dispatch.

absetz- ['apzɛts] zW: ~en vt (niederstellen, aussteigen lassen) put down; (abnehmen) take off; (COMM: verkaufen) sell; (FIN: abziehen) deduct; (entlassen) dismiss; (König) depose; (streichen) drop; (hervorheben) pick out // vr (sich entfernen) clear off; (sich ablagern) be deposited; A~ung f (FIN: Abzug) deduction; (Entlassung) dismissal; (von König) deposing; (Streichung) dropping.

absichern ['apzɪçərn] vtr make safe; (schützen) safeguard.

Absicht ['apzɪçt] f intention; mit ~ on purpose; a~lich a intentional, deliberate.

absinken ['apzɪŋkən] vi unreg sink; (Temperatur, Geschwindigkeit) decrease.

absitzen ['apzɪtsən] unreg vi dismount // vt (Strafe) serve.

absolut [apzo'luːt] a absolute;

A~ismus [-'tɪsmʊs] m absolutism.

absolvieren [apzɔl'viːrən] vt (SCH) complete.

absonder- ['apzɔndər] zW: ~lich [ap'zɔndərlɪç] a odd, strange; ~n vt separate; (ausscheiden) give off, secrete // vr cut o.s. off; A~ung f separation; (MED) secretion.

abspalten ['apʃpaltən] vt split off.

abspeisen ['apʃpaizən] vt (fig) fob off.

abspenstig ['apʃpɛnstɪç] a: ~ machen lure away (jdm from sb).

absperren ['apʃpɛrən] vt block od close off; (Tür) lock.

Absperrung f (Vorgang) blocking od closing off; (Sperre) barricade.

abspielen ['apʃpiːlən] vt (Platte, Tonband) play; (SPORT: Ball) pass // vr happen.

absplittern ['apʃplɪtərn] vt chip off.

Absprache ['apʃpraːxə] f arrangement.

absprechen ['apʃprɛçən] vt unreg (vereinbaren) arrange; jdm etw ~ deny sb sth.

abspringen ['apʃprɪŋən] vi unreg jump down/off; (Farbe, Lack) flake off; (AVIAT) bale out; (sich distanzieren) back out.

Absprung ['apʃprʊŋ] m jump.

abspülen ['apʃpyːlən] vt rinse; (Geschirr) wash up.

abstammen ['apʃtamən] vi be descended; (Wort) be derived.

Abstammung f descent; derivation.

Abstand ['apʃtant] m distance; (zeitlich) interval; davon ~ nehmen, etw zu tun refrain from doing sth; ~ halten (AUT) keep one's distance; mit ~ der beste by far the best.

abstatten ['apʃtatən] vt (Dank) give; (Besuch) pay.

abstauben ['apʃtaubən] vti dust; (umg: stehlen) pinch.

Abstecher ['apʃtɛçər] m -s, - detour.

abstehen ['apʃteːən] vi unreg (Ohren, Haare) stick out; (entfernt sein) stand away.

absteigen ['apʃtaigən] vi unreg (vom Rad etc) get off, dismount; (in Gasthof) put up (in +dat at); (SPORT) be relegated (in +akk to).

abstellen ['apʃtɛlən] vt (niederstellen) put down; (entfernt stellen) pull out; (hinstellen: Auto) park; (ausschalten) turn od switch off; (Mißstand, Unsitte) stop; (ausrichten) gear (auf +akk to).

Abstellgleis nt siding.

abstempeln ['apʃtɛmpəln] vt stamp.

absterben ['apʃtɛrbən] vi unreg die; (Körperteil) go numb.

Abstieg ['apʃtiːk] m -(e)s, -e descent; (SPORT) relegation; (fig) decline.

abstimmen ['apʃtɪmən] vi vote // vt

(*Instrument*) tune (*auf +akk* to); (*Interessen*) match (*auf +akk* with); (*Termine, Ziele*) fit in (*auf +akk* with) // *vr* agree.

Abstimmung *f* vote.

Abstinenz [apsti'nɛnts] *f* abstinence; teetotalism; ~**ler(in** *f*) *m* -s, - teetotaller.

abstoßen ['apʃtoːsən] *vt unreg* push off *od* away; (*verkaufen*) unload; (*anekeln*) repel, repulse; ~**d** *a* repulsive.

abstrakt [ap'strakt] *a* abstract // *ad* abstractly, in the abstract.

abstreiten ['apʃtraitən] *vt unreg* deny.

Abstrich ['apʃtriç] *m* (*Abzug*) cut; (*MED*) smear; ~**e machen** lower one's sights.

abstufen ['apʃtuːfən] *vt* (*Hang*) terrace; (*Farben*) shade; (*Gehälter*) grade.

abstumpfen ['apʃtumpfən] *vt* (*lit, fig*) dull, blunt // *vi* (*lit, fig*) become dulled.

Absturz ['apʃturts] *m* fall; (*AVIAT*) crash.

abstürzen ['apʃtyrtsən] *vi* fall; (*AVIAT*) crash.

absuchen ['apzuːxən] *vt* scour, search.

absurd [ap'zurt] *a* absurd.

Abszeß [aps'tsɛs] *m* -**sses, -sse** abscess.

Abt [apt] *m* -**(e)s, -e** abbot.

Abt. *abk* (= *Abteilung*) dept.

abtasten ['aptastən] *vt* feel, probe.

abtauen ['aptauən] *vti* thaw.

Abtei [ap'tai] *f* -, -**en** abbey.

Abteil [ap'tail] *nt* -**(e)s, -e** compartment; '**a~en** *vt* divide up; (*abtrennen*) divide off; ~**ung** *f* (*in Firma, Kaufhaus*) department; (*in Krankenhaus*) section; (*MIL*) unit.

abtönen ['aptøːnən] *vt* (*PHOT*) tone down.

abtransportieren ['aptransportiːrən] *vt* take away, remove.

abtreiben ['aptraibən] *unreg vt* (*Boot, Flugzeug*) drive off course; (*Kind*) abort // *vi* be driven off course; abort.

Abtreibung *f* abortion.

abtrennen ['aptrɛnən] *vt* (*lostrennen*) detach; (*entfernen*) take off; (*abteilen*) separate off.

abtreten ['aptreːtən] *unreg vt* wear out; (*überlassen*) hand over, cede (*jdm to sb*) // *vi* go off; (*zurücktreten*) step down.

Abtritt ['aptrit] *m* resignation.

abtrocknen ['aptrɔknən] *vti* dry.

abtun ['aptuːn] *vt unreg* take off; (*fig*) dismiss.

abverlangen ['apfɛrlaŋən] *vt*: **jdm etw ~** demand sth from sb.

abwägen ['apvɛːgən] *vt unreg* weigh

up.

abwandeln ['apvandəln] *vt* adapt.

abwandern ['apvandərn] *vi* move away.

abwarten ['apvartən] *vt* wait for // *vi* wait.

abwärts ['apvɛrts] *ad* down.

Abwasch ['apvaʃ] *m* -**(e)s** washing-up; **a~en** *vt unreg* (*Schmutz*) wash off; (*Geschirr*) wash (up).

Abwasser ['apvasər] *nt* -**s, -wässer** sewage.

abwechseln ['apvɛksəln] *vir* alternate; (*Personen*) take turns; ~**d** *a* alternate.

Abwechslung *f* change.

Abweg ['apveːk] *m*: **auf ~e geraten/führen** go/lead astray; **a~ig** ['apveːgiç] *a* wrong.

Abwehr ['apveːr] *f* - defence; (*Schutz*) protection; (~*dienst*) counter intelligence (service); **a~en** *vt* ward off; (*Ball*) stop.

abweichen ['apvaiçən] *vi unreg* deviate; (*Meinung*) differ; ~**d** *a* deviant; differing.

abweisen ['apvaizən] *vt unreg* turn away; (*Antrag*) turn down; ~**d** *a* (*Haltung*) cold.

abwenden ['apvɛndən] *unreg vt* avert // *vr* turn away.

abwerfen ['apvɛrfən] *vt unreg* throw off; (*Profit*) yield; (*aus Flugzeug*) drop; (*Spielkarte*) discard.

abwerten ['apvɛrtən] *vt* (*FIN*) devalue.

abwesend ['apveːzənt] *a* absent.

Abwesenheit ['apveːzənhait] *f* absence.

abwickeln ['apvikəln] *vt* unwind; (*Geschäft*) wind up.

abwiegen ['apviːgən] *vt unreg* weigh out.

abwischen ['apviʃən] *vt* wipe off *od* away; (*putzen*) wipe.

Abwurf ['apvurf] *m* throwing off; (*von Bomben etc*) dropping; (*von Reiter, SPORT*) throw.

abwürgen ['apvyrgən] *vt* (*umg*) scotch; (*Motor*) stall.

abzahlen ['aptsaːlən] *vt* pay off.

abzählen ['aptsɛːlən] *vti* count (up).

Abzahlung *f* repayment; **auf ~** kaufen buy on hire purchase.

abzapfen ['aptsapfən] *vt* draw off; **jdm Blut ~** take blood from sb.

abzäunen ['aptsɔynən] *vt* fence off.

Abzeichen ['aptsaiçən] *nt* badge; (*Orden*) decoration.

abzeichnen ['aptsaiçnən] *vt* draw, copy; (*Dokument*) initial // *vr* stand out; (*fig: bevorstehen*) loom.

Abziehbild *nt* transfer.

abziehen ['aptsiːən] *unreg vt* take off; (*Tier*) skin; (*Bett*) strip; (*Truppen*) withdraw; (*subtrahieren*) take away, subtract; (*kopieren*) run off // *vi* go away; (*Truppen*) withdraw.

abzielen ['aptsi:lən] *vi* be aimed (*auf* +*akk* at).

Abzug ['aptsu:k] *m* departure; (*von Truppen*) withdrawal; (*Kopie*) copy; (*Subtraktion*) subtraction; (*Betrag*) deduction; (*Rauch~*) flue; (*von Waffen*) trigger.

abzüglich ['aptsy:klıç] *präp* +*gen* less.

abzweigen ['aptsvaıgən] *vi* branch off // *vt* set aside.

Abzweigung *f* junction.

ach [ax] *interj* oh; ~ **ja!** (oh) yes; ~ **so!** I see; **mit A~ und Krach** by the skin of one's teeth.

Achse ['aksə] *f* -, -n axis; (*AUT*) axle.

Achsel ['aksəl] *f* -, -n shoulder; ~**höhle** *f* armpit; ~**zucken** *nt* shrug (of one's shoulders).

acht [axt] *num* eight; **sich in ~ nehmen** be careful (*vor* +*dat* of), watch out (*vor* +*dat* for); **etw außer ~ lassen** disregard sth; ~ **Tage** a week; ~**bar** a worthy; ~**e(r, s)** a eighth; ~**el** *num* eighth; ~**en** *vt* respect // *vi* pay attention (*auf* +*akk* to); **darauf ~en, daß** ... be careful that ...

ächten ['ɛçtən] *vt* outlaw, ban.

Achter- ['axtər] *zW*: ~**bahn** *f* roller coaster; ~**deck** *nt* (*NAUT*) afterdeck.

acht- *zW*: ~**fach** a eightfold; ~**geben** *vi unreg* take care (*auf* +*akk* of); ~**los** a careless; ~**mal** *ad* eight times; ~**sam** a attentive.

Achtung ['axtʊŋ] *f* attention; (*Ehrfurcht*) respect; **alle ~!** good for you/him *etc* // *interj* look out!; (*MIL*) attention!

achtzehn *num* eighteen.

achtzig *num* eighty.

ächzen ['ɛçtsən] *vi* groan (*vor* +*dat* with).

Acker ['akər] *m* -s, ⁻ field; ~**bau** *m* agriculture; **a~n** *vti* plough; (*umg*) slog away.

ADAC [a:de:'a'tse:] *abk* (= *Allgemeiner Deutscher Automobil-Club*) ≈ AA, RAC.

addieren [a'di:rən] *vt* add (up).

Addition [aditsi'o:n] *f* addition.

Adel ['a:dəl] *m* -s nobility; **a~ig, adlig** a noble.

Ader ['a:dər] *f* -, -n vein.

Adler ['a:dlər] *m* -s, - eagle.

Admiral [atmi'ra:l] *m* -s, -e admiral; **Admiralität** *f* admiralty.

adopt- *zW*: ~**ieren** [adɔp'ti:rən] *vt* adopt; **A~ion** [adɔptsi'o:n] *f* adoption; **A~iveltern** [adɔp'ti:f-] *pl* adoptive parents *pl*; **A~ivkind** *nt* adopted child.

Adress- *zW*: ~**ant** [adrɛ'sant] *m* sender; ~**at** [adrɛ'sa:t] *m* -en, -en addressee; ~**e** [a'drɛsə] *f* -, -n address; **a~ieren** [adrɛ'si:rən] *vt* address (*an* +*akk* to).

Adria ['a:dria] *f* - Adriatic.

Advent [at'vɛnt] *m* -(e)s, -e Advent; **Adventskranz** *m* Advent wreath.

aero- [aero] *präf* aero-.

Aerobic [ae'rɔbık] *nt* aerobics.

Affäre [a'fɛ:rə] *f* -, -n affair.

Affe ['afə] *m* -n, -n monkey.

affektiert [afɛk'ti:rt] a affected.

Affen- *zW*: **a~artig** a like a monkey; **mit a~artiger Geschwindigkeit** like a flash; ~**hitze** *f* (*umg*) incredible heat; ~**schande** *f* (*umg*) crying shame.

affig ['afıç] a affected.

Afrika ['a:frika] *nt* -s Africa; ~**ner(in** *f*) [-'ka:nər(ın)] *m* -s, - African; **a~nisch** [-'ka:nıʃ] a African.

After ['aftər] *m* -s, - anus.

AG [a:'ge:] *abk* (= *Aktiengesellschaft*) (*Brit*) (public) limited company, Ltd; (*US*) corporation, Inc.

ägäisch [ɛ'gɛ:ıʃ] a: ~**es Meer** Aegean.

Agent [a'gɛnt] *m* agent; **Agentur** [agen'tu:r] *f* agency.

Aggregat [agre'ga:t] *nt* -(e)s, -e aggregate; (*TECH*) unit; ~**zustand** *m* (*PHYS*) state.

Aggress- *zW*: ~**ion** [agrɛsi'o:n] *f* aggression; **a~iv** [agrɛ'si:f] a aggressive; ~**ivität** [agrɛsivi'tɛ:t] *f* aggressiveness.

Agitation [agitatsi'o:n] *f* agitation.

Agrar- [a'gra:r] *zW*: ~**politik** *f* agricultural policy; ~**staat** *m* agrarian state.

Ägypt- [ɛ'gypt] *zW*: ~**en** *nt* -s Egypt; ~**er(in** *f*) *m* -s, - Egyptian; **ä~isch** a Egyptian.

ah [a:] *interj* ah.

aha [a'ha:] *interj* aha.

Ahn [a:n] *m* -en, -en forebear.

ähneln ['ɛ:nəln] *vi* (+*dat*) be like, resemble // *vr* be alike od similar.

ahnen ['a:nən] *vt* suspect; (*Tod, Gefahr*) have a presentiment of.

ähnlich ['ɛ:nlıç] a similar (*dat* to); **Ä~keit** *f* similarity.

Ahnung ['a:nʊŋ] *f* idea, suspicion; presentiment; **a~slos** a unsuspecting.

Ahorn ['a:hɔrn] *m* -s, -e maple.

Ähre ['ɛ:rə] *f* -, -n ear.

Aids [e:dz] *nt* AIDS.

Akademie [akade'mi:] *f* academy.

Akademiker(in *f*) [aka'de:mikər(ın)] *m* -s, - university graduate.

akademisch a academic.

akklimatisieren [aklimati'zi:rən] *vr* become acclimatized.

Akkord [a'kɔrt] *m* -(e)s, -e (*MUS*) chord; **im ~ arbeiten** do piecework; ~**arbeit** *f* piecework; **Akkordeon**

[a'kɔrdeon] nt -s, -s accordion.
Akrobat(in f) [akro'baːt(ın)] m -en,
-en acrobat.
Akt [akt] m -(e)s, -e act; (KUNST)
nude.
Akte ['aktə] f -, -n file; **aktenkundig** a
on the files; **Aktenschrank** m filing
cabinet; **Aktentasche** f briefcase.
Aktie ['aktsiə] f -, -n share.
Aktien- zW: ~**emission** f share issue;
~**gesellschaft** f joint-stock company;
~**kurs** m share price.
Aktion [aktsi'oːn] f campaign; (Poli-
zei~, Such~) action; ~**är** [-'nɛːr] m
-s, -e shareholder.
aktiv [ak'tiːf] a active; (MIL) regular;
~**ieren** [-'viːrən] vt activate; **A~i'tät** f
activity.
Aktualität [aktualiˈtɛːt] f topicality;
(einer Mode) up-to-dateness.
aktuell [aktuˈel] a topical; up-to-date.
Akustik [aˈkʊstɪk] f acoustics pl.
akut [aˈkuːt] a acute.
AKW [aːkaˈveː] nt abk von **Atomkraft-
werk.**
Akzent [akˈtsɛnt] m accent; (Betonung) stress.
akzeptieren [aktsepˈtiːrən] vt accept.
Alarm [aˈlarm] m -(e)s, -e alarm;
a~bereit a standing by; ~**bereitschaft** f stand-by; **a~ieren** [-ˈmiːrən]
vt alarm.
Alban- [alˈbaːn] zW: ~**ien** nt -s - Albania; ~**ier(in** f) m -s, - Albanian;
a~isch a Albanian.
albern ['albərn] a silly.
Album ['albʊm] nt -s, **Alben** album.
Algebra ['algebra] f - algebra.
Alger- [alˈgeːr] zW: ~**ien** nt -s Algeria; ~**ier(in** f) m -s, - Algerian;
a~isch a Algerian.
alias ['aːliɑs] ad alias.
Alibi ['aːlibi] nt -s, -s alibi.
Alimente [aliˈmɛntə] pl alimony.
Alkohol ['alkohoːl] m -s, -e alcohol;
a~frei a non-alcoholic; ~**iker(in** f)
[alkoˈhoːlikər(ın)] m -s, - alcoholic;
a~isch a alcoholic; ~**verbot** nt ban
on alcohol.
All [al] nt -s universe; **a~ˈabendlich** a
every evening; **'a~bekannt** a uni-
versally known.
alle(r, s) ['alə(r, s)] ♦**a 1** (sämtliche)
all; **wir** ~ all of us; ~ **Kinder waren
da** all the children were there; ~
Kinder mögen ... all children like ...;
~ **beide** both of us/them; **sie kamen**
~ they all came; ~**s Gute** all the
best; ~**s in** ~**m** all in all
2 (mit Zeit- oder Maßangaben)
every; ~ **vier Jahre** every four
years; ~ **fünf Meter** every five
metres
♦**pron** everything; ~**s was er sagt**
everything he says, all that he says

♦**ad** (zu Ende, aufgebraucht)
finished; **die Milch ist** ~ the milk's
all gone, there's no milk left; **etw** ~
machen finish sth up.
Allee [aˈleː] f -, -n avenue.
allein [aˈlaın] ad alone; (ohne Hilfe)
on one's own, by oneself; **nicht** ~
(nicht nur) not only // kj but, only
A~erziehende(r) mf single parent;
A~gang m: **im A~gang** on one's
own; **A~herrscher** m autocrat;
~**stehend** a single.
allemal ['aləˈmaːl] ad (jedesmal) always; (ohne weiteres) with no
bother; **ein für** ~**mal** once and for
all.
allenfalls ['alənfals] ad at all events;
(höchstens) at most.
aller- ['alər] zW: ~**beste(r, s)** a very
best; ~**dings** ad (zwar) admittedly;
(gewiß) certainly.
Allergie [alerˈgiː] f allergy; **allergisch**
[aˈlergɪʃ] a allergic.
aller- zW: ~**hand** a inv (umg) all
sorts of; **das ist doch** ~**hand!** that's a
bit much; ~**hand!** (lobend) good
show!; **A~heiligen** nt All Saints'
Day; ~**höchstens** ad at the very
most; ~**lei** a inv all sorts of;
~**letzte(r, s)** a very last; ~**seits** ad
on all sides; **prost** ~**seits!** cheers
everyone!; ~**wenigste(r, s)** a very
least.
alles pron everything; ~ **in allem** all
in all; ~ **Gute!** all the best!
allgemein ['algəˈmaın] a general; **im**
~**en** in general; ~**gültig** a generally
accepted; **A~heit** f (Menschen) general public; (pl: Redensarten) general remarks pl.
Alliierte(r) [aliˈiːrtə(r)] m ally.
all- zW: ~**jährlich** a annual; ~**mählich**
a gradual; **A~tag** m everyday life;
~**täglich** a,ad daily; (gewöhnlich)
commonplace; ~**tags** ad on week-
days; ~**wissend** a omniscient; ~**zu**
ad all too; ~**zuoft** ad all too often;
~**zuviel** ad too much.
Almosen ['almoːzən] nt -s, - alms pl.
Alpen ['alpən] pl Alps pl.
Alphabet [alfaˈbeːt] nt -(e)s, -e alphabet; **a~isch** a alphabetical.
Alptraum ['alptraum] m nightmare.
als [als] kj **1** (zeitlich) when; (gleichzeitig) as; **damals,** ~ ... (in the days)
when ...; **gerade,** ~ ... just as ...
2 (in der Eigenschaft) as; ~ **Antwort**
as an answer; ~ **Kind** as a child
3 (bei Vergleichen) than; **ich kam
später** ~ **er** I came later than he
(did) od later than him; **lieber** ... ~
rather ... than; **nichts** ~ **Ärger** nothing but trouble
4: ~ **ob/wenn** as if.
also ['alzoː] kj so; (folglich) therefore;

~ **gut** *od* **schön!** okay then; ~, so **was!** well really!; **na** ~! there you are then!

alt [alt] *a* old; **alles beim** ~**en lassen** leave everything as it was; **A**~ *m* **-s, -e** (*MUS*) alto; **Altar** [al'ta:r] *m* **-(e)s, -äre** altar; ~**bekannt** *a* long-known; **A**~'**eisen** *nt* scrap iron.

Alter ['altər] *nt* **-s, -** age; (*hohes*) old age; **im** ~ **von** at the age of; **a**~**n** *vi* grow old, age.

Alternativ- [alterna'ti:f] *in zW* alternative; ~**e** *f* alternative.

Alters- *zW*: ~**grenze** *f* age limit; ~**heim** *nt* old people's home; ~**versorgung** *f* old age pension.

Altertum *nt* antiquity.

alt- *zW*: **A**~**glascontainer** *m* bottle bank; ~'**hergebracht** *a* traditional; ~**klug** *a* precocious; ~**modisch** *a* old-fashioned; **A**~**papier** *nt* waste paper; **A**~**stadt** *f* old town.

Aluminium [alu'mi:niʊm] *nt* **-s** aluminium, aluminum (*US*); ~**folie** *f* tinfoil.

am [am] = **an dem;** ~ **Schlafen** (*umg*) sleeping; ~ **15. März** on March 15th; ~ **besten/schönsten** best/ most beautiful.

Amateur [ama'tø:r] *m* amateur.

Amboß ['ambɔs] *m* **-sses, -sse** anvil.

ambulant [ambu'lant] *a* outpatient.

Ambulanz [ambu'lants] *f* outpatients *sing.*

Ameise ['a:maizə] *f* **-, -n** ant.

Amerika [a'me:rika] *nt* **-s** America; ~**ner(in** *f*) [-'ka:nər(ɪn)] *m* **-s, -** American; **a**~**nisch** [-'ka:nɪʃ] *a* American.

Ampel ['ampəl] *f* **-, -n** traffic lights *pl.*

amputieren [ampu'ti:rən] *vt* amputate.

Amsel ['amzəl] *f* **-, -n** blackbird.

Amt [amt] *nt* **-(e)s, -er** office; (*Pflicht*) duty; (*TEL*) exchange; **a**~**ieren** [am'ti:rən] *vi* hold office; **a**~**lich** *a* official.

Amts- *zW*: ~**person** *f* official; ~**richter** *m* district judge; ~**stunden** *pl* office hours *pl*; ~**zeit** *f* period of office.

amüsant [amy'zant] *a* amusing.

amüsieren [amy'zi:rən] *vt* amuse // *vr* enjoy o.s.

an [an] ♦*präp +dat* **1** (*räumlich: wo?*) at; (*auf, bei*) on; (*nahe bei*) near; ~ **diesem Ort** at this place; ~ **der Wand** on the wall; **zu nahe** ~ **etw** too near to sth; **unten am Fluß** down by the river; **Köln liegt am Rhein** Cologne is on the Rhine.

2 (*zeitlich: wann?*) on; ~ **diesem Tag** on this day; ~ **Ostern** at Easter

3: **arm** ~ **Fett** low in fat; ~ **etw sterben** die of sth; ~ (**und für**) **sich** actually

♦*präp +akk* **1** (*räumlich: wohin?*) to; **er ging** ~**s Fenster** he went (over) to the window; **etw** ~ **die Wand hängen/schreiben** hang/write sth on the wall

2 (*zeitlich: woran?*): ~ **etw denken** think of sth

3 (*gerichtet* ~) to; **ein Gruß/eine Frage** ~ **dich** greetings/a question to you

♦*ad* **1** (*ungefähr*) about: ~ **die hundert** about a hundred

2 (*auf Fahrplänen*): **Frankfurt** ~ **18.30** arriving Frankfurt 18.30

3 (*ab*): **von dort/heute** ~ from there/ today onwards

4 (~**geschaltet,** ~**gezogen**) on; **das Licht ist** ~ the light is on; **ohne etwas** ~ with nothing on

♦*siehe auch* **am.**

analog [ana'lo:k] *a* analogous; **A**~**ie** [-'gi:] *f* analogy.

Analyse [ana'ly:zə] *f* **-, -n** analysis.

analysieren [analy'zi:rən] *vt* analyse.

Ananas ['ananas] *f* **-, -** *od* **-se** pineapple.

Anarchie [anar'çi:] *f* anarchy.

Anatomie [anato'mi:] *f* anatomy.

anbahnen ['anba:nən] *vtr* open up.

Anbau ['anbau] *m* (*AGR*) cultivation; (*Gebäude*) extension; **a**~**en** *vt* (*AGR*) cultivate; (*Gebäudeteil*) build on.

anbehalten ['anbəhaltən] *vt unreg* keep on.

anbei [an'bai] *ad* enclosed.

anbeißen ['anbaisən] *unreg vt* bite into // *vi* (*lit*) bite; (*fig*) swallow the bait; **zum A**~ (*umg*) good enough to eat.

anbelangen ['anbəlaŋən] *vt* concern; **was mich anbelangt** as far as I am concerned.

anbeten ['anbe:tən] *vt* worship.

Anbetracht ['anbətraxt] *m:* **in** ~ (+*gen*) in view of.

anbiedern ['anbi:dərn] *vr* make up (*bei* to).

anbieten ['anbi:tən] *unreg vt* offer // *vr* volunteer.

anbinden ['anbındən] *vt unreg* tie up; **kurz angebunden** (*fig*) curt.

Anblick ['anblık] *m* sight; **a**~**en** *vt* look at.

anbrechen ['anbreçən] *unreg vt* start; (*Vorräte*) break into // *vi* start; (*Tag*) break; (*Nacht*) fall.

anbrennen ['anbrenən] *vi unreg* catch fire; (*KOCH*) burn.

anbringen ['anbrıŋən] *vt unreg* bring; (*Ware*) sell; (*festmachen*) fasten.

Anbruch ['anbrʊx] *m* beginning; ~ **des Tages/der Nacht** dawn/ nightfall.

anbrüllen ['anbrylən] *vt* roar at.

Andacht ['andaxt] *f* **-, -en** devotion; (*Gottesdienst*) prayers *pl.*

andächtig ['andɛçtɪç] *a* devout.

andauern ['andauərn] *vi* last, go on; ~**d** *a* continual.

Anden ['andən] *pl* Andes.

Andenken ['andɛŋkən] *nt* -s, - memory; souvenir.

andere(r, s) ['andərə(r,z)] *a* other; (*verschieden*) different; **ein** ~**s Mal** another time; **kein** ~**r** nobody else; **von etw** ~**m sprechen** talk about sth else; **andererseits** *ad* on the other hand.

ändern ['ɛndərn] *vt* alter, change // *vr* change.

andernfalls ['andərnfals] *ad* otherwise.

anders ['andərs] *ad* differently (*als from*); **wer** ~**?** who else?; **jd/ irgendwo** ~ sb/somewhere else; ~ **aussehen/klingen** look/sound different; ~**artig** *a* different; ~**farbig** *a* of a different colour; ~**herum** *ad* the other way round; ~**wo** *ad* somewhere else; ~**woher** *ad* from somewhere else.

anderthalb ['andərt'halp] *a* one and a half.

Änderung ['ɛndərʊŋ] *f* alteration, change.

anderweitig ['andər'vaɪtɪç] *a* other // *ad* otherwise; (*anderswo*) elsewhere.

andeuten ['andɔytən] *vt* indicate; (*Wink geben*) hint at.

Andeutung *f* indication; hint.

Andrang ['andraŋ] *m* crush.

andrehen ['andre:ən] *vt* turn *od* switch on; (*umg*) **jdm etw** ~ unload sth onto sb.

androhen ['andro:ən] *vt:* **jdm etw** ~ threaten sb with sth.

aneignen ['an'aɪgnən] *vt:* **sich** (*dat*) **etw** ~ acquire sth; (*widerrechtlich*) appropriate sth.

aneinander [an'aɪ'nandər] *ad* at/on/to *etc* one another *od* each other; ~**fügen** *vt* put together; ~**geraten** *vi unreg* clash.

anekeln ['an'e:kəln] *vt* disgust.

Anemone [ane'mo:nə] *f* -, -n anemone.

anerkannt ['an'ɛrkant] *a* recognized, acknowledged.

anerkennen ['an'ɛrkɛnən] *vt unreg* recognize, acknowledge; (*würdigen*) appreciate; ~**d** *a* appreciative; **anerkennenswert** *a* praiseworthy.

Anerkennung *f* recognition, acknowledgement; appreciation.

anfachen ['anfaxən] *vt* (*lit*) fan into flame; (*fig*) kindle.

anfahren ['anfa:rən] *unreg vt* deliver; (*fahren gegen*) hit; (*Hafen*) put into; (*fig*) bawl out // *vi* drive up; (*losfahren*) drive off.

Anfall ['anfal] *m* (*MED*) attack; **a**~**en** *unreg vt* attack; (*fig*) overcome // *vi* (*Arbeit*) come up; (*Produkt*) be ob-

tained.

anfällig ['anfɛlɪç] *a* delicate; ~ **für etw** prone to sth.

Anfang ['anfaŋ] *m* -(e)s, -fänge beginning, start; **von** ~ **an** right from the beginning; **zu** ~ at the beginning; ~ **Mai** at the beginning of May; **a**~**en** *vti unreg* begin, start; (*machen*) do.

Anfänger(in *f*) ['anfɛŋər(ɪn)] *m* -s, - beginner.

anfänglich ['anfɛŋlɪç] *a* initial.

anfangs *ad* at first; **A**~**buchstabe** *m* initial *od* first letter; **A**~**stadium** *nt* initial stages *pl*.

anfassen ['anfasən] *vt* handle; (*berühren*) touch // *vi* lend a hand // *vr* feel.

anfechten ['anfɛçtən] *vt unreg* dispute; (*beunruhigen*) trouble.

anfertigen ['anfɛrtɪgən] *vt* make.

anfeuern ['anfɔyərn] *vt* (*fig*) spur on.

anflehen ['anfle:ən] *vt* implore.

anfliegen ['anfli:gən] *vt unreg* fly to.

Anflug ['anflu:k] *m* (*AVIAT*) approach; (*Spur*) trace.

anfordern ['anfɔrdərn] *vt* demand; (*COMM*) requisition.

Anforderung *f* demand (*gen* for).

Anfrage ['anfra:gə] *f* inquiry; **a**~**n** *vi* inquire.

anfreunden ['anfrɔyndən] *vr* make friends.

anfügen ['anfy:gən] *vt* add; (*beifügen*) enclose.

anfühlen ['anfy:lən] *vtr* feel.

anführen ['anfy:rən] *vt* lead; (*zitieren*) quote; (*umg: betrügen*) lead up the garden path.

Anführer *m* leader.

Anführung *f* leadership; (*Zitat*) quotation; **Anführungszeichen** *pl* quotation marks *pl*, inverted commas *pl*.

Angabe ['anga:bə] *f* statement; (*TECH*) specification; (*umg: Prahlerei*) boasting; (*SPORT*) service; ~**n** *pl* (*Auskunft*) particulars *pl*.

angeben ['ange:bən] *unreg vt* give; (*anzeigen*) inform on; (*bestimmen*) set // *vi* (*umg*) boast; (*SPORT*) serve.

Angeber *m* -s, - (*umg*) show-off; ~**ei** [-'raɪ] *f* (*umg*) showing off.

angeblich ['ange:plɪç] *a* alleged.

angeboren ['angəbo:rən] *a* inborn, innate (*jdm* in sb).

Angebot ['angəbo:t] *nt* offer; (*COMM*) supply (*an* +*dat* of).

angebracht ['angəbraxt] *a* appropriate, in order.

angegriffen ['angəgrɪfən] *a* exhausted.

angeheitert ['angəhaɪtərt] *a* tipsy.

angehen ['ange:ən] *unreg vt* concern; (*angreifen*) attack; (*bitten*) approach (*um* for) // *vi* (*Feuer*) light; (*umg: beginnen*) begin; ~**d** *a* prospective.

angehören ['angəhø:rən] *vi* belong (*dat* to).

Angehörige(r) *mf* relative.
Angeklagte(r) ['angəkla:ktə(r)] *mf* accused.
Angel ['aŋəl] *f* -, -n fishing rod; (*Tür~*) hinge.
Angelegenheit ['angəle:gənhaıt] *f* affair, matter.
Angel- *zW*: **~haken** *m* fish hook; **a~n** *vt* catch // *vi* fish; **~n** *nt* -s angling, fishing; **~rute** *f* fishing rod.
angemessen ['angəmesən] *a* appropriate, suitable.
angenehm ['angəne:m] *a* pleasant; **~!** (*bei Vorstellung*) pleased to meet you.
angenommen ['angənɔmən] *a* assumed; **~, wir …** assuming we …
angesehen ['angəze:ən] *a* respected.
angesichts ['angəzıçts] *präp +gen* in view of, considering.
angespannt ['angəʃpant] *a* (*Aufmerksamkeit*) close; (*Arbeit*) hard.
Angestellte(r) ['angəʃtɛltə(r)] *mf* employee.
angetan ['angəta:n] *a*: **von jdm/etw ~ sein** be impressed by sb/sth; **es jdm ~ haben** appeal to sb.
angewiesen ['angəvi:zən] *a*: **auf jdn/ etw ~ sein** be dependent on sb/sth.
angewöhnen ['angəvø:nən] *vt*: **jdm/ sich etw ~** get sb/become accustomed to sth.
Angewohnheit ['angəvo:nhaıt] *f* habit.
angleichen ['anglaıçən] *vtr unreg* adjust (*dat* to).
Angler ['aŋlər] *m* -s, - angler.
angreifen ['angraıfən] *vt unreg* attack; (*anfassen*) touch; (*Arbeit*) tackle; (*beschädigen*) damage.
Angreifer *m* -s, - attacker.
Angriff ['angrıf] *m* attack; **etw in ~ nehmen** make a start on sth.
Angst [aŋst] *f* -, ⁻e fear; **~ haben** be afraid *od* scared (*vor +dat od*); **~ haben um jdn/etw** be worried about sb/sth; **a~**: **jdm ist a~** sb is afraid *od* scared; **jdm a~ machen** scare sb; **~hase** *m* (*umg*) chicken, scaredy-cat.
ängst- [ɛŋst] *zW*: **~igen** *vt* frighten // *vr* worry (*o.s.*) (*vor +dat, um* about); **~lich** *a* nervous; (*besorgt*) worried; **Ä~lichkeit** *f* nervousness.
anhaben ['anha:bən] *vt unreg* have on; **er kann mir nichts ~** he can't hurt me.
anhalt- ['anhalt] *zW*: **~en** *unreg vt* stop; (*gegen etw halten*) hold up (*jdm* against sb); **jdn zur Arbeit/ Höflichkeit ~en** make sb work/be polite // *vi* stop; (*andauern*) persist; **~end** *a* persistent; **A~er** *m* -s, - hitch-hiker; **per A~er fahren** hitchhike; **Anhaltspunkt** *m* clue.
anhand [an'hant] *präp +gen* with.

Anhang ['anhaŋ] *m* appendix; (*Leute*) family; supporters *pl*.
anhäng- ['anhɛŋ] *zW*: **~en** *vt unreg* hang up; (*Wagen*) couple up; (*Zusatz*) add (on); **A~er** *m* -s, - supporter; (*AUT*) trailer; (*am Koffer*) tag; (*Schmuck*) pendant; **A~erschaft** *f* supporters *pl*; **~lich** *a* devoted; **A~lichkeit** *f* devotion; **A~sel** *nt* -s, - appendage.
Anhäufung ['anhɔyfuŋ] *f* accumulation.
anheben ['anhe:bən] *vt unreg* lift up; (*Preise*) raise.
Anhieb ['anhi:b] *m*: **auf ~** at the very first go; (*kurz entschlossen*) on the spur of the moment.
Anhöhe ['anhø:ə] *f* hill.
anhören ['anhø:rən] *vt* listen to; (*anmerken*) hear // *vr* sound.
animieren [ani'mi:rən] *vt* encourage, urge on.
Anis [a'ni:s] *m* -es, -e aniseed.
Ank. *abk* (= *Ankunft*) arr.
ankaufen ['ankaufən] *vt* purchase, buy.
Anker ['aŋkər] *m* -s, - anchor; **vor ~ gehen** drop anchor; **a~n** *vti* anchor; **~platz** *m* anchorage.
Anklage ['ankla:gə] *f* accusation; (*JUR*) charge; **~bank** *f* dock; **a~n** *vt* accuse; (*JUR*) charge (*gen* with).
Ankläger ['anklɛ:gər] *m* accuser.
Anklang ['anklaŋ] *m*: **bei jdm ~ finden** meet with sb's approval.
Ankleide- ['anklaıdə] *zW*: **~kabine** *f* changing cubicle; **a~n** *vtr* dress.
anklopfen ['anklɔpfən] *vi* knock.
anknüpfen ['anknypfən] *vt* fasten *od* tie on; (*fig*) start // *vi* (*anschließen*) refer (*an +akk* to).
ankommen ['ankɔmən] *vi unreg* arrive; (*näherkommen*) approach; (*Anklang finden*) go down (*bei* with); **es kommt darauf an it** depends; (*wichtig sein*) that (is what) matters; **es darauf ~ lassen** let things take their course; **gegen jdn/etw ~** cope with sb/sth.
ankündigen ['ankyndıgən] *vt* announce.
Ankündigung *f* announcement.
Ankunft ['ankunft] *f* -, -künfte arrival; **Ankunftszeit** *f* time of arrival.
ankurbeln ['ankurbəln] *vt* (*AUT*) crank; (*fig*) boost.
Anlage ['anla:gə] *f* disposition; (*Begabung*) talent; (*Park*) gardens *pl*; (*Beilage*) enclosure; (*TECH*) plant; (*FIN*) investment; (*Entwurf*) layout.
Anlaß ['anlas] *m* -sses, -lässe cause (*zu* for); (*Ereignis*) occasion; **aus ~ (+gen)** on the occasion of; **~ zu etw geben** give rise to sth; **etw zum ~ nehmen** take the opportunity of sth.

anlassen *unreg vt* leave on; (*Motor*) start // *vr* (*umg*) start off.

Anlasser *m* -s, - (*AUT*) starter.

anläßlich ['anlɛslɪç] *präp* +*gen* on the occasion of.

Anlauf ['anlaʊf] *m* run-up; **a~en** *unreg vi* begin; (*Film*) show; (*SPORT*) run up; (*Fenster*) mist up; (*Metall*) tarnish; **rot a~en** colour; **angelaufen kommen** come running up // *vt* call at.

anlegen ['anleːgən] *vt* put (*an* +*akk* against/on); (*anziehen*) put on; (*gestalten*) lay out; (*Geld*) invest; (*Gewehr*) aim (*auf* +*akk* at); **es auf etw** (*akk*) ~ **be out for sth/to do sth; sich mit jdm** ~ (*umg*) quarrel with sb // *vi* dock.

Anlegestelle *f*, landing place.

anlehnen ['anleːnən] *vt* lean (*an* +*akk* against); (*Tür*) leave ajar // *vr* lean (*an* +*akk* on).

anleiten ['anlaɪtən] *vt* instruct.

Anleitung *f* instructions *pl*.

anlernen ['anlɛrnən] *vt* teach, instruct.

anliegen ['anliːgən] *vi unreg* (*Kleidung*) cling; **A~** *nt* -s, - matter; (*Wunsch*) wish; **~d** *a* adjacent; (*beigefügt*) enclosed.

Anlieger *m* -s, - resident; **'~ frei'** 'residents only'.

anlügen ['anlyːgən] *vt unreg* lie to.

anmachen ['anmaxən] *vt* attach; (*Elektrisches*) put on; (*Zigarette*) light; (*Salat*) dress.

anmaßen ['anmaːsən] *vt*: **sich** (*dat*) **etw** ~ (*Recht*) lay claim to sth; **~d** *a* arrogant.

Anmaßung *f* presumption.

anmelden ['anmɛldən] *vt* announce // *vr* (*sich ankündigen*) make an appointment; (*polizeilich, für Kurs etc*) register.

Anmeldung *f* announcement; appointment; registration.

anmerken ['anmɛrkən] *vt* observe; (*anstreichen*) mark; **sich** (*dat*) **nichts** ~ **lassen** not give anything away.

Anmerkung *f* note.

Anmut ['anmuːt] *f* - grace; **a~en** *vt* give a feeling; **a~ig** *a* charming.

annähern ['annɛːərn] *vr* get closer; **~d** *a* approximate.

Annäherung *f* approach; **Annäherungsversuch** *m* advances *pl*.

Annahme ['annaːmə] *f* -, -n acceptance; (*Vermutung*) assumption.

annehm- ['annɛːm] *vt*: **~bar** *a* acceptable; **~en** *unreg vt* accept; (*Namen*) take; (*Kind*) adopt; (*vermuten*) suppose, assume // *vr* take care (*gen* of); **A~lichkeit** *f* comfort.

Annonce [a'nõːsə] *f* -, -n advertisement.

annoncieren [anõ'siːrən] *vti* advertise.

annullieren [anʊ'liːrən] *vt* annul.

anöden ['anˈøːdən] *vt* (*umg*) bore stiff.

anonym [ano'nyːm] *a* anonymous.

Anorak ['anorak] *m* -s, -s anorak.

anordnen ['anˈɔrdnən] *vt* arrange; (*befehlen*) order.

Anordnung *f* arrangement; order.

anpacken ['anpakən] *vt* grasp; (*fig*) tackle; **mit** ~ lend a hand.

anpassen ['anpasən] *vt* fit (*jdm* on sb); (*fig*) adapt (*dat* to) // *vr* adapt.

Anpassung *f* fitting; adaptation; **anpassungsfähig** *a* adaptable.

Anpfiff ['anpfɪf] *m* (*SPORT*) (starting) whistle; kick-off; (*umg*) rocket.

Anprall ['anpral] *m* collision (*gegen, an* +*akk* with).

anprangern ['anpraŋərn] *vt* denounce.

anpreisen ['anpraɪzən] *vt unreg* extol.

Anprobe ['anproːbə] *f* trying on.

anprobieren ['anprobiːrən] *vt* try on.

anrechnen ['anrɛçnən] *vt* charge; (*fig*) count; **jdm etw hoch** ~ value sb's sth greatly.

Anrecht ['anrɛçt] *nt* right (*auf* +*akk* to).

Anrede ['anreːdə] *f* form of address; **a~n** *vt* address; (*belästigen*) accost.

anregen ['anreːgən] *vt* stimulate; **angeregte Unterhaltung** lively discussion; **~d** *a* stimulating.

Anregung *f* stimulation; (*Vorschlag*) suggestion.

anreichern ['anraɪçərn] *vt* enrich.

Anreise ['anraɪzə] *f* journey; **a~n** *vi* arrive.

Anreiz ['anraɪts] *m* incentive.

Anrichte ['anrɪçtə] *f* -, -n sideboard; **a~n** *vt* serve up; **Unheil a~n** make mischief.

anrüchig ['anrʏçɪç] *a* dubious.

anrücken ['anrʏkən] *vi* approach; (*MIL*) advance.

Anruf ['anruːf] *m* call; **a~en** *vt unreg* call out to; (*bitten*) call on; (*TEL*) ring up, phone, call.

ans [ans] = **an das**.

Ansage ['anzaːgə] *f* -, -n announcement; **a~n** *vt* announce // *vr* say one will come; **Ansager(in** *f*) *m* -s, - announcer.

Ansammlung *f* collection; (*Leute*) crowd.

ansässig ['anzɛsɪç] *a* resident.

Ansatz ['anzats] *m* start; (*Haar~*) hairline; (*Hals~*) base; (*Verlängerungsstück*) extension; (*Veranschlagung*) estimate; **~punkt** *m* starting point.

anschaffen ['anʃafən] *vt* buy, purchase.

Anschaffung *f* purchase.

anschalten ['anʃaltən] *vt* switch on.

anschau- ['anʃaʊ] *zW*: **~en** *vt* look at;

~**lich** *a* illustrative; **A~ung** *f* (*Meinung*) view; **aus eigener A~ung** from one's own experience.

Anschein ['anʃaın] *m* appearance; **allem ~ nach** to all appearances; **den ~ haben** seem, appear; **a~end** *a* apparent.

Anschlag ['anʃlɑːk] *m* notice; (*Attentat*) attack; (*COMM*) estimate; (*auf Klavier*) touch; (*Schreibmaschine*) character; **a~en** ['anʃlɑːgən] *unreg vt* put up; (*beschädigen*) chip; (*Akkord*) strike; (*Kosten*) estimate // *vi* hit (*an +akk* against); (*wirken*) have an effect; (*Glocke*) ring; (*Hund*) bark.

anschließen ['anʃliːsən] *unreg vt* connect up; (*Sender*) link up // *vr*: (**sich**) **an etw** (*akk*) ~ adjoin sth; (*zeitlich*) follow sth // *vr* join (*jdm/ etw* sb/sth); (*beipflichten*) agree (*jdm/etw* with sb/sth); ~**d** *a* adjacent; (*zeitlich*) subsequent // *ad* afterwards.

Anschluß ['anʃlus] *m* (*ELEK, EISENB*) connection; (*von Wasser etc*) supply; **im ~ an** (*+akk*) following; **~ finden** make friends.

anschmiegsam ['anʃmiːkzɑːm] *a* affectionate.

anschnallen ['anʃnalən] *vt* buckle on // *vr* fasten one's seat belt.

anschneiden ['anʃnaıdən] *vt unreg* cut into; (*Thema*) introduce.

anschreiben ['anʃraıbən] *vt unreg* write (up); (*COMM*) charge up; (*benachrichtigen*) write to.

anschreien ['anʃraıən] *vt unreg* shout at.

Anschrift ['anʃrıft] *f* address.

Anschuldigung ['anʃuldıguŋ] *f* accusation.

anschwellen ['anʃvɛlən] *vi unreg* swell (up).

anschwemmen ['anʃvɛmən] *vt* wash ashore.

anschwindeln ['anʃvındəln] *vt* lie to.

ansehen ['anzeːən] *vt unreg* look at; **jdm etw ~** see sth (from sb's face); **jdn/etw als etw ~** look on sb/sth as sth; **~ für** consider; **A~** *nt* **-s** respect; (*Ruf*) reputation.

ansehnlich ['anzeːnlıç] *a* fine-looking; (*beträchtlich*) considerable.

ansetzen ['anzɛtsən] *vt* (*anfügen*) fix on (*an +akk* to); (*anlegen, an Mund etc*) put (*an +akk* to); (*festlegen*) fix; (*entwickeln*) develop; (*Fett*) put on; (*Blätter*) grow; (*zubereiten*) prepare // *vi* (*anfangen*) start, begin; (*Entwicklung*) set in; (*dick werden*) put on weight // *vr* (*Rost etc*) start to develop.

Ansicht ['anzıçt] *f* (*Anblick*) sight; (*Meinung*) view, opinion; **zur ~** on approval; **meiner ~ nach** in my opinion; **Ansichtskarte** *f* picture postcard; **Ansichtssache** *f* matter of opinion.

anspannen ['anʃpanən] *vt* harness; (*Muskel*) strain.

Anspannung *f* strain.

Anspiel ['anʃpiːl] *nt* (*SPORT*) start; **a~en** *vi* (*SPORT*) start play; **auf etw** (*akk*) **a~en** refer *od* allude to sth; **~ung** *f* reference, allusion (*auf +akk* to).

Ansporn ['anʃpɔrn] *m* **-(e)s** incentive.

Ansprache ['anʃprɑːxə] *f* address.

ansprechen ['anʃprɛçən] *unreg vt* speak to; (*bitten, gefallen*) appeal to; **jdn auf etw** (*akk*) (**hin**) ~ ask sb about sth // *vi* react (*auf +akk* to); ~**d** *a* attractive.

anspringen ['anʃprıŋən] *unreg vi* (*AUT*) start // *vt* jump at.

Anspruch ['anʃprux] *m* (*Recht*) claim (*auf +akk* to); **hohe Ansprüche stellen/haben** demand/expect a lot; **jdn/etw in ~ nehmen** occupy sb/take up sth; **anspruchslos** *a* undemanding; **anspruchsvoll** *a* demanding.

anstacheln ['anʃtaxəln] *vt* spur on.

Anstalt ['anʃtalt] *f* **-, -en** institution; **~en machen, etw zu tun** prepare to do sth.

Anstand ['anʃtant] *m* decency.

anständig ['anʃtɛndıç] *a* decent; (*umg*) proper; (*groß*) considerable.

anstandslos *ad* without any ado.

anstarren ['anʃtarən] *vt* stare at.

anstatt [an'ʃtat] *präp +gen* instead of // *kj*: ~ **etw zu tun** instead of doing sth.

Ansteck- ['anʃtɛk-] *zW*: **a~en** *vt* pin on; (*MED*) infect; (*Pfeife*) light; (*Haus*) set fire to // *vr*: **ich habe mich bei ihm angesteckt** I caught it from him // *vi* (*fig*) be infectious; **a~end** *a* infectious; **~ung** *f* infection.

anstehen ['anʃteːən] *vi unreg* queue (up) (*Brit*), line up (*US*).

anstelle [an'ʃtɛlə] *präp +gen* in place of; **~n** ['an-] *vt* (*einschalten*) turn on; (*Arbeit geben*) employ; (*machen*) do // *vr* queue (up) (*Brit*), line up (*US*); (*umg*) act.

Anstellung *f* employment; (*Posten*) post, position.

Anstieg ['anʃtiːk] *m* **-(e)s, -e** climb; (*fig: von Preisen etc*) increase (*gen* in).

anstift- ['anʃtıft] *zW*: **~en** *vt* (*Unglück*) cause; **jdn zu etw ~en** put sb up to sth; **A~er** *m* **-s, -** instigator.

anstimmen ['anʃtımən] *vt* (*Lied*) strike up with; (*Geschrei*) set up.

Anstoß ['anʃtoːs] *m* impetus; (*Ärgernis*) offence; (*SPORT*) kick-off; **der erste ~** the initiative; **~ nehmen an** (*+dat*) take offence at; **a~en** *unreg* *vt* push; (*mit Fuß*) kick // *vi* knock, bump; (*mit der Zunge*) lisp; (*mit Gläsern*) drink (a toast) (*auf +akk* to).

anstößig ['anʃtøːsɪç] *a* offensive, indecent; **A~keit** *f* indecency, offensiveness.

anstreichen ['anʃtraɪçən] *vt unreg* paint.

Anstreicher *m* -s, - painter.

anstrengen ['anʃtrɛŋən] *vt* strain; (*JUR*) bring // *vr* make an effort; **angestrengt** *ad* as hard as one can; **~d** *a* tiring.

Anstrengung *f* effort.

Anstrich ['anʃtrɪç] *m* coat of paint.

Ansturm ['anʃturm] *m* rush; (*MIL*) attack.

Antarktis [ant''arktɪs] *f* - Antarctic.

antasten ['antastən] *vt* touch; (*Recht*) infringe upon; (*Ehre*) question.

Anteil ['antaɪl] *m* -s, -e share (*an +dat* in); (*Mitgefühl*) sympathy; **~ nehmen an** (+*dat*) share in; (*sich interessieren*) take an interest in; **~nahme** *f* - sympathy.

Antenne [an'tɛnə] *f* -, -n aerial.

Anti- ['anti] *in zW* anti; **~alko'holiker** *m* teetotaller; **a~autori'tär** *a* anti-authoritarian; **~biotikum** [anti-bi'oːtikʊm] *nt* -s, **-ka** antibiotic.

antik [an'tiːk] *a* antique; **A~e** *f* -, - (*Zeitalter*) ancient world; (*Kunstgegenstand*) antique.

Antilope [anti'loːpə] *f* -, -n antelope.

Antipathie [antipa'tiː] *f* antipathy.

Antiquariat [antikvari'aːt] *nt* -(e)s, -e secondhand bookshop.

Antiquitäten [antikvi'tɛːtən] *pl* antiques *pl*; **~händler** *m* antique dealer.

Antrag ['antraːk] *m* -(e)s, **-träge** proposal; (*PARL*) motion; (*Gesuch*) application.

antreffen ['antrɛfən] *vt unreg* meet.

antreiben ['antraɪbən] *unreg vt* drive on; (*Motor*) drive; (*anschwemmen*) wash up // *vi* be washed up.

antreten ['antreːtən] *unreg vt* (*Amt*) take up; (*Erbschaft*) come into; (*Beweis*) offer; (*Reise*) start, begin // *vi* (*MIL*) fall in; (*SPORT*) line up; **gegen jdn ~** play/fight against sb.

Antrieb ['antriːp] *m* (*lit, fig*) drive; **aus eigenem ~** of one's own accord.

antrinken ['antrɪŋkən] *vt unreg* (*Flasche, Glas*) start to drink from; **sich** (*dat*) **Mut/einen Rausch ~** give oneself Dutch courage/get drunk; **angetrunken sein** be tipsy.

Antritt ['antrɪt] *m* beginning, commencement; (*eines Amts*) taking up.

antun ['antuːn] *vt unreg*: **jdm etw ~** do sth to sb; **sich** (*dat*) **Zwang ~** force o.s.; **sich** (*dat*) **etwas ~** (try to)

take one's own life.

Antwort ['antvɔrt] *f* -, **-en** answer, reply; **a~en** *vi* answer, reply.

anvertrauen ['anfɛrtrauən] *vt*: **jdm etw ~** entrust sb with sth; **sich jdm ~** confide in sb.

anwachsen ['anvaksən] *vi unreg* grow; (*Pflanze*) take root.

Anwalt ['anvalt] *m* -(e)s, **-wälte**, **Anwältin** ['anvɛltɪn] *f* solicitor; lawyer; (*fig*) champion.

Anwärter ['anvɛrtər] *m* candidate.

anweisen ['anvaɪzən] *vt unreg* instruct; (*zuteilen*) assign (*jdm etw* sth to sb).

Anweisung *f* instruction; (*COMM*) remittance; (*Post~, Zahlungs~*) money order.

anwend- ['anvɛnd] *zW*: **~bar** ['anvɛnt-] *a* practicable, applicable; **~en** *vt unreg* use, employ; (*Gesetz, Regel*) apply; **A~ung** *f* use; application.

Anwesen- ['anveːzən] *zW*: **a~d** *a* present; **die ~den** those present; **~heit** *f* presence.

anwidern ['anviːdərn] *vt* disgust.

Anzahl ['antsaːl] *f* number (*an +dat* of); **a~en** *vt* pay on account; **~ung** *f* deposit, payment on account.

Anzeichen ['antsaɪçən] *nt* sign, indication.

Anzeige ['antsaɪgə] *f* -, -n (*Zeitungs~*) announcement; (*Werbung*) advertisement; (*bei Polizei*) report; **~ erstatten gegen jdn** report sb (to the police); **a~n** *vt* (*zu erkennen geben*) show; (*bekanntgeben*) announce; (*bei Polizei*) report; **~r** *m* indicator.

anziehen ['antsiːən] *unreg vt* attract; (*Kleidung*) put on; (*Mensch*) dress; (*Schraube, Seil*) pull tight; (*Knie*) draw up; (*Feuchtigkeit*) absorb // *vr* get dressed; **~d** *a* attractive.

Anziehung *f* (*Reiz*) attraction; **Anziehungskraft** *f* power of attraction; (*PHYS*) force of gravitation.

Anzug ['antsuːk] *m* suit; **im ~ sein** be approaching.

anzüglich ['antsyːklɪç] *a* personal; (*anstößig*) offensive; **A~keit** *f* offensiveness; (*Bemerkung*) personal remark.

anzünden ['antsyndən] *vt* light.

Anzünder *m* lighter.

anzweifeln ['antsvaɪfəln] *vt* doubt.

Apathie [apa'tiː] *f* apathy.

apathisch [a'paːtɪʃ] *a* apathetic.

Apfel ['apfəl] *m* -s, ⁻ apple; **~saft** *m* apple juice; **Apfelsine** [apfəl'ziːnə] *f* -, -n orange; **~wein** *m* cider.

Apostel [a'pɔstəl] *m* -s, - apostle.

Apostroph [apo'stroːf] *m* -s, -e apostrophe.

Apotheke [apo'teːkə] *f* -, -n chemist's

(shop), drugstore (*US*); **Apotheker(in** *f*) *m* -s, - chemist, druggist (*US*).
Apparat [apa'ra:t] *m* -(e)s, -e piece of apparatus; camera; telephone; (*RAD. TV*) set; **am ~!** speaking!; **~ur** [-'tu:r] *f* apparatus.
Appartement [apartə'mã:] *nt* -s, -s flat.
Appell [a'pɛl] *m* -s, -e (*MIL*) muster, parade; (*fig*) appeal; **a~ieren** [ape'li:rən] *vi* appeal (*an* +*akk* to).
Appetit [ape'ti:t] *m* -(e)s, -e appetite; **guten ~** enjoy your meal; **a~lich** *a* appetizing; **~losigkeit** *f* lack of appetite.
Applaus [ap'laus] *m* -es, -e applause.
Aprikose [apri'ko:zə] *f* -, -n apricot.
April [a'prɪl] *m* -(s), -e April.
Aquarell [akva'rɛl] *nt* -s, -e watercolour.
Aquarium [a'kva:rium] *nt* aquarium.
Äquator [ɛ'kva:tɔr] *m* -s equator.
Arab- ['arab] *zW:* **~er(in** *f*) *m* -s, - Arab; **~ien** [a'ra:biən] *nt* -s Arabia; **a~isch** [a'ra:bɪʃ] *a* Arabian.
Arbeit ['arbait] *f* -, -en work (*no art*); (*Stelle*) job; (*Erzeugnis*) piece of work; (*wissenschaftliche*) dissertation; (*Klassen~*) test; **das war eine ~** that was a hard job; **a~en** *vi* work // *vt* work, make; **~er(in** *f*) *m* -s, - worker; (*ungelernt*) labourer; **~erschaft** *f* workers *pl*, labour force; **~geber** *m* -s, - employer; **~nehmer** *m* -s, - employee; **a~sam** *a* industrious.
Arbeits- *in zW* labour; **~amt** *nt* employment exchange; **a~fähig** *a* fit for work; **~gericht** *nt* industrial tribunal; **~gang** *m* operation; **~kräfte** *pl* workers *pl*, labour; **a~los** *a* unemployed, out-of-work; **~losigkeit** *f* unemployment; **~platz** *m* job; place of work; (*Großraumbüro*) workstation; **a~scheu** *a* work-shy; **~tag** *m* work(ing) day; **a~unfähig** *a* unfit for work; **~zeit** *f* working hours *pl*.
Archäologe [arçɛo'lo:gə] *m* -n, -n archaeologist.
Architekt(in *f*) [arçi'tɛkt(ɪn)] *m* -en, -en architect; **~ur** [-'tu:r] *f* architecture.
Archiv [ar'çi:f] *nt* -s, -e archive.
arg [ark] *a* bad, awful // *ad* awfully, very.
Argentin- [argen'ti:n] *zW:* **~ien** *nt* -s Argentina, the Argentine; **~ier(in** *f*) *m* -s, - Argentinian; **a~isch** *a* Argentinian.
Ärger ['ɛrgər] *m* -s (*Wut*) anger; (*Unannehmlichkeit*) trouble; **ä~lich** *a* (*zornig*) angry; (*lästig*) annoying, aggravating; **ä~n** *vt* annoy // *vr* get annoyed; **~nis** *nt* -ses, -se annoyance.

arg- *zW:* **~listig** *a* cunning, insidious; **~los** *a* guileless, innocent; **A~losigkeit** *f* guilelessness, innocence; **Argument** [argu'mɛnt] *nt* argument; **A~wohn** *m* suspicion; **~wöhnisch** *a* suspicious.
Arie ['a:riə] *f* -, -n aria.
Aristokrat [aristo'kra:t] *m* -en, -en aristocrat; **~ie** [-'ti:] *f* aristocracy; **a~isch** *a* aristocratic.
Arktis ['arktɪs] *f* - Arctic.
arm [arm] *a* poor; **A~** *m* -(e)s, -e arm; (*Fluß~*) branch; **Arma'tur** (*ELEK*) armature; **Arma'turenbrett** *nt* instrument panel; (*AUT*) dashboard; **A~band** *nt* bracelet; **A~banduhr** *f* (wrist) watch; **A~e(r)** *mf* poor man/woman; **die A~en** the poor; **Armee** [ar'me:] *f* -, -n army.
Ärmel ['ɛrməl] *m* -s, - sleeve; **etw aus dem ~ schütteln** (*fig*) produce sth just like that; **~kanal** *m* English Channel.
ärmlich ['ɛrmlɪç] *a* poor.
armselig *a* wretched, miserable.
Armut ['armu:t] *f* - poverty.
Aroma [a'ro:ma] *nt* -s, **Aromen** aroma; **aromatisch** [aro'ma:tɪʃ] *a* aromatic.
arrangieren [arã'ʒi:rən] *vt* arrange // *vr* come to an arrangement.
Arrest [a'rɛst] *m* -(e)s, -e detention.
arrogant [aro'gant] *a* arrogant.
Arroganz *f* arrogance.
Arsch [arʃ] *m* -es, ⁻e (*umg*) arse, bum.
Art [a:rt] *f* -, -en (*Weise*) way; (*Sorte*) kind, sort; (*BIOL*) species; **eine ~ (von) Frucht** a kind of fruit; **Häuser aller ~** houses of all kinds; **es ist nicht seine ~, das zu tun** it's not like him to do that; **ich mache das auf meine ~** I do that my (own) way.
Arterie [ar'te:riə] *f* artery; **Arterienverkalkung** *f* arteriosclerosis.
artig ['a:rtɪç] *a* good, well-behaved.
Artikel [ar'ti:kəl] *m* -s, - article.
Artillerie [artɪlə'ri:] *f* artillery.
Arznei [a:rts'nai] *f* medicine; **~mittel** *nt* medicine, medicament.
Arzt [a:rtst] *m* -es, ⁻e, **Ärztin** ['ɛrtstɪn] *f* doctor.
ärztlich ['ɛrtstlɪç] *a* medical.
As [as] *nt* -ses, -se ace.
Asbest [as'bɛst] *m* -(e)s, -e asbestos.
Asche ['aʃə] *f* -, -n ash, cinder; **Aschenbahn** *f* cinder track; **Aschenbecher** *m* ashtray; **Aschermittwoch** *m* Ash Wednesday.
Asi- ['a:zi] *zW:* **~en** *nt* -s Asia; **~at(in** *f*) [azi'a:t(ɪn)] *m* -en, -en Asian; **a~atisch** [-'a:tɪʃ] *a* Asian.
asozial ['azotsia:l] *a* antisocial; (*Familien*) asocial.
Aspekt [as'pɛkt] *m* -(e)s, -e aspect.

Asphalt [as'falt] *m* -(e)s, -e asphalt; **a~ieren** [-'ti:rən] *vt* asphalt.

aß *v siehe* **essen.**

Assistent(in *f)* [asɪs'tɛnt(ɪn)] *m* assistant.

Assoziation [asotsiatsi'o:n] *f* association.

Ast [ast] *m* -(e)s, ¨e bough, branch; **~er** *f* -, -n aster.

ästhetisch [ɛs'te:tɪʃ] *a* aesthetic.

Asthma ['astma] *nt* -s asthma; **~tiker(in** *f)* [ast'ma:tikər(ɪn)] *m* -s, - asthmatic.

Astro- [astro] *zW:* **~'loge** *m* -n, -n astrologer; **~lo'gie** *f* astrology; **~'naut** *m* -en, -en astronaut; **~'nom** *m* -en, -en astronomer; **~no'mie** *f* astronomy.

Asyl [a'zy:l] *nt* -s, -e asylum; (*Heim*) home; (*Obdachlosen~*) shelter.

Atelier [atəli'e:] *nt* -s, -s studio.

Atem ['a:təm] *m* -s breath; **den ~ anhalten** hold one's breath; **außer ~** out of breath; **a~beraubend** *a* breathtaking; **a~los** *a* breathless; **~pause** *f* breather; **~zug** *m* breath.

Atheismus [ate'ɪsmʊs] *m* atheism.

Atheist *m* atheist; **a~isch** *a* atheistic.

Athen [a'te:n] *nt* -s Athens; **A~er(in** *f)* *m* -s, - Athenian; **a~isch** *a* Athenian.

Äther ['ɛ:tər] *m* -s, - ether.

Äthiop- [ɛti'o:p] *zW:* **~ien** *nt* -s Ethiopia; **~ier(in** *f)* *m* -s, - Ethiopian; **ä~isch** *a* Ethiopian.

Athlet [at'le:t] *m* -en, -en athlete.

Atlant- [at'lant] *zW:* **~ik** *m* -s Atlantic (Ocean); **a~isch** *a* Atlantic.

Atlas ['atlas] *m* - *od* -ses, -se *od* **At'lanten** atlas.

atmen ['a:tmən] *vti* breathe.

Atmosphäre [atmo'sfɛ:rə] *f* -, -n atmosphere.

atmosphärisch *a* atmospheric.

Atmung ['a:tmʊŋ] *f* respiration.

Atom [a'to:m] *nt* -s, -e atom; **a~ar** [ato'ma:r] *a* atomic; **~bombe** *f* atom bomb; **~energie** *f* atomic *od* nuclear energy; **~kraftgegner** *m* opponent of nuclear power; **~kraftwerk** *nt* nuclear power station; **~krieg** *m* nuclear *od* atomic war; **~macht** *f* nuclear *od* atomic power; **~müll** *m* atomic waste; **~sperrvertrag** *m* (*POL*) nuclear non-proliferation treaty; **~strom** (electricity generated by) nuclear power; **~versuch** *m* atomic test; **~waffen** *pl* atomic weapons *pl*; **a~waffenfrei** *a* nuclear-free; **~zeitalter** *nt* atomic age.

Attentat ['atənta:t] *nt* -(e)s, -e (attempted) assassination (*auf* +*akk* of).

Attentäter ['atəntɛ:tər] *m* (would-be) assassin.

Attest [a'tɛst] *nt* -(e)s, -e certificate.

attraktiv [atrak'ti:f] *a* attractive.

Attrappe [a'trapə] *f* -, -n dummy.

Attribut [atri'bu:t] *nt* -(e)s, -e (*GRAM*) attribute.

ätzen ['ɛtsən] *vi* be caustic.

au [au] *interj* ouch!; **~ja!** oh yes!

auch [aux] *ad* **1** (*ebenfalls*) also, too, as well; **das ist ~ schön** that's nice too *od* as well; **er kommt — ich ~** he's coming — so am I, me too; **~ nicht** not ... either; **ich ~ nicht** nor I, me neither; **oder ~** or; **~ das noch!** not that as well!

2 (*selbst, sogar*) even; **~ wenn das Wetter schlecht ist** even if the weather is bad; **ohne ~ nur zu fragen** without even asking

3 (*wirklich*) really; **du siehst müde aus — bin ich ~** you look tired — (so) I am; **so sieht es ~ aus** it looks like it too

4 (**~ immer**): **wer ~** whoever; **was ~** whatever; **wie dem ~ sei** be that as it may; **wie sehr er sich ~ bemühte** however much he tried.

auf [auf] ◆*präp* + *dat* (*wo?*) on; **~ dem Tisch** on the table; **~ der Reise** on the way; **~ der Post/dem Fest** at the post office/party; **~ der Straße** on the road; **~ dem Land/der ganzen Welt** in the country/the whole world

◆*präp* +*akk* (*wohin?*) on(to); **~ den Tisch** on(to) the table; **~ die Post gehen** go to the post office; **~ das Land** into the country; **etw ~ einen Zettel schreiben** write sth on a piece of paper

2: **~ deutsch** in German; **~ Lebenszeit** for my/his lifetime; **bis ~ ihn** except for him; **~ einmal** at once; **~ seinen Vorschlag (hin)** at his suggestion

◆*ad* **1** (*offen*) open; **das Fenster ist ~** the window is open

2 (*hinauf*) up; **~ und ab** up and down; **~ und davon** up and away; **~!** (*los!*) come on!

3 (*gestanden*) up; **ist er schon ~?** is he up yet?

◆*kj:* **~ daß** (so) that.

aufatmen ['auf?a:tmən] *vi* heave a sigh of relief.

aufbahren ['aufba:rən] *vt* lay out.

Aufbau ['aufbau] *m* (*Bauen*) building, construction; (*Struktur*) structure; (*aufgebautes Teil*) superstructure; **a~en** *vt* erect, build (up); (*Existenz*) make; (*gestalten*) construct; (*gründen*) found, base (*auf* +*dat* on).

aufbauschen ['aufbauʃən] *vt* puff out; (*fig*) exaggerate.

aufbekommen ['aufbəkɔmən] *vt unreg* (*öffnen*) get open; (*Hausaufgaben*) be given.

aufbessern ['aufbɛsərn] *vt* (*Gehalt*) increase.

aufbewahren ['aʊfbəvaːrən] *vt* keep; (*Gepäck*) put in the left-luggage office.

Aufbewahrung *f* (safe)keeping; (*Gepäck~*) left-luggage office (*Brit*), baggage check (*US*).

aufbieten ['aʊfbiːtən] *vt unreg* (*Kraft*) summon (up), exert; (*Armee, Polizei*) mobilize; (*Brautpaar*) publish the banns of.

aufblasen ['aʊfblaːzən] *unreg vt* blow up, inflate // *vr* (*umg*) become big-headed.

aufbleiben ['aʊfblaɪbən] *vi unreg* (*Laden*) remain open; (*Person*) stay up.

aufblicken ['aʊfblɪkən] *vi* (*lit, fig*) look up (*zu* (*lit*) at, (*fig*) to).

aufblühen ['aʊfblyːən] *vi* blossom, flourish.

aufbrauchen ['aʊfbraʊxən] *vt* use up.

aufbrausen ['aʊfbraʊzən] *vi* (*fig*) flare up; **~d** *a* hot-tempered.

aufbrechen ['aʊfbrɛçən] *unreg vt* break *od* prize (*Brit*) open // *vi* burst open; (*gehen*) start, set off.

aufbringen ['aʊfbrɪŋən] *vt unreg* (*öffnen*) open; (*in Mode*) bring into fashion; (*beschaffen*) procure; (*FIN*) raise; (*ärgern*) irritate; **Verständnis für etw ~** be able to understand sth.

Aufbruch ['aʊfbrʊx] *m* departure.

aufbrühen ['aʊfbryːən] *vt* (*Tee*) make.

aufbürden ['aʊfbʏrdən] *vt* burden (*jdm etw* sb with sth).

aufdecken ['aʊfdɛkən] *vt* uncover.

aufdringlich ['aʊfdrɪŋlɪç] *a* pushy.

aufeinander [aʊfaɪˈnandər] *ad* on top of each other; (*schießen*) at each other; (*vertrauen*) each other; **~folgen** *vi* follow one another; **~folgend** *a* consecutive; **~legen** *vt* lay on top of one another; **~prallen** *vi* hit one another.

Aufenthalt ['aʊfʔɛnthalt] *m* stay; (*Verzögerung*) delay; (*EISENB*: *Halten*) stop; (*Ort*) haunt; **Aufenthaltsgenehmigung** *f* residence permit.

auferlegen ['aʊfʔɛrleːgən] *vt* impose (*jdm etw* sth upon sb).

Auferstehung ['aʊfʔɛrʃteːʊŋ] *f* resurrection.

aufessen ['aʊfʔɛsən] *vt unreg* eat up.

auffahr- ['aʊffaːr] *zW*: **~en** *unreg vi* (*Auto*) run, crash (*auf* +*akk* into); (*herankommen*) draw up; (*hochfahren*) jump up; (*wütend werden*) flare up; (*in den Himmel*) ascend // *vt* (*Kanonen, Geschütz*) bring up; **~end** *a* hot-tempered; **A~t** *f* (*Haus~*) drive; (*Autobahn~*) slip road (*Brit*), (*freeway*) entrance (*US*); **A~unfall** *m* pile-up.

auffallen ['aʊffalən] *vi unreg* be noticeable; **jdm ~** strike sb; **~d** *a* strik-

ing.

auffällig ['aʊffɛlɪç] *a* conspicuous, striking.

auffangen ['aʊffaŋən] *vt unreg* catch; (*Funkspruch*) intercept; (*Preise*) peg.

auffassen ['aʊffasən] *vt* understand, comprehend; (*auslegen*) see, view.

Auffassung *f* (*Meinung*) opinion; (*Auslegung*) view, concept; (*also* **Auffassungsgabe**) grasp.

auffindbar ['aʊffɪntbaːr] *a* to be found.

auffordern ['aʊffɔrdərn] *vt* (*befehlen*) call upon, order; (*bitten*) ask.

Aufforderung *f* (*Befehl*) order; (*Einladung*) invitation.

auffrischen ['aʊffrɪʃən] *vt* freshen up; (*Kenntnisse*) brush up; (*Erinnerungen*) reawaken // *vi* (*Wind*) freshen.

aufführen ['aʊffyːrən] *vt* (*THEAT*) perform; (*in einem Verzeichnis*) list, specify // *vr* (*sich benehmen*) behave.

Aufführung *f* (*THEAT*) performance; (*Liste*) specification.

Aufgabe ['aʊfgaːbə] *f* -, **-n** task; (*SCH*) exercise; (*Haus~*) homework; (*Verzicht*) giving up; (*von Gepäck*) registration; (*von Post*) posting; (*von Inserat*) insertion.

Aufgang ['aʊfgaŋ] *m* ascent; (*Sonnen~*) rise; (*Treppe*) staircase.

aufgeben ['aʊfgeːbən] *unreg vt* (*verzichten*) give up; (*Paket*) send, post; (*Gepäck*) register; (*Bestellung*) give; (*Inserat*) insert; (*Rätsel, Problem*) set // *vi* give up.

Aufgebot ['aʊfgəboːt] *nt* supply; (*Ehe~*) banns *pl*.

aufgedunsen ['aʊfgədʊnzən] *a* swollen, puffed up.

aufgehen ['aʊfgeːən] *vi unreg* (*Sonne, Teig*) rise; (*sich öffnen*) open; (*klar werden*) become clear (*jdm* to sb); (*MATH*) come out exactly; (*sich widmen*) be absorbed (*in* +*dat* in); **in Rauch/Flammen ~** go up in smoke/flames.

aufgelegt ['aʊfgəleːkt] *a*: **gut/ schlecht ~ sein** be in a good/bad mood; **zu etw ~ sein** be in the mood for sth.

aufgeregt ['aʊfgəreːkt] *a* excited.

aufgeschlossen ['aʊfgəʃlɔsən] *a* open, open-minded.

aufgeweckt ['aʊfgəvɛkt] *a* bright, intelligent.

aufgießen ['aʊfgiːsən] *vt unreg* (*Wasser*) pour over; (*Tee*) infuse.

aufgreifen ['aʊfgraɪfən] *vt unreg* (*Thema*) take up; (*Verdächtige*) pick up, seize.

aufgrund [aʊfˈgrʊnt] *präp* +*gen* on the basis of; (*wegen*) because of.

aufhaben ['aʊfhaːbən] *vt unreg* have on; (*Arbeit*) have to do.

aufhalsen ['aʊfhalzən] *vt* (*umg*) **jdm**

etw ~ saddle *od* lumber sb with sth.

aufhalten ['aʊfhaltən] *unreg vt* (*Person*) detain; (*Entwicklung*) check; (*Tür, Hand*) hold open; (*Augen*) keep open // *vr* (*wohnen*) live; (*bleiben*) stay; **sich mit etw ~** waste time over.

aufhängen ['aʊfhɛŋən] *unreg vt* (*Wäsche*) hang up; (*Menschen*) hang // *vr* hang o.s.

Aufhänger *m* **-s, -** (*am Mantel*) hook; (*fig*) peg.

aufheben ['aʊfheːbən] *unreg vt* (*hochheben*) raise, lift; (*Sitzung*) wind up; (*Urteil*) annul; (*Gesetz*) repeal, abolish; (*aufbewahren*) keep; **bei jdm gut aufgehoben sein** be well looked after at sb's // *vr* cancel itself out; **viel A~(s) machen** make a fuss (*von* about).

aufheitern ['aʊfhaɪtərn] *vtr* (*Himmel, Miene*) brighten; (*Mensch*) cheer up.

aufhellen ['aʊfhɛlən] *vtr* clear up; (*Farbe, Haare*) lighten.

aufhetzen ['aʊfhɛtsən] *vt* stir up (*gegen* against).

aufholen ['aʊfhoːlən] *vt* make up // *vi* catch up.

aufhorchen ['aʊfhɔrçən] *vi* prick up one's ears.

aufhören ['aʊfhøːrən] *vi* stop; **~ etw zu tun** stop doing sth.

aufklappen ['aʊfklapən] *vt* open.

aufklären ['aʊfklɛːrən] *vt* (*Geheimnis etc*) clear up; (*Person*) enlighten; (*sexuell*) tell the facts of life to; (*MIL*) reconnoitre // *vr* clear up.

Aufklärung *f* (*von Geheimnis*) clearing up; (*Unterrichtung, Zeitalter*) enlightenment; (*sexuell*) sex education; (*MIL. AVIAT*) reconnaissance.

aufkleben ['aʊfkleːbən] *vt* stick on.

Aufkleber *m* **-s, -** sticker.

aufknöpfen ['aʊfknœpfən] *vt* unbutton.

aufkommen ['aʊfkɔmən] *vi unreg* (*Wind*) come up; (*Zweifel, Gefühl*) arise; (*Mode*) start; **für jdn/etw ~ be** liable *od* responsible for sb/sth.

aufladen ['aʊflaːdən] *vt unreg* load.

Auflage ['aʊflaːgə] *f* edition; (*Zeitung*) circulation; (*Bedingung*) condition; **jdm etw zur ~ machen** make sth a condition for sb.

auflassen ['aʊflasən] *vt unreg* (*offen*) leave open; (*aufgesetzt*) leave on.

auflauern ['aʊflaʊərn] *vi*: **jdm ~** lie in wait for sb.

Auflauf ['aʊflaʊf] *m* (*KOCH*) pudding; (*Menschen~*) crowd.

auflegen ['aʊfleːgən] *vt* put on; (*Telefon*) hang up; (*TYP*) print.

auflehnen ['aʊfleːnən] *vt* lean on // *vr* rebel (*gegen* against).

Auflehnung *f* rebellion.

auflesen ['aʊfleːzən] *vt unreg* pick up.

aufleuchten ['aʊflɔʏçtən] *vi* light up.

auflockern ['aʊflɔkərn] *vt* loosen; (*fig: Eintönigkeit etc*) liven up.

auflösen ['aʊfløːzən] *vtr* dissolve; (*Haare etc*) loosen; (*Mißverständnis*) sort out; (**in Tränen**) **aufgelöst sein** be in tears.

Auflösung *f* dissolving; (*fig*) solution.

aufmachen ['aʊfmaxən] *vt* open; (*Kleidung*) undo; (*zurechtmachen*) do up // *vr* set out.

Aufmachung *f* (*Kleidung*) outfit, get-up; (*Gestaltung*) format.

aufmerksam ['aʊfmɛrkzaːm] *a* attentive; **jdn auf etw** (*akk*) **~ machen** point sth out to sb; **A~keit** *f* attention, attentiveness.

aufmuntern ['aʊfmʊntərn] *vt* (*ermutigen*) encourage; (*erheitern*) cheer up.

Aufnahme ['aʊfnaːmə] *f* **-, -n** reception; (*Beginn*) beginning; (*in Verein etc*) admission; (*in Liste etc*) inclusion; (*Notieren*) taking down; (*PHOT*) shot; (*auf Tonband etc*) recording; **a~fähig** *a* receptive; **~prüfung** *f* entrance test.

aufnehmen ['aʊfneːmən] *vt unreg* receive; (*hochheben*) pick up; (*beginnen*) take up; (*in Verein etc*) admit; (*in Liste etc*) include; (*fassen*) hold; (*notieren*) take down; (*fotografieren*) photograph; (*auf Tonband, Platte*) record; (*FIN: leihen*) take out; **es mit jdm ~ können** be able to compete with sb.

aufopfern ['aʊfʔɔpfərn] *vtr* sacrifice; **~d** *a* selfless.

aufpassen ['aʊfpasən] *vi* (*aufmerksam sein*) pay attention; **auf jdn/etw ~** look after *od* watch sb/sth; **aufgepaßt!** look out!

Aufprall ['aʊfpral] *m* **-s, -e** impact; **a~en** *vi* hit, strike.

Aufpreis ['aʊfpraɪs] *m* extra charge.

aufpumpen ['aʊfpʊmpən] *vt* pump up.

aufraffen ['aʊfrafən] *vr* rouse o.s.

aufräumen ['aʊfrɔʏmən] *vti* (*Dinge*) clear away; (*Zimmer*) tidy up.

aufrecht ['aʊfrɛçt] *a* (*lit, fig*) upright; **~erhalten** *vt unreg* maintain.

aufreg- ['aʊfreːg] *zW*: **~en** *vt* excite // *vr* get excited; **~end** *a* exciting; **A~ung** *f* excitement.

aufreibend ['aʊfraɪbənd] *a* strenuous.

aufreißen ['aʊfraɪsən] *vt unreg* (*Umschlag*) tear open; (*Augen*) open wide; (*Tür*) throw open; (*Straße*) take up.

aufreizen ['aʊfraɪtsən] *vt* incite, stir up; **~d** *a* exciting, stimulating.

aufrichten ['aʊfrɪçtən] *vt* put up, erect; (*moralisch*) console // *vr* rise; (*moralisch*) take heart (*an* +*dat* from).

aufrichtig ['aufrɪçtɪç] a sincere, honest; **A~keit** f sincerity.

aufrücken ['aufrʏkən] vi move up; (beruflich) be promoted.

Aufruf ['aufru:f] m summons; (zur Hilfe) call; (des Namens) calling out; **a~en** vt unreg (auffordern) call upon (zu for); (Namen) call out.

Aufruhr ['aufru:r] m -(e)s, -e uprising, revolt.

aufrührerisch ['aufry:rərɪʃ] a rebellious.

aufrunden ['aufrʊndən] vt (Summe) round up.

Aufrüstung ['aufrʏstʊŋ] f rearmament.

aufrütteln ['aufrʏtəln] vt (lit, fig) shake up.

aufs [aufs] = **auf das**.

aufsagen ['aufza:gən] vt (Gedicht) recite.

aufsammeln ['aufzaməln] vt gather up.

aufsässig ['aufzɛsɪç] a rebellious.

Aufsatz ['aufzats] m (Geschriebenes) essay; (auf Schrank etc) top.

aufsaugen ['aufzaugən] vt unreg soak up.

aufschauen ['aufʃauən] vi look up.

aufscheuchen ['aufʃɔʏçən] vt scare od frighten away.

aufschieben ['aufʃi:bən] vt unreg push open; (verzögern) put off, postpone.

Aufschlag ['aufʃla:k] m (Ärmel~) cuff; (Jacken~) lapel; (Hosen~) turn-up; (Aufprall) impact; (Preis~) surcharge; (Tennis) service; **a~en** [-gən] unreg vt (öffnen) open; (verwunden) cut; (hochschlagen) turn up; (aufbauen: Zelt, Lager) pitch, erect; (Wohnsitz) take up // vi (aufprallen) hit; (teurer werden) go up; (Tennis) serve.

aufschließen ['aufʃli:sən] unreg vt open up, unlock // vi (aufrücken) close up.

Aufschluß ['aufʃlʊs] m information; **a~reich** a informative, illuminating.

aufschnappen ['aufʃnapən] vt (umg) pick up // vi fly open.

aufschneiden ['aufʃnaɪdən] unreg vt (Geschwür) cut open; (Brot) cut up; (MED) lance // vi brag.

Aufschneider m -s, - boaster, braggart.

Aufschnitt ['aufʃnɪt] m (slices of) cold meat.

aufschrecken ['aufʃrɛkən] vt startle // vi unreg start up.

Aufschrei ['aufʃraɪ] m cry; **a~en** vi unreg cry out.

aufschreiben ['aufʃraɪbən] vt unreg write down.

Aufschrift ['aufʃrɪft] f (Inschrift) inscription; (auf Etikett) label.

Aufschub ['aufʃu:p] m -(e)s, -schübe delay, postponement.

Aufschwung ['aufʃvʊŋ] n (Elan) boost; (wirtschaftlich) upturn, boom; (SPORT) circle.

aufsehen ['aufze:ən] vi unreg (lit, fig) look up (zu (lit) at, (fig) to); **A~** nt -s sensation, stir; **~erregend** a sensational.

Aufseher(in f) m -s, - guard; (im Betrieb) supervisor; (Museums~) attendant; (Park~) keeper.

aufsetzen ['aufzɛtsən] vt put on; (Flugzeug) put down; (Dokument) draw up // vr sit upright // vi (Flugzeug) touch down.

Aufsicht ['aufzɪçt] f supervision; **die ~ haben** be in charge.

aufsitzen ['aufzɪtsən] vi unreg (aufrecht hinsitzen) sit up; (aufs Pferd, Motorrad) mount, get on; (Schiff) run aground; **jdm ~** (umg) be taken in by sb.

aufsparen ['aufʃpa:rən] vt save (up).

aufsperren ['aufʃpɛrən] vt unlock; (Mund) open wide.

aufspielen ['aufʃpi:lən] vr show off.

aufspießen ['aufʃpi:sən] vt spear.

aufspringen ['aufʃprɪŋən] vi unreg jump (auf +akk onto); (hochspringen) jump up; (sich öffnen) spring open; (Hände, Lippen) become chapped.

aufspüren ['aufʃpy:rən] vt track down, trace.

aufstacheln ['aufʃtaxəln] vt incite.

Aufstand ['aufʃtant] m insurrection, rebellion.

aufständisch ['aufʃtɛndɪʃ] a rebellious, mutinous.

aufstecken ['aufʃtɛkən] vt stick on, pin up; (umg) give up.

aufstehen ['aufʃte:ən] vi unreg get up; (Tür) be open.

aufsteigen ['aufʃtaɪgən] vi unreg (auf etw) get onto; (hochsteigen) climb; (Rauch) rise.

aufstellen ['aufʃtɛlən] vt (aufrecht stellen) put up; (aufreihen) line up; (nominieren) put up; (formulieren: Programm etc) draw up; (leisten: Rekord) set up.

Aufstellung f (SPORT) line-up; (Liste) list.

Aufstieg ['aufʃti:k] m -(e)s, -e (auf Berg) ascent; (Fortschritt) rise; (beruflich, SPORT) promotion.

aufstoßen ['aufʃto:sən] unreg vt push open // vi belch.

aufstützen ['aufʃtʏtsən] vr lean (auf +akk on) // vt (Körperteil) prop, lean; (Person) prop up.

aufsuchen ['aufzu:xən] vt (besuchen) visit; (konsultieren) consult.

Auftakt ['auftakt] m (MUS) upbeat;

(fig) prelude.

auftanken ['aoftaŋkən] *vi* get petrol *(Brit)* od gas *(US)* // *vt* refuel.

auftauchen ['aoftaoxən] *vi* appear; *(aus Wasser etc)* emerge; *(U-Boot)* surface; *(Zweifel)* arise.

auftauen ['aoftaoən] *vti* thaw; *(fig)* relax.

aufteilen ['aoftailən] *vt* divide up; *(Raum)* partition.

Aufteilung *f* division; partition.

Auftrag ['aoftra:k] *m* -(e)s, -träge order; *(Anweisung)* commission; *(Aufgabe)* mission; **im ~ von** on behalf of; **a~en** [-gən] *vt unreg (Essen)* serve; *(Farbe)* put on; *(Kleidung)* wear out; **jdm etw a~en** tell sb sth; **dick a~en** *(fig)* exaggerate; **~geber** *m* -s, - *(COMM)* purchaser, customer.

auftreiben ['aoftraibən] *vt unreg (umg: beschaffen)* raise.

auftreten ['aoftre:tən] *unreg vt* kick open // *vi* appear; *(mit Füßen)* tread; *(sich verhalten)* behave; **A~** *nt* -s *(Vorkommen)* appearance; *(Benehmen)* behaviour.

Auftrieb ['aoftri:p] *m* (*PHYS*) buoyancy, lift; *(fig)* impetus.

Auftritt ['aoftrɪt] *m (des Schauspielers)* entrance; *(lit, fig: Szene)* scene.

auftun ['aoftu:n] *unreg vt* open // *vr* open up.

aufwachen ['aofvaxən] *vi* wake up.

aufwachsen ['aofvaksən] *vi unreg* grow up.

Aufwand ['aofvant] *m* -(e)s expenditure; *(Kosten auch)* expense; *(Luxus)* show.

aufwärmen ['aofvɛrmən] *vt* warm up; *(alte Geschichten)* rake up.

aufwärts ['aofvɛrts] *ad* upwards; **A~entwicklung** *f* upward trend.

aufwecken ['aofvɛkən] *vt* wake up, waken up.

aufweisen ['aofvaizən] *vt unreg* show.

aufwenden ['aofvɛndən] *vt unreg* expend; *(Geld)* spend; *(Sorgfalt)* devote.

aufwendig *a* costly.

aufwerfen ['aofvɛrfən] *vt unreg (Fenster etc)* throw open; *(Probleme)* throw up, raise.

aufwerten ['aofvɛːrtən] *vt (FIN)* revalue; *(fig)* raise in value.

aufwiegeln ['aofvi:gəln] *vt* stir up, incite.

aufwiegen ['aofvi:gən] *vt unreg* make up for.

Aufwind ['aofvɪnt] *m* up-current.

aufwirbeln ['aofvɪrbəln] *vt* whirl up; **Staub ~** *(fig)* create a stir.

aufwischen ['aofvɪʃən] *vt* wipe up.

aufzählen ['aoftsɛːlən] *vt* list.

aufzeichnen ['aoftsaiçnən] *vt* sketch; *(schriftlich)* jot down; *(auf Band)* re-

cord.

Aufzeichnung *f (schriftlich)* note; *(Tonband~)* recording; *(Film~)* record.

aufzeigen ['aoftsaigən] *vt* show, demonstrate.

aufziehen ['aoftsi:ən] *vt unreg (hochziehen)* raise, draw up; *(öffnen)* pull open; *(Uhr)* wind; *(umg: necken)* tease; *(großziehen: Kinder)* raise, bring up; *(Tiere)* rear.

Aufzug ['aoftsu:k] *m (Fahrstuhl)* lift, elevator; *(Aufmarsch)* procession, parade; *(Kleidung)* get-up; *(THEAT)* act.

aufzwingen ['aoftsvɪŋən] *vt unreg:* **jdm etw ~** force sth upon sb.

Aug- ['aog] *zW:* **~apfel** *m* eyeball; *(fig)* apple of one's eye; **~e** *nt* -s, -n eye; *(Fett~)* globule of fat; **unter vier ~en** in private; **~enblick** *m* moment; **im ~enblick** at the moment; **a~enblicklich** *a (sofort)* instantaneous; *(gegenwärtig)* present; **~enbraue** *f* eyebrow; **~enweide** *f* sight for sore eyes; **~enzeuge** *m* eye witness.

August [ao'gost] *m* -(e)s od -, -e August.

Auktion [aoktsi'o:n] *f* auction.

Aula ['aola] *f* -, **Aulen** od -s assembly hall.

aus [aos] ◆*präp + dat* **1** *(räumlich)* out of; *(von ... her)* from; **er ist ~ Berlin** he's from Berlin; **~ dem Fenster** out of the window

2 *(gemacht/hergestellt ~)* made of; **ein Herz ~ Stein** a heart of stone

3 *(auf Ursache deutend)* out of; **~ Mitleid** out of sympathy; **~ Erfahrung** from experience; **~ Spaß** for fun

4: **~ ihr wird nie etwas** she'll never get anywhere

◆*ad* **1** *(zu Ende)* finished, over; **~ und vorbei** over and done with

2 *(~geschaltet, ~gezogen)* out; *(Aufschrift an Geräten)* off; **Licht ~!** lights out!

3 *(in Verbindung mit von):* **von Rom ~** from Rome; **vom Fenster ~** out of the window; **von sich ~** *(selbständig)* of one's own accord; **von ihm ~** as far as he's concerned.

ausarbeiten ['aos'arbaitən] *vt* work out.

ausarten ['aos'artən] *vi* degenerate; *(Kind)* become overexcited.

ausatmen ['aos'a:tmən] *vi* breathe out.

ausbaden ['aosba:dən] *vt:* **etw ~ müssen** *(umg)* carry the can for sth.

Ausbau ['aosbao] *m* extension, expansion; removal; **a~en** *vt* extend, expand; *(herausnehmen)* take out, remove; **a~fähig** *a (fig)* worth developing.

ausbessern ['ausbɛsərn] vt mend, repair.

ausbeulen ['ausbɔylən] vt beat out.

Ausbeute ['ausbɔytə] f yield; (Fische) catch; a~n vt exploit; (MIN) work.

ausbild- ['ausbild] zW: ~en vt educate; (Lehrling, Soldat) instruct, train; (Fähigkeiten) develop; (Geschmack) cultivate; A~er m -s, - instructor; A~ung f education; training, instruction; development, cultivation.

ausbleiben ['ausblaibən] vi unreg (Personen) stay away, not come; (Ereignisse) fail to happen, not happen.

Ausblick ['ausblik] m (lit, fig) prospect, outlook, view.

ausbrechen ['ausbrɛçən] unreg vi break out; in Tränen/Gelächter ~ burst into tears/out laughing // vt break off.

ausbreiten ['ausbraitən] vt spread (out); (Arme) stretch out // vr spread; (über Thema) expand, enlarge (über +akk on).

ausbrennen ['ausbrɛnən] unreg vt scorch; (Wunde) cauterize // vi burn out.

Ausbruch ['ausbrux] m outbreak; (von Vulkan) eruption; (Gefühls~) outburst; (von Gefangenen) escape.

ausbrüten ['ausbry:tən] vt (lit, fig) hatch.

Ausdauer ['ausdauər] f perseverance, stamina; **ausdauernd** a persevering.

ausdehnen ['ausde:nən] vtr (räumlich) expand; (Gummi) stretch; (Nebel) extend; (zeitlich) stretch; (fig: Macht) extend.

ausdenken ['ausdɛŋkən] vt unreg: sich (dat) etw ~ think sth up.

Ausdruck ['ausdruk] m expression, phrase; (Kundgabe, Gesichts~) expression; (COMPUT) print-out, hard copy; a~en vt (COMPUT) print out.

ausdrücken ['ausdrykən] vt (auch vr: formulieren, zeigen) express; (Zigarette) put out; (Zitrone) squeeze.

ausdrücklich a express, explicit.

ausdrucks- zW: ~los a expressionless, blank; ~voll a expressive; A~weise f mode of expression.

auseinander [aus'ai'nandər] ad (getrennt) apart; ~ schreiben write as separate words; ~bringen vt unreg separate; ~fallen vi unreg fall apart; ~gehen vi unreg (Menschen) separate; (Meinungen) differ; (Gegenstand) fall apart; (umg: dick werden) put on weight; ~halten vt unreg tell apart; ~nehmen vt unreg take to pieces, dismantle; ~setzen vt (erklären) set forth, explain // vr (sich

verständigen) come to terms, settle; (sich befassen) concern o.s.; A~setzung f argument.

auserlesen ['aus'ɛrle:zən] a select, choice.

Ausfahrt ['ausfa:rt] f (des Zuges etc) leaving, departure; (Autobahn~, Garagen~) exit, way out; (Spazierfahrt) drive, excursion.

Ausfall ['ausfal] m loss; (Nichtstattfinden) cancellation; (MIL) sortie; (Fechten) lunge; (radioaktiv) fallout; a~en vi unreg (Zähne, Haare) fall od come out; (nicht stattfinden) be cancelled; (wegbleiben) be omitted; (Person) drop out; (Lohn) be stopped; (nicht funktionieren) break down; (Resultat haben) turn out; a~end a impertinent; ~straße f arterial road.

Ausfertigung ['ausfɛrtigun] f drawing up; making out; (Exemplar) copy.

ausfindig machen ['ausfindiç maxən] vt discover.

ausflippen ['ausflipən] vi (umg) freak out.

Ausflucht ['ausfluxt] f -, -flüchte excuse.

Ausflug ['ausflu:k] m excursion, outing.

Ausflügler ['ausfly:klər] m -s, - tripper.

Ausfluß ['ausflus] m outlet; (MED) discharge.

ausfragen ['ausfra:gən] vt interrogate, question.

ausfressen ['ausfrɛsən] vt unreg eat up; (aushöhlen) corrode; (umg: anstellen) be up to.

Ausfuhr ['ausfu:r] f -, -en export, exportation; in zW export.

ausführ- ['ausfy:r] zW: ~en vt (verwirklichen) carry out; (Person) take out; (Hund) take for a walk; (COMM) export; (erklären) give details of; ~lich a detailed // ad in detail; A~lichkeit f detail; A~ung f execution, performance; (Durchführung) completion; (Herstellungsart) version; (Erklärung) explanation.

ausfüllen ['ausfylən] vt fill up; (Fragebogen etc) fill in; (Beruf) be fulfilling for.

Ausgabe ['ausga:bə] f (Geld) expenditure, outlay; (Aushändigung) giving out; (Gepäck~) left-luggage office; (Buch) edition; (Nummer) issue; (COMPUT) output.

Ausgang ['ausgan] m way out, exit; (Ende) end; (Ausgangspunkt) starting point; (Ergebnis) result; (Ausgehtag) free time, time off; kein ~ no exit.

Ausgangs- zW: ~basis f, ~punkt m starting point; ~sperre f curfew.

ausgeben ['aʊsge:bən] *unreg vt Geld* spend; *(austeilen)* issue, distribute // *vr:* **sich für etw/jdn ~** pass o.s. off as sth/sb.

ausgedient ['aʊsgədi:nt] *a (Soldat)* discharged; *(verbraucht)* no longer in use; **~ haben** have done good service.

ausgefallen ['aʊsgəfalən] *a (ungewöhnlich)* exceptional.

ausgeglichen ['aʊsgəglıçən] *a* (well-) balanced; **A~heit** *f* balance; *(von Mensch)* even-temperedness.

Ausgeh- ['aʊsge:] *zW:* **a~en** *vi unreg* go out; *(zu Ende gehen)* come to an end; *(Benzin)* run out; *(Haare, Zähne)* fall od come out; *(Feuer, Ofen, Licht)* go out; *(Strom)* go off; *(Resultat haben)* turn out; **mir ging das Benzin aus** I ran out of petrol *(Brit) od* gas *(US)*; **auf etw** *(akk)* **a~en** aim at sth; **von etw a~en** *(wegführen)* lead away from sth; *(herrühren)* come from sth; *(zugrunde legen)* proceed from sth; **wir können davon a~en, daß** ... we can take as our starting point that ...; **leer a~en** get nothing; **schlecht a~en** turn out badly; **~verbot** *nt* curfew.

ausgelassen ['aʊsgəlasən] *a* boisterous, high-spirited; **A~heit** *f* boisterousness, high spirits *pl*, exuberance.

ausgelastet ['aʊsgəlastət] *a* fully occupied.

ausgelernt ['aʊsgəlɛrnt] *a* trained, qualified.

ausgemacht ['aʊsgəmaxt] *a (umg)* settled; *(Dummkopf etc)* out-and-out, downright; **es war eine ~e Sache, daß** ... it was a foregone conclusion that ...

ausgenommen ['aʊsgənɔmən] *präp +gen od dat, kj* except; **Anwesende sind ~** present company excepted.

ausgeprägt ['aʊsgəprɛ:kt] *a* prominent.

ausgerechnet ['aʊsgərɛçnət] *ad* just, precisely; **~ du/heute** you of all people/today of all days.

ausgeschlossen ['aʊsgəʃlɔsən] *a (unmöglich)* impossible, out of the question.

ausgeschnitten ['aʊsgəʃnıtən] *a (Kleid)* low-necked.

ausgesprochen ['aʊsgəʃprɔxən] *a (Faulheit, Lüge etc)* out-and-out; *(unverkennbar)* marked // *ad* decidedly.

ausgezeichnet ['aʊsgətsaıçnət] *a* excellent.

ausgiebig ['aʊsgi:bıç] *a (Gebrauch)* thorough, good; *(Essen)* generous, lavish; **~ schlafen** have a good sleep.

Ausgleich ['aʊsglaıç] *m* **-(e)s, -e** balance; *(Vermittlung)* reconciliation; *(SPORT)* equalization; **zum ~** *(+gen)*

in order to offset; **a~en** *unreg vt* balance *(out)*; reconcile; *(Höhe)* even up // *vi (SPORT)* equalize.

ausgraben ['aʊsgra:bən] *vt unreg* dig up; *(Leichen)* exhume; *(fig)* unearth.

Ausgrabung *f* excavation; *(Ausgraben auch)* digging up.

Ausguß ['aʊsgʊs] *m (Spüle)* sink; *(Abfluß)* outlet; *(Tülle)* spout.

aushalten ['aʊshaltən] *unreg vt* bear, stand; *(Geliebte)* keep // *vi* hold out; **das ist nicht zum A~** that is unbearable.

aushandeln ['aʊshandəln] *vt* negotiate.

aushändigen ['aʊshɛndıgən] *vt:* **jdm etw ~** hand sth over to sb.

Aushang ['aʊshaŋ] *m* notice.

aushängen ['aʊshɛŋən] *unreg vt (Meldung)* put up; *(Fenster)* take off its hinges // *vi* be displayed // *vr* hang out.

ausharren ['aʊsharən] *vi* hold out.

ausheben ['aʊshe:bən] *vt unreg (Erde)* lift out; *(Grube)* hollow out; *(Tür)* take off its hinges; *(Diebesnest)* clear out; *(MIL)* enlist.

aushelfen ['aʊshɛlfən] *vi unreg:* **jdm ~** help sb out.

Aushilfe ['aʊshılfə] *f* help, assistance; *(Person)* (temporary) worker.

Aushilfskraft *f* temporary worker.

aushilfsweise *ad* temporarily, as a stopgap.

ausholen ['aʊsho:lən] *vi* swing one's arm back; *(zur Ohrfeige)* raise one's hand; *(beim Gehen)* take long strides; **weit ~** *(fig)* be expansive.

aushorchen ['aʊshɔrçən] *vt* sound out, pump.

aushungern ['aʊshʊŋərn] *vt* starve out.

auskennen ['aʊskɛnən] *vr unreg* know thoroughly; *(an einem Ort)* know one's way about; *(in Fragen etc)* be knowledgeable.

Ausklang ['aʊsklaŋ] *m* end.

auskleiden ['aʊsklaıdən] *vr* undress // *vt (Wand)* line.

ausklingen ['aʊsklıŋən] *vi unreg (Ton, Lied)* die away; *(Fest)* peter out.

ausklopfen ['aʊsklɔpfən] *vt (Teppich)* beat; *(Pfeife)* knock out.

auskochen ['aʊskɔxən] *vt* boil; *(MED)* sterilize; **ausgekocht** *(fig)* out-and-out.

auskommen ['aʊskɔmən] *vi unreg:* **mit jdm ~** get on with sb; **mit etw ~** get by with sth; **A~** *nt* **-s:** **sein A~ haben** get by.

auskosten ['aʊskɔstən] *vt* enjoy to the full.

auskundschaften ['aʊskʊntʃaftən] *vt* spy out; *(Gebiet)* reconnoitre.

Auskunft ['aʊskʊnft] *f* **-, -künfte** information; *(nähere)* details *pl*, particulars *pl*; (*Stelle*) information office; (*TEL*) inquiries.

auslachen ['aʊslaxən] *vt* laugh at, mock.

ausladen ['aʊslɑːdən] *vt unreg* unload; (*umg*: *Gäste*) cancel an invitation to.

Auslage ['aʊslɑːgə] *f* shop window (display); **~n** *pl* outlay, expenditure.

Ausland ['aʊslant] *nt* foreign countries *pl*; im/ins ~ abroad.

Ausländer(in *f*) ['aʊslɛndər(ɪn)] *m* **-s,** - foreigner.

ausländisch *a* foreign.

Auslands- *zW*: **~gespräch** *nt* international call; **~korrespondent(in** *f*) *m* foreign correspondent; **~reise** *f* trip abroad.

auslassen ['aʊslasən] *unreg vt* leave out; (*Wort etc auch*) omit; (*Fett*) melt; (*Kleidungsstück*) let out; (*Wut, Ärger*) vent (*an* +*dat* on) // *vr*: sich über etw (*akk*) ~ speak one's mind about sth.

Auslassung *f* omission.

Auslauf ['aʊslaʊf] *m* (*für Tiere*) run; (*Ausfluß*) outflow, outlet; **a~en** *vi unreg* run out; (*Behälter*) leak; (*NAUT*) put out (to sea); (*langsam aufhören*) run down.

Ausläufer ['aʊslɔyfər] *m* (*von Gebirge*) spur; (*Pflanze*) runner; (*MET*: *von Hoch*) ridge; (*von Tief*) trough.

ausleeren ['aʊsleːrən] *vt* empty.

auslegen ['aʊsleːgən] *vt* (*Waren*) lay out; (*Köder*) put down; (*Geld*) lend; (*bedecken*) cover; (*Text etc*) interpret.

Auslegung *f* interpretation.

Ausleihe ['aʊslaɪə] *f* **-, -n** issuing; (*Stelle*) issue desk; **a~n** *vt unreg* (*verleihen*) lend; sich (*dat*) etw a~en borrow sth.

Auslese ['aʊsleːzə] *f* **-, -n** selection; (*Elite*) elite; (*Wein*) choice wine; **a~n** *vt unreg* select; (*umg*: *zu Ende lesen*) finish.

ausliefern ['aʊsliːfərn] *vt* deliver (up), hand over; (*COMM*) deliver; jdm/etw ausgeliefert sein be at the mercy of sb/sth.

auslöschen ['aʊslœʃən] *vt* extinguish; (*fig*) wipe out, obliterate.

auslosen ['aʊsloːzən] *vt* draw lots for.

auslösen ['aʊsløːzən] *vt* (*Explosion, Schuß*) set off; (*hervorrufen*) cause, produce; (*Gefangene*) ransom; (*Pfand*) redeem.

Auslöser *m* **-s,** - (*PHOT*) release.

ausmachen ['aʊsmaxən] *vt* (*Licht, Radio*) turn off; (*Feuer*) put out; (*entdecken*) make out; (*vereinbaren*) agree; (*beilegen*) settle; (*Anteil darstellen, betragen*) represent; (*bedeuten*) matter; macht es Ihnen etwas aus, wenn ...? would you mind if ...?

ausmalen ['aʊsmɑːlən] *vt* paint; (*fig*) describe; sich (*dat*) etw ~ imagine sth.

Ausmaß ['aʊsmɑːs] *nt* dimension; (*fig auch*) scale.

ausmerzen ['aʊsmɛrtsən] *vt* eliminate.

ausmessen ['aʊsmɛsən] *vt unreg* measure.

Ausnahme ['aʊsnɑːmə] *f* **-, -n** exception; **~fall** *m* exceptional case; **~zustand** *m* state of emergency.

ausnahmslos *ad* without exception.

ausnahmsweise *ad* by way of exception, for once.

ausnehmen ['aʊsneːmən] *unreg vt* take out, remove; (*Tier*) gut; (*Nest*) rob; (*umg*: *Geld abnehmen*) clean out; (*ausschließen*) make an exception of // *vr* look, appear; **~d** *a* exceptional.

ausnützen ['aʊsnytsən] *vt* (*Zeit, Gelegenheit*) use, turn to good account; (*Einfluß*) use; (*Mensch, Gutmütigkeit*) exploit.

auspacken ['aʊspakən] *vt* unpack.

auspfeifen ['aʊspfaɪfən] *vt unreg* hiss/boo at.

ausplaudern ['aʊsplaʊdərn] *vt* (*Geheimnis*) blab.

ausprobieren ['aʊsprobiːrən] *vt* try (out).

Auspuff ['aʊspʊf] *m* **-(e)s, -e** (*TECH*) exhaust; **~rohr** *nt* exhaust (pipe); **~topf** *m* (*AUT*) silencer.

ausradieren ['aʊsradiːrən] *vt* erase, rub out; (*fig*) annihilate.

ausrangieren ['aʊsrãʒiːrən] *vt* (*umg*) chuck out.

ausrauben ['aʊsraʊbən] *vt* rob.

ausräumen ['aʊsrɔymən] *vt* (*Dinge*) clear away; (*Schrank, Zimmer*) empty; (*Bedenken*) put aside.

ausrechnen ['aʊsrɛçnən] *vt* calculate, reckon.

Ausrede ['aʊsreːdə] *f* excuse; **a~n** *vi* have one's say // *vt*: jdm etw a~n talk sb out of sth.

ausreichen ['aʊsraɪçən] *vi* suffice, be enough; **~d** *a* sufficient, adequate; (*SCH*) adequate.

Ausreise ['aʊsraɪzə] *f* departure; bei der ~ when leaving the country; **~erlaubnis** *f* exit visa; **a~n** *vi* leave the country.

ausreißen ['aʊsraɪsən] *unreg vt* tear od pull out // *vi* (*Riß bekommen*) tear; (*umg*) make off, scram.

ausrenken ['aʊsrɛŋkən] *vt* dislocate.

ausrichten ['aʊsrɪçtən] *vt* (*Botschaft*) deliver; (*Gruß*) pass on; (*Hochzeit etc*) arrange; (*erreichen*) get anywhere (*bei* with); (*in gerade Linie bringen*) get in a straight line; (*angleichen*) bring into line; (*TYP*) justify; ich werde es ihm ~ I'll tell him.

ausrotten ['ausrɔtən] *vt* stamp out, exterminate.

ausrücken ['ausrʏkən] *vi* (*MIL*) move off; (*Feuerwehr, Polizei*) be called out; (*umg: weglaufen*) run away.

Ausruf ['ausru:f] *m* (*Schrei*) cry, exclamation; (*Verkünden*) proclamation; **a~en** *vt unreg* cry out, exclaim; call out; **Ausrufezeichen** *nt* exclamation mark.

ausruhen ['ausru:ən] *vtr* rest.

ausrüsten ['ausrʏstən] *vt* equip, fit out.

Ausrüstung *f* equipment.

ausrutschen ['ausrutʃən] *vi* slip.

Aussage ['ausza:gə] *f* -, **-n** (*JUR*) statement; **a~n** *vt* say, state // *vi* (*JUR*) give evidence.

ausschalten ['ausʃaltən] *vt* switch off; (*fig*) eliminate.

Ausschank ['ausʃaŋk] *m* **-(e)s, -schänke** dispensing, giving out; (*COMM*) selling; (*Theke*) bar.

Ausschau ['ausʃau] *f*: **~ halten** look out, watch (*nach* for); **a~en** *vi* look out (*nach* for), be on the look-out.

ausscheiden ['ausʃaidən] *unreg vt* separate; (*MED*) give off, secrete // *vi* leave (*aus etw* sth); (*SPORT*) be eliminated *od* knocked out.

Ausscheidung *f* separation; secretion; (*aus Amt*) retiral; elimination.

ausschimpfen ['ausʃimpfən] *vt* scold, tell off.

ausschlafen ['ausʃla:fən] *unreg vir* have a long lie (in) // *vt* sleep off; **ich bin nicht ausgeschlafen** I didn't have *od* get enough sleep.

Ausschlag ['ausʃla:k] *m* (*MED*) rash; (*Pendel~*) swing; (*Nadel*) deflection; **den ~ geben** (*fig*) tip the balance; **a~en** [-gən] *unreg vt* knock out; (*auskleiden*) deck out; (*verweigern*) decline // *vi* (*Pferd*) kick out; (*BOT*) sprout; **a~gebend** *a* decisive.

ausschließen ['ausʃli:sən] *vt unreg* shut *od* lock out; (*fig*) exclude.

ausschließlich *a, ad* exclusive(ly) // *präp* +*gen* excluding, exclusive of.

Ausschluß ['ausʃlus] *m* exclusion.

ausschmücken ['ausʃmʏkən] *vt* decorate; (*fig*) embellish.

ausschneiden ['ausʃnaidən] *vt unreg* cut out; (*Büsche*) trim.

Ausschnitt ['ausʃnit] *m* (*Teil*) section; (*von Kleid*) neckline; (*Zeitungs~*) cutting; (*aus Film etc*) excerpt.

ausschreiben ['ausʃraibən] *vt unreg* (*ganz schreiben*) write out (in full); (*ausstellen*) write (out); (*Stelle, Wettbewerb etc*) announce, advertise.

Ausschreitung ['ausʃraituŋ] *f* excess.

Ausschuß ['ausʃus] *m* committee, board; (*Abfall*) waste, scraps *pl*; (*COMM: auch ~ware f*) reject.

ausschütten ['ausʃʏtən] *vt* pour out;

(*Eimer*) empty; (*Geld*) pay // *vr* shake (with laughter).

ausschweifend ['ausʃvaifənt] *a* (*Leben*) dissipated, debauched; (*Phantasie*) extravagant.

Ausschweifung *f* excess.

aussehen ['ausze:ən] *vi unreg* look; **es sieht nach Regen aus** it looks like rain; **es sieht schlecht aus** things look bad; **A~** *nt* **-s** appearance.

außen ['ausən] *ad* outside; (*nach ~*) outwards; **~ ist es rot** it's red (on the) outside.

Außen- *zW*: **~bordmotor** *m* outboard motor; **~dienst** *m*: **im ~dienst sein** work outside the office; **~handel** *m* foreign trade; **~minister** *m* foreign minister; **~ministerium** *nt* foreign office; **~politik** *f* foreign policy; **~seite** *f* outside; **~seiter** *m* **-s,** - outsider; **~welt** *f* outside world.

außer ['ausər] *präp* +*dat* (*räumlich*) out of; (*abgesehen von*) except; **~ Gefahr** out of danger; **~ Zweifel** beyond any doubt; **~ Betrieb** out of order; **~ sich** (*dat*) **sein/geraten** be beside o.s.; **~ Dienst** retired; **~ Landes** abroad // *kj* (*ausgenommen*) except; **~ wenn** unless; **~ daß** except; **~dem** *kj* besides, in addition.

äußere(r, s) ['ɔʏsərə(r,z)] *a* outer, external.

außer- *zW*: **~ehelich** *a* extramarital; **~gewöhnlich** *a* unusual; **~halb** *präp* +*gen, ad* outside.

äußerlich *a, ad* external.

äußern ['ɔʏsərn] *vt* utter, express; (*zeigen*) show // *vr* give one's opinion; (*sich zeigen*) show itself.

außer- *zW*: **~ordentlich** *a* extraordinary; **~planmäßig** *a* unscheduled; **~'stande** *ad* not in a position, unable.

äußerst ['ɔʏsərst] *ad* extremely, most; **~e(r, s)** *a* utmost; (*räumlich*) farthest; (*Termin*) last possible; (*Preis*) highest.

aussetzen ['auszɛtsən] *vt* (*Kind, Tier*) abandon; (*Boote*) lower; (*Belohnung*) offer; (*Urteil, Verfahren*) postpone; **jdm/etw ausgesetzt sein** be exposed to sb/sth; **an jdm/etw etwas ~** find fault with sb/sth // *vi* (*aufhören*) stop; (*Pause machen*) drop out.

Aussicht ['ausziçt] *f* view; (*in Zukunft*) prospect; **etw in ~ haben** have sth in view.

Aussichts- *zW*: **a~los** *a* hopeless; **~punkt** *m* viewpoint; **a~reich** *a* promising; **~turm** *m* observation tower.

aussöhnen ['auszø:nən] *vt* reconcile // *vr* reconcile o.s., become reconciled.

Aussöhnung *f* reconciliation.

aussondern ['auszɔndərn] *vt* separate, select.

aussortieren ['auszɔrti:rən] *vt* sort out.

ausspannen ['aʊsʃpanən] vt spread od
stretch out; (Pferd) unharness;
(umg: Mädchen) steal (jdm from sb)
// vi relax.

aussperren ['aʊsʃpɛrən] vt lock out.

Aussperrung f lock-out.

ausspielen ['aʊsʃpiːlən] vt (Karte)
lead; (Geldprämie) offer as a prize;
jdn gegen jdn ~ play sb off against
sb // vi (KARTEN) lead; **ausgespielt
haben** be finished.

Aussprache ['aʊsʃpraːxə] f pronunciation; (Unterredung) (frank) discussion.

aussprechen ['aʊsʃprɛçən] unreg vt
pronounce; (äußern) say, express //
vr (sich äußern) speak (über +akk
about); (sich anvertrauen) unburden
o.s.; (diskutieren) discuss // vi (zu
Ende sprechen) finish speaking.

Ausspruch ['aʊsʃprʊx] m saying, remark.

ausspülen ['aʊsʃpyːlən] vt wash out;
(Mund) rinse.

Ausstand ['aʊsʃtant] m strike; **in den
~ treten** go on strike.

ausstatten ['aʊsʃtatən] vt (Zimmer
etc) furnish; **jdn mit etw ~** equip sb
od kit sb out with sth.

Ausstattung f (Ausstatten) provision;
(Kleidung) outfit; (Aussteuer) dowry;
(Aufmachung) make-up; (Einrich-
tung) furnishing.

ausstechen ['aʊsʃtɛçən] vt unreg
(Augen, Rasen, Graben) dig out;
(Kekse) cut out; (übertreffen) out-
shine.

ausstehen ['aʊsʃteːən] unreg vt stand,
endure // vi (noch nicht dasein) be
outstanding.

aussteigen ['aʊsʃtaɪɡən] vi unreg get
out, alight.

ausstellen ['aʊsʃtɛlən] vt exhibit, dis-
play; (umg: ausschalten) switch off;
(Rechnung etc) make out; (Paß,
Zeugnis) issue.

Ausstellung f exhibition; (FIN) drawing up; (einer Rechnung) making
out; (eines Passes etc) issuing.

aussterben ['aʊsʃtɛrbən] vi unreg die
out.

Aussteuer ['aʊsʃtɔyər] f dowry.

Ausstieg ['aʊsʃtiːk] m -(e)s, -e exit.

ausstopfen ['aʊsʃtɔpfən] vt stuff.

ausstoßen ['aʊsʃtoːsən] vt unreg
(Luft, Rauch) give off, emit; (aus
Verein etc) expel, exclude; (Auge)
poke out.

ausstrahlen ['aʊsʃtraːlən] vti radiate;
(RAD) broadcast.

Ausstrahlung f radiation; (fig) cha-
risma.

ausstrecken ['aʊsʃtrɛkən] vtr stretch
out.

ausstreichen ['aʊsʃtraɪçən] vt unreg

cross out; (glätten) smooth out.

ausströmen ['aʊsʃtrøːmən] vi (Gas)
pour out, escape // vt give off; (fig)
radiate.

aussuchen ['aʊszuːxən] vt select, pick
out.

Austausch ['aʊstaʊʃ] m exchange;
a~bar a exchangeable; **a~en** vt exchange, swop; **~motor** m recondi-
tioned engine.

austeilen ['aʊstaɪlən] vt distribute,
give out.

Auster ['aʊstər] f -, -n oyster.

austoben ['aʊstoːbən] vr (Kind) run
wild; (Erwachsene) sow one's wild
oats.

austragen ['aʊstraːɡən] vt unreg
(Post) deliver; (Streit etc) decide;
(Wettkämpfe) hold.

Austral- [aʊs'traːl] zW: **~ien** nt -s
Australia; **~ier(in** f) m -s, - Australian; **a~isch** a Australian.

austreiben ['aʊstraɪbən] vt unreg
drive out, expel; (Geister) exorcize.

austreten ['aʊstreːtən] unreg vi (zur
Toilette) be excused; **aus etw ~** leave
sth // vt (Feuer) tread out, trample;
(Schuhe) wear out; (Treppe) wear
down.

austrinken ['aʊstrɪŋkən] unreg vt
(Glas) drain; (Getränk) drink up // vi
finish one's drink, drink up.

Austritt ['aʊstrɪt] m emission; (aus
Verein, Partei etc) retirement, withdrawal.

austrocknen ['aʊstrɔknən] vti dry up.

ausüben ['aʊsʔyːbən] vt (Beruf) practise, carry out; (Funktion) perform;
(Einfluß) exert; (Reiz, Wirkung) exercise, have (auf jdn on sb).

Ausverkauf ['aʊsfɛrkaʊf] m sale;
a~en vt sell out; (Geschäft) sell up;
a~t a (Karten, Artikel) sold out;
(THEAT: Haus) full.

Auswahl ['aʊsvaːl] f selection, choice
(an +dat of).

auswählen ['aʊsvɛːlən] vt select,
choose.

Auswander- ['aʊsvandər] zW: **~er** m
emigrant; **a~n** vi emigrate; **~ung** f
emigration.

auswärtig ['aʊsvɛrtɪç] a (nicht am/
vom Ort) out-of-town; (ausländisch)
foreign.

auswärts ['aʊsvɛrts] ad outside; (nach
außen) outwards; **~ essen** eat out;
A~spiel nt away game.

auswechseln ['aʊsvɛksəln] vt change,
substitute.

Ausweg ['aʊsveːk] m way out; **a~los**
a hopeless.

ausweichen ['aʊsvaɪçən] vi unreg:
jdm/etw ~ (lit) move aside od make
way for sb/sth; (fig) side-step sb/sth;
~d a evasive.

ausweinen ['ausvainən] *vr* have a (good) cry.

Ausweis ['ausvais] *m* **-es, -e** identity card, passport; (*Mitglieds~*, *Bibliotheks~ etc*) card; **a~en** [-zən] *unreg vt* expel, banish // *vr* prove one's identity; **~papiere** *pl* identity papers *pl*; **~ung** *f* expulsion.

ausweiten ['ausvaitən] *vt* stretch.

auswendig ['ausvɛndıç] *ad* by heart; **~ lernen** *vt* learn by heart.

auswert- ['ausvɛrt] *zW*: **~en** *vt* evaluate; **A~ung** *f* evaluation, analysis; (*Nutzung*) utilization.

auswirk- ['ausvırk] *zW*: **~en** *vr* have an effect; **A~ung** *f* effect.

auswischen ['ausvıʃən] *vt* wipe out; **jdm eins ~** (*umg*) put one over on sb.

Auswuchs ['ausvu:ks] *m* (out)growth; (*fig*) product.

auswuchten ['ausvuxtən] *vt* (*AUT*) balance.

auszahlen ['austsa:lən] *vt* (*Lohn, Summe*) pay out; (*Arbeiter*) pay off; (*Miterbe*) buy out // *vr* (*sich lohnen*) pay.

auszählen ['austsɛ:lən] *vt* (*Stimmen*) count; (*BOXEN*) count out.

auszeichnen ['austsaıçnən] *vt* honour; (*MIL*) decorate; (*COMM*) price // *vr* distinguish o.s.

Auszeichnung *f* distinction; (*COMM*) pricing; (*Ehrung*) awarding of decoration; (*Ehre*) honour; (*Orden*) decoration; **mit ~** with distinction.

ausziehen ['austsi:ən] *unreg vt* (*Kleidung*) take off; (*Haare, Zähne, Tisch etc*) pull out; (*nachmalen*) trace // *vr* undress // *vi* (*aufbrechen*) leave; (*aus Wohnung*) move out.

Auszug ['austsu:k] *m* (*aus Wohnung*) removal; (*aus Buch etc*) extract; (*Konto~*) statement; (*Ausmarsch*) departure.

Auto ['auto] *nt* **-s, -s** (motor-) car; **~ fahren** drive; **~bahn** *f* motorway; **~bahndreieck** *nt* motorway junction; **~bahnkreuz** *nt* motorway intersection; **~fähre** *f* car ferry; **~fahrer(in** *f*) *m* motorist, driver; **~fahrt** *f* drive; **autogen** [-'ge:n] *a* autogenous; **~'gramm** *nt* autograph; **Auto'mat** *m* **-en, -en** machine; **auto'matisch** *a* automatic; **autonom** [-'no:m] *a* autonomous.

Autor ['autɔr] *m* **-s, -en, Autorin** [au'to:rin] *f* author.

Auto- *zW*: **~radio** *nt* car radio; **~reifen** *m* car tyre; **~rennen** *nt* motor racing.

autoritär [autori'tɛ:r] *a* authoritarian.

Autorität *f* authority.

Auto- *zW*: **~stopp** *m*: **per ~stopp fahren** hitch-hike; **~unfall** *m* car *od* motor accident; **~verleih** *m* car hire

(*Brit*) *od* rental (*US*); **~wäsche** *f* car wash.

Axt [akst] *f* **-, ⁻e** axe.

B

B, b [be:] *nt* B, b.

Baby ['be:bi] *nt* **-s, -s** baby; **~ausstattung** *f* layette; **~sitter** ['be:bizitər] *m* **-s, -** baby-sitter.

Bach [bax] *m* **-(e)s, ⁻e** stream, brook.

Back- [bak] *zW*: **~bord** *nt* **-(e)s, -e** (*NAUT*) port; **~e** *f* **-, -n** cheek; **b~en** *vti unreg* bake; **~enbart** *m* sideboards *pl*; **~enzahn** *m* molar.

Bäcker ['bɛkər] *m* **-s, -** baker; **~ei** [-'raı] *f* bakery; (*~laden*) baker's (shop).

Back- *zW*: **~obst** *nt* dried fruit; **~ofen** *m* oven; **~pflaume** *f* prune; **~pulver** *nt* baking powder; **~stein** *m* brick.

Bad [ba:t] *nt* **-(e)s, ⁻er** bath; (*Schwimmen*) bathe; (*Ort*) spa.

Bade- ['ba:də] *zW*: **~anstalt** *f* (swimming) baths *pl*; **~anzug** *m* bathing suit; **~hose** *f* bathing *od* swimming trunks *pl*; **~kappe** *f* bathing cap; **~mantel** *m* bath(ing) robe; **~meister** *m* baths attendant; **~mütze** *f* bathing cap; **b~n** *vi* bathe, have a bath // *vt* bath; **~ort** *m* spa; **~tuch** *nt* bath towel; **~wanne** *f* bath (tub); **~zimmer** *nt* bathroom.

Bagatelle [baga'tɛlə] *f* **-, -n** trifle.

Bagger ['bagər] *m* **-s, -** excavator; (*NAUT*) dredger; **b~n** *vti* excavate; (*NAUT*) dredge.

Bahn [ba:n] *f* **-, -en** railway, railroad (*US*); (*Weg*) road, way; (*Spur*) lane; (*Renn~*) track; (*ASTRON*) orbit; (*Stoff~*) length; **b~brechend** *a* pioneering; **~damm** *m* railway embankment; **b~en** *vt*: **sich/jdm einen Weg b~en** clear a way/a way for sb; **~fahrt** *f* railway journey; **~hof** *m* station; **auf dem ~hof** at the station; **~hofsvorsteher** *m* station-master; **~linie** *f* (railway) line; **~steig** *m* platform; **~steigkarte** *f* platform ticket; **~strecke** *f* (railway) line; **~übergang** *m* level crossing, grade crossing (*US*); **~wärter** *m* signalman.

Bahre ['ba:rə] *f* **-, -n** stretcher.

Bajonett [bajo'nɛt] *nt* **-(e)s, -e** bayonet.

Bakterien [bak'te:riən] *pl* bacteria *pl*.

Balance [ba'lã:sə] *f* **-, -n** balance, equilibrium.

balan'cieren *vti* balance.

bald [balt] *ad* (*zeitlich*) soon; (*beinahe*) almost; **~ig** ['baldıç] *a* early, speedy; **~möglichst** *ad* as soon as possible.

Baldrian ['baldriaːn] *m* -s, -e valerian.

Balkan ['balkaːn] *m*: der ~ the Balkans *pl*.

Balken ['balkən] *m* -s, - beam; (*Trag~*) girder; (*Stütz~*) prop.

Balkon [bal'kõː] *m* -s, -s *od* -e balcony; (*THEAT*) (dress) circle.

Ball [bal] *m* -(e)s, ⁻s ball; (*Tanz*) dance, ball.

Ballade [ba'laːdə] *f* -, -n ballad.

Ballast ['balast] *m* -(e)s, -e ballast; (*fig*) weight, burden.

Ballen ['balən] *m* -s, - bale; (*ANAT*) ball; **b~** *vt* (*formen*) make into a ball; (*Faust*) clench // *vr* build up; (*Menschen*) gather.

Ballett [ba'lɛt] *nt* -(e)s, -e ballet.

Ballkleid *nt* evening dress.

Ballon [ba'lõː] *m* -s, -s *od* -e balloon.

Ballspiel *nt* ball game.

Bambus ['bambus] *m* -ses, -se bamboo; **~rohr** *nt* bamboo cane.

banal [ba'naːl] *a* banal.

Banane [ba'naːnə] *f* -, -n banana.

band *etc v siehe* **binden.**

Band [bant] *m* -(e)s, ⁻e (*Buch~*) volume // *nt* -(e)s, ⁻er (*Stoff~*) ribbon, tape; (*Fließ~*) production line; (*Faß~*) hoop; (*Ton~*) tape; (*ANAT*) ligament; etw auf ~ aufnehmen tape sth; am laufenden ~ (*umg*) non-stop // nt -(e)s, -e (*Freundschafts~ etc*) bond // [bɛnt] *f* -, -s band, group.

Bandage [ban'daːʒə] *f* -, -n bandage.

banda'gieren *vt* bandage.

Bande ['bandə] *f* -, -n band; (*Straßen~*) gang.

bändigen ['bɛndɪgən] *vt* (*Tier*) tame; (*Trieb, Leidenschaft*) control, restrain.

Bandit [ban'diːt] *m* -en, -en bandit.

Band- *zW*: **~maß** *nt* tape measure; **~scheibe** *f* (*ANAT*) disc; **~wurm** *m* tapeworm.

bange ['baŋə] *a* scared; (*besorgt*) anxious; jdm wird es ~ sb is becoming scared; jdm ~ machen scare sb; **~n** *vi*: um jdn/etw ~n be anxious *od* worried about sth/sb.

Banjo ['banjo, 'bɛndʒo] *nt* -s, -s banjo.

Bank [baŋk] *f* -, ⁻e (*Sitz~*) bench; (*Sand~ etc*) (sand)bank *od* -bar // *f* -, -en (*Geld~*) bank; **~anweisung** *f* banker's order; **~beamte(r)** *m* bank clerk.

Bankett [baŋ'kɛt] *nt* -(e)s, -e (*Essen*) banquet; (*Straßenrand*) verge (*Brit*), shoulder (*US*).

Bankier [baŋki'eː] *m* -s, -s banker.

Bank- *zW*: **~konto** *nt* bank account; **~note** *f* banknote; **~raub** *m* bank robbery.

Bankrott [baŋ'krɔt] *m* -(e)s, -e bankruptcy; ~ machen go bankrupt; **b~** *a*

bankrupt.

Bann [ban] *m* -(e)s, -e (*HIST*) ban; (*Kirchen~*) excommunication; (*fig*: *Zauber*) spell; **b~en** *vt* (*Geister*) exorcise; (*Gefahr*) avert; (*bezaubern*) enchant; (*HIST*) banish; **~er** *nt* -s, - banner, flag.

bar [baːr] *a* (*unbedeckt*) bare; (*frei von*) lacking (*gen* in); (*offenkundig*) utter, sheer; ~e(s) Geld cash; etw (in) ~ bezahlen pay sth (in) cash; etw für ~e Münze nehmen (*fig*) take sth at its face value; **B~** *f* -, -s bar.

Bär [bɛːr] *m* -en, -en bear.

Baracke [ba'rakə] *f* -, -n hut, barracks.

barbarisch [bar'baːrɪʃ] *a* barbaric, barbarous.

Bar- *zW*: **b~fuß** *a* barefoot; **~geld** *nt* cash, ready money; **b~geldlos** *a* non-cash; **~hocker** *m* bar stool; **~kauf** *m* cash purchase; **~keeper** ['baːrkiːpər] *m* -s, - barman, bartender.

barmherzig [barm'hɛrtsɪç] *a* merciful, compassionate; **B~keit** *f* mercy, compassion.

Barometer [baro'meːtər] *nt* -s, - barometer.

Baron [ba'roːn] *m* -s, -e baron; **~esse** [baro'nɛsə] *f* -, -n, ~in *f* baroness.

Barren ['barən] *m* -s, - parallel bars *pl*; (*Gold~*) ingot.

Barriere [bari'eːrə] *f* -, -n barrier.

Barrikade [bari'kaːdə] *f* -, -n barricade.

Barsch [barʃ] *m* -(e)s, -e perch; **b~** *a* brusque, gruff.

Bar- *zW*: **~schaft** *f* ready money; **~scheck** *m* open *od* uncrossed cheque (*Brit*), open check (*US*).

Bart [baːrt] *m* -(e)s, ⁻e beard; (*Schlüssel~*) bit.

bärtig ['bɛːrtɪç] *a* bearded.

Barzahlung *f* cash payment.

Base ['baːzə] *f* -, -n (*CHEM*) base; (*Kusine*) cousin.

Basel ['baːzəl] *nt* Basle.

BASIC ['beːsik] (*COMPUT*) BASIC.

basieren [ba'ziːrən] *vt* base // *vi* be based.

Basis ['baːzɪs] *f* -, Basen basis.

Baß [bas] *m* Basses, Bässe bass; **~stimme** *f* bass voice.

Bassin [ba'sɛ̃ː] *nt* -s, -s pool.

Bassist [ba'sɪst] *m* bass.

Bast [bast] *m* -(e)s, -e raffia.

basteln *vt* make // *vi* do handicrafts.

bat *etc v siehe* **bitten.**

Bataillon [batal'joːn] *nt* -s, -e battalion.

Batist [ba'tɪst] *m* -(e)s, -e batiste.

Batterie [batə'riː] *f* battery.

Bau [bau] *m* -(e)s (*Bauen*) building, construction; (*Aufbau*) structure; (*Körper~*) frame; (*Baustelle*) building site; pl ~e (Tier~) hole, burrow; (MIN) working(s); pl ~ten (Gebäude) building; **sich im ~ befinden** be under construction; ~arbeiter m building worker.

Bauch [baʊx] m -(e)s, **Bäuche** belly; (ANAT auch) stomach, abdomen; ~fell nt peritoneum; **b~ig** a bulging; ~redner m ventriloquist; ~tanz m belly dance; belly dancing; ~schmerzen pl, ~weh nt stomachache.

bauen ['baʊən] vti build; (TECH) construct; **auf jdn/etw ~** depend od count upon sb/sth.

Bauer ['baʊər] m -n od -s, -n farmer; (Schach) pawn // nt od m -s, - (Vogel~) cage.

Bäuerin ['bɔʏərɪn] f farmer; (Frau des Bauers) farmer's wife.

bäuerlich a rustic.

Bauern- zW: ~fänge'rei f deception; ~haus nt farmhouse; ~hof m farm(yard).

Bau- zW: **b~fällig** a dilapidated; ~fälligkeit f dilapidation; ~gelände nt building site; ~genehmigung f building permit; ~herr m purchaser; ~kasten m box of bricks; ~kosten pl construction costs pl; ~land nt building land; **b~lich** a structural.

Baum [baʊm] m -(e)s, **Bäume** tree.

baumeln ['baʊməln] vi dangle.

bäumen ['bɔʏmən] vr rear (up).

Baum- zW: ~schule f nursery; ~stamm m tree trunk; ~stumpf m tree stump; ~wolle f cotton.

Bau- zW: ~plan m architect's plan; ~platz m building site; ~sparkasse f building society; ~stein m building stone, freestone; ~stelle f building site; ~teil nt prefabricated part (of building); ~unternehmer m contractor, builder; ~weise f (method of) construction; ~werk nt building; ~zaun m hoarding.

Bayer(in f) ['baɪər(ɪn)] m Bavarian.

Bayern ['baɪərn] nt Bavaria.

bayrisch ['baɪrɪʃ] a Bavarian.

Bazillus [ba'tsɪlʊs] m -, **Bazillen** bacillus.

beabsichtigen [bə'apzɪçtɪgən] vt intend.

beachten [bə''axtən] vt take note of; (Vorschrift) obey; (Vorfahrt) observe.

beachtlich a considerable.

Beachtung f notice, attention, observation.

Beamte(r) [bə''amtə(r)] m -n, -n, **Beamtin** f official, civil servant; (Bank~ etc) employee.

beängstigend [bə''ɛŋstɪgənt] a alarming.

beanspruchen [bə''anʃprʊxən] vt

claim; (Zeit, Platz) take up, occupy; (Mensch) take up sb's time.

beanstanden [bə''anʃtandən] vt complain about, object to.

Beanstandung f complaint.

beantragen [bə''antra:gən] vt apply for, ask for.

beantworten [bə''antvɔrtən] vt answer.

Beantwortung f reply (gen to).

bearbeiten [bə''arbaɪtən] vt work; (Material) process; (Thema) deal with; (Land) cultivate; (CHEM) treat; (Buch) revise; (umg: beeinflussen wollen) work on.

Bearbeitung f processing; treatment; cultivation; revision.

Beatmung [bə''a:tmʊŋ] f respiration.

beaufsichtigen [bə''aʊfzɪçtɪgən] vt supervise.

Beaufsichtigung f supervision.

beauftragen [bə''aʊftra:gən] vt instruct; **jdn mit etw ~** entrust sb with sth.

bebauen [bə'baʊən] vt build on; (AGR) cultivate.

beben ['be:bən] vi tremble, shake; **B~** nt -s, - earthquake.

Becher ['bɛçər] m -s, - mug; (ohne Henkel) tumbler.

Becken ['bɛkən] nt -s, - basin; (MUS) cymbal; (ANAT) pelvis.

bedacht [bə'daxt] a thoughtful, careful; **auf etw** (akk) ~ **sein** be concerned about sth.

bedächtig [bə'dɛçtɪç] a (umsichtig) thoughtful, reflective; (langsam) slow, deliberate.

bedanken [bə'daŋkən] vr say thank you (bei jdm to sb).

Bedarf [bə'darf] m -(e)s need, requirement; (COMM) demand; supply; **je nach ~** according to demand; **bei ~** if necessary; ~ **an etw** (dat) **haben** be in need of sth.

Bedarfs- zW: ~artikel m requisite; ~fall m case of need; ~haltestelle f request stop.

bedauerlich [bə'daʊərlɪç] a regrettable.

bedauern [bə'daʊərn] vt be sorry for; (bemitleiden) pity; **B~** nt -s regret; **bedauernswert** a (Zustände) regrettable; (Mensch) pitiable, unfortunate.

bedecken [bə'dɛkən] vt cover.

bedeckt a covered; (Himmel) overcast.

bedenken [bə'dɛŋkən] vt unreg think (over), consider; **B~** nt -s, - (Überlegen) consideration; (Zweifel) doubt; (Skrupel) scruple.

bedenklich a doubtful; (bedrohlich) dangerous, risky.

bedeuten [bə'dɔʏtən] vt mean; signify; (wichtig sein) be of importance; **~d** *a* important; (*beträchtlich*) considerable.

Bedeutung *f* meaning; significance; (*Wichtigkeit*) importance; **bedeutungslos** *a* insignificant, unimportant; **bedeutungsvoll** *a* momentous, significant.

bedienen [bə'di:nən] *vt* serve; (*Maschine*) work, operate // *vr* (*beim Essen*) help o.s.; (*gebrauchen*) make use (*gen* of).

Bedienung *f* service; (*Kellnerin*) waitress; (*Verkäuferin*) shop assistant; (*Zuschlag*) service (charge).

Bedingung *f* condition; (*Voraussetzung*) stipulation; **bedingungslos** *a* unconditional.

bedrängen [bə'drɛŋən] *vt* pester, harass.

bedrohen [bə'dro:ən] *vt* threaten.
bedrohlich *a* ominous, threatening.
Bedrohung *f* threat, menace.
bedrücken [bədrʏkən] *vt* oppress, trouble.

bedürf- [bə'dʏrf] *zW:* **~en** *vi unreg* +*gen* need, require; **B~nis** *nt* -ses, -se need; **B~nisanstalt** *f* public convenience, comfort station (*US*); **~tig** *a* in need (*gen* of), poor, needy.

beeilen [bə''aılən] *vr* hurry.
beeindrucken [bə''aındrʊkən] *vt* impress, make an impression on.

beeinflussen [bə''aınflʊsən] *vt* influence.

beeinträchtigen [bə''aıntrɛçtıgən] *vt* affect adversely; (*Freiheit*) infringe upon.

beend(ig)en [bə''ɛnd(ıg)ən] *vt* end, finish, terminate.

beengen [bə''ɛŋən] *vt* cramp; (*fig*) hamper, oppress.

beerben [bə''ɛrbən] *vt* inherit from.
beerdigen [bə''e:rdıgən] *vt* bury.
Beerdigung *f* funeral, burial; **Beerdigungsunternehmer** *m* undertaker.

Beere ['be:rə] *f* -, -n berry; (*Trauben~*) grape.

Beet [be:t] *nt* -(e)s, -e bed.
befähigen [bə'fɛ:ıgən] *vt* enable.
befähigt *a* (*begabt*) talented; (*fähig*) capable (*für* of).

Befähigung *f* capability; (*Begabung*) talent, aptitude.

befahrbar [bə'fa:rba:r] *a* passable; (*NAUT*) navigable.

befahren [bə'fa:rən] *vt unreg* use, drive over; (*NAUT*) navigate // *a* used.

befallen [bə'falən] *vt unreg* come over.

befangen [bə'faŋən] *a* (*schüchtern*) shy, self-conscious; (*voreingenommen*) biased; **B~heit** *f* shyness; bias.

befassen [bə'fasən] *vr* concern o.s.

Befehl [bə'fe:l] *m* -(e)s, -e command, order; **b~en** *vt unreg vt* order; **jdm etw b~en** order sb to do sth // *vi* give orders; **Befehlshaber** *m* -s, - commanding officer; **Befehlsverweigerung** *f* insubordination.

befestigen [bə'fɛstıgən] *vt* fasten (*an* +*dat* to); (*stärken*) strengthen; (*MIL*) fortify.

Befestigung *f* fastening; strengthening; (*MIL*) fortification.

befeuchten [bə'fɔʏçtən] *vt* damp(en), moisten.

befinden [bə'fındən] *unreg vr* be; (*sich fühlen*) feel // *vt:* **jdn/etw für** *od* **als etw ~** deem sb/sth to be sth // *vi* decide (*über* +*akk* on), adjudicate; **B~** *nt* -s health, condition; (*Meinung*) view, opinion.

befolgen [bə'fɔlgən] *vt* comply with, follow.

befördern [bə'fœrdərn] *vt* (*senden*) transport, send; (*beruflich*) promote.

Beförderung *f* transport, conveyance; promotion.

befragen [bə'fra:gən] *vt* question.
befreien [bə'fraıən] *vt* set free; (*erlassen*) exempt.

Befreier *m* -s, - liberator.
Befreiung *f* liberation, release; (*Erlassen*) exemption.

befremden [bə'frɛmdən] *vt* surprise, disturb; **B~** *nt* -s surprise, astonishment.

befreunden [bə'frɔʏndən] *vr* make friends; (*mit Idee etc*) acquaint o.s.

befreundet *a* friendly.
befriedigen [bə'fri:dıgən] *vt* satisfy; **~d** *a* satisfactory.

Befriedigung *f* satisfaction, gratification.

befristet [bə'frıstət] *a* limited.
befruchten [bə'frʊxtən] *vt* fertilize; (*fig*) stimulate.

Befruchtung *f:* **künstliche ~** artificial insemination.

Befugnis [bə'fu:knıs] *f* -, -se authorization, powers *pl*.

befugt *a* authorized, entitled.
Befund [bə'fʊnt] *m* -(e)s, -e findings *pl*; (*MED*) diagnosis.

befürchten [bə'fʏrçtən] *vt* fear.
Befürchtung *f* fear, apprehension.
befürwort- [bə'fy:rvɔrt] *zW:* **~en** *vt* support, speak in favour of; **B~er** *m* -s, - supporter, advocate.

begabt [bə'ga:pt] *a* gifted.
Begabung [bə'ga:bʊŋ] *f* talent, gift.
begann *etc vt siehe* **beginnen**.
begeben [bə'ge:bən] *vr unreg* (*gehen*) proceed (*zu, nach* to); (*geschehen*) occur; **B~heit** *f* occurrence.

begegnen [bə'ge:gnən] *vi* meet (*jdm* sb); meet with (*etw* (*dat*) sth); (*behandeln*) treat (*jdm* sb).

Begegnung f meeting.

begehen [bə'ge:ən] vt unreg (Straftat) commit; (abschreiten) cover; (Straße etc) use, negotiate; (Feier) celebrate.

begehren [bə'ge:rən] vt desire; **begehrenswert** a desirable.

begehrt a in demand; (Junggeselle) eligible.

begeistern [bə'gaɪstərn] vt fill with enthusiasm, inspire // vr: **sich für etw ~** get enthusiastic about sth.

begeistert a enthusiastic.

Begeisterung f enthusiasm.

Begierde [bə'gi:rdə] f -, -n desire, passion.

begierig [bə'gi:rɪç] a eager, keen.

begießen [bə'gi:sən] vt unreg water; (mit Alkohol) drink to.

Beginn [bə'gɪn] m -(e)s beginning; **zu ~** at the beginning; **b~en** vti unreg start, begin.

beglaubigen [bə'glaubɪgən] vt countersign.

Beglaubigung f countersignature.

begleichen [bə'glaɪçən] vt unreg settle, pay.

Begleit- [bə'glaɪt] zW: **b~en** vt accompany; (MIL) escort; **~er** m -s, - companion; (Freund) escort; (MUS) accompanist; **~erscheinung** f concomitant (occurrence); **~schreiben** nt covering letter; **~umstände** pl concomitant circumstances pl; **~ung** f company; (MIL) escort; (MUS) accompaniment.

beglücken [bə'glʏkən] vt make happy, delight.

beglückwünschen [bə'glʏkvʏnʃən] vt congratulate (zu on).

begnadigen [bə'gna:dɪgən] vt pardon.

Begnadigung f pardon, amnesty.

begnügen [bə'gny:gən] vr be satisfied, content o.s.

Begonie [bə'go:niə] f begonia.

begonnen v siehe **beginnen**.

begraben [bə'gra:bən] vt unreg bury.

Begräbnis [bə'grɛ:pnɪs] nt -ses, -se burial, funeral.

begreifen [bə'graɪfən] vt unreg understand, comprehend.

begreiflich [bə'graɪflɪç] a understandable.

Begrenztheit [bə'grɛntsthaɪt] f limitation, restriction; (fig) narrowness.

Begriff [bə'grɪf] m -(e)s, -e concept, idea; **im ~ sein, etw zu tun** be about to do sth; **schwer von ~** (umg) slow, dense; **begriffsstutzig** a dense, slow.

begründ- [bə'grʏnd] zW: **~en** vt (Gründe geben) justify; **begründet** a well-founded, justified; **B~ung** f justification, reason.

begrüßen [bə'gry:sən] vt greet, welcome.

Begrüßung f greeting, welcome.

begünstigen [bə'gʏnstɪgən] vt (Person) favour; (Sache) further, promote.

begutachten [bə'gu:t'axtən] vt assess.

begütert [bə'gy:tərt] a wealthy, well-to-do.

behaart [bə'ha:rt] a hairy.

behäbig [bə'hɛ:bɪç] a (dick) portly, stout; (geruhsam) comfortable.

behagen [bə'ha:gən] vi: **das behagt ihm nicht** he does not like it; **B~** nt -s comfort, ease.

behaglich [bə'ha:klɪç] a comfortable, cosy; **B~keit** f comfort, cosiness.

behalten [bə'haltən] vt unreg keep, retain; (im Gedächtnis) remember.

Behälter [bə'hɛltər] m -s, - container, receptacle.

behandeln [bə'handəln] vt treat; (Thema) deal with; (Maschine) handle.

Behandlung f treatment; (von Maschine) handling.

beharren [bə'harən] vi: **auf etw** (dat) **~** stick od keep to sth.

beharrlich [bə'harlɪç] a (ausdauernd) steadfast, unwavering; (hartnäckig) tenacious, dogged; **B~keit** f steadfastness; tenacity.

behaupten [bə'hauptən] vt claim, assert, maintain; (sein Recht) defend // vr assert o.s.

Behauptung f claim, assertion.

beheizen [bə'haɪtsən] vt heat.

behelfen [bə'hɛlfən] vr unreg: **sich mit etw ~** make do with sth; **behelfsmäßig** a improvised, makeshift; (vorübergehend) temporary.

behelligen [bə'hɛlɪgən] vt trouble, bother.

beherbergen [bə'hɛrbergən] vt put up, house.

beherrschen [bə'hɛrʃən] vt (Volk) rule, govern; (Situation) control; (Sprache, Gefühle) master // vr control o.s.

beherrscht a controlled.

Beherrschung f rule; control; mastery.

beherzigen [bə'hɛrtsɪgən] vt take to heart.

beherzt a spirited, brave.

behilflich [bə'hɪlflɪç] a helpful; **jdm ~ sein** help sb (bei with).

behindern [bə'hɪndərn] vt hinder, impede.

Behinderte(r) mf disabled person.

Behinderung f hindrance; (Körper~) handicap.

Behörde [bə'hø:rdə] f -, -n authorities pl.

behördlich [bə'hø:rtlɪç] a official.

behüten [bə'hy:tən] vt guard; **jdn vor etw** (dat) **~** preserve sb from sth.

behutsam [bə'huːtzaːm] *a* cautious, careful; **B~keit** *f* caution, carefulness.

bei [baɪ] *präp + dat* **1** (*nahe ~*) near; (*zum Aufenthalt*) at, with; (*unter, zwischen*) among; **~ München** near Munich; **~ uns** at our place; **~m Friseur** at the hairdresser's; **~ seinen Eltern wohnen** live with one's parents; **~ einer Firma arbeiten** work for a firm; **etw ~ sich haben** have sth on one; **jdn ~ sich haben** have sb with one; **~ Goethe** in Goethe; **~m Militär** in the army **2** (*zeitlich*) at, on; (*während*) during; (*Zustand, Umstand*) in; **~ Nacht** at night; **~ Nebel** in fog; **~ Regen** if it rains; **~ solcher Hitze** in such heat; **~ meiner Ankuft** on my arrival; **~ der Arbeit** when I'm *etc* working; **~m Fahren** while driving.

beibehalten ['baɪbəhaltən] *vt unreg* keep, retain.

beibringen ['baɪbrɪŋən] *vt unreg* (*Beweis, Zeugen*) bring forward; (*Gründe*) adduce; **jdm etw ~** (*zufügen*) inflict sth on sb; (*zu verstehen geben*) make sb understand sth; (*lehren*) teach sb sth.

Beichte ['baɪçtə] *f* -, **-n** confession; **b~n** *vt* confess // *vi* go to confession.

Beichtstuhl *m* confessional.

beide(s) ['baɪdə(s)] *pron, a* both; **meine ~n Brüder** my two brothers, both my brothers; **die ersten ~n** the first two; **wir ~** we two; **einer von ~n** one of the two; **alles ~s** both (of them).

beider- ['baɪdər] *zW*: **~lei** *a inv* of both; **~seitig** *a* mutual, reciprocal; **~seits** *ad* mutually // *präp +gen* on both sides of.

beieinander [baɪaɪ'nandər] *ad* together.

Beifahrer ['baɪfaːrər] *m* passenger; **~sitz** *m* passenger seat.

Beifall ['baɪfal] *m* -(e)s applause; (*Zustimmung*) approval.

beifällig ['baɪfɛlɪç] *a* approving; (*Kommentar*) favourable.

beifügen ['baɪfyːgən] *vt* enclose.

beige ['beːʒ] *a* beige, fawn.

beigeben ['baɪgeːbən] *unreg vt* (*zufügen*) add; (*mitgeben*) give // *vi* (*nachgeben*) give in (*dat* to).

Beigeschmack ['baɪgəʃmak] *m* aftertaste.

Beihilfe ['baɪhɪlfə] *f* aid, assistance; (*Studien~*) grant; (*JUR*) aiding and abetting.

beikommen ['baɪkɔmən] *vi unreg* (*+dat*) get at; (*einem Problem*) deal with.

Beil [baɪl] *nt* -(e)s, **-e** axe, hatchet.

Beilage [baɪlaːgə] *f* (*Buch~ etc*) sup-

plement; (*KOCH*) vegetables and potatoes *pl*.

beiläufig ['baɪlɔyfɪç] *a* casual, incidental // *ad* casually, by the way.

beilegen ['baɪleːgən] *vt* (*hinzufügen*) enclose, add; (*beimessen*) attribute, ascribe; (*Streit*) settle.

Beileid ['baɪlaɪt] *nt* condolence, sympathy; **herzliches ~** deepest sympathy.

beiliegend ['baɪliːgənt] *a* (*COMM*) enclosed.

beim [baɪm] = **bei dem**.

beimessen ['baɪmɛsən] *vt unreg* attribute, ascribe (*dat* to).

Bein [baɪn] *nt* -(e)s, **-e** leg; **~bruch** *m* fracture of the leg.

beinah(e) ['baɪna:(ə)] *ad* almost, nearly.

beinhalten [bə'ɪnhaltən] *vt* contain.

beipflichten ['baɪpflɪçtən] *vi*: **jdm/etw ~** agree with sb/sth.

beirren [bə'ɪrən] *vt* confuse, muddle; **sich nicht ~ lassen** not let o.s. be confused.

beisammen [baɪ'zamən] *ad* together; **B~sein** *nt* **-s** get-together.

Beischlaf ['baɪʃlaːf] *m* sexual intercourse.

Beisein ['baɪzaɪn] *nt* **-s** presence.

beiseite [baɪ'zaɪtə] *ad* to one side, aside; (*stehen*) on one side, aside; **etw ~ legen** (*sparen*) put sth by; **jdn/etw ~ schaffen** put sb/get sth out of the way.

beisetzen ['baɪzɛtsən] *vt* bury.

Beisetzung *f* funeral.

Beisitzer ['baɪzɪtsər] *m* **-s, -** (*bei Prüfung*) assessor.

Beispiel ['baɪʃpiːl] *nt* -(e)s, **-e** example; **sich an jdm ein ~ nehmen** take sb as an example; **zum ~** for example; **b~haft** *a* exemplary; **b~los** *a* unprecedented, unexampled; **beispielsweise** *ad* for instance *od* example.

beißen ['baɪsən] *unreg vti* bite; (*stechen: Rauch, Säure*) burn // *vr* (*Farben*) clash; **~d** *a* biting, caustic; (*fig auch*) sarcastic.

Beistand ['baɪʃtant] *m* -(e)s, **⁻e** support, help; (*JUR*) adviser.

beistehen ['baɪʃteːən] *vi unreg*: **jdm ~** stand by sb.

beisteuern ['baɪʃtɔyərn] *vt* contribute.

beistimmen ['baɪʃtɪmən] *vi* (*+dat*) agree with.

Beitrag ['baɪtraːk] *m* -(e)s, **⁻e** contribution; (*Zahlung*) fee, subscription; (*Versicherungs~*) premium; **b~en** ['baɪtraːgən] *vt unreg* contribute (*zu* to); (*mithelfen*) help (*zu* with).

beitreten ['baɪtreːtən] *vi unreg* join (*einem Verein* a club).

Beitritt ['baɪtrɪt] *m* joining, membership.

beiwohnen ['baivo:nən] *vi:* einer Sache (*dat*) ~ attend *od* be present at sth.

Beize ['baitsə] *f* -, -n (*Holz*~) stain; (*KOCH*) marinade.

beizeiten [bai'tsaitən] *ad* in time.

bejahen [bə'ja:ən] *vt* (*Frage*) say yes to, answer in the affirmative; (*gutheißen*) agree with.

bejahrt [bə'ja:rt] *a* aged, elderly.

bekämpfen [bə'kɛmpfən] *vt* (*Gegner*) fight; (*Seuche*) combat // *vr* fight.

Bekämpfung *f* fight *od* struggle against.

bekannt [bə'kant] *a* (well-) known; (*nicht fremd*) familiar; **mit jdm ~ sein** know sb; **jdn mit jdm ~ machen** introduce sb to sb; **das ist mir ~** I know that; **es/sie kommt mir ~ vor** it/she seems familiar; **B~e(r)** *mf* friend, acquaintance; **B~enkreis** *m* circle of friends; **B~gabe** *f* announcement; **~geben** *vt unreg* announce publicly; **~lich** *ad* as is well known, as you know; **~machen** *vt* announce; **B~machung** *f* publication; announcement; **B~schaft** *f* acquaintance.

bekehren [bə'ke:rən] *vt* convert // *vr* become converted.

bekennen [bə'kɛnən] *vt unreg* confess; (*Glauben*) profess; **Farbe ~** (*umg*) show where one stands.

Bekenntnis [bə'kɛntnis] *nt* -ses, -se admission, confession; (*Religion*) confession, denomination.

beklagen [bə'kla:gən] *vt* deplore, lament // *vr* complain; **beklagenswert** *a* lamentable, pathetic.

bekleiden [bə'klaidən] *vt* clothe; (*Amt*) occupy, fill.

Bekleidung *f* clothing.

beklemmen [bə'klɛmən] *vt* oppress.

beklommen [bə'kləmən] *a* anxious, uneasy; **B~heit** *f* anxiety, uneasiness.

bekommen [bə'kəmən] *unreg vt* get, receive; (*Kind*) have; (*Zug*) catch, get // *vi:* **jdm ~** agree with sb.

bekömmlich [bə'kœmlıç] *a* wholesome, easily digestible.

bekräftigen [bə'krɛftıgən] *vt* confirm, corroborate.

Bekräftigung *f* corroboration.

bekreuzigen [bə'krɔytsıgən] *vr* cross o.s.

bekümmern [bə'kymərn] *vt* worry, trouble.

bekunden [bə'kundən] *vt* (*sagen*) state; (*zeigen*) show.

belächeln [bə'lɛçəln] *vt* laugh at.

beladen [bə'la:dən] *vt unreg* load.

Belag [bə'la:k] *m* -(e)s, -̈e covering, coating; (*Brot*~) spread; (*Zahn*~) tartar; (*auf Zunge*) fur; (*Brems*~)

lining.

belagern [bə'la:gərn] *vt* besiege.

Belagerung *f* siege.

Belang [bə'laŋ] *m* -(e)s importance; **~e** *pl* interests *pl*, concerns *pl*; **b~en** *vt* (*JUR*) take to court; **b~los** *a* trivial, unimportant; **~losigkeit** *f* triviality.

belassen [bə'lasən] *vt unreg* (*in Zustand, Glauben*) leave; (*in Stellung*) retain.

belasten [bə'lastən] *vt* (*lit*) burden; (*fig: bedrücken*) trouble, worry; (*COMM: Konto*) debit; (*JUR*) incriminate // *vr* weigh o.s. down; (*JUR*) incriminate o.s.; **~d** *a* (*JUR*) incriminating.

belästigen [bə'lɛstıgən] *vt* annoy, pester.

Belästigung *f* annoyance, pestering.

Belastung [bə'lastuŋ] *f* (*lit*) load; (*fig: Sorge etc*) weight; (*COMM*) charge, debit(ing); (*JUR*) incriminatory evidence; **Belastungsprobe** *f* capacity test; (*fig*) test; **Belastungszeuge** *m* witness for prosecution.

belaufen [bə'laufən] *vr unreg* amount (*auf* +*akk* to).

belebt [bə'le:pt] *a* (*Straße*) crowded.

Beleg [bə'le:k] *m* -(e)s, -e (*COMM*) receipt; (*Beweis*) documentary evidence, proof; (*Beispiel*) example; **b~en** [bə'le:gən] *vt* cover; (*Kuchen, Brot*) spread; (*Platz*) reserve, book; (*Kurs, Vorlesung*) register for; (*beweisen*) verify, prove; (*MIL: mit Bomben*) bomb; **~schaft** *f* personnel, staff; **belegt** *a:* **belegtes Brot** open sandwich.

belehren [bə'le:rən] *vt* instruct, teach.

Belehrung *f* instruction.

beleibt [bə'laipt] *a* stout, corpulent.

beleidigen [bə'laidıgən] *vt* insult, offend.

Beleidigung *f* insult; (*JUR*) slander, libel.

belesen [bə'le:zən] *a* well-read.

beleuchten [bə'lɔyçtən] *vt* light, illuminate; (*fig*) throw light on.

Beleuchtung *f* lighting, illumination.

Belg- ['bɛlg] *zW:* **~ien** [-ıən] *nt* Belgium; **~ier(in** *f)* *m* Belgian; **b~isch** *a* Belgian.

belichten [bə'lıçtən] *vt* expose.

Belichtung *f* exposure; **Belichtungsmesser** *m* exposure meter.

Belieben [bə'li:bən] *nt:* (**ganz**) **nach ~** (just) as you wish.

beliebig [bə'li:bıç] *a* any you like, as you like; **~** viel as many as you like; **ein ~es Thema** any subject you like *od* want.

beliebt [bə'li:pt] *a* popular; **sich bei jdm ~ machen** make o.s. popular with sb; **B~heit** *f* popularity.

beliefern [bə'li:fərn] *vt* supply.
bellen ['bɛlən] *vi* bark.
Belletristik [belɛ'trɪstɪk] *f* fiction and poetry.
belohnen [bə'lo:nən] *vt* reward.
Belohnung *f* reward.
belügen [bə'ly:gən] *vt unreg* lie to, deceive.
belustigen [bə'lʊstɪgən] *vt* amuse.
Belustigung *f* amusement.
bemalen [bə'ma:lən] *vt* paint.
bemängeln [bə'mɛŋəln] *vt* criticize.
bemannen [bə'manən] *vt* man.
bemerk- [bə'mɛrk] *zW:* ~**bar** *a* perceptible, noticeable; **sich** ~**bar machen** (*Person*) make *od* get o.s. noticed; (*Unruhe*) become noticeable; ~**en** *vt* (*wahrnehmen*) notice, observe; (*sagen*) say, mention; ~**enswert** *a* remarkable, noteworthy; **B**~**ung** *f* remark; (*schriftlich auch*) note.
bemitleiden [bə'mɪtlaɪdən] *vt* pity.
bemühen [bə'my:ən] *vr* take trouble *od* pains.
Bemühung *f* trouble, pains *pl*, effort.
benachbart [bə'naxba:rt] *a* neighbouring.
benachrichtigen [bə'na:xrɪçtɪgən] *vt* inform.
Benachrichtigung *f* notification, information.
benachteiligen [bə'na:xtaɪlɪgən] *vt* disadvantage, victimize.
benehmen [bə'ne:mən] *vr unreg* behave; **B**~ *nt* -**s** behaviour.
beneiden [bə'naɪdən] *vt* envy; **beneidenswert** *a* enviable.
benennen [bə'nɛnən] *vt unreg* name.
Bengel ['bɛŋəl] *m* -**s**, - (little) rascal *od* rogue.
benommen [bə'nɔmən] *a* dazed.
benötigen [bə'nø:tɪgən] *vt* need.
benutzen [bə'nʊtsən], **benützen** [bə'nʏtsən] *vt* use.
Benutzer *m* -**s**, - user; **b**~**freundlich** *a* user-friendly.
Benutzung *f* utilization, use.
Benzin [bɛnt'si:n] *nt* -**s**, -**e** (*AUT*) petrol (*Brit*), gas(oline) (*US*); ~**kanister** *m* petrol can (*Brit*), gas can (*US*); ~**tank** *m* petrol tank (*Brit*), gas tank (*US*); ~**uhr** *f* petrol gauge (*Brit*), gas gauge (*US*).
beobacht- [bə'o:baxt] *zW:* ~**en** *vt* observe; **B**~**er** *m* -**s**, - observer; (*eines Unfalls*) witness; (*PRESSE, TV*) correspondent; **B**~**ung** *f* observation.
bepacken [bə'pakən] *vt* load, pack.
bequem [bə'kve:m] *a* comfortable; (*Ausrede*) convenient; (*Person*) lazy, indolent; ~**en** *vr* condescend (*zu* to); **B**~**lichkeit** *f* convenience, comfort; (*Faulheit*) laziness, indolence.
beraten [bə'ra:tən] *unreg vt* advise;

(*besprechen*) discuss, debate // *vr* consult; **gut/schlecht** ~ **sein** be well/ill advised; **sich** ~ **lassen** get advice.
Berater *m* -**s**, - adviser.
Beratung *f* advice, consultation; (*Besprechung*) consultation; **Beratungsstelle** *f* advice centre.
berauben [bə'raubən] *vt* rob.
berechenbar [bə'rɛçənba:r] *a* calculable.
berechnen [bə'rɛçnən] *vt* calculate; (*COMM: anrechnen*) charge; ~**d** *a* (*Mensch*) calculating, scheming.
Berechnung *f* calculation; (*COMM*) charge.
berechtig- [bə'rɛçtɪg] *zW:* ~**en** *vt* entitle, authorize; (*fig*) justify; ~**t** [bə'rɛçtɪçt] *a* justifiable, justified; **B**~**ung** *f* authorization; (*fig*) justification.
bereden [bə're:dən] *vtr* (*besprechen*) discuss; (*überreden*) persuade.
Bereich [bə'raɪç] *m* -**(e)s**, -**e** (*Bezirk*) area; (*PHYS*) range; (*Ressort, Gebiet*) sphere.
bereichern [bə'raɪçərn] *vt* enrich // *vr* get rich.
bereinigen [bə'raɪnɪgən] *vt* settle.
bereit [bə'raɪt] *a* ready, prepared; **zu etw** ~ **sein** be ready for sth; **sich** ~ **erklären** declare o.s. willing; ~**en** *vt* prepare, make ready; (*Kummer, Freude*) cause; ~**halten** *vt unreg* keep in readiness; ~**legen** *vt* lay out; ~**machen** *vtr* prepare, get ready; ~**s** *ad* already; **B**~**schaft** *f* readiness; (*Polizei*) alert; **B**~**schaftsdienst** *m* emergency service; ~**stehen** *vi unreg* (*Person*) be prepared; (*Ding*) be ready; ~**stellen** *vt* (*Kisten, Pakete etc*) put ready; (*Geld etc*) make available; (*Truppen, Maschinen*) put at the ready; ~**willig** *a* willing, ready; **B**~**willigkeit** *f* willingness, readiness.
bereuen [bə'rɔyən] *vt* regret.
Berg [bɛrk] *m* -**(e)s**, -**e** mountain, hill; **b**~**ab** *ad* downhill; **b**~**auf** *ad* uphill; ~**arbeiter** *m* miner; ~**bahn** *f* mountain railway; ~**bau** *m* mining; **b**~**en** ['bɛrgən] *vt unreg* (*retten*) rescue; (*Ladung*) salvage; (*enthalten*) contain; ~**führer** *m* mountain guide; **b**~**ig** ['bɛrgɪç] *a* mountainous, hilly; ~**kette** *f* mountain range; ~**mann** *m*, *pl* ~**leute** miner; ~**rutsch** *m* landslide; ~**steigen** *nt* mountaineering; ~**steiger(in** *f*) *m* -**s**, - mountaineer, climber; ~**ung** ['bɛrgʊŋ] *f* (*von Menschen*) rescue; (*von Material*) recovery; (*NAUT*) salvage; ~**wacht** *f* mountain rescue service; ~**werk** *nt* mine.
Bericht [bə'rɪçt] *m* -**(e)s**, -**e** report, account; **b**~**en** *vti* report; ~**erstatter**

m **-s, -** reporter, (newspaper) correspondent.
berichtigen [bə'rıçtıgən] *vt* correct.
Berichtigung *f* correction.
Bernstein ['bɛrnʃtaın] *m* amber.
bersten ['bɛrstən] *vi unreg* burst, split.
berüchtigt [bə'rүçtıçt] *a* notorious, infamous.
berücksichtigen [bə'rүkzıçtıgən] *vt* consider, bear in mind.
Berücksichtigung *f* consideration.
Beruf [bə'ru:f] *m* **-(e)s, -e** occupation, profession; (*Gewerbe*) trade; **b~en** *unreg vt* (*in Amt*) appoint (*in +akk* to; *zu* as) // *vr*: **sich auf jdn/etw b~en** refer *od* appeal to sb/sth; **b~en** *a* competent, qualified; **b~lich** *a* professional.
Berufs- *zW*: **~berater** *m* careers adviser; **~beratung** *f* vocational guidance; **~geheimnis** *nt* professional secret; **~leben** *nt* professional life; **b~mäßig** *a* professional; **~schule** *f* vocational *od* trade school; **~sportler** *m* professional (sportsman); **b~tätig** *a* employed; **~verkehr** *m* commuter traffic.
Berufung *f* vocation, calling; (*Ernennung*) appointment; (*JUR*) appeal; **~ einlegen** appeal.
beruhen [bə'ru:ən] *vi*: **auf etw** (*dat*) **~** be based on sth; **etw auf sich ~ lassen** leave sth at that.
beruhigen [bə'ru:ıgən] *vt* calm, pacify, soothe // *vr* (*Mensch*) calm (o.s.) down; (*Situation*) calm down.
Beruhigung *f* reassurance; (*der Nerven*) calming; **zu jds ~** to reassure sb; **Beruhigungsmittel** *nt* sedative.
berühmt [bə'ry:mt] *a* famous; **B~heit** *f* (*Ruf*) fame; (*Mensch*) celebrity.
berühren [bə'ry:rən] *vt* touch; (*gefühlsmäßig bewegen*) affect; (*flüchtig erwähnen*) mention, touch on // *vr* meet, touch.
Berührung *f* contact.
besagen [bə'za:gən] *vt* mean.
besagt *a* (*Tag etc*) in question.
besänftig- [bə'zɛnftıg] *zW*: **~en** *vt* soothe, calm; **~end** *a* soothing; **B~ung** *f* soothing, calming.
Besatz [bə'zats] *m* **-es, -e** trimming, edging; **~ung** *f* garrison; (*NAUT. AVIAT*) crew; **~ungsmacht** *f* occupying power.
beschädig- [bə'ʃɛːdıg] *zW*: **~en** *vt* damage; **B~ung** *f* damage; (*Stelle*) damaged spot.
beschaffen [bə'ʃafən] *vt* get, acquire // *a* constituted; **B~heit** *f* constitution, nature.
Beschaffung *f* acquisition.
beschäftigen [bə'ʃɛftıgən] *vt* occupy; (*beruflich*) employ // *vr* occupy *od* concern o.s.

beschäftigt *a* busy, occupied.
Beschäftigung *f* (*Beruf*) employment; (*Tätigkeit*) occupation; (*Befassen*) concern.
beschämen [bə'ʃɛːmən] *vt* put to shame; **~d** *a* shameful; (*Hilfsbereitschaft*) shaming.
beschämt *a* ashamed.
beschatten [bə'ʃatən] *vt* shade; (*Verdächtige*) shadow.
Bescheid [bə'ʃaıt] *m* **-(e)s, -e** information; (*Weisung*) directions *pl*; **~ wissen** be well-informed (*über +akk* about); **ich weiß ~** I know; **jdm ~ geben** *od* **sagen** let sb know.
bescheiden [bə'ʃaıdən] *vr unreg* content o.s. // *a* modest; **B~heit** *f* modesty.
bescheinen [bə'ʃaınən] *vt unreg* shine on.
bescheinigen [bə'ʃaınıgən] *vt* certify; (*bestätigen*) acknowledge.
Bescheinigung *f* certificate; (*Quittung*) receipt.
bescheren [bə'ʃeːrən] *vt*: **jdm etw ~** give sb sth as a present; **jdn ~** give presents to sb.
Bescherung *f* giving of presents; (*umg*) mess.
beschildern [bə'ʃıldərn] *vt* signpost.
beschimpfen [bə'ʃımpfən] *vt* abuse.
Beschimpfung *f* abuse, insult.
Beschlag [bə'ʃla:k] *m* **-(e)s, -e** (*Metallband*) fitting; (*auf Fenster*) condensation; (*auf Metall*) tarnish; finish; (*Hufeisen*) horseshoe; **jdn/etw in ~ nehmen** *od* **mit ~ belegen** monopolize sb/sth; **b~en** [bə'ʃla:gən] *unreg vt* cover; (*Pferd*) shoe; (*Fenster, Metall*) cover // **b~en sein** be well versed (*in od auf +dat* in) // *vir* (*Fenster etc*) mist over; **b~nahmen** *vt* seize, confiscate; requisition; **~nahmung** *f* confiscation, sequestration.
beschleunigen [bə'ʃlɔynıgən] *vt* accelerate, speed up // *vi* (*AUT*) accelerate.
Beschleunigung *f* acceleration.
beschließen [bə'ʃliːsən] *vt unreg* decide on; (*beenden*) end, close.
Beschluß [bə'ʃlus] *m* **-sses, -schlüsse** decision, conclusion; (*Ende*) close, end.
beschmutzen [bə'ʃmutsən] *vt* dirty, soil.
beschönigen [bə'ʃøːnıgən] *vt* gloss over.
beschränken [bə'ʃrɛŋkən] *vt* limit, restrict (*auf +akk* to) // *vr* restrict o.s.
beschränk- *zW*: **~t** *a* confined, narrow; (*Mensch*) limited, narrowminded; **Beschränktheit** *f* narrowness; **B~ung** *f* limitation.
beschreiben [bə'ʃraıbən] *vt unreg* de-

scribe; (*Papier*) write on.
Beschreibung *f* description.
beschriften [bə'ʃrɪftən] *vt* mark, label.
Beschriftung *f* lettering.
beschuldigen [bə'ʃʊldɪgən] *vt* accuse.
Beschuldigung *f* accusation.
beschütz- [bə'ʃʏts] *zW:* ~**en** *vt* protect (*vor +dat* from); **B~er** *m* -**s**, - protector.
Beschwerde [bə'ʃveːrdə] *f* -, -**n** complaint; (*Mühe*) hardship; (*pl: Leiden*) pain.
beschweren [bə'ʃveːrən] *vt* weight down; (*fig*) burden // *vr* complain.
beschwerlich *a* tiring, exhausting.
beschwichtigen [bə'ʃvɪçtɪgən] *vt* soothe, pacify.
beschwindeln [bə'ʃvɪndəln] *vt* (*betrügen*) cheat; (*belügen*) fib to.
beschwingt [bə'ʃvɪŋt] *a* a cheery, in high spirits.
beschwören [bə'ʃvøːrən] *vt* unreg (*Aussage*) swear to; (*anflehen*) implore; (*Geister*) conjure up.
beseitigen [bə'zaɪtɪgən] *vt* remove.
Beseitigung *f* removal.
Besen ['beːzən] *m* -**s**, - broom; ~**stiel** *m* broomstick.
besessen [bə'zɛsən] *a* possessed.
besetz- [bə'zɛts] *zW:* ~**en** *vt* (*Haus, Land*) occupy; (*Platz*) take, fill; (*Posten*) fill; (*Rolle*) cast; (*mit Edelsteinen*) set; ~**t** *a* full; (*TEL*) engaged, busy; (*Platz*) taken; (*WC*) engaged; **Besetztzeichen** *nt* engaged tone; **B~ung** *f* occupation; filling; (*von Rolle*) casting; (*die Schauspieler*) cast.
besichtigen [bə'zɪçtɪgən] *vt* visit, look at.
Besichtigung *f* visit.
Besied(e)lung [bə'ziːd(ə)lʊŋ] *f* population.
besiegen [bə'ziːgən] *vt* defeat, overcome.
besinnen [bə'zɪnən] *vr* unreg (*nachdenken*) think, reflect; (*erinnern*) remember; **sich anders** ~ change one's mind.
besinnlich *a* contemplative.
Besinnung *f* consciousness; **zur** ~ **kommen** recover consciousness; (*fig*) come to one's senses; **besinnungslos** *a* unconscious.
Besitz [bə'zɪts] *m* -**es** possession; (*Eigentum*) property; **b~en** *vt* unreg possess, own; (*Eigenschaft*) have; ~**er(in** *f*) *m* -**s**, - owner, proprietor; ~**ergreifung** *f* occupation, seizure.
besoffen [bə'zɔfən] *a* (*umg*) drunk.
besohlen [bə'zoːlən] *vt* sole.
Besoldung [bə'zɔldʊŋ] *f* salary, pay.
besondere(r, s) [bə'zɔndərə(r,z)] *a* special; (*eigen*) particular; (*gesondert*) separate; (*eigentümlich*) pecu-

liar.
Besonderheit [bə'zɔndərhaɪt] *f* peculiarity.
besonders [bə'zɔndərs] *ad* especially, particularly; (*getrennt*) separately.
besonnen [bə'zɔnən] *a* sensible, level-headed; **B~heit** *f* prudence.
besorg- [bə'zɔrg] *zW:* ~**en** *vt* (*beschaffen*) acquire; (*kaufen auch*) purchase; (*erledigen: Geschäfte*) deal with; (*sich kümmern um*) take care of; **B~nis** *f* -, -**se** anxiety, concern; ~**t** [bə'zɔrçt] *a* anxious, worried; **Besorgtheit** *f* anxiety, worry; **B~ung** *f* acquisition; (*Kauf*) purchase.
bespielen [bə'ʃpiːlən] *vt* record.
bespitzeln [bə'ʃpɪtsəln] *vt* spy on.
besprechen [bə'ʃprɛçən] *unreg vt* discuss; (*Tonband etc*) record, speak onto; (*Buch*) review // *vr* discuss, consult.
Besprechung *f* meeting, discussion; (*von Buch*) review.
besser ['bɛsər] *a* better; ~**n** *vt* make better, improve // *vr* improve; (*Menschen*) reform; **B~ung** *f* improvement; **gute B~ung!** get well soon; **B~wisser** *m* -**s**, - know-all.
Bestand [bə'ʃtant] *m* -**(e)s**, ¨**e** (*Fortbestehen*) duration, stability; (*Kassen~*) amount, balance; (*Vorrat*) stock; ~ **haben, von** ~ **sein** last long, endure.
beständig [bə'ʃtɛndɪç] *a* (*ausdauernd*) constant (*auch fig*); (*Wetter*) settled; (*Stoffe*) resistant; (*Klagen etc*) continual.
Bestandsaufnahme *f* stocktaking.
Bestandteil *m* part, component; (*Zutat*) ingredient.
bestärken [bə'ʃtɛrkən] *vt:* **jdn in etw** (*dat*) ~ strengthen *od* confirm sb in sth.
bestätigen [bə'ʃtɛːtɪgən] *vt* confirm; (*anerkennen, COMM*) acknowledge.
Bestätigung *f* confirmation; acknowledgement.
bestatt- [bə'ʃtat] *zW:* ~**en** *vt* bury; **B~er** *m* -**s**, - undertaker; **B~ung** *f* funeral.
beste(r, s) ['bɛstə(r, s)] *a* best; **so ist es am** ~**n** it's best that way; **am** ~**n gehst du gleich** you'd better go at once; **jdn zum** ~**n haben** pull sb's leg; **etw zum** ~**n geben** tell a joke/story *etc*; **aufs** ~ in the best possible way; **zu jds B~n** for the benefit of sb.
bestechen [bə'ʃtɛçən] *vt* unreg bribe.
bestechlich *a* corruptible.
Bestechung *f* bribery, corruption.
Besteck [bə'ʃtɛk] *nt* -**(e)s**, -**e** knife, fork and spoon, cutlery; (*MED*) set of instruments.
bestehen [bə'ʃteːən] *unreg vi* be; ex-

ist; (andauern) last // vt (Kampf, Probe, Prüfung) pass; ~ auf (+dat) insist on; ~ aus consist of.

bestehlen [bə'ʃteːlən] vt unreg rob.

besteigen [bə'ʃtaɪgən] vt unreg climb, ascend; (Pferd) mount; (Thron) ascend.

Bestell- [bə'ʃtɛl] zW: ~buch nt order book; b~en vt order; (kommen lassen) arrange to see; (nominieren) name; (Acker) cultivate; (Grüße, Auftrag) pass on; ~schein m order coupon; ~ung f (COMM) order; (Bestellen) ordering.

bestenfalls ['bɛstən'fals] ad at best.

bestens ['bɛstəns] ad very well.

Bestie ['bɛstiə] f (lit, fig) beast.

bestimm- [bə'ʃtɪm] zW: ~en vt (Regeln) lay down; (Tag, Ort) fix; (beherrschen) characterize; (ausersehen) mean; (ernennen) appoint; (definieren) define; (veranlassen) induce; ~t a (entschlossen) firm; (gewiß) certain, definite; (Artikel) definite; suchen Sie etwas B~tes? are you looking for something in particular? // ad (gewiß) definitely, for sure; **Bestimmtheit** f certainty; **B~ung** f (Verordnung) regulation; (Festsetzen) determining; (Verwendungszweck) purpose; (Schicksal) fate; (Definition) definition; B~ungsort m destination.

Bestleistung f best performance.

bestmöglich a best possible.

bestrafen [bə'ʃtraːfən] vt punish.

Bestrafung f punishment.

bestrahlen [bə'ʃtraːlən] vt shine on; (MED) treat with X-rays.

Bestrahlung f (MED) X-ray treatment, radiotherapy.

Bestreben [bə'ʃtreːbən] nt -s endeavour, effort.

bestreichen [bə'ʃtraɪçən] vt unreg (Brot) spread.

bestreiten [bə'ʃtraɪtən] vt unreg (abstreiten) dispute; (finanzieren) pay for, finance.

bestreuen [bə'ʃtrɔyən] vt sprinkle, dust; (Straße) grit.

bestürmen [bə'ʃtʏrmən] vt (mit Fragen, Bitten etc) overwhelm, swamp.

bestürzt [bə'ʃtʏrtst] a dismayed.

Bestürzung f consternation.

Besuch [bə'zuːx] m -(e)s, -e visit; (Person) visitor; einen ~ machen bei jdm pay sb a visit od call; ~ haben have visitors; bei jdm auf or zu ~ sein be visiting sb; b~en vt visit; (SCH etc) attend; gut ~t well-attended; ~er(in f) m -s, - visitor, guest; **Besuchszeit** f visiting hours pl.

betagt [bə'taːkt] a aged.

betätigen [bə'tɛːtɪgən] vt (bedienen) work, operate // vr involve o.s.; sich als etw ~ work as sth.

Betätigung f activity; (beruflich) occupation; (TECH) operation.

betäuben [bə'tɔybən] vt stun; (fig: Gewissen) still; (MED) anaesthetize.

Betäubungsmittel nt anaesthetic.

Bete ['beːtə] f -, -n: rote ~ beetroot (Brit), beet (US).

beteiligen [bə'taɪlɪgən] vr (an +dat) take part, participate, share; (an Geschäft: finanziell) have a share // vt: jdn ~ give sb a share od interest (an +dat in).

Beteiligung f participation; (Anteil) share, interest; (Besucherzahl) attendance.

beten ['beːtən] vti pray.

beteuern [bə'tɔyərn] vt assert; (Unschuld) protest.

Beteuerung f assertion, protest(ation), assurance.

Beton [be'tõː] m -s, -s concrete.

betonen [bə'toːnən] vt stress.

betonieren [beto'niːrən] vt concrete.

Betonung f stress, emphasis.

betören [bə'tøːrən] vt beguile.

Betr. abk (= Betreff; betrifft) re.

Betracht [bə'traxt] m: in ~ kommen be concerned od relevant; etw in ~ ziehen consider sth; außer ~ bleiben not be considered; b~en vt look at; (fig auch) consider; ~er(in f) m -s, - onlooker.

beträchtlich [bə'trɛçtlıç] a considerable.

Betrachtung f (Ansehen) examination; (Erwägung) consideration.

Betrag [bə'traːk] m -(e)s, ⁻e amount; b~en [bə'traːgən] unreg vt amount to // vr behave; ~en nt -s behaviour.

betreffen [bə'trɛfən] vt unreg concern, affect; was mich betrifft as for me; ~d a relevant, in question.

betreffs [bə'trɛfs] präp +gen concerning, regarding.

betreiben [bə'traɪbən] vt unreg (ausüben) practise; (Politik) follow; (Studien) pursue; (vorantreiben) push ahead; (TECH: antreiben) drive.

betreten [bə'treːtən] vt unreg enter; (Bühne etc) step onto; B~ verboten keep off/out // a embarrassed.

Betrieb [bə'triːp] m -(e)s, -e (Firma) firm, concern; (Anlage) plant; (Tätigkeit) operation; (Treiben) traffic; außer ~ sein be out of order; in ~ sein be in operation.

Betriebs- zW: b~fähig a in working order; ~ferien pl company holidays pl (Brit), company vacation (US); ~klima nt (working) atmosphere; ~kosten pl running costs pl; ~rat m workers' council; b~sicher a safe, reliable; **~störung** f breakdown; **~unfall** m industrial accident; **~wirtschaft** f economics.

betrinken [bə'trıŋkən] vr unreg get drunk.

betroffen [bə'trɔfən] a (bestürzt) amazed, perplexed; **von etw ~ werden** od **sein** be affected by sth.

betrüben [bə'try:bən] vt grieve.

betrübt [bə'try:pt] a sorrowful, grieved.

Betrug [bə'tru:k] m -(e)s deception; (JUR) fraud.

betrügen [bə'try:gən] unreg vt cheat; (JUR) defraud; (Ehepartner) be unfaithful to // vr deceive o.s.

Betrüger m -s, - cheat, deceiver; **b~isch** a deceitful; (JUR) fraudulent.

betrunken [bə'trʊŋkən] a drunk.

Bett [bɛt] nt -(e)s, -en bed; **ins** od **zu ~ gehen** go to bed; **~bezug** m duvet cover; **~decke** f blanket; (Daunen~) quilt; (Überwurf) bedspread.

Bettel- ['bɛtəl] zW: **b~arm** a very poor, destitute; **~ei** [bɛtə'laı] f begging; **b~n** vi beg.

bettlägerig ['bɛtlɛːgərıç] a bedridden.

Bettlaken nt sheet.

Bettler(in f) ['bɛtlər(ın)] m -s, - beggar.

Bett- zW: **~vorleger** m bedside rug; **~(t)uch** nt, **~wäsche** f, **~zeug** nt bedclothes pl, bedding.

beugen ['bɔʏgən] vt bend; (GRAM) inflect // vr (sich fügen) bow (dat to).

Beule ['bɔʏlə] f -, -n bump, swelling.

beunruhigen [bə''ʊnruːıgən] vt disturb, alarm // vr become worried.

Beunruhigung f worry, alarm.

beurlauben [bə''uːrlaʊbən] vt give leave od holiday to (Brit), grant vacation time to (US).

beurteilen [bə''ʊrtaılən] vt judge; (Buch etc) review.

Beurteilung f judgement; review; (Note) mark.

Beute ['bɔʏtə] f - booty, loot; **~l** m -s, - bag; (Geld~) purse; (Tabak~) pouch.

Bevölkerung [bə'fœlkərʊŋ] f population.

bevollmächtigen [bə'fɔlmɛçtıgən] vt authorize.

Bevollmächtigte(r) mf authorized agent.

bevor [bə'foːr] kj before; **~munden** vt insep dominate; **~stehen** vi unreg be in store (dat for); **~stehend** a imminent, approaching; **~zugen** vt insep prefer; **B~zugung** f preference.

bewachen [bə'vaxən] vt watch, guard.

Bewachung f (Bewachen) guarding; (Leute) guard, watch.

bewaffnen [bə'vafnən] vt arm.

Bewaffnung f (Vorgang) arming; (Ausrüstung) armament, arms pl.

bewahren [bə'vaːrən] vt keep; **jdn vor jdm/etw ~** save sb from sb/sth.

bewähren [bə'vɛːrən] vr prove o.s.; (Maschine) prove its worth.

bewahrheiten [bə'vaːrhaıtən] vr come true.

bewährt a reliable.

Bewährung f (JUR) probation; **Bewährungsfrist** f (period of) probation.

bewältigen [bə'vɛltıgən] vt overcome; (Arbeit) finish; (Portion) manage.

bewandert [bə'vandərt] a expert, knowledgeable.

bewässern [bə'vɛsərn] vt irrigate.

Bewässerung f irrigation.

Beweg- [bə'veːg] zW: **b~en** vtr move; **jdn zu etw b~en** induce sb to (do) sth; **~grund** [bə'veːk-] m motive; **b~lich** a movable, mobile; (flink) quick; **b~t** a (Leben) eventful; (Meer) rough; (ergriffen) touched; **~ung** f movement, motion; (innere) emotion; (körperlich) exercise; **~ungsfreiheit** f freedom of movement od action; **b~ungslos** a motionless.

Beweis [bə'vaıs] m -es, -e proof; (Zeichen) sign; **b~bar** [bə'vaız-] a provable; **b~en** vt unreg prove; (zeigen) show; **~mittel** nt evidence.

Bewerb- [bə'vɛrb] zW: **b~en** vr unreg apply (um for); **~er(in** f) m -s, - applicant; **~ung** f application.

bewerkstelligen [bə'vɛrkʃtɛlıgən] vt manage, accomplish.

bewerten [bə'veːrtən] vt assess.

bewilligen [bə'vılıgən] vt grant, allow.

Bewilligung f granting.

bewirken [bə'vırkən] vt cause, bring about.

bewirten [bə'vırtən] vt entertain.

bewirtschaften [bə'vırtʃaftən] vt manage.

Bewirtung f hospitality.

bewog etc v siehe **bewegen**.

bewohn- [bə'voːn] zW: **~bar** a inhabitable; **~en** vt inhabit, live in; **B~er(in** f) m -s, - inhabitant; (von Haus) resident.

bewölkt [bə'vœlkt] a cloudy, overcast.

Bewölkung f clouds pl.

Bewunder- [bə'vʊndər] zW: **~er** m -s, - admirer; **b~n** vt admire; **b~nswert** a admirable, wonderful; **~ung** f admiration.

bewußt [bə'vʊst] a conscious; (absichtlich) deliberate; **sich** (dat) **einer Sache ~ sein** be aware of sth; **~los** a unconscious; **B~losigkeit** f unconsciousness; **B~sein** nt consciousness; **bei B~sein** conscious.

bezahlen [bə'tsaːlən] vt pay (for).

Bezahlung f payment.

bezaubern [bə'tsaubərn] *vt* enchant, charm.

bezeichnen [bə'tsaıçnən] *vt* (*kennzeichnen*) mark; (*nennen*) call; (*beschreiben*) describe; (*zeigen*) show, indicate; ~**d** *a* characteristic, typical (*für* of).

Bezeichnung *f* (*Zeichen*) mark, sign; (*Beschreibung*) description.

Bezichtigung [bə'tsıçtıguŋ] *f* accusation.

beziehen [bə'tsi:ən] *unreg vt* (*mit Überzug*) cover; (*Bett*) make; (*Haus, Position*) move into; (*Standpunkt*) take up; (*erhalten*) receive; (*Zeitung*) subscribe to, take; **etw auf jdn/etw** ~ relate sth to sb/sth // *vr* refer (*auf* +*akk* to); (*Himmel*) cloud over.

Beziehung *f* (*Verbindung*) connection; (*Zusammenhang*) relation; (*Verhältnis*) relationship; (*Hinsicht*) respect; ~**en haben** (*vorteilhaft*) have connections *od* contacts; **b~sweise** *ad* or; (*genauer gesagt auch*) that is, or rather.

Bezirk [bə'tsɪrk] *m* -(**e**)**s**, -**e** district.

Bezug [bə'tsu:k] *m* -(**e**)**s**, ¨**e** (*Hülle*) covering; (*COMM*) ordering; (*Gehalt*) income, salary; (*Beziehung*) relationship (*zu* to); **in b~ auf** (+*akk*) with reference to; ~ **nehmen auf** (+*akk*) refer to.

bezüglich [bə'tsy:klıç] *präp* +*gen* concerning, referring to // *a* concerning; (*GRAM*) relative.

bezwecken [bə'tsvɛkən] *vt* aim at.

bezweifeln [bə'tsvaıfəln] *vt* doubt, query.

Bhf. *abk* (= *Bahnhof*) station.

Bibel ['bi:bəl] *f* -, -**n** Bible.

Biber ['bi:bər] *m* -**s**, - beaver.

Biblio- *zW*: ~**graphie** [bibliogra'fi:] *f* bibliography; ~**thek** [biblio'te:k] *f* -, -**en** library; ~**thekar(in** *f*) [bibliote'ka:r(ın)] *m* -**s**, -**e** librarian.

biblisch ['bi:blıʃ] *a* biblical.

bieder ['bi:dər] *a* upright, worthy; (*Kleid etc*) plain.

bieg- [bi:g] *zW*: ~**en** *unreg vtr* bend // *vi* turn; ~**sam** ['bi:k-] *a* supple; **B~ung** *f* bend, curve.

Biene ['bi:nə] *f* -, -**n** bee.

Bienenhonig *m* honey.

Bier [bi:r] *nt* -(**e**)**s**, -**e** beer; ~**deckel** *m* beer mat; ~**krug** *m* beer mug.

bieten ['bi:tən] *unreg vt* offer; (*bei Versteigerung*) bid // *vr* (*Gelegenheit*) be open (*dat* to); **sich** (*dat*) **etw** ~ **lassen** put up with sth.

Bikini [bi'ki:ni] *m* -**s**, -**s** bikini.

Bilanz [bi'lants] *f* balance; (*fig*) outcome; ~ **ziehen** take stock (*aus* of).

Bild [bɪlt] *nt* -(**e**)**s**, -**er** (*lit, fig*) picture; photo; (*Spiegel*~) reflection; ~**bericht**

m pictorial report.

bilden ['bɪldən] *vt* form; (*erziehen*) educate; (*ausmachen*) constitute // *vr* arise; (*erziehen*) educate o.s.

Bilder- ['bɪldər] *zW*: ~**buch** *nt* picture book; ~**rahmen** *m* picture frame.

Bild- *zW*: ~**fläche** *f* screen; (*fig*) scene; ~**hauer** *m* -**s**, - sculptor; **b~hübsch** *a* lovely, pretty as a picture; **b~lich** *a* figurative; pictorial; ~**schirm** *m* television screen; (*COMPUT*) monitor; **b~schön** *a* lovely; ~**sichtgerät** *n* visual display unit, VDU; ~**ung** ['bɪlduŋ] *f* formation; (*Wissen, Benehmen*) education; ~**ungslücke** *f* gap in one's education; ~**ungspolitik** *f* educational policy.

Billard ['bɪljart] *nt* -**s**, -**e** billiards; ~**kugel** *f* billiard ball.

billig ['bɪlıç] *a* cheap; (*gerecht*) fair, reasonable; ~**en** ['bɪlıgən] *vt* approve of; **B~laden** *m* (*umg*) discount store; **B~ung** *f* approval.

Billion [bɪli'o:n] *f* billion, trillion (*US*).

Binde ['bɪndə] *f* -, -**n** bandage; (*Arm*~) band; (*MED*) sanitary towel; ~**glied** *nt* connecting link; **b~n** *vt* *unreg* bind, tie; ~**strich** *m* hyphen; ~**wort** *nt* conjunction.

Bind- *zW*: ~**faden** *m* string; ~**ung** *f* bond, tie; (*Ski*~) binding.

binnen ['bɪnən] *präp* +*dat od gen* within; **B~hafen** *m* inland harbour; **B~handel** *m* internal trade.

Binse ['bɪnzə] *f* -, -**n** rush, reed; **Binsenwahrheit** *f* truism.

Bio- [bio] *zW* bio-; ~**graphie** [-gra'fi:] *f* biography; ~**loge** ['lo:gə] *m* -**n**, -**n** biologist; ~**logie** [-lo'gi:] *f* biology; **b~logisch** [-'lo:gıʃ] *a* biological.

Birke ['bɪrkə] *f* -, -**n** birch.

Birma ['bɪrma] *nt* Burma.

Birnbaum *m* pear tree.

Birne ['bɪrnə] *f* -, -**n** pear; (*ELEK*) (light) bulb.

bis [bɪs] ♦*präp* +*akk, ad* **1** (*zeitlich*) till, until; (~ *spätestens*) by; **Sie haben** ~ **Dienstag Zeit** you have until *od* till Tuesday; ~ **Dienstag muß es fertig sein** it must be ready by Tuesday; ~ **auf weiteres** until further notice; ~ **in die Nacht** into the night; ~ **bald/gleich** see you later/soon

2 (*räumlich*) (up) to; **ich fahre** ~ **Köln** I'm going to *od* I'm going as far as Cologne; ~ **an unser Grundstück** (right *od* up) to our plot; ~ **hierher** this far

3 (*bei Zahlen*) up to; ~ **zu** up to

4: ~ **auf etw** (*akk*) (*außer*) except sth; (*einschließlich*) including sth.

♦*kj* **1** (*mit Zahlen*) to; **10** ~ **20** 10 to 20

2 (*zeitlich*) till, until; ~ **es dunkel wird** till *od* until it gets dark; **von** ...

~ ... from ... to ...

Bischof ['bɪʃɔf] *m* -s, ⁻e bishop.

bischöflich ['bɪʃøːflɪç] *a* episcopal.

bisher [bɪs'heːr]· *ad*, ~**ig** *a* till now, hitherto.

Biskuit [bɪs'kviːt] *m od nt* -(e)s, -s *od* -e biscuit; ~**teig** *m* sponge mixture.

biß *etc v siehe* **beißen.**

Biß [bɪs] *m* -sses, -sse bite.

bißchen ['bɪsçən] *a*, *ad* bit.

Bissen ['bɪsən] *m* -s, - bite, morsel.

bissig ['bɪsɪç] *a* (*Hund*) snappy; (*Bemerkung*) cutting, biting.

bist *v siehe* **sein.**

bisweilen [bɪs'vaɪlən] *ad* at times, occasionally.

Bit [bɪt] *nt* (COMPUT) bit.

Bitte ['bɪtə] *f* -, -n request; **b~** *interj* please; (*wie b~?*) (I beg your) pardon; (*als Antwort auf Dank*) you're welcome; **darf ich?** — **aber ~!** may I? — please do; **b~ schön!** it was a pleasure; **b~n** *vti unreg* ask (*um* for); **b~nd** *a* pleading, imploring.

bitter ['bɪtər] *a* bitter; ~**böse** *a* very angry; **B~keit** *f* bitterness; ~**lich** *a* bitter.

Blähungen ['blɛːʊŋən] *pl* (MED) wind.

blamabel [bla'maːbəl] *a* disgraceful.

Blamage [bla'maːʒə] *f* -, -n disgrace.

blamieren [bla'miːrən] *vr* make a fool of o.s., disgrace o.s. // *vt* let down, disgrace.

blank [blaŋk] *a* bright; (*unbedeckt*) bare; (*sauber*) clean, polished; (*umg: ohne Geld*) broke; (*offensichtlich*) blatant.

blanko ['blaŋko] *ad* blank; **B~scheck** *m* blank cheque.

Bläschen ['blɛːsçən] *nt* bubble; (MED) spot, blister.

Blase ['blaːzə] *f* -, -n bubble; (MED) blister; (ANAT) bladder; ~**balg** *m* -(e)s, -bälge bellows *pl*; **b~n** *vti unreg* blow.

Blas- ['blaːs] *zW*: ~**instrument** *nt* wind instrument; ~**kapelle** *f* brass band; ~**musik** *f* brass band music.

blaß [blas] *a* pale.

Blässe ['blɛsə] *f* - paleness, pallor.

Blatt [blat] *nt* -(e)s, ⁻er leaf; newspaper; (*von Papier*) sheet; (KARTEN) hand.

blättern ['blɛtərn] *vi*: **in etw** (*dat*) ~ leaf through sth.

Blätterteig *m* flaky *od* puff pastry.

blau [blaʊ] *a* blue; (*umg*) drunk, stoned; (KOCH) boiled; (*Auge*) black; ~**er Fleck** bruise; **Fahrt ins B~e** mystery tour; ~**äugig** *a* blue-eyed; **B~licht** *nt* flashing blue light; ~**machen** *vi* (*umg*) skive off work.

Blech [blɛç] *nt* -(e)s, -e tin, sheet metal; (*Back~*) baking tray; ~**büchse** *f*, ~**dose** *f* tin, can; **b~en** *vti* (*umg*)

pay; ~**schaden** *m* (AUT) damage to bodywork.

Blei [blaɪ] *nt* -(e)s, -e lead.

Bleibe ['blaɪbə] *f* -, -n roof over one's head; **b~n** *vi unreg* stay, remain; **bleibenlassen** *vt unreg* leave (alone).

bleich [blaɪç] *a* faded, pale; ~**en** *vt* bleach.

Blei- *zW*: **b~ern** *a* leaden; **b~frei** *a* (*Benzin*) lead-free; ~**stift** *m* pencil; ~**stiftspitzer** *m* pencil sharpener.

Blende ['blɛndə] *f* -, -n (PHOT) aperture; **b~n** *vt* blind, dazzle; (*fig*) hoodwink; **b~nd** *a* (*umg*) grand; **b~nd aussehen** look smashing.

Blick [blɪk] *m* -(e)s, -e (*kurz*) glance, glimpse; (*Anschauen*) look, gaze; (*Aussicht*) view; **b~en** *vi* look; **sich b~en lassen** put in an appearance; ~**fang** *m* eye-catching object; ~**feld** *nt* range of vision (*auch fig*).

blieb *etc v siehe* **bleiben.**

blind [blɪnt] *a* blind; (*Glas etc*) dull; ~**er Passagier** stowaway; **B~darm** *m* appendix; **B~darmentzündung** *f* appendicitis; **B~enschrift** ['blɪndən-] *f* braille; **B~heit** *f* blindness; ~**lings** *ad* blindly; **B~schleiche** *f* slow worm.

blink- [blɪŋk] *zW*: ~**en** *vi* twinkle, sparkle; (*Licht*) flash, signal; (AUT) indicate // *vt* flash, signal; **B~er** *m* -s, - (AUT) indicator.

blinzeln ['blɪntsəln] *vi* blink, wink.

Blitz [blɪts] *m* -es, -e (flash of) lightning; ~**ableiter** *m* lightning conductor; **b~en** *vi* (*aufleuchten*) glint, shine; **es blitzt** (MET) there's a flash of lightning; ~**licht** *nt* flashlight; **b~schnell** *a, ad* as quick as a flash.

Block [blɔk] *m* -(e)s, ⁻e (*lit, fig*) block; (*von Papier*) pad; **Blockade** [blɔ'kaːdə] *f* -, -n blockade; **b~flöte** *f* recorder; **b~frei** *a* (POL) unaligned; **b~ieren** [blɔ'kiːrən] *vt* block // *vi* (*Räder*) jam; ~**schrift** *f* block letters *pl*.

blöd [bløːt] *a* silly, stupid; **B~sinn** *m* nonsense; ~**sinnig** *a* silly, idiotic.

blond [blɔnt] *a* blond, fair-haired.

bloß [bloːs] ◆ *a* **1** (*unbedeckt*) bare; (*nackt*) naked; **mit der** ~**en Hand** with one's bare hand; **mit** ~**em Auge** with the naked eye

2 (*alleinig, nur*) mere; **der** ~**e Gedanke** the very thought; ~**er Neid** sheer envy

◆ *ad* only, merely; **laß das** ~**!** just don't do that!; **wie ist das** ~ **passiert?** how on earth did that happen?

Blöße ['bløːsə] *f* -, -n bareness; nakedness; (*fig*) weakness.

bloß- *zW*: ~**legen** *vt* expose; ~**stellen** *vt* show up.

blühen ['blyːən] *vi* (*lit*) bloom, be in

bloom; *(fig)* flourish.

Blume ['blu:mə] *f* -, -n flower; *(von Wein)* bouquet; **Blumenkohl** *m* cauliflower; **Blumentopf** *m* flowerpot; **Blumenzwiebel** *f* bulb.

Bluse ['blu:zə] *f* -, -n blouse.

Blut [blu:t] *nt* -(e)s blood; **b~arm** *a* anaemic; *(fig)* penniless; **b~befleckt** *a* bloodstained; **~druck** *m* blood pressure.

Blüte ['bly:tə] *f* -, -n blossom; *(fig)* prime; **~zeit** *f* flowering period; *(fig)* prime.

Blutegel *m* leech.

bluten *vi* bleed.

Blütenstaub *m* pollen.

Blut- *zW:* **~er** *m* -s, - *(MED)* haemophiliac; **~erguß** *m* haemorrhage; *(auf Haut)* bruise; **~gruppe** *f* blood group; **b~ig** *a* bloody; **b~jung** *a* very young; **~probe** *f* blood test; **~spender** *m* blood donor; **~übertragung** *f* blood transfusion; **~ung** *f* bleeding, haemorrhage; **~vergiftung** *f* blood poisoning; **~wurst** *f* black pudding.

Bö(e) ['bø:(ə)] *f* -, -en squall.

Bock [bɔk] *m* -(e)s, ⸚e buck, ram; *(Gestell)* trestle, support; *(SPORT)* buck; **~wurst** *f* type of pork sausage.

Boden ['bo:dən] *m* -s, ⸚ ground; *(Fuß~)* floor; *(Meeres~, Faß~)* bottom; *(Speicher)* attic; **~see** *m*: der ~see Lake Constance; **b~los** *a* bottomless; *(umg)* incredible; **~schätze** *pl* mineral wealth; **~turnen** *nt* floor exercises *pl*.

Bogen ['bo:gən] *m* -s, - *(Biegung)* curve; *(ARCHIT)* arch; *(Waffe, MUS)* bow; *(Papier)* sheet; **~gang** *m* arcade.

Bohle ['bo:lə] *f* -, -n plank.

Bohne ['bo:nə] *f* -, -n bean; **Bohnenkaffee** *m* pure coffee; **bohnern** *vt* wax, polish; **Bohnerwachs** *nt* floor polish.

Bohr- ['bo:r] *zW:* **b~en** *vt* bore; **~er** *m* -s, - drill; **~insel** *f* oil rig; **~maschine** *f* drill; **~turm** *m* derrick.

Boje ['bo:jə] *f* -, -n buoy.

Bolivien [bo'li:viən] *nt* Bolivia.

Bolzen ['bɔltsən] *m* -s, - bolt.

bombardieren [bɔmbar'di:rən] *vt* bombard; *(aus der Luft)* bomb.

Bombe ['bɔmbə] *f* -, -n bomb.

Bombenangriff *m* bombing raid.

Bombenerfolg *m (umg)* huge success.

Bonbon [bõ'bõ:] *m od nt* -s, -s sweet.

Boot [bo:t] *nt* -(e)s, -e boat.

Bord [bɔrt] *m* -(e)s, -e *(AVIAT, NAUT)* board; **an ~** on board // *nt (Brett)* shelf; **Bordell** [bɔr'dɛl] *nt* -s, -e brothel; **~stein** *m* kerb(stone).

borgen ['bɔrgən] *vt* borrow; **jdm etw**

~ **lend sb sth.**

borniert [bɔr'ni:rt] *a* narrow-minded.

Börse ['bœrzə] *f* -, -n stock exchange; *(Geld~)* purse.

Borste ['bɔrstə] *f* -, -n bristle.

Borte ['bɔrtə] *f* -, -n edging; *(Band)* trimming.

bös(e) [bø:s, 'bø:zə] *a* bad, evil; *(zornig)* angry.

bösartig ['bø:s-] *a* malicious.

Böschung ['bœʃʊŋ] *f* slope; *(Ufer~ etc)* embankment.

bos- ['bo:s] *zW:* **~haft** *a* malicious, spiteful; **B~heit** *f* malice, spite.

böswillig ['bø:svɪlɪç] *a* malicious.

bot *etc v siehe* **bieten.**

Botanik [bo'ta:nɪk] *f* botany.

botanisch [bo'ta:nɪʃ] *a* botanical.

Bot- ['bo:t] *zW:* **~e** *m* -n, *an* messenger; **~schaft** *f* message, news; *(POL)* embassy; **~schafter** *m* -s, - ambassador.

Bottich ['bɔtɪç] *m* -(e)s, -e vat, tub.

Bouillon [bʊ'ljõ:] *f* -, -s consommé.

Bowle ['bo:lə] *f* -, -n punch.

Box- ['bɔks] *zW:* **b~en** *vi* box; **~er** *m* -s, - boxer; **~handschuh** *m* boxing glove; **~kampf** *m* boxing match.

boykottieren [bɔykɔ'ti:rən] *vt* boycott.

brach *etc v siehe* **brechen.**

brachte *etc v siehe* **bringen.**

Branche ['brã:ʃə] *f* -, -n line of business; **Branchenverzeichnis** *nt* yellow pages *pl.*

Brand [brant] *m* -(e)s, ⸚e fire; *(MED)* gangrene; **b~en** [brandən] *vi* surge; *(Meer)* break; **b~marken** *vt* brand; *(fig)* stigmatize; **~salbe** *f* ointment for burns; **~stifter** *m* arsonist, fire-raiser; **~stiftung** *f* arson; **~ung** *f* surf; **~wunde** *f* burn.

Branntwein ['brantvaɪn] *m* brandy.

Brasil- [bra'zi:l] *zW:* **~ien** *[-iən] nt* Brazil; **~ianer(in** *f)* [-i'a:nər(ɪn)] *m* Brazilian; **b~ianisch** *a* Brazilian.

Brat- [bra:t] *zW:* **~apfel** *m* baked apple; **b~en** *vt unreg* roast, fry; **~en** *m* -s, - roast, joint; **~hähnchen** *nt*, **~huhn** *nt* roast chicken; **~kartoffeln** *pl* fried *od* roast potatoes *pl*; **~pfanne** *f* frying pan.

Bratsche ['bra:tʃə] *f* -, -n viola.

Brat- *zW:* **~spieß** *m* spit; **~wurst** *f* grilled sausage.

Brauch [braʊx] *m* -(e)s, Bräuche custom; **b~bar** *a* usable, serviceable; *(Person)* capable; **b~en** *vt (bedürfen)* need; *(müssen)* have to; *(verwenden)* use.

Braue ['braʊə] *f* -, -n brow; **b~n** *vt* brew; **Braue'rei** *f* brewery.

braun [braʊn] *a* brown; *(von Sonne auch)* tanned.

Bräune ['brɔynə] *f* - brownness; *(Sonnen~)* tan; **b~n** *vt* make brown;

(*Sonne*) tan.

braungebrannt *a* tanned.

Brause ['brauzə] *f* -, -n shower bath; (*von Gießkanne*) rose; (*Getränk*) lemonade; **b~n** *vi* roar; (*auch vr: duschen*) take a shower.

Braut [braut] *f* -, **Bräute** bride; (*Verlobte*) fiancée.

Bräutigam ['brɔytɪgam] *m* -s, -e bridegroom; fiancé.

Brautpaar *nt* bride and bridegroom, bridal pair.

brav [braːf] *a* (*artig*) good; (*ehrenhaft*) worthy, honest.

bravo ['braːvo] *interj* well done.

BRD ['beːˈɛrˈdeː] *f* *abk* *von* **Bundesrepublik Deutschland.**

Brech- ['brɛç] *zW*: **~eisen** *nt* crowbar; **b~en** *vti* *unreg* break; (*Licht*) refract; (*fig: Mensch*) crush; (*speien*) vomit; **~reiz** *m* nausea, retching.

Brei [brai] *m* -(e)s, -e (*Masse*) pulp; (*KOCH*) gruel; (*Hafer~*) porridge (*Brit*), oat meal (*US*).

breit [brait] *a* wide, broad; **B~e** *f* -, -n width; breadth; (*GEOG*) latitude; **~en** *vt*: etw über etw (*akk*) **~en** spread sth over sth; **B~engrad** *m* degree of latitude; **~machen** *vr* spread o.s. out; **~treten** *vt* *unreg* (*umg*) enlarge upon.

Brems- ['brɛms] *zW*: **~belag** *m* brake lining; **~e** [-zə] *f* -, -n brake; (*ZOOL*) horsefly; **b~en** [-zən] *vi* brake, apply the brakes // *vt* (*Auto*) brake; (*fig*) slow down; **~licht** *nt* brake light; **~pedal** *nt* brake pedal; **~spur** *f* tyre (*Brit*) *od* tire (*US*) marks *pl*; **~weg** *m* braking distance.

Brenn- ['brɛn] *zW*: **b~bar** *a* inflammable; **b~en** *unreg* *vi* burn, be on fire; (*Licht, Kerze etc*) burn // *vt* (*Holz etc*) burn; (*Ziegel, Ton*) fire; (*Kaffee*) roast; darauf b~en, etw zu tun be dying to do sth; **~(n)essel** *f* nettle; **~spiritus** *m* methylated spirits; **~stoff** *m* liquid fuel.

brenzlig ['brɛntslɪç] *a* (*fig*) precarious.

Brett [brɛt] *nt* -(e)s, -er board, plank; (*Bord*) shelf; (*Spiel~*) board; Schwarze(s) ~ notice board; **~er** *pl* (*SKI*) skis *pl*; (*THEAT*) boards *pl*; **~erzaun** *m* wooden fence.

Brezel ['breːtsəl] *f* -, -n pretzel.

brichst *etc* *v* *siehe* **brechen.**

Brief [briːf] *m* -(e)s, -e letter; **~freund** *m* penfriend; **~kasten** *m* letterbox; **~kopf** *m* letterhead; **b~lich** *a,ad* by letter; **~marke** *f* postage stamp; **~öffner** *m* letter opener; **~papier** *nt* notepaper; **~tasche** *f* wallet; **~träger** *m* postman; **~umschlag** *m* envelope; **~wechsel** *m* correspondence.

briet *etc* *v* *siehe* **braten.**

Brikett [briˈkɛt] *nt* -s, -s briquette.

brillant [brɪlˈjant] *a* (*fig*) sparkling, brilliant; **B~** *m* -en, -en brilliant, diamond.

Brille ['brɪlə] *f* -, -n spectacles *pl*; (*Schutz~*) goggles *pl*; (*Toiletten~*) (toilet) seat.

bringen ['brɪŋən] *vt* *unreg* bring; (*mitnehmen, begleiten*) take; (*einbringen: Profit*) bring in; (*veröffentlichen*) publish; (*THEAT, CINE*) show; (*RAD, TV*) broadcast; (*in einen Zustand versetzen*) get; (*umg: tun können*) manage; jdn dazu ~, etw zu tun make sb do sth; jdn nach Hause ~ take sb home; jdn um etw ~ make sb lose sth; jdn auf eine Idee ~ give sb an idea.

Brise ['briːzə] *f* -, -n breeze.

Brit- ['briːt] *zW*: **~e** *m*, **~in** *f* Briton; **b~isch** *a* British.

bröckelig ['brœkəlɪç] *a* crumbly.

Brocken ['brɔkən] *m* -s, - piece, bit; (*Fels~*) lump of rock.

brodeln ['broːdəln] *vi* bubble.

Brokat [broˈkaːt] *m* -(e)s, -e brocade.

Brombeere ['brɔmbeːrə] *f* blackberry, bramble (*Brit*).

Bronchien ['brɔnçiən] *pl* bronchia(l tubes) *pl*.

Bronze ['brõːsə] *f* -, -n bronze.

Brosche ['brɔʃə] *f* -, -n brooch.

Broschüre [brɔˈʃyːrə] *f* -, -n pamphlet.

Brot [broːt] *nt* -(e)s, -e bread; (*~laib*) loaf.

Brötchen ['brøːtçən] *nt* roll.

Bruch [brʊx] *m* -(e)s, ˡe breakage; (*zerbrochene Stelle*) break; (*fig*) split, breach; (*MED: Eingeweide~*) rupture, hernia; (*Bein~ etc*) fracture; (*MATH*) fraction.

brüchig ['brʏçɪç] *a* brittle, fragile; (*Haus*) dilapidated.

Bruch- *zW*: **~landung** *f* crash landing; **~strich** *m* (*MATH*) line; **~stück** *nt* fragment; **~teil** *m* fraction.

Brücke ['brʏkə] *f* -, -n bridge; (*Teppich*) rug.

Bruder ['bruːdər] *m* -s, ˡ brother.

brüderlich ['brʏːdərlɪç] *a* brotherly.

Brühe ['brʏːə] *f* -, -n broth, stock; (*pej*) muck.

brüllen ['brʏlən] *vi* bellow, scream.

brummen ['brʊmən] *vi* (*Bär, Mensch etc*) growl; (*Insekt, Radio*) buzz; (*Motoren*) roar; (*murren*) grumble // *vt* growl.

brünett [brʏˈnɛt] *a* brunette, dark-haired.

Brunnen ['brʊnən] *m* -s, - fountain; (*tief*) well; (*natürlich*) spring.

brüsk [brʏsk] *a* abrupt, brusque.

Brüssel ['brʏsəl] *nt* Brussels.

Brust [brʊst] *f* -, ˡe breast; (*Männer~*) chest.

brüsten ['brystən] *vr* boast.

Brust- *zW:* **~fellentzündung** *f* pleurisy; **~kasten** *m* chest; **~schwimmen** *nt* breast-stroke; **~warze** *f* nipple.

Brüstung ['brystʊŋ] *f* parapet.

Brut [bru:t] *f* -, **-en** brood; (*Brüten*) hatching; **brutal** [bru'ta:l] *a* brutal; **Brutali'tät** *f* brutality; **~kasten** *m* incubator.

brüten ['bry:tən] *vi* hatch, brood (*auch fig*).

brutto ['brʊto] *ad* gross; **B~einkommen** *nt*, **B~gehalt** *nt* gross salary; **B~gewicht** *nt* gross weight; **B~lohn** *m* gross wages *pl*.

Bube ['bu:bə] *m* **-n**, **-n** (*Schurke*) rogue; (*KARTEN*) jack.

Buch [bu:x] *nt* **-(e)s**, **-̈er** book; (*COMM*) account book; **~binder** *m* bookbinder; **~drucker** *m* printer; **~e** *f* -, **-n** beech tree; **b~en** *vt* book; (*Betrag*) enter.

Bücher- ['by:çər] *zW:* **~brett** *nt* bookshelf; **~ei** [-'rai] *f* library; **~regal** *nt* bookshelves *pl*, bookcase; **~schrank** *m* bookcase.

Buch- *zW:* **~fink** *m* chaffinch; **~führung** *f* book-keeping, accounting; **~halter(in** *f*) *m* **-s**, - bookkeeper; **~handel** *m* book trade; **~händler(in** *f*) *m* bookseller; **~handlung** *f* bookshop.

Büchse ['bʏksə] *f* -, **-n** tin, can; (*Holz~*) box; (*Gewehr*) rifle; **Büchsenfleisch** *nt* tinned meat; **Büchsenöffner** *m* tin *od* can opener.

Buch- *zW:* **~stabe** *m* **-ns**, **-n** letter (of the alphabet); **b~stabieren** [bu:xʃta'bi:rən] *vt* spell; **b~stäblich** ['bu:xʃtɛ:pliç] *a* literal.

Bucht ['bʊxt] *f* -, **-en** bay.

Buchung ['bu:xʊŋ] *f* booking; (*COMM*) entry.

Buckel ['bʊkəl] *m* **-s**, - hump.

bücken ['bʏkən] *vr* bend.

Bückling ['bʏklɪŋ] *m* (*Fisch*) kipper; (*Verbeugung*) bow.

Bude ['bu:də] *f* -, **-n** booth, stall; (*umg*) digs *pl* (*Brit*).

Büfett [by'fe:] *nt* **-s**, **-s** (*Anrichte*) sideboard; (*Geschirrschrank*) dresser; **kaltes** ~ cold buffet.

Büffel ['bʏfəl] *m* **-s**, - buffalo.

Bug [bu:k] *m* **-(e)s**, **-e** (*NAUT*) bow; (*AVIAT*) nose.

Bügel ['by:gəl] *m* **-s**, - (*Kleider~*) hanger; (*Steig~*) stirrup; (*Brillen~*) arm; **~brett** *nt* ironing board; **~eisen** *nt* iron; **~falte** *f* crease; **b~n** *vti* iron.

Bühne ['by:nə] *f* -, **-n** stage; **Bühnenbild** *nt* set, scenery.

Buhruf ['bu:ru:f] *m* boo.

buk *etc v siehe* **backen**.

Bulgarien [bʊl'ga:riən] *nt* Bulgaria.

Bull- ['bʊl] *zW:* **~dogge** *f* bulldog; **~dozer** ['bʊldo:zər] *m* **-s**, - bulldozer; **~e** *m* **-n**, **-n** bull.

Bummel ['bʊməl] *m* **-s**, - stroll; (*Schaufenster~*) window-shopping; **~ant** [-'lant] *m* slowcoach; **~ei** [-'lai] *f* wandering; dawdling; skiving; **b~n** *vi* wander, stroll; (*trödeln*) dawdle; (*faulenzen*) skive, loaf around; **~streik** *m* go-slow; **~zug** *m* slow train.

Bund [bʊnt] *m* **-(e)s**, **-̈e** (*Freundschafts~ etc*) bond; (*Organisation*) union; (*POL*) confederacy; (*Hosen~*, *Rock~*) waistband // *nt* **-(e)s**, **-e** bunch; (*Stroh~*) bundle.

Bündel ['bʏndəl] *nt* **-s**, - bundle, bale; **b~n** *vt* bundle.

Bundes- ['bʊndəs] *in zW* Federal (*bes* West German); **~bahn** *f* Federal Railways *pl*; **~hauptstadt** *f* Federal capital; **~kanzler** *m* Federal Chancellor; **~land** *nt* Land; **~liga** *f* football league; **~präsident** *m* Federal President; **~rat** *m* upper house of West German Parliament; **~republik** *f* Federal Republic (of West Germany); **~staat** *m* Federal state; **~tag** *m* West German Parliament; **~verfassungsgericht** *nt* Federal Constitutional Court; **~wehr** *f* West German Armed Forces *pl*.

Bünd- *zW:* **b~ig** *a* (*kurz*) concise; **~nis** *nt* **-ses**, **-se** alliance.

Bunker ['bʊŋkər] *m* **-s**, - bunker.

bunt [bʊnt] *a* coloured; (*gemischt*) mixed; **jdm wird es zu** ~ it's getting too much for sb; **B~stift** *m* coloured pencil, crayon.

Burg [bʊrk] *f* -, **-en** castle, fort.

Bürge ['bʏrgə] *m* **-n**, **-n** guarantor; **b~n** *vi* vouch (*für* for).

Bürger(in *f*) ['bʏrgər(ɪn)] *m* **-s**, - citizen; member of the middle class; **~krieg** *m* civil war; **b~lich** *a* (*Rechte*) civil; (*Klasse*) middleclass; (*pej*) bourgeois; **~meister** *m* mayor; **~recht** *nt* civil rights *pl*; **~schaft** *f* population, citizens *pl*; **~steig** *m* pavement; **~tum** *nt* citizens *pl*.

Bürgschaft *f* surety; ~ **leisten** give security.

Büro [by'ro:] *nt* **-s**, **-s** office; **~angestellte(r)** *mf* office worker; **~automatisierung** *f* office automation, OA; **~klammer** *f* paper clip; **~krat** [byro'kra:t] *m* **-en**, **-en** bureaucrat; **~kra'tie** *f* bureaucracy; **b~kratisch** *a* bureaucratic; **~schluß** *m* office closing time.

Bursch(e) [bʊrʃ(ə)] *m* **-en**, **-en** lad, fellow; (*Diener*) servant.

Bürste ['bʏrstə] *f* -, **-n** brush; **b~n** *vt* brush.

Bus [bʊs] *m* **-ses, -se** bus.
Busch [bʊʃ] *m* **-(e)s, ⸚e** bush, shrub.
Büschel ['bʏʃəl] *nt* **-s, -** tuft.
buschig *a* bushy.
Busen ['bu:zən] *m* **-s, -** bosom; (*Meer~*) inlet, bay.
Buße ['bu:sə] *f* **-, -n** atonement, penance; (*Geld*) fine.
büßen ['by:sən] *vti* do penance (for), atone (for).
Bußgeld ['bu:sgelt] *nt* fine.
Büste ['bʏstə] *f* **-, -n** bust; **Büstenhalter** *m* bra.
Butter ['bʊtər] *f* **-** butter; **~blume** *f* buttercup; **~brot** *nt* (piece of) bread and butter; **~brotpapier** *nt* greaseproof paper; **~dose** *f* butter dish; **b~weich** *a* soft as butter; (*fig, umg*) soft.
b.w. *abk* (= *bitte wenden*) p.t.o.
Byte [baɪt] *nt* **-s** byte.
bzgl. *abk* (= *bezüglich*) re.
bzw. *abk von* **beziehungsweise.**

C

(*siehe auch* **K**, **Z**;
für **CH** *siehe auch* **SCH**)

C, c [tse:] *nt* C, c.
ca. *abk* (= *circa*) approx.
Café [ka'fe:] *nt* **-s, -s** café.
Cafeteria [kafete'ri:a] *f* **-, -s** cafeteria.
Camp- [kɛmp] *zW*: **c~en** *vi* camp; **~er(in** *f***)** *m* **-s, -** camper; **~ing** *nt* **-s** camping; **~ingkocher** *m* camping stove; **~ingplatz** *m* camp(ing) site.
CDU [tse:de:''u:] *f abk* (= *Christlich-Demokratische Union*) Christian Democratic Union.
Cellist [tʃɛ'lɪst] *m* cellist.
Cello ['tʃɛlo] *nt* **-s, -s** *od* **Celli** cello.
Chamäleon [ka'mɛ:leɔn] *nt* **-s, -s** chameleon.
Champagner [ʃam'panjər] *m* **-s, -** champagne.
Champignon ['ʃampɪnjõ] *m* **-s, -s** button mushroom.
Chance ['ʃã:s(ə)] *f* **-, -n** chance, opportunity.
Chaos ['ka:ɔs] *nt* **-, -** chaos.
chaotisch [ka'o:tɪʃ] *a* chaotic.
Charakter [ka'raktər] *m* **-s, -e** [karak'te:rə] character; **c~fest** *a* of firm character, strong; **c~i'sieren** *vt* characterize; **c~istisch** [karakte'rɪstɪʃ] *a* characteristic, typical (*für* of); **c~los** *a* unprincipled; **~losigkeit** *f* lack of principle; **~schwäche** *f* weakness of character; **~stärke** *f* strength of character; **~zug** *m* characteristic, trait.
charmant [ʃar'mant] *a* charming.
Charme [ʃarm] *m* **-s** charm.
Charterflug ['(t)ʃa:rtərflu:k] *m* charter flight.
Chassis [ʃa'si:] *nt* **-, -** chassis.
Chauffeur [ʃɔ'fø:r] *m* chauffeur.
Chauvinist [ʃovi'nɪst] *m* chauvinist, jingoist.
Chef [ʃɛf] *m* **-s, -s** head; (*umg*) boss; **~arzt** *m* head physician; **~in** *f* (*umg*) boss.
Chemie [çe'mi:] *f* **-** chemistry; **~faser** *f* man-made fibre.
Chemikalie [çemi'ka:liə] *f* **-, -n** chemical.
Chemiker(in *f***)** ['çe:mikər(ɪn)] *m* **-s, -** (industrial) chemist.
chemisch ['çe:mɪʃ] *a* chemical; **~e** Reinigung dry cleaning.
Chiffre ['ʃɪfrə] *f* **-, -n** (*Geheimzeichen*) cipher; (*in Zeitung*) box number.
Chile ['çi:le, 'tʃi:le] *nt* Chile; **~ne** [-'le:nə] *m*, **~nin** *f* Chilean; **c~nisch** *a* Chilean.
Chin- ['çi:n] *zW*: **~a** *nt* China; **~ese** [-'ne:zə] *m*, **~esin** *f* Chinese; **c~esisch** *a* Chinese.
Chips [tʃɪps] *pl* crisps *pl*, chips *pl* (*US*).
Chirurg [çi'rʊrk] *m* **-en, -en** surgeon; **~ie** [-'gi:] *f* surgery; **c~isch** *a* surgical.
Chlor [klo:r] *nt* **-s** chlorine; **Chloro'form** *nt* **-s** chloroform.
Cholera ['ko:lera] *f* **-** cholera.
cholerisch [ko'le:rɪʃ] *a* choleric.
Chor [ko:r] *m* **-(e)s, ⸚e** choir; (*Musikstück*, *THEAT*) chorus; **~al** [ko'ra:l] *m* **-s, -äle** chorale.
Choreograph [koreo'gra:f] *m* **-en, -en** choreographer; **~ie** [-'fi:] *f* choreography.
Chorknabe *m* choirboy.
Christ ['krɪst] *m* **-en, -en** Christian; **~baum** *m* Christmas tree; **~entum** *nt* Christianity; **~in** *f* Christian; **~kind** *nt* ≈ Father Christmas; (*Jesus*) baby Jesus; **c~lich** *a* Christian; **Christus** *m* **-** Christ.
Chrom [kro:m] *nt* **-s** (*CHEM*) chromium; chrome.
Chron- ['kro:n] *zW*: **~ik** *f* chronicle; **c~isch** *a* chronic; **c~ologisch** [-'lo:gɪʃ] *a* chronological.
Chrysantheme [kryzan'te:mə] *f* **-, -n** chrysanthemum.
circa ['tsɪrka] *ad* about, approximately.
Clown [klaʊn] *m* **-s, -s** clown.
cm *abk von* **Zentimeter.**
COBOL ['ko:bɔl] (*COMPUT*) COBOL.
Cola ['ko:la] *f* **-, -s** Coke ®.
Computer [kɔm'pju:tər] *m* **-s, -** computer.
Conférencier [kõferãsi'e:] *m* **-s, -s** compère.
Coupé [ku'pe:] *nt* **-s, -s** (*AUT*) coupé, sports version.
Coupon [ku'põ:] *m* **-s, -s** coupon;

(Stoff~) length of cloth.

Cousin [ku'zɛ:] *m* **-s, -s** cousin; **~e** [ku'zi:nə] *f* **-, -n** cousin.

Creme [krɛ:m] *f* **-, -s** *(lit, fig)* cream; *(Schuh~)* polish; *(Zahn~)* paste; *(KOCH)* mousse; **c~farben** *a* cream(-coloured).

CSU [tse:'ɛs''u:] *f abk* (= *Christlich-Soziale Union*) Christian Social Union.

Curry(pulver *nt)* ['kœri(pʊlfər)] *m od nt* **-s** curry powder.

Cursor ['kœrsər] *m* cursor.

Cutter(in *f)* ['katər(ɪn)] *m* **-s, -** *(CINE)* editor.

D

D, d [de:] *nt* D, d.

da [da:] ◆*ad* **1** *(örtlich)* there; *(hier)* here; **~ draußen** out there; **~ bin ich** here I am; **~, wo** where; **ist noch Milch ~?** is there any milk left? **2** *(zeitlich)* then; *(folglich)* so **3**: **~ haben wir Glück gehabt** we were lucky there; **~ kann man nichts machen** nothing can be done about it ◆*kj (weil)* as, since.

dabehalten *vt unreg* keep.

dabei [da'baɪ] *ad (räumlich)* close to it; *(noch dazu)* besides; *(zusammen mit)* with them; *(zeitlich)* during this; *(obwohl doch)* but, however; **was ist schon ~?** what of it?; **es ist doch nichts ~, wenn ...** it doesn't matter if ...; **bleiben wir ~** let's leave it at that; **es bleibt ~** that's settled; **das Dumme/Schwierige ~** the stupid/difficult part of it; **er war gerade ~, zu gehen** he was just leaving; **~sein** *vi unreg (anwesend)* be present; *(beteiligt)* be involved; **~stehen** *vi unreg* stand around.

Dach [dax] *nt* **-(e)s, ⁻er** roof; **~boden** *m* attic, loft; **~decker** *m* **-s, -** slater, tiler; **~fenster** *nt,* **~luke** *f* skylight; **~pappe** *f* roofing felt; **~rinne** *f* gutter; **~ziegel** *m* roof tile.

Dachs [daks] *m* **-es, -e** badger.

dachte *etc v siehe* **denken**.

Dackel ['dakəl] *m* **-s, -** dachshund.

dadurch [da'dʊrç] *ad (räumlich)* through it; *(durch diesen Umstand)* thereby, in that way; *(deshalb)* because of that, for that reason // *kj*: **~, daß** because.

dafür [da'fy:r] *ad* for it; *(anstatt)* instead; **er kann nichts ~** he can't help it; **er ist bekannt ~** he is well-known for that; **was bekomme ich ~?** what will I get for it?

dagegen [da'ge:gən] *ad* against it; *(im Vergleich damit)* in comparison with it; *(bei Tausch)* to it; **ich habe**

nichts **~** I don't mind; **ich war ~** I was against it; **~ kann man nichts tun** one can't do anything about it // *kj* however; **~halten** *vt unreg (vergleichen)* compare with it; *(entgegnen)* object to it.

daheim [da'haɪm] *ad* at home; **D~** *nt* **-s** home.

daher [da'he:r] *ad (räumlich)* from there; *(Ursache)* from that // *kj (deshalb)* that's why.

dahin [da'hɪn] *ad (räumlich)* there; *(zeitlich)* then; *(vergangen)* gone; **~gegen** *kj* on the other hand; **~gehend** *ad* on this matter; **~gestellt** *ad*: **~gestellt bleiben** remain to be seen; **~gestellt sein lassen** leave sth open *od* undecided.

dahinten [da'hɪntən] *ad* over there.

dahinter [da'hɪntər] *ad* behind it; **~kommen** *vi unreg* get to the bottom of sth.

Dahlie ['da:liə] *f* **-, -n** dahlia.

dalli ['dali] *adv (umg)* chop chop.

damalig ['da:ma:lɪç] *a* of that time, then.

damals ['da:ma:ls] *ad* at that time, then.

Damast [da'mast] *m* **-(e)s, -e** damask.

Dame ['da:mə] *f* **-, -n** lady; *(SCHACH, KARTEN)* queen; *(Spiel)* draughts; **damenhaft** *a* ladylike; **Damenwahl** *f* ladies' excuse-me.

damit [da'mɪt] *ad* with it; *(begründend)* by that; **was meint er ~?** what does he mean by that?; **genug ~!** that's enough; **~ eilt es nicht** there's no hurry // *kj* in order that *od* to.

dämlich ['dɛ:mlɪç] *a (umg)* silly, stupid.

Damm [dam] *m* **-(e)s, ⁻e** dyke; *(Stau~)* dam; *(Hafen~)* mole; *(Bahn~, Straßen~)* embankment.

Dämm- ['dɛm] *zW*: **d~en** *vt (Wasser)* dam up; *(Schmerzen)* keep back; **d~erig** *a* dim, faint; **d~ern** *vi (Tag)* dawn; *(Abend)* fall; **~erung** *f* twilight; *(Morgen~)* dawn; *(Abend~)* dusk.

dämonisch [dɛ'mo:nɪʃ] *a* demoniacal.

Dampf [dampf] *m* **-(e)s, ⁻e** steam; *(Dunst)* vapour; **d~en** *vi* steam.

dämpfen ['dɛmpfən] *vt (KOCH)* steam; *(bügeln auch)* iron with a damp cloth; *(fig)* dampen, subdue.

Dampf- *zW*: **~er** *m* **-s, -** steamer; **~kochtopf** *m* pressure cooker; **~schiff** *nt* steamship; **~walze** *f* steamroller.

danach [da'na:x] *ad* after that; *(zeitlich auch)* afterwards; *(gemäß)* accordingly; according to which *od* that; **er sieht ~ aus** he looks it.

daneben [da'ne:bən] *ad* beside it; *(im Vergleich)* in comparison;

~**benehmen** *vr unreg* misbehave; ~**gehen** *vi unreg* miss; (*Plan*) fail.

Dän- ['dɛːn] *zW:* ~**e** *m*, ~**in** *f* Dane; ~**emark** *nt* Denmark; **d~isch** *a* Danish.

Dank [daŋk] *m* **-(e)s** thanks *pl*; **vielen** *od* **schönen** ~ many thanks; **jdm** ~ **sagen** thank sb; **d~** *präp* +*dat od gen* thanks to; **d~bar** *a* grateful; (*Aufgabe*) rewarding; ~**barkeit** *f* gratitude; **d~e** *interj* thank you, thanks; **d~en** *vi* (+*dat*) thank; **d~enswert** *a* (*Arbeit*) worthwhile; rewarding; (*Bemühung*) kind; **d~sagen** *vi* express one's thanks.

dann [dan] *ad* then; ~ **und wann** now and then.

daran [da'ran] *ad* on it; (*stoßen*) against it; **es liegt** ~, **daß** ... the cause of it is that ...; **gut/schlecht** ~ **sein** to be well-/badly off; **das Beste/Dümmste** ~ the best/stupidest thing about it; **ich war nahe** ~, **zu** ... I was on the point of ...; **er ist** ~ **gestorben** he died from *od* of it; ~**gehen** *vi unreg* start; ~**setzen** *vt* stake; **er hat alles** ~**gesetzt, von Glasgow wegzukommen** he has done his utmost to get away from Glasgow.

darauf [da'rauf] *ad* (*räumlich*) on it; (*zielgerichtet*) towards it; (*danach*) afterwards; **es kommt ganz** ~ **an, ob** ... it depends whether ...; **die Tage** ~ the days following *od* thereafter; **am Tag** ~ the next day; ~**folgend** *a* (*Tag, Jahr*) next, following; ~**legen** *vt* lay *od* put on top.

daraus [da'raus] *ad* from it; **was ist** ~ **geworden?** what became of it?; ~ **geht hervor, daß** ... this means that ...

Darbietung ['daːrbiːtʊŋ] *f* performance.

darf *etc v siehe* **dürfen**.

darin [da'rɪn] *ad* in (there), in it.

Dar- ['daːr] *zW:* **d~legen** *vt* explain, expound, set forth; ~**legung** *f* explanation; ~**leh(e)n** *nt* **-s,** - loan.

Darm [darm] *m* **-(e)s, ˆe** intestine; (*Wurst~*) skin; ~**saite** *f* gut string.

Darstell- ['daːrʃtɛl] *zW:* **d~en** *vt* (*abbilden, bedeuten*) represent; (*THEAT*) act; (*beschreiben*) describe // *vr* appear to be; ~**er(in** *f*) *m* **-s,** - actor/actress; ~**ung** *f* portrayal, depiction.

darüber [da'ryːbər] *ad* (*räumlich*) over/above it; (*fahren*) over it; (*mehr*) more; (*währenddessen*) meanwhile; (*sprechen, streiten*) about it; ~ **geht nichts** there's nothing like it.

darum [da'rʊm] *ad* (*räumlich*) round it; **er bittet** ~ he is pleading for it; **es geht** ~, **daß** ... the thing is that ...;

er würde viel ~ **geben, wenn** ... he would give a lot to ... // *kj* that's why; **ich tue es** ~, **weil** ... I am doing it because ...

darunter [da'rʊntər] *ad* (*räumlich*) under it; (*dazwischen*) among them; (*weniger*) less; **ein Stockwerk** ~ one floor below (it); **was verstehen Sie** ~? what do you understand by that?.

das [das] *def art* the // *pron* that.

Dasein ['daːzain] *nt* **-s** (*Leben*) life; (*Anwesenheit*) presence; (*Bestehen*) existence; **d~** *vi unreg* be there.

daß [das] *kj* that.

dasselbe [das'zɛlbə] *art, pron* the same.

dastehen ['daːʃteːən] *vi unreg* stand there.

Datei [da'tai] *f* file.

Daten- ['daːtən] *zW:* ~**bank** *f* data base; ~**sichtgerät** *nt* visual display unit, VDU.

datieren [da'tiːrən] *vt* date.

Dattel ['datəl] *f* -, **-n** date.

Datum ['daːtʊm] *nt* **-s, Daten** date; (*pl: Angaben*) data *pl*.

Dauer ['dauər] *f* -, **-n** duration; (*gewisse Zeitspanne*) length; (*Bestand, Fortbestehen*) permanence; **es war nur von kurzer** ~ it didn't last long; **auf die** ~ in the long run; (*auf längere Zeit*) indefinitely; ~**auftrag** *m* standing order; **d~haft** *a* lasting, durable; ~**karte** *f* season ticket; ~**lauf** *m* long-distance run; **d~n** *vi* last; **es hat sehr lang gedauert, bis er** ... it took him a long time to ...;

dauernd *a* constant; ~**welle** *f* perm(anent wave); ~**wurst** *f* German salami; ~**zustand** *m* permanent condition.

Daumen ['daumən] *m* **-s,** - thumb.

Daune ['daunə] *f* -, **-n** down; **Daunendecke** *f* down duvet *od* quilt.

davon [da'fɔn] *ad* of it; (*räumlich*) away; (*weg von*) from it; (*Grund*) because of it; **das kommt** ~! that's what you get; ~ **abgesehen** apart from that; ~ **sprechen/wissen** talk/know of *od* about it; **was habe ich** ~? what's the point?; ~**gehen** *vi unreg* leave, go away; ~**laufen** *vi unreg* run away.

davor [da'foːr] *ad* (*räumlich*) in front of it; (*zeitlich*) before (that); ~ **warnen** warn about it.

dazu [da'tsuː] *ad* (*legen, stellen*) by it; (*essen, singen*) with it; **und** ~ **noch** and in addition; **ein Beispiel/seine Gedanken** ~ one example for/his thoughts on this; **wie komme ich denn** ~? why should I?; ~ **fähig sein** be capable of it; **sich** ~ **äußern** say sth on it; ~**gehören** *vi* belong to it; ~**kommen** *vi unreg* (*Ereignisse*) happen too; (an einen Ort) come along.

dazwischen [da'tsvɪʃən] ad in between; (räumlich auch) between (them); (zusammen mit) among them; **der Unterschied ~** the difference between them; **~kommen** vi unreg (hineingeraten) get caught in it; **es ist etwas ~gekommen** something cropped up; **~reden** vi (unterbrechen) interrupt; (sich einmischen) interfere; **~treten** vi unreg intervene.

DB abk (= Deutsche Bundesbahn) Federal Railways.

DDR [de:de:'ɛr] f abk (= Deutsche Demokratische Republik) GDR.

Debatte [de'batə] f -, -n debate.

Deck [dɛk] nt -(e)s, -s od -e deck; **an ~ gehen** go on deck; **~e** f -, -n cover; (Bett~) blanket; (Tisch~) tablecloth; (Zimmer~) ceiling; **unter einer ~e stecken** be hand in glove; **~el** m -s, - lid; **d~en** vt cover // vr coincide; **~ung** f (Schützen) covering; (Schutz) cover; (SPORT) defence; (Übereinstimmen) agreement; **d~ungsgleich** a congruent.

Defekt [de'fɛkt] m -(e)s, -e fault, defect; **d~** a faulty.

defensiv [defɛn'siːf] a defensive.

definieren [defi'niːrən] vt define.

Definition [definitsi'oːn] f definition.

Defizit [ˈdeːfitsit] nt -s, -e deficit.

deftig [ˈdɛftɪç] a (Essen) large; (Witz) coarse.

Degen [ˈdeːɡən] m -s, - sword.

degenerieren [deɡeneˈriːrən] vi degenerate.

Dehn- [ˈdeːn] zW: **d~bar** a elastic; (fig: Begriff) loose; **~barkeit** f elasticity; looseness; **d~en** vtr stretch.

Deich [daɪç] m -(e)s, -e dyke, dike.

Deichsel [ˈdaɪksəl] f -, -n shaft; **d~n** vt (fig, umg) wangle.

dein [daɪn] pron (**D~** in Briefen) your; **~e(r, s)** yours; **~er** pron gen of **du** of you; **~erseits** ad on your part; **~esgleichen** pron people like you; **~etwegen**, **~etwillen** ad (für dich) for your sake; (wegen dir) on your account; **~ige** pron: **der/die/das ~ige** yours.

dekadent [dekaˈdɛnt] a decadent.

Dekadenz f decadence.

Deklination [deklinatsiˈoːn] f declension.

deklinieren [dekliˈniːrən] vt decline.

Dekolleté [dekɔlˈteː] nt -s, -s low neckline.

Deko- [deko] zW: **~rateur** [-raˈtøːr] m window dresser; **~ration** [-ratsiˈoːn] f decoration; (in Laden) window dressing; **d~rativ** [-raˈtiːf] a decorative; **d~rieren** [-ˈriːrən] vt decorate;

(Schaufenster) dress.

Delegation [delegatsiˈoːn] f delegation.

delikat [deliˈkaːt] a (zart, heikel) delicate; (köstlich) delicious.

Delikatesse [delikaˈtɛsə] f -, -n delicacy; (pl: Feinkost) delicatessen food; **Delikatessengeschäft** nt delicatessen.

Delikt [deˈlɪkt] nt -(e)s, -e (JUR) offence.

Delle [ˈdɛlə] f -, -n (umg) dent.

Delphin [dɛlˈfiːn] m -s, -e dolphin.

dem [de(ː)m] art dat von **der**.

Demagoge [demaˈɡoːɡə] m -n, -n demagogue.

dementieren [demɛnˈtiːrən] vt deny.

dem- zW: **~gemäß**, **~nach** ad accordingly; **~nächst** ad shortly.

Demokrat [demoˈkraːt] m -en, -en democrat; **~ie** [-ˈtiː] f democracy; **d~isch** a democratic; **d~isieren** [-iˈziːrən] vt democratize.

demolieren [demoˈliːrən] vt demolish.

Demon- [demɔn] zW: **~strant(in** f) [-ˈstrant(ɪn)] m demonstrator; **~stration** [-stratsiˈoːn] f demonstration; **d~strativ** [-straˈtiːf] a demonstrative; (Protest) pointed; **d~strieren** [-ˈstriːrən] vti demonstrate.

Demoskopie [demoskoˈpiː] f public opinion research.

Demut [ˈdeːmuːt] f - humility.

demütig [ˈdeːmyːtɪç] a humble; **~en** [ˈdeːmyːtɪɡən] vt humiliate; **D~ung** f humiliation.

demzufolge [ˈdeːmtsuˈfɔlɡə] ad accordingly.

den [de(ː)n] art akk von **der**.

denen [ˈdeːnən] pron dat pl von **der**, **die**, **das**.

Denk- [ˈdɛŋk] zW: **d~bar** a conceivable; **d~en** vti unreg think; **~en** nt -s thinking; **~fähigkeit** f intelligence; **d~faul** a lazy; **~fehler** m logical error; **~mal** nt -s, ⁻er monument; **d~würdig** a memorable; **~zettel** m: **jdm einen ~zettel verpassen** teach sb a lesson.

denn [dɛn] kj for // ad then; (nach Komparativ) than; **warum ~?** why?

dennoch [ˈdɛnɔx] kj nevertheless.

Denunziant [denuntsiˈant] m informer.

deponieren [depoˈniːrən] vt (COMM) deposit.

Depot [deˈpoː] nt -s, -s warehouse; (Bus~, EISENB) depot; (Bank~) strongroom, safe (US).

Depression [deprɛsiˈoːn] f depression.

deprimieren [depriˈmiːrən] vt depress.

der, die, das [deːr, diː, das] ◆ def art gen **des**, **der**, **des**, dat **dem**, **der**, **dem** akk **den**, **die**, **das**, pl **die** the; **der Rhein** the Rhine; **der Klaus** (umg) Klaus; **die Frau** (im allgemeinen) women; **der Tod/das Leben** death/life; **der Fuß des Berges** the foot of the hill; **gib es der Frau** give it to the woman; **er hat sich die Hand verletzt** he has hurt his hand

◆*rel pron* (*bei Menschen*) who, that; (*bei Tieren, Sachen*) which, that; **der Mann, den ich gesehen habe** the man who *od* whom *od* that I saw

◆*dem pron* he/she/it; (*jener, dieser*) that; *pl* those; **der/die war es** it was him/her; **der mit der Brille** the one with glasses; **ich will den (da)** I want that one.

derart ['deːrʔaːrt] *ad* so; (*solcher Art*) such; **~ig** *a* such, this sort of.

derb [dɛrp] *a* sturdy; (*Kost*) solid; (*grob*) coarse; **D~heit** *f* sturdiness; solidity; coarseness.

der- *zW:* **'~'gleichen** *pron* such; **'~jenige** *pron* he; she; it; (*rel*) the one (who); that (which); **'~'maßen** *ad* to such an extent, so; **~'selbe** *art*, *pron* the same; **'~weil(en)** *ad* in the meantime; **'~zeitig** *a* present, current; (*damalig*) then.

des [dɛs] *art gen von* **der.**

desertieren [dɛzɛr'tiːrən] *vi* desert.

desgleichen ['dɛs'glaɪçən] *pron* the same.

deshalb ['dɛs'halp] *ad* therefore, that's why.

Desinfektion [dɛzɪnfɛktsi'oːn] *f* disinfection; **Desinfektionsmittel** *nt* disinfectant.

desinfizieren [dɛzɪnfi'tsiːrən] *vt* disinfect.

dessen ['dɛsən] *pron gen von* **der**, **das**; **~'ungeachtet** *ad* nevertheless, regardless.

Dessert [dɛ'sɛːr] *nt* **-s, -s** dessert.

destillieren [dɛstɪ'liːrən] *vt* distil.

desto ['dɛsto] *ad* all *od* so much the; **~ besser** all the better.

deswegen ['dɛs've:gən] *kj* therefore, hence.

Detail [de'taɪ] *nt* **-s, -s** detail.

Detektiv [detɛk'tiːf] *m* **-s, -e** detective.

deut- ['dɔyt] *zW:* **~en** *vt* interpret, explain // *vi* point (*auf +akk* to *od* at); **~lich** *a* clear; (*Unterschied*) distinct; **D~lichkeit** *f* clarity; distinctness.

deutsch [dɔytʃ] *a* German; **auf ~** in German; **D~e Demokratische Republik** German Democratic Republic, East Germany; **~es Beefsteak** *nt* ≈ hamburger; **D~** *nt* German; **D~e** *f*, **D~er** *m* German; **ich bin D~er** I am German; **D~land** *nt* Germany.

Devise [de'viːzə] *f* **-, -n** motto, device; (*pl: FIN*) foreign currency *od* exchange.

Dezember [de'tsɛmbər] *m* **-(s), -** December.

dezent [de'tsɛnt] *a* discreet.

dezimal [detsi'maːl] *a* decimal; **D~bruch** *m* decimal (fraction); **D~system** *nt* decimal system.

d.h. *abk* (= *das heißt*) i.e.

Dia ['diːa] *nt* **-s, -s** (*PHOT*) slide, transparency.

Diabetes [dia'beːtɛs] *m* **-, -** (*MED*) diabetes.

Diagnose [dia'gnoːzə] *f* **-, -n** diagnosis.

diagonal [diago'naːl] *a* diagonal; **D~e** *f* **-, -n** diagonal.

Dialekt [dia'lɛkt] *m* **-(e)s, -e** dialect; **d~isch** *a* dialectal; (*Logik*) dialectical.

Dialog [dia'loːk] *m* **-(e)s, -e** dialogue.

Diamant [dia'mant] *m* diamond.

Diät [di'ɛːt] *f* **-** diet; **~en** *pl* (*POL*) allowance.

dich [dɪç] *pron akk von* **du** you; yourself.

dicht [dɪçt] *a* dense; (*Nebel*) thick; (*Gewebe*) close; (*undurchlässig*) (water)tight; (*fig*) concise // *ad:* **~ an/bei** close to; **~bevölkert** *a* densely *od* heavily populated; **D~e** *f* **-, -n** density; thickness; closeness; (water)tightness; (*fig*) conciseness; **~en** *vt* (*dicht machen*) make watertight; seal; (*NAUT*) caulk // *vti* (*LITER*) compose, write; **D~er(in** *f*) *m* **-s, -** poet; (*Autor*) writer; **~erisch** *a* poetical; **~halten** *vi unreg* (*umg*) keep one's mouth shut; **D~ung** *f* (*TECH*) washer; (*AUT*) gasket; (*Gedichte*) poetry; (*Prosa*) (piece of) writing.

dick [dɪk] *a* thick; (*fett*) fat; **durch ~ und dünn** through thick and thin; **D~e** *f* **-, -n** thickness; fatness; **~flüssig** *a* viscous; **D~icht** *nt* **-s, -e** thicket; **D~kopf** *m* mule; **D~milch** *f* soured milk.

die [diː] *def art siehe* **der.**

Dieb(in *f*) [diːp/diːbɪn] *m* **-(e)s, -e** thief; **d~isch** *a* thieving; (*umg*) immense; **~stahl** *m* **-(e)s, -e** theft.

Diele ['diːlə] *f* **-, -n** (*Brett*) board; (*Flur*) hall, lobby.

dienen ['diːnən] *vi* serve (*jdm* sb).

Diener *m* **-s, -** servant; **~in** *f* (*maid*)servant; **~schaft** *f* servants *pl*.

Dienst [diːnst] *m* **-(e)s, -e** service; **außer ~** retired; **~ haben** be on duty.

Dienstag ['diːnstaːk] *m* Tuesday; **d~s** *ad* on Tuesdays.

Dienst- *zW:* **~geheimnis** *nt* professional secret; **~gespräch** *nt* business call; **d~habend** *a* (*Arzt*) on duty; **~leistungsgewerbe** *nt* service industries *pl*; **d~lich** *a* official; **~mädchen** *nt* domestic servant; **~reise** *f* business trip; **~stelle** *f* office; **~vorschrift** *f* service regulations *pl*; **~weg** *m* official channels *pl*; **~zeit** *f* office hours *pl*; (*MIL*) period of service.

dies- [di:s] *zW*: **~bezüglich** *a* (*Frage*) on this matter; **~e**(*r, s*) [di:zə(r,z)] *pron* this (one); **dieselbe** [di:'zɛlbə] *pron, art* the same.

Dieselöl ['di:zəl'ø:l] *nt* diesel oil.

diesig ['di:zɪç] *a* drizzly.

dies- *zW*: **~jährig** *a* this year's; **~mal** *ad* this time; **~seits** *präp* +*gen* on this side; **D~seits** *nt* - this life.

Dietrich ['di:trɪç] *m* -s, -e picklock.

differential [dɪfɛrɛntsi'a:l] *a* differential; **D~getriebe** *nt* differential gear; **D~rechnung** *f* differential calculus.

differenzieren [dɪfɛrɛn'tsi:rən] *vt* make differences in; **differenziert** complex.

Dikt- [dɪkt] *zW*: **~aphon** [-a'fo:n] *nt* dictaphone; **~at** [-'ta:t] *nt* -(e)s, -e dictation; **~ator** [-'ta:tɔr] *m* dictator; **d~atorisch** [-a'to:rɪʃ] *a* dictatorial; **~atur** [-a'tu:r] *f* dictatorship; **d~ieren** [-'ti:rən] *vt* dictate.

Dilemma [di'lɛma] *nt* -s, -s *od* -ta dilemma.

Dilettant [dilɛ'tant] *m* dilettante, amateur; **d~isch** *a* amateurish, dilettante.

Dimension [dimɛnzi'o:n] *f* dimension.

Ding [dɪŋ] *nt* -(e)s, -e thing, object; **d~lich** *a* real, concrete; **Dings, Dingsbums** ['dɪŋksbums] *nt* - (*umg*) thingummybob.

Diözese [diø'tse:zə] *f* -, -n diocese.

Diphtherie [dɪfte'ri:] *f* diphtheria.

Diplom [di'plo:m] *nt* -(e)s, -e diploma, certificate; **~at** [-a't] *m* -en, -en diplomat; **~atie** [-a'ti:] *f* diplomacy; **d~atisch** [-'ma:tɪʃ] *a* diplomatic; **~ingenieur** *m* qualified engineer.

dir [di:r] *pron dat von* **du** (to) you.

direkt [di'rɛkt] *a* direct; **D~or** *m* director; (*SCH*) principal, headmaster; **D~übertragung** *f* live broadcast.

Dirigent [diri'gɛnt] *m* conductor.

dirigieren [diri'gi:rən] *vt* direct; (*MUS*) conduct.

Dirne ['dɪrnə] *f* -, -n prostitute.

Diskette [dɪs'kɛtə] *f* diskette, floppy disk.

Diskont [dɪs'kɔnt] *m* -s, -e discount; **~satz** *m* rate of discount.

Diskothek [dɪsko'te:k] *f* -, -en disco(theque).

diskret [dɪs'kre:t] *a* discreet; **D~ion** [-tsi'o:n] *f* discretion.

Diskussion [dɪskusi'o:n] *f* discussion; debate; **zur ~ stehen** be under discussion.

diskutabel [dɪsku'ta:bəl] *a* debatable.

diskutieren [dɪsku'ti:rən] *vti* discuss; debate.

Distanz [dɪs'tants] *f* distance.

Distel ['dɪstəl] *f* -, -n thistle.

Disziplin [dɪstsi'pli:n] *f* discipline.

Dividende [divi'dɛndə] *f* -, -n dividend.

dividieren [divi'di:rən] *vt* divide (*durch* by).

DM [de:'ɛm] *abk* (= *Deutsche Mark*) German Mark.

D-Mark ['de:mark] *f* D Mark, German Mark.

doch [dɔx] ◆ *ad* **1** (*dennoch*) after all; (*sowieso*) anyway; **er kam ~ noch** he came after all; **du weißt es ja ~ besser** you know better than I do anyway; **und ~ ... and yet ...**

2 (*als bejahende Antwort*) yes I do/it does *etc*; **das ist nicht wahr — ~!** that's not true — yes it is!

3 (*auffordernd*): **komm ~** do come; **laß ihn ~** just leave him; **nicht ~!** oh no!

4: **sie ist ~ noch so jung** but she's still so young; **Sie wissen ~, wie das ist** you know how it is(, don't you?); **wenn ~** if only

◆ *kj* (*aber*) but; (*trotzdem*) all the same; **und ~ hat er es getan** but still he did it.

Docht [dɔxt] *m* -(e)s, -e wick.

Dogge ['dɔgə] *f* -, -n bulldog.

Dogma ['dɔgma] *nt* -s, -men dogma; **d~tisch** [dɔg'ma:tɪʃ] *a* dogmatic.

Doktor ['dɔktɔr] *m* -s, -en [-'to:rən] doctor; **Doktorand** [-'rant] *m* -en, -en candidate for a doctorate; **~arbeit** *f* doctoral thesis.

Dokument [doku'mɛnt] *nt* document.

Dokumentar- [dokumen'ta:r] *zW*: **~bericht** [-'ta:rbərɪçt] *m* documentary; **~film** *m* documentary (film); **d~isch** *a* documentary.

Dolch [dɔlç] *m* -(e)s, -e dagger.

dolmetschen ['dɔlmɛtʃən] *vti* interpret.

Dolmetscher(in *f)* *m* -s, - interpreter.

Dom [do:m] *m* -(e)s, -e cathedral.

dominieren [domi'ni:rən] *vt* dominate // *vi* predominate.

Dompfaff ['do:mpfaf] *m* bullfinch.

Donau ['do:nau] *f* Danube.

Donner ['dɔnər] *m* -s, - thunder; **d~n** *vi unpers* thunder.

Donnerstag ['dɔnərsta:k] *m* Thursday.

doof [do:f] *a* (*umg*) daft, stupid.

Doppel ['dɔpəl] *nt* -s, - duplicate; (*SPORT*) doubles; **~- in** *zW* double; **~bett** *nt* double bed; **~fenster** *nt* double glazing; **~gänger** *m* -s, - double; **~haus** *nt* semi-detached house; **~punkt** *m* colon; **~stecker** *m* two-way adaptor; **d~t** *a* double; **in d~ter Ausführung** in duplicate; **~zentner** *m* 100 kilograms; **~zimmer** *nt* double room.

Dorf [dɔrf] *nt* -(e)s, ¨er village; **~bewohner** *m* villager.

Dorn [dɔrn] *m* -(e)s, -en (*BOT*) thorn;

pl **-e** (*Schnallen*~) tongue; pin; **d~ig** *a* thorny.

dörren ['dœrən] *vt* dry.

Dörrobst ['dœr'o:pst] *nt* dried fruit.

Dorsch [dɔrʃ] *m* **-(e)s, -e** cod.

dort [dɔrt] *ad* there; ~ **drüben** over there; ~**her** from there; ~**hin** (to) there; ~**ig** *a* of that place; in that town.

Dose ['do:zə] *f* -, **-n** box; (*Blech*~) tin, can; **Dosenöffner** *m* tin od can opener.

Dosis ['do:zɪs] *f* -, **Dosen** dose.

Dotter ['dɔtər] *m* **-s,** - egg yolk.

Dozent [do'tsɛnt] *m* university lecturer.

Drache ['draxə] *m* **-n, -n** (*Tier*) dragon; ~**n** *m* **-s,** - kite.

Draht [dra:t] *m* **-(e)s, ⁻e** wire; **auf** ~ **sein** be on the ball; ~**gitter** *nt* wire grating; ~**seil** *nt* cable; ~**seilbahn** *f* cable railway, funicular; ~**zange** *f* pliers *pl.*

Drama ['dra:ma] *nt* **-s, Dramen** drama, play; ~**tiker** [-'ma:tikər] *m* **-s,** - dramatist; **d~tisch** [-'ma:tɪʃ] *a* dramatic.

dran [dran] *ad* (*umg*) **jetzt bin ich** ~! it's my turn now; *siehe* **daran.**

Drang [draŋ] *m* **-(e)s, ⁻e** (*Trieb*) impulse, urge, desire (*nach* for); (*Druck*) pressure.

drängeln ['drɛŋəln] *vti* push, jostle.

drängen ['drɛŋən] *vt* (*schieben*) push, press; (*antreiben*) urge // *vi* (*eilig sein*) be urgent; (*Zeit*) press; **auf etw** (*akk*) ~ press for sth.

drastisch ['drastɪʃ] *a* drastic.

drauf [drauf] *ad* (*umg*) *siehe* **darauf; D~gänger** *m* **-s,** - daredevil.

draußen ['drausən] *ad* outside, out-of-doors.

Dreck [drɛk] *m* **-(e)s** mud, dirt; **d~ig** *a* dirty, filthy.

Dreh- ['dre:] *zW:* ~**arbeiten** *pl* (*CINE*) shooting; ~**bank** *f* lathe; **d~bar** *a* revolving; ~**buch** *nt* (*CINE*) script; **d~en** *vti* turn, rotate; (*Zigaretten*) roll; (*Film*) shoot // *vr* turn; (*handeln von*) be (*um* about); ~**orgel** *f* barrel organ; ~**tür** *f* revolving door; ~**ung** *f* (*Rotation*) rotation; (*Um*~, *Wendung*) turn; ~**zahl** *f* rate of revolutions; ~**zahlmesser** *m* rev(olution) counter.

drei [drai] *num* three; **D~eck** *nt* triangle; ~**eckig** *a* triangular; ~**einhalb** *num* three and a half; ~**erlei** *a inv* of three kinds; ~**fach** *a,ad* triple, treble; ~**hundert** *num* three hundred; **D~'königsfest** *nt* Epiphany; ~**mal** *ad* three times; ~**malig** *a* three times.

dreinreden ['drainre:dən] *vi:* **jdm** ~ (*dazwischenreden*) interrupt sb; (*sich einmischen*) interfere with sb.

dreißig ['draisiç] *num* thirty.

dreist [draist] *a* bold, audacious; **D~igkeit** *f* boldness, audacity.

drei- *zW:* ~**viertel** *num* three-quarters; **D~viertelstunde** *f* three-quarters of an hour; ~**zehn** *num* thirteen.

dressieren [drɛ'si:rən] *vt* train.

Drill- ['drɪl] *zW:* ~**bohrer** *m* light drill; **d~en** *vt* (*bohren*) drill, bore; (*MIL*) drill; (*fig*) train; **Drilling** *m* triplet.

drin [drɪn] *ad* (*umg*) *siehe* **darin.**

dringen ['drɪŋən] *vi unreg* (*Wasser, Licht, Kälte*) penetrate (*durch* through; *in* +*akk* into); **auf etw** (*akk*) ~ insist on sth.

dringend ['drɪŋənt], **dringlich** ['drɪŋlɪç] *a* urgent.

Dringlichkeit *f* urgency.

drinnen ['drɪnən] *ad* inside, indoors.

dritte(r, s) ['drɪtə(r, s)] *a* third; ~ **Welt** Third World; **D~s Reich** Third Reich; **Drittel** *nt* **-s,** - third; **drittens** *ad* thirdly.

droben ['dro:bən] *ad* above, up there.

Droge ['dro:gə] *f* -, **-n** drug; **drogenabhängig** *a* addicted to drugs; **Drogenhändler** *m* drug pedlar, pusher; **Drogerie** [dro:gə'ri:] *f* chemist's shop.

Drogist [dro'gɪst] *m* pharmacist, chemist.

drohen ['dro:ən] *vi* threaten (*jdm* sb).

dröhnen ['drø:nən] *vi* (*Motor*) roar; (*Stimme, Musik*) ring, resound.

Drohung ['dro:uŋ] *f* threat.

drollig ['drɔlɪç] *a* droll.

Drossel ['drɔsəl] *f* -, **-n** thrush.

drüben ['dry:bən] *ad* over there, on the other side.

drüber ['dry:bər] *ad* (*umg*) *siehe* **darüber.**

Druck [druk] *m* **-(e)s, -e** (*PHYS, Zwang*) pressure; (*TYP: Vorgang*) printing; (: *Produkt*) print; (*fig: Belastung*) burden, weight; ~**buchstabe** *m* block letter; ~**er** *m* printer.

Drück- ['dryk] *zW:* **d~en** *vti* (*Knopf, Hand*) press; (*zu eng sein*) pinch; (*fig: Preise*) keep down; (*fig: belasten*) oppress, weigh down // *vr:* **sich vor etw** (*dat*) **d~en** get out of (doing) sth; **d~end** *a* oppressive; ~**er** *m* **-s,** - button; (*Tür*~) handle; (*Gewehr*~) trigger.

Druck- *zW:* ~**er** *m* **-s,** - printer. **Drucke'rei** *f* printing works, press; ~**erschwärze** *f* printer's ink; ~**fehler** *m* misprint; ~**knopf** *m* press stud, snap fastener; ~**sache** *f* printed matter; ~**schrift** *f* block od printed letters *pl.*

drum [drum] *ad* (*umg*) *siehe* **darum.**

drunten ['druntən] *ad* below, down there.

Drüse ['dry:zə] *f* -, -**n** gland.

Dschungel ['dʒʊŋəl] *m* -**s**, - jungle.

du [du:] *pron* (**D~** *in Briefen*) you; **D~** sagen *siehe* **duzen**.

ducken ['dukən] *vt* (*Kopf, Person*) duck; (*fig*) take down a peg or two // *vr* duck.

Duckmäuser ['dukmɔyzər] *m* -**s**, - yes-man.

Dudelsack ['du:dəlzak] *m* bagpipes *pl*.

Duell [du'ɛl] *nt* -**s**, -**e** duel.

Duett [du'ɛt] *nt* -(**e**)**s**, -**e** duet.

Duft [duft] *m* -(**e**)**s**, ⁻**e** scent, odour; **d~en** *vi* smell, be fragrant; **d~ig** *a* (*Stoff, Kleid*) delicate, diaphanous.

duld- ['dold] *zW*: **~en** *vti* suffer; (*zulassen*) tolerate; **~sam** *a* tolerant.

dumm [dum] *a* stupid; (*ärgerlich*) annoying; **der D~e** sein be the loser; **~erweise** *ad* stupidly; **D~heit** *f* stupidity; (*Tat*) blunder, stupid mistake; **D~kopf** *m* blockhead.

dumpf [dumpf] *a* (*Ton*) hollow, dull; (*Luft*) close; (*Erinnerung, Schmerz*) vague; **~ig** *a* musty.

Düne ['dy:nə] *f* -, -**n** dune.

düngen ['dyŋən] *vt* manure.

Dünger *m* -**s**, - dung, manure; (*künstlich*) fertilizer.

dunkel ['duŋkəl] *a* dark; (*Stimme*) deep; (*Ahnung*) vague; (*rätselhaft*) obscure; (*verdächtig*) dubious, shady; **im ~n tappen** (*fig*) grope in the dark.

Dunkel- *zW*: **~heit** *f* darkness; (*fig*) obscurity; **~kammer** *f* (*PHOT*) dark room; **d~n** *vi* *unpers* grow dark; **~ziffer** *f* estimated number of unreported cases.

dünn [dyn] *a* thin; **~flüssig** *a* watery, thin.

Dunst [dunst] *m* -**es**, ⁻**e** vapour; (*Wetter*) haze.

dünsten ['dynstən] *vt* steam.

dunstig ['dunstiç] *a* vaporous; (*Wetter*) hazy, misty.

Duplikat [dupli'ka:t] *nt* -(**e**)**s**, -**e** duplicate.

Dur [du:r] *nt* -, - (*MUS*) major.

durch [durç] *◆präp + akk* **1** (*hin~*) through; **~ den Urwald** through the jungle; **~ die ganze Welt reisen** travel all over the world
2 (*mittels*) through, by (means of); (*aufgrund*) due to, owing to; **Tod ~ Herzschlag/den Strang** death from a heart attack/by hanging; **~ die Post** by post; **~ seine Bemühungen** through his efforts
◆ad 1 (*hin~*) through; **die ganze Nacht ~** all through the night; **den Sommer ~** during the summer; **8 Uhr ~** past 8 o'clock; **~ und ~** completely
2 (*~gebraten etc*): (**gut**) **~** well-done.

durch- *zW*: **~arbeiten** *vti* work through // *vr* work one's way through; **~'aus** *ad* completely; (*unbedingt*) definitely; **~aus nicht** absolutely not; **~blättern** *vt* leaf through.

Durchblick ['durçblɪk] *m* view; (*fig*) comprehension; **d~en** *vi* look through; (*umg: verstehen*) understand (*bei etw* sth); **etw d~en lassen** (*fig*) hint at sth.

durchbrechen ['durçbrɛçən] *vti unreg* break; [durç'brɛçən] *vt unreg insep* (*Schranken*) break through; (*Schallmauer*) break; (*Gewohnheit*) break free from.

durchbrennen ['durçbrɛnən] *vi unreg* (*Draht, Sicherung*) burn through; (*umg*) run away.

Durchbruch ['durçbrux] *m* (*Öffnung*) opening; (*MIL*) breach; (*von Gefühlen etc*) eruption; (*der Zähne*) cutting; (*fig*) breakthrough; **zum ~ kommen** break through.

durch- *zW*: **~dacht** [durç'daxt] *a* well thought-out; **~'denken** *vt unreg insep* think out; **'~drehen** *vt* (*Fleisch*) mince // *vi* (*umg*) crack up.

durcheinander [durç'ai'nandər] *ad* in a mess, in confusion; (*umg: verwirrt*) confused; **~ trinken** mix one's drinks; **D~** *nt* -**s** (*Verwirrung*) confusion; (*Unordnung*) mess; **~bringen** *vt unreg* mess up; (*verwirren*) confuse; **~reden** *vi* talk at the same time.

durch- *zW*: **D~fahrt** *f* transit; (*Verkehr*) thoroughfare; **D~fall** *m* (*MED*) diarrhoea; **~fallen** *vi unreg* fall through; (*in Prüfung*) fail; **~finden** *vr unreg* find one's way through; **~'forschen** *vt insep* explore; **~fragen** *vr* find one's way by asking.

durchführ- ['durçfy:r] *zW*: **~bar** *a* feasible, practicable; **~en** *vt* carry out; **D~ung** *f* execution, performance.

Durchgang ['durçgaŋ] *m* passage(way); (*bei Produktion, Versuch*) run; (*SPORT*) round; (*bei Wahl*) ballot; **~ verboten** no thoroughfare.

Durchgangs- *zW*: **~handel** *m* transit trade; **~lager** *nt* transit camp; **~verkehr** *m* through traffic.

durchgefroren ['durçgefro:rən] *a* (*Mensch*) frozen stiff.

durchgehen ['durçge:ən] *unreg vt* (*behandeln*) go over // *vi* go through; (*ausreißen: Pferd*) break loose; (*Mensch*) run away; **mein Temperament ging mit mir durch** my temper got the better of me; **jdm etw ~ lassen** let sb get away with sth; **~d** *a* (*Zug*) through; (*Öffnungszeiten*) continuous.

durch- *zW*: **~greifen** *vi unreg* take

strong action; **~halten** *unreg vi* last out // *vt* keep up; **~kommen** *vi unreg* get through; (*überleben*) pull through.

durch'kreuzen *vt insep* thwart, frustrate.

durch- *zW:* **~lassen** *vt unreg* (*Person*) let through; (*Wasser*) let in; **~lässig** *a* leaky; **D~lauferhitzer** *m* **-s**, - (hot water) geyser.

durch- *zW:* **~'leben** *vt insep* live *od* go through, experience; '**~lesen** *vt unreg* read through; **~'leuchten** *vt insep* X-ray; '**~machen** *vt* go through; **die Nacht ~machen** make a night of it.

Durch- *zW:* **~marsch** *m* march through; **~messer** *m* **-s**, - diameter.

durch'nässen *vt insep* soak (through).

durch- *zW:* **~nehmen** *vt unreg* go over; **~numerieren** *vt* number consecutively.

durchqueren [durç'kve:rən] *vt insep* cross.

durch- *zW:* **D~reiche** *f* -, **-n** (serving) hatch; **D~reise** *f* transit; **auf der D~reise** passing through; (*Güter*) in transit; **~ringen** *vr unreg* reach after a long struggle; **~rosten** *vi* rust through.

durchs [durçs] = **durch das**.

Durchsage ['durçza:gə] *f* -, **-n** intercom *od* radio announcement.

Durchsatz ['durçzats] *m* throughput.

durchschauen ['durçʃauən] *vi* (*lit*) look *od* see through // [durç'ʃauən] *vt insep* (*Person, Lüge*) see through.

durchscheinen ['durçʃainən] *vi unreg* shine through; **~d** *a* translucent.

Durchschlag ['durçʃla:k] *m* (*Doppel*) carbon copy; (*Sieb*) strainer; **d~en** *unreg vt* (*entzweischlagen*) split (in two); (*sieben*) sieve // *vi* (*zum Vorschein kommen*) emerge, come out // *vr* get by; **d~end** *a* resounding.

durchschneiden ['durçʃnaidən] *vt unreg* cut through.

Durchschnitt ['durçʃnit] *m* (*Mittelwert*) average; **über/unter dem** ~ above/below average; **im ~** on average; **d~lich** *a* average // *ad* on average.

Durchschnitts- *zW:* **~geschwindigkeit** *f* average speed; **~mensch** *m* average man, man in the street; **~wert** *m* average.

durch- *zW:* **D~schrift** *f* copy; **~sehen** *vt unreg* look through; **~setzen** *vt* enforce; **seinen Kopf ~setzen** get one's own way // *vr* (*Erfolg haben*) succeed; (*sich behaupten*) get one's way // [durç'zɛtsən] *vt insep* mix.

Durchsicht ['durçzıçt] *f* looking through, checking; **d~ig** *a* transpar-

ent; **~igkeit** *f* transparence.

durch- *zW:* '**~sprechen** *vt unreg* talk over; '**~stehen** *vt unreg* live through; '**~streichen** *vt unreg* cross out; **~'suchen** *vt insep* search; **D~'suchung** *f* search; **~trieben** [-'tri:bən] *a* cunning, wily; **~'wachsen** *a* (*lit: Speck*) streaky; (*fig: mittelmäßig*) so-so.

durch- *zW:* **~weg** *ad* throughout, completely; **~ziehen** *unreg vt* (*Faden*) draw through // *vi* pass through; **D~zug** *m* (*Luft*) draught; (*von Truppen, Vögeln*) passage.

dürfen ['dyrfən] *vi unreg* **1** (*Erlaubnis haben*) be allowed to; **ich darf das** I'm allowed to (do that); **darf ich?** may I?; **darf ich ins Kino?** can *od* may I go to the cinema?; **es darf geraucht werden** you may smoke **2** (*in Verneinungen*): **er darf das nicht** he's not allowed to (do that); **das darf nicht geschehen** that must not happen; **da darf sie sich nicht wundern** that shouldn't surprise her **3** (*in Höflichkeitsformeln*): **darf ich Sie bitten, das zu tun?** may *od* could I ask you to do that?; **was darf es sein?** what can I do for you? **4** (*können*): **das ~ Sie mir glauben** you can believe me **5** (*Möglichkeit*): **das dürfte genug sein** that should be enough; **es dürfte Ihnen bekannt sein, daß** ... as you will probably know ...

dürftig ['dyrftıç] *a* (*ärmlich*) needy, poor; (*unzulänglich*) inadequate.

dürr [dyr] *a* dried-up; (*Land*) arid; (*mager*) skinny, gaunt; **D~e** *f* -, **-n** aridity; (*Zeit*) drought; (*Magerkeit*) skinniness.

Durst [durst] *m* **-(e)s** thirst; **~ haben** be thirsty; **d~ig** *a* thirsty.

Dusche ['duʃə] *f* -, **-n** shower; **d~n** *vir* have a shower.

Düse ['dy:zə] *f* -, **-n** nozzle; (*Flugzeug~*) jet.

Düsen- *zW:* **~antrieb** *m* jet propulsion; **~flugzeug** *nt* jet (plane); **~jäger** *m* jet fighter.

Dussel ['dusəl] *m* **-s**, - (*umg*) twit.

düster ['dy:stər] *a* dark; (*Gedanken, Zukunft*) gloomy.

Dutzend ['dutsənt] *nt* **-s**, **-e** dozen; **d~(e)mal** *ad* a dozen times; **d~weise** *ad* by the dozen.

duzen ['du:tsən] *vtr* use the familiar form of address *od* 'du' (*jdn* to *od* with sb).

Dynamik [dy'na:mık] *f* (*PHYS*) dynamics; (*fig: Schwung*) momentum; (*von Mensch*) dynamism.

dynamisch [dy'na:mıʃ] *a* (*lit, fig*) dynamic.

Dynamit [dyna'mi:t] *nt* **-s** dynamite.

Dynamo [dy'na:mo] *m* **-s, -s** dynamo.
D-Zug ['dɛ:tsu:k] *m* through train.

E

E, e [e:] *nt* E, e.
Ebbe ['ɛbə] *f* -, **-n** low tide.
eben ['e:bən] *a* level; (*glatt*) smooth // *ad* just; (*bestätigend*) exactly; ~ **deswegen** just because of that; **ebenbürtig** *a*: jdm ebenbürtig sein be sb's peer; **E~e** *f* -, **-n** plain; ~**falls** *ad* likewise; ~**so** *ad* just as; ~**sogut** *ad* just as well; ~**sooft** *ad* just as often; ~**soweit** *ad* just as far; ~**sowenig** *ad* just as little.
Eber ['e:bər] *m* **-s,** - boar; ~**esche** *f* mountain ash, rowan.
ebnen ['e:bnən] *vt* level.
Echo ['ɛço] *nt* **-s, -s** echo.
echt [ɛçt] *a* genuine; (*typisch*) typical; **E~heit** *f* genuineness.
Eck- ['ɛk] *zW*: ~**ball** *m* corner (kick); ~**e** *f* -, **-n** corner; (*MATH*) angle; **e~ig** *a* angular; ~**zahn** *m* eye tooth.
edel ['e:dəl] *a* noble; **E~metall** *nt* rare metal; **E~stein** *m* precious stone.
EDV [e:de:'fau] *abk* (= *elektronische Datenverarbeitung*) electronic data processing.
Efeu ['e:fɔy] *m* **-s** ivy.
Effekten [ɛ'fɛktən] *pl* stocks *pl*.
effektiv [ɛfɛk'ti:f] *a* effective, actual.
EG ['e:'ge:] *abk* (= *Europäische Gemeinschaft*) European Community.
egal [e'ga:l] *a* all the same.
Ego- [e:go] *zW*: ~**ismus** [-'ɪsmʊs] *m* selfishness, egoism; ~**ist** [-'ɪst] *m* egoist; **e~istisch** *a* selfish, egoistic.
Ehe ['e:ə] *f* -, **-n** marriage; **e~** *kj* before; ~**bruch** *m* adultery; ~**frau** *f* married woman, wife; ~**leute** *pl* married people *pl*; **e~lich** *a* matrimonial; (*Kind*) legitimate; **e~malig** *a* former; **e~mals** *ad* formerly; ~**mann** *m* married man; husband; ~**paar** *nt* married couple.
eher ['e:ər] *ad* (*früher*) sooner; (*lieber*) rather; (*mehr*) more.
eheste(r, s) ['e:əstə(r, s)] *a* (*früheste*) first, earliest; **am** ~**n** (*liebsten*) soonest; (*meist*) most; (*wahrscheinlichst*) most probably.
Ehr- ['e:r] *zW*: **e~bar** *a* honourable, respectable; **e~e** *f* -, **-n** honour; **e~en** *vt* honour.
Ehren- ['e:rən] *zW*: ~**gast** *m* guest of honour; **e~haft** *a* honourable; ~**runde** *f* lap of honour; ~**sache** *f* point of honour; **e~voll** *a* honourable; ~**wort** *nt* word of honour.
Ehr- *zW*: ~**furcht** *f* awe, deep respect; ~**gefühl** *nt* sense of honour; ~**geiz** *m* ambition; **e~geizig** *a* ambitious;

e~lich *a* honest; ~**lichkeit** *f* honesty; **e~los** *a* dishonourable; ~**ung** *f* honour(ing); **e~würdig** *a* venerable.
Ei [aɪ] *nt* **-(e)s, -er** egg; **e~** *interj* well, well.
Eich- ['aɪç] *zW*: ~**amt** *nt* Office of Weights and Measures; ~**e** *f* -, **-n** oak (tree); ~**el** *f* -, **-n** acorn; **e~en** *vt* standardize; ~**hörnchen** *nt* squirrel; ~**maß** *nt* standard.
Eid ['aɪt] *m* **-(e)s, -e** oath; ~**echse** ['aɪdɛksə] *f* -, **-n** lizard; **e~esstattlich** *a*: e~esstattliche Erklärung affidavit; ~**genosse** *m* Swiss.
Eidotter ['aɪdɔtər] *nt* egg yolk.
Eier- *zW*: ~**becher** *m* eggcup; ~**kuchen** *m* omelette; pancake; ~**likör** *m* advocaat; ~**schale** *f* eggshell; ~**stock** *m* ovary; ~**uhr** *f* egg timer.
Eifer ['aɪfər] *m* **-s** zeal, enthusiasm; ~**sucht** *f* jealousy; **e~süchtig** *a* jealous (*auf +akk* of).
eifrig ['aɪfrɪç] *a* zealous, enthusiastic.
Eigelb ['aɪgɛlp] *nt* **-(e)s,** - egg yolk.
eigen ['aɪgən] *a* own; (~*artig*) peculiar; **mit der/dem ihm** ~**en** ... with that ... peculiar to him; **sich** (*dat*) **etw zu** ~ **machen** make sth one's own; **E~art** *f* peculiarity; characteristic; ~**artig** *a* peculiar; ~**händig** *a* with one's own hand; **E~heim** *nt* owner-occupied house; **E~heit** *f* peculiarity; ~**mächtig** *a* high-handed; **E~name** *m* proper name; ~**s** *ad* expressly, on purpose; **E~schaft** *f* quality, property, attribute; **E~schaftswort** *nt* adjective; **E~sinn** *m* obstinacy; ~**sinnig** *a* obstinate; **eigentlich** *a* actual, real // *ad* actually, really; **E~tor** *nt* own goal; **E~tum** *nt* property; **E~tümer(in** *f*) *m* **-s,** - owner, proprietor; ~**tümlich** *a* peculiar; **E~tümlichkeit** *f* peculiarity; **E~tumswohnung** *f* freehold flat.
eignen ['aɪgnən] *vr* be suited.
Eignung *f* suitability.
Eil- ['aɪl] *zW*: ~**bote** *m* courier; ~**brief** *m* express letter; ~**e** *f* - haste; **es hat keine** ~ there's no hurry; **e~en** *vi* (*Mensch*) hurry; (*dringend sein*) be urgent; **e~ends** *ad* hastily; ~**gut** *nt* express goods *pl*, fast freight (*US*); **e~ig** *a* hasty, hurried; (*dringlich*) urgent; **es** ~**ig haben** be in a hurry; ~**zug** *m* semi-fast train, limited stop train.
Eimer ['aɪmər] *m* **-s,** - bucket, pail.
ein(e) [aɪn(ə)] *num* one // *indef art* a, an // *ad*: **nicht** ~ **noch aus wissen** not know what to do; ~**e(r, s)** *pron* one; (*jemand*) someone.
einander [aɪ'nandər] *pron* one another, each other.
einarbeiten ['aɪnarbaɪtən] *vr* familiar-

ize o.s. (*in +akk* with).

einatmen ['aɪnaːtmən] *vti* inhale, breathe in.

Einbahnstraße ['aɪnbaːnʃtraːsə] *f* one-way street.

Einband ['aɪnbant] *m* binding, cover.

einbau- ['aɪnbaʊ] *zW:* ~**en** *vt* build in; (*Motor*) install, fit; **E**~**möbel** *pl* built-in furniture.

einberufen ['aɪnbəruːfən] *vt unreg* convene; (*MIL*) call up.

einbeziehen ['aɪnbətsiːən] *vt unreg* include.

einbiegen ['aɪnbiːgən] *vi unreg* turn.

einbilden ['aɪnbɪldən] *vt:* **sich** (*dat*) **etw** ~ imagine sth.

Einbildung *f* imagination; (*Dünkel*) conceit; **Einbildungskraft** *f* imagination.

Einblick ['aɪnblɪk] *m* insight.

einbrechen ['aɪnbrɛçən] *vi unreg* (*in Haus*) break in; (*in Land etc*) invade; (*Nacht*) fall; (*Winter*) set in; (*durchbrechen*) break.

Einbrecher *m* -**s**, - burglar.

einbringen ['aɪnbrɪŋən] *vt unreg* bring in; (*Geld, Vorteil*) yield; (*mitbringen*) contribute.

Einbruch ['aɪnbrʊx] *m* (*Haus*~) break-in, burglary; (*Eindringen*) invasion; (*des Winters*) onset; (*Durchbrechen*) break; (*MET*) approach; (*MIL*) penetration; ~ **der Nacht** nightfall; **einbruchssicher** *a* burglar-proof.

einbürgern ['aɪnbʏrgərn] *vt* naturalize // *vr* become adopted.

Einbürgerung *f* naturalization.

Einbuße ['aɪnbuːsə] *f* loss, forfeiture.

einbüßen ['aɪnbyːsən] *vt* lose, forfeit.

einchecken ['aɪntʃɛkən] *vti* check in.

eindecken ['aɪndɛkən] *vr* lay in stocks (*mit* of).

eindeutig ['aɪndɔʏtɪç] *a* unequivocal.

eindring- ['aɪndrɪŋ] *zW:* ~**en** *vi unreg* (*in +akk*) force one's way in(to); (*in Haus*) break in(to); (*in Land*) invade; (*Gas, Wasser*) penetrate; (*mit Bitten*) pester (*auf jdn* sb); ~**lich** *a* forcible, urgent; **E**~**ling** *m* intruder.

Eindruck ['aɪndrʊk] *m* impression; **eindrucksvoll** *a* impressive.

eindrücken ['aɪndrʏkən] *vt* press in.

eineiig ['aɪn'aɪɪç] *a* (*Zwillinge*) identical.

eineinhalb ['aɪn'aɪn'halp] *num* one and a half.

einengen ['aɪn'ɛŋən] *vt* confine, restrict.

einer- ['aɪnər] *zW:* '**E**~**'lei** *nt* -**s** sameness; '~**'lei** *a* (*gleichartig*) the same kind of; **es ist mir** ~**lei** it is all the same to me; ~**seits** *ad* on the one hand.

einfach ['aɪnfax] *a* simple; (*nicht*

mehrfach) single // *ad* simply; **E**~**heit** *f* simplicity.

einfahren ['aɪnfaːrən] *unreg vt* bring in; (*Barriere*) knock down; (*Auto*) run in // *vi* drive in; (*Zug*) pull in; (*MIN*) go down.

Einfahrt *f* (*Vorgang*) driving in; pulling in; (*MIN*) descent; (*Ort*) entrance.

Einfall ['aɪnfal] *m* (*Idee*) idea, notion; (*Licht*~) incidence; (*MIL*) raid; **e**~**en** *vi unreg* (*Licht*) fall; (*MIL*) raid; (*einstimmen*) join in (*in +akk* with); (*einstürzen*) fall in, collapse; **etw fällt jdm ein** sth occurs to sb; **das fällt mir gar nicht ein** I wouldn't dream of it; **sich** (*dat*) **etwas e**~**en lassen** have a good idea.

einfältig ['aɪnfɛltɪç] *a* simple(-minded).

Einfamilienhaus [aɪnfaˈmiːliənhaʊs] *nt* detached house.

einfarbig ['aɪnfarbɪç] *a* all one colour; (*Stoff etc*) self-coloured.

einfetten ['aɪnfɛtən] *vt* grease.

einfinden ['aɪnfɪndən] *vr unreg* come, turn up.

einfließen ['aɪnfliːsən] *vi unreg* flow in.

einflößen ['aɪnfløːsən] *vt:* **jdm etw** ~ (*lit*) give sb sth; (*fig*) instil sth in sb.

Einfluß ['aɪnflʊs] *m* influence; ~**bereich** *m* sphere of influence; **e**~**reich** *a* influential.

einförmig ['aɪnfœrmɪç] *a* uniform; **E**~**keit** *f* uniformity.

einfrieren ['aɪnfriːrən] *unreg vi* freeze (in) // *vt* freeze.

einfügen ['aɪnfyːgən] *vt* fit in; (*zusätzlich*) add.

Einfuhr ['aɪnfuːr] *f* - import; ~**artikel** *m* imported article.

einführ- ['aɪnfyːr] *zW:* ~**en** *vt* bring in; (*Mensch, Sitten*) introduce; (*Ware*) import; **E**~**ung** *f* introduction.

Eingabe ['aɪngaːbə] *f* petition; (*COMPUT*) input.

Eingang ['aɪngaŋ] *m* entrance; (*COMM: Ankunft*) arrival; (*Sendung*) post; **e**~**s** *ad, präp +gen* at the outset (of).

eingeben ['aɪngeːbən] *vt unreg* (*Arznei*) give; (*Daten etc*) enter; (*Gedanken*) inspire.

eingebildet ['aɪngəbɪldət] *a* imaginary; (*eitel*) conceited.

Eingeborene(r) ['aɪngəboːrənə(r)] *mf* native.

Eingebung *f* inspiration.

eingedenk ['aɪngədɛŋk] *präp +gen* bearing in mind.

eingefroren ['aɪngəfroːrən] *a* frozen.

eingehen ['aɪngeːən] *unreg vi* (*Aufnahme finden*) come in; (*verständlich sein*) be comprehensible (*jdm* to sb); (*Sendung, Geld*) be received;

(Tier, Pflanze) die; *(Firma)* fold; *(schrumpfen)* shrink; **auf etw** *(akk)* ~ go into sth; **auf jdn** ~ respond to sb // *vt* enter into; *(Wette)* make; **~d** *a* exhaustive, thorough.

Eingemachte(s) ['aɪŋəmaxtə(s)] *nt* preserves *pl.*

eingenommen ['aɪŋənɔmən] *a (von)* fond (of), partial (to); *(gegen)* prejudiced.

eingeschrieben ['aɪŋəʃriːbən] *a* registered.

eingespielt ['aɪŋəʃpiːlt] *a*: **aufeinander** ~ **sein** be in tune with each other.

Eingeständnis ['aɪŋəʃtɛntnɪs] *nt* **-ses, -se** admission, confession.

eingestehen ['aɪŋəʃteːən] *vt unreg* confess.

eingetragen ['aɪŋətraːgən] *a (COMM)* registered.

Eingeweide ['aɪŋəwaɪdə] *nt* **-s, -** innards *pl*, intestines *pl.*

Eingeweihte(r) ['aɪŋəwaɪtə(r)] *mf* initiate.

eingleisig ['aɪŋlaɪzɪç] *a* single-track.

eingreifen ['aɪŋraɪfən] *vi unreg* intervene, interfere; *(Zahnrad)* mesh.

Eingriff ['aɪŋrɪf] *m* intervention, interference; *(Operation)* operation.

einhaken ['aɪnhaːkən] *vt* hook in // *vr*: **sich bei jdm** ~ link arms with sb // *vi (sich einmischen)* intervene.

Einhalt ['aɪnhalt] *m*: ~ **gebieten** (+*dat*) put a stop to; **e~en** *unreg vt (Regel)* keep // *vi* stop.

einhändigen ['aɪnhɛndɪgən] *vt* hand in.

einhängen ['aɪnhɛŋən] *vt* hang; *(Telefon: auch vi)* hang up; **sich bei jdm** ~ link arms with sb.

einheimisch ['aɪnhaɪmɪʃ] *a* native.

Einheit ['aɪnhaɪt] *f* unity; *(Maß, MIL)* unit; **e~lich** *a* uniform; **Einheitspreis** *m* uniform price.

einholen ['aɪnhoːlən] *vt (Tau)* haul in; *(Fahne, Segel)* lower; *(Vorsprung aufholen)* catch up with; *(Verspätung)* make up; *(Rat, Erlaubnis)* ask // *vi (einkaufen)* buy, shop.

Einhorn ['aɪnhɔrn] *nt* unicorn.

einhüllen ['aɪnhʏlən] *vt* wrap up.

einig ['aɪnɪç] *a (vereint)* united; **sich** *(dat)* ~ **sein** be in agreement; ~ **werden** agree; **~e** ['aɪnɪgə] *pl* some; *(mehrere)* several; **~e(r, s)** *a* some; **einigemal** *ad* a few times; **~en** *vt* unite // *vr* agree *(auf +akk* on); **~ermaßen** *ad* somewhat; *(leidlich)* reasonably; **~es** *pron* something; **~gehen** *vi unreg* agree; **E~keit** *f* unity; *(Übereinstimmung)* agreement; **E~ung** *f* agreement; *(Vereinigung)* unification.

einkalkulieren ['aɪnkalkuliːrən] *vt* take

into account, allow for.

Einkauf ['aɪnkauf] *m* purchase; **e~en** *vt* buy // *vi* go shopping.

Einkaufs- *zW*: **~bummel** *m* shopping spree; **~korb** *m* shopping basket; **~netz** *nt* string bag; **~wagen** *m* shopping trolley; **~preis** *m* cost price; **~zentrum** *nt* shopping centre.

einklammern ['aɪnklamərn] *vt* put in brackets, bracket.

Einklang ['aɪnklaŋ] *m* harmony.

einklemmen ['aɪnklɛmən] *vt* jam.

einkochen ['aɪnkɔxən] *vt* boil down; *(Obst)* preserve, bottle.

Einkommen ['aɪnkɔmən] *nt* **-s, -** income; **~(s)steuer** *f* income tax.

Einkünfte ['aɪnkʏnftə] *pl* income, revenue.

einlad- ['aɪnlaːd] *zW*: **~en** *vt unreg (Person)* invite; *(Gegenstände)* load; **jdn ins Kino ~en** take sb to the cinema; **E~ung** *f* invitation.

Einlage ['aɪnlaːgə] *f (Programm~)* interlude; *(Spar~)* deposit; *(Schuh~)* insole; *(Fußstütze)* support; *(Zahn~)* temporary filling; *(KOCH)* noodles *pl*, vegetables *pl* etc in soup.

einlagern *vt* store.

einlassen ['aɪnlasən] *unreg vt* let in; *(einsetzen)* set in // *vr*: **sich mit jdm/ auf etw** *(akk)* ~ get involved with sb/sth.

Einlauf ['aɪnlauf] *m* arrival; *(von Pferden)* finish; *(MED)* enema; **e~en** *unreg vi* arrive, come in; *(in Hafen)* enter; *(SPORT)* finish; *(Wasser)* run in; *(Stoff)* shrink // *vt (Schuhe)* break in; **jdm das Haus e~en** invade sb's house // *vr (SPORT)* warm up; *(Motor, Maschine)* run in.

einleben ['aɪnleːbən] *vr* settle down.

einlegen ['aɪnleːgən] *vt (einfügen: Blatt, Sohle)* insert; *(KOCH)* pickle; *(Pause)* have; *(Protest)* make; *(Veto)* use; *(Berufung)* lodge.

einleiten ['aɪnlaɪtən] *vt* introduce, start; *(Geburt)* induce.

Einleitung *f* introduction; induction.

einleuchten ['aɪnlɔʏçtən] *vi* be clear *od* evident *(jdm* to sb); **~d** *a* clear.

einliefern ['aɪnliːfərn] *vt* take *(in +akk* into).

einlösen ['aɪnløːzən] *vt (Scheck)* cash; *(Schuldschein, Pfand)* redeem; *(Versprechen)* keep.

einmachen ['aɪnmaxən] *vt* preserve.

einmal ['aɪnmaːl] *ad* once; *(erstens)* first; *(zukünftig)* sometime; **nehmen wir ~** an just let's suppose; **noch ~** once more; **nicht ~** not even; **auf ~** all at once; **es war ~** once upon a time there was/were; **E~eins** *nt* multiplication tables *pl*; **~ig** *a* unique; *(einmal geschehend)* single; *(prima)* fantastic.

Einmannbetrieb [aɪn'manbətri:p] *m* one-man business.

Einmarsch ['aɪnmarʃ] *m* entry; (*MIL*) invasion; **e~ieren** *vi* march in.

einmischen ['aɪnmɪʃən] *vr* interfere (*in* + *akk* with).

einmütig ['aɪnmy:tɪç] *a* unanimous.

Einnahme ['aɪnna:mə] *f* -, **-n** (*Geld*) takings *pl*, revenue; (*von Medizin*) taking; (*MIL*) capture, taking; **~quelle** *f* source of income.

einnehmen ['aɪnne:mən] *vt unreg* take; (*Stellung, Raum*) take up; **~ für/gegen** persuade in favour of/ against; **~d** *a* charming.

Einöde ['aɪn'ø:də] *f* desert, wilderness.

einordnen ['aɪn'ɔrdnən] *vt* arrange, fit in // *vr* adapt; (*AUT*) get into lane.

einpacken ['aɪnpakən] *vt* pack (up).

einparken ['aɪnparkən] *vt* park.

einpendeln ['aɪnpendəln] *vr* even out.

einpflanzen ['aɪnpflantsən] *vt* plant; (*MED*) implant.

einplanen ['aɪnpla:nən] *vt* plan for.

einprägen ['aɪnprɛ:gən] *vt* impress, imprint; (*beibringen*) impress (*jdm* on sb): **sich** (*dat*) **etw ~** memorize sth.

einrahmen ['aɪnra:mən] *vt* frame.

einräumen ['aɪnrɔymən] *vt* (*ordnend*) put away; (*überlassen: Platz*) give up; (*zugestehen*) admit, concede.

einreden ['aɪnre:dən] *vt*: **jdm/sich etw ~** talk sb/o.s. into believing sth.

einreiben ['aɪnraɪbən] *vt unreg* rub in.

einreichen ['aɪnraɪçən] *vt* hand in; (*Antrag*) submit.

Einreise ['aɪnraɪzə] *f* entry; **~bestimmungen** *pl* entry regulations *pl*; **~erlaubnis** *f*, **~genehmigung** *f* entry permit; **e~n** *vi* enter (*in ein Land* a country).

einrichten ['aɪnrɪçtən] *vt* (*Haus*) furnish; (*schaffen*) establish, set up; (*arrangieren*) arrange; (*möglich machen*) manage // *vr* (*in Haus*) furnish one's house; (*sich vorbereiten*) prepare o.s. (*auf* +*akk* for); (*sich anpassen*) adapt (*auf* +*akk* to).

Einrichtung *f* (*Wohnungs~*) furnishings *pl*; (*öffentliche Anstalt*) organization; (*Dienste*) service.

einrosten ['aɪnrɔstən] *vi* get rusty.

Eins [aɪns] *f* -, **-en** one; **e~** *num* one; **es ist mir alles e~** it's all one to me.

einsam ['aɪnza:m] *a* lonely, solitary; **E~keit** *f* loneliness, solitude.

einsammeln ['aɪnzaməln] *vt* collect.

Einsatz ['aɪnzats] *m* (*Teil*) inset; (*an Kleid*) insertion; (*Verwendung*) use, employment; (*Spiel~*) stake; (*Risiko*) risk; (*MIL*) operation; (*MUS*) entry; **im ~** in action; **e~bereit** *a* ready for action.

einschalten ['aɪnʃaltən] *vt* (*einfügen*)

insert; (*Pause*) make; (*ELEK*) switch on; (*AUT: Gang*) engage; (*Anwalt*) bring in // *vr* (*dazwischentreten*) intervene.

einschätzen ['aɪnʃɛtsən] *vt* estimate, assess // *vr* rate o.s.

einschenken ['aɪnʃɛŋkən] *vt* pour out.

einschicken ['aɪnʃɪkən] *vt* send in.

einschl. *abk* (= *einschließlich*) incl.

einschlafen ['aɪnʃla:fən] *vi unreg* fall asleep, go to sleep.

einschläfernd ['aɪnʃlɛ:fərnt] *a* (*MED*) soporific; (*langweilig*) boring; (*Stimme*) lulling.

Einschlag ['aɪnʃla:k] *m* impact; (*fig: Beimischung*) touch, hint; **e~en** *unreg vt* knock in; (*Fenster*) smash, break; (*Zähne, Schädel*) smash in; (*Steuer*) turn; (*kürzer machen*) take up; (*Ware*) pack, wrap up; (*Weg, Richtung*) *vi* hit (*in etw* (*akk*) *sth*, *auf jdn* sb); (*sich einigen*) agree; (*Anklang finden*) work, succeed.

einschlägig ['aɪnʃlɛ:gɪç] *a* relevant.

einschließen ['aɪnʃli:sən] *unreg vt* (*Kind*) lock in; (*Häftling*) lock up; (*Gegenstand*) lock away; (*Bergleute*) cut off; (*umgeben*) surround; (*MIL*) encircle; (*fig*) include, comprise // *vr* lock o.s. in.

einschließlich *ad* inclusive // *präp* +*gen* inclusive of, including.

einschmeicheln ['aɪnʃmaɪçəln] *vr* ingratiate o.s. (*bei* with).

einschnappen ['aɪnʃnapən] *vi* (*Tür*) click to; (*fig*) be touchy; **eingeschnappt sein** be in a huff.

einschneidend ['aɪnʃnaɪdənt] *a* incisive.

Einschnitt ['aɪnʃnɪt] *m* cutting; (*MED*) incision; (*Ereignis*) incident.

einschränken ['aɪnʃrɛŋkən] *vt* limit, restrict; (*Kosten*) cut down, reduce // *vr* cut down (on expenditure); **~d** *a* restrictive.

Einschränkung *f* restriction, limitation; reduction; (*von Behauptung*) qualification.

Einschreib- ['aɪnʃraɪb] *zW*: **~(e)brief** *m* recorded delivery letter; **e~en** *unreg vt* write in; (*Post*) send recorded delivery // *vr* register; (*UNIV*) enrol; **~en** *nt* recorded delivery letter.

einschreiten ['aɪnʃraɪtən] *vi unreg* step in, intervene; **~ gegen** take action against.

einschüchtern ['aɪnʃʏçtərn] *vt* intimidate.

einschweißen ['aɪnʃvaɪsən] *vt* shrinkwrap.

einsehen ['aɪnze:ən] *vt unreg* (*hineinsehen in*) realize; (*Akten*) have a look at; (*verstehen*) see; **E~** *nt* -s understanding; **ein E~ haben** show understanding.

einseitig ['aɪnzaɪtɪç] a one-sided.

Einsend- ['aɪnzɛnd] zW: **e~en** vt unreg send in; **~er** m -s, - sender, contributor; **~ung** f sending in.

einsetzen ['aɪnzɛtsən] vt put (in); (in Amt) appoint, install; (Geld) stake; (verwenden) use; (MIL) employ // vi (beginnen) set in; (MUS) enter, come in // vr work hard; **sich für jdn/etw ~** support sb/sth.

Einsicht ['aɪnzɪçt] f insight; (in Akten) look, inspection; **zu der ~ kommen, daß ...** come to the conclusion that ...; **e~ig** a (Mensch) judicious; **~nahme** f -, -n examination; **einsichtslos** a unreasonable; **einsichtsvoll** a understanding.

Einsiedler ['aɪnziːdlər] m hermit.

einsilbig ['aɪnzɪlbɪç] a (lit, fig) monosyllabic.

einsperren ['aɪnʃpɛrən] vt lock up.

einspielen ['aɪnʃpiːlən] vr (SPORT) warm up; **sich aufeinander ~** become attuned to each other // vt (Film: Geld) bring in; (Instrument) play in; **gut eingespielt** smoothly running.

einspringen ['aɪnʃprɪŋən] vi unreg (aushelfen) help out, step into the breach.

Einspritzmotor ['aɪnʃprɪtsmoːtɔr] m fuel injection engine.

Einspruch ['aɪnʃprʊx] m protest, objection; **Einspruchsrecht** nt veto.

einspurig ['aɪnʃpuːrɪç] a single-lane.

einst [aɪnst] ad once; (zukünftig) one od some day.

Einstand ['aɪnʃtant] m (TENNIS) deuce; (Antritt) entrance (to office).

einstecken ['aɪnʃtɛkən] vt stick in, insert; (Brief) post; (ELEK: Stecker) plug in; (Geld) pocket; (mitnehmen) take; (überlegen sein) put in the shade; (hinnehmen) swallow.

einstehen ['aɪnʃteːən] vi unreg guarantee (für jdn/etw sb/sth); (verantworten) answer (für for).

einsteigen ['aɪnʃtaɪgən] vi unreg get in od on; (in Schiff) go on board; (sich beteiligen) come in; (hineinklettern) climb in.

einstell- ['aɪnʃtɛl] zW: **~en** vti (aufhören) stop; (Geräte) adjust; (Kamera etc) focus; (Sender, Radio) tune in; (unterstellen) put; (in Firma) employ, take on // vr (anfangen) set in; (kommen) arrive; **sich auf jdn/etw ~en** adapt to sb/prepare o.s. for sth; **E~ung** f (Aufhören) suspension, cessation; adjustment; focusing; (von Arbeiter etc) appointment; (Haltung) attitude.

Einstieg ['aɪnʃtiːk] m -(e)s, -e entry; (fig) approach.

einstig ['aɪnstɪç] a former.

einstimmig ['aɪnʃtɪmɪç] a unanimous; (MUS) for one voice.

einst- ['aɪnst] zW: **~malig** a former; **~mals** ad once, formerly.

einstöckig ['aɪnʃtœkɪç] a single-storeyed.

Einsturz ['aɪnʃtʊrts] m collapse; **~gefahr** f danger of collapse.

einstürzen ['aɪnʃtʏrtsən] vi fall in, collapse.

einst- ['aɪnst] zW: **~weilen** ad meanwhile; (vorläufig) temporarily, for the time being; **~weilig** a temporary.

eintägig ['aɪntɛːgɪç] a one-day.

eintasten ['aɪntastən] vt key (in).

eintauschen ['aɪntaʊʃən] vt exchange.

eintausend ['aɪntaʊzənt] num one thousand.

einteil- ['aɪntaɪl] zW: **~en** vt (in Teile) divide (up); (Menschen) assign; **~ig** a one-piece.

eintönig ['aɪntøːnɪç] a monotonous; **E~keit** f monotony.

Eintopf(gericht nt) ['aɪntɔpf(gərɪçt)] m stew.

Eintracht ['aɪntraxt] f - concord, harmony.

einträchtig ['aɪntrɛçtɪç] a harmonious.

Eintrag ['aɪntraːk] m -(e)s, ¨e entry; **amtlicher ~** entry in the register; **e~en** unreg vt (in Buch) enter; (Profit) yield; **jdm etw e~en** bring sb sth // vr put one's name down.

einträglich ['aɪntrɛːklɪç] a profitable.

eintreffen ['aɪntrɛfən] vi unreg happen; (ankommen) arrive.

eintreten ['aɪntreːtən] unreg vi occur; (hineingehen) enter (in etw (akk) sth); (sich einsetzen) intercede; (in Club, Partei) join (in etw (akk) sth); (in Stadium etc) enter // vt (Tür) kick open.

Eintritt ['aɪntrɪt] m (Betreten) entrance; (Anfang) commencement; (in Club etc) joining.

Eintritts- zW: **~geld** nt, **~preis** m charge for admission; **~karte** f (admission) ticket.

einüben ['aɪnyːbən] vt practise, drill.

Einvernehmen ['aɪnfɛrneːmən] nt -s, - agreement, understanding.

einverstanden ['aɪnfɛrʃtandən] interj agreed // a: **~ sein** agree, be agreed.

Einverständnis ['aɪnfɛrʃtɛntnɪs] nt understanding; (gleiche Meinung) agreement.

Einwand ['aɪnvant] m -(e)s, ¨e objection.

Einwanderer ['aɪnvandərər] m immigrant.

einwandern vi immigrate.

Einwanderung f immigration.

einwandfrei a perfect // ad absolutely.

Einwegflasche ['aɪnveːɡflaʃə] f no-deposit bottle.

einweichen ['aɪnvaɪçən] vt soak.

einweih- ['aɪnvaɪ] zW: **~en** vt (Kirche) consecrate; (Brücke) open; (Gebäude) inaugurate; (Person) initiate (in +akk in); **E~ung** f consecration; opening; inauguration; initiation.

einweisen ['aɪnvaɪzən] vt unreg (in Amt) install; (in Arbeit) introduce; (in Anstalt) send.

einwenden ['aɪnvɛndən] vt unreg object, oppose (gegen to).

einwerfen ['aɪnvɛrfən] vt unreg throw in; (Brief) post; (Geld) put in, insert; (Fenster) smash; (äußern) interpose.

einwickeln ['aɪnvɪkəln] vt wrap up; (fig umg) outsmart.

einwillig- ['aɪnvɪlɪɡ] zW: **~en** vi consent, agree (in +akk to); **E~ung** f consent.

einwirken ['aɪnvɪrkən] vi: auf jdn/etw **~en** influence sb/sth.

Einwohner ['aɪnvoːnər] m -s, - inhabitant; **~'meldeamt** nt registration office; **~schaft** f population, inhabitants pl.

Einwurf ['aɪnvʊrf] m (Öffnung) slot; (Einwand) objection; (SPORT) throw-in.

Einzahl ['aɪntsaːl] f singular; **e~en** vt pay in; **~ung** f paying in.

einzäunen ['aɪntsɔynən] vt fence in.

Einzel ['aɪntsəl] nt -s, - (TENNIS) singles // in zW: **~** individual; single; **~fall** m single instance, individual case; **~handel** m retail trade; **~handelspreis** m retail price; **~haft** f solitary confinement; **~heit** f particular, detail; **~karte** f single ticket; **e~n** a single; (vereinzelt) the odd // ad singly; **e~ne** the individual; **der/die e~ne** the individual; **das e~ne** the particular; **ins e~ne gehen** go into detail(s); **~teil** nt component (part); **~zimmer** nt single room.

einziehen ['aɪntsiːən] unreg vt draw in, take in; (Kopf) duck; (Fühler, Antenne, Fahrgestell) retract; (Steuern, Erkundigungen) collect; (MIL) draft, call up; (aus dem Verkehr ziehen) withdraw; (konfiszieren) confiscate // vi move in(to); (Friede, Ruhe) come; (Flüssigkeit) penetrate.

einzig ['aɪntsɪç] a only; (ohnegleichen) unique; **das ~e** the only thing; **der/die ~e** the only one; **~artig** a unique.

Einzug ['aɪntsuːk] m entry, moving in.

Eis [aɪs] -es, - ice; (Speise~) ice cream; **~bahn** f ice od skating rink; **~bär** m polar bear; **~becher** m sundae; **~bein** nt pig's trotters pl;

~berg m iceberg; **~decke** f sheet of ice; **~diele** f ice-cream parlour.

Eisen ['aɪzən] nt -s, - iron; **~bahn** f railway, railroad (US); **~bahner** m -s, - railwayman, railway employee, railroader (US); **~bahnschaffner** m railway guard; **~bahnübergang** m level crossing, grade crossing (US); **~bahnwagen** m railway carriage; **~erz** nt iron ore; **e~haltig** a containing iron.

eisern ['aɪzərn] a iron; (Gesundheit) robust; (Energie) unrelenting; (Reserve) emergency.

Eis- zW: **e~frei** a clear of ice; **~hockey** nt ice hockey; **e~ig** ['aɪzɪç] a icy; **e~kalt** a icy cold; **~kunstlauf** m figure skating; **~laufen** nt ice skating; **~läufer(in** f) m ice-skater; **~pickel** m ice-axe; **~schießen** nt ≈ curling; **~schrank** m fridge, ice-box (US); **~zapfen** m icicle; **~zeit** f ice age.

eitel ['aɪtəl] a vain; **E~keit** f vanity.

Eiter ['aɪtər] m -s pus; **e~ig** a suppurating; **e~n** vi suppurate.

Ei- [aɪ] zW: **~weiß** nt -es, -e white of an egg; **~zelle** f ovum.

Ekel ['eːkəl] m -s nausea, disgust // nt -s, - (umg: Mensch) nauseating person; **e~erregend, e~haft, ek(e)lig** a nauseating, disgusting; **e~n** vt disgust; **es ekelt jdn** od **jdm** sb is disgusted // vr loathe, be disgusted (vor +dat at).

Ekstase [ɛk'staːzə] f -, -n ecstasy.

Ekzem [ɛk'tseːm] nt -s, -e (MED) eczema.

Elan [e'laːn] m -s elan.

elastisch [e'lastɪʃ] a elastic.

Elastizität [elastitsi'tɛːt] f elasticity.

Elch [ɛlç] m -(e)s, -e elk.

Elefant [ele'fant] m elephant.

elegant [ele'ɡant] a elegant.

Eleganz [ele'ɡants] f elegance.

Elek- [e'lɛk] zW: **~triker** [-trɪkər] m -s, - electrician; **e~trisch** [-trɪʃ] a electric; **e~trisieren** [-tri'ziːrən] vt (lit, fig) electrify; (Mensch) give an electric shock to // vr get an electric shock; **~trizität** [-tritsi'tɛːt] f electricity; **~trizitätswerk** nt electricity works, power plant.

Elektro- [e'lɛktro] zW: **~de** [elɛk'troːdə] f -, -n electrode; **~herd** m electric cooker; **~n** [-ɔn] nt -s, -en electron; **~nen(ge)hirn** [elɛk'troːnən-] nt electronic brain; **~nenrechner** m computer; **e~nisch** a electronic; **e~nische Post** electronic mail; **e~nischer Briefkasten** electronic mailbox; **~rasierer** m electric razor.

Element [ele'mɛnt] nt -s, -e element; (ELEK) cell, battery; **e~ar** [-'taːr] a elementary; (naturhaft) elemental.

Elend ['e:lɛnt] *nt* -(e)s misery; **e~** *a* miserable; **Elendsviertel** *nt* slum.

elf [ɛlf] *num* eleven; **E~** *f* -, -en (*SPORT*) eleven; **E~e** *f* -, -n elf; **E~enbein** *nt* ivory; **E~meter** *m* (*SPORT*) penalty (kick).

Elite [e'li:tə] *f* -, -n elite.

Elixier [eli'ksi:r] *nt* -s, -e elixir.

Ell- *zW*: **~e** ['ɛlə] *f* -, -n ell; (*Maß*) yard; **~(en)bogen** *m* elbow; **Ellipse** [ɛ'lɪpsə] *f* -, -n ellipse.

Elsaß ['ɛlzas] *nt*: das ~ Alsace.

Elster ['ɛlstər] *f* -, -n magpie.

elterlich ['ɛltərlɪç] *a* parental.

Eltern ['ɛltərn] *pl* parents *pl*; **~haus** *nt* home; **e~los** *a* parentless.

Email [e'ma:j] *nt* -s, -s enamel; **e~lieren** [ema'ji:rən] *vt* enamel.

Emanzipation [emantsipatsi'o:n] *f* emancipation.

emanzi'pieren *vt* emancipate.

Embryo ['ɛmbryo] *m* -s, -s *od* -nen embryo.

Emi- [emi] *zW*: **~gration** [-gratsi'o:n] *f* emigration; **e~grieren** [-'gri:rən] *vi* emigrate.

empfahl *etc v siehe* **empfehlen.**

Empfang [ɛm'pfaŋ] *m* -(e)s, ⁻e reception; (*Erhalten*) receipt; **in ~ nehmen** receive; **e~en** *unreg vt* receive // *vi* (*schwanger werden*) conceive.

Empfäng- [ɛm'pfɛŋ] *zW*: **~er** *m* -s, - receiver; (*COMM*) addressee, consignee; **e~lich** *a* receptive, susceptible; **~nis** *f* -, -se conception; **~nisverhütung** *f* contraception.

Empfangs- *zW*: **~bestätigung** *f* acknowledgement; **~dame** *f* receptionist; **~schein** *m* receipt; **~zimmer** *nt* reception room.

empfehlen [ɛm'pfe:lən] *unreg vt* recommend // *vr* take one's leave; **~swert** *a* recommendable.

Empfehlung *f* recommendation.

empfiehlst *etc v siehe* **empfehlen.**

empfind- [ɛm'pfɪnt] *zW*: **~en** [ɛm'pfɪndən] *vt unreg* feel; **~lich** *a* sensitive; (*Stelle*) sore; (*reizbar*) touchy; **~sam** *a* sentimental; **E~ung** *f* feeling, sentiment.

empfohlen *v siehe* **empfehlen.**

empor [ɛm'po:r] *ad* up, upwards.

empören [ɛm'pø:rən] *vt* make indignant; shock // *vr* become indignant; **~d** *a* outrageous.

Emporkömmling [ɛm'po:rkœmlɪŋ] *m* upstart, parvenu.

Empörung *f* indignation.

emsig ['ɛmzɪç] *a* diligent, busy.

End- ['ɛnt] *in zW* final; **~e** *nt* -s, -n end; **am ~e** at the end; (*schließlich*) in the end; **am ~e sein** be at the end of one's tether; **~e Dezember** at the end of December; **zu ~e sein** be finished; **e~en** *vi* end; **e~gültig** *a* final, definite; **Endivie** [ɛn'di:viə] *f* endive; **e~lich** *a* final; (*MATH*) finite // *ad* finally; **e~lich!** at last!; **komm e~lich!** come on!; **e~los** *a* endless, infinite; **~lospapier** *nt* continuous stationery; **~spiel** *nt* final(s); **~spurt** *m* (*SPORT*) final spurt; **~station** *f* terminus; **~ung** *f* ending.

Energie [enɛr'gi:] *f* energy; **~einsparung** *f* energy saving; **e~los** *a* lacking in energy, weak; **~wirtschaft** *f* energy industry.

energisch [e'nɛrgɪʃ] *a* energetic.

eng [ɛŋ] *a* narrow; (*Kleidung*) tight; (*fig: Horizont auch*) limited; (*Freundschaft, Verhältnis*) close; **~ an etw** (*dat*) close to sth.

Engagement [ãgaʒə'mã:] *nt* -s, -s engagement; (*Verpflichtung*) commitment.

engagieren [ãga'ʒi:rən] *vt* engage; **ein engagierter Schriftsteller** a committed writer // *vr* commit o.s.

Enge ['ɛŋə] *f* -, -n (*lit,fig*) narrowness; (*Land~*) defile; (*Meer~*) straits *pl*; **jdn in die ~ treiben** drive sb into a corner.

Engel ['ɛŋəl] *m* -s, - angel; **e~haft** *a* angelic; **~macher(in** *f*) *m* -s, - (*umg*) backstreet abortionist.

eng- *zW*: **~herzig** *a* petty; **E~land** *nt* England; **E~länder** *m* Englishman; **E~länderin** *f* Englishwoman; **~lisch** *a* English; **E~paß** *m* defile, pass; (*fig, Verkehr*) bottleneck.

en gros [ã'gro:] *ad* wholesale.

engstirnig ['ɛŋʃtɪrnɪç] *a* narrow-minded.

Enkel ['ɛŋkəl] *m* -s, - grandson; **~in** *f* granddaughter.

enorm [e'nɔrm] *a* enormous.

Ensemble [ã'sãbəl] *nt* -s, -s company, ensemble.

entbehr- [ɛnt'be:r] *zW*: **~en** *vt* do without, dispense with; **~lich** *a* superfluous.

entbinden [ɛnt'bɪndən] *unreg vt* release (*gen* from); (*MED*) deliver // *vi* (*MED*) give birth.

Entbindung *f* release; (*MED*) confinement; **Entbindungsheim** *nt* maternity hospital.

entdeck- [ɛnt'dɛk] *zW*: **~en** *vt* discover. **E~er** *m* -s, - discoverer; **E~ung** *f* discovery.

Ente ['ɛntə] *f* -, -n duck; (*fig*) canard, false report.

enteignen [ɛnt'aignən] *vt* expropriate; (*Besitzer*) dispossess.

enteisen [ɛnt'aizən] *vt* de-ice, defrost.

enterben [ɛnt'ɛrbən] *vt* disinherit.

entfallen [ɛnt'falən] *vi unreg* drop, fall; (*wegfallen*) be dropped; **jdm ~** (*vergessen*) slip sb's memory; **auf**

jdn ~ be allotted to sb.

entfalten [ɛnt'faltən] *vt* unfold; (*Talente*) develop // *vr* open; (*Mensch*) develop one's potential.

Entfaltung *f* unfolding; (*von Talenten*) development.

entfern- [ɛnt'fɛrn] *zW*: **~en** *vt* remove; (*hinauswerfen*) expel // *vr* go away, withdraw; **~t** *a* distant; weit davon **~t** sein, etw zu tun be far from doing sth; **E~ung** *f* distance; (*Wegschaffen*) removal; **E~ungsmesser** *m* -s, - (*PHOT*) rangefinder.

entfremd- [ɛnt'frɛmd] *zW*: **~en** *vt* estrange, alienate; **E~ung** *f* alienation, estrangement.

entfrost- [ɛnt'frɔst] *zW*: **~en** *vt* defrost; **E~er** *m* -s, - (*AUT*) defroster.

entführ- [ɛnt'fyːr] *zW*: **~en** *vt* carry off, abduct; kidnap; **E~er** *m* kidnapper; **E~ung** *f* abduction; kidnapping.

entgegen [ɛnt'geːgən] *präp* +*dat* contrary to, against // *ad* towards; **~bringen** *vt unreg* bring; (*fig*) show (*jdm etw* sb sth); **~gehen** *vi unreg* (+*dat*) go to meet, go towards; **~gesetzt** *a* opposite; (*widersprechend*) opposed; **~halten** *vt unreg* (*fig*) object; **~kommen** *vi unreg* approach; meet (*jdm* sb); (*fig*) accommodate (*jdm* sb); **E~kommen** *nt* obligingness; **~kommend** *a* obliging; **~nehmen** *vt unreg* receive, accept; **~sehen** *vi unreg* (+*dat*) await; **~setzen** *vt* oppose (*dat* to); **~treten** *vi unreg* (+*dat*: *lit*) step up to; (*fig*) oppose, counter; **~wirken** *vi* (+*dat*) counteract.

entgegnen [ɛnt'geːgnən] *vt* reply, retort.

entgehen [ɛnt'geːən] *vi unreg* (*fig*) jdm ~ escape sb's notice; sich (*dat*) etw ~ lassen miss sth.

entgeistert [ɛnt'gaɪstərt] *a* thunderstruck.

Entgelt [ɛnt'gɛlt] *nt* -(e)s, -e compensation, remuneration.

entgleisen [ɛnt'glaɪzən] *vi* (*EISENB*) be derailed; (*fig: Person*) misbehave; ~ lassen derail.

entgräten [ɛnt'grɛːtən] *vt* fillet, bone.

Enthaarungsmittel [ɛnt'haːrʊŋsmɪtəl] *nt* depilatory.

enthalten [ɛnt'haltən] *unreg vt* contain // *vr* abstain, refrain (*gen* from).

enthaltsam [ɛnt'haltzaːm] *a* abstinent, abstemious; **E~keit** *f* abstinence.

enthemmen [ɛnt'hɛmən] *vt*: jdn ~ free sb from his inhibitions.

enthüllen [ɛnt'hylən] *vt* reveal, unveil.

Enthusiasmus [ɛntuzi'asmʊs] *m* enthusiasm.

entkommen [ɛnt'kɔmən] *vi unreg* get away, escape (*dat, aus* from).

entkräften [ɛnt'krɛftən] *vt* weaken, exhaust; (*Argument*) refute.

entladen [ɛnt'laːdən] *unreg vt* unload; (*ELEK*) discharge // *vr* (*ELEK, Gewehr*) discharge; (*Ärger etc*) vent itself.

entlang [ɛnt'laŋ] *präp* +*akk od dat*, ad along; ~ dem Fluß, den Fluß ~ along the river; **~gehen** *vi unreg* walk along.

entlarven [ɛnt'larfən] *vt* unmask, expose.

entlassen [ɛnt'lasən] *vt unreg* discharge; (*Arbeiter*) dismiss.

Entlassung *f* discharge; dismissal; **Entlassungsabfindung** *f* redundancy payment.

entlasten [ɛnt'lastən] *vt* relieve; (*Achse*) relieve the load on; (*Angeklagten*) exonerate; (*Konto*) clear.

Entlastung *f* relief; (*COMM*) crediting.

entlegen [ɛnt'leːgən] *a* remote.

entlocken [ɛnt'lɔkən] *vt* elicit (*jdm etw* sth from sb).

entmachten [ɛnt'maxtən] *vt* deprive of power.

entmilitarisiert [ɛntmilitari'ziːrt] *a* demilitarized.

entmündigen [ɛnt'mʏndɪgən] *vt* certify.

entmutigen [ɛnt'muːtɪgən] *vt* discourage.

entnehmen [ɛnt'neːmən] *vt unreg* (+*dat*) take out (of), take (from); (*folgern*) infer (from).

entrahmen [ɛnt'raːmən] *vt* skim.

entreißen [ɛnt'raɪsən] *vt unreg* snatch (away) (*jdm etw* sth from sb).

entrichten [ɛnt'rɪçtən] *vt* pay.

entrosten [ɛnt'rɔstən] *vt* derust.

entrüst- [ɛnt'rʏst] *zW*: **~en** *vt* incense, outrage // *vr* be filled with indignation; **~et** *a* indignant, outraged; **E~ung** *f* indignation.

entschädigen [ɛnt'ʃɛːdɪgən] *vt* compensate.

Entschädigung *f* compensation.

entschärfen [ɛnt'ʃɛrfən] *vt* defuse; (*Kritik*) tone down.

Entscheid [ɛnt'ʃaɪt] *m* -(e)s, -e decision; **e~en** *vtir unreg* decide; **e~end** *a* decisive; (*Stimme*) casting; **~ung** *f* decision.

entschieden [ɛnt'ʃiːdən] *a* decided; (*entschlossen*) resolute; **E~heit** *f* firmness, determination.

entschließen [ɛnt'ʃliːsən] *vr unreg* decide.

entschlossen [ɛnt'ʃlɔsən] *a* determined, resolute; **E~heit** *f* determination.

Entschluß [ɛnt'ʃlʊs] *m* decision; **e~freudig** *a* decisive; **~kraft** *f* determination, decisiveness.

entschuld- [ɛntˈʃʊld] zW: **~igen** vt excuse // vr apologize; **E~igung** f apology; (Grund) excuse; **jdn um E~igung bitten** apologize to sb; **E~igung! excuse me;** (Verzeihung) sorry.

entsetz- [ɛntˈzɛts] zW: **~en** vt horrify; (MIL) relieve // vr be horrified od appalled; **E~en** nt **-s** horror, dismay; **~lich** a dreadful, appalling; **~t** a horrified.

entsinnen [ɛntˈzɪnən] vr unreg remember (gen sth).

entspannen [ɛntˈʃpanən] vtr (Körper) relax; (POL: Lage) ease.

Entspannung f relaxation, rest, (POL) détente; **Entspannungspolitik** f policy of détente.

entsprechen [ɛntˈʃprɛçən] vi unreg (+dat) correspond to; (Anforderungen, Wünschen) meet, comply with; **~d** a appropriate // ad accordingly.

entspringen [ɛntˈʃprɪŋən] vi unreg spring (from).

entstehen [ɛntˈʃteːən] vi unreg arise, result.

Entstehung f genesis, origin.

entstellen [ɛntˈʃtɛlən] vt disfigure; (Wahrheit) distort.

entstören [ɛntˈʃtøːrən] vt (RAD) eliminate interference from; (AUT) suppress.

enttäuschen [ɛntˈtɔyʃən] vt disappoint.

Enttäuschung f disappointment.

Entwarnung [ɛntˈvarnʊŋ] f all clear (signal).

entwässern [ɛntˈvɛsərn] vt drain.

entweder [ˈɛntveːdər] kj either.

entwenden [ɛntˈvɛndən] vt unreg purloin, steal.

entwerfen [ɛntˈvɛrfən] vt unreg (Zeichnung) sketch; (Modell) design; (Vortrag, Gesetz etc) draft.

entwerten [ɛntˈveːrtən] vt devalue; (stempeln) cancel.

Entwerter m **-s,** - ticket punching machine.

entwickeln [ɛntˈvɪkəln] vtr develop (auch PHOT); (Mut, Energie) show, display.

Entwickler m **-s,** - developer.

Entwicklung [ɛntˈvɪklʊŋ] f development; (PHOT) developing.

Entwicklungs- zW: **~hilfe** f aid for developing countries; **~jahre** pl adolescence sing; **~land** nt developing country.

entwöhnen [ɛntˈvøːnən] vt wean; (Süchtige) cure (dat, von of).

Entwöhnung f weaning; cure, curing.

entwürdigend [ɛntˈvyrdɪɡənt] a degrading.

Entwurf [ɛntˈvʊrf] m outline, design;

(Vertrags~, Konzept) draft.

entziehen [ɛntˈtsiːən] unreg vt withdraw, take away (dat from); (Flüssigkeit) draw, extract // vr escape (dat from); (jds Kenntnis) be outside; (der Pflicht) shirk.

Entziehung f withdrawal.

Entziehungs- zW: **~anstalt** f drug addiction/alcoholism treatment centre; **~kur** f treatment for drug addiction/alcoholism.

entziffern [ɛntˈtsɪfərn] vt decipher; decode.

entzücken [ɛntˈtsykən] vt delight; **E~** nt **-s** delight; **~d** a delightful, charming.

entzünden [ɛntˈtsyndən] vt light, set light to; (fig, MED) inflame; (Streit) spark off // vr (lit, fig) catch fire; (Streit) start; (MED) become inflamed.

Entzündung f (MED) inflammation.

entzwei [ɛntˈtsvaɪ] ad broken; in two; **~brechen** vti unreg break in two; **~en** vt set at odds // vr fall out; **~gehen** vi unreg break (in two).

Enzian [ˈɛntsiaːn] m **-s, -e** gentian.

Enzym [ɛnˈtsyːm] nt **-s, -e** enzyme.

Epidemie [epideˈmiː] f epidemic.

Epilepsie [epilɛpˈsiː] f epilepsy.

Episode [epiˈzoːdə] f **-, -n** episode.

Epoche [eˈpɔxə] f **-, -n** epoch; **e~machend** a epoch-making.

Epos [ˈeːpɔs] nt **-s, Epen** epic (poem).

er [eːr] pron he; it.

erachten [ɛrˈaxtən] vt: **~ für** od **als** consider (to be); **meines E~s** in my opinion.

erarbeiten [ɛrˈarbaɪtən] vt (auch sich (dat) ~) work for, acquire; (Theorie) work out.

erbarmen [ɛrˈbarmən] vr have pity od mercy (gen on); **E~** nt **-s** pity.

erbärmlich [ɛrˈbɛrmlɪç] a wretched, pitiful; **E~keit** f wretchedness.

erbarmungslos [ɛrˈbarmʊŋsloːs] a pitiless, merciless.

erbau- [ɛrˈbau] zW: **~en** vt build, erect; (fig) edify; **E~er** m **-s,** - builder; **~lich** a edifying; **E~ung** f construction; (fig) edification.

Erbe [ˈɛrbə] m **-n, -n** heir // nt **-s** inheritance; (fig) heritage; **e~n** vt inherit.

erbeuten [ɛrˈbɔytən] vt carry off; (MIL) capture.

Erb- [ɛrb] zW: **~faktor** m gene; **~folge** f (line of) succession; **~in** f heiress.

erbittern [ɛrˈbɪtərn] vt embitter; (erzürnen) incense.

erbittert [ɛrˈbɪtərt] a (Kampf) fierce, bitter.

erblassen [ɛrˈblasən] vi, **erbleichen** [ɛrˈblaɪçən] vi unreg (turn) pale.

erblich ['ɛrplɪç] *a* hereditary.

erbosen [ɛr'boːzən] *vt* anger // *vr* grow angry.

erbrechen [ɛr'brɛçən] *vtr unreg* vomit.

Erbschaft *f* inheritance, legacy.

Erbse ['ɛrpsə] *f* -, -n pea.

Erd- ['ɛːrd] *zW:* ~**achse** *f* earth's axis; ~**atmosphäre** *f* earth's atmosphere; ~**beben** *nt* earthquake; ~**beere** *f* strawberry; ~**boden** *m* ground; ~**e** *f* -, -n earth; **zu ebener** ~**e** at ground level; **e**~**en** *vt* (*ELEK*) earth.

erdenklich [ɛr'dɛŋklɪç] *a* conceivable.

Erd- *zW:* ~**gas** *nt* natural gas; ~**geschoß** *nt* ground floor; ~**kunde** *f* geography; ~**nuß** *f* peanut; ~**oberfläche** *f* surface of the earth; ~**öl** *nt* (mineral) oil.

erdrosseln [ɛr'drɔsəln] *vt* strangle, throttle.

erdrücken [ɛr'drykən] *vt* crush.

Erd- *zW:* ~**rutsch** *m* landslide; ~**teil** *m* continent.

erdulden [ɛr'dʊldən] *vt* endure, suffer.

ereifern [ɛr'aɪfərn] *vr* get excited.

ereignen [ɛr'aɪɡnən] *vr* happen.

Ereignis [ɛr'aɪɡnɪs] *nt* -ses, -se event; **e**~**reich** *a* eventful.

erfahren [ɛr'faːrən] *vt unreg* learn, find out; (*erleben*) experience // *a* experienced.

Erfahrung *f* experience; **erfahrungsgemäß** *ad* according to experience.

erfassen [ɛr'fasən] *vt* seize; (*fig: einbeziehen*) include, register; (*verstehen*) grasp.

erfind- [ɛr'fɪnd] *zW:* ~**en** *vt unreg* invent; **E**~**er** *m* -s, - inventor; ~**erisch** *a* inventive; **E**~**ung** *f* invention.

Erfolg [ɛr'fɔlk] *m* -(e)s, -e success; (*Folge*) result; **e**~**en** *vi* follow; (*sich ergeben*) result; (*stattfinden*) take place; (*Zahlung*) be effected; **e**~**los** *a* unsuccessful; ~**losigkeit** *f* lack of success; **e**~**reich** *a* successful; **e**~**versprechend** *a* promising.

erforder- [ɛr'fɔrdər] *zW:* ~**lich** *a* requisite, necessary; ~**n** *vt* require, demand.

erforsch- [ɛr'fɔrʃ] *zW:* ~**en** *vt* (*Land*) explore; (*Problem*) investigate; (*Gewissen*) search; **E**~**ung** *f* exploration; investigation; searching.

erfreuen [ɛr'frɔyən] *vr:* **sich** ~ **an** (+*dat*) enjoy; **sich einer Sache** (*gen*) ~ enjoy sth // *vt* delight.

erfreulich [ɛr'frɔylɪç] *a* pleasing, gratifying; ~**erweise** *ad* happily, luckily.

erfrieren [ɛr'friːrən] *vi unreg* freeze (to death); (*Glieder*) get frostbitten; (*Pflanzen*) be killed by frost.

erfrischen [ɛr'frɪʃən] *vt* refresh.

Erfrischung *f* refreshment; **Erfrischungsraum** *m* snack bar, cafeteria.

erfüllen [ɛr'fʏlən] *vt* (*Raum etc*) fill; (*fig: Bitte etc*) fulfil // *vr* come true.

ergänzen [ɛr'ɡɛntsən] *vt* supplement, complete // *vr* complement one another.

Ergänzung *f* completion; (*Zusatz*) supplement.

ergeben [ɛr'ɡeːbən] *unreg vt* yield, produce // *vr* surrender; (*sich hingeben*) give o.s. up, yield (*dat* to); (*folgen*) result // *a* devoted, humble; (*dem Trunk*) addicted (to); **E**~**heit** *f* devotion, humility.

Ergebnis [ɛr'ɡeːpnɪs] *nt* -ses, -se result; **e**~**los** *a* without result, fruitless.

ergehen [ɛr'ɡeːən] *unreg vi* be issued, go out; **etw über sich** ~ **lassen** put up with sth // *vi unpers:* **es ergeht ihm gut/schlecht** he's faring *od* getting on well/badly // *vr:* **sich in etw** (*dat*) ~ indulge in sth.

ergiebig [ɛr'ɡiːbɪç] *a* productive.

ergreifen [ɛr'ɡraɪfən] *vt unreg* (*lit, fig*) seize; (*Beruf*) take up; (*Maßnahmen*) resort to; (*rühren*) move.

ergriffen [ɛr'ɡrɪfən] *a* deeply moved.

Erguß [ɛr'ɡʊs] *m* discharge; (*fig*) outpouring, effusion.

erhaben [ɛr'haːbən] *a* (*lit*) raised, embossed; (*fig*) exalted, lofty; **über etw** (*akk*) ~ **sein** be above sth.

erhalten [ɛr'haltən] *vt unreg* receive; (*bewahren*) preserve, maintain; **gut** ~ in good condition.

erhältlich [ɛr'hɛltlɪç] *a* obtainable, available.

Erhaltung *f* maintenance, preservation.

erhärten [ɛr'hɛrtən] *vt* harden; (*These*) substantiate, corroborate.

erheben [ɛr'heːbən] *unreg vt* raise; (*Protest, Forderungen*) make; (*Fakten*) ascertain, establish // *vr* rise (up); **sich über etw** (*akk*) ~ rise above sth.

erheblich [ɛr'heːplɪç] *a* considerable.

erheitern [ɛr'haɪtərn] *vt* amuse, cheer (up).

Erheiterung *f* exhilaration; **zur allgemeinen** ~ to everybody's amusement.

erhitzen [ɛr'hɪtsən] *vt* heat // *vr* heat up; (*fig*) become heated.

erhoffen [ɛr'hɔfən] *vt* hope for.

erhöhen [ɛr'høːən] *vt* raise; (*verstärken*) increase.

erhol- [ɛr'hoːl] *zW:* ~**en** *vr* recover; (*entspannen*) have a rest; ~**sam** *a* restful; **E**~**ung** *f* recovery; relaxation, rest; ~**ungsbedürftig** *a* in need of a rest, run-down; **E**~**ungsheim** *nt* convalescent/rest home.

erhören [ɛr'høːrən] *vt* (*Gebet etc*) hear; (*Bitte etc*) yield to.

erinnern [ɛr'ʔɪnərn] *vt* remind (*an +akk* of) // *vr* remember (*an etw (akk)* sth).

Erinnerung *f* memory; (*Andenken*) reminder.

erkält- [ɛr'kɛlt] *zW:* ~**en** *vr* catch cold; ~**et** *a* with a cold; ~**et sein** have a cold; **E~ung** *f* cold.

erkenn- [ɛr'kɛn] *zW:* ~**bar** *a* recognizable; ~**en** *vt unreg* recognize; (*sehen, verstehen*) see.

erkennt- *zW:* ~**lich** *a:* sich ~**lich zeigen** show one's appreciation; **E~lichkeit** *f* gratitude; (*Geschenk*) token of one's gratitude; **E~nis** *f -, -se** knowledge; (*das Erkennen*) recognition; (*Einsicht*) insight; **zur E~t- nis kommen** realize.

Erkennung *f* recognition.

Erker ['ɛrkər] *m* **-s, -** bay; ~**fenster** *nt* bay window.

erklär- [ɛr'klɛːr] *zW:* ~**bar** *a* explicable; ~**en** *vt* explain; ~**lich** *a* explicable; (*verständlich*) understandable; **E~ung** *f* explanation; (*Aussage*) declaration.

erkranken [ɛr'kraŋkən] *vi* fall ill.

Erkrankung *f* illness.

erkund- [ɛr'kʊnd] *zW:* ~**en** *vt* find out, ascertain; (*bes MIL*) reconnoitre, scout; ~**igen** *vr* inquire (*nach* about); **E~igung** *f* inquiry; **E~ung** *f* reconnaissance, scouting.

erlahmen [ɛr'laːmən] *vi* tire; (*nachlassen*) flag, wane.

erlangen [ɛr'laŋən] *vt* attain, achieve.

Erlaß [ɛr'las] *m* **-sses, -lässe** decree; (*Aufhebung*) remission.

erlassen *vt unreg* (*Verfügung*) issue; (*Gesetz*) enact; (*Strafe*) remit; **jdm etw ~** release sb from sth.

erlauben [ɛr'laubən] *vt* allow, permit (*jdm etw* sb to do sth) // *vr* permit o.s., venture.

Erlaubnis [ɛr'laupnɪs] *f -, -se** permission; (*Schriftstück*) permit.

erläutern [ɛr'lɔytərn] *vt* explain.

Erläuterung *f* explanation.

Erle ['ɛrlə] *f -, -n** alder.

erleben [ɛr'leːbən] *vt* experience; (*Zeit*) live through; (*mit~*) witness; (*noch mit~*) live to see.

Erlebnis [ɛr'leːpnɪs] *nt* **-ses, -se** experience.

erledigen [ɛr'leːdɪgən] *vt* take care of, deal with; (*Antrag etc*) process; (*umg: erschöpfen*) wear out; (*umg: ruinieren*) finish; (*umg: umbringen*) do in.

erleichter- [ɛr'laɪçtər] *zW:* ~**n** *vt* make easier; (*fig: Last*) lighten; (*lindern, beruhigen*) relieve; ~**t** *a* relieved; **E~ung** *f* facilitation; lightening; relief.

erleiden [ɛr'laɪdən] *vt unreg* suffer, endure.

erlernen [ɛr'lɛrnən] *vt* learn, acquire.

erlesen [ɛr'leːzən] *a* select, choice.

erleuchten [ɛr'lɔyçtən] *vt* illuminate; (*fig*) inspire.

Erleuchtung *f* (*Einfall*) inspiration.

Erlös [ɛr'løːs] *m* **-es, -e** proceeds *pl*.

erlösen [ɛr'løːzən] *vt* redeem, save.

Erlösung *f* release; (*REL*) redemption.

ermächtigen [ɛr'mɛçtɪgən] *vt* authorize, empower.

Ermächtigung *f* authorization; authority.

ermahnen [ɛr'maːnən] *vt* exhort, admonish.

Ermahnung *f* admonition, exhortation.

ermäßigen [ɛr'mɛːsɪgən] *vt* reduce.

Ermäßigung *f* reduction.

ermessen [ɛr'mɛsən] *vt unreg* estimate, gauge; **E~** *nt* **-s** estimation; discretion; **in jds E~ liegen** lie within sb's discretion.

ermitteln [ɛr'mɪtəln] *vt* determine; (*Täter*) trace // *vi:* **gegen jdn ~** investigate sb.

Ermittlung [ɛr'mɪtlʊŋ] *f* determination; (*Polizei~*) investigation.

ermöglichen [ɛr'møːklɪçən] *vt* make possible (*dat* for).

ermorden [ɛr'mɔrdən] *vt* murder.

Ermordung *f* murder.

ermüden [ɛr'myːdən] *vti* tire; (*TECH*) fatigue; ~**d** *a* tiring; (*fig*) wearisome.

Ermüdung *f* fatigue; **Ermüdungserscheinung** *f* sign of fatigue.

ermutigen [ɛr'muːtɪgən] *vt* encourage.

ernähr- [ɛr'nɛːr] *zW:* ~**en** *vt* feed, nourish; (*Familie*) support // *vr* support o.s., earn a living; **sich ~en von** live on; **E~er** *m* **-s, -** breadwinner; **E~ung** *f* nourishment; nutrition; (*Unterhalt*) maintenance.

ernennen [ɛr'nɛnən] *vt unreg* appoint.

Ernennung *f* appointment.

erneu- [ɛr'nɔy] *zW:* ~**ern** *vt* renew; restore; renovate; **E~erung** *f* renewal; restoration; renovation; ~**t** *a* renewed, fresh // *ad* once more.

Ernst [ɛrnst] *m* **-es** seriousness; **das ist mein ~** I'm quite serious; **im ~** in earnest; ~ **machen mit etw** put sth into practice; **e~** *a* serious; ~**fall** *m* emergency; **e~gemeint** *a* meant in earnest, serious; **e~haft** *a* serious; ~**haftigkeit** *f* seriousness; **e~lich** *a* serious.

Ernte ['ɛrntə] *f -, -n** harvest; **e~n** *vt* harvest; (*Lob etc*) earn.

ernüchtern [ɛr'nʏçtərn] *vt* sober up; (*fig*) bring down to earth.

Erober- [ɛr'oːbər] *zW:* ~**er** *m* **-s, -** conqueror; **e~n** *vt* conquer; ~**ung** *f* conquest.

eröffnen [ɛr''œfnən] *vt* open; **jdm etw ~** disclose sth to sb // *vr* present itself.

Eröffnung *f* opening.

erörtern [ɛr''œrtərn] *vt* discuss.

Erörterung *f* discussion.

Erotik [e'ro:tɪk] *f* eroticism.

erotisch *a* erotic.

erpress- [ɛr'prɛs] *zW:* **~en** *vt (Geld etc)* extort; *(Mensch)* blackmail; **E~er** *m* **-s, -** blackmailer; **E~ung** *f* blackmail; extortion.

erraten [ɛr'ra:tən] *vt unreg* guess.

erreg- [ɛr're:g] *zW:* **~en** *vt* excite; *(ärgern)* infuriate; *(hervorrufen)* arouse, provoke *vr* get excited *od* worked up; **E~er** *m* **-s, -** causative agent; **E~ung** *f* excitement.

erreichbar *a* accessible, within reach.

erreichen [ɛr'raɪçən] *vt* reach; *(Zweck)* achieve; *(Zug)* catch.

errichten [ɛr'rɪçtən] *vt* erect, put up; *(gründen)* establish, set up.

erringen [ɛr'rɪŋən] *vt unreg* gain, win.

erröten [ɛr'rø:tən] *vi* blush, flush.

Errungenschaft [ɛr'rʊŋənʃaft] *f* achievement; *(umg: Anschaffung)* acquisition.

Ersatz [ɛr'zats] *m* **-es** substitute; replacement; *(Schaden~)* compensation; *(MIL)* reinforcements *pl*; **~dienst** *m (MIL)* alternative service; **~reifen** *m (AUT)* spare tyre; **~teil** *nt* spare (part).

erschaffen [ɛr'ʃafən] *vt unreg* create.

erscheinen [ɛr'ʃaɪnən] *vi unreg* appear.

Erscheinung *f* appearance; *(Geist)* apparition; *(Gegebenheit)* phenomenon; *(Gestalt)* figure.

erschießen [ɛr'ʃi:sən] *vt unreg* shoot (dead).

erschlagen [ɛr'ʃla:gən] *vt unreg* strike dead.

erschöpf- [ɛr'ʃœpf] *zW:* **~en** *vt* exhaust; **~end** *a* exhaustive, thorough; **~t** *a* exhausted; **E~ung** *f* exhaustion.

erschrecken [ɛr'ʃrɛkən] *vt* startle, frighten // *vi unreg* be frightened *od* startled; **~d** *a* alarming, frightening.

erschrocken [ɛr'ʃrɔkən] *a* frightened, startled.

erschüttern [ɛr'ʃʏtərn] *vt* shake; *(ergreifen)* move deeply.

Erschütterung *f* shaking; shock.

erschweren [ɛr'ʃve:rən] *vt* complicate.

erschwingen [ɛr'ʃvɪŋən] *vt unreg* afford.

erschwinglich *a* within one's means.

ersehen [ɛr'ze:ən] *vt unreg:* **aus etw ~, daß** gather from sth that.

ersetzen [ɛr'zɛtsən] *vt* replace; **jdm Unkosten** *etc* **~** pay sb's expenses *etc*.

ersichtlich [ɛr'zɪçtlɪç] *a* evident, obvious.

ersparen [ɛr'ʃpa:rən] *vt (Ärger etc)* spare; *(Geld)* save.

Ersparnis *f* **-, -se** saving.

erst ['e:rst] *ad* **1** first; **mach ~ mal die Arbeit fertig** finish your work first; **wenn du das ~ mal hinter dir hast** once you've got that behind you **2** *(nicht früher als, nur)* only; *(nicht bis)* not till; **~ gestern** only yesterday; **~ morgen** not until tomorrow; **~ als** only when, not until; **wir fahren ~ später** we're not going until later; **er ist (gerade) ~ angekommen** he's only just arrived **3: wäre er doch ~ zurück!** if only he were back!

erstatten [ɛr'ʃtatən] *vt (Kosten)* (re)pay; **Anzeige** *etc* **~** report sb; **Bericht ~** make a report.

Erstaufführung ['e:rst'aʊffy:rʊŋ] *f* first performance.

erstaunen [ɛr'ʃtaʊnən] *vt* astonish // *vi* be astonished; **E~** *nt* **-s** astonishment.

erstaunlich *a* astonishing.

erst- ['e:rst] *zW:* **E~ausgabe** *f* first edition; **~beste(r, s)** *a* first that comes along; **~e(r, s)** *a* first.

erstechen [ɛr'ʃtɛçən] *vt unreg* stab (to death).

erstehen [ɛr'ʃte:ən] *vt unreg* buy // *vi* (a)rise.

erstens ['e:rstəns] *ad* firstly, in the first place.

ersticken [ɛr'ʃtɪkən] *vt (lit, fig)* stifle; *(Mensch)* suffocate; *(Flammen)* smother // *vi (Mensch)* suffocate; *(Feuer)* be smothered; **in Arbeit ~** be snowed under with work.

erst- *zW:* **~klassig** *a* first-class; **E~kommunion** *f* first communion; **~malig** *a* first; **~mals** *ad* for the first time.

erstrebenswert [ɛr'ʃtre:bənsve:rt] *a* desirable, worthwhile.

erstrecken [ɛr'ʃtrɛkən] *vr* extend, stretch.

ersuchen [ɛr'zu:xən] *vt* request.

ertappen [ɛr'tapən] *vt* catch, detect.

erteilen [ɛr'taɪlən] *vt* give.

Ertrag [ɛr'tra:k] *m* **-(e)s, -̈e** yield; *(Gewinn)* proceeds *pl*; **e~en** *vt unreg* bear, stand.

erträglich [ɛr'trɛ:klɪç] *a* tolerable, bearable.

ertrinken [ɛr'trɪŋkən] *vi unreg* drown; **E~** *nt* **-s** drowning.

erübrigen [ɛr''y:brɪgən] *vt* spare // *vr* be unnecessary.

erwachen [ɛr'vaxən] *vi* awake.

erwachsen [ɛr'vaksən] *a* grown-up; **E~e(r)** *mf* adult; **E~enbildung** *f* adult education.

erwägen [ɛr'vɛ:gən] *vt unreg* consider.

Erwägung *f* consideration.

erwähn- [ɛr'vɛ:n] *zW*: ~**en** *vt* mention; ~**enswert** *a* worth mentioning; **E~ung** *f* mention.

erwärmen [ɛr'vɛrmən] *vt* warm, heat // *vr* get warm, warm up; **sich** ~ **für** warm to.

erwarten [ɛr'vartən] *vt* expect; (*warten auf*) wait for; **etw kaum** ~ **können** hardly be able to wait for sth.

Erwartung *f* expectation; **erwartungsgemäß** *ad* as expected; **erwartungsvoll** *a* expectant.

erwecken [ɛr'vɛkən] *vt* rouse, awake; **den Anschein** ~ give the impression.

Erweis [ɛr'vais] *m* -es, -e proof; **e~en** *unreg vt* prove; (*Ehre, Dienst*) do (*jdm sb*) // *vr* prove (*als* to be).

Erwerb [ɛr'vɛrp] *m* -(e)s, -e acquisition; (*Beruf*) trade; **e~en** *vt unreg* acquire.

erwerbs- *zW*: ~**los** *a* unemployed; **E~quelle** *f* source of income; ~**tätig** *a* (gainfully) employed; ~**unfähig** *a* unemployable.

erwidern [ɛr'vi:dərn] *vt* reply; (*vergelten*) return.

erwiesen [ɛr'vi:zən] *a* proven.

erwischen [ɛr'vɪʃən] *vt* (*umg*) catch, get.

erwünscht [ɛr'vʏnʃt] *a* desired.

erwürgen [ɛr'vʏrgən] *vt* strangle.

Erz [ɛːrts] *nt* -es, -e ore.

erzähl- [ɛr'tsɛːl] *zW*: ~**en** *vt* tell // *vi*: **sie kann gut** ~**en** she's a good storyteller; **E~er** *m* -s, - narrator; **E~ung** *f* story, tale.

Erz- *zW*: ~**bischof** *m* archbishop; ~**engel** *m* archangel.

erzeug- [ɛr'tsɔyg] *zW*: ~**en** *vt* produce; (*Strom*) generate; **E~nis** *nt* -ses, -se product, produce; **E~ung** *f* production; generation.

erziehen [ɛr'tsi:ən] *vt unreg* bring up; (*bilden*) educate, train.

Erziehung *f* bringing up; (*Bildung*) education.

Erziehungs- *zW*: ~**beihilfe** *f* educational grant; ~**berechtigte(r)** *mf* parent; guardian; ~**heim** *nt* approved school.

erzielen [ɛr'tsi:lən] *vt* achieve, obtain; (*Tor*) score.

erzwingen [ɛr'tsvɪŋən] *vt unreg* force, obtain by force.

es [ɛs] *pron nom, akk* it.

Esche ['ɛʃə] *f* -, -n ash.

Esel ['e:zəl] *m* -s, - donkey, ass.

Eskalation [ɛskalatsi'oːn] *f* escalation.

eßbar ['ɛsbaːr] *a* eatable, edible.

essen ['ɛsən] *vti unreg* eat; **E~** *nt* -s, - meal; food; **Essenszeit** *f* mealtime; dinner time.

Essig ['ɛsɪç] *m* -s, -e vinegar; ~**gurke** *f* gherkin.

Eß- ['ɛs] *zW*: ~**kastanie** *f* sweet chestnut; ~**löffel** *m* tablespoon; ~**tisch** *m* dining table; ~**waren** *pl* food stuffs *pl*, provisions *pl*; ~**zimmer** *nt* dining room.

etablieren [eta'bliːrən] *vr* become established; set up in business.

Etage [e'ta:ʒə] *f* -, -n floor, storey; **Etagenbetten** *pl* bunk beds *pl*; **Etagenwohnung** *f* flat.

Etappe [e'tapə] *f* -, -n stage.

Etat [e'ta:] *m* -s, -s budget.

etepetete [e:təpe'te:tə] *a* (*umg*) fussy.

Ethik ['e:tɪk] *f* ethics *sing*.

ethisch ['e:tɪʃ] *a* ethical.

Etikett [eti'kɛt] *nt* -(e)s, -e label; tag; ~**e** *f* etiquette, manners *pl*; **e~ieren** [-'tiːrən] *vt* label; tag.

etliche ['ɛtlɪçə] *pron pl* some, quite a few; ~**s** a thing or two.

Etui [ɛt'vi:] *nt* -s, -s case.

etwa ['ɛtva] *ad* (*ungefähr*) about; (*vielleicht*) perhaps; (*beispielsweise*) for instance; **nicht** ~ by no means; ~**ig** ['ɛtvaɪç] *a* possible; **etwas** *pron* something; anything; (*ein wenig*) a little // *ad* a little.

euch [ɔyç] *pron akk von* **ihr** you; yourselves // *dat von* **ihr** (to) you.

euer ['ɔyər] *pron gen von* **ihr** of you // *pron* your; ~**e(r, s)** yours.

Eule ['ɔylə] *f* -, -n owl.

eure(r, s) ['ɔyrə(r, s)] *pron* your; yours; **eurerseits** *ad* on your part; **euresgleichen** *pron* people like you; **euretwegen, euretwillen** *ad* (*für euch*) for your sakes; (*wegen euch*) on your account.

eurige ['ɔyrigə] *pron*: **der/die/das** ~ yours.

Euro- *zW*: ~**pa** [ɔy'ro:pa] *nt* Europe; ~**päer(in)** [ɔyro'pɛ:ər(ɪn)] *mf* European; **e~päisch** *a* European; ~**pameister** [ɔy'ro:pa-] *m* European champion.

Euter ['ɔytər] *nt* -s, - udder.

ev. *abk von* **evangelisch.**

evakuieren [evaku'i:rən] *vt* evacuate.

evangelisch [evaŋ'ge:lɪʃ] *a* Protestant.

Evangelium [evaŋ'ge:liʊm] *nt* gospel.

eventuell [evɛntu'ɛl] *a* possible // *ad* possibly, perhaps.

evtl. *abk von* **eventuell.**

EWG [e:ve:'ge:] *f* - *abk* (= *Europäische Wirtschaftsgemeinschaft*) EEC, Common Market.

ewig ['e:vɪç] *a* eternal; **E~keit** *f* eternity.

Ex- [ɛks] *in zW* ex-.

exakt [ɛ'ksakt] *a* exact.

Examen [ɛ'ksa:mən] *nt* -s, - *od* **Examina** examination.

Exemplar [ɛksɛm'plaːr] *nt* -s, -e specimen; (*Buch~*) copy; **e~isch** *a* exemplary.

exerzieren [ɛksɛr'tsiːrən] *vi* drill.

Exil [ɛ'ksiːl] *nt* **-s, -e** exile.

Existenz [ɛksɪs'tɛnts] *f* existence; (*Unterhalt*) livelihood, living; (*pej: Mensch*) character; **~kampf** *m* struggle for existence; **~minimum** *nt* **-s** subsistence level.

existieren [ɛksɪs'tiːrən] *vi* exist.

exklusiv [ɛksklu'ziːf] *a* exclusive; **~e** [-'ziːvə] *ad, präp +gen* exclusive of, not including.

exotisch [ɛ'ksoːtɪʃ] *a* exotic.

Expedition [ɛkspeditsi'oːn] *f* expedition.

Experiment [ɛksperi'mɛnt] *nt* experiment; **e~ell** [-'tɛl] *a* experimental; **e~ieren** [-'tiːrən] *vi* experiment.

Experte [ɛks'pɛrtə] *m* **-n, -n, Expertin** *f* expert, specialist.

explo- [ɛksploː] *zW:* **~dieren** [-'diːrən] *vi* explode; **E~sion** [ɛksplozi'oːn] *f* explosion; **~siv** [-'ziːf] *a* explosive.

Export [ɛks'pɔrt] *m* **-(e)s, -e** export; **Exporteur** [-'tøːr] *m* exporter; **~handel** *m* export trade; **e~ieren** [-'tiːrən] *vt* export; **~land** *nt* exporting country.

Expreß- [ɛks'prɛs] *zW:* **~gut** *nt* express goods *pl od* freight; **~zug** *m* express (train).

extra ['ɛkstra] *a inv* (*umg: gesondert*) separate; (*besondere*) extra // *ad* (*gesondert*) separately; (*speziell*) specially; (*absichtlich*) on purpose; (*vor Adjektiven, zusätzlich*) extra; **E~** *nt* **-s, -s** extra; **E~ausgabe** *f*, **E~blatt** *nt* special edition.

Extrakt [ɛks'trakt] *m* **-(e)s, -e** extract.

extrem [ɛks'treːm] *a* extreme; **~istisch** [-'mɪstɪʃ] *a* (*POL*) extremist; **E~itäten** [-'tɛːtən] *pl* extremities *pl*.

exzentrisch [ɛks'tsɛntrɪʃ] *a* eccentric.

Exzeß [ɛks'tsɛs] *m* **-sses, -sse** excess.

F

F, f [ɛf] *nt* F, f.

Fa. *abk* (= *Firma*) firm; (*in Briefen*) Messrs.

Fabel ['faːbəl] *f* **-, -n** fable; **f~haft** *a* fabulous, marvellous.

Fabrik [fa'briːk] *f* factory; **~ant** [-'kant] *m* (*Hersteller*) manufacturer; (*Besitzer*) industrialist; **~arbeiter** *m* factory worker; **~at** [-'kaːt] *nt* **-(e)s, -e** manufacture, product; **~ation** [-atsi'oːn] *f* manufacture, production; **~gelände** *nt* factory premises *pl*.

Fach [fax] *nt* **-(e)s, ¨er** compartment; (*Sachgebiet*) subject; **ein Mann vom ~** an expert; **~arbeiter** *m* skilled worker; **~arzt** *m* (medical) special-

ist; **~ausdruck** *m* technical term.

Fächer ['fɛçər] *m* **-s, -** fan.

Fach- *zW:* **~hochschule** *f* ≈ technical college; **f~kundig** *a* expert, specialist; **f~lich** *a* professional; expert; **~mann** *m*, *pl* **-leute** specialist; **f~männisch** *a* professional; **~schule** *f* technical college; **f~simpeln** *vi* talk shop; **~werk** *nt* timber frame.

Fackel ['fakəl] *f* **-, -n** torch.

fad(e) ['faɪt, faːdə] *a* insipid; (*langweilig*) dull.

Faden ['faːdən] *m* **-s, ¨** thread; **f~scheinig** *a* (*lit, fig*) threadbare.

fähig ['fɛːɪç] *a* capable (*zu, gen* of); able; **F~keit** *f* ability.

fahnden ['faːndən] *vi:* **~ nach** search for.

Fahndung *f* search; **Fahndungsliste** *f* list of wanted criminals, wanted list.

Fahne ['faːnə] *f* **-, -n** flag, standard; **eine ~ haben** (*umg*) smell of drink; **Fahnenflucht** *f* desertion.

Fahr- ['faːr] *zW:* **~ausweis** *m* ticket; **~bahn** *f* carriageway (*Brit*), roadway.

Fähre ['fɛːrə] *f* **-, -n** ferry.

fahren ['faːrən] *unreg vt* drive; (*Rad*) ride; (*befördern*) drive, take; (*Rennen*) drive in // *vi* (*sich bewegen*) go; (*Schiff*) sail; (*abfahren*) leave; **mit dem Auto/Zug ~** go *od* travel by car/train; **mit der Hand ~ über** (*+akk*) pass one's hand over.

Fahr- *zW:* **~er(in** *f)* *m* **-s, -** driver; **~erflucht** *f* hit-and-run; **~gast** *m* passenger; **~geld** *nt* fare; **~gestell** *nt* chassis; (*AVIAT*) undercarriage; **~karte** *f* ticket; **~kartenausgabe** *f*, **~kartenschalter** *m* ticket office; **f~lässig** *a* negligent; **f~lässige Tötung** manslaughter; **~lässigkeit** *f* negligence; **~lehrer** *m* driving instructor; **~plan** *m* timetable; **f~planmäßig** *a* (*EISENB*) scheduled; **~preis** *m* fare; **~prüfung** *f* driving test; **~rad** *nt* bicycle; **~schein** *m* ticket; **~schule** *f* driving school; **~stuhl** *m* lift (*Brit*), elevator (*US*).

Fahrt [faːrt] *f* **-, -en** journey; (*kurz*) trip; (*AUT*) drive; (*Geschwindigkeit*) speed; **gute ~!** have a good journey.

Fährte ['fɛːrtə] *f* **-, -n** track, trail.

Fahrtkosten *pl* travelling expenses *pl*.

Fahrtrichtung *f* course, direction.

Fahrzeug *nt* vehicle; **~halter** *m* **-s, -** owner of a vehicle.

Faksimile [fak'ziːmile] *nt* facsimile.

Faktor ['faktɔr] *m* factor.

Faktum ['faktum] *nt* **-s, -ten** fact.

Fakultät [fakʊl'tɛːt] *f* faculty.

Falke ['falkə] *m* **-n, -n** falcon.

Fall [fal] *m* **-(e)s, ¨er** (*Sturz*) fall; (*Sachverhalt, JUR, GRAM*) case; **auf jeden ~, auf alle ¨e** in any case; (*be-*

stimmt) definitely; **auf keinen ~!** no way!; **~e** *f* -, **-n** trap; **f~en lassen** drop sth.
fällen ['fɛlən] *vt (Baum)* fell; *(Urteil)* pass.
fallenlassen *vt unreg (Bemerkung)* make; *(Plan)* abandon, drop.
fällig ['fɛlıç] *a* due.
falls [fals] *ad* in case, if.
Fall- *zW:* **~schirm** *m* parachute; **~schirmjäger** *pl* paratroops *pl*; **~schirmspringer** *m* parachutist.
falsch [falʃ] *a* false; *(unrichtig)* wrong.
fälschen ['fɛlʃən] *vt* forge.
Falschgeld *nt* counterfeit money.
fälsch- *zW:* **~lich** *a* false; **~licherweise** *ad* mistakenly; **F~ung** *f* forgery.
Falte ['faltə] *f* -, **-n** *(Knick)* fold, crease; *(Haut~)* wrinkle; *(Rock~)* pleat; **f~n** *vt* fold; *(Stirn)* wrinkle.
familiär [familı'εːr] *a* familiar.
Familie [fa'miːliə] *f* family.
Familien- *zW:* **~kreis** *m* family circle; **~name** *m* surname; **~stand** *m* marital status.
Fanatiker [fa'naːtikər] *m* -**s**, - fanatic.
fanatisch *a* fanatical.
Fanatismus [fana'tısmʊs] *m* fanaticism.
fand *etc v siehe* **finden.**
Fang [faŋ] *m* -(e)s, ⁻e catch; *(Jagen)* hunting; *(Kralle)* talon, claw; **f~en** *unreg vt* catch *// vr* get caught; *(Flugzeug)* level out; *(Mensch: nicht fallen)* steady o.s.; *(fig)* compose o.s.; *(in Leistung)* get back on form.
Farb- ['farb] *zW:* **~aufnahme** *f* colour photograph; **~band** *m* typewriter ribbon; **~e** *f* -, **-n** colour; *(zum Malen etc)* paint; *(Stoff~)* dye; **f~echt** *a* colourfast.
färben ['fεrbən] *vt* colour; *(Stoff, Haar)* dye.
farben- ['farbən] *zW:* **~blind** *a* colourblind; **~froh** *a* colourful, gay.
Farb- *zW:* **~fernsehen** *nt* colour television; **~film** *m* colour film; **~foto** *nt* colour photograph; **f~ig** *a* coloured; **~ige(r)** *mf* coloured; **~kasten** *m* paint-box; **f~los** *a* colourless; **~stift** *m* coloured pencil; **~stoff** *m* dye; **~ton** *m* hue, tone.
Färbung ['fɛrbʊŋ] *f* colouring; *(Tendenz)* bias.
Farn [farn] *m* -(e)s, -e, **~kraut** *nt* fern; bracken.
Fasan [fa'zaːn] *m* -(e)s, -e(n) pheasant.
Fasching ['faʃıŋ] *m* -**s**, -e *od* -s carnival.
Faschismus [fa'ʃısmʊs] *m* fascism.
Faschist *m* fascist.
Faser ['faːzər] *f* -, **-n** fibre; **f~n** *vi* fray.

Faß [fas] *nt* -sses, **Fässer** vat, barrel; *(für Öl)* drum; **Bier vom ~** draught beer.
Fassade [fa'saːdə] *f* facade.
faßbar ['fasbaːr] *a* comprehensible.
fassen ['fasən] *vt (ergreifen)* grasp, take; *(inhaltlich)* hold; *(Entschluß etc)* take; *(verstehen)* understand; *(Ring etc)* set; *(formulieren)* formulate, phrase; **nicht zu ~** unbelievable *// vr* calm down.
Fassung ['fasʊŋ] *f* *(Umrahmung)* mounting; *(Lampen~)* socket; *(Wortlaut)* version; *(Beherrschung)* composure; **jdn aus der ~ bringen** upset sb; **fassungslos** *a* speechless.
fast [fast] *ad* almost, nearly.
fasten ['fastən] *vi* fast; **F~zeit** *f* Lent.
Fastnacht *f* Shrove Tuesday; carnival.
fatal [fa'taːl] *a* fatal; *(peinlich)* embarrassing.
faul [faʊl] *a* rotten; *(Person)* lazy; *(Ausreden)* lame; **daran ist etwas ~** there's sth fishy about it; **~en** *vi* rot; **faulenzen** *vi* idle; **Faulenzer** *m* -**s**, - idler, loafer; **F~heit** *f* laziness; **~ig** *a* putrid.
Fäulnis ['fɔʏlnıs] *f* - decay, putrefaction.
Faust ['faʊst] *f* -, **Fäuste** fist; **auf eigene ~** off one's own bat; **~handschuh** *m* mitten.
Favorit [favo'riːt] *m* -en, -en favourite.
FDP [εfdeː'peː] *f abk* (= *Freie Demokratische Partei)* Free Democratic Party.
Februar ['feːbruaːr] *m* -(s), -e February.
fechten ['fεçtən] *vi unreg* fence.
Feder ['feːdər] *f* -, **-n** feather; *(Schreib~)* pen nib; *(TECH)* spring; **~ball** *m* shuttlecock; **~bett** *nt* continental quilt; **~halter** *m* penholder, pen; **f~leicht** *a* light as a feather; **f~n** *vi (nachgeben)* be springy; *(sich bewegen)* bounce *// vt* spring; **~ung** *f* suspension.
Fege- ['feːgə] *zW:* **~feuer** *nt* purgatory; **f~n** *vt* sweep.
fehl [feːl] *a:* **~ am Platz** *od* **Ort** out of place; **~en** *vi* be wanting *od* missing; *(abwesend sein)* be absent; **etw fehlt jdm** sb lacks sth; **du fehlst mir** I miss you; **was fehlt ihm?** what's wrong with him?; **F~er** *m* -**s**, - mistake, error; *(Mangel, Schwäche)* fault; **~erfrei** *a* faultless; without any mistakes; **~erhaft** *a* incorrect; faulty; **F~geburt** *f* miscarriage; **~gehen** *vi unreg* go astray; **F~griff** *m* blunder; **F~konstruktion** *f* badly designed thing; **F~schlag** *m* failure; **~schlagen** *vi unreg* fail; **F~start** *m*

(*SPORT*) false start; **F~zündung** *f*
(*AUT*) misfire, backfire.
Feier ['faɪər] *f* -, -n celebration;
~abend *m* time to stop work;
~abend machen stop, knock off; jetzt
ist **~abend**! that's enough!; **f~lich** *a*
solemn; **~lichkeit** *f* solemnity;
~lichkeiten *pl* festivities *pl*; **f~n** *vti*
celebrate; **~tag** *m* holiday.
feig(e) ['faɪg(ə)] *a* cowardly; **F~e** *f* -,
-n *fig*; **F~heit** *f* cowardice; **F~ling** *m*
coward.
Feil- [faɪl] *zW*: **~e** *f* -, -n file; **f~schen**
vi haggle.
fein [faɪn] *a* fine; (*vornehm*) refined;
(*Gehör etc*) keen; **~**! great!
Feind [faɪnt] *m* -(e)s, -e enemy; **f~lich**
a hostile; **~schaft** *f* enmity; **f~selig**
a hostile; **~seligkeit** *f* hostility.
Fein- *zW*: **f~fühlend**, **f~fühlig** *a* sensitive; **~gefühl** *nt* delicacy, tact;
~heit *f* fineness; refinement; keen-
ness; **~kostgeschäft** *nt* delicatessen
(shop); **~schmecker** *m* -s, - gourmet.
Feld [fɛlt] *nt* -(e)s, -er field; (*SCHACH*)
square; (*SPORT*) pitch; **~herr** *m*
commander; **~stecher** *m* -s, - binoculars *pl*; **~webel** *m* -s, - sergeant;
~weg *m* path.
Felge ['fɛlgə] *f* -, -n (wheel) rim.
Fell [fɛl] *nt* -(e)s, -e fur; coat; (*von
Schaf*) fleece; (*von toten Tieren*)
skin.
Fels [fɛls] *m* -en, -en, **Felsen** ['fɛlzən]
m -s, - rock; (*Klippe*) cliff; **f~enfest**
a firm; **~envorsprung** *m* ledge; **f~ig**
a rocky; **~spalte** *f* crevice.
feminin [femi'ni:n] *a* feminine; (*pej*)
effeminate.
Fenster ['fɛnstər] *nt* -s, - window;
~brett *nt* windowsill; **~ platz** *m* window seat; **~putzer** *m* -s, - window
cleaner; **~scheibe** *f* windowpane;
~sims *m* windowsill.
Ferien ['fe:riən] *pl* holidays *pl*, vacation (*US*); **~ haben** be on holiday;
~kurs *m* holiday course; **~reise** *f*
holiday; **~zeit** *f* holiday period.
Ferkel ['fɛrkəl] *nt* -s, - piglet.
fern [fɛrn] *a,ad* far-off, distant; **~ von
hier** a long way (away) from here;
der F~e Osten the Far East; **F~amt**
nt (*TEL*) exchange; **F~bedienung** *f*
remote control; **F~e** *f* -, -n distance;
~er *a,ad* further; (*weiterhin*) in future; **F~gespräch** *nt* trunk call;
F~glas *nt* binoculars *pl*; **~halten** *vtr
unreg* keep away; **F~lenkung** *f* remote control; **F~meldeamt** *nt* international exchange; **F~rohr** *nt* telescope; **F~schreiben** *nt* telex;
F~sehapparat *m* television set;
~sehen *vi unreg* watch television;
F~sehen *nt* -s television; im

F~sehen on television; **F~seher** *m*
television; **F~sehüberwachungsan-
lage** *f* closed-circuit television; **F~-
sprecher** *m* telephone; **F~sprechzelle**
f telephone box *od* booth (*US*).
Ferse ['fɛrzə] *f* -, -n heel.
fertig ['fɛrtɪç] *a* (*bereit*) ready; (*been-
det*) finished; (*gebrauchs~*) ready-
made; **F~bau** *m* prefab(ricated
house); **F~keit** *f* skill; **~machen** *vt*
(*beenden*) finish; (*umg: Person*)
finish; (: *körperlich*) exhaust; (:
moralisch) get down // *vr* get ready;
~stellen *vt* complete.
Fessel ['fɛsəl] *f* -, -n fetter; **f~n** *vt*
bind; (*mit Fesseln*) fetter; (*fig*) spell-
bind; **f~nd** *a* fascinating, captivat-
ing.
fest [fɛst] *a* firm; (*Nahrung*) solid;
(*Gehalt*) regular; **f~e Kosten** fixed
cost // *ad* (*schlafen*) soundly; **F~** *nt*
-(e)s, -e party; festival; **frohes ~**!
Happy Christmas!; **~angestellt** *a*
permanently employed; **~binden** *vt
unreg* tie, fasten; **~bleiben** *vi unreg*
stand firm; **F~essen** *nt* banquet;
~halten *unreg vt* seize, hold fast;
(*Ereignis*) record // *vr* hold on (*an
+dat* to); **~igen** *vt* strengthen;
F~igkeit *f* strength; **Festival**
['fɛstival] *nt* -s, -s festival; **F~land** *nt*
mainland; **~legen** *vt* fix // *vr* commit
o.s.; **~lich** *a* festive; **~machen** *vt*
fasten; (*Termin etc*) fix; **F~nahme** *f*
-, -n capture; **~nehmen** *vt unreg*
capture, arrest; **F~rede** *f* address;
~setzen *vt* fix, settle; **F~spiel** *nt,
F~spiele** *pl* festival; **~stehen** *vi
unreg* be certain; **~stellen** *vt* establish; (*sagen*) remark; **F~ung** *f* fortress; **F~wochen** *pl* festival.
Fett [fɛt] *nt* -(e)s, -e fat, grease; **f~** *a*
fat; (*Essen etc*) greasy; **f~arm** *a* low
fat; **f~en** *vt* grease; **f~ig** *a* greasy,
fatty; **~näpfchen** *nt*: **ins ~näpfchen
treten** put one's foot in it.
Fetzen ['fɛtsən] *m* -s, - scrap.
feucht [fɔyçt] *a* damp; (*Luft*) humid;
F~igkeit *f* dampness; humidity.
Feuer ['fɔyər] *nt* -s, - fire; (*zum
Rauchen*) a light; (*fig: Schwung*)
spirit; **~alarm** *nt* fire alarm; **~eifer**
m zeal; **f~fest** *a* fireproof; **~gefahr** *f*
danger of fire; **f~gefährlich** *a* inflammable; **~leiter** *f* fire escape ladder;
~löscher *m* -s, - fire extinguisher;
~melder *m* -s, - fire alarm; **f~n** *vti*
(*lit, fig*) fire; **~stein** *m* flint; **~wehr**
f -, -en fire brigade; **~wehrwagen** *m*
fire engine; **~werk** *nt* fireworks *pl*;
~zeug *nt* (cigarette) lighter.
Fichte ['fɪçtə] *f* -, -n spruce, pine.
Fieber ['fi:bər] *nt* -s, - fever, temperature; **f~haft** *a* feverish; **~messer** *m*,
~thermometer *nt* thermometer.

fiel *etc v siehe* **fallen.**
fies [fi:s] *a* (*umg*) nasty.
Figur [fi'gu:r] *f* -, **-en** figure; (*Schach~*) chessman, chess piece.
Filiale [fili'a:lə] *f* -, **-n** (*COMM*) branch.
Film [fɪlm] *m* -(e)s, -e film; **~aufnahme** *f* shooting; **f~en** *vti* film; **~kamera** *f* cine-camera.
Filter ['fɪltər] *m* -s, - filter; **f~n** *vt* filter; **~papier** *nt* filter paper; **~zigarette** *f* tipped cigarette.
Filz [fɪlts] *m* -es, -e felt; **f~en** *vt* (*umg*) frisk // *vi* (*Wolle*) mat; **~stift** *m* felt-tip pen.
Finale [fi'na:lə] *nt* -s, -(s) finale; (*SPORT*) final(s).
Finanz [fi'nants] *f* finance; **~amt** *nt* Inland Revenue Office; **~beamte(r)** *m* revenue officer; **f~iell** [-tsi'ɛl] *a* financial; **f~ieren** [-'tsi:rən] *vt* finance; **~minister** *m* Chancellor of the Exchequer (*Brit*), Minister of Finance.
Find- ['fɪnd] *zW:* **f~en** *unreg vt* find; (*meinen*) think // *vr* be (found); (*sich fassen*) compose o.s.; **ich finde nichts dabei, wenn ...** I don't see what's wrong if ...; **das wird sich f~en** things will work out; **~er** *m* -s, - finder; **f~ig** *a* resourceful.
fing *etc v siehe* **fangen.**
Finger ['fɪŋər] *m* -s, - finger; **~abdruck** *m* fingerprint; **~hut** *m* thimble; (*BOT*) foxglove; **~nagel** *m* fingernail; **~spitze** *f* fingertip.
fingieren [fɪŋ'gi:rən] *vt* feign.
fingiert *a* made-up, fictitious.
Fink ['fɪŋk] *m* -en, -en finch.
Finn- [fɪn] *zW:* **~e** *m*, **~in** *f* Finn; **f~isch** *a* Finnish; **~land** *nt* Finland.
finster ['fɪnstər] *a* dark, gloomy; (*verdächtig*) dubious; (*verdrossen*) grim; (*Gedanke*) dark; **F~nis** *f* - darkness, gloom.
Finte ['fɪntə] *f* -, **-n** feint, trick.
Firma ['fɪrma] *f* -, **-men** firm.
Firmen- ['fɪrmən] *zW:* **~inhaber.** *m* owner of firm; **~schild** *nt* (shop) sign; **~zeichen** *nt* registered trademark.
Firnis ['fɪrnɪs] *m* -ses, -se varnish.
Fisch [fɪʃ] *m* -(e)s, -e fish // *pl* (*ASTROL*) Pisces; **f~en** *vti* fish; **~er** *m* -s, - fisherman; **~e'rei** *f* fishing, fishery; **~fang** *m* fishing; **~geschäft** *nt* fishmonger's (shop); **~gräte** *f* fishbone.
fix [fɪks] *a* fixed; (*Person*) alert, smart; **~ und fertig** finished; (*erschöpft*) done in; **~ieren** [fɪ'ksi:rən] *vt* fix; (*anstarren*) stare at.
flach [flax] *a* flat; (*Gefäß*) shallow.
Fläche ['flɛçə] *f* -, **-n** area; (*Ober~*) surface; **~ninhalt** *m* surface area.
Flachland *nt* lowland.
flackern ['flakərn] *vi* flare, flicker.

Flagge ['flagə] *f* -, **-n** flag.
Flamme ['flamə] *f* -, **-n** flame.
Flanell [fla'nɛl] *m* -s, -e flannel.
Flanke ['flaŋkə] *f* -, **-n** flank; (*SPORT: Seite*) wing.
Flasche ['flaʃə] *f* -, **-n** bottle; (*umg: Versager*) wash-out.
Flaschen- *zW:* **~bier** *nt* bottled beer; **~öffner** *m* bottle opener; **~zug** *m* pulley.
flatterhaft *a* flighty, fickle.
flattern ['flatərn] *vi* flutter.
flau [flau] *a* weak, listless; (*Nachfrage*) slack; **jdm ist ~** sb feels queasy.
Flaum [flaum] *m* -(e)s (*Feder*) down; (*Haare*) fluff.
flauschig ['flauʃɪç] *a* fluffy.
Flausen ['flauzən] *pl* silly ideas *pl*; (*Ausflüchte*) weak excuses *pl*.
Flaute ['flautə] *f* -, **-n** calm; (*COMM*) recession.
Flechte ['flɛçtə] *f* -, **-n** plait; (*MED*) dry scab; (*BOT*) lichen; **f~n** *vt unreg* plait; (*Kranz*) twine.
Fleck [flɛk] *m* -(e)s, -e, **Flecken** *m* -s, - spot; (*Schmutz~*) stain; (*Stoff~*) patch; (*Makel*) blemish; **nicht vom ~ kommen** (*lit, fig*) not get any further; **vom ~ weg** straight away; **f~enlos** *a* spotless; **~enmittel** *nt*, **~enwasser** *nt* stain remover; **f~ig** *a* spotted; stained.
Fledermaus ['fle:dərmaus] *f* bat.
Flegel ['fle:gəl] *m* -s, - (*Mensch*) lout; **f~haft** *a* loutish, unmannerly; **~jahre** *pl* adolescence.
flehen ['fle:ən] *vi* implore; **flehentlich** *a* imploring.
Fleisch ['flaiʃ] *nt* -(e)s flesh; (*Essen*) meat; **~brühe** *f* beef tea, stock; **~er** *m* -s, - butcher; **~e'rei** *f* butcher's (shop); **~wolf** *m* mincer; **~wunde** *f* flesh wound.
Fleiß ['flais] *m* -es diligence, industry; **f~ig** *a* diligent, industrious.
fletschen ['flɛtʃən] *vt* (*Zähne*) show.
flexibel [flɛ'ksi:bəl] *a* flexible.
Flicken ['flɪkən] *m* -s, - patch; **f~** *vt* mend.
Flieder ['fli:dər] *m* -s, - lilac.
Fliege ['fli:gə] *f* -, **-n** fly; (*Kleidung*) bow tie; **f~n** *vti unreg* fly; **auf jdn/ etw f~en** (*umg*) be mad about sb/sth; **Fliegenpilz** *m* toadstool; **~r** *m* -s, - flier, airman.
fliehen ['fli:ən] *vi unreg* flee.
Fliese ['fli:zə] *f* -, **-n** tile.
Fließ- ['fli:s] *zW:* **~band** *nt* production *od* assembly line; **f~en** *vi unreg* flow; **f~end** *a* flowing; (*Rede, Deutsch*) fluent; (*Übergänge*) smooth.
flimmern ['flɪmərn] *vi* glimmer.
flink [flɪŋk] *a* nimble, lively.

Flinte ['flɪntə] f -, -n rifle; shotgun.
Flitter ['flɪtər] m -s, - spangle, tinsel; ~**wochen** pl honeymoon.
flitzen ['flɪtsən] vi flit.
Flocke ['flɔkə] f -, -n flake.
flog etc v siehe **fliegen**.
Floh ['floː] m -(e)s, ⁻e flea; ~**markt** m flea market.
florieren [flo'riːrən] vi flourish.
Floskel ['flɔskəl] f -, -n empty phrase.
floß etc v siehe **fließen**.
Floß [floːs] nt -es, ⁻e raft, float.
Flosse ['flɔsə] f -, -n fin.
Flöte ['fløːtə] f -, -n flute; (Block~) recorder.
Flötist(in f) [fløː'tɪst(ɪn)] m flautist.
flott [flɔt] a lively; (elegant) smart; (NAUT) afloat; **F~e** f -, -n fleet, navy.
Fluch [fluːx] m -(e)s, ⁻e curse; **f~en** vi curse, swear.
Flucht [fluxt] f -, -en flight; (Fenster~) row; (Reihe) range; (Zimmer~) suite; **f~artig** a hasty.
flücht- ['flʏçt] zW: ~**en** vir flee, escape; ~**ig** a fugitive; (vergänglich) transitory; (oberflächlich) superficial; (eilig) fleeting; **F~igkeit** f transitoriness; superficiality; **F~igkeitsfehler** m careless slip; **F~ling** m fugitive, refugee.
Flug [fluːk] m -(e)s, ⁻e flight; im ~ airborne, in flight; ~**blatt** nt pamphlet.
Flügel ['flyːgəl] m -s, - wing; (MUS) grand piano.
Fluggast m airline passenger.
flügge ['flʏgə] a (fully-)fledged.
Flug- zW: ~**geschwindigkeit** f flying od air speed; ~**gesellschaft** f airline (company); ~**hafen** m airport; ~**höhe** f altitude (of flight); ~**plan** m flight schedule; ~**platz** m airport; (klein) airfield; ~**schein** m plane ticket; ~**verkehr** m air traffic; ~**zeug** nt (aero)plane, airplane (US); ~**zeugentführung** f hijacking of a plane; ~**zeughangar** f hangar; ~**zeugträger** m aircraft carrier.
Flunder ['flʊndər] f -, -n flounder.
flunkern ['flʊŋkərn] vi fib, tell stories.
Fluor ['fluːor] nt -s fluorine.
Flur [fluːr] m -(e)s, -e hall; (Treppen~) staircase.
Fluß [flʊs] -sses, ⁻sse river; (Fließen) flow; im ~ sein (fig) be in a state of flux.
flüssig ['flʏsɪç] a liquid; **F~keit** f liquid; (Zustand) liquidity; ~**machen** vt (Geld) make available.
flüstern ['flʏstərn] vti whisper.
Flut [fluːt] f -, -en (lit, fig) flood; (Gezeiten) high tide; **f~en** vi flood; ~**licht** nt floodlight.
Fohlen ['foːlən] nt -s, - foal.
Föhre ['føːrə] f -, -n Scots pine.
Folge ['fɔlgə] f -, -n series, sequence;

(Fortsetzung) instalment; (Auswirkung) result; **in rascher** ~ in quick succession; **etw zur** ~ **haben** result in sth; ~**n haben** have consequences; **einer Sache** ~ **leisten** comply with sth; **f~n** vi follow (jdm sb); (gehorchen) obey (jdm sb); **jdm f~n können** (fig) follow od understand sb; **f~nd** a following; **f~nde(r, s)** a following; **f~ndermaßen** ad as follows, in the following way; **f~nschwer** a momentous; **f~rn** vt conclude (aus +dat from); ~**rung** f conclusion.
folglich ad consequently.
folgsam a obedient.
Folie ['foːliə] f -, -n foil.
Folter ['fɔltər] f -, -n torture; (Gerät) rack; **f~n** vt torture.
Fön ® [føːn] m -(e)s, -e hair-dryer; **f~en** vt (blow) dry.
Fontäne [fɔn'tɛːnə] f -, -n fountain.
Förder- ['fœrdər] zW: ~**band** nt conveyor belt; ~**gebiet** nt development area; ~**korb** m pit cage; **f~lich** a beneficial.
fordern ['fɔrdərn] vt demand.
Förder- zW: **f~n** vt promote; (unterstützen) help; (Kohle) extract; ~**ung** f promotion; help; extraction.
Forderung ['fɔrdəruŋ] f demand.
Forelle [fo'rɛlə] f trout.
Form [fɔrm] f -, -en shape; (Gestaltung) form; (Guß~) mould; (Back~) baking tin; **in** ~ **sein** be in good form od shape; **in** ~ **von** in the shape of; ~**alität** f formality; ~**at** [-'maːt] nt -(e)s, -e format; (fig) distinction; **f~atieren** vt format; ~**ati'on** f formation; **f~bar** a malleable; ~**el** f -, -n formula; **f~ell** [-'mɛl] a formal; **f~en** vt form, shape; ~**fehler** m faux-pas, gaffe; (JUR) irregularity; **f~ieren** [-'miːrən] vt form // vr form up.
förmlich ['fœrmlɪç] a formal; (umg) real; **F~keit** f formality.
Form- zW: **f~los** a shapeless; (Benehmen etc) informal; ~**u'lar** nt -s, -e form; **f~u'lieren** vt formulate.
forsch [fɔrʃ] a energetic, vigorous; ~**en** vt search (nach for) // vi (wissenschaftlich) (do) research; ~**end** a searching; **F~er** m -s, - research scientist; (Natur~) explorer.
Forschung ['fɔrʃuŋ] f research; **Forschungsreise** f scientific expedition.
Forst [fɔrst] m -(e)s, -e forest.
Förster ['fœrstər] m -s, - forester; (für Wild) gamekeeper.
fort [fɔrt] ad away; (verschwunden) gone; (vorwärts) on; **und so** ~ and so on; **in einem** ~ on and on; ~**bestehen** vi unreg survive; ~**bewegen** vtr move away; ~**bilden** vr continue one's education;

~**bleiben** vi unreg stay away; **F~dauer** f continuance; ~**fahren** vi unreg depart; (fortsetzen) go on, continue; ~**führen** vt continue, carry on; ~**gehen** vi unreg go away; ~**geschritten** a advanced; ~**müssen** vi unreg have to go; ~**pflanzen** vr reproduce; **F~pflanzung** f reproduction; ~**schaffen** vt remove; ~**schreiten** vi unreg advance.

Forts. abk (= Fortsetzung) cont(d).

Fortschritt ['fɔrtʃrɪt] m advance; ~**e machen** make progress; **f~lich** a progressive.

fort- zW: ~**setzen** vt continue; **F~setzung** f continuation; (folgender Teil) instalment; **F~setzung folgt** to be continued; ~**während** a incessant, continual.

Foto ['fo:to] nt -s, -s photo(graph); ~**apparat** m camera; ~'**graf** m photographer; ~**gra'fie** f photography; (Bild) photograph; **f~gra'fieren** vt photograph // vi take photographs; ~**kopie** f photocopy; **f~kopieren** vt photocopy.

Foul [faʊl] nt -s, -s foul.

Fr. abk (= Frau) Mrs., Ms.

Fracht [fraxt] f -, -en freight; (NAUT) cargo; (Preis) carriage; ~ **zahlt Empfänger** (COMM) carriage forward; ~**er** m -s, - freighter, cargo boat; ~**gut** nt freight.

Frack [frak] m -(e)s, ~e tails pl.

Frage ['fra:gə] f -, -n question; **etw in ~ stellen** question sth; **jdm eine ~ stellen** ask sb a question, put a question to sb; **nicht in ~ kommen** be out of the question; ~**bogen** m questionnaire; **f~n** vti ask; ~**zeichen** nt question mark.

fraglich a questionable, doubtful.

fraglos ad unquestionably.

Fragment [fra'gmɛnt] nt fragment.

fragwürdig ['fra:kvʏrdɪç] a questionable, dubious.

Fraktion [fraktsi'o:n] f parliamentary party.

frankieren [fraŋ'ki:rən] vt stamp, frank.

Frankiermaschine f franking machine.

franko ['fraŋko] ad post-paid; carriage paid.

Frankreich ['fraŋkraɪç] nt -s France.

Franse ['franzə] f -, -n fringe.

Franzose [fran'tso:zə] m Frenchman.

Französ- [fran'tsø:z] zW: ~**in** f Frenchwoman; **f~isch** a French.

fraß etc v siehe **fressen**.

Fratze ['fratsə] f -, -n grimace.

Frau [fraʊ] f -, -en woman; (Ehe~) wife; (Anrede) Mrs., Ms.; ~ **Doktor** Doctor; ~**enarzt** m gynaecologist; ~**enbewegung** f feminist movement;

f~enfeindlich a anti-women; ~**enzimmer** nt female, broad (US).

Fräulein ['frɔʏlaɪn] nt young lady; (Anrede) Miss, Ms.

fraulich ['fraʊlɪç] a womanly.

frech [frɛç] a cheeky, impudent; **F~dachs** m cheeky monkey; **F~heit** f cheek, impudence.

Fregatte [fre'gatə] f frigate.

frei [fraɪ] a free; (Stelle, Sitzplatz auch) vacant; (Mitarbeiter) freelance; (unbekleidet) bare; **sich** (dat) **einen Tag ~ nehmen** take a day off; **von etw ~ sein** be free of sth; **im F~en** in the open air; ~ **sprechen** talk without notes; ~ **Haus** (COMM) carriage paid; ~**er Wettbewerb** (COMM) fair/open competition; **F~bad** nt open-air swimming pool; ~**bekommen** vt unreg: **jdn/einen Tag ~bekommen** get sb freed/get a day off; ~**gebig** a generous; ~**halten** vt unreg keep free; ~**händig** ad (fahren) with no hands; **F~heit** f freedom; ~**heitlich** a liberal; **F~heitsstrafe** f prison sentence; **F~karte** f free ticket; ~**lassen** vt unreg (set) free; ~**legen** vt expose; ~**lich** ad certainly, admittedly; **ja ~lich** yes of course; **F~lichtbühne** f open-air theatre; ~**machen** vt (Post) frank; **Tage ~machen** take days off // vr arrange to be free; (entkleiden) undress; ~**sprechen** vt unreg acquit (von of); **F~spruch** m acquittal; ~**stellen** vt: **jdm etw ~stellen** leave sth (up) to sb; **F~stoß** m free kick; **F~tag** m Friday; ~**tags** ad on Fridays; ~**willig** a voluntary; **F~zeit** f spare od free time; ~**zeitbeschäftigung** f leisure pursuit; ~**zügig** a liberal, broad-minded; (mit Geld) generous.

fremd [frɛmt] a (unvertraut) strange; (ausländisch) foreign; (nicht eigen) someone else's; **etw ist jdm ~** sth is foreign to sb; ~**artig** a strange; **F~e(r)** ['frɛmdə(r)] mf stranger; (Ausländer) foreigner; **F~enführer** m (tourist) guide; **F~enlegion** f foreign legion; **F~enverkehr** m tourism; **F~enzimmer** nt guest room; **F~körper** m foreign body; ~**ländisch** a foreign; **F~ling** m stranger; **F~sprache** f foreign language; **F~wort** nt foreign od loan word.

Frequenz [fre'kvɛnts] f (RAD) frequency.

fressen ['frɛsən] vti unreg eat.

Freude ['frɔʏdə] f -, -n joy, delight.

freudig a joyful, happy.

freuen ['frɔʏən] vt unpers make happy od pleased; **freut mich!** pleased to meet you // vr be glad od happy; **sich auf etw** (akk) ~ look forward to sth;

sich über etw (akk) ~ be pleased about sth.

Freund [frɔynt] m -(e)s, -e friend; boyfriend; ~in [-dɪn] f friend; girlfriend; f~lich a kind, friendly; f~licherweise ad kindly; ~lichkeit f friendliness, kindness; ~schaft f friendship; f~schaftlich a friendly.

Frieden ['friːdən] m -s, - peace; im ~ in peacetime.

Friedens- zW: ~schluß m peace agreement; ~vertrag m peace treaty; ~zeit f peacetime.

fried- ['friːt] zW: ~fertig a peaceable; F~hof m cemetery; ~lich a peaceful.

frieren ['friːrən] vti unreg freeze; ich friere, es friert mich I am freezing, I'm cold.

Fries [friːs] m -es, -e (ARCHIT) frieze.

frigid(e) [fri'giːt, fri'giːdə] a frigid.

Frikadelle [frika'dɛlə] f meatball.

frisch [frɪʃ] a fresh; (lebhaft) lively; ~ gestrichen! wet paint!; sich ~ machen freshen (o.s.) up; F~e f - freshness; liveliness.

Friseur [fri'zøːr] m, **Friseuse** [fri'zøːzə] f hairdresser.

Frisier- [fri'ziːr] zW: f~en vtr do (one's hair); (fig: Abrechnung) fiddle, doctor; ~salon m hairdressing salon; ~tisch m dressing table.

frißt etc v siehe **fressen**.

Frist [frɪst] f -, -en period; (Termin) deadline; f~los a (Entlassung) instant.

Frisur [fri'zuːr] f hairdo, hairstyle.

frivol [fri'voːl] a frivolous.

froh [froː] a happy, cheerful; ich bin ~, daß ... I'm glad that ...

fröhlich ['frøːlɪç] a merry, happy; F~keit f merriness, gaiety.

Frohsinn m cheerfulness.

fromm [frɔm] a pious, good; (Wunsch) idle.

Frömmigkeit ['frœmɪçkaɪt] f piety.

Fronleichnam [froːn'laɪçnaːm] m -(e)s Corpus Christi.

Front [frɔnt] f -, -en front; f~al [frɔn'taːl] a frontal.

fror etc v siehe **frieren**.

Frosch [frɔʃ] m -(e)s, -e frog; (Feuerwerk) squib; ~mann m frogman; ~schenkel m frog's leg.

Frost [frɔst] m -(e)s, -e frost; ~beule f chilblain.

frösteln ['frœstəln] vi shiver.

Frost- zW: ~gefahr f icy conditions; f~ig a frosty; ~schutzmittel nt antifreeze.

Frottee [frɔ'teː] nt od m -(s), -s towelling.

Frottier(hand)tuch [frɔ'tiːr(hant)tuːx] nt towel.

Frucht [fruxt] f -, -e (lit, fig) fruit; (Getreide) corn; f~bar a fruitful,

fertile; ~barkeit f fertility; f~en vi be of use; f~los a fruitless; ~saft m fruit juice.

früh [fryː] a,ad early; heute ~ this morning; F~aufsteher m -s, - early riser; F~e f - early morning; ~er a earlier; (ehemalig) former // ad formerly; ~er war das anders that used to be different; ~estens ad at the earliest; F~geburt f premature birth/baby; F~jahr nt, F~ling m spring; ~reif a precocious; F~stück nt breakfast; ~stücken vi (have) breakfast; ~zeitig a early; (pej) untimely.

frustrieren [frus'triːrən] vt frustrate.

Fuchs [fuks] m -es, -e fox; f~en (umg) vt rile, annoy; f~teufelswild a hopping mad.

Füchsin ['fʏksɪn] f vixen.

fuchteln ['fuxtəln] vi gesticulate wildly.

Fuge ['fuːgə] f -, -n joint; (MUS) fugue.

fügen ['fyːgən] vt place, join // vr be obedient (in +akk to); (anpassen) adapt oneself (in +akk to) // vr unpers happen.

fügsam ['fyːkzaːm] a obedient.

fühl- ['fyːl] zW: ~bar a perceptible, noticeable; ~en vtir feel; F~er m -s, - feeler.

fuhr etc v siehe **fahren**.

führen ['fyːrən] vt lead; (Geschäft) run; (Name) bear; (Buch) keep // vi lead // vr behave.

Führer ['fyːrər] m -s, - leader; (Fremden~) guide; ~schein m driving licence.

Führung ['fyːruŋ] f leadership; (eines Unternehmens) management; (MIL) command; (Benehmen) conduct; (Museums~) conducted tour; **Führungskraft** f executive; **Führungszeugnis** nt certificate of good conduct.

Fülle ['fʏlə] f - wealth, abundance; f~n vtr fill; (KOCH) stuff; ~n nt -s, - foal; ~r m -s, -, **Füllfederhalter** m fountain pen.

Füllung ['fʏluŋ] f (Holz~) panel.

fummeln ['fuməln] vi (umg) fumble.

Fund [funt] m -(e)s, -e find; ~ament [-da'mɛnt] nt foundation; f~amen'tal a fundamental; ~büro nt lost property office, lost and found; ~grube f (fig) treasure trove; f~ieren [-'diːrən] vt back up; f~iert a sound.

fünf [fynf] num five; ~hundert num five hundred; F~kampf m pentathlon; ~te(r, s) a fifth; F~tel nt -s, - fifth; ~zehn num fifteen; ~zig num fifty.

Funk [fuŋk] m -s radio, wireless; ~e(n) m -ns, -n (lit, fig) spark;

f~eln vi sparkle; **~er** m **-s,** - radio operator; **~gerät** nt radio set; **~spruch** m radio signal; **~station** f radio station; **~streife** f police radio patrol.

Funktion [fʊŋktsi'oːn] f function; **f~ieren** [-'niːrən] vi work, function.

für [fyːr] präp +akk for; **was ~** what kind od sort of; **das F~ und Wider** the pros and cons pl; **Schritt ~ Schritt** step by step; **F~bitte** f intercession.

Furche ['fʊrçə] f -, **-n** furrow.

Furcht [fʊrçt] f - fear; **f~bar** a terrible, frightful.

fürcht- ['fʏrçt] zW: **~en** vt be afraid of, fear // vr be afraid (vor +dat of); **~erlich** a awful.

furchtlos a fearless.

furchtsam a timid.

füreinander [fyːr'aɪ'nandər] ad for each other.

Furnier [fur'niːr] nt **-s,** -e veneer.

fürs [fyːrs] = **für das.**

Fürsorge ['fyːrzɔrgə] f care; (Sozial~) welfare; **~r(in f)** m **-s,** - welfare worker; **~unterstützung** f social security, welfare benefit (US).

Fürsprache f recommendation; (um Gnade) intercession.

Fürsprecher m advocate.

Fürst [fʏrst] m **-en, -en** prince; **~entum** nt principality; **~in** f princess; **f~lich** a princely.

Fusion [fuzi'oːn] f merger.

Fuß [fuːs] m **-es,** ᵉe foot; (von Glas, Säule etc) base; (von Möbel) leg; **zu ~** on foot; **~ball** m football; **~ballplatz** m football pitch; **~ballspiel** nt football match; **~ballspieler** m footballer; **~boden** m floor; **~bremse** f (AUT) footbrake; **~ende** nt foot; **~gänger(in f)** m **-s,** - pedestrian; **~gängerzone** f pedestrian precinct; **~note** f footnote; **~spur** f footprint; **~tritt** m kick; (Spur) footstep; **~weg** m footpath.

Futter ['fʊtər] nt **-s,** - fodder, feed; (Stoff) lining; **~al** [-'raːl] nt **-s, -e** case.

füttern ['fʏtərn] vt feed; (Kleidung) line.

Futur [fu'tuːr] nt **-s, -e** future.

G

G, g [geː] nt G, g.

g abk von **Gramm.**

gab etc v siehe **geben.**

Gabe ['gaːbə] f -, **-n** gift.

Gabel ['gaːbəl] f -, **-n** fork; **~ung** f fork.

gackern ['gakərn] vi cackle.

gaffen ['gafən] vi gape.

Gage ['gaːʒə] f -, **-n** fee; salary.

gähnen ['gɛːnən] vi yawn.

galant [ga'lant] a gallant, courteous.

Galerie [galə'riː] f gallery.

Galgen ['galgən] m **-s,** - gallows pl; **~frist** f respite; **~humor** m macabre humour.

Galle ['galə] f -, **-n** gall; (Organ) gallbladder.

Galopp [ga'lɔp] m **-s, -s** od **-e** gallop; **g~ieren** [-'piːrən] vi gallop.

Gamasche [ga'maʃə] f -, **-n** gaiter; (kurz) spat.

gammeln ['gaməln] vi (umg) bum around.

Gang [gaŋ] m **-(e)s,** ᵉe walk; (Boten~) errand; (~art) gait; (Abschnitt eines Vorgangs) operation; (Essens~, Ablauf) course; (Flur etc) corridor; (Durch~) passage; (TECH) gear; **in ~ bringen** start up; (fig) get off the ground; **in ~ sein** be in operation; (fig) be underway; **g~** a: **g~ und gäbe** usual, normal.

gängig ['gɛŋɪç] a common, current; (Ware) in demand, selling well.

Ganove [ga'noːvə] m **-n, -n** (umg) crook.

Gans [gans] f -, ᵉe goose.

Gänse- ['gɛnzə] zW: **~blümchen** nt daisy; **~braten** m roast goose; **~haut** f goose pimples pl; **~marsch** m: **im ~marsch** in single file; **Gänserich** m **-s, -e** gander.

ganz [gants] a whole; (vollständig) complete; **~ Europa** all Europe; **sein ~es Geld** all his money // ad quite; (völlig) completely; **~ und gar nicht** not at all; **es sieht ~ so aus** it really looks like it; **aufs G~e gehen** go for the lot.

gänzlich ['gɛntslɪç] a,ad complete(ly), entire(ly).

gar [gaːr] a cooked, done // ad quite; **~ nicht/nichts/keiner** not/nothing/nobody at all; **~ nicht schlecht** not bad at all.

Garage [ga'raːʒə] f -, **-n** garage.

Garantie [garan'tiː] f guarantee; **g~ren** vt guarantee; **er kommt garantiert** he's guaranteed to come.

Garbe ['garbə] f -, **-n** sheaf; (MIL) burst of fire.

Garderobe [gardə'roːbə] f -, **-n** wardrobe; (Abgabe) cloakroom; **Garderobenfrau** f cloakroom attendant; **Garderobenständer** m hallstand.

Gardine [gar'diːnə] f curtain.

gären ['gɛːrən] vi unreg ferment.

Garn [garn] nt **-(e)s, -e** thread; yarn (auch fig).

Garnele [gar'neːlə] f -, **-n** shrimp, prawn.

garnieren [gar'niːrən] vt decorate; (Speisen) garnish.

Garnitur [garni'tuːr] f (Satz) set; (Unterwäsche) set of (matching) underwear; (fig) **erste ~** top rank; **zweite ~** second rate.

garstig ['garstɪç] a nasty, horrid.

Garten ['gartən] m -s, ⁼ garden; **~arbeit** f gardening; **~gerät** nt gardening tool; **~schere** f pruning shears pl; **~tür** f garden gate.

Gärtner(in f) ['gɛrtnər(ɪn)] m -s, - gardener; **~ei** [-'raɪ] f nursery; (Gemüse~) market garden (Brit), truck farm (US).

Gärung ['gɛːrʊŋ] f fermentation.

Gas [gaːs] nt -es, -e gas; **~ geben** (AUT) accelerate, step on the gas; **~herd** m, **~kocher** m gas cooker; **~leitung** f gas pipeline; **~maske** f gasmask; **~pedal** nt accelerator, gas pedal.

Gasse ['gasə] f -, -n lane, alley; **Gassenjunge** m street urchin.

Gast [gast] m -es, ⁼e guest; (in Lokal) patron; **bei jdm zu ~ sein** be a guest at sb's place; **~arbeiter(in** f) m foreign worker.

Gästebuch ['gɛstəbuːx] nt visitors' book, guest book.

Gast- zW: **g~freundlich** a hospitable; **~geber** m -s, - host; **~geberin** f hostess; **~haus** nt, **~hof** m hotel, inn; **g~ieren** [-'tiːrən] vi (THEAT) (appear as a) guest; **g~lich** a hospitable; **~rolle** f guest role.

gastronomisch [gastro'noːmɪʃ] a gastronomic(al).

Gast- zW: **~spiel** nt (THEAT) guest performance; **~stätte** f restaurant; pub; **~wirt** m innkeeper; **~wirtschaft** f hotel, inn; **~zimmer** nt (guest) room.

Gas- zW: **~vergiftung** f gas poisoning; **~werk** nt gasworks sing od pl; **~zähler** m gas meter.

Gatte ['gatə] m -n, -n husband, spouse.

Gatter ['gatər] nt -s, - railing, grating; (Eingang) gate.

Gattin f wife, spouse.

Gattung ['gatʊŋ] f genus; kind.

Gaul [gaʊl] m -(e)s, **Gäule** horse; nag.

Gaumen ['gaʊmən] m -s, - palate.

Gauner ['gaʊnər] m -s, - rogue; **~ei** [-'raɪ] f swindle.

Gaze ['gaːzə] f -, -n gauze.

geb. abk von geboren.

Gebäck [gə'bɛk] nt -(e)s, -e pastry.

gebacken [gə'bakən] a baked; (gebraten) fried.

Gebälk [gə'bɛlk] nt -(e)s timberwork.

Gebärde [gə'bɛːrdə] f -, -n gesture; **g~n** vr behave.

gebären [gə'bɛːrən] vt unreg give birth to, bear.

Gebärmutter f uterus, womb.

Gebäude [gə'bɔʏdə] nt -s, - building; **~komplex** m (building) complex.

Gebell [gə'bɛl] nt -(e)s barking.

geben ['geːbən] unreg vti (jdm etw) give (sb sth od sth to sb); (Karten) deal; **ein Wort gab das andere** one angry word led to another // v unpers **es gibt** there is/are; there will be; **was gibt's?** what's up?; **was gibt es im Kino?** what's on at the cinema?; **gegeben** given; **zu gegebener Zeit** in good time // vr (sich verhalten) behave, act; (aufhören) abate; **sich geschlagen ~** admit defeat; **das wird sich schon ~** that'll soon sort itself out.

Gebet [gə'beːt] nt -(e)s, -e prayer.

gebeten v siehe bitten.

Gebiet [gə'biːt] nt -(e)s, -e area; (Hoheits~) territory; (fig) field; **g~en** vt unreg command, demand; **g~erisch** a imperious.

Gebilde [gə'bɪldə] nt -s, - object, structure; **g~t** a cultured, educated.

Gebirge [gə'bɪrgə] nt -s, - mountain chain.

Gebiß [gə'bɪs] nt -sses, -sse teeth pl; (künstlich) dentures pl.

gebissen v siehe beißen.

geblieben v siehe bleiben.

geboren [gə'boːrən] a born; (Frau) née.

geborgen [gə'bɔrgən] a secure, safe.

Gebot [gə'boːt] nt -(e)s, -e command(ment REL); (bei Auktion) bid.

geboten v siehe bieten.

Gebr. abk (= Gebrüder) Bros.

gebracht v siehe bringen.

gebraten [gə'braːtən] a fried.

Gebrauch [gə'braʊx] m -(e)s, **Gebräuche** use; (Sitte) custom; **g~en** vt use.

gebräuchlich [gə'brɔʏçlɪç] a usual, customary.

Gebrauchs- zW: **~anweisung** f directions pl for use; **~artikel** m article of everyday use; **g~fertig** a ready for use; **~gegenstand** m commodity.

gebraucht [gə'braʊxt] a used; **G~wagen** m secondhand od used car.

gebrechlich [gə'brɛçlɪç] a frail.

gebrochen [gə'brɔxən] a broken.

Gebrüder [gə'bryːdər] pl brothers pl.

Gebrüll [gə'brYl] nt -(e)s roaring.

Gebühr [gə'byːr] f -, -en charge, fee; **nach ~** fittingly; **über ~** unduly; **g~en** vi: **jdm g~en** be sb's due od due to sb // vr be fitting; **g~end** a,ad fitting(ly), appropriate(ly).

Gebühren- zW: **~erlaß** m remission of fees; **~ermäßigung** f reduction of fees; **g~frei** a free of charge; **g~pflichtig** a subject to charges.

gebunden v siehe binden.

Geburt [gə'bu:rt] *f* **-, -en** birth.
Geburten- *zW*: **~beschränkung** *f*, **~kontrolle** *f*, **~reglung** *f* birth control; **~ziffer** *f* birth-rate.
gebürtig [gə'bʏrtɪç] *a* born in, native of; **~e Schweizerin** native of Switzerland.
Geburts- *zW*: **~anzeige** *f* birth notice; **~datum** *nt* date of birth; **~jahr** *nt* year of birth; **~ort** *m* birthplace; **~tag** *m* birthday; **~urkunde** *f* birth certificate.
Gebüsch [gə'bʏʃ] *nt* **-(e)s, -e** bushes *pl*.
gedacht *v siehe* **denken.**
Gedächtnis [gə'dɛçtnɪs] *nt* **-ses, -se** memory; **~feier** *f* commemoration.
Gedanke [gə'daŋkə] *m* **-ns, -n** thought; **sich über etw** (*akk*) **~n machen** think about sth.
Gedanken- *zW*: **~austausch** *m* exchange of ideas; **g~los** *a* thoughtless; **~losigkeit** *f* thoughtlessness; **~strich** *m* dash; **~übertragung** *f* thought transference, telepathy; **g~voll** *a* thoughtful.
Gedeck [gə'dɛk] *nt* **-(e)s, -e** cover(ing); (*Speisenfolge*) menu; **ein ~ auflegen** lay a place.
gedeihen [gə'daɪən] *vi unreg* thrive, prosper.
gedenken [gə'dɛŋkən] *vi unreg* (*sich erinnern*: *+gen*) remember; (*beabsichtigen*) intend.
Gedenk- *zW*: **~feier** *f* commemoration; **~minute** *f* minute's silence; **~tag** *m* remembrance day.
Gedicht [gə'dɪçt] *nt* **-(e)s, -e** poem.
gediegen [gə'di:gən] *a* (good) quality; (*Mensch*) reliable, honest.
Gedränge [gə'drɛŋə] *nt* **-s** crush, crowd; **ins ~ kommen** (*fig*) get into difficulties.
gedrängt *a* compressed; **~ voll** packed.
gedrungen [gə'drʊŋən] *a* thickset, stocky.
Geduld [gə'dʊlt] *f* **-** patience; **g~en** [gə'dʊldən] *vr* be patient; **g~ig** *a* patient, forbearing; **Geduldsprobe** *f* trial of (one's) patience.
gedurft *v siehe* **dürfen.**
geehrt [gə'e:rt] *a*: **sehr ~e Frau X** dear Mrs X.
geeignet [gə''aɪgnət] *a* suitable.
Gefahr [gə'fa:r] *f* **-, -en** danger; **~ laufen, etw zu tun** run the risk of doing sth; **auf eigene ~** at one's own risk.
gefährden [gə'fɛ:rdən] *vt* endanger.
Gefahrenquelle *f* source of danger.
Gefahrenzulage *f* danger money.
gefährlich [gə'fɛ:rlɪç] *a* dangerous.
Gefälle [gə'fɛlə] *nt* **-s, -** gradient, incline.
Gefallen [gə'falən] *m* **-s, -** favour // *nt* **-s** pleasure; **an etw** (*dat*) **~ finden** derive pleasure from sth; **g~** *vi unreg*: **jdm g~** please sb; **er/es gefällt mir** I like him/it; **das gefällt mir an ihm** that's one thing I like about him; **sich** (*dat*) **etw g~ lassen** put up with sth // *ptp von* **fallen.**
gefällig [gə'fɛlɪç] *a* (*hilfsbereit*) obliging; (*erfreulich*) pleasant; **G~keit** *f* favour; helpfulness; **etw aus G~keit tun** do sth as a favour.
gefälligst *ad* kindly.
gefangen [gə'faŋən] *a* captured; (*fig*) captivated; **G~e(r)** *m* prisoner, captive; **~halten** *vt unreg* keep prisoner; **G~nahme** *f* **-, -n** capture; **~nehmen** *vt unreg* take prisoner; **G~schaft** *f* captivity.
Gefängnis [gə'fɛŋnɪs] *nt* **-ses, -se** prison; **~strafe** *f* prison sentence; **~wärter** *m* prison warder.
Gefäß [gə'fɛ:s] *nt* **-es, -e** vessel (*auch* ANAT), container.
gefaßt [gə'fast] *a* composed, calm; **auf etw** (*akk*) **~ sein** be prepared *od* ready for sth.
Gefecht [gə'fɛçt] *nt* **-(e)s, -e** fight; (MIL) engagement.
Gefieder [gə'fi:dər] *nt* **-s, -** plumage, feathers *pl*.
gefleckt [gə'flɛkt] *a* spotted, mottled.
geflogen *v siehe* **fliegen.**
geflossen *v siehe* **fließen.**
Geflügel [gə'fly:gəl] *nt* **-s** poultry.
Gefolge [gə'fɔlgə] *nt* **-s, -** retinue.
Gefolgschaft *f* following.
gefragt [ge'fra:kt] *a* in demand.
gefräßig [gə'frɛ:sɪç] *a* voracious.
Gefreite(r) [gə'fraɪtə(r)] *m* **-n, -n** lance corporal; (NAUT) able seaman; (AVIAT) aircraftman.
gefrieren [gə'fri:rən] *vi unreg* freeze.
Gefrier- *zW*: **~fach** *nt* icebox; **~fleisch** *nt* frozen meat; **g~getrocknet** *a* freeze-dried; **~punkt** *m* freezing point; **~schutzmittel** *nt* antifreeze; **~truhe** *f* deep-freeze.
gefroren *v siehe* **frieren.**
gefügig [gə'fy:gɪç] *a* pliant; (*Mensch*) obedient.
Gefühl [gə'fy:l] *nt* **-(e)s, -e** feeling; **etw im ~ haben** have a feel for sth; **g~los** *a* unfeeling.
gefühls- *zW*: **~betont** *a* emotional; **G~duselei** [-du:zə'laɪ] *f* emotionalism; **~mäßig** *a* instinctive.
gefunden *v siehe* **finden.**
gegangen *v siehe* **gehen.**
gegebenenfalls [gə'ge:bənənfals] *ad* if need be.
gegen ['ge:gən] *präp +akk* **1** against; **nichts ~ jdn haben** have nothing against sb; **X ~ Y** (SPORT, JUR) X

versus Y; **ein Mittel ~ Schnupfen** something for colds
2 (*in Richtung auf*) towards; **~ Osten** to(wards) the east; **~ Abend** towards evening; **~ einen Baum fahren** drive into a tree
3 (*ungefähr*) round about, around; **~ 3 Uhr** around 3 o'clock
4 (*gegenüber*) towards; **gerecht ~ alle** fair to all
5 (*im Austausch für*) for; **~ bar** for cash; **~ Quittung** against a receipt
6 (*verglichen mit*) compared with.
Gegenangriff *m* counter-attack.
Gegenbeweis *m* counter-evidence.
Gegend ['ge:gənt] *f* -, -en area, district.
Gegen- *zW:* **g~ei'nander** *ad* against one another; **~fahrbahn** *f* oncoming carriageway; **~frage** *f* counterquestion; **~gewicht** *nt* counterbalance; **~gift** *nt* antidote; **~leistung** *f* service in return; **~satz** *m* contrast; **~sätze überbrücken** overcome differences; **g~sätzlich** *a* contrary, opposite; (*widersprüchlich*) contradictory; **g~seitig** *a* mutual, reciprocal; **sich g~seitig helfen** help each other; **~seitigkeit** *f* reciprocity; **~spieler** *m* opponent; **~stand** *m* object; **g~ständlich** *a* objective, concrete; **~stimme** *f* vote against; **~stoß** *m* counterblow; **~stück** *nt* counterpart; **~teil** *nt* opposite; **im ~teil** on the contrary; **g~teilig** *a* opposite, contrary.
gegenüber [ge:gən''y:bər] *präp* +*dat* opposite; (*zu*) to(wards); (*angesichts*) in the face of // *ad* opposite; **G~** *nt* -s, - person opposite; **~liegen** *vr unreg* face each other; **~stehen** *vr unreg* be opposed (to each other); **~stellen** *vt* confront; (*fig*) contrast; **G~stellung** *f* confrontation; (*fig*) contrast; **~treten** *vi unreg* (+*dat*) face.
Gegen- *zW:* **~verkehr** *m* oncoming traffic; **~vorschlag** *m* counterproposal; **~wart** *f* present; **g~wärtig** *a* present; **das ist mir nicht mehr g~wärtig** that has slipped my mind // *ad* at present; **~wert** *m* equivalent; **~wind** *m* headwind; **g~zeichnen** *vti* countersign.
gegessen *v siehe* essen.
Gegner ['ge:gnər] *m* -s, - opponent; **g~isch** *a* opposing; **~schaft** *f* opposition.
gegrillt [gə'grɪlt] *a* grilled.
Gehackte(s) [gə'haktə(s)] *nt* mince(d meat).
Gehalt [gə'halt] *m* -(e)s, -e content // *nt* -(e)s, ⁻er salary.
Gehalts- *zW:* **~empfänger** *m* salary earner; **~erhöhung** *f* salary increase; **~zulage** *f* salary increment.

gehaltvoll *a* (*nahrhaft*) nutritious.
gehässig [gə'hɛsɪç] *a* spiteful, nasty; **G~keit** *f* spite(fulness).
Gehäuse [gə'hɔyzə] *nt* -s, - case; casing; (*von Apfel etc*) core.
geheim [gə'haɪm] *a* secret; **G~dienst** *m* secret service, intelligence service; **~halten** *vt unreg* keep secret; **G~nis** *nt* -ses, -se secret; mystery; **~nisvoll** *a* mysterious; **G~nummer** *f* (*TEL*) ex-directory (*Brit*) *or* unlisted (*US*) number; **G~polizei** *f* secret police.
gehen ['ge:ən] *unreg vti* go; (*zu Fuß ~*) walk; **~ nach** (*Fenster*) face // *v unpers*: **wie geht es (dir)?** how are you *od* things?; **mir/ihm geht es gut** I'm/he's (doing) fine; **geht das?** is that possible?; **geht's noch?** can you manage?; **es geht not too bad, O.K.; das geht nicht** that's not on; **es geht um etw sth** is concerned, it's about sth.
geheuer [gə'hɔyər] *a*: **nicht ~** eerie; (*fragwürdig*) dubious.
Gehilfe [gə'hɪlfə] *m* -n, -n, **Gehilfin** *f* assistant.
Gehirn [gə'hɪrn] *nt* -(e)s, -e brain; **~erschütterung** *f* concussion; **~wäsche** *f* brainwashing.
geholfen *v siehe* helfen.
Gehör [gə'hø:r] *nt* -(e)s hearing; **musikalisches ~ ear**; **~ finden** gain a hearing; **jdm ~ schenken** give sb a hearing.
gehorchen [gə'hɔrçən] *vi* obey (*jdm sb*).
gehören [gə'hø:rən] *vi* belong // *vr unpers* be right *od* proper.
gehörig *a* proper; **~ zu** *od* +*dat* belonging to; part of.
gehorsam [gə'ho:rza:m] *a* obedient; **G~** *m* -s obedience.
Gehsteig [ge:ʃtaɪk] *m*, **Gehweg** *m* ['ge:ve:k] pavement, sidewalk (*US*).
Geier ['gaɪər] *m* -s, - vulture.
Geige ['gaɪgə] *f* -, -n violin.
Geiger *m* -s, - violinist; **~zähler** *m* geiger counter.
geil [gaɪl] *a* randy (*Brit*), horny (*US*).
Geisel ['gaɪzəl] *f* -, -n hostage.
Geist [gaɪst] *m* -(e)s, -er spirit; (*Gespenst*) ghost; (*Verstand*) mind.
geisterhaft *a* ghostly.
Geistes- *zW:* **g~abwesend** *a* absentminded; **~blitz** *m* brainwave; **~gegenwart** *f* presence of mind; **g~krank** *a* mentally ill; **~kranke(r)** *mf* mentally ill person; **~krankheit** *f* mental illness; **~zustand** *m* state of mind.
geist- *zW:* **~ig** *a* intellectual; mental; (*Getränke*) alcoholic; **~ig behindert** mentally handicapped; **~lich** *a* spiritual, religious; clerical; **G~liche(r)**

m clergyman; **G~lichkeit** *f* clergy; **~los** *a* uninspired, dull; **~reich** *a* clever; witty; **~voll** *a* intellectual; (*weise*) wise.

Geiz [gaɪts] *m* **-es** miserliness, meanness; **g~en** *vi* be miserly; **~hals** *m*, **~kragen** *m* miser; **g~ig** *a* miserly, mean.

gekannt *v siehe* **kennen**.

geknickt [gə'knɪkt] *a* (*fig*) dejected.

gekocht [gə'kɔxt] *a* boiled.

gekonnt [gə'kɔnt] *a* skilful // *v siehe* **können**.

Gekritzel [gə'krɪtsəl] *nt* **-s** scrawl, scribble.

gekünstelt [ge'kynstəlt] *a* artificial, affected.

Gelächter [gə'lɛçtər] *nt* **-s**, **-** laughter.

geladen [ge'la:dən] *a* loaded; (*ELEK*) live; (*fig*) furious.

gelähmt [gə'lɛːmt] *a* paralysed.

Gelände [gə'lɛndə] *nt* **-s**, **-** land, terrain; (*von Fabrik, Sport~*) grounds *pl*; (*Bau~*) site; **~lauf** *m* cross-country race.

Geländer [gə'lɛndər] *nt* **-s**, **-** railing; (*Treppen~*) banister(s).

gelangen [gə'laŋən] *vi* (*an +akk od zu*) reach; (*erwerben*) attain; **in jds Besitz ~** come into sb's possession.

gelassen [gə'lasən] *a* calm, composed; **G~heit** *f* calmness, composure.

Gelatine [ʒela'tiːnə] *f* gelatine.

geläufig [gə'lɔyfɪç] *a* (*üblich*) common; **das ist mir nicht ~** I'm not familiar with that.

gelaunt [gə'laʊnt] *a*: **schlecht/gut ~** in a bad/good mood; **wie ist er ~?** what sort of mood is he in?

gelb [gɛlp] *a* yellow; (*Ampellicht*) amber; **~lich** *a* yellowish; **G~sucht** *f* jaundice.

Geld [gɛlt] *nt* **-(e)s**, **-er** money; **etw zu ~ machen** sell sth off; **~anlage** *f* investment; **~automat** *m* cash dispenser; **~beutel** *m*, **~börse** *f* purse; **~geber** *m* **-s**, **-** financial backer; **g~gierig** *a* avaricious; **~schein** *m* banknote; **~schrank** *m* safe, strongbox; **~strafe** *f* fine; **~stück** *nt* coin; **~wechsel** *m* exchange (of money).

Gelee [ʒe'leː] *nt od m* **-s**, **-s** jelly.

gelegen [gə'leːgən] *a* situated; (*passend*) convenient, opportune; **etw kommt jdm ~** sth is convenient for sb // *v siehe* **liegen**.

Gelegenheit [gə'leːgənhaɪt] *f* opportunity; (*Anlaß*) occasion; **bei jeder ~** at every opportunity.

Gelegenheits- *zW*: **~arbeit** *f* casual work; **~arbeiter** *m* casual worker; **~kauf** *m* bargain.

gelegentlich [gə'leːgəntlɪç] *a* occasional // *ad* occasionally; (*bei Gelegenheit*) some time (or other) // *präp*

+gen on the occasion of.

gelehrt [gə'leːrt] *a* learned; **G~e(r)** *mf* scholar; **G~heit** *f* scholarliness.

Geleise [gə'laɪzə] *nt* **-s**, **-** *siehe* **Gleis**.

Geleit [gə'laɪt] *nt* **-(e)s**, **-e** escort; **g~en** *vt* escort; **~schutz** *m* escort.

Gelenk [gə'lɛŋk] *nt* **-(e)s**, **-e** joint; **g~ig** *a* supple.

gelernt [gə'lɛrnt] *a* skilled.

Geliebte(r) [gə'liːptə(r)] *mf* sweetheart, beloved.

geliehen *v siehe* **leihen**.

gelind(e) [gə'lɪnt, gə'lɪndə] *a* mild, light; (*fig: Wut*) fierce; **~e gesagt** to put it mildly.

gelingen [gə'lɪŋən] *vi unreg* succeed; **es ist mir gelungen, etw zu tun** I succeeded in doing sth.

gell [gɛl] *interj* isn't it?; aren't you? *etc*.

geloben [gə'loːbən] *vt* vow, swear.

gelten ['gɛltən] *unreg vt* (*wert sein*) be worth; **jdm viel/wenig ~** mean a lot/not mean much to sb; **was gilt die Wette?** do you want to bet? // *vi* (*gültig sein*) be valid; (*erlaubt sein*) be allowed; **jdm ~** (*gemünzt sein auf*) be meant for *od* aimed at sb; **etw ~ lassen** accept sth; **als** *od* **für etw ~** be considered to be sth; **jdm** *od* **für jdn ~** (*betreffen*) apply to *od* for sb // *v unpers*: **es gilt, etw zu tun** it is necessary to do sth; **~d** *a* prevailing; **etw ~d machen** to assert sth; **sich ~d machen** make itself/o.s. felt.

Geltung ['gɛltʊŋ] *f*: **~ haben** have validity; **sich/etw** *od* **verschaffen** establish oneself/sth; **etw zur ~ bringen** show sth to its best advantage; **zur ~ kommen** be seen/heard *etc* to its best advantage.

Geltungsbedürfnis *nt* desire for admiration.

Gelübde [gə'lypdə] *nt* **-s**, **-** vow.

gelungen [gə'lʊŋən] *a* successful.

gem. *abk von* **gemischt**.

gemächlich [gə'mɛːçlɪç] *a* leisurely.

Gemahl [gə'maːl] *m* **-(e)s**, **-e** husband; **~in** *f* wife.

Gemälde [gə'mɛːldə] *nt* **-s**, **-** picture, painting.

gemäß [gə'mɛːs] *präp +dat* in accordance with // *a* appropriate (*dat* to).

gemäßigt *a* moderate; (*Klima*) temperate.

gemein [gə'maɪn] *a* common; (*niederträchtig*) mean; **etw ~ haben (mit)** have sth in common (with).

Gemeinde [gə'maɪndə] *f* **-**, **-n** district, community; (*Pfarr~*) parish; (*Kirchen~*) congregation; **~steuer** *f* local rates *pl*; **~verwaltung** *f* local administration; **~wahl** *f* local election.

Gemein- *zW:* **g~gefährlich** *a* dangerous to the public; **~heit** *f* commonness; mean thing to do/to say; **~platz** *m* commonplace, platitude; **g~sam** *a* joint, common (*auch MATH*); **g~same Sache mit jdm machen** be in cahoots with sb // *ad* together, jointly; **etw g~sam haben** have sth in common; **~samkeit** *f* community, having in common; **~schaft** *f* community; **in ~schaft mit** jointly od together with; **g~schaftlich** *a siehe* **g~sam**; **~schaftsarbeit** *f* teamwork; team effort; **~sinn** *m* public spirit; **~wohl** *nt* common good.

Gemenge [gəˈmɛŋə] *nt* **-s,** - mixture; (*Hand~*) scuffle.

gemessen [gəˈmɛsən] *a* measured.

Gemetzel [gəˈmɛtsəl] *nt* **-s,** - slaughter, carnage, butchery.

Gemisch [gəˈmɪʃ] *nt* **-es, -e** mixture; **g~t** *a* mixed.

gemocht *v siehe* **mögen.**

Gemse [ˈgɛmzə] *f -,* -n chamois.

Gemunkel [gəˈmʊŋkəl] *nt* **-s** gossip.

Gemurmel [gəˈmʊrməl] *nt* **-s** murmur(ing).

Gemüse [gəˈmyːzə] *nt* **-s,** - vegetables *pl;* **~garten** *m* vegetable garden; **~händler** *m* greengrocer.

gemußt *v siehe* **müssen.**

Gemüt [gəˈmyːt] *nt* **-(e)s, -er** disposition, nature; person; **sich** (*dat*) **etw zu ~e führen** (*umg*) indulge in sth; **die ~er erregen** arouse strong feelings; **g~lich** *a* comfortable, cosy; (*Person*) good-natured; **~lichkeit** *f* comfortableness, cosiness; amiability.

Gemüts- *zW:* **~mensch** *m* sentimental person; **~ruhe** *f* composure; **~szustand** *m* state of mind.

gemütvoll *a* warm, tender.

genannt *v siehe* **nennen.**

genau [gəˈnaʊ] *a,ad* exact(ly), precise(ly); **etw ~ nehmen** take sth seriously; **~genommen** *ad* strictly speaking; **G~igkeit** *f* exactness, accuracy; **~so** *ad* just the same; **~so gut** just as good.

genehm [gəˈneːm] *a* agreeable, acceptable; **~igen** *vt* approve, authorize; **sich** (*dat*) **etw ~igen** indulge in sth; **G~igung** *f* approval, authorization; (*Schriftstück*) permit.

General [genəˈraːl] *m* **-s, -e** *od* **-e** general; **~direktor** *m* director general; **~konsulat** *nt* consulate general; **~probe** *f* dress rehearsal; **~streik** *m* general strike; **g~überholen** *vt* thoroughly overhaul.

Generation [generatsiˈoːn] *f* generation.

Generator [geneˈraːtɔr] *m* generator, dynamo.

generell [geneˈrɛl] *a* general.

genesen [geˈneːzən] *vi unreg* convalesce, recover, get well.

Genesung *f* recovery, convalescence.

genetisch [geˈneːtɪʃ] *a* genetic.

Genf [gɛnf] *nt* Geneva; **~er** See Lake Geneva.

genial [geniˈaːl] *a* brilliant; **G~i'tät** *f* brilliance, genius.

Genick [gəˈnɪk] *nt* **-(e)s, -e** (back of the) neck; **~starre** *f* stiff neck.

Genie [ʒeˈniː] *nt* **-s, -s** genius.

genieren [ʒeˈniːrən] *vt* bother; **geniert es Sie, wenn ...?** do you mind if ...? // *vr* feel awkward *od* self-conscious.

genießbar *a* edible; drinkable.

genießen [gəˈniːsən] *vt unreg* enjoy; eat; drink.

Genießer *m* **-s,** - epicure; pleasure lover; **g~isch** *a* appreciative // *ad* with relish.

genommen *v siehe* **nehmen.**

Genosse [gəˈnɔsə] *m* **-n, -n, Genossin** *f* comrade (*bes POL*), companion; **Genossenschaft** *f* cooperative (association).

genug [gəˈnuːk] *ad* enough.

Genüge [gəˈnyːgə] *f -:* **jdm/etw ~ tun** *od* **leisten** satisfy sb/sth; **g~n** *vi* be enough (+*dat* for); **g~nd** *a* sufficient.

genügsam [gəˈnyːkzam] *a* modest, easily satisfied; **G~keit** *f* moderation.

Genugtuung [gəˈnuːktuːʊŋ] *f* satisfaction.

Genuß [gəˈnʊs] *m* **-sses, ¨sse** pleasure; (*Zusichnehmen*) consumption; **in den ~ von etw kommen** receive the benefit of sth; **~mittel** *pl* (semi-) luxury items *pl.*

genüßlich [gəˈnʏslɪç] *ad* with relish.

geöffnet [gəˈœfnət] *a* open.

Geograph [geoˈgraːf] *m* **-en, -en** geographer; **~ie** [-ˈfiː] *f* geography; **g~isch** *a* geographical.

Geologe [geoˈloːgə] *m* **-n, -n** geologist; **Geolo'gie** *f* geology.

Geometrie [geomeˈtriː] *f* geometry.

Gepäck [gəˈpɛk] *nt* **-(e)s** luggage, baggage; **~abfertigung** *f,* **~annahme** *f,* **~aufgabe** *f,* **~ausgabe** *f* luggage office; **~aufbewahrung** *f* left-luggage office (*Brit*), baggage check (*US*); **~netz** *nt* luggage-rack; **~rückgabe** *f* luggage office; **~träger** *m* porter; (*Fahrrad*) carrier; **~wagen** *m* luggage van (*Brit*), baggage car (*US*).

gepflegt [gəˈpfleːkt] *a* well-groomed; (*Park etc*) well looked after.

gerade [gəˈraːdə] ♦ *a* straight; (*aufrecht*) upright; **eine ~ Zahl** an even number

♦ *ad* **1** (*genau*) just, exactly; (*speziell*) especially; **~ deshalb** that's just od exactly why; **das ist es ja ~!** that's just it!; **~ du** you especially;

warum ~ ich? why me (of all people)?; jetzt ~ nicht! not now!; ~ neben right next to

2 (eben, soeben) just; er wollte ~ aufstehen he was just about to get up; ~ erst only just; ~ noch (only) just.

Gerade f -n, -n straight line; **g~aus** ad straight ahead; **g~heraus** ad straight out, bluntly; **g~zu** ad (beinahe) virtually, almost.

gerannt v siehe **rennen**.

Gerät [gə'rɛːt] nt -(e)s, -e device; (Werkzeug) tool; (SPORT) apparatus; (Zubehör) equipment no pl.

geraten [gə'raːtən] vi unreg (gelingen) turn out well (jdm for sb); (gedeihen) thrive; **gut/schlecht** ~ turn out well/badly; **an jdn** ~ come across sb; **in etw** (akk) ~ get into sth; **in Angst** ~ get frightened; **nach jdm** ~ take after sb.

Geratewohl [gəraːtə'voːl] nt: **aufs** ~ on the off chance; (bei Wahl) at random.

geräumig [gə'rɔɪmɪç] a roomy.

Geräusch [gə'rɔɪʃ] nt -(e)s, -e sound, noise; **g~los** a silent.

gerben ['gɛrbən] vt tan.

gerecht [gə'rɛçt] a just, fair; **jdm/etw** ~ **werden** do justice to sb/sth; **G~igkeit** f justice, fairness.

Gerede [gə'reːdə] nt -s talk, gossip.

gereizt [gə'raɪtst] a irritable; **G~heit** f irritation.

Gericht [gə'rɪçt] nt -(e)s, -e court; (Essen) dish; **mit jdm ins** ~ **gehen** (fig) judge sb harshly; **das Jüngste** ~ the Last Judgement; **g~lich** a,ad judicial(ly), legal(ly).

Gerichts- zW: **~barkeit** f jurisdiction; **~hof** m court (of law); **~kosten** pl (legal) costs pl; **~saal** m courtroom; **~verfahren** nt legal proceedings pl; **~verhandlung** f court proceedings pl; **~svollzieher** m bailiff.

gerieben [gə'riːbən] a grated; (umg: schlau) smart, wily // v siehe **reiben**.

gering [gə'rɪŋ] a slight, small; (niedrig) low; (Zeit) short; **~fügig** a slight, trivial; **~schätzig** a disparaging.

geringste(r, -s) a slightest, least; **~nfalls** ad at the very least.

gerinnen [gə'rɪnən] vi unreg congeal; (Blut) clot; (Milch) curdle.

Gerippe [gə'rɪpə] nt -s, - skeleton.

gerissen [gə'rɪsən] a wily, smart.

geritten v siehe **reiten**.

gern(e) ['gɛrn(ə)] ad willingly, gladly; ~ haben, ~ mögen like; **etwas** ~ **tun** like doing something; **ich möchte** ~ ... I'd like ...; **ja**, ~ yes, please; yes, I'd like to; ~ **geschehen** it's a pleasure.

gerochen v siehe **riechen**.

Geröll [gə'rœl] nt -(e)s, -e scree.

Gerste ['gɛrstə] f -, -n barley; **Gerstenkorn** nt (im Auge) stye.

Geruch [gə'rux] m -(e)s, -e smell, odour; **g~los** a odourless; **g~tilgend** a deodorant.

Gerücht [gə'rʏçt] nt -(e)s, -e rumour.

geruhen [gə'ruːən] vi deign.

Gerümpel [gə'rʏmpəl] nt -s junk.

Gerüst [gə'rʏst] nt -(e)s, -e (Bau~) scaffold(ing); frame.

gesamt [gə'zamt] a whole, entire; (Kosten) total; (Werke) complete; **im** ~**en** all in all; **~deutsch** a all-German; **G~eindruck** m general impression; **G~heit** f totality, whole; **G~schule** f ≈ comprehensive school.

gesandt v siehe **senden**.

Gesandte(r) [gə'zantə(r)] m envoy.

Gesandtschaft [gə'zantʃaft] f legation.

Gesang [gə'zaŋ] m -(e)s, -e song; (Singen) singing; **~buch** nt (REL) hymn book.

Gesäß [gə'zɛːs] nt -es, -e seat, bottom.

Geschäft [gə'ʃɛft] nt -(e)s, -e business; (Laden) shop; (~sabschluß) deal; **~emacher** m -s, wheeler-dealer; **g~ig** a active, busy; (pej) officious; **g~lich** a commercial // ad on business.

Geschäfts- zW: **~bericht** m financial report; **~essen** nt business lunch; **~führer** m manager; (Klub) secretary; **~geheimnis** nt trade secret; **~jahr** nt financial year; **~lage** f business conditions pl; **~mann** m businessman; **g~mäßig** a businesslike; **~reise** f business trip; **~schluß** m closing time; **~stelle** f office, place of business; **g~tüchtig** a efficient; **~viertel** nt business quarter; shopping centre; **~wagen** m company car; **~zeiten** pl business hours.

geschehen [gə'ʃeːən] vi unreg happen; **es war um ihn** ~ that was the end of him.

gescheit [gə'ʃaɪt] a clever.

Geschenk [gə'ʃɛŋk] nt -(e)s, -e present, gift.

Geschichte [gə'ʃɪçtə] f -, -n story; (Sache) affair; (Historie) history.

geschichtlich a historical.

Geschick [gə'ʃɪk] nt -(e)s, -e aptitude; (Schicksal) fate; **~lichkeit** f skill, dexterity; **g~t** a skilful.

geschieden [gə'ʃiːdən] a divorced.

geschienen v siehe **scheinen**.

Geschirr [gə'ʃɪr] nt -(e)s, -e crockery; pots and pans pl; (Pferd) harness; **~spülmaschine** f dishwashing machine; **~tuch** nt dish cloth.

Geschlecht [gə'ʃlɛçt] nt -(e)s, -er sex; (GRAM) gender; (KUNST) species; family; **g~lich** a sexual.

Geschlechts- *zW*: **~krankheit** *f* venereal disease; **~teil** *nt* genitals *pl*; **~verkehr** *m* sexual intercourse.

geschlossen [gə'ʃlɔsən] *a* shut // *v siehe* **schließen.**

Geschmack [gə'ʃmak] *m* **-(e)s, ⁻e** taste; **nach jds ~** to sb's taste; **~ finden an etw** (*dat*) (come to) like sth; **g~los** *a* tasteless; (*fig*) in bad taste; **~(s)sache** *f* matter of taste; **~sinn** *m* sense of taste; **g~voll** *a* tasteful.

geschmeidig [gə'ʃmaɪdɪç] *a* supple; (*formbar*) malleable.

geschnitten *v siehe* **schneiden.**

Geschöpf [gə'ʃœpf] *nt* **-(e)s, -e** creature.

Geschoß [gə'ʃɔs] *nt* **-sses, -sse** (*MIL*) projectile, missile; (*Stockwerk*) floor.

geschossen *v siehe* **schießen.**

geschraubt [gə'ʃraʊpt] *a* stilted, artificial.

Geschrei [gə'ʃraɪ] *nt* **-s** cries *pl*, shouting; (*fig*: *Aufheben*) noise, fuss.

geschrieben *v siehe* **schreiben.**

Geschütz [gə'ʃʏts] *nt* **-es, -e** gun, cannon; **ein schweres ~ auffahren** (*fig*) bring out the big guns; **~feuer** *nt* artillery fire, gunfire; **g~t** *a* protected.

Geschwader [gə'ʃvaːdər] *nt* **-s, -** (*NAUT*) squadron; (*AVIAT*) group.

Geschwafel [gə'ʃvaːfəl] *nt* **-s** silly talk.

Geschwätz [gə'ʃvɛts] *nt* **-es** chatter, gossip; **g~ig** *a* talkative.

geschweige [gə'ʃvaɪgə] *ad*: **~ (denn)** let alone, not to mention.

geschwind [gə'ʃvɪnt] *a* quick, swift; **G~igkeit** [-dɪçkaɪt] *f* speed, velocity; **G~igkeitsbegrenzung** *f* speed limit; **G~igkeitsüberschreitung** *f* exceeding the speed limit.

Geschwister [gə'ʃvɪstər] *pl* brothers and sisters *pl*.

geschwollen [gə'ʃvɔlən] *a* pompous.

geschwommen *v siehe* **schwimmen.**

Geschworene(r) [gə'ʃvoːrənə(r)] *mf* juror // *pl* jury.

Geschwulst [gə'ʃvʊlst] *f* **-, ⁻e** swelling; growth, tumour.

Geschwür [gə'ʃvyːr] *nt* **-(e)s, -e** ulcer.

Gesell- [gə'zɛl-] *zW*: **~e** *m* **-n, -n** fellow; (*Handwerk~*) journeyman; **g~ig** *a* sociable; **~igkeit** *f* sociability; **~schaft** *f* society; (*Begleitung*, *COMM*) company; (*Abend~schaft etc*) party; **g~schaftlich** *a* social; **~schaftsordnung** *f* social structure; **~schaftsschicht** *f* social stratum.

gesessen *v siehe* **sitzen.**

Gesetz [gə'zɛts] *nt* **-es, -e** law; **~buch** *nt* statute book; **~entwurf** *m*, **~esvorlage** *f* bill; **g~gebend** *a* legislative; **~gebung** *f* legislation; **g~lich** *a* legal, lawful; **~lichkeit** *f* legality,

lawfulness; **g~los** *a* lawless; **g~mäßig** *a* lawful; **g~t** *a* (*Mensch*) sedate; **g~widrig** *a* illegal, unlawful.

ges. gesch. *abk* (= *gesetzlich geschützt*) registered.

Gesicht [gə'zɪçt] *nt* **-(e)s, -er** face; **das zweite ~** second sight; **das ist mir nie zu ~ gekommen** I've never laid eyes on that.

Gesichts- *zW*: **~ausdruck** *m* (facial) expression; **~farbe** *f* complexion; **~punkt** *m* point of view; **~züge** *pl* features *pl*.

Gesindel [gə'zɪndəl] *nt* **-s** rabble.

gesinnt [gə'zɪnt] *a* disposed, minded.

Gesinnung [gə'zɪnʊŋ] *f* disposition; (*Ansicht*) views *pl*; **Gesinnungswandel** *m* change of opinion, volteface.

gesittet [gə'zɪtət] *a* well-mannered.

Gespann [gə'ʃpan] *nt* **-(e)s, -e** team; (*umg*) couple; **g~t** *a* tense, strained; (*begierig*) eager; **ich bin g~t, ob I** wonder if *od* whether; **auf etw/jdn g~t sein** look forward to sth/meeting sb.

Gespenst [gə'ʃpɛnst] *nt* **-(e)s, -er** ghost, spectre; **g~erhaft** *a* ghostly.

gesperrt [gə'ʃpɛrt] *a* closed off.

Gespött [gə'ʃpœt] *nt* **-(e)s** mockery; **zum ~ werden** become a laughing stock.

Gespräch [gə'ʃprɛːç] *nt* **-(e)s, -e** conversation; discussion(s); (*Anruf*) call; **g~ig** *a* talkative; **~igkeit** *f* talkativeness; **Gesprächsthema** *nt* subject *od* topic (of conversation).

gesprochen *v siehe* **sprechen.**

gesprungen *v siehe* **springen.**

Gespür [gə'ʃpyːr] *nt* **-s** feeling.

Gestalt [gə'ʃtalt] *f* **-, -en** form, shape; (*Person*) figure; **in ~ von** in the form of; **~ annehmen** take shape; **g~en** *vt* (*formen*) shape, form; (*organisieren*) arrange, organize // *vr* turn out (*zu* to be); **~ung** *f* formation; organization.

gestanden *v siehe* **stehen.**

Geständnis [gə'ʃtɛntnɪs] *nt* **-ses, -se** confession.

Gestank [gə'ʃtaŋk] *m* **-(e)s** stench.

gestatten [gə'ʃtatən] *vt* permit, allow; **~ Sie? may I?; sich** (*dat*) **, etw zu tun** take the liberty of doing sth.

Geste ['gɛstə] *f* **-, -n** gesture.

gestehen [gə'ʃteːən] *vt ut unreg* confess.

Gestein [gə'ʃtaɪn] *nt* **-(e)s, -e** rock.

Gestell [gə'ʃtɛl] *nt* **-(e)s, -e** frame; (*Regal*) rack, stand.

gestern ['gɛstərn] *ad* yesterday; **~ abend/morgen** yesterday evening/ morning.

Gestirn [gə'ʃtɪrn] *nt* **-(e)s, -e** star; (*Sternbild*) constellation.

gestohlen *v siehe* **stehlen.**

gestorben *v siehe* **sterben.**

gestreift [gə'ʃtraift] a striped.

gestrichen [gə'ʃtriçən] a cancelled.

gestrig ['gɛstriç] a yesterday's.

Gestrüpp [gə'ʃtryp] nt -(e)s, -e undergrowth.

Gestüt [gə'ʃtyːt] nt -(e)s, -e stud farm.

Gesuch [gə'zuːx] nt -(e)s, -e petition; (Antrag) application; **g~t** a (COMM) in demand; wanted; (fig) contrived.

gesund [gə'zʊnt] a healthy; **wieder ~ werden** get better; **G~heit** f health(iness); **G~heit!** bless you!; **~heitlich** a,ad health attr, physical; **wie geht es Ihnen ~heitlich?** how's your health?; **~heitsschädlich** a unhealthy; **G~heitswesen** nt health service; **G~heitszustand** m state of health.

gesungen v siehe **singen**.

getan v siehe **tun**.

Getöse [gə'tøːzə] nt -s din, racket.

Getränk [gə'trɛŋk] nt -(e)s, -e drink; **Getränkekarte** f wine list.

getrauen [gə'trauən] vr dare, venture.

Getreide [gə'traidə] nt -s, - cereals pl, grain; **~speicher** m granary.

getrennt [gə'trɛnt] a separate.

Getriebe [gə'triːbə] nt -s, - (Leute) bustle; (AUT) gearbox.

getrieben v siehe **treiben**.

getroffen v siehe **treffen**.

getrost [gə'troːst] ad without any bother.

getrunken v siehe **trinken**.

Getue [gə'tuːə] nt -s fuss.

geübt [gə''yːpt] a experienced.

Gewächs [gə'vɛks] nt -es, -e growth; (Pflanze) plant.

gewachsen [gə'vaksən] a: **jdm/etw ~ sein** be sb's equal/equal to sth.

Gewächshaus nt greenhouse.

gewagt [gə'vaːkt] a daring, risky.

gewählt [gə'vɛːlt] a (Sprache) refined, elegant.

Gewähr [gə'vɛːr] f - guarantee; **keine ~ übernehmen für** accept no responsibility for; **g~en** vt grant; (geben) provide; **g~leisten** vt guarantee.

Gewahrsam [gə'vaːrzaːm] m -s, - safekeeping; (Polizei~) custody.

Gewährsmann m informant, source.

Gewährung f granting.

Gewalt [gə'valt] f -, -en power; (große Kraft) force; (~taten) violence; **mit aller ~** with all one's might; **~anwendung** f use of force; **g~ig** a tremendous; (Irrtum) huge; **~marsch** m forced march; **g~sam** a forcible; **g~tätig** a violent.

gewandt [gə'vant] a deft, skilful; (erfahren) experienced; **G~heit** f dexterity, skill.

gewann etc v siehe **gewinnen**.

Gewässer [gə'vɛsɐ] nt -s, - waters pl.

Gewebe [gə'veːbə] nt -s, - (Stoff) fabric; (BIOL) tissue.

Gewehr [gə'veːr] nt -(e)s, -e gun; rifle; **~lauf** m rifle barrel.

Geweih [gə'vai] nt -(e)s, -e antlers pl.

Gewerb- [gə'vɛrp] zW: **~e** nt -s, - trade, occupation; **Handel und ~e** trade and industry; **~eschule** f technical school; **g~lich** a industrial; trade attr; **gewerbsmäßig** a professional; **Gewerbszweig** m line of trade.

Gewerkschaft [gə'vɛrkʃaft] f trade union; **~ler** m -s, - trade unionist; **Gewerkschaftsbund** m trade unions federation.

Gewicht [gə'viçt] nt -(e)s, -e weight; (fig) importance; **g~ig** a weighty.

gewieft [gə'viːft] a, **gewiegt** [gə'viːkt] a shrewd, cunning.

gewillt [gə'vilt] a willing, prepared.

Gewimmel [gə'viməl] nt -s swarm.

Gewinde [gə'vində] nt -s, - (Kranz) wreath; (von Schraube) thread.

Gewinn [gə'vin] m -(e)s, -e profit; (bei Spiel) winnings pl; **etw mit ~ verkaufen** sell sth at a profit; **~- und Verlustrechnung** (COMM) profit and loss account; **~beteiligung** f profitsharing; **g~bringend** a profitable; **g~en** unreg vt win; (erwerben) gain; (Kohle, Öl) extract // vi win; (profitieren) gain; **an etw** (dat) **g~en** gain in sth; **~er(in f)** m -s, - winner; **~spanne** f profit margin; **~(n)ummer** f winning number; **~ung** f winning; gaining; (von Kohle etc) extraction.

Gewirr [gə'vir] nt -(e)s, -e tangle; (von Straßen) maze.

gewiß [gə'vis] a,ad certain(ly).

Gewissen [gə'visən] nt -s, - conscience; **g~haft** a conscientious; **~haftigkeit** f conscientiousness; **g~los** a unscrupulous.

Gewissens- zW: **~bisse** pl pangs of conscience pl, qualms pl; **~frage** f matter of conscience; **~freiheit** f freedom of conscience; **~konflikt** m moral conflict.

gewissermaßen [gəvisɐ'maːsən] ad more or less, in a way.

Gewißheit [gə'vishait] f certainty.

Gewitter [gə'vitɐ] nt -s, - thunderstorm; **g~n** vi unpers: **es gewittert** there's a thunderstorm.

gewitzt [gə'vitst] a shrewd, cunning.

gewogen [gə'voːgən] a well-disposed (+dat towards).

gewöhnen [gə'vøːnən] vt: **jdn an etw** (akk) **~** accustom sb to sth; (erziehen zu) teach sb sth // vr: **sich an etw** (akk) **~** get used or accustomed to sth.

Gewohnheit [gə'voːnhait] f habit; (Brauch) custom; **aus ~** from habit;

zur ~ werden become a habit.
Gewohnheits- *in zW* habitual;
  ~mensch *m* creature of habit;
  ~recht *nt* common law.
gewöhnlich [gə'vø:nlıç] *a* usual; ordinary; (*pej*) common; **wie ~** as usual.
gewohnt [gə'vo:nt] *a* usual; **etw ~
sein** be used to sth.
Gewöhnung *f* getting accustomed
(*an +akk* to).
Gewölbe [gə'vœlbə] *nt* -s, - vault.
gewonnen *v siehe* **gewinnen.**
geworden *v siehe* **werden.**
geworfen *v siehe* **werfen.**
Gewühl [gə'vy:l] *nt* -(e)s throng.
Gewürz [gə'vʏrts] *nt* -es, -e spice, seasoning; **~nelke** *f* clove; **~t** *a* spiced.
gewußt *v siehe* **wissen.**
Gezeiten [gə'tsaɪtən] *pl* tides *pl*.
gezielt [gə'tsi:lt] *a* with a particular
aim in mind, purposeful; (*Kritik*)
pointed.
geziert [gə'tsi:rt] *a* affected.
gezogen *v siehe* **ziehen.**
Gezwitscher [gə'tsvɪtʃər] *nt* -s twit-
ter(ing), chirping.
gezwungen [gə'tsvʊŋən] *a* forced;
  ~ermaßen *ad* of necessity.
gibst *etc v siehe* **geben.**
Gicht [gıçt] *f* - gout; **g~isch** *a* gouty.
Giebel ['gi:bəl] *m* -s, - gable; **~dach**
nt gable(d) roof; **~fenster** *nt* gable
window.
Gier [gi:r] *f* - greed; **g~ig** *a* greedy.
Gieß- ['gi:s] *zW*: **g~en** *vt unreg* pour;
(*Blumen*) water; (*Metall*) cast;
(*Wachs*) mould; **~kanne** *f* watering
can.
Gift [gıft] *nt* -(e)s, -e poison; **g~ig** *a*
poisonous; (*fig: boshaft*) venomous;
  ~zahn *m* fang.
ging *etc v siehe* **gehen.**
Ginster ['gınstər] *m* -s, - broom.
Gipfel ['gıpfəl] *m* -s, - summit, peak;
(*fig*) height; **g~n** *vi* culminate;
  ~treffen *nt* summit (meeting).
Gips [gıps] *m* -es, -e plaster; (*MED*)
plaster (of Paris); **~abdruck** *m* plaster cast; **g~en** *vt* plaster; **~verband**
m plaster (cast).
Giraffe [gi'rafə] *f* -, -n giraffe.
Girlande [gır'landə] *f* -, -n garland.
Giro ['ʒi:ro] *nt* -s, -s giro; **~konto** *nt*
current account.
Gischt [gıʃt] *m* -(e)s, -e spray, foam.
Gitarre [gi'tarə] *f* -, -n guitar.
Gitter ['gıtər] *nt* -s, - grating, bars *pl*;
(*für Pflanzen*) trellis; (*Zaun*) rail-
ing(s); **~bett** *nt* cot; **~fenster** *nt*
barred window; **~zaun** *m* railing(s).
Glacéhandschuh [gla'se:hantʃu:] *m*
kid glove.
Gladiole [gladi'o:lə] *f* -, -n gladiolus.
Glanz [glants] *m* -es shine, lustre;
(*fig*) splendour.

glänzen ['glɛntsən] *vi* shine (*also fig*),
gleam // *vt* polish; **~d** *a* shining;
(*fig*) brilliant.
Glanz- *zW*: **~leistung** *f* brilliant
achievement; **g~los** *a* dull; **~zeit** *f*
heyday.
Glas [gla:s] *nt* -es, ⁻er glass; **~bläser**
m -s, - glass blower; **~er** *m* -s, -
glazier; **~faser** *f* fibreglass; **g~ieren**
[gla'zi:rən] *vt* glaze; **g~ig** *a* glassy;
  ~scheibe *f* pane; **~ur** [gla'zu:r] *f*
glaze; (*KOCH*) icing.
glatt [glat] *a* smooth; (*rutschig*) slippery; (*Absage*) flat; (*Lüge*) downright; **G~eis** *nt* (black) ice; **jdn aufs
G~eis führen** (*fig*) take sb for a ride.
Glätte ['glɛtə] *f* -, -n smoothness; slipperiness; **g~n** *vt* smooth out.
Glatze ['glatsə] *f* -, -n bald head; **eine
~ bekommen** go bald.
Glaube ['glaubə] *m* -ns, -n faith (*an
+akk* in); belief (*an +akk* in); **g~n**
vti believe (*an +akk* in, *jdm* sb);
think; **daran g~n müssen** (*umg*) be
for it; **Glaubensbekenntnis** *nt* creed.
glaubhaft ['glaubhaft] *a* credible.
gläubig ['glɔʏbıç] *a* (*REL*) devout;
(*vertrauensvoll*) trustful; **G~e(r)** *mf*
believer; **die G~en** the faithful; **G~er**
m -s, - creditor.
glaubwürdig ['glaubvʏrdıç] *a* credible; (*Mensch*) trustworthy; **G~keit** *f*
credibility; trustworthiness.
gleich [glaɪç] *a* equal; (*identisch*)
(the) same, identical; **es ist mir ~**
it's all the same to me; **2 mal 2 ~ 4** 2
times 2 is *od* equals 4 // *ad* equally;
(*sofort*) straight away; (*bald*) in a
minute; **~ groß** the same size; **~
nach/an** right after/at; **~altrig** *a* of
the same age; **~artig** *a* similar;
  ~bedeutend *a* synonymous; **~be-
rechtigt** *a* having equal rights;
G~berechtigung *f* equal rights *pl*;
  ~bleibend *a* constant; **~en** *unreg vi*:
jdm/etw ~en be like sb/sth // *vr* be
alike; **~falls** *ad* likewise; **danke
~falls!** the same to you; **G~-
förmigkeit** *f* uniformity; **~gesinnt**
a like-minded; **G~gewicht** *nt* equilibrium, balance; **~gültig** *a* indifferent; (*unbedeutend*) unimportant;
G~gültigkeit *f* indifference; **G~heit** *f*
equality; **~kommen** *vi unreg* +*dat*
be equal to; **~mäßig** *a* even, equal;
G~mut *m* equanimity; **G~nis** *nt*
-ses, -se parable; **~sam** *ad* as it
were; **G~strom** *m* (*ELEK*) direct
current; **~tun** *vi unreg*: **es jdm ~tun**
match sb; **G~ung** *f* equation; **~viel**
ad no matter; **~zeitig** *a* simultaneous.
Gleis [glaɪs] *nt* -es, -e track, rails *pl*;
(*Bahnsteig*) platform.
gleiten ['glaɪtən] *vi unreg* glide;

(rutschen) slide.

Gletscher ['glɛtʃər] m -s, - glacier; ~**spalte** f crevasse.

Glied [gliːt] nt -(e)s, -er member; (Arm, Bein) limb; (von Kette) link; (MIL) rank(s); **g~ern** vt organize, structure; ~**erung** f structure, organization; ~**maßen** pl limbs pl.

glimmen ['glɪmən] vi unreg glow, gleam.

glimpflich ['glɪmpflɪç] a mild, lenient; ~ **davonkommen** get off lightly.

glitzern ['glɪtsərn] vi glitter, twinkle.

Globus ['gloːbus] m - od -ses, **Globen** od -se globe.

Glocke ['glɔkə] f -, -n bell; etw an die große ~ hängen (fig) shout sth from the rooftops.

Glocken- zW: ~**geläut** nt peal of bells; ~**spiel** nt chime(s); (MUS) glockenspiel; ~**turm** m bell tower.

Glosse ['glɔsə] f -, -n comment.

glotzen ['glɔtsən] vi (umg) stare.

Glück [glʏk] nt -(e)s luck, fortune; (Freude) happiness; ~ **haben** be lucky; **viel ~** good luck; **zum ~** fortunately; **g~en** vi succeed; **es glückte ihm, es zu bekommen** he succeeded in getting it.

gluckern ['glukərn] vi glug.

Glück- zW: **g~lich** a fortunate; (froh) happy; **g~licherweise** ad fortunately; **Glücksbringer** m -s, - lucky charm; **g~'selig** a blissful.

Glücks- zW: ~**fall** m stroke of luck; ~**kind** nt lucky person; ~**sache** f matter of luck; ~**spiel** nt game of chance.

Glückwunsch m congratulations pl, best wishes pl.

Glüh- ['glyː] zW: ~**birne** f light bulb; **g~en** vi glow; ~**wein** m mulled wine; ~**würmchen** nt glow-worm.

Glut [gluːt] f -, -en (Röte) glow; (Feuers~) fire; (Hitze) heat; (fig) ardour.

GmbH ['geːʔɛmbeːˈhaː] f abk (= Gesellschaft mit beschränkter Haftung) (private) limited company, Ltd. (Brit); corporation, inc. (US).

Gnade ['gnaːdə] f -, -n (Gunst) favour; (Erbarmen) mercy; (Milde) clemency.

Gnaden- zW: ~**frist** f reprieve, respite; **g~los** a merciless; ~**stoß** m coup de grâce.

gnädig ['gnɛːdɪç] a gracious; (voll Erbarmen) merciful.

Gold [gɔlt] nt -(e)s gold; **g~en** a golden; ~**fisch** m goldfish; ~**grube** f goldmine; ~**regen** m laburnum.

Golf [gɔlf] m -(e)s, -e gulf // nt -s golf; ~**platz** m golf course; ~**schläger** m golf club; ~**spieler** m golfer; ~**strom** m Gulf Stream.

Gondel ['gɔndəl] f -, -n gondola; (Seilbahn) cable-car.

gönnen ['gœnən] vt: jdm etw ~ not begrudge sb sth; sich (dat) etw ~ allow oneself sth.

Gönner m -s, - patron; **g~haft** a patronizing.

Gosse ['gɔsə] f -, -n gutter.

Gott [gɔt] m -es, ⁻er god; mein ~, um ~es Willen! for heaven's sake!; grüß ~! hello; ~ sei Dank! thank God!; ~**esdienst** m service; ~**eslästerung** f blasphemy; ~**heit** f deity.

Gött- [gœt] zW: ~**in** f goddess; **g~lich** a divine.

gottlos a godless.

Götze ['gœtsə] m -n, -n idol.

Grab [graːp] nt -(e)s, ⁻er grave; **g~en** ['graːbən] vt unreg dig; ~**en** m -s, ⁻ ditch; (MIL) trench; ~**stein** m gravestone.

Grad [graːt] m -(e)s, -e degree; ~**einteilung** f graduation.

Graf [graːf] m -en, -en count, earl; ~**schaft** f county.

Gräfin ['grɛːfɪn] f countess.

Gram [graːm] m -(e)s grief, sorrow.

grämen ['grɛːmən] vr grieve.

Gramm [gram] nt -s, -e gram(me).

Grammatik [gra'matɪk] f grammar.

grammatisch a grammatical.

Grammophon [gramo'foːn] nt -s, -e gramophone.

Granat [gra'naːt] m -(e)s, -e (Stein) garnet; ~**e** f -, -n (MIL) shell; (Hand~) grenade.

Granit [gra'niːt] m -s, -e granite.

graphisch ['graːfɪʃ] a graphic.

Gras [graːs] nt -es, ⁻er grass; **g~en** vi graze; ~**halm** m blade of grass.

grassieren [gra'siːrən] vi be rampant, rage.

gräßlich ['grɛslɪç] a horrible.

Grat [graːt] m -(e)s, -e ridge.

Gräte ['grɛːtə] f -, -n fishbone.

gratis ['graːtɪs] a,ad free (of charge); **G~probe** f free sample.

Gratulation [gratulatsi'oːn] f congratulation(s).

gratulieren [gratu'liːrən] vi: jdm ~ (zu etw) congratulate sb (on sth); (ich) gratuliere! congratulations!

grau [grau] a grey; ~**en** vi unpers: es graut jdm vor etw sb dreads sth, sb is afraid of sth // vr: sich ~**en** vor dread, have a horror of; **G~en** nt -s horror; ~**enhaft** a horrible; ~**haarig** a grey-haired.

grausam ['grauzaːm] a cruel; **G~keit** f cruelty.

Grausen ['grauzən] nt -s horror; **g~** vi unpers, vr siehe **grauen**.

gravieren [gra'viːrən] vt engrave; ~**d** a grave.

Grazie ['graːtsiə] f -, -n grace.

graziös [gratsi'ø:s] *a* graceful.

greif- [graɪf] *zW:* **~bar** *a* tangible, concrete; **in ~barer Nähe** within reach; **~en** *vt unreg* seize; grip; **nach etw ~en** reach for sth; **um sich ~en** (*fig*) spread; **zu etw ~en** (*fig*) turn to sth.

Greis [graɪs] *m* **-es, -e** old man; **~enalter** *nt* old age; **g~enhaft** *a* senile; **~in** *f* old woman.

grell [grɛl] *a* harsh.

Grenz- ['grɛnts] *zW:* **~beamte(r)** *m* frontier official; **~e** *f* **-, -n** boundary; (*Staats~*) frontier; (*Schranke*) limit; **g~en** *vi* border (*an* +*akk* on); **g~enlos** *a* boundless; **~fall** *m* borderline case; **~übergang** *m* frontier crossing.

Greuel ['grɔʏəl] *m* **-s, -** horror, revulsion; **etw ist jdm ein ~** sb loathes sth; **~tat** *f* atrocity.

greulich ['grɔʏlɪç] *a* horrible.

Griech- [gri:ç] *zW:* **~e** *m*, **~in** *f* Greek; **~enland** *nt* Greece; **g~isch** *a* Greek.

griesgrämig ['gri:sgrɛːmɪç] *a* grumpy.

Grieß [gri:s] *m* **-es, -e** (*KOCH*) semolina.

Griff [grɪf] *m* **-(e)s, -e** grip; (*Vorrichtung*) handle; **g~bereit** *a* handy.

Grill [grɪl] *m* grill; **~e** *f* **-, -n** cricket; **g~en** *vt* grill.

Grimasse [gri'masə] *f* **-, -n** grimace.

grimmig ['grɪmɪç] *a* furious; (*heftig*) fierce, severe.

grinsen ['grɪnzən] *vi* grin.

Grippe ['grɪpə] *f* **-, -n** influenza, flu.

grob [gro:p] *a* coarse, gross; (*Fehler, Verstoß*) gross; **G~heit** *f* coarseness; coarse expression.

Groll [grɔl] *m* **-(e)s** resentment; **g~en** *vi* bear ill will (+*dat od mit* towards); (*Donner*) rumble.

Groschen ['grɔʃən] *m* 10 pfennig piece.

groß [gro:s] *a* big, large; (*hoch*) tall; (*fig*) great; **im ~en und ganzen** on the whole // *ad* greatly; **~artig** *a* great, splendid; **G~aufnahme** *f* (*CINE*) close-up; **G~britannien** *nt* Great Britain.

Größe ['grø:sə] *f* **-, -n** size; (*fig*) greatness; (*Länge*) height.

Groß- *zW:* **~einkauf** *m* bulk purchase; **~eltern** *pl* grandparents *pl*; **g~enteils** *ad* mostly.

Größenwahn ['grø:sənvaːn] *m* megalomania.

Groß- *zW:* **~format** *nt* large size; **~handel** *m* wholesale trade; **~händler** *m* wholesaler; **~macht** *f* great power; **~maul** *m* braggart; **g~mütig** *a* magnanimous; **~mutter** *f* grandmother; **~rechner** *m* mainframe (computer); **g~spurig** *a* pompous; **~stadt** *f* city, large town.

größte(r, s) [grø:stə(r, s)] *a superl von* **groß**; **größtenteils** *ad* for the most part.

Groß- *zW:* **g~tun** *vi unreg* boast; **~vater** *m* grandfather; **g~ziehen** *vt unreg* raise; **g~zügig** *a* generous; (*Planung*) on a large scale.

grotesk [gro'tɛsk] *a* grotesque.

Grotte ['grɔtə] *f* **-, -n** grotto.

Grübchen ['gry:pçən] *nt* dimple.

Grube ['gru:bə] *f* **-, -n** pit; mine; **Grubenarbeiter** *m* miner.

grübeln ['gry:bəln] *vi* brood.

Gruft [gruft] *f* **-, ⁻e** tomb, vault.

grün [gry:n] *a* green; **die G~en** (*POL*) the Greens; **G~anlage** *f* park.

Grund [grunt] *m* **-(e)s, ⁻e** ground; (*von See, Gefäß*) bottom; (*fig*) reason; **im ~e genommen** basically; **~ausbildung** *f* basic training; **~besitz** *m* land(ed property), real estate; **~buch** *nt* land register.

gründ- [grynd] *zW:* **~en** *vt* found; **~en auf** (+*akk*) base on // *vr* be based (*auf* +*dat* on); **G~er** *m* **-s, -** founder.

Grund- *zW:* **~gebühr** *f* basic charge; **~gesetz** *nt* constitution; **~lage** *f* foundation; **g~legend** *a* fundamental.

gründlich *a* thorough.

Grund- *zW:* **g~los** *a* groundless; **~regel** *f* basic rule; **~riß** *m* plan; (*fig*) outline; **~satz** *m* principle; **g~sätzlich** *a,ad* fundamental(ly); (*Frage*) of principle; (*prinzipiell*) on principle; **~schule** *f* elementary school; **~stein** *m* foundation stone; **~stück** *nt* estate; plot.

Gründung *f* foundation.

Grundzug *m* characteristic.

Grün- *zW:* **~kohl** *m* kale; **~schnabel** *m* greenhorn; **~span** *m* verdigris; **~streifen** *m* central reservation.

grunzen ['gruntsən] *vi* grunt.

Gruppe ['grupə] *f* **-, -n** group; **g~nweise** *ad* in groups.

gruppieren [gru'pi:rən] *vtr* group.

gruselig *a* creepy.

gruseln ['gru:zəln] *vi unpers:* **es gruselt jdm vor etw** sth gives sb the creeps // *vr* have the creeps.

Gruß [gru:s] *m* **-es, ⁻e** greeting; (*MIL*) salute; **viele ~e** best wishes; **mit freundlichen ~en** yours sincerely; **~e an** (+*akk*) regards to.

grüßen ['gry:sən] *vt* greet; (*MIL*) salute; **jdn von jdm ~** give sb sb's regards; **jdn ~ lassen** send sb one's regards.

gucken ['gukən] *vi* look.

Gulasch ['gu:laʃ] *nt* **-(e)s, -e** goulash.

gültig ['gyltɪç] *a* valid; **G~keit** *f* validity.

Gummi ['gumi] *nt od m* **-s, -s** rubber; (*~harze*) gum; **~band** *nt* rubber od elastic band; (*Hosen~*) elastic; **~baum** *m* rubber plant; **gummieren** [gʊ'miːrən] *vt* gum; **~knüppel** *m* rubber truncheon; **~strumpf** *m* elastic stocking.

günstig ['gʏnstɪç] *a* convenient; (*Gelegenheit*) favourable; **das habe ich ~ bekommen** it was a bargain.

Gurgel ['gʊrgəl] *f -, -n* throat; **g~n** *vi* gurgle; (*im Mund*) gargle.

Gurke ['gʊrkə] *f -, -n* cucumber; **saure ~** pickled cucumber, gherkin.

Gurt [gʊrt] *m -(e)s, -e* belt.

Gürtel ['gʏrtəl] *m -s, -* belt; (*GEOG*) zone; **~reifen** *m* radial tyre.

Guß [gʊs] *m -sses, Güsse* casting; (*Regen~*) downpour; (*KOCH*) glazing; **~eisen** *nt* cast iron.

gut [guːt] *a* good; **alles G~e** all the best; **also ~** all right then

◆ *ad* well; **~ schmecken** taste good; **~, aber ...** ok, but ...; (na) **~, ich komme** all right, I'll come; **~ drei Stunden** a good three hours; **das kann ~ sein** that may well be; **laß es ~ sein** that'll do.

Gut [guːt] *nt -(e)s, -er* (*Besitz*) possession; (*pl: Waren*) goods *pl*; **laß es g~ sein** that'll do; **~achten** *nt -s, -* (expert) opinion; **~achter** *m -s, -* expert; **g~artig** *a* good-natured; (*MED*) benign; **g~bürgerlich** *a* (*Küche*) (good) plain; **~dünken** *nt*: **nach ~dünken** at one's discretion.

Güte ['gyːtə] *f -* goodness, kindness; (*Qualität*) quality.

Güter- *zW*: **~abfertigung** *f* (*EISENB*) goods office; **~bahnhof** *m* goods station; **~wagen** *m* goods waggon (*Brit*), freight car (*US*); **~zug** *m* goods train (*Brit*), freight train (*US*).

Gut- *zW*: **g~gehen** *v unpers unreg* work, come off; **es geht jdm g~** sb's doing fine; **g~gemeint** *a* well meant; **g~gläubig** *a* trusting; **~haben** *nt -s* credit; **g~heißen** *vt unreg* approve (of).

gütig ['gyːtɪç] *a* kind.

Gut- *zW*: **g~mütig** *a* good-natured; **~mütigkeit** *f* good nature; **~schein** *m* voucher; **g~schreiben** *vt unreg* credit; **~schrift** *f* credit; **g~tun** *vi unreg*: **jdm g~tun** do sb good; **g~willig** *a* willing.

Gymnasium [gym'naːziʊm] *nt* grammar school (*Brit*), high school (*US*).

Gymnastik [gym'nastɪk] *f* exercises *pl*, keep fit.

H

H, h [haː] *nt* H, h.

Haag [haːg] *m*: **Den ~** the Hague.

Haar [haːr] *nt -(e)s, -e* hair; **um ein ~** nearly; **an den ~en herbeigezogen** (*umg: Vergleich*) very far-fetched; **~bürste** *f* hairbrush; **h~en** *vir* lose hair; **~esbreite** *f*: **um ~esbreite** by a hair's-breadth; **h~genau** *ad* precisely; **h~ig** *a* hairy; (*fig*) nasty; **~klemme** *f* hair grip; **~nadel** *f* hairpin; **h~scharf** *ad* (*beobachten*) very sharply; (*daneben*) by a hair's breadth; **~schnitt** *m* haircut; **~shampoo** *nt* shampoo; **~spange** *f* hair slide; **h~sträubend** *a* hairraising; **~teil** *nt* hairpiece; **~waschmittel** *nt* shampoo.

Habe ['haːbə] *f -* property.

haben ['haːbən] *vt, v aux unreg* have; **Hunger/Angst ~** be hungry/afraid; **woher hast du das?** where did you get that from?; **was hast du denn?** what's the matter (with you)?; **du hast zu schweigen** you're to be quiet; **ich hätte gern** I would like; **H~** *nt -s, -* credit.

Habgier *f* avarice; **h~ig** *a* avaricious.

Habicht ['haːbɪçt] *m -s, -e* hawk.

Habseligkeiten *pl* belongings *pl*.

Hachse ['haksə] *f -, -n* (*KOCH*) knuckle.

Hacke ['hakə] *f -, -n* hoe; (*Ferse*) heel; **h~n** *vt* hack, chop; (*Erde*) hoe.

Hackfleisch *nt* mince, minced meat.

Hafen ['haːfən] *m -s, ⁻* harbour, port; **~arbeiter** *m* docker; **~damm** *m* jetty, mole; **~stadt** *f* port.

Hafer ['haːfər] *m -s, -* oats *pl*; **~flocken** *pl* rolled oats *pl*; **~schleim** *m* gruel.

Haft [haft] *f -* custody; **h~bar** *a* liable, responsible; **~befehl** *m* warrant (of arrest); **h~en** *vi* stick, cling; **h~en für** be liable *od* responsible for; **h~enbleiben** *vi unreg* stick (*an* +*dat* to); **~pflicht** *f* liability; **~pflichtversicherung** *f* third party insurance; **~schalen** *pl* contact lenses *pl*; **~ung** *f* liability.

Hage- ['haːgə] *zW*: **~butte** *f -, -n* rose hip; **~dorn** *m* hawthorn.

Hagel ['haːgəl] *m -s* hail; **h~n** *vi unpers* hail.

hager ['haːgər] *a* gaunt.

Hahn [haːn] *m -(e)s, ⁻e* cock; (*Wasser~*) tap, faucet (*US*).

Hähnchen ['hɛːnçən] *nt* cockerel; (*KOCH*) chicken.

Hai(fisch) ['haɪ(fɪʃ)] *m -(e)s, -e* shark.

Häkchen ['hɛːkçən] *nt* small hook.

Häkel- ['hɛːkəl] *zW*: **~arbeit** *f* crochet work; **h~n** *vt* crochet; **~nadel** *f* crochet hook.

Haken ['haːkən] *m -s, -* hook; (*fig*) catch; **~kreuz** *nt* swastika; **~nase** *f* hooked nose.

halb [halp] *a* half; **~ eins** half past twelve; **ein ~es Dutzend** half a doz-

en; **H~dunkel** nt semi-darkness.
halber ['halbər] präp +gen (wegen) on account of; (für) for the sake of.
Halb- zW: **~heit** f half-measure; **h~ieren** vt halve; **~insel** f peninsula; **h~jährlich** a half-yearly; **~kreis** m semicircle; **~kugel** f hemisphere; **~leiter** m semiconductor; **h~links** a (SPORT) inside left; **~mond** m half-moon; (fig) crescent; **h~offen** a half-open; **~pension** f half-board; **h~rechts** a (SPORT) inside right; **~schuh** m shoe; **~tagsarbeit** f part-time work; **h~wegs** ad half-way; **h~wegs besser** more or less better; **~wertzeit** f half-life; **~wüchsige(r)** mf adolescent; **~zeit** f (SPORT) half; (Pause) half-time.
half etc v siehe **helfen.**
Hälfte ['hɛlftə] -, **-n** f half.
Halfter ['halftər] f -, **-n,** od nt **-s,** - halter; (Pistolen~) holster.
Halle ['halə] f -, **-n** hall; (AVIAT) hangar; **h~n** vi echo, resound; **Hallenbad** nt indoor swimming pool.
hallo [ha'loː] interj hello.
Halluzination [halutsinatsi'oːn] f hallucination.
Halm [halm] m **-(e)s, -e** blade, stalk.
Hals [hals] m **-es, ⁻e** neck; (Kehle) throat; **~ über Kopf** in a rush; **~kette** f necklace; **~-Nasen-Ohren-Arzt** m ear nose and throat specialist; **~schlagader** f carotid artery; **~schmerzen** pl sore throat; **~tuch** nt scarf; **~wirbel** m cervical vertebra.
Halt [halt] m **-(e)s, -e** stop; (fester ~) hold; (innerer ~) stability; **h~** interj stop!, halt! // ad just; **h~bar** a durable; (Lebensmittel) non-perishable; (MIL, fig) tenable; **~barkeit** f durability; (non-)perishability.
halten ['haltən] unreg vt keep; (fest~) hold; **~ für** regard as; **~ von** think of // vi hold; (frisch bleiben) keep; (stoppen) stop; **an sich ~** restrain oneself // vr (frisch bleiben) keep; (sich behaupten) hold out; **sich rechts/links ~** keep to the right/left.
Haltestelle f stop.
Halteverbot nt: **hier ist ~** it's no waiting here.
Halt- zW: **h~los** a unstable; **h~machen** vi stop; **~ung** f posture; (fig) attitude; (Selbstbeherrschung) composure.
Halunke [ha'luŋkə] m **-n, -n** rascal.
hämisch ['hɛːmɪʃ] a malicious.
Hammel ['haməl] m **-s, ⁻ od** - wether; **~fleisch** nt mutton.
Hammer ['hamər] m **-s, ⁻** hammer.
hämmern ['hɛmərn] vti hammer.
Hämorrhoiden [hɛmɔro'iːdən] pl haemorrhoids.
Hampelmann ['hampəlman] m (lit,

fig) puppet.
Hamster ['hamstər] m **-s,** - hamster; **~ei** [-'raɪ] f hoarding; **h~n** vi hoard.
Hand [hant] f -, **⁻e** hand; **~arbeit** f manual work; (Nadelarbeit) needlework; **~arbeiter** m manual worker; **~bremse** f handbrake; **~buch** nt handbook, manual.
Händedruck ['hɛndədruk] m handshake.
Handel ['handəl] m **-s** trade; (Geschäft) transaction.
handeln ['handəln] vi trade; act; **~ von** be about // vr unpers: **sich ~ um** be a question of, be about; **H~** nt **-s** action.
Handels- zW: **~bilanz** f balance of trade; **~kammer** f chamber of commerce; **~name** m trade name; **~reisende(r)** m commercial traveller; **~schule** f business school; **h~üblich** a customary; (Preis) going attr; **~vertreter** m sales representative.
Hand- zW: **~feger** m **-s,** - brush; **h~fest** a hefty; **h~gearbeitet** a handmade; **~gelenk** nt wrist; **~gemenge** nt scuffle; **~gepäck** nt hand-luggage; **h~greiflich** a palpable; **h~greiflich werden** become violent; **~griff** m flick of the wrist; **h~haben** vt insep handle.
Händler ['hɛndlər] m **-s,** - trader, dealer.
handlich ['hantlɪç] a handy.
Handlung ['handluŋ] f -, **-en** act(ion); (in Buch) plot; (Geschäft) shop; **Handlungsweise** f manner of dealing.
Hand- zW: **~pflege** f manicure; **~schelle** f handcuff; **~schlag** m handshake; **~schrift** f handwriting; (Text) manuscript; **~schuh** m glove; **~tasche** f handbag; **~tuch** nt towel; **~werk** nt trade, craft; **~werker** m **-s,** - craftsman, artisan; **~werkzeug** nt tools pl.
Hanf [hanf] m **-(e)s** hemp.
Hang [haŋ] m **-(e)s, ⁻e** inclination; (Ab~) slope.
Hänge- ['hɛŋə] in zW hanging; **~brücke** f suspension bridge; **~matte** f hammock.
hängen ['hɛŋən] vi unreg hang; **~ an** (fig) be attached to // vt hang (an +akk on(to)); **sich ~ an** (+akk) hang on to, cling to; **~bleiben** vi unreg be caught (an +dat on); (fig) remain, stick; **~lassen** vt unreg (vergessen) leave; **den Kopf ~lassen** get downhearted.
Hannover [ha'noːfər] nt **-s** Hanover.
hänseln ['hɛnzəln] vt tease.
hantieren [han'tiːrən] vi work, be busy; **mit etw ~** handle sth.

hapern ['ha:pərn] *vi unpers*: es hapert an etw (*dat*) there is a lack of sth.

Happen ['hapən] *m* -s, - mouthful.

Hardware ['ha:dwɛə] *f* hardware.

Harfe ['harfə] *f* -, -n harp.

Harke ['harkə] *f* -, -n rake; **h~n** *vti* rake.

harmlos ['harmlo:s] *a* harmless; **H~igkeit** *f* harmlessness.

Harmonie [harmo'ni:] *f* harmony; **h~ren** *vi* harmonize.

Harmonika [har'mo:nika] *f* -, -s (*Zieh~*) concertina.

harmonisch [har'mo:nɪʃ] *a* harmonious.

Harmonium [har'mo:niʊm] *nt* -s, -nien *od* -s harmonium.

Harn [harn] *m* -(e)s, -e urine; **~blase** *f* bladder.

Harpune [har'pu:nə] *f* -, -n harpoon.

harren ['harən] *vi* wait (*auf* +*akk* for).

hart [ha:t] *a* hard; (*fig*) harsh.

Härte ['hertə] *f* -, -n hardness; (*fig*) harshness.

hart- *zW*: **~gekocht** *a* hard-boiled; **~herzig** *a* hard-hearted; **~näckig** *a* stubborn; **H~näckigkeit** *f* stubbornness; **H~platte** *f* hard disk.

Harz [ha:rts] *nt* -es, -e resin.

Haschee [ha'ʃe:] *nt* -s, -s hash.

Haschisch ['haʃɪʃ] *nt* - hashish.

Hase ['ha:zə] *m* -n, -n hare.

Haselnuß ['ha:zəlnʊs] *f* hazelnut.

Hasenfuß *m* coward.

Hasenscharte *f* harelip.

Haß [has] *m* -sses hate, hatred.

hassen ['hasən] *vt* hate.

häßlich ['heslɪç] *a* ugly; (*gemein*) nasty; **H~keit** *f* ugliness; nastiness.

hast *v siehe* **haben.**

Hast [hast] *f* - haste; **h~en** *vi* rush; **h~ig** *a* hasty.

hat, hatte *etc v siehe* **haben.**

Haube ['haʊbə] *f* -, -n hood; (*Mütze*) cap; (*AUT*) bonnet, hood (*US*).

Hauch [haʊx] *m* -(e)s, -e breath; (*Luft~*) breeze; (*fig*) trace; **h~dünn** *a* very thin; **h~en** *vi* breathe.

Haue ['haʊə] *f* -, -n hoe, pick; (*umg*) hiding; **h~n** *vt unreg* hew, cut; (*umg*) thrash.

Haufen ['haʊfən] *m* -s, - heap; (*Leute*) crowd; **ein ~ (x)** (*umg*) loads *od* a lot (of x); **auf einem ~** in one heap.

häufen ['hɔyfən] *vt* pile up // *vr* accumulate.

haufenweise *ad* in heaps; in droves; **etw ~ haben** have piles of sth.

häufig ['hɔyfɪç] *a,ad* frequent(ly); **H~keit** *f* frequency.

Haupt [haʊpt] *nt* -(e)s, **Häupter** head; (*Ober~*) chief; (*in zW*) main; **~bahnhof** *m* central station; **h~beruflich** *ad* as one's main occupation; **~darsteller(in** *f*) *m* leading

actor/actress; **~eingang** *m* main entrance; **~film** *m* main film.

Häuptling ['hɔyptlɪŋ] *m* chief, chieftain.

Haupt- *zW*: **~mann** *m, pl* -**leute** (*MIL*) captain; **~person** *f* central figure; **~quartier** *nt* headquarters *pl*; **~rolle** *f* leading part; **~sache** *f* main thing; **h~sächlich** *a,ad* chief(ly); **~satz** *m* main clause; **~schlagader** *f* aorta; **~schule** *f* ≈ secondary school; **~sendezeit** *f* (*TV*) prime time; **~stadt** *f* capital; **~straße** *f* main street; **~wort** *nt* noun.

Haus [haʊs] *nt* -es, **Häuser** house; **nach ~e** home; **zu ~e** at home; **~angestellte** *f* domestic servant; **~arbeit** *f* housework; (*SCH*) homework; **~arzt** *m* family doctor; **~aufgabe** *f* (*SCH*) homework; **~besitzer(in** *f*) *m*, **~eigentümer(in** *f*) *m* house-owner.

Häuser- ['hɔyzər] *zW*: **~block** *m* block (of houses); **~makler** *m* estate agent (*Brit*), real estate agent (*US*).

Haus- *zW*: **~frau** *f* housewife; **h~gemacht** *a* home-made; **~halt** *m* household; (*POL*) budget; **h~halten** *vi unreg* (*sparen*) economize; **~hälterin** *f* housekeeper; **~haltsgeld** *nt* housekeeping (money); **~haltsgerät** *nt* domestic appliance; **~herr** *m* host; (*Vermieter*) landlord; **h~hoch** *ad*: **h~hoch verlieren** lose by a mile.

hausieren [haʊ'zi:rən] *vi* peddle.

Hausierer *m* -s, - peddlar.

häuslich ['hɔyslɪç] *a* domestic.

Haus- *zW*: **~meister** *m* caretaker, janitor; **~nummer** *f* street number; **~ordnung** *f* house rules *pl*; **~putz** *m* house cleaning; **~schlüssel** *m* front-door key; **~schuh** *m* slipper; **~suchung** *f* police raid; **~tier** *nt* domestic animal; **~wirt** *m* landlord; **~wirtschaft** *f* domestic science.

Haut [haʊt] *f* -, **Häute** skin; (*Tier~*) hide.

Haut- *zW*: **h~eng** *a* skin-tight; **~farbe** *f* complexion.

Haxe ['haksə] *f* -, -n *siehe* **Hachse.**

Hbf *abk von* **Hauptbahnhof.**

he [he:] *interj* hey.

Hebamme ['he:p'amə] *f* -, -n midwife.

Hebel ['he:bəl] *m* -s, - lever.

heben ['he:bən] *vt unreg* raise, lift.

Hecht [heçt] *m* -(e)s, -e pike.

Heck [hɛk] *nt* -(e)s, -e stern; (*von Auto*) rear.

Hecke ['hɛkə] *f* -, -n hedge.

Heckenrose *f* dog rose.

Heckenschütze *m* sniper.

Heer [he:r] *nt* -(e)s, -e army.

Hefe ['he:fə] *f* -, -n yeast.

Heft [heft] *nt* -(e)s, -e exercise book; (*Zeitschrift*) number; (*von Messer*)

haft; **h~en** vt fasten (an +akk to);
(nähen) tack; **~er** m -s, - folder.

heftig a fierce, violent; **H~keit** f
fierceness, violence.

Heft- zW: **~klammer** f paper clip;
~maschine f stapling machine;
~pflaster nt sticking plaster;
~zwecke f drawing pin.

Hehl [he:l] m od nt: **kein(en) ~ aus
etw** (dat) **machen** make no secret of
sth; **~er** m -s, - receiver (of stolen
goods), fence.

Heide ['haɪdə] f -, -n heath, moor;
(~kraut) heather // m -n, -n, **Heidin** f
heathen, pagan; **~kraut** nt heather;
Heidelbeere f bilberry; **Heidentum**
nt paganism.

heikel ['haɪkəl] a awkward, thorny;
(wählerisch) fussy.

Heil [haɪl] nt -(e)s well-being; (See-
len~) salvation; **h~** a in one piece,
intact; **~and** m -(e)s, -e saviour;
h~bar a curable; **h~en** vt cure // vi
heal; **h~froh** a very relieved.

heilig ['haɪlɪç] a holy; **H~abend** m
Christmas Eve; **H~e(r)** mf saint;
~en vt sanctify, hallow; **H~enschein**
m halo; **H~keit** f holiness;
~sprechen vt unreg canonize;
H~tum nt shrine; (Gegenstand) relic.

Heil- zW: **h~los** a unholy; **~mittel** nt
remedy; **h~sam** a (fig) salutary;
Heilsarmee f Salvation Army; **~ung**
f cure.

Heim [haɪm] nt -(e)s, -e home; **h~** ad
home.

Heimat ['haɪmɑ:t] f -, -en home
(town/country etc); **~land** nt home-
land; **h~lich** a native, home attr;
(Gefühle) nostalgic; **h~los** a homeless; **~ort** m home town/area;
~vertriebene(r) mf displaced person.

Heim- zW: **~computer** m home computer; **h~fahren** vi unreg drive/go
home; **~fahrt** f journey home;
h~gehen vi unreg go home; (sterben) pass away; **h~isch** a (gebürtig)
native; **sich h~isch fühlen** feel at
home; **~kehr** f -, -en homecoming;
h~kehren vi return home; **h~lich** a
secret; **~lichkeit** f secrecy; **~reise** f
journey home; **h~suchen** vt afflict;
(Geist) haunt; **h~tückisch** a malicious; **~weg** m way home; **~weh** nt
homesickness; **~weh haben** be home-
sick; **h~zahlen** vt: **jdm etw
h~zahlen** pay back sb for sth.

Heirat ['haɪrɑ:t] f -, -en marriage;
h~en vti marry.

Heiratsantrag m proposal.

heiser ['haɪzər] a hoarse; **H~keit** f
hoarseness.

heiß [haɪs] a hot; **~e(r) Draht** hot
line; **~es Eisen** (umg) hot potato;

~blütig a hot-blooded.

heißen ['haɪsən] unreg vi be called;
(bedeuten) mean; **das heißt** that is to
say // vt command; (nennen) name //
vi unpers it says; it is said.

Heißhunger m ravenous hunger.

heißlaufen vir unreg overheat.

heiter ['haɪtər] a cheerful; (Wetter)
bright; **H~keit** f cheerfulness; (Belustigung) amusement.

Heiz- ['haɪts] zW: **h~bar** a heated;
(Raum) with heating; **~decke** f electric blanket; **h~en** vt heat; **~er** m
-s, - stoker; **~körper** m radiator;
~öl nt fuel oil; **~sonne** f electric
fire; **~ung** f heating; **~ungsanlage** f
heating system.

hektisch ['hɛktɪʃ] a hectic.

Held [hɛlt] m -en, -en hero; **~in** f
heroine.

helfen ['hɛlfən] unreg vi help (jdm sb,
bei with); (nützen) be of use; **sich**
(dat) **zu ~ wissen** be resourceful // v
unpers: **es hilft nichts, du mußt ...**
it's no use, you have to ...

Helfer m -s, - helper, assistant;
Helfershelfer m accomplice.

hell [hɛl] a clear, bright; (Farbe,
Bier) light; **~blau** a light blue;
~blond a ash-blond; **H~e** f - clear-
ness, brightness; **H~seher** m clairvoyant; **~wach** a wide-awake.

Helm [hɛlm] m -(e)s, -e (auf Kopf)
helmet.

Hemd [hɛmt] nt -(e)s, -en shirt; (Un-
ter~) vest; **~bluse** f blouse.

hemmen ['hɛmən] vt check, hold up;
gehemmt sein be inhibited.

Hemmung f check; (PSYCH) inhibi-
tion; **hemmungslos** a unrestrained,
without restraint.

Hengst [hɛŋst] m -es, -e stallion.

Henkel ['hɛŋkəl] m -s, - handle.

Henker m -s, - hangman.

Henne ['hɛnə] f -, -n hen.

her [he:r] ad **1** (Richtung) **komm ~ zu
mir** come here (to me); **von England
~** from England; **von weit ~** from a
long way away; **~ damit!** hand it
over!; **wo hat er das ~?** where did he
get that from?
2 (Blickpunkt): **von der Form ~** as
far as the form is concerned
3 (zeitlich): **das ist 5 Jahre ~** that
was 5 years ago; **wo bist du ~?**
where do you come from? **ich kenne
ihn von früher ~** I know him from
before.

herab [hɛ'rap] ad down(ward(s));
~hängen vi unreg hang down;
~lassen unreg vt let down // vr condescend; **~lassend** a condescending;
~setzen vt lower, reduce; (fig) belittle, disparage; **~würdigen** vt belittle,
disparage.

heran [hɛ'ran] *ad*: näher ~! come up closer!; ~ **zu mir**! come up to me!; ~**bringen** *vt unreg* bring up (*an* +*akk* to); ~**fahren** *vi unreg* drive up (*an* +*akk* to); ~**kommen** *vi unreg* (*an* +*akk*) approach, come near; ~**machen** *vr*: sich an jdn ~**machen** make up to sb; ~**wachsen** *vi unreg* grow up; ~**ziehen** *vt unreg* pull nearer; (*aufziehen*) raise; (*ausbilden*) train; jdn zu etw ~**ziehen** call upon sb to help in sth.

herauf [hɛ'raʊf] *ad* up(ward(s)), up here; ~**beschwören** *vt unreg* conjure up, evoke; ~**bringen** *vt unreg* bring up.

heraus [hɛ'raʊs] *ad* out; outside; from; ~**bekommen** *vt unreg* get out; (*fig*) find *od* figure out; ~**bringen** *vt unreg* bring out; (*Geheimnis*) elicit; ~**finden** *vt unreg* find out; ~**fordern** *vt* challenge; **H~forderung** *f* challenge; provocation; ~**geben** *vt unreg* give up, surrender; (*Geld*) give back; (*Buch*) edit; (*veröffentlichen*) publish; ~**geber** *m* -s, - editor; (*Verleger*) publisher; ~**halten** *vr unreg*: sich aus etw ~**halten** keep out of sth; ~**hängen** *vti unreg* hang out; ~**holen** *vt* get out (*aus* of); ~**kommen** *vi unreg* come out; dabei kommt nichts ~ nothing will come of it; ~**reißen** *vt unreg* tear out; pull out; ~**rücken** *vt* (*Geld*) fork out, hand over; mit etw ~**rücken** (*fig*) come out with sth; ~**stellen** *vr* turn out (*als* to be); ~**ziehen** *vt unreg* pull out, extract.

herb [hɛrp] *a* (slightly) bitter, acid; (*Wein*) dry; (*fig: schmerzlich*) bitter; (: *streng*) stern, austere.

herbei [hɛr'baɪ] *ad* (over) here; ~**führen** *vt* bring about; ~**schaffen** *vt* procure.

herbemühen ['hɛːrbəmyːən] *vr* take the trouble to come.

Herberge ['hɛrbɛrgə] *f* -, -n shelter; hostel, inn.

Herbergsmutter *f*, **Herbergsvater** *m* warden.

her- *zW*: ~**bitten** *vt unreg* ask to come (here); ~**bringen** *vt unreg* bring here.

Herbst [hɛrpst] *m* -(e)s, -e autumn, fall (*US*); **h~lich** *a* autumnal.

Herd [hɛːrt] *m* -(e)s, -e cooker; (*fig, MED*) focus, centre.

Herde ['hɛːrdə] *f* -, -n herd; (*Schaf~*) flock.

herein [hɛ'raɪn] *ad* in (here), here; ~! come in!; ~**bitten** *vt unreg* ask in; ~**brechen** *vi unreg* set in; ~**bringen** *vt unreg* bring in; ~**dürfen** *vi unreg* have permission to enter; ~**fallen** *vi unreg* be caught, taken in; ~**fallen auf** (+*akk*) fall for; ~**kommen** *vi*

unreg come in; ~**lassen** *vt unreg* admit; ~**legen** *vt*: jdn ~**legen** take sb in.

Her- *zW*: ~**fahrt** *f* journey here; **h~fallen** *vi unreg*: **h~fallen über** fall upon; ~**gang** *m* course of events, circumstances *pl*; **h~geben** *vt unreg* give, hand (over); sich zu etw **h~geben** lend one's name to sth; **h~gehen** *vi unreg*: hinter jdm **h~gehen** follow sb; es geht hoch **h~** there are a lot of goings-on; **h~halten** *vt unreg* hold out; **h~halten müssen** (*umg*) have to suffer; **h~hören** *vi* listen.

Hering ['heːrɪŋ] *m* -s, -e herring.

her- *zW*: ~**kommen** *vi unreg* come; komm mal ~! come here!; ~**kömmlich** *a* traditional; **H~kunft** *f* -, -künfte origin; ~**laufen** *vi unreg*: ~**laufen hinter** (+*dat*) run after.

Hermelin [hɛrmə'liːn] *m od nt* -s, -e ermine.

hermetisch [hɛr'meːtɪʃ] *a,ad* hermetic(ally).

her- [hɛr] *zW*: ~'**nach** *ad* afterwards; ~'**nieder** *ad* down.

Herr [hɛr] *m* -(e)n, -en master; (*Mann*) gentleman; (*REL*) Lord; (*vor Namen*) Mr.; mein ~! sir!; meine ~en! gentlemen!; ~**endoppel** *nt* men's doubles; ~**enhaus** *nt* mansion; ~**eneinzel** *nt* men's singles; ~**enhaus** *nt* mansion; ~**enkonfektion** *f* menswear; **h~enlos** *a* ownerless.

herrichten ['heːrrɪçtən] *vt* prepare.

Herr- *zW*: ~**in** *f* mistress; **h~isch** *a* domineering; **h~lich** *a* marvellous, splendid; ~**lichkeit** *f* splendour, magnificence; ~**schaft** *f* power, rule; (*Herr und Herrin*) master and mistress; meine ~**schaften**! ladies and gentlemen!

herrschen ['hɛrʃən] *vi* rule; (*bestehen*) prevail, be.

Herrscher(in *f*) *m* -s, - ruler.

her- *zW*: ~**rühren** *vi* arise, originate; ~**sagen** *vt* recite; ~**stellen** *vt* make, manufacture; **H~steller** *m* -s, - manufacturer; **H~stellung** *f* manufacture.

herüber [hɛ'ryːbər] *ad* over (here), across.

herum [hɛ'rʊm] *ad* about, (a)round; um etw ~ around sth; ~**führen** *vt* show around; ~**gehen** *vi unreg* walk *od* go round (um *etw* sth); walk about; ~**irren** *vi* wander about; ~**kriegen** *vt* (*umg*) bring *od* talk around; ~**sprechen** *vr unreg* get around, be spread; ~**treiben** *vir unreg* drift about; ~**ziehen** *vir unreg* wander about.

herunter [hɛ'rʊntər] *ad* downward(s), down (there); ~**gekommen** *a* run-

down; **~hängen** vi unreg hang down;
~holen vt bring down; **~kommen** vi
unreg come down; (fig) come down
in the world; **~machen** vt take
down; (schimpfen) have a go at.

hervor [hɛr'foːr] ad out, forth;
~bringen vt unreg produce; (Wort)
utter; **~gehen** vi unreg emerge, result; **~heben** vt unreg stress; (als
Kontrast) set off; **~ragend** a (fig)
excellent; **~rufen** vt unreg cause,
give rise to.

Herz [hɛrts] nt **-ens, -en** heart; (KAR-
TEN) hearts; **~anfall** m heart attack;
~enslust f: nach **~enslust** to one's
heart's content; **~fehler** m heart defect; **h~haft** a hearty; **~infarkt** m
heart attack; **~klopfen** nt palpitation; **h~lich** a cordial; **h~lichen**
Glückwunsch congratulations pl;
h~liche Grüße best wishes; **h~los** a
heartless.

Herzog [ˈhɛrtsoːk] m **-(e)s, ⸚e** duke;
~in f duchess; **h~lich** a ducal; **~tum**
nt duchy.

Herzschlag m heartbeat; (MED) heart
attack.

herzzerreißend a heartrending.

heterogen [hetero'geːn] a hetero-
geneous.

Hetze [ˈhɛtsə] f -, -n (Eile) rush; **h~n**
vt hunt; (verfolgen) chase; **jdn/etw**
auf jdn/etw **h~n** set sb/sth on sb/sth //
vi (eilen) rush; **h~n gegen** stir up
feeling against; **h~n zu** agitate for;
Hetze'rei f agitation; (Eile) rush.

Heu [hɔy] nt **-(e)s** hay; **Geld wie ~**
stacks of money; **~boden** m hayloft.

Heuchelei [hɔyçəˈlaɪ] f hypocrisy.

heucheln [ˈhɔyçəln] vt pretend, feign //
vi be hypocritical.

Heuchler(in f) [ˈhɔyçlər(ɪn)] m **-s, -**
hypocrite; **h~isch** a hypocritical.

heulen [ˈhɔylən] vi howl; cry; das **~de**
Elend bekommen get the blues.

Heuschnupfen m hay fever.

Heuschrecke [ˈhɔyʃrɛkə] f grass-
hopper, locust.

heute [ˈhɔytə] ad today; **~ abend/früh**
this evening/morning.

heutig [ˈhɔytɪç] a today's.

heutzutage [ˈhɔytsuːtaːgə] ad nowa-
days.

Hexe [ˈhɛksə] f -, -n witch; **h~n** vi
practise witchcraft; **ich kann doch**
nicht h~n I can't work miracles;
Hexenkessel m (lit, fig) cauldron;
Hexenschuß m lumbago; **Hexe'rei** f
witchcraft.

Hieb [hiːp] m **-(e)s, -e** blow; (Wunde)
cut, gash; (Stichelei) cutting remark;
~e bekommen get a thrashing.

hielt etc v siehe **halten.**

hier [hiːr] ad here; **~auf** ad there-
upon; (danach) after that; **~be-**

halten vt unreg keep here; **~bei** ad
herewith, enclosed; **~bleiben** vi
unreg stay here; **~durch** ad by this
means; (örtlich) through here; **~her**
ad this way, here; **~hin** ad here;
~lassen vt unreg leave here; **~mit**
ad hereby; **~nach** ad hereafter;
~von ad about this, hereof;
~zulande ad in this country.

hiesig [ˈhiːzɪç] a of this place, local.

hieß etc v siehe **heißen.**

Hilfe [ˈhɪlfə] f -, -n help; aid; **Erste ~**
first aid; **~!** help!.

Hilf- zW: **~los** a helpless; **~losigkeit**
f helplessness; **h~reich** a helpful.

Hilfs- zW: **~arbeiter** m labourer;
h~bedürftig a needy; **h~bereit** a
ready to help; **~kraft** f assistant,
helper; **~schule** f school for backward children.

hilfst etc v siehe **helfen.**

Himbeere [ˈhɪmbeːrə] f -, -n raspberry.

Himmel [ˈhɪməl] m **-s, -** sky; (REL, liter) heaven; **h~blau** a sky-blue;
~fahrt f Ascension; **h~schreiend** a
outrageous; **Himmelsrichtung** f direction.

himmlisch [ˈhɪmlɪʃ] a heavenly.

hin [hɪn] ad **1** (Richtung) **~ und zu-**
rück there and back; **~ und her** to and
fro; **bis zur Mauer ~** up to the wall;
wo ist er ~? where has he gone?;
Geld ~, Geld her money or no money
2 (auf ... ~): **auf meine Bitte ~** at
my request; **auf seinen Rat ~** on the
basis of his advice
3: **mein Glück ist ~** my happiness
has gone.

hinab [hɪˈnap] ad down; **~gehen** vi
unreg go down; **~sehen** vi unreg
look down.

hinauf [hɪˈnauf] ad up; **~arbeiten** vr
work one's way up; **~steigen** vi
unreg climb.

hinaus [hɪˈnaus] ad out; **~gehen** vi
unreg go out; **~gehen über** (+akk)
exceed; **~laufen** vi unreg run out;
~laufen auf (+akk) come to, amount
to; **~lehnen** vr lean out; **~schieben**
vt unreg put off, postpone; **~wollen**
vi want to go out; **~wollen auf**
(+akk) drive at, get at.

Hinblick [ˈhɪnblɪk] m: in od im **~ auf**
(+akk) in view of.

hinder- [ˈhɪndər] zW: **~lich** a awkward; **~n** vt hinder, hamper; **jdn an**
etw (dat) **~n** prevent sb from doing
sth; **H~nis** nt **-ses, -se** obstacle;
H~nisrennen nt steeple chase.

hindeuten [ˈhɪndɔytən] vi point (auf
+akk to).

hindurch [hɪnˈdʊrç] ad through;
across; (zeitlich) over.

hinein [hɪˈnaɪn] ad in; **~fallen** vi

unreg fall in; **~fallen in** (+*akk*) fall into; **~gehen** *vi unreg* go in; **~gehen in** (+*akk*) go into, enter; **~geraten** *vi unreg*: **~geraten in** (+*akk*) get into; **~passen** *vi* fit in; **~passen in** (+*akk*) fit into; **~steigern** *vr* get worked up; **~versetzen** *vr*: **sich ~versetzen in** (+*akk*) put oneself in the position of.

hin- ['hin] *zW*: **~fahren** *unreg vi* go; drive // *vt* take; drive; **H~fahrt** *f* journey there; **~fallen** *vi unreg* fall down; **~fällig** *a* frail, decrepit; (*Regel etc*) unnecessary, otiose; **H~gabe** *f* devotion; **~geben** *vr unreg* +*dat* give oneself up to, devote oneself to; **~gehen** *vi unreg* go; (*Zeit*) pass; **~halten** *vt unreg* hold out; (*warten lassen*) put off, stall.

hinken ['hɪŋkən] *vi* limp; (*Vergleich*) be unconvincing.

hin- ['hin] *zW*: **~legen** *vt* put down // *vr* lie down; **~nehmen** *vt unreg* (*fig*) put up with, take; **H~reise** *f* journey out; **~reißen** *vt unreg* carry away, enrapture; **sich ~reißen lassen, etw zu tun** get carried away and do sth; **~richten** *vt* execute; **H~richtung** *f* execution; **~setzen** *vt* put down // *vr* sit down; **~sichtlich** *präp* +*gen* with regard to; **H~spiel** *nt* (*SPORT*) first leg; **~stellen** *vt* put (down) // *vr* place o.s.

hintanstellen [hɪnt''anʃtɛlən] *vt* (*fig*) ignore.

hinten ['hɪntən] *ad* at the back; behind; **~herum** *ad* round the back; (*fig*) secretly.

hinter ['hɪntər] *präp* +*dat od akk* behind; (*nach*) after; **~ jdm hersein** be after sb; **H~achse** *f* rear axle; **H~bliebene(r)** *mf* surviving relative; **~e(r, s)** *a* rear, back; **~einander** *ad* one after the other; **H~gedanke** *m* ulterior motive; **~gehen** *vt unreg* deceive; **H~grund** *m* background; **H~halt** *m* ambush; **~hältig** *a* underhand, sneaky; **~her** *ad* afterwards; after; **H~hof** *m* backyard; **H~kopf** *m* back of one's head; **~'lassen** *vt unreg* leave; **~'legen** *vt* deposit; **H~list** *f* cunning, trickery; (*Handlung*) trick, dodge; **~listig** *a* cunning, crafty; **H~mann** *m*, *pl* **~männer** person behind; **H~rad** *nt* back wheel; **H~radantrieb** *m* (*AUT*) rear wheel drive; **~rücks** *ad* from behind; **H~tür** *f* back door; (*fig*: *Ausweg*) escape, loophole; **~'ziehen** *vt unreg* (*Steuern*) evade (paying).

hinüber [hɪ'ny:bər] *ad* across, over; **~gehen** *vi unreg* go over *od* across.

hinunter [hɪ'nʊntər] *ad* down; **~bringen** *vt unreg* take down; **~schlucken** *vt* (*lit, fig*) swallow; **~steigen** *vi unreg* descend.

Hinweg ['hɪnve:k] *m* journey out.

hinweg- [hɪn'vɛk] *zW*: **~helfen** *vi unreg*: **jdm über etw** (*akk*) **~helfen** help sb to get over sth; **~'setzen** *vr*: **sich ~setzen über** (+*akk*) disregard.

hin- ['hin] *zW*: **H~weis** *m* -es, -e (*Andeutung*) hint; (*Anweisung*) instruction; (*Verweis*) reference; **~weisen** *vi unreg* (*auf* +*akk*: *anzeigen*) point to; (*sagen*) point out, refer to; **~werfen** *vt unreg* throw down; **~ziehen** *vr unreg* (*fig*) drag on.

hinzu [hɪn'tsu:] *ad* in addition; **~fügen** *vt* add.

Hirn [hɪrn] *nt* -(e)s, -e brain(s); **~gespinst** *nt* -(e)s, -e fantasy; **h~verbrannt** *a* half-baked, crazy.

Hirsch [hɪrʃ] *m* -(e)s, -e stag.

Hirse ['hɪrzə] *f* -, -n millet.

Hirt ['hɪrt] *m* -en, -en herdsman; (*Schaf~, fig*) shepherd.

hissen ['hɪsən] *vt* hoist.

Historiker [hɪs'to:rikər] *m* -s, - historian.

historisch [hɪs'to:rɪʃ] *a* historical.

Hitze ['hɪtsə] *f* - heat; **h~beständig** *a* heat-resistant; **h~frei** *a*: **h~frei haben** have time off from school on account of excessively hot weather; **~welle** *f* heatwave.

hitzig ['hɪtsɪç] *a* hot-tempered; (*Debatte*) heated.

Hitz- *zW*: **~kopf** *m* hothead; **h~köpfig** *a* fiery, hotheaded; **~schlag** *m* heatstroke.

hm [(h)m] *interj* hm.

Hobby ['hɔbi] *nt* hobby.

Hobel ['ho:bəl] *m* -s, - plane; **~bank** *f* carpenter's bench; **h~n** *vti* plane; **~späne** *pl* wood shavings *pl*.

hoch [ho:x] *a* high; **H~** *nt* -s, -s (*Ruf*) cheer; (*MET*) anticyclone; **~achten** *vt* respect; **H~achtung** *f* respect, esteem; **~achtungsvoll** *ad* yours faithfully; **H~amt** *nt* high mass; **~begabt** *a* extremely gifted; **H~betrieb** *m* intense activity; (*COMM*) peak time; **H~burg** *f* stronghold; **H~deutsch** *nt* High German; **~dotiert** *a* highly paid; **H~druck** *m* high pressure; **H~ebene** *f* plateau; **~erfreut** *a* highly delighted; **H~form** *f* top form; **~halten** *vt unreg* hold up; (*fig*) uphold, cherish; **H~haus** *nt* multistorey building; **~heben** *vt unreg* lift (up); **H~konjunktur** *f* boom; **H~land** *nt* highlands *pl*; **~leben** *vi*: **jdn ~leben lassen** give sb three cheers; **H~mut** *m* pride; **~mütig** *a* proud, haughty; **~näsig** *a* stuck-up, snooty; **H~ofen** *m* blast furnace; **~prozentig** *a* (*Alkohol*) strong; **H~rechnung** *f* projected result; **H~saison** *f* high season; **H~schätzung** *f* high esteem; **H~schule** *f* college; university;

H~sommer *m* middle of summer; **H~spannung** *f* high tension; **H~sprung** *m* high jump.

höchst [høːçst] *ad* highly, extremely; **~e(r, s)** *a* highest; *(äußerste)* extreme.

Hochstapler ['hoːxstaːplər] *m* -s, - swindler.

Höchst- *zW:* **h~ens** *ad* at the most; **~geschwindigkeit** *f* maximum speed; **h~persönlich** *ad* in person; **~preis** *m* maximum price; **h~wahrscheinlich** *ad* most probably.

Hoch- *zW:* **~verrat** *m* high treason; **~wasser** *nt* high water; *(Überschwemmung)* floods *pl;* **~würden** *m* Reverend; **~zahl** *f* (MATH) exponent.

Hochzeit ['hɔxtsaɪt] *f* -, -en wedding; **Hochzeitsreise** *f* honeymoon.

hocken ['hɔkən] *vir* squat, crouch.

Hocker *m* -s, - stool.

Höcker ['hœkər] *m* -s, - hump.

Hoden ['hoːdən] *m* -s, - testicle.

Hof [hoːf] *m* -(e)s, *"e (Hinter~)* yard; *(Bauern~)* farm; *(Königs~)* court.

hoffen ['hɔfən] *vi* hope *(auf +akk* for).

hoffentlich ['hɔfəntlıç] *ad* I hope, hopefully.

Hoffnung ['hɔfnʊŋ] *f* -, -en hope.

Hoffnungs- *zW:* **h~los** *a* hopeless; **~losigkeit** *f* hopelessness; **~schimmer** *m* glimmer of hope; **h~voll** *a* hopeful.

höflich ['høːflıç] *a* polite, courteous; **H~keit** *f* courtesy, politeness.

hohe(r, s) ['hoːə(r, s)] *a siehe* **hoch.**

Höhe ['høːə] *f* -, -n height; *(An~)* hill.

Hoheit ['hoːhaɪt] *f* (POL) sovereignty; *(Titel)* Highness.

Hoheitsgebiet *nt* sovereign territory.

Hoheitsgewässer *nt* territorial waters *pl.*

Höhen- ['høːən] *zW:* **~angabe** *f* altitude reading; *(auf Karte)* height marking; **~messer** *m* -s, - altimeter; **~sonne** *f* sun lamp; **~unterschied** *m* difference in altitude.

Höhepunkt *m* climax.

höher *a,ad* higher.

hohl [hoːl] *a* hollow.

Höhle ['høːlə] *f* -, -n cave, hole; *(Mund~)* cavity; *(fig, ZOOL)* den.

Hohlheit *f* hollowness.

Hohlmaß *nt* measure of volume.

Hohn [hoːn] *m* -(e)s scorn.

höhnisch *a* scornful, taunting.

holen ['hoːlən] *vt* get, fetch; *(Atem)* take; **jdn/etw ~ lassen** send for sb/sth.

Holl- ['hɔl] *zW:* **~and** *nt* Holland; **~änder** *m* Dutchman; **~änderin** *f* Dutchwoman; **h~ändisch** *a* Dutch.

Hölle ['hœlə] *f* -, -n hell.

höllisch ['hœlıʃ] *a* hellish, infernal.

holperig ['hɔlpərıç] *a* rough, bumpy.

Holz [hɔlts] *nt* -es, *"er* wood.

hölzern ['hœltsərn] *a (lit, fig)* wooden.

Holz- *zW:* **~fäller** *m* -s, - lumberjack, woodcutter; **h~ig** *a* woody; **~kohle** *f* charcoal; **~scheit** *nt* log; **~schuh** *m* clog; **~weg** *m (fig)* wrong track; **~wolle** *f* fine wood shavings *pl.*

homosexuell [homozɛksuˈɛl] *a* homosexual.

Honig ['hoːnıç] *m* -s, -e honey; **~wabe** *f* honeycomb.

Honorar [honoˈraːr] *nt* -s, -e fee.

honorieren [honoˈriːrən] *vt* remunerate; *(Scheck)* honour.

Hopfen ['hɔpfən] *m* -s, - hops *pl.*

hopsen ['hɔpsən] *vi* hop.

Hör- ['høːr] *zW:* **~apparat** *m* hearing aid; **h~bar** *a* audible.

horch [hɔrç] *interj* listen; **~en** *vi* listen; *(pej)* eavesdrop.

Horde ['hɔrdə] *f* -, -n horde.

hören ['høːrən] *vti* hear; **Musik/Radio ~** listen to music/the radio.

Hörer *m* -s, - hearer; (RAD) listener; (UNIV) student; *(Telefon~)* receiver.

Horizont [horiˈtsɔnt] *m* -(e)s, -e horizon; **h~al** [-ˈtaːl] *a* horizontal.

Hormon [hɔrˈmoːn] *nt* -s, -e hormone.

Hörmuschel *f* (TEL) earpiece.

Horn [hɔrn] *nt* -(e)s, *"er* horn; **~haut** *f* horny skin.

Hornisse [hɔrˈnɪsə] *f* -, -n hornet.

Horoskop [horoˈskoːp] *nt* -s, -e horoscope.

Hörsaal *m* lecture room.

horten ['hɔrtən] *vt* hoard.

Hose ['hoːzə] *f* -, -n trousers *pl,* pants (US) *pl.*

Hosen- *zW:* **~anzug** *m* trouser suit; **~rock** *m* culottes *pl;* **~tasche** *f* (trouser) pocket; **~träger** *m* braces *pl (Brit),* suspenders (US) *pl.*

Hostie ['hɔstiə] *f* (REL) host.

Hotel [hoˈtɛl] *nt* -s, -s hotel.

Hotelier [hoteliˈeː] *m* -s, -s hotelkeeper, hotelier.

Hubraum *m* (AUT) cubic capacity.

hübsch [hypʃ] *a* pretty, nice.

Hubschrauber ['huːbʃraʊbər] *m* -s, - helicopter.

Huf ['huːf] *m* -(e)s, -e hoof; **~eisen** *nt* horseshoe; **~nagel** *m* horseshoe nail.

Hüft- ['hyft] *zW:* **~e** *f* -, -n hip; **~gürtel** *m,* **~halter** *m* -s, - girdle.

Hügel ['hyːgəl] *m* -s, - hill; **h~ig** *a* hilly.

Huhn [huːn] *nt* -(e)s, *"er* hen; (KOCH) chicken.

Hühner- ['hyːnər] *zW:* **~auge** *nt* corn; **~brühe** *f* chicken broth.

Hülle ['hylə] *f* -, -n cover(ing); wrapping; **in ~ und Fülle** galore; **h~n** *vt* cover, wrap *(in +akk* with).

Hülse ['hylzə] *f* -, -n husk, shell; **Hülsenfrucht** *f* pulse.

human [huˈmaːn] *a* humane; **~iˈtär** *a* humanitarian; **H~iˈtät** *f* humanity.
Hummel [ˈhʊməl] *f* -, -n bumblebee.
Hummer [ˈhʊmər] *m* -s, - lobster.
Humor [huˈmoːr] *m* -s, -e humour; **~ haben** have a sense of humour; **~ist** [-ˈrɪst] *m* humorist; **h~istisch** *a*, **h~voll** *a* humorous.
humpeln [ˈhʊmpəln] *vi* hobble.
Humpen [ˈhʊmpən] *m* -s, - tankard.
Hund [hʊnt] *m* -(e)s, -e dog.
Hunde- [ˈhʊndə] *zW*: **~hütte** *f* (dog) kennel; **~kuchen** *m* dog biscuit; **h~müde** *a* (umg) dog-tired.
hundert [ˈhʊndərt] *num* hundred; **H~jahrfeier** *f* centenary; **~prozentig** *a,ad* one hundred per cent.
Hündin [ˈhʏndɪn] *f* bitch.
Hunger [ˈhʊŋər] *m* -s hunger; **~ haben** be hungry; **h~n** *vi* starve; **Hungersnot** *f* famine; **~streik** *m* hunger strike.
hungrig [ˈhʊŋrɪç] *a* hungry.
Hupe [ˈhuːpə] *f* -, -n horn; **h~n** *vi* hoot, sound one's horn.
hüpfen [ˈhʏpfən] *vi* hop, jump.
Hürde [ˈhʏrdə] *f* -, -n hurdle; (für Schafe) pen; **Hürdenlauf** *m* hurdling.
Hure [ˈhuːrə] *f* -, -n whore.
hurra [huˈra:] *inter* hooray.
hurtig [ˈhʊrtɪç] *a,ad* brisk(ly), quick-(ly).
huschen [ˈhʊʃən] *vi* flit, scurry.
Husten [ˈhuːstən] *m* -s cough; **h~** *vi* cough; **~anfall** *m* coughing fit; **~bonbon** *m od nt* cough drop; **~saft** *m* cough mixture.
Hut [huːt] *m* -(e)s, -e hat // *f* - care; **auf der ~ sein** be on one's guard.
hüten [ˈhyːtən] *vt* guard //. *vr* watch out; **sich ~, zu** take care not to; **sich ~ vor** beware of.
Hütte [ˈhʏtə] *f* -, -n hut, cottage; (Eisen~) forge.
Hyäne [hyˈɛːnə] *f* -, -n hyena.
Hyazinthe [hyaˈtsɪntə] *f* -, -n hyacinth.
Hydrant [hyˈdrant] *m* hydrant.
hydraulisch [hyˈdraʊlɪf] *a* hydraulic.
Hygiene [hygiˈeːnə] *f* - hygiene.
hygienisch [hygiˈeːnɪʃ] *a* hygienic.
Hymne [ˈhʏmnə] *f* -, -n hymn, anthem.
hyper- [ˈhypər] *präf* hyper-.
Hypno- [hʏpˈnoː] *zW*: **~se** *f* -, -n hypnosis; **h~tisch** *a* hypnotic; **~tiseur** [-tiˈzøːr] hypnotist; **h~tiˈsieren** *vt* hypnotize.
Hypothek [hypoˈteːk] *f* -, -en mortgage.
Hypothese [hypoˈteːzə] *f* -, -n hypothesis.
hypothetisch [hypoˈteːtɪʃ] *a* hypothetical.
Hysterie [hysteˈriː] *f* hysteria.
hysterisch [hʏsˈteːrɪʃ] *a* hysterical.

I

I, i [iː] *nt* I, i.
i.A. *abk* (= im Auftrag) for; (in Briefen auch) pp.
ich [ɪç] *pron* I; **~ bin's!** it's me!; **I~** *nt* -(s), -(s) self; (PSYCH) ego.
Ideal [ideˈaːl] *nt* -s, -e ideal; **i~** *a* ideal; **~ist** [-ˈlɪst] *m* idealist; **i~istisch** [-ˈlɪstɪʃ] *a* idealistic.
Idee [iˈdeː] *f* -, -n [iˈdeːən] idea.
identifizieren [iˈdɛntifiˈtsiːrən] *vt* identify.
identisch [iˈdɛntɪʃ] *a* identical.
Identität [idɛntiˈtɛːt] *f* identity.
Ideo- [ideo] *zW*: **~loge** [-ˈloːgə] *m* -n, -n ideologist; **~logie** [-loˈgiː] *f* ideology; **i~logisch** [-ˈloːgɪʃ] *a* ideological.
Idiot [idiˈoːt] *m* -en, -en idiot; **i~isch** *a* idiotic.
idyllisch [iˈdʏlɪʃ] *a* idyllic.
Igel [ˈiːgəl] *m* -s, - hedgehog.
ignorieren [ɪgnoˈriːrən] *vt* ignore.
ihm [iːm] *pron dat von* **er, es** (to) him, (to) it.
ihn [iːn] *pron akk von* **er** him; it; **~en** *pron dat von* **sie** *pl* (to) them; **I~en** *pron dat von* **Sie** (to) you.
ihr [iːr] ◆*pron* **1** *nom pl* you; **~ seid es** it's you
2 *dat von* **sie** *sing* to her; **gib es ~** give it to her; **er steht neben ~** he is standing beside her
◆*poss pron* **1** *sing* her; (bei Tieren, Dingen) its; **~ Mann** her husband
2 *pl* their; **die Bäume und ~e Blätter** the trees and their leaves
ihr(e) [iːr(ə)] *poss pron* your; **~e(r, s)** *poss pron sing* hers; // *pl* theirs; **I~e(r, s)** *poss pron* yours; **~er** *pron gen von* **sie** *sing/pl* of her/them; **I~er** *pron gen von* **Sie** of you; **~erseits** *ad* for her/their part; **~esgleichen** *pron* people like her/them; (von Dingen) others like it; **~etwegen, ~etwillen** *ad* (für sie) for her/its/their sake; (wegen ihr) on her/its/their account; **~ige** *pron*: **der/die/das ~ige** hers; its; theirs.
illegal [ˈɪlegaːl] *a* illegal.
Illusion [ɪluziˈoːn] *f* illusion.
illusorisch [ɪluˈzoːrɪʃ] *a* illusory.
illustrieren [ɪlusˈtriːrən] *vt* illustrate.
Illustrierte *f* -n, -n picture magazine.
Iltis [ˈɪltɪs] *m* -ses, -se polecat.
im [ɪm] = **in dem**.
Imbiß [ˈɪmbɪs] *m* -sses, -sse snack; **~halle** *f*, **~stube** *f* snack bar.
imitieren [ɪmiˈtiːrən] *vt* imitate.
immatrikulieren [ɪmatrikuˈliːrən] *vir* register.
immer [ˈɪmər] *ad* always; **~ wieder** again and again; **~ noch** still; **~ noch**

nicht still not; **für** ~ forever; ~ **wenn ich ...** everytime I ...; ~ **schöner/trauriger** more and more beautiful/sadder and sadder; **was/wer (auch)** ~ whatever/whoever; **~hin** ad all the same; **~zu** ad all the time.

Immobilien [ımo'bi:liən] pl real estate.

immun [ı'mu:n] a immune; **I~ität** [-i'tɛ:t] f immunity.

Imperfekt ['ımperfɛkt] nt -s, -e imperfect (tense).

Impf- ['ımpf] zW: **i~en** vt vaccinate; **~stoff** m vaccine, serum; **~ung** f vaccination; **~zwang** m compulsory vaccination.

imponieren [ımpo'ni:rən] vi impress (jdm sb).

Import [ım'pɔrt] m -(e)s, -e import; **i~ieren** [-'ti:rən] vt import.

impotent ['ımpotɛnt] a impotent.

imprägnieren [ımprɛ'gni:rən] vt (water)proof.

improvisieren [ımprovi'zi:rən] vti improvize.

Impuls [ım'pʊls] m -es, -e impulse; **i~iv** [-'zi:f] a impulsive.

imstande [ım'ʃtandə] a: ~ **sein** be in a position; (fähig) be able.

in [ın] ◆präp +akk **1** (räumlich: wohin?) in, into; ~ **die Stadt** into town; ~ **die Schule gehen** go to school
2 (zeitlich): **bis ~s 20. Jahrhundert** into od up to the 20th century
◆präp +dat **1** (räumlich: wo) in; ~ **der Stadt** in town; ~ **der Schule sein** be at school
2 (zeitlich: wann): ~ **diesem Jahr** this year; (~ jenem Jahr) in that year; **heute** ~ **zwei Wochen** two weeks today.

Inanspruchnahme [ın''anʃpruxna:mə] f -, -n demands pl (gen on).

Inbegriff ['ınbəgrıf] m embodiment, personification; **i~en** ad included.

indem [ın'de:m] kj while; ~ **man etw macht** (dadurch) by doing sth.

Inder(in f) ['ındər(ın)] m Indian.

Indianer(in f) [ındi'a:nər(ın)] m -s, - Red Indian.

indianisch a Red Indian.

Indien ['ındiən] nt India.

indirekt ['ındırɛkt] a indirect.

indisch ['ındıʃ] a Indian.

indiskret ['ındıskre:t] a indiscreet.

indiskutabel ['ındısku'ta:bəl] a out of the question.

Individu- [ındividu] zW: **~alist** [-a'lıst] m individualist; **~alität** [-ali'tɛ:t] f individuality; **i~ell** [-'ɛl] a individual; **~um** [ındi'vi:duʊm] nt -s, -en individual.

Indiz [ın'di:ts] nt -es, -ien sign (für of); (JUR) clue.

Indonesien [ındo'ne:ziən] nt Indonesia.

industrialisieren [ındustriali'zi:rən] vt industrialize.

Industrie [ındʊs'tri:] f industry; in zW industrial; **~gebiet** nt industrial area; **~gelände** nt industrial od trading estate; **industriell** [ındustri'ɛl] a industrial; **~zweig** m branch of industry.

ineinander [ın'aı'nandər] ad in(to) one another od each other.

Infarkt [ın'farkt] m -(e)s, -e coronary (thrombosis).

Infektion [ınfɛktsi'o:n] f infection; **Infektionskrankheit** f infectious disease.

Infinitiv ['ınfiniti:f] m -s, -e infinitive.

infizieren [ınfi'tsi:rən] vt infect // vr be infected (bei by).

Inflation [ınflatsi'o:n] f inflation.

inflationär [ınflatsio'nɛ:r] a inflationary.

infolge [ın'fɔlgə] präp +gen as a result of, owing to; **~dessen** [-'dɛsən] ad consequently.

Informatik [ınfor'ma:tık] f information studies pl.

Information [ınfɔrmatsi'o:n] f information no pl.

informieren [ınfor'mi:rən] vt inform // vr find out (über +akk about).

Infusion [ınfuzi'o:n] f infusion.

Ingenieur [ınʒeni'ø:r] m engineer; **~schule** f school of engineering.

Ingwer ['ıŋvər] m -s ginger.

Inh. abk (= Inhaber) prop.; (= Inhalt) contents.

Inhaber(in f) ['ınha:bər(ın)] m -s, - owner; (Haus~) occupier; (Lizenz~) licensee, holder; (FIN) bearer.

inhalieren [ınha'li:rən] vti inhale.

Inhalt ['ınhalt] m -(e)s, -e contents pl; (eines Buchs etc) content; (MATH) area; volume; **i~lich** a as regards content.

Inhalts- zW: **~angabe** f summary; **i~los** a empty; **~sverzeichnis** nt table of contents.

inhuman ['ınhuma:n] a inhuman.

Initiative [ınitsia'ti:və] f initiative.

Injektion [ınjɛktsi'o:n] f injection.

inklusive [ınklu'zi:və] präp, ad inclusive (gen of).

inkognito [ın'kɔgnito] ad incognito.

Inkrafttreten [ın'krafttre:tən] nt -s coming into force.

Inland ['ınlant] nt -(e)s (GEOG) inland; (POL, COMM) home (country).

inmitten [ın'mıtən] präp +gen in the middle of; ~ **von** amongst.

innehaben ['ınəha:bən] vt unreg hold.

innen ['ınən] ad inside; **I~architekt** m interior designer; **I~einrichtung** f (interior) furnishings pl; **I~minister** m minister of the interior, Home Secretary (*Brit*); l~politik *f* domestic policy; l~stadt *f* town/city centre.

inner- ['ɪnər] *zW*: ~e(r, s) *a* inner; (*im Körper, inländisch*) internal; l~e(s) *nt* inside; (*Mitte*) centre; (*fig*) heart; Innereien [-'raɪən] *pl* innards *pl*; ~halb *ad, präp* +*gen* within; (*räumlich*) inside; ~lich *a* internal; (*geistig*) inward; l~ste(s) *nt* heart; ~ste(r, s) *a* innermost.

inoffiziell ['ɪn'ɔfitsiel] *a* unofficial.

ins [ɪns] = in das.

Insasse ['ɪnzasə] *m* -n, -n (*Anstalt*) inmate; (*AUT*) passenger.

insbesondere [ɪnsbə'zɔndərə] *ad* (e)specially.

Inschrift ['ɪnʃrɪft] *f* inscription.

Insekt [ɪn'zɛkt] *nt* -(e)s, -en insect.

Insel ['ɪnzəl] *f* -, -n island.

Inser- *zW*: ~at [ɪnzeˈraːt] *nt* -(e)s, -e advertisement; ~ent [ɪnzeˈrɛnt] *m* advertiser; i~ieren [ɪnzeˈriːrən] *vti* advertise.

insgeheim [ɪnsgəˈhaɪm] *ad* secretly.

insgesamt [ɪnsgəˈzamt] *ad* altogether, all in all.

insofern ['ɪnzoˈfɛrn], insoweit ['ɪnzoˈvaɪt] *ad* in this respect; ~ als in so far as // *kj* if; (*deshalb*) (and) so.

Installateur [ɪnstalaˈtøːr] *m* electrician; plumber.

Instand- [ɪn'ʃtant] *zW*: ~haltung *f* maintenance; ~setzung *f* overhaul; (*eines Gebäudes*) restoration.

Instanz [ɪn'ʃtants] *f* authority; (*JUR*) court; ~enweg *m* official channels *pl*.

Instinkt [ɪn'ʃtɪŋkt] *m* -(e)s, -e instinct; i~iv [-'tiːf] *a* instinctive.

Institut [ɪnstiˈtuːt] *nt* -(e)s, -e institute.

Instrument [ɪnstruˈmɛnt] *nt* instrument.

Intell- [ɪntɛl] *zW*: i~ektuell [-ɛktuˈɛl] *a* intellectual; i~igent [-iˈgɛnt] *a* intelligent; ~igenz [-iˈgɛnts] *f* intelligence; (*Leute*) intelligentsia *pl*.

Intendant [ɪntɛnˈdant] *m* director.

intensiv [ɪntɛnˈziːf] *a* intensive.

Interess- *zW*: i~ant [ɪntɛreˈsant] *a* interesting; i~anterweise *ad* interestingly enough; ~e [ɪnteˈresə] *nt* -s, -n interest; ~e haben be interested (*an* +*dat* in); ~ent [ɪntɛreˈsɛnt] *m* interested party; i~ieren [ɪntɛreˈsiːrən] *vt* interest // *vr* be interested (*für* in).

Inter- [ɪnter] *zW*: ~nat [-'naːt] *nt* -(e)s, -e boarding school; i~national [-natsioˈnaːl] *a* international; i~pretieren [-preˈtiːrən] *vt* interpret; ~vall [-'val] *nt* -s, -e interval; ~view ['-vjuː] *nt* -s, -s interview; i~viewen [-'vjuːən] *vt* interview.

intim [ɪn'tiːm] *a* intimate; l~ität [ɪntimiˈtɛːt] *f* intimacy.

intolerant ['ɪntolerant] *a* intolerant.

intransitiv ['ɪntranzitiːf] *a* (*GRAM*) intransitive.

Intrige [ɪn'triːgə] *f* -, -n intrigue, plot.

Invasion [ɪnvaziˈoːn] *f* invasion.

Inventar [ɪnvɛnˈtaːr] *nt* -s, -e inventory.

Inventur [ɪnvɛnˈtuːr] *f* stocktaking; ~ machen stocktake.

investieren [ɪnvɛstiˈrən] *vt* invest.

Investition [ɪnvɛstitsiˈoːn] *f* investment.

Investmentgesellschaft [ɪn'vɛstmɛntgəzɛlʃaft] *f* unit trust.

inwiefern [ɪnviˈfɛrn], inwieweit [ɪnviˈvaɪt] *ad* how far, to what extent.

inzwischen [ɪn'tsvɪʃən] *ad* meanwhile.

Irak [i'raːk] *m* -s: der ~ Iraq; i~sch *a* Iraqi.

Iran [i'raːn] *n* -s: der ~ Iran; i~isch *a* Iranian.

irdisch ['ɪrdɪʃ] *a* earthly.

Ire ['iːrə] *m* -n, -n Irishman.

irgend ['ɪrgənt] *ad* at all; wann/was/wer ~ whenever/whatever/whoever; ~ jemand/etwas somebody/something; anybody/anything; ~ein(e,s) *a* some, any; ~einmal *ad* sometime or other; (*fragend*) ever; ~wann *ad* sometime; ~wer *ad* (*umg*) somebody; anybody; ~wie *ad* somehow; ~wo *ad* somewhere; anywhere; ~wohin *ad* somewhere (or other).

Irin ['iːrɪn] *f* Irishwoman.

Irland ['ɪrlant] *nt* -s Ireland.

Ironie [iroˈniː] *f* irony.

ironisch [i'roːnɪʃ] *a* ironic(al).

irre ['ɪrə] *a* crazy, mad; l~(r) *mf* lunatic; ~führen *vt* mislead; ~machen *vt* confuse; ~n *vir* be mistaken; (*umher~*) wander, stray; Irrenanstalt *f* lunatic asylum.

irrig ['ɪrɪç] *a* incorrect, wrong.

Irr- *zW*: i~sinnig *a* mad, crazy; (*umg*) terrific; ~tum *m* -s, -tümer mistake, error; i~tümlich *a* mistaken.

Island ['iːslant] *nt* -s Iceland.

Isolation [izolatsiˈoːn] *f* isolation; (*ELEK*) insulation.

Isolator [izoˈlaːtor] *m* insulator.

Isolier- [izoˈliːr] *zW*: ~band *nt* insulating tape; i~en *vt* isolate; (*ELEK*) insulate; ~station *f* (*MED*) isolation ward; ~ung *f* isolation; (*ELEK*) insulation.

Israel ['ɪsraeːl] *nt* -s Israel; ~i [-'eːli] *m* -s, -s Israeli; ~isch *a* Israeli.

ißt *v siehe* essen.

ist *v siehe* sein.

Italien [i'taːliən] *nt* -s Italy; ~er(in *f*) [-liˈeːnər(ɪn)] *m* -s Italian; i~isch *a* Italian.

i.V. *abk von* in Vertretung.

J

J, j [jɔt] *nt* J, j.
ja [jaː] *adv* **1** yes; **haben Sie das gesehen?** — ~ **did you see it?** — yes(, I did); **ich glaube** ~ (yes) I think so
2 (*fragend*) really?; **ich habe gekündigt** — ~? I've quit — have you?; **du kommst,** ~? you're coming, aren't you?
3 sei ~ **vorsichtig** do be careful; **Sie wissen** ~, **daß** ... as you know, ...; **tu das** ~ **nicht!** don't do that!; **ich habe es** ~ **gewußt** I just knew it; ~, **also,** ... well you see ...
Jacht [jaxt] *f* -, **-en** yacht.
Jacke ['jakə] *f* -, **-n** jacket; (*Woll*~) cardigan.
Jackett [ʒa'kɛt] *nt* **-s, -e** *od* **-e** jacket.
Jagd [jaːkt] *f* -, **-en** hunt; (*Jagen*) hunting; ~**beute** *f* kill; ~**flugzeug** *nt* fighter; ~**gewehr** *nt* sporting gun.
jagen ['jaːgən] *vi* hunt; (*eilen*) race // *vt* hunt; (*weg*~) drive (off); (*verfolgen*) chase.
Jäger ['jɛːgər] *m* **-s, -** hunter.
jäh [jɛː] *a* sudden, abrupt; (*steil*) steep, precipitous.
Jahr [jaːr] *nt* **-(e)s, -e** year; **j**~**elang** *ad* for years.
Jahres- *zW:* ~**abonnement** *nt* annual subscription; ~**abschluß** *m* end of the year; (*COMM*) annual statement of account; ~**bericht** *m* annual report; ~**hauptversammlung** *f* annual general meeting, AGM; ~**wechsel** *m* turn of the year; ~**zahl** *f* date, year; ~**zeit** *f* season.
Jahr- *zW:* ~**gang** *m* age group; (*von Wein*) vintage; ~**hundert** *nt* **-s, -e** century; ~'**hundertfeier** *f* centenary.
jährlich ['jɛːrlıç] *a,ad* yearly.
Jahrmarkt *m* fair.
Jahr'zehnt *nt* decade.
Jähzorn ['jɛːtsɔrn] *m* sudden anger; hot temper; **j**~**ig** *a* hot-tempered.
Jalousie [ʒalu'ziː] *f* venetian blind.
Jammer ['jamər] *m* **-s** misery; **es ist ein** ~, **daß** ... it is a crying shame that ...
jämmerlich ['jɛmərlıç] *a* wretched, pathetic.
jammern *vi* wail // *vt* *unpers:* **es jammert jdn** it makes sb feel sorry.
jammerschade *a:* **es ist** ~ it is a crying shame.
Januar ['januaːr] *m* **-s, -e** January.
Japan ['jaːpan] *nt* **-s** Japan; ~**er(in** *f*) [-'paːnər(ın)] *m* **-s** Japanese; **j**~**isch** *a* Japanese.
Jargon [ʒar'gõː] *m* **-s, -s** jargon.
jäten ['jɛːtən] *vt:* **Unkraut** ~ weed.

jauchzen ['jauxtsən] *vi* rejoice, shout (with joy).
jaulen ['jaulən] *vi* howl.
jawohl [ja'voːl] *ad* yes (of course).
Jawort ['jaːvɔrt] *nt* consent.
Jazz [dʒɛs] *m* - Jazz.
je [jeː] ◆*ad* **1** (*jemals*) ever; **hast du so was** ~ **gesehen?** did you ever see anything like it?
2 (*jeweils*) every, each; **sie zahlten** ~ **3 Mark** they paid 3 marks each
◆*kj* **1:** ~ **nach** depending on; ~ **nachdem** it depends; ~ **nachdem, ob** ... depending on whether ...
2: ~ **eher, desto** *od* **um so besser** the sooner the better.
Jeans [dʒiːnz] *pl* jeans.
jede(r, s) ['jeːdə(r, s)] *a* every, each // *pron* everybody; (~ *einzelne*) each; **ohne** ~ **x** without any x.
jedenfalls *ad* in any case.
jedermann *pron* everyone.
jederzeit *ad* at any time.
jedesmal *ad* every time, each time.
jedoch [je'dɔx] *ad* however.
jemals ['jeːmaːls] *ad* ever.
jemand ['jeːmant] *pron* somebody; anybody.
Jemen ['jeːmən] *m* **-s:** **der** ~ the Yemen.
jene(r, s) ['jeːnə(r, s)] *a* that // *pron* that one.
jenseits ['jeːnzaıts] *ad* on the other side // *präp* +*gen* on the other side of, beyond; **das J**~ the hereafter, the beyond.
jetzig ['jɛtsıç] *a* present.
jetzt [jɛtst] *ad* now.
je- *zW:* ~**weilig** *a* respective; ~**weils** *ad:* ~**weils zwei zusammen** two at a time; **zu** ~**weils 5 DM** at 5 marks each; ~**weils das erste** the first each time.
Jh. *abk von* **Jahrhundert.**
Jockei ['dʒɔke] *m* **-s, -s** jockey.
Jod [joːt] *nt* **-(e)s** iodine.
jodeln ['joːdəln] *vi* yodel.
joggen ['dʒɔgən] *vi* jog.
Joghurt ['joːgurt] *m* *od* *nt* **-s, -s** yogurt.
Johannisbeere [jo'hanısbeːrə] *f* redcurrant; **schwarze** ~ blackcurrant.
johlen ['joːlən] *vi* yell.
Jolle ['jɔlə] *f* -, **-n** dinghy.
jonglieren [ʒõ'gliːrən] *vi* juggle.
Jordanien [jɔr'daːniən] *nt* **-s** Jordan.
Journal- *zW:* ~**ismus** [-'lısmus] *m* journalism; ~**ist(in** *f*) [-'lıst] *m* journalist; **j**~**istisch** *a* journalistic.
Jubel ['juːbəl] *m* **-s** rejoicing; **j**~**n** *vi* rejoice.
Jubiläum [jubi'lɛːum] *nt* **-s, Jubiläen** anniversary, jubilee.
jucken ['jukən] *vi* itch // *vt* **es juckt**

mich am Arm my arm is itching; das juckt mich that's itchy.

Juckreiz ['jokraɪts] *m* itch.

Jude ['juːdə] *m* -n, -n Jew.

Judentum *nt* - Judaism; Jewry.

Judenverfolgung *f* persecution of the Jews.

Jüd- ['jyːd] *zW*: ~in *f* Jewess; **j~isch** *a* Jewish.

Judo ['juːdo] *nt* -(s) judo.

Jugend ['juːgənt] *f* - youth; ~**club** *m* youth club; ~**herberge** *f* youth hostel; ~**kriminalität** *f* juvenile crime; **j~lich** *a* youthful; ~**liche(r)** *mf* teenager, young person.

Jugoslaw- [jugɔ'slaːv] *zW*: ~e *m*, ~in *f* Yugoslavian; ~**ien** *nt* Yugoslavia; **j~isch** *a* Yugoslavian.

Juli ['juːli] *m* -(s), -s July.

jun. *abk* (= *junior*) jr.

jung [joŋ] *a* young; **J~e** *m* -n, -n boy, lad; **J~e(s)** *nt* young animal; (*pl*) young *pl*.

Jünger ['jyŋər] *m* -s, - disciple; **j~** *a* younger.

Jungfer ['joŋfər] *f* -, -n: alte ~ old maid.

Jungfernfahrt *f* maiden voyage.

Jung- *zW*: ~**frau** *f* virgin; (*ASTROL*) Virgo; ~**geselle** *m* bachelor; ~**gesellin** *f* unmarried woman.

jüngst ['jyŋst] *ad* lately, recently; ~**e(r, s)** *a* youngest; (*neueste*) latest.

Juni ['juːni] *m* -(s), -s June.

Junior ['juːniɔr] *m* -s, -en [-'oːrən] junior.

Jurist [ju'rɪst] *m* jurist, lawyer; **j~isch** *a* legal.

Justiz [jos'tiːts] *f* - justice; ~**beamte(r)** *m* judicial officer; ~**irrtum** *m* miscarriage of justice.

Juwel [ju'veːl] *nt od m* -s, -en jewel.

Juwelier [juve'liːr] *m* -s, -e jeweller; ~**geschäft** *nt* jeweller's (shop).

Jux [joks] *m* -es, -e joke, lark.

K

K, k [kaː] *nt* K, k.

Kabarett [kaba'rɛt] *nt* -s, -e *od* -s cabaret; ~**ist** [-'tɪst] *m* cabaret artiste.

Kabel ['kaːbəl] *nt* -s, - (*ELEK*) wire; (*stark*) cable; ~**fernsehen** *nt* cable television.

Kabeljau ['kaːbəljau] *m* -s, -e *od* -s cod.

kabeln *vti* cable.

Kabine [ka'biːnə] *f* cabin; (*Zelle*) cubicle.

Kabinett [kabi'nɛt] *nt* -s, -e (*POL*) cabinet.

Kachel ['kaxəl] *f* -, -n tile; **k~n** *vt* tile; ~**ofen** *m* tiled stove.

Käfer ['kɛːfər] *m* -s, - beetle.

Kaffee ['kafe] *m* -s, -s coffee; ~**kanne** *f* coffeepot; ~**klatsch** *m*, ~**kränzchen** *nt* hen party; coffee morning; ~**löffel** *m* coffee spoon; ~**satz** *m* coffee grounds *pl*.

Käfig ['kɛːfɪç] *m* -s, -e cage.

kahl [kaːl] *a* bald; ~**geschoren** *a* shaven, shorn; **K~heit** *f* baldness; ~**köpfig** *a* bald-headed.

Kahn [kaːn] *m* -s, -e boat, barge.

Kai [kaɪ] *m* -s, -e *od* -s quay.

Kaiser ['kaɪzər] *m* -s, - emperor; ~**in** *f* empress; **k~lich** *a* imperial; ~**reich** *nt* empire; ~**schnitt** *m* (*MED*) Caesarian (section).

Kakao [ka'kao] *m* -s, -s cocoa.

Kaktee [kak'teː(ə)] *f* -, -n, **Kaktus** ['kaktos] *m* -, -se cactus.

Kalb [kalp] *nt* -(e)s, -er calf; **k~en** ['kalbən] *vi* calve; ~**fleisch** *nt* veal; **Kalbsleder** *nt* calf(skin).

Kalender [ka'lɛndər] *m* -s, - calendar; (*Taschen~*) diary.

Kaliber [ka'liːbər] *nt* -s, - (*lit, fig*) calibre.

Kalk [kalk] *m* -(e)s, -e lime; (*BIOL*) calcium; ~**stein** *m* limestone.

kalkulieren [kalku'liːrən] *vt* calculate.

Kalorie [kalo'riː] *f* calorie.

kalt [kalt] *a* cold; **mir ist (es)** ~ I am cold; ~**bleiben** *vi unreg* be unmoved; ~**blütig** *a* cold-blooded; (*ruhig*) cool.

Kälte ['kɛltə] *f* - cold; coldness; ~**grad** *m* degree of frost *od* below zero; ~**welle** *f* cold spell.

kalt- *zW*: ~**herzig** *a* cold-hearted; ~**schnäuzig** *a* cold, unfeeling; ~**stellen** *vt* chill; (*fig*) leave out in the cold.

kam *etc v siehe* **kommen**

Kamel [ka'meːl] *nt* -(e)s, -e camel.

Kamera ['kamera] *f* -, -s camera.

Kamerad [kamə'raːt] *m* -en, -en comrade, friend; ~**schaft** *f* comradeship; **k~schaftlich** *a* comradely.

Kamille [ka'mɪlə] *f* -, -n camomile; **Kamillentee** *m* camomile tea.

Kamin [ka'miːn] *m* -s, -e (*außen*) chimney; (*innen*) fireside, fireplace; ~**feger**, ~**kehrer** *m* -s, - chimney sweep.

Kamm [kam] *m* -(e)s, -e comb; (*Berg~*) ridge; (*Hahnen~*) crest.

kämmen ['kɛmən] *vt* comb // *vr* comb one's hair.

Kammer ['kamər] *f* -, -n chamber; small bedroom; ~**diener** *m* valet.

Kampagne [kam'panjə] *f* -, -n campaign.

Kampf [kampf] *m* -(e)s, -e fight, battle; (*Wettbewerb*) contest; (*fig: Anstrengung*) struggle; **k~bereit** *a* ready for action.

kämpfen ['kɛmpfən] *vi* fight.

Kämpfer *m* -s, - fighter, combatant.

Kampf- *zW:* **~handlung** *f* action; **k~los** *a* without a fight; **~richter** *m* (*SPORT*) referee; (*Tennis*) umpire.

Kanada ['kanada] *nt* **-s** Canada.

Kanadier(in *f*) [ka'na:diər(in)] *m* **-s**, - Canadian.

kanadisch [ka'na:dıʃ] *a* Canadian.

Kanal [ka'na:l] *m* **-s, Kanäle** (*Fluß*) canal; (*Rinne, Ärmel~*) channel; (*für Abfluß*) drain; **~inseln** *pl* Channel Islands; **~isation** [-izatsi'o:n] *f* sewage system.

Kanarienvogel [ka'na:riənfo:gəl] *m* canary.

kanarisch [ka'na:rıʃ] *a*: K~e Inseln Canary Islands, Canaries.

Kandi- [kandi] *zW:* **~dat** [-'da:t] *m* **-en, -en** candidate; **~datur** [-da'tu:r] *f* candidature, candidacy; **k~dieren** [-'di:rən] *vi* stand, run.

Kandis(zucker) ['kandıs(tsʊkər)] *m* - candy.

Känguruh ['kɛnguru] *nt* **-s, -s** kangaroo.

Kaninchen [ka'ni:nçən] *nt* rabbit.

Kanister [ka'nıstər] *m* **-s**, - can, canister.

Kännchen ['kɛnçən] *nt* pot.

Kanne ['kanə] *f* **-, -n** (*Krug*) jug; (*Kaffee~*) pot; (*Milch~*) churn; (*Gieß~*) can.

kannst *etc v siehe* **können**.

Kanon ['ka:nɔn] *m* **-s, -s** canon.

Kanone [ka'no:nə] *f* **-, -n** gun; (*HIST*) cannon; (*fig: Mensch*) ace.

Kantate [kan'ta:tə] *f* **-, -n** cantata.

Kante ['kantə] *f* **-, -n** edge.

Kantine [kan'ti:nə] *f* canteen.

Kanu ['ka:nu] *nt* **-s, -s** canoe.

Kanzel ['kantsəl] *f* **-, -n** pulpit.

Kanzler ['kantslər] *m* **-s**, - chancellor.

Kap [kap] *nt* **-s, -s** cape; ~ der Guten Hoffnung Cape of Good Hope.

Kapazität [kapatsi'tɛ:t] *f* capacity; (*Fachmann*) authority.

Kapelle [ka'pɛlə] *f* (*Gebäude*) chapel; (*MUS*) band.

kapieren [ka'pi:rən] *vti* (*umg*) understand.

Kapital [kapi'ta:l] *nt* **-s, -e** *od* **-ien** capital; **~anlage** *f* investment; **~ismus** [-'lısmʊs] *m* capitalism; **~ist** [-'lıst] *m* capitalist; **k~istisch** *a* capitalist.

Kapitän [kapi'tɛ:n] *m* **-s, -e** captain.

Kapitel [ka'pıtəl] *nt* **-s**, - chapter.

Kapitulation [kapitulatsi'o:n] *f* capitulation.

kapitulieren [kapitu'li:rən] *vi* capitulate.

Kaplan [ka'pla:n] *m* **-s, Kapläne** chaplain.

Kappe ['kapə] *f* **-, -n** cap; (*Kapuze*) hood; **k~n** *vt* cut.

Kapsel ['kapsəl] *f* **-, -n** capsule.

Kapstadt ['kapʃtat] *nt* **-s** Cape Town.

kaputt [ka'pʊt] *a* (*umg*) kaput, broken; (*Person*) exhausted, finished; am Auto ist etwas ~ there's something wrong with the car; **~gehen** *vi* *unreg* break; (*Schuhe*) fall apart; (*Firma*) go bust; (*Stoff*) wear out; (*sterben*) cop it; **~machen** *vt* break; (*Mensch*) exhaust, wear out.

Kapuze [ka'pu:tsə] *f* **-, -n** hood.

Karaffe [ka'rafə] *f* **-, -n** carafe; (*geschliffen*) decanter.

Karamel [kara'mɛl] *m* **-s** caramel; **~bonbon** *m* *od* *nt* toffee.

Karat [ka'ra:t] *nt* **-(e)s, -e** carat.

Karate [ka'ra:tə] *nt* **-s** karate.

Karawane [kara'va:nə] *f* **-, -n** caravan.

Kardinal [kardi'na:l] *m* **-s, Kardinäle** cardinal; **~zahl** *f* cardinal number.

Karfreitag [ka:r'fraıta:k] *m* Good Friday.

kärglich ['kɛrklıç] *a* poor, scanty.

karibisch [ka'ri:bıʃ] *a*: K~e Inseln Caribbean Islands.

kariert [ka'ri:rt] *a* (*Stoff*) checked; (*Papier*) squared.

Karies ['ka:ries] *f* - caries.

Karikatur [karika'tu:r] *f* caricature; **~ist** [-'rıst] *m* cartoonist.

Karneval ['karnəval] *m* **-s, -e** *od* **-s** carnival.

Karo ['ka:ro] *nt* **-s, -s** square; (*KARTEN*) diamonds; **~-As** *nt* ace of diamonds.

Karosserie [karosə'ri:] *f* (*AUT*) body(work).

Karotte [ka'rɔtə] *f* **-, -n** carrot.

Karpaten [kar'pa:tən] *pl* Carpathians.

Karpfen ['karpfən] *m* **-s**, - carp.

Karre ['karə] *f* **-, -n, ~n** *m* **-s**, - cart, barrow.

Karriere [kari'ɛ:rə] *f* **-, -n** career; ~ machen get on, get to the top; **~macher** *m* **-s**, - careerist.

Karte ['kartə] *f* **-, -n** card; (*Land~*) map; (*Speise~*) menu; (*Eintritts~, Fahr~*) ticket; alles auf eine ~ setzen put all one's eggs in one basket.

Kartei [kar'taı] *f* card index; **~karte** *f* index card.

Kartell [kar'tɛl] *nt* **-s, -e** cartel.

Kartenspiel *nt* card game; pack of cards.

Kartoffel [kar'tɔfəl] *f* **-, -n** potato; **~brei** *m*, **~mus** *nt*, **~püree** *nt* mashed potatoes *pl*; **~salat** *m* potato salad.

Karton [kar'tõ:] *m* **-s, -s** cardboard; (*Schachtel*) cardboard box; **k~iert** [karto'ni:rt] *a* hardback.

Karussell [karu'sɛl] *nt* **-s, -s** roundabout (*Brit*), merry-go-round.

Karwoche ['ka:rvɔxə] *f* Holy Week.

Käse ['kɛ:zə] *m* **-s**, - cheese; **~blatt** *nt* (*umg*) (local) rag; **~kuchen** *m* cheesecake.

Kaserne [ka'zɛrnə] f -, -n barracks pl; **Kasernenhof** m parade ground.

Kasino [ka'zi:no] nt -s, -s club; (MIL) officers' mess; (Spiel~) casino.

kaspisch ['kaspɪʃ] a: K~es Meer Caspian Sea.

Kasse ['kasə] f -, -n (Geldkasten) cashbox; (in Geschäft) till, cash register; (Kino~, Theater~ etc) box office; ticket office; (Kranken~) health insurance; (Spar~) savings bank; ~ machen count the money; getrennte ~ führen pay separately; an der ~ (in Geschäft) at the desk; gut bei ~ sein be in the money.

Kassen- zW: ~arzt m panel doctor (Brit); ~bestand m cash balance; ~patient m panel patient (Brit); ~prüfung f audit; ~sturz m: ~sturz machen check one's money; ~zettel m receipt.

Kassette [ka'sɛtə] f small box; (Tonband, PHOT) cassette; (Bücher~) case.

Kassettengerät nt, **Kassettenrecorder** m -s, - cassette recorder.

kassieren [ka'si:rən] vt take // vi: darf ich ~? would you like to pay now?

Kassierer [ka'si:rər] m -s, - cashier; (von Klub) treasurer.

Kastanie [kas'ta:niə] f chestnut; (Baum) chestnut tree.

Kasten ['kastən] m -s, ⁻ box (Sport auch), case; (Truhe) chest; ~wagen m van.

kastrieren [kas'tri:rən] vt castrate.

Katalog [kata'lo:k] m -(e)s, -e catalogue.

Katalysator [kataly'za:tər] m catalyst.

Katarrh [ka'tar] m -s, -e catarrh.

katastrophal [katastro'fa:l] a catastrophic.

Katastrophe [kata'stro:fə] f -, -n catastrophe, disaster.

Kat-Auto ['kat'auto] n car fitted with a device for purifying exhaust fumes.

Kategorie [katego'ri:] f category.

kategorisch [kate'go:rɪʃ] a categorical.

Kater ['ka:tər] m -s, - tomcat; (umg) hangover.

kath. abk (= katholisch) Cath.

Kathedrale [kate'dra:lə] f -, -n cathedral.

Kathode [ka'to:də] f -, -n cathode.

Katholik [kato'li:k] m -en, -en Catholic.

katholisch [ka'to:lɪʃ] a Catholic.

Kätzchen ['kɛtsçən] nt kitten.

Katze ['katsə] f -, -n cat; für die Katz (umg) in vain, for nothing.

Katzen- zW: ~auge nt cat's eye; (Fahrrad) rear light; ~jammer m (umg) hangover; ~sprung m (umg)

stone's throw; short journey.

Kauderwelsch ['kaudərvɛlʃ] nt -(s) jargon; (umg) double Dutch.

kauen ['kauən] vti chew.

Kauf [kauf] m -(e)s, **Käufe** purchase, buy; (Kaufen) buying; ein guter ~ a bargain; etw in ~ nehmen put up with sth; k~en vt buy.

Käufer(in f) ['kɔyfər(ın)] m -s, - buyer.

Kaufhaus nt department store.

Kaufkraft f purchasing power.

käuflich ['kɔyflɪç] a,ad purchasable, for sale; (pej) venal; ~ erwerben purchase.

Kauf- zW: k~lustig a interested in buying; ~mann m, pl -leute businessman; shopkeeper; k~männisch a commercial; ~männischer Angestellter office worker.

Kaugummi ['kaugumi] m chewing gum.

Kaulquappe ['kaulkvapə] f -, -n tadpole.

kaum [kaum] ad hardly, scarcely.

Kaution [kautsi'o:n] f deposit; (JUR) bail.

Kauz [kauts] m -es, **Käuze** owl; (fig) queer fellow.

Kavalier [kava'li:r] m -s, -e gentleman, cavalier; **Kavaliersdelikt** nt peccadillo.

Kaviar ['ka:viar] m caviar.

keck [kɛk] a daring, bold; K~heit f daring, boldness.

Kegel ['ke:gəl] m -s, - skittle; (MATH) cone; ~bahn f skittle alley; bowling alley; k~n vi play skittles.

Kehle ['ke:lə] f -, -n throat.

Kehlkopf m larynx.

Kehre ['ke:rə] f -, -n turn(ing), bend; k~n vti (wenden) turn; (mit Besen) sweep; sich an etw (dat) nicht k~n not heed sth.

Kehricht ['ke:rɪçt] m -s sweepings pl.

Kehrmaschine f sweeper.

Kehrseite f reverse, other side; wrong side; bad side.

kehrtmachen vi turn about, aboutturn.

keifen ['kaifən] vi scold, nag.

Keil ['kail] m -(e)s, -e wedge; (MIL) arrowhead; ~riemen m (AUT) fan belt.

Keim [kaim] m -(e)s, -e bud; (MED, fig) germ; k~en vi germinate; k~frei a sterile; ~zelle f (fig) nucleus.

kein [kain] a no, not ... any; ~e(r, s) pron no one, nobody; none.

keinesfalls ad on no account.

keineswegs ad by no means.

keinmal ad not once.

Keks [ke:ks] m od nt -es, -e biscuit.

Kelch [kɛlç] m -(e)s, -e cup, goblet, chalice.

Kelle ['kɛlə] *f* -, -n ladle; (*Maurer~*) trowel.

Keller ['kɛlər] *m* -s, - cellar; **~assel** *f* -, -n woodlouse.

Kellner ['kɛlnər] *m* -s, - waiter; **~in** *f* waitress.

keltern ['kɛltərn] *vt* press.

kennen ['kɛnən] *vt unreg* know; **~lernen** *vt* get to know; sich ~lernen get to know each other; (*zum ersten-mal*) meet.

Kenner *m* -s, - connoisseur.

kenntlich *a* distinguishable, discernible; etw ~ **machen** mark sth.

Kenntnis *f* -, -se knowledge *no pl*; etw zur ~ **nehmen** note sth; von etw ~ **nehmen** take notice of sth; jdn in ~ **setzen** inform sb.

Kenn- *zW:* **~zeichen** *nt* mark, characteristic; **k~zeichnen** *vt insep* characterize; **~ziffer** *f* reference number.

kentern ['kɛntərn] *vi* capsize.

Keramik [ke'raːmɪk] *f* -, -en ceramics *pl*, pottery.

Kerb- ['kɛrb] *zW:* **~e** *f* -, -n notch, groove; **k~en** *vt* notch; **~holz** *nt:* etw auf dem ~holz haben have done sth wrong.

Kerker ['kɛrkər] *m* -s, - prison.

Kerl [kɛrl] *m* -s, -e chap, bloke (*Brit*), guy; sie ist ein netter ~ she's a good sort.

Kern [kɛrn] *m* -(e)s, -e (*Obst~*) pip, stone; (*Nuß~*) kernel; (*Atom~*) nucleus; (*fig*) heart, core; **~energie** *f* nuclear energy; **~forschung** *f* nuclear research; **~frage** *f* central issue; **k~gesund** *a* thoroughly healthy, fit as a fiddle; **k~ig** *a* robust; (*Aus-spruch*) pithy; **~kraftwerk** *nt* nuclear power station; **k~los** *a* seedless, pipless; **~physik** *f* nuclear physics; **~reaktion** *f* nuclear reaction; **~schmelze** *f* meltdown; **~spaltung** *f* nuclear fission; **~waffen** *pl* nuclear weapons *pl*.

Kerze ['kɛrtsə] *f* -, -n candle; (*Zünd~*) plug; **kerzengerade** *a* straight as a die; **Kerzenständer** *m* candle holder.

keß [kɛs] *a* saucy.

Kessel ['kɛsəl] *m* -s, - kettle; (*von Lokomotive etc*) boiler; (*GEOG*) depression; (*MIL*) encirclement.

Kette ['kɛtə] *f* -, -n chain; **k~n** *vt* chain.

Ketten- *zW:* **~laden** *m* chain store; **~rauchen** *nt* chain smoking; **~reaktion** *f* chain reaction.

Ketzer ['kɛtsər] *m* -s, - heretic.

keuchen ['kɔyçən] *vi* pant, gasp.

Keuchhusten *m* whooping cough.

Keule ['kɔylə] *f* -, -n club; (*KOCH*) leg.

keusch [kɔyʃ] *a* chaste; **K~heit** *f* chastity.

kfm. *abk von* **kaufmännisch.**

Kfz [kaː'ɛf'tsɛt] *abk von* **Kraftfahrzeug.**

KG [kaː'geː] *abk* (= *Kommandit-gesellschaft*) limited partnership.

kg *abk von* **Kilogramm.**

kichern ['kɪçərn] *vi* giggle.

kidnappen ['kɪdnɛpən] *vt* kidnap.

Kiefer ['kiːfər] *m* -s, - jaw // *f* -, -n pine; **Kiefernzapfen** *m* pine cone.

Kiel [kiːl] *m* -(e)s, -e (*Feder~*) quill; (*NAUT*) keel.

Kieme ['kiːmə] *f* -, -n gill.

Kies [kiːs] *m* -es, -e gravel; **Kieselstein** ['kiːzəlʃtaɪn] *m* pebble.

Kilo ['kiːlo] kilo; **~gramm** [kilo'gram] *nt* -s, -e kilogram; **~meter** [kilo-'meːtər] *m* kilometre; **~meterzähler** *m* ≈ milometer.

Kind [kɪnt] *nt* -(e)s, -er child; von ~ auf from childhood.

Kinder- ['kɪndər] *zW:* **~ei** *f* childishness; **~garten** *m* nursery school, playgroup; **~geld** *nt* family allowance; **~lähmung** *f* poliomyelitis; **k~leicht** *a* childishly easy; **k~los** *a* childless; **~mädchen** *nt* nursemaid; **k~reich** *a* with a lot of children; **~spiel** *nt* child's play; **~tagesstätte** *f* day-nursery; **~wagen** *m* pram, baby carriage (*US*).

Kind- *zW:* **~heit** *f* childhood; **k~isch** *a* childish; **k~lich** *a* childlike.

Kinn [kɪn] *nt* -(e)s, -e chin; **~haken** *m* (*Boxen*) uppercut; **~lade** *f* jaw.

Kino ['kiːno] *nt* -s, -s cinema; **~besucher** *m* cinema-goer; **~programm** *nt* film programme.

Kiosk ['kiːɔsk] *m* -(e)s, -e kiosk.

Kipp- ['kɪp] *zW:* **~e** *f* -, -n cigarette end; (*umg*) fag; auf der ~e stehen (*fig*) be touch and go; **k~en** *vi* topple over, overturn // *vt* tip.

Kirch- ['kɪrç] *zW:* **~e** *f* -, -n church; **~enlied** *nt* hymn; **~gänger** *m* -s, - churchgoer; **~hof** *m* churchyard; **k~lich** *a* ecclesiastical; **~turm** *m* church tower, steeple.

Kirmes ['kɪrmɛs] *f* -, -sen fair.

Kirsche ['kɪrʃə] *f* -, -n cherry.

Kissen ['kɪsən] *nt* -s, - cushion; (*Kopf~*) pillow; **~bezug** *m* pillow-slip.

Kiste ['kɪstə] *f* -, -n box; chest.

Kitsch [kɪtʃ] *m* -(e)s trash; **k~ig** *a* trashy.

Kitt [kɪt] *m* -(e)s, -e putty; **Kittel** *m* -s, - overall, smock; **kitten** *vt* putty; (*fig: Ehe etc*) cement.

Kitz [kɪts] *nt* -es, -e kid; (*Reh~*) fawn.

kitzel- ['kɪtsəl] *zW:* **~ig** *a* (*lit, fig*) ticklish; **~n** *vi* tickle.

KKW [kaːkaː'veː] *nt abk von* **Kernkraftwerk.**

kläffen ['klɛfən] *vi* yelp.

Klage ['klaːgə] *f* -, -n complaint; (*JUR*) action; **k~n** *vi* (*weh~*) lament, wail;

(sich beschweren) complain; *(JUR)* take legal action.

Kläger(in f) ['klɛːgər(ɪn)] m -s, - plaintiff.

kläglich ['klɛːklɪç] a wretched.

klamm [klam] a *(Finger)* numb; *(feucht)* damp.

Klammer ['klamər] f -, -n clamp; *(in Text)* bracket; *(Büro~)* clip; *(Wäsche~)* peg; *(Zahn~)* brace; **k~n** vr cling *(an +akk* to*)*.

Klang [klaŋ] m -(e)s, ⁻e sound; **k~voll** a sonorous.

Klappe ['klapə] f -, -n valve; *(Ofen~)* damper; *(umg: Mund)* trap; **k~n** vi *(Geräusch)* click // vti *(Sitz etc)* tip // v unpers work; **Klappentext** m blurb.

Klapper ['klapər] f -, -n rattle; **k~ig** a run-down, worn-out; **k~n** vi clatter, rattle; **~schlange** f rattlesnake; **~storch** m stork.

Klapp- zW: **~messer** nt jack-knife; **~rad** nt collapsible bicycle; **~stuhl** m folding chair; **~tisch** m folding table.

klar [klaːr] a clear; *(NAUT)* ready for sea; *(MIL)* ready for action; **sich** *(dat)* **im ~en sein über** *(+akk)* be clear about; **ins ~e kommen** get clear; **(na) ~!** of course.

Klär- ['klɛːr] zW: **~anlage** f purification plant; **k~en** vt *(Flüssigkeit)* purify; *(Probleme)* clarify // vr clear (itself) up.

Klarheit f clarity.

Klarinette [klari'nɛtə] f clarinet.

klar- zW: **~legen** vt clear up, explain; **~machen** vt *(Schiff)* get ready for sea; **jdm etw ~machen** make sth clear to sb; **~sehen** vi unreg see clearly; **K~sichtfolie** f transparent film; **~stellen** vt clarify.

Klärung ['klɛːruŋ] f purification; clarification.

Klasse ['klasə] f -, -n class; *(SCH auch)* form; **k~** a *(umg)* smashing.

Klassen- zW: **~arbeit** f test; **~bewußtsein** nt class consciousness; **~gesellschaft** f class society; **~kampf** m class conflict; **~lehrer** m form master; **k~los** a classless; **~sprecher(in** f) m form prefect; **~zimmer** nt classroom.

klassifizieren [klasifi'tsiːrən] vt classify.

Klassik ['klasɪk] f *(Zeit)* classical period; *(Stil)* classicism; **~er** m -s, - classic.

klassisch a *(lit, fig)* classical.

Klatsch [klatʃ] m -(e)s, -e smack, crack; *(Gerede)* gossip; **~base** f gossip, scandalmonger; **~e** f -, -n *(umg)* crib; **k~en** vi *(Geräusch)* clash; *(reden)* gossip; *(Beifall)* applaud, clap; **~mohn** m (corn) poppy; **k~naß** a

soaking wet.

Klaue ['klauə] f -, -n claw; *(umg: Schrift)* scrawl; **k~n** vt claw; *(umg)* pinch.

Klausel ['klauzəl] f -, -n clause.

Klausur [klau'zuːr] f seclusion; **~arbeit** f examination paper.

Klaviatur [klavia'tuːr] f keyboard.

Klavier [kla'viːr] nt -s, -e piano.

Kleb- ['klɛːb] zW: **k~en** vt stick *(an +akk* to*)*; **k~rig** a sticky; **~stoff** m glue; **~streifen** m adhesive tape.

Klecks [klɛks] m -es, -e blot, stain; **k~en** vi blot; *(pej)* daub.

Klee [kleː] m -s clover; **~blatt** nt cloverleaf; *(fig)* trio.

Kleid [klait] nt -(e)s, -er garment; *(Frauen~)* dress // pl clothes pl; **k~en** ['klaidən] vt clothe, dress; *(auch vi)* suit // vr dress.

Kleider- ['klaidər] zW: **~bügel** m coat hanger; **~bürste** f clothes brush; **~schrank** m wardrobe.

Kleid- zW: **k~sam** a becoming; **~ung** f clothing; **~ungsstück** nt garment.

Kleie ['klaiə] f -, -n bran.

klein [klain] a little, small; **K~asien** nt Asia Minor; **K~e(r, s)** little one; **K~format** nt small size; **im K~format** small-scale; **K~geld** nt small change; **~hacken** vt chop up, mince; **K~igkeit** f trifle; **K~kind** nt infant; **K~kram** m details pl; **~laut** a dejected, quiet; **~lich** a petty, paltry; **Kleinod** ['klainoːt] nt -s, -odien gem, jewel; treasure; **~schneiden** vt unreg chop up; **~städtisch** a provincial; **kleinstmöglich** a smallest possible.

Kleister ['klaistər] m -s, - paste; **k~n** vt paste.

Klemme ['klɛmə] f -, -n clip; *(MED)* clamp; *(fig)* jam; **k~n** vt *(festhalten)* jam; *(quetschen)* pinch, nip // vr catch o.s.; *(sich hineinzwängen)* squeeze o.s.; **sich hinter jdn/etw k~n** get on to sb/get down to sth // vi *(Tür)* stick, jam.

Klempner ['klɛmpnər] m -s, - plumber.

Kleptomanie [klɛptoma'niː] f kleptomania.

Klerus ['kleːrus] m - clergy.

Klette ['klɛtə] f -, -n burr.

Kletter- ['klɛtər] zW: **~er** m -s, - climber; **k~n** vi climb; **~pflanze** f creeper.

Klient(in f) [kli'ɛnt(ɪn)] m client.

Klima ['kliːma] nt -s, -s od -te [kli'maːtə] climate; **~anlage** f air conditioning; **~wechsel** m change of air.

Klinge ['klɪŋə] f -, -n blade, sword.

Klingel ['klɪŋəl] f -, -n bell; **~beutel** m collection bag; **k~n** vi ring.

klingen ['klɪŋən] *vi unreg* sound; (*Gläser*) clink.

Klinik ['kliːnɪk] *f* hospital, clinic.

Klinke ['klɪŋkə] *f* -, -n handle.

Klippe ['klɪpə] *f* -, -n cliff; (*im Meer*) reef; (*fig*) hurdle.

klipp und klar ['klɪp'ʊntklaːr] *a* clear and concise.

Klips [klɪps] *m* -es, -e clip; (*Ohr~*) earring.

klirren ['klɪrən] *vi* clank, jangle; (*Gläser*) clink; **~de Kälte** biting cold.

Klischee [klɪ'ʃeː] *nt* -s, -s (*Druckplatte*) plate, block; (*fig*) cliché; **~vorstellung** *f* stereotyped idea.

Klo [kloː] *nt* -s, -s (*umg*) loo (*Brit*), john (*US*).

Kloake [klo'aːkə] *f* -, -n sewer.

klobig ['kloːbɪç] *a* clumsy.

klopfen ['klɔpfən] *vti* knock; (*Herz*) thump; **es klopft** somebody's knocking; **jdm auf die Schulter ~** tap sb on the shoulder // *vt* beat.

Klopfer *m* -s, - (*Teppich~*) beater; (*Tür~*) knocker.

Klops [klɔps] *m* -es, -e meatball.

Klosett [klo'zɛt] *nt* -s, -e *od* -s lavatory, toilet; **~papier** *nt* toilet paper.

Kloß [kloːs] *m* -es, ⁻e (*Erd~*) clod; (*im Hals*) lump; (*KOCH*) dumpling.

Kloster ['kloːstər] *nt* -s, ⁻ (*Männer~*) monastery; (*Frauen~*) convent.

klösterlich ['kløːstərlɪç] *a* monastic; convent.

Klotz [klɔts] *m* -es, ⁻e log; (*Hack~*) block; **ein ~ am Bein** (*fig*) drag, millstone round (sb's) neck.

Klub [klʊp] *m* -s, -s club; **~sessel** *m* easy chair.

Kluft [klʊft] *f* -, ⁻e cleft, gap; (*GEOL*) gorge, chasm.

klug [kluːk] *a* clever, intelligent; **K~heit** *f* cleverness, intelligence.

Klumpen ['klʊmpən] *m* -s, - (*Erd~*) clod; (*Blut~*) lump, clot; (*Gold~*) nugget; (*KOCH*) lump; **k~** *vi* go lumpy, clot.

km *abk von* **Kilometer**.

km/h *abk* (= *Kilometer je Stunde*) kph, ≈ mph.

knabbern ['knabərn] *vti* nibble.

Knabe ['knaːbə] *m* -n, -n boy; **knabenhaft** *a* boyish.

Knäckebrot ['knɛkəbroːt] *nt* crispbread.

knacken ['knakən] *vti* (*lit, fig*) crack.

Knall [knal] *m* -(e)s, -e bang; (*Peitschen~*) crack; **~ und Fall** (*umg*) unexpectedly; **~bonbon** *nt* cracker; **k~en** *vi* bang; crack; **k~rot** *a* bright red.

knapp [knap] *a* tight; (*Geld*) scarce; (*Sprache*) concise; **eine ~e Stunde** just under an hour; **~ unter/neben** just under/by; **~halten** *vt unreg*

stint; **K~heit** *f* tightness; scarcity; conciseness.

knarren ['knarən] *vi* creak.

knattern ['knatərn] *vi* rattle; (*MG*) chatter.

Knäuel ['knɔyəl] *m od nt* -s, - (*Woll~*) ball; (*Menschen~*) knot.

Knauf [knauf] *m* -(e)s, **Knäufe** knob; (*Schwert~*) pommel.

knautschen ['knautʃən] *vti* crumple.

Knebel ['kneːbəl] *m* -s, - gag; **k~n** *vt* gag; (*NAUT*) fasten.

kneifen ['knaɪfən] *vti unreg* pinch; (*sich drücken*) back out; **vor etw ~** dodge sth.

Kneipe ['knaɪpə] *f* -, -n (*umg*) pub.

kneten ['kneːtən] *vt* knead; (*Wachs*) mould.

Knick [knɪk] *m* -(e)s, -e (*Sprung*) crack; (*Kurve*) bend; (*Falte*) fold; **k~en** *vti* (*springen*) crack; (*brechen*) break; (*Papier*) fold; **geknickt sein** be downcast.

Knicks [knɪks] *m* -es, -e curtsey; **k~en** *vi* curtsey.

Knie [kniː] *nt* -s, - knee; **~beuge** *f* -, -n knee bend; **~fall** *m* genuflection; **~gelenk** *nt* knee joint; **~kehle** *f* back of the knee; **k~n** *vi* kneel; **~scheibe** *f* kneecap; **~strumpf** *m* knee-length sock.

Kniff [knɪf] *m* -(e)s, -e (*fig*) trick, knack; **kniffelig** *a* tricky.

knipsen ['knɪpsən] *vti* (*Fahrkarte*) punch; (*PHOT*) take a snap (of), snap.

Knirps [knɪrps] *m* -es, -e little chap; ® (*Schirm*) telescopic umbrella.

knirschen ['knɪrʃən] *vi* crunch; **mit den Zähnen ~** grind one's teeth.

knistern ['knɪstərn] *vi* crackle.

Knitter- ['knɪtər] *zW*: **~falte** *f* crease; **k~frei** *a* non-crease; **k~n** *vi* crease.

Knoblauch ['knoːplaux] *m* -(e)s garlic.

Knöchel ['knœçəl] *m* -s, - knuckle; (*Fuß~*) ankle.

Knochen ['knɔxən] *m* -s, - bone; **~bau** *m* bone structure; **~bruch** *m* fracture; **~gerüst** *nt* skeleton.

knöchern ['knœçərn] *a* bone.

knochig ['knɔxɪç] *a* bony.

Knödel ['knøːdəl] *m* -s, - dumpling.

Knolle ['knɔlə] *f* -, -n bulb.

Knopf [knɔpf] *m* -(e)s, ⁻e button; (*Kragen~*) stud; **~loch** *nt* buttonhole.

knöpfen ['knœpfən] *vt* button.

Knorpel ['knɔrpəl] *m* -s, - cartilage, gristle; **k~ig** *a* gristly.

Knospe ['knɔspə] *f* -, -n bud.

Knoten ['knoːtən] *m* -s, - knot; (*BOT*) node; (*MED*) lump; **k~** *vt* knot; **~punkt** *m* junction.

Knüller ['knylər] *m* -s, - (*umg*) hit; (*Reportage*) scoop.

knüpfen ['knʏpfən] *vt* tie; (*Teppich*) knot; (*Freundschaft*) form.

Knüppel ['knʏpəl] *m* **-s**, **-** cudgel; (*Polizei~*) baton, truncheon; (*AVIAT*) (joy)stick; **~schaltung** *f* (*AUT*) floor-mounted gear change.

knurren ['knʊrən] *vi* (*Hund*) snarl, growl; (*Magen*) rumble; (*Mensch*) mutter.

knusperig ['knʊspərɪç] *a* crisp; (*Keks*) crunchy.

k.o. [kaː'oː] *a* (*lit*) knocked out; (*fig*) done in.

Koalition [koalitsi'oːn] *f* coalition.

Kobalt ['koːbalt] *nt* **-s** cobalt.

Kobold ['koːbɔlt] *m* **-(e)s**, **-e** goblin, imp.

Kobra ['koːbra] *f* **-**, **-s** cobra.

Koch [kɔx] *m* **-(e)s**, **⁻e** cook; **~buch** *nt* cook(ery) book; **k~en** *vti* cook; (*Wasser*) boil; **~er** *m* **-s**, **-** stove, cooker.

Köcher ['kœçər] *m* **-s**, **-** quiver.

Kochgelegenheit ['kɔxgəleːgənhaɪt] *f* cooking facilities *pl*.

Köchin ['kœçɪn] *f* cook.

Koch- *zW*: **~löffel** *m* kitchen spoon; **~nische** *f* kitchenette; **~platte** *f* boiling ring, hotplate; **~salz** *nt* cooking salt; **~topf** *m* saucepan, pot.

Köder ['køːdər] *m* **-s**, **-** bait, lure.

Koexistenz [kɔɛksɪs'tɛnts] *f* coexistence.

Koffein [kɔfe'iːn] *nt* **-s** caffeine; **k~frei** *a* decaffeinated.

Koffer ['kɔfər] *m* **-s**, **-** suitcase; (*Schrank~*) trunk; **~radio** *nt* portable radio; **~raum** *m* (*AUT*) boot (*Brit*), trunk (*US*).

Kognak ['kɔnjak] *m* **-s**, **-s** brandy, cognac.

Kohl [koːl] *m* **-(e)s**, **-e** cabbage.

Kohle ['koːlə] *f* **-**, **-n** coal; (*Holz~*) charcoal; (*CHEM*) carbon; **~hydrat** *nt* **-(e)s**, **-e** carbohydrate.

Kohlen- *zW*: **~dioxyd** *nt* **-(e)s**, **-e** carbon dioxide; **~händler** *m* coal merchant, coalman; **~säure** *f* carbon dioxide; **~stoff** *m* carbon.

Kohlepapier *nt* carbon paper.

kohlrübe *f* turnip.

Koje ['koːjə] *f* **-**, **-n** cabin; (*Bett*) bunk.

Kokain [koka'iːn] *nt* **-s** cocaine.

kokett [ko'kɛt] *a* coquettish, flirtatious.

Kokosnuß ['koːkɔsnʊs] *f* coconut.

Koks [koːks] *m* **-es**, **-e** coke.

Kolben ['kɔlbən] *m* **-s**, **-** (*Gewehr~*) rifle butt; (*Keule*) club; (*CHEM*) flask; (*TECH*) piston; (*Mais~*) cob.

Kolchose [kɔl'çoːzə] *f* **-**, **-n** collective farm.

Kolik ['koːlɪk] *f* colic, gripe.

Kollaps [kɔ'laps] *m* **-es**, **-e** collapse.

Kolleg [kɔl'eːk] *nt* **-s**, **-s** *od* **-ien** lecture course; **~e** [kɔ'leːgə] *m* **-n**, **-n**, **~in** *f* colleague; **~ium** *nt* board; (*SCH*) staff.

Kollekte [kɔ'lɛktə] *f* **-**, **-n** (*REL*) collection.

kollektiv [kɔlɛk'tiːf] *a* collective.

Kollision [kɔlizi'oːn] *f* collision; (*zeitlich*) clash.

Köln [kœln] *nt* **-s** Cologne.

Kolonie [kolo'niː] *f* colony.

kolonisieren [koloni'ziːrən] *vt* colonize.

Kolonne [ko'lɔnə] *f* **-**, **-n** column; (*von Fahrzeugen*) convoy.

Koloß [ko'lɔs] *m* **-sses**, **-sse** colossus.

kolossal [kolɔ'saːl] *a* colossal.

Kombi- ['kɔmbi] *zW*: **~nation** [-natsi'oːn] *f* combination; (*Vermutung*) conjecture; (*Hemdhose*) combinations *pl*; **~nationsschloß** *nt* combination lock; **k~nieren** [-'niːrən] *vt* combine // *vi* deduce, work out; (*vermuten*) guess; **~wagen** *m* station wagon; **~zange** *f* (pair of) pliers.

Komet [ko'meːt] *m* **-en**, **-en** comet.

Komfort [kɔm'foːr] *m* **-s** luxury.

Komik ['koːmɪk] *f* humour, comedy; **~er** *m* **-s**, **-** comedian.

komisch ['koːmɪʃ] *a* funny.

Komitee [komi'teː] *nt* **-s**, **-s** committee.

Komma ['kɔma] *nt* **-s**, **-s** *od* **-ta** comma; 2 ~ 3 2 point 3.

Kommand- [kɔ'mand] *zW*: **~ant** [-'dant] *m* commander, commanding officer; **~eur** [-'døːr] *m* commanding officer; **k~ieren** [-'diːrən] *vti* command; **Kommando** *nt* **-s**, **-s** command, order; (*Truppe*) detachment, squad; **auf Kommando** to order.

kommen ['kɔmən] *vi unreg* come; (*näher~*) approach; (*passieren*) happen; (*gelangen*, *geraten*) get; (*Blumen*, *Zähne*, *Tränen etc*) appear; (*in die Schule*, *das Zuchthaus etc*) go; ~ **lassen** send for; **das kommt in den Schrank** that goes in the cupboard; **zu sich** ~ come round *od* to; **zu etw** ~ acquire sth; **um etw** ~ lose sth; **nichts auf jdn/etw** ~ **lassen** have nothing said against sb/sth; **jdm frech** ~ get cheeky with sb; **auf jeden vierten kommt ein Platz** there's one place for every fourth person; **wer kommt zuerst?** who's first?; **unter ein Auto** ~ be run over by a car; **wie hoch kommt das?** what does that cost?; **komm gut nach Hause!** safe journey (home); **~den Sonntag** next Sunday; **K~** *nt* **-s** coming.

Kommentar [kɔmɛn'taːr] *m* commentary; **kein** ~ no comment; **k~los** *a* without comment.

Kommentator [kɔmɛn'taːtɔr] *m* (*TV*) commentator.

kommentieren [kɔmɛn'ti:rən] vt comment on.

kommerziell [kɔmɛrtsi'ɛl] a commercial.

kommilitone [kɔmili'to:nə] m -n, -n fellow student.

Kommissar [kɔmɪ'sa:r] m police inspector.

Kommission [kɔmɪsɪ'o:n] f (COMM) commission; (Ausschuß) committee.

Kommode [kɔ'mo:də] f -, -n (chest of) drawers.

Kommunalsteuer [kɔmʊ'na:lʃtɔʏər] f rates pl.

Kommune [kɔ'mu:nə] f -, -n commune.

Kommunikation [kɔmunɪkatsɪ'o:n] f communication.

Kommunion [kɔmuni'o:n] f communion.

Kommuniqué [kɔmyni'ke:] nt -s, -s communiqué.

Kommunismus [kɔmu'nɪsmʊs] m communism.

Kommunist(in f) [kɔmu'nɪst(ɪn)] m communist; k~isch a communist.

kommunizieren [kɔmuni'tsi:rən] vi communicate; (ECCL) receive communion.

Komödie [ko'mø:diə] f comedy.

Kompagnon [kɔmpaɲ'jõ:] m -s, -s (COMM) partner.

kompakt [kɔm'pakt] a compact.

Kompanie [kɔmpa'ni:] f company.

Kompaß ['kɔmpas] m -sses, -sse compass.

kompatibel [kɔmpa'ti:bəl] a compatible.

kompetent [kɔmpe'tɛnt] a competent.

Kompetenz f competence, authority.

komplett [kɔm'plɛt] a complete.

Komplikation [kɔmplikatsɪ'o:n] f complication.

Kompliment [kɔmpli'mɛnt] nt compliment.

Komplize [kɔm'pli:tsə] m -n, -n accomplice.

kompliziert [kɔmpli'tsi:rt] a complicated.

komponieren [kɔmpo'ni:rən] vt compose.

Komponist [kɔmpo'nɪst] m composer.

Komposition [kɔmpozitsɪ'o:n] f composition.

Kompost [kɔm'pɔst] m -(e)s, -e compost.

Kompott [kɔm'pɔt] nt -(e)s, -e stewed fruit.

Kompromiß [kɔmpro'mɪs] m -sses, -sse compromise; k~bereit a willing to compromise; ~lösung f compromise solution.

Kondens- [kɔn'dɛns] zW: ~ation [kɔndɛnzatsɪ'o:n] f condensation; ~ator [kɔndɛn'za:tɔr] m condenser;

k~ieren [kɔndɛn'zi:rən] vt condense; ~milch f condensed milk.

Konditionstraining [kɔnditsɪ'o:nstrɛ:nɪŋ] nt fitness training.

Konditor [kɔn'di:tɔr] m pastrycook; **Konditorei** [kɔndɪto'raɪ] f café; cake shop.

Kondom [kɔn'do:m] nt -s, -e condom.

Konferenz [kɔnfe'rɛnts] f conference, meeting.

Konfession [kɔnfɛsɪ'o:n] f religion; (christlich) denomination; k~ell [-'nɛl] a denominational; konfessionslos a non-denominational.

Konfetti [kɔn'fɛti] nt -(s) confetti.

Konfirmand [kɔnfɪr'mant] m candidate for confirmation.

Konfirmation [kɔnfɪrmatsɪ'o:n] f (ECCL) confirmation.

konfirmieren [kɔnfɪr'mi:rən] vt confirm.

konfiszieren [kɔnfɪs'tsi:rən] vt confiscate.

Konfitüre [kɔnfi'ty:rə] f -, -n jam.

Konflikt [kɔn'flɪkt] m -(e)s, -e conflict.

konfrontieren [kɔnfrɔn'ti:rən] vt confront.

konfus [kɔn'fu:s] a confused.

Kongreß [kɔn'grɛs] m -sses, -sse congress.

Kongruenz [kɔngru'ɛnts] f agreement, congruence.

König ['kø:nɪç] m -(e)s, -e king; ~in ['kø:nɪgɪn] f queen; k~lich a royal; ~reich nt kingdom; ~tum nt -(e)s, -tümer kingship.

Konjugation [kɔnjugatsɪ'o:n] f conjugation.

konjugieren [kɔnju'gi:rən] vt conjugate.

Konjunktion [kɔnjʊŋktsɪ'o:n] f conjunction.

Konjunktiv ['kɔnjʊŋkti:f] m -s, -e subjunctive.

Konjunktur [kɔnjʊŋk'tu:r] f economic situation; (Hoch~) boom.

konkav [kɔn'ka:f] a concave.

konkret [kɔn'kre:t] a concrete.

Konkurrent(in f) [kɔnkʊ'rɛnt(ɪn)] m competitor.

Konkurrenz [kɔnkʊ'rɛnts] f competition; k~fähig a competitive; ~kampf m competition; (umg) rat race.

konkurrieren [kɔnkʊ'ri:rən] vi compete.

Konkurs [kɔn'kʊrs] m -es, -e bankruptcy.

können ['kœnən] vti pt konnte, ptp gekonnt od (als Hilfsverb) können I be able to; ich kann es machen I can do it, I am able to do it; ich kann es nicht machen I can't do it, I'm not able to do it; ich kann nicht ... I can't ..., I cannot ...; ich kann nicht

mehr I can't go on
2 (*wissen, beherrschen*) know; ~ **Sie Deutsch?** can you speak German?; **er kann gut Englisch** he speaks English well; **sie kann keine Mathematik** she can't do mathematics
3 (*dürfen*) to be allowed to; **kann ich gehen?** can I go?; **könnte ich ...? could I ...?; kann ich mit?** (*umg*) can I come with you?
4 (*möglich sein*): **Sie könnten recht haben** you may be right; **das kann sein** that's possible; **kann sein** maybe.
Können ['kœnən] *nt* -s ability.
konnte *etc v siehe* **können**.
konsequent [kɔnze'kvɛnt] *a* consistent.
Konsequenz [kɔnze'kvɛnts] *f* consistency; (*Folgerung*) conclusion.
Konserv- [kɔn'zɛrv] *zW:* **k~ativ** [-a'tiːf] *a* conservative; **~ative(r)** [-a'tiːvə(r)] *mf* (*POL*) conservative; **~e** *f* -, **-n** tinned food; **~enbüchse** *f* tin, can; **k~ieren** [-'viːrən] *vt* preserve; **~ierung** *f* preservation; **~ierungsmittel** *nt* preservative.
Konsonant [kɔnzo'nant] *m* consonant.
konstant [kɔn'stant] *a* constant.
konstruieren [kɔnstru'iːrən] *vt* construct.
Konstrukteur [kɔnstrʊk'tøːr] *m* engineer, designer.
Konstruktion [kɔnstrʊktsi'oːn] *f* construction.
konstruktiv [kɔnstrʊk'tiːf] *a* constructive.
Konsul ['kɔnzʊl] *m* -s, -n consul; **~at** [-'laːt] *nt* consulate.
konsultieren [kɔnzʊl'tiːrən] *vt* consult.
Konsum [kɔn'zuːm] *m* -s consumption; **~artikel** *m* consumer article; **~ent** [-'mɛnt] *m* consumer; **k~ieren** [-'miːrən] *vt* consume.
Kontakt [kɔn'takt] *m* -(e)s, -e contact; **k~arm** *a* unsociable; **k~freudig** *a* sociable; **~linsen** *pl* contact lenses *pl*.
kontern ['kɔntərn] *vti* counter.
Kontinent ['kɔntinɛnt] *m* continent.
Kontingent [kɔntiŋ'gɛnt] *nt* -(e)s, -e quota; (*Truppen~*) contingent.
kontinuierlich [kɔntinu'iːrlɪç] *a* continuous.
Konto ['kɔnto] *nt* -s, **Konten** account; **~auszug** *m* statement (of account); **~inhaber(in** *f*) *m* account holder; **~stand** *m* balance.
Kontra ['kɔntra] *nt* -s, -s (*KARTEN*) double; **jdm ~ geben** (*fig*) contradict sb; **~baß** *m* double bass; **Kontrahent** [-'hɛnt] *m* contracting party; **~punkt** *m* counterpoint.
Kontrast [kɔn'trast] *m* -(e)s, -e contrast.
Kontroll- [kɔn'trɔl] *zW:* **~e** *f* -, -n con-

trol, supervision; (*Paß~*) passport control; **~eur** [-'løːr] *m* inspector; **k~ieren** [-'liːrən] *vt* control, supervise; (*nachprüfen*) check.
Kontur [kɔn'tuːr] *f* contour.
Konvention [kɔnvɛntsi'oːn] *f* convention; **k~ell** [-'nɛl] *a* conventional.
Konversation [kɔnvɛrzatsi'oːn] *f* conversation; **Konversationslexikon** *nt* encyclopaedia.
konvex [kɔn'vɛks] *a* convex.
Konvoi ['kɔnvɔy] *m* -s, -s convoy.
Konzentration [kɔntsɛntratsi'oːn] *f* concentration.
konzentrieren [kɔntsɛn'triːrən] *vtr* concentrate.
konzentriert *a* concentrated // *ad* (*zuhören, arbeiten*) intently.
Konzept [kɔn'tsɛpt] *nt* -(e)s, -e rough draft; **jdn aus dem ~ bringen** confuse sb.
Konzern [kɔn'tsɛrn] *m* -s, -e combine.
Konzert [kɔn'tsɛrt] *nt* -(e)s, -e concert; (*Stück*) concerto; **~saal** *m* concert hall.
Konzession [kɔntsɛsi'oːn] *f* licence; (*Zugeständnis*) concession.
Konzil [kɔn'tsiːl] *nt* -s, -e *od* -ien council.
kooperativ [ko'opera'tiːf] *a* cooperative.
koordinieren [ko'ɔrdi'niːrən] *vt* coordinate.
Kopf [kɔpf] *m* -(e)s, ⁻e head; **~bedeckung** *f* headgear; **~ haut** *f* scalp; **~hörer** *m* headphones *pl*; **~kissen** *nt* pillow; **k~los** *a* panic-stricken; **k~rechnen** *vi* do mental arithmetic; **~salat** *m* lettuce; **~schmerzen** *pl* headache; **~sprung** *m* header, dive; **~tuch** *nt* headscarf; **~weh** *nt* headache; **~zerbrechen** *nt:* **jdm ~zerbrechen machen** give sb a lot of headaches.
Kopie [ko'piː] *f* copy; **k~ren** *vt* copy.
Koppel ['kɔpəl] *f* -, -n (*Weide*) enclosure // *nt* -s, - (*Gürtel*) belt; **k~n** *vt* couple; **~ung** *f* coupling.
Koralle [ko'ralə] *f* -, -n coral; **Korallenriff** *nt* coral reef.
Korb [kɔrp] *m* -(e)s, ⁻e basket; **jdm einen ~ geben** (*fig*) turn sb down; **~ball** *m* basketball; **~stuhl** *m* wicker chair.
Kord [kɔrt] *m* -(e)s, -e corduroy.
Kordel ['kɔrdəl] *f* -, -n cord, string.
Kork [kɔrk] *m* -(e)s, -e cork; **~en** *m* -s, - stopper, cork; **~enzieher** *m* -s, - corkscrew.
Korn [kɔrn] *nt* -(e)s, ⁻er corn, grain; (*Gewehr*) sight; **~blume** *f* cornflower.
Körper ['kœrpər] *m* -s, - body; **~bau** *m* build; **k~behindert** *a* disabled; **~gewicht** *nt* weight; **~größe** *f*

height; **k~lich** *a* physical; **~pflege** *f* personal hygiene; **~schaft** *f* corporation; **~schaftssteuer** *f* corporation tax; **~teil** *m* part of the body.

korpulent [kɔrpu'lɛnt] *a* corpulent.

korrekt [kɔ'rɛkt] *a* correct; **K~or** *m* proofreader; **K~ur** [-'tuːr] *f* (*eines Textes*) proofreading; (*Text*) proof; (*SCH*) marking, correction.

Korrespond- [kɔrɛspɔnd] *zW:* **~ent(in** *f*) [-'dɛnt(ın)] *m* correspondent; **~enz** [-'dɛnts] *f* correspondence; **k~ieren** [-'diːrən] *vi* correspond.

Korridor ['kɔridoːr] *m* -s, -e corridor.

korrigieren [kɔri'giːrən] *vt* correct.

Korruption [kɔruptsi'oːn] *f* corruption.

Korsett [kɔr'zɛt] *nt* -(e)s, -e corset.

Kose- ['koːzə] *zW:* **~form** *f* pet form; **~name** *m* pet name; **~wort** *nt* term of endearment.

Kosmetik [kɔs'meːtık] *f* cosmetics *pl;* **~erin** *f* beautician.

kosmetisch *a* cosmetic; (*Chirurgie*) plastic.

kosmisch ['kɔsmıʃ] *a* cosmic.

Kosmo- [kɔsmo] *zW:* **~naut** [-'naut] *m* -en, -en cosmonaut; **~polit** [-po'liːt] *m* -en, -en cosmopolitan; **k~politisch** [-po'liːtıʃ] *a* cosmopolitan; **Kosmos** ['kɔsmɔs] *m* - cosmos.

Kost [kɔst] *f* - (*Nahrung*) food; (*Verpflegung*) board; **k~bar** *a* precious; (*teuer*) costly, expensive; **~barkeit** *f* preciousness; costliness, expensiveness; (*Wertstück*) valuable.

Kosten *pl* cost(s); (*Ausgaben*) expenses *pl;* **auf ~ von** at the expense of; **k~** *vt* **cost was kostet ...?** what does ... cost?, how much is ...? // *vti* (*versuchen*) taste; **~anschlag** *m* estimate; **k~los** *a* free (of charge).

köstlich ['kœstlıç] *a* precious; (*Einfall*) delightful; (*Essen*) delicious; **sich ~ amüsieren** have a marvellous time.

Kost- *zW:* **~probe** *f* taste; (*fig*) sample; **k~spielig** *a* expensive.

Kostüm [kɔs'tyːm] *nt* -s, -e costume; (*Damen~*) suit; **~fest** *nt* fancy-dress party; **k~ieren** [kɔsty'miːrən] *vtr* dress up; **~verleih** *m* costume agency.

Kot [koːt] *m* -(e)s excrement.

Kotelett [kɔtə'lɛt] *nt* -(e)s, -e *od* -s cutlet, chop; **~en** *pl* sideboards *pl.*

Köter ['køːtər] *m* -s, - cur.

Kotflügel *m* (*AUT*) wing.

Krabbe ['krabə] *f* -, -n shrimp; **krabbeln** *vi* crawl.

Krach [krax] *m* -(e)s, -s *od* -e crash; (*andauernd*) noise; (*umg: Streit*) quarrel, argument; **k~en** *vi* crash; (*beim Brechen*) crack // *vr* (*umg*) argue, quarrel.

krächzen ['krɛçtsən] *vi* croak.

Kraft [kraft] *f* -, ⁻e strength, power, force; (*Arbeits~*) worker; **in ~ treten** come into effect; **k~** *präp* +*gen* by virtue of; **~fahrer** *m* motor driver; **~fahrzeug** *nt* motor vehicle; **~fahrzeugbrief** *m* logbook; **~fahrzeugsteuer** *f* ≈ road tax.

kräftig ['krɛftıç] *a* strong; **~en** [krɛftıgən] *vt* strengthen.

Kraft- *zW:* **k~los** *a* weak; powerless; (*JUR*) invalid; **~probe** *f* trial of strength; **k~voll** *a* vigorous; **~wagen** *m* motor vehicle; **~werk** *nt* power station.

Kragen ['kraːgən] *m* -s, - collar; **~weite** *f* collar size.

Krähe ['krɛːə] *f* -, -n crow; **k~n** *vi* crow.

Kralle ['kralə] *f* -, -n claw; (*Vogel~*) talon; **k~n** *vt* clutch; (*krampfhaft*) claw.

Kram [kraːm] *m* -(e)s stuff, rubbish; **k~en** *vi* rummage; **~laden** *m* (*pej*) small shop.

Krampf [krampf] *m* -(e)s, ⁻e cramp; (*zuckend*) spasm; **~ader** *f* varicose vein; **k~haft** *a* convulsive; (*fig: Versuche*) desperate.

Kran [kraːn] *m* -(e)s, ⁻e crane; (*Wasser~*) tap.

Kranich ['kraːnıç] *m* -s, -e (*ZOOL*) crane.

krank [kraŋk] *a* ill, sick; **K~e(r)** *mf* sick person; invalid, patient.

kranken ['kraŋkən] *vi:* **an etw** (*dat*) **~** (*fig*) suffer from sth.

kränken ['krɛŋkən] *vt* hurt.

Kranken- *zW:* **~bericht** *m* medical report; **~geld** *nt* sick pay; **~haus** *nt* hospital; **~kasse** *f* health insurance; **~pfleger** *m* nursing orderly; **~schwester** *f* nurse; **~schein** *m* health insurance card; **~versicherung** *f* health insurance; **~wagen** *m* ambulance.

Krank- *zW:* **k~haft** *a* diseased; (*Angst etc*) morbid; **~heit** *f* illness, disease; **~heitserreger** *m* disease-carrying agent.

kränk- ['krɛŋk] *zW:* **~lich** *a* sickly; **K~ung** *f* insult, offence.

Kranz [krants] *m* -es, ⁻e wreath, garland.

kraß [kras] *a* crass.

Krater ['kraːtər] *m* -s, - crater.

Kratz- ['krats] *zW:* **~bürste** *f* (*fig*) crosspatch; **k~en** *vti* scratch; **~er** *m* -s, - scratch; (*Werkzeug*) scraper.

Kraul ['kraʊl] *nt* -s crawl; **~ schwimmen** do the crawl; **k~en** *vi* (*schwimmen*) do the crawl // *vt* (*streicheln*) tickle.

kraus [kraʊs] *a* crinkly; (*Haar*) frizzy; (*Stirn*) wrinkled; **K~e** ['kraʊzə] *f* -, -n frill, ruffle.

Kraut [kraʊt] nt -(e)s, **Kräuter** plant; (Gewürz) herb; (Gemüse) cabbage.
Krawall [kra'val] m -s, -e row, uproar.
Krawatte [kra'vatə] f -, -n tie.
Krebs [kre:ps] m -es, -e crab; (MED, ASTROL) cancer.
Kredit [kre'di:t] m -(e)s, -e credit; ~**karte** f credit card.
Kreide ['kraɪdə] f -, -n chalk; **k~bleich** a as white as a sheet.
Kreis [kraɪs] m -es, -e circle; (Stadt~ etc) district; **im ~ gehen** (lit, fig) go round in circles.
kreischen ['kraɪʃən] vi shriek, screech.
Kreis- zW: ~**el** ['kraɪzəl] m -s, - top; (Verkehrs~) roundabout; **k~en** ['kraɪzən] vi spin; ~**lauf** m (MED) circulation; (fig: der Natur etc) cycle; ~**säge** f circular saw; ~**stadt** f county town; ~**verkehr** m roundabout traffic.
Kreißsaal ['kraɪs-za:l] m delivery room.
Krematorium [krema'to:riʊm] nt crematorium.
Kreml ['krem(ə)l] m -s Kremlin.
krepieren [kre'pi:rən] vi (umg: sterben) die, kick the bucket.
Krepp [krep] m -s, -s od -e crepe; ~**(p)apier** nt crepe paper; ~**sohle** f crepe sole.
Kresse ['krɛsə] f -, -n cress.
Kreta ['kre:ta] nt -s Crete.
Kreuz [krɔʏts] nt -es, -e cross; (ANAT) small of the back; (KARTEN) clubs; **k~en** vtr cross // vi (NAUT) cruise; ~**er** m -s, - (Schiff) cruiser; ~**fahrt** f cruise; ~**gang** m cloisters pl; **k~igen** vt crucify; ~**igung** f crucifixion; ~**otter** f adder; ~**ung** f (Verkehrs~) crossing, junction; (Züchten) cross; ~**verhör** nt cross-examination; ~**weg** m crossroads; (REL) Way of the Cross; ~**worträtsel** nt crossword puzzle; ~**zug** m crusade.
Kriech- ['kri:ç] zW: **k~en** vi unreg crawl, creep; (pej) grovel, crawl; ~**er** m -s, - crawler; ~**spur** f crawler lane; ~**tier** nt reptile.
Krieg [kri:k] m -(e)s, -e war.
kriegen ['kri:gən] vt (umg) get.
Kriegs- zW: ~**dienstverweigerer** m conscientious objector; ~**erklärung** f declaration of war; ~**fuß** m: mit jdm/etw auf ~**fuß stehen** be at loggerheads with sb/not get on with sth; ~**gefangene(r)** m prisoner of war; ~**gefangenschaft** f captivity; ~**gericht** nt court-martial; ~**schiff** nt warship; ~**verbrecher** m war criminal; ~**versehrte(r)** m person disabled in the war; ~**zustand** m state of war.
Krim [krɪm] f - Crimea.

Krimi ['kri:mi] m -s, -s (umg) thriller.
Kriminal- [krimi'na:l] zW: ~**beamte(r)** m detective; ~**i'tät** f criminality; ~'**polizei** f ≈ Criminal Investigation Department, CID (Brit), Federal Bureau of Investigation, FBI (US); ~'**roman** m detective story.
kriminell [krimi'nɛl] a criminal; **K~e(r)** m criminal.
Krippe ['krɪpə] f -, -n manger, crib; (Kinder~) crèche.
Krise ['kri:zə] f -, -n crisis; **k~ln** vi: es kriselt there's a crisis.
Kristall [krɪs'tal] m -s, -e crystal // nt -s (Glas) crystal.
Kriterium [kri'te:riʊm] nt criterion.
Kritik [kri'ti:k] f criticism; (Zeitungs~) review, write-up; ~**er** ['kri:tikər] m -s, - critic; **k~los** a uncritical.
kritisch ['kri:tɪʃ] a critical.
kritisieren [kriti'zi:rən] vti criticize.
kritzeln ['krɪtsəln] vti scribble, scrawl.
Krokodil [kroko'di:l] nt -s, -e crocodile.
Krokus ['kro:kʊs] m -, - od -se crocus.
Krone ['kro:nə] f -, -n crown; (Baum~) top.
krönen ['krø:nən] vt crown.
Kron- zW: ~**korken** m bottle top; ~**leuchter** m chandelier; ~**prinz** m crown prince.
Krönung ['krø:nʊŋ] f coronation.
Kropf [krɔpf] m -(e)s, ⁻e (MED) goitre; (von Vogel) crop.
Kröte ['krø:tə] f -, -n toad.
Krücke ['krykə] f -, -n crutch.
Krug [kru:k] m -(e)s, ⁻e jug; (Bier~) mug.
Krümel ['kry:məl] m -s, - crumb; **k~n** vti crumble.
krumm [krʊm] a (lit, fig) crooked; (kurvig) curved; ~**beinig** a bandy-legged; ~**lachen** vr (umg) laugh o.s. silly; ~**nehmen** vt unreg (umg): jdm etw ~**nehmen** take sth amiss.
Krümmung ['krymʊŋ] f bend, curve.
Krüppel ['krypəl] m -s, - cripple.
Kruste ['krʊstə] f -, -n crust.
Kruzifix [krutsi'fɪks] nt -es, -e crucifix.
Kübel ['ky:bəl] m -s, - tub; (Eimer) pail.
Kubikmeter [kʊ'bi:kme:tər] m cubic metre.
Küche ['kyçə] f -, -n kitchen; (Kochen) cooking, cuisine.
Kuchen ['ku:xən] m -s, - cake; ~**form** f baking tin; ~**gabel** f pastry fork.
Küchen- zW: ~**herd** m range; (Gas, ELEK) cooker, stove; ~**schabe** f cockroach; ~**schrank** m kitchen cabinet.
Kuckuck ['kʊkʊk] m -s, -e cuckoo; **Kuckucksuhr** f cuckoo clock.
Kufe ['ku:fə] f -, -n (Faß) vat; (Schlit-

ten~) runner; (*AVIAT*) skid.

Kugel ['ku:gəl] *f -, -n* ball; (*MATH*) sphere; (*MIL*) bullet; (*Erd~*) globe; (*SPORT*) shot; **k~förmig** *a* spherical; **~kopf** *m* golf ball; **~lager** *nt* ball bearing; **k~rund** *a* (*Gegenstand*) round; (*umg: Person*) tubby; **~schreiber** *m* ball-point (pen), biro ®; **k~sicher** *a* bulletproof; **~stoßen** *nt* -s shot-put.

Kuh [ku:] *f -, ¨e* cow.

kühl [ky:l] *a* (*lit, fig*) cool; **K~anlage** *f* refrigerating plant; **K~e** *f* - coolness; **~en** *vt* cool; **K~er** *m* -s, - (*AUT*) radiator; **K~erhaube** *f* (*AUT*) bonnet (*Brit*), hood (*US*); **K~raum** *m* cold-storage chamber; **K~schrank** *m* refrigerator; **K~truhe** *f* freezer; **K~ung** *f* cooling; **K~wasser** *nt* cooling water.

kühn [ky:n] *a* bold, daring; **K~heit** *f* boldness.

Küken ['ky:kən] *nt -s, -* chicken.

kulant [ku'lant] *a* obliging.

Kuli ['ku:li] *m -s, -s* coolie; (*umg: Kugelschreiber*) biro ®.

Kulisse [ku'lisə] *f -, -n* scene.

kullern ['kʊlərn] *vi* roll.

Kult [kʊlt] *m* -(e)s, -e worship, cult; **mit etw einen ~ treiben** make a cult out of sth; **k~ivieren** [-i'vi:rən] *vt* cultivate; **k~iviert** *a* cultivated, refined.

Kultur [kʊl'tu:r] *f* culture; civilization; (*des Bodens*) cultivation; **~banause** *m* (*umg*) philistine, low-brow; **k~ell** [-u'rɛl] *a* cultural.

Kümmel ['kyməl] *m -s, -* caraway seed; (*Branntwein*) kümmel.

Kummer ['kʊmər] *m -s* grief, sorrow.

kümmer- ['kymər] *zW*: **~lich** *a* miserable, wretched; **~n** *vr*: **sich um jdn ~n** look after sb; **sich um etw ~n** see to sth // *vt* concern; **das kümmert mich nicht** that doesn't worry me.

Kumpel ['kʊmpəl] *m -s, -* (*umg*) mate.

kündbar ['kyntba:r] *a* redeemable, recallable; (*Vertrag*) terminable.

Kunde ['kʊndə] *m -n, -n*, **Kundin** *f* customer // *f -, -n* (*Botschaft*) news; **Kundendienst** *m* after-sales service; **Kundenkonto** *nt* charge account.

Kund- *zW*: **~gabe** *f* announcement; **k~geben** *vt unreg* announce; **~gebung** *f* announcement; (*Versammlung*) rally.

Künd- *zW*: **k~igen** *vi* give in one's notice; **jdm k~igen** give sb his notice // *vt* cancel; (jdm) **die Stellung/Wohnung k~igen** give (sb) notice; **~igung** *f* notice; **~igungsfrist** *f* period of notice.

Kundschaft *f* customers *pl*, clientele.

künftig ['kynftıç] *a* future // *ad* in future.

Kunst [kʊnst] *f -, ¨e* art; (*Können*) skill; **das ist doch keine ~** it's easy; **~dünger** *m* artificial manure; **~faser** *f* synthetic fibre; **~fertigkeit** *f* skilfulness; **~geschichte** *f* history of art; **~gewerbe** *nt* arts and crafts *pl*; **~griff** *m* trick, knack; **~händler** *m* art dealer.

Künstler(in *f)* ['kynstlər(ın)] *m -s, -* artist; **k~isch** *a* artistic; **~name** *m* stagename; pseudonym.

künstlich ['kynstlıç] *a* artificial.

Kunst- *zW*: **~sammler** *m -s, -* art collector; **~seide** *f* artificial silk; **~stoff** *m* synthetic material; **~stück** *nt* trick; **~turnen** *nt* gymnastics; **k~voll** *a* ingenious, artistic; **~werk** *nt* work of art.

kunterbunt ['kʊntərbʊnt] *a* higgledy-piggledy.

Kupfer ['kʊpfər] *nt -s, -* copper; **~geld** *nt* coppers *pl*; **k~n** *a* copper.

Kuppe ['kʊpə] *f -, -n* (*Berg~*) top; (*Finger~*) tip.

Kupp- ['kʊp] *zW*: **Kuppelei** *f* (*JUR*) procuring; **kuppeln** *vi* (*JUR*) procure; (*AUT*) declutch // *vt* join; **~lung** *f* coupling; (*AUT*) clutch.

Kur [ku:r] *f -, -en* cure, treatment.

Kür [ky:r] *f -, -en* (*SPORT*) free skating/exercises *pl*.

Kurbel ['kʊrbəl] *f -, -n* crank, winch; (*AUT*) starting handle; **~welle** *f* crankshaft.

Kürbis ['kyrbıs] *m -ses, -se* pumpkin; (*exotisch*) gourd.

Kur- ['ku:r] *zW*: **~gast** *m* visitor (to a health resort); **k~ieren** [ku'ri:rən] *vt* cure; **k~ios** [kuri'o:s] *a* curious, odd; **~iosität** *f* curiosity; **~ort** *m* health resort; **~pfuscher** *m* quack.

Kurs [kʊrs] *m -es, -e* course; (*FIN*) rate; **~buch** *nt* timetable; **k~ieren** [kʊr'zi:rən] *vi* circulate; **k~iv** *ad* in italics; **~us** ['kʊrzʊs] *m -, Kurse** course; **~wagen** *m* (*EISENB*) through carriage.

Kurve ['kʊrvə] *f -, -n* curve; (*Straßen~ auch*) bend; **kurvenreich, kurvig** *a* (*Straße*) bendy.

kurz [kʊrts] *a* short; **~ gesagt** in short; **zu ~ kommen** come off badly; **den ~eren ziehen** get the worst of it; **K~arbeit** *f* short-time work; **~ärm(e)lig** *a* short-sleeved.

Kürze ['kyrtsə] *f -, -n* shortness, brevity; **k~n** *vt* cut short; (*in der Länge*) shorten; (*Gehalt*) reduce.

kurz- *zW*: **~erhand** *ad* on the spot; **~fristig** *a* short-term; **K~geschichte** *f* short story; **~halten** *vt unreg* keep short; **~lebig** *a* short-lived.

kürzlich ['kyrtslıç] *ad* lately, recently.

Kurz- *zW*: **~schluß** *m* (*ELEK*) short circuit; **~schrift** *f* shorthand; **k~sichtig** *a* short-sighted; **~welle** *f* shortwave.

kuscheln ['kuʃəln] *vr* snuggle up.

Kusine [ku'ziːnə] *f* cousin.

Kuß [kʊs] *m* -sses, ¨sse kiss.

küssen ['kʏsən] *vtr* kiss.

Küste ['kʏstə] *f* -, -n coast, shore; **Küstenwache** *f* coastguard (station).

Küster ['kʏstər] *m* -s, - sexton, verger.

Kutsche ['kʊtʃə] *f* -, -n coach, carriage; **~r** *m* -s, - coachman.

Kutte ['kʊtə] *f* -, -n cowl.

Kuvert [ku'veːr] *nt* -s, -e *od* -s envelope; cover.

Kybernetik [kybɛr'neːtɪk] *f* cybernetics.

L

L, l [ɛl] *nt* L, l // **l.** *abk von* **Liter.**

Labor [la'boːr] *nt* -s, -e *od* -s lab; **~ant(in** *f)* [labo'rant(ɪn)] *m* lab(oratory) assistant; **~atorium** [labora'toːriʊm] *nt* laboratory.

Labyrinth [laby'rɪnt] *nt* -s, -e labyrinth.

lächeln ['lɛçəln] *vi* smile; **L~** *nt* -s smile.

lachen ['laxən] *vi* laugh.

lächerlich ['lɛçərlɪç] *a* ridiculous.

Lachgas *nt* laughing gas.

lachhaft *a* laughable.

Lachs [laks] *m* -es, -e salmon.

Lack [lak] *m* -(e)s, -e lacquer, varnish; *(von Auto)* paint; **l~ieren** [la'kiːrən] *vt* varnish; *(Auto)* spray; **~ierer** [la'kiːrər] *m* -s, - varnisher.

Lackmus ['lakmʊs] *m od nt* - litmus.

laden ['laːdən] *vt unreg (Lasten)* load; *(JUR)* summon; *(einladen)* invite.

Laden ['laːdən] *m* -s, ¨ shop; *(Fenster~)* shutter; **~dieb** *m* shoplifter; **~diebstahl** *m* shoplifting; **~schluß** *m* closing time; **~tisch** *m* counter.

Ladung ['laːdʊŋ] *f (Last)* cargo, load; *(Beladen)* loading; *(JUR)* summons; *(Einladung)* invitation; *(Spreng~)* charge.

lag *etc v siehe* **liegen.**

Lage ['laːgə] *f* -, -n position, situation; *(Schicht)* layer; **in der ~ sein** be in a position.

Lager ['laːgər] *nt* -s, - camp; *(COMM)* warehouse; *(Schlaf~)* bed; *(von Tier)* lair; *(TECH)* bearing; **~bestand** *m* stocks *pl*; **~haus** *nt* warehouse, store.

lagern ['laːgərn] *vi (Dinge)* be stored; *(Menschen)* camp // *vt* store; *(betten)* lay down; *(Maschine)* bed.

Lagune [la'guːnə] *f* -, -n lagoon.

lahm [laːm] *a* lame; **~en** *vi* be lame, limp.

lähmen ['lɛːmən] *vt* paralyse.

lahmlegen *vt* paralyse.

Lähmung *f* paralysis.

Laib [laip] *m* -s, -e loaf.

Laie ['laiə] *m* -n, -n layman; **laienhaft** *a* amateurish.

Laken ['laːkən] *nt* -s, - sheet.

Lakritze [la'krɪtsə] *f* -, -n liquorice.

lallen ['lalən] *vti* slur; *(Baby)* babble.

Lamelle [la'mɛlə] *f* lamella; *(ELEK)* lamina; *(TECH)* plate.

Lametta [la'mɛta] *nt* -s tinsel.

Lamm [lam] *nt* -(e)s, ¨er lamb; **~fell** *nt* lambskin.

Lampe ['lampə] *f* -, -n lamp; **Lampenfieber** *nt* stage fright; **Lampenschirm** *m* lampshade.

Lampion [lampi'õː] *m* -s, -s Chinese lantern.

Land [lant] *nt* -(e)s, ¨er land; *(Nation, nicht Stadt)* country; *(Bundes~)* state; **auf dem ~(e)** in the country; **~besitz** *m* landed property; **Landebahn** *f* runway; **l~en** ['landən] *vti* land.

Landes- ['landəs] *zW:* **~farben** *pl* national colours *pl*; **~innere(s)** *nt* inland region; **~sprache** *f* national language; **l~üblich** *a* customary; **~verrat** *m* high treason; **~währung** *f* national currency.

Land- *zW:* **~haus** *nt* country house; **~karte** *f* map; **~kreis** *m* administrative region; **l~läufig** *a* customary.

ländlich ['lɛntlɪç] *a* rural.

Land- *zW:* **~schaft** *f* countryside; *(KUNST)* landscape; **l~schaftlich** *a* scenic; regional; **~straße** *f* country road; **~streicher** *m* -s, - tramp; **~strich** *m* region; **~tag** *m (POL)* regional parliament.

Landung ['landʊŋ] *f* landing.

Landungs- *zW:* **~boot** *nt* landing craft; **~brücke** *f* jetty, pier; **~stelle** *f* landing place.

Land- *zW:* **~wirt** *m* farmer; **~wirtschaft** *f* agriculture; **~zunge** *f* spit.

lang [laŋ] *a* long; *(Mensch)* tall; **~atmig** *a* long-winded; **~e** *ad* for a long time; *(dauern, brauchen)* a long time.

Länge ['lɛŋə] *f* -, -n length; *(GEOG)* longitude.

langen ['laŋən] *vi (ausreichen)* do, suffice; *(fassen)* reach *(nach* for); **es langt mir** I've had enough.

Länge- *zW:* **Längengrad** *m* longitude; **Längenmaß** *nt* linear measure.

lang- *zW:* **L~eweile** *f* boredom; **~fristig** *a* long-term; **~lebig** *a* long-lived.

länglich *a* longish.

längs [lɛŋs] *präp +gen od dat* along // *ad* lengthwise.

lang- *zW:* **~sam** *a* slow; **L~samkeit** *f*

slowness; **L~schläfer(in** f) m late riser; **L~spielplatte** f long-playing record.

längst ['lɛŋst] ad: das ist ~ fertig that was finished a long time ago, that has been finished for a long time; **~e(r, s)** a longest.

lang- zW: **~weilen** vt bore // vr be bored; **~weilig** a boring, tedious; **L~welle** f long wave; **~wierig** a lengthy, long-drawn-out.

Lanze ['lantsə] f -, -n lance.

Lappalie [la'pa:liə] f trifle.

Lappen ['lapən] m -s, - cloth, rag; (ANAT) lobe.

läppisch ['lɛpɪʃ] a foolish.

Lappland ['laplant] nt -s Lapland.

Lapsus ['lapsʊs] m -, - slip.

Lärche ['lɛrçə] f -, -n larch.

Lärm [lɛrm] m -(e)s noise; **l~en** vi be noisy, make a noise.

Larve ['larfə] f -, -n (BIOL) larva.

las etc v siehe **lesen**.

lasch [laʃ] a slack.

Lasche ['laʃə] f -, -n (Schuh~) tongue.

Laser ['leɪzə] m -s, - laser.

lassen ['lasən] ◆vt pt ließ, ptp gelassen 1 (unterlassen) stop; (momentan) leave; (sein) laß das (do it)!; (hör auf) stop it!; laß mich! leave me alone; ~ wir das! let's leave it; er kann das Trinken nicht ~ he can't stop drinking
2 (zurücklassen) leave; etw ~, wie es ist leave sth (just) as it is
3 (überlassen): jdm etw ~ let sb have sth
4 (zulassen): jdn ins Haus ~ let sb into the house
◆vi: laß mal, ich mache das schon leave it, I'll do it
◆ (als Hilfsverb) pt ließ, ptp lassen 1 (veranlassen): etw machen ~ have od get sth done; sich dat etw schicken ~ have sth sent (to one)
2 (zulassen): jdn etw wissen ~ let sb know sth; das Licht brennen ~ leave the light on; jdn warten ~ keep sb waiting; das läßt sich machen that can be done
3: laß uns gehen let's go.

lässig ['lɛsɪç] a casual; **L~keit** f casualness.

Last [last] f -, -en load, burden; (NAUT, AVIAT) cargo; (meist pl: Gebühr) charge; jdm zur ~ fallen be a burden to sb; **~auto** nt lorry, truck; **l~en** vi (auf +dat) weigh on.

Laster ['lastər] nt -s, - vice.

lästern ['lɛstərn] vti (Gott) blaspheme; (schlecht sprechen) mock.

Lästerung f jibe; (Gottes~) blasphemy.

lästig ['lɛstɪç] a troublesome, tiresome.

Last- zW: **~kahn** m barge; **~-**

kraftwagen m heavy goods vehicle; **~schrift** f debit; **~wagen** m lorry, truck.

Latein [la'taɪn] nt -s Latin; **~amerika** nt Latin America.

latent [la'tɛnt] a latent.

Laterne [la'tɛrnə] f -, -n lantern; (Straßen~) lamp, light; **Laternenpfahl** m lamppost.

latschen ['la:tʃən] vi (umg: gehen) wander, go; (lässig) slouch.

Latte ['latə] f -, -n lath; (SPORT) goalpost; (quer) crossbar.

Latzhose ['latsho:zə] f dungarees pl.

lau [lau] a (Nacht) balmy; (Wasser) lukewarm.

Laub [laup] nt -(e)s foliage; **~baum** m deciduous tree; **~frosch** m tree frog; **~säge** f fretsaw.

Lauch [laux] m -(e)s, -e leek.

Lauer ['lauər] f: auf der ~ sein od liegen, **l~n** vi lie in wait; (Gefahr) lurk.

Lauf [lauf] m -(e)s, Läufe run; (Wett~) race; (Entwicklung, ASTRON) course; (Gewehr) barrel; einer Sache ihren ~ lassen let sth take its course; **~bahn** f career.

laufen ['laufən] vti unreg run; (umg: gehen) walk; **~d** a running; (Monat, Ausgaben) current; auf dem **~den** sein/halten be/keep up to date; am **~den Band** (fig) continuously.

Läufer ['lɔyfər] m -s, - (Teppich, SPORT) runner; (Fußball) half-back; (Schach) bishop.

Lauf- zW: **~masche** f run, ladder (Brit); **~stall** m playpen; **~steg** m catwalk; **~werk** nt (COMPUT) disk drive; **~zettel** m circular.

Lauge ['laugə] f -, -n soapy water; (CHEM) alkaline solution.

Laune ['launə] f -, -n mood, humour; (Einfall) caprice; (schlechte) temper; **l~nhaft** a capricious, changeable.

launisch a moody; bad-tempered.

Laus [laus] f -, Läuse louse; **~bub** m rascal, imp.

lauschen ['lauʃən] vi eavesdrop, listen in.

lauschig ['lauʃɪç] a snug.

laut [laut] a loud // ad loudly; (lesen) aloud // präp +gen od dat according to; **L~** m -(e)s, -e sound.

Laute ['lautə] f -, -n lute.

lauten ['lautən] vi say; (Urteil) be.

läuten ['lɔytən] vti ring, sound.

lauter ['lautər] a (Wasser) clear, pure; (Wahrheit, Charakter) honest; inv (Freude, Dummheit etc) sheer; (mit pl) nothing but, only.

läutern ['lɔytərn] vt purify.

Läuterung f purification.

laut- zW: **~hals** ad at the top of one's

voice; ~**los** *a* noiseless, silent; **L~schrift** *f* phonetics *pl*; **L~sprecher** *m* loudspeaker; **L~sprecherwagen** *m* loudspeaker van; ~**stark** *a* vociferous; **L~stärke** *f* (RAD) volume.

lauwarm ['lauvarm] *a* (lit, fig) lukewarm.

Lava ['la:va] *f* -, **Laven** lava.

Lavendel [la'vɛndəl] *m* -s, - lavender.

Lawine [la'vi:nə] *f* avalanche; **Lawinengefahr** *f* danger of avalanches.

lax [laks] *a* lax.

Lazarett [latsa'rɛt] *nt* -(e)s, -e (MIL) hospital, infirmary.

leben ['le:bən] *vti* live; **L~** *nt* -s, - life; ~**d** *a* living; **lebendig** [le'bɛndɪç] *a* living, alive; (lebhaft) lively; **Lebendigkeit** *f* liveliness.

Lebens- *zW*: ~**alter** *nt* age; ~**art** *f* way of life; ~**erwartung** *f* life expectancy; **l~fähig** *a* able to live; ~**gefahr** *f*: ~**gefahr!** danger!; in ~**gefahr** dangerously ill; **l~gefährlich** *a* dangerous; (Verletzung) critical; ~**haltungskosten** *pl* cost of living *sing*; ~**jahr** *nt* year of life; **l~lustig** *a* cheerful, lively; ~**mittel** *pl* food *sing*; ~**mittelgeschäft** *nt* grocer's; **l~müde** *a* tired of life; ~**retter** *m* lifesaver; ~**standard** *m* standard of living; ~**unterhalt** *m* livelihood; ~**versicherung** *f* life insurance; ~**wandel** *m* way of life; ~**zeichen** *nt* sign of life.

Leber ['le:bər] *f* -, -n liver; ~**fleck** *m* mole; ~**tran** *m* cod-liver oil; ~**wurst** *f* liver sausage.

Lebewesen *nt* creature.

Lebewohl *nt* farewell, goodbye.

leb- ['le:p] *zW*: ~**haft** *a* lively, vivacious; **L~kuchen** *m* gingerbread; ~**los** *a* lifeless.

leck [lɛk] *a* leaky, leaking; **L~** *nt* -(e)s, -e leak; ~**en** *vi* (Loch haben) leak // *vti* (schlecken) lick.

lecker ['lɛkər] *a* delicious, tasty; **L~bissen** *m* dainty morsel.

led. *abk von* ledig.

Leder ['le:dər] *nt* -s, - leather; **l~n** *a* leather; ~**waren** *pl* leather goods *pl*.

ledig ['le:dɪç] *a* single; **einer Sache** ~ **sein** be free of sth; ~**lich** *ad* merely, solely.

leer [le:r] *a* empty; vacant; ~ **machen** empty; **L~e** *f* - emptiness; ~**en** *vt* empty // *vr* empty; **L~gewicht** *nt* weight when empty; ~**lauf** *m* neutral; ~**stehend** *a* empty; **L~ung** *f* emptying; (Post) collection.

legal [le'ga:l] *a* legal, lawful; ~**i'sieren** *vt* legalize; **L~i'tät** *f* legality.

legen ['le:gən] *vt* lay, put, place; (Ei) lay // *vr* lie down; (fig) subside.

Legende [le'gɛndə] *f* -, -n legend.

leger [le'ʒe:r] *a* casual.

legieren [le'gi:rən] *vt* alloy.

Legierung *f* alloy.

Legislative [legɪsla'ti:və] *f* legislature.

legitim [legi'ti:m] *a* legitimate; **L~ation** [-atsi'o:n] *f* legitimation; ~**ieren** [-'mi:rən] *vt* legitimate // *vr* prove one's identity.

Lehm [le:m] *m* -(e)s, -e loam; **l~ig** *a* loamy.

Lehne ['le:nə] *f* -, -n arm; back; **l~n** *vtr* lean.

Lehnstuhl *m* armchair.

Lehr- *zW*: ~**amt** *nt* teaching profession; ~**brief** *m* indentures *pl*; ~**buch** *nt* textbook.

Lehre ['le:rə] *f* -, -n teaching, doctrine; (beruflich) apprenticeship; (moralisch) lesson; (TECH) gauge; **l~n** *vt* teach; ~**r(in** *f*) *m* -s, - teacher; **Lehrerzimmer** *nt* staff room.

Lehr- *zW*: ~**gang** *m* course; ~**jahre** *pl* apprenticeship; ~**ling** *m* apprentice; **l~reich** *a* instructive; ~**stelle** *f* apprenticeship; ~**stuhl** *m* chair; ~**zeit** *f* apprenticeship.

Leib [laip] *m* -(e)s, -er body; **halt ihn mir vom** ~! keep him away from me; **l~haftig** *a* personified; (Teufel) incarnate; ~**lich** *a* bodily; (Vater etc) own; ~**wache** *f* bodyguard.

Leiche ['laiçə] *f* -, -n corpse.

Leichen- *zW*: ~ **haus** *nt* mortuary; ~**träger** *m* bearer; ~**wagen** *m* hearse.

Leichnam ['laiçna:m] *m* -(e)s, -e corpse.

leicht [laiçt] *a* light; (einfach) easy; **L~athletik** *f* athletics *sing*; ~**fallen** *vi unreg*: **jdm** ~**fallen** be easy for sb; ~**fertig** *a* frivolous; ~**gläubig** *a* gullible, credulous; **L~gläubigkeit** *f* gullibility, credulity; ~**hin** *ad* lightly; **L~igkeit** *f* easiness; **mit L~igkeit** with ease; ~**machen** *vt*: **es sich** (dat) ~**machen** make things easy for oneself; **L~sinn** *m* carelessness; ~**sinnig** *a* careless.

Leid [lait] *nt* -(e)s grief, sorrow; **l~** *a*: **etw l~ haben** *od* **sein** be tired of sth; **es tut mir/ihm l~** I am/he is sorry; **er/das tut mir l~** I am sorry for him/ it; **l~en** ['laidən] *unreg vt* suffer; (erlauben) permit; **jdn/etw nicht l~en können** not be able to stand sb/sth // *vi* suffer; ~**en** *nt* -s, - suffering; (Krankheit) complaint; ~**enschaft** *f* passion; **l~enschaftlich** *a* passionate.

leider ['laidər] *ad* unfortunately; **ja,** ~ yes, I'm afraid so; ~ **nicht** I'm afraid not.

Leidtragende(r) *mf* bereaved; (Benachteiligter) one who suffers.

Leidwesen *nt*: **zu jds** ~ to sb's dismay.

Leier ['laıәr] *f* -, **-n** lyre; (*fig*) old story; **~kasten** *m* barrel organ.

Leihbibliothek *f* lending library.

leihen ['laıәn] *vt unreg* lend; **sich** (*dat*) **etw ~** borrow sth.

Leih- *zW:* **~gebühr** *f* hire charge; **~haus** *nt* pawnshop; **~schein** *m* pawn ticket; (*Buch~ etc*) borrowing slip; **~wagen** *m* hired car.

Leim [laım] *m* **-(e)s, -e** glue; **l~en** *vt* glue.

Leine ['laınә] *f* -, **-n** line, cord; (*Hunde~*) leash, lead; **~n** *nt* **-s, -** linen; **l~n** *a* linen.

Leintuch *nt* (*Bett~*) sheet; linen cloth.

Leinwand *f* (*KUNST*) canvas; (*CINE*) screen.

leise ['laızә] *a* quiet; (*sanft*) soft, gentle.

Leiste ['laıstә] *f* -, **-n** ledge; (*Zier~*) strip; (*ANAT*) groin.

leisten ['laıstәn] *vt* (*Arbeit*) do; (*Gesellschaft*) keep; (*Ersatz*) supply; (*vollbringen*) achieve; **sich** (*dat*) **etw ~ können** be able to afford sth.

Leistung *f* performance; (*gute*) achievement.

Leistungs- *zW:* **~druck** *m* pressure; **l~fähig** *a* efficient; **~fähigkeit** *f* efficiency; **~sport** *m* competitive sport; **~zulage** *f* productivity bonus.

Leitartikel *m* leading article.

Leitbild *nt* model.

leiten ['laıtәn] *vt* lead; (*Firma*) manage; (*in eine Richtung*) direct; (*ELEK*) conduct.

Leiter ['laıtәr] *m* **-s, -** leader, head; (*ELEK*) conductor // *f* -, **-n** ladder.

Leit- *zW:* **~faden** *m* guide; **~motiv** *nt* leitmotiv; **~planke** *f* crash barrier.

Leitung *f* (*Führung*) direction; (*CINE, THEAT etc*) production; (*von Firma*) management; directors *pl*; (*Wasser~*) pipe; (*Kabel*) cable; **eine lange ~ haben** be slow on the uptake.

Leitungs- *zW:* **~draht** *m* wire; **~rohr** *nt* pipe; **~wasser** *nt* tap water.

Lektion [lɛktsi'oːn] *f* lesson.

Lektüre [lɛk'tyːrә] *f* -, **-n** (*Lesen*) reading; (*Lesestoff*) reading matter.

Lende ['lɛndә] *f* -, **-n** loin; **Lendenstück** *nt* fillet.

lenk- ['lɛŋk] *zW:* **~bar** *a* (*Fahrzeug*) steerable; (*Kind*) manageable; **~en** *vt* steer; (*Kind*) guide; (*Blick, Aufmerksamkeit*) direct (*auf +akk* at); **L~rad** *nt* steering wheel; **L~stange** *f* handlebars *pl*.

Leopard [leo'part] *m* **-en, -en** leopard.

Lepra ['leːpra] *f* - leprosy.

Lerche ['lɛrçә] *f* -, **-n** lark.

lern- ['lɛrn] *zW:* **~begierig** *a* eager to learn; **~en** *vt* learn.

lesbar ['leːsbaːr] *a* legible.

Lesbierin ['lɛsbiәrın] *f* lesbian.

lesbisch ['lɛsbıʃ] *a* lesbian.

Lese ['leːzә] *f* -, **-n** (*Wein*) harvest; **~buch** *nt* reading book, reader; **l~n** *vti unreg* read; (*ernten*) gather, pick.

Leser(in *f*) *m* **-s, -** reader; **~brief** *m* reader's letter; **l~lich** *a* legible.

Lesung ['leːzʊŋ] *f* (*PARL*) reading.

letzte(r, s) ['lɛtstә(r, s)] *a* last; (*neueste*) latest; **zum ~nmal** *ad* for the last time; **~ns** *ad* lately; **~re(r, s)** *a* latter.

Leuchte ['lɔyçtә] *f* -, **-n** lamp, light; **l~n** *vi* shine, gleam; **~r** *m* **-s, -** candlestick.

Leucht- *zW:* **~farbe** *f* fluorescent colour; **~kugel** *f*, **~rakete** *f* flare; **~reklame** *f* neon sign; **~röhre** *f* strip light; **~turm** *m* lighthouse; **~zifferblatt** *nt* luminous dial.

leugnen ['lɔygnәn] *vti* deny.

Leugnung *f* denial.

Leukämie [lɔyke'miː] *f* leukaemia.

Leukoplast ® [lɔyko'plast] *nt* **-(e)s, -e** elastoplast ®.

Leumund ['lɔymʊnt] *m* **-(e)s, -e** reputation.

Leumundszeugnis *nt* character reference.

Leute ['lɔytә] *pl* people *pl*.

Leutnant ['lɔytnant] *m* **-s, -s** *od* **-e** lieutenant.

Lexikon ['lɛksikɔn] *nt* **-s, Lexiken** *od* **Lexika** encyclopaedia.

libanesisch [liːba'neːzıʃ] *a* Lebanese.

Libanon ['liːbanɔn] *n* **-s: (der) ~** the Lebanon.

Libelle [li'bɛlә] *f* -, **-n** dragonfly; (*TECH*) spirit level.

liberal [libe'aːl] *a* liberal; **L~e(r)** *mf* liberal; **L~ismus** [libera'lısmʊs] *m* liberalism.

Libero ['liːbero] *m* **-s, -s** (*Fußball*) sweeper.

Libyen ['liːbiәn] *nt* **-s** Libya.

libysch ['liːbıʃ] *a* Libyan.

Licht [lıçt] *nt* **-(e)s, -er** light; **~bild** *nt* photograph; (*Dia*) slide; **~blick** *m* cheering prospect; **l~empfindlich** *a* sensitive to light; **l~en** *vt* clear; (*Anker*) weigh // *vr* clear up; (*Haar*) thin; **~hupe** *f* flashing of headlights; **~jahr** *nt* light year; **~maschine** *f* dynamo; **~schalter** *m* light switch.

Lichtung *f* clearing, glade.

Lid [liːt] *nt* **-(e)s, -er** eyelid; **~schatten** *m* eyeshadow.

lieb [liːp] *a* dear; **das ist ~ von dir** that's kind of you; **~äugeln** *vi insep* ogle (*mit jdm/etw* sb/sth).

Liebe ['liːbә] *f* -, **-n** love; **l~bedürftig** *a*: **l~bedürftig sein** need love; **~'lei** *f* flirtation; **l~n** *vt* love; like.

liebens- *zW:* **~wert** *a* loveable; **~würdig** *a* kind; **~würdigerweise** *ad*

kindly; **L~würdigkeit** *f* kindness.
lieber ['li:bər] *ad* rather, preferably; ich gehe ~ nicht I'd rather not go // *siehe* **gern, lieb.**
Liebes- *zW:* **~brief** *m* love letter; **~kummer** *m:* **~kummer haben** be lovesick; **~paar** *nt* courting couple, lovers *pl.*
liebevoll *a* loving.
lieb- ['li:p] *zW:* **~gewinnen** *vt unreg* get fond of; **~haben** *vt unreg* be fond of; **L~haber** *m* -s, - lover; **L~habe'rei** *f* hobby; **~kosen** [li:p'ko:zən] *vt insep* caress; **~lich** *a* lovely, charming; **L~ling** *m* darling; **L~lings-** *in zW* favourite; **~los** *a* unloving; **L~schaft** *f* love affair; **~ste(r, s)** *a* favourite; **etw am ~sten mögen** like sth best.
Lied [li:t] *nt* -(e)s, -er song; (*ECCL*) hymn; **~erbuch** *nt* songbook; hymn book.
liederlich ['li:dərlıç] *a* slovenly; (*Lebenswandel*) loose, immoral; **L~keit** *f* slovenliness; immorality.
lief *etc v siehe* **laufen.**
Lieferant [lifə'rant] *m* supplier.
liefern ['li:fərn] *vt* deliver; (*versorgen mit*) supply; (*Beweis*) produce.
Liefer- *zW:* **~schein** *m* delivery note; **~termin** *m* delivery date; **~ung** *f* delivery; supply; **~wagen** *m* van.
Liege ['li:gə] *f* -, -n bed.
liegen ['li:gən] *vi unreg* lie; (*sich befinden*) be; **mir liegt nichts/viel daran** it doesn't matter to me/it matters a lot to me; **es liegt bei Ihnen, ob** ... it's up to you whether ...; **Sprachen ~ mir nicht** languages are not my line; **woran liegt es?** what's the cause?; **~bleiben** *vi unreg* (*Person*) stay in bed; stay lying down; (*Ding*) be left (behind); **~lassen** *vt unreg* (*vergessen*) leave behind.
Liege- *zW:* **~sitz** *m* (*AUT*) reclining seat; **~stuhl** *m* deck chair; **~wagen** *m* (*EISENB*) couchette.
lieh *etc v siehe* **leihen.**
ließ *etc v siehe* **lassen.**
liest *etc v siehe* **lesen.**
Lift [lıft] *m* -(e)s, -e *od* -s lift.
Likör [li'kø:r] *m* -s, -e liqueur.
lila ['li:la] *a inv* purple, lilac; **L~** *nt* -s, -s (*Farbe*) purple, lilac.
Lilie ['li:liə] *f* lily.
Limonade [limo'na:də] *f* lemonade.
Linde ['lındə] *f* -, -n lime tree, linden.
lindern ['lındərn] *vt* alleviate, soothe.
Linderung *f* alleviation.
Lineal [line'a:l] *nt* -s, -e ruler.
Linie ['li:niə] *f* line.
Linien- *zW:* **~blatt** *nt* ruled sheet; **~flug** *m* scheduled flight; **~richter** *m* linesman; **l~treu** *a* (*POL*) loyal to the party line.

linieren [lini'i:rən] *vt* line.
Linke ['lıŋkə] *f* -, -n left side; left hand; (*POL*) left; **l~(r, s)** *a* left; **ein L~r** (*POL*) a left-winger; **l~ Masche** purl.
linkisch *a* awkward, gauche.
links [lıŋks] *ad* left; to *od* on the left; **~ von mir** on *od* to my left; **L~außen** [lıŋks''ausən] *m* -s, - (*SPORT*) outside left; **L~händer(in** *f*) *m* -s, - left-handed person; **L~kurve** *f* left-hand bend; **L~verkehr** *m* traffic on the left.
Linoleum [li'no:leum] *nt* -s lino(leum).
Linse ['lınzə] *f* -, -n lentil; (*optisch*) lens.
Lippe ['lıpə] *f* -, -n lip; **Lippenstift** *m* lipstick.
lispeln ['lıspəln] *vi* lisp.
Lissabon ['lısabɔn] *nt* -s Lisbon.
List [lıst] *f* -, -en cunning; trick, ruse.
Liste ['lıstə] *f* -, -n list.
listig ['lıstıç] *a* cunning, sly.
Litanei [lita'nai] *f* litany.
Liter ['li:tər] *nt od m* -s, - litre.
literarisch [lite'ra:rıʃ] *a* literary.
Literatur [litera'tu:r] *f* literature.
Litfaßsäule ['lıtfaszɔylə] *f* advertising pillar.
Lithographie [litogra'fi:] *f* lithography.
Liturgie [litur'gi:] *f* liturgy.
liturgisch [li'turgıʃ] *a* liturgical.
Litze ['lıtsə] *f* -, -n braid; (*ELEK*) flex.
live [laıf] *ad* (*RAD, TV*) live.
Livree [li'vre:] *f* -, -n livery.
Lizenz [li'tsɛnts] *f* licence.
Lkw [ɛlka:'ve:] *m abk von* **Lastkraftwagen.**
Lob [lo:p] *nt* -(e)s praise.
Lobby ['lɔbi] *f* lobby.
loben ['lo:bən] *vt* praise; **lobenswert** *a* praiseworthy.
löblich ['lø:plıç] *a* praiseworthy, laudable.
Loch [lɔx] *nt* -(e)s, ¨er hole; **l~en** *vt* punch holes in; **~er** *m* -s, - punch.
löcherig ['lœçərıç] *a* full of holes.
Lochkarte *f* punch card.
Lochstreifen *m* punch tape.
Locke ['lɔkə] *f* -, -n lock, curl; **l~n** *vt* entice; (*Haare*) curl; **Lockenwickler** *m* -s, - curler.
locker ['lɔkər] *a* loose; **~lassen** *vi unreg:* **nicht ~lassen** not let up; **~n** *vt* loosen.
lockig ['lɔkıç] *a* curly.
Lodenmantel ['lo:dənmantəl] *m* thick woollen coat.
lodern ['lo:dərn] *vi* blaze.
Löffel ['lœfəl] *m* -s, - spoon.
Logarithmus [loga'rıtmus] *m* logarithm.
Loge ['lo:ʒə] *f* -, -n (*THEAT*) box; (*Freimaurer*) (masonic) lodge; (*Pförtner~*) office.

Logik ['lo:gɪk] *f* logic.
logisch ['lo:gɪʃ] *a* logical.
Lohn [lo:n] *m* -(e)s, ⁻e reward; (*Arbeits~*) pay, wages *pl*; **~büro** *nt* wages office; **~empfänger** *m* wage earner.
lohnen ['lo:nən] *vt* (*liter*) reward (*jdm etw* sb for sth) // *vr unpers* be worth it; **~d** *a* worthwhile.
Lohn- *zW*: **~steuer** *f* income tax; **~streifen** *m* pay slip; **~tüte** *f* pay packet.
lokal [lo'ka:l] *a* local; **L~** *nt* -(e)s, -e pub(lic house); **~i'sieren** *vt* localize.
Lokomotive [lokomo'ti:və] *f* -, -n locomotive.
Lokomotivführer *m* engine driver.
Lorbeer ['lɔrbe:r] *m* -s, -en (*lit, fig*) laurel; **~blatt** *nt* (*KOCH*) bay leaf.
Lore ['lo:rə] *f* -, -n (*MIN*) truck.
Los [lo:s] *nt* -es, -e (*Schicksal*) lot, fate; (*Lotterie~*) lottery ticket.
los [lo:s] *a* (*locker*) loose; **~!** go on!; *etw* ~ *sein* be rid of sth; *was ist* ~? what's the matter?; *dort ist nichts/viel* ~ there's nothing/a lot going on there; *etw* ~ *haben* (*umg*) be clever; **~binden** *vt unreg* untie.
löschen ['lœʃən] *vt* (*Feuer, Licht*) put out, extinguish; (*Durst*) quench; (*COMM*) cancel; (*COMPUT*) delete; (*Tonband*) erase; (*Fracht*) unload // *vi* (*Feuerwehr*) put out a fire; (*Papier*) blot.
Lösch- *zW*: **~fahrzeug** *nt* fire engine; fire boat; **~gerät** *nt* fire extinguisher; **~papier** *nt* blotting paper.
lose ['lo:zə] *a* loose.
Lösegeld *nt* ransom.
losen ['lo:zən] *vi* draw lots.
lösen ['lø:zən] *vt* loosen; (*Rätsel etc*) solve; (*Verlobung*) call off; (*CHEM*) dissolve; (*Partnerschaft*) break up; (*Fahrkarte*) buy // *vr* (*aufgehen*) come loose; (*Zucker etc*) dissolve; (*Problem, Schwierigkeit*) (re)solve itself.
los- *zW*: **~fahren** *vi unreg* leave; **~gehen** *vi unreg* set out; (*anfangen*) start; (*Bombe*) go off; *auf jdn* **~gehen** go for sb; **~kaufen** *vt* (*Gefangene, Geißeln*) pay ransom for; **~kommen** *vi unreg*: *von etw* **~kommen** get away from sth; **~lassen** *vt unreg* (*Seil*) let go of; (*Schimpfe*) let loose; **~laufen** *vi unreg* run off.
löslich ['lø:slɪç] *a* soluble; **L~keit** *f* solubility.
los- *zW*: **~lösen** *vtr* free; **~machen** *vt* loosen; (*Boot*) unmoor // *vr* get free; **~schrauben** *vt* unscrew; **~sprechen** *vt unreg* absolve.
Losung ['lo:zʊŋ] *f* watchword, slogan.
Lösung ['lø:zʊŋ] *f* (*Lockermachen*) loosening; (*eines Rätsels, CHEM*) solution; **Lösungsmittel** *nt* solvent.
loswerden *vt unreg* get rid of.
Lot [lo:t] *nt* -(e)s, -e plummet; *im* ~ vertical; (*fig*) on an even keel.
löten [lø:tən] *vt* solder.
Lothringen ['lo:trɪŋən] *nt* -s Lorraine.
Lötkolben *m* soldering iron.
Lotse ['lo:tsə] *m* -n, -n pilot; (*AVIAT*) air traffic controller; **l~n** *vt* pilot; (*umg*) lure.
Lotterie [lɔtə'ri:] *f* lottery.
Löwe ['lø:və] *m* -n, -n lion; (*ASTROL*) Leo; **Löwenanteil** *m* lion's share; **Löwenzahn** *m* dandelion.
loyal [loa'ja:l] *a* loyal.
lt. *abk* (= *laut*) according to.
Luchs ['lʊks] *m* -es, -e lynx.
Lücke ['lʏkə] *f* -, -n gap; **Lückenbüßer** *m* -s, - stopgap; **lückenlos** *a* complete.
Luder ['lu:dər] *nt* -s, - (*pej: Frau*) hussy; (*bedauernswert*) poor wretch.
Luft [lʊft] *f* -, ⁻e air; (*Atem*) breath; *in der* ~ *liegen* be in the air; *jdn wie* ~ *behandeln* ignore sb; **~angriff** *m* air raid; **~ballon** *m* balloon; **~blase** *f* air bubble; **l~dicht** *a* airtight; **~druck** *m* atmospheric pressure.
lüften ['lʏftən] *vti* air; (*Hut*) lift, raise.
Luft- *zW*: **~fahrt** *f* aviation; **l~gekühlt** *a* air-cooled; **l~ig** *a* (*Ort*) breezy; (*Raum*) airy; (*Kleider*) summery; **~kissenfahrzeug** *nt* hovercraft; **~kurort** *m* health resort; **l~leer** *a*: **~leerer Raum** vacuum; **~linie** *f*: *in der* **~linie** as the crow flies; **~loch** *nt* air-hole; (*AVIAT*) airpocket; **~matratze** *f* lilo ® (*Brit*), air mattress; **~pirat** *m* hijacker; **~post** *f* airmail; **~röhre** *f* (*ANAT*) wind pipe; **~schlange** *f* streamer; **~schutzkeller** *m* air-raid shelter.
Lüftung ['lʏftʊŋ] *f* ventilation.
Luft- *zW*: **~verkehr** *m* air traffic; **~waffe** *f* air force; **~zug** *m* draught.
Lüge ['ly:gə] *f* -, -n lie; *jdn/etw* **~n** *strafen* give the lie to sb/sth; **l~n** *vi unreg* lie.
Lügner(in *f*) *m* -s, - liar.
Luke ['lu:kə] *f* -, -n dormer window, hatch.
Lümmel ['lʏməl] *m* -s, - lout; **l~n** *vr* lounge (about).
Lump [lʊmp] *m* -en, -en scamp, rascal.
Lumpen ['lʊmpən] *m* -s, - rag; *sich nicht* **l~** *lassen* not be mean.
lumpig ['lʊmpɪç] *a* shabby.
Lunge ['lʊŋə] *f* -, -n lung; **Lungenentzündung** *f* pneumonia; **lungenkrank** *a* consumptive.
lungern ['lʊŋərn] *vi* hang about.
Lupe ['lu:pə] *f* -, -n magnifying glass;

unter die ~ **nehmen** (*fig*) scrutinize.
Lupine [lu'pi:nə] *f* lupin.
Lust [lʊst] *f* -, ¨e joy, delight; (*Neigung*) desire; ~ **haben zu** *od* **auf etw** (*akk*)/**etw zu tun** feel like sth/doing sth.
lüstern ['lʏstərn] *a* lustful, lecherous.
lustig ['lʊstɪç] *a* (*komisch*) amusing, funny; (*fröhlich*) cheerful.
Lüstling *m* lecher.
Lust- *zW:* **l~los** *a* unenthusiastic; **~mord** *m* sex(ual) murder; **~spiel** *nt* comedy.
lutschen ['lʊtʃən] *vti* suck; **am Daumen** ~ suck one's thumb.
Lutscher *m* -s, - lollipop.
Luxemburg ['lʊksəmbʊrk] *nt* -s Luxembourg.
luxuriös [lʊksuri'ø:s] *a* luxurious.
Luxus ['lʊksʊs] *m* - luxury; **~artikel** *pl* luxury goods *pl*; **~hotel** *nt* luxury hotel.
Lymphe ['lʏmfə] *f* -, -n lymph.
lynchen ['lʏnçən] *vt* lynch.
Lyrik ['ly:rɪk] *f* lyric poetry; **~er** *m* -s, - lyric poet.
lyrisch ['ly:rɪʃ] *a* lyrical.

M

M, m [ɛm] *nt* M, m // **m** *abk von* **Meter.**
Maas [ma:s] *f* - Meuse.
Mach- [max]' *zW:* **~art** *f* make; **m~bar** *a* feasible; **~e** *f* - (*umg*) show, sham.
machen ['maxən] ◆ *vt* **1** do; (*herstellen, zubereiten*) make; **was machst du da?** what are you doing (there)?; **das ist nicht zu ~** that can't be done; **das Radio leiser ~** turn the radio down; **aus Holz gemacht** made of wood
2 (*verursachen, bewirken*) make; **jdm Angst ~** make sb afraid; **das macht die Kälte** it's the cold that does that
3 (*ausmachen*) matter; **das macht nichts** that doesn't matter; **die Kälte macht mir nichts** I don't mind the cold
4 (*kosten, ergeben*) be; **3 und 5 macht 8** 3 and 5 is *od* are 8; **was** *od* **wieviel macht das?** how much does that make?
5: **was macht die Arbeit?** how's the work going?; **was macht dein Bruder?** how is your brother doing?; **das Auto ~ lassen** have the car done; **mach's gut!** take care! (*viel Glück*) good luck!
◆ *vi:* **mach schnell** hurry up!; **Schluß ~** finish (off); **mach schon!** come on!; **das macht müde** it makes you

tired; **in etw** (*dat*) ~ be *od* deal in sth
◆ *vr* come along (nicely); **sich an etw** (*akk*) ~ set about sth; **sich verständlich** ~ make oneself understood; **sich** (*dat*) **viel aus jdm/etw** ~ like sb/ sth.
Macht [maxt] *f* -, ¨e power; **~haber** *m* -s, - ruler.
mächtig ['mɛçtɪç] *a* powerful, mighty; (*umg: ungeheuer*) enormous.
Macht- *zW:* **m~los** *a* powerless; **~probe** *f* trial of strength; **~stellung** *f* position of power; **~wort** *nt:* **ein ~wort sprechen** lay down the law.
Machwerk *nt* work; (*schlechte Arbeit*) botched-up job.
Mädchen ['mɛ:tçən] *nt* girl; **m~haft** *a* girlish; **~name** *m* maiden name.
Made ['ma:də] *f* -, -n maggot.
madig ['ma:dɪç] *a* maggoty; **jdm etw ~ machen** spoil sth for sb.
mag *etc v siehe* **mögen.**
Magazin [maga'tsi:n] *nt* -s, -e magazine.
Magen ['ma:gən] *m* -s, - *od* ¨ stomach; **~schmerzen** *pl* stomachache.
mager ['ma:gər] *a* lean; (*dünn*) thin; **M~keit** *f* leanness; thinness.
Magie [ma'gi:] *f* magic.
Magier ['ma:giər] *m* -s, - magician.
magisch ['ma:gɪʃ] *a* magical.
Magnet [ma'gne:t] *m* -s *od* -en, -en magnet; **~band** *nt* magnetic tape; **m~isch** *a* magnetic; **m~i'sieren** *vt* magnetize; **~nadel** *f* magnetic needle.
Mahagoni [maha'go:ni] *nt* -s mahogany.
mähen ['mɛ:ən] *vti* mow.
Mahl [ma:l] *nt* -(e)s, -e meal; **m~en** *vt unreg* grind; **~zeit** *f* meal // *interj* enjoy your meal.
Mahnbrief *m* reminder.
Mähne ['mɛ:nə] *f* -, -n mane.
Mahn- ['ma:n] *zW:* **m~en** *vt* remind; (*warnend*) warn; (*wegen Schuld*) demand payment from; **~ung** *f* reminder; admonition, warning.
Mähren ['mɛ:rən] *nt* -s Moravia.
Mai [mai] *m* -(e)s, -e May; **~glöckchen** *nt* lily of the valley; **~käfer** *m* cockchafer; **~land** *nt* Milan; **m~ländisch** *a* Milanese.
Mais [mais] *m* -es, -e maize, corn (*US*); **~kolben** *m* corncob.
Majestät [majes'tɛ:t] *f* majesty; **m~isch** *a* majestic.
Major [ma'jo:r] *m* -s, -e (*MIL*) major; (*AVIAT*) squadron leader.
Majoran [majo'ra:n] *m* -s, -e marjoram.
makaber [ma'ka:bər] *a* macabre.
Makel ['ma:kəl] *m* -s, - blemish; (*moralisch*) stain; **m~los** *a* immaculate,

spotless.

mäkeln ['mɛːkəln] *vi* find fault.

Makkaroni [maka'roːni] *pl* macaroni *sing*.

Makler(in *f*) ['maːklər(ɪn)] *m* -s, - broker.

Makrele [ma'kreːlə] *f* -, -n mackerel.

Makrone [ma'kroːnə] *f* -, -n macaroon.

Mal [maːl] *nt* -(e)s, -e mark, sign; (*Zeitpunkt*) time; **m~** *ad* times; (*umg*) siehe **einmal**; **-m~** *suff* -times; **m~en** *vti* paint; **~er** *m* -s, - painter; **~e'rei** *f* painting; **m~erisch** *a* picturesque; **~kasten** *m* paintbox.

Mallorca [ma'lɔrka] *nt* -s Majorca.

malnehmen *vti unreg* multiply.

Malz [malts] *nt* -es malt; **~bonbon** *nt* cough drop; **~kaffee** *m* malt coffee.

Mama ['mamaː] *f* -, -s, **Mami** ['mami] *f* -, -s (*umg*) mum(my).

Mammut ['mamʊt] *nt* -s, -e *od* -s mammoth.

man [man] *pron* one, you; **~** sagt, ... they *od* people say ...; **wie schreibt ~ das?** how do you write it? how is it written?

manche(r, s) ['mançə(r, s)] *a* many a; (*pl*) a number of // *pron* some.

mancherlei *a inv* various // *pron* a variety of things.

manchmal *ad* sometimes.

Mandant(in *f*) [man'dant(ɪn)] *m* (*JUR*) client.

Mandarine [manda'riːnə] *f* mandarin, tangerine.

Mandat [man'daːt] *nt* -(e)s, -e mandate.

Mandel ['mandəl] *f* -, -n almond; (*ANAT*) tonsil.

Manege [ma'nɛːʒə] *f* -, -n ring, arena.

Mangel ['maŋəl] *f* -, -n mangle // *m* -s, ⁼ lack; (*Knappheit*) shortage (*an* +*dat* of); (*Fehler*) defect, fault; **~erscheinung** *f* deficiency symptom; **m~haft** *a* poor; (*fehlerhaft*) defective, faulty; **m~n** *vi unpers*: **es mangelt jdm an etw** (*dat*) sb lacks sth // *vt* (*Wäsche*) mangle; **m~s** *präp* +*gen* for lack of.

Manie [ma'niː] *f* mania.

Manier [ma'niːr] *f* - manner; style; (*pej*) mannerism; **~en** *pl* manners *pl*.

Manifest [mani'fɛst] *nt* -es, -e manifesto.

Maniküre [mani'kyːrə] *f* -, -n manicure; **m~n** *vt* manicure.

manipulieren [manipu'liːrən] *vt* manipulate.

Manko ['maŋko] *nt* -s, -s deficiency; (*COMM*) deficit.

Mann [man] *m* -(e)s, ⁼er man; (*Ehe~*) husband; (*NAUT*) hand; **seinen ~ stehen** hold one's own.

Männchen ['mɛnçən] *nt* little man;

(*Tier*) male.

Mannequin [manə'kɛː] *nt* -s, -s fashion model.

männlich ['mɛnlɪç] *a* (*BIOL*) male; (*fig*, *GRAM*) masculine.

Mannschaft *f* (*SPORT*, *fig*) team; (*NAUT*, *AVIAT*) crew; (*MIL*) other ranks *pl*.

Manöver [ma'nøːvər] *nt* -s, - manoeuvre.

manövrieren [manøˈvriːrən] *vti* manoeuvre.

Mansarde [man'zardə] *f* -, -n attic.

Manschette [man'ʃɛtə] *f* cuff; (*TECH*) collar; sleeve; **Manschettenknopf** *m* cufflink.

Mantel ['mantəl] *m* -s, ⁼ coat; (*TECH*) casing, jacket.

Manuskript [manu'skrɪpt] *nt* -(e)s, -e manuscript.

Mappe ['mapə] *f* -, -n briefcase; (*Akten~*) folder.

Märchen ['mɛːrçən] *nt* fairy tale; **m~haft** *a* fabulous; **~prinz** *m* Prince Charming.

Marder ['mardər] *m* -s, - marten.

Margarine [marga'riːnə] *f* margarine.

Marienkäfer [ma'riːənkɛːfər] *m* ladybird.

Marine [ma'riːnə] *f* navy; **m~blau** *a* navy-blue.

marinieren [mari'niːrən] *vt* marinate.

Marionette [mario'nɛtə] *f* puppet.

Mark [mark] *f* -, - (*Münze*) mark // *nt* -(e)s (*Knochen~*) marrow; **durch ~ und Bein gehen** go right through sb; **m~ant** [mar'kant] *a* striking.

Marke ['markə] *f* -, -n mark; (*Warensorte*) brand; (*Fabrikat*) make; (*Rabatt~*, *Brief~*) stamp; (*Essens~*) ticket; (*aus Metall etc*) token, disc.

Mark- *zW*: **m~ieren** [mar'kiːrən] *vt* mark // *vti* (*umg*) act; **~ierung** *f* marking; **~ise** [mar'kiːzə] *f* -, -n awning; **~stück** *nt* one-mark piece.

Markt [markt] *m* -(e)s, ⁼e market; **~forschung** *f* market research; **m~gängig** *a* marketable; **~platz** *m* market place; **~wirtschaft** *f* market economy.

Marmelade [marmə'laːdə] *f* -, -n jam.

Marmor ['marmɔr] *m* -s, -e marble; **m~ieren** [-'riːrən] *vt* marble; **m~n** *a* marble.

Marokk- [ma'rɔk] *zW*: **~o** *nt* -s Morocco; **~aner(in** *f*) [marɔ'kaːnər(ɪn)] *m* -s, - Moroccan; **m~'anisch** *a* Moroccan.

Marone [ma'roːnə] *f* -, -n *od* **Maroni** chestnut.

Marotte [ma'rɔtə] *f* -, -n fad, quirk.

Marsch [marʃ] *m* -(e)s, ⁼e march; **m~** *interj* march // *f* -, -en marsh; **~befehl** *m* marching orders *pl*; **m~bereit** *a* ready to move; **m~ieren**

[mar'ʃiːrən] *vi* march.

Märtyrer(in *f*) ['mɛrtyrər(ın)] *m* **-s, -** martyr.

März [mɛrts] *m* **-(es), -e** March.

Marzipan [martsi'paːn] *nt* **-s, -e** marzipan.

Masche ['maʃə] *f* **-, -n** mesh; (*Strick~*) stitch; **das ist die neueste ~** that's the latest thing; **Maschendraht** *m* wire mesh; **maschenfest** *a* runproof.

Maschine [ma'ʃiːnə] *f* machine; (*Motor*) engine; (*Schreib~*) typewriter; **maschinell** [maʃi'nɛl] *a* machine(-); mechanical.

Maschinen- *zW*: **~bauer** *m* mechanical engineer; **~gewehr** *nt* machine gun; **~pistole** *f* submachine gun; **~schaden** *m* mechanical fault; **~schlosser** *m* fitter; **~schrift** *f* typescript.

machineschreiben *vi unreg* type.

Maschinist [maʃi'nıst] *m* engineer.

Maser ['maːzər] *f* **-, -n** grain; speckle; **~n** *pl* (*MED*) measles *sing*; **~ung** *f* grain(ing).

Maske ['maskə] *f* **-, -n** mask.

Maskenball *m* fancy-dress ball.

Maskerade [maskə'raːdə] *f* masquerade.

maskieren [mas'kiːrən] *vt* mask; (*verkleiden*) dress up // *vr* disguise o.s., dress up.

Maß [maːs] *nt* **-es, -e** measure; (*Mäßigung*) moderation; (*Grad*) degree, extent // *f* **-, -(e)** litre of beer.

Massage [ma'saːʒə] *f* **-, -n** massage.

Maßanzug *m* made-to-measure suit.

Maßarbeit *f* (*fig*) neat piece of work.

Masse ['masə] *f* **-, -n** mass.

Massen- *zW*: **~artikel** *m* mass-produced article; **~grab** *nt* mass grave; **m~haft** *a* loads of; **~medien** *pl* mass media *pl*; **~veranstaltung** *f* mass meeting.

Masseur [ma'søːr] *m* masseur.

Masseuse [ma'søːzə] *f* masseuse.

maßgebend *a* authoritative.

maßhalten *vi unreg* exercise moderation.

massieren [ma'siːrən] *vt* massage; (*MIL*) mass.

massig ['masıç] *a* massive; (*umg*) massive amount of.

mäßig ['mɛːsıç] *a* moderate; **~en** ['mɛːsıgən] *vt* restrain, moderate; **M~keit** *f* moderation.

massiv [ma'siːf] *a* solid; (*fig*) heavy, rough; **M~** *nt* **-s, -e** massif.

Maß- *zW*: **~krug** *m* tankard; **m~los** *a* extreme; **~nahme** *f* **-, -n** measure, step; **m~regeln** *vt insep* reprimand; **~stab** *m* rule, measure; (*fig*) standard; (*GEOG*) scale; **m~voll** *a* moderate.

Mast ['mast] *m* **-(e)s, -e(n)** mast; (*ELEK*) pylon.

mästen ['mɛstən] *vt* fatten.

Material [materi'aːl] *nt* **-s, -ien** material(s); **~fehler** *m* material defect; **~ismus** [-'lismʊs] *m* materialism; **~ist** [-'list] *m* materialist; **m~istisch** [-'listıʃ] *a* materialistic.

Materie [ma'teːriə] *f* matter, substance.

materiell [materi'ɛl] *a* material.

Mathematik [matema'tiːk] *f* mathematics *sing*; **~er(in** *f*) [mate-'maːtikər(ın)] *m* **-s, -** mathematician.

mathematisch [mate'maːtıʃ] *a* mathematical.

Matratze [ma'tratsə] *f* **-, -n** mattress.

Matrixdrucker ['maːtriksdrʊkər] dot-matrix printer.

Matrize [ma'triːtsə] *f* **-, -n** matrix; (*zum Abziehen*) stencil.

Matrose [ma'troːzə] *m* **-n, -n** sailor.

Matsch [matʃ] *m* **-(e)s** mud; (*Schnee~*) slush; **m~ig** *a* muddy; slushy.

matt [mat] *a* weak; (*glanzlos*) dull; (*PHOT*) matt; (*Schach*) mate.

Matte ['matə] *f* **-, -n** mat.

Mattscheibe *f* (*TV*) screen; **~haben** (*umg*) not be quite with it.

Mauer ['mauər] *f* **-, -n** wall; **m~n** *vti* build; lay bricks.

Maul [maʊl] *nt* **-(e)s, Mäuler** mouth; **m~en** *vi* (*umg*) grumble; **~esel** *m* mule; **~korb** *m* muzzle; **~sperre** *f* lockjaw; **~tier** *nt* mule; **~wurf** *m* mole.

Maurer ['maʊrər] *m* **-s, -** bricklayer.

Maus [maʊs] *f* **-, Mäuse** (*auch COMPUT*) mouse.

Mause- ['maʊzə] *zW*: **~falle** *f* mousetrap; **m~n** *vt* (*umg*) flinch // *vi* catch mice; **m~tot** *a* stone dead.

maximal [maksi'maːl] *a* maximum.

Maximum ['maksimʊm] *nt* maximum.

Maxi-Single ['maksi'sıŋgl] *f* **-, -s** 12-inch single.

Mayonnaise [majɔ'nɛːzə] *f* **-, -n** mayonnaise.

m.E. *abk* (= *meines Erachtens*) in my opinion.

Mechan- [meʧaːn] *zW*: **~ik** *f* mechanics *sing*; (*Getriebe*) mechanics *pl*; **~iker** *m* **-s, -** mechanic, engineer; **m~isch** *a* mechanical; **~ismus** [meʧa'nısmʊs] *m* mechanism.

meckern ['mɛkərn] *vi* bleat; (*umg*) moan.

Medaille [me'daljə] *f* **-, -n** medal.

Medaillon [medal'jõː] *nt* **-s, -s** (*Schmuck*) locket.

Medikament [medika'mɛnt] *nt* medicine.

meditieren [medi'tiːrən] *vi* meditate.

Medizin [medi'tsiːn] *f* **-, -en** medicine;

m~isch *a* medical.
Meer [me:r] *nt* -(e)s, -e sea; **~busen** *m* bay, gulf; **~enge** *f* straits *pl*; **Meeresspiegel** *m* sea level; **~rettich** *m* horseradish; **~schweinchen** *nt* guinea-pig.
Megaphon [mega'fo:n] *nt* -s, -e megaphone.
Mehl ['me:l] *nt* -(e)s, -e flour; **m~ig** *a* floury.
mehr [me:r] *a,ad* more; **~deutig** *a* ambiguous; **~ere** *a* several; **~eres** *pron* several things; **~fach** *a* multiple; (*wiederholt*) repeated; **M~heit** *f* majority; **~malig** *a* repeated; **~mals** *ad* repeatedly; **~stimmig** *a* for several voices; **~stimmig singen** harmonize; **M~wertsteuer** *f* value added tax, VAT; **M~zahl** *f* majority; (*GRAM*) plural.
meiden ['maɪdən] *vt unreg* avoid.
Meile ['maɪlə] *f* -, -n mile; **Meilenstein** *m* milestone; **meilenweit** *a* for miles.
mein [maɪn] *pron* my; **~e(r, s)** mine.
Meineid ['maɪn'aɪt] *m* perjury.
meinen ['maɪnən] *vti* think; (*sagen*) say; (*sagen wollen*) mean; **das will ich ~** I should think so.
mein-: **~erseits** *ad* for my part; **~esgleichen** *pron* people like me; **~etwegen** *ad* (*für mich*) for my sake; (*wegen mir*) on my account; (*von mir aus*) as far as I'm concerned; I don't care *od* mind.
Meinung ['maɪnʊŋ] *f* opinion; **ganz meine ~** I quite agree; **jdm die ~ sagen** give sb a piece of one's mind.
Meinungs- *zW*: **~austausch** *m* exchange of views; **~umfrage** *f* opinion poll; **~verschiedenheit** *f* difference of opinion.
Meise ['maɪzə] *f* -, -n tit(mouse).
Meißel ['maɪsəl] *m* -s, - chisel; **m~n** *vt* chisel.
meist ['maɪst] *a,ad* most(ly); **am ~en** the most; **~ens** *ad* generally, usually.
Meister ['maɪstər] *m* -s, - master; (*SPORT*) champion; **m~haft** *a* masterly; **~schaft** *f* mastery; (*SPORT*) championship; **~stück** *nt*, **~werk** *nt* masterpiece.
Melancholie [melaŋko'li:] *f* melancholy.
melancholisch [melaŋ'ko:lɪʃ] *a* melancholy.
Melde- ['mɛldə] *zW*: **~frist** *f* registration period; **m~n** *vt* report // *vr* report (*bei* to); (*SCH*) put one's hand up; (*freiwillig*) volunteer; (*auf etw, am Telefon*) answer; **sich zu Wort m~n** ask to speak; **~pflicht** *f* obligation to register with the police; **~stelle** *f* registration office.

Meldung ['mɛldʊŋ] *f* announcement; (*Bericht*) report.
meliert [me'li:rt] *a* mottled, speckled.
melken ['mɛlkən] *vt unreg* milk.
Melodie [melo'di:] *f* melody, tune.
melodisch [me'lo:dɪʃ] *a* melodious, tuneful.
Melone [me'lo:nə] *f* -, -n melon; (*Hut*) bowler (hat).
Membran(e) [mem'bra:n(ə)] *f* -, -en (*TECH*) diaphragm.
Memoiren [memo'a:rən] *pl* memoirs *pl.*
Menge ['mɛŋə] *f* -, -n quantity; (*Menschen~*) crowd; (*große Anzahl*) lot (of); **m~n** *vt* mix // *vr*: **sich m~n in** (+*akk*) meddle with; **Mengenlehre** *f* (*MATH*) set theory; **Mengenrabatt** *m* bulk discount.
Mensch [mɛnʃ] *m* -en, -en human being, man; person; **kein ~** nobody // *interj* hey.
Menschen- *zW*: **~feind** *m* misanthrope; **m~freundlich** *a* philanthropical; **~kenner** *m* -s, - judge of human nature; **m~möglich** *a* humanly possible; **~recht** *nt* human rights *pl*; **m~unwürdig** *a* degrading; **~verstand** *m*: **gesunder ~verstand** common sense.
Mensch- *zW*: **~heit** *f* humanity, mankind; **m~lich** *a* human; (*human*) humane; **~lichkeit** *f* humanity.
Menstruation [mɛnstruatsi'o:n] *f* menstruation.
Mentalität [mɛntali'tɛ:t] *f* mentality.
Menü [me'ny:] *nt* -s, -s (*auch COMPUT*) menu.
Merk- [mɛrk] *zW*: **~blatt** *nt* instruction sheet *od* leaflet; **m~en** *vt* notice; **sich** (*dat*) **etw m~en** remember sth; **m~lich** *a* noticeable; **~mal** *nt* sign, characteristic; **m~würdig** *a* odd.
meßbar ['mɛsba:r] *a* measurable.
Messe ['mɛsə] *f* -, -n fair; (*ECCL*) mass; **m~n** *unreg vt* measure // *vr* compete.
Messer *nt* -s, - knife; **~spitze** *f* knife point; (*in Rezept*) pinch.
Meßgerät *nt* measuring device, gauge.
Messing ['mɛsɪŋ] *nt* -s brass.
Metall [me'tal] *nt* -s, -e metal; **m~en**, **m~isch** *a* metallic.
Meteor [mete'o:r] *m* -s, -e meteor.
Meter ['me:tər] *nt od m* -s, - metre; **~maß** *nt* tape measure.
Methode [me'to:də] *f* -, -n method.
methodisch [me'to:dɪʃ] *a* methodical.
Metropole [metro'po:lə] *f* -, -n metropolis.
Metzger ['mɛtsgər] *m* -s, - butcher; **~ei** [-'raɪ] *f* butcher's (shop).
Meuchelmord ['mɔʏçəlmɔrt] *m* assassination.

Meute ['mɔytə] f -, -n pack; ~'**rei** f mutiny; **m~rn** vi mutiny.

miauen [mi'auən] vi miaow.

mich [mɪç] pron akk von **ich** me; myself.

Miene ['miːnə] f -, -n look, expression.

mies [miːs] a (umg) lousy.

Miet- ['miːt] zW: ~**auto** nt hired car; ~**e** f -, -n rent; **zur ~e wohnen** live in rented accommodation; **m~en** vt rent; (Auto) hire; ~**er(in** f) m -s, - tenant; **Mietshaus** nt tenement, block of flats; ~**vertrag** m tenancy agreement.

Migräne [mi'grɛːnə] f -, -n migraine.

Mikro- ['mikro] zW: ~**computer** m microcomputer; ~**fon,** ~**phon** [-'foːn] nt -s, -e microphone; ~**skop** [-'skoːp] nt -s, -e microscope; **m~skopisch** a microscopic; ~**wellenherd** m microwave (oven).

Milch [mɪlç] f - milk; ~**glas** nt frosted glass; **m~ig** a milky; ~**kaffee** m white coffee; ~**pulver** nt powdered milk; ~**straße** f Milky Way; ~**zahn** m milk tooth.

mild [mɪlt] a mild; (Richter) lenient; (freundlich) kind, charitable; **M~e** ['mɪldə] f -, -n mildness; leniency; ~**ern** vt mitigate, soften; (Schmerz) alleviate; ~**ernde Umstände** extenuating circumstances.

Milieu [mili'øː] nt -s, -s background, environment; **m~geschädigt** a maladjusted.

Mili- [mili] zW: **m~tant** [-'tant] a militant; ~**tär** [-'tɛːr] nt -s military, army; ~'**tärgericht** nt military court; **m~'tärisch** a military.

Milli- ['mɪli] zW: **m~ardär** [-ar'dɛːr] m multimillionaire; ~**arde** [-'ardə] f -, -n milliard; billion (bes US); ~**meter** m millimetre; ~**on** [-'oːn] f -, -en million; ~**onär** [-o'nɛːr] m millionaire.

Milz [mɪlts] f -, -en spleen.

Mimik ['miːmɪk] f mime.

Mimose [mi'moːzə] f -, -n mimosa; (fig) sensitive person.

minder ['mɪndər] a inferior // ad less; **M~heit** f minority; ~**jährig** a minor; **M~jährigkeit** f minority; ~**n** vtr decrease, diminish; **M~ung** f decrease; ~**wertig** a inferior; **M~wertigkeitskomplex** m inferiority complex.

Mindest- ['mɪndəst] zW: ~**alter** nt minimum age; ~**betrag** m minimum amount; **m~e(r, s)** a least; **m~ens, zum m~en** ad at least; ~**lohn** m minimum wage; ~**maß** nt minimum.

Mine ['miːnə] f -, -n mine; (Bleistift~) lead; (Kugelschreiber~) refill; **Minenfeld** nt minefield.

Mineral [mine'raːl] nt -s, -e od -ien mineral; **m~isch** a mineral;

~**wasser** nt mineral water.

Miniatur [minia'tuːr] f miniature.

minimal [mini'maːl] a minimal.

Minimum ['minimʊm] nt minimum.

Minister [mi'nɪstər] m -s, - minister; **m~iell** [mɪnɪsteri'ɛl] a ministerial; ~**ium** [mɪnɪs'teːriʊm] nt ministry; ~**präsident** m prime minister.

minus ['miːnʊs] ad minus; **M~** nt -, - deficit; **M~pol** m negative pole; **M~zeichen** nt minus sign.

Minute [mi'nuːtə] f -, -n minute; **Minutenzeiger** m minute hand.

Mio. abk (= Million(en)) million(s).

mir [miːr] pron dat von **ich** (to) me; ~ **nichts, dir nichts** just like that.

Misch- ['mɪʃ] zW: ~**ehe** f mixed marriage; **m~en** vt mix; ~**ling** m halfcaste; ~**ung** f mixture.

Miß- ['mɪs] zW: **m~'achten** vt insep disregard; ~'**achtung** f disregard; ~**behagen** nt discomfort, uneasiness; ~**bildung** f deformity; **m~'billigen** vt insep disapprove of; ~**billigung** f disapproval; ~**brauch** m abuse; (falscher Gebrauch) misuse; **m~'brauchen** vt insep abuse; misuse (zu for); ~**erfolg** m failure; **m~'fallen** vi unreg insep displease (jdm sb); ~**fallen** nt -s displeasure; ~**geburt** f freak; (fig) abortion; ~**geschick** nt misfortune; **m~glücken** [mɪs'glʏkən] vi insep fail; **jdm m~glückt etw** sb does not succeed with sth; ~**griff** m mistake; ~**gunst** f envy; **m~günstig** a envious; **m~'handeln** vt insep ill-treat; ~'**handlung** f ill-treatment.

Mission [mɪsi'oːn] f mission; ~**ar** [mɪsio'naːr] m missionary.

Miß- zW: ~**klang** m discord; ~**kredit** m discredit; **m~lingen** [mɪs'lɪŋən] vi unreg insep fail; ~**mut** m bad temper; **m~mutig** a cross; **m~'raten** vi (unreg insep) turn out badly // a illbred; ~**stand** m bad state of affairs; abuse; ~**stimmung** f ill-humour, discord; **m~'trauen** vi insep mistrust; ~**trauen** nt -s distrust, suspicion (of); ~**trauensantrag** m (POL) motion of no confidence; ~**trauensvotum** nt -s, -voten (POL) vote of no confidence; **m~trauisch** a distrustful, suspicious; ~**verhältnis** nt disproportion; ~**verständnis** nt misunderstanding; **m~verstehen** vt unreg insep misunderstand.

Mist [mɪst] m -(e)s dung; dirt; (umg) rubbish; ~**el** f -, -n mistletoe; ~**haufen** m dungheap.

mit [mɪt] präp +dat with; (mittels) by; ~ **der Bahn** by train; ~ **10 Jahren** at the age of 10 // ad along, too; **wollen Sie ~?** do you want to come along?

Mitarbeit ['mit'arbait] f cooperation; **m~en** vi cooperate, collaborate; **~er(in** f) m collaborator; co-worker // pl staff.

Mit- zW: **~bestimmung** f participation in decision-making; **m~bringen** vt unreg bring along; **~bürger(in** f) m fellow citizen.

miteinander [mit'ai'nandər] ad together, with one another.

Mit- zW: **m~erleben** vt see, witness; **~esser** ['mit'ɛsər] m **-s**, - blackhead; **m~geben** vt unreg give; **~gefühl** nt sympathy; **m~gehen** vi unreg go/ come along; **m~genommen** a done in, in a bad way; **~gift** f dowry.

Mitglied ['mitgli:t] nt member; **Mitgliedsbeitrag** m membership fee; **~schaft** f membership.

Mit- zW: **m~halten** vi unreg keep up; **~hilfe** f help, assistance; **m~hören** vt listen in to; **m~kommen** vi unreg come along; (verstehen) keep up, follow; **~läufer** m hanger-on; (POL) fellow-traveller.

Mitleid nt sympathy; (Erbarmen) compassion; **~enschaft** f: in **~enschaft ziehen** affect; **m~ig** a sympathetic; **m~slos** a pitiless, merciless.

Mit- zW: **m~machen** vt join in, take part in; **~mensch** m fellow man; **m~nehmen** vt unreg take along/ away; (anstrengen) wear out, exhaust; **zum M~nehmen** to take away.

mitsamt [mit'zamt] präp +dat together with.

Mitschuld f complicity; **m~ig** a also guilty (an +dat of).

Mit- zW: **~schüler(in** f) m schoolmate; **m~spielen** vi join in, take part; **~spieler(in** f) m partner; **~spracherecht** ['mitʃpra:xəreçt] nt voice, say.

Mittag ['mita:k] m **-(e)s**, **-e** midday, lunchtime; **(zu)** ~ **essen** have lunch; **m~** ad at lunchtime od noon; **~essen** nt lunch, dinner.

mittags ad at lunchtime od noon; **M~pause** f lunch break; **M~schlaf** m early afternoon nap, siesta.

Mittäter(in f) ['mittɛ:tər(in)] m accomplice.

Mitte ['mitə] f **-**, **-n** middle; (POL) centre; **aus unserer** ~ from our midst.

mitteil- ['mittail] zW: **~en** vt: jdm etw **~en** inform sb of sth, communicate sth to sb; **M~ung** f communication.

Mittel ['mitəl] nt **-s** - means; method; (MATH) average; (MED) medicine; **ein** ~ **zum Zweck** a means to an end; **~alter** nt Middle Ages pl; **m~alterlich** a mediaeval; **~amerika**

nt Central America; **m~bar** a indirect; **~ding** nt cross; **~europa** nt Central Europe; **m~los** a without means; **m~mäßig** a mediocre, middling; **~mäßigkeit** f mediocrity; **~meer** nt Mediterranean; **~punkt** m centre; **m~s** präp +gen by means of; **~stand** m middle class; **~streckenrakete** f medium-range missile; **~streifen** m central reservation; **~stürmer** m centre-forward; **~weg** m middle course; **~welle** f (RAD) medium wave.

mitten ['mitən] ad in the middle; ~ **auf der Straße/in der Nacht** in the middle of the street/night.

Mitternacht ['mitərnaxt] f midnight.

mittlere(r, s) ['mitlərə(r, s)] a middle; (durchschnittlich) medium, average.

mittlerweile ['mitlər'vailə] ad meanwhile.

Mittwoch ['mitvɔx] m **-(e)s**, **-e** Wednesday; **m~s** ad on Wednesdays.

mitunter [mit''untər] ad occasionally, sometimes.

Mit- zW: **m~verantwortlich** a also responsible; **m~wirken** vi contribute (bei to); (THEAT) take part (bei in); **~wirkung** f contribution; participation.

Möbel ['mø:bəl] pl furniture; **~wagen** m furniture od removal van.

mobil [mo'bi:l] a mobile; (MIL) mobilized; **M~iar** [mobili'a:r] nt **-s**, **-e** movable assets pl; **M~machung** f mobilization.

möblieren [mø'bli:rən] vt furnish; **möbliert wohnen** live in furnished accommodation.

möchte(n) ['møçtə(n)] v siehe **mögen**.

Mode ['mo:də] f **-**, **-n** fashion.

Modell [mo'dɛl] nt **-s**, **-e** model; **m~ieren** [-'li:rən] vt model.

Mode(n)schau f fashion show.

modern [mo'dɛrn] a modern; (modisch) fashionable; **modernisieren** vt modernize.

Mode- zW: **~schmuck** m fashion jewellery; **~schöpfer(in** f) m fashion designer; **~wort** nt fashionable word, buzz word.

modisch ['mo:diʃ] a fashionable.

Mofa ['mo:fa] nt **-s**, **-s** small moped.

mogeln ['mo:gəln] vi (umg) cheat.

mögen ['mø:gən] ♦vti pt **mochte**, ptp **gemocht** like; **magst du/mögen Sie ihn?** do you like him?; **ich möchte ...** I would like ..., I'd like ...; **er möchte in die Stadt** he'd like to go into town; **ich möchte nicht, daß du ...** I wouldn't like you to ...; **ich mag nicht mehr** I've had enough

♦ (als Hilfsverb) pt **mochte**, ptp **mögen** like to; (wollen) want; **möchtest du etwas essen?** would you like something to eat?; **sie mag nicht bleiben** she doesn't want to stay; **das mag wohl sein** that may well be; **was mag das heißen?** what might that mean?; **Sie möchten zu Hause anrufen?** could you please call home?

möglich ['møːklɪç] *a* possible; **~erweise** *ad* possibly; **M~keit** *f* possibility; **nach M~keit** if possible; **~st** *ad* as ... as possible.

Mohn [moːn] *m* -(e)s, -e (~*blume*) poppy; (~*samen*) poppy seed.

Möhre ['møːrə] *f* -, -n, **Mohrrübe** *f* carrot.

mokieren [mo'kiːrən] *vr* make fun (*über* +*akk* of).

Moldau ['mɔldau] *f* - Moldavia.

Mole ['moːlə] *f* -, -n (harbour) mole.

Molekül [mole'kyːl] *nt* -s, -e molecule.

Molkerei [mɔlkə'rai] *f* dairy.

Moll [mɔl] *nt* -, - (*MUS*) minor (key); **m~ig** *a* cosy; (*dicklich*) plump.

Moment [mo'mɛnt] *m* -(e)s, -e moment; **im ~** at the moment; **~ (mal)!** just a moment // *nt* factor, element; **m~an** [-'taːn] *a* momentary // *ad* at the moment.

Monarch [mo'narç] *m* -en, -en monarch; **~ie** [monar'çiː] *f* monarchy.

Monat ['moːnat] *m* -(e)s, -e month; **m~elang** *ad* for months; **m~lich** *a* monthly; **~skarte** *f* monthly ticket.

Mönch [mœnç] *m* -(e)s, -e monk.

Mond [moːnt] *m* -(e)s, -e moon; **~finsternis** *f* eclipse of the moon; **m~hell** *a* moonlit; **~landung** *f* moon landing; **~schein** *m* moonlight; **~sonde** *f* moon probe.

Mono- [mono] *in zW* mono; **~log** [-'loːk] *m* -s, -e monologue; **~pol** [-'poːl] *nt* -s, -e monopoly; **m~polisieren** [-poli'ziːrən] *vt* monopolize; **m~ton** [-'toːn] *a* monotonous; **~tonie** [-to'niː] *f* monotony.

Monsun [mɔn'zuːn] *m* -s, -e monsoon.

Montag ['moːntaːk] *m* -(e)s, -e Monday; **m~s** *ad* on Mondays.

Montage [mɔn'taːʒə] *f* -, -n (*PHOT etc*) montage; (*TECH*) assembly; (*Einbauen*) fitting.

Monteur [mɔn'tøːr] *m* fitter.

montieren [mɔn'tiːrən] *vt* assemble.

Monument [monu'mɛnt] *nt* monument; **m~al** [-'taːl] *a* monumental.

Moor [moːr] *nt* -(e)s, -e moor.

Moos [moːs] *nt* -es, -e moss.

Moped ['moːpɛt] *nt* -s, -s moped.

Mops [mɔps] *m* -es, -e pug.

Moral [mo'raːl] *f* -, -en morality; (*einer Geschichte*) moral; **m~isch** *a* moral.

Moräne [mo'rɛːnə] *f* -, -n moraine.

Morast [mo'rast] *m* -(e)s, -e morass, mire; **m~ig** *a* boggy.

Mord [mɔrt] *m* -(e)s, -e murder; **~anschlag** *m* murder attempt.

Mörder ['mœrdər] *m* -s, - murderer; **~in** *f* murderess.

Mord- *zW:* **~kommission** *f* murder squad; **Mordsglück** *nt* (*umg*) amazing luck; **mordsmäßig** *a* (*umg*) terrific, enormous; **Mordsschreck** *m* (*umg*) terrible fright; **~verdacht** *m* suspicion of murder; **~waffe** *f* murder weapon.

morgen ['mɔrgən] *ad*, **M~** *nt* tomorrow; **~ früh** tomorrow morning; **M~** *m* -s, - morning; **M~mantel** *m*, **M~rock** *m* dressing gown; **M~röte** *f* dawn; **~s** *ad* in the morning.

morgig ['mɔrgɪç] *a* tomorrow's; **der ~e Tag** tomorrow.

Morphium ['mɔrfiʊm] *nt* morphine.

morsch [mɔrʃ] *a* rotten.

Morse- ['mɔrzə] *zW:* **~alphabet** *nt* Morse code; **m~n** *vi* send a message by Morse code.

Mörtel ['mœrtəl] *m* -s, - mortar.

Mosaik [moza'iːk] *nt* -s, -en *od* -e mosaic.

Moschee [mɔ'ʃeː] *f* -, -n [mɔ'ʃeːən] mosque.

Moskau ['mɔskau] *nt* -s Moscow; **~er** *a* Muscovite.

Moskito [mɔs'kiːto] *m* -s, -s mosquito.

Most [mɔst] *m* -(e)s, -e (unfermented) fruit juice; (*Apfelwein*) cider.

Motel [mo'tɛl] *nt* -s, -s motel.

Motiv [mo'tiːf] *nt* -s, -e motive; (*MUS*) theme; **m~ieren** [moti'viːrən] *vt* motivate; **~ierung** *f* motivation.

Motor ['moːtɔr] *m* -s, -en [mo'toːrən] engine; (*bes ELEK*) motor; **~boot** *nt* motorboat; **~enöl** *nt* motor oil; **m~isieren** [motori'ziːrən] *vt* motorize; **~rad** *nt* motorcycle; **~schaden** *m* engine trouble *od* failure.

Motte ['mɔtə] *f* -, -n moth; **Mottenkugel** *f* mothball(s).

Motto ['mɔto] *nt* -s, -s motto.

Möwe ['møːvə] *f* -, -n seagull.

Mrd. *abk* (= *Milliarde(n)*) thousand millions, billion(s) (*US*).

Mücke ['mʏkə] *f* -, -n midge, gnat; **Mückenstich** *m* midge *od* gnat bite.

müde ['myːdə] *a* tired.

Müdigkeit ['myːdɪçkait] *f* tiredness.

Muff [mʊf] *m* -(e)s, -e (*Handwärmer*) muff; **~el** *m* -s, - (*umg*) killjoy, sourpuss; **m~ig** *a* (*Luft*) musty.

Mühe ['myːə] *f* -, -n trouble, pains *pl*; **mit Müh und Not** with great difficulty; **sich** (*dat*) **~ geben** go to a lot of trouble; **m~los** *a* without trouble, easy.

mühevoll *a* laborious, arduous.

Mühle ['my:lə] *f* -, -n mill; (*Kaffee~*) grinder.

Müh- *zW:* **~sal** *f* -, -e hardship, tribulation; **m~sam** *a* arduous, troublesome; **m~selig** *a* arduous, laborious.

Mulde ['muldə] *f* -, -n hollow, depression.

Mull [mul] *m* -(e)s, -e thin muslin; **~binde** *f* gauze bandage.

Müll [myl] *m* -(e)s refuse; **~abfuhr** *f* rubbish disposal; (*Leute*) dustmen *pl*; **~abladeplatz** *m* rubbish dump; **~eimer** *m* dustbin, garbage can (*US*); **~haufen** *m* rubbish heap; **~schlucker** *m* -s, - garbage disposal unit; **~verbrennungsanlage** *f* incinerator; **~wagen** *m* dustcart, garbage truck (*US*).

mulmig ['mulmɪç] *a* rotten; (*umg*) dodgy; **jdm ist ~** sb feels funny.

multiplizieren [multipli'tsi:rən] *vt* multiply.

Mumie ['mu:mɪə] *f* mummy.

Mumm [mum] *m* -s (*umg*) gumption, nerve.

München ['mynçən] *nt* -s Munich.

Mund [munt] *m* -(e)s, ⁻er ['myndər] mouth; **~art** *f* dialect.

Mündel ['myndəl] *nt* -s, - ward.

münden ['myndən] *vi* flow (*in* +akk into).

Mund- *zW:* **m~faul** *a* taciturn; **~geruch** *m* bad breath; **~harmonika** *f* mouth organ.

mündig ['myndɪç] *a* of age; **M~keit** *f* majority.

mündlich ['myntlɪç] *a* oral.

Mundstück *nt* mouthpiece; (*Zigaretten~*) tip.

Mündung ['myndʊŋ] *f* mouth; (*Gewehr*) muzzle.

Mund- *zW:* **~wasser** *nt* mouthwash; **~werk** *nt*: **ein großes ~werk haben** have a big mouth; **~winkel** *m* corner of the mouth.

Munition [munitsi'o:n] *f* ammunition; **Munitionslager** *nt* ammunition dump.

munkeln ['muŋkəln] *vi* whisper, mutter.

Münster ['mynstər] *nt* -s, - minster.

munter ['muntər] *a* lively; **M~keit** *f* liveliness.

Münze ['myntsə] *f* -, -n coin; **m~n** *vt* coin, mint; **auf jdn gemünzt sein** be aimed at sb.

Münzfernsprecher ['myntsfernʃpreçər] *m* callbox (*Brit*), pay phone.

mürb(e) ['myrb(ə)] *a* (*Gestein*) crumbly; (*Holz*) rotten; (*Gebäck*) crisp; **jdn ~ machen** wear sb down; **M~(e)teig** *m* shortcrust pastry.

murmeln ['murməln] *vti* murmer, mutter.

Murmeltier ['murməlti:r] *nt* marmot.

murren ['murən] *vi* grumble, grouse.

mürrisch ['myrɪʃ] *a* sullen.

Mus [mu:s] *nt* -es, -e purée.

Muschel ['muʃəl] *f* -, -n mussel; (*~schale*) shell; (*Telefon~*) receiver.

Muse ['mu:zə] *f* -, -n muse.

Museum [mu'ze:um] *nt* -s, **Museen** museum.

Musik [mu'zi:k] *f* music; (*Kapelle*) band; **m~alisch** [-'ka:lɪʃ] *a* musical; **~box** *f* jukebox; **~er** ['mu:zikər] *m* -s, - musician; **~hochschule** *f* music school; **~instrument** *nt* musical instrument; **~truhe** *f* radiogram.

musizieren [muzi'tsi:rən] *vi* make music.

Muskat [mus'ka:t] *m* -(e)s, -e nutmeg.

Muskel ['muskəl] *m* -s, -n muscle; **~kater** *m*: **einen ~kater haben** be stiff.

Muskulatur [muskula'tu:r] *f* muscular system.

muskulös [musku'lø:s] *a* muscular.

Muß [mus] *nt* - necessity, must.

Muße ['mu:sə] *f* - leisure.

müssen ['mysən] *vi pt* **mußte,** *ptp* **gemußt** *od* (*als Hilfsverb*) **müssen 1** (*Zwang*) must (*nur im Präsens*), have to; **ich muß es tun** I must do it, I have to do it; **ich mußte es tun** I had to do it; **er muß es nicht tun** he doesn't have to do it; **muß ich?** must I?, do I have to?; **wann müßt ihr zur Schule?** when do you have to go to school?; **er hat gehen ~** he (has) had to go; **muß das sein?** is that really necessary?; **ich muß mal** (*umg*) I need the toilet

2 (*sollen*): **das mußt du nicht tun!** you oughtn't to *od* shouldn't do that!; **Sie hätten ihn fragen ~** you should have asked him

3 (*Vermutung*): **es muß geregnet haben** it must have rained; **es muß nicht wahr sein** it needn't be true.

müßig ['my:sɪç] *a* idle; **M~gang** *m* idleness.

Muster ['mustər] *nt* -s, - model; (*Dessin*) pattern; (*Probe*) sample; **m~gültig** *a* exemplary; **m~n** *vt* (*Tapete*) pattern; (*fig, MIL*) examine; (*Truppen*) inspect; **~ung** *f* (*von Stoff*) pattern; (*MIL*) inspection.

Mut [mu:t] *m* courage; **nur ~!** cheer up!; **jdm ~ machen** encourage sb; **m~ig** *a* courageous; **m~los** *a* discouraged, despondent.

mutmaßlich ['mu:tma:slɪç] *a* presumed // *ad* probably.

Mutter ['mutər] *f* -, ⁻ mother; *pl* **~n** (*Schrauben~*) nut; **~gesellschaft** *f* parent company.

mütterlich ['mytərlɪç] *a* motherly; **~erseits** *ad* on the mother's side.

Mutter- *zW:* **~liebe** *f* motherly love; **~mal** *nt* birthmark, mole; **~schaft** *f*

motherhood, maternity; ~**schutz** m
maternity regulations; '**m~'seelena'l-
lein** a all alone; ~**sprache** f native
language; ~**tag** m Mother's Day.
Mutti ['muti] f -, -s mum(my) (Brit),
mom(my) (US).
mutwillig ['muːtvɪlɪç] a malicious, deliberate.
Mütze ['mʏtsə] f -, -n cap.
MwSt abk (= Mehrwertsteuer) VAT.
mysteriös [mʏsteri'øːs] a mysterious.
Mythos ['myːtɔs] m -, **Mythen** myth.

N

N, n [ɛn] nt N, n.
na [na] interj well; ~ **gut** okay then.
Nabel ['naːbəl] m -s, - navel; ~**schnur**
f umbilical cord.
nach [naːx] ◆präp +dat **1** (örtlich) to;
~ Berlin to Berlin; ~ **links/rechts** (to
the) left/right; ~ **oben/hinten** up/back
2 (zeitlich) after; **einer** ~ **dem anderen** one after the other; ~ **Ihnen!**
after you!; **zehn (Minuten)** ~ **drei** ten
(minutes) past three
3 (gemäß) according to; ~ **dem Gesetz** according to the law; **dem
Namen** ~ judging by his/her name; ~
allem, was ich weiß as far as I know
◆adv: **ihm** ~! after him!; ~ **und** ~
gradually, little by little; ~ **wie vor**
still.
nachahmen ['naːxʔaːmən] vt imitate.
Nachahmung f imitation.
Nachbar(in f) ['naxbaːr(ɪn)] m -s, -n
neighbour; ~**haus** nt: im ~haus next
door; **n~lich** a neighbourly; ~**schaft**
f neighbourhood; ~**staat** m neighbouring state.
nach- zW: ~**bestellen** vt: 50 Stück
~**bestellen** order another 50;
N~bestellung f (COMM) repeat order; ~**bilden** vt copy; **N~bildung** f
imitation, copy; ~**blicken** vi gaze
after; ~**datieren** vt postdate.
nachdem [naːx'deːm] kj after; (weil)
since; **je** ~ **(ob)** it depends
(whether).
nach- zW: ~**denken** vi unreg think
(über +akk about); **N~denken** nt -s
reflection, meditation; ~**denklich** a
thoughtful, pensive.
Nachdruck ['naːxdrʊk] m emphasis;
(TYP) reprint, reproduction.
nachdrücklich ['naːxdrʏklɪç] a emphatic.
nacheinander [naːx'aɪ'nandər] ad one
after the other.
nachempfinden ['naːxʔɛmpfɪndən] vt
unreg: jdm etw ~ feel sth with sb.
Nacherzählung [naːx'ɛrtsɛːlʊŋ] f reproduction (of a story).
Nachfahr ['naːxfaːr] m -s, -en de-

scendant.
Nachfolge ['naːxfɔlgə] f succession;
n~n vi (lit) follow (jdm/etw sb/sth);
~**r(in** f) m -s, - successor.
nachforschen vti investigate.
Nachforschung f investigation.
Nachfrage ['naːxfraːgə] f inquiry;
(COMM) demand; **n~n** vi inquire.
nach- zW: ~**fühlen** vt siehe
~**empfinden**; ~**füllen** vt refill; ~
geben vi unreg give way, yield;
N~gebühr f surcharge; (Post) excess postage; **N~geburt** f afterbirth.
nachgehen ['naːxgeːən] vi unreg follow (jdm sb); (erforschen) inquire
(einer Sache into sth); (Uhr) be
slow.
Nachgeschmack ['naːxgəʃmak] m
aftertaste.
nachgiebig ['naːxgiːbɪç] a soft, accommodating; **N~keit** f softness.
nachhaltig ['naːxhaltɪç] a lasting;
(Widerstand) persistent.
nachhelfen ['naːxhɛlfən] vi unreg assist, help (jdm sb).
nachher [naːx'heːr] ad afterwards.
Nachhilfeunterricht ['naːxhɪlfə-
ʊntərrɪçt] m extra tuition.
nachholen ['naːxhoːlən] vt catch up
with; (Versäumtes) make up for.
Nachkomme ['naːxkɔmə] m -, -n de-
scendant.
nachkommen vi unreg follow; (einer
Verpflichtung) fulfil; **N~schaft** f de-
scendants pl.
Nachkriegs- ['naːxkriːks] in zW postwar; ~**zeit** f postwar period.
Nach- zW: ~**laß** m -lasses, -lässe
(COMM) discount, rebate; (Erbe) estate; **n~lassen** unreg vt (Strafe) remit; (Summe) take off; (Schulden)
cancel // vi decrease, ease off;
(Sturm auch) die down; (schlechter
werden) deteriorate; **er hat
n~gelassen** he has got worse;
n~lässig a negligent, careless;
~**lässigkeit** f negligence, carelessness.
nachlaufen ['naːxlaʊfən] vi unreg run
after, chase (jdm sb).
nachmachen ['naːxmaxən] vt imitate,
copy (jdm etw sth from sb);
(fälschen) counterfeit.
Nachmittag ['naːxmɪtaːk] m afternoon; **am** ~, **n~s** ad in the afternoon.
Nach- zW: ~**nahme** f -, -n cash on delivery; **per** ~**nahme** C.O.D.; ~**name**
m surname; ~**porto** nt excess postage.
nachprüfen ['naːxpryːfən] vt check,
verify.
nachrechnen ['naːxrɛçnən] vt check.
Nachrede ['naːxreːdə] f: **üble** ~ libel;
slander.

Nachricht ['naːxrɪçt] f -, -en (piece of) news; (*Mitteilung*) message; ~en pl news; ~enagentur f news agency; ~endienst m (*MIL*) intelligence service; ~ensprecher(in f) m newsreader; ~entechnik f telecommunications sing.

Nachruf ['naːxruːf] m obituary.

nachsagen ['naːxzaːgən] vt repeat; jdm etw ~ say sth of sb.

nachschicken ['naːxʃɪkən] vt forward.

Nachschlag- ['naːxʃlaːg] zW: **n~en** vt unreg look up; **Nachschlagewerk** nt reference book.

Nach- zW: **~schlüssel** m master key; **~schub** m supplies pl; (*Truppen*) reinforcements pl.

nachsehen ['naːxzeːən] unreg vt (*prüfen*) check; jdm etw ~ forgive sb sth // vi (*erforschen*) look and see; das N~ haben come off worst.

nachsenden ['naːxzɛndən] vt unreg send on, forward.

Nachsicht ['naːxzɪçt] f - indulgence, leniency; **n~ig** a indulgent, lenient.

nachsitzen ['naːxzɪtsən] vi unreg: ~(müssen) (*SCH*) be kept in.

Nachspeise ['naːxʃpaɪzə] f dessert, sweet, pudding.

Nachspiel ['naːxʃpiːl] nt epilogue; (*fig*) sequel.

nachsprechen ['naːxʃprɛçən] vt unreg repeat (jdm after sb).

nächst [nɛːçst] präp +dat (*räumlich*) next to; (*außer*) apart from; **~beste(r, s)** a first that comes along; (*zweitbeste*) next best; **N~e(r)** mf neighbour; **~e(r, s)** a next; (*nächstgelegen*) nearest; **N~enliebe** f love for one's fellow men; **~ens** ad shortly, soon; **~liegend** a (*lit*) nearest; (*fig*) obvious; **~möglich** a next possible.

nachsuchen ['naːxzuːxən] vi: um etw ~ ask od apply for sth.

Nacht [naxt] f -, -e night.

Nachteil ['naːxtaɪl] m disadvantage; **n~ig** a disadvantageous.

Nachthemd nt nightshirt; nightdress.

Nachtigall ['naxtɪgal] f -, -en nightingale.

Nachtisch ['naːxtɪʃ] m siehe **Nachspeise**.

Nachtklub m night club.

nächtlich ['nɛçtlɪç] a nightly.

Nachtlokal nt night club.

Nach- zW: **~trag** m -(e)s, -träge supplement; **n~tragen** vt unreg carry (jdm after sb); (*zufügen*) add; jdm etw n~tragen hold sth against sb; **n~träglich** a,ad later, subsequent(ly); additional(ly); **n~trauern** vi: jdm/etw n~trauern mourn the loss of sb/sth.

Nacht- zW: **~ruhe** f sleep; **n~s** ad by

night; **~schicht** f nightshift; **nachts-über** ad during the night; **~tarif** m off-peak tariff; **~tisch** m bedside table; **~wächter** m night watchman.

Nach- zW: **~untersuchung** f checkup; **n~wachsen** vi unreg grow again; **~wehen** pl afterpains pl; (*fig*) after-effects pl.

Nachweis ['naːxvaɪs] m -es, -e proof; **n~bar** a provable, demonstrable; **n~en** ['naːxvaɪzən] vt unreg prove; jdm etw n~en point sth out to sb; **n~lich** a evident, demonstrable.

nach- zW: **~wirken** vi have after-effects; **N~wirkung** f after-effect; **N~wort** nt appendix; **N~wuchs** m offspring; (*beruflich etc*) new recruits pl; **~zahlen** vti pay extra; **N~zahlung** f additional payment; (*zurückdatiert*) back pay; **~zählen** vt count again; **N~zügler** m -s, - straggler.

Nacken ['nakən] m -s, - nape of the neck.

nackt [nakt] a naked; (*Tatsachen*) plain, bare; **N~heit** f nakedness.

Nadel ['naːdəl] f -, -n needle; (*Steck~*) pin; **~kissen** nt pincushion; **~öhr** nt eye of a needle; **~wald** m coniferous forest.

Nagel ['naːgəl] m -s, - nail; **~feile** f nailfile; **~haut** f cuticle; **~lack** m nail varnish; **n~n** vti nail; **n~neu** a brand-new; **~schere** f nail scissors pl.

nagen ['naːgən] vti gnaw.

Nagetier ['naːgətiːr] nt rodent.

nah(e) ['naː(ə)] a,ad (*räumlich*) near(by); (*Verwandte*) near; (*Freunde*) close; (*zeitlich*) near, close; der N~e Osten the Near East // präp +dat near (to), close to; **N~aufnahme** f close-up.

Nähe ['nɛːə] f - nearness, proximity; (*Umgebung*) vicinity; in der ~ close by; at hand; aus der ~ from close to.

nahe- zW: **~bei** ad nearby; **~gehen** vi unreg grieve (jdm sb); **~kommen** vi unreg get close (jdm to sb); **~legen** vt: jdm etw ~legen suggest sth to sb; **~liegen** vi unreg be obvious; **~liegend** a obvious; **~n** vir approach, draw near.

Näh- ['nɛː] zW: **n~en** vti sew; **n~er** a,ad nearer; (*Erklärung, Erkundigung*) more detailed; **~ere(s)** nt details pl, particulars pl; **~erei** f sewing, needlework; **~erin** f seamstress; **n~erkommen** vir unreg get closer; **n~ern** vr approach.

nahe- zW: **~stehen** vi unreg be close (jdm to sb); einer Sache **~stehen** sympathize with sth; **~stehend** a close; **~treten** vi unreg: jdm (zu) **~treten** offend sb; **~zu** ad nearly.

Nähgarn nt thread.
nahm etc v siehe **nehmen**.
Näh- zW: **~maschine** f sewing machine; **~nadel** f needle.
nähren ['nɛːrən] vtr feed.
nahrhaft ['naːrhaft] a nourishing, nutritious.
Nahrung [naːrʊŋ] f food; (fig auch) sustenance.
Nahrungs- zW: **~mittel** nt foodstuffs pl; **~mittelindustrie** f food industry; **~suche** f search for food.
Nährwert m nutritional value.
Naht [naːt] f -, ⁻e seam; (MED) suture; (TECH) join; **n~los** a seamless; **n~los ineinander übergehen** follow without a gap.
Nah- zW: **~verkehr** m local traffic; **~verkehrszug** m local train; **~ziel** nt immediate objective.
naiv [na'iːf] a naive; **N~ität** [naivi'tɛːt] f naivety.
Name ['naːmə] m -ns, -n name; im **~n von** on behalf of; **n~ns** ad by the name of; (namstag m name day, saint's day; **n~ntlich** a by name // ad particularly, especially.
namhaft ['naːmhaft] a (berühmt) famed, renowned; (beträchtlich) considerable; **~ machen** name.
nämlich ['nɛːmlɪç] ad that is to say, namely; (denn) since.
nannte etc v siehe **nennen**.
nanu [na'nuː] interj well, well!
Napf [napf] m -(e)s, ⁻e bowl, dish.
Narbe ['narbə] f -, -n scar.
narbig ['narbɪç] a scarred.
Narkose [nar'koːzə] f -, -n anaesthetic.
Narr [nar] m -en, -en fool; **n~en** vt fool; **~heit** f foolishness.
Närr- ['nɛr] zW: **~in** f fool; **n~isch** a foolish, crazy.
Narzisse [nar'tsɪsə] f -, -n narcissus; daffodil.
nasch- ['naʃ] zW: **~en** vti nibble; eat secretly; **~haft** a sweet-toothed.
Nase ['naːzə] f -, -n nose.
Nasen- zW: **~bluten** nt -s nosebleed; **~loch** nt nostril; **~tropfen** pl nose drops pl.
naseweis a pert, cheeky; (neugierig) nosey.
Nashorn ['naːshɔrn] nt rhinoceros.
naß [nas] a wet.
Nässe ['nɛsə] f - wetness; **n~n** vt wet.
naßkalt a wet and cold.
Naßrasur f wet shave.
Nation [natsi'oːn] f nation.
national [natsio'naːl] a national; **N~hymne** f national anthem; **~isieren** [-i'ziːrən] vt nationalize; **N~i'sierung** f nationalization; **N~ismus** [-'lɪsmʊs] m nationalism; **~istisch** [-'lɪstɪʃ] a nationalistic; **N~i'tät** f nationality; **N~mannschaft**

f national team; **N~sozialismus** m national socialism.
Natron ['naːtrɔn] nt -s soda.
Natter ['natər] f -, -n adder.
Natur [na'tuːr] f nature; (körperlich) constitution; **~a'lismus** m naturalism; **~erscheinung** f natural phenomenon od event; **~farben** a natural coloured; **n~gemäß** a natural; **~gesetz** nt law of nature; **~katastrophe** f natural disaster.
natürlich [na'tyːrlɪç] a natural // ad naturally; ja, ~! yes, of course; **N~keit** f naturalness.
Natur- zW: **~produkt** nt natural product; **n~rein** a natural, pure; **~schutzgebiet** nt nature reserve; **~wissenschaft** f natural science; **~wissenschaftler(in** f) m scientist; **~zustand** m natural state.
nautisch ['nautɪʃ] a nautical.
Nazi ['naːtsi] m -s, -s Nazi.
n.Chr. abk (= nach Christus) AD.
Neapel [ne'aːpəl] nt -s Naples.
Nebel ['neːbəl] m -s, - fog, mist; **n~ig** a foggy, misty; **~scheinwerfer** m foglamp.
neben ['neːbən] präp +akk od dat next to; (außer) apart from, besides; **~an** [neːbən'ʔan] ad next door; **N~anschluß** m (TEL) extension; **~bei** [neːbən'baɪ] ad at the same time; (außerdem) additionally; (beiläufig) incidentally; **N~beschäftigung** f second job; **N~buhler(in** f) m -s, - rival; **~einander** [neːbən'aɪ'nandər] ad side by side; **~einanderlegen** vt put next to each other; **N~eingang** m side entrance; **N~erscheinung** f side effect; **N~fach** nt subsidiary subject; **N~fluß** m tributary; **N~geräusch** nt (RAD) atmospherics pl, interference; **~her** [neːbən'heːr] ad (zusätzlich) besides; (gleichzeitig) at the same time; (daneben) alongside; **~herfahren** vi unreg drive alongside; **N~kosten** pl extra charges pl, extras pl; **N~produkt** nt by-product; **N~rolle** f minor part; **N~sache** f trifle, side issue; **~sächlich** a minor, peripheral; **N~straße** f side street.
neblig ['neːblɪç] a = **nebelig**.
Necessaire [nesɛ'sɛːr] nt -s, -s (Näh~) needlework box; (Nagel~) manicure case.
neck- ['nɛk] zW: **~en** vt tease; **N~e'rei** f teasing; **~isch** a coy; (Einfall, Lied) amusing.
Neffe ['nɛfə] m -n, -n nephew.
negativ [nega'tiːf] a negative; **N~** nt -s, -e (PHOT) negative.
Neger ['neːgər] m -s, - negro; **~in** f negress.
nehmen ['neːmən] vt unreg take; jdn

zu sich ~ take sb in; **sich ernst** ~ take o.s. seriously; **nimm dir noch einmal** help yourself.

Neid [naɪt] *m* -(e)s envy; ~**er** *m* -s, - envier; **n~isch** *a* envious, jealous.

neigen ['naɪgən] *vt* incline, lean; (*Kopf*) bow // *vi:* **zu etw** ~ tend to sth.

Neigung *f* (*des Geländes*) slope; (*Tendenz*) tendency, inclination; (*Vorliebe*) liking; (*Zuneigung*) affection.

nein [naɪn] *ad* no.

Nelke ['nɛlkə] *f* -, -n carnation, pink; (*Gewürz*) clove.

Nenn- ['nɛn] *zW:* **n~en** *vt unreg* name; (*mit Namen*) call; **wie** ~**t man ...?** what do you call ...?; **n~enswert** *a* worth mentioning; ~**er** *m* -s, - denominator; ~**wert** *m* nominal value; (*COMM*) par.

Neon ['neːɔn] *nt* -s neon; ~**licht** *nt* neon light; ~**röhre** *f* neon tube.

Nerv [nɛrf] *m* -s, -en nerve; **jdm auf die** ~**en gehen** get on sb's nerves; **n~enaufreibend** *a* nerve-racking; ~**enbündel** *nt* bundle of nerves; ~**enheilanstalt** *f* mental home; **n~enkrank** *a* mentally ill; ~**enschwäche** *f* neurasthenia; ~**ensystem** *nt* nervous system; ~**enzusammenbruch** *m* nervous breakdown; **n~ös** [nɛr'vøːs] *a* nervous; ~**osi'tät** *f* nervousness; **n~tötend** *a* nerve-racking; (*Arbeit*) soul-destroying.

Nerz [nɛrts] *m* -es, -e mink.

Nessel ['nɛsəl] *f* -, -n nettle.

Nest [nɛst] *nt* -(e)s, -er nest; (*umg: Ort*) dump.

nett [nɛt] *a* nice; (*freundlich auch*) kind; ~**erweise** *ad* kindly.

netto ['nɛtoː] *ad* net.

Netz [nɛts] *nt* -es, -e net; (*Gepäck~*) rack; (*Einkaufs~*) string bag; (*Spinnen~*) web; (*System*) network; **jdm ins** ~ **gehen** (*fig*) fall into sb's trap; ~**anschluß** *m* mains connection; ~**haut** *f* retina.

neu [nɔy] *a* new; (*Sprache, Geschichte*) modern; **seit** ~**estem** (since) recently; **die** ~**esten Nachrichten** the latest news; ~ **schreiben** rewrite, write again; **N~anschaffung** *f* new purchase *od* acquisition; ~**artig** *a* new kind of; **N~auflage** *f* new edition; **N~bau** *m* new building; ~**erdings** *ad* (*kürzlich*) (since) recently; (*von neuem*) again; **N~erung** *f* innovation, new departure; **N~fundland** *nt* Newfoundland; **N~gier** *f* curiosity; ~**gierig** *a* curious; **N~guinea** *nt* New Guinea; **N~heit** *f* newness; novelty; **N~igkeit** *f* news; **N~jahr** *nt* New Year; ~**lich**

ad recently, the other day; **N~ling** *m* novice; **N~mond** *m* new moon.

neun [nɔyn] *num* nine; ~**zehn** *num* nineteen; ~**zig** *num* ninety.

neureich *a* nouveau riche; **N~e(r)** *mf* nouveau riche.

Neur- *zW:* ~**ose** [nɔy'roːzə] *f* -, -n neurosis; ~**otiker** [nɔy'roːtikər] *m* -s, - neurotic; **n~otisch** *a* neurotic.

Neusee- [nɔy'zeː] *zW:* ~**land** *nt* New Zealand; ~**länder(in** *f*) *m* New Zealander; **n~ländisch** *a* New Zealand.

Neutr- *zW:* **n~al** [nɔy'traːl] *a* neutral; **n~ali'sieren** *vt* neutralize; ~**ali'tät** *f* neutrality; ~**on** ['nɔytrɔn] *nt* -s, -en neutron; ~**um** ['nɔytrʊm] *nt* -s, -a *od* -en neuter.

Neu- *zW:* ~**wert** *m* purchase price; ~**zeit** *f* modern age; **n~zeitlich** *a* modern, recent.

nicht [nɪçt] *ad* **1** (*Verneinung*) not; **er ist es** ~ it's not him, it isn't him; **er raucht** ~ (*gerade*) he isn't smoking; (*gewöhnlich*) he doesn't smoke; **ich kann das** ~ — **und ich kann's auch** ~ I can't do it — neither *od* nor can I; **es regnet** ~ **mehr** it's not raining any more **2** (*Bitte, Verbot*): ~! don't!, no!; ~ **berühren!** do not touch!; ~ **doch!** don't! **3** (*rhetorisch*): **du bist müde,** ~ (**wahr**)? you're tired, aren't you?; **das ist schön,** ~ (**wahr**)? it's nice, isn't it? **4**: **was du** ~ **sagst!** the things you say!

Nichtangriffspakt [nɪçt''angrifspakt] *m* non-aggression pact.

Nichte ['nɪçtə] *f* -, -n niece.

nichtig ['nɪçtɪç] *a* (*ungültig*) null, void; (*wertlos*) futile; **N~keit** *f* nullity, invalidity; (*Sinnlosigkeit*) futility.

Nichtraucher(in *f*) *m* non-smoker.

nichtrostend *a* stainless.

nichts [nɪçts] *pron* nothing; **für** ~ **und wieder** ~ for nothing at all; **N~** *nt* - nothingness; (*pej: Person*) nonentity; ~**destoweniger** *ad* nevertheless; **N~nutz** *m* -es, -e good-for-nothing; ~**nutzig** *a* worthless, useless; ~**sagend** *a* meaningless; **N~tun** *nt* -s idleness.

Nickel ['nɪkəl] *nt* -s nickel.

nicken ['nɪkən] *vi* nod.

Nickerchen ['nɪkərçən] *nt* nap.

nie [niː] *ad* never; ~ **wieder** *od* **mehr** never again; ~ **und nimmer** never ever.

nieder ['niːdər] *a* low; (*gering*) inferior // *ad* down; **N~gang** *m* decline; ~**gehen** *vi unreg* descend; (*AVIAT*) come down; (*Regen*) fall; (*Boxer*) go down; ~**geschlagen** *a* depressed, dejected; **N~geschlagenheit** *f* depression, dejection; **N~lage** *f* defeat;

N~lande *pl* Netherlands; **N~länder(in** *f)* *m* Dutchman; Dutchwoman; **~ländisch** *a* Dutch; **~lassen** *vr unreg* (*sich setzen*) sit down; (*an Ort*) settle (down); (*Arzt, Rechtsanwalt*) set up a practice; **N~lassung** *f* settlement; (*COMM*) branch; **~legen** *vt* lay down; (*Arbeit*) stop; (*Amt*) resign; **N~rhein** *nt* Lower Rhine; **N~sachsen** *nt* Lower Saxony; **N~schlag** *m* (*MET*) precipitation; rainfall; **~schlagen** *unreg vt* (*Gegner*) beat down; (*Gegenstand*) knock down; (*Augen*) lower; (*Aufstand*) put down // *vr* (*CHEM*) precipitate; **N~schrift** *f* transcription; **~trächtig** *a* base, mean; **N~trächtigkeit** *f* meanness, baseness; outrage; **N~ung** *f* (*GEOG*) depression; flats *pl*.

niedlich ['ni:tlıç] *a* sweet, cute.

niedrig ['ni:drıç] *a* low; (*Stand*) lowly, humble; (*Gesinnung*) mean.

niemals ['ni:ma:ls] *ad* never.

niemand ['ni:mant] *pron* nobody, no one; **Niemandsland** *nt* no-man's land.

Niere ['ni:rə] *f* -, -n kidney; **Nierenentzündung** *f* kidney infection.

nieseln ['ni:zəln] *vi* drizzle.

niesen ['ni:zən] *vi* sneeze.

Niete ['ni:tə] *f* -, -n (*TECH*) rivet; (*Los*) blank; (*Reinfall*) flop; (*Mensch*) failure; **n~en** *vt* rivet.

Nikotin [niko'ti:n] *nt* -s nicotine.

Nil [ni:l] *m* Nile; **~pferd** *nt* hippopotamus.

Nimmersatt ['nımərzat] *m* -(e)s, -e glutton.

nimmst *etc v siehe* **nehmen**.

nippen ['nıpən] *vti* sip.

nirgend- ['nırgənt] *zW*: **~s, ~wo** *ad* nowhere; **~wohin** *ad* nowhere.

Nische ['ni:ʃə] *f* -, -n niche.

nisten ['nıstən] *vi* nest.

Nitrat [ni'tra:t] *nt* -(e)s, -e nitrate.

Niveau [ni'vo:] *nt* -s, -s level.

Nixe ['nıksə] *f* -, -n water nymph.

noch [nɔx] ◆*ad* **1** (*weiterhin*) still; ~ nicht not yet; ~ nie never (yet); ~ immer, immer ~ still; bleiben Sie doch ~ stay a bit longer

2 (*in Zukunft*) still, yet; das kann ~ passieren that might still happen; er wird ~ kommen he'll come (yet)

3 (*nicht später als*): ~ vor einer Woche only a week ago; ~ am selben Tag the very same day; ~ im 19. Jahrhundert as late as the 19th century; ~ heute today

4 (*zusätzlich*): wer war ~ da? who else was there?; ~ einmal once more, again; ~ dreimal three times; ~ einer another one

5 (*bei Vergleichen*): ~ größer even bigger; das ist ~ besser that's better still; und wenn es ~ so schwer ist

however hard it is

6: Geld ~ und ~ heaps (and heaps) of money; sie hat ~ und ~ versucht, ... she tried again and again to ...

◆*kj* weder A ~ B neither A nor B.

nochmal(s) ['nɔxma:l(s)] *ad* again, once more.

nochmalig ['nɔxma:lıç] *a* repeated.

Nominativ ['no:minati:f] *m* -s, -e nominative.

nominell [nomi'nɛl] *a* nominal.

Nonne ['nɔnə] *f* -, -n nun.

Nord(en) ['nɔrd(ən)] *m* -s north; **N~irland** *nt* Northern Ireland; **n~isch** *a* northern.

nördlich ['nœrtlıç] *a* northerly, northern; ~ von, ~ präp +gen (to the) north of.

Nord- *zW*: **~pol** *m* North Pole; **~rhein-Westfalen** *nt* North Rhine-Westphalia; **~see** *f* North Sea; **n~wärts** *ad* northwards.

Nörg- ['nœrg] *zW*: **~elei** *f* grumbling; **n~eln** *vi* grumble; **~ler** *m* -s, -grumbler.

Norm [nɔrm] *f* -, -en norm; (*Größenvorschrift*) standard; **n~al** [nɔr'ma:l] *a* normal; **n~alerweise** *ad* normally; **n~ali'sieren** *vt* normalize // *vr* return to normal; **n~en** *vt* standardize.

Norweg- ['nɔrve:g] *zW*: **~en** *nt* Norway; **~er(in** *f)* *m* -s, - Norwegian; **n~isch** *a* Norwegian.

Not [no:t] *f* -, ⁻e need; (*Mangel*) want; (*Mühe*) trouble; (*Zwang*) necessity; zur ~ if necessary; (*gerade noch*) just about.

Notar [no'ta:r] *m* -s, -e notary; **n~i'ell** *a* notarial.

Not- *zW*: **~ausgang** *m* emergency exit; **~behelf** *m* -s, -e makeshift; **~bremse** *f* emergency brake; **n~dürftig** *a* scanty; (*behelfsmäßig*) makeshift.

Note ['no:tə] *f* -, -n note; (*SCH*) mark (*Brit*), grade (*US*).

Noten- *zW*: **~blatt** *nt* sheet of music; **~schlüssel** *m* clef; **~ständer** *m* music stand.

Not- *zW*: **~fall** *m* (case of) emergency; **n~falls** *ad* if need be; **n~gedrungen** *a* necessary, unavoidable; etw **n~gedrungen** machen be forced to do sth.

notieren [no'ti:rən] *vt* note; (*COMM*) quote.

Notierung *f* (*COMM*) quotation.

nötig ['nø:tıç] *a* necessary; etw ~ haben need sth; **~en** *vt* compel, force; **~enfalls** *ad* if necessary.

Notiz [no'ti:ts] *f* -, -en note; (*Zeitungs~*) item; ~ nehmen take notice; **~buch** *nt* notebook.

Not- *zW*: **~lage** *f* crisis, emergency;

n~landen vi make a forced od emergency landing; **n~leidend** a needy; **~lösung** f temporary solution; **~lüge** f white lie.

notorisch [no'to:rɪʃ] a notorious.

Not- zW: **~ruf** m emergency call; **~stand** m state of emergency; **~unterkunft** f emergency accommodation; **~verband** m emergency dressing; **~wehr** f - self-defence; **n~wendig** a necessary; **~wendigkeit** f necessity; **~zucht** f rape.

Novelle [no'vɛlə] f -, -n short story; (JUR) amendment.

November [no'vɛmbər] m -(s), - November.

Nr. abk (= Nummer) no.

Nu [nu:] m: im ~ in an instant.

Nuance [ny'ã:sə] f -, -n nuance.

nüchtern ['nʏçtərn] a sober; (Magen) empty; (Urteil) prudent; **N~heit** f sobriety.

Nudel ['nu:dəl] f -, -n noodle; **~n** pasta; (in Suppe) noodles.

Null [nʊl] f -, -en nought, zero; (pej: Mensch) washout; **n~** num zero; (Fehler) no; **n~ Uhr** midnight; **n~ und nichtig** null and void; **~punkt** m zero; **auf dem ~punkt** at zero.

numerieren [nume'ri:rən] vt number.

numerisch [nu'me:rɪʃ] a numerical.

Nummer ['nʊmər] f -, -n number; (Größe) size; **Nummernschild** nt (AUT) number od license (US) plate.

nun [nu:n] ad now; das ist ~ mal so that's the way it is // interj well.

nur [nu:r] ad just, only; wo bleibt er ~? (just) where is he?.

Nürnberg ['nʏrnbɛrk] nt -s Nuremberg.

Nuß [nʊs] f -, **Nüsse** nut; **~baum** m walnut tree; hazelnut tree; **~knacker** m -s, - nutcracker.

Nüster ['nʏstər] f -, -n nostril.

Nutte ['nʊtə] f -, -n tart.

nutz [nʊts], **nütze** ['nʏtsə] a: zu nichts ~ sein be useless; **~en, nützen** vt use (zu etw for sth) // vi be of use; was nützt es? what's the use?, what use is it?; **N~en** m -s usefulness; profit; **von N~en** useful.

nützlich ['nʏtslɪç] a useful; **N~keit** f usefulness.

Nutz- zW: **n~los** a useless; **~losigkeit** f uselessness; **~nießer** m -s, - beneficiary.

Nylon ['naɪlɔn] nt nylon.

O

O, o [o:] nt O, o.

Oase [o'a:zə] f -, -n oasis.

ob [ɔp] kj if, whether; ~ das wohl wahr ist? can that be true?; und ~! you bet!

Obdach ['ɔpdax] nt -(e)s shelter, lodging; **o~los** a homeless; **~lose(r)** mf homeless person.

Obduktion [ɔpdʊktsi'o:n] f postmortem.

obduzieren [ɔpdu'tsi:rən] vt do a post-mortem on.

O-Beine ['o:baɪnə] pl bow od bandy legs pl.

oben ['o:bən] ad above; (in Haus) upstairs; nach ~ up; von ~ down; ~ ohne topless; jdn von ~ bis unten ansehen look sb up and down; Befehl von ~ orders from above; **~an** ad at the top; **~auf** ad up above, on the top // a (munter) in form; **~drein** ad into the bargain; **~erwähnt, ~genannt** a above-mentioned.

Ober ['o:bər] m -s, - waiter; **~arm** m upper arm; **~arzt** m senior physician; **~aufsicht** f supervision; **~bayern** nt Upper Bavaria; **~befehl** m supreme command; **~befehlshaber** m commander-in-chief; **~bekleidung** f outer clothing; **~'bürgermeister** m lord mayor; **~deck** nt upper od top deck; **o~e(r, s)** a upper; die **~en** the bosses; (ECCL) the superiors; **~fläche** f surface; **o~flächlich** a superficial; **~geschoß** nt upper storey; **o~halb** ad, präp +gen above; **~haupt** nt head, chief; **~haus** nt upper house; House of Lords; **~hemd** nt shirt; **~herrschaft** f supremacy, sovereignty; **~in** f matron; (ECCL) Mother Superior; **~kellner** m head waiter; **~kiefer** m upper jaw; **~körper** m trunk, upper part of body; **~leitung** f direction; (ELEK) overhead cable; **~licht** nt skylight; **~lippe** f upper lip; **~schenkel** m thigh; **~schicht** f upper classes pl; **~schule** f grammar school (Brit), high school (US); **~schwester** f (MED) matron.

Oberst ['o:bərst] m -en od -s, -en od -e colonel; **o~e(r, s)** a very top, topmost.

Ober- zW: **~stufe** f upper school; **~teil** nt upper part; **~weite** f bust/chest measurement.

obgleich [ɔp'glaɪç] kj although.

Obhut ['ɔphu:t] f - care, protection; in jds ~ sein be in sb's care.

obig ['o:bɪç] a above.

Objekt [ɔp'jɛkt] nt -(e)s, -e object; **~iv** [-'ti:f] nt -s, -e lens; **o~iv** a objective; **~ivi'tät** f objectivity.

Oblate [o'bla:tə] f -, -n (Gebäck) wafer; (ECCL) host.

Obligation [ɔbligatsi'o:n] f bond.

obligatorisch [obliga'to:rɪʃ] a compulsory, obligatory.

Oboe [o'bo:ə] f -, -n oboe.

Obrigkeit ['o:brɪçkaɪt] f (Behörden) authorities pl, administration; (Regierung) government.

obschon [ɔp'ʃo:n] kj although.

Observatorium [ɔpzɛrva'to:riʊm] nt observatory.

obskur [ɔps'ku:r] a obscure; (verdächtig) dubious.

Obst [o:pst] nt -(e)s fruit; ~baum m fruit tree; ~garten m orchard; ~händler m fruiterer, fruit merchant; ~kuchen m fruit tart.

obszön [ɔps'tsø:n] a obscene; **O~ität** f obscenity.

obwohl [ɔp'vo:l] kj although.

Ochse ['ɔksə] m -n, -n ox; (umg) cram, swot (Brit); **Ochsenschwanzsuppe** f oxtail soup; **Ochsenzunge** f oxtongue.

öd(e) ['ø:d(ə)] a (Land) waste, barren; (fig) dull; **O~e** f -, -n desert, waste(land); (fig) tedium.

oder ['o:dər] kj or; das stimmt, ~? that's right, isn't it?

Ofen ['o:fən] m -s, ⁓ oven; (Heiz~) fire, heater; (Kohlen~) stove; (Hoch~) furnace; (Herd) cooker, stove; ~rohr nt stovepipe.

offen ['ɔfən] a open; (aufrichtig) frank; (Stelle) vacant; ~ gesagt to be honest; ~bar a obvious; ~baren [ɔfən'ba:rən] vt reveal, manifest; **O~'barung** f (REL) revelation; ~bleiben vi unreg (Fenster) stay open; (Frage, Entscheidung) remain open; ~halten vt unreg keep open; **O~heit** f candour, frankness; ~herzig a candid, frank; (Kleid) revealing; ~kundig a well-known; (klar) evident; ~lassen vt unreg leave open; ~sichtlich a evident, obvious.

offensiv [ɔfɛn'zi:f] a offensive; **O~e** [-'zi:və] f -, -n offensive.

offenstehen vi unreg be open; (Rechnung) be unpaid; es steht Ihnen offen, es zu tun you are at liberty to do it.

öffentlich ['œfəntlɪç] a public; **Ö~keit** f (Leute) public; (einer Versammlung etc) public nature; in aller Ö~keit in public; an die Ö~keit dringen reach the public ear.

offiziell [ɔfitsi'ɛl] a official.

Offizier [ɔfi'tsi:r] m -s, -e officer; **Offizierskasino** nt officers' mess.

öffnen ['œfnən] vtr open; jdm die Tür ~ open the door for sb.

Öffner ['œfnər] m -s, - opener.

Öffnung ['œfnʊŋ] f opening; **Öffnungszeiten** pl opening times pl.

oft [ɔft] ad often.

öfter ['œftər] ad more often od frequently; ~s ad often, frequently.

oftmals ad often, frequently.

oh [o:] interj oh; ~ je! oh dear.

OHG [o:ha'ge:] abk (= Offene Handelsgesellschaft) general partnership.

ohne ['o:nə] präp +akk, kj without; das ist nicht ~ (umg) it's not bad; ~ weiteres without a second thought; ~ zu fragen without asking; ~ daß er es wußte without him knowing it; (sofort) immediately; ~dies [o:nə-'di:s] ad anyway; ~einander [o:nə'aɪ'nandər] ad without each other; ~gleichen [o:nə'glaɪçən] a unsurpassed, without equal; ~hin [o:nə'hɪn] ad anyway, in any case.

Ohnmacht ['o:nmaxt] f faint; (fig) impotence; in ~ fallen faint.

ohnmächtig ['o:nmɛçtɪç] a in a faint, unconscious; (fig) weak, impotent; sie ist ~ she has fainted.

Ohr [o:r] nt -(e)s, -en ear; (Gehör) hearing.

Öhr [ø:r] nt -(e)s, -e eye.

Ohren- zW: ~arzt m ear specialist; **o~betäubend** a deafening; ~schmalz nt earwax; ~schmerzen pl earache; ~schützer m -s, - earmuff.

Ohr- zW: ~feige f slap on the face; box on the ears; **o~feigen** vt slap sb's face; box sb's ears; ~läppchen nt ear lobe; ~ringe pl earrings pl; ~wurm m earwig; (MUS) catchy tune.

ökonomisch [øko'no:mɪʃ] a economical.

Oktave [ɔk'ta:və] f -, -n octave.

Oktober [ɔk'to:bər] m -(s), - October.

ökumenisch [øku'me:nɪʃ] a ecumenical.

Öl [ø:l] nt -(e)s, -e oil; ~baum m olive tree; **ö~en** vt oil; (TECH) lubricate; ~farbe f oil paint; ~feld nt oilfield; ~film m film of oil; ~heizung f oil-fired central heating; **ö~ig** a oily.

oliv [o'li:f] a olive-green; **O~e** [o'li:və] f -, -n olive.

Öl- zW: ~meßstab m dipstick; ~sardine f sardine; ~standanzeiger m (AUT) oil gauge; ~ung f lubrication; oiling; (ECCL) anointment; die Letzte ~ung Extreme Unction; ~wechsel m oil change; ~zeug nt oilskins pl.

Olymp- [o'lɪmp] zW: ~iade f -i'a:də] f Olympic Games pl; ~iasieger(in f) [-iazi:gər(ɪn)] m Olympic champion; ~iateilnehmer(in f) m Olympic competitor; **o~isch** a Olympic.

Oma ['o:ma] f -, -s (umg) granny.

Omelett [ɔm(ə)'lɛt] nt -(e)s, -s omelet(te).

Omen ['o:mɛn] nt -s, - omen.

Omnibus ['ɔmnibʊs] m (omni)bus.

Onanie [ona'ni:] f masturbation; **o~ren** vi masturbate.

Onkel ['ɔŋkəl] m -s, - uncle.

Opa ['ɔːpa] *m* -s, -s (*umg*) grandpa.

Opal [o'paːl] *m* -s, -e opal.

Oper ['oːpər] *f* -, -n opera; opera house.

Operation [operatsi'oːn] *f* operation; **Operationssaal** *m* operating theatre.

Operette [ope'rɛtə] *f* operetta.

operieren [ope'riːrən] *vti* operate.

Opern- *zW:* **~glas** *nt* opera glasses *pl;* **~haus** *nt* opera house; **~sänger(in** *f*) *m* operatic singer.

Opfer ['ɔpfər] *nt* -s, - sacrifice; (*Mensch*) victim; **o~n** *vt* sacrifice; **~stock** *m* (*ECCL*) offertory box; **~ung** *f* sacrifice.

Opium ['oːpiʊm] *nt* -s opium.

opponieren [ɔpo'niːrən] *vi* oppose (*gegen jdn/etw* sb/sth).

opportun [ɔpɔr'tuːn] *a* opportune; **O~ist** [-'nɪst] *m* opportunist.

Opposition [ɔpozitsi'oːn] *f* opposition; **o~ell** [-'nɛl] *a* opposing.

Optik ['ɔptɪk] *f* optics *sing;* **~er** *m* -s, - optician.

optimal [ɔpti'maːl] *a* optimal, optimum.

Optimismus [ɔpti'mɪsmʊs] *m* optimism.

Optimist [ɔpti'mɪst] *m* optimist; **o~isch** *a* optimistic.

optisch ['ɔptɪʃ] *a* optical.

Orakel [o'raːkəl] *nt* -s, - oracle.

Orange [o'raːʒə] *f* -, -n orange; **o~** *a* orange; **Orangeade** [orã'ʒaːdə] *f* orangeade; **Orangeat** [orã'ʒaːt] *nt* -s, -e candied peel; **Orangensaft** *m* orange juice.

Orchester [ɔr'kɛstər] *nt* -s, - orchestra.

Orchidee [ɔrçi'deːə] *f* -, -n orchid.

Orden ['ɔrdən] *m* -s, - (*ECCL*) order; (*MIL*) decoration; **Ordensschwester** *f* nun.

ordentlich ['ɔrdəntlɪç] *a* (*anständig*) decent, respectable; (*geordnet*) tidy, neat; (*umg: annehmbar*) not bad; (*umg: tüchtig*) real, proper; **~er** **Professor** (full) professor // *ad* properly; **O~keit** *f* respectability; tidiness, neatness.

ordinär [ɔrdi'nɛːr] *a* common, vulgar.

ordnen ['ɔrdnən] *vt* order, put in order.

Ordner *m* -s, - steward; (*COMM*) file.

Ordnung *f* order; (*Ordnen*) ordering; (*Geordnetsein*) tidiness; **~ machen** tidy up; **in ~!** okay.

Ordnungs- *zW:* **o~gemäß** *a* proper, according to the rules; **o~halber** *ad* as a matter of form; **~strafe** *f* fine; **o~widrig** *a* contrary to the rules, irregular; **~zahl** *f* ordinal number.

Organ [ɔr'gaːn] *nt* -s, -e organ; (*Stimme*) voice; **~isation** [-izatsi'oːn] *f* organisation; **~isator** [-i'zaːtɔr] *m*

organizer; **o~isch** *a* organic; **o~isieren** [-i'ziːrən] *vt* organize, arrange; (*umg: beschaffen*) acquire // *vr* organize; **~ismus** [-'nɪsmʊs] *m* organism; **~ist** [-'nɪst] *m* organist.

Orgasmus [ɔr'gasmʊs] *m* orgasm.

Orgel ['ɔrgəl] *f* -, -n organ.

Orgie ['ɔrgiə] *f* orgy.

Orient ['oːriɛnt] *m* -s Orient, east; **~ale** [-'taːlə] *m* -n, -n Oriental; **o~alisch** [-'taːlɪʃ] *a* oriental; **o~ieren** [-'tiːrən] *vt* (*örtlich*) locate; (*fig*) inform // *vr* find one's way *od* bearings; inform oneself; **~ierung** [-'tiːrʊŋ] *f* orientation; (*fig*) information; **~ierungssinn** *m* sense of direction.

original [origi'naːl] *a* original; **O~** *nt* -s, -e original; **O~fassung** *f* original version; **O~i'tät** *f* originality.

originell [origi'nɛl] *a* original.

Orkan [ɔr'kaːn] *m* -(e)s, -e hurricane.

Ornament [ɔrna'mɛnt] *nt* decoration, ornament; **o~al** [-'taːl] *a* decorative, ornamental.

Ort [ɔrt] *m* -(e)s, -e *od* ˝-er place; **an ~ und Stelle** on the spot; **o~en** *vt* locate.

ortho- [ɔrto] *zW:* **~dox** [-'dɔks] *a* orthodox; **O~graphie** [-gra'fiː] *f* spelling, orthography; **o~'graphisch** *a* orthographic; **O~päde** [-'pɛːdə] *m* -n, -n orthopaedic specialist, orthopaedist; **O~pädie** [-pɛ'diː] *f* orthopaedics *sing;* **o~'pädisch** *a* orthopaedic.

örtlich ['œrtlɪç] *a* local; **Ö~keit** *f* locality.

Ortschaft *f* village, small town.

Orts- *zW:* **o~fremd** *a* non-local; **~gespräch** *nt* local (phone) call; **~name** *m* place-name; **~netz** *nt* (*TEL*) local telephone exchange area; **~zeit** *f* local time.

Ortung *f* locating.

Öse ['øːzə] *f* -, -n loop, eye.

Ost- [ɔst] *zW:* **o~'asien** *nt* Eastern Asia; **~block** *m* (*POL*) Eastern bloc; **~en** *m* -s east; **o~'ende** *nt* Ostend.

Oster- ['oːstər] *zW:* **~ei** *nt* Easter egg; **~fest** *nt* Easter; **~glocke** *f* daffodil; **~hase** *m* Easter bunny; **~montag** *m* Easter Monday; **~n** *nt* -s, - Easter.

Österreich ['øːstərraiç] *nt* -s Austria; **~er(in** *f*) *m* -s, - Austrian; **ö~isch** *a* Austrian.

Ostersonntag *m* Easter Day *od* Sunday.

östlich ['œstlɪç] *a* eastern, easterly.

Ost- *zW:* **~see** *f* Baltic Sea; **o~wärts** *ad* eastwards; **~wind** *m* east wind.

Otter ['ɔtər] *m* -s, - otter // *f* -, -n (*Schlange*) adder.

Ouvertüre [uver'tyːrə] *f* -, -n overture.

oval [o'vaːl] *a* oval.

Ovation [ovatsi'oːn] *f* ovation.

Ovulation [ovulatsi'o:n] f ovulation.

Oxyd [ɔ'ksy:t] nt -(e)s, -e oxide; **o~ieren** [ɔksy'di:rən] vti oxidize; **~ierung** f oxidization.

Ozean ['o:tsea:n] m -s, -e ocean; **~dampfer** m (ocean-going) liner.

Ozon [o'tso:n] nt -s ozone.

P

P, p [pe:] nt P, p.

Paar [pa:r] nt -(e)s, -e pair; (Ehe~) couple; ein p~ a few; **p~en** vtr couple; (Tiere) mate; **~lauf** m pair skating; **p~mal** ad: ein p~mal a few times; **~ung** f combination; mating; **p~weise** ad in pairs; in couples.

Pacht [paxt] f -, -en lease; **p~en** vt lease.

Pächter ['pɛçtər] m -s, - leaseholder, tenant.

Pack [pak] m -(e)s, -e od ⁼e bundle, pack // nt -(e)s (pej) mob, rabble.

Päckchen ['pɛkçən] nt small package; (Zigaretten) packet; (Post~) small parcel.

Pack- zW: **p~en** vt pack; (fassen) grasp, seize; (umg: schaffen) manage; (fig: fesseln) grip; **~en** m -s, - bundle; (fig: Menge) heaps of; **~esel** m (lit, fig) packhorse; **~papier** nt brown paper, wrapping paper; **~ung** f packet; (Pralinen~) box; (MED) compress.

Pädagog- [pɛda'go:g] zW: **~e** m -n, -n teacher; **~ik** f education; **p~isch** a educational, pedagogical.

Paddel ['padəl] nt -s, - paddle; **~boot** nt canoe; **p~n** vi paddle.

Page ['pa:ʒə] m -n, -n page; **Pagenkopf** m pageboy.

Paket [pa'ke:t] nt -(e)s, -e packet; (Post~) parcel; **~karte** f dispatch note; **~post** f parcel post; **~schalter** m parcels counter.

Pakt [pakt] m -(e)s, -e pact.

Palast [pa'last] m -es, **Paläste** palace.

Palästin- [palɛs'ti:n] zW: **~a** nt -s Palestine; **~enser(in** f) [palɛsti'nɛnzər(in)] m -s, - Palestinian; **p~'ensisch** a Palestinian.

Palme ['palmə] f -, -n palm (tree).

Palmsonntag m Palm Sunday.

Pampelmuse ['pampəlmu:zə] f -, -n grapefruit.

pampig ['pampiç] a (umg: frech) fresh.

panieren [pa'ni:rən] vt (KOCH) bread.

Paniermehl [pa'ni:rme:l] nt breadcrumbs pl.

Panik ['pa:nik] f panic.

panisch ['pa:niʃ] a panic-stricken.

Panne ['panə] f -, -n (AUT etc) breakdown; (Mißgeschick) slip; **Pannen-**

hilfe f breakdown service.

panschen ['panʃən] vi splash about // vt water down.

Panther ['pantər] m -s, - panther.

Pantoffel [pan'tɔfəl] m -s, -n slipper; **~held** m (umg) henpecked husband.

Pantomime [panto'mi:mə] f -, -n mime.

Panzer ['pantsər] m -s, - armour; (Platte) armour plate; (Fahrzeug) tank; **~glas** nt bulletproof glass; **p~n** vtr armour; (fig) arm o.s.

Papa [pa'pa:] m -s, -s (umg) dad, daddy.

Papagei [papa'gai] m -s, -en parrot.

Papier [pa'pi:r] nt -s, -e paper; (Wert~) share; **~fabrik** f paper mill; **~geld** nt paper money; **~korb** m wastepaper basket; **~tüte** f paper bag.

Papp- [pap] zW: **~deckel** m, **~e** f -, -n cardboard; **Pappel** f -, -n poplar; **p~en** vti (umg) stick; **p~ig** a sticky; **~maché** [-ma'ʃe:] nt -s, -s papiermâché.

Paprika ['paprika] m -s, -s (Gewürz) paprika; (~schote) pepper.

Papst [pa:pst] m -(e)s, ⁼e pope.

päpstlich ['pɛ:pstliç] a papal.

Parabel [pa'ra:bəl] f -, -n parable; (MATH) parabola.

Parade [pa'ra:də] f (MIL) parade, review; (SPORT) parry; **~marsch** m march-past; **~schritt** m goose-step.

Paradies [para'di:s] nt -es, -e paradise; **p~isch** a heavenly.

paradox [para'dɔks] a paradoxical; **P~** nt -es, -e paradox.

Paragraph [para'gra:f] m -en, -en paragraph; (JUR) section.

parallel [para'le:l] a parallel; **P~e** f parallel.

Paranuß ['pa:ranus] f Brazil nut.

Parasit [para'zi:t] m -en, -en (lit, fig) parasite.

parat [pa'ra:t] a ready.

Pärchen ['pɛ:rçən] nt couple.

Parfüm [par'fy:m] nt -s, -s od -e perfume; **~erie** [-ə'ri:] f perfumery; **~flasche** f scent bottle; **p~ieren** [-'mi:rən] vt scent, perfume.

parieren [pa'ri:rən] vt parry // vi (umg) obey.

Paris [pa'ri:s] nt - Paris; **~er(in** f) m Parisian // a Parisian.

Park [park] m -s, -s park; **~anlage** f park; (um Gebäude) grounds pl; **p~en** vti park; **Parkett** [par'kɛt] f -(e)s, -e parquet (floor); (THEAT) stalls pl; **~haus** nt multi-storey car park; **~lücke** f parking space; **~platz** m parking place; car park, parking lot (US); **~scheibe** f parking disc; **~uhr** f parking meter; **~verbot** nt no parking.

Parlament [parla'mɛnt] *nt* parliament; ~arier [-'ta:riər] *m* -s, - parliamentarian; p~arisch [-'ta:rɪʃ] *a* parliamentary.

Parlaments- *zW:* ~beschluß *m* vote of parliament; ~mitglied *nt* member of parliament; ~sitzung *f* sitting (of parliament).

Parodie [paro'di:] *f* parody; p~ren *vt* parody.

Parole [pa'ro:lə] *f* -, -n password; (*Wahlspruch*) motto.

Partei [par'taɪ] *f* party; ~ ergreifen für jdn take sb's side; p~isch *a* partial, biased; ~nahme *f* -, -n support, taking the part of; ~tag *m* party conference.

Parterre [par'tɛr(ə)] *nt* -s, -s ground floor; (*THEAT*) stalls *pl*.

Partie [par'ti:] *f* part; (*Spiel*) game; (*Ausflug*) outing; (*Mann, Frau*) catch; (*COMM*) lot; mit von der ~ sein join in.

Partisan [parti'za:n] *m* -s *od* -en, -en partisan.

Partitur [parti'tu:r] *f* (*MUS*) score.

Partizip [parti'tsi:p] *nt* -s, -ien participle.

Partner(in *f)* ['partnər(ɪn)] *m* -s, - partner; p~schaftlich *a* as partners.

Party ['pa:rti] *f* -, -s *od* Parties party.

Paß [pas] *m* -sses, -sse pass; (*Ausweis*) passport.

Pass- *zW:* p~abel [pa'sa:bəl] *a* passable, reasonable; ~age [pa'sa:ʒə] *f* -, -n passage; ~agier [pasa'ʒi:r] *m* -s, -e passenger; p~agierflugzeug *nt* airliner; ~ant [pa'sant] *m* passer-by.

Paßamt *nt* passport office.

Paßbild *nt* passport photograph.

passen ['pasən] *vi* fit; (*Farbe*) go (*zu* with); (*auf Frage, KARTEN, SPORT*) pass; das paßt mir nicht that doesn't suit me; er paßt nicht zu dir he's not right for you; ~d *a* suitable; (*zusammen~d*) matching; (*angebracht*) fitting; (*Zeit*) convenient.

passier- [pa'si:r] *zW:* ~bar *a* passable; ~en *vt* pass; (*durch Sieb*) strain // *vi* happen; P~schein *m* pass, permit.

Passion [pasi'o:n] *f* passion; p~iert [-'ni:rt] *a* enthusiastic, passionate; **Passionsspiel** *nt* Passion Play.

passiv ['pasi:f] *a* passive; P~ *nt* -s, -e passive; **Passiva** *pl* (*COMM*) liabilities *pl*; P~i'tät *f* passiveness.

Paß- *zW:* ~kontrolle *f* passport control; ~stelle *f* passport office; ~straße *f* (mountain) pass.

Paste ['pastə] *f* -, -n paste.

Pastell [pas'tɛl] *nt* -(e)s, -e pastel.

Pastete [pas'te:tə] *f* -, -n pie.

pasteurisieren [pastøri'zi:rən] *vt* pasteurize.

Pastor ['pastɔr] *m* vicar; pastor, minister.

Pate ['pa:tə] *m* -n, -n godfather; **Patenkind** *nt* godchild.

Patent [pa'tɛnt] *nt* -(e)s, -e patent; (*MIL*) commission; p~ *a* clever; ~amt *nt* ˔patent office; p~ieren [-'ti:rən] *vt* patent; ~inhaber *m* patentee.

Pater ['pa:tər] *m* -s, - *od* **Patres** (*ECCL*) Father.

pathetisch [pa'te:tɪʃ] *a* emotional; bombastic.

Pathologe [pato'lo:gə] *m* -n, -n pathologist.

pathologisch *a* pathological.

Pathos ['pa:tɔs] *nt* - emotiveness, emotionalism.

Patient(in *f)* [patsi'ent(ɪn)] *m* patient.

Patin ['pa:tɪn] *f* godmother.

Patina ['pa:tina] *f* - patina.

Patriot [patri'o:t] *m* -en, -en patriot; p~isch *a* patriotic; ~ismus [-'tɪsmʊs] *m* patriotism.

Patrone [pa'tro:nə] *f* -, -n cartridge.

patrouillieren [patrul'ji:rən] *vi* patrol.

patsch [patʃ] *interj* splash; P~e *f* -, -n (*umg: Bedrängnis*) mess, jam; ~en *vti* smack, slap; (*im Wasser*) splash; ~naß *a* soaking wet.

patzig ['patsɪç] *a* (*umg*) cheeky, saucy.

Pauke ['paukə] *f* -, -n kettledrum; auf die ~ hauen live it up.

pausbäckig ['pausbɛkɪç] *a* chubby-cheeked.

pauschal [pau'ʃa:l] *a* (*Kosten*) inclusive; (*Urteil*) sweeping; P~e *f* -, -n, P~gebühr *f* flat rate; P~preis *m* all-in price; P~reise *f* package tour; P~summe *f* lump sum.

Pause ['pauzə] *f* -, -n break; (*THEAT*) interval; (*Innehalten*) pause; (*Kopie*) tracing.

pausen *vt* trace; ~los *a* non-stop; P~zeichen *nt* call sign; (*MUS*) rest.

Pauspapier ['pauspapi:r] *nt* tracing paper.

Pavian ['pa:via:n] *m* -s, -e baboon.

Pazif- [pa'tsi:f] *zW:* ~ik *m* ~s Pacific; p~isch *a:* P~ischer Ozean Pacific; ~ist [patsi'fɪst] *m* pacifist; p~istisch *a* pacifist.

Pech ['pɛç] *nt* -s, -e pitch; (*fig*) bad luck; ~ haben be unlucky; p~schwarz *a* pitch-black; ~strähne *m* (*umg*) unlucky patch; ~vogel *m* (*umg*) unlucky person.

Pedal [pe'da:l] *nt* -s, -e pedal.

Pedant [pe'dant] *m* pedant; ~e'rie *f* pedantry; p~isch *a* pedantic.

Pegel ['pe:gəl] *m* -s, - water gauge; ~stand *m* water level.

peilen ['pailən] *vt* get a fix on.

Pein [pain] *f* - agony, pain; p~igen *vt*

torture; (*plagen*) torment; **p~lich** *a* (*unangenehm*) embarrassing, awkward, painful; (*genau*) painstaking; **P~lichkeit** *f* painfulness, awkwardness; scrupulousness.

Peitsche ['paɪtʃə] *f* -, -n whip; **p~n** *vt* whip; (*Regen*) lash.

Pelikan ['peːlikaːn] *m* -s, -e pelican.

Pelle ['pɛlə] *f* -, -n skin; **p~n** *vt* skin, peel.

Pellkartoffeln *pl* jacket potatoes *pl.*

Pelz [pɛlts] *m* -es, -e fur.

Pendel ['pɛndəl] *nt* -s, - pendulum; **~verkehr** *m* shuttle traffic; (*für Pendler*) commuter traffic.

Pendler ['pɛndlər] *m* -s, - commuter.

penetrant [pene'trant] *a* sharp; (*Person*) pushing.

Penis ['peːnɪs] *m* -, -se penis.

pennen ['pɛnən] *vi* (*umg*) kip.

Pension [pɛnzi'oːn] *f* (*Geld*) pension; (*Ruhestand*) retirement; (*für Gäste*) boarding *od* guest-house; **~är(in** *f)* [-'nɛr(ɪn)] *m* -s, -e pensioner; **~at** [-'naːt] *nt* -(e)s, -e boarding school; **p~ieren** [-'niːrən] *vt* pension (off); **p~iert** *a* retired; **~ierung** *f* retirement; **Pensionsgast** *m* boarder, paying guest.

Pensum ['pɛnzum] *nt* -s, **Pensen** quota; (*SCH*) curriculum.

per [pɛr] *präp* +*akk* by, per; (*pro*) per; (*bis*) by.

Perfekt ['pɛrfɛkt] *nt* -(e)s, -e perfect; **p~** [pɛr'fɛkt] *a* perfect; **~ionismus** [pɛrfɛktsio'nɪsmus] *m* perfectionism.

perforieren [pɛrfo'riːrən] *vt* perforate.

Pergament [pɛrga'mɛnt] *nt* parchment; **~papier** *nt* greaseproof paper.

Periode [peri'oːdə] *f* -, -n period.

periodisch [peri'oːdɪʃ] *a* periodic; (*dezimal*) recurring.

peripher [peri'feːr] *a* peripheral; **~es Gerät** peripheral.

Perle ['pɛrlə] *f* -, -n (*lit, fig*) pearl; **p~n** *vi* sparkle; (*Tropfen*) trickle.

Perlmutt ['pɛrlmut] *nt* -s mother-of-pearl.

perplex [pɛr'plɛks] *a* dumbfounded.

Pers- ['pɛrz] *zW:* **~er(in** *f)* **m s-,** - Persian; **~i'aner** *m* -s, - Persian lamb; **~ien** [-iən] *nt* -s Persia; **p~isch** *a* Persian.

Person [pɛr'zoːn] *f* -, -en person; **ich für meine ~** personally I.

Personal [pɛrzo'naːl] *nt* -s personnel; (*Bedienung*) servants *pl;* **~ausweis** *m* identity card; **~computer** *m* personal computer, PC; **~ien** [iən] *pl* particulars *pl;* **~i'tät** *f* personality; **~mangel** *m* undermanning; **~pronomen** *nt* personal pronoun.

Personen- *zW:* **~aufzug** *m* lift, elevator (*US*); **~gesellschaft** *f* partnership; **~kraftwagen** *m* private motor-

car; **~schaden** *m* injury to persons; **~zug** *m* stopping train; passenger train.

personifizieren [pɛrzonifi'tsiːrən] *vt* personify.

persönlich [pɛr'zøːnlɪç] *a* personal // *ad* in person; personally; **P~keit** *f* personality.

Perspektive [pɛrspɛk'tiːvə] *f* perspective.

Perücke [pe'rʏkə] *f* -, -n wig.

pervers [pɛr'vɛrs] *a* perverse; **P~i'tät** *f* perversity.

Pessimismus [pɛsi'mɪsmus] *m* pessimism.

Pessimist [pɛsi'mɪst] *m* pessimist; **p~isch** *a* pessimistic.

Pest [pɛst] *f* - plague.

Petersilie [petər'ziːliə] *f* parsley.

Petroleum [pe'troːleum] *nt* -s paraffin, kerosene (*US*).

Pfad [pfaːt] *m* -(e)s, -e path; **~finder** *m* -s, - boy scout; **~finderin** *f* girl guide.

Pfahl [pfaːl] *m* -(e)s, ⁻e post, stake.

Pfand [pfant] *nt* -(e)s, ⁻er pledge, security; (*Flaschen~*) deposit; (*im Spiel*) forfeit; **~brief** *m* bond.

pfänden ['pfɛndən] *vt* seize, distrain.

Pfänderspiel *nt* game of forfeits.

Pfandhaus *nt* pawnshop.

Pfandschein *m* pawn ticket.

Pfändung ['pfɛnduŋ] *f* seizure, distraint.

Pfanne ['pfanə] *f* -, -n (frying) pan.

Pfannkuchen *m* pancake; (*Berliner*) doughnut.

Pfarr- ['pfar] *zW:* **~ei** [-'raɪ] *f* parish; **~er** *m* -s, - priest; (*evangelisch*) vicar; minister; **~haus** *nt* vicarage; manse.

Pfau [pfau] *m* -(e)s, -en peacock; **~enauge** *nt* peacock butterfly.

Pfeffer ['pfefər] *m* -s, - pepper; **~korn** *nt* peppercorn; **~kuchen** *m* gingerbread; **~minz** *nt* -es, -e peppermint; **~mühle** *f* pepper-mill; **p~n** *vt* pepper; (*umg: werfen*) fling; **gepfefferte Preise/Witze** steep prices/spicy jokes.

Pfeife ['pfaɪfə] *f* -, -n whistle; (*Tabak~, Orgel~*) pipe; **p~n** *vti unreg* whistle; **~r** *m* -s, - piper.

Pfeil [pfaɪl] *m* -(e)s, -e arrow.

Pfeiler ['pfaɪlər] *m* -s, - pillar, prop; (*Brücken~*) pier.

Pfennig ['pfɛnɪç] *m* -(e)s, -e pfennig (*hundredth part of a mark*).

Pferd [pfeːrt] *nt* -(e)s, -e horse.

Pferde- ['pfeːrdə] *zW:* **~rennen** *nt* horse-race; horse-racing; **~schwanz** *m* (*Frisur*) ponytail; **~stall** *m* stable.

Pfiff [pfɪf] *m* -(e)s, -e whistle.

Pfifferling ['pfɪfərlɪŋ] *m* yellow chanterelle (*mushroom*); **keinen ~ wert**

not worth a thing.
pfiffig *a* sly, sharp.
Pfingsten ['pfɪŋstən] *nt* -, - Whitsun.
Pfingstrose ['pfɪŋstroːzə] *f* peony.
Pfirsich ['pfɪrzɪç] *m* -s, -e peach.
Pflanz- ['pflants] *zW*: **~e** *f* -, -n plant; **p~en** *vt* plant; **~enfett** *nt* vegetable fat; **p~lich** *a* vegetable; **~ung** *f* plantation.
Pflaster ['pflastər] *nt* -s, - plaster; (*Straße*) pavement; **p~n** *vt* pave; **~stein** *m* paving stone.
Pflaume ['pflaumə] *f* -, -n plum.
Pflege ['pfleːgə] *f* -, -n care; (*von Idee*) cultivation; (*Kranken~*) nursing; in ~ sein (*Kind*) be fostered out; **p~bedürftig** *a* needing care; **~eltern** *pl* foster parents *pl*; **~kind** *nt* foster child; **p~leicht** *a* easy-care; **~mutter** *f* foster mother; **p~n** *vt* look after; (*Kranke*) nurse; (*Beziehungen*) foster; **~r** *m* -s, - orderly; male nurse; **~rin** *f* nurse, attendant; **~vater** *m* foster father.
Pflicht [pflɪçt] *f* -, -en duty; (*SPORT*) compulsory section; **p~bewußt** *a* conscientious; **~fach** *nt* (*SCH*) compulsory subject; **~gefühl** *nt* sense of duty; **p~gemäß** *a* dutiful // *ad* as in duty bound; **~versicherung** *f* compulsory insurance.
pflücken ['pflʏkən] *vt* pick; (*Blumen auch*) pluck.
Pflug [pfluːk] *m* -(e)s, ⁻e plough.
pflügen ['pflyːgən] *vt* plough.
Pforte ['pfɔrtə] *f* -, -n gate; door.
Pförtner ['pfœrtnər] *m* -s, - porter, doorkeeper, doorman.
Pfosten ['pfɔstən] *m* -s, - post.
Pfote ['pfoːtə] *f* -, -n paw; (*umg: Schrift*) scrawl.
Pfropfen ['pfrɔpfən] *m* -s, - (*Flaschen~*) stopper; (*Blut~*) clot; **p~** *vt* (*stopfen*) cram; (*Baum*) graft.
pfui [pfʊi] *interj* ugh.
Pfund [pfʊnt] *nt* -(e)s, -e pound; **p~ig** *a* (*umg*) great.
pfuschen ['pfʊʃən] *vi* (*umg*) be sloppy; **jdm in etw** (*akk*) ~ interfere in sth.
Pfuscher ['pfʊʃər] *m* -s, - (*umg*) sloppy worker; (*Kur~*) quack; **~ei** [-'raɪ] *f* (*umg*) sloppy work; (*Kur~*) quackery.
Pfütze ['pfʏtsə] *f* -, -n puddle.
Phänomen [fɛno'meːn] *nt* -s, -e phenomenon; **p~al** [-'naːl] *a* phenomenal.
Phantasie [fanta'ziː] *f* imagination; **p~los** *a* unimaginative; **p~ren** *vi* fantasize; **p~voll** *a* imaginative.
phantastisch [fan'tastɪʃ] *a* fantastic.
Pharmazeut(in *f)* [farma'tsɔʏt(ɪn)] *m* -en, -en pharmacist.
Phase ['faːzə] *f* -, -n phase.
Philippinen [fɪlɪ'piːnən] *pl* Philippines.

Philologe [filo'loːgə] *m* -n, -n philologist.
Philologie [filolo'giː] *f* philology.
Philosoph [filo'zoːf] *m* -en, -en philosopher; **~ie** [-'fiː] *f* philosophy; **p~isch** *a* philosophical.
Phlegma ['flɛgma] *nt* -s lethargy; **p~tisch** [flɛ'gmatɪʃ] *a* lethargic.
Phonet- [fo'neːt] *zW*: **~ik** *f* phonetics *sing*; **p~isch** *a* phonetic.
Phosphor ['fɔsfɔr] *m* -s phosphorus.
Photo ['foːto] *nt* -s, -s *etc siehe* Foto.
Phrase ['fraːzə] *f* -, -n phrase; (*pej*) hollow phrase.
Physik [fy'ziːk] *f* physics *sing*; **p~alisch** [-'kaːlɪʃ] *a* of physics; **~er(in** *f)* ['fyːzikər(ɪn)] *m* -s, - physicist.
Physiologe [fyzio'loːgə] *m* -n, -n physiologist.
Physiologie [fyziolo'giː] *f* physiology.
physisch ['fyːzɪʃ] *a* physical.
Pianist(in *f)* [pia'nɪst(ɪn)] *m* pianist.
Pickel ['pɪkəl] *m* -s, - pimple; (*Werkzeug*) pickaxe; (*Berg~*) ice-axe; **p~ig** *a* pimply.
picken ['pɪkən] *vi* pick, peck.
Picknick ['pɪknɪk] *nt* -s, -e *od* -s picnic; ~ **machen** have a picnic.
piepen ['piːpən], **piepsen** ['piːpsən] *vi* chirp.
Pietät [pie'tɛːt] *f* piety, reverence; **p~los** *a* impious, irreverent.
Pigment [pɪ'gmɛnt] *nt* pigment.
Pik [piːk] *nt* -s, -e (*KARTEN*) spades; **p~ant** [pi'kant] *a* spicy, piquant; (*anzüglich*) suggestive.
Pilger ['pɪlgər] *m* -s, - pilgrim; **~fahrt** *f* pilgrimage.
Pille ['pɪlə] *f* -, -n pill.
Pilot [pi'loːt] *m* -en, -en pilot.
Pils [pɪls] *nt* -, - lager.
Pilz [pɪlts] *m* -es, -e fungus; (*eßbar*) mushroom; (*giftig*) toadstool; **~krankheit** *f* fungal disease.
pingelig ['pɪŋəlɪç] *a* (*umg*) fussy.
Pinguin ['pɪŋguiːn] *m* -s, -e penguin.
Pinie ['piːniə] *f* pine.
pinkeln ['pɪŋkəln] *vi* (*umg*) pee.
Pinsel ['pɪnzəl] *m* -s, - paintbrush.
Pinzette [pɪn'tsɛtə] *f* tweezers *pl*.
Pionier [pio'niːr] *m* -s, -e pioneer; **~ensender** *m* pirate radio station.
Pirat [pi'raːt] *m* -en, -en pirate; **~ensender** *m* pirate radio station.
Piste ['pɪstə] *f* -, -n (*SKI*) run, piste; (*AVIAT*) runway.
Pistole [pɪs'toːlə] *f* -, -n pistol.
Pizza ['pɪtsa] *f* -, -s pizza.
Pkw [peːkaː'veː] *m* -(s), -(s) *abk von* Personenkraftwagen.
plädieren [plɛ'diːrən] *vi* plead.
Plädoyer [plɛdoa'jeː] *nt* -s, -s speech for the defence; (*fig*) plea.
Plage ['plaːgə] *f* -, -n plague; (*Mühe*)

nuisance; ~**geist** m pest, nuisance;
p~n vt torment // vr toil, slave.
Plakat [pla'ka:t] nt -(e)s, -e placard;
poster.
Plan [pla:n] -(e)s, ⁻e plan; (Karte)
map; ~**e** f -, -n tarpaulin; **p~en** vt
plan; (Mord etc) plot; ~**er** m -s, -
planner; **Planet** [pla'ne:t] m -en -en
planet; **p~gemäß** ad according to
schedule od plan; (EISENB) on time;
p~ieren [pla'ni:rən] vt plane, level.
Planke ['plaŋkə] f -, -n plank.
planlos a (Vorgehen) unsystematic;
(Umherlaufen) aimless.
planmäßig a according to plan; systematic; (EISENB) scheduled.
Plansch- ['planʃ] zW: ~**becken** nt paddling pool; **p~en** vi splash.
Plansoll nt -s output target.
Planstelle f post.
Plantage [plan'ta:ʒə] f -, -n plantation.
Planung f planning.
Planwirtschaft f planned economy.
plappern ['plapərn] vi chatter.
plärren ['plɛrən] vi (Mensch) cry,
whine; (Radio) blare.
Plasma ['plasma] nt -s, **Plasmen** plasma.
Plastik ['plastɪk] f sculpture // nt -s
(Kunststoff) plastic; ~**folie** f plastic
film.
plastisch ['plastɪʃ] a plastic; **stell dir
das ~ vor!** just picture it!
Platane [pla'ta:nə] f -, -n plane (tree).
Platin ['pla:ti:n] nt -s platinum.
Platitüde [plati'ty:də] f -, -n platitude.
platonisch [pla'to:nɪʃ] a platonic.
platsch [platʃ] interj splash; ~**en** vi
splash; ~**naß** a drenched.
plätschern ['plɛtʃərn] vi babble.
platt [plat] a flat; (umg: überrascht)
flabbergasted; (fig: geistlos) flat, boring; ~**deutsch** a low German; **P~e**
f -, -n (Speisen~, PHOT, TECH)
plate; (Stein~) flag; (Kachel) tile;
(Schall~) record; **P~enspieler** m
record player; **P~enteller** m turntable; **P~fuß** m flat foot.
Platz [plats] m -es, ⁻e place; (Sitz~)
seat; (Raum) space, room; (in
Stadt) square; (SPORT~) playing
field; ~ **nehmen** take a seat; **jdm ~
machen** make room for sb; ~**angst** f
(MED) agoraphobia; (umg) claustrophobia; ~**anweiser(in** f) m -s, - ush-
er(ette).
Plätzchen ['plɛtsçən] nt spot; (Gebäck) biscuit.
Platz- zW: **p~en** vi burst; (Bombe)
explode; **vor Wut p~en** (umg) be
bursting with anger; ~**karte** f seat
reservation; ~**mangel** m lack of
space; ~**patrone** f blank cartridge;
~**regen** m downpour; ~**wunde** f cut.
Plauderei [plaudə'raɪ] f chat, conver-

sation; (RAD) talk.
plaudern ['plaudərn] vi chat, talk.
plausibel [plau'zi:bəl] a plausible.
plazieren [pla'tsi:rən] vt place // vr
(SPORT) be placed; (Tennis) be
seeded.
pleite ['plaɪtə] a (umg) broke; **P~** f -,
-n bankruptcy; (umg: Reinfall) flop;
P~ machen go bust.
Plenum ['ple:nʊm] nt -s plenum.
Plombe ['plɔmbə] f -, -n lead seal;
(Zahn~) filling.
plombieren [plɔm'bi:rən] vt seal;
(Zahn) fill.
plötzlich ['plœtslɪç] a sudden // ad suddenly.
plump [plʊmp] a clumsy; (Hände)
coarse; (Körper) shapeless; ~**sen** vi
(umg) plump down, fall.
Plunder ['plʊndər] m -s rubbish.
plündern ['plʏndərn] vti plunder;
(Stadt) sack.
Plünderung ['plʏndərʊŋ] f plundering,
sack, pillage.
Plural [plu'ra:l] m -s, -e plural;
p~istisch [plura'lɪstɪʃ] a pluralistic.
Plus [plʊs] nt -, - plus; (FIN) profit;
(Vorteil) advantage; **p~** ad plus.
Plüsch [ply:ʃ] m -(e)s, -e plush.
Plus- zW: ~**pol** m (ELEK) positive
pole; ~**punkt** m point; (fig) point in
sb's favour.
PLZ abk von **Postleitzahl.**
Po [po:] m -s, -s (umg) bottom, bum.
Pöbel ['pø:bəl] m -s mob, rabble; ~**ei**
[-'laɪ] f vulgarity; **p~haft** a low, vul-
gar.
pochen ['pɔxən] vi knock; (Herz)
pound; **auf etw** (akk) ~ (fig) insist on
sth.
Pocken ['pɔkən] pl smallpox.
Podium ['po:dium] nt podium;
Podiumsdiskussion f panel discus-
sion.
Poesie [poe'zi:] f poetry.
Poet [po'e:t] m -en, -en poet; **p~isch**
a poetic.
Pointe [po'ɛːtə] f -, -n point.
Pokal [po'ka:l] m -s, -e goblet;
(SPORT) cup; ~**spiel** nt cup-tie.
Pökel- ['pø:kəl] zW: ~**fleisch** nt salt
meat; **p~n** vt pickle, salt.
Pol [po:l] m -s, -e pole; **p~ar** [po'la:r]
a polar; ~**arkreis** m arctic circle; ~**e**
m -n, -n, ~**in** f Pole; ~**en** nt -s Po-
land.
polemisch [po'le:mɪʃ] a polemical.
Police [po'li:s(ə)] f -, -n insurance
policy.
Polier [po'li:r] m -s, -e foreman; **p~en**
vt polish.
Poliklinik ['po:likli:nɪk] f outpatients.
Politik [poli'ti:k] f politics sing; (eine
bestimmte) policy; ~**er(in** f) [po'li:-
tikər(ɪn)] m -s, - politician.

politisch [po'li:tɪʃ] *a* political.
Politur [poli'tu:r] *f* polish.
Polizei [poli'tsai] *f* police; **~beamte(r)** *m* police officer; **p~lich** *a* police; **sich p~lich melden** register with the police; **~revier** *nt* police station; **~staat** *m* police state; **~streife** *f* police patrol; **~stunde** *f* closing time; **~wache** *f* = **~revier**.
Polizist [poli'tsɪst] *m* -en, -en policeman; **~in** *f* policewoman.
Pollen ['pɔlən] *m* -s, - pollen.
polnisch ['pɔlnɪʃ] *a* Polish.
Polster ['pɔlstər] *nt* -s, - cushion; (*Polsterung*) upholstery; (*in Kleidung*) padding; (*fig: Geld*) reserves *pl*; **~er** *m* -s, - upholsterer; **~möbel** *pl* upholstered furniture; **p~n** *vt* upholster; pad; **~ung** *f* upholstery.
Polter- ['pɔltər] *zW:* **~abend** *m* party on eve of wedding; **p~n** *vi* (*Krach machen*) crash; (*schimpfen*) rant.
Polyp [po'ly:p] *m* -en -en polyp; (*pl: MED*) adenoids *pl*; (*umg*) cop.
Pomade [po'ma:də] *f* pomade.
Pommes frites [pɔm'frɪt] *pl* chips *pl*, French fried potatoes *pl*.
Pomp [pɔmp] *m* -(e)s pomp.
Pony ['pɔni] *m* -s, -s (*Frisur*) fringe // *nt* -s, -s (*Pferd*) pony.
Popmusik ['pɔpmuzi:k] *f* pop music.
Popo [po'po:] *m* -s, -s bottom, bum.
populär [popu'lɛ:r] *a* popular.
Popularität [populari'tɛ:t] *f* popularity.
Pore ['po:rə] *f* -, -n pore.
Pornographie [pɔrnogra'fi:] *f* pornography.
porös [po'rø:s] *a* porous.
Porree ['pɔre] *m* -s, -s leek.
Portal [pɔr'ta:l] *nt* -s, -e portal.
Portefeuille [pɔrt'fø:j] *nt* (*POL, FIN*) portfolio.
Portemonnaie [pɔrtmɔ'nɛ:] *nt* -s, -s purse.
Portier [pɔrti'e:] *m* -s, -s porter.
Portion [pɔrtsi'o:n] *f* portion, helping; (*umg: Anteil*) amount.
Porto ['pɔrto] *nt* -s, -s postage; **p~frei** *a* post-free, (postage) prepaid.
Porträt [pɔr'trɛ:] *nt* -s, -s portrait; **p~ieren** [pɔrtrɛ'ti:rən] *vt* paint, portray.
Portug- [pɔrtug] *zW:* **~al** *nt* **~s** Portugal; **~iese** [pɔrtu'gi:zə] *m* -n, -n, **~'iesin** *f* Portuguese; **p~'iesisch** *a* Portuguese.
Porzellan [pɔrtse'la:n] *nt* -s, -e china, porcelain; (*Geschirr*) china.
Posaune [po'zaunə] *f* -, -n trombone.
Pose ['po:zə] *f* -, -n pose.
posieren [po'zi:rən] *vi* pose.
Position [pozitsi'o:n] *f* position.
positiv ['po:ziti:f] *a* positive; **P~** *nt* -s, -e (*PHOT*) positive.
possessiv ['pɔsɛsi:f] *a* possessive;

P~pronomen *nt* -s, -e possessive pronoun.
possierlich [pɔ'si:rlɪç] *a* funny.
Post [pɔst] *f* -, -en post (office); (*Briefe*) mail; **~amt** *nt* post office; **~anweisung** *f* postal order, money order; **~bote** *m* postman; **~en** *m* -s, - post, position; (*COMM*) item; (*auf Liste*) entry; (*MIL*) sentry; (*Streik~*) picket; **~er** *nt* -s, -(s) poster; **~fach** *nt* post-office box; **~karte** *f* postcard; **p~lagernd** *ad* poste restante; **~leitzahl** *f* postal code; **~scheckkonto** *nt* postal giro account; **~sparkasse** *f* post office savings bank; **~stempel** *m* postmark; **~wertzeichen** *nt* postage stamp.
potent [po'tɛnt] *a* potent.
Potential [potɛntsi'a:l] *nt* -s, -e potential.
potentiell [potɛntsi'ɛl] *a* potential.
Potenz [po'tɛnts] *f* power; (*eines Mannes*) potency.
Pracht [praxt] *f* - splendour, magnificence.
prächtig ['prɛçtɪç] *a* splendid.
Prachtstück *nt* showpiece.
prachtvoll *a* splendid, magnificent.
Prädikat [prɛdi'ka:t] *nt* -(e)s, -e title; (*GRAM*) predicate; (*Zensur*) distinction.
Prag [pra:k] *nt* -s Prague.
prägen ['prɛ:gən] *vt* stamp; (*Münze*) mint; (*Ausdruck*) coin; (*Charakter*) form.
prägnant [prɛ'gnant] *a* precise, terse.
Prägung ['prɛ:guŋ] *f* minting; forming; (*Eigenart*) character, stamp.
prahlen ['pra:lən] *vi* boast, brag.
Prahlerei [pra:lə'rai] *f* boasting.
Praktik ['praktɪk] *f* practice; **p~abel** [-'ka:bəl] *a* practicable; **~ant(in** *f*) [-'kant(ɪn)] *m* trainee; **~um** *nt* -s, **Praktika** *od* **Praktiken** practical training.
praktisch ['praktɪʃ] *a* practical, handy; **~er Arzt** general practitioner.
praktizieren [prakti'tsi:rən] *vti* practise.
Praline [pra'li:nə] *f* chocolate.
prall [pral] *a* firmly rounded; (*Segel*) taut; (*Arme*) plump; (*Sonne*) blazing; **~en** *vi* bounce, rebound; (*Sonne*) blaze.
Prämie ['prɛ:miə] *f* premium; (*Belohnung*) award, prize; **p~ren** [prɛ'mi:rən] *vt* give an award to.
Pranger ['praŋər] *m* -s, - (*HIST*) pillory; **jdn an den ~ stellen** (*fig*) pillory sb.
Präparat [prɛpa'ra:t] *nt* -(e)s, -e (*BIOL*) preparation; (*MED*) medicine.
Präposition [prɛpozitsi'o:n] *f* preposition.

Präsens ['prɛːzɛns] nt - present tense.
präsentieren [prɛzɛn'tiːrən] vt present.
Präservativ [prɛzɛrva'tiːf] nt -s, -e contraceptive.
Präsident(in f) [prɛzi'dɛnt(ɪn)] m president; **~schaft** f presidency.
Präsidium [prɛ'ziːdiʊm] nt presidency, chair(manship); (Polizei~) police headquarters pl.
prasseln ['prasəln] vi (Feuer) crackle; (Hagel) drum; (Wörter) rain down.
Praxis ['praksɪs] f -, **Praxen** practice; (Behandlungsraum) surgery; (von Anwalt) office.
präzis [prɛ'tsiːs] a precise; **P~ion** [prɛtsizi'oːn] f precision.
predigen ['preːdɪgən] vti preach.
Prediger m -s, - preacher.
Predigt ['preːdɪçt] f -, -en sermon.
Preis [praɪs] m -es, -e price; (Sieges~) prize; **um keinen ~** not at any price; **Preiselbeere** f cranberry; **p~en** [praɪzən] vi unreg praise; **p~geben** vt unreg abandon; (opfern) sacrifice; (zeigen) expose; **p~gekrönt** a prize-winning; **~gericht** nt jury; **p~günstig** a inexpensive; **~lage** f price range; **~träger(in** f) m prizewinner; **p~wert** a inexpensive.
prekär [pre'kɛːr] a precarious.
Prell- [prɛl] zW: **~bock** m buffers pl; **p~en** vt bump; (fig) cheat, swindle; **~ung** f bruise.
Premiere [prəmi'ɛːrə] f -, -n premiere.
Premierminister [prəmi'eːmɪnɪstər] m prime minister, premier.
Presse ['prɛsə] f -, -n press; **~freiheit** f freedom of the press; **p~n** vt press; **~verlautbarung** f press release.
pressieren [prɛ'siːrən] vi (be in a) hurry.
Preßluft ['prɛslʊft] f compressed air; **~bohrer** m pneumatic drill.
Prestige [prɛs'tiːʒə] nt -s prestige.
Preuß- [prɔʏs] zW: **~e** m -n, -n, **~in** f Prussian; **~en** nt -s Prussia; **p~isch** a Prussian.
prickeln ['prɪkəln] vti tingle, tickle.
Priester ['priːstər] m -s, - priest.
prima ['priːma] a inv first-class, excellent; **P~** f -, **Primen** sixth form, top class.
primär [pri'mɛːr] a primary.
Primel ['priːməl] f -, -n primrose.
primitiv [primi'tiːf] a primitive.
Prinz [prɪnts] m -en, -en prince; **Prinzessin** [prɪn'tsɛsɪn] f princess.
Prinzip [prɪn'tsiːp] nt -s, -ien principle; **p~iell** [-i'ɛl] a,ad on principle; **p~ienlos** a unprincipled.
Priorität [priori'tɛːt] f priority.
Prise ['priːzə] f -, -n pinch.
Prisma ['prɪsma] nt -s, **Prismen** prism.

privat [pri'vaːt] a private.
pro [proː] präp +akk per; **P~** nt - pro.
Probe ['proːbə] f -, -n test; (Test-stück) sample; (THEAT) rehearsal; **jdn auf die ~ stellen** put sb to the test; **~exemplar** nt specimen copy; **~fahrt** f test drive; **p~n** vt try; (THEAT) rehearse; **p~weise** ad on approval; **~zeit** f probation period.
probieren [pro'biːrən] vti try; (Wein, Speise) taste, sample.
Problem [pro'bleːm] nt -s, -e problem; **~atik** [-'maːtɪk] f problem; **p~atisch** [-'maːtɪʃ] a problematic; **p~los** a problem-free.
Produkt [pro'dʊkt] nt -(e)s, -e product; (AGR) produce no pl; **~ion** [prodʊktsi'oːn] f production; output; **p~iv** [-'tiːf] a productive; **~ivität** f productivity.
Produzent [produ'tsɛnt] m manufacturer; (Film) producer.
produzieren [produ'tsiːrən] vt produce.
Professor [pro'fɛsɔr] m professor.
Profi ['proːfi] m -s, -s (umg, SPORT) pro.
Profil [pro'fiːl] nt -s, -e profile; (fig) image; **p~ieren** [profi'liːrən] vr create an image for o.s.
Profit [pro'fiːt] m -(e)s, -e profit; **p~ieren** [profi'tiːrən] vi profit (von from).
Prognose [pro'gnoːzə] f -; -n prediction, prognosis.
Programm [pro'gram] nt -s, -e programme; (COMPUT) program; **p~ieren** [-'miːrən] vt programme; (COMPUT) program; **~ierer(in** f) m -s, - programmer.
progressiv [progrɛ'siːf] a progressive.
Projekt [pro'jɛkt] nt -(e)s, -e project; **~or** [pro'jɛktɔr] m projector.
proklamieren [prokla'miːrən] vt proclaim.
Prolet [pro'leːt] m -en, -en prole, pleb; **~ariat** [-ari'aːt] nt -(e)s, -e proletariat; **~arier** [-'taːriər] m -s, - proletarian.
Prolog [pro'loːk] m -(e)s, -e prologue.
Promenade [promə'naːdə] f promenade.
Promille [pro'mɪlə] nt -(s), - alcohol level.
prominent [promi'nɛnt] a prominent.
Prominenz [promi'nɛnts] f VIPs pl.
Promotion [promotsi'oːn] f doctorate, Ph.D.
promovieren [promo'viːrən] vi do a doctorate od Ph.D.
prompt [prɔmpt] a prompt.
Pronomen [pro'noːmɛn] nt -s, - pronoun.
Propaganda [propa'ganda] f - propaganda.

Propeller [pro'pɛlər] *m* -s, - propeller.

Prophet [pro'feːt] *m* -en, -en prophet.

prophezeien [profe'tsaıən] *vt* prophesy.

Prophezeiung *f* prophecy.

Proportion [proportsi'oːn] *f* proportion; **p~al** [-'naːl] *a* proportional.

Prosa [pro'zaː] *f* - prose; **p~isch** [pro'zaːıʃ] *a* prosaic.

prosit ['proːzɪt] *interj* cheers.

Prospekt [pro'spɛkt] *m* -(e)s, -e leaflet, brochure.

prost [proːst] *interj* cheers.

Prostituierte [prostitu'iːrtə] *f* -n, -n prostitute.

Prostitution [prostitutsi'oːn] *f* prostitution.

Protest [pro'tɛst] *m* -(e)s, -e protest; **~ant(in** *f)* [protes'tant] *m* Protestant; **p~antisch** [protes'tantıʃ] *a* Protestant; **p~ieren** [protes'tiːrən] *vi* protest.

Prothese [pro'teːzə] *f* -, -n artificial limb; (*Zahn~*) dentures *pl*.

Protokoll [proto'kɔl] *nt* -s, -e register; (*von Sitzung*) minutes *pl*; (*diplomatisch*) protocol; (*Polizei~*) statement; **p~ieren** [-'liːrən] *vt* take down in the minutes.

protz- ['prɔts] *zW*: **~en** *vi* show off; **~ig** *a* ostentatious.

Proviant [provi'ant] *m* -s, -e provisions *pl*, supplies *pl*.

Provinz [pro'vɪnts] *f* -, -en province; **p~i'ell** *a* provincial.

Provision [provizi'oːn] *f* (*COMM*) commission.

provisorisch [provi'zoːrıʃ] *a* provisional.

Provokation [provokatsi'oːn] *f* provocation.

provozieren [provo'tsiːrən] *vt* provoke.

Prozedur [protse'duːr] *f* procedure; (*pej*) carry-on.

Prozent [pro'tsɛnt] *nt* -(e)s, -e per cent, percentage; **~satz** *m* percentage; **p~ual** [-u'aːl] *a* percentage; as a percentage.

Prozeß [pro'tsɛs] *m* -sses, -sse trial, case.

Prozession [protsɛsi'oːn] *f* procession.

prüde ['pryːdə] *a* prudish; **P~rie** [-'riː] *f* prudery.

Prüf- ['pryːf] *zW*: **p~en** *vt* examine, test; (*nach~*) check; **~er** *m* -s, - examiner; **~ling** *m* examinee; **~ung** *f* examination; checking; **~ungsausschuß** *m* examining board.

Prügel ['pryːgəl] *m* -s, - cudgel // *pl* beating; **~ei** [-'laı] *f* fight; **~knabe** *m* scapegoat; **p~n** *vt* beat // *vr* fight; **~strafe** *f* corporal punishment.

Prunk [prʊŋk] *m* -(e)s pomp, show; **p~voll** *a* splendid, magnificent.

PS [peː'ɛs] *abk* (= *Pferdestärke*) horsepower, HP.

Psalm [psalm] *m* -s, -en psalm.

pseudo- ['psɔydo] *in zW* pseudo.

pst [pst] *interj* psst.

Psych- ['psyç] *zW*: **~iater** [-i'aːtər] *m* -s, - psychiatrist; **p~isch** *a* psychological; **~oanalyse** [-o'ana'lyːzə] *f* psychoanalysis; **~ologe** [-o'loːgə] *m* -n, -n psychologist; **~olo'gie** *f* psychology; **p~ologisch** *a* psychological.

Pubertät [puber'tɛːt] *f* puberty.

Publikum ['puːblikʊm] *nt* -s audience; (*SPORT*) crowd.

publizieren [publi'tsiːrən] *vt* publish, publicize.

Pudding ['pʊdɪŋ] *m* -s, -e *od* -s blancmange.

Pudel ['puːdəl] *m* -s poodle.

Puder ['puːdər] *m* -s, - powder; **~dose** *f* powder compact; **p~n** *vt* powder; **~zucker** *m* icing sugar.

Puff [pʊf] *m* -s, -e (*Wäsche~*) linen basket; (*Sitz~*) pouf; *pl* -e (*umg: Stoß*) push; *pl* -s (*umg: Bordell*) brothel; **~er** *m* -s, - buffer; **~erspeicher** *m* (*COMPUT*) buffer.

Pullover [pʊ'loːvər] *m* -s, - pullover, jumper.

Puls [pʊls] *m* -es, -e pulse; **~ader** *f* artery; **p~ieren** [pʊl'ziːrən] *vi* throb, pulsate.

Pult [pʊlt] *nt* -(e)s, -e desk.

Pulver ['pʊlfər] *nt* -s, - powder; **p~ig** *a* powdery; **~schnee** *m* powdery snow.

pummelig ['pʊməlıç] *a* chubby.

Pumpe ['pʊmpə] *f* -, -n pump; **p~n** *vt* pump; (*umg*) lend; borrow.

Punkt [pʊŋkt] *m* -(e)s, -e point; (*bei Muster*) dot; (*Satzzeichen*) full stop; **p~ieren** [-'tiːrən] *vt* dot; (*MED*) aspirate.

pünktlich ['pʏŋktlıç] *a* punctual; **P~keit** *f* punctuality.

Punktsieg *m* victory on points.

Punktzahl *f* score.

Punsch [pʊnʃ] *m* -(e)s, -e punch.

Pupille [pu'pılə] *f* -, -n pupil.

Puppe ['pʊpə] *f* -, -n doll; (*Marionette*) puppet; (*Insekten~*) pupa, chrysalis; **~nspieler** *m* puppeteer.

pur [puːr] *a* pure; (*völlig*) sheer; (*Whisky*) neat.

Püree [py'reː] *nt* -s, -s mashed potatoes *pl*.

Purzel- ['pʊrtsəl] *zW*: **~baum** *m* somersault; **p~n** *vi* tumble.

Puste ['puːstə] *f* - (*umg*) puff; (*fig*) steam; **p~n** *vi* puff, blow.

Pute ['puːtə] *f* -, -n turkey-hen; **~r** *m* -s, - turkey-cock.

Putsch [pʊtʃ] *m* -(e)s, -e revolt, putsch.

Putz [pʊts] *m* -es (*Mörtel*) plaster, roughcast; **p~en** *vt* clean; (*Nase*) wipe, blow // vr clean oneself; dress oneself up; **~frau** f charwoman; **p~ig** a quaint, funny; **~lappen** m cloth.

Puzzle ['pasəl] nt -s, -es jigsaw.

Pyjama [py'dʒaːma] m -s, -s pyjamas pl.

Pyramide [pyra'miːdə] f -, -n pyramid.

Pyrenäen [pyre'nɛːən] pl Pyrenees pl.

Q

Q, q [kuː] nt Q, q.

Quacksalber ['kvakzalbər] m -s, - quack (doctor).

Quader ['kvaːdər] m -s, - square stone; (MATH) cuboid.

Quadrat [kva'draːt] nt -(e)s, -e square; **q~isch** a square; **~meter** m square metre.

quaken ['kvaːkən] vi croak; (Ente) quack.

quäken ['kvɛːkən] vi screech.

Qual [kvaːl] f -, -en pain, agony; (see-lisch) anguish.

Quäl- [kvɛːl] zW: **q~en** vt torment // vr struggle; (geistig) torment oneself; **~erei** [-ə'raɪ] f torture, torment; **~geist** m pest.

qualifizieren [kvalifi'tsiːrən] vtr qualify; (einstufen) label.

Qualität [kvali'tɛːt] f quality; **Qualitätsware** f article of high quality.

Qualle ['kvalə] f -, -n jellyfish.

Qualm [kvalm] m -(e)s thick smoke; **q~en** vti smoke.

qualvoll ['kvaːlfɔl] a excruciating, painful, agonizing.

Quant- ['kvant] zW: **~entheorie** f quantum theory; **~ität** [-i'tɛːt] f quantity; **q~itativ** [-ita'tiːf] a quantitative; **~um** nt -s, **Quanten** quantity, amount.

Quarantäne [karan'tɛːnə] f -, -n quarantine.

Quark [kvark] m -s curd cheese; (umg) rubbish.

Quarta ['kvarta] f -, **Quarten** third year of secondary school; **Quartal** [kvar'taːl] nt -s, -e quarter (year).

Quartier [kvar'tiːr] nt -s, -e accommodation; (MIL) quarters pl; (Stadt~) district.

Quarz [kvaːrts] m -es, -e quartz.

quasseln ['kvasəln] vi (umg) natter.

Quatsch [kvatʃ] m -es rubbish; **q~en** vi chat, natter.

Quecksilber ['kvɛkzɪlbər] nt mercury.

Quelle ['kvɛlə] f -, -n spring; (eines Flusses) source; **q~n** vi (hervor~) pour od gush forth; (schwellen) swell.

quer [kveːr] ad crossways, diagonally; (rechtwinklig) at right angles; **~ auf**

dem Bett across the bed; **Q~balken** m crossbeam; **~feldein** ad across country; **Q~flöte** f flute; **Q~schnitt** m cross-section; **~schnittsgelähmt** a paralysed below the waist; **Q~straße** f intersecting road.

quetschen ['kvɛtʃən] vt squash, crush; (MED) bruise.

Quetschung f bruise, contusion.

quieken ['kviːkən] vi squeak.

quietschen ['kviːtʃən] vi squeak.

Quint- ['kvɪnt] zW: **~a** f -, -en second form in secondary school; **~essenz** [-'ɛsɛnts] f quintessence; **~ett** [-'tɛt] nt -(e)s, -e quintet.

Quirl [kvɪrl] m -(e)s, -e whisk.

quitt [kvɪt] a quits, even; **Q~e** f -, -n quince; **~ieren** [-'tiːrən] vt give a receipt for; (Dienst) leave; **Q~ung** f receipt.

Quiz [kvɪs] nt -, - quiz.

Quote ['kvoːtə] f -, -n number, rate.

R

R, r [ɛr] nt R, r.

Rabatt [ra'bat] m -(e)s, -e discount; **~e** f -, -n flowerbed, border; **~marke** f trading stamp.

Rabe ['raːbə] m -n, -n raven.

rabiat [rabi'aːt] a furious.

Rache ['raxə] f - revenge, vengeance; **~n** m -s, - throat.

rächen ['rɛçən] vt avenge, revenge // vr take (one's) revenge; **das wird sich ~** you'll pay for that.

Rachitis [ra'xiːtɪs] f - rickets sing.

Rad [raːt] nt -(e)s, -er wheel; (Fahr~) bike; **Radar** ['raːdaːr] m od nt -s radar; **Radarfalle** f speed trap; **Radarkontrolle** f radar-controlled speed trap; **Radau** [ra'dau] m -s (umg) row; **~dampfer** m paddle steamer; **radebrechen** vi insep: **deutsch** etc **radebrechen** speak broken German etc; **r~fahren** vi unreg cycle; **~fahrer(in** f) m cyclist; **~fahrweg** m cycle track od path.

Radier- [ra'diːr] zW: **r~en** vt rub out, erase; (ART) etch; **~gummi** m rubber, eraser; **~ung** f etching.

Radieschen [ra'diːsçən] nt radish.

radikal [radi'kaːl] a, **R~e(r)** mf radical.

Radio ['raːdio] nt -s, -s radio, wireless; **r~ak'tiv** a radioactive; **~aktivi'tät** f radioactivity; **~apparat** m radio, wireless set.

Radius ['raːdius] m -, **Radien** radius.

Rad- zW: **~kappe** f (AUT) hub cap; **~rennen** nt cycle race; cycle racing; **~sport** m cycling.

raff- [raf] zW: **~en** vt snatch, pick up; (Stoff) gather (up); (Geld) pile up,

rake in; **R~inade** [-i'na:də] f refined
sugar; **~i'niert** a crafty, cunning.
ragen ['ra:gən] vi tower, rise.
Rahm [ra:m] m -s cream; **~en** m -s, -
frame(work); **im ~en des Möglichen**
within the bounds of possibility; **r~en**
vt frame; **~enplan** m outline plan;
r~ig a creamy.
Rakete [ra'ke:tə] f -, -n rocket;
Raketenstützpunkt m missile base.
rammen ['ramən] vt ram.
Rampe ['rampə] f -, -n ramp;
Rampenlicht vt (THEAT) footlights
pl.
ramponieren [rampo'ni:rən] vt (umg)
damage.
Ramsch [ramʃ] m -(e)s, -e junk.
ran [ran] ad (umg) = **heran.**
Rand [rant] m -(e)s, ⁻er edge; (von
Brille, Tasse etc) rim; (Hut~) brim;
(auf Papier) margin; (Schmutz~,
unter Augen) ring; (fig) verge,
brink; **außer ~ und Band** wild; **am
~e bemerkt** mentioned in passing;
r~alieren [randa'li:rən] vi (go on the)
rampage.
Rang [raŋ] m -(e)s, ⁻e rank; (Stand)
standing; (Wert) quality; (THEAT)
circle.
Rangier- [rãʒiːr] zW: **~bahnhof** m
marshalling yard; **r~en** vt (EISENB)
shunt, switch (US) // vi rank, be
classed; **~gleis** nt siding.
Ranke ['raŋkə] f -, -n tendril, shoot.
rannte etc v siehe **rennen.**
ranzig ['rantsɪç] a rancid.
Rappe ['rapə] m -n, -n black horse.
Rappen ['rapən] m (FIN) rappen, cen-
time.
rar [ra:r] a rare; **sich ~ machen**
(umg) keep oneself to oneself;
R~i'tät f rarity; (Sammelobjekt) cu-
rio.
rasant [ra'zant] a quick, rapid.
rasch [raʃ] a quick; **~eln** vi rustle.
Rasen ['ra:zən] m -s, - lawn; grass;
r~ vi rave; (schnell) race; **r~d** a
furious; **r~de Kopfschmerzen** a splitting headache; **~mäher** m -s, - f
lawnmower; **~platz** m lawn.
Rasier- [ra'zi:r] zW: **~apparat** m shaver; **~creme** f shaving cream; **r~en**
vtr shave; **~klinge** f razor blade;
~messer nt razor; **~pinsel** m shaving brush; **~seife** f shaving soap od
stick; **~wasser** nt shaving lotion.
Rasse ['rasə] f -, -n race; (Tier~)
breed; **~hund** m thoroughbred dog;
Rassenhaß m race od racial hatred;
Rassentrennung f racial segregation.
Rassismus [ra'sɪsmʊs] m racism.
Rast [rast] f -, -en rest; **r~en** vi rest;
~haus nt, **~hof** m (AUT) service station; **r~los** a tireless; (unruhig) restless; **~platz** m (AUT) layby; **~stätte**

f (AUT) service station.
Rasur [ra'zu:r] f shaving.
Rat [ra:t] m -(e)s, -schläge advice no
pl; **ein ~** a piece of advice; **jdn zu ~e
ziehen** consult sb; **keinen ~ wissen**
not know what to do; **~e** f -, -n instalment; **r~en** vti unreg guess;
(empfehlen) advise (jdm sb);
~enzahlung f hire purchase; **~geber**
m -s, - adviser; **~haus** nt town hall.
ratifizieren [ratifi'tsi:rən] vt ratify.
Ration [ratsi'o:n] f ration; **r~al** [-'na:l]
a rational; **r~ali'sieren** vt rational-
ize; **r~ell** [-'nɛl] a efficient; **r~ieren**
[-'ni:rən] vt ration.
Rat- zW: **r~los** a at a loss, helpless;
r~sam a advisable; **~schlag** m
(piece of) advice.
Rätsel ['rɛːtsəl] nt -s, - puzzle;
(Wort~) riddle; **r~haft** a mysterious; **es ist mir r~haft** it's a mystery
to me.
Ratte ['ratə] f -, -n rat; **Rattenfänger**
m -s, - ratcatcher.
rattern ['ratərn] vi rattle, clatter.
Raub [raʊp] m -(e)s robbery; (Beute)
loot, booty; **~bau** m ruthless exploi-
tation; **r~en** [raʊbən] vt rob;
(Mensch) kidnap, abduct.
Räuber ['rɔybər] m -s, - robber.
Raub- zW: **~mord** m robbery with
murder; **~tier** nt predator; **~überfall**
m robbery with violence; **~vogel** m
bird of prey.
Rauch [raʊx] m -(e)s smoke; **r~en** vti
smoke; **~er** m -s, - smoker;
~erabteil nt (EISENB) smoker.
räuchern ['rɔyçərn] vt smoke, cure.
Rauchfleisch nt smoked meat.
rauchig a smoky.
rauf [raʊf] ad (umg) = **herauf, hinauf;**
~en vt (Haare) pull out // vir fight;
R~e'rei f brawl, fight.
rauh [raʊ] a rough, coarse; (Wetter)
harsh; **R~reif** m hoarfrost.
Raum [raʊm] m -(e)s, Räume space;
(Zimmer, Platz) room; (Gebiet)
area.
räumen ['rɔymən] vt clear; (Wohnung,
Platz) vacate; (wegbringen) shift,
move; (in Schrank etc) put away.
Raum- zW: **~fähre** f space shuttle;
~fahrt f space travel; **~inhalt** m cubic capacity, volume.
räumlich ['rɔymlɪç] a spatial;
R~keiten pl premises pl.
Raum- zW: **~mangel** m lack of
space; **~pflegerin** f cleaner; **~schiff**
nt spaceship; **~schiffahrt** f space
travel.
Räumung ['rɔymʊŋ] f vacating,
evacuation; clearing (away); **Räu-
mungsverkauf** m clearance sale;
(bei Geschäftsaufgabe) closing down
sale.

Raupe ['raʊpə] f -, -n caterpillar; (~nkette) (caterpillar) track; **Raupenschlepper** m caterpillar tractor.

raus [raʊs] ad (umg) = **heraus, hinaus.**

Rausch [raʊʃ] m -(e)s, **Räusche** intoxication; **r~en** vi (Wasser) rush; (Baum) rustle; (Radio etc) hiss; (Mensch) sweep, sail; **r~end** a (Beifall) thunderous; (Fest) sumptuous; **~gift** nt drug; **~gifthandel** m drug traffic; **~giftsüchtige(r)** mf drug addict.

räuspern ['rɔyspərn] vr clear one's throat.

Razzia ['ratsia] f -, **Razzien** raid.

Reagenzglas [rea'gɛntsglaːs] nt test tube.

reagieren [rea'giːrən] vi react (auf +akk to).

Reakt- zW: **~ion** [reaktsi'oːn] f reaction; **r~io'när** a reactionary; **~or** [re'aktɔr] m reactor.

real [re'aːl] a real, material; **R~ismus** [-'lɪsmʊs] m realism; **~istisch** a realistic; **R~schule** f secondary school.

Rebe ['reːbə] f -, -n vine.

Rebell [re'bɛl] m -en, -en rebel; **~i'on** f rebellion; **r~isch** a rebellious.

Rechen ['rɛçən] m -s, - rake; **r~** vti rake; **~fehler** m miscalculation; **~maschine** f calculating machine; **~schaft** f account; für etw **~schaft ablegen** account for sth; **~schieber** m slide rule.

Rech- ['rɛç] zW: **r~nen** vti calculate; jdn/etw **r~nen zu** count sb/sth among; **r~nen mit** reckon with; **r~nen auf** (+akk) count on; **~nen** nt arithmetic; **~ner** m -s, - calculator; (COMPUT) computer; **~nung** f calculation(s); (COMM) bill, check (US); jdm/etw **~nung tragen** take sb/sth into account; **~nungsjahr** nt financial year; **~nungsprüfer** m auditor.

recht [rɛçt] a, ad right; (vor Adjektiv) really, quite; das ist mir ~ that suits me; jetzt erst ~ now more than ever; ~ **haben be right**; jdm ~ **geben agree with sb**; **R~** nt -(e)s, -e right; (JUR) law; mit **R~** rightly, justly; von **R~s wegen** by rights; **R~e** f -n, -n right (hand); (POL) Right; **~e(r, s)** a right; (POL) right-wing; **ein R~r** a right-winger; **R~e(s)** nt right thing; etwas/nichts **R~es** something/nothing proper; **R~eck** nt -s, -e rectangle; **~eckig** a rectangular; **~fertigen** vtr insep justify (o.s.); **R~fertigung** f justification; **~mäßig** a legal, lawful.

rechts [rɛçts] ad on/to the right; **R~anwalt** m, **R~anwältin** f lawyer, barrister; **R~'außen** m -, - (SPORT) outside right.

rechtschaffen a upright.

Rechtschreibung f spelling.

Rechts- zW: **~fall** m (law) case; **~händer** m -s, - right-handed person; **r~kräftig** a valid, legal; **~kurve** f right-hand bend; **~streit** m law-suit; **r~verbindlich** a legally binding; **~verkehr** m driving on the right; **r~widrig** a illegal; **~wissenschaft** f jurisprudence.

rechtwinklig a right-angled.

rechtzeitig a timely // ad in time.

Reck [rɛk] nt -(e)s, -e horizontal bar; **r~en** vtr stretch.

Redakteur [redak'tøːr] m editor.

Redaktion [redaktsi'oːn] f editing; (Leute) editorial staff; (Büro) editorial office(s).

Rede ['reːdə] f -, -n speech; (Gespräch) talk; jdn zur ~ **stellen** take sb to task; **~freiheit** f freedom of speech; **r~gewandt** a eloquent; **r~n** vi talk, speak // vt say; (Unsinn etc) talk; **Redensart** f set phrase; **~wendung** f expression, idiom.

red- ['reːd] zW: **~lich** a honest; **R~ner** m -s, - speaker, orator; **~selig** a talkative, loquacious.

reduzieren [redu'tsiːrən] vt reduce.

Reede ['reːdə] f -, -n protected anchorage; **~r** m -s, - shipowner; **~'rei** f shipping line od firm.

reell [re'ɛl] a fair, honest; (MATH) real.

Refer- zW: **~at** [refe'raːt] nt -(e)s, -e report; (Vortrag) paper; (Gebiet) section; **~ent** [refe'rɛnt] m speaker; (Berichterstatter) reporter; (Sachbearbeiter) expert; **~enz** [refe'rɛnts] f reference; **r~ieren** [refe'riːrən] vi: **r~ieren über** (+akk) speak od talk on.

Reflex [re'flɛks] m -es, -e reflex; **~bewegung** f reflex action; **r~iv** [-'ksiːf] a (GRAM) reflexive.

Reform [re'fɔrm] f -, -en reform; **~ati'on** f reformation; **~haus** nt health food shop; **r~ieren** [-'miːrən] vt reform.

Regal [re'gaːl] nt -s, -e (book)shelves pl, bookcase; stand, rack.

Regel ['reːgəl] f -, -n rule; (MED) period; **r~mäßig** a regular; **~mäßigkeit** f regularity; **r~n** vt regulate, control; (Angelegenheit) settle // vr: sich von selbst **r~n** take care of itself; **r~recht** a regular, proper, thorough; **~ung** f regulation; settlement; **r~widrig** a irregular, against the rules.

Regen ['reːgən] m -s, - rain; **R~bogen** m rainbow; **R~bogenpresse** f tabloids pl; **R~mantel** m raincoat, mac(kintosh); **R~schauer** m shower (of rain); **R~schirm** m umbrella; **~wurm** m earthworm.

Regie [re'ʒiː] f (Film etc) direction; (THEAT) production.

Regier- [re'giːr] zW: **r~en** vti govern, rule; **~ung** f government; (Monarchie) reign; **~ungswechsel** m change of government; **~ungszeit** f period in government; (von König) reign.

Regiment [regi'ment] nt **-s, -er** regiment.

Region [regi'oːn] f region.

Regisseur [reʒɪ'søːr] m director; (THEAT) (stage) producer.

Register [re'gɪstər] nt **-s, -** register; (in Buch) table of contents, index.

registrieren [regɪs'triːrən] vt register.

reg- ['reːg] zW: **R~ler** m **-s, -** regulator, governor; **~los** ['reːkloːs] a motionless; **regnen** vi unpers rain; **regnerisch** a rainy.

regulär [regu'lɛːr] a regular.

regulieren [regu'liːrən] vt regulate; (COMM) settle.

Regung ['reːgʊŋ] f motion; (Gefühl) feeling, impulse; **regungslos** a motionless.

Reh [reː] nt **-(e)s, -e** deer, roe; **~bock** m roebuck; **~kalb** nt, **~kitz** nt fawn.

Reib- ['raɪb] zW: **~e** f **-, -n**, **~eisen** nt grater; **r~en** vt unreg rub; (KOCH) grate; **~e'rei** f friction no pl; **~fläche** f rough surface; **~ung** f friction; **r~ungslos** a smooth.

reich [raɪç] a rich; **R~** nt **-(e)s, -e** empire, kingdom; (fig) realm; das Dritte R~ the Third Reich; **~en** vi reach; (genügen) be enough od sufficient (jdm for sb) // vt hold out; (geben) pass, hand; (anbieten) offer; **~haltig** a ample, rich; **~lich** a ample, plenty of; **R~tum** m **-s, -tümer** wealth; **R~weite** f range.

reif [raɪf] a ripe; (Mensch, Urteil) mature; **R~** m **-(e)s** hoarfrost // **-(e)s, -e** (Ring) ring, hoop; **R~e** f **-** ripeness; maturity; **~en** vi mature; ripen; **R~en** m **-s, -** ring, hoop; (Fahrzeug~) tyre; **R~endruck** m tyre pressure; **R~enpanne** f puncture.

Reihe ['raɪə] f **-, -n** row; (von Tagen etc, umg: Anzahl) series sing; der ~ nach in turn; er ist an der ~ it's his turn; an die ~ kommen have one's turn; **Reihenfolge** f sequence; alphabetische Reihenfolge alphabetical order; **~nhaus** nt terraced house.

Reim [raɪm] m **-(e)s, -e** rhyme; **r~en** vt rhyme.

rein [raɪn] ad (umg) = **herein, hinein** // a, ad pure(ly); (sauber) clean; etw ins ~e schreiben make a fair copy of sth; etw ins ~e bringen clear up sth; **R~fall** m (umg) let-down; **R~gewinn** m net profit; **R~heit** f purity; cleanness; **~igen** vt clean; (Wasser) puri-

fy; **R~igung** f cleaning; purification; (Geschäft) cleaners; **chemische R~igung** dry cleaning; dry cleaners; **~lich** a clean; **~rassig** a pedigree; **R~schrift** f fair copy.

Reis [raɪs] m **-es, -e** rice.

Reise ['raɪzə] f **-, -n** journey; (Schiffs~) voyage; gute ~! have a good journey; **~n** pl travels pl; **~andenken** nt souvenir; **~büro** nt travel agency; **r~fertig** a ready to start; **~führer** m guide(book); (Mensch) travel guide; **~gepäck** nt luggage; **~gesellschaft** f party of travellers; **~kosten** pl travelling expenses pl; **~leiter** m courier; **~lektüre** f reading matter for the journey; **r~n** vi travel; go (nach to); **Reisende(r)** mf traveller; **~paß** m passport; **~proviant** m food and drink for the journey; **~scheck** m traveller's cheque; **~ziel** nt destination.

Reiß- ['raɪs] zW: **r~en** vti unreg tear; (ziehen) pull, drag; (Witz) crack; etw an sich r~en snatch sth up; (fig) take over sth; sich um etw r~en scramble for sth; **~nagel** m drawing pin (Brit), thumbtack (US); **~verschluß** m zip(per), zip fastener; **~wolf** m shredder; **~zwecke** f = **~nagel**.

Reit- ['raɪt] zW: **r~en** vti unreg ride; **~er(in** f) m **-s, -** rider; (MIL) cavalryman, trooper; **~hose** f riding breeches pl; **~pferd** nt saddle horse; **~stiefel** m riding boot; **~zeug** nt riding outfit.

Reiz [raɪts] m **-es, -e** stimulus; (angenehm) charm; (Verlockung) attraction; **r~bar** a irritable; **~barkeit** f irritability; **r~en** vt stimulate; (unangenehm) irritate; (verlocken) appeal to, attract; **r~end** a charming; **r~voll** a attractive.

rekeln ['reːkəln] vr stretch out; (lümmeln) lounge od loll about.

Reklamation [reklamatsi'oːn] f complaint.

Reklame [re'klaːmə] f **-, -n** advertising; advertisement; ~ machen für etw advertise sth.

rekonstruieren [rekɔnstru'iːrən] vt reconstruct.

Rekord [re'kɔrt] m **-(e)s, -e** record; **~leistung** f record performance.

Rektor ['rektɔr] m (UNIV) rector, vice-chancellor; (SCH) headteacher (Brit), principal (US); **~at** [-'raːt] nt **-(e)s, -e** rectorate, vice-chancellorship; headship; (Zimmer) rector's etc office.

Relais [rə'lɛː] nt **-, -** relay.

relativ [rela'tiːf] a relative; **R~ität** [relativi'tɛːt] f relativity.

relevant [rele'vant] a relevant.
Relief [reli'ɛf] nt -s, -s relief.
Religion [religi'o:n] f religion.
religiös [religi'ø:s] a religious.
Reling ['re:lɪŋ] f -, -s (NAUT) rail.
Remoulade [remu'la:də] f remoulade.
Rendezvous [rãde'vu:] nt -, - rendezvous.
Renn- ['rɛn] zW: **~bahn** f racecourse; (AUT) circuit, race track; **r~en** vti unreg run, race; **~en** vt -s, - running; (Wettbewerb) race; **~fahrer** m racing driver; **~pferd** nt racehorse; **~wagen** m racing car.
renovier- [reno'vi:r] zW: **~en** vt renovate; **R~ung** f renovation.
rentabel [rɛn'ta:bəl] a profitable, lucrative.
Rentabilität [rɛntabili'tɛ:t] f profitability.
Rente ['rɛntə] f -, -n pension; **rentendynamisch** a index-linked; **Rentenversicherung** f pension scheme.
Rentier ['rɛnti:r] nt reindeer.
rentieren [rɛn'ti:rən] vr pay, be profitable.
Rentner(in f) ['rɛntnər(ɪn)] m -s, - pensioner.
Reparatur [repara'tu:r] f repairing; repair; **~werkstatt** f repair shop; (AUT) garage.
reparieren [repa'ri:rən] vt repair.
Reportage [repɔr'ta:ʒə] f -, -n (on-the-spot) report; (TV, RAD) live commentary od coverage.
Reporter [re'pɔrtər] m -s, - reporter, commentator.
Repressalien [reprɛ'sa:liən] pl reprisals pl.
Reprivatisierung [reprivati'zi:rʊŋ] f denationalisation.
Reproduktion [reprodʊkts'io:n] f reproduction.
reproduzieren [reprodu'tsi:rən] vt reproduce.
Reptil [rɛp'ti:l] nt -s, -ien reptile.
Republik [repu'bli:k] f republic; **r~anisch** [-'ka:nɪʃ] a republican.
Reservat [rezɛr'va:t] nt -(e)s, -e reservation.
Reserve [re'zɛrvə] f -, -n reserve; **~rad** nt (AUT) spare wheel; **~spieler** m reserve; **~tank** m reserve tank.
reservieren [rezɛr'vi:rən] vt reserve.
Reservoir [rezɛrvo'a:r] nt -s, -e reservoir.
Residenz [rezi'dɛnts] f residence, seat.
resignieren [rezi'gni:rən] vi resign.
resolut [rezo'lu:t] a resolute.
Resonanz [rezo'nants] f (lit) resonance; (fig) response.
Resopal ® [rezo'pa:l] nt -s Formica ®.
Resozialisierung [rezotsiali'zi:rʊŋ] f rehabilitation.

Respekt [re'spɛkt] m -(e)s respect; **r~ieren** [-'ti:rən] vt respect; **r~los** a disrespectful; **r~voll** a respectful.
Ressort [rɛ'so:r] nt -s, -s department.
Rest [rɛst] m -(e)s, -e remainder, rest; (Über~) remains pl.
Restaurant [rɛsto'rã:] nt -s, -s restaurant.
restaurieren [rɛstau'ri:rən] vt restore.
Rest- zW: **~betrag** m remainder, outstanding sum; **r~lich** a remaining; **r~los** a complete.
Resultat [rezul'ta:t] nt -(e)s, -e result.
Retorte [re'tɔrtə] f -, -n retort.
Retouren [re'tu:rən] pl (COMM) returns pl.
retten ['rɛtən] vt save, rescue.
Rettich ['rɛtɪç] m -s, -e radish.
Rettung f rescue; (Hilfe) help; **seine letzte ~** his last hope.
Rettungs- zW: **~boot** nt lifeboat; **r~los** a hopeless; **~ring** m lifebelt, life preserver (US).
retuschieren [retu'ʃi:rən] vt (PHOT) retouch.
Reue ['rɔyə] f - remorse; (Bedauern) regret; **r~n** vt: **es reut ihn** he regrets (it) od is sorry (about it).
reuig ['rɔyɪç] a penitent.
Revanche [re'vã:ʃə] f -, -n revenge; (SPORT) return match.
revanchieren [revã'ʃi:rən] vr (sich rächen) get one's own back, have one's revenge; (erwidern) reciprocate, return the compliment.
Revier [re'vi:r] nt -s, -e district; (Jagd~) preserve; police station/beat.
Revolte [re'vɔltə] f -, -n revolt.
Revolution [revolutsi'o:n] f revolution; **~är** [-'nɛ:r] m -s, -e revolutionary; **r~ieren** [-'ni:rən] vt revolutionize.
Rezept [re'tsɛpt] nt -(e)s, -e recipe; (MED) prescription; **~ion** [retsɛp-tsi'o:n] f reception; **r~pflichtig** a available only on prescription.
rezitieren [retsi'ti:rən] vt recite.
R-Gespräch ['ɛrgəʃprɛ:ç] nt reverse charge call (Brit), collect call (US).
Rhabarber [ra'barbər] m -s rhubarb.
Rhein [raɪn] m -s Rhine; **r~isch** a Rhenish.
Rhesusfaktor ['re:zusfaktɔr] m rhesus factor.
rhetorisch [re'to:rɪʃ] a rhetorical.
Rheuma ['rɔyma] nt -s, **Rheumatismus** [rɔyma'tɪsmus] m rheumatism.
Rhinozeros [ri'no:tserɔs] nt - od -ses, -se rhinoceros.
rhyth- ['rʏt] zW: **~misch** a rhythmical; **R~mus** m rhythm.
Richt- ['rɪçt] zW: **r~en** vt direct (an +akk to); (fig) (an +akk to); (Waffe) aim (auf +akk at); (einstellen) adjust;

(instandsetzen) repair; *(zurechtmachen)* prepare; *(bestrafen)* pass judgement on // *vr:* **sich r~en nach go by;** **~er(in** *f)* *m* **-s,** - judge; **r~erlich** *a* judicial; **r~ig** *a* right, correct; *(echt)* proper; **bin ich hier r~ig?** am I in the right place? // *ad (umg: sehr)* really; **der/die ~ige** the right one/person; **das ~ige** the right thing; **~igkeit** *f* correctness; **~igstellung** *f* correction, rectification; **~preis** *m* recommended price; **~ung** *f* direction; tendency, orientation.

rieb *etc v siehe* **reiben.**

riechen ['riːçən] *vti unreg* smell *(an etw (dat)* sth; *nach* of); **ich kann das/ihn nicht ~** *(umg)* I can't stand it/him.

rief *etc v siehe* **rufen.**

Riegel ['riːgəl] *m* **-s,** - bolt, bar.

Riemen ['riːmən] *m* **-s,** - strap; *(Gürtel, TECH)* belt; *(NAUT)* oar.

Riese ['riːzə] *m* **-n,** -n giant; **rieseln** *vi* trickle; *(Schnee)* fall gently; **Riesenerfolg** *m* enormous success; **r~ngroß** *a* colossal, gigantic, huge.

riesig ['riːzɪç] *a* enormous, huge, vast.

riet *etc v siehe* **raten.**

Riff [rɪf] *nt* **-(e)s,** -e reef.

Rille ['rɪlə] *f* **-,** -n groove.

Rind [rɪnt] *nt* **-(e)s,** -er ox; cow; cattle *pl;* *(KOCH)* beef; **~e** *f* ['rɪndə] **-,** -n rind; *(Baum~)* bark; *(Brot~)* crust; **~fleisch** *nt* beef; **~vieh** *nt* cattle *pl;* *(umg)* blockhead, stupid oaf.

Ring [rɪŋ] *m* **-(e)s,** -e ring; **~buch** *nt* ring binder; **Ringelnatter** *f* grass snake; **r~en** *vi unreg* wrestle; **~en** *nt* **-s** wrestling; **~finger** *m* ring finger; **~kampf** *m* wrestling bout; **~richter** *m* referee; **rings um** *ad* round; **ringsherum** *ad* round about; **~straße** *f* ring road; **ringsum(her)** *ad (rundherum)* round about; *(überall)* all round.

Rinn- ['rɪn] *zW:* **~e** *f* **-,** -n gutter, drain; **r~en** *vi unreg* run, trickle; **~stein** *m* gutter.

Rippchen ['rɪpçən] *nt* small rib; cutlet.

Rippe ['rɪpə] *f* **-,** -n rib; **Rippenfellentzündung** *f* pleurisy.

Risiko ['riːziko] *nt* **-s,** -s *od* **Risiken** risk.

riskant [rɪs'kant] *a* risky, hazardous.

riskieren [rɪs'kiːrən] *vt* risk.

Riß [rɪs] *m* **-sses,** -sse tear; *(in Mauer, Tasse etc)* crack; *(in Haut)* scratch; *(TECH)* design.

rissig ['rɪsɪç] *a* torn; cracked; scratched.

ritt *etc v siehe* **reiten.**

Ritt [rɪt] *m* **-(e)s,** -e ride; **~er** *m* **-s,** - knight; **r~erlich** *a* chivalrous.

Ritze ['rɪtsə] *f* **-,** -n crack, chink.

Rivale [ri'vaːlə] *m* **-n,** -n rival.

Rivalität [rivali'tɛːt] *f* rivalry.

Rizinusöl ['riːtsinʊsøːl] *nt* castor oil.

Robbe ['rɔbə] *f* **-,** -n seal.

Roboter ['rɔbɔtər] *m* **-s,** - robot.

roch *etc v siehe* **riechen.**

Rock [rɔk] *m* **-(e)s,** ⁻e skirt; *(Jackett)* jacket; *(Uniform~)* tunic.

Rodel ['roːdəl] *m* **-s,** - toboggan; **~bahn** *f* toboggan run; **r~n** *vi* toboggan.

roden ['roːdən] *vti* clear.

Rogen ['roːgən] *m* **-s,** - roe, spawn.

Roggen ['rɔgən] *m* **-s,** - rye.

roh [roː] *a* raw; *(Mensch)* coarse, crude; **R~bau** *m* shell of a building; **R~material** *nt* raw material; **R~öl** *nt* crude oil.

Rohr ['roːr] *nt* **-(e)s,** -e pipe, tube; *(BOT)* cane; *(Schilf)* reed; *(Gewehr~)* barrel; **~bruch** *m* burst pipe.

Röhre ['røːrə] *f* **-,** -n tube, pipe; *(RAD etc)* valve; *(Back~)* oven.

Rohr- *zW:* **~leitung** *f* pipeline; **~post** *f* pneumatic post; **~zucker** *m* cane sugar.

Rohstoff *m* raw material.

Rokoko ['rɔkoko] *nt* **-s** rococo.

Roll- ['rɔl] *zW:* **~(l)aden** *m* shutter; **~bahn** *f,* **~feld** *nt (AVIAT)* runway.

Rolle ['rɔlə] *f* **-,** -n roll; *(THEAT, soziologisch)* role; *(Garn~ etc)* reel, spool; *(Walze)* roller; *(Wäsche~)* mangle; **keine ~ spielen** not matter; **eine (wichtige) ~ spielen bei** play a (major) part *od* role in; **r~n** *vti* roll; *(AVIAT)* taxi; **~r** *m* **-s,** - scooter; *(Welle)* roller.

Roll- *zW:* **~mops** *m* pickled herring; **~schuh** *m* roller skate; **~stuhl** *m* wheelchair; **~treppe** *f* escalator.

Rom [roːm] *nt* **-s** Rome.

Roman [ro'maːn] *m* **-s,** -e novel; **~tik** [ro'mantɪk] *f* romanticism; **~tiker** [ro'mantɪkər] *m* **-s,** - romanticist; **r~tisch** [ro'mantɪʃ] *a* romantic; **Romanze** [ro'mantsə] *f* **-,** -n romance.

Röm- ['røːm] *zW:* **~er** *m* **-s,** - wineglass; *(Mensch)* Roman; **r~isch** *a* Roman.

röntgen ['rœntgən] *vt* X-ray; **R~aufnahme** *f,* **R~bild** *nt* X-ray; **R~strahlen** *pl* X-rays *pl.*

rosa ['roːza] *a inv* pink, rose(-coloured).

Rose ['roːzə] *f* **-,** -n rose; **Rosenkohl** *m* Brussels sprouts *pl;* **Rosenkranz** *m* rosary.

rosig ['roːzɪç] *a* rosy.

Rosine [ro'ziːnə] *f* raisin, currant.

Roß [rɔs] *nt* **-sses,** -sse horse, steed; **~kastanie** *f* horse chestnut.

Rost [rɔst] *m* **-(e)s,** -e rust; *(Gitter)* grill, gridiron; *(Bett~)* springs *pl;*

~braten *m* roast(ed) meat, joint; **r~en** *vi* rust.
rösten ['røːstən] *vt* roast; toast; grill.
Rost- *zW:* **r~frei** *a* rust-free; rustproof; stainless; **r~ig** *a* rusty; **~schutz** *m* rust-proofing.
rot [roːt] *a* red; **in den ~en Zahlen** in the red; **das R~e Meer** the Red Sea.
Röte ['røːtə] *f* - redness; **Röteln** *pl* German measles *sing*; **r~n** *vtr* redden.
rot- *zW:* **~haarig** *a* red-haired; **~ieren** [ro'tiːrən] *vi* rotate; **R~kehlchen** *nt* robin; **R~stift** *m* red pencil; **R~wein** *m* red wine.
Rouge [ruːʒ] *nt* blusher.
Roulade [ru'laːdə] *f* (*KOCH*) beef olive.
Route ['ruːtə] *f* -, **-n** route.
Routine [ru'tiːnə] *f* experience; routine.
Rübe ['ryːbə] *f* -, **-n** turnip; **gelbe ~** carrot; **rote ~** beetroot (*Brit*), beet (*US*).
rüber ['ryːbər] *ad* (*umg*) = **herüber, hinüber.**
Rubin [ru'biːn] *m* -s, **-e** ruby. ✓
Rubrik [ru'briːk] *f* heading; (*Spalte*) column.
Ruck [rʊk] *m* -(e)s, **-e** jerk, jolt.
Rück- ['rʏk] *zW:* **~antwort** *f* reply, answer; **r~bezüglich** *a* reflexive; **r~blickend** *a* retrospective.
rücken ['rʏkən] *vti* move; **R~** *m* -s, **-** back; (*Berg~*) ridge; **R~mark** *nt* spinal cord; **R~schwimmen** *nt* backstroke; **R~wind** *m* following wind.
Rück- *zW:* **~erstattung** *f* return, restitution; **~fahrkarte** *f* return; **~fahrt** *f* return journey; **~fall** *m* relapse; **r~fällig** *a* relapsing; **r~fällig werden** relapse; **~flug** *m* return flight; **~frage** *f* question; **~gabe** *f* return; **~gang** *m* decline, fall; **r~gängig** *a:* **etw r~gängig machen** cancel sth; **~grat** *nt* -(e)s, **-e** spine, backbone; **~kehr** *f* -, **-en** return; **~licht** *nt* back light; **r~lings** *ad* from behind; backwards; **~nahme** *f* -, **-n** taking back; **~porto** *nt* return postage; **~reise** *f* return journey; (*NAUT*) home voyage; **~ruf** *m* recall.
Rucksack ['rʊkzak] *m* rucksack.
Rück- *zW:* **~schau** *f* reflection; **~schluß** *m* conclusion; **~schritt** *m* retrogression; **r~schrittlich** *a* reactionary; retrograde; **~seite** *f* back; (*von Münze etc*) reverse; **~sicht** *f* consideration; **~sicht nehmen auf** (+*akk*) show consideration for; **r~sichtslos** *a* inconsiderate; (*Fahren*) reckless; (*unbarmherzig*) ruthless; **r~sichtsvoll** *a* considerate; **~sitz** *m* back seat; **~spiegel** *m* (*AUT*) rear-view mirror; **~spiel** *nt*

return match; **~sprache** *f* further discussion od talk; **~stand** *m* arrears *pl*; **r~ständig** *a* backward, out-of-date; (*Zahlungen*) in arrears; **~stoß** *m* recoil; **~strahler** *m* -s, **-** rear reflector; **~tritt** *m* resignation; **~trittbremse** *f* pedal brake; **~vergütung** *f* repayment; (*COMM*) refund; **~versicherung** *f* reinsurance; **r~wärtig** *a* rear; **r~wärts** *ad* backward(s), back; **~wärtsgang** *m* (*AUT*) reverse gear; **~weg** *m* return journey, way back; **r~wirkend** *a* retroactive; **~wirkung** *f* reaction; retrospective effect; **~zahlung** *f* repayment; **~zug** *m* retreat.
Rudel ['ruːdəl] *nt* -s, **-** pack; herd.
Ruder ['ruːdər] *nt* -s, **-** oar; (*Steuer*) rudder; **~boot** *nt* rowing boat; **r~n** *vti* row.
Ruf [ruːf] *m* -(e)s, **-e** call, cry; (*Ansehen*) reputation; **r~en** *vti unreg* call; cry; **~name** *m* usual (first) name; **~nummer** *f* (tele)phone number; **~zeichen** *nt* (*RAD*) call sign; (*TEL*) ringing tone.
Rüge ['ryːgə] *f* -, **-n** reprimand, rebuke.
Ruhe ['ruːə] *f* - rest; (*Ungestörtheit*) peace, quiet; (*Gelassenheit, Stille*) calm; (*Schweigen*) silence; **jdn in ~ lassen** leave sb alone; **sich zur ~ setzen** retire; **~!** be quiet!, silence!; **r~n** *vi* rest; **~pause** *f* break; **~platz** *m* resting place; **~stand** *m* retirement; **letzte ~stätte** *f* final resting place; **~störung** *f* breach of the peace; **~tag** *m* closing day.
ruhig ['ruːɪç] *a* quiet; (*bewegungslos*) still; (*Hand*) steady; (*gelassen, friedlich*) calm; (*Gewissen*) clear; **kommen Sie ~ herein** just come on in; **tu das ~** feel free to do that.
Ruhm [ruːm] *m* -(e)s fame, glory.
rühmen ['ryːmən] *vt* praise // *vr* boast.
Ruhr ['ruːr] *f* - dysentery.
Rühr- ['ryːr] *zW:* **~ei** *nt* scrambled egg; **r~en** *vtr* (*lit, fig*) move, stir (*auch KOCH*) // *vi:* **r~en von** come *od* stem from; **r~en an** (+*akk*) touch; (*fig*) touch on; **r~end** *a* touching, moving; **r~ig** *a* active, lively; **r~selig** *a* sentimental, emotional; **~ung** *f* emotion.
Ruin [ru'iːn] *m* -s, **~e**, *f* -, **-n** ruin; **r~ieren** [rui'niːrən] *vt* ruin.
rülpsen ['rʏlpsən] *vi* burp, belch.
rum [rʊm] *ad* (*umg*) = **herum.**
Rum [rʊm] *m* -s, **-s** rum.
Rumän- [ru'mɛːn] *zW:* **~e** *m* -n, **-n**, **~in** *f* Ro(u)manian; **~ien** *nt* -s Ro(u)mania; **r~isch** *a* Ro(u)manian.
Rummel ['rʊməl] *m* -s (*umg*) hubbub; (*Jahrmarkt*) fair; **~platz** *m* fairground, fair.

Rumpf [rumpf] *m* -(e)s, ⁝e trunk, torso; (*AVIAT*) fuselage; (*NAUT*) hull.

rümpfen ['rympfən] *vt* (*Nase*) turn up.

rund [runt] *a* round // *ad* (*etwa*) around; ~ **um etw** round sth; **R~brief** *m* circular; **R~e** ['rundə] *f* -, -n round; (*in Rennen*) lap; (*Gesellschaft*) circle; **R~fahrt** *f* (round) trip.

Rundfunk ['runtfuŋk] *m* -(e)s broadcasting; **im ~** on the radio; ~**gerät** *nt* wireless set; ~**sendung** *f* broadcast, radio programme.

Rund- *zW*: **r~heraus** *ad* straight out, bluntly; **r~herum** *ad* round about; all round; **r~lich** *a* plump, rounded; ~**reise** *f* round trip; ~**schreiben** *nt* (*COMM*) circular.

runter ['runtər] *ad* (*umg*) = **herunter, hinunter.**

Runzel ['runtsəl] *f* -, -n wrinkle; **r~ig** *a* wrinkled; **r~n** *vt* wrinkle; **die Stirn r~n** frown.

rupfen ['rupfən] *vt* pluck; **R~** *m* -s, - sackcloth.

ruppig ['rupiç] *a* rough, gruff.

Rüsche ['ry:ʃə] *f* -, -n frill.

Ruß [ru:s] *m* -es soot.

Russe ['rusə] *m* -n, -n Russian.

Rüssel ['rysəl] *m* -s, - snout; (*Elefanten~*) trunk.

rußig ['ru:sıç] *a* sooty.

Russ- [rus] *zW*: ~**in** *f* Russian; **r~isch** *a* Russian.

Rußland ['ruslant] *nt* -s Russia.

rüsten ['rystən] *vtri* prepare; (*MIL*) arm.

rüstig ['rystiç] *a* sprightly, vigorous.

Rüstung ['rystuŋ] *f* preparation; arming; (*Ritter~*) armour; (*Waffen etc*) armaments *pl*; **Rüstungskontrolle** *f* arms control.

Rute ['ru:tə] *f* -, -n rod.

Rutsch [rutʃ] *m* -(e)s, -e slide; (*Erd~*) landslide; ~**bahn** *f* slide; **r~en** *vi* slide; (*ausr~en*) slip; **r~ig** *a* slippery.

rütteln ['rytəln] *vti* shake, jolt.

S

S, s [ɛs] *nt* S, s.
S. *abk* (= *Seite*) p. // *abk von* **Schilling.**
s. *abk* (= *siehe*) see.
Saal [za:l] *m* -(e)s, **Säle** hall; room.
Saarland ['za:rlant] *nt*: **das ~** the Saar(land).
Saat [za:t] *f* -, -en seed; (*Pflanzen*) crop; (*Säen*) sowing.
Säbel ['zɛ:bəl] *m* -s, - sabre, sword.
Sabotage [zabo'ta:ʒə] *f* -, -n sabotage.
sabotieren [zabo'ti:rən] *vt* sabotage.
Sach- [zax] *zW*: ~**bearbeiter** *m* spe-

cialist; **s~dienlich** *a* relevant, helpful; ~**e** *f* -, -n thing; (*Angelegenheit*) affair, business; (*Frage*) matter; (*Pflicht*) task; **zur ~e** to the point; **s~kundig** *a* expert; **s~lich** *a* matter-of-fact, objective; (*Irrtum, Angabe*) factual.

sächlich ['zɛxlıç] *a* neuter.

Sachschaden *m* material damage.

Sachsen ['zaksən] *nt* -s Saxony.

sächsisch ['zɛksıʃ] *a* Saxon.

sacht(e) ['zaxt(ə)] *ad* softly, gently.

Sachverständige(r) *mf* expert.

Sack [zak] *m* -(e)s, ⁝e sack; ~**gasse** *f* cul-de-sac, dead-end street (*US*).

Sadismus [za'dısmus] *m* sadism.

Sadist [za'dıst] *m* sadist; **s~isch** *a* sadistic.

säen ['zɛ:ən] *vti* sow.

Saft [zaft] *m* -(e)s, ⁝e juice; (*BOT*) sap; **s~ig** *a* juicy; **s~los** *a* dry.

Sage ['za:gə] *f* -, -n saga.

Säge ['zɛ:gə] *f* -, -n saw; ~**mehl** *nt* sawdust; **s~n** *vti* saw.

sagen ['za:gən] *vti* say (*jdm* to sb); (*mitteilen*), tell (*jdm* sb); ~ **Sie ihm, daß ...** tell him ...; ~**haft** *a* legendary; (*umg*) great, smashing.

sah *etc v siehe* **sehen.**

Sahne ['za:nə] *f* - cream.

Saison [zɛ'ző] *f* -, -s season; ~**arbeiter** *m* seasonal worker.

Saite ['zaıtə] *f* -, -n string; **Saiteninstrument** *nt* string instrument.

Sakko ['zako] *m od nt* -s, -s jacket.

Sakrament [zakra'mɛnt] *nt* sacrament.

Sakristei [zakrıs'taı] *f* sacristy.

Salat [za'la:t] *m* -(e)s, -e salad; (*Kopfsalat*) lettuce; ~**soße** *f* salad dressing.

Salb- ['zalb] *zW*: ~**e** *f* -, -n ointment; ~**ei** [zal'baı] *m od f* -s od - sage; **s~en** *vt* anoint.

Saldo ['zaldo] *m* -s, **Salden** balance.

Salmiak [zalmi'ak] *m* -s sal ammoniac; ~**geist** *m* liquid ammonia.

salopp [za'lɔp] *a* casual.

Salpeter [zal'pe:tər] *m* -s saltpetre; ~**säure** *f* nitric acid.

Salve ['zalvə] *f* -, -n salvo.

Salz [zalts] *nt* -es, -e salt; **s~en** *vt unreg* salt; **s~ig** *a* salty; ~**kartoffeln** *pl* boiled potatoes *pl*; ~**säure** *f* hydrochloric acid.

Samen ['za:mən] *m* -s, - seed; (*ANAT*) sperm.

Sammel- ['zaməl] *zW*: ~**band** *m* anthology; **s~n** *vt* collect // *vr* assemble, gather; (*konzentrieren*) concentrate.

Sammlung ['zamluŋ] *f* collection; assembly, gathering; concentration.

Samstag ['zamsta:k] *m* Saturday; **s~s** *ad* (on) Saturdays.

Samt [zamt] *m* -(e)s, -e velvet; **s~**

präp +*dat* (along) with, together with; s~ **und sonders** each and every one (of them).

sämtlich ['zɛmtliç] *a* all (the), entire.

Sand [zant] *m* -(e)s, -e sand; **Sandale** [zan'da:lə] *f* -, -n sandal; ~**bank** *f* sandbank; s~**ig** ['zandɪç] *a* sandy; ~**kasten** *m* sandpit; ~**kuchen** *m* Madeira cake; ~**papier** *nt* sandpaper; ~**stein** *m* sandstone; s~**strahlen** *vti insep* sandblast.

sandte *etc v siehe* **senden**.

Sanduhr *f* hourglass.

sanft [zanft] *a* soft, gentle; ~**mütig** *a* gentle, meek.

sang *etc v siehe* **singen**.

Sänger(in *f)* ['zɛŋər(ɪn)] *m* -s, - singer.

Sani- *zW:* s~**eren** [za'ni:rən] *vt* re-develop; (*Betrieb*) make financially sound // *vr* line one's pockets; become financially sound; s~**tär** [zani'tɛːr] *a* sanitary; s~**täre Anlagen** sanitation; ~**täter** [zani'tɛːtər] *m* -s, - first-aid attendant; (*MIL*) (medical) orderly.

sanktionieren [zaŋktsio'ni:rən] *vt* sanction.

Saphir ['za:fiːr] *m* -s, -e sapphire.

Sardelle [zar'dɛlə] *f* anchovy.

Sardin- [zar'di:n] *zW:* ~**e** *f* sardine; ~**ien** [-ɪən] *nt* -s Sardinia.

Sarg [zark] *m* -(e)s, ⁻e coffin.

Sarkasmus [zar'kasmus] *m* sarcasm.

sarkastisch [zar'kastɪʃ] *a* sarcastic.

saß *etc v siehe* **sitzen**.

Satan ['za:tan] *m* -s, -e Satan; devil.

Satellit [zatɛ'li:t] *m* -en, -en satellite; ~**enfoto** *nt* satellite picture.

Satire [za'ti:rə] *f* -, -n satire.

satirisch [za'ti:rɪʃ] *a* satirical.

satt [zat] *a* full; (*Farbe*) rich, deep; **jdn/etw ~ sein** *od* **haben** be fed up with sb/sth; **sich ~ hören/sehen an** (+*dat*) see/hear enough of; **sich ~ essen** eat one's fill; ~ **machen** be filling.

Sattel ['zatəl] *m* -s, ⁻ saddle; (*Berg*) ridge; s~**n** *vt* saddle; ~**schlepper** *m* articulated lorry.

sättigen ['zɛtɪgən] *vt* satisfy; (*CHEM*) saturate.

Satz [zats] *m* -es, ⁻e (*GRAM*) sentence; (*Neben~, Adverbial~*) clause; (*Theorem*) theorem; (*MUS*) movement; (*TENNIS, Briefmarken etc*) set; (*Kaffee*) grounds *pl*; (*COMM*) rate; (*Sprung*) jump; ~**teil** *m* part of a sentence; ~**zeichen** *nt* punctuation mark.

Sau [zau] *f* -, **Säue** sow; (*umg*) dirty pig.

sauber ['zaubər] *a* clean; (*ironisch*) fine; ~**halten** *vt unreg* keep clean; **S~keit** *f* cleanness; (*einer Person*) cleanliness.

säuberlich ['zɔybərlɪç] *ad* neatly.

saubermachen *vti* clean.

säubern *vt* clean; (*POL etc*) purge.

Säuberung *f* cleaning; purge.

Sauce ['zo:sə] *f* -, -n sauce, gravy.

sauer ['zauər] *a* sour; (*CHEM*) acid; (*umg*) cross; **Saurer Regen** acid rain.

Sauerei [zauə'rai] *f* (*umg*) rotten state of affairs, scandal; (*Schmutz etc*) mess; (*Unanständigkeit*) obscenity.

Sauer- *zW:* ~**milch** *f* sour milk; ~**stoff** *m* oxygen; ~**teig** *m* leaven.

saufen ['zaufən] *vti unreg* (*umg*) drink, booze.

Säufer ['zɔyfər] *m* -s, - (*umg*) boozer.

saugen ['zaugən] *vti unreg* suck.

Sauger ['zaugər] *m* -s, - dummy, comforter (*US*); (*auf Flasche*) teat; (*Staub~*) vacuum cleaner, hoover ®.

Säug- ['zɔyg] *zW:* **Säugetier** *nt* mammal; ~**ling** *m* infant, baby.

Säule ['zɔylə] *f* -, -n column, pillar.

Saum [zaum] *m* -(e)s, **Säume** hem; (*Naht*) seam.

säumen ['zɔymən] *vt* hem; seam // *vi* delay, hesitate.

Sauna ['zauna] *f* -, -s sauna.

Säure ['zɔyrə] *f* -, -n acid; (*Geschmack*) sourness, acidity.

sausen ['zauzən] *vi* blow; (*umg: eilen*) rush; (*Ohren*) buzz; **etw ~ lassen** (*umg*) not bother with sth.

Saustall ['zauʃtal] *m* (*umg*) pigsty.

Saxophon [zakso'fo:n] *nt* -s, -e saxophone.

SB *abk von* **Selbstbedienung**.

S-Bahn *abk* (= *Schnellbahn*) high speed railway; (= *Stadtbahn*) suburban railway.

schaben ['ʃa:bən] *vt* scrape.

schäbig ['ʃɛːbɪç] *a* shabby.

Schablone [ʃa'blo:nə] *f* -, -n stencil; (*Muster*) pattern; (*fig*) convention.

Schach [ʃax] *nt* -s, -s chess; (*Stellung*) check; ~**brett** *nt* chessboard; ~**figur** *f* chessman; **'s~'matt** *a* checkmate; ~**spiel** *nt* game of chess.

Schacht [ʃaxt] *m* -(e)s, ⁻e shaft.

Schachtel *f* -, -n box; (*pej: Frau*) bag, cow.

schade ['ʃa:də] *a* a pity *od* shame; **sich** (*dat*) **zu ~ sein für etw** consider oneself too good for sth // *interj*: (**wie**) ~! what a pity *od* shame.

Schädel ['ʃɛːdəl] *m* -s, - skull; ~**bruch** *m* fractured skull.

Schaden ['ʃa:dən] *m* -s, ⁻ damage; (*Verletzung*) injury; (*Nachteil*) disadvantage; s~ *vi* (+*dat*) hurt; **einer Sache** s~ damage sth; ~**ersatz** *m* compensation, damages *pl*; ~**freude** *f* malicious glee.

schadhaft ['ʃa:thaft] *a* faulty, damaged.

schäd- ['ʃɛːt] *zW*: **~igen** ['ʃɛdɪgən] *vt* damage; (*Person*) do harm to, harm; **~lich** *a* harmful (*für* to); **S~lichkeit** *f* harmfulness; **S~ling** *m* pest.

Schadstoff ['ʃaːtʃtɔf] *m* harmful substance.

Schaf [ʃaːf] *nt* -(e)s, -e sheep; **~bock** *m* ram.

Schäfer ['ʃɛːfər] *m* -s, -e shepherd; **~hund** *m* Alsatian.

schaffen ['ʃafən] *vt unreg* create; (*Platz*) make; *sich* (*dat*) *etw* ~ get o.s. sth // *vt* (*erreichen*) manage, do; (*erledigen*) finish; (*Prüfung*) pass; (*transportieren*) take // *vi* (*umg*: *arbeiten*) work; *sich an etw* (*dat*) *zu* ~ *machen* busy oneself with sth; **S~** *nt* -s (creative) activity.

Schaffner(in *f*) ['ʃafnər(ɪn)] *m* -s, - (*Bus~*) conductor/conductress; (*EISENB*) guard.

Schaft [ʃaft] *m* -(e)s, ⁻e shaft; (*von Gewehr*) stock; (*von Stiefel*) leg; (*BOT*) stalk; tree trunk; **~stiefel** *m* high boot.

Schakal [ʃa'kaːl] *m* -s, -e jackal.

schal [ʃaːl] *a* flat; (*fig*) insipid; **S~** *m* -s, -e *od* -s scarf.

Schälchen ['ʃɛːlçən] *nt* cup, bowl.

Schale ['ʃaːlə] *f* -, -n skin; (*abgeschält*) peel; (*Nuß~*, *Muschel~*, *Ei~*) shell; (*Geschirr*) dish, bowl.

schälen ['ʃɛːlən] *vt* peel; shell // *vr* peel.

Schall [ʃal] *m* -(e)s, -e sound; **~dämpfer** *m* -s, - (*AUT*) silencer; **s~dicht** *a* soundproof; **s~en** *vi* (re)sound; **s~end** *a* resounding, loud; **~mauer** *f* sound barrier; **~platte** *f* (gramophone) record.

Schalt- ['ʃalt] *zW*: **~bild** *nt* circuit diagram; **~brett** *nt* switchboard; **s~en** *vt* switch, turn // *vi* (*AUT*) change (gear); (*umg*: *begreifen*) catch on; **~er** *m* -s, - counter; (*an Gerät*) switch; **~erbeamte(r)** *m* counter clerk; **~hebel** *m* switch; (*AUT*) gear-lever; **~jahr** *nt* leap year; **~ung** *f* switching; (*ELEK*) circuit; (*AUT*) gear change.

Scham [ʃaːm] *f* - shame; (*~gefühl*) modesty; (*Organe*) private parts *pl*.

schämen ['ʃɛːmən] *vr* be ashamed.

schamlos *a* shameless.

Schande ['ʃandə] *f* - disgrace.

schändlich ['ʃɛntlɪç] *a* disgraceful, shameful.

Schändung ['ʃɛnduŋ] *f* violation, defilement.

Schank- ['ʃaŋk] *zW*: **~erlaubnis** *f* (publican's) licence; **~tisch** *m* bar.

Schanze ['ʃantsə] *f* -, -n (*Sprung~*) skijump.

Schar [ʃaːr] *f* -, -en band, company; (*Vögel*) flock; (*Menge*) crowd; in

~en in droves; **s~en** *vr* assemble, rally.

scharf [ʃarf] *a* sharp; (*Essen*) hot; (*Munition*) live; ~ *nachdenken* think hard; *auf etw* (*acc*) ~ *sein* (*umg*) be keen on sth.

Schärf- ['ʃɛrf] *zW*: **~e** *f* -, -n sharpness; (*Strenge*) rigour; **s~en** *vt* sharpen.

Scharf- *zW*: **s~machen** *vt* (*umg*) stir up; **~richter** *m* executioner; **~schütze** *m* marksman, sharpshooter; **~sinn** *m* penetration, astuteness; **s~sinnig** *a* astute, shrewd.

Scharnier [ʃar'niːr] *nt* -s, -e hinge.

Schärpe ['ʃɛrpə] *f* -, -n sash.

scharren ['ʃarən] *vti* scrape, scratch.

Schaschlik ['ʃaʃlɪk] *m od nt* -s, -e (shish) kebab.

Schatten ['ʃatən] *m* -s, - shadow; **~bild** *nt*, **~riß** *m* silhouette; **~seite** *f* shady side, dark side; **~wirtschaft** *f* black economy.

schattieren [ʃa'tiːrən] *vti* shade.

schattig ['ʃatɪç] *a* shady.

Schatulle [ʃa'tulə] *f* -, -n casket; (*Geld~*) coffer.

Schatz [ʃats] *m* -es, ⁻e treasure; (*Person*) darling.

schätz- ['ʃɛts] *zW*: **~bar** *a* assessable; **S~chen** *nt* darling, love; **~en** *vt* (*abschätzen*) estimate; (*Gegenstand*) value; (*würdigen*) value, esteem; (*vermuten*) reckon; **S~ung** *f* estimate; estimation; valuation; *nach meiner* S~ung... I reckon that...; **~ungsweise** *ad* approximately; it is thought.

Schau [ʃau] *f* - show; (*Ausstellung*) display, exhibition; *etw zur* ~ *stellen* make a show of sth, show sth off; **~bild** *nt* diagram.

Schauder ['ʃaudər] *m* -s, -s shudder; (*wegen Kälte*) shiver; **s~haft** *a* horrible; **s~n** *vi* shudder; shiver.

schauen ['ʃauən] *vi* look.

Schauer ['ʃauər] *m* -s, - (*Regen~*) shower; (*Schreck*) shudder; **~geschichte** *f* horror story; **s~lich** *a* horrific, spine-chilling.

Schaufel ['ʃaufəl] *f* -, -n shovel; (*NAUT*) paddle; (*TECH*) scoop; **s~n** *vt* shovel, scoop.

Schau- *zW*: **~fenster** *nt* shop window; **~fensterbummel** *m* window shopping (expedition); **~kasten** *m* showcase.

Schaukel ['ʃaukəl] *f* -, -n swing; **s~n** *vi* swing, rock; **~pferd** *nt* rocking horse; **~stuhl** *m* rocking chair.

Schaum [ʃaum] *m* -(e)s, **Schäume** foam; (*Seifen~*) lather.

schäumen ['ʃɔymən] *vi* foam.

Schaum- *zW*: **~gummi** *m* foam (rubber); **s~ig** *a* frothy, foamy; **~wein** *m* sparkling wine.

Schau- *zW:* **~platz** *m* scene; **s~rig** *a* horrific, dreadful; **~spiel** *nt* spectacle; (*THEAT*) play; **~spieler** *m* actor; **~spielerin** *f* actress; **s~spielern** *vi insep* act; **~spielhaus** *nt* theatre.

Scheck [ʃɛk] *m* **-s, -s** cheque; **~heft** *m* cheque book; **~karte** *f* cheque card.

scheffeln ['ʃɛfəln] *vt* amass.

Scheibe ['ʃaıbə] *f* **-, -n** disc; (*Brot etc*) slice; (*Glas~*) pane; (*MIL*) target.

Scheiben- *zW:* **~bremse** *f* (*AUT*) disc brake; **~waschanlage** *f* (*AUT*) windscreen washers *pl*; **~wischer** *m* (*AUT*) windscreen wiper.

Scheich [ʃaıç] *m* **-s, -e** *od* **-s** sheik(h).

Scheide ['ʃaıdə] *f* **-, -n** sheath; (*Grenze*) boundary; (*ANAT*) vagina; **s~n** *unreg vt* separate; (*Ehe*) dissolve; **sich s~n lassen** get a divorce // *vi* (de)part.

Scheidung *f* (*Ehe~*) divorce.

Schein [ʃaın] *m* **-(e)s, -e** light; (*An~*) appearance; (*Geld*) (bank)note; (*Bescheinigung*) certificate; **zum ~** in pretence; **s~bar** *a* apparent; **s~en** *vi unreg* shine; (*Anschein haben*) seem; **s~heilig** *a* hypocritical; **~werfer** *m* **-s, -** floodlight; spotlight; (*Such~*) searchlight; (*AUT*) headlamp.

Scheiß- ['ʃaıs] *in zW* (*umg*) bloody; **~e** *f* - (*umg*) shit.

Scheit [ʃaıt] *nt* **-(e)s, -e** *od* **-er** log, billet.

Scheitel ['ʃaıtəl] *m* **-s, -** top; (*Haar*) parting; **s~n** *vt* part.

scheitern ['ʃaıtərn] *vi* fail.

Schelle ['ʃɛlə] *f* **-, -n** small bell; **s~n** *vi* ring.

Schellfisch ['ʃɛlfıʃ] *m* haddock.

Schelm [ʃɛlm] *m* **-(e)s, -e** rogue; **s~isch** *a* mischievous, roguish.

Schelte ['ʃɛltə] *f* **-, -n** scolding; **s~n** *vt unreg* scold.

Schema ['ʃeːma] *nt* **-s, -s** *od* **-ta** scheme, plan; (*Darstellung*) schema; **nach ~** quite mechanically; **s~tisch** [ʃe'maːtıʃ] *a* schematic; (*pej*) mechanical.

Schemel ['ʃeːməl] *m* **-s, -** (foot)stool.

Schenkel ['ʃɛŋkəl] *m* **-s, -** thigh.

schenken ['ʃɛŋkən] *vt* (*lit, fig*) give; (*Getränk*) pour; **sich** (*dat*) **etw ~** (*umg*) skip sth; **das ist geschenkt!** (*billig*) that's a giveaway!; (*nichts wert*) that's worthless!

Scherbe ['ʃɛrbə] *f* **-, -n** broken piece, fragment; (*archäologisch*) potsherd.

Schere ['ʃeːrə] *f* **-, -n** scissors *pl*; (*groß*) shears *pl*; **s~n** *vt unreg* cut; (*Schaf*) shear; (*kümmern*) bother // *vr* care; **scher dich zum Teufel!** get lost!; **~'rei** *f* (*umg*) bother, trouble.

Scherz [ʃɛrts] *m* **-es, -e** joke; fun;

~frage *f* conundrum; **s~haft** *a* joking, jocular.

scheu [ʃɔy] *a* shy; **S~** *f* - shyness; (*Angst*) fear (*vor +dat* of); (*Ehrfurcht*) awe; **~en** *vr:* **sich ~en vor** (+*dat*) be afraid of, shrink from // *vt* shun // *vi* (*Pferd*) shy.

scheuern ['ʃɔyərn] *vt* scour, scrub.

Scheuklappe *f* blinker.

Scheune ['ʃɔynə] *f* **-, -n** barn.

Scheusal ['ʃɔyzaːl] *nt* **-s, -e** monster.

scheußlich ['ʃɔyslıç] *a* dreadful, frightful; **S~keit** *f* dreadfulness.

Schi [ʃiː] *m siehe* **Ski**.

Schicht [ʃıçt] *f* **-, -en** layer; (*Klasse*) class, level; (*in Fabrik etc*) shift; **~arbeit** *f* shift work; **s~en** *vt* layer, stack.

schick [ʃık] *a* stylish, chic; **~en** *vt* send // *vr* resign oneself (*in +akk* to) // *v unpers* (*anständig sein*) be fitting; **~lich** *a* proper, fitting; **S~sal** *nt* **-s, -e** fate; **S~salsschlag** *m* great misfortune, blow.

Schieb- ['ʃiːp] *zW:* **Schiebedach** *nt* (*AUT*) sun roof; **s~en** *vti unreg* (*auch Drogen*) push; (*Schuld*) put (*auf jdn* on sb); **Schiebetür** *f* sliding door; **~ung** *f* fiddle.

Schieds- ['ʃiːts] *zW:* **~gericht** *nt* court of arbitration; **~richter** *m* referee; umpire; (*Schlichter*) arbitrator; **~verfahren** *nt* arbitration.

schief [ʃiːf] *a* crooked; (*Ebene*) sloping; (*Turm*) leaning; (*Winkel*) oblique; (*Blick*) funny; (*Vergleich*) distorted // *ad* crooked(ly); (*ansehen*) askance; **etw ~ stellen** slope sth.

Schiefer ['ʃiːfər] *m* **-s, -** slate; **~dach** *nt* slate roof; **~tafel** *f* (child's) slate.

schiefgehen *vi unreg* (*umg*) go wrong.

schielen ['ʃiːlən] *vi* squint; **nach etw ~** (*fig*) eye sth.

schien *etc v siehe* **scheinen**.

Schienbein *nt* shinbone.

Schiene ['ʃiːnə] *f* **-, -n** rail; (*MED*) splint; **s~n** *vt* put in splints.

schier [ʃiːr] *a* (*fig*) sheer // *ad* nearly, almost.

Schieß- ['ʃiːs] *zW:* **~bude** *f* shooting gallery; **s~en** *vti unreg* shoot (*auf +akk* at); (*Salat etc*) run to seed; (*Ball*) kick; (*Geschoß*) fire; **~e'rei** *f* shooting incident, shoot-up; **~pulver** *nt* gunpowder; **~scharte** *f* embrasure.

Schiff [ʃıf] *nt* **-(e)s, -e** ship, vessel; (*Kirchen~*) nave; **~bau** *m* shipbuilding; **~bruch** *m* shipwreck; **s~brüchig** *a* shipwrecked; **~chen** *nt* small boat; (*Weben*) shuttle; (*Mütze*) forage cap; **~er** *m* **-s, -** bargeman, boatman; **~(f)ahrt** *f* shipping;

(*Reise*) voyage; ~**(f)ahrtslinie** *f* shipping route.

Schikane [ʃi'kaːnə] *f* -, -n harassment; dirty trick; **mit allen** ~n with all the trimmings.

schikanieren [ʃika'niːrən] *vt* harass, torment.

Schild [ʃɪlt] *m* -(e)s, -e shield; **etw im** ~**e führen** be up to sth // *nt* -(e)s, -er sign; nameplate; (*Etikett*) label; ~**drüse** *f* thyroid gland; **s~ern** ['ʃɪldərn] *vt* depict, portray; ~**erung** *f* description, portrayal; ~**kröte** *f* tortoise; (*Wasser~*) turtle.

Schilf [ʃɪlf] *nt* -(e)s, -e, ~**rohr** *nt* (*Pflanze*) reed; (*Material*) reeds *pl*, rushes *pl*.

schillern ['ʃɪlərn] *vi* shimmer; ~**d** *a* iridescent.

Schilling ['ʃɪlɪŋ] *m* schilling.

Schimmel ['ʃɪməl] *m* -s, - mould; (*Pferd*) white horse; **s~ig** *a* mouldy; **s~n** *vi* get mouldy.

schimmern ['ʃɪmərn] *vi* glimmer, shimmer.

Schimpanse [ʃɪm'panzə] *m* -n, -n chimpanzee.

Schimpf- [ʃɪmpf] *zW*: **s~en** *vti* scold // *vi* curse, complain; ~**wort** *nt* term of abuse.

Schind- ['ʃɪnd] *zW*: **s~en** *unreg vt* maltreat, drive too hard; **Eindruck s~en** (*umg*) create an impression // *vr* sweat and strain, toil away (*mit at*); ~**e'rei** *f* grind, drudgery.

Schinken ['ʃɪŋkən] *m* -s, - ham.

Schippe ['ʃɪpə] *f* -, -n shovel; **s~n** *vt* shovel.

Schirm [ʃɪrm] *m* -(e)s, -e (*Regen~*) umbrella; (*Sonnen~*) parasol, sunshade; (*Wand~*, *Bild~*) screen; (*Lampen~*) (lamp)shade; (*Mützen~*) peak; (*Pilz~*) cap; ~**mütze** *f* peaked cap; ~**ständer** *m* umbrella stand.

schizophren [ʃitso'freːn] *a* schizophrenic.

Schlacht [ʃlaxt] *f* -, -en battle; **s~en** *vt* slaughter, kill; ~**enbummler** *m* football supporter; ~**er** *m* -s, - butcher; ~**feld** *nt* battlefield; ~**haus** *nt*, ~**hof** *m* slaughterhouse, abattoir; ~**schiff** *nt* battleship; ~**vieh** *nt* animals kept for meat; beef cattle.

Schlacke ['ʃlakə] *f* -, -n slag.

Schlaf [ʃlaːf] *m* -(e)s sleep; ~**anzug** *m* pyjamas *pl*.

Schläfe ['ʃlɛːfə] *f* -, -n temple.

schlafen ['ʃlaːfən] *vi unreg* sleep; ~ **gehen** g to bed; **S~gehen** *nt* -s going to bed; **Schlafenszeit** *f* bedtime.

schlaff [ʃlaf] *a* slack; (*energielos*) limp; (*erschöpft*) exhausted.

Schlaf- *zW*: ~**gelegenheit** *f* sleeping accommodation; ~**lied** *nt* lullaby;

s~los *a* sleepless; ~**losigkeit** *f* sleeplessness, insomnia; ~**mittel** *nt* sleeping pill.

schläfrig ['ʃlɛːfrɪç] *a* sleepy.

Schlaf- *zW*: ~**saal** *m* dormitory; ~**sack** *m* sleeping bag; ~**tablette** *f* sleeping pill; ~**wagen** *m* sleeping car, sleeper; **s~wandeln** *vi insep* sleepwalk; ~**zimmer** *nt* bedroom.

Schlag [ʃlaːk] *m* -(e)s, ⸚e (*lit*, *fig*) blow; stroke (*auch MED*); (*Puls~*, *Herz~*) beat; (*pl*: *Tracht Prügel*) beating; (*ELEK*) shock; (*Blitz~*) bolt, stroke; (*Autotür*) car door; (*umg*: *Portion*) helping; (*Art*) kind, type; **mit einem** ~ all at once; ~ **auf** ~ in rapid succession; ~**ader** *f* artery; ~**anfall** *m* stroke; **s~artig** *a* sudden, without warning; ~**baum** *m* barrier; **s~en** ['ʃlaːgən] *unreg vti* strike, hit; (*wiederholt s~en*, *besiegen*) beat; (*Glocke*) ring; (*Stunde*) strike; (*Sahne*) whip; (*Schlacht*) fight; **nach jdm s~en** (*fig*) take after sb // *vr* fight; **sich gut s~en** (*fig*) do well; ~**er** ['ʃlaːgər] *m* -s, - (*lit*, *fig*) hit; ~**ersänger(in** *f*) *m* pop singer.

Schläg- ['ʃlɛːg] *zW*: ~**er** *m* -s, - brawler; (*SPORT*) bat; (*TENNIS etc*) racket; (*Golf*) club; hockey stick; (*Waffe*) rapier; ~**e'rei** *f* fight, punch-up.

Schlag- *zW*: **s~fertig** *a* quick-witted; ~**fertigkeit** *f* ready wit, quickness of repartee; ~**loch** *nt* pothole; ~**sahne** *f* (whipped) cream; ~**seite** *f* (*NAUT*) list; ~**wort** *nt* slogan, catch phrase; ~**zeile** *f* headline; ~**zeug** *nt* percussion; drums *pl*; ~**zeuger** *m* -s, - drummer.

Schlamassel [ʃla'masəl] *m* -s, - (*umg*) mess.

Schlamm [ʃlam] *m* -(e)s, -e mud; **s~ig** *a* muddy.

Schlamp- ['ʃlamp] *zW*: ~**e** *f* -, -n (*umg*) slut; **s~en** *vi* (*umg*) be sloppy; ~**e'rei** *f* (*umg*) disorder, untidiness; sloppy work.

Schlange ['ʃlaŋə] *f* -, -n snake; (*Menschen~*) queue (*Brit*), line-up (*US*); ~ **stehen** (form a) queue, line up.

Schlangen- *zW*: ~**biß** *m* snake bite; ~**gift** *nt* snake venom; ~**linie** *f* wavy line.

schlank [ʃlaŋk] *a* slim, slender; **S~heit** *f* slimness, slenderness; **S~heitskur** *f* diet.

schlapp [ʃlap] *a* limp; (*locker*) slack; **S~e** *f* -, -n (*umg*) setback.

Schlaraffenland [ʃla'rafənlant] *nt* land of milk and honey.

schlau [ʃlau] *a* crafty, cunning.

Schlauch [ʃlaux] *m* -(e)s, **Schläuche** hose; (*in Reifen*) inner tube; (*umg*:

Anstrengung) grind; **~boot** *nt* rubber dinghy; **s~en** *vt* (*umg*) tell on, exhaust; **s~los** *a* (*Reifen*) tubeless.

Schlau- *zW:* **~heit** *f*, **Schläue** ['ʃlɔyə] *f* - cunning; **~kopf** *m* clever dick.

schlecht [ʃlɛçt] *a* bad; **es geht ihr ~** she's in a bad way; **~ gelaunt** in a bad mood; **~ und recht** after a fashion; **jdm ist ~** sb feels sick *od* bad; **~gehen** *vi unpers unreg:* **jdm geht es ~** sb is in a bad way; **S~igkeit** *f* badness; bad deed; **~machen** *vt* run down; **etw ~ machen** do sth badly.

schlecken ['ʃlɛkən] *vti* lick.

Schlegel ['ʃleːgəl] *m* **-s**, - (drum)stick; (*Hammer*) mallet, hammer; (*KOCH*) leg.

schleichen ['ʃlaɪçən] *vi unreg* creep, crawl; **~d** *a* gradual; creeping.

Schleier ['ʃlaɪər] *m* **-s**, - veil; **s~haft** *a* (*umg*): **jdm s~haft sein** be a mystery to sb.

Schleif- ['ʃlaɪf] *zW:* **~e** *f* -, **-n** loop; (*Band*) bow; **s~en** *vti* drag // *vt unreg* grind; (*Edelstein*) cut; (*MIL: Soldaten*) drill; **~stein** *m* grindstone.

Schleim [ʃlaɪm] *m* **-(e)s**, **-e** slime; (*MED*) mucus; (*KOCH*) gruel; **s~ig** *a* slimy.

Schlemm- ['ʃlɛm] *zW:* **s~en** *vi* feast; **~er** *m* **-s**, - gourmet; **~e'rei** *f* gluttony, feasting.

schlendern ['ʃlɛndərn] *vi* stroll.

schlenkern ['ʃlɛŋkərn] *vti* swing, dangle.

Schlepp- ['ʃlɛp] *zW:* **~e** *f* -, **-n** train; **s~en** *vt* drag; (*Auto, Schiff*) tow; (*tragen*) lug; **s~end** *a* dragging, slow; **~er** *m* **-s**, - tractor; (*Schiff*) tug.

Schleuder ['ʃlɔydər] *f* -, **-n** catapult; (*Wäsche~*) spin-drier; (*Butter~ etc*) centrifuge; **s~n** *vt* hurl; (*Wäsche*) spin-dry // *vi* (*AUT*) skid; **~preis** *m* give-away price; **~sitz** *m* (*AVIAT*) ejector seat; (*fig*) hot seat; **~ware** *f* cheap *od* cut-price goods *pl*.

schleunigst ['ʃlɔynɪçst] *ad* straight away.

Schleuse ['ʃlɔyzə] *f* -, **-n** lock; (*Schleusentor*) sluice.

schlicht [ʃlɪçt] *a* simple, plain; **~en** *vt* smooth, dress; (*Streit*) settle; **S~er** *m* **-s**, - mediator, arbitrator; **S~ung** *f* settlement; arbitration.

Schlick [ʃlɪk] *m* **-(e)s**, **-e** mud; (*Öl~*) slick.

schlief *etc v siehe* **schlafen**.

Schließ- ['ʃliːs] *zW:* **~e** *f* -, **-n** fastener; **s~en** *vtir unreg* close, shut; (*beenden*) close; (*Freundschaft, Bündnis, Ehe*) enter into; (*folgern*) infer (*aus +dat* from); **etw in sich s~en** include sth; **~fach** *nt* locker; **s~lich** *ad* finally; (*s~lich doch*) after

all.

Schliff [ʃlɪf] *m* **-(e)s**, **-e** cut(ting); (*fig*) polish.

schlimm [ʃlɪm] *a* bad; **~er** *a* worse; **~ste(r, s)** *a* worst; **~stenfalls** *ad* at (the) worst.

Schling- ['ʃlɪŋ] *zW:* **~e** *f* -, **-n** loop; (*des Henkers*) noose; (*Falle*) snare; (*MED*) sling; **~el** *m* **-s**, - rascal; **s~en** *unreg vt* wind; *vti* (*essen*) bolt (one's food), gobble; **s~ern** *vi* roll.

Schlips [ʃlɪps] *m* **-es**, **-e** tie.

Schlitten ['ʃlɪtən] *m* **-s**, - sledge, sleigh; **~bahn** *f* toboggan run; **~fahren** *nt* **-s** tobogganing.

schlittern ['ʃlɪtərn] *vi* slide.

Schlittschuh ['ʃlɪt-ʃuː] *m* skate; **~ laufen** skate; **~bahn** *f* skating rink; **~läufer(in** *f*) *m* skater.

Schlitz [ʃlɪts] *m* **-es**, **-e** slit; (*für Münze*) slot; (*Hosen~*) flies *pl*; **s~äugig** *a* slant-eyed; **s~en** *vt* slit.

schloß *etc v siehe* **schließen**.

Schloß [ʃlɔs] *nt* **-sses**, **-sser** lock; (*an Schmuck etc*) clasp; (*Bau*) castle, chateau.

Schlosser ['ʃlɔsər] *m* **-s**, - (*Auto~*) fitter; (*für Schlüssel etc*) locksmith; **~ei** [-'raɪ] *f* metal (working) shop.

Schlot ['ʃloːt] *m* **-(e)s**, **-e** chimney; (*NAUT*) funnel.

schlottern ['ʃlɔtərn] *vi* shake, tremble; (*Kleidung*) be baggy.

Schlucht [ʃluxt] *f* -, **-en** gorge, ravine.

schluchzen ['ʃluxtsən] *vi* sob.

Schluck [ʃluk] *m* **-(e)s**, **-e** swallow; (*Menge*) drop; **~auf** *m* **-s**, **-s** hiccups *pl*; **s~en** *vti* swallow.

schludern ['ʃluːdərn] *vi* skimp, do sloppy work.

schlug *etc v siehe* **schlagen**.

Schlummer ['ʃlumər] *m* **-s** slumber; **s~n** *vi* slumber.

Schlund [ʃlunt] *m* **-(e)s**, **-̈e** gullet; (*fig*) jaw.

schlüpfen ['ʃlYpfən] *vi* slip; (*Vogel etc*) hatch (out).

Schlüpfer ['ʃlYpfər] *m* **-s**, - panties *pl*, knickers *pl*.

schlüpfrig ['ʃlYpfrɪç] *a* slippery; (*fig*) lewd; **S~keit** *f* slipperiness; (*fig*) lewdness.

schlurfen ['ʃlurfən] *vi* shuffle.

schlürfen ['ʃlYrfən] *vti* slurp.

Schluß [ʃlus] *m* **-sses**, **-̈sse** end; (*~folgerung*) conclusion; **am ~** at the end; **~ machen mit** finish with.

Schlüssel ['ʃlYsəl] *m* **-s**, - (*lit, fig*) key; (*Schraub~*) spanner, wrench; (*MUS*) clef; **~bein** *nt* collarbone; **~blume** *f* cowslip, primrose; **~bund** *m* bunch of keys; **~loch** *nt* keyhole; **~position** *f* key position; **~wort** *nt* keyword.

schlüssig ['ʃlʏsɪç] *a* conclusive.
Schluß- *zW*: **~licht** *nt* taillight; (*fig*) tailender; **~strich** *m* (*fig*) final stroke; **~verkauf** *m* clearance sale.
schmächtig ['ʃmɛçtɪç] *a* slight.
schmackhaft ['ʃmakhaft] *a* tasty.
schmal [ʃmaːl] *a* narrow; (*Person, Buch etc*) slender, slim; (*karg*) meagre.
schmälern ['ʃmɛːlərn] *vt* diminish; (*fig*) belittle.
Schmalfilm *m* cine film.
Schmalz [ʃmalts] *nt* **-es**, **-e** dripping, lard; (*fig*) sentiment, schmaltz; **s~ig** *a* (*fig*) schmaltzy.
schmarotzen [ʃma'rɔtsən] *vi* sponge; (*BOT*) be parasitic.
Schmarotzer *m* **-s**, - parasite; sponger.
Schmarren ['ʃmarən] *m* **-s**, - (*Aus*) small piece of pancake; (*fig*) rubbish, tripe.
schmatzen ['ʃmatsən] *vi* smack one's lips; eat noisily.
schmecken ['ʃmɛkən] *vti* taste; es schmeckt ihm he likes it.
Schmeichel- ['ʃmaɪçəl] *zW*: **~ei** [-'laɪ] *f* flattery; **s~haft** *a* flattering; **s~n** *vi* flatter.
schmeißen ['ʃmaɪsən] *vt unreg* (*umg*) throw, chuck.
Schmeißfliege *f* bluebottle.
Schmelz [ʃmɛlts] *m* **-es**, **-e** enamel; (*Glasur*) glaze; (*von Stimme*) melodiousness; **s~bar** *a* fusible; **s~en** *vti unreg* melt; (*Erz*) smelt; **~punkt** *m* melting point; **~wasser** *nt* melted snow.
Schmerz [ʃmɛrts] *m* **-es**, **-en** pain; (*Trauer*) grief; **s~empfindlich** *a* sensitive to pain; **s~en** *vti* hurt; **Schmerzensgeld** *nt* compensation; **s~haft**, **s~lich** *a* painful; **s~los** *a* painless; **s~stillend** *a* soothing; **~tablette** *f* painkiller.
Schmetterling ['ʃmɛtərlɪŋ] *m* butterfly.
Schmied [ʃmiːt] *m* **-(e)s**, **-e** blacksmith; **~e** ['ʃmiːdə] *f* -, **-n** smithy, forge; **Schmiedeeisen** *nt* wrought iron; **s~en** *vt* forge; (*Pläne*) devise, concoct.
schmiegen ['ʃmiːgən] *vt* press, nestle // *vr* cling, nestle (up) (*an +akk* to).
Schmier- ['ʃmiːr] *zW*: **~e** *f* -, **-n** grease; (*THEAT*) greasepaint, make-up; **s~en** *vt* smear; (*ölen*) lubricate, grease; (*bestechen*) bribe // *vti* (*schreiben*) scrawl; **~fett** *nt* grease; **~fink** *m* messy person; **~geld** *nt* bribe; **s~ig** *a* greasy; **~seife** *f* soft soap.
Schminke ['ʃmɪŋkə] *f* -, **-n** make-up; **s~n** *vtr* make up.
schmirgel- ['ʃmɪrgəl] *zW*: **~n** *vt* sand

(down); **S~papier** *nt* emery paper.
schmollen ['ʃmɔlən] *vi* sulk, pout.
Schmor- ['ʃmoːr] *zW*: **~braten** *m* stewed *od* braised meat; **s~en** *vt* stew, braise.
Schmuck [ʃmʊk] *m* **-(e)s**, **-e** jewellery; (*Verzierung*) decoration.
schmücken ['ʃmʏkən] *vt* decorate.
Schmuck- *zW*: **s~los** *a* unadorned, plain; **~losigkeit** *f* simplicity; **~sachen** *pl* jewels *pl*, jewellery.
Schmuggel ['ʃmʊgəl] *m* **-s** smuggling; **s~n** *vti* smuggle.
Schmuggler *m* **-s**, - smuggler.
schmunzeln ['ʃmʊntsəln] *vi* smile benignly.
Schmutz [ʃmʊts] *m* **-es** dirt, filth; **~fink** *m* filthy creature; **~fleck** *m* stain; **s~ig** *a* dirty.
Schnabel ['ʃnaːbəl] *m* **-s**, ¨ beak, bill; (*Ausguß*) spout.
Schnake ['ʃnaːkə] *f* -, **-n** cranefly; (*Stechmücke*) gnat.
Schnalle ['ʃnalə] *f* -, **-n** buckle, clasp; **s~n** *vt* buckle.
Schnapp- ['ʃnap] *zW*: **s~en** *vt* grab, catch // *vi* snap; **~schloß** *nt* spring lock; **~schuß** *m* (*PHOT*) snapshot.
Schnaps [ʃnaps] *m* **-es**, ¨e spirits *pl*; schnapps.
schnarchen ['ʃnarçən] *vi* snore.
schnauben ['ʃnaʊbən] *vi* snort // *vr* blow one's nose.
schnaufen ['ʃnaʊfən] *vi* puff, pant.
Schnauz- ['ʃnaʊts] *zW*: **~bart** *m* moustache; **~e** *f* -, **-n** snout, muzzle; (*Ausguß*) spout; (*umg*) gob.
Schnecke ['ʃnɛkə] *f* -, **-n** snail; **Schneckenhaus** *nt* snail's shell.
Schnee [ʃneː] *m* **-s** snow; (*Ei~*) beaten egg white; **~ball** *m* snowball; **~flocke** *f* snowflake; **~gestöber** *nt* snowstorm; **~glöckchen** *nt* snowdrop; **~kette** *f* (*AUT*) snow chain; **~pflug** *m* snowplough; **~schmelze** *f* -, **-n** thaw; **~wehe** *f* snowdrift.
Schneid [ʃnaɪt] *m* **-(e)s** (*umg*) pluck; **~e** ['ʃnaɪdə] *f* -, **-n** edge; (*Klinge*) blade; **s~en** *vtr unreg* cut (o.s.); (*kreuzen*) cross, intersect; **s~end** *a* cutting; **~er** *m* **-s**, - tailor; **~erin** *f* dressmaker; **s~ern** *vt* make // *vi* be a tailor; **Schneidezahn** *m* incisor.
schneien ['ʃnaɪən] *vi unpers* snow.
Schneise ['ʃnaɪzə] *f* -, **-n** clearing.
schnell [ʃnɛl] *a*, *ad* quick(ly), fast; **S~hefter** *m* **-s**, - loose-leaf binder; **S~igkeit** *f* speed; **S~imbiß** *m* (*Lokal*) snack bar; **S~kochtopf** *m* (*Dampfkochtopf*) pressure cooker; **S~reinigung** *f* dry cleaner's; **~stens** *ad* as quickly as possible; **S~straße** *f* expressway; **S~zug** *m* fast *od* express train.
schneuzen ['ʃnɔʏtsən] *vr* blow one's

nose.

schnippisch ['ʃnɪpɪʃ] *a* sharp-tongued.

schnitt *etc v siehe* schneiden.

Schnitt [ʃnɪt] *m* -(e)s, -e cut(ting); (~*punkt*) intersection; (*Quer*~) (cross) section; (*Durch*~) average; (~*muster*) pattern; (*an Buch*) edge; (*umg: Gewinn*) profit; ~**blumen** *pl* cut flowers *pl*; ~**e** *f* -, -n slice; (*belegt*) sandwich; ~**fläche** *f* section; ~**lauch** *m* chive; ~**muster** *nt* pattern; ~**punkt** *m* (point of) intersection; ~**stelle** *f* (*COMPUT*) interface; ~**wunde** *f* cut.

Schnitz- [ʃnɪts] *zW*: ~**arbeit** *f* wood carving; ~**el** *nt* -s, - chip; (*KOCH*) escalope; **s~en** *vt* carve; ~**er** *m* -s, - carver; (*umg*) blunder; ~**e'rei** *f* carving; carved woodwork.

schnodderig ['ʃnɔdərɪç] *a* (*umg*) snotty.

Schnorchel ['ʃnɔrçəl] *m* -s, - snorkel.

Schnörkel ['ʃnœrkəl] *m* -s, - flourish; (*ARCHIT*) scroll.

schnorren ['ʃnɔrən] *vti* cadge.

schnüffeln ['ʃnʏfəln] *vi* sniff. **S~** *nt* (*umg: von Klebstoff etc*) glue-sniffing.

Schnüffler *m* -s, - snooper.

Schnuller ['ʃnʊlər] *m* -s, - dummy, comforter (*US*).

Schnupfen ['ʃnʊpfən] *m* -s, - cold.

schnuppern ['ʃnʊpərn] *vi* sniff.

Schnur [ʃnuːr] *f* -, "-e string, cord; (*ELEK*) flex; **s~gerade** *a* straight (as a die).

schnüren ['ʃnyːrən] *vt* tie.

Schnurr- ['ʃnʊr] *zW*: ~**bart** *m* moustache; **s~en** *vi* purr; (*Kreisel*) hum.

Schnür- ['ʃnyːr] *zW*: ~**schuh** *m* lace-up (shoe); ~**senkel** *m* shoelace.

schnurstracks *ad* straight (away).

Schock [ʃɔk] *m* -(e)s, -e shock; **s~ieren** [ʃɔ'kiːrən] *vt* shock, outrage.

Schöffe ['ʃœfə] *m* -n, - lay magistrate.

Schokolade [ʃoko'laːdə] *f* -, -n chocolate.

Scholle ['ʃɔlə] *f* -, -n clod; (*Eis*~) ice floe; (*Fisch*) plaice.

schon [ʃoːn] *ad* **1** (*bereits*) already; er ist ~ da he's there already, he's already there; ist er ~ da? is he there yet?; warst du ~ einmal da? have you ever been there?; ich war ~ einmal da I've been there before; das war ~ immer so that has always been the case; ~ oft often; hast du ~ gehört? have you heard?

2 (*bestimmt*) all right; du wirst ~ sehen you'll see (all right); das wird ~ noch gut that'll be OK

3 (*bloß*) just; allein ~ das Gefühl ... just the very feeling ...; ~ der Gedanke the very thought; wenn ich

das ~ höre I only have to hear that

4 (*einschränkend*): ja ~, aber ... yes (well), but ...

5: ~ möglich possible; ~ gut! OK!; du weißt ~ you know; komm ~! come on!

schön [ʃøːn] *a* beautiful; (*nett*) nice; ~**e** Grüße best wishes; ~**e** Ferien have a nice holiday; ~**en** Dank (many) thanks.

schonen ['ʃoːnən] *vt* look after // *vr* take it easy; ~**d** *a* careful, gentle.

Schön- *zW*: ~**heit** *f* beauty; ~**heitsfehler** *m* blemish, flaw; ~**heitsoperation** *f* cosmetic plastic surgery; **s~machen** *vr* make oneself look nice.

Schon- *zW*: ~**ung** *f* good care; (*Nachsicht*) consideration; (*Forst*) plantation of young trees; **s~ungslos** *a* unsparing, harsh; ~**zeit** *f* close season.

Schöpf- ['ʃœpf] *zW*: **s~en** *vt* scoop, ladle; (*Mut*) summon up; (*Luft*) breathe in; ~**er** *m* -s, - creator; **s~erisch** *a* creative; ~**kelle** *f* ladle; ~**löffel** *m* skimmer, scoop; ~**ung** *f* creation.

Schorf [ʃɔrf] *m* -(e)s, -e scab.

Schornstein ['ʃɔrnʃtain] *m* chimney; (*NAUT*) funnel; ~**feger** *m* -s, - chimney sweep.

schoß *etc v siehe* schießen.

Schoß [ʃoːs] *m* -es, "-e lap; (*Rock*~) coat tail; ~**hund** *m* pet dog, lapdog.

Schote ['ʃoːtə] *f* -, -n pod.

Schotte ['ʃɔtə] *m* Scot, Scotsman.

Schotter ['ʃɔtər] *m* -s, - broken stone, road metal; (*EISENB*) ballast.

Schott- ['ʃɔt] *zW*: ~**in** *f* Scotswoman; **s~isch** *a* Scottish, Scots; ~**land** *nt* Scotland.

schraffieren [ʃra'fiːrən] *vt* hatch.

schräg [ʃrɛːk] *a* slanting, not straight; etw ~ stellen put sth at an angle; ~ gegenüber diagonally opposite; **S~e** *f* -, -n slant; **S~strich** *m* oblique stroke.

Schramme ['ʃramə] *f* -, -n scratch; **s~n** *vt* scratch.

Schrank [ʃraŋk] *m* -(e)s, "-e cupboard; (*Kleider*~) wardrobe; ~**e** *f* -, -n barrier; ~**enwärter** *m* (*EISENB*) level crossing attendant; ~**koffer** *m* trunk.

Schraube ['ʃraubə] *f* -, -n screw.

schrauben *vt* screw; **S~schlüssel** *m* spanner; **S~zieher** *m* -s, - screwdriver.

Schraubstock ['ʃraubʃtɔk] *m* (*TECH*) vice.

Schreck [ʃrɛk] *m* -(e)s, -e, ~**en** *m* -s, - terror; fright; **s~en** *vt* frighten, scare; ~**gespenst** *nt* spectre, nightmare; **s~haft** *a* jumpy, easily frightened; **s~lich** *a* terrible, dreadful.

Schrei [ʃraɪ] m -(e)s, -e scream; (Ruf) shout.

Schreib- ['ʃraɪb] zW: ~**block** m writing pad; ~**dichte** f: einfache/doppelte ~**dichte** (Diskette) single/double density; **s~en** vti unreg write; (buchstabieren) spell; ~**en** nt -s, - letter, communication; **s~faul** a bad about writing letters; ~**fehler** m spelling mistake; ~**maschine** f typewriter; ~**papier** nt notepaper; ~**tisch** m desk; ~**ung** f spelling; ~**waren** pl stationery; ~**warenhandlung** f stationer's; ~**weise** f spelling; way of writing; ~**zentrale** f typing pool; ~**zeug** nt writing materials pl.

schreien ['ʃraɪən] vti unreg scream; (rufen) shout; ~**d** a (fig) glaring; (Farbe) loud.

Schreiner ['ʃraɪnər] m -s, - joiner; (Zimmermann) carpenter; (Möbel~) cabinetmaker; ~**ei** [-'raɪ] f joiner's workshop.

schreiten ['ʃraɪtən] vi unreg stride.

schrieb etc v siehe **schreiben**.

Schrift [ʃrɪft] f -, -en writing; handwriting; (~art) script; (Gedrucktes) pamphlet, work; ~**deutsch** nt written German; ~**führer** m secretary; **s~lich** a written // ad in writing; ~**setzer** m compositor; ~**sprache** f written language; ~**steller(in** f) m -s, - writer; ~**stück** nt document.

schrill [ʃrɪl] a shrill.

Schritt [ʃrɪt] m -(e)s, -e step; (Gangart) walk; (Tempo) pace; (von Hose) crutch; ~ **fahren** drive at walking pace; ~**macher** m -s, - pacemaker; ~**(t)empo** nt: im ~**(t)empo** at a walking pace.

schroff [ʃrɔf] a steep; (zackig) jagged; (fig) brusque; (ungeduldig) abrupt.

schröpfen ['ʃrœpfən] vt (fig) fleece.

Schrot [ʃroːt] m od nt -(e)s, -e (Blei) (small) shot; (Getreide) coarsely ground grain, groats pl; ~**flinte** f shotgun.

Schrott [ʃrɔt] m -(e)s, -e scrap metal; ~**haufen** m scrap heap; **s~reif** a ready for the scrap heap.

schrubben ['ʃrʊbən] vt scrub.

Schrubber m -s, - scrubbing brush.

schrumpfen ['ʃrʊmpfən] vi shrink; (Apfel) shrivel.

Schub- ['ʃuːb] zW: ~**fach** nt drawer; ~**karren** m wheelbarrow; ~**lade** f drawer.

schüchtern ['ʃʏçtərn] a shy; **S~heit** f shyness.

Schuft [ʃʊft] m -(e)s, -e scoundrel; **s~en** vi (umg) graft, slave away.

Schuh [ʃuː] m -(e)s, -e shoe; ~**band** nt shoelace; ~**creme** f shoe polish; ~**löffel** m shoehorn; ~**macher** m -s, - shoemaker.

Schul- ['ʃuːl] zW: ~**aufgaben** pl homework; ~**besuch** m school attendance; ~**buch** nt school book.

Schuld [ʃʊlt] f -, -en guilt; (FIN) debt; (Verschulden) fault; **s~** a: **s~ sein** od **haben** be to blame (an +dat for); er ist od hat **s~** it's his fault; **jdm s~ geben** blame sb; **s~en** ['ʃʊldən] vt owe; **s~enfrei** a free from debt; ~**gefühl** nt feeling of guilt; **s~ig** a guilty (an +dat of); (gebührend) due; **jdm etw s~ig sein** owe sb sth; **jdm etw s~ig bleiben** not provide sb with sth; **s~los** a innocent, without guilt; ~**ner** m -s, - debtor; ~**schein** m promissory note, IOU; ~**spruch** m verdict of guilty.

Schule ['ʃuːlə] f -, -n school; **s~n** vt train, school.

Schüler(in f) ['ʃyːlər(ɪn)] m -s, - pupil; ~**lotse** m pupil acting as road crossing warden.

Schul- ['ʃuːl] zW: ~**ferien** pl school holidays pl; **s~frei** a: **s~freier Tag** holiday; **s~frei sein** be a holiday; ~**hof** m playground; ~**jahr** nt school year; ~**junge** m schoolboy; ~**mädchen** nt schoolgirl; **s~pflichtig** a of school age; ~**schiff** nt (NAUT) training ship; ~**stunde** f period, lesson; ~**tasche** f school bag.

Schulter ['ʃʊltər] f -, -n shoulder; ~**blatt** nt shoulder blade; **s~n** vt shoulder.

Schul- zW: ~**ung** f education, schooling; ~**zeugnis** nt school report.

Schund [ʃʊnt] m -(e)s trash, garbage; ~**roman** m trashy novel.

Schuppe ['ʃʊpə] f -, -n scale; ~**n** pl (Haar~) dandruff; **s~n** vt scale // vr peel; ~**n** m -s, - shed.

schuppig ['ʃʊpɪç] a scaly.

Schur [ʃuːr] f -, -en shearing.

Schür- ['ʃyːr] zW: **s~en** vt rake; (fig) stir up; **schürfen** ['ʃʏrfən] vti scrape, scratch; (MIN) prospect, dig.

Schurke ['ʃʊrkə] m -n, -n rogue.

Schürze ['ʃʏrtsə] f -, -n apron.

Schuß [ʃʊs] m -sses, -sse shot; (WEBEN) woof; ~**bereich** m effective range.

Schüssel ['ʃʏsəl] f -, -n bowl.

Schuß- zW: ~**linie** f line of fire; ~**verletzung** f bullet wound; ~**waffe** f firearm; ~**weite** f range (of fire).

Schuster ['ʃuːstər] m -s, - cobbler, shoemaker.

Schutt [ʃʊt] m -(e)s rubbish; (Bau~) rubble; ~**abladeplatz** m refuse dump.

Schütt- ['ʃʏt] zW: **Schüttelfrost** m shivering; **s~eln** vtr shake; **s~en** vt pour; (Zucker, Kies etc) tip; (ver~en) spill // vi unpers pour (down).

Schutthalde f dump.

Schutthaufen m heap of rubble.

Schutz [ʃʊts] m -es protection; (*Unterschlupf*) shelter; jdn in ~ nehmen stand up for sb; **~anzug** m overalls pl; **~blech** nt mudguard; **~brille** f goggles pl.

Schütze ['ʃʏtsə] m -n, -n gunman; (*Gewehr~*) rifleman; (*Scharf~, Sport~*) marksman; (ASTROL) Sagittarius; **s~n** vt protect (*vor* +dat, *gegen* from); **Schützenfest** nt fair *featuring shooting matches.*

Schutz- zW: **~engel** m guardian angel; **~gebiet** nt protectorate; (*Natur~*) reserve; **~impfung** f immunisation; **s~los** a defenceless; **~mann** m, pl **-leute** od **-männer** policeman; **~patron** m patron saint.

Schwaben ['ʃvaːbən] nt Swabia.

schwäbisch ['ʃvɛːbɪʃ] a Swabian.

schwach [ʃvax] a weak, feeble.

Schwäche ['ʃvɛçə] f -, -n weakness; **s~n** vt weaken.

Schwachheit f weakness.

schwächlich a weakly, delicate.

Schwächling m weakling.

Schwach- zW: **~sinn** m imbecility; **s~sinnig** a mentally deficient; (*Idee*) idiotic; **~strom** m weak current.

Schwächung ['ʃvɛçʊŋ] f weakening.

schwafeln ['ʃvaːfəln] vti drivel.

Schwager ['ʃvaːɡər] m -s, ⁻ brother-in-law.

Schwägerin ['ʃvɛːɡərɪn] f sister-in-law.

Schwalbe ['ʃvalbə] f -, -n swallow.

Schwall [ʃval] m -(e)s, -e surge; (*Worte*) flood, torrent.

schwamm etc v siehe **schwimmen**.

Schwamm [ʃvam] m -(e)s, ⁻e sponge; (*Pilz*) fungus; **s~ig** a spongy; (*Gesicht*) puffy.

Schwan [ʃvaːn] m -(e)s, ⁻e swan; **s~en** vi unpers: jdm schwant etw sb has a foreboding of sth.

schwanger ['ʃvaŋər] a pregnant.

schwängern ['ʃvɛŋərn] vt make pregnant.

Schwangerschaft f pregnancy.

Schwank [ʃvaŋk] m -(e)s, ⁻e funny story; **s~en** vi sway; (*taumeln*) stagger, reel; (*Preise, Zahlen*) fluctuate; (*zögern*) hesitate, vacillate; **~ung** f fluctuation.

Schwanz [ʃvants] m -es, ⁻e tail.

schwänzen ['ʃvɛntsən] (*umg*) vt skip, cut // vi play truant.

Schwarm [ʃvarm] m -(e)s, ⁻e swarm; (*umg*) heart-throb, idol.

schwärm- ['ʃvɛrm] zW: **~en** vi swarm; **~en für** be mad od wild about; **S~erei** f [-əˈraɪ] enthusiasm; **~erisch** a impassioned, effusive.

Schwarte ['ʃvartə] f -, -n hard skin; (*Speck~*) rind.

schwarz [ʃvarts] a black; **~es Brett** notice board; ins S~e treffen (*lit, fig*) hit the bull's eye; in den **~en Zahlen** in the black; **S~arbeit** f illicit work, moonlighting; **S~brot** nt black bread.

Schwärze ['ʃvɛrtsə] f -, -n blackness; (*Farbe*) blacking; (*Drucker~*) printer's ink; **s~n** vt blacken.

Schwarz- zW: **s~fahren** vi unreg travel without paying; drive without a licence; **~handel** m black-market (trade); **s~hören** vi listen to the radio without a licence; **~markt** m black market; **s~sehen** vi unreg (*umg*) see the gloomy side of things; (TV) watch TV without a licence; **~seher** m pessimist; (TV) viewer without a licence; **~wald** m Black Forest; **s~weiß** a black and white.

schwatzen ['ʃvatsən], **schwätzen** ['ʃvɛtsən] vi chatter.

Schwätzer ['ʃvɛtsər] m -s, - gasbag; **~in** f chatterbox, gossip.

schwatzhaft a talkative, gossipy.

Schwebe ['ʃveːbə] f: in der ~ (*fig*) in abeyance; **~bahn** f overhead railway; **~balken** m (SPORT) beam; **s~n** vi drift, float; (*hoch*) soar.

Schwed- ['ʃveːd] zW: **~e** m Swede; **~en** nt Sweden; **~in** f Swede; **s~isch** a Swedish.

Schwefel ['ʃveːfəl] m -s sulphur; **s~ig** a sulphurous; **~säure** f sulphuric acid.

Schweig- ['ʃvaɪɡ] zW: **Schweigegeld** nt hush money; **s~en** vi unreg be silent; stop talking; **~en** nt -s silence; **s~sam** ['ʃvaɪkzaːm] a silent, taciturn; **~samkeit** f taciturnity, quietness.

Schwein [ʃvaɪn] nt -(e)s, -e pig; (*umg*) (good) luck.

Schweine- zW: **~fleisch** nt pork; **~rei** f mess; (*Gemeinheit*) dirty trick; **~stall** m pigsty.

schweinisch a filthy.

Schweinsleder nt pigskin.

Schweiß [ʃvaɪs] m -es sweat, perspiration; **s~en** vti weld; **~er** m -s, - welder; **~füße** pl sweaty feet pl; **~naht** f weld.

Schweiz [ʃvaɪts] f Switzerland; **~er(in** f) m Swiss; **s~erisch** a Swiss.

schwelgen ['ʃvɛlɡən] vi indulge.

Schwelle ['ʃvɛlə] f -, -n threshold (*auch fig*); doorstep; (EISENB) sleeper; **s~n** vi unreg swell.

Schwellung f swelling.

Schwenk- ['ʃvɛŋk] zW: **s~bar** a swivel-mounted; **s~en** vt swing; (*Fahne*) wave; (*abspülen*) rinse // vi turn, swivel; (MIL) wheel; **~ung** f turn; wheel.

schwer [ʃveːr] a heavy; (schwierig) difficult, hard; (schlimm) serious, bad // ad (sehr) very (much) // (verletzt etc) seriously, badly; **S~arbeiter** m manual worker, labourer; **S~e** f -, -n weight, heaviness; (PHYS) gravity; **schwerelos** a weightless; (Kammer) zero-G; **~erziehbar** a difficult (to bring up); **~fallen** vi unreg: jdm ~fallen be difficult for sb; **~fällig** a ponderous; **S~gewicht** nt heavyweight; (fig) emphasis; **~hörig** a hard of hearing; **S~industrie** f heavy industry; **S~kraft** f gravity; **S~kranke(r)** mf person who is seriously ill; **~lich** ad hardly; **~machen** vt: jdm/sich etw ~machen make sth difficult for sb/o.s.; **~mütig** a melancholy; **~nehmen** vt unreg take to heart; **S~punkt** m centre of gravity; (fig) emphasis, crucial point.

Schwert [ʃveːrt] nt -(e)s, -er sword; **~lilie** f iris.

schwer- zW: **~tun** vi unreg: sich (dat od akk) ~tun have difficulties; **S~verbrecher(in** f) m criminal, serious offender; **~verdaulich** a indigestible, heavy; **~verletzt** a badly injured; **~wiegend** a weighty, important.

Schwester [ˈʃvɛstər] f -, -n sister; (MED) nurse; **~lich** a sisterly.

Schwieger- [ˈʃviːɡər] zW: **~eltern** pl parents-in-law pl; **~mutter** f mother-in-law; **~sohn** m son-in-law; **~tochter** f daughter-in-law; **~vater** m father-in-law.

Schwiele [ˈʃviːlə] f -, -n callus.

schwierig [ˈʃviːrɪç] a difficult, hard; **S~keit** f difficulty.

Schwimm- [ˈʃvɪm] zW: **~bad** nt swimming baths pl; **~becken** nt swimming pool; **~en** vi unreg swim; (treiben, nicht sinken) float; (fig: unsicher sein) be all at sea; **~er** m -s, - swimmer; (Angeln) float; **~lehrer** m swimming instructor; **~weste** f life jacket.

Schwindel [ˈʃvɪndəl] m -s giddiness; dizzy spell; (Betrug) swindle, fraud; (Zeug) stuff; **s~frei** a; s~frei sein have a good head for heights; **s~n** vi (umg: lügen) fib; jdm schwindelt es sb feels dizzy.

schwinden [ˈʃvɪndən] vi unreg disappear; (sich verringern) decrease; (Kräfte) decline.

Schwind- [ʃvɪnt] zW: **~ler** m -s, - swindler; (Lügner) liar; **s~lig** a dizzy; mir ist s~lig I feel dizzy.

Schwing- [ˈʃvɪŋ] zW: **s~en** vti unreg swing; (Waffe etc) brandish; (vibrieren) vibrate; (klingen) sound; **~tür** f swing door(s); **~ung** f vibration; (PHYS) oscillation.

Schwips [ʃvɪps] m -es, -e: einen ~ haben be tipsy.

schwirren [ˈʃvɪrən] vi buzz.

schwitzen [ˈʃvɪtsən] vi sweat, perspire.

schwören [ˈʃvøːrən] vti unreg swear.

schwul [ʃvuːl] a (umg) gay, queer.

schwül [ʃvyːl] a sultry, close; **S~e** f - sultriness, closeness.

schwülstig [ˈʃvʏlstɪç] a pompous.

Schwung [ʃvʊŋ] m -(e)s, ⁻e swing; (Triebkraft) momentum; (fig: Energie) verve, energy; (umg: Menge) batch; **s~haft** a brisk, lively; **s~voll** a vigorous.

Schwur [ʃvuːr] m -(e)s, ⁻e oath; **~gericht** nt court with a jury.

sechs [zɛks] num six; **~hundert** num six hundred; **~te(r, s)** a sixth; **S~tel** nt -s - sixth.

sechzehn [ˈzɛçtseːn] num sixteen.

sechzig [ˈzɛçtsɪç] num sixty.

See [zeː] f -, -n sea // m -s, -n lake; **~bad** nt seaside resort; **~fahrt** f seafaring; (Reise) voyage; **~gang** m (motion of the) sea; **~hund** m seal; **~igel** [ˈzeːʔiːɡəl] m sea urchin; **s~krank** a seasick; **~krankheit** f seasickness; **~lachs** m rock salmon.

Seele [ˈzeːlə] f -, -n soul; **seelenruhig** ad calmly.

Seeleute [ˈzeːlɔʏtə] pl seamen pl.

Seel- zW: **s~isch** a mental; **~sorge** f pastoral duties pl; **~sorger** m -s, - clergyman.

See- zW: **~macht** f naval power; **~mann** m, pl -leute seaman, sailor; **~meile** f nautical mile; **~not** f distress; **~pferd(chen)** nt sea horse; **~räuber** m pirate; **~rose** f water lily; **~stern** m starfish; **s~tüchtig** a seaworthy; **~weg** m sea route; auf dem ~weg by sea; **~zunge** f sole.

Segel [ˈzeːɡəl] nt -s, - sail; **~boot** nt yacht; **~fliegen** nt -s gliding; **~flieger** m glider pilot; **~flugzeug** nt glider; **s~n** vti sail; **~schiff** nt sailing vessel; **~sport** m sailing; **~tuch** nt canvas.

Segen [ˈzeːɡən] m -s, - blessing; **segensreich** a beneficial.

Segler [ˈzeːɡlər] m -s, - sailor, yachtsman.

segnen [ˈzeːɡnən] vt bless.

Seh- [ˈzeː] zW: **s~en** vti unreg see; mal s~en(, ob ...) let's see (if ...); (in bestimmte Richtung) look; **s~enswert** a worth seeing; **~enswürdigkeiten** pl sights pl (of a town); **~er** m -s, - seer; **~fehler** m sight defect.

Sehn- [ˈzeː] zW: **~e** f -, -n sinew; (an Bogen) string; **s~en** vr long, yearn (nach for); **s~ig** a sinewy;

s~lich *a* ardent; **~sucht** *f* longing; **s~süchtig** *a* longing.

sehr [zeːr] *ad* very; (*mit Verben*) a lot, (very) much; **zu ~** too much; **~ geehrte(r)** ... dear ....

seicht [zaıçt] *a* (*lit, fig*) shallow.

Seide ['zaıdə] *f* -, **-n** silk; **s~n** *a* silk; **Seidenpapier** *nt* tissue paper.

seidig ['zaıdıç] *a* silky.

Seife ['zaıfə] *f* -, **-n** soap.

Seifen- *zW*: **~lauge** *f* soapsuds *pl*; **~schale** *f* soap dish; **~schaum** *m* lather.

seihen ['zaıən] *vt* strain, filter.

Seil [zaıl] *nt* **-(e)s, -e** rope; cable; **~bahn** *f* cable railway; **~hüpfen** *nt* **-s,** **~springen** *nt* **-s** skipping; **~tänzer(in** *f*) *m* tightrope walker.

sein [zaın] *vi pt* **war,** *ptp* **gewesen 1** be; **ich bin** I am; **du bist** you are; **er/sie/es ist** he/she/it is; **wir sind/ihr seid/sie sind** we/you/they are; **wir waren** we were; **wir sind gewesen** we have been

2: **seien Sie nicht böse** don't be angry; **sei so gut und ...** be so kind as to ...; **das wäre gut** that would *od* that'd be a good thing; **wenn ich Sie wäre** if I were *od* was you; **das wär's** that's all, that's it; **morgen bin ich in Rom** tomorrow I'll *od* I will *od* I shall be in Rome; **waren Sie mal in Rom?** have you ever been to Rome?

3: **wie ist das zu verstehen?** how is that to be understood?; **er ist nicht zu ersetzen** he cannot be replaced; **mit ihr ist nicht zu reden** you can't talk to her

4: **mir ist kalt** I'm cold; **was ist?** what's the matter?, what is it?; **ist was?** is something the matter?; **es sei denn, daß ...** unless ...; **wie dem auch sei** be that as it may; **wie wäre es mit ...?** how *od* what about ...?; **laß das ~!** stop that!

sein [zaın] *pron* his; its; **~e(r, s)** his; its; **~er** *pron gen von* **er** of him; **~erseits** *ad* for his part; **~erzeit** *ad* in those days, formerly; **~esgleichen** *pron* people like him; **~etwegen,** **~etwillen** *ad* (*für ihn*) for his sake; (*wegen ihm*) on his account; (*von ihm aus*) as far as he is concerned; **~ige** *pron*: **der/die/das ~ige** his.

Seismograph [zaısmoˈgraːf] *m* **-en,** **-en** seismograph.

seit [zaıt] *präp, kj* since; **er ist ~ einer Woche hier** he has been here for a week; **~ langem** for a long time; **~dem** [zaıtˈdeːm] *ad, kj* since.

Seite ['zaıtə] *f* -, **-n** side; (*Buch~*) page; (*MIL*) flank.

Seiten- *zW*: **~ansicht** *f* side view; **~hieb** *m* (*fig*) passing shot, dig; **seitens** *präp* (+*gen*) on the part of;

~schiff *nt* aisle; **~sprung** *m* extramarital escapade; **~stechen** *nt* (a) stitch; **~straße** *f* side road.

seit- *zW*: **~her** [zaıtˈheːr] *ad, kj* since (then); **~lich** *a* on one *od* the side; side; **~wärts** *ad* sideways.

Sekretär [zekreˈtɛːr] *m* secretary; (*Möbel*) bureau; **~in** *f* secretary.

Sekretariat [zekretariˈaːt] *nt* **-(e)s, -e** secretary's office, secretariat.

Sekt [zɛkt] *m* **-(e)s, -e** champagne.

Sekte ['zɛktə] *f* -, **-n** sect.

Sekunde [zeˈkʊndə] *f* -, **-n** second.

selber ['zɛlbər] = **selbst.**

selbst [zɛlpst] ◆*pron* **1**: **ich/er/wir ~** I myself/he himself/we ourselves; **sie ist die Tugend ~** she's virtue itself; **er braut sein Bier ~** he brews his own beer; **wie geht's? — gut, und ~?** how are things? — fine, and yourself? **2** (*ohne Hilfe*) alone, on my/his/one's *etc* own; **von ~** by itself; **er kam von ~** he came of his own accord

◆*ad* even; **~ wenn** even if; **~ Gott** even God (himself).

Selbst [zɛlpst] *nt* - self; **~achtung** *f* self-respect; **selbständig** ['zɛlpʃtɛndıç] *a* independent; **Selbständigkeit** *f* independence; **~auslöser** *m* (*PHOT*) delayed-action shutter release; **~bedienung** *f* self-service; **~befriedigung** *f* masturbation; **~beherrschung** *f* self-control; **~bewußt** *a* (self-)confident; **~bewußtsein** *nt* self-confidence; **~erhaltung** *f* self-preservation; **~erkenntnis** *f* self-knowledge; **s~gefällig** *a* smug, self-satisfied; **s~gemacht** *a* home-made; **~gespräch** *nt* conversation with oneself; **~kostenpreis** *m* cost price; **s~los** *a* unselfish, selfless; **~mord** *m* suicide; **~mörder(in** *f*) *m* suicide; **s~mörderisch** *a* suicidal; **s~sicher** *a* self-assured; **s~tätig** *a* automatic; **s~verständlich** *a* obvious *od* naturally; **ich halte das für s~verständlich** I take that for granted; **~vertrauen** *nt* self-confidence; **~verwaltung** *f* autonomy, self-government.

selig ['zeːlıç] *a* happy, blissful; (*REL*) blessed; (*tot*) late; **S~keit** *f* bliss.

Sellerie ['zɛləriː] *m* **-s, -(s)** *od f* -, - celery.

selten ['zɛltən] *a* rare // *ad* seldom, rarely; **S~heit** *f* rarity.

Selterswasser ['zɛltərsvasər] *nt* soda water.

seltsam ['zɛltzaːm] *a* strange, curious; **~erweise** *ad* curiously, strangely; **S~keit** *f* strangeness.

Semester [zeˈmɛstər] *nt* **-s,** - semester.

Semi- [zemi] *in zW* semi-; **~kolon** [-ˈkoːlɔn] *nt* **-s, -s** semicolon; **~nar**

[-'na:r] nt -s, -e seminary; (Kurs) seminar; (UNIV: Ort) department building.

Semmel ['zɛməl] f -, -n roll.

sen. abk (= senior) sen.

Senat [ze'na:t] m -(e)s, -e senate, council.

Sende- ['zɛndə] zW: ~bereich m transmission range; ~folge f (Serie) series; s~n vt unreg send // vti (RAD, TV) transmit, broadcast; ~r m -s, - station; (Anlage) transmitter; ~reihe f series (of broadcasts).

Sendung ['zɛnduŋ] f consignment; (Aufgabe) mission; (RAD, TV) transmission; (Programm) programme.

Senf [zɛnf] m -(e)s, -e mustard.

Senk- ['zɛŋk] zW: ~blei nt plumb; ~e f -, -n depression; s~en vt lower // vr sink, drop gradually; s~recht a vertical, perpendicular; ~rechte f -n, -n perpendicular; ~rechtstarter m (AVIAT) vertical take-off plane; (fig) high-flyer.

Sensation [zɛnzatsi'o:n] f sensation; s~ell [-'nɛl] a sensational.

Sense ['zɛnzə] f -, -n scythe.

sensibel [zɛn'zi:bəl] a sensitive.

sentimental [zɛntimɛn'ta:l] a sentimental; S~i'tät f sentimentality.

separat [zepa'ra:t] a separate.

September [zɛp'tɛmbər] m -(s), - September.

Serie ['ze:riə] f series; **serienweise** ad in series.

seriös [zeri'ø:s] a serious, bona fide.

Serum ['ze:rum] nt -s, Seren serum.

Service [zɛr'vi:s] nt -(s), - set, service // ['sø:rvɪs] m -, -s service.

servieren [zɛr'vi:rən] vti serve.

Serviette [zɛrvi'ɛtə] f napkin, serviette.

Sessel ['zɛsəl] m -s, - armchair; ~lift m chairlift.

seßhaft ['zɛshaft] a settled; (ansässig) resident.

setzen ['zɛtsən] vt put, set; (Baum etc) plant; (Segel, TYP) set // vr settle; (Person) sit down // vi (springen) leap; (wetten) bet.

Setz- [zɛts] zW: ~er m -s, - (TYP) compositor; ~e'rei f caseroom; ~ling m young plant.

Seuche ['zɔyçə] f -, -n epidemic; **Seuchengebiet** nt infected area.

seufzen ['zɔyftsən] vti sigh.

Seufzer ['zɔyftsər] m -s, - sigh.

Sex [zɛks] m -(es) sex; ~ualität [-uali'tɛt] f sex, sexuality; s~uell [-u'ɛl] a sexual.

sezieren [ze'tsi:rən] vt dissect.

Shampoo [ʃam'pu:] nt shampoo.

Sibirien [zi'bi:riən] nt Siberia.

sibirisch [zi'bi:rɪʃ] a Siberian.

sich [zɪç] pron (mit Infinitiv) **1** (akk):

er/sie/es ... ~ he/she/it ... himself/herself/itself; sie (pl)/man ... ~ they/one ... themselves/oneself; Sie ... ~ you ... yourself/(pl) yourselves; ~ wiederholen repeat oneself/itself

2 (dat): er/sie/es ... ~ he/she/it ... to himself/herself/itself; sie (pl)/man ... ~ they/one ... to themselves/oneself; Sie ... ~ you ... to yourself/(pl) yourselves; sie hat ~ einen Pullover gekauft she bought herself a jumper; ~ die Haare waschen wash one's hair

3 (mit Präposition): haben Sie Ihren Ausweis bei ~? do you have your pass on you?; er hat nichts bei ~ he's got nothing on him; sie bleiben gern unter ~ they keep themselves to themselves

4 (einander) each other, one another; sie bekämpfen ~ they fight each other od one another

5: dieses Auto fährt ~ gut this car drives well; hier sitzt es ~ gut it's good to sit here.

Sichel ['zɪçəl] f -, -n sickle; (Mond~) crescent.

sicher ['zɪçər] a safe (vor +dat from); (gewiß) certain (+gen of); (zuverlässig) secure, reliable; (selbst~) confident; ich bin nicht ~ I'm not sure od certain; ~ nicht surely not; aber ~! of course; ~gehen vi unreg make sure.

Sicherheit ['zɪçərhaɪt] f safety; security (auch FIN); (Gewißheit) certainty; (Selbst~) confidence.

Sicherheits- zW: ~abstand m safe distance; ~glas nt safety glass; ~gurt m safety belt; s~halber ad for safety; to be on the safe side; ~nadel f safety pin; ~vorkehrung f safety precaution.

sicher- zW: ~lich ad certainly, surely; ~n vt secure; (schützen) protect; (Waffe) put the safety catch on; jdm/sich etw ~n secure sth for sb/for o.s.; ~stellen vt impound; (COMPUT) save; S~ung f (Sichern) securing; (Vorrichtung) safety device; (an Waffen) safety catch; (ELEK) fuse; S~ungskopie f back-up copy.

Sicht [zɪçt] f - sight; (Aus~) view; auf od nach ~ (FIN) at sight; auf lange ~ on a long-term basis; s~bar a visible; ~en vt sight; (auswählen) sort out; s~lich a evident, obvious; ~verhältnisse pl visibility; ~vermerk m visa.

sickern ['zɪkərn] vi trickle, seep.

Sie [zi:] pron sing, pl, nom, akk you.

sie [zi:] pron sing nom she // akk her // pl nom they // akk them.

Sieb [zi:p] nt -(e)s, -e sieve; (KOCH) strainer; s~en ['zi:bən] vt sift; (Flüssigkeit) strain.

sieben ['zi:bən] *num* seven; ~**hundert** *num* seven hundred; **S~sachen** *pl* belongings *pl*.

siebte(r, s) ['zi:ptə(r,s)] *a* seventh; **Siebtel** *nt* -s, - seventh.

siebzehn ['zi:ptse:n] *num* seventeen.

siebzig ['zi:ptsɪç] *num* seventy.

sied- [zi:d] *zW*: ~**en** *vti* boil, simmer; **Siedepunkt** *m* boiling point; **S~lung** *f* settlement; (*Häuser~lung*) housing estate.

Sieg [zi:k] *m* -(e)s, -e victory.

Siegel ['zi:gəl] *nt* -s, - seal; ~**lack** *m* sealing wax; ~**ring** *m* signet ring.

Sieg- *zW*: **s~en** *vi* be victorious; (*SPORT*) win; ~**er** *m* -s, - victor; (*SPORT etc*) winner; **siegessicher** *a* sure of victory; **s~reich** *a* victorious.

siehe [zi:ə] (*Imperativ*) see.

siehst *etc* v **siehe sehen**.

siezen ['zi:tsən] *vt* address as 'Sie'.

Signal [zɪ'gna:l] *nt* -s, -e signal.

Silbe ['zɪlbə] *f* -, -n syllable.

Silber ['zɪlbər] *nt* -s silver; **s~n** *a* silver; ~**papier** *nt* silver paper.

Silhouette [zilu'ɛtə] *f* silhouette.

Silo ['zi:lo] *nt od m* -s, -s silo.

Silvester(abend *m***)** [zɪl'vɛstər(a:bənt)] *nt* -s, - New Year's Eve, Hogmanay (*Scot*).

simpel ['zɪmpəl] *a* simple.

Sims [zɪms] *nt od m* -es, -e (*Kamin~*) mantelpiece; (*Fenster~*) (window)-sill.

simulieren [zimu'li:rən] *vti* simulate; (*vortäuschen*) feign.

simultan [zimul'ta:n] *a* simultaneous.

Sinfonie [zɪnfo'ni:] *f* symphony.

singen ['zɪŋən] *vti unreg* sing.

Singular ['zɪŋgula:r] *m* singular.

Singvogel ['zɪŋfo:gəl] *m* songbird.

sinken ['zɪŋkən] *vi unreg* sink; (*Preise etc*) fall, go down.

Sinn [zɪn] *m* -(e)s, -e mind; (*Wahrnehmungs~*) sense; (*Bedeutung*) sense, meaning; ~ **für etw** sense of sth; **von ~en sein** be out of one's mind; **es hat keinen ~** there's no point; ~**bild** *nt* symbol; **s~en** *vi unreg* ponder; **auf etw** (*akk*) **s~en** contemplate sth; **Sinnestäuschung** *f* illusion; **s~gemäß** *a* faithful; (*Wiedergabe*) in one's own words; **s~ig** *a* clever; **s~lich** *a* sensual, sensuous; (*Wahrnehmung*) sensory; ~**lichkeit** *f* sensuality; **s~los** *a* senseless; meaningless; ~**losigkeit** *f* senselessness; meaninglessness; **s~voll** *a* meaningful; (*vernünftig*) sensible.

Sintflut ['zɪntflu:t] *f* Flood.

Siphon [zi'fõ:] *m* -s, -e siphon.

Sippe ['zɪpə] *f* -, -n clan, kin.

Sippschaft ['zɪpʃaft] *f* (*pej*) relations *pl*, tribe; (*Bande*) gang.

Sirene [zi're:nə] *f* -, -n siren.

Sirup ['zi:rup] *m* -s, -e syrup.

Sitt- [zɪt] *zW*: ~**e** *f* -, -n custom // *pl* morals *pl*; **Sittenpolizei** *f* vice squad; **s~lich** *a* moral; ~**lichkeit** *f* morality; ~**lichkeitsverbrechen** *nt* sex offence; **s~sam** *a* modest, demure.

Situation [zituatsi'o:n] *f* situation.

Sitz [zɪts] *m* -es, -e seat; **der Anzug hat einen guten** ~ the suit is a good fit; **s~en** *vi unreg* sit; (*Bemerkung, Schlag*) strike home, tell; (*Gelerntes*) have sunk in; **s~en bleiben** remain seated; **s~enbleiben** *vi unreg* (*SCH*) have to repeat a year; **auf etw** (*dat*) **s~enbleiben** be lumbered with sth; **s~end** *a* (*Tätigkeit*) sedentary; **s~enlassen** *vt unreg* (*SCH*) make (*sb*) repeat a year; (*Mädchen*) jilt; (*Wartenden*) stand up; **etw auf sich** (*dat*) **s~enlassen** take sth lying down; ~**gelegenheit** *f* place to sit down; ~**platz** *m* seat; ~**streik** *m* sit-down strike; ~**ung** *f* meeting.

Sizilien [zi'tsi:liən] *nt* Sicily.

Skala ['ska:la] *f* -, **Skalen** scale.

Skalpell [skal'pɛl] *nt* -s, -e scalpel.

Skandal [skan'da:l] *m* -s, -e scandal; **s~ös** [skanda'lø:s] *a* scandalous.

Skandinav- [skandi'na:v] *zW*: ~**ien** [-iən] *nt* Scandinavia; ~**ier(in** *f***)** *m* Scandinavian; **s~isch** *a* Scandinavian.

Skelett [ske'lɛt] *nt* -(e)s, -e skeleton.

Skepsis ['skɛpsɪs] *f* - scepticism.

skeptisch ['skɛptɪʃ] *a* sceptical.

Ski, Schi [ʃi:] *m* -s, -er ski; ~ **laufen** *od* **fahren** ski; ~**fahrer** *m*, ~**läufer** *m* skier; ~**lehrer** *m* ski instructor; ~**lift** *m* ski-lift; ~**springen** *nt* ski-jumping; ~**stock** *m* ski-pole.

Skizze ['skɪtsə] *f* -, -n sketch.

skizzieren [skɪ'tsi:rən] *vti* sketch.

Sklave ['skla:və] *m* -n, -n, **Sklavin** *f* slave; ~**rei** *f* slavery.

Skonto ['skɔnto] *m od nt* -s, -s discount.

Skorpion [skɔrpi'o:n] *m* -s, -e scorpion; (*ASTROL*) Scorpio.

Skrupel ['skru:pəl] *m* -s, - scruple; **s~los** *a* unscrupulous.

Slalom ['sla:lɔm] *m* -s, -s slalom.

Smaragd [sma'rakt] *m* -(e)s, -e emerald.

Smoking ['smo:kɪŋ] *m* -s, -s dinner jacket.

s.o. *abk* = **siehe oben**.

so [zo:] ♦ *ad* **1** (*~sehr*) so; ~ **groß/schön** *etc* so big/nice *etc*; ~ **groß/schön wie ...** as big/nice as ...; **das hat ihn** ~ **geärgert, daß ...** that annoyed him so much that ...; ~ **einer wie ich** somebody like me; **na** ~ **was!** well, well!

2 (*auf diese Weise*) like this; **mach es nicht** ~ don't do it like that; ~

oder ~ in one way or the other; **und ~ weiter** and so on; **... oder ~ was ...** or something like that; **das ist gut ~** that's fine

3 (*umg: umsonst*): **ich habe es ~ bekommen** I got it for nothing

◆*kj:* ~ **daß** so that; ~ **wie es jetzt ist** as things are at the moment

◆*interj:* ~? really?; ~, **das wär's so,** that's it then.

sobald [zo'balt] *kj* as soon as.

Socke ['zɔkə] *f* -, -n sock.

Sockel ['zɔkəl] *m* -s, - pedestal, base.

Sodawasser ['zo:davasər] *nt* soda water.

Sodbrennen ['zo:tbrɛnən] *nt* -s, - heartburn.

soeben [zo''e:bən] *ad* just (now).

Sofa ['zo:fa] *nt* -s, -s sofa.

sofern [zo'fɛrn] *kj* if, provided (that).

sofort [zo'fɔrt] *ad* immediately, at once; ~**ig** *a* immediate.

Software ['sɔftwɛər] *f* software.

so- *zW:* ~**gar** [zo'ga:r] *ad* even; ~**genannt** ['zo:gənant] *a* so-called; ~**gleich** [zo'glaɪç] *ad* straight away, at once.

Sohle ['zo:lə] *f* -, -n sole; (*Tal~ etc*) bottom; (*MIN*) level.

Sohn [zo:n] *m* -(e)s, -e son.

solang(e) [zo'laŋ(ə)] *kj* as *od* so long as.

solch [zɔlç] *pron* such; **ein ~e(r, s)...** such a...

Sold [zɔlt] *m* -(e)s, -e pay; **Soldat** [zɔl'da:t] *m* -en, -en soldier.

Söldner ['zœldnər] *m* -s, - mercenary.

solid(e) [zo'li:d(ə)] *a* solid; (*Leben, Person*) respectable; ~**arisch** [zoli'da:rɪʃ] *a* in/with solidarity; **sich ~arisch erklären** declare one's solidarity.

Solist(in *f*) [zo'lɪst(ɪn)] *m* soloist.

Soll [zɔl] *nt* -(s), -(s) (*FIN*) debit (side); (*Arbeitsmenge*) quota, target.

sollen ['zɔlən] ◆(*als Hilfsverb*) *pt* **sollte,** *ptp* **sollen 1** (*Pflicht, Befehl*) be supposed to; **du hättest nicht gehen ~** you shouldn't have gone, you oughtn't to have gone; **soll ich?** shall I?; **soll ich dir helfen?** shall I help you?; **sag ihm, er soll warten** tell him he's to wait; **was soll ich machen?** what should I do?

2 (*Vermutung*): **sie soll verheiratet sein** she's said to be married; **was soll das heißen?** what's that supposed to mean?; **man sollte glauben, daß ...** you would think that ...; **sollte das passieren, ...** if that should happen ...

◆*vti pt* **sollte,** *ptp* **gesollt: was soll das?** what's all this?; **das sollst du nicht** you shouldn't do that; **was soll's?** what the hell!

Solo ['zo:lo] *nt* -s, -s *od* **Soli** solo.

somit [zo'mɪt] *kj* and so, therefore.

Sommer ['zɔmər] *m* -s, - summer; **s~lich** *a* summery; summer; ~**schlußverkauf** *m* summer sale; ~**sprossen** *pl* freckles *pl*.

Sonate [zo'na:tə] *f* -, -n sonata.

Sonde ['zɔndə] *f* -, -n probe.

Sonder- ['zɔndər] *in zW* special; ~**angebot** *nt* special offer; **s~bar** *a* strange, odd; ~**fahrt** *f* special trip; ~**fall** *m* special case; **s~gleichen** *a inv* without parallel, unparalleled; **s~lich** *a* particular; (*außergewöhnlich*) remarkable; (*eigenartig*) peculiar; **s~n** *kj* but; **nicht nur ...,** **s~n auch** not only..., but also // *vt* separate; ~**preis** *m* special price; ~**zug** *m* special train.

Sonett [zo'nɛt] *nt* -(e)s, -e sonnet.

Sonnabend ['zɔn'a:bənt] *m* Saturday.

Sonne ['zɔnə] *f* -, -n sun; **s~n** *vr* sun oneself.

Sonnen- *zW:* ~**aufgang** *m* sunrise; **s~baden** *vi* sunbathe; ~**brand** *m* sunburn; ~**brille** *f* sunglasses *pl*; ~**creme** *f* suntan lotion; ~**energie** *f* solar energy; ~**finsternis** *f* solar eclipse; ~**schein** *m* sunshine; ~**schirm** *m* parasol, sunshade; ~**stich** *m* sunstroke; ~**uhr** *f* sundial; ~**untergang** *m* sunset; ~**wende** *f* solstice.

sonnig ['zɔnɪç] *a* sunny.

Sonntag ['zɔnta:k] *m* Sunday; **s~s** *ad* (on) Sundays.

sonst [zɔnst] *ad* otherwise (*auch kj*); (*mit pron, in Fragen*) else; (*zu anderer Zeit*) at other times, normally; ~ **noch etwas?** anything else?; ~ **nichts** nothing else; ~**ig** *a* other; ~**jemand** *pron* anybody (at all); ~**wo(hin)** *ad* somewhere else; ~**woher** *ad* from somewhere else.

sooft [zo''ɔft] *kj* whenever.

Sopran [zo'pra:n] *m* -s, -e soprano.

Sorge ['zɔrgə] *f* -, care, worry.

sorgen *vi:* **für jdn ~** look after sb; **für etw ~** take care of *od* see to sth // *vr* worry (*um* about); ~**frei** *a* carefree; **S~kind** *nt* problem child; ~**voll** *a* troubled, worried.

Sorgerecht *nt* custody (of a child).

Sorg- [zɔrk] *zW:* ~**falt** *f* - care(fulness); **s~fältig** *a* careful; **s~los** *a* careless; (*ohne Sorgen*) carefree; **s~sam** *a* careful.

Sorte ['zɔrtə] *f* -, -n sort; (*Waren~*) brand; ~**n** *pl* (*FIN*) foreign currency.

sortieren [zɔr'ti:rən] *vt* sort (out).

Sortiment [zɔrti'mɛnt] *nt* assortment.

sosehr [zo'ze:r] *kj* as much as.

Soße ['zo:sə] *f* -, -n sauce; (*Braten~*) gravy.

Souffleur [zu'flø:r] *m*, **Souffleuse**

[zu'fløːzə] f prompter.

soufflieren [zu'fliːrən] vti prompt.

souverän [zuvə'rɛːn] a sovereign; (überlegen) superior.

so- zW: ~**viel** [zo'fiːl] kj: ~**viel ich weiß** as far as I know // pron as much (wie as); **rede nicht ~viel** don't talk so much; ~**weit** [zo'vaɪt] kj as far as // a: ~**weit sein** to be ready; ~**weit wie** od **als möglich** as far as possible; **ich bin ~weit zufrieden** by and large I'm quite satisfied; ~**wenig** [zo'veːnɪç] kj little as // pron as little (wie as); ~**wie** [zo'viː] kj (sobald) as soon as; (ebenso) as well as; ~**wieso** [zovi'zoː] ad anyway.

Sowjet- [zɔ'vjet] zW: **s~isch** a Soviet; ~**union** f Soviet Union.

sowohl [zo'voːl] kj: ~ ... **als** od **wie auch** both ... and.

sozial [zotsi'aːl] a social; **S~abgaben** pl national insurance contributions pl; **S~demokrat** m social democrat; ~**demokratisch** a social democratic; ~**i'sieren** vt socialize; **S~ismus** [-'lɪsmʊs] m socialism; **S~ist** [-'lɪst] m socialist; ~**istisch** a socialist; **S~politik** f social welfare policy; **S~produkt** nt (gross/net) national product; **S~staat** m welfare state.

Sozio- [zotsiɔ] zW: ~**loge** [-'loːgə] m -n, -n sociologist; ~**logie** [-lo'giː] f sociology; **s~logisch** [-'loːgɪʃ] a sociological.

sozusagen [zotsu'zaːgən] ad so to speak.

Spachtel ['ʃpaxtəl] m -s, - spatula.

spähen ['ʃpɛːən] vi peep, peek.

Spalier [ʃpa'liːr] nt -s, -e (Gerüst) trellis; (Leute) guard of honour.

Spalt [ʃpalt] m -(e)s, -e crack; (Tür~) chink; (fig: Kluft) split; ~**e** f -, -n crack, fissure; (Gletscher~) crevasse; (in Text) column; **s~en** vtr (lit, fig) split; ~**ung** f splitting.

Span [ʃpaːn] m -(e)s, ⁻e shaving; ~**ferkel** nt sucking-pig; ~**ien** nt Spain; ~**ier(in** f) m Spaniard; **s~isch** a Spanish.

Spange ['ʃpaŋə] f -, -n clasp; (Haar~) hair slide; (Schnalle) buckle; (Armreif) bangle.

Spann- ['ʃpan] zW: ~**beton** m prestressed concrete; ~**e** f -, -n (Zeit~e) space; (Differenz) gap; **s~en** vt (straffen) tighten, tauten; (befestigen) brace // vi be tight; **s~end** a exciting, gripping; ~**ung** f tension; (ELEK) voltage; (fig) suspense; (unangenehm) tension.

Spar- ['ʃpaːr] zW: ~**buch** nt savings book; ~**büchse** f moneybox; **s~en** vti save; **sich** (dat) **etw s~en** save oneself sth; (Bemerkung) keep sth to oneself; **mit etw** (dat) **s~en** be spar-

ing with sth; **an etw** (dat) **s~en** economize on sth; ~**er** m -s, - saver.

Spargel ['ʃpargəl] m -s, - asparagus.

Spar- zW: ~**kasse** f savings bank; ~**konto** nt savings account.

spärlich ['ʃpɛːrlɪç] a meagre; (Bekleidung) scanty.

Spar- zW: ~**maßnahme** f economy measure, cut; **s~sam** a economical, thrifty; ~**samkeit** f thrift, economizing; ~**schwein** nt piggy bank.

Sparte ['ʃpartə] f -, -n field; line of business; (PRESSE) column.

Spaß [ʃpaːs] m -es, ⁻e joke; (Freude) fun; **jdm ~ machen** be fun (for sb); **viel ~!** have fun!; ~**s~ mit ihm ist nicht zu s~en** you can't take liberties with him; **s~haft, s~ig** a funny, droll; ~**verderber** m -s, - spoilsport.

spät [ʃpɛːt] a, ad late; **wie ~ ist es?** what's the time?

Spaten ['ʃpaːtən] m -s, - spade.

spät- zW: ~**er** a, ad later; ~**estens** ad at the latest.

Spatz [ʃpats] m -en, -en sparrow.

spazier- [ʃpa'tsiːr] zW: ~**en** vi stroll, walk; ~**enfahren** vi unreg go for a drive; ~**engehen** vi unreg go for a walk; **S~gang** m walk; **S~stock** m walking stick; **S~weg** m path, walk.

SPD [ɛspeː'deː] f abk (= Sozialdemokratische Partei Deutschlands) Social Democratic Party.

Specht [ʃpɛçt] m -(e)s, -e woodpecker.

Speck [ʃpɛk] m -(e)s, -e bacon.

Spediteur [ʃpedi'tøːr] m carrier; (Möbel~) furniture remover.

Spedition [ʃpeditsi'oːn] f carriage; (~sfirma) road haulage contractor; removal firm.

Speer [ʃpeːr] m -(e)s, -e spear; (SPORT) javelin.

Speiche ['ʃpaɪçə] f -, -n spoke.

Speichel ['ʃpaɪçəl] m -s saliva, spit(tle).

Speicher ['ʃpaɪçər] m -s, - storehouse; (Dach~) attic, loft; (Korn~) granary; (Wasser~) tank; (TECH) store; (COMPUT) memory; **s~n** vt store; (COMPUT) save.

speien ['ʃpaɪən] vti unreg spit; (erbrechen) vomit; (Vulkan) spew.

Speise ['ʃpaɪzə] f -, -n food; ~**eis** ['-'aɪs] nt ice-cream; ~**kammer** f larder, pantry; ~**karte** f menu; **s~n** vt feed; eat // vi dine; ~**röhre** f gullet, oesophagus; ~**saal** m dining room; ~**wagen** m dining car.

Speku- [ʃpeku] zW: ~**lant** [-'lant] m speculator; ~**lation** [-latsi'oːn] f speculation; **s~lieren** [-'liːrən] vi (fig) speculate; **auf etw** (akk) **s~lieren** have hopes of sth.

Spelunke [ʃpe'lʊŋkə] f -, -n dive.

Spende ['ʃpɛndə] f -, -n donation; s~n vt donate, give; ~r m -s, - donor, donator.

spendieren [ʃpɛn'diːrən] vt pay for, buy; jdm etw ~ treat sb to sth, stand sb sth.

Sperling ['ʃpɛrlɪŋ] m sparrow.

Sperma ['ʃpɛrma] nt -s, **Spermen** sperm.

Sperr- ['ʃpɛr] zW: ~e f -, -n barrier; (Verbot) ban; s~en vt block; (SPORT) suspend, bar; (vom Ball) obstruct; (einschließen) lock; (verbieten) ban // vr baulk, jib(e); ~gebiet nt prohibited area; ~holz nt plywood; s~ig a bulky; ~sitz m (THEAT) stalls pl; ~stunde f closing time.

Spesen ['ʃpeːzən] pl expenses pl; ~abrechnung f expense account.

Spezial- [ʃpetsi'aːl] in zW special; s~angefertigt a custom-built; (Kleidung) tailor-made; s~i'sieren vr specialize; ~i'sierung f specialization; ~ist [-'lɪst] m specialist; ~i'tät f speciality.

speziell [ʃpetsi'ɛl] a special.

spezifisch [ʃpe'tsiːfɪʃ] a specific.

Sphäre ['sfɛːrə] f -, -n sphere.

Spiegel ['ʃpiːgəl] m -s, - mirror; (Wasser~) level; (MIL) tab; ~bild nt reflection; s~bildlich a reversed; ~ei ['-'aı] nt fried egg; s~n vt mirror, reflect // vr be reflected // vi gleam; (wider~n) be reflective; ~schrift f mirror-writing; ~ung f reflection.

Spiel [ʃpiːl] nt -(e)s, -e game; (Schau~) play; (Tätigkeit) play(ing); (KARTEN) deck; (TECH) (free) play; s~en vti play; (um Geld) gamble; (THEAT) perform, act; s~end ad easily; ~er m -s, - player; (um Geld) gambler; ~e'rei f trifling pastime; ~feld nt pitch, field; ~film m feature film; ~plan m (THEAT) programme; ~platz m playground; ~raum m room to manoeuvre, scope; ~regel f rule; ~sachen pl toys pl; ~verderber m -s, - spoilsport; ~waren pl, ~zeug nt toys pl.

Spieß [ʃpiːs] m -es, -e spear; (Brat~) spit; ~bürger m, ~er m -s, - bourgeois; ~rutenlaufen nt running the gauntlet.

Spikes [spaıks] pl spikes pl; (AUT) studs pl.

Spinat [ʃpi'naːt] m -(e)s, -e spinach.

Spind [ʃpɪnt] m od nt -(e)s, -e locker.

Spinn- [ʃpɪn] zW: ~e f -, -n spider; s~en vti unreg spin; (umg) talk rubbish; (verrückt) be crazy od mad; ~e'rei f spinning mill; ~rad nt spinning-wheel; ~webe f cobweb.

Spion [ʃpi'oːn] m -s, -e spy; (in Tür)

spyhole; ~age [ʃpio'naːʒə] f -, -n espionage; s~ieren [ʃpio'niːrən] vi spy.

Spirale [ʃpi'raːlə] f -, -n spiral.

Spirituosen [ʃpiritu'oːzən] pl spirits pl.

Spiritus ['ʃpiːritʊs] m -, -se (methylated) spirit.

Spital [ʃpi'taːl] nt -s, ⁻er hospital.

spitz [ʃpɪts] a pointed; (Winkel) acute; (fig: Zunge) sharp; (: Bemerkung) caustic; S~bogen m pointed arch; S~bube m rogue; S~e f -, -n point, tip; (Berg~) peak; (Bemerkung) taunt, dig; (erster Platz) lead, top; (meist pl: Gewebe) lace; S~el m -s, - police informer; ~en vt sharpen.

Spitzen- zW: ~leistung f top performance; ~lohn m top wages pl; ~marke f brand leader; ~sportler m top-class sportsman.

spitzfindig a (over)subtle.

Spitzname m nickname.

Splitter ['ʃplɪtər] m -s, - splinter; s~nackt a stark naked.

sponsern ['sponzərn, 'ʃponzərn] vt sponsor.

spontan [ʃpon'taːn] a spontaneous.

Sport ['ʃport] m -(e)s, -e sport; (fig) hobby; ~lehrer(in f) m games od P.E. teacher; ~ler(in f) m -s, - sportsman/woman; s~lich a sporting; (Mensch) sporty; ~platz m playing od sports field; ~verein m sports club; ~wagen m sports car.

Spott [ʃpot] m -(e)s mockery, ridicule; s~billig a dirt-cheap; s~en vi mock (über +akk at), ridicule.

spöttisch ['ʃpœtɪʃ] a mocking.

sprach etc v siehe **sprechen**.

Sprach- ['ʃpraːx] zW: s~begabt a good at languages; ~e f -, -n language; ~fehler m speech defect; ~führer m phrasebook; ~gefühl nt feeling for language; ~labor nt language laboratory; s~lich a linguistic; s~los a speechless.

sprang etc v siehe **springen**.

Spray [spreː] m od nt -s, -s spray.

Sprech- ['ʃprɛç] zW: ~anlage f intercom; s~en unreg vi speak, talk (mit to); das spricht für ihn that's a point in his favour // vt say; (Sprache) speak; (Person) speak to; ~er(in f) m -s, - speaker; (für Gruppe) spokesman; (RAD, TV) announcer; ~stunde f consultation (hour); (doctor's) surgery; ~stundenhilfe f (doctor's) receptionist; ~zimmer nt consulting room, surgery.

Spreng- ['ʃprɛŋ] zW: ~arbeiten pl blasting operations pl; s~en vt sprinkle; (mit Sprengstoff) blow up; (Gestein) blast; (Versammlung) break up; **~kopf** *m* warhead; **~ladung** *f* explosive charge; **~stoff** *m* explosive(s).

Spreu [ʃprɔy] *f* - chaff.

sprichst *etc v siehe* **sprechen.**

Sprich- ['ʃpriç] *zW:* **~wort** *nt* proverb; **s~wörtlich** *a* proverbial.

Spring- ['ʃpriŋ] *zW:* **~brunnen** *m* fountain; **s~en** *vi unreg* jump; (*Glas*) crack; (*mit Kopfsprung*) dive; **~er** *m* **-s,** - jumper; (*Schach*) knight.

Spritz- ['ʃprits] *zW:* **~e** *f* -, **-n** syringe; injection; (*an Schlauch*) nozzle; **s~en** *vt* spray; (*MED*) inject / *vi* splash; (*heraus~en*) spurt; (*MED*) give injections; **~pistole** *f* spray gun.

spröde ['ʃprøːdə] *a* brittle; (*Person*) reserved, coy.

Sprosse ['ʃprɔsə] *f* -, **-n** rung.

Spruch [ʃprux] *m* **-(e)s,** ⁻e saying, maxim; (*JUR*) judgement.

Sprudel ['ʃpruːdəl] *m* **-s,** - mineral water; lemonade; **s~n** *vi* bubble.

Sprüh- ['ʃpryː] *zW:* **~dose** *f* aerosol (can); **s~en** *vti* spray; (*fig*) sparkle; **~regen** *m* drizzle.

Sprung [ʃprʊŋ] *m* **-(e)s,** ⁻e jump; (*Riß*) crack; **~brett** *nt* springboard; **s~haft** *a* erratic; (*Aufstieg*) rapid; **~schanze** *f* skijump.

Spucke ['ʃpʊkə] *f* - spit; **s~n** *vti* spit.

Spuk [ʃpuːk] *m* **-(e)s,** **-e** haunting; (*fig*) nightmare; **s~en** *vi* (*Geist*) walk; **hier spukt es** this place is haunted.

Spule ['ʃpuːlə] *f* -, **-n** spool; (*ELEK*) coil.

Spül- ['ʃpyːl] *zW:* **~e** *f* -, **-n** (kitchen) sink; **s~en** *vti* rinse; (*Geschirr*) wash up; (*Toilette*) flush; **~maschine** *f* dishwasher; **~mittel** *nt* washing-up liquid; **~stein** *m* sink; **~ung** *f* rinsing; flush; (*MED*) irrigation.

Spur [ʃpuːr] *f* -, **-en** trace; (*Fuß~, Rad~, Tonband~*) track; (*Fährte*) trail; (*Fahr~*) lane.

spür- ['ʃpyːr] *zW:* **~bar** *a* noticeable, perceptible; **~en** *vt* feel.

spurlos *ad* without (a) trace.

Spurt [ʃpʊrt] *m* **-(e)s,** **-s** *od* **-e** spurt.

sputen ['ʃpuːtən] *vr* make haste.

St. *abk von* **Stück** // *abk* (= *Sankt*) St.

Staat [ʃtaːt] *m* **-(e)s,** **-en** state; (*Prunk*) show; (*Kleidung*) finery; **mit etw ~ machen** show off *od* parade sth; **s~enlos** *a* stateless; **s~lich** *a* state(-); state-run.

Staats- *zW:* **~angehörigkeit** *f* nationality; **~anwalt** *m* public prosecutor; **~bürger** *m* citizen; **~dienst** *m* civil service; **s~feindlich** *a* subversive; **~mann,** *pl* **-männer** statesman; **~sekretär** *m* secretary of state.

Stab [ʃtaːp] *m* **-(e)s,** ⁻e rod; (*Gitter~*) bar; (*Menschen*) staff; **~hochsprung** *m* pole vault; **stabil** *a* stable; (*Möbel*) sturdy; **stabili'sieren** *vt* stabilize.

Stachel ['ʃtaxəl] *m* **-s,** **-n** spike; (*von Tier*) spine; (*von Insekten*) sting; **~beere** *f* gooseberry; **~draht** *m* barbed wire; **s~ig** *a* prickly; **~schwein** *nt* porcupine.

Stadion ['ʃtaːdiɔn] *nt* **-s,** **Stadien** stadium.

Stadium ['ʃtaːdiʊm] *nt* stage, phase.

Stadt [ʃtat] *f* -, ⁻e town.

Städt- ['ʃtɛːt] *zW:* **~chen** *nt* small town; **Städtebau** *m* town planning; **~er(in** *f*) *m* **-s,** - town dweller; **s~isch** *a* municipal; (*nicht ländlich*) urban.

Stadt- *zW:* **~mauer** *f* city wall(s); **~mitte** *f* town centre; **~plan** *m* street map; **~rand** *m* outskirts *pl*; **~rundfahrt** *f* tour of a/the city; **~teil** *m* district, part of town; **~zentrum** *nt* town centre.

Staffel ['ʃtafəl] *f* -, **-n** rung; (*SPORT*) relay (team); (*AVIAT*) squadron; **s~n** *vt* graduate.

stahl *etc v siehe* **stehlen.**

Stahl [ʃtaːl] *m* **-(e)s,** ⁻e steel.

stak *etc v siehe* **stecken.**

Stall [ʃtal] *m* **-(e)s,** ⁻e stable; (*Kaninchen~*) hutch; (*Schweine~*) sty; (*Hühner~*) henhouse.

Stamm [ʃtam] *m* **-(e)s,** ⁻e (*Baum~*) trunk; (*Menschen~*) tribe; (*GRAM*) stem; **~baum** *m* family tree; (*von Tier*) pedigree; **s~eln** *vti* stammer; **s~en** *vi:* **s~en von** *od* **aus** come from; **~gast** *m* regular (customer).

stämmig ['ʃtɛmiç] *a* sturdy; (*Mensch*) stocky.

Stammtisch ['ʃtamtiʃ] *m* table for the regulars.

stampfen ['ʃtampfən] *vti* stamp; (*stapfen*) tramp; (*mit Werkzeug*) pound.

stand *etc v siehe* **stehen.**

Stand [ʃtant] *m* **-(e)s,** ⁻e position; (*Wasser~, Benzin~ etc*) level; (*Stehen*) standing position; (*Zustand*) state; (*Spiel~*) score; (*Messe~ etc*) stand; (*Klasse*) class; (*Beruf*) profession.

Standard ['ʃtandart] *m* **-s,** **-s** standard.

Ständer ['ʃtɛndər] *m* **-s,** - stand.

Standes- ['ʃtandəs] *zW:* **~amt** *nt* registry office; **~beamte(r)** *m* registrar; **s~gemäß** *a, ad* according to one's social position; **~unterschied** *m* social difference.

Stand- *zW:* **s~haft** *a* steadfast; **~haftigkeit** *f* steadfastness; **s~halten** *vi unreg* stand firm (*jdm/etw* against sb/sth), resist (*jdm/etw* sb/sth).

ständig ['ʃtɛndɪç] *a* permanent; (*ununterbrochen*) constant, continual.

Stand- *zW:* ~**licht** *nt* sidelights *pl*, parking lights *pl* (*US*); ~**ort** *m* location; (*MIL*) garrison; ~**punkt** *m* standpoint.

Stange ['ʃtaŋə] *f* -, -n stick; (*Stab*) pole, bar; rod; (*Zigaretten*) carton; **von der ~** (*COMM*) off the peg; **eine ~ Geld** quite a packet.

Stanniol [ʃtani'oːl] *nt* -s, -e tinfoil.

Stapel ['ʃtaːpəl] *m* -s, - pile; (*NAUT*) stocks *pl*; ~**lauf** *m* launch; **s~n** *vt* pile (up).

Star [ʃtaːr] *m* -(e)s, -e starling; (*MED*) cataract // *m* -s, -s (*Film etc*) star.

starb *etc v siehe* **sterben**.

stark [ʃtark] *a* strong; (*heftig, groß*) heavy; (*Maßangabe*) thick.

Stärke ['ʃtɛrkə] *f* -, -n strength; heaviness; thickness; (*KOCH, Wäsche~*) starch; **s~n** *vt* strengthen; (*Wäsche*) starch.

Starkstrom *m* heavy current.

Stärkung ['ʃtɛrkʊŋ] *f* strengthening; (*Essen*) refreshment.

starr [ʃtar] *a* stiff; (*unnachgiebig*) rigid; (*Blick*) staring; ~**en** *vi* stare; ~**en vor** *od* **von** be covered in; (*Waffen*) be bristling with; **S~heit** *f* rigidity; ~**köpfig** *a* stubborn; **S~sinn** *m* obstinacy.

Start [ʃtart] *m* -(e)s, -e start; (*AVIAT*) takeoff; ~**automatik** *f* (*AUT*) automatic choke; ~**bahn** *f* runway; **s~en** *vti* start; take off; ~**er** *m* -s, - starter; ~**erlaubnis** *f* takeoff clearance.

Station [ʃtatsi'oːn] *f* station; hospital ward; **s~ieren** [-'niːrən] *vt* station.

Statist [ʃta'tɪst] *m* extra, supernumerary; ~**ik** *f* statistics; ~**iker** *m* -s, - statistician; **s~isch** *a* statistical.

Stativ [ʃta'tiːf] *nt* -s, -e tripod.

statt [ʃtat] *kj, präp* +*gen od dat* instead of.

Stätte ['ʃtɛtə] *f* -, -n place.

statt- *zW:* ~**finden** *vi unreg* take place; ~**haft** *a* admissible; ~**lich** *a* imposing, handsome.

Statue ['ʃtaːtuə] *f* -, -n statue.

Status ['ʃtaːtʊs] *m* -, - status; ~**symbol** *nt* status symbol.

Statuten [ʃta'tuːtən] *pl* rules *pl*.

Stau [ʃtaʊ] *m* -(e)s, -e blockage; (*Verkehrs~*) (traffic) jam.

Staub [ʃtaʊp] *m* -(e)s dust; **s~en** ['ʃtaʊbən] *vi* be dusty; **s~ig** *a* dusty; ~**sauger** *m* vacuum cleaner; ~**tuch** *nt* duster.

Staudamm *m* dam.

Staude ['ʃtaʊdə] *f* -, -n shrub.

stauen ['ʃtaʊən] *vt* (*Wasser*) dam up; (*Blut*) stop the flow of // *vr* (*Wasser*) become dammed up; (*MED, Verkehr*)

become congested; (*Menschen*) collect together; (*Gefühle*) build up.

staunen ['ʃtaʊnən] *vi* be astonished; **S~** *nt* -s amazement.

Stauung ['ʃtaʊʊŋ] *f* (*von Wasser*) damming-up; (*von Blut, Verkehr*) congestion.

Std. *abk* (= *Stunde*) hr.

Steak [steːk] *nt* steak.

Stech- ['ʃtɛç] *zW:* **s~en** *vt unreg* (*mit Nadel etc*) prick; (*mit Messer*) stab; (*mit Finger*) poke; (*Biene etc*) sting; (*Mücke*) bite; (*Sonne*) burn; (*KARTEN*) take; (*ART*) engrave; (*Torf, Spargel*) cut; **in See s~en** put to sea; ~**en** *nt* -s, - (*SPORT*) play-off; jump-off; **s~end** *a* piercing, stabbing; (*Geruch*) pungent; ~**palme** *f* holly; ~**uhr** *f* time clock.

Steck- ['ʃtɛk] *zW:* ~**brief** *m* 'wanted' poster; ~**dose** *f* (wall) socket; **s~en** *vt* put, insert; (*Nadel*) stick; (*Pflanzen*) plant; (*beim Nähen*) pin // *vi* (*auch unreg*) be; (*festsitzen*) be stuck; (*Nadeln*) stick; **s~enbleiben** *vi unreg* get stuck; **s~enlassen** *vt unreg* leave in; ~**enpferd** *nt* hobby-horse; ~**er** *m* -s, - plug; ~**nadel** *f* pin; ~**rübe** *f* turnip.

Steg [ʃteːk] *m* -(e)s, -e small bridge; (*Anlege~*) landing stage; ~**reif** *m*: **aus dem ~reif** just like that.

stehen ['ʃteːən] *unreg vi* stand (*zu* by); (*sich befinden*) be; (*in Zeitung*) say; (*still~*) have stopped; **jdm ~** suit sb // *vi unpers*: **es steht schlecht um** things are bad for; **wie steht's?** how are things?; (*SPORT*) what's the score?; **~ bleiben** remain standing; ~**bleiben** *vi unreg* (*Uhr*) stop; (*Fehler*) stay as it is; ~**lassen** *vt unreg* leave; (*Bart*) grow.

Stehlampe ['ʃteːlampə] *f* standard lamp.

stehlen ['ʃteːlən] *vt unreg* steal.

Stehplatz ['ʃteːplats] *m* standing place.

steif [ʃtaɪf] *a* stiff; **S~heit** *f* stiffness.

Steig- [ʃtaɪk] *zW:* ~**bügel** *m* stirrup; ~**eisen** *nt* crampon; **s~en** *vi unreg* rise; (*klettern*) climb; **s~en in** (+*akk*)/**auf** (+*akk*) get in/on; **s~ern** *vt* raise; (*GRAM*) compare // *vi* (*Auktion*) bid // *vr* increase; ~**erung** *f* raising; (*GRAM*) comparison; ~**ung** *f* incline, gradient, rise.

steil [ʃtaɪl] *a* steep.

Stein [ʃtaɪn] *m* -(e)s, -e stone; (*in Uhr*) jewel; ~**bock** *m* (*ASTROL*) Capricorn; ~**bruch** *m* quarry; **s~butt** *m* -s, -e turbot; **s~ern** *a* (made of) stone; (*fig*) stony; ~**gut** *nt* stoneware; **s~hart** *a* hard as stone; **s~ig** *a* stony; **s~igen** *vt* stone; ~**kohle** *f* mineral coal.

Stelle ['ʃtɛlə] *f* -, -n place; (*Arbeit*) post, job; (*Amt*) office; **an lhrer/ meiner ~** in your/my place.

stellen *vt* put; (*Uhr etc*) set; (*zur Verfügung ~*) supply; (*fassen: Dieb*) apprehend // *vr* (*sich aufstellen*) stand; (*sich einfinden*) present oneself; (*bei Polizei*) give oneself up; (*vorgeben*) pretend (to be); **sich zu etw ~** have an opinion of sth; **S~angebot** *nt* offer of a post; (*Zeitung*) vacancies; **S~gesuch** *nt* application for a post; **S~vermittlung** *f* employment agency.

Stell- *zW:* **~ung** *f* position; (*MIL*) line; **~ung nehmen zu** comment on; **~ungnahme** *f* -, -n comment; **s~vertretend** *a* deputy, acting; **~vertreter** *m* deputy; **~werk** *nt* (*EISENB*) signal box.

Stelze ['ʃtɛltsə] *f* -, -n stilt.

Stemm- ['ʃtɛm] *zW:* **~bogen** *m* (*SKI*) stem turn; **s~en** *vt* lift (up); (*drükken*) press; **sich s~en gegen** (*fig*) resist, oppose.

Stempel ['ʃtɛmpəl] *m* -s, - stamp; (*BOT*) pistil; **~kissen** *nt* inkpad; **s~n** *vt* stamp; (*Briefmarke*) cancel; **s~n gehen** (*umg*) be/go on the dole.

Stengel ['ʃtɛŋəl] *m* -s, - stalk.

Steno- ['ʃteno] *zW:* **~gramm** [-'gram] *nt* shorthand report; **~graphie** [-gra'fi:] *f* shorthand; **~graphieren** [-gra'fi:rən] *vti* write (in) shorthand; **~typist(in** *f)* [-ty'pɪst(ɪn)] *m* shorthand typist.

Stepp- ['ʃtɛp] *zW:* **~decke** *f* quilt; **~e** *f* -, -n prairie; steppe; **s~en** *vt* stitch // *vi* tap-dance.

Sterb- ['ʃtɛrb] *zW:* **Sterbefall** *m* death; **s~en** *vi unreg* die; **s~lich** ['ʃtɛrplɪç] *a* mortal; **~lichkeit** *f* mortality; **~lichkeitsziffer** *f* death rate.

stereo- ['ʃteːreo] *in zW* stereo(-); **S~anlage** *f* stereo (system); **~typ** [ʃtereo'tyːp] *a* stereotype.

steril [ʃteˈriːl] *a* sterile; **~isieren** *vt* sterilize; **S~isierung** *f* sterilization.

Stern [ʃtɛrn] *m* -(e)s, -e star; **~bild** *nt* constellation; **~schnuppe** *f* -, -n meteor, falling star; **~stunde** *f* historic moment.

stet [ʃteːt] *a* steady; **~ig** *a* constant, continual; **~s** *ad* continually, always.

Steuer ['ʃtɔyər] *nt* -s, - (*NAUT*) helm; (*~ruder*) rudder; (*AUT*) steering wheel // *f* -, -n tax; **~erklärung** *f* tax return; **~freibetrag** *m* tax allowance; **~klasse** *f* tax group; **~knüppel** *m* control column; (*AVIAT, COMPUT*) joystick; **~mann** *m, pl* -männer *od* -leute helmsman; **s~n** *vti* steer; (*Flugzeug*) pilot; (*Entwicklung, Tonstärke*) control; **~paradies** *nt* tax haven; **~rad** *nt* steering wheel; **~ung** *f*

steering (*auch AUT*); piloting; control; (*Vorrichtung*) controls *pl*; **~vergünstigung** *f* tax relief; **~zahler** *m* -s, - taxpayer.

Steward ['stjuːərt] *m* -s, -s steward; **Stewardeß** ['stjuːərdɛs] *f* -, -essen stewardess; air hostess.

Stich [ʃtɪç] *m* -(e)s, -e (*Insekten~*) sting; (*Messer~*) stab; (*beim Nähen*) stitch; (*Färbung*) tinge; (*KARTEN*) trick; (*ART*) engraving; **jdn im ~ lassen** leave sb in the lurch; **s~eln** *vi* (*fig*) jibe; **s~haltig** *a* sound, tenable; **~probe** *f* spot check; **~wahl** *f* final ballot; **~wort** *nt* cue; (*in Wörterbuch*) headword; (*für Vortrag*) note.

Stick- [ʃtɪk] *zW:* **s~en** *vti* embroider; **~e'rei** *f* embroidery; **s~ig** *a* stuffy, close; **~stoff** *m* nitrogen.

Stiefel ['ʃtiːfəl] *m* -s, - boot.

Stief- ['ʃtiːf] *in zW* step; **~kind** *nt* stepchild; (*fig*) Cinderella; **~mutter** *f* stepmother; **~mütterchen** *nt* pansy.

Stiege ['ʃtiːgə] *f* -, -n staircase.

stiehlst *etc v siehe* **stehlen**.

Stiel [ʃtiːl] *m* -(e)s, -e handle; (*BOT*) stalk.

stier [ʃtiːr] *a* staring, fixed; **S~** *m* -(e)s, -e bull; (*ASTROL*) Taurus; **~en** *vi* stare.

Stift [ʃtɪft] *m* -(e)s, -e peg; (*Nagel*) tack; (*Farb~*) crayon; (*Blei~*) pencil // *nt* -(e)s, -e (*charitable*) foundation; (*ECCL*) religious institution; **s~en** *vt* found; (*Unruhe*) cause; (*spenden*) contribute; **~er(in** *f)* *m* -s, - founder; **~ung** *f* donation; (*Organisation*) foundation; **~zahn** *m* crown tooth.

Stil [ʃtiːl] *m* -(e)s, -e style.

still [ʃtɪl] *a* quiet; (*unbewegt*) still; (*heimlich*) secret; **S~er Ozean** Pacific; **S~e** *f* -, -n stillness, quietness; **in aller S~e** quietly; **~en** *vt* stop; (*befriedigen*) satisfy; (*Säugling*) breast-feed; **~halten** *vi unreg* keep still; **~(l)egen** *vt* close down; **S~(l)egung** *f* shut-down; **~schweigen** *vi unreg* be silent; **S~schweigen** *nt* silence; **~schweigend** *a, ad* silent(ly); (*Einverständnis*) tacit(ly); **S~stand** *m* standstill; **~stehen** *vi unreg* stand still.

Stimm- ['ʃtɪm] *zW:* **~bänder** *pl* vocal chords *pl*; **s~berechtigt** *a* entitled to vote; **~e** *f* -, -n voice; (*Wahl~e*) vote; **s~en** *vt* (*MUS*) tune; **das stimmte ihn traurig** that made him feel sad // *vi* be right; **s~en für/gegen** vote for/against; **stimmt so!** that's right; **~enmehrheit** *f* majority (of votes); **~enthaltung** *f* abstention; **~gabel** *f* tuning fork; **~recht** *nt* right to vote; **~ung** *f* mood; atmosphere;

s~**ungsvoll** *a* enjoyable; full of atmosphere; ~**zettel** *m* ballot paper.
stinken [ʃtɪŋkən] *vi unreg* stink.
Stipendium [ʃtiˈpɔndium] *nt* grant.
stirbst *etc v siehe* **sterben**.
Stirn [ʃtɪrn] *f* -, -**en** forehead, brow; (*Frechheit*) impudence; ~**höhle** *f* sinus; ~**runzeln** *nt* -**s** frown(ing).
stöbern [ʃtøbərn] *vi* rummage.
stochern [ʃtɔxərn] *vi* poke (about).
Stock [ʃtɔk] *m* -(**e**)**s**, ⁻e stick; (*BOT*) stock // *pl* -**werke** storey; **s**~**en** *vi* stop, pause; **s**~**end** *a* halting; ~**ung** *f* stoppage; ~**werk** *nt* storey, floor.
Stoff [ʃtɔf] *m* -(**e**)**s**, -**e** (*Gewebe*) material, cloth; (*Materie*) matter; (*von Buch etc*) subject (matter); **s**~**lich** *a* material; ~**wechsel** *m* metabolism.
stöhnen [ʃtøːnən] *vi* groan.
stoisch [ʃtoːɪʃ] *a* stoical.
Stollen [ʃtɔlən] *m* -**s**, - (*MIN*) gallery; (*KOCH*) cake eaten at Christmas; (*von Schuhen*) stud.
stolpern [ʃtɔlpərn] *vi* stumble, trip.
Stolz [ʃtɔlts] *m* -**es** pride; **s**~ *a* proud; **s**~**ieren** [ʃtɔlˈtsiːrən] *vi* strut.
Stopf- [ʃtɔpf] *zW:* **s**~**en** *vt* (*hinein~en*) stuff; (*voll~en*) fill (up); (*nähen*) darn // *vi* (*MED*) cause constipation; ~**garn** *nt* darning thread.
Stoppel [ʃtɔpəl] *f* -, -**n** stubble.
Stopp- [ʃtɔp] *zW:* **s**~**en** *vti* stop; (*mit Uhr*) time; ~**schild** *nt* stop sign; ~**uhr** *f* stopwatch.
Stöpsel [ʃtœpsəl] *m* -**s**, - plug; (*für Flaschen*) stopper.
Storch [ʃtɔrç] *m* -(**e**)**s**, ⁻e stork.
Stör- [ʃtøːr] *zW:* **s**~**en** *vt* disturb; (*behindern*, *RAD*) interfere with // *vr* **sich an etw** (*dat*) **s**~**en** let sth bother one; **s**~**end** *a* disturbing, annoying; ~**enfried** *m* -(**e**)**s**, -**e** troublemaker.
störrisch [ʃtœrɪʃ] *a* stubborn, perverse.
Störsender *m* jammer.
Störung *f* disturbance; interference.
Stoß [ʃtoːs] *m* -**es**, ⁻e (*Schub*) push; (*Schlag*) blow; knock; (*mit Schwert*) thrust; (*mit Fuß*) kick; (*Erd~*) shock; (*Haufen*) pile; ~**dämpfer** *m* -**s**, - shock absorber; **s**~**en** *unreg vt* (*mit Druck*) shove, push; (*mit Schlag*) knock, bump; (*mit Fuß*) kick; (*Schwert etc*) thrust; (*an~en*: *Kopf etc*) bump; // *vr* get a knock, **sich s**~**en an** (+*dat*) (*fig*) take exception to // *vi:* **s**~**en an** *od* **auf** (+*akk*) bump into; (*finden*) come across; (*angrenzen*) be next to; ~**stange** *f* (*AUT*) bumper.
stottern [ʃtɔtərn] *vti* stutter.
Str. *abk* (= *Straße*) St.
Straf- [ʃtraːf] *zW:* ~**anstalt** *f* penal institution; ~**arbeit** *f* (*SCH*) punishment; lines *pl*; **s**~**bar** *a* punishable;

~**barkeit** *f* criminal nature; ~**e** *f* -, -**n** punishment; (*JUR*) penalty; (*Gefängnis~e*) sentence; (*Geld~e*) fine; **s**~**en** *vt* punish.
straff [ʃtraf] *a* tight; (*streng*) strict; (*Stil etc*) concise; (*Haltung*) erect; ~**en** *vt* tighten, tauten.
Straf- *zW:* ~**gefangene(r)** *mf* prisoner, convict; ~**gesetzbuch** *nt* penal code.
Sträf- [ʃtrɛːf] *zW:* **s**~**lich** *a* criminal; ~**ling** *m* convict.
Straf- *zW:* ~**porto** *nt* excess postage (charge); ~**predigt** *f* telling-off; ~**raum** *m* (*SPORT*) penalty area; ~**recht** *nt* criminal law; ~**stoß** *m* (*SPORT*) penalty (kick); ~**tat** *f* punishable act; ~**zettel** *m* ticket.
Strahl [ʃtraːl] *m* -**s**, -**en** ray, beam; (*Wasser~*) jet; **s**~**en** *vi* radiate; (*fig*) beam; ~**entherapie** *f* radiotherapy; ~**ung** *f* radiation.
Strähne [ʃtrɛːnə] *f* -, -**n** strand.
stramm [ʃtram] *a* tight; (*Haltung*) erect; (*Mensch*) robust.
strampeln [ʃtrampəln] *vi* kick (about), fidget.
Strand [ʃtrant] *m* -(**e**)**s**, ⁻e shore; (*mit Sand*) beach; ~**bad** *nt* open-air swimming pool, lido; **s**~**en** [ʃtrandən] *vi* run aground; (*fig: Mensch*) fail; ~**gut** *nt* flotsam; ~**korb** *m* beach chair.
Strang [ʃtraŋ] *m* -(**e**)**s**, ⁻e cord, rope; (*Bündel*) skein.
Strapaz- *zW:* ~**e** [ʃtraˈpaːtsə] *f* -, -**n** strain, exertion; **s**~**ieren** [ʃtrapaˈtsiːrən] *vt* (*Material*) treat roughly, punish; (*Mensch, Kräfte*) wear out, exhaust; **s**~**ierfähig** *a* hard-wearing; **s**~**iös** [ʃtrapatsiˈøːs] *a* exhausting, tough.
Straße [ʃtraːsə] *f* -, -**n** street, road.
Straßen- *zW:* ~**e** *f* tram, streetcar (*US*); ~**beleuchtung** *f* street lighting; ~**feger**, ~**kehrer** *m* -**s**, - roadsweeper; ~**sperre** *f* roadblock; ~**verkehrsordnung** *f* highway code.
Strateg- [ʃtraˈteːg] *zW:* ~**e** *m* -**n**, -**n** strategist; ~**ie** [ʃtrateˈgiː] *f* strategy; **s**~**isch** *a* strategic.
sträuben [ʃtrɔybən] *vt* ruffle // *vr* bristle; (*Mensch*) resist (*gegen etw* sth).
Strauch [ʃtraux] *m* -(**e**)**s**, **Sträucher** bush, shrub.
Strauß [ʃtraus] *m* -**es**, **Sträuße** bunch; bouquet // *pl* -**e** ostrich.
Streb- [ʃtreːb] *zW:* **s**~**en** *vi* strive (*nach* for), endeavour; ~**er** *m* -**s**, - (*pej*) pusher, climber; (*SCH*) swot (*Brit*), bootlicker (*US*); **s**~**sam** *a* industrious.
Strecke [ʃtrɛkə] *f* -, -**n** stretch; (*Entfernung*) distance; (*EISENB*)

line; (*MATH*) line; **s~n** vt stretch; (*Waffen*) lay down; (*KOCH*) eke out // vr stretch (oneself).

Streich [ʃtraɪç] m -(e)s, -e trick, prank; (*Hieb*) blow; **s~eln** vt stroke; **s~en** unreg vt (*berühren*) stroke; (*auftragen*) spread; (*anmalen*) paint; (*durch~en*) delete; (*nicht genehmigen*) cancel // vi (*berühren*) brush; (*schleichen*) prowl; **~holz** nt match; **~instrument** nt string instrument.

Streif- [ʃtraɪf] zW: **~e** f -, -n patrol; **s~en** vt (*leicht berühren*) brush against, graze; (*Blick*) skim over; (*Thema, Problem*) touch on; (*ab~en*) take off // vi (*gehen*) roam; **~en** m -s, - (*Linie*) stripe; (*Stück*) strip; (*Film*) film; **~endienst** m patrol duty; **~enwagen** m patrol car; **~schuß** m graze, grazing shot; **~zug** m scouting trip.

Streik [ʃtraɪk] m -(e)s, -s strike; **~brecher** m -s, - blackleg, strikebreaker; **s~en** vi strike; **~kasse** f strike fund; **~posten** m (strike) picket.

Streit [ʃtraɪt] m -(e)s, -e argument; dispute; **s~en** vir unreg argue; dispute; **~frage** f point at issue; **s~ig** a: jdm etw s~ig machen dispute sb's right to sth; **~igkeiten** pl quarrel, dispute; **~kräfte** pl (*MIL*) armed forces pl.

streng [ʃtrɛŋ] a severe; (*Lehrer, Maßnahme*) strict; (*Geruch etc*) sharp; **S~e** f - severity; strictness; sharpness; **~genommen** ad strictly speaking; **~gläubig** a orthodox, strict; **~stens** ad strictly.

Streu [ʃtrɔy] f -, -en litter, bed of straw; **s~en** vt strew, scatter, spread; **~ung** f dispersion.

Strich [ʃtrɪç] m -(e)s, -e (*Linie*) line; (*Feder~, Pinsel~*) stroke; (*von Geweben*) nap; (*von Fell*) pile; auf den ~ gehen (*umg*) walk the streets; jdm gegen den ~ gehen rub sb up the wrong way; einen ~ machen durch (*lit*) cross out; (*fig*) foil; **~mädchen** nt streetwalker; **~punkt** m semicolon; **s~weise** ad here and there.

Strick [ʃtrɪk] m -(e)s, -e rope; **s~en** vti knit; **~jacke** f cardigan; **~leiter** f rope ladder; **~nadel** f knitting needle; **~waren** pl knitwear.

strikt [ʃtrɪkt] a strict.

strittig [ʃtrɪtɪç] a disputed, in dispute.

Stroh [ʃtroː] nt -(e)s straw; **~blume** f everlasting flower; **~dach** nt thatched roof; **~halm** m (drinking) straw.

Strom [ʃtroːm] m -(e)s, ⁻e river; (*fig*) stream; (*ELEK*) current; **s~abwärts** [-'ʔapvɛrts] ad downstream; **s~aufwärts** [-'ʔaufvɛrts] ad upstream.

strömen [ˈʃtrøːmən] vi stream, pour.

Strom- zW: **~kreis** m circuit; **s~linienförmig** a streamlined; **~rechnung** f electricity bill; **~sperre** f power cut.

Strömung [ˈʃtrøːmʊŋ] f current.

Strophe [ˈʃtroːfə] f -, -n verse.

strotzen [ˈʃtrɔtsən] vi: ~ vor od von abound in, be full of.

Strudel [ˈʃtruːdəl] m -s, - whirlpool, vortex; (*KOCH*) strudel.

Struktur [ʃtrʊkˈtuːr] f structure.

Strumpf [ʃtrʊmpf] m -(e)s, ⁻e stocking; **~band** nt garter; **~hose** f (pair of) tights.

Stube [ˈʃtuːbə] f -, -n room.

Stuben- zW: **~arrest** m confinement to one's room; (*MIL*) confinement to quarters; **~hocker** m (*umg*) stay-at-home; **s~rein** a house-trained.

Stuck [ʃtʊk] m -(e)s stucco.

Stück [ʃtʏk] nt -(e)s, -e piece; (*etwas*) bit; (*THEAT*) play; **~chen** nt little piece; **~lohn** m piecework wages pl; **s~weise** ad bit by bit, piecemeal; (*COMM*) individually; **~werk** nt bits and pieces pl.

Student(in f) [ʃtuˈdɛnt(ɪn)] m student; **s~isch** a student, academic.

Studie [ˈʃtuːdiə] f study.

studieren [ʃtuˈdiːrən] vti study.

Studio [ˈʃtuːdio] nt -s, -s studio.

Studium [ˈʃtuːdiʊm] nt studies pl.

Stufe [ˈʃtuːfə] f -, -n step; (*Entwicklungs~*) stage; **stufenweise** ad gradually.

Stuhl [ʃtuːl] m -(e)s, ⁻e chair; **~gang** m bowel movement.

stülpen [ˈʃtʏlpən] vt (*umdrehen*) turn upside down; (*bedecken*) put.

stumm [ʃtʊm] a silent; (*MED*) dumb.

Stummel m -s, - stump; (*Zigaretten~*) stub; **~film** m silent film; **S~heit** f silence; dumbness.

Stümper [ˈʃtʏmpər] m -s, - incompetent, duffer; **s~haft** a bungling, incompetent; **s~n** vi (*umg*) bungle.

stumpf [ʃtʊmpf] a blunt; (*teilnahmslos, glanzlos*) dull; (*Winkel*) obtuse; **S~** m -(e)s, ⁻e stump; **S~sinn** m tediousness; **~sinnig** a dull.

Stunde [ˈʃtʊndə] f -, -n hour; (*SCH*) lesson.

stunden vt: jdm etw ~ give sb time to pay sth; **S~geschwindigkeit** f average speed per hour; **S~kilometer** pl kilometres per hour; **~lang** a for hours; **S~lohn** m hourly wage; **S~plan** m timetable; **~weise** a by the hour; every hour.

stündlich [ˈʃtʏntlɪç] a hourly.

Stups [ʃtʊps] m -es, -e (*umg*) push; **~nase** f snub nose.

stur [ʃtuːr] a obstinate, pigheaded.

Sturm [ʃtʊrm] *m* -(e)s, ⁻e storm, gale; (*MIL etc*) attack, assault.
stürm- ['ʃtʏrm] *zW:* ∼**en** *vi* (*Wind*) blow hard, rage; (*rennen*) storm // *vt* (*MIL, fig*) storm // *v unpers* es ∼t there's a gale blowing; **S∼er** *m* -s, - (*SPORT*) forward, striker; ∼**isch** *a* stormy.
Sturmwarnung *f* gale warning.
Sturz [ʃtʊrts] *m* -es, ⁻e fall; (*POL*) overthrow.
stürzen ['ʃtʏrtsən] *vt* (*werfen*) hurl; (*POL*) overthrow; (*umkehren*) overturn // *vr* rush; (*hinein∼*) plunge // *vi* fall; (*AVIAT*) dive; (*rennen*) dash.
Sturz- *zW:* ∼**flug** *m* nose-dive; ∼**helm** *m* crash helmet.
Stute ['ʃtuːtə] *f* -, -n mare.
Stütz- ['ʃtʏts] *zW:* ∼**balken** *m* brace, joist; ∼**e** *f* -, -n support; help; **s∼en** *vt* (*lit, fig*) support; (*Ellbogen etc*) prop up.
stutz- ['ʃtʊts] *zW:* ∼**en** *vt* trim; (*Ohr, Schwanz*) dock; (*Flügel*) clip // *vi* hesitate; become suspicious; ∼**ig** *a* perplexed, puzzled; (*mißtrauisch*) suspicious.
Stützpunkt *m* point of support; (*von Hebel*) fulcrum; (*MIL, fig*) base.
Styropor ® [ʃtyro'poːr] *nt* -s polystyrene.
s.u. *abk* = siehe unten.
Subjekt [zʊp'jɛkt] *nt* -(e)s, -e subject; **s∼iv** [-'tiːf] *a* subjective; ∼**ivi'tät** *f* subjectivity.
Substantiv ['zʊpstantiːf] *nt* -s, -e noun.
Substanz [zʊp'stants] *f* substance.
subtil [zʊp'tiːl] *a* subtle.
subtrahieren [zʊptra'hiːrən] *vt* subtract.
Subvention [zʊpvɛntsi'oːn] *f* subsidy; **s∼ieren** [-'niːrən] *vt* subsidize.
Such- ['zuːx] *zW:* ∼**aktion** *f* search; ∼**e** *f* -, -n search; **s∼en** *vti* look (for), seek; (*ver∼en*) try; ∼**er** *m* -s, - seeker, searcher; (*PHOT*) viewfinder.
Sucht [zʊxt] *f* -, ⁻e mania; (*MED*) addiction, craving.
süchtig ['zʏçtɪç] *a* addicted; **S∼e(r)** *mf* addict.
Süd- ['zyːt] *zW:* ∼**en** ['zyːdən] *m* -s south; ∼**früchte** *pl* Mediterranean fruit; **s∼lich** *a* southern; **s∼lich von** (to the) south of; ∼**pol** *m* South Pole; **s∼wärts** *ad* southwards.
süffig ['zʏfɪç] *a* (*Wein*) pleasant to the taste.
süffisant [zyfi'zant] *a* smug.
suggerieren [zʊge'riːrən] *vt* suggest (*jdm etw* sth to sb).
Sühne ['zyːnə] *f* -, -n atonement, expiation; **s∼n** *vt* atone for, expiate.
Sultan ['zʊltan] *m* -s, -e sultan; ∼**ine** [zʊlta'niːnə] *f* sultana.

Sülze ['zʏltsə] *f* -, -n brawn.
Summ- ['zʊm] *zW:* ∼**e** *f* -, -n sum, total; **s∼en** *vti* buzz; (*Lied*) hum.
Sumpf [zʊmpf] *m* -(e)s, ⁻e swamp, marsh; **s∼ig** *a* marshy.
Sünde ['zʏndə] *f* -, -n sin; **Sündenbock** *m* (*umg*) scapegoat; **Sündenfall** *m* Fall (of man); ∼**r(in** *f)* *m* -s, - sinner.
Super ['zuːpər] *nt* -s (*Benzin*) four star (petrol); **Superlativ** [-latiːf] *m* -s, -e superlative; ∼**markt** *m* supermarket.
Suppe ['zʊpə] *f* -, -n soup.
süß [zyːs] *a* sweet; **S∼e** *f* - sweetness; ∼**en** *vt* sweeten; **S∼igkeit** *f* sweetness; (*Bonbon etc*) sweet (*Brit*), candy (*US*); ∼**lich** *a* sweetish; (*fig*) sugary; **S∼speise** *f* pudding, sweet; **S∼stoff** *m* sweetener; **S∼wasser** *nt* fresh water.
Sylvester [zyl'vɛstər] *nt* -s, - *siehe* **Silvester.**
Symbol [zym'boːl] *nt* -s, -e symbol; **s∼isch** *a* symbolic(al).
Symmetrie [zyme'triː] *f* symmetry.
symmetrisch [zy'meːtrɪʃ] *a* symmetrical.
Sympath- *zW:* ∼**ie** [zympa'tiː] *f* liking, sympathy; **s∼isch** [zym'paːtɪʃ] *a* likeable; er ist mir **s∼isch** I like him; **s∼i'sieren** *vi* sympathize.
Symptom [zymp'toːm] *nt* -s, -e symptom; **s∼atisch** [zympto'maːtɪʃ] *a* symptomatic.
Synagoge [zyna'goːgə] *f* -, -n synagogue.
synchron [zyn'kroːn] *a* synchronous; **S∼getriebe** *nt* synchromesh (gears *pl*); ∼**i'sieren** *vt* synchronize; (*Film*) dub.
Synonym [zyno'nyːm] *nt* -s, -e synonym; **s∼** *a* synonymous.
Synthese [zyn'teːzə] *f* -, -n synthesis.
synthetisch [zyn'teːtɪʃ] *a* synthetic.
Syphilis ['zyːfilɪs] *f* - syphilis.
Syr- ['zyːr] *zW:* ∼**er(in** *f)* *m* Syrian; ∼**ien** *nt* Syria; **s∼isch** *a* Syrian.
System [zys'teːm] *nt* -s, -e system; **s∼atisch** [zystɛ'maːtɪʃ] *a* systematic; **s∼ati'sieren** *vt* systematize; ∼**platte** *f* system disk.
Szene ['stseːnə] *f* -, -n scene; **Szenerie** [stsenə'riː] *f* scenery.

T

T, t [teː] T, t.
t *abk* (= *Tonne*) t.
Tabak ['taːbak] *m* -s, -e tobacco.
Tabell- [ta'bɛl] *zW:* **t∼arisch** [tabɛ'laːrɪʃ] *a* tabular; ∼**e** *f* table; **Tabellenführer** *m* top of the table, league leader.

Tablett [ta'blɛt] *nt* tray; ~**e** *f* tablet, pill.

Tabu [ta'bu:] *nt* taboo; **t~** *a* taboo.

Tachometer [taxo'me:tər] *m* -s, - (*AUT*) speedometer.

Tadel ['ta:dəl] *m* -s, - censure, scolding; (*Fehler*) fault, blemish; **t~los** *a* faultless, irreproachable; **t~n** *vt* scold; **t~nswert** *a* blameworthy.

Tafel ['ta:fəl] *f* -, -n table (*auch MATH*); (*Anschlag~*) board; (*Wand~*) blackboard; (*Schiefer~*) slate; (*Gedenk~*) plaque; (*Illustration*) plate; (*Schalt~*) panel; (*Schokolade etc*) bar.

Taft [taft] *m* -(e)s, -e taffeta.

Tag [ta:k] *m* -(e)s, -e day; daylight; **unter/über** ~**e** (*MIN*) underground/on the surface; **an den** ~ **kommen** come to light; **guten** ~! good morning/afternoon!; **t~aus, t~ein** *ad* day in, day out; ~**dienst** *m* day duty.

Tage- ['ta:gə] *zW*: ~**buch** ['ta:gəbu:x] *nt* diary, journal; ~**geld** *nt* daily allowance; **t~lang** *ad* for days; **t~n** *vi* sit, meet // *v unpers*: **es tagt** dawn is breaking.

Tages- *zW*: ~**ablauf** *m* course of the day; ~**anbruch** *m* dawn; ~**karte** *f* menu of the day; (*Fahrkarte*) day ticket; ~**licht** *nt* daylight; ~**ordnung** *f* agenda; ~**zeit** *f* time of day; ~**zeitung** *f* daily (paper).

täglich ['tɛ:klɪç] *a, ad* daily.

tagsüber ['ta:ks'y:bər] *ad* during the day.

Tagung *f* conference.

Taille ['taljə] *f* -, -n waist.

Takt [takt] *m* -(e)s, -e tact; (*MUS*) time; ~**gefühl** *nt* tact; ~**ik** *f* tactics *pl*; **t~isch** *a* tactical; **t~los** *a* tactless; ~**losigkeit** *f* tactlessness; ~**stock** *m* (conductor's) baton; **t~voll** *a* tactful.

Tal [ta:l] *nt* -(e)s, ⁻er valley.

Talent [ta'lɛnt] *nt* -(e)s, -e talent; **t~iert** [talɛn'ti:rt] *a* talented, gifted.

Talisman ['ta:lɪsman] *m* -s, -e talisman.

Tal- *zW*: ~**sohle** *f* bottom of a valley; ~**sperre** *f* dam.

Tamburin [tambu'ri:n] *nt* -s, -e tambourine.

Tampon ['tampɔn] *m* -s, -s tampon.

Tang [taŋ] *m* -(e)s, -e seaweed.

Tangente [taŋ'gɛntə] *f* -, -n tangent.

tangieren [taŋ'gi:rən] *vt* (*lit*) touch; (*fig*) affect.

Tank [taŋk] *m* -s, -s tank; **t~en** *vi* fill up with petrol (*Brit*) *od* gas (*US*); (*AVIAT*) refuel; ~**er** *m* -s, -, ~**schiff** *nt* tanker; ~**stelle** *f* petrol (*Brit*) *od* gas (*US*) station; ~**wart** *m* petrol pump (*Brit*) *od* gas station (*US*) attendant.

Tanne ['tanə] *f* -, -n fir; **Tannenbaum** *m* fir tree; **Tannenzapfen** *m* fir cone.

Tante ['tantə] *f* -, -n aunt.

Tanz [tants] *m* -es, ⁻e dance; **t~en** *vti* dance.

Tänzer(in *f*) ['tɛntsər(ɪn)] *m* -s, - dancer.

Tanz- *zW*: ~**fläche** *f* (dance) floor; ~**schule** *f* dancing school.

Tapete [ta'pe:tə] *f* -, -n wallpaper; **Tapetenwechsel** *m* (*fig*) change of scenery.

tapezieren [tape'tsi:rən] *vt* (wall)-paper.

Tapezierer [tape'tsi:rər] *m* -s, - (interior) decorator.

tapfer ['tapfər] *a* brave; **T~keit** *f* courage, bravery.

Tarif [ta'ri:f] *m* -s, -e tariff, (scale of) fares/charges; ~**lohn** *m* standard wage rate; ~**verhandlungen** *pl* wage negotiations *pl*.

Tarn- ['tarn] *zW*: **t~en** *vt* camouflage; (*Person, Absicht*) disguise; ~**farbe** *f* camouflage paint; ~**ung** *f* camouflaging; disguising.

Tasche ['taʃə] *f* -, -n pocket; handbag.

Taschen- *in zW* pocket; ~**buch** *nt* paperback; ~**dieb** *m* pickpocket; ~**geld** *nt* pocket money; ~**lampe** *f* (electric) torch, flashlight (*US*); ~**messer** *nt* penknife; ~**tuch** *nt* handkerchief.

Tasse ['tasə] *f* -, -n cup.

Tastatur [tasta'tu:r] *f* keyboard.

Taste ['tastə] *f* -, -n push-button control; (*an Schreibmaschine*) key; **t~n** *vt* feel, touch // *vi* feel, grope // *vr* feel one's way.

tat *etc v siehe* **tun**.

Tat [ta:t] *f* -, -en act, deed, action; **in der** ~ indeed, as a matter of fact; ~**bestand** *m* facts *pl* of the case; **t~enlos** *a* inactive.

Tät- ['tɛ:t] *zW*: ~**er(in** *f*) *m* -s, - perpetrator, culprit; **t~ig** *a* active; **in einer Firma t~ig sein** work for a firm; ~**igkeit** *f* activity; (*Beruf*) occupation; **t~lich** *a* violent; ~**lichkeit** *f* violence // *pl* blows *pl*.

tätowieren [tɛto'vi:rən] *vt* tattoo.

Tat- *zW*: ~**sache** *f* fact; **t~sächlich** *a* actual // *ad* really.

Tau [tau] *nt* -(e)s, -e rope // *m* -(e)s dew.

taub [taup] *a* deaf; (*Nuß*) hollow; **T~heit** *f* deafness; ~**stumm** *a* deaf-and-dumb.

Taube ['taubə] *f* -, -n dove; pigeon; **Taubenschlag** *m* dovecote; **hier geht es zu wie in einem Taubenschlag** it's a hive of activity here.

Tauch- ['taux] *zW*: **t~en** *vt* dip // *vi* dive; (*NAUT*) submerge; ~**er** *m* -s, - diver; ~**eranzug** *m* diving suit; ~**sieder** *m* -s, - immersion coil (for *boiling water*).

tauen ['tauən] *vti, v unpers* thaw.

Tauf- ['tauf] *zW:* **~becken** *nt* font; **~e** *f* -, **-n** baptism; **t~en** *vt* christen, baptize; **~name** *m* Christian name; **~pate** *m* godfather; **~patin** *f* godmother; **~schein** *m* certificate of baptism.

Taug- ['taug] *zW:* **t~en** *vi* be of use; **t~en für** do *od* be good for; **nicht t~en** be no good *od* useless; **Taugenichts** *m* -es, -e good-for-nothing; **t~lich** ['tauklıç] *a* suitable; (*MIL*) fit (for service).

Taumel ['tauməl] *m* -s dizziness; (*fig*) frenzy; **t~n** *vi* reel, stagger.

Tausch [tauʃ] *m* -(e)s, -e exchange; **t~en** *vt* exchange, swap; **~handel** *m* barter.

täuschen ['tɔyʃən] *vt* deceive // *vi* be deceptive // *vr* be wrong; **~d** *a* deceptive.

Täuschung *f* deception; (*optisch*) illusion.

tausend ['tauzənt] *num* (a) thousand; **T~füßler** *m* -s, - centipede; millipede.

Tauwetter *nt* thaw.

Taxi ['taksi] *nt* -(s), -(s) taxi; **~fahrer** *m* taxi driver; **~stand** *m* taxi rank.

Tech- ['tɛç] *zW:* **~nik** *f* technology; (*Methode, Kunstfertigkeit*) technique; **~niker** *m* -s, - technician; **t~nisch** *a* technical; **~nolo'gie** *f* technology; **t~no'logisch** *a* technological.

TEE [teː'eː''eː] *m abk* (= *Trans-Europ-Express*) Trans-European Express.

Tee [teː] *m* -s, -s tea; **~kanne** *f* teapot; **~löffel** *m* teaspoon.

Teer [teːr] *m* -(e)s, -e tar; **t~en** *vt* tar.

Teesieb *nt* tea strainer.

Teich [taıç] *m* -(e)s, -e pond.

Teig [taık] *m* -(e)s, -e dough; **t~ig** *a* doughy; **~waren** *pl* pasta *sing*.

Teil [taıl] *m od nt* -(e)s, -e part; (*An~*) share; (*Bestand~*) component; **zum ~** partly; **t~bar** *a* divisible; **~betrag** *m* instalment; **~chen** *nt* (atomic) particle; **t~en** *vtr* divide; (*mit jdm*) share; **t~haben** *vi unreg* share (*an* +*dat* in); **~haber** *m* -s, - partner; **~kaskoversicherung** *f* third party, fire and theft insurance; **~nahme** *f* -, -n participation; (*Mitleid*) sympathy; **t~nahmslos** *a* disinterested, apathetic; **t~nehmen** *vi unreg* take part (*an* +*dat* in); **~nehmer** *m* -s, - participant; **t~s** *ad* partly; **~ung** *f* division; **t~weise** *ad* partially, in part; **~zahlung** *f* payment by instalments.

Teint [tɛ̃ː] *m* -s, -s complexion.

Telefax ['telefaks] *nt* fax.

Telefon [tele'foːn] *nt* -s, -e telephone; **~amt** *nt* telephone exchange; **~anruf** *m*, **~at** [telefo'naːt] *nt* -(e)s, -e (tele)phone call; **~buch** *nt* telephone directory; **t~ieren** [telefo'niːrən] *vi* telephone; **t~isch** [-ıʃ] *a* telephone; (*Benachrichtigung*) by telephone; **~ist(in** *f*) [telefo'nıst(ın)] *m* telephonist; **~nummer** *f* (tele)phone number; **~verbindung** *f* telephone connection; **~zelle** *f* telephone kiosk, callbox; **~zentrale** *f* telephone exchange.

Telegraf [tele'graːf] *m* -en, -en telegraph; **~enleitung** *f* telegraph line; **~enmast** *m* telegraph pole; **~ie** [-'fiː] *f* telegraphy; **t~ieren** [-'fiːrən] *vti* telegraph, wire; **t~isch** *a* telegraphic.

Telegramm [tele'gram] *nt* -s, -e telegram, cable; **~adresse** *f* telegraphic address.

Tele- *zW:* **~objektiv** ['teːlɛ'ɔpjɛktiːf] *nt* telephoto lens; **~pathie** [telepa'tiː] *f* telepathy; **t~pathisch** [tele'paːtıʃ] *a* telepathic; **~skop** [tele'skoːp] *nt* -s, -e telescope.

Telex ['teleks] *nt* -es, -e telex.

Teller ['tɛlɔr] *m* -s, - plate.

Tempel ['tɛmpəl] *m* -s, - temple.

Temperament [tɛmpera'mɛnt] *nt* temperament; (*Schwung*) vivacity, liveliness; **t~los** *a* spiritless; **t~voll** *a* high-spirited, lively.

Temperatur [tɛmpera'tuːr] *f* temperature.

Tempo ['tɛmpo] *nt* -s, -s speed, pace // *pl* **Tempi** (*MUS*) tempo; **~!** get a move on!

Tendenz [tɛn'dɛnts] *f* tendency; (*Absicht*) intention; **t~iös** [-i'øːs] *a* biased, tendentious.

tendieren [tɛn'diːrən] *vi* show a tendency, incline (*zu* to(wards)).

Tennis ['tɛnis] *nt* - tennis; **~platz** *m* tennis court; **~schläger** *m* tennis racket; **~spieler(in** *f*) *m* tennis player.

Tenor [te'noːr] *m* -s, ⁻e tenor.

Teppich ['tɛpıç] *m* -s, -e carpet; **~boden** *m* wall-to-wall carpeting.

Termin [tɛr'miːn] *m* -s, -e (*Zeitpunkt*) date; (*Frist*) time limit, deadline; (*Arzt~ etc*) appointment; **~kalender** *m* diary, appointments book.

Termite [tɛr'miːtə] *f* -, -n termite.

Terpentin [tɛrpɛn'tiːn] *nt* -s, -e turpentine, turps *sing*.

Terrasse [tɛ'rasə] *f* -, -n terrace.

Terrine [tɛ'riːnə] *f* tureen.

territorial [tɛritori'aːl] *a* territorial.

Territorium [tɛri'toːriʊm] *nt* territory.

Terror ['tɛrɔr] *m* -s terror; reign of terror; **t~isieren** [tɛrori'ziːrən] *vt* terrorize; **~ismus** [-'rısmʊs] *m* terrorism; ~**ist** [-'rɪst] m terrorist.

Terz [tɛrts] f -, -en (MUS) third; ~**ett** [tɛr'tsɛt] nt -(e)s, -e trio.

Tesafilm ® ['te:zafilm] m sellotape (Brit), Scotch tape ® (US).

Test [tɛst] m -s, -s test.

Testament [tɛsta'mɛnt] nt will, testament; (REL) Testament; **t~arisch** [-'ta:rɪʃ] a testamentary; **Testamentsvollstrecker** m executor (of a will).

Testbild nt (TV) test card.

testen vt test.

Tetanus ['te:tanʊs] m - tetanus; ~**impfung** f (anti-)tetanus injection.

teuer ['tɔʏər] a dear, expensive; **T~ung** f increase in prices; **T~ungszulage** f cost of living bonus.

Teufel ['tɔʏfəl] m -s, - devil.

teuflisch ['tɔʏflɪʃ] a fiendish, diabolical.

Text [tɛkst] m -(e)s, -e text; (Lieder~) words pl; **t~en** vi write the words.

textil [tɛks'ti:l] a textile; **T~ien** pl textiles pl; **T~industrie** f textile industry; **T~waren** pl textiles pl.

Theater [te'a:tər] nt -s, - theatre; (umg) fuss; ~ **spielen** (lit, fig) playact; ~**besucher** m playgoer; ~**kasse** f box office; ~**stück** nt (stage-)play.

Theke ['te:kə] f -, -n (Schanktisch) bar; (Ladentisch) counter.

Thema ['te:ma] nt -s, **Themen** od -ta theme, topic, subject.

Themse ['tɛmzə] f Thames.

Theo- [teo] zW: ~**loge** [-'lo:gə] m -n, -n theologian; ~**logie** [-lo'gi:] f theology; **t~logisch** [-'lo:gɪʃ] a theological; ~**retiker** [-'re:tikər] m -s, - theorist; **t~retisch** [-'re:tɪʃ] a theoretical; ~**rie** [-'ri:] f theory.

Thera- [tera] zW: ~**peut** [-'pɔʏt] m -en, -en therapist; **t~peutisch** [-'pɔʏtɪʃ] a therapeutic; ~**pie** [-'pi:] f therapy.

Therm- zW: ~**albad** [tɛrm'a:lba:t] nt thermal bath; thermal spa; ~**odrucker** ['tɛrmo-] m thermal printer; ~**ometer** [tɛrmo'me:tər] nt -s, - thermometer; ~**osflasche** ['tɛrmɔsflaʃə] f Thermos ® flask; ~**ostat** [tɛrmo'sta:t] m -(e)s od -en, -e(n) thermostat.

These ['te:zə] f -, -n thesis.

Thrombose [trɔm'bo:zə] f -, -n thrombosis.

Thron [tro:n] m -(e)s, -e throne; ~**folge** f succession (to the throne).

Thunfisch ['tu:nfɪʃ] m tuna.

Thymian ['ty:mia:n] m -s, -e thyme.

Tick [tɪk] m -(e)s, -s tic; (Eigenart) quirk; (Fimmel) craze; **t~en** vi tick.

tief [ti:f] a deep; (tiefsinnig) profound; (Ausschnitt, Preis, Ton) low; **T~** nt -s, -s (MET) depression; **T~druck** m

low pressure; **T~e** f -, -n depth; **T~ebene** f plain; **Tiefenpsychologie** f depth psychology; **Tiefenschärfe** f (PHOT) depth of focus; **T~garage** f underground garage; ~**gekühlt** a frozen; ~**greifend** a far-reaching; **T~kühlfach** nt deep-freeze compartment; **T~kühltruhe** f deep-freeze, freezer; **T~land** nt lowlands pl; **T~punkt** m low point; (fig) low ebb; **T~schlag** m (Boxen, fig) blow below the belt; ~**schürfend** a profound; **T~see** f deep sea; ~**sinnig** a profound; melancholy; **T~stand** m low level; **Tiefstwert** m minimum od lowest value.

Tier [ti:r] nt -(e)s, -e animal; ~**arzt** m vet(erinary surgeon); ~**garten** m zoo(logical gardens pl); **t~isch** a animal; (lit, fig) brutish; (fig: Ernst etc) deadly; ~**kreis** m zodiac; ~**kunde** f zoology; **t~liebend** a fond of animals; ~**quälerei** [-kvɛ:lə'raɪ] f cruelty to animals; ~**schutzverein** m society for the prevention of cruelty to animals.

Tiger ['ti:gər] m -s, - tiger; ~**in** f tigress.

tilgen ['tɪlgən] vt erase; (Sünden) expiate; (Schulden) pay off.

Tinte ['tɪntə] f -, -n ink.

Tinten- zW: ~**fisch** m cuttlefish; ~**stift** m copying od indelible pencil.

Tip [tɪp] m tip; **tippen** vti tap, touch; (umg: schreiben) type; (umg: raten) tip (auf jdn sb); (im Lotto etc) bet (on).

Tipp- ['tɪp] zW: ~**fehler** m (umg) typing error; **t~topp** a (umg) tip-top; ~**zettel** m (pools) coupon.

Tirol [ti'ro:l] nt the Tyrol; ~**er(in** f) m Tyrolean; **t~isch** a Tyrolean.

Tisch [tɪʃ] m -(e)s, -e table; **bei ~** at table; **vor/nach ~** before/after eating; **unter den ~ fallen** (fig) be dropped; ~**decke** f tablecloth; ~**ler** m -s, - carpenter, joiner; ~**le'rei** f joiner's workshop; (Arbeit) carpentry, joinery; **t~lern** vi do carpentry etc; ~**rede** f after-dinner speech; ~**tennis** nt table tennis.

Titel ['ti:təl] m -s, - title; ~**anwärter** m (SPORT) challenger; ~**bild** nt cover (picture); (von Buch) frontispiece; ~**geschichte** f main story; ~**rolle** f title role; ~**seite** f cover; (Buch~) title page; ~**verteidiger** m defending champion, title holder.

Toast [to:st] m -(e)s, -s od -e toast; ~**er** m -s, - toaster.

tob- ['to:b] zW: ~**en** vi rage; (Kinder) romp about; **T~sucht** f raving madness; ~**süchtig** a maniacal.

Tochter ['tɔxtər] f -, ⁻ daughter; ~**gesellschaft** f subsidiary (company).

Tod [to:t] *m* -(e)s, -e death; **t~ernst** *a* deadly serious // *ad* in dead earnest.

Todes- ['to:dəs] *zW:* **~angst** [-aŋst] *f* mortal fear; **~anzeige** *f* obituary (notice); **~fall** *m* death; **~strafe** *f* death penalty; **~ursache** *f* cause of death; **~urteil** *nt* death sentence; **~verachtung** *f* utter disgust.

todkrank *a* dangerously ill.

tödlich ['tø:tlıç] *a* deadly, fatal.

tod- *zW:* **~müde** *a* dead tired; **~schick** *a* (*umg*) smart, classy; **~sicher** *a* (*umg*) absolutely *od* dead certain; **T~sünde** *f* deadly sin.

Toilette [toa'lɛtə] *f* toilet, lavatory; (*Frisiertisch*) dressing table; (*Kleidung*) outfit.

Toiletten- *zW:* **~artikel** *pl* toiletries *pl*, toilet articles *pl*; **~papier** *nt* toilet paper; **~tisch** *m* dressing table.

toi, toi, toi ['tɔy, 'tɔy, 'tɔy] *interj* touch wood.

tolerant [tole'rant] *a* tolerant.

Toleranz [tole'rants] *f* tolerance.

tolerieren [tole'ri:rən] *vt* tolerate.

toll [tɔl] *a* mad; (*Treiben*) wild; (*umg*) terrific; **~en** *vi* romp; **T~kirsche** *f* deadly nightshade; **~kühn** *a* daring; **T~wut** *f* rabies.

Tomate [to'ma:tə] *f* -, -n tomato; **Tomatenmark** *nt* tomato puree.

Ton [to:n] *m* -(e)s, -e (*Erde*) clay // *m* -e (*Laut*) sound; (*MUS*), note; (*Redeweise*) tone; (*Farb~, Nuance*) shade; (*Betonung*) stress; **~abnehmer** *m* pick-up; **t~angebend** *a* leading; **~art** *f* (musical) key; **~band** *nt* tape; **~bandgerät** *nt* tape recorder.

tönen ['tø:nən] *vi* sound // *vt* shade; (*Haare*) tint.

tönern ['tø:nərn] *a* clay.

Ton- *zW:* **~fall** *m* intonation; **~film** *m* sound film; **~leiter** *f* (*MUS*) scale; **t~los** *a* soundless.

Tonne ['tɔnə] *f* -, -n barrel; (*Maß*) ton.

Ton- *zW:* **~spur** *f* soundtrack; **~taube** *f* clay pigeon; **~waren** *pl* pottery, earthenware.

Topf [tɔpf] *m* -(e)s, -e pot; **~blume** *f* pot plant.

Töpfer ['tœpfər] *m* -s, - potter; **~ei** [-'raı] *f* piece of pottery; potter's workshop; **~scheibe** *f* potter's wheel.

topographisch [topo'gra:fıʃ] *a* topographic.

Tor [to:r] *m* -en, -en fool // *nt* -(e)s, -e gate; (*SPORT*) goal; **~bogen** *m* archway.

Torf [tɔrf] *m* -(e)s peat.

Tor- *zW:* **~heit** *f* foolishness; foolish deed; **~hüter** *m* -s, - goalkeeper.

töricht ['tø:rıçt] *a* foolish.

torkeln ['tɔrkəln] *vi* stagger, reel.

Torpedo [tɔr'pe:do] *m* -s, -s torpedo.

Torte ['tɔrtə] *f* -, -n cake; (*Obst~*) flan, tart.

Tortur [tɔr'tu:r] *f* ordeal.

Torwart *m* -(e)s, -e goalkeeper.

tosen ['to:zən] *vi* roar.

tot [to:t] *a* dead.

total [to'ta:l] *a* total; **~itär** [totali'tɛ:r] *a* totalitarian; **T~schaden** *m* (*AUT*) complete write-off.

töten ['tø:tən] *vti* kill.

Toten- ['to:tən] *zW:* **~bett** *nt* death bed; **t~blaß** *a* deathly pale, white as a sheet; **~kopf** *m* skull; **~schein** *m* death certificate; **~stille** *f* deathly silence.

Tot- *zW:* **~e(r)** *mf* dead person; **t~fahren** *vt unreg* run over; **t~geboren** *a* stillborn; **t~lachen** *vr* (*umg*) laugh one's head off.

Toto ['to:to] *m od nt* -s, -s pools *pl*; **~schein** *m* pools coupon.

tot- *zW:* **~sagen** *vt*: jdn ~sagen say that sb is dead; **T~schlag** *m* manslaughter; **~schlagen** *vt unreg* (*lit, fig*) kill; **~schweigen** *vt unreg* hush up; **~stellen** *vr* pretend to be dead.

Tötung ['tø:tuŋ] *f* killing.

Toupet [tu'pe:] *nt* -s, -s toupee.

toupieren [tu'pi:rən] *vt* back-comb.

Tour [tu:r] *f* -, -en tour, trip; (*Umdrehung*) revolution; (*Verhaltensart*) way; in einer ~ incessantly; **Tourenzähler** *m* rev counter; **~ismus** [tu'rısmʊs] *m* tourism; **~ist** [tu'rıst] *m* tourist; **~istenklasse** *f* tourist class; **Tournee** [tʊr'ne:] *f* -, -n (*THEAT etc*) tour; auf Tournee gehen go on tour.

Trab [tra:p] *m* -(e)s trot; **~ant** [tra'bant] *m* satellite; **~antenstadt** *f* satellite town; **t~en** *vi* trot.

Tracht [traxt] *f* -, -en (*Kleidung*) costume, dress; eine ~ Prügel a sound thrashing; **t~en** *vi* strive (*nach* for), endeavour; jdm nach dem Leben t~en seek to kill sb.

trächtig ['trɛçtıç] *a* (*Tier*) pregnant.

Tradition [traditsi'o:n] *f* tradition; **t~ell** [-'nɛl] *a* traditional.

traf *etc v siehe* **treffen**.

Trag- ['tra:g] *zW:* **~bahre** *f* stretcher; **t~bar** *a* (*Gerät*) portable; (*Kleidung*) wearable; (*erträglich*) bearable.

träge ['trɛ:gə] *a* sluggish, slow; (*PHYS*) inert.

tragen ['tra:gən] *unreg vt* carry; (*Kleidung, Brille*) wear; (*Namen, Früchte*) bear; (*erdulden*) endure; sich mit einem Gedanken ~ have an idea in mind // *vi* (*schwanger sein*) be pregnant; (*Eis*) hold; zum T~ kommen have an effect.

Träger ['trɛ:gər] *m* -s, - carrier; wearer; bearer; (*Ordens~*) holder; (*an*

Kleidung) (shoulder) strap; (*Körperschaft etc*) sponsor; ~**rakete** f launch vehicle; ~**rock** m skirt with shoulder straps.

Trag- ['traːk] *zW*: ~**fläche** f (*AVIAT*) wing; ~**flügelboot** nt hydrofoil.

Trägheit ['trɛːkhaɪt] f laziness; (*PHYS*) inertia.

Tragik ['traːgɪk] f tragedy.

tragisch ['traːgɪʃ] a tragic.

Tragödie [tra'gøːdiə] f tragedy.

Tragweite f range; (*fig*) scope.

Train- [trɛːn] *zW*: ~**er** m -s, - (*SPORT*) trainer, coach; (*Fußball*) manager; **t~ieren** [trɛ'niːrən] vti train; (*Mensch auch*) coach; (*Übung*) practise; ~**ing** nt -s, -s training; ~**ingsanzug** m track suit.

Traktor ['traktɔr] m -s, -en tractor; (*von Drucker*) tractor feed.

trällern ['trɛlərn] vti trill, sing.

trampeln ['trampəln] vti trample, stamp.

trampen ['trɛmpən] vi hitch-hike.

Tran [traːn] m -(e)s, -e train oil, blubber.

Tranchierbesteck [trãˈʃiːrbəʃtɛk] nt (pair of) carvers.

tranchieren [trãˈʃiːrən] vt carve.

Träne ['trɛːnə] f -, -n tear; **t~n** vi water; **Tränengas** nt teargas.

trank *etc* v *siehe* **trinken**.

tränken ['trɛŋkən] vt (*Tiere*) water.

Trans- *zW*: ~**formator** [transfɔr'maːtɔr] m transformer; ~**istor** [tran'zistɔr] m transistor; **t~itiv** ['tranzitiːf] a transitive; **Transitverkehr** m transit traffic; **Transitvisum** nt transit visa; **t~parent** [transpaˈrɛnt] a transparent; ~**parent** nt -(e)s, -e (*Bild*) transparency; (*Spruchband*) banner; **t~pirieren** [transpiˈriːrən] vi perspire; ~**plantation** [transplantatsiˈoːn] f transplantation; (*Haut~plantation*) graft(ing).

Transport [transˈpɔrt] m -(e)s, -e transport; **t~ieren** [transpɔrˈtiːrən] vt transport; ~**kosten** pl transport charges pl, carriage; ~**mittel** nt means of transportation; ~**unternehmen** nt carrier.

Trapez [traˈpeːts] nt -es, -e trapeze; (*MATH*) trapezium.

Traube ['traubə] f -, -n grape; bunch (of grapes); **Traubenzucker** m glucose.

trauen ['trauən] vi: jdm/etw ~ trust sb/sth // vr dare // vt marry.

Trauer ['trauər] f - sorrow; (*für Verstorbenen*) mourning; ~**fall** m death, bereavement; ~**kleidung** f mourning; **t~n** vi mourn (*um* for); ~**rand** m black border; ~**spiel** nt tragedy.

traulich ['traulɪç] a cosy, intimate.

Traum [traum] m -(e)s, **Träume** dream; **Trauma** nt -s, -men trauma.

träum- ['trɔym] *zW*: ~**en** vti dream; **T~er** m -s, - dreamer; **T~e'rei** f dreaming; ~**erisch** a dreamy.

traumhaft a dreamlike; (*fig*) wonderful.

traurig ['trauriç] a sad; **T~keit** f sadness.

Trau- ['trau] *zW*: ~**ring** m wedding ring; ~**schein** m marriage certificate; ~**ung** f wedding ceremony; ~**zeuge** m witness (to a marriage).

treffen ['trɛfən] unreg vti strike, hit; (*Bemerkung*) hurt; (*begegnen*) meet; (*Entscheidung etc*) make; (*Maßnahmen*) take; **er hat es gut getroffen** he did well; ~ **auf** (+akk) come across, meet with // vr meet; **es traf sich, daß...** it so happened that...; **es trifft sich gut** it's convenient; **wie es so trifft** as these things happen; **T~** nt -s, - meeting; ~**d** a pertinent, apposite.

Treffer m -s, - hit; (*Tor*) goal; (*Los*) winner.

Treffpunkt m meeting place.

Treib- ['traɪb] *zW*: ~**eis** nt drift ice; **t~en** unreg vt drive; (*Studien etc*) pursue; (*Sport*) do, go in for; **Unsinn t~en** fool around // vi (*Schiff etc*) drift; (*Pflanzen*) sprout; (*KOCH: aufgehen*) rise; (*Tee, Kaffee*) be diuretic; ~**haus** nt greenhouse; ~**stoff** m fuel.

Trend [trɛnt] m -s, -s trend; ~**wende** f trend away (from sth).

trenn- ['trɛn] *zW*: ~**bar** a separable; ~**en** vt separate; (*teilen*) divide // vr separate; **sich ~en von** part with; **T~schärfe** f (*RAD*) selectivity; **T~ung** f separation; **T~wand** f partition (wall).

Trepp- [trɛp] *zW*: **t~ab** ad downstairs; **t~auf** ad upstairs; ~**e** f -, -n stair(case); **Treppengeländer** nt banister; **Treppenhaus** nt staircase.

Tresor [treˈzoːr] m -s, -e safe.

treten ['treːtən] unreg vi step; (*Tränen, Schweiß*) appear; ~ **nach** kick at; ~ **in** (+akk) step in(to); **in Verbindung** ~ get in contact; **in Erscheinung** ~ appear // vt (*mit Fußtritt*) kick; (*nieder~*) tread, trample.

treu [trɔy] a faithful, true; **T~e** f - loyalty, faithfulness; **T~händer** m -s, - trustee; **T~handgesellschaft** f trust company; ~**herzig** a innocent; ~**los** a faithless.

Tribüne [triˈbyːnə] f -, -n grandstand; (*Redner~*) platform.

Trichter ['trɪçtər] m -s, - funnel; (*in Boden*) crater.

Trick [trɪk] m -s, -e od -s trick; ~**film**

m cartoon.

trieb *etc v siehe* **trieben**.

Trieb [tri:p] *m* -(e)s, -e urge, drive; (*Neigung*) inclination; (*an Baum etc*) shoot; ~**feder** *f* (*fig*) motivating force; ~**kraft** *f* (*fig*) drive; ~**täter** *m* sex offender; ~**werk** *nt* engine.

triefen ['tri:fən] *vi* drip.

triffst *etc v siehe* **treffen**.

triftig ['trɪftɪç] *a* good, convincing.

Trikot [tri'ko:] *nt* -s, -s vest; (*SPORT*) shirt.

Trimester [tri'mɛstər] *nt* -s, - term.

trimmen ['trɪmən] *vr* do keep fit exercises.

trink- ['trɪŋk] *zW:* ~**bar** *a* drinkable; ~**en** *vti unreg* drink; **T**~**er** *m* -s, - drinker; **T**~**geld** *nt* tip; **T**~**spruch** *m* toast; **T**~**wasser** *nt* drinking water.

Tripper ['trɪpər] *m* -s, - gonorrhoea.

Tritt [trɪt] *m* -(e)s, -e step; (*Fuß*~) kick; ~**brett** *nt* (*EISENB*) step; (*AUT*) running-board.

Triumph [tri'ʊmf] *m* -(e)s, -e triumph; ~**bogen** *m* triumphal arch; **t**~**ieren** [-'fi:rən] *vi* triumph; (*jubeln*) exult.

trocken ['trɔkən] *a* dry; **T**~**element** *nt* dry cell; **T**~**haube** *f* hair-dryer; **T**~**heit** *f* dryness; ~**legen** *vt* (*Sumpf*) drain; (*Kind*) put a clean nappy on; **T**~**milch** *f* dried milk.

trocknen ['trɔknən] *vti* dry.

Trödel ['trø:dəl] *m* -s (*umg*) junk; ~**markt** *m* flea market; **t**~**n** *vi* (*umg*) dawdle.

Trog [tro:k] *m* -(e)s, ⁻e trough.

Trommel ['trɔməl] *f* -, -n drum; ~**fell** *nt* eardrum; **t**~**n** *vti* drum.

Trommler ['trɔmlər] *m* -s, - drummer.

Trompete [trɔm'pe:tə] *f* -, -n trumpet; ~**r** *m* -s, - trumpeter.

Tropen ['tro:pən] *pl* tropics *pl*; ~**helm** *m* sun helmet.

tröpfeln ['trœpfəln] *vi* drop, trickle.

Tropfen ['trɔpfən] *m* -s, - drop; **t**~ *vti* drip // *v unpers:* es tropft a few raindrops are falling; **t**~**weise** *ad* in drops.

Tropfsteinhöhle *f* stalactite cave.

tropisch ['tro:pɪʃ] *a* tropical.

Trost [tro:st] *m* -es consolation, comfort; **t**~**bedürftig** *a* in need of consolation.

tröst- ['trø:st] *zW:* ~**en** *vt* console, comfort; **T**~**er(in** *f)* *m* -s, - comfort(er); ~**lich** *a* comforting.

trost- *zW:* ~**los** *a* bleak; (*Verhältnisse*) wretched; **T**~**preis** *m* consolation prize; ~**reich** *a* comforting.

Trott [trɔt] *m* -s, -e trot; (*Routine*) routine; **Trottel** *m* -s, - (*umg*) fool, dope; **t**~**en** *vi* trot; **Trottoir** [trɔto'a:r] *nt* -s, -s *od* -e pavement, sidewalk (*US*).

Trotz [trɔts] *m* -es pigheadedness; etw aus ~ tun do sth just to show them; jdm zum ~ in defiance of sb; **t**~ *präp* +*gen od dat* in spite of; **t**~**dem** *ad* nevertheless, all the same // *kj* although; **t**~**ig** *a* defiant, pig-headed; ~**kopf** *m* obstinate child; ~**reaktion** *f* fit of pique.

trüb [try:p] *a* dull; (*Flüssigkeit, Glas*) cloudy; (*fig*) gloomy.

Trubel ['tru:bəl] *m* -s, - hurly-burly.

trüb- *zW:* ~**en** ['try:bən] *vt* cloud // *vr* become clouded; **T**~**heit** *f* dullness; cloudiness; gloom; **T**~**sal** *f* -, -e distress; ~**selig** *a* sad, melancholy; **T**~**sinn** *m* depression; ~**sinnig** *a* depressed, gloomy.

Trüffel ['trʏfəl] *f* -, -n truffle.

trug *etc v siehe* **tragen**.

trüg- ['try:g] *zW:* ~**en** *unreg vt* deceive // *vi* be deceptive; ~**erisch** *a* deceptive.

Trugschluß ['tru:gʃlʊs] *m* false conclusion.

Truhe ['tru:ə] *f* -, -n chest.

Trümmer ['trʏmər] *pl* wreckage; (*Bau*~) ruins *pl*; ~**haufen** *m* heap of rubble.

Trumpf [trʊmpf] *m* -(e)s, ⁻e (*lit, fig*) trump; **t**~**en** *vti* trump.

Trunk [trʊŋk] *m* -(e)s, ⁻e drink; **t**~**en** *a* intoxicated; ~**enheit** *f* intoxication; ~**enheit am Steuer** drunken driving; ~**sucht** *f* alcoholism.

Trupp [trʊp] *m* -s, -s troop; ~**e** *f* -, -n troop; (*Waffengattung*) force; (*Schauspiel*~) troupe; ~**en** *pl* troops *pl*; ~**enübungsplatz** *m* training area.

Truthahn ['tru:tha:n] *m* turkey.

Tschech- [tʃɛç] *zW:* ~**e** *m*, ~**in** *f*, ~**oslowake** [-oslo'va:kə] *m*, ~**oslowakin** *f* Czech, Czechoslovak(ian); **t**~**isch**, **t**~**oslowakisch** [-oslo'va:kɪʃ] *a* Czech, Czechoslovak(ian).

tschüs [tʃy:s] *interj* cheerio.

T-Shirt ['ti:ʃœrt] *nt* T-shirt.

Tube ['tu:bə] *f* -, -n tube.

Tuberkulose [tuberku'lo:zə] *f* -, -n tuberculosis.

Tuch [tu:x] *nt* -(e)s, ⁻er cloth; (*Hals*~) scarf; (*Kopf*~) headscarf; (*Hand*~) towel.

tüchtig ['tʏçtɪç] *a* efficient, (cap)able; (*umg: kräftig*) good, sound; **T**~**keit** *f* efficiency, ability.

Tücke ['tʏkə] *f* -, -n (*Arglist*) malice; (*Trick*) trick; (*Schwierigkeit*) difficulty, problem; seine ~**n** haben be temperamental.

tückisch ['tʏkɪʃ] *a* treacherous; (*böswillig*) malicious.

Tugend ['tu:gənt] *f* -, -en virtue; **t**~**haft** *a* virtuous.

Tüll [tʏl] *m* -s, -e tulle; ~**e** *f* -, -n

spout.

Tulpe ['tulpə] f -, -n tulip.

Tumor ['tu:mɔr] m -s, -e tumour.

Tümpel ['tʏmpəl] m -s, - pool, pond.

Tumult [tu'mult] m -(e)s, -e tumult.

tun [tu:n] unreg vt (machen) do; (legen) put; jdm etw ~ (antun) do sth to sb; etw tut es auch sth will do; das tut nichts that doesn't matter; das tut nichts zur Sache that's neither here nor there // vi act; so ~, als ob act as if // vr: es tut sich etwas/viel something/a lot is happening.

tünchen ['tʏnçən] vt whitewash.

Tunesien [tu'ne:ziən] nt Tunisia.

Tunke ['tuŋkə] f -, -n sauce; **t~n** vt dip, dunk.

tunlichst ['tu:nliçst] ad if at all possible; ~ bald as soon as possible.

Tunnel ['tunəl] m -s, -s od - tunnel.

tupfen ['tupfən] vti dab; (mit Farbe) dot; **T~** m -s, - dot, spot.

Tür [ty:r] f -, -en door.

Turban ['turban] m -s, -e turban.

Turbine [tur'bi:nə] f turbine.

Türk- [tʏrk] zW: **~e** m Turk; **~ei** [tʏr'kaɪ] f: die **~ei** Turkey.

Türkis [tʏr'ki:s] m -es, -e turquoise; **t~** a turquoise.

türkisch ['tʏrkɪʃ] a Turkish.

Turm [turm] m -(e)s, -̈e tower; (Kirch~) steeple; (Sprung~) diving platform; (SCHACH) castle, rook.

türmen ['tʏrmən] vr tower up // vt heap up // vi (umg) scarper, bolt.

Turn- ['turn] zW: **t~en** vi do gymnastic exercises // vt perform; **~en** nt -s gymnastics; (SCH) physical education, P.E.; **~er(in f)** m -s, - gymnast; **~halle** f gym(nasium); **~hose** f gym shorts pl.

Turnier [tur'ni:r] nt -s, -e tournament.

Turn- zW: **~verein** m gymnastics club; **~schuh** m gym shoe; **~zeug** nt gym things pl.

Tusche ['tuʃə] f -, -n Indian ink.

tuscheln ['tuʃəln] vti whisper.

Tuschkasten m paintbox.

Tüte ['ty:tə] f -, -n bag.

tuten ['tu:tən] vi (AUT) hoot (Brit), honk (US).

TÜV [tʏf] m abk (= Technischer Überwachungsverein) MOT.

Typ [ty:p] m -s, -en type; **~e** f -, -n (TYP) type; **Typenraddrucker** m daisy-wheel printer.

Typhus ['ty:fus] m - typhoid (fever).

typisch ['ty:piʃ] a typical (für of).

Tyrann [ty'ran] m -en, -en tyrant; **~ei** [-'naɪ] f tyranny; **t~isch** a tyrannical; **t~i'sieren** vt tyrannize.

U

U, u [u:] nt U, u.

u. abk von und.

u.a. abk von unter anderem.

U-Bahn ['u:ba:n] f underground, tube.

übel ['y:bəl] a bad; (moralisch auch) wicked; jdm ist ~ sb feels sick; **Ü~nt** -s, - evil; (Krankheit) disease; **~gelaunt** a bad-tempered; **Ü~keit** f nausea; **~nehmen** vt unreg: jdm eine Bemerkung ~nehmen be offended at sb's remark etc.

üben ['y:bən] vti exercise, practise.

über ['y:bər] ◆präp +dat 1 (räumlich) over, above; zwei Grad ~ Null two degrees above zero.

2 (zeitlich) over; ~ der Arbeit einschlafen fall asleep over one's work ◆präp +akk 1 (räumlich) over; (hoch ~ auch) above; (quer ~ auch) across.

2 (zeitlich) over; ~ Weihnachten over Christmas; ~ kurz oder lang sooner or later

3 (mit Zahlen): Kinder ~ 12 Jahren children over od above 12 years of age; ein Scheck ~ 200 Mark a cheque for 200 marks

4 (auf dem Wege) via; nach Köln ~ Aachen to Cologne via Aachen; ich habe es ~ die Auskunft erfahren I found out from information

5 (betreffend) ein Buch ~ ... a book about od on ...; ~ jdn/etw lachen laugh about od at sb/sth

6: Macht ~ jdn haben have power over sb; sie liebt ihn ~ alles she loves him more than everything ◆ad over; ~ und ~ over and over; den ganzen Tag ~ all day long; jdm in etw (dat) ~ sein be superior to sb in sth.

überall [y:bər'?al] ad everywhere; **~'hin** ad everywhere.

überanstrengen [y:bər'?anʃtrɛŋən] vtr insep overexert (o.s.).

überarbeiten [y:bər'?arbaɪtn] vt insep revise, rework // vr overwork (o.s.).

überaus ['y:bər?aus] ad exceedingly.

überbelichten ['y:bərbəliçtən] vt (PHOT) overexpose.

über'bieten vt unreg insep outbid; (übertreffen) surpass; (Rekord) break.

Überbleibsel ['y:bərblaɪpsəl] nt -s, - residue, remainder.

Überblick ['y:bərblɪk] m view; (fig: Darstellung) survey, overview; (Fähigkeit) overall view, grasp (über +akk of); **ü~en** [-'blɪkən] vt insep survey.

überbring- [y:bər'brɪŋ] zW: **~en**

vt unreg insep deliver, hand over; **Ü~er** *m* **-s,** - bearer; **Ü~ung** *f* delivery.

überbrücken [y:bər'brykən] *vt insep* bridge (over).

über'dauern *vt insep* outlast.

über'denken *vt unreg insep* think over.

überdies [y:bər'di:s] *ad* besides.

überdimensional ['y:bərdimɛnziona:l] *a* oversize.

Überdruß ['y:bərdrus] *m* **-sses** weariness; **bis zum ~** ad nauseam.

überdrüssig ['y:bərdrysıç] *a* tired, sick (*gen* of).

übereifrig ['y:bəraifrıç] *a* overkeen.

übereilt [y:bər'ailt] *a* (over)hasty, premature.

überein- [y:bər'ain] *zW:* **~ander** [y:bər'ai'nandər] *ad* one upon the other; (*sprechen*) about each other; **~kommen** *vi unreg* agree; **Ü~kunft** *f* -, **-künfte** agreement; **~stimmen** *vi* agree; **Ü~stimmung** *f* agreement.

überempfindlich ['y:bərɛmpfintlıç] *a* hypersensitive.

überfahren [y:bər'fa:rən] *vt unreg insep* (*AUT*) run over; (*fig*) walk all over.

Überfahrt ['y:bərfa:rt] *f* crossing.

Überfall ['y:bərfal] *m* (*Bank~*, *MIL*) raid; (*auf jdn*) assault; **ü~en** [-'falən] *vt unreg insep* attack; (*Bank*) raid; (*besuchen*) surprise.

überfällig ['y:bərfɛlıç] *a* overdue.

über'fliegen *vt unreg insep* fly over, overfly; (*Buch*) skim through.

Überfluß ['y:bərflus] *m* (*super*)-abundance, excess (*an* +*dat* of).

überflüssig ['y:bərflysıç] *a* superfluous.

über'fordern *vt insep* demand too much of; (*Kräfte etc*) overtax.

über'führen *vt insep* (*Leiche etc*) transport; (*Täter*) have convicted (*gen* of).

Über'führung *f* transport; conviction; (*Brücke*) bridge, overpass.

Übergabe ['y:bərga:bə] *f* handing over; (*MIL*) surrender.

Übergang ['y:bərgaŋ] *m* crossing; (*Wandel, Überleitung*) transition.

Übergangs- *zW:* **~erscheinung** *f* transitory phenomenon; **~lösung** *f* provisional solution, stopgap; **~stadium** *nt* transitional stage; **~zeit** *f* transitional period.

über'geben *unreg insep vt* hand over; (*MIL*) surrender; **dem Verkehr ~** open to traffic // *vr* be sick.

übergehen ['y:bərge:ən] *unreg vi* (*Besitz*) pass; (*zum Feind etc*) go over, defect; (*überleiten*) go on (*zu* to); (*sich verwandeln*) turn (*in* +*akk* into) // [-'ge:ən] *vt insep* pass over, omit.

Übergewicht ['y:bərgəvıçt] *nt* excess weight; (*fig*) preponderance.

überglücklich ['y:bərglyklıç] *a* overjoyed.

übergroß ['y:bərgro:s] *a* outsize, huge.

überhandnehmen [y:bər'hantne:mən] *vi unreg* gain the ascendancy.

überhaupt [y:bər'haupt] *ad* at all; (*im allgemeinen*) in general; (*besonders*) especially; **~ nicht/keine** not/none at all.

überheblich [y:bər'he:plıç] *a* arrogant; **Ü~keit** *f* arrogance.

über'holen *vt insep* overtake; (*TECH*) overhaul.

überholt *a* out-of-date, obsolete.

über'hören *vt insep* not hear; (*absichtlich*) ignore.

überirdisch ['y:bər'ırdıʃ] *a* supernatural, unearthly.

über'laden *vt unreg insep* overload // *a* (*fig*) cluttered.

über'lassen *unreg insep vt:* **jdm etw ~** leave sth to sb // *vr:* **sich etw** (*dat*) **~** give o.s. over to sth.

über'lasten *vt insep* overload; (*Mensch*) overtax.

überlaufen ['y:bərlaufən] *unreg vi* (*Flüssigkeit*) flow over; (*zum Feind etc*) go over, defect // [-'laufən] *vt insep* (*Schauer etc*) come over; **~ sein** be inundated *od* besieged.

Überläufer ['y:bərloyfər] *m* deserter.

über'leben *vt insep* survive; **Ü~de(r)** *mf* survivor.

über'legen *vt insep* consider; **ich muß es mir ~** I'll have to think about it // *a* superior; **Ü~heit** *f* superiority.

Überlegung *f* consideration, deliberation.

über'liefern *vt insep* hand down, transmit.

Überlieferung *f* tradition.

überlisten [y:bər'lıstən] *vt insep* outwit.

überm ['y:bərm] = **über dem**.

Übermacht ['y:bərmaxt] *f* superior force, superiority.

übermächtig ['y:bərmɛçtıç] *a* superior (in strength); (*Gefühl etc*) overwhelming.

übermannen [y:bər'manən] *vt insep* overcome.

Übermaß ['y:bərma:s] *nt* excess (*an* +*dat* of).

übermäßig ['y:bərmɛ:sıç] *a* excessive.

Übermensch ['y:bərmɛnʃ] *m* superman; **ü~lich** *a* superhuman.

übermitteln [y:bər'mıtəln] *vt insep* convey.

übermorgen ['y:bərmɔrgən] *ad* the day after tomorrow.

Übermüdung [y:bər'my:duŋ] *f* fatigue, overtiredness.

Übermut ['y:bərmu:t] *m* exuberance.

übermütig ['y:bərmy:tıç] a exuberant, high-spirited; ~ **werden** get overconfident.

übernachten [y:bər'naxtən] vi insep spend the night (bei jdm at sb's place).

Übernachtung [y:bər'naxtʊŋ] f overnight stay.

Übernahme ['y:bərna:mə] f -, -n taking over od on, acceptance.

über'nehmen unreg insep vt take on, accept; (Amt, Geschäft) take over // vr take on too much.

über'prüfen vt insep examine, check.

Überprüfung f examination.

überqueren [y:bər'kve:rən] vt insep cross.

überragen [y:bər'ra:gən] vt insep tower above; (fig) surpass.

überraschen [y:bər'raʃən] vt insep surprise.

Überraschung f surprise.

überreden [y:bər're:dən] vt insep persuade.

überreichen [y:bər'raiçən] vt insep present, hand over.

Überreste ['y:bərrɛstə] pl remains pl, remnants pl.

überrumpeln [y:bər'rʊmpəln] vt insep take by surprise.

überrunden [y:bər'rʊndən] vt insep lap.

übers ['y:bərs] = über das.

Überschall- ['y:bərʃal] zW: ~**flugzeug** nt supersonic jet; ~**geschwindigkeit** f supersonic speed.

über'schätzen vtr insep overestimate.

Überschlag ['y:bərʃla:k] m (FIN) estimate; (SPORT) somersault; **ü~en** [-'ʃla:gən] unreg insep vt (berechnen) estimate; (auslassen: Seite) omit // vr somersault; (Stimme) crack; (AVIAT) loop the loop // ['y:bərʃla:gən] unreg vt (Beine) cross // vi (Wellen) break over; (Funken) flash over.

überschnappen ['y:bərʃnapən] vi (Stimme) crack; (umg: Mensch) flip one's lid.

über'schneiden vr unreg insep (lit, fig) overlap; (Linien) intersect.

über'schreiben vt unreg insep provide with a heading; **jdm etw** ~ transfer od make over sth to sb.

über'schreiten vt unreg insep cross over; (fig) exceed; (verletzen) transgress.

Überschrift ['y:bərʃrıft] f heading, title.

Überschuß ['y:bərʃʊs] m surplus (an +dat of).

überschüssig ['y:bərʃysıç] a surplus, excess.

über'schütten vt insep: jdn/etw mit etw ~ (lit) pour sth over sb/sth; jdn mit etw ~ (fig) shower sb with sth.

überschwemmen [y:bər'ʃvɛmən] vt insep flood.

Überschwemmung f flood.

überschwenglich ['y:bərʃvɛŋlıç] a effusive.

Übersee ['y:bərze:] f: nach/in ~ overseas; **ü~isch** a overseas.

über'sehen vt unreg insep look (out) over; (fig: Folgen) see, get an over: all view of; (: nicht beachten) overlook.

über'senden vt unreg insep send, forward.

übersetz- zW: ~**en** [y:bər'zɛtsən] vt insep translate // ['y:bərzɛtsən] vi cross; **Ü~er(in** f) [-'zɛtsər(ın)] m -s, -translator; **Ü~ung** [-zɛtsʊŋ] f translation; (TECH) gear ratio.

Übersicht ['y:bərzıçt] f overall view; (Darstellung) survey; **ü~lich** a clear; (Gelände) open; ~**lichkeit** f clarity, lucidity.

übersiedeln ['y:bərzi:dəln] od [y:bər'zi:dəln] vi sep od insep move.

über'spannen vt insep (zu sehr spannen) overstretch; (überdecken) cover.

über'spannt a eccentric; (Idee) wild, crazy; **Ü~heit** f eccentricity.

überspitzt [y:bər'ʃpıtst] a exaggerated.

über'springen vt unreg insep jump over; (fig) skip.

überstehen [y:bər'ʃte:ən] unreg vt insep overcome, get over; (Winter etc) survive, get through // ['y:bərʃte:ən] vi project.

über'steigen vt unreg insep climb over; (fig) exceed.

über'stimmen vt insep outvote.

Überstunden ['y:bərʃtʊndən] pl overtime.

über'stürzen insep vt rush // vr follow (one another) in rapid succession.

überstürzt a (over)hasty.

über'tönen vt insep drown (out).

Übertrag ['y:bərtra:k] m -(e)s, -träge (COMM) amount brought forward; **ü~bar** [-'tra:kba:r] a transferable; (MED) infectious; **ü~en** [-'tra:gən] unreg insep vt transfer (auf +akk to); (RAD) broadcast; (übersetzen) render; (Krankheit) transmit; jdm etw **ü~en** assign sth to sb // vr spread (auf +akk to) // a figurative; ~**ung** [-'tra:gʊŋ] f transfer(ence); (RAD) broadcast; rendering; transmission.

über'treffen vt unreg insep surpass.

über'treiben vt unreg insep exaggerate.

Übertreibung f exaggeration.

übertreten [y:bər'tre:tən] unreg vt

insep cross; (*Gebot etc*) break //
['y:bǝrtre:tǝn] *vi* (*über Linie, Gebiet*)
step (over); (*SPORT*) overstep; (*in
andere Partei*) go over (*in +akk* to);
(*zu anderem Glauben*) be converted.

Über'tretung *f* violation, transgres-
sion.

übertrieben [y:bǝr'tri:bǝn] *a* exaggerated, excessive.

übervölkert [y:bǝr'fœlkǝrt] *a* over-
populated.

übervoll ['y:bǝrfɔl] *a* overfull.

übervorteilen [y:bǝr'fɔrtailǝn] *vt insep*
dupe, cheat.

über'wachen *vt insep* supervise;
(*Verdächtigen*) keep under surveillance.

Überwachung *f* supervision; surveillance.

überwältigen [y:bǝr'vɛltigǝn] *vt insep*
overpower; ~**d** *a* overwhelming.

überweisen [y:bǝr'vaizǝn] *vt unreg
insep* transfer.

Überweisung *f* transfer.

über'wiegen *vi unreg insep* predominate; ~**d** *a* predominant.

über'winden *unreg insep vt* overcome // *vr* make an effort, bring oneself (to do sth).

Überwindung *f* effort, strength of
mind.

Überzahl ['y:bǝrtsa:l] *f* superiority,
superior numbers *pl*; **in der ~ sein**
outnumber sb, be numerically superior.

überzählig ['y:bǝrtsɛ:lɪç] *a* surplus.

über'zeugen *vt insep* convince (*von
etw* of sth); ~**d** *a* convincing.

Überzeugung *f* conviction; **Über-
zeugungskraft** *f* power of persuasion.

überziehen ['y:bǝrtsi:ǝn] *unreg vt* put
on // [-'tsi:ǝn] *vt insep* cover; (*Konto*)
overdraw.

Überzug ['y:bǝrtsu:k] *m* cover; (*Belag*) coating.

üblich ['y:plɪç] *a* usual.

U-Boot ['u:bo:t] *nt* submarine.

übrig ['y:brɪç] *a* remaining; **für jdn
etwas ~ haben** (*umg*) be fond of sb;
die ~en ['y:brɪgǝn] the others; **das
~e** the rest; **im ~en** besides;
~**bleiben** *vi unreg* remain, be left
(over); **übrigens** *ad* besides;
(*nebenbei bemerkt*) by the way;
~**lassen** *vt unreg* leave (over).

Übung ['y:buŋ] *f* practice; (*Turn~,
Aufgabe etc*) exercise; ~ **macht den
Meister** practice makes perfect.

UdSSR [u:de:'ɛs'ɛs'ɛr] *f abk* (=
*Union der Sozialistischen Sowjetrepu-
bliken*) USSR.

Ufer ['u:fǝr] *nt* -s, - bank; (*Meeres~*)
shore.

Uhr [u:r] *f* -, -en clock; (*Armband~*)
watch; **wieviel ~ ist es?** what time is

it?; **1 ~ 1** o'clock; **20 ~ 8** o'clock,
20.00 (twenty hundred) hours; ~**band**
nt watch strap; ~**kette** *f* watch
chain; ~**macher** *m* **-s,** - watch-
maker; ~**werk** *nt* clockwork; works
of a watch; ~**zeiger** *m* hand;
~**zeigersinn** *m*: **im** ~**zeigersinn**
clockwise; **entgegen dem ~zeigersinn**
anticlockwise; ~**zeit** *f* time (of day).

Uhu ['u:hu] *m* **-s, -s** eagle owl.

UKW [u:ka:'ve:] *abk* (= *Ultrakurz-
welle*) VHF.

Ulk [ʊlk] *m* **-s, -e** lark; **u~ig** *a* funny.

Ulme ['ʊlmǝ] *f* -, -n elm.

Ultimatum [ʊlti'ma:tʊm] *nt* **-s,**
Ultimaten ultimatum.

ultraviolett ['ʊltravio'let] *a* ultraviolet.

um [ʊm] ♦*präp* +*akk* **1** (~ *herum*)
(a)round; ~ **Weihnachten** around
Christmas; **er schlug ~ sich** he hit
about him

2 (*mit Zeitangabe*) at; ~ **acht** (**Uhr**)
at eight (o'clock)

3 (*mit Größenangabe*) by; **etw ~ 4
cm kürzen** shorten sth by 4 cm; ~
10% teurer 10% more expensive; ~
vieles besser better by far; ~ **nichts
besser** not in the least bit better; ~
so besser so much the better

4: **der Kampf ~ den Titel** the battle
for the title; ~ **Geld spielen** play for
money; **Stunde ~ Stunde** hour after
hour; **Auge ~ Auge** an eye for an eye
♦*präp* +*gen*: ~ **... willen** for the
sake of ...; ~ **Gottes willen** for goodness *od* (*stärker*) God's sake

♦*kj*: ~ **... zu** (in order) to; **zu klug,**
~ **zu ...** too clever to ...; ~ **so
besser/schlimmer** so much the
better/worse

♦*ad* **1** (*ungefähr*) about; ~ (**die**) **30
Leute** about *od* around 30 people

2 (*vorbei*): **die 2 Stunden sind ~** the
two hours are up

umänder- ['um'ɛndǝr] *zW*: ~**n** *vt* alter; **U~ung** *f* alteration.

umarbeiten ['um'arbaitǝn] *vt* re-
model; (*Buch etc*) revise, rework.

umarmen [um'armǝn] *vt insep* embrace.

Umbau ['umbau] *m* -(e)s, -e *od* -ten
reconstruction, alteration(s); **u~en**
vt rebuild, reconstruct.

umbenennen ['umbǝnɛnǝn] *vt unreg*
rename.

umbilden ['umbɪldǝn] *vt* reorganize;
(*POL: Kabinett*) reshuffle.

umbinden ['umbɪndǝn] *vt unreg*
(*Krawatte etc*) put on.

umblättern ['umblɛtǝrn] *vt* turn over.

umblicken ['umblɪkǝn] *vr* look around.

umbringen ['umbrɪŋǝn] *vt unreg* kill.

Umbruch ['umbrʊx] *m* radical
change; (*TYP*) make-up.

umbuchen ['umbu:xǝn] *vti* change

one's reservation/flight *etc.*
umdenken ['umdɛŋkən] *vi unreg* adjust one's views.
umdrehen ['umdre:ən] *vtr* turn (round); (*Hals*) wring.
Um'drehung *f* revolution; rotation.
umeinander [um'aɪ'nandər] *ad* round one another; (*füreinander*) for one another.
umfahren ['umfa:rən] *vt unreg* run over // [-'fa:rən] *insep* drive/sail round.
umfallen ['umfalən] *vi unreg* fall down *od* over.
Umfang ['umfaŋ] *m* extent; (*von Buch*) size; (*Reichweite*) range; (*Fläche*) area; (*MATH*) circumference; **u~reich** *a* extensive; (*Buch etc*) voluminous.
um'fassen *vt insep* embrace; (*umgeben*) surround; (*enthalten*) include; **~d** *a* comprehensive, extensive.
umform- ['umform] *zW:* **~en** *vi* transform; **U~er** *m* **-s,** - (*ELEK*) transformer, converter.
Umfrage ['umfra:gə] *f* poll.
umfüllen ['umfʏlən] *vt* transfer; (*Wein*) decant.
umfunktionieren ['umfuŋktsioni:rən] *vt* convert, transform.
Umgang ['umgaŋ] *m* company; (*mit jdm*) dealings *pl;* (*Behandlung*) way of behaving.
umgänglich ['umgɛŋlıç] *a* sociable.
Umgangs- *zW:* **~formen** *pl* manners *pl;* **~sprache** *f* colloquial language.
umgeb- [um'ge:b] *zW:* **~en** *vt unreg insep* surround; **U~ung** *f* surroundings *pl;* (*Milieu*) environment; (*Personen*) people in one's circle.
umgehen ['umge:ən] *unreg vi* go (a)round; **im Schlosse ~** haunt the castle; **mit jdm grob** *etc* **~** treat sb roughly *etc;* **mit Geld sparsam ~** be careful with one's money // [-'ge:ən] *vt insep* bypass; (*MIL*) outflank; (*Gesetz etc*) circumvent; (*vermeiden*) avoid; **'~d** *a* immediate.
Um'gehung *f* bypassing; outflanking; circumvention; avoidance; **Umgehungsstraße** *f* bypass.
umgekehrt ['umgəke:rt] *a* reverse(d); (*gegenteilig*) opposite // *ad* the other way around; **und ~** and vice versa.
umgraben ['umgra:bən] *vt unreg* dig up.
Umhang ['umhaŋ] *m* wrap, cape.
umhauen ['umhauən] *vt* fell; (*fig*) bowl over.
umher [um'he:r] *ad* about, around; **~gehen** *vi unreg* walk about; **~ziehen** *vi unreg* wander from place to place.
umhinkönnen [um'hınkœnən] *vi unreg:* **ich kann nicht umhin, das zu tun**

I can't help doing it.
umhören ['umhø:rən] *vr* ask around.
Umkehr ['umke:r] *f* - turning back; (*Änderung*) change; **u~en** *vi* turn back // *vt* turn round, reverse; (*Tasche etc*) turn inside out; (*Gefäß etc*) turn upside down.
umkippen ['umkıpən] *vt* tip over // *vi* overturn; (*fig: Meinung ändern*) change one's mind; (*umg: Mensch*) keel over.
Umkleideraum ['umklaɪdəraum] *m* changing- *od* dressing room.
umkommen ['umkɔmən] *vi unreg* die, perish; (*Lebensmittel*) go bad.
Umkreis ['umkraɪs] *m* neighbourhood; **im ~ von** within a radius of.
Umlage ['umla:gə] *f* share of the costs.
Umlauf ['umlauf] *m* (*Geld~*) circulation; (*von Gestirn*) revolution; **~bahn** *f* orbit.
Umlaut ['umlaut] *m* umlaut.
umlegen ['umle:gən] *vt* put on; (*verlegen*) move, shift; (*Kosten*) share out; (*umkippen*) tip over; (*umg: töten*) bump off.
umleiten ['umlaɪtən] *vt* divert.
Umleitung *f* diversion.
umliegend ['umli:gənt] *a* surrounding.
um'rahmen *vt insep* frame.
um'randen *vt insep* border, edge.
umrechnen ['umrɛçnən] *vt* convert.
Umrechnung *f* conversion; **Umrechnungskurs** *m* rate of exchange.
um'reißen *vt unreg insep* outline, sketch.
um'ringen *vt insep* surround.
Umriß ['umrıs] *m* outline.
umrühren ['umry:rən] *vti* stir.
ums [ums] **= um das.**
Umsatz ['umzats] *m* turnover.
umschalten ['umʃaltən] *vt* switch.
Umschau ['umʃau] *f* look(ing) round; **~ halten nach** look around for; **u~en** *vr* look round.
Umschlag ['umʃla:k] *m* cover; (*Buch~ auch*) jacket; (*MED*) compress; (*Brief~*) envelope; (*Wechsel*) change; (*von Hose*) turn-up; **u~en** ['umʃla:gən] *unreg vi* change; (*NAUT*) capsize // *vt* knock over; (*Ärmel*) turn up; (*Seite*) turn over; (*Waren*) transfer; **~platz** *m* (*COMM*) distribution centre.
umschreiben *vt unreg* ['umʃraɪbən] (*neu~*) rewrite; (*übertragen*) transfer (*auf +akk* to) // [-'ʃraɪbən] *insep* paraphrase; (*abgrenzen*) define.
umschulen ['umʃu:lən] *vt* retrain; (*Kind*) send to another school.
Umschweife ['umʃvaɪfə] *pl:* **ohne ~** without beating about the bush, straight out.
Umschwung ['umʃvuŋ] *m* change

(around), revolution.

umsehen ['ʊmzeːən] vr unreg look around od about; (suchen) look out (nach for).

umseitig ['ʊmzaɪtɪç] ad overleaf.

Umsicht ['ʊmzɪçt] f prudence, caution; **u~ig** a cautious, prudent.

umsonst [ʊm'zɔnst] ad in vain; (gratis) for nothing.

umspringen ['ʊmʃprɪŋən] vi unreg change; (Wind auch) veer; **mit jdm ~** treat sb badly.

Umstand ['ʊmʃtant] m circumstance; **Umstände** pl (fig: Schwierigkeiten) fuss; **in anderen Umständen sein** be pregnant; **Umstände machen** go to a lot of trouble; **unter Umständen** possibly.

umständlich ['ʊmʃtɛntlɪç] a, ad (Methode) cumbersome, complicated; (Ausdrucksweise, Erklärung auch) long-winded; (Mensch) ponderous.

Umstandskleid nt maternity dress.

Umstehende(n) ['ʊmʃteːəndə(n)] pl bystanders pl.

umsteigen ['ʊmʃtaɪgən] vi unreg (EISENB) change.

umstellen ['ʊmʃtɛlən] vt (an anderen Ort) change round, rearrange; (TECH) convert // vr adapt o.s. (auf +akk to) // [ʊm'ʃtɛlən] vt insep surround.

Umstellung ['ʊmʃtɛlʊŋ] f change; (Umgewöhnung) adjustment; (TECH) conversion.

umstimmen ['ʊmʃtɪmən] vt (MUS) retune; **jdn ~** make sb change his mind.

umstoßen ['ʊmʃtoːsən] vt unreg (lit) overturn; (Plan etc) change, upset.

umstritten [ʊm'ʃtrɪtən] a disputed.

Umsturz ['ʊmʃtʊrts] m overthrow.

umstürzen ['ʊmʃtʏrtsən] vt (umwerfen) overturn // vi collapse, fall down; (Wagen) overturn.

Umtausch ['ʊmtaʊʃ] m exchange; **u~en** vt exchange.

umwandeln ['ʊmvandəln] vt change, convert; (ELEK) transform.

umwechseln ['ʊmvɛksəln] vt change.

Umweg ['ʊmveːk] m detour, roundabout way.

Umwelt ['ʊmvɛlt] f environment; **u~freundlich** a not harmful to the environment; **u~feindlich** a ecologically harmful; **~schutz** m conservation; **~schützer** m environmentalist; **~verschmutzung** f environmental pollution.

umwenden ['ʊmvɛndən] vtr unreg turn (round).

um'werben vt unreg insep court, woo.

umwerfen ['ʊmvɛrfən] vt unreg (lit)

upset, overturn; (Mantel) throw on; (fig: erschüttern) upset, throw.

umziehen ['ʊmtsiːən] unreg vtr change // vi move.

umzingeln [ʊm'tsɪŋəln] vt insep surround, encircle.

Umzug ['ʊmtsuːk] m procession; (Wohnungs~) move, removal.

unab- ['ʊnʔap] zW: **~änderlich** a irreversible, unalterable; **~hängig** a independent; **U~hängigkeit** f independence; **~kömmlich** a indispensable; **zur Zeit ~kömmlich** not free at the moment; **~lässig** a incessant, constant; **~sehbar** a immeasurable; (Folgen) unforeseeable; (Kosten) incalculable; **~sichtlich** a unintentional; **~'wendbar** a inevitable.

unachtsam ['ʊnʔaxtzaːm] a careless; **U~keit** f carelessness.

unan- ['ʊnʔan] zW: **~'fechtbar** a indisputable; **~gebracht** a uncalled-for; **~gemessen** a inadequate; **~genehm** a unpleasant; **~gepaßt** a nonconformist; **U~nehmlichkeit** f inconvenience // pl trouble; **~sehnlich** a unsightly; **~ständig** a indecent, improper.

unappetitlich ['ʊnʔapetiːtlɪç] a unsavoury.

Unart ['ʊnʔaːrt] f bad manners pl; (Angewohnheit) bad habit; **u~ig** a naughty, badly behaved.

unauf- ['ʊnʔaʊf] zW: **~fällig** a unobtrusive; (Kleidung) inconspicuous; **~'findbar** a not to be found; **~gefordert** a unasked // ad spontaneously; **~haltsam** a irresistible; **~'hörlich** a incessant, continuous; **~merksam** a inattentive; **~richtig** a insincere.

unaus- ['ʊnʔaʊs] zW: **~'bleiblich** a inevitable, unavoidable; **~geglichen** a unbalanced; **~'sprechlich** a inexpressible; **~'stehlich** a intolerable.

unbarmherzig ['ʊnbarmhɛrtsɪç] a pitiless, merciless.

unbeabsichtigt ['ʊnbəʔapzɪçtɪçt] a unintentional.

unbeachtet ['ʊnbəʔaxtət] a unnoticed, ignored.

unbedenklich ['ʊnbədɛŋklɪç] a (Plan) unobjectionable // ad without hesitation.

unbedeutend ['ʊnbədɔʏtənt] a insignificant, unimportant; (Fehler) slight.

unbedingt ['ʊnbədɪŋt] a unconditional // ad absolutely; **mußt du ~ gehen?** do you really have to go?

unbefangen ['ʊnbəfaŋən] a impartial, unprejudiced; (ohne Hemmungen) uninhibited; **U~heit** f impartiality; uninhibitedness.

unbefriedig- ['ʊnbəfriːdɪg] zW: **~end**

a unsatisfactory; **~t** [-dıçt] *a* unsatisfied, dissatisfied.

unbefugt ['ʊnbəfuːkt] *a* unauthorized.

unbegreiflich [ʊnbə'graıflıç] *a* inconceivable.

unbegrenzt ['ʊnbəgrɛntst] *a* unlimited.

unbegründet ['ʊnbəgryndət] *a* unfounded.

Unbehag- ['ʊnbəhaːg] *zW:* **~en** *nt* discomfort; **u~lich** [-klıç] *a* uncomfortable; *(Gefühl)* uneasy.

unbeholfen ['ʊnbəhɔlfən] *a* awkward, clumsy; **U~heit** *f* awkwardness, clumsiness.

unbeirrt ['ʊnbəʔırt] *a* imperturbable.

unbekannt ['ʊnbəkant] *a* unknown.

unbekümmert ['ʊnbəkymərt] *a* unconcerned.

unbeliebt ['ʊnbəliːpt] *a* unpopular.

unbequem ['ʊnbəkveːm] *a (Stuhl)* uncomfortable; *(Mensch)* bothersome; *(Regelung)* inconvenient.

unberech- *zW:* **~enbar** [ʊnbə'rɛçənbaːr] *a* incalculable; *(Mensch, Verhalten)* unpredictable; **~tigt** [ʊnbərɛçtıçt] *a* unjustified; *(nicht erlaubt)* unauthorized.

unberührt ['ʊnbəryːrt] *a* untouched, intact; **sie ist noch ~** she is still a virgin.

unbescheiden ['ʊnbəʃaıdən] *a* presumptuous.

unbeschreiblich [ʊnbə'ʃraıplıç] *a* indescribable.

unbesonnen ['ʊnbəzɔnən] *a* unwise, rash, imprudent.

unbeständig ['ʊnbəʃtɛndıç] *a (Mensch)* inconstant; *(Wetter)* unsettled; *(Lage)* unstable.

unbestechlich [ʊnbə'ʃtɛçlıç] *a* incorruptible.

unbestimmt ['ʊnbəʃtımt] *a* indefinite; *(Zukunft auch)* uncertain.

unbeteiligt ['ʊnbətaılıçt] *a* unconcerned, indifferent.

unbewacht ['ʊnbəvaxt] *a* unguarded, unwatched.

unbeweglich ['ʊnbəveːklıç] *a* immovable.

unbewußt ['ʊnbəvʊst] *a* unconscious.

unbrauchbar ['ʊnbrauxbaːr] *a (Arbeit)* useless; *(Gerät auch)* unusable.

und [ʊnt] *kj* and; **~ so weiter** and so on.

Undank ['ʊndaŋk] *m* ingratitude; **u~bar** *a* ungrateful; **~barkeit** *f* ingratitude.

undefinierbar [ʊndefi'niːrbaːr] *a* indefinable.

undenkbar [ʊn'dɛŋkbaːr] *a* inconceivable.

undeutlich ['ʊndɔytlıç] *a* indistinct.

undicht ['ʊndıçt] *a* leaky.

Unding ['ʊndıŋ] *nt* absurdity.

undurch- ['ʊndʊrç] *zW:* **~führbar**

~- ['fyːrbaːr] *a* impracticable; **~lässig** [-lɛsıç] *a* waterproof, impermeable; **~sichtig** [-zıçtıç] *a* opaque; *(fig)* obscure.

uneben ['ʊnʔeːbən] *a* uneven.

unehelich ['ʊnʔeːəlıç] *a* illegitimate.

uneigennützig ['ʊnʔaıgənnytsıç] *a* unselfish.

uneinig ['ʊnʔaınıç] *a* divided; **~ sein** disagree; **U~keit** *f* discord, dissension.

uneins ['ʊnʔaıns] *a* at variance, at odds.

unempfindlich ['ʊnʔɛmpfıntlıç] *a* insensitive; *(Stoff)* practical.

unendlich [ʊn'ʔɛntlıç] *a* infinite; **U~keit** *f* infinity.

unent- ['ʊnʔɛnt] *zW:* **~behrlich** [-'beːrlıç] *a* indispensable; **~geltlich** [-gɛltlıç] *a* free (of charge); **~schieden** [-'ʃiːdən] *a* undecided; **~schieden enden** *(SPORT)* end in a draw; **~schlossen** [-'ʃlɔsən] *a* undecided; irresolute; **~wegt** [-'veːkt] *a* unswerving; *(unaufhörlich)* incessant.

uner- ['ʊnʔer] *zW:* **~bittlich** ['bıtlıç] *a* unyielding, inexorable; **~fahren** [-'faːrən] *a* inexperienced; **~freulich** [-'frɔylıç] *a* unpleasant; **~gründlich** [-'gryntlıç] *a* unfathomable; **~heblich** [-'heːplıç] *a* unimportant; **~hört** [-'høːrt] *a* unheard-of; *(Bitte)* outrageous; **~läßlich** [-'lɛslıç] *a* indispensable; **~laubt** [-laupt] *a* unauthorized; **~meßlich** [-'mɛslıç] *a* immeasurable, immense; **~müdlich** [-'myːtlıç] *a* indefatigable; **~sättlich** [-'zɛtlıç] *a* insatiable; **~schöpflich** [-'ʃœpflıç] *a* inexhaustible; **~schütterlich** [-'ʃʏtərlıç] *a* unshakeable; **~schwinglich** [-'ʃvıŋlıç] *a (Preis)* exorbitant; too expensive; **~träglich** [-'trɛːklıç] *a (Frechheit)* insufferable; **~wartet** [-vartət] *a* unexpected; **~wünscht** [-vʏnʃt] *a* undesirable, unwelcome.

unfähig ['ʊnfɛːıç] *a* incapable *(zu of)*; incompetent; **U~keit** *f* incapacity; incompetence.

unfair ['ʊnfɛːr] *a* unfair.

Unfall ['ʊnfal] *m* accident; **~flucht** *f* hit-and-run (driving); **~stelle** *f* scene of the accident; **~versicherung** *f* accident insurance.

unfaßbar [ʊn'fasbaːr] *a* inconceivable.

unfehlbar [ʊn'feːlbaːr] *a* infallible // *ad* inevitably; **U~keit** *f* infallibility.

unfit ['ʊnfıt] *a* unfit.

unfrei ['ʊnfraı] *a* not free, unfree; *(Paket)* unfranked; **~willig** *a* involuntary, against one's will.

unfreundlich ['ʊnfrɔyntlıç] *a* unfriendly; **U~keit** *f* unfriendliness.

Unfriede(n) ['ʊnfriːdə(n)] *m* dissension, strife.

unfruchtbar ['ʊnfrʊxtbaːr] *a* infertile;

(*Gespräche*) unfruitful; **U~keit** *f* infertility; unfruitfulness.

Unfug ['ʊnfuːk] *m* **-s** (*Benehmen*) mischief; (*Unsinn*) nonsense; grober ~ (*JUR*) gross misconduct; malicious damage.

Ungar(in *f*) ['ʊŋgar(ɪn)] *m* Hungarian; **~n** *nt* Hungary; **u~isch** *a* Hungarian.

ungeachtet ['ʊngə'axtət] *präp* +*gen* notwithstanding.

ungeahnt ['ʊngə'a:nt] *a* unsuspected, undreamt-of.

ungebeten ['ʊngəbe:tən] *a* uninvited.

ungebildet ['ʊngəbɪldət] *a* uneducated; uncultured.

ungedeckt ['ʊngədɛkt] *a* (*Scheck*) uncovered.

Ungeduld ['ʊngədʊlt] *f* impatience; **u~ig** [-dɪç] *a* impatient.

ungeeignet ['ʊngə'aɪgnət] *a* unsuitable.

ungefähr ['ʊngəfɛːr] *a* rough, approximate; **das kommt nicht von ~** that's hardly surprising; **~lich** *a* not dangerous, harmless.

ungehalten ['ʊngəhaltən] *a* indignant.

ungeheuer ['ʊngəhɔʏər] *a* huge // *ad* (*umg*) enormously; **U~** *nt* **-s**, **-** monster; **~lich** [-'hɔʏərlɪç] *a* monstrous.

ungehobelt ['ʊngəho:bəlt] *a* (*fig*) uncouth.

ungehörig ['ʊngəhøːrɪç] *a* impertinent, improper; **U~keit** *f* impertinence.

ungehorsam ['ʊngəhɔrza:m] *a* disobedient; **U~** *m* disobedience.

ungeklärt ['ʊngəklɛːrt] *a* not cleared up; (*Rätsel*) unsolved.

ungeladen ['ʊngəla:dən] *a* not loaded; (*Gast*) uninvited.

ungelegen ['ʊngəle:gən] *a* inconvenient.

ungelernt ['ʊngəlɛrnt] *a* unskilled.

ungelogen ['ʊngəlo:gən] *ad* really, honestly.

ungemein ['ʊngəmaɪn] *a* uncommon.

ungemütlich ['ʊngəmyːtlɪç] *a* uncomfortable; (*Person*) disagreeable.

ungenau ['ʊngənaʊ] *a* inaccurate; **U~igkeit** *f* inaccuracy.

ungeniert ['ʊnʒeni:rt] *a* free and easy, unceremonious // *ad* without embarrassment, freely.

ungenießbar ['ʊngəni:sba:r] *a* inedible; undrinkable; (*umg*) unbearable.

ungenügend ['ʊngəny:gənt] *a* insufficient, inadequate.

ungepflegt ['ʊngəpfle:kt] *a* (*Garten etc*) untended; (*Person*) unkempt; (*Hände*) neglected.

ungerade ['ʊngəra:də] *a* uneven, odd.

ungerecht ['ʊngərɛçt] *a* unjust; **~fertigt** *a* unjustified; **U~igkeit** *f* injustice, unfairness.

ungern ['ʊngɛrn] *ad* unwillingly, reluctantly.

ungeschehen ['ʊngəʃe:ən] *a*: ~ **machen** undo.

Ungeschick- ['ʊngəʃɪk] *zW*: **~lichkeit** *f* clumsiness; **u~t** *a* awkward, clumsy.

ungeschminkt ['ʊngəʃmɪŋkt] *a* without make-up; (*fig*) unvarnished.

ungesetzlich ['ʊngəzɛtslɪç] *a* illegal.

ungestört ['ʊngəʃtøːrt] *a* undisturbed.

ungestraft ['ʊngəʃtra:ft] *ad* with impunity.

ungestüm ['ʊngəʃty:m] *a* impetuous; tempestuous; **U~** *nt* **-(e)s** impetuosity; passion.

ungesund ['ʊngəzʊnt] *a* unhealthy.

ungetrübt ['ʊngətry:pt] *a* clear; (*fig*) untroubled; (*Freude*) unalloyed.

Ungetüm ['ʊngəty:m] *nt* **-(e)s**, **-e** monster.

ungewiß ['ʊngəvɪs] *a* uncertain; **U~heit** *f* uncertainty.

ungewöhnlich ['ʊngəvøːnlɪç] *a* unusual.

ungewohnt ['ʊngəvo:nt] *a* unaccustomed.

Ungeziefer ['ʊngətsi:fər] *nt* **-s** vermin.

ungezogen ['ʊngətso:gən] *a* rude, impertinent; **U~heit** *f* rudeness, impertinence.

ungezwungen ['ʊngətsvʊŋən] *a* natural, unconstrained.

ungläubig ['ʊnglɔʏbɪç] *a* unbelieving; **die U~en** the infidel(s).

unglaublich [ʊn'glaʊplɪç] *a* incredible.

ungleich ['ʊnglaɪç] *a* dissimilar; unequal // *ad* incomparably; **~artig** *a* different; **U~heit** *f* dissimilarity; inequality.

Unglück ['ʊnglʏk] *nt* **-(e)s**, **-e** misfortune; (*Pech*) bad luck; (*~sfall*) calamity, disaster; (*Verkehrs~*) accident; **u~lich** *a* unhappy; (*erfolglos*) unlucky; (*unerfreulich*) unfortunate; **u~licherweise** [-'vaɪzə] *ad* unfortunately; **u~selig** *a* calamitous; (*Person*) unfortunate; **Unglücksfall** *m* accident, calamity.

ungültig ['ʊngʏltɪç] *a* invalid; **U~keit** *f* invalidity.

ungünstig ['ʊngʏnstɪç] *a* unfavourable.

ungut ['ʊngu:t] *a* (*Gefühl*) uneasy; **nichts für ~** no offence.

unhaltbar ['ʊnhaltba:r] *a* untenable.

Unheil ['ʊnhaɪl] *nt* evil; (*Unglück*) misfortune; ~ **anrichten** cause mischief; **u~bar** *a* incurable; **u~bringend** *a* fatal, fateful; **u~voll** *a* disastrous.

unheimlich ['ʊnhaɪmlɪç] *a* weird, uncanny // *ad* (*umg*) tremendously.

unhöflich ['ʊnhøːflɪç] *a* impolite; **U~keit** *f* impoliteness.

unhygienisch ['ʊnhygi'e:nɪʃ] *a* unhygienic.

Uni ['uni] f -, -s (umg) university; u~ [y'ni:] a self-coloured.

Uniform [uni'fɔrm] f uniform; u~iert [-'mi:rt] a uniformed.

uninteressant ['ʊnɪnteresant] a uninteresting.

Universität [univerzi'tɛːt] f university.

unkenntlich ['ʊnkɛntlıç] a unrecognizable.

Unkenntnis ['ʊnkɛntnıs] f ignorance.

unklar ['ʊnklaːr] a unclear; im ~en sein über (+akk) be in the dark about; **U~heit** f unclarity; (Unentschiedenheit) uncertainty.

unklug ['ʊnkluːk] a unwise.

Unkosten ['ʊnkɔstən] pl expense(s).

Unkraut ['ʊnkraʊt] nt weed; weeds pl.

unlängst ['ʊnlɛŋst] ad not long ago.

unlauter ['ʊnlaʊtər] a unfair.

unleserlich ['ʊnleːzərlıç] a illegible.

unlogisch ['ʊnloːgıʃ] a illogical.

unlösbar [ʊn'løːsbar], **unlöslich** [ʊn'løːslıç] a insoluble.

Unlust ['ʊnlʊst] f lack of enthusiasm; **u~ig** a unenthusiastic.

unmäßig ['ʊnmɛːsıç] a immoderate.

Unmenge ['ʊnmɛŋə] f tremendous number, hundreds pl.

Unmensch ['ʊnmɛnʃ] m ogre, brute; **u~lich** a inhuman, brutal; (ungeheuer) awful.

unmerklich [ʊn'mɛrklıç] a imperceptible.

unmißverständlich ['ʊnmɪsfɛrʃtɛntlıç] a unmistakable.

unmittelbar ['ʊnmɪtəlbaːr] a immediate.

unmöbliert ['ʊnmøbliːrt] a unfurnished.

unmöglich ['ʊnmøːklıç] a impossible; **U~keit** f impossibility.

unmoralisch ['ʊnmoraːlıʃ] a immoral.

Unmut ['ʊnmuːt] m ill humour.

unnachgiebig ['ʊnnaːxgiːbıç] a unyielding.

unnahbar [ʊn'naːbaːr] a unapproachable.

unnötig ['ʊnnøːtıç] a unnecessary.

unnütz ['ʊnnʏts] a useless.

unordentlich ['ʊn'ɔrdəntlıç] a untidy.

Unordnung ['ʊn'ɔrdnʊŋ] f disorder.

unparteiisch ['ʊnpartaıʃ] a impartial; **U~e(r)** m umpire; (Fußball) referee.

unpassend ['ʊnpasənt] a inappropriate; (Zeit) inopportune.

unpäßlich ['ʊnpɛslıç] a unwell.

unpersönlich ['ʊnpɛrzøːnlıç] a impersonal.

unpolitisch ['ʊnpoliːtıʃ] a apolitical.

unpraktisch ['ʊnpraktıʃ] a unpractical.

unpünktlich ['ʊnpʏnktlıç] a unpunctual.

unrationell ['ʊnratsionɛl] a inefficient.

unrecht ['ʊnrɛçt] a wrong; **U~** nt wrong; zu U~ wrongly; U~ haben be wrong; **~mäßig** a unlawful, illegal.

unregelmäßig ['ʊnreːgəlmɛsıç] a irregular; **U~keit** f irregularity.

unreif ['ʊnraıf] a (Obst) unripe; (fig) immature.

unrentabel ['ʊnrɛntaːbəl] a unprofitable.

unrichtig ['ʊnrıçtıç] a incorrect, wrong.

Unruhe ['ʊnruːə] f -, -n unrest; **~stifter** m troublemaker.

unruhig ['ʊnruːıç] a restless.

uns [ʊns] pron akk, dat von wir us; ourselves.

unsachlich ['ʊnzaxlıç] a not to the point, irrelevant.

unsagbar [ʊn'zaːkbaːr] a indescribable.

unsanft ['ʊnzanft] a rough.

unsauber ['ʊnzaʊbər] a unclean, dirty; (fig) crooked; (MUS) fuzzy.

unschädlich ['ʊnʃɛːtlıç] a harmless; jdn/etw ~ machen render sb/sth harmless.

unscharf ['ʊnʃarf] a indistinct; (Bild etc) out of focus, blurred.

unscheinbar ['ʊnʃaınbaːr] a insignificant; (Aussehen, Haus etc) unprepossessing.

unschlagbar [ʊn'ʃlaːkbaːr] a invincible.

unschlüssig ['ʊnʃlʏsıç] a undecided.

Unschuld ['ʊnʃʊlt] f innocence; **u~ig** [-dıç] a innocent.

unselbständig ['ʊnzɛlpʃtɛndıç] a dependent, over-reliant on others.

unser ['ʊnzər] pron our; ~e(r, s) ours; ~einer, ~eins pron people like us; **unsererseits** ad on our part; **unsertwegen, um unsertwillen** ad (für uns) for our sake; (wegen uns) on our account.

unsicher ['ʊnzıçər] a uncertain; (Mensch) insecure; **U~heit** f uncertainty; insecurity.

unsichtbar ['ʊnzıçtbaːr] a invisible.

Unsinn ['ʊnzın] m nonsense; **u~ig** a nonsensical.

Unsitte ['ʊnzıtə] f deplorable habit.

unsittlich ['ʊnzıtlıç] a indecent.

unsportlich ['ʊnʃpɔrtlıç] a not sporty; unfit; (Verhalten) unsporting.

unsre ['ʊnzrə] = unsere.

unsterblich ['ʊnʃtɛrplıç] a immortal; **U~keit** f immortality.

Unstimmigkeit ['ʊnʃtımıçkaıt] f inconsistency; (Streit) disagreement.

unsympathisch ['ʊnzʏmpaːtıʃ] a unpleasant; er ist mir ~ I don't like him.

untätig ['ʊntɛːtıç] a idle.

untauglich ['ʊntaʊklıç] a unsuitable; (MIL) unfit.

unteilbar [ʊn'taılbaːr] a indivisible.

unten ['ʊntən] *ad* below; (*im Haus*) downstairs; (*an der Treppe etc*) at the bottom; **nach ~** down; **~ am Berg** *etc* at the bottom of the mountain *etc;* **ich bin bei ihm ~ durch** (*umg*) he's through with me.

unter [ʊntər] ◆*präp* +*dat* **1** (*räumlich, mit Zahlen*) under; (*drunter*) underneath, below; **~ 18 Jahren** under 18 years

2 (*zwischen*) among(st); **sie waren ~ sich** they were by themselves; **einer ~ ihnen** one of them; **~ anderem** among other things

◆*präp* +*akk* under, below.

Unterarm ['ʊntər'arm] *m* forearm.

unter *zW:* **~belichten** *vt* (*PHOT*) underexpose; **U~bewußtsein** *nt* subconscious; **~bezahlt** *a* underpaid.

unterbieten [ʊntər'biːtən] *vt unreg insep* (*COMM*) undercut; (*Rekord*) lower.

unterbinden [ʊntər'bɪndən] *vt unreg insep* stop, call a halt to.

unterbrech- [ʊntər'brɛç] *zW:* **~en** *vt unreg insep* interrupt; **U~ung** *f* interruption.

unterbringen ['ʊntərbrɪŋən] *vt unreg* (*in Koffer*) stow; (*in Zeitung*) place; (*Person: in Hotel etc*) accommodate, put up; (: *beruflich*) fix up (*auf, in* with).

unterdessen [ʊntər'dɛsən] *ad* meanwhile.

Unterdruck ['ʊntərdrʊk] *m* low pressure.

unterdrücken [ʊntər'drykən] *vt insep* suppress; (*Leute*) oppress.

untere(r, s) ['ʊntərə(r, s)] *a* lower.

untereinander [ʊntər'aɪ'nandər] *ad* with each other; among themselves *etc.*

unterentwickelt ['ʊntər'ɛntvɪkəlt] *a* underdeveloped.

unterernährt ['ʊntər'ɛrnɛːrt] *a* undernourished, underfed.

Unterernährung *f* malnutrition.

Unter'führung *f* subway, underpass.

Untergang ['ʊntərgaŋ] *m* (down)fall, decline; (*NAUT*) sinking; (*von Gestirn*) setting.

unter'geben *a* subordinate.

untergehen ['ʊntərgeːən] *vi unreg* go down; (*Sonne auch*) set; (*Staat*) fall; (*Volk*) perish; (*Welt*) come to an end; (*im Lärm*) be drowned.

Untergeschoß ['ʊntərgəʃɔs] *nt* basement.

unter'gliedern *vt insep* subdivide.

Untergrund ['ʊntərgrʊnt] *m* foundation; (*POL*) underground; **~bahn** *f* underground, tube, subway (*US*); **~bewegung** *f* underground (movement).

unterhalb ['ʊntərhalp] *präp* +*gen, ad*

below; **~ von** below.

Unterhalt ['ʊntərhalt] *m* maintenance; **u~en** [ʊntər'haltən] *unreg insep vt* maintain; (*belustigen*) entertain // *vr* talk; (*sich belustigen*) enjoy o.s.; **~ung** *f* maintenance; (*Belustigung*) entertainment, amusement; (*Gespräch*) talk.

Unterhemd ['ʊntərhɛmt] *nt* vest, undershirt (*US*).

Unterhose ['ʊntərhoːzə] *f* underpants *pl.*

unterirdisch ['ʊntər'ɪrdɪʃ] *a* underground.

Unterkiefer ['ʊntərkiːfər] *m* lower jaw.

unterkommen ['ʊntərkɔmən] *vi unreg* find shelter; find work; **das ist mir noch nie untergekommen** I've never met with that.

Unterkunft ['ʊntərkʊnft] *f* -, **-künfte** accommodation.

Unterlage ['ʊntərlaːgə] *f* foundation; (*Beleg*) document; (*Schreib~ etc*) pad.

unter'lassen *vt unreg insep* (*versäumen*) fail (to do); (*sich enthalten*) refrain from.

unterlaufen [ʊntər'laʊfən] *vi unreg insep* happen // *a:* **mit Blut ~** suffused with blood; (*Augen*) bloodshot.

unterlegen ['ʊntərleːgən] *vt* lay *od* put under // [ʊntər'leːgən] *a* inferior (*dat* to); (*besiegt*) defeated.

Unterleib ['ʊntərlaɪp] *m* abdomen.

unter'liegen *vi unreg insep* be defeated *od* overcome (*jdm* by *sb*); (*unterworfen sein*) be subject to.

Untermiete ['ʊntərmiːtə] *f:* **zur ~ wohnen** be a subtenant *od* lodger; **~r(in** *f*) *m* subtenant, lodger.

unter'nehmen *vt unreg insep* undertake; **U~** *nt* -s, - undertaking, enterprise (*auch COMM*).

Unternehmer [ʊntər'neːmər] *m* -s, - entrepreneur, businessman.

Unterredung [ʊntər'reːdʊŋ] *f* discussion, talk.

Unterricht ['ʊntərrɪçt] *m* -(e)s, -e instruction, lessons *pl;* **u~en** [ʊntər'rɪçtən] *insep vt* instruct; (*SCH*) teach // *vr* inform o.s. (*über* +*akk* about).

Unterrock ['ʊntərrɔk] *m* petticoat, slip.

unter'sagen *vt insep* forbid (*jdm etw* sb to do sth).

unter'schätzen *vt insep* underestimate.

unter'scheiden *unreg insep vt* distinguish // *vr* differ.

Unter'scheidung *f* (*Unterschied*) distinction; (*Unterscheiden*) differentiation.

Unterschied ['ʊntərʃiːt] *m* -(e)s, -e difference, distinction; **im ~ zu** as distinct from; **u~lich** a varying, differing; (*diskriminierend*) discriminatory; **unterschiedslos** ad indiscriminately.

unter'schlagen vt unreg insep embezzle; (*verheimlichen*) suppress.

Unter'schlagung f embezzlement.

Unterschlupf ['ʊntərʃlʊpf] m -(e)s, -schlüpfe refuge.

unter'schreiben vt unreg insep sign.

Unterschrift ['ʊntərʃrɪft] f signature.

Unterseeboot ['ʊntərzeːboːt] nt submarine.

Untersetzer ['ʊntərzɛtsər] m tablemat; (*für Gläser*) coaster.

untersetzt [ʊntər'zɛtst] a stocky.

unterste(r, s) ['ʊntərstə(r, s)] a lowest, bottom.

unterstehen [ʊntər'ʃteːən] unreg vi insep be under (*jdm* sb) // vr dare // ['ʊntərʃteːən] vi shelter.

unterstellen [ʊntər'ʃtɛlən] vt insep subordinate (*dat* to); (*fig*) impute (*jdm etw* sth to sb) // ['ʊntərʃtɛlən] vt (*Auto*) garage, park // vr take shelter.

unter'streichen vt unreg insep (*lit, fig*) underline.

Unterstufe ['ʊntərʃtuːfə] f lower grade.

unter'stützen vt insep support.

Unter'stützung f support, assistance.

unter'suchen vt insep (*MED*) examine; (*Polizei*) investigate.

Unter'suchung f examination; investigation, inquiry; **Untersuchungsausschuß** m committee of inquiry; **Untersuchungshaft** f imprisonment on remand.

Untertan ['ʊntərtaːn] m -s, -en subject.

untertänig ['ʊntərtɛːnɪç] a submissive, humble.

Untertasse ['ʊntərtasə] f saucer.

untertauchen ['ʊntərtaʊxən] vi dive; (*fig*) disappear, go underground.

Unterteil ['ʊntərtaɪl] nt od m lower part, bottom; **u~en** [ʊntər'taɪlən] vt insep divide up.

Unterwäsche ['ʊntərvɛʃə] f underwear.

unterwegs [ʊntər'veːks] ad on the way.

unter'weisen vt unreg insep instruct.

unter'werfen unreg insep vt subject; (*Volk*) subjugate // vr submit (*dat* to).

unterwürfig ['ʊntərvʏrfɪç] a obsequious, servile.

unter'zeichnen vt insep sign.

unter'ziehen unreg insep vt subject (*dat* to) // vr undergo (*etw* (*dat*) sth); (*einer Prüfung*) take.

untreu ['ʊntrɔʏ] a unfaithful; **U~e** f unfaithfulness.

untröstlich [ʊn'trøːstlɪç] a inconsolable.

unüber- ['ʊn'yːbər] zW: **~legt** [-leːkt] a ill-considered // ad without thinking; **~sehbar** [-'zeːbaːr] a incalculable.

unum- [ʊn'ʊm] zW: **~gänglich** [-'gɛŋlɪç] a indispensable, vital; absolutely necessary; **~wunden** [-'vʊndən] a candid // ad straight out.

ununterbrochen ['ʊn'ʊntərbrɔxən] a uninterrupted.

unver- [ʊnfɛr] zW: **~änderlich** [-'ɛndərlɪç] a unchangeable; **~antwortlich** [-'antvɔrtlɪç] a irresponsible; (*unentschuldbar*) inexcusable; **~besserlich** [-'bɛsərlɪç] a incorrigible; **~bindlich** ['-bɪntlɪç] a not binding; (*Antwort*) curt // ad (*COMM*) without obligation; **~blümt** [-'blyːmt] a, ad plain(ly), blunt(ly); **~daulich** ['-daʊlɪç] a indigestible; **~dorben** ['-dɔrbən] a unspoilt; **~einbar** [-'aɪnbaːr] a incompatible; **~fänglich** [-'fɛŋlɪç] a harmless; **~froren** ['-froːrən] a impudent; **~hofft** ['-hɔft] a unexpected; **~kennbar** [-'kɛnbaːr] a unmistakable; **~meidlich** [-'maɪtlɪç] a unavoidable; **~mutet** ['-muːtət] a unexpected; **~nünftig** ['-nʏnftɪç] a foolish; **~schämt** ['-ʃɛːmt] a impudent; **U~schämtheit** f impudence, insolence; **~sehens** ['-zeːəns] ad all of a sudden; **~sehrt** ['-zeːrt] a uninjured; **~söhnlich** ['-zøːnlɪç] a irrecocilable; **~ständlich** [-'ʃtɛntlɪç] a unintelligible; **~träglich** ['-trɛːklɪç] a quarrelsome; (*Meinungen*, *MED*) incompatible; **~wüstlich** [-'vyːstlɪç] a indestructible; (*Mensch*) irrepressible; **~zeihlich** [-'tsaɪlɪç] a unpardonable; **~züglich** [-'tsyːklɪç] a immediate.

unvoll- ['ʊnfɔl] zW: **~kommen** a imperfect; **~ständig** a incomplete.

unvor- [ʊnfoːr] zW: **~bereitet** a unprepared; **~eingenommen** a unbiased; **~hergesehen** [-hɛːrgəzeːən] a unforeseen; **~sichtig** [-zɪçtɪç] a careless, imprudent; **~stellbar** [-'ʃtɛlbaːr] a inconceivable; **~teilhaft** [-taɪlhaft] a disadvantageous.

unwahr ['ʊnvaːr] a untrue; **~scheinlich** a improbable, unlikely // ad (*umg*) incredibly.

unweigerlich [ʊn'vaɪɡərlɪç] a unquestioning // ad without fail.

Unwesen ['ʊnveːzən] nt nuisance; (*Unfug*) mischief; sein ~ treiben wreak havoc; **unwesentlich** a inessential, unimportant; **unwesentlich besser** marginally better.

Unwetter ['ʊnvɛtər] nt thunderstorm.

unwichtig ['ʊnvɪçtɪç] a unimportant.

unwider- [ʊnviːdər] zW: **~legbar** [-'leːkbaːr] a irrefutable; **~ruflich**

[-'ruːflıç] *a* irrevocable; **~stéhlich**
[-'ʃteːlıç] *a* irresistible.

unwill- ['ʊnvıl] *zW*: **U~e(n)** *m* indignation; **~ig** *a* indignant; (*widerwillig*) reluctant; **~kürlich** [-kyːrlıç] *a*
involuntary // *ad* instinctively;
(*lachen*) involuntarily.

unwirklich ['ʊnvırklıç] *a* unreal.

unwirsch ['ʊnvırʃ] *a* cross, surly.

unwirtschaftlich ['ʊnvırtʃaftlıç] *a* un-
economical.

unwissen- ['ʊnvısən] *zW*: **~d** *a* ignorant; **U~heit** *f* ignorance; **~schaft-
lich** *a* unscientific.

unwohl ['ʊnvoːl] *a* unwell, ill; **U~sein**
nt -s indisposition.

unwürdig ['ʊnvyrdıç] *a* unworthy (*jds
of sb*).

unzählig [ʊn'tsɛːlıç] *a* innumerable,
countless.

unzer- [ʊntsɛr] *zW*: **~brechlich**
[-'brɛçlıç] *a* unbreakable; **~störbar**
[-'ʃtøːrbaːr] *a* indestructible; **~trenn-
lich** [-'trɛnlıç] *a* inseparable.

Unzucht ['ʊntsʊxt] *f* sexual offence.

unzüchtig ['ʊntsyçtıç] *a* immoral;
lewd.

unzu- ['ʊntsu] *zW*: **~frieden** *a* dissatisfied; **U~friedenheit** *f* discontent;
~länglich ['ʊntsuːlɛŋlıç] *a* inadequate;
~lässig ['ʊntsuːlɛsıç] *a* inadmissible;
~rechnungsfähig ['ʊntsuːrɛçnʊŋsfɛːıç]
a irresponsible; **~treffend** ['ʊntsuː-] *a*
incorrect; **~verlässig** ['ʊntsuː-] *a* unreliable.

unzweideutig ['ʊntsvaıdɔytıç] *a* unam-
biguous.

üppig ['ʏpıç] *a* (*Frau*) curvaceous;
(*Busen*) full, ample; (*Essen*) sumptuous; (*Vegetation*) luxuriant, lush.

uralt ['uːr'alt] *a* ancient, very old.

Uran [u'raːn] *nt* -s uranium.

Ur- ['uːr] *in zW* original; **~aufführung**
f first performance; **~einwohner** *m*
original inhabitant; **~eltern** *pl* ances-
tors *pl*; **~enkel(in** *f)* *m* great-
grandchild; **~großmutter** *f* great-
grandmother; **~großvater** *m* great-
grandfather; **~heber** *m* -s, - origina-
tor; (*Autor*) author.

Urin [u'riːn] *m* -s, -e urine.

Urkunde ['uːrkʊndə] *f* -, -n document,
deed.

Urlaub ['uːrlaʊp] *m* -(e)s, -e holiday(s
pl) (*Brit*), vacation (*US*); (*MIL etc*)
leave; **~er** [-laʊbər] *m* -s, - holiday-
maker (*Brit*), vacationer (*US*).

Urne ['ʊrnə] *f* -, -n urn.

Ursache ['uːrzaxə] *f* cause; keine ~
that's all right.

Ursprung ['uːrʃprʊŋ] *m* origin,
source; (*von Fluß*) source.

ursprünglich [uːr'ʃprʏŋlıç] *a*, *ad* origi-
nal(ly).

Urteil ['ʊrtaıl] *nt* -s, -e opinion; (*JUR*)

sentence, judgement; **u~en** *vi* judge;
Urteilsspruch *m* sentence, verdict.

Ur- *zW*: **~wald** *m* jungle; **~zeit** *f* pre-
historic times *pl*.

USA [uːˈɛsˈaː] *f abk* (= *Vereinigte
Staaten von Amerika*) USA.

usw. [uːɛsvɛː] *abk* (= *und so weiter*)
etc.

Utensilien [utɛn'ziːliən] *pl* utensils *pl*.

Utopie [uto'piː] *f* pipedream.

utopisch [u'toːpıʃ] *a* utopian.

u.U. *abk von* **unter Umständen**.

V

V, v [faʊ] *nt* V, v.

vag(e) [vaːk, 'vaːgə] *a* vague.

Vagina [va'giːna] *f* -, **Vaginen** vagina.

Vakuum ['vaːkuʊm] *nt* -s, **Vakua** *od*
Vakuen vacuum.

Vanille [va'nıljə] *f* - vanilla.

Variation [variatsi'oːn] *f* variation.

variieren [vari'iːrən] *vti* vary.

Vase ['vaːzə] *f* -, -n vase.

Vater ['faːtər] *m* -s, ᵉ father; **~land** *nt*
native country; Fatherland.

väterlich ['fɛːtərlıç] *a* fatherly; **väterli-
cherseits** *ad* on the father's side.

Vater- *zW*: **~schaft** *f* paternity;
~unser *nt* -s, - Lord's prayer.

Vati ['faːti] *m* daddy.

v.Chr. *abk* (= *vor Christus*) BC.

Vegetarier(in *f)* [vege'taːriər(ın)] *m* -s,
- vegetarian.

Veilchen ['faılçən] *nt* violet.

Vene ['veːnə] *f* -, -n vein.

Venedig [ve'neːdıç] *nt* Venice.

Ventil [vɛn'tiːl] *nt* -s, -e valve; **~ator**
[vɛnti'laːtər] *m* ventilator.

verab- [fɛr'ap] *zW*: **~reden** *vt* agree,
arrange; **mit jdm ~redet sein** have
arranged to meet sb // *vr* arrange to
meet (*mit jdm* sb); **V~redung** *f* arrangement; (*Treffen*) appointment;
~scheuen *vt* detest, abhor;
~schieden *vt* (*Gäste*) say goodbye
to; (*entlassen*) discharge; (*Gesetz*)
pass // *vr* take one's leave (*von* of);
V~schiedung *f* leave-taking; discharge; passing.

ver- [fɛr] *zW*: **~achten** [-'axtən] *vt*
despise; **~ächtlich** [-'ɛçtlıç] *a* con-
temptuous; (*verachtenswert*) contemptible; **jdn ~ächtlich machen** run
sb down; **V~achtung** *f* contempt.

verallgemein- [fɛr'algə'maın] *zW*:
~ern *vt* generalize; **V~erung** *f* gen-
eralization.

veralten [fɛr'altən] *vi* become obsolete
od out-of-date.

Veranda [ve'randa] *f* -, **Veranden** veranda.

veränder- [fɛr'ɛndər] *zW*: **~lich** *a*
changeable; **~n** *vtr* change, alter;

V~ung f change, alteration.
veran- [fɛr''an] zW: **~lagt** a with a ... nature; **V~lagung** f disposition; **~lassen** vt cause; **Maßnahmen ~lassen** take measures; **sich ~laßt sehen** feel prompted; **~schaulichen** vt illustrate; **~schlagen** vt estimate; **~stalten** vt organize, arrange; **V~stalter** m **-s,** - organizer; **V~staltung** f (Veranstalten) organizing; (Konzert etc) event, function.
verantwort- [fɛr''antvɔrt] zW: **~en** vt answer for // vr justify o.s.; **~lich** a responsible; **V~ung** f responsibility; **~ungsbewußt** a responsible; **~ungslos** a irresponsible.
verarbeiten [fɛr''arbaɪtən] vt process; (geistig) assimilate; **etw zu etw ~** make sth into sth.
Verarbeitung f processing; assimilation.
verärgern [fɛr''ɛrgərn] vt annoy.
verausgaben [fɛr''ausga:bən] vr run out of money; (fig) exhaust o.s.
veräußern [fɛr''ɔysərn] vt dispose of, sell.
Verb [vɛrp] nt **-s, -en** verb.
Verband [fɛr'bant] m **-(e)s, ⁻e** (MED) bandage, dressing; (Bund) association, society; (MIL) unit; **~kasten** m medicine chest, first-aid box; **~zeug** nt bandage.
verbannen [fɛr'banən] vt banish.
Verbannung f exile.
verbergen [fɛr'bɛrgən] vtr unreg hide (vor +dat from).
verbessern [fɛr'bɛsərn] vtr improve; (berichtigen) correct (o.s.).
Verbesserung f improvement; correction.
verbeugen [fɛr'bɔygən] vr bow.
Verbeugung f bow.
ver'biegen vi unreg bend.
ver'bieten vt unreg forbid (jdm etw sb to do sth).
verbilligt [fɛr'bɪlɪçt] a reduced.
ver'binden unreg vt connect; (kombinieren) combine; (MED) bandage; **jdm die Augen ~** blindfold sb // vr combine (auch CHEM), join.
verbindlich [fɛr'bɪntlɪç] a binding; (freundlich) friendly; **V~keit** f obligation; (Höflichkeit) civility.
Ver'bindung f connection; (Zusammensetzung) combination; (CHEM) compound; (UNIV) club.
ver'bitten vt unreg: **sich** (dat) **etw ~** not tolerate sth, not stand for sth.
verblassen [fɛr'blasən] vi fade.
Verbleib [fɛr'blaɪp] m **-(e)s** whereabouts; **v~en** [fɛr'blaɪbən] vi unreg remain.
verblüffen [fɛr'blʏfən] vt stagger, amaze.
Verblüffung f stupefaction.

ver'blühen vi wither, fade.
ver'bluten vi bleed to death.
verborgen [fɛr'bɔrgən] a hidden.
Verbot [fɛr'bo:t] nt **-(e)s, -e** prohibition, ban; **v~en** a forbidden; **Rauchen v~en!** no smoking; **Verbotsschild** nt prohibitory sign.
Verbrauch [fɛr'braux] m **-(e)s** consumption; **v~en** vt use up; **~er** m **-s,** - consumer; **v~t** a used up, finished; (Luft) stale; (Mensch) worn-out.
Verbrechen [fɛr'brɛçən] nt **-s,** - crime; **v~** vt unreg perpetrate.
Verbrecher [fɛr'brɛçər] m **-s,** - criminal; **v~isch** a criminal.
ver'breiten vt spread; **sich über etw** (akk) **~** expound on sth.
verbreitern [fɛr'braɪtərn] vt broaden.
Verbreitung f spread(ing), propagation.
verbrenn- [fɛr'brɛn] zW: **~bar** a combustible; **~en** unreg vt burn; (Leiche) cremate; **V~ung** f burning; (in Motor) combustion; (von Leiche) cremation; **V~ungsmotor** m internal combustion engine.
ver'bringen vt unreg spend.
verbrühen [fɛr'bry:ən] vt scald.
verbuchen [fɛr'bu:xən] vt (FIN) register; (Erfolg) enjoy; (Mißerfolg) suffer.
verbunden [fɛr'bʊndən] a connected; **jdm ~ sein** be obliged od indebted to sb; **falsch ~** (TEL) wrong number; **V~heit** f bond, relationship.
verbünden [fɛr'bʏndən] vr ally o.s.
Verbündete(r) [fɛr'bʏndətə(r)] mf ally.
ver'bürgen vr: **sich ~ für** vouch for.
ver'büßen vt: **eine Strafe ~** serve a sentence.
Verdacht [fɛr'daxt] m **-(e)s** suspicion.
verdächtig [fɛr'dɛçtɪç] a suspicious, suspect; **~en** [fɛr'dɛçtɪgən] vt suspect.
verdammen [fɛr'damən] vt damn, condemn; **verdammt!** damn!
ver'dampfen vi vaporize, evaporate.
ver'danken vt: **jdm etw ~** owe sb sth.
verdauen [fɛr'dauən] vt (lit, fig) digest.
verdaulich [fɛr'daulɪç] a digestible; **das ist schwer ~** that is hard to digest.
Verdauung f digestion.
Verdeck [fɛr'dɛk] nt **-(e)s, -e** (AUT) hood; (NAUT) deck; **v~en** vt cover (up); (verbergen) hide.
ver'denken vt unreg: **jdm etw ~** blame sb for sth, hold sth against sb.
Verderb- [fɛr'dɛrp] zW: **~en** [fɛr'dɛrbən] nt **-s** ruin; **v~en** unreg vt spoil; (schädigen) ruin; (moralisch) corrupt; **es mit jdm v~en** get into sb's bad books // vi (Essen) spoil,

rot; (*Mensch*) go to the bad; **v~lich**
a (*Einfluß*) pernicious; (*Lebensmittel*) perishable.
verdeutlichen [fɛr'dɔʏtlɪçən] *vt* make
clear.
ver'dichten *vtr* condense.
ver'dienen *vt* earn; (*moralisch*) deserve.
Ver'dienst *m* -(e)s, -e earnings *pl* // *nt*
-(e)s, -e merit; (*Leistung*) service
(*um* to).
verdient [fɛr'diːnt] *a* well-earned;
(*Person*) deserving of esteem; **sich**
um etw ~ machen do a lot for sth.
verdoppeln [fɛr'dɔpəln] *vt* double.
verdorben [fɛr'dɔrbən] *a* spoilt; (*geschädigt*) ruined; (*moralisch*) corrupt.
verdrängen [fɛr'drɛŋən] *vt* oust, displace (*auch PHYS*); (*PSYCH*) repress.
ver'drehen *vt* (*lit, fig*) twist; (*Augen*)
roll; **jdm den Kopf ~** (*fig*) turn sb's
head.
verdreifachen [fɛr'draɪfaxən] *vt* treble.
verdrießlich [fɛr'driːslɪç] *a* peevish,
annoyed.
Verdruß [fɛr'drʊs] *m* -sses, -sse annoyance, worry.
verdummen [fɛr'dʊmən] *vt* make stupid // *vi* grow stupid.
verdunkeln [fɛr'dʊŋkəln] *vtr* darken;
(*fig*) obscure.
Verdunk(e)lung *f* blackout; (*fig*) obscuring.
verdünnen [fɛr'dʏnən] *vt* dilute.
verdunsten [fɛr'dʊnstən] *vi* evaporate.
verdursten [fɛr'dʊrstən] *vi* die of
thirst.
verdutzt [fɛr'dʊtst] *a* nonplussed,
taken aback.
verehr- [fɛr''eːr] *zW*: **~en** *vt* venerate,
worship (*auch REL*); **jdm etw ~en**
present sb with sth; **V~er(in** *f*) *m* -s,
- admirer, worshipper (*auch REL*);
~t *a* esteemed; **V~ung** *f* respect;
(*REL*) worship.
Verein [fɛr''aɪn] *m* -(e)s, -e club, association; **v~bar** *a* compatible;
v~baren [-baːrən] *vt* agree upon;
~barung *f* agreement; **v~fachen**
[-faxən] *vt* simplify; **v~igen** [-ɪɡən]
vtr unite; **V~igte Staaten** *pl* United
States; **~igung** *f* union; (*Verein*) association; **v~t** *a* united; **vereinzelt** *a*
isolated.
vereiteln [fɛr''aɪtəln] *vt* frustrate.
ver'eitern *vi* suppurate, fester.
verengen [fɛr''ɛŋən] *vr* narrow.
vererb- [fɛr'ɛrb] *zW*: **~en** *vt* bequeath; (*BIOL*) transmit // *vr* be hereditary; **~lich** [fɛr''ɛrplɪç] *a* hereditary; **V~ung** *f* bequeathing; (*BIOL*)
transmission; (*Lehre*) heredity.
verewigen [fɛr''eːvɪɡən] *vt* immortalize // *vr* (*umg*) leave one's name.

ver'fahren *unreg vi* act; **~ mit** deal
with // *vr* get lost // *a* tangled; **V~** *nt*
-s, - procedure; (*TECH*) process;
(*JUR*) proceedings *pl*.
Verfall [fɛr'fal] *m* -(e)s decline; (*von
Haus*) dilapidation; (*FIN*) expiry;
v~en *vi unreg* decline; (*Haus*) be
falling down; (*FIN*) lapse; **v~en in**
(+*acc*) lapse into; **v~en auf** (+*acc*)
hit upon; **einem Laster v~en sein** be
addicted to a vice.
ver'färben *vr* change colour.
Verfasser(in *f*) [fɛr'fasər(ɪn)] *m* -s, -
author, writer.
Verfassung *f* constitution (*auch POL*).
Verfassungs- *zW*: **v~gericht** *nt* constitutional court; **v~mäßig** *a* constitutional; **v~widrig** *a* unconstitutional.
ver'faulen *vi* rot.
ver'fehlen *vt* miss; **etw für verfehlt**
halten regard sth as mistaken.
verfeinern [fɛr'faɪnərn] *vt* refine.
ver'filmen *vt* film.
ver'fluchen *vt* curse.
verfolg- [fɛr'fɔlɡ] *zW*: **~en** *vt* pursue;
(*gerichtlich*) prosecute; (*grausam,
bes POL*) persecute; **V~er** *m* -s, -
pursuer; **V~ung** *f* pursuit; prosecution; persecution.
verfremden [fɛr'frɛmdən] *vt* alienate,
distance.
verfrüht [fɛr'fryːt] *a* premature.
verfüg- [fɛr'fyːɡ] *zW*: **~bar** *a* available; **~en** *vt* direct, order // *vr* proceed // *vi*: **~en über** (+*akk*) have at
one's disposal; **V~ung** *f* direction, order; **zur V~ung** at one's disposal;
jdm zur V~ung stehen be available to
sb.
verführ- [fɛr'fyːr] *zW*: **~en** *vt* tempt;
(*sexuell*) seduce; **V~er** *m* tempter;
seducer; **~erisch** *a* seductive;
V~ung *f* seduction; (*Versuchung*)
temptation.
ver'gammeln *vi* (*umg*) go to seed;
(*Nahrung*) go off.
vergangen [fɛr'ɡaŋən] *a* past; **V~heit**
f past.
vergänglich [fɛr'ɡɛŋlɪç] *a* transitory;
V~keit *f* transitoriness, impermanence.
vergasen [fɛr'ɡaːzən] *vt* (*töten*) gas.
Vergaser *m* -s, - (*AUT*) carburettor.
vergaß *etc v siehe* **vergessen**.
vergeb- [fɛr'ɡeːb] *zW*: **~en** *vt unreg*
forgive (*jdm etw* sb for sth); (*weggeben*) give away; **~ens** *ad* in vain;
~lich [fɛr'ɡeːplɪç] *ad* in vain // *a* vain,
futile; **V~ung** *f* forgiveness.
ver'gehen *unreg vi* pass by *od* away;
jdm vergeht etw sb loses sth // *vr*
commit an offence (*gegen etw*
against sth); **sich an jdm ~** (*sexually*) assault sb; **V~** *nt* -s, - offence.
ver'gelten *vt unreg* pay back (*jdm*

etw sb for sth), repay.

Ver'geltung *f* retaliation, reprisal; **Vergeltungsschlag** *m* (*MIL*) reprisal.

vergessen [fɛr'gɛsən] *vt unreg* forget; **V~heit** *f* oblivion.

vergeßlich [fɛr'gɛslɪç] *a* forgetful; **V~keit** *f* forgetfulness.

vergeuden [fɛr'gɔʏdən] *vt* squander, waste.

vergewaltigen [fɛrgə'valtɪgən] *vt* rape; (*fig*) violate.

Vergewaltigung *f* rape.

vergewissern [fɛrgə'vɪsərn] *vr* make sure.

ver'gießen *vt unreg* shed.

vergiften [fɛr'gɪftən] *vt* poison.

Vergiftung *f* poisoning.

Vergißmeinnicht [fɛr'gɪsmaɪnnɪçt] *nt* -(e)s, -e forget-me-not.

vergißt *etc v siehe* **vergessen**.

Vergleich [fɛr'glaɪç] *m* -(e)s, -e comparison; (*JUR*) settlement; im ~ mit *od* zu compared with *od* to; **v~bar** *a* comparable; **v~en** *unreg vt* compare // *vr* reach a settlement.

vergnügen [fɛr'gnyːgən] *vr* enjoy *od* amuse o.s.; **V~** *nt* -s, - pleasure; viel **V~!** enjoy yourself!

vergnügt [fɛr'gnyːkt] *a* cheerful.

Vergnügung *f* pleasure, amusement; **Vergnügungspark** *m* amusement park; **vergnügungssüchtig** *a* pleasure-loving.

vergolden [fɛr'gɔldən] *vt* gild.

vergöttern [fɛr'gœtərn] *vt* idolize.

ver'graben *vt* bury.

ver'greifen *vr unreg*: sich an jdm ~ lay hands on sb; sich an etw ~ misappropriate sth; sich im Ton ~ say the wrong thing.

vergriffen [fɛr'grɪfən] *a* (*Buch*) out of print; (*Ware*) out of stock.

vergrößern [fɛr'grøːsərn] *vt* enlarge; (*mengenmäßig*) increase; (*Lupe*) magnify.

Vergrößerung *f* enlargement; increase; magnification; **Vergrößerungsglas** *nt* magnifying glass.

Vergünstigung [fɛr'gynstɪgʊŋ] *f* concession, privilege.

vergüten [fɛr'gyːtən] *vt*: jdm etw ~ compensate sb for sth.

Vergütung *f* compensation.

verhaften [fɛr'haftən] *vt* arrest.

Verhaftung *f* arrest.

ver'hallen *vi* die away.

ver'halten *unreg vr* be, stand; (*sich benehmen*) behave; (*MATH*) be in proportion to // *vt* hold *od* keep back; (*Schritt*) check; **V~** *nt* -s behaviour.

Verhältnis [fɛr'hɛltnɪs] *nt* -ses, -se relationship; (*MATH*) proportion, ratio // *pl* (*Umstände*) conditions *pl*; über seine ~se leben live beyond one's means; **v~mäßig** *a, ad* relative(ly),

comparative(ly).

verhandeln [fɛr'handəln] *vi* negotiate (*über etw* (*akk*) sth); (*JUR*) hold proceedings // *vt* discuss; (*JUR*) hear.

Verhandlung *f* negotiation; (*JUR*) proceedings *pl*; **Verhandlungspaket** *nt* package (of proposals).

ver'hängen *vt* (*fig*) impose, inflict.

Verhängnis [fɛr'hɛŋnɪs] *nt* -ses, -se fate, doom; jdm zum ~ werden be sb's undoing; **v~voll** *a* fatal, disastrous.

verharmlosen [fɛr'harmloːzən] *vt* make light of, play down.

verhärten [fɛr'hɛrtən] *vr* harden.

verhaßt [fɛr'hast] *a* odious, hateful.

verheerend [fɛr'heːrənt] *a* disastrous, devastating.

verheimlichen [fɛr'haɪmlɪçən] *vt* keep secret (*jdm* from sb).

verheiratet [fɛr'haɪraːtət] *a* married.

ver'helfen *vi unreg*: jdm ~ zu help sb to get.

verherrlichen [fɛr'hɛrlɪçən] *vt* glorify.

ver'hexen *vt* bewitch; es ist wie verhext it's jinxed.

ver'hindern *vt* prevent; verhindert sein be unable to make it.

verhöhnen [fɛr'høːnən] *vt* mock, sneer at.

Verhör [fɛr'høːr] *nt* -(e)s, -e interrogation; (*gerichtlich*) (cross-)examination; **v~en** *vt* interrogate; (cross-)examine // *vr* misunderstand, mishear.

ver'hungern *vi* starve, die of hunger.

ver'hüten *vt* prevent, avert.

Ver'hütung *f* prevention; **Verhütungsmittel** *nt* contraceptive.

verirren [fɛr'ɪrən] *vr* go astray.

ver'jagen *vt* drive away *od* out.

verkalken [fɛr'kalkən] *vi* calcify; (*umg*) become senile.

verkannt [fɛr'kant] *a* unappreciated.

Verkauf [fɛr'kaʊf] *m* sale; **v~en** *vt* sell.

Verkäufer(in *f*) [fɛr'kɔʏfər(ɪn)] *m* -s, - seller; salesman; (*in Laden*) shop assistant.

verkäuflich [fɛr'kɔʏflɪç] *a* saleable.

Verkaufsbedingungen *pl* terms and conditions of sale.

Verkehr [fɛr'keːr] *m* -s, -e traffic; (*Umgang, bes sexuell*) intercourse; (*Umlauf*) circulation; **v~en** *vi* (*Fahrzeug*) ply, run; (*besuchen*) visit regularly (*bei jdm* sb); **v~en mit** associate with // *vtr* turn, transform.

Verkehrs- *zW*: **~ampel** *f* traffic lights *pl*; **~amt** *nt* tourist office; **~delikt** *nt* traffic offence; **~stauung** *f*, **~stockung** *f* traffic jam, stoppage; **~teilnehmer** *m* road-user; **~unfall** *m* traffic accident; **~zeichen** *nt* traffic sign.

verkehrt a wrong; (*umgekehrt*) the wrong way round.
ver'kennen vt unreg misjudge, not appreciate.
ver'klagen vt take to court.
verkleiden [fɛr'klaɪdən] vtr disguise (o.s.), dress up.
Verkleidung f disguise; (*ARCHIT*) wainscoting.
verkleinern [fɛr'klaɪnərn] vt make smaller, reduce in size.
verklemmt [fɛr'klɛmt] a (*fig*) inhibited.
ver'klingen vi unreg die away.
ver'kneifen vt (*umg*): **sich** (*dat*) **etw** ~ (*Lachen*) stifle; (*Schmerz*) hide; (*sich versagen*) do without.
verknüpfen [fɛr'knʏpfən] vt tie (up), knot; (*fig*) connect.
ver'kommen vi unreg deteriorate, decay; (*Mensch*) go downhill, come down in the world // a (*moralisch*) dissolute, depraved.
verkörpern [fɛr'kœrpərn] vt embody, personify.
verkraften [fɛr'kraftən] vt cope with.
ver'kriechen vr unreg creep away, creep into a corner.
Verkrümmung f bend, warp; (*ANAT*) curvature.
verkrüppelt [fɛr'krʏpəlt] a crippled.
verkrustet [fɛr'krʊstət] a encrusted.
ver'kühlen vr get a chill.
ver'kümmern vi waste away.
verkünden [fɛr'kʏndən] vt proclaim; (*Urteil*) pronounce.
verkürzen [fɛr'kʏrtsən] vt shorten; (*Wort*) abbreviate; **sich** (*dat*) **die Zeit** ~ while away the time.
Verkürzung f shortening; abbreviation.
Verlag [fɛr'la:k] m -(e)s, -e publishing firm.
verlangen [fɛr'laŋən] vt demand; desire; ~ **Sie Herrn X** ask for Mr X // vi: ~ **nach** ask for, desire; **V**~ nt -s, - desire (*nach* for); **auf jds V**~ (*hin*) at sb's request.
verlängern [fɛr'lɛŋərn] vt extend; (*länger machen*) lengthen.
Verlängerung f extension; (*SPORT*) extra time; **Verlängerungsschnur** f extension cable.
verlangsamen [fɛr'laŋza:mən] vtr decelerate, slow down.
Verlaß [fɛr'las] m: **auf ihn/das ist kein** ~ he/it cannot be relied upon.
ver'lassen unreg vt leave // vr depend (*auf* +*akk* on) // a desolate; (*Mensch*) abandoned; **V**~**heit** f loneliness.
verläßlich [fɛr'lɛslɪç] a reliable.
Verlauf [fɛr'lauf] m course; **v**~**en** unreg vi (*zeitlich*) pass; (*Farben*) run // vr get lost; (*Menschenmenge*)

disperse.
ver'lauten vi: **etw** ~ **lassen** disclose sth; **wie verlautet** as reported.
ver'legen vt move; (*verlieren*) mislay; (*Buch*) publish // vr: **sich auf etw** (*akk*) ~ take up od to sth // a embarrassed; **nicht** ~ **um** never at a loss for; **V**~**heit** f embarrassment; (*Situation*) difficulty, scrape.
Verleger [fɛr'le:gər] m -s, - publisher.
Verleih [fɛr'laɪ] m -(e)s, -e hire service; **v**~**en** vt unreg lend; (*Kraft, Anschein*) confer, bestow; (*Preis, Medaille*) award; ~**ung** f lending; bestowal; award.
ver'leiten vt lead astray; ~ **zu** talk into, tempt into.
ver'lernen vt forget, unlearn.
ver'lesen unreg vt read out; (*aussondern*) sort out // vr make a mistake in reading.
verletz- [fɛr'lɛts] zW: ~**en** vt (*lit, fig*) injure, hurt; (*Gesetz etc*) violate; ~**end** a (*fig: Worte*) hurtful; ~**lich** a vulnerable, sensitive; **V**~**te(r)** mf injured person; **V**~**ung** f injury; (*Verstoß*) violation, infringement.
verleumd- [fɛr'lɔʏmd] zW: ~**en** vt slander; **V**~**ung** f slander, libel.
ver'lieben vr fall in love (*in jdn* with sb).
verliebt [fɛr'li:pt] a in love; **V**~**heit** f being in love.
verlieren [fɛr'li:rən] unreg vti lose // vr get lost.
verlob- [fɛr'lo:b] zW: ~**en** vr get engaged (*mit* to); **V**~**te(r)** [fɛr'lo:ptə(r)] mf fiancé(e); **V**~**ung** f engagement.
ver'locken vt entice, lure.
Ver'lockung f temptation, attraction.
verlogen [fɛr'lo:gən] a untruthful; **V**~**heit** f untruthfulness.
verlor etc v siehe **verlieren**.
verloren [fɛr'lo:rən] a lost; (*Eier*) poached; **etw** ~ **geben** give sth up for lost // v seihe **verlieren**; ~**gehen** vi unreg get lost.
verlosen [fɛr'lo:zən] vt raffle, draw lots for.
Verlosung f raffle, lottery.
verlottern [fɛr'lɔtərn], **verludern** [fɛr'lu:dərn] vi (*umg*) go to the dogs.
Verlust [fɛr'lʊst] m -(e)s, -e loss; (*MIL*) casualty.
ver'machen vt bequeath, leave.
Vermächtnis [fɛr'mɛçtnɪs] nt -ses, -se legacy.
Vermählung f wedding, marriage.
vermehren [fɛr'me:rən] vtr multiply; (*Menge*) increase.
Vermehrung f multiplying; increase.
ver'meiden vt unreg avoid.
vermeintlich [fɛr'maɪntlɪç] a supposed.
Vermerk [fɛr'mɛrk] m -(e)s, -e note; (*in Ausweis*) endorsement; **v**~**en** vt

note.

ver'messen unreg vt survey // a presumptuous, bold; **V~heit** f presumptuousness; recklessness.

Ver'messung f survey(ing).

ver'mieten vt let, rent (out); (Auto) hire out, rent.

Ver'mieter(in f) m -s, - landlord/landlady.

Ver'mietung f letting, renting (out); (von Autos) hiring (out).

vermindern [fɛr'mɪndərn] vtr lessen, decrease; (Preise) reduce.

Verminderung f reduction.

ver'mischen vtr mix, blend.

vermissen [fɛr'mɪsən] vt miss.

vermißt [fɛr'mɪst] a missing.

vermitteln [fɛr'mɪtəln] vi mediate // vt (Gespräch) connect; jdm etw ~ help sb to obtain sth.

Vermittler [fɛr'mɪtlər] m -s, - (Schlichter) agent, mediator.

Vermittlung f procurement; (Stellen~) agency; (TEL) exchange; (Schlichtung) mediation.

ver'mögen vt unreg be capable of; ~ zu be able to; **V~** nt -s, - wealth; (Fähigkeit) ability; ein **V~** kosten cost a fortune; **~d** a wealthy.

vermuten [fɛr'mu:tən] vt suppose, guess; (argwöhnen) suspect.

vermutlich a supposed, presumed // ad probably.

Vermutung f supposition; suspicion.

vernachlässigen [fɛr'na:xlɛsɪgən] vt neglect.

ver'nehmen vt unreg perceive, hear; (erfahren) learn; (JUR) (cross-)examine; dem **V~** nach from what I/we etc hear.

vernehmlich [fɛr'ne:mlɪç] a audible.

Vernehmung f (cross-)examination.

verneigen [fɛr'naɪgən] vr bow.

verneinen [fɛr'naɪnən] vt (Frage) answer in the negative; (ablehnen) deny; (GRAM) negate; **~d** a negative.

Verneinung f negation.

vernichten [fɛr'nɪçtən] vt annihilate, destroy; **~d** a (fig) crushing; (Blick) withering; (Kritik) scathing.

Vernichtung f destruction, annihilation.

verniedlichen [fɛr'ni:tlɪçən] vt play down.

Vernunft [fɛr'nʊnft] f - reason, understanding.

vernünftig [fɛr'nynftɪç] a sensible, reasonable.

veröffentlichen [fɛr'œfəntlɪçən] vt publish.

Veröffentlichung f publication.

verordnen [fɛr'ɔrdnən] vt (MED) prescribe.

Verordnung f order, decree; (MED)

prescription.

ver'pachten vt lease (out).

ver'packen vt pack.

Ver'packung f, **Verpackungsmaterial** nt packing, wrapping.

ver'passen vt miss; jdm eine Ohrfeige ~ (umg) give sb a clip round the ear.

ver'pflanzen vt transplant.

Ver'pflanzung f transplant(ing).

ver'pflegen vt feed, cater for.

Ver'pflegung f feeding, catering; (Kost) food; (in Hotel) board.

verpflichten [fɛr'pflɪçtən] vt oblige, bind; (anstellen) engage // vr undertake; (MIL) sign on // vi carry obligations; jdm zu Dank verpflichtet sein be obliged to sb.

Verpflichtung f obligation, duty.

verpönt [fɛr'pø:nt] a disapproved (of), taboo.

ver'prügeln vt (umg) beat up, do over.

Verputz [fɛr'pʊts] m plaster, roughcast; **v~en** vt plaster; (umg: Essen) put away.

Verrat [fɛr'ra:t] m -(e)s treachery; (POL) treason; **v~en** unreg vt betray; (Geheimnis) divulge // vr give o.s. away.

Verräter [fɛr'rɛːtər] m -s, - traitor; **~in** f traitress; **v~isch** a treacherous.

ver'rechnen vt: ~ mit set off against // vr miscalculate.

Verrechnungsscheck [fɛr'rɛçnʊŋsʃɛk] m crossed cheque.

verregnet [fɛr'reːgnət] a spoilt by rain, rainy.

ver'reisen vi go away (on a journey).

verrenken [fɛr'rɛŋkən] vt contort; (MED) dislocate; sich (dat) den Knöchel ~ sprain one's ankle.

ver'richten vt do, perform.

verriegeln [fɛr'ri:gəln] vt bolt up, lock.

verringern [fɛr'rɪŋərn] vt reduce // vr diminish.

Verringerung f reduction; lessening.

ver'rinnen vi unreg run out od away; (Zeit) elapse.

ver'rosten vi rust.

verrotten [fɛr'rɔtən] vi rot.

ver'rücken vt move, shift.

verrückt [fɛr'rʏkt] a crazy, mad; **V~e(r)** mf lunatic; **V~heit** f madness, lunacy.

Verruf [fɛr'ruːf] m: in ~ geraten/bringen fall/bring into disrepute; **v~en** a notorious, disreputable.

Vers [fɛrs] m -es, -e verse.

ver'sagen vt: jdm/sich (dat) etw ~ deny sb/o.s. sth // vi fail; **V~** nt -s failure.

Versager [fɛr'za:gər] m -s, - failure.

ver'salzen vt unreg put too much salt

in; (*fig*) spoil.

ver'sammeln *vtr* assemble, gather.

Ver'sammlung *f* meeting, gathering.

Versand [fɛr'zant] *m* -(e)s forwarding; dispatch; (~*abteilung*) dispatch department; ~**haus** *nt* mail-order firm.

versäumen [fɛr'zɔʏmən] *vt* miss; (*unterlassen*) neglect, fail.

ver'schaffen *vt*: **jdm/sich etw ~** get *od* procure sth for sb/o.s.

verschämt [fɛr'ʃɛːmt] *a* bashful.

verschandeln [fɛr'ʃandəln] *vt* (*umg*) spoil.

verschärfen [fɛr'ʃɛrfən] *vtr* intensify; (*Lage*) aggravate.

ver'schätzen *vr* be out in one's reckoning.

ver'schenken *vt* give away.

ver'schicken *vt* send off.

ver'schieben *vt unreg* shift; (*EISENB*) shunt; (*Termin*) postpone.

verschieden [fɛr'ʃiːdən] *a* different; (*pl: mehrere*) various; **sie sind ~ groß** they are of different sizes; ~**e** *pl* various people/things *pl*; ~**es** *pron* various things *pl*; **etwas V~es** something different; **V~heit** *f* difference; **verschiedentlich** *ad* several times.

verschlafen [fɛr'ʃlaːfən] *unreg vt* sleep through; (*fig: versäumen*) miss // *vir* oversleep // *a* sleepy.

Verschlag [fɛr'ʃlaːk] *m* shed; **v~en** [fɛr'ʃlaːgən] *vt unreg* board up; **jdm den Atem v~en** take sb's breath away; **an einen Ort v~en werden** wind up in a place // *a* cunning.

verschlechtern [fɛr'ʃlɛçtərn] *vt* make worse // *vr* deteriorate, get worse.

Verschlechterung *f* deterioration.

Verschleiß [fɛr'ʃlaɪs] *m* -es, -e wear and tear; **v~en** *unreg vt* wear out.

ver'schleppen *vt* carry off, abduct; (*Krankheit*) protract; (*zeitlich*) drag out.

ver'schleudern *vt* squander; (*COMM*) sell dirt-cheap.

verschließ- [fɛr'ʃliːs] *zW*: ~**bar** *a* lockable; ~**en** *unreg vt* close; lock // *vr*: **sich einer Sache ~en** close one's mind to sth.

verschlimmern [fɛr'ʃlɪmərn] *vt* make worse, aggravate // *vr* get worse, deteriorate.

verschlingen [fɛr'ʃlɪŋən] *vt unreg* devour, swallow up; (*Fäden*) twist.

verschlossen [fɛr'ʃlɔsən] *a* locked; (*fig*) reserved; **V~heit** *f* reserve.

ver'schlucken *vt* swallow // *vr* choke.

Verschluß [fɛr'ʃlʊs] *m* lock; (*von Kleid etc*) fastener; (*PHOT*) shutter; (*Stöpsel*) plug; **unter ~ halten** keep under lock and key.

verschlüsseln [fɛr'ʃlʏsəln] *vt* encode.

verschmähen [fɛr'ʃmɛːən] *vt* disdain, scorn.

verschmerzen [fɛr'ʃmɛrtsən] *vt* get over.

verschmutzen [fɛr'ʃmʊtsən] *vt* soil; (*Umwelt*) pollute.

verschneit [fɛr'ʃnaɪt] *a* snowed up, covered in snow.

verschollen [fɛr'ʃɔlən] *a* lost, missing.

ver'schonen *vt* spare (*jdn mit etw* sb sth).

verschönern [fɛr'ʃøːnərn] *vt* decorate; (*verbessern*) improve.

ver'schreiben *unreg vt* (*MED*) prescribe // *vr* make a mistake (in writing); **sich einer Sache ~** devote oneself to sth.

verschroben [fɛr'ʃroːbən] *a* eccentric, odd.

verschrotten [fɛr'ʃrɔtən] *vt* scrap.

verschuld- [fɛr'ʃʊld] *zW*: ~**en** *vt* be guilty of; **V~en** *nt* -s fault, guilt; ~**et** *a* in debt; **V~ung** *f* fault; (*Geld*) debts *pl*.

ver'schütten *vt* spill; (*zuschütten*) fill; (*unter Trümmern*) bury.

ver'schweigen *vt unreg* keep secret; **jdm etw ~** keep sth from sb.

verschwend- [fɛr'ʃvɛnd] *zW*: ~**en** *vt* squander; **V~er** *m* -s, - spendthrift; ~**erisch** *a* wasteful, extravagant; **V~ung** *f* waste; extravagance.

verschwiegen [fɛr'ʃviːgən] *a* discreet; (*Ort*) secluded; **V~heit** *f* discretion; seclusion.

ver'schwimmen *vi unreg* grow hazy, become blurred.

ver'schwinden *vi unreg* disappear, vanish; **V~** *nt* -s disappearance.

verschwommen [fɛr'ʃvɔmən] *a* hazy, vague.

verschwör- [fɛr'ʃvøːr] *zW*: ~**en** *vr unreg* plot, conspire; **V~er** *m* -s, - conspirator; **V~ung** *f* conspiracy, plot.

ver'sehen *unreg vt* supply, provide; (*Pflicht*) carry out; (*Amt*) fill; (*Haushalt*) keep // *vr* (*fig*) make a mistake; **ehe er (es) sich ~ hatte...** before he knew it...; **V~** *nt* -s, - oversight; **aus V~** by mistake; **versehentlich** *ad* by mistake.

Versehrte(r) [fɛr'zeːrtə(r)] *mf* disabled person.

ver'senden *vt unreg* forward, dispatch.

ver'senken *vt* sink // *vr* become engrossed (*in +akk* in).

versessen [fɛr'zɛsən] *a*: ~ **auf** (+*akk*) mad about.

ver'setzen *vt* transfer; (*verpfänden*) pawn; (*umg*) stand up; **jdm einen Tritt/Schlag ~** kick/hit sb; **etw mit etw ~** mix sth with sth; **jdn in gute Laune ~** put sb in a good mood // *vr*: **sich in jdn** *od* **in jds Lage ~** put o.s. in sb's place.

Ver'setzung f transfer.

verseuchen [fɛr'zɔyçən] vt contaminate.

versichern [fɛr'zɪçərn] vt assure; (mit Geld) insure.

Versicherung f assurance; insurance; **Versicherungsgesellschaft** f insurance company; **Versicherungspolice** f insurance policy.

ver'siegen vi dry up.

ver'sinken vi unreg sink.

versöhnen [fɛr'zøːnən] vt reconcile // vr become reconciled.

Versöhnung f reconciliation.

ver'sorgen vt provide, supply (mit with); (Familie etc) look after.

Ver'sorgung f provision; (Unterhalt) maintenance; (Alters~ etc) benefit, assistance.

verspäten [fɛr'ʃpɛːtən] vr be late.

Verspätung f delay; ~ haben be late.

ver'sperren vt bar, obstruct.

ver'spotten vt ridicule, scoff at.

ver'sprechen vt unreg promise; sich (dat) etw von etw ~ expect sth from sth; **V~** nt -s, - promise.

verstaatlichen [fɛr'ʃtaːtlıçən] vt nationalize.

Verstand [fɛr'ʃtant] m intelligence; mind; den ~ verlieren go out of one's mind; über jds ~ gehen go beyond sb.

verständig [fɛr'ʃtɛndıç] a sensible; **~en** [fɛr'ʃtɛndıgən] vt inform // vr communicate; (sich einigen) come to an understanding; **V~ung** f communication; (Benachrichtigung) informing; (Einigung) agreement.

verständ- [fɛr'ʃtɛnt] zW: **~lich** a understandable, comprehensible; **V~lichkeit** f clarity, intelligibility; **V~nis** nt -ses, -se understanding; **~nislos** a uncomprehending; **~nisvoll** a understanding, sympathetic.

verstärk- [fɛr'ʃtɛrk] zW: **~en** vt strengthen; (Ton) amplify; (erhöhen) intensify // vr intensify; **V~er** m -s, - amplifier; **V~ung** f strengthening; (Hilfe) reinforcements pl; (von Ton) amplification.

verstauchen [fɛr'ʃtauxən] vt sprain.

verstauen [fɛr'ʃtauən] vt stow away.

Versteck [fɛr'ʃtɛk] nt -(e)s, -e hiding (place); **v~en** vtr hide; **v~t** a hidden.

ver'stehen unreg vt understand // vr get on; das versteht sich (von selbst) that goes without saying.

versteigern [fɛr'ʃtaɪgərn] vt auction.

Versteigerung f auction.

verstell- [fɛr'ʃtɛl] zW: **~bar** a adjustable, variable; **~en** vt move, shift; (Uhr) adjust; (versperren) block; (fig) disguise // vr pretend, put

on an act; **V~ung** f pretence.

verstiegen [fɛr'ʃtiːgən] a exaggerated.

verstimmt [fɛr'ʃtɪmt] a out of tune; (fig) cross, put out; (Magen) upset.

verstohlen [fɛr'ʃtoːlən] a stealthy.

ver'stopfen vt block, stop up; (MED) constipate.

Ver'stopfung f obstruction; (MED) constipation.

verstorben [fɛr'ʃtɔrbən] a deceased, late.

verstört [fɛr'ʃtøːrt] a (Mensch) distraught.

Verstoß [fɛr'ʃtoːs] m infringement, violation (gegen of); **v~en** unreg vt disown, reject // vi: **v~en gegen** offend against.

ver'streichen unreg vt spread // vi elapse.

ver'streuen vt scatter (about).

verstümmeln [fɛr'ʃtʏməln] vt maim, mutilate (auch fig).

verstummen [fɛr'ʃtʊmən] vi go silent; (Lärm) die away.

Versuch [fɛr'zuːx] m -(e)s, -e attempt; (SCI) experiment; **v~en** vt try; (verlocken) tempt // vr: sich an etw (dat) **v~en** try one's hand at sth; **Versuchskaninchen** nt guinea-pig; **versuchsweise** ad tentatively; **~ung** f temptation.

versumpfen [fɛr'zʊmpfən] vi (fig umg) get into a booze-up.

versunken [fɛr'zʊnkən] a sunken; ~ sein in (+acc) be absorbed od engrossed in.

vertagen [fɛr'taːgən] vti adjourn.

ver'tauschen vt exchange; (versehentlich) mix up.

verteidig- [fɛr'taɪdıç] zW: **~en** vt defend; **V~er** m -s, - defender; (JUR) defence counsel; **V~ung** f defence.

ver'teilen vt distribute; (Rollen) assign; (Salbe) spread.

Verteilung f distribution, allotment.

vertiefen [fɛr'tiːfən] vt deepen // vr: sich in etw (akk) ~ become engrossed od absorbed in sth.

Vertiefung f depression.

vertikal [vɛrti'kaːl] a vertical.

vertilgen [fɛr'tɪlgən] vt exterminate; (umg) eat up, consume.

vertonen vt set to music.

Vertrag [fɛr'traːk] m -(e)s, -̈e contract, agreement; (POL) treaty; **v~en** [fɛr'traːgən] unreg vt tolerate, stand // vr get along; (sich aussöhnen) become reconciled; **v~lich** a contractual.

verträglich [fɛr'trɛːklıç] a good-natured, sociable; (Speisen) easily digested; (MED) easily tolerated; **V~keit** f sociability; good nature; digestibility.

Vertrags- zW: **~bruch** m breach of

contract; **~partner** *m* party to a contract; **v~widrig** *a* contrary to contract.

vertrauen [fɛr'trauən] *vi* trust (*jdm* sb); **~ auf** (+*akk*) rely on; **V~ nt -s** confidence; **~erweckend** *a* inspiring trust; **vertrauensvoll** *a* trustful; **vertrauenswürdig** *a* trustworthy.

vertraulich [fɛr'trauliç] *a* familiar; (*geheim*) confidential.

vertraut [fɛr'traut] *a* familiar; **V~heit** *f* familiarity.

ver'treiben *vt unreg* drive away; (*aus Land*) expel; (*COMM*) sell; (*Zeit*) pass.

vertret- [fɛr'treːt] *zW:* **~en** *vt unreg* represent; (*Ansicht*) hold, advocate; **sich** (*dat*) **die Beine ~en** stretch one's legs; **V~er** *m* **-s, -** representative; (*Verfechter*) advocate; **V~ung** *f* representation; advocacy.

Vertrieb [fɛr'triːp] *m* **-(e)s, -e** marketing.

ver'trocknen *vi* dry up.

ver'trösten *vt* put off.

vertun [fɛr'tuːn] *unreg vt* (*umg*) waste // *vr* make a mistake.

vertuschen [fɛr'tuʃən] *vt* hush *od* cover up.

verübeln [fɛr''yːbəln] *vt:* **jdm etw ~** be cross *od* offended with sb on account of sth.

verüben [fɛr''yːbən] *vt* commit.

verun- [fɛr''un] *zW:* **~glimpfen** [-glimpfən] *vt* disparage; **~glücken** [-glʏkən] *vi* have an accident; **tödlich ~glücken** be killed in an accident; **~reinigen** *vt* soil; (*Umwelt*) pollute; **~sichern** *vt* rattle; **~treuen** [-trɔyən] *vt* embezzle.

verur- [fɛr''uːr] *zW:* **~sachen** [-zaxən] *vt* cause; **~teilen** [-tailən] *vt* condemn; **V~teilung** *f* condemnation; (*JUR*) sentence.

verviel- [fɛr'fiːl] *zW:* **~fachen** [-faxən] *vt* multiply; **~fältigen** [-fɛltɪgən] *vt* duplicate, copy; **V~fältigung** *f* duplication, copying.

vervoll- [fɛr'fɔl] *zW:* **~kommnen** [-kɔmnən] *vt* perfect; **~ständigen** [-ʃtɛndɪgən] *vt* complete.

ver'wackeln *vt* (*PHOTO*) blur.

ver'wählen *vr* (*TEL*) dial the wrong number.

verwahr- [fɛr'vaːr] *zW:* **~en** *vt* keep, lock away // *vr* protest; **~losen** [-loːzən] *vi* become neglected; (*moralisch*) go to the bad; **~lost** [-loːst] *a* neglected; wayward.

verwalt- [fɛr'valt] *zW:* **~en** *vt* manage; administer; **V~er** *m* **-s, -** manager; (*Vermögens~er*) trustee; **V~ung** *f* administration; management; **V~ungsbezirk** *m* administrative district.

ver'wandeln *vtr* change, transform.

Ver'wandlung *f* change, transformation.

verwandt [fɛr'vant] *a* related (*mit* to); **V~e(r)** *mf* relative, relation; **V~schaft** *f* relationship; (*Menschen*) relations *pl*.

ver'warnen *vt* caution.

Ver'warnung *f* caution.

ver'wechseln *vt* confuse (*mit* with); mistake (*mit* for); **zum V~ ähnlich** as like as two peas.

Ver'wechslung *f* confusion, mixing up.

verwegen [fɛr've:gən] *a* daring, bold.

Verwehung [fɛr've:uŋ] *f* snow-/sanddrift.

verweichlicht [fɛr'vaiçlıçt] *a* effeminate, soft.

ver'weigern *vt* refuse (*jdm etw* sb sth); **den Gehorsam/die Aussage ~** refuse to obey/testify.

Ver'weigerung *f* refusal.

Verweis [fɛr'vais] *m* **-es, -e** reprimand, rebuke; (*Hinweis*) reference; **v~en** [fɛr'vaizən] *vt unreg* refer; **jdn von der Schule v~en** expel sb (from school); **jdn des Landes v~en** deport *od* expel sb.

ver'welken *vi* fade.

ver'wenden *unreg vt* use; (*Mühe, Zeit, Arbeit*) spend // *vr* intercede.

Ver'wendung *f* use.

ver'werfen *vt unreg* reject.

verwerflich [fɛr'vɛrflıç] *a* reprehensible.

ver'werten *vt* utilize.

Ver'wertung *f* utilization.

verwesen [fɛr've:zən] *vi* decay.

ver'wickeln *vt* tangle (up); (*fig*) involve (*in* +*akk* in) // *vr* get tangled (up); **sich ~ in** (+*acc*) (*fig*) get involved in.

verwildern [fɛr'vildərn] *vi* run wild.

ver'winden *vt unreg* get over.

verwirklichen [fɛr'virklıçən] *vt* realize, put into effect.

Verwirklichung *f* realization.

verwirren [fɛr'virən] *vt* tangle (up); (*fig*) confuse.

Verwirrung *f* confusion.

verwittern [fɛr'vitərn] *vi* weather.

verwitwet [fɛr'vitvət] *a* widowed.

verwöhnen [fɛr'vø:nən] *vt* spoil.

verworfen [fɛr'vɔrfən] *a* depraved.

verworren [fɛr'vɔrən] *a* confused.

verwund- *zW:* **~bar** [fɛr'vuntbaːr] *a* vulnerable; **~en** [fɛr'vundən] *vt* wound; **~erlich** [fɛr'vundərlıç] *a* surprising; **V~erung** [fɛr'vundəruŋ] *f* astonishment; **V~ete(r)** *mf* injured (person); **V~ung** *f* wound, injury.

ver'wünschen *vt* curse.

verwüsten [fɛr'vy:stən] *vt* devastate.

verzagen [fɛr'tsa:gən] *vi* despair.

ver'zählen vr miscount.

verzehren [fɛr'tseːrən] vt consume.

ver'zeichnen vt list; (Niederlage, Verlust) register.

Verzeichnis [fɛr'tsaiçnis] nt **-ses, -se** list, catalogue; (in Buch) index.

verzeih- [fɛr'tsai] zW: ~**en** vti unreg forgive (jdm etw sb for sth); ~**lich** a pardonable; **V~ung** f forgiveness, pardon; **V~ung!** sorry!, excuse me!

Verzicht [fɛr'tsiçt] m **-(e)s, -e** renunciation (auf +akk of); **v~en** vi forgo, give up (auf etw (acc) sth).

ver'ziehen unreg vi move // vt put out of shape; (Kind) spoil; (Pflanzen) thin out; **das Gesicht** ~ pull a face // vr go out of shape; (Gesicht) contort; (verschwinden) disappear.

verzieren [fɛr'tsiːrən] vt decorate, ornament.

verzinsen [fɛr'tsinzən] vt pay interest on.

ver'zögern vt delay.

Ver'zögerung f delay, time-lag; **Verzögerungstaktik** f delaying tactics pl.

verzollen [fɛr'tsɔlən] vt declare, pay duty on.

verzück- [fɛr'tsyk] zW: ~**t** a enraptured; **V~ung** f ecstasy.

verzweif- [fɛr'tsvaif] zW: ~**eln** vi despair; ~**elt** a desperate; **V~lung** f despair.

verzwickt [fɛr'tsvikt] a (umg) awkward, complicated.

Vesuv [ve'zuːf] m Vesuvius.

Veto ['veːto] nt **-s, -s** veto.

Vetter ['fɛtər] m **-s, -n** cousin.

vgl. abk (= vergleiche) cf.

v.H. abk (= vom Hundert) pc.

vibrieren [vi'briːrən] vi vibrate.

Video ['viːdeo] nt video; ~**gerät** nt, ~**recorder** m video recorder.

Vieh [fiː] nt **-(e)s** cattle pl; **v~isch** a bestial.

viel [fiːl] a a lot of, much; ~**e** pl a lot of, many // ad a lot, much; ~ **zuwenig** much too little; ~**erlei** a a great variety of; ~**es** a a lot; ~**fach** a, ad many times; **auf ~fachen Wunsch** at the request of many people; **V~falt** f - variety; ~**fältig** a varied, many-sided.

vielleicht [fi'laiçt] ad perhaps.

viel- zW: ~**mal(s)** ad many times; **danke ~mals** many thanks; ~**mehr** ad rather, on the contrary; ~**sagend** a significant; ~**seitig** a many-sided; ~**versprechend** a promising.

vier [fiːr] num four; **V~eck** nt **-(e)s, -e** four-sided figure; (gleichseitig) square; ~**eckig** a four-sided; square; **V~taktmotor** m four-stroke engine; ~**te(r, s)** ['fiːrtə(r,z)] a fourth; **V~tel** ['fɪrtəl] nt **-s, -** quarter; ~**teljährlich** a quarterly; **V~telnote** f crotchet;

V~telstunde ['fɪrtəl'ʃtundə] f quarter of an hour; ~**zehn** ['fɪrtseːn] num fourteen; **in ~zehn Tagen** in a fortnight; ~**zehntägig** a fortnightly; ~**zig** ['fɪrtsiç] num forty.

Villa ['vila] f -, **Villen** villa.

violett [vio'lɛt] a violet.

Violin- [vio'liːn] zW: ~**e** f -, **-n** violin; ~**konzert** nt violin concerto; ~**schlüssel** m treble clef.

Virus ['viːrus] m od nt -, **Viren** virus.

vis-à-vis [viza'viː] ad opposite.

Visier [vi'ziːr] nt **-s, -e** gunsight; (am Helm) visor.

Visite [vi'ziːtə] f -, **-n** (MED) visit; **Visitenkarte** f visiting card.

Visum ['viːzum] nt **-s, Visa** od **Visen** visa.

vital [vi'taːl] a lively, full of life, vital.

Vitamin [vita'miːn] nt **-s, -e** vitamin.

Vogel ['foːgəl] m **-s, ⁻** bird; **einen ~ haben** (umg) have bats in the belfry; **jdm den ~ zeigen** (umg) tap one's forehead (to indicate that one thinks sb stupid); ~**bauer** nt birdcage; ~**scheuche** f -, **-n** scarecrow.

Vogesen [vo'geːzən] pl Vosges pl.

Vokabel [vo'kaːbəl] f -, **-n** word.

Vokabular [vokabu'laːr] nt **-s, -e** vocabulary.

Vokal [vo'kaːl] m **-s, -e** vowel.

Volk [fɔlk] nt **-(e)s, ⁻er** people; nation.

Völker- ['fœlkər] zW: ~**recht** nt international law; **v~rechtlich** a according to international law; ~**verständigung** f international understanding.

Volks- zW: ~**abstimmung** f referendum; **v~eigen** a state-owned; ~**fest** nt fair; ~**hochschule** f adult education classes pl; ~**lied** nt folksong; ~**republik** f people's republic; **die ~republik China** the People's Republic of China; ~**schule** f elementary school; ~**tanz** m folk dance; **v~tümlich** ['fɔlkstyːmliç] a popular; ~**wirtschaft** f economics; ~**zählung** f (national) census.

voll [fɔl] a full; **etw ~ machen** fill sth up; ~ **und ganz** completely; **jdn für ~ nehmen** (umg) take sb seriously; ~**auf** [fɔl'auf] ad amply; **V~bart** m full beard; ~'**bringen** vt unreg insep accomplish; ~'**enden** vt insep finish, complete; **vollends** ['fɔlɛnts] ad completely; **V~endung** f completion; ~**er** a fuller; (+gen) full of.

Volleyball ['vɔlibal] m volleyball.

Vollgas nt: **mit ~** at full throttle; ~ **geben** step on it.

völlig ['fœliç] a, ad complete(ly).

voll- zW: ~**jährig** a of age; **V~kaskoversicherung** f fully comprehensive insurance; ~'**kommen** a perfect; **V~kommenheit** f perfection; **V~kornbrot** nt wholemeal bread; **V~macht** *f* -, **-en** authority, full powers *pl*; **V~mond** *m* full moon; **V~pension** *f* full board; **~schlank** *a*: Kleidung für V~schlanke clothes for the fuller figure; **~ständig** *a* complete; **~'strecken** *vt insep* execute; **~tanken** *vti* fill up; **~zählig** *a* complete; in full number; **~'ziehen** *vt unreg insep* carry out // *vr* happen; **V~'zug** *m* execution.

Volt [vɔlt] *nt - od* **-(e)s, -** volt.

Volumen [vo'lu:mən] *nt* **-s, -** *od* **Volumina** volume.

vom [fɔm] = **von dem**.

von [fɔn] *präp* +*dat* **1** (*Ausgangspunkt*) from; **~** ... **bis** from ... to; **~ morgens bis abends** from morning till night; **~** ... **nach** ... from ... to ...; **~** ... **an** from ...; **~** ... **aus** from ...; **~ dort aus** from there; **etw ~ sich aus tun** do sth of one's own accord; **~ mir aus** (*umg*) if you like, I don't mind; **~ wo/wann** ...? where/when ... from?

2 (*Ursache, im Passiv*) by; **ein Gedicht ~ Schiller** a poem by Schiller; **~ etw müde** tired from sth

3 (*als Genitiv*) of; **ein Freund ~ mir** a friend of mine; **nett ~ dir** nice of you; **jeweils zwei ~ zehn** two out of every ten

4 (*über*) about; **er erzählte vom Urlaub** he talked about his holiday

5: **~ wegen!** (*umg*) no way!

vonei'nander [fɔnaɪ'nandər] *ad* from each other.

vonstatten [fɔn'ʃtatən] *ad*: **~ gehen** proceed, go.

vor [fo:r] ◆*präp* +*dat* **1** (*räumlich*) in front of; **~ der Kirche links abbiegen** turn left before the church

2 (*zeitlich*) before; **ich war ~ ihm da** I was there before him; **~ 2 Tagen** 2 days ago; **5** (**Minuten**) **~ 4** 5 (minutes) to 4; **~ kurzem** a little while ago

3 (*Ursache*) with; **~ Wut/Liebe** with rage/love; **~ Hunger sterben** die of hunger; **~ lauter Arbeit** because of work

4: **~ allem, ~ allen Dingen** most of all

◆*präp* +*akk* (*räumlich*) in front of

◆*ad*: **~ und zurück** backwards and forwards.

Vorabend ['fo:r'a:bənt] *m* evening before, eve.

voran [fo'ran] *ad* before, ahead; **mach ~!** get on with it!; **~gehen** *vi unreg* go ahead; **einer Sache** (*dat*) **~gehen** precede sth; **~gehend** *a* previous; **~kommen** *vi unreg* come along, make progress.

Vor- ['fo:r] *zW*: **~anschlag** *m* esti-

mate; **~arbeiter** *m* foreman.

voraus [fo'raus] *ad* ahead; (*zeitlich*) in advance; **jdm ~ sein** be ahead of sb; **im ~** in advance; **~gehen** *vi unreg* go (on) ahead; (*fig*) precede; **~haben** *vt unreg*: **jdm etw ~haben** have the edge on sb in sth; **V~sage** *f* -, **-n** prediction; **~sagen** *vt* predict; **~sehen** *vt unreg* foresee; **~setzen** *vt* assume; **~gesetzt, daß** ... provided that ...; **V~setzung** *f* requirement, prerequisite; **V~sicht** *f* foresight; **aller V~sicht nach** in all probability; **~sichtlich** *ad* probably.

Vorbehalt ['fo:rbəhalt] *m* **-(e)s, -e** reservation, proviso; **~en** *vt unreg*: **sich/jdm etw ~en** reserve sth (for o.s.)/for sb; **v~los** *a, ad* unconditional(ly).

vorbei [for'baɪ] *ad* by, past; **das ist ~** that's over; **~gehen** *vi unreg* pass by, go past.

vorbe- *zW*: **~lastet** ['fo:rbəlastət] *a* (*fig*) handicapped; **~reiten** ['fo:rbəraɪtən] *vt* prepare; **V~reitung** *f* preparation; **~straft** ['fo:rbəʃtraft] *a* previously convicted, with a record.

vorbeugen ['fo:rbɔʏgən] *vtr* lean forward // *vi* prevent (*einer Sache* (*dat*) sth); **~d** *a* preventive.

Vorbeugung *f* prevention; **zur ~ gegen** for the prevention of.

Vorbild ['fo:rbɪlt] *nt* model; **sich** (*dat*) **jdn zum ~ nehmen** model o.s. on sb; **v~lich** *a* model, ideal.

vorbringen ['fo:rbrɪŋən] *vt unreg* advance, state.

Vorder- ['fɔrdər] *zW*: **~achse** *f* front axle; **~asien** *nt* the Near East; **v~e(r, s)** *a* front; **~grund** *m* foreground; **v~hand** *ad* for the present; **~mann** *m, pl* **-männer** man in front; **jdn auf ~mann bringen** (*umg*) get sb to shape up; **~seite** *f* front (side); **v~ste(r, s)** *a* front.

vordrängen ['fo:rdrɛŋən] *vr* push to the front.

voreilig ['fo:r'aɪlɪç] *a* hasty, rash.

voreingenommen ['fo:r'aɪngənɔmən] *a* biased; **V~heit** *f* bias.

vorenthalten ['fo:r'ɛnthaltən] *vt unreg*: **jdm etw ~** withhold sth from sb.

vorerst ['fo:r'e:rst] *ad* for the moment *od* present.

Vorfahr ['fo:rfa:r] *m* **-en, -en** ancestor; **v~en** *vi unreg* drive (on) ahead; (*vors Haus etc*) drive up.

Vorfahrt *f* (*AUT*) right of way; **~ achten!** give way!

Vorfahrts- *zW*: **~regel** *f* right of way; **~schild** *nt* give way sign; **~straße** *f* major road.

Vorfall ['fo:rfal] *m* incident; **v~en** *vi unreg* occur.

vorfinden ['fo:rfɪndən] *vt unreg* find.

vorführen ['fo:rfy:rən] *vt* show, display; **dem Gericht ~** bring before the court.

Vorgabe ['fo:rga:bə] *f* (*SPORT*) start, handicap; **Vorgabe-** *in zW* (*COMPUT*) default.

Vorgang ['fo:rgaŋ] *m* course of events; (*bes SCI*) process.

Vorgänger(in *f*) ['fo:rgɛŋər(ın)] *m* **-s, -** predecessor.

vorgeben ['fo:rge:bən] *vt unreg* pretend, use as a pretext; (*SPORT*) give an advantage *od* a start of.

vorge- ['fo:rgə] *zW*: **~faßt** [-fast] *a* preconceived; **~fertigt** [-fɛrtıçt] *a* prefabricated.

vorgehen ['fo:rge:ən] *vi unreg* (*voraus*) go (on) ahead; (*nach vorn*) go up front; (*handeln*) act, proceed; (*Uhr*) be fast; (*Vorrang haben*) take precedence; (*passieren*) go on; **V~** *nt* **-s** action.

Vorgeschmack ['fo:rgəʃmak] *m* foretaste.

Vorgesetzte(r) ['fo:rgəzɛtstə(r)] *mf* superior.

vorgestern ['fo:rgɛstərn] *ad* the day before yesterday.

vorhaben ['fo:rha:bən] *vt unreg* intend; **hast du schon was vor?** have you got anything on?; **V~** *nt* **-s, -** intention.

vorhalten ['fo:rhaltən] *unreg vt* hold *od* put up; (*fig*) reproach (*jdm etw* sb for sth) // *vi* last.

Vorhaltung *f* reproach.

vorhanden [fo:r'handən] *a* existing; (*erhältlich*) available.

Vorhang ['fo:rhaŋ] *m* curtain.

Vorhängeschloß ['fo:rhɛŋəʃlɔs] *nt* padlock.

vorher [fo:r'he:r] *ad* before(hand); **~bestimmen** *vt* (*Schicksal*) preordain; **~gehen** *vi unreg* precede; **~ig** [fo:r'he:rıç] *a* previous.

Vorherrschaft ['fo:rhɛrʃaft] *f* predominance, supremacy.

vorherrschen ['fo:rhɛrʃən] *vi* predominate.

vorher- [fo:r'he:r] *zW*: **V~sage** *f* **-, -n** forecast; **~sagen** *vt* forecast, predict; **~sehbar** *a* predictable; **~sehen** *vt unreg* foresee.

vorhin [fo:r'hın] *ad* not long ago, just now; **vorhinein** [fo:r'hınaın] *ad*: **im vorhinein** beforehand.

vorig ['fo:rıç] *a* previous, last.

Vorkaufsrecht ['fo:rkaufsrɛçt] *nt* option to buy.

Vorkehrung ['fo:rke:ruŋ] *f* precaution.

vorkommen ['fo:rkɔmən] *vi unreg* come forward; (*geschehen, sich finden*) occur; (*scheinen*) seem (to be); **sich** (*dat*) **dumm** *etc* **~** feel stupid *etc*; **V~** *nt* **-s, -** occurrence.

Vorkriegs- ['fo:rkri:ks] *in zW* prewar.

Vorladung ['fo:rla:duŋ] *f* summons.

Vorlage ['fo:rla:gə] *f* model, pattern; (*Gesetzes~*) bill; (*SPORT*) pass.

vorlassen ['fo:rlasən] *vt unreg* admit; (*vorgehen lassen*) allow to go in front.

vorläufig ['fo:rlɔyfıç] *a* temporary, provisional.

vorlaut ['fo:rlaut] *a* impertinent, cheeky.

vorlesen ['fo:rle:zən] *vt unreg* read (out).

Vorlesung *f* (*UNIV*) lecture.

vorletzte(r, s) ['fo:rlɛtstə(r, s)] *a* last but one.

Vorliebe ['fo:rli:bə] *f* preference, partiality.

vorliebnehmen [fo:r'li:pne:mən] *vi unreg*: **~ mit** make do with.

vorliegen ['fo:rli:gən] *vi unreg* be (here); **etw liegt jdm vor** sb has sth; **~d** *a* present, at issue.

vormachen ['fo:rmaxən] *vt*: **jdm etw ~** show sb how to do sth; (*fig*) fool sb; **have** sb on.

Vormachtstellung ['fo:rmaxtʃtɛluŋ] *f* supremacy, hegemony.

Vormarsch ['fo:rmarʃ] *m* advance.

vormerken ['fo:rmɛrkən] *vt* book.

Vormittag ['fo:rmıta:k] *m* morning; **v~s** *ad* in the morning, before noon.

Vormund ['fo:rmʊnt] *m* **-(e)s, -e** *od* **-münder** guardian.

vorn(e) ['fɔrn(ə)] *ad* in front; **von ~ anfangen** start at the beginning; **nach ~ to** the front.

Vorname ['fo:rna:mə] *m* first or Christian name.

vornehm ['fo:rne:m] *a* distinguished; refined; elegant; **~en** *vt unreg* (*fig*) carry out; **sich** (*dat*) **etw ~en** start on sth; (*beschließen*) decide to do sth; **sich** (*dat*) **jdn ~en** tell sb off; **~lich** *ad* chiefly, specially.

vornherein ['fɔrnhɛraın] *ad*: **von ~** from the start.

Vorort ['fo:r'ɔrt] *m* suburb.

Vorrang ['fo:rraŋ] *m* precedence, priority; **v~ig** *a* of prime importance, primary.

Vorrat ['fo:rra:t] *m* stock, supply; **Vorratskammer** *f* pantry.

vorrätig ['fo:rrɛ:tıç] *a* in stock.

Vorrecht ['fo:rrɛçt] *nt* privilege.

Vorrichtung ['fo:rrıçtuŋ] *f* device, contrivance.

vorrücken ['fo:rrʏkən] *vi* advance // *vt* move forward.

Vorsatz ['fo:rzats] *m* intention; (*JUR*) intent; **einen ~ fassen** make a resolution.

vorsätzlich ['fo:rzɛtslıç] *a, ad* intentional(ly); (*JUR*) premeditated.

Vorschau ['fo:rʃau] *f* (*RAD, TV*) (programme) preview; (*Film*) trailer.

Vorschlag ['fo:rʃla:k] *m* suggestion, proposal; **v~en** *vt unreg* suggest, propose.

vorschnell ['fo:rʃnɛl] *ad* hastily, too quickly.

vorschreiben ['fo:rʃraɪbən] *vt unreg* prescribe, specify.

Vorschrift ['fo:rʃrɪft] *f* regulation(s); rule(s); (*Anweisungen*) instruction(s); **Dienst nach ~** work-to-rule; **vorschriftsmäßig** *a* as per regulations/instructions.

Vorschuß ['fo:rʃus] *m* advance.

vorsehen ['fo:rze:ən] *unreg vt* provide for, plan // *vr* take care, be careful // *vi* be visible.

Vorsehung *f* providence.

vorsetzen ['fo:rzɛtsən] *vt* move forward; (*vor etw*) put in front; (*anbieten*) offer.

Vorsicht ['fo:rzɪçt] *f* caution, care; **~!** look out!, take care!; (*auf Schildern*) caution!, danger!; **~, Stufe!** mind the step!; **v~ig** *a* cautious, careful; **vorsichtshalber** *ad* just in case.

Vorsilbe ['fo:rzɪlbə] *f* prefix.

Vorsitz ['fo:rzɪts] *m* chair(manship); **~ende(r)** *mf* chairman/-woman.

Vorsorge ['fo:rzɔrgə] *f* precaution(s), provision(s); **v~n** *vi*: **v~n für** make provision(s) for; **~untersuchung** *f* check-up.

vorsorglich ['fo:rzɔrklɪç] *ad* as a precaution.

Vorspeise ['fo:rʃpaɪzə] *f* hors d'oeuvre, appetizer.

Vorspiel ['fo:rʃpi:l] *nt* prelude.

vorsprechen ['fo:rʃprɛçən] *unreg vt* say out loud, recite // *vi*: **bei jdm ~** call on sb.

Vorsprung ['fo:rʃpruŋ] *m* projection, ledge; (*fig*) advantage, start.

Vorstadt ['fo:rʃtat] *f* suburbs *pl*.

Vorstand ['fo:rʃtant] *m* executive committee; (*COMM*) board (of directors); (*Person*) director, head.

vorstehen ['fo:rʃte:ən] *vi unreg* project; **etw** (*dat*) **~** (*fig*) be the head of sth.

vorstell- ['fo:rʃtɛl] *zW*: **~bar** *a* conceivable; **~en** *vt* put forward; (*vor etw*) put in front; (*bekannt machen*) introduce; (*darstellen*) represent; **sich** (*dat*) **etw ~en** imagine sth; **V~ung** *f* (*Bekanntmachen*) introduction; (*THEAT etc*) performance; (*Gedanke*) idea, thought.

Vorstrafe ['fo:rʃtra:fə] *f* previous conviction.

Vortag ['fo:rtak] *m* day before (*einer Sache* sth).

vortäuschen ['fo:rtɔyʃən] *vt* feign, pretend.

Vorteil ['fɔrtaɪl] *m* **-s, -e** advantage

(*gegenüber* over); **im ~ sein** have the advantage; **v~haft** *a* advantageous.

Vortrag ['fo:rtra:k] *m* **-(e)s, Vorträge** talk, lecture; **v~en** *vt unreg* carry forward; (*fig*) recite; (*Rede*) deliver; (*Lied*) perform; (*Meinung etc*) express.

vortrefflich [fo:rtrɛflɪç] *a* excellent.

vortreten ['fo:rtre:tən] *vi unreg* step forward; (*Augen etc*) protrude.

vorüber [fo'ry:bər] *ad* past, over; **~gehen** *vi unreg* pass (by); **~gehen an** (+*dat*) (*fig*) pass over; **~gehend** *a* temporary, passing.

Vorurteil ['fo:rʊrtaɪl] *nt* prejudice.

Vorverkauf ['fo:rfɛrkaʊf] *m* advance booking.

Vorwahl ['fo:rva:l] *f* preliminary election; (*TEL*) dialling code.

Vorwand ['fo:rvant] *m* **-(e)s, Vorwände** pretext.

vorwärts ['fo:rvɛrts] *ad* forward; **V~gang** *m* (*AUT etc*) forward gear; **~gehen** *vi unreg* progress; **~kommen** *vi unreg* get on, make progress.

vorweg [fo:r'vɛk] *ad* in advance; **V~nahme** *f* **-, -n** anticipation; **~nehmen** *vt unreg* anticipate.

vorweisen ['fo:rvaɪzən] *vt unreg* show, produce.

vorwerfen ['fo:rvɛrfən] *vt unreg*: **jdm etw ~** reproach sb for sth, accuse sb of sth; **sich** (*dat*) **nichts vorzuwerfen haben** have nothing to reproach o.s. with.

vorwiegend ['fo:rvi:gənt] *a, ad* predominant(ly).

Vorwort ['fo:rvɔrt] *nt* **-(e)s, -e** preface.

Vorwurf ['fo:rvʊrf] *m* reproach; **jdm/sich Vorwürfe machen** reproach sb/o.s.; **vorwurfsvoll** *a* reproachful.

vorzeigen ['fo:rtsaɪgən] *vt* show, produce.

vorzeitig ['fo:rtsaɪtɪç] *a* premature.

vorziehen ['fo:rtsi:ən] *vt unreg* pull forward; (*Gardinen*) draw; (*lieber haben*) prefer.

Vorzug ['fo:rtsu:k] *m* preference; (*gute Eigenschaft*) merit, good quality; (*Vorteil*) advantage.

vorzüglich [fo:r'tsy:klɪç] *a* excellent.

vulgär [vʊl'gɛ:r] *a* vulgar.

Vulkan [vʊl'ka:n] *m* **-s, -e** volcano.

W

W, w [ve:] *nt* W, w.

Waage ['va:gə] *f* **-, -n** scales *pl*; (*ASTROL*) Libra; **w~recht** *a* horizontal.

Wabe ['va:bə] *f* **-, -n** honeycomb.

wach [vax] *a* awake; (*fig*) alert; **W~e**

f -, **-n** guard, watch; **W~e halten** keep watch; **W~e stehen** stand guard; **~en** *vi* be awake; (*W~e halten*) guard.

Wacholder [va'xɔldər] *m* **-s**, - juniper.

Wachs [vaks] *nt* **-es**, **-e** wax.

wachsam ['vaxza:m] *a* watchful, vigilant, alert; **W~keit** *f* vigilance.

Wachs- *zW*: **w~en** *vi unreg* grow // *vt* (*Skier*) wax; **~tuch** *nt* oilcloth; **~tum** *nt* **-s** growth.

Wächter ['vɛçtər] *m* **-s**, - guard, warden, keeper; (*Parkplatz~*) attendant.

wackel- ['vakəl] *zW*: **~ig** *a* shaky, wobbly; **W~kontakt** *m* loose connection; **~n** *vi* shake; (*fig: Position*) be shaky.

wacker ['vakər] *a* valiant, stout // *ad* well, bravely.

Wade ['va:də] *f* -, **-n** (*ANAT*) calf.

Waffe ['vafə] *f* -, **-n** weapon.

Waffel *f* -, **-n** waffle; wafer.

Waffen- *zW*: **~schein** *m* gun licence; **~schieber** *m* gun-runner; **~stillstand** *m* armistice, truce.

Wagemut ['va:gəmu:t] *m* daring.

wagen ['va:gən] *vt* venture, dare.

Wagen ['va:gən] *m* **-s**, - vehicle; (*Auto*) car; (*EISENB*) carriage; (*Pferde~*) cart; **~heber** *m* **-s**, - jack.

Waggon [va'gõ:] *m* **-s**, **-s** carriage; (*Güter~*) goods van, freight truck (*US*).

waghalsig ['va:khalzɪç] *a* foolhardy.

Wagnis ['va:knɪs] *nt* **-ses**, **-se** risk.

Wahl [va:l] *f* -, **-en** choice; (*POL*) election; **zweite ~** seconds *pl*.

wähl- ['vɛ:l] *zW*: **~bar** *a* eligible; **~en** *vti* choose; (*POL*) elect, vote (for); (*TEL*) dial; **W~er(in** *f*) *m* **-s**, - voter; **~erisch** *a* fastidious, particular.

Wahl- *zW*: **~fach** *nt* optional subject; **~gang** *m* ballot; **~kabine** *f* polling booth; **~kampf** *m* election campaign; **~kreis** *m* constituency; **~lokal** *nt* polling station; **w~los** *ad* at random; **~recht** *nt* franchise; **~spruch** *m* motto; **~urne** *f* ballot box.

Wahn [va:n] *m* **-(e)s** delusion; folly; **~sinn** *m* madness; **w~sinnig** *a* insane, mad // *ad* (*umg*) incredibly.

wahr [va:r] *a* true; **~en** *vt* maintain, keep.

während ['vɛ:rənd] *präp* +*gen* during // *kj* while; **~dessen** [vɛ:rənt'dɛsən] *ad* meanwhile.

wahr- *zW*: **~haben** *vt unreg*: etw nicht **~haben wollen** refuse to admit sth; **~haft** *ad* (*tatsächlich*) truly; **~haftig** [va:r'haftɪç] *a* true, real // *ad* really; **W~heit** *f* truth; **~nehmen** *vt unreg* perceive, observe; **W~nehmung** *f* perception; **~sagen** *vi* prophesy, tell fortunes; **W~sager(in** *f*) *m* **-s**, - fortune teller;

~scheinlich [va:r'ʃaɪnlɪç] *a* probable // *ad* probably; **W~'scheinlichkeit** *f* probability; **aller W~scheinlichkeit nach** in all probability; **W~zeichen** *nt* emblem.

Währung ['vɛ:rʊŋ] *f* currency.

Waise ['vaɪzə] *f* -, **-n** orphan; **Waisenhaus** *nt* orphanage.

Wald [valt] *m* **-(e)s**, **=er** wood(s); (*groß*) forest; **~sterben** *nt* dying of trees due to pollution.

Wal(fisch) ['va:l(fɪʃ)] *m* **-(e)s**, **-e** whale.

Wall [val] *m* **-(e)s**, **=e** embankment; (*Bollwerk*) rampart; **w~fahren** *vi unreg insep* go on a pilgrimage; **~fahrer(in** *f*) *m* pilgrim; **~fahrt** *f* pilgrimage.

Wal- ['val] *zW*: **~nuß** *f* walnut; **~roß** *nt* walrus.

Walze ['valtsə] *f* -, **-n** (*Gerät*) cylinder; (*Fahrzeug*) roller; **w~n** *vt* roll (out).

wälzen ['vɛltsən] *vt* roll (over); (*Bücher*) hunt through; (*Probleme*) deliberate on // *vr* wallow; (*vor Schmerzen*) roll about; (*im Bett*) toss and turn.

Walzer ['valtsər] *m* **-s**, - waltz.

Wand [vant] *f* -, **=e** wall; (*Trenn~*) partition; (*Berg~*) precipice.

Wandel ['vandəl] *m* **-s** change; **w~bar** *a* changeable, variable; **w~n** *vtr* change // *vi* (*gehen*) walk.

Wander- ['vandər] *zW*: **~er** *m* **-s**, - hiker, rambler; **w~n** *vi* hike; (*Blick*) wander; (*Gedanken*) stray; **~schaft** *f* travelling; **~ung** *f* walking tour, hike.

Wandlung *f* change, transformation.

Wange ['vaŋə] *f* -, **-n** cheek.

wankelmütig ['vaŋkəlmy:tɪç] *a* vacillating, inconstant.

wanken ['vaŋkən] *vi* stagger; (*fig*) waver.

wann [van] *ad* when.

Wanne ['vanə] *f* -, **-n** tub.

Wanze ['vantsə] *f* -, **-n** bug.

Wappen ['vapən] *nt* **-s**, - coat of arms, crest; **~kunde** *f* heraldry.

war *etc v siehe* **sein**.

Ware ['va:rə] *f* -, **-n** ware.

Waren- *zW*: **~haus** *nt*: department store; **~lager** *nt* stock, store; **~probe** *f* sample; **~zeichen** *nt*: (eingetragenes) **~zeichen** (registered) trademark.

warf *etc v siehe* **werfen**.

warm [varm] *a* warm; (*Essen*) hot.

Wärm- ['vɛrm] *zW*: **~e** *f* -, **-n** warmth; **w~en** *vtr* warm, heat; **~flasche** *f* hot-water bottle.

warnen ['varnən] *vt* warn.

Warnung *f* warning.

Warschau ['varʃaʊ] *nt* Warsaw; **~er**

Pakt Warsaw Pact.

warten ['vartən] *vi* wait (*auf* +*akk* for); **auf sich ~ lassen** take a long time.

Wärter(in *f*) ['vɛrtər(ɪn)] *m* **-s**, - attendant.

Warte- ['vartə] *zW*: **~raum**, **~saal** *m* (*EISENB*), **~zimmer** *nt* waiting room.

Wartung *f* servicing; service; **~ und Instandhaltung** maintenance.

warum [va'rʊm] *ad* why.

Warze ['vartsə] *f* -, **-n** wart.

was [vas] *pron* what; (*umg: etwas*) something; **~ für (ein)** ... what sort of ....

Wasch- [vaʃ] *zW*: **w~bar** *a* washable; **~becken** *nt* washbasin; **w~echt** *a* colourfast; (*fig*) genuine.

Wäsche ['vɛʃə] *f* -, **-n** wash(ing); (*Bett~*) linen; (*Unter~*) underclothing; **~klammer** *f* clothes peg (*Brit*), clothespin (*US*); **~leine** *f* washing line (*Brit*), clothesline (*US*).

waschen ['vaʃən] *unreg vti* wash // *vr* (have a) wash; **sich** (*dat*) **die Hände ~** wash one's hands.

Wäsche'rei *f* laundry.

Wasch- *zW*: **~küche** *f* laundry room; **~lappen** *m* face flannel, washcloth (*US*); (*umg*) sissy; **~maschine** *f* washing machine; **~mittel** *nt*, **~pulver** *nt* detergent, washing powder; **~raum** *m* washroom.

Wasser ['vasər] *nt* **-s**, - water; **~ball** *m* water polo; **w~dicht** *a* waterproof; **~fall** *m* waterfall; **~farbe** *f* watercolour; **w~gekühlt** *a* (*AUT*) water-cooled; **~hahn** *m* tap, faucet (*US*); **~kraftwerk** *nt* hydroelectric power station; **~leitung** *f* water pipe; **~mann** *n* (*ASTROL*) Aquarius.

wässern ['vɛsərn] *vti* water.

Wasser- *zW*: **w~scheu** *a* afraid of the water; **~ski** *nt* water-skiing; **~stoff** *m* hydrogen; **~stoffbombe** *f* hydrogen bomb; **~waage** *f* spirit level; **~zeichen** *nt* watermark.

wäßrig ['vɛsrɪç] *a* watery.

waten ['vatən] *vi* wade.

watscheln ['vatʃəln] *vi* waddle.

Watt [vat] *nt* **-(e)s**, **-en** mud flats *pl* // *nt* **-s**, - (*ELEK*) watt; **~e** *f* -, **-n** cotton wool, absorbent cotton (*US*).

WC ['veː'tseː] *nt abk* (= *water closet*) WC.

Web- ['veːb] *zW*: **w~en** *vt unreg* weave; **~er** *m* **-s**, - weaver; **~e'rei** *f* (*Betrieb*) weaving mill; **~stuhl** *m* loom.

Wechsel ['vɛksəl] *m* **-s**, - change; (*COMM*) bill of exchange; **~beziehung** *f* correlation; **~geld** *nt* change; **w~haft** *a* (*Wetter*) variable; **~jahre** *pl* change of life; **~kurs** *m* rate of exchange; **w~n** *vt* change;

(*Blicke*) exchange // *vi* change; vary; (*Geld* **w~n**) have change; **~sprechanlage** two-way intercom; **~strom** *m* alternating current; **~stube** *f* bureau de change; **~wirkung** *f* interaction.

wecken ['vɛkən] *vt* wake (up); call.

Wecker ['vɛkər] *m* **-s**, - alarm clock.

wedeln ['veːdəln] *vi* (*mit Schwanz*) wag; (*mit Fächer etc*) wave.

weder ['veːdər] *kj* neither; **~** ... **noch** ... neither ... nor ...

weg [vɛk] *ad* away, off; **über etw** (*akk*) **~ sein** be over sth; **er war schon ~** he had already left; **Finger ~**! hands off!; **W~** [veːk] *m* **-(e)s**, **-e** way; (*Pfad*) path; (*Route*) route; **sich auf den W~ machen** be on one's way; **jdm aus dem W~ gehen** keep out of sb's way; **W~bereiter** *m* **-s**, - pioneer; **~bleiben** *vi unreg* stay away.

wegen ['veːgən] *präp* +*gen od* (*umg*) *dat* because of.

weg- ['vɛk] *zW*: **~fahren** *vi unreg* drive away; leave; **~fallen** *vi unreg* be left out; (*aufhören*) cease; **~gehen** *vi unreg* go away; leave; **~lassen** *vt unreg* leave out; **~laufen** *vi unreg* run away od off; **~legen** *vt* put aside; **~machen** *vt* (*umg*) get rid of; **~müssen** *vi unreg* (*umg*) have to go; **~nehmen** *vt unreg* take away; **~tun** *vt unreg* put away; **W~weiser** ['veːgvaɪzər] *m* **-s**, - road sign, signpost; **~werfen** *vt unreg* throw away; **~werfend** *a* disparaging; **W~werfgesellschaft** *f* throw-away society.

weh [veː] *a* sore; **~ tun** hurt, be sore; **jdm/sich ~ tun** hurt sb/o.s.; **~(e)** *interj*: **~(e)**, **wenn du**... woe betide you if...; **o ~**! oh dear!; **~e**! just you dare!; **~en** *vti* blow; (*Fahnen*) flutter; **W~en** *pl* (*MED*) labour pains *pl*; **~leidig** *a* whiny, whining; **W~mut** *f* - melancholy; **~mütig** *a* melancholy.

Wehr [veːr] *nt* **-(e)s**, **-e** weir // *f*: **sich zur ~ setzen** defend o.s.; **~dienst** *m* military service; **w~en** *vr* defend o.s.; **w~los** *a* defenceless; **~pflicht** *f* compulsory military service; **w~pflichtig** *a* liable for military service.

Weib [vaɪp] *nt* **-(e)s**, **-er** woman, female; wife; **~chen** *nt* female; **w~lich** *a* feminine.

weich [vaɪç] *a* soft; **W~e** *f* -, **-n** (*EISENB*) points *pl*; **~en** *vi unreg* yield, give way; **W~heit** *f* softness; **~lich** *a* soft, namby-pamby; **W~ling** *m* weakling.

Weide ['vaɪdə] *f* -, **-n** (*Baum*) willow; (*Gras*) pasture; **w~n** *vi* graze // *vr*: **sich an etw** (*dat*) **w~n** delight in sth.

weidlich ['vaɪtlɪç] *ad* thoroughly.
weigern ['vaɪgərn] *vr* refuse.
Weigerung ['vaɪgərʊŋ] *f* refusal.
Weih- ['vaɪ] *zW:* ~e *f* -, -n consecration; (*Priester*~) ordination; **w~en** *vt* consecrate; ordain; ~er *m* -s, - pond; ~**nachten** *nt* -, - Christmas; **w~nachtlich** *a* Christmas; ~**nachtsabend** *m* Christmas Eve; ~**nachtslied** *nt* Christmas carol; ~**nachtsmann** *m* Father Christmas, Santa Claus; ~**nachtstag** *m* Christmas Day; **zweiter** ~**nachtstag** *m* Boxing Day; ~**rauch** *m* incense; ~**wasser** *nt* holy water.
weil [vaɪl] *kj* because.
Weile ['vaɪlə] *f* - while, short time.
Wein [vaɪn] *m* -(e)s, -e wine; (*Pflanze*) vine; ~**bau** *m* cultivation of vines; ~**beere** *f* grape; ~**berg** *m* vineyard; ~**bergschnecke** *f* snail; ~**brand** *m* brandy; **w~en** *vti* cry; **das ist zum** ~ en it's enough to make you cry *od* weep; ~**karte** *f* wine list; ~**lese** *f* vintage; ~**rebe** *f* vine; ~**stock** *m* vine; ~**traube** *f* grape.
weise ['vaɪzə] *a* wise; **W~(r)** *mf* wise old man/woman, sage.
Weise ['vaɪzə] *f* -, -n manner, way; (*Lied*) tune; **auf diese** ~ in this way; **w~n** *vt unreg* show.
Weisheit ['vaɪshaɪt] *f* wisdom; **Weisheitszahn** *m* wisdom tooth.
weiß [vaɪs] *a* white // *v siehe* **wissen**; **W~brot** *nt* white bread; ~**en** *vt* whitewash; **W~glut** *f* (*TECH*) incandescence; **jdn bis zur W~glut bringen** (*fig*) make sb see red; **W~kohl** *m* (white) cabbage; **W~wein** *m* white wine.
weit [vaɪt] *a* wide; (*Begriff*) broad; (*Reise, Wurf*) long; **wie** ~ **ist es ...?** how far is it ...?; **in** ~ **er Ferne** in the far distance; **das geht zu** ~ that's going too far // *ad* far; ~**aus** *ad* by far; ~**blickend** *a* far-seeing; **W~e** *f* -, -n width; (*Raum*) space; (*von Entfernung*) distance; ~**en** *vtr* widen.
weiter ['vaɪtər] *a* wider; broader; farther (away); (*zusätzlich*) further; **ohne** ~**es** without further ado; just like that // *ad* further; ~ **nichts/niemand** nothing/nobody else; ~**arbeiten** *vi* go on working; ~**empfehlen** *vt unreg* recommend (to others); **W~fahrt** *f* continuation of the journey; ~**gehen** *vi unreg* go on; ~**hin** *ad:* **etw** ~**hin tun** go on doing sth; ~**leiten** *vt* pass on; ~**machen** *vti* continue.
weit- *zW:* ~**gehend** *a* considerable // *ad* largely; ~**läufig** *a* (*Gebäude*) spacious; (*Erklärung*) lengthy; (*Verwandter*) distant; ~**schweifig** *a* long-winded; ~**sichtig** *a* (*MED*) long-

sighted; (*fig*) far-sighted; **W~sprung** *m* long jump; ~**verbreitet** *a* widespread; **W~winkelobjektiv** *nt* (*PHOT*) wide-angle lens.
Weizen [vaɪtsən] *m* -s, - wheat.
welche(r, s) ['vɛlçə(r, s)] ♦*interrog pron* which; ~**r von beiden?** which (one) of the two?; ~**n hast du genommen?** which (one) did you take?; **welch eine ... what a ...!;** ~ **Freude!** what joy!
♦*indef pron* some; (*in Fragen*) any; **ich habe** ~ I have some; **haben Sie** ~? do you have any?
♦*rel pron* (*bei Menschen*) who; (*bei Sachen*) which, that; ~**(r, s) auch immer** whoever/whichever/whatever.
welk [vɛlk] *a* withered; ~**en** *vi* wither.
Well- [vɛl] *zW:* ~**blech** *nt* corrugated iron; ~**e** *f* -, -n wave; (*TECH*) shaft.
Wellen- *zW:* ~**bereich** *m* waveband; ~**länge** *f* (*lit, fig*) wavelength; ~**sittich** *m* budgerigar.
Welt [vɛlt] *f* -, -en world; ~**all** *nt* universe; ~**anschauung** *f* philosophy of life; **w~berühmt** *a* world-famous; **w~fremd** *a* unworldly; ~**krieg** *m* world war; **w~lich** *a* worldly; (*nicht kirchlich*) secular; ~**macht** *f* world power; ~**meister** *m* world champion; ~**meisterschaft** *f* world championships *pl*; ~**raum** *m* space; ~**reise** *f* trip round the world; ~**stadt** *f* metropolis; **w~weit** *a* world-wide.
wem [ve:m] *pron* (*dat*) to whom.
wen [ve:n] *pron* (*akk*) whom.
Wende ['vɛndə] *f* -, -n turn; (*Veränderung*) change; ~**kreis** *m* (*GEOG*) tropic; (*AUT*) turning circle; **Wendeltreppe** *f* spiral staircase; **w~n** *vtir unreg* turn; **sich an jdn w~n** go/come to sb; ~**punkt** *m* turning point.
Wendung *f* turn; (*Rede*~) idiom.
wenig ['ve:nɪç] *a* little; ~**e** ['ve:nɪgə] *pl* few *pl*; ~**er** *a* less; (*mit pl*) fewer // *ad* less; ~**ste(r, s)** *a* least; **am** ~**sten** least; ~**stens** *ad* at least.
wenn [vɛn] *kj* **1** (*falls, bei Wünschen*) if; ~ **auch ..., selbst** ~ ... even if ...; ~ **ich doch ...** if only I ... **2** (*zeitlich*) when; **immer** ~ whenever.
wennschon ['vɛnʃo:n] *ad:* **na** ~ so what?; ~, **dennschon!** in for a penny, in for a pound.
wer [ve:r] *pron* who.
Werbe- ['vɛrbə] *zW:* ~**fernsehen** *nt* commercial television; **w~n** *unreg vt* win; (*Mitglied*) recruit // *vi* advertise; **um jdn/etw w~n** try to win sb/sth; **für jdn/etw w~n** promote sb/sth; ~**spot** *m* TV ad(vertisement).
Werbung *f* advertising; (*von Mitgliedern*) recruitment; (*um jdn/etw*) pro-

motion (um of).

werden ['veːrdən] ◆vi pt **wurde,** ptp **geworden** become; **was ist aus ihm/ aus der Sache geworden?** what became of him/it?; **es ist nichts/gut geworden** it came to nothing/turned out well; **es wird Nacht/Tag** it's getting dark/light; **mir wird kalt** I'm getting cold; **mir wird schlecht** I feel ill; **Erster ~** come od be first; **das muß anders ~** that'll have to change; **rot/zu Eis ~** turn red/to ice; **was willst du (mal) ~?** what do you want to be?; **die Fotos sind gut geworden** the photos have come out nicely
◆ (als Hilfsverb) **1** (bei Futur): **er wird es tun** he will od he'll do it; **er wird das nicht tun** he will not od won't do it; **es wird gleich regnen** it's going to rain
2 (bei Konjunktiv): **ich würde ...** I would ...; **er würde gern ...** he would od he'd like to; **ich würde lieber ...** I would od I'd rather ...
3 (bei Vermutung): **sie wird in der Küche sein** she will be in the kitchen
4 (bei Passiv) ptp **worden:** gebraucht ~ be used; **er ist erschossen worden** he has od he's been shot; **mir wurde gesagt, daß ...** I was told that ...

werfen ['verfən] vt unreg throw.

Werft [verft] f -, -en shipyard, dockyard.

Werk [verk] nt -(e)s, -e work; (Tätigkeit) job; (Fabrik, Mechanismus) works pl; **ans ~ gehen** set to work; **~statt** f -, **-stätten** workshop; (AUT) garage; **~tag** m working day; **w~tags** ad on working days; **w~tätig** a working; **~zeug** nt tool.

Wermut ['veːrmuːt] m -(e)s wormwood; (Wein) vermouth.

Wert [veːrt] m -(e)s, -e worth; (FIN) value; **~ legen auf** (+akk) attach importance to; **es hat doch keinen ~** it's useless; **w~** a worth; (geschätzt) dear; worthy; **das ist nichts/viel w~** it's not worth anything/it's worth a lot; **das ist es/er mir w~** it's/he's worth that to me; **w~en** vt rate; **w~los** a worthless; **~papier** nt security; **w~voll** a valuable.

Wesen ['veːzən] nt -s, - (Geschöpf) being; (Natur, Character) nature; **wesentlich** a significant; (beträchtlich) considerable.

weshalb [ves'halp] ad why.

Wespe ['vespə] f -, -n wasp.

wessen ['vesən] pron (gen) whose.

West- [vest] zW: **~deutschland** nt West Germany; **~e** f -, -n waistcoat, vest (US); (Woll~e) cardigan; **~en** m -s west; **~europa** nt Western Europe; **Westfalen** nt Westphalia;

~indien nt the West Indies; **w~lich** a western // ad to the west.

weswegen [ves've:gən] ad why.

wett [vet] a even; **W~bewerb** m competition; **W~e** f -, -n bet, wager; **~en** vti bet.

Wetter ['vetər] nt -s, - weather; **~bericht** m weather report; **~dienst** m meteorological service; **~lage** f (weather) situation; **~vorhersage** f weather forecast; **~warte** f -, -n weather station.

Wett- zW: **~kampf** m contest; **~lauf** m race; **w~machen** vt make good; **~streit** m contest.

wichtig ['viçtiç] a important; **W~keit** f importance.

wickeln ['vikəln] vt wind; (Haare) set; (Kind) change; **jdn/etw in etw** (akk) ~ wrap sb/sth in sth.

Widder ['vidər] m -s, - ram; (ASTROL) Aries.

wider ['viːdər] präp +akk against; **~'fahren** vi unreg happen (jdm to sb); **~'legen** vt refute.

widerlich ['viːdərliç] a disgusting, repulsive.

wider- ['viːdər] zW: **~rechtlich** a unlawful; **W~rede** f contradiction; **W~ruf** m retraction; countermanding; **w~'rufen** vt unreg insep retract; (Anordnung) revoke; (Befehl) countermand; **~setzen** vr insep oppose (jdm/etw sb/sth).

widerspenstig ['viːdərʃpenstiç] a wilful.

wider'sprechen vi unreg insep contradict (jdm sb).

Widerspruch ['viːdərʃprux] m contradiction; **widerspruchslos** ad without arguing.

Widerstand ['viːdərʃtant] m resistance.

Widerstands- zW: **~bewegung** f resistance (movement); **w~fähig** a resistant, tough; **w~los** a unresisting.

wider'stehen vi unreg insep withstand (jdm/etw sb/sth).

Wider- ['viːdər] zW: **w~wärtig** a nasty, horrid; **~wille** m aversion (gegen to); **w~willig** a unwilling, reluctant.

widmen ['vitmən] vt dedicate // vtr devote (o.s.).

widrig ['viːdriç] a (Umstände) adverse.

wie [viː] ◆ad how; **~ groß/schnell?** how big/fast?; **~ wär's?** how about it?; **~ ist er?** what's he like?; **~ gut du das kannst!** you're very good at it; **~ bitte?** pardon?; (entrüstet) I beg your pardon!; **und ~!** and how!
◆kj **1** (bei Vergleichen): **so schön ~ ...** as beautiful as ...; **~ ich schon sagte** as I said; **~ du** like you; **singen**

~ **ein** ... sing like a ...; ~ (**zum Beispiel**) such as (for example)
2 (*zeitlich*): ~ er das hörte, ging er when he heard that he left; **er hörte, ~ der Regen fiel** he heard the rain falling.

wieder ['viːdər] *ad* again; ~ **da sein** be back (again); **gehst du schon ~?** are you off again?; ~ **ein(e)...** another...; **W~aufbau** [-'ʔaʊfbaʊ] *m* rebuilding; **~aufnehmen** *vt unreg* resume; **~bekommen** *vt unreg* get back; **~bringen** *vt unreg* bring back; **~erkennen** *vt unreg* recognize; **W~gabe** *f* reproduction; **~geben** *vt unreg* (*zurückgeben*) return; (*Erzählung etc*) repeat; (*Gefühle etc*) convey; **~gutmachen** [-'guːtmaxən] *vt* make up for; (*Fehler*) put right; **W~'gutmachung** *f* reparation; **~'herstellen** *vt* restore; **~'holen** *vt insep* repeat; **W~'holung** *f* repetition; **W~hören** *nt*: **auf W~hören** (*TEL*) goodbye; **W~kehr** *f* - return; (*von Vorfall*) repetition, recurrence; **~sehen** *vt unreg* see again; **auf W~sehen** goodbye; **~um** *ad* again; (*andererseits*) on the other hand; **W~wahl** *f* re-election.

Wiege ['viːgə] *f* -, -**n** cradle; **w~n** *vt* (*schaukeln*) rock // *vti unreg* (*Gewicht*) weigh.

wiehern ['viːərn] *vi* neigh, whinny.

Wien [viːn] *nt* Vienna; **~er** *a* Viennese; **~er(in** *f*) *m* Viennese; **~er Schnitzel** Wiener schnitzel.

Wiese ['viːzə] *f* -, -**n** meadow.

Wiesel ['viːzəl] *nt* -**s**, - weasel.

wieso [viˈzoː] *ad* why.

wieviel [viˈfiːl] *a* how much; ~ **Menschen** how many people; **~mal** *ad* how often; **~te(r, s)** *a*: **zum ~ten Mal?** how many times?; **den W~ten haben wir?** what's the date?; **an ~ter Stelle?** in what place?; **der ~te Besucher war er?** how many visitors were there before him?

wieweit [viːˈvait] *ad* to what extent.

wild [vilt] *a* wild; **W~** *nt* -(**e**)**s** game; **~ern** ['vildərn] *vi* poach; **~'fremd** *a* (*umg*) quite strange *od* unknown; **W~heit** *f* wildness; **W~leder** *nt* suede; **W~nis** *f* -, -**se** wilderness; **W~schwein** *nt* (wild) boar.

will *etc v siehe* **wollen**.

Wille ['vilə] *m* -**ns**, -**n** will; **w~n** *präp* +*gen*: **um... w~n** for the sake of...; **willensstark** *a* strong-willed.

will- *zW*: **~ig** *a* willing; **~kommen** [vilˈkɔmən] *a* welcome; **jdn ~kommen heißen** welcome sb; **W~kommen** *nt* -**s**, - welcome; **~kürlich** *a* arbitrary; (*Bewegung*) voluntary.

wimmeln ['viməln] *vi* swarm (*von* with).

wimmern ['vimərn] *vi* whimper.

Wimper ['vimpər] *f* -, -**n** eyelash.

Wind [vint] *m* -(**e**)**s**, -**e** wind; **~beutel** *m* cream puff; (*fig*) windbag; **~e** ['vində] *f* -, -**n** (*TECH*) winch, windlass; (*BOT*) bindweed; **Windel** ['vindəl] *f* -, -**n** nappy, diaper (*US*); **w~en** ['vindən] *vi unpers* be windy // *unreg vt* wind; (*Kranz*) weave; (*ent~en*) twist // *vr* wind; (*Person*) writhe; **~hund** *m* greyhound; (*Mensch*) fly-by-night; **w~ig** ['vindiç] *a* windy; (*fig*) dubious; **~mühle** *f* windmill; **~pocken** *pl* chickenpox; **~schutzscheibe** *f* (*AUT*) windscreen, windshield (*US*); **~stille** *f* calm; **~stoß** *m* gust of wind.

Wink [viŋk] *m* -(**e**)**s**, -**e** hint; (*mit Kopf*) nod; (*mit Hand*) wave.

Winkel ['viŋkəl] *m* -**s**, - (*MATH*) angle; (*Gerät*) set square; (*in Raum*) corner.

winken ['viŋkən] *vti* wave.

winseln ['vinzəln] *vi* whine.

Winter ['vintər] *m* -**s**, - winter; **w~lich** *a* wintry; **~sport** *m* winter sports *pl*.

Winzer ['vintsər] *m* -**s**, - vine grower.

winzig ['vintsiç] *a* tiny.

Wipfel ['vipfəl] *m* -**s**, - treetop.

wir [viːr] *pron we*; ~ **alle** all of us, we all.

Wirbel ['virbəl] *m* -**s**, - whirl, swirl; (*Trubel*) hurly-burly; (*Aufsehen*) fuss; (*ANAT*) vertebra; **w~n** *vi* whirl, swirl; **~säule** *f* spine.

wird *v siehe* **werden**.

wirfst *etc v siehe* **werfen**.

wirken ['virkən] *vi* have an effect; (*erfolgreich sein*) work; (*scheinen*) seem // *vt* (*Wunder*) work.

wirklich ['virkliç] *a* real // *ad* really; **W~keit** *f* reality.

wirksam ['virkzaːm] *a* effective; **W~keit** *f* effectiveness, efficacy.

Wirkung ['virkuŋ] *f* effect; **wirkungslos** *a* ineffective; **wirkungslos bleiben** have no effect; **wirkungsvoll** *a* effective.

wirr [vir] *a* confused, wild; **W~warr** [-var] *m* -**s** disorder, chaos.

Wirsing ['virziŋ] *m* -**s** savoy cabbage.

wirst *v siehe* **werden**.

Wirt [virt] *m* -(**e**)**s**, -**e** landlord; **~in** *f* landlady; **~schaft** *f* (*Gaststätte*) pub; (*Haushalt*) housekeeping; (*eines Landes*) economy; (*umg: Durcheinander*) mess; **w~schaftlich** *a* economical; (*POL*) economic.

Wirtschafts- *zW*: **~krise** *f* economic crisis; **~prüfer** *m* chartered accountant; **~wunder** *nt* economic miracle.

Wirtshaus *nt* inn.

Wisch [viʃ] *m* -(**e**)**s**, -**e** scrap of paper; **w~en** *vt* wipe; **~er** *m* -**s**, - (*AUT*) wiper.

wispern ['vɪspərn] *vti* whisper.

Wißbegier(de) ['vɪsbəgiːr(də)] *f* thirst for knowledge; **w~ig** *a* inquisitive, eager for knowledge.

wissen ['vɪsən] *vt unreg* know; **was weiß ich!** I don't know!; **W~** *nt* **-s** knowledge; **W~schaft** *f* science; **W~schaftler(in** *f)* *m* **-s,** - scientist; **~schaftlich** *a* scientific; **wissenswert** *a* worth knowing; **wissentlich** *a* knowing.

wittern ['vɪtərn] *vt* scent; *(fig)* suspect.

Witterung *f* weather; *(Geruch)* scent.

Witwe ['vɪtvə] *f* -, **-n** widow; **~r** *m* **-s,** - widower.

Witz [vɪts] *m* **-(e)s, -e** joke; **~blatt** *nt* comic (paper); **~bold** *m* **-(e)s, -e** joker, wit; **w~ig** *a* funny.

wo [voː] *ad* where; *(umg: irgendwo)* somewhere; **im Augenblick, ~ ...** the moment (that) ...; **die Zeit, ~ ...** the time when ...; **~anders** [voːˈandərs] *ad* elsewhere; **~andershin** *ad* somewhere else; **~bei** [voːˈbaɪ] *ad (rel)* by/with which; *(interrog)* what ... in/ by/with.

Woche ['vɔxə] *f* -, **-n** week.

Wochen- *zW:* **~ende** *nt* weekend; **w~lang** *a, ad* for weeks; **~schau** *f* newsreel.

wöchentlich ['vœçəntlɪç] *a, ad* weekly.

wo- *zW:* **~durch** [voːˈdʊrç] *ad (rel)* through which; *(interrog)* what ... through; **~für** [voːˈfyːr] *ad (rel)* for which; *(interrog)* what ... for.

wog *etc v siehe* **wiegen.**

Woge ['voːgə] *f* -, **-n** wave.

wo- *zW:* **~gegen** [voːˈgeːgən] *ad (rel)* against which; *(interrog)* what ... against; **~her** [voːˈheːr] *ad* where ... from; **~hin** [voːˈhɪn] *ad* where ... to.

wohl [voːl] *ad* **1: sich ~ fühlen** *(zufrieden)* feel happy; *(gesundheitlich)* feel well; **~ oder übel** whether one likes it or not
2 *(wahrscheinlich)* probably; *(gewiß)* certainly; *(vielleicht)* perhaps; **sie ist ~ zu Hause** she's probably at home; **das ist doch ~ nicht dein Ernst!** surely you're not serious! **das mag ~ sein** that may well be; **ob das ~ stimmt?** I wonder if that's true; **er weiß das sehr ~** he knows that perfectly well.

Wohl [voːl] *nt* **-(e)s** welfare; **zum ~!** cheers!; **w~auf** [voːlˈʔaʊf] *ad* well; **~behagen** *nt* comfort; **~fahrt** *f* welfare; **~fahrtsstaat** *m* welfare state; **w~habend** *a* wealthy; **w~ig** *a* contented, comfortable; **w~schmeckend** *a* delicious; **~stand** *m* prosperity; **~standsgesellschaft** *f* affluent society; **~tat** *f* relief; act of charity;

~täter(in *f)* *m* benefactor; **w~tätig** *a* charitable; **w~tun** *vi unreg* do good *(jdm sb)*; **w~verdient** *a* well-earned, well-deserved; **w~weislich** *ad* prudently; **~wollen** *nt* **-s** good will; **w~wollend** *a* benevolent.

wohn- ['voːn] *zW:* **~en** *vi* live; **W~gemeinschaft** *f (Menschen)* people sharing a flat; **~haft** *a* resident; **~lich** *a* comfortable; **W~ort** *m* domicile; **W~sitz** *m* place of residence; **W~ung** *f* house; *(Etagen~ung)* flat, apartment *(US)*; **W~wagen** *m* caravan; **W~zimmer** *nt* living room.

wölben ['vœlbən] *vtr* curve.

Wölbung *f* curve.

Wolf [vɔlf] *m* **-(e)s, ⁻e** wolf.

Wolke ['vɔlkə] *f* -, **-n** cloud; **Wolkenkratzer** *m* skyscraper.

wolkig ['vɔlkɪç] *a* cloudy.

Wolle ['vɔlə] *f* -, **-n** wool; **w~n** *a* woollen.

wollen ['vɔlən] ◆ *vti* want; **ich will nach Hause** I want to go home; **er will nicht** he doesn't want to; **er wollte das nicht** he didn't want it; **wenn du willst** if you like; **ich will, daß du mir zuhörst** I want you to listen to me
◆ *(als Hilfsverb) ptp* **wollen: er will ein Haus kaufen** he wants to buy a house; **ich wollte, ich wäre ...** I wish I were ...; **etw gerade tun ~** be going to do sth.

wollüstig ['vɔlʏstɪç] *a* lusty, sensual.

wo- *zW:* **~mit** [voːˈmɪt] *ad (rel)* with which; *(interrog)* what ... with; **~möglich** [voːˈmøːklɪç] *ad* probably, I suppose; **~nach** [voːˈnaːx] *ad (rel)* after/for which; *(interrog)* what ... for/after; **~ran** [voːˈran] *ad (rel)* on/ at which; *(interrog)* what ... on/at; **~rauf** [voːˈraʊf] *ad (rel)* on which; *(interrog)* what ... on; **~raus** [voːˈraʊs] *ad (rel)* from/out of which; *(interrog)* what ... from/out of; **~rin** [voːˈrɪn] *ad (rel)* in which; *(interrog)* what ... in.

Wort [vɔrt] *nt* **-(e)s, ⁻er** *od* **-e** word; **jdn beim ~ nehmen** take sb at his word; **mit anderen ~en** in other words; **w~brüchig** *a* not true to one's word.

Wörterbuch ['vœrtərbuːx] *nt* dictionary.

Wort- *zW:* **~führer** *m* spokesman; **w~karg** *a* taciturn; **~laut** *m* wording.

wörtlich ['vœrtlɪç] *a* literal.

Wort- *zW:* **~los** *a* mute; **w~reich** *a* wordy, verbose; **~schatz** *m* vocabulary; **~spiel** *nt* play on words, pun.

wo- *zW:* **~rüber** [voːˈryːbər] *ad (rel)* over/about which; *(interrog)* what ...

over/about; ~**rum** [voːˈrʊm] *ad* (*rel*)
about/round which; (*interrog*) what
... about/round; ~**runter** [voːˈrʊntər]
ad (*rel*) under which; (*interrog*)
what ... under; ~**von** [voːˈfɔn] *ad*
(*rel*) from which; (*interrog*) what ...
from; ~**vor** [voːˈfɔːr] *ad* (*rel*) in front
of/before which; (*interrog*) in front
of/before what; of what; ~**zu**
[voːˈtsuː] *ad* (*rel*) to/for which; (*interrog*) what ... for/to; (*warum*) why.
Wrack [vrak] *nt* -(e)s, -s wreck.
wringen [ˈvrɪŋən] *vt* *unreg* wring.
Wucher [ˈvuːxər] *m* -s profiteering;
~**er** *m* -s, - profiteer; **w~isch** *a* profiteering; **w~n** *vi* (*Pflanzen*) grow
wild; ~**ung** *f* (*MED*) growth, tumour.
Wuchs [vuːks] *m* -es (*Wachstum*)
growth; (*Statur*) build.
Wucht [vʊxt] *f* - force.
wühlen [ˈvyːlən] *vi* scrabble; (*Tier*)
root; (*Maulwurf*) burrow; (*umg:
arbeiten*) slave away // *vt* dig.
Wulst [vʊlst] *m* -es, ⁻e bulge; (*an
Wunde*) swelling.
wund [vʊnt] *a* sore, raw; **W~e**
[ˈvʊndə] *f* -, -n wound.
Wunder [ˈvʊndər] *nt* -s, - miracle; **es
ist kein ~** it's no wonder; **w~bar** *a*
wonderful, marvellous; ~**kind** *nt* infant prodigy; **w~lich** *a* odd, peculiar;
w~n *vr* be surprised (*über +akk* at)
// *vt* surprise; **w~schön** *a* beautiful;
w~voll *a* wonderful.
Wundstarrkrampf [ˈvʊntʃtarkrampf]
m tetanus, lockjaw.
Wunsch [vʊnʃ] *m* -(e)s, ⁻e wish.
wünschen [ˈvʏnʃən] *vt* wish; **sich**
(*dat*) **etw ~** want sth, wish for sth;
wünschenswert *a* desirable.
wurde *etc v siehe* **werden**.
Würde [ˈvʏrdə] *f* -, -n dignity; (*Stellung*) honour; **w~voll** *a* dignified.
würdig [ˈvʏrdɪç] *a* worthy; (*würdevoll*) dignified; ~**en** [ˈvʏrdɪgən] *vt* appreciate; **jdn keines Blickes ~en** not
so much as look at sb.
Wurf [vʊrf] *m* -s, ⁻e throw; (*Junge*)
litter.
Würfel [ˈvʏrfəl] *m* -s, - dice; (*MATH*)
cube; ~**becher** *m* (dice) cup; **w~n**
vi play dice // *vt* dice; ~**zucker** *m*
lump sugar.
würgen [ˈvʏrgən] *vti* choke.
Wurm [vʊrm] *m* -(e)s, ⁻er worm;
w~en *vt* (*umg*) rile, nettle; ~**stichig**
a worm-ridden.
Wurst [vʊrst] *f* -, ⁻e sausage; **das ist
mir ~** (*umg*) I don't care, I don't
give a damn.
Würstchen [ˈvʏrstçən] *nt* sausage.
Würze [ˈvʏrtsə] *f* -, -n seasoning,
spice.
Wurzel [ˈvʊrtsəl] *f* -, -n root.
würz- [ˈvʏrts] *zW*: ~**en** *vt* season,

spice; ~**ig** *a* spicy.
wusch *etc v siehe* **waschen**.
wußte *etc v siehe* **wissen**.
wüst [vyːst] *a* untidy, messy; (*ausschweifend*) wild; (*öde*) waste;
(*umg: heftig*) terrible; **W~e** *f* -, -n
desert.
Wut [vuːt] *f* - rage, fury; ~**anfall** *m* fit
of rage.
wüten [ˈvyːtən] *vi* rage; ~**d** *a* furious,
mad.

X

X, x [ɪks] *nt* X, x.
X-Beine [ˈɪksbaɪnə] *pl* knock-knees *pl*.
x-beliebig [ɪksbəˈliːbɪç] *a* any (whatever).
xerokopieren [kseroːkoˈpiːrən] *vt* xer-
ox, photocopy.
x-mal [ˈɪksmaːl] *ad* any number of
times, n times.
Xylophon [ksyloˈfoːn] *nt* -s, -e xylo-
phone.

Y

Y, y [ˈʏpsilɔn] *nt* Y, y.
Ypsilon *nt* -(s), -s the letter Y.

Z

Z, z [tsɛt] *nt* Z, z.
Zacke [ˈtsakə] *f* -, -n point; (*Berg~*)
jagged peak; (*Gabel~*) prong;
(*Kamm~*) tooth.
zackig [ˈtsakɪç] *a* jagged; (*umg*)
smart; (*Tempo*) brisk.
zaghaft [ˈtsaːkhaft] *a* timid.
zäh [tsɛː] *a* tough; (*Mensch*) tenacious; (*Flüssigkeit*) thick; (*schleppend*) sluggish; **Z~igkeit** *f* tough-
ness; tenacity.
Zahl [tsaːl] *f* -, -en number; **z~bar** *a*
payable; **z~en** *vti* pay; **z~en bitte!**
the bill please!
zählen [ˈtsɛːlən] *vti* count (*auf +akk*
on); ~ **zu** be numbered among.
Zähler [ˈtsɛːlər] *m* -s, - (*TECH*) meter;
(*MATH*) numerator.
Zahl- *zW*: **z~los** *a* countless; **z~reich**
a numerous; ~**tag** *m* payday; ~**ung**
f payment; **z~ungsfähig** *a* solvent;
~**ungsrückstände** *pl* arrears *pl*;
~**wort** *nt* numeral.
zahm [tsaːm] *a* tame.
zähmen [ˈtsɛːmən] *vt* tame; (*fig*)
curb.
Zahn [tsaːn] *m* -(e)s, ⁻e tooth; ~**arzt**
m dentist; ~**bürste** *f* toothbrush;
~**creme** *f* toothpaste; ~**fleisch** *nt*
gums *pl*; ~**pasta** *f* toothpaste; ~**rad**

nt cog(wheel); ~**schmerzen** *pl* toothache; ~**stein** *m* tartar; ~**stocher** *m* -s, - toothpick.

Zange ['tsaŋə] *f* -, -n pliers *pl*; (*Zucker~* etc) tongs *pl*; (*Beiß~*, *ZOOL*) pincers *pl*; (*MED*) forceps *pl*.

zanken ['tsaŋkən] *vir* quarrel.

zänkisch ['tsɛŋkɪʃ] *a* quarrelsome.

Zäpfchen ['tsɛpfçən] *nt* (*ANAT*) uvula; (*MED*) suppository.

Zapfen ['tsapfən] *m* -s, - plug; (*BOT*) cone; (*Eis~*) icicle; **z~** *vt* tap; ~**streich** *m* (*MIL*) tattoo.

zappeln ['tsapəln] *vi* wriggle; fidget.

zart [tsart] *a* (*weich*, *leise*) soft; (*Fleisch*) tender; (*fein*, *schwächlich*) delicate; **Z~gefühl** *nt* tact; **Z~heit** *f* softness; tenderness; delicacy.

zärtlich ['tsɛːrtlɪç] *a* tender, affectionate; **Z~keit** *f* tenderness; **Z~keiten** *pl* caresses *pl*.

Zauber ['tsaubər] *m* -s, - magic; (*~bann*) spell; ~**ei** [-'raɪ] *f* magic; ~**er** *m* -s, - magician; conjuror; **z~haft** *a* magical, enchanting; ~**künstler** *m* conjuror; **z~n** *vi* conjure, practise magic.

zaudern ['tsaudərn] *vi* hesitate.

Zaum [tsaum] *m* -(e)s, Zäume bridle; etw im ~ halten keep sth in check.

Zaun [tsaun] *m* -(e)s, Zäune fence; ~**könig** *m* wren.

z.B. *abk* (= *zum Beispiel*) e.g.

Zebra ['tseːbra] *nt* zebra; ~**streifen** *m* zebra crossing.

Zeche ['tsɛçə] *f* -, -n bill; (*Bergbau*) mine.

Zehe ['tseːə] *f* -, -n toe; (*Knoblauch~*) clove.

zehn [tseːn] *num* ten; ~**te(r, s)** *a* tenth; **Z~tel** *nt* -s, - tenth (part).

Zeich- ['tsaɪç] *zW:* ~**en** *nt* -s, - sign; **z~nen** *vti* draw; (*kenn~nen*) mark; (*unter~nen*) sign; ~**ner** *m* -s, - artist; **technischer** ~**ner** draughtsman; ~**nung** *f* drawing; (*Markierung*) markings *pl*.

Zeige- ['tsaɪgə] *zW:* ~**finger** *m* index finger; **z~n** *vi* show // *vi* point (*auf* +*akk* to, at) // *vr* show o.s.; es wird sich **z~n** time will tell; es zeigte sich, daß ... it turned out that ...; ~**r** *m* -s, - pointer; (*Uhr~r*) hand.

Zeile ['tsaɪlə] *f* -, -n line; (*Häuser~*) row.

Zeit [tsaɪt] *f* -, -en time; (*GRAM*) tense; **zur** ~ at the moment; sich (*dat*) ~ **lassen** take one's time; **von** ~ **zu** ~ from time to time; ~**alter** *nt* age; **z~gemäß** *a* in keeping with the times; ~**genosse** *m* contemporary; **z~ig** *a* early; ~**lich** *a* temporal; ~**lupe** *f* slow motion; **z~raubend** *a* time-consuming; ~**raum** *m* period; ~**rechnung** *f* time, era; **nach/vor**

unserer ~**rechnung** A.D./B.C.; ~**schrift** *f* periodical; ~**ung** *f* newspaper; ~**verschwendung** *f* waste of time; ~**vertreib** *m* pastime, diversion; **z~weilig** *a* temporary; **z~weise** *ad* for a time; ~**wort** *nt* verb; ~**zünder** *m* time fuse.

Zell- ['tsɛl] *zW:* ~**e** *f* -, -n cell; (*Telefon~e*) callbox; ~**stoff** *m* cellulose.

Zelt [tsɛlt] *nt* -(e)s, -e tent; **z~en** *vi* camp.

Zement [tse'mɛnt] *m* -(e)s, -e cement; **z~ieren** [-'tiːrən] *vt* cement.

zensieren [tsɛn'ziːrən] *vt* censor; (*SCH*) mark.

Zensur [tsɛn'zuːr] *f* censorship; (*SCH*) mark.

Zentimeter [tsɛnti'meːtər] *m od nt* centimetre.

Zentner ['tsɛntnər] *m* -s, - hundredweight.

zentral [tsɛn'traːl] *a* central; **Z~e** *f* -, -n central office; (*TEL*) exchange; **Z~einheit** *f* central processing unit, CPU; **Z~heizung** *f* central heating.

Zentrum ['tsɛntrum] *nt* -s, Zentren centre.

zerbrech- [tsɛr'brɛç] *zW:* ~**en** *vti* *unreg* break; ~**lich** *a* fragile.

zer'drücken *vt* squash, crush; (*Kartoffeln*) mash.

Zeremonie [tseremo'niː] *f* ceremony.

Zerfall [tsɛr'fal] *m* decay; **z~en** *vi* *unreg* disintegrate, decay; (*sich gliedern*) fall (*in* +*akk* into).

zer'gehen *vi* *unreg* melt, dissolve.

zerkleinern [tsɛr'klaɪnərn] *vt* reduce to small pieces.

zerleg- [tsɛr'leːg] *zW:* ~**bar** *a* able to be dismantled; ~**en** *vt* take to pieces; (*Fleisch*) carve; (*Satz*) analyse.

zermürben [tsɛr'myrbən] *vt* wear down.

zerquetschen [tsɛr'kvɛtʃən] *vt* squash.

Zerrbild ['tsɛrbɪlt] *nt* caricature, distorted picture.

zer'reißen *unreg* *vt* tear to pieces // *vi* tear, rip.

zerren ['tsɛrən] *vt* drag // *vi* tug (*an* +*dat* at).

zer'rinnen *vi* *unreg* melt away.

zerrissen [tsɛr'rɪsən] *a* torn, tattered; **Z~heit** *f* tattered state; (*POL*) disunion, discord; (*innere Z~heit*) disintegration.

zerrütten [tsɛr'rytən] *vt* wreck, destroy.

zerrüttet *a* wrecked, shattered.

zer'schlagen *unreg* *vt* shatter, smash // *vr* fall through.

zer'schneiden *vt* *unreg* cut up.

zer'setzen *vtr* decompose, dissolve.

zer'springen *vi* *unreg* shatter, burst.

Zerstäuber [tsɛr'ʃtɔybər] *m* -s, - atomizer-

zerstör- [tsɛr'ʃtøːr] zW: **~en** vt destroy; **Z~ung** f destruction.

zerstreu- [tsɛr'ʃtrɔy] zW: **~en** vtr disperse, scatter; (*unterhalten*) divert; (*Zweifel etc*) dispel; **~t** a scattered; (*Mensch*) absent-minded; **Zerstreutheit** f absent-mindedness; **Z~ung** f dispersion; (*Ablenkung*) diversion.

zerstückeln [tsər'ʃtykəln] vt cut into pieces.

zer'teilen vt divide into parts.

Zertifikat [tsɛrtifi'kaːt] nt certificate.

zer'treten vt unreg crush underfoot.

zertrümmern [tsɛr'trymərn] vt shatter; (*Gebäude etc*) demolish.

zerzausen [tsɛr'tsauzən] vt (*Haare*) ruffle up, tousle.

zetern ['tseːtərn] vi shout, shriek.

Zettel ['tsɛtəl] m -s, - piece of paper, slip; (*Notiz~*) note; (*Formular*) form.

Zeug [tsɔyk] nt -(e)s, -e (*umg*) stuff; (*Ausrüstung*) gear; **dummes ~** (stupid) nonsense; **das ~ haben zu** have the makings of; **sich ins ~ legen** put one's shoulder to the wheel.

Zeuge ['tsɔygə] m -n, -n, **Zeugin** ['tsɔygɪn] f witness; **z~n** vi bear witness, testify; **es zeugt von ...** it testifies to ... // zt vt (*Kind*) father; **Zeugenaussage** f evidence.

Zeugnis ['tsɔygnɪs] nt -ses, -se certificate; (*SCH*) report; (*Referenz*) reference; (*Aussage*) evidence, testimony; **~ geben von** be evidence of, testify to.

z.H(d). abk (= zu Händen) attn.

Zickzack ['tsɪktsak] m -(e)s, -e zigzag.

Ziege ['tsiːgə] f -, -n goat; **Ziegenleder** nt kid.

Ziegel ['tsiːgəl] m -s, - brick; (*Dach~*) tile.

ziehen ['tsiːən] unreg vt draw; (*zerren*) pull; (*SCHACH etc*) move; (*züchten*) rear; **etw nach sich ~** lead to sth, entail sth // vi draw; (*um~, wandern*) move; (*Rauch, Wolke etc*) drift; (*reißen*) pull // v unpers: **es zieht** there is a draught, it's draughty // vr (*Gummi*) stretch; (*Grenze etc*) run; (*Gespräche*) be drawn out.

Ziehharmonika ['tsiːharmoːnika] f concertina; accordion.

Ziehung ['tsiːuŋ] f (*Los~*) drawing.

Ziel [tsiːl] nt -(e)s, -e (*einer Reise*) destination; (*SPORT*) finish; (*MIL*) target; (*Absicht*) goal, aim; **z~en** vi aim (*auf +akk* at); **z~los** a aimless; **~scheibe** f target; **z~strebig** a purposeful.

ziemlich ['tsiːmlɪç] a quite a; fair // ad rather; quite a bit.

Zierde ['tsiːrdə] f ornament.

zieren ['tsiːrən] vr act coy.

zierlich ['tsiːrlɪç] a dainty; **Z~keit** f daintiness.

Ziffer ['tsɪfər] f -, -n figure, digit; **~blatt** nt dial, clock-face.

zig [tsɪç] a (*umg*) umpteen.

Zigarette [tsigaˈrɛtə] f cigarette.

Zigaretten- zW: **~automat** m cigarette machine; **~schachtel** f cigarette packet; **~spitze** f cigarette holder.

Zigarillo [tsigaˈrɪlo] nt od m -s, -s cigarillo.

Zigarre [tsiˈgarə] f -, -n cigar.

Zigeuner(in f) [tsiˈgɔynər(ɪn)] m -s, - gipsy.

Zimmer ['tsɪmər] nt -s, - room; **~lautstärke** f reasonable volume; **~mädchen** nt chambermaid; **~mann** m carpenter; **z~n** vt make, carpenter; **~nachweis** m accommodation office; **~pflanze** f indoor plant.

zimperlich ['tsɪmpərlɪç] a squeamish; (*pingelig*) fussy, finicky.

Zimt [tsɪmt] m -(e)s, -e cinnamon.

Zink [tsɪŋk] nt -(e)s zinc.

Zinn [tsɪn] nt -(e)s (*Element*) tin; (*in ~waren*) pewter; **~soldat** m tin soldier.

Zins [tsɪns] m -es, -en interest; **Zinseszins** m compound interest; **~fuß** m, **~satz** m rate of interest; **z~los** a interest-free.

Zipfel ['tsɪpfəl] m -s, - corner; (*spitz*) tip; (*Hemd~*) tail; (*Wurst~*) end; **~mütze** f stocking cap; nightcap.

zirka ['tsɪrka] ad (round) about.

Zirkel ['tsɪrkəl] m -s, - circle; (*MATH*) pair of compasses.

Zirkus ['tsɪrkʊs] m -, -se circus.

zischen ['tsɪʃən] vi hiss.

Zitat [tsiˈtaːt] nt -(e)s, -e quotation, quote.

zitieren [tsiˈtiːrən] vt quote.

Zitronat [tsitroˈnaːt] nt -(e)s, -e candied lemon peel.

Zitrone [tsiˈtroːnə] f -, -n lemon; **Zitronenlimonade** f lemonade; **Zitronensaft** m lemon juice.

zittern ['tsɪtərn] vi tremble.

zivil [tsiˈviːl] a civil; (*Preis*) moderate; **Z~** nt -s plain clothes pl; (*MIL*) civilian clothing; **Z~bevölkerung** f civilian population; **Z~courage** f courage of one's convictions; **Z~dienstleistende(r)** f conscientious objector doing alternative service (in the community); **Z~isation** [tsivilizatsi'oːn] f civilization; **Z~isationskrankheit** f disease peculiar to civilization; **~i'sieren** vt civilize; **Z~ist** [tsivi'lɪst] m civilian.

zog etc v siehe ziehen.

zögern ['tsøːgərn] vi hesitate.

Zoll [tsɔl] m -(e)s, ⁻e customs pl; (*Abgabe*) duty; **~abfertigung** f customs clearance; **~amt** nt customs office;

~**beamte(r)** *m* customs official; ~**erklärung** *f* customs declaration; **z~frei** *a* duty-free; ~**kontrolle** *f* customs check; **z~pflichtig** *a* liable to duty, dutiable.

Zone ['tso:nə] *f* -, -n zone.

Zoo [tso:] *m* -s, -s zoo; ~**loge** [tsoo'lo:gə] *m* -n, -n zoologist; ~**lo'gie** *f* zoology; **z~logisch** *a* zoological.

Zopf [tsɔpf] *m* -(e)s, ⁻e plait; pigtail; **alter** ~ antiquated custom.

Zorn [tsɔrn] *m* -(e)s anger; **z~ig** *a* angry.

zottig ['tsɔtiç] *a* shaggy.

z.T. *abk von* zum Teil.

zu [tsu:] ◆*präp* +*dat* **1** (*örtlich*) to; ~**m Bahnhof/Arzt gehen** go to the station/doctor; ~**r Schule/Kirche gehen** go to school/church; **sollen wir** ~ **euch gehen?** shall we go to your place?; **sie sah** ~ **ihm hin** she looked towards him; ~**m Fenster herein** through the window; ~ **meiner Linken** to *od* on my left

2 (*zeitlich*) at; ~ **Ostern** at Easter; **bis** ~**m 1. Mai** until May 1st; (*nicht später als*) by May 1st; ~ **meiner Zeit** in my time

3 (*Zusatz*) with; **Wein** ~**m Essen trinken** drink wine with one's meal; **sich** ~ **jdm setzen** sit down beside sb; **setz dich doch** ~ **uns** (come and) sit with us; **Anmerkungen** ~ **etw** notes on sth

4 (*Zweck*) for; **Wasser** ~**m Waschen** water for washing; **Papier** ~**m Schreiben** paper to write on; **etw** ~**m Geburtstag bekommen** get sth for one's birthday

5 (*Veränderung*) into; ~ **etw werden** turn into sth; **jdn** ~ **etw machen** make sb (into) sth; ~ **Asche verbrennen** burn to ashes

6 (*mit Zahlen*): **3** ~ **2** (*SPORT*) 3-2; **das Stück** ~ **2 Mark** at 2 marks each; ~**m ersten Mal** for the first time

7: ~ **meiner Freude** *etc* to my joy *etc*; ~**m Glück** luckily; ~ **Fuß** on foot; **es ist** ~**m Weinen** it's enough to make you cry

◆*kj* to; **etw** ~ **essen** sth to eat; **um besser sehen** ~ **können** in order to see better; **ohne es** ~ **wissen** without knowing it; **noch** ~ **bezahlende Rechnungen** bills that are still to be paid

◆*ad* **1** (*allzu*) too; ~ **sehr** too much **2** (*örtlich*) toward(s); **er kam auf mich** ~ he came up to me **3** (*geschlossen*) shut, closed; **die Geschäfte haben** ~ the shops are closed; **'auf/~'** (*Wasserhahn etc*) 'on/off'

4 (*umg*: *los*): **nur** ~! just keep on!; **mach** ~! hurry up!

zualler- [tsu''alər] *zW*: ~**erst** *ad* first of all; ~**letzt** *ad* last of all.

Zubehör ['tsu:bəhø:r] *nt* -(e)s, -e accessories *pl*.

zubereiten ['tsu:bəraitən] *vt* prepare.

zubilligen ['tsu:biligən] *vt* grant.

zubinden ['tsu:bindən] *vt unreg* tie up.

zubringen ['tsu:briŋən] *vt unreg* (*Zeit*) spend.

Zubringer *m* -s, - (*Straße*) approach *od* slip road.

Zucht [tsuxt] *f* -, -en (*von Tieren*) breed(ing); (*von Pflanzen*) cultivation; (*Rasse*) breed; (*Erziehung*) raising; (*Disziplin*) discipline.

züchten ['tsyçtən] *vt* (*Tiere*) breed; (*Pflanzen*) cultivate, grow.

Züchter *m* -s, - breeder; grower.

Zuchthaus *nt* prison, penitentiary (*US*).

züchtigen ['tsyçtigən] *vt* chastise.

zucken ['tsukən] *vi* jerk, twitch; (*Strahl etc*) flicker // *vt* (*Schultern*) shrug.

Zucker ['tsukər] *m* -s, - sugar; (*MED*) diabetes; ~**dose** *f* sugar bowl; ~**guß** *m* icing; **z~krank** *a* diabetic; **z~n** *vt* sugar; ~**rohr** *nt* sugar cane; ~**rübe** *f* sugar beet.

Zuckung ['tsukuŋ] *f* convulsion, spasm; (*leicht*) twitch.

zudecken ['tsu:dekən] *vt* cover (up).

zudem [tsu'de:m] *ad* in addition (to this).

zudringlich ['tsu:driŋliç] *a* forward, pushing, obtrusive.

zudrücken ['tsu:drykən] *vt* close; **ein Auge** ~ turn a blind eye.

zueinander [tsu'ai'nandər] *ad* to one other; (*in Verbverbindung*) together.

zuerkennen ['tsu:'ɛrkɛnən] *vt unreg* award (*jdm etw* to sb, sb sth).

zuerst [tsu''e:rst] *ad* first; (*zu Anfang*) at first; ~ **einmal** first of all.

Zufahrt ['tsu:fa:rt] *f* approach; **Zufahrtsstraße** *f* approach road; (*von Autobahn etc*) slip road.

Zufall ['tsu:fal] *m* chance; (*Ereignis*) coincidence; **durch** ~ by accident; **so ein** ~ what a coincidence; **z~en** *vi unreg* close, shut itself; (*Anteil, Aufgabe*) fall (*jdm* to sb).

zufällig ['tsu:fɛliç] *a* chance // *ad* by chance; (*in Frage*) by any chance.

Zuflucht ['tsu:fluxt] *f* recourse; (*Ort*) refuge.

zufolge [tsu'fɔlgə] *präp* +*dat od gen* judging by; (*laut*) according to.

zufrieden [tsu'fri:dən] *a* content(ed), satisfied; **Z~heit** *f* satisfaction, contentedness; ~**stellen** *vt* satisfy.

zufrieren ['tsu:fri:rən] *vi unreg* freeze up *od* over.

zufügen ['tsu:fy:gən] *vt* add (*dat* to); (*Leid etc*) cause (*jdm etw* sth to sb).

Zufuhr ['tsu:fu:r] f -, -en (Herbeibringen) supplying; (MET) influx.

Zug [tsu:k] m -(e)s, ˝e (EISENB) train; (Luft~) draught; (Ziehen) pull(ing); (Gesichts~) feature; (SCHACH etc) move; (Klingel~) pull; (Schrift~) stroke; (Atem~) breath; (Charakter~) trait; (an Zigarette) puff, pull, drag; (Schluck) gulp; (Menschengruppe) procession; (von Vögeln) flight; (MIL) platoon; **etw in vollen ~en genießen** enjoy sth to the full.

Zu- ['tsu:] zW: **~gabe** f extra; (in Konzert etc) encore; **~gang** m access, approach; **z~gänglich** a accessible; (Mensch) approachable.

zugeben ['tsu:ge:bən] vt unreg (beifügen) add, throw in; (zugestehen) admit; (erlauben) permit.

zugehen ['tsu:ge:ən] vi unreg (schließen) shut; **es geht dort seltsam zu** there are strange goings-on there; **auf jdn/etw ~** walk towards sb/sth; **dem Ende ~** be finishing.

Zugehörigkeit ['tsu:gəhø:rɪçkaɪt] f membership (zu of), belonging (zu to).

Zügel ['tsy:gəl] m -s, - rein(s); (fig auch) curb; **z~n** vt curb; (Pferd auch) rein in.

zuge- ['tsu:gə] zW: **Z~ständnis** nt -ses, -se concession; **~stehen** vt unreg admit; (Rechte) concede (jdm to sb); **~stiegen** a: **noch jemand ~stiegen?** tickets please.

zugig ['tsu:gɪç] a draughty.

zügig ['tsy:gɪç] a speedy, swift.

zugreifen ['tsu:graɪfən] vi unreg seize od grab at; (helfen) help; (beim Essen) help o.s.

Zugriff ['tsu:grɪf] m (COMPUT) access.

zugrunde [tsu:grʊndə] ad: **~ gehen** collapse; (Mensch) perish; **einer Sache etw ~ legen** base sth on sth; **einer Sache ~ liegen** be based on sth; **~ richten** ruin, destroy.

zugunsten [tsu:gʊnstən] präp +gen od dat in favour of.

zugute [tsu:gu:tə] ad: **jdm etw ~ halten** concede sth; **jdm ~ kommen** be of assistance to sb.

Zugvogel m migratory bird.

Zuhälter ['tsu:hɛltər] m -s, - pimp.

Zuhause [tsu:hausə] nt - home.

zuhören ['tsu:hø:rən] vi listen (dat to).

Zuhörer m -s, - listener; **~schaft** f audience.

zukleben ['tsu:kle:bən] vt paste up.

zukommen ['tsu:kɔmən] vi unreg come up (auf +akk to); (sich gehören) be fitting (jdm for sb); (Recht haben auf) be entitled to; **jdm etw ~ lassen** give sb sth; **etw auf sich ~ lassen** wait and see.

Zukunft ['tsu:kʊnft] f -, Zukünfte fu-

ture.

zukünftig ['tsu:kʏnftɪç] a future; **mein ~er Mann** my husband to be // ad in future.

Zulage ['tsu:la:gə] f bonus, allowance.

zulassen ['tsu:lasən] vt unreg (hereinlassen) admit; (erlauben) permit; (Auto) license; (umg: nicht öffnen) (keep) shut.

zulässig ['tsu:lɛsɪç] a permissible, permitted.

zuleide [tsu:laɪdə] a: **jdm etw ~ tun** hurt od harm sb.

zuletzt [tsu:lɛtst] ad finally, at last.

zuliebe [tsu:li:bə] ad: **jdm ~ to please sb.**

zum [tsum] = **zu dem**; **~ dritten Mal** for the third time; **~ Scherz** as a joke; **~ Trinken** for drinking.

zumachen ['tsu:maxən] vt shut; (Kleidung) do up, fasten // vi shut; (umg) hurry up.

zumal [tsu:ma:l] kj especially (as).

zumeist [tsu:maɪst] ad mostly.

zumindest [tsu:mɪndəst] ad at least.

zumut- zW: **~bar** ['tsu:mu:tba:r] a reasonable; **~e** ad: **wie ist ihm ~e?** how does he feel?; **~en** ['tsu:mu:tən] vt expect, ask (jdm of sb); **Z~ung** ['tsu:mu:tʊŋ] f unreasonable expectation od demand, impertinence.

zunächst [tsu:nɛ:çst] ad first of all; **~ einmal** to start with.

Zunahme ['tsu:na:mə] f -, -n increase.

Zuname ['tsu:na:mə] m surname.

Zünd- [tsʏnd] zW: **z~en** vi (Feuer) light, ignite; (Motor) fire; (begeistern) fire (with enthusiasm) (bei jdm sb); **z~end** a fiery; **~er** m -s, - fuse; (MIL) detonator; **~holz** ['tsʏnt-] nt match; **~kerze** f (AUT) spark(ing) plug; **~schlüssel** m ignition key; **~schnur** f fuse wire; **~ung** f ignition.

zunehmen ['tsu:ne:mən] vi unreg increase, grow; (Mensch) put on weight.

Zuneigung f affection.

Zunft [tsʊnft] f -, ˝e guild.

zünftig ['tsʏnftɪç] a proper, real; (Handwerk) decent.

Zunge ['tsʊŋə] f -, -n tongue.

zunichte [tsu:nɪçtə] ad: **~ machen** ruin, destroy; **~ werden** come to nothing.

zunutze [tsu:nʊtsə] ad: **sich (dat) etw ~ machen** make use of sth.

zuoberst [tsu:ɔ:bərst] ad at the top.

zupfen ['tsʊpfən] vt pull, pick, pluck; (Gitarre) pluck.

zur [tsu:r] = **zu der.**

zurechnungsfähig ['tsu:rɛçnʊŋsfɛ:ɪç] a responsible, accountable; **Z~keit** f responsibility, accountability.

zurecht- [tsu:rɛçt] zW: **~finden** vr

unreg find one's way (about); **~kommen** *vi unreg* (be able to) deal (*mit* with), manage; **~legen** *vt* get ready; (*Ausrede etc*) have ready; **~machen** *vt* prepare // *vr* get ready; **~weisen** *vt unreg* reprimand; **Z~weisung** *f* reprimand, rebuff.

zureden ['tsu:re:dən] *vi* persuade, urge (*jdm* sb).

zurück [tsu'rʏk] *ad* back; **~behalten** *vt unreg* keep back; **~bekommen** *vt unreg* get back; **~bleiben** *vi unreg* (*Mensch*) remain behind; (*nicht nachkommen*) fall behind, lag; (*Schaden*) remain; **~bringen** *vt unreg* bring back; **~fahren** *unreg vi* travel back; (*vor Schreck*) recoil, start // *vt* drive back; **~finden** *vi unreg* find one's way back; **~fordern** *vt* demand back; **~führen** *vt* lead back; etw auf etw (*akk*) **~führen** trace sth back to sth; **~geben** *vt unreg* give back; (*antworten*) retort with; **~geblieben** *a* retarded; **~gehen** *vi unreg* go back; (*zeitlich*) date back (*auf +akk* to); (*fallen*) go down, fall; **~gezogen** *a* retired, withdrawn; **~halten** *unreg vt* hold back; (*Mensch*) restrain; (*hindern*) prevent // *vr* (*reserviert sein*) be reserved; (*im Essen*) hold back; **~haltend** *a* reserved; **Z~haltung** *f* reserve; **~kehren** *vi* return; **~kommen** *vi unreg* come back; auf etw (*akk*) **~kommen** return to sth; **~lassen** *vt unreg* leave behind; **~legen** *vt* put back; (*Geld*) put by; (*reservieren*) keep back; (*Strecke*) cover; **~nehmen** *vt unreg* take back; **~schrecken** *vi* shrink (*vor +dat* from); **~stellen** *vt* put back, replace; (*aufschieben*) put off, postpone; (*MIL*) turn down; (*Interessen*) defer; (*Ware*) keep; **~treten** *vi unreg* step back; (*vom Amt*) retire; **gegenüber** *od* **hinter etw ~treten** diminish in importance in view of sth; **~weisen** *vt unreg* turn down; (*Mensch*) reject; **~zahlen** *vt* repay, pay back; **~ziehen** *unreg vt* pull back; (*Angebot*) withdraw // *vr* retire.

Zuruf ['tsu:ru:f] *m* shout, cry.

Zusage ['tsu:za:gə] *f* -, -n promise; (*Annahme*) consent; **z~n** *vt* promise // *vi* accept; jdm **z~n** (*gefallen*) agree with *od* please sb.

zusammen [tsu'zamən] *ad* together; **Z~arbeit** *f* cooperation; **~arbeiten** *vi* cooperate; **~beißen** *vt unreg* (*Zähne*) clench; **~bleiben** *vi unreg* stay together; **~brechen** *vi unreg* collapse; (*Mensch auch*) break down; **~bringen** *vt unreg* bring *od* get together; (*Geld*) get; (*Sätze*) put together; **Z~bruch** *m* collapse;

~fassen *vt* summarize; (*vereinigen*) unite; **Z~fassung** *f* summary, résumé; **~fügen** *vt* join (together), unite; **~halten** *vi unreg* stick together; **Z~hang** *m* connection; im/aus dem Z~hang in/out of context; **~hängen** *vi unreg* be connected *od* linked; **~kommen** *vi unreg* meet, assemble; (*sich ereignen*) occur at once *od* together; **~legen** *vt* put together; (*stapeln*) pile up; (*falten*) fold; (*verbinden*) combine, unite; (*Termine, Fest*) amalgamate; (*Geld*) collect; **~nehmen** *unreg vt* summon up; alles **~genommen** all in all // *vr* pull o.s. together; **~passen** *vi* go well together, match; **~schließen** *vtr unreg* join (together); **Z~schluß** *m* amalgamation; **~schreiben** *vt unreg* write as one word; (*Bericht*) put together; **Z~sein** *nt* -s get-together; **~setzen** *vt* put together // *vr* (*Stoff*) be composed of; (*Menschen*) get together; **Z~setzung** *f* composition; **~stellen** *vt* put together; compile; **Z~stoß** *m* collision; **~stoßen** *vi unreg* collide; **~treffen** *vi unreg* coincide; (*Menschen*) meet; **Z~treffen** *nt* meeting; coincidence; **~zählen** *vt* add up; **~ziehen** *unreg vt* (*verengern*) draw together; (*vereinigen*) bring together; (*addieren*) add up // *vr* shrink; (*sich bilden*) form, develop.

zusätzlich ['tsu:zɛtslɪç] *a* additional // *ad* in addition.

zuschauen ['tsu:ʃauən] *vi* watch, look on.

Zuschauer(in *f*) *m* -s, - spectator // *pl* (*THEAT*) audience.

zuschicken ['tsu:ʃɪkən] *vt* send, forward (*jdm etw* sth to sb).

Zuschlag ['tsu:ʃla:k] *m* extra charge, surcharge; **z~en** ['tsu:ʃla:gən] *unreg vt* (*Tür*) slam; (*Ball*) hit (*jdm* to sb); (*bei Auktion*) knock down; (*Steine etc*) knock into shape // *vi* (*Fenster, Tür*) shut; (*Mensch*) hit, punch; **~karte** *f* (*EISENB*) surcharge ticket; **z~pflichtig** *a* subject to surcharge.

zuschneiden ['tsu:ʃnaɪdən] *vt unreg* cut out *od* to size.

zuschrauben ['tsu:ʃraubən] *vt* screw down *od* up.

zuschreiben ['tsu:ʃraɪbən] *vt unreg* (*fig*) ascribe, attribute; (*COMM*) credit.

Zuschrift ['tsu:ʃrɪft] *f* letter, reply.

zuschulden [tsu'ʃuldən] *ad*: sich (*dat*) etw ~ kommen lassen make o.s. guilty of sth.

Zuschuß ['tsu:ʃus] *m* subsidy, allowance.

zusehen ['tsu:ze:ən] *vi unreg* watch

(jdm/etw sb/sth); (dafür sorgen) take care; **zusehends** ad visibly.

zusenden ['tsu:zɛndən] vt unreg forward, send on (jdm etw sth to sb).

zusichern ['tsu:zɪçərn] vt assure (jdm etw sb of sth).

zuspielen ['tsu:ʃpiːlən] vti pass (jdm to sb).

zuspitzen ['tsu:ʃpɪtsən] vt sharpen // vr (Lage) become critical.

zusprechen ['tsu:ʃprɛçən] unreg vt (zuerkennen) award (jdm etw sb sth, sth to sb); **jdm Trost** ~ comfort sb // vi speak (jdm to sb); **dem Essen/Alkohol** ~ eat/drink a lot.

Zustand ['tsu:ʃtant] m state, condition; **z~e** [tsu:ʃtandə] ad: **z~e bringen** vt unreg bring about; **z~e kommen** vi unreg come about.

zuständig ['tsu:ʃtɛndɪç] a responsible; **Z~keit** f competence, responsibility.

zustehen ['tsu:ʃteːən] vi unreg: **jdm** ~ be sb's right.

zustellen ['tsu:ʃtɛlən] vt (verstellen) block; (Post etc) send.

zustimmen ['tsu:ʃtɪmən] vi agree (dat to).

Zustimmung f agreement, consent.

zustoßen ['tsu:ʃtoːsən] vi unreg (fig) happen (jdm to sb).

zutage [tsu:ta:gə] ad: ~ **bringen** bring to light; ~ **treten** come to light.

Zutaten [tsu:ta:tən] pl ingredients pl.

zutiefst [tsu:ti:fst] ad deeply.

zutragen ['tsu:tra:gən] unreg vt bring (jdm etw sth to sb); (Klatsch) tell // vr happen.

zutrau- ['tsu:trau] zW: ~**en** vt credit (jdm etw sb with sth); **Z~en** nt -s trust (zu in); ~**lich** a trusting, friendly; **Z~lichkeit** f trust.

zutreffen ['tsu:trɛfən] vi unreg be correct; apply; **Z~des bitte unterstreichen** please underline where applicable.

Zutritt ['tsu:trɪt] m access, admittance.

Zutun ['tsu:tu:n] nt -s assistance.

zuverlässig ['tsu:fɛrlɛsɪç] a reliable; **Z~keit** f reliability.

Zuversicht ['tsu:fɛrzɪçt] f - confidence; **z~lich** a confident.

zuviel [tsu:fi:l] ad too much.

zuvor [tsu'fo:r] ad before, previously; ~**kommen** vi unreg anticipate (jdm sb), beat (sb) to it; ~**kommend** a obliging, courteous.

Zuwachs ['tsu:vaks] m -es increase, growth; (umg) addition; **z~en** vi unreg become overgrown; (Wunde) heal (up).

zuwege [tsu've:gə] ad: etw ~ **bringen** accomplish sth.

zuweilen [tsu'vaɪlən] ad at times, now and then.

zuweisen ['tsu:vaɪzən] vt unreg assign, allocate (jdm to sb).

zuwenden ['tsu:vɛndən] unreg vt turn (dat towards); **jdm seine Aufmerksamkeit** ~ give sb one's attention // vr devote o.s., turn (dat to).

zuwenig [tsu've:nɪç] ad too little.

zuwider [tsu'vi:dər] ad: etw ist jdm ~ sb loathes sth, sb finds sth repugnant // präp +dat contrary to; ~**handeln** vi act contrary (dat to); **einem Gesetz ~handeln** contravene a law.

zuziehen ['tsu:tsi:ən] unreg vt (schließen: Vorhang) draw, close; (herbeirufen: Experten) call in; **sich** (dat) etw ~ (Krankheit) catch; (Zorn) incur // vi move in, come.

zuzüglich ['tsu:tsy:klɪç] präp +gen plus, with the addition of.

Zwang [tsvaŋ] m -(e)s, ⁻e compulsion, coercion.

zwängen ['tsvɛŋən] vtr squeeze.

zwanglos a informal.

Zwangs- zW: ~**arbeit** f forced labour; (Strafe) hard labour; ~**jacke** f straightjacket; ~**lage** f predicament, tight corner; **z~läufig** a necessary, inevitable.

zwanzig ['tsvantsɪç] num twenty.

zwar [tsva:r] ad to be sure, indeed; **das ist** ~ ..., **aber** ... that may be ... but ...; **und** ~ **am Sonntag** on Sunday to be precise; **und** ~ **so schnell, daß** ... in fact so quickly that ...

Zweck [tsvɛk] m -(e)s, -e purpose, aim; **es hat keinen** ~ there's no point; **z~dienlich** a practical; expedient; ~**e** f -, -n hobnail; (Heft~e) drawing pin, thumbtack (US); **z~los** a pointless; **z~mäßig** a suitable, appropriate; **zwecks** präp +gen for the purpose of.

zwei [tsvaɪ] num two; ~**deutig** a ambiguous; (unanständig) suggestive; ~**erlei** a: ~**erlei Stoff** two different kinds of material; ~**erlei Meinung** of differing opinions; ~**fach** a double.

Zweifel ['tsvaɪfəl] m -s, - doubt; **z~haft** a doubtful, dubious; **z~los** a doubtless; **z~n** vi doubt (an etw (dat) sth).

Zweig [tsvaɪk] m -(e)s, -e branch; ~**stelle** f branch (office).

zwei- zW: ~**hundert** num two hundred; **Z~kampf** m duel; ~**mal** ad twice; ~**sprachig** a bilingual; ~**spurig** a (AUT) two-lane; ~**stimmig** a for two voices; **Z~taktmotor** m two-stroke engine.

zweit- [tsvaɪt] ad: **zu** ~ together; (bei mehreren Paaren) in twos; ~**beste(r, s)** a second best; ~**e(r, s)** a second; ~**ens** ad secondly; ~**größte(r, s)** a second largest; ~**klassig** a second-class; ~**letzte(r, s)** a last but one, pe-

nultimate; **~rangig** *a* second-rate.
Zwerchfell ['tsvɛrçfɛl] *nt* diaphragm.
Zwerg [tsvɛrk] *m* -(e)s, -e dwarf.
Zwetsch(g)e ['tsvɛtʃ(g)ə] *f* -, -n plum.
Zwieback ['tsviːbak] *m* -(e)s, -e rusk.
Zwiebel ['tsviːbəl] *f* -, -n onion; (*Blumen~*) bulb.
Zwie- ['tsviː] *zW*: **z~lichtig** *a* shady, dubious; **z~spältig** *a* (*Gefühle*) conflicting; (*Charakter*) contradictory; **~tracht** *f* discord, dissension.
Zwilling ['tsvɪlɪŋ] *m* -s, -e twin; **~e** *pl* (*ASTROL*) Gemini.
zwingen ['tsvɪŋən] *vt unreg* force; **~d** *a* (*Grund etc*) compelling.
zwinkern ['tsvɪŋkərn] *vi* blink; (*absichtlich*) wink.
Zwirn [tsvɪrn] *m* -(e)s, -e thread.
zwischen ['tsvɪʃən] *präp* +*akk od dat* between; **Z~bemerkung** *f* (incidental) remark; **Z~ding** *nt* cross; **~durch** [-'dʊrç] *ad* in between; (*räumlich*) here and there; **Z~ergebnis** *nt* intermediate result;

Z~fall *m* incident; **Z~frage** *f* question; **Z~handel** *m* middlemen *pl*; middleman's trade; **Z~landung** *f* stop, intermediate landing; **~menschlich** *a* interpersonal; **Z~raum** *m* space; **Z~ruf** *m* interjection, **Z~station** *f* intermediate station; **Z~zeit** *f* interval; **in der Z~zeit** in the interim, meanwhile.
Zwist [tsvɪst] *m* -es, -e dispute, feud.
zwitschern ['tsvɪtʃərn] *vti* twitter, chirp.
zwo [tsvoː] *num* two.
zwölf [tsvœlf] *num* twelve.
Zyklus ['tsyːklʊs] *m* -, **Zyklen** cycle.
Zylinder [tsi'lɪndər] *m* -s, - cylinder; (*Hut*) top hat; **z~förmig** *a* cylindrical.
Zyniker ['tsyːnikər] *m* -s, - cynic.
zynisch ['tsyːnɪʃ] *a* cynical.
Zynismus [tsy'nɪsmʊs] *m* cynicism.
Zypern ['tsyːpərn] *nt* Cyprus.
Zyste ['tsystə] *f* -, -n cyst.
z.Z(t). *abk von* **zur Zeit.**

ENGLISH - GERMAN
ENGLISCH - DEUTSCH

A

A [eɪ] *n* (*MUS*) A *nt*; ~ **road** Hauptverkehrsstraße *f*.

a [eɪ, ə] *indef art* (*before vowel or silent h*: **an**) **1** ein; eine; ~ **woman** eine Frau; ~ **book** ein Buch; **an apple** ein Apfel; **she's** ~ **doctor** sie ist Ärztin
2 (*instead of the number 'one'*) ein; eine; ~ **year ago** vor einem Jahr; ~ **hundred/thousand** *etc* **pounds** (ein)hundert/(ein)tausend *etc* Pfund
3 (*in expressing ratios, prices etc*) pro; **3** ~ **day/week** 3 pro Tag/Woche, 3 am Tag/in der Woche; **10 km an hour** 10 km pro Stunde/in der Stunde.

A.A. *n abbr* = **Automobile Association** (*Brit*); **Alcoholics Anonymous.**

A.A.A. *n abbr* (*US*) = **American Automobile Association.**

aback [ə'bæk] *ad*: **to be taken** ~ verblüfft sein.

abandon [ə'bændən] *vt* (*give up*) aufgeben; (*desert*) verlassen // *n* Hingabe *f*.

abashed [ə'bæʃt] *a* verlegen.

abate [ə'beɪt] *vi* nachlassen, sich legen.

abattoir ['æbətwɑː*] *n* (*Brit*) Schlachthaus *nt*.

abbey ['æbɪ] *n* Abtei *f*.

abbot ['æbət] *n* Abt *m*.

abbreviate [ə'briːvɪeɪt] *vt* abkürzen.

abbreviation [əbriːvɪ'eɪʃən] *n* Abkürzung *f*.

abdicate ['æbdɪkeɪt] *vt* aufgeben // *vi* abdanken.

abdomen ['æbdəmən] *n* Unterleib *m*.

abduct [æb'dʌkt] *vt* entführen.

aberration [æbə'reɪʃən] *n* (geistige) Verwirrung *f*.

abet [ə'bet] *vt see* **aid.**

abeyance [ə'beɪəns] *n*: **in** ~ in der Schwebe; (*disuse*) außer Kraft.

abhor [əb'hɔː*] *vt* verabscheuen.

abide [ə'baɪd] *vt* vertragen; leiden; ~ **by** *vt* sich halten an (+*acc*).

ability [ə'bɪlɪtɪ] *n* (*power*) Fähigkeit *f*; (*skill*) Geschicklichkeit *f*.

abject ['æbdʒekt] *a* (*liar*) übel; (*poverty*) größte(r, s); (*apology*) zerknirscht.

ablaze [ə'bleɪz] *a* in Flammen.

able ['eɪbl] *a* geschickt, fähig; **to be** ~ **to do sth** etw tun können; ~-**bodied** *a* kräftig; (*seaman*) Voll-.

ably ['eɪblɪ] *ad* geschickt.

abnormal [æb'nɔːməl] *a* regelwidrig, abnorm.

aboard [ə'bɔːd] *ad, prep* an Bord

(+*gen*).

abode [ə'bəud] *n*: **of no fixed** ~ ohne festen Wohnsitz.

abolish [ə'bɒlɪʃ] *vt* abschaffen.

abolition [æbə'lɪʃən] *n* Abschaffung *f*.

abominable [ə'bɒmɪnəbl] *a* scheußlich.

aborigine [æbə'rɪdʒɪniː] *n* Ureinwohner *m*.

abort [ə'bɔːt] *vt* abtreiben; fehlgebären; ~**ion** [ə'bɔːʃən] *n* Abtreibung *f*; (*miscarriage*) Fehlgeburt *f*; ~**ive** *a* mißlungen.

abound [ə'baund] *vi* im Überfluß vorhanden sein; **to** ~ **in** Überfluß haben an (+*dat*).

about [ə'baut] ◆*ad* **1** (*approximately*) etwa, ungefähr; ~ **a hundred/thousand** *etc* etwa hundert/tausend *etc*; **at** ~ **2 o'clock** etwa um 2 Uhr; **I've just** ~ **finished** ich bin gerade fertig
2 (*referring to place*): herum, umher; **to leave things lying** ~ Sachen herumliegen lassen; **to run/walk** *etc* ~ herumrennen/gehen *etc*
3: **to be** ~ **to do sth** im Begriff sein, etw zu tun; **he was** ~ **to go to bed** er wollte gerade ins Bett gehen
◆*prep* **1** (*relating to*) über (+*acc*); **a book** ~ **London** ein Buch über London; **what is it** ~? worum geht es?; (*book etc*) wovon handelt es?; **we talked** ~ **it** wir haben darüber geredet; **what** *or* **how** ~ **doing this?** wollen wir das machen?
2 (*referring to place*) um (... herum); **to walk** ~ **the town** in der Stadt herumgehen; **her clothes were scattered** ~ **the room** ihre Kleider waren über das ganze Zimmer verstreut.

about-face [ə'baut'feɪs] *n*, **about-turn** [ə'baut'tɜːn] *n* Kehrtwendung *f*.

above [ə'bʌv] *ad* oben // *prep* über; ~ **all** vor allem; ~ **board** *a* offen, ehrlich.

abrasive [ə'breɪzɪv] *a* Abschleif-; (*personality*) zermürbend, aufreibend.

abreast [ə'brest] *ad* nebeneinander; **to keep** ~ **of** Schritt halten mit.

abridge [ə'brɪdʒ] *vt* (ab)kürzen.

abroad [ə'brɔːd] *ad* (*be*) im Ausland; (*go*) ins Ausland.

abrupt [ə'brʌpt] *a* (*sudden*) abrupt, jäh; (*curt*) schroff.

abscess ['æbsɪs] *n* Geschwür *nt*.

abscond [əb'skɒnd] *vi* flüchten, sich davonmachen.

abseil ['æbsaɪl] *vi* (*also*: ~ **down**) sich abseilen.

absence ['æbsəns] n Abwesenheit f.

absent ['æbsənt] a abwesend, nicht da; (lost in thought) geistesabwesend; ~ee [æbsən'ti:] n Abwesende(r) m; ~eeism [æbsən'ti:ɪzəm] n Fehlen nt (am Arbeitsplatz/in der Schule); ~-minded a zerstreut.

absolute ['æbsəlu:t] a absolut; (power) unumschränkt; (rubbish) vollkommen, rein; ~ly [æbsə'lu:tlɪ] ad absolut, vollkommen; ~ly! ganz bestimmt!

absolve [əb'zɒlv] vt entbinden; freisprechen.

absorb [əb'zɔ:b] vt aufsaugen, absorbieren; (fig) ganz in Anspruch nehmen, fesseln; to be ~ed in a book vertieft in ein Buch vertieft sein; ~ent a absorbierend; ~ent cotton n (US) Verbandwatte f; ~ing a aufsaugend; (fig) packend.

abstain [əb'steɪn] vi (in vote) sich enthalten; to ~ from (keep from) sich enthalten (+gen).

abstemious [əb'sti:mɪəs] a enthaltsam.

abstention [əb'stenʃən] n (in vote) (Stimm)enthaltung f.

abstinence ['æbstɪnəns] n Enthaltsamkeit f.

abstract ['æbstrækt] a abstrakt.

absurd [əb'sɜ:d] a absurd.

abundance [ə'bʌndəns] n Überfluß m (of an +dat).

abundant [ə'bʌndənt] a reichlich.

abuse [ə'bju:s] n (rude language) Beschimpfung f; (ill usage) Mißbrauch m; (bad practice) (Amts)mißbrauch m // [ə'bju:z] vt (misuse) mißbrauchen.

abusive [ə'bju:sɪv] a beleidigend, Schimpf-.

abysmal [ə'bɪzməl] a scheußlich; (ignorance) bodenlos.

abyss [ə'bɪs] n Abgrund m.

AC abbr of alternating current.

academic [ækə'demɪk] a akademisch; (theoretical) theoretisch // n Akademiker(in f) m.

academy [ə'kædəmɪ] n (school) Hochschule f; (society) Akademie f.

accelerate [æk'seləreɪt] vi schneller werden; (AUT) Gas geben // vt beschleunigen.

acceleration [ækselə'reɪʃən] n Beschleunigung f.

accelerator [ək'seləreɪtə*] n Gas(pedal) nt.

accent ['æksent] n Akzent m, Tonfall m; (mark) Akzent m; (stress) Betonung f.

accept [ək'sept] vt (take) annehmen; (agree to) akzeptieren; ~able a annehmbar; ~ance n Annahme f.

access ['ækses] n Zugang m; ~ible [æk'sesɪbl] a (easy to approach) zugänglich; (within reach) (leicht) erreichbar.

accessory [æk'sesərɪ] n Zubehörteil nt; **accessories** pl Zubehör nt; **toilet ac-**

cessories pl Toilettenartikel pl.

accident ['æksɪdənt] n Unfall m; (coincidence) Zufall m; by ~ zufällig; ~al [æksɪ'dentl] a unbeabsichtigt; ~ally [æksɪ'dentəlɪ] ad zufällig; ~-prone a: to be ~-prone zu Unfällen neigen.

acclaim [ə'kleɪm] vt zujubeln (+dat) // n Beifall m.

acclimatize [ə'klaɪmətaɪz], (US) **acclimate** [ə'klaɪmət] vt: to become ~d sich gewöhnen (to an +acc), sich akklimatisieren.

accolade ['ækəleɪd] n Auszeichnung f.

accommodate [ə'kɒmədeɪt] vt unterbringen; (hold) Platz haben für; (oblige) (aus)helfen (+dat).

accommodating [ə'kɒmədeɪtɪŋ] a entgegenkommend.

accommodation [ə'kɒmə'deɪʃən] n (US: ~s) Unterkunft f.

accompaniment [ə'kʌmpənɪmənt] n Begleitung f.

accompany [ə'kʌmpənɪ] vt begleiten.

accomplice [ə'kʌmplɪs] n Helfershelfer m, Komplize m.

accomplish [ə'kʌmplɪʃ] vt (fulfil) durchführen; (finish) vollenden; (aim) erreichen; ~ed a vollendet, ausgezeichnet; ~ment n (skill) Fähigkeit f; (completion) Vollendung f; (feat) Leistung f.

accord [ə'kɔ:d] n Übereinstimmung f; of one's own ~ freiwillig // vt gewähren; ~ance n: in ~ance with in Übereinstimmung mit; ~ing to prep nach, laut (+gen); ~ingly ad danach, dementsprechend.

accordion [ə'kɔ:dɪən] n Akkordeon nt.

accost [ə'kɒst] vt ansprechen.

account [ə'kaʊnt] n (bill) Rechnung f; (narrative) Bericht m; (report) Rechenschaftsbericht m; (in bank) Konto nt; (importance) Geltung f; ~s pl Bücher pl; on ~ auf Rechnung; of no ~ ohne Bedeutung; on no ~ keinesfalls; on ~ of wegen; to take into ~ berücksichtigen; ~ for (expenditure) Rechenschaft ablegen für; how do you ~ for that? wie erklären Sie (sich) das?; ~able a verantwortlich; ~ancy n Buchhaltung f; ~ant n Wirtschaftsprüfer(in f) m; ~ number n Kontonummer f.

accredited [ə'kredɪtɪd] a (offiziell) zugelassen.

accrue [ə'kru:] vi sich ansammeln.

accumulate [ə'kju:mjuleɪt] vt ansammeln // vi sich ansammeln.

accuracy ['ækjʊrəsɪ] n Genauigkeit f.

accurate ['ækjʊrɪt] a genau; ~ly ad genau, richtig.

accusation [ækju:'zeɪʃən] n Anklage f, Beschuldigung f.

accuse [ə'kju:z] vt anklagen, beschuldigen; ~d n Angeklagte(r) mf.

accustom [ə'kʌstəm] vt gewöhnen (to

an +*acc*); ~ed *a* gewohnt.
ace [eɪs] *n* As *nt*; (*col*) As *nt*, Kanone *f*.
ache [eɪk] *n* Schmerz *m* // *vi* (*be sore*) schmerzen, weh tun.
achieve [ə'tʃiːv] *vt* zustande bringen; (*aim*) erreichen; ~ment *n* Leistung *f*; (*act*) Erreichen *nt*.
acid ['æsɪd] *n* Säure *f* // *a* sauer, scharf; ~ rain *n* Saure(r) Regen *m*.
acknowledge [ək'nɒlɪdʒ] *vt* (*receipt*) bestätigen; (*admit*) zugeben; ~ment *n* Anerkennung *f*; (*letter*) Empfangsbestätigung *f*.
acne ['ækni] *n* Akne *f*.
acorn ['eɪkɔːn] *n* Eichel *f*.
acoustic [ə'kuːstɪk] *a* akustisch; ~s *npl* Akustik *f*.
acquaint [ə'kweɪnt] *vt* vertraut machen; to be ~ed with sb mit jdm bekannt sein; ~ance *n* (*person*) Bekannte(r) *mf*; (*knowledge*) Kenntnis *f*.
acquiesce [ækwi'es] *vi* sich abfinden (*in* mit).
acquire [ə'kwaɪə*] *vt* erwerben.
acquisition [ækwɪ'zɪʃən] *n* Errungenschaft *f*; (*act*) Erwerb *m*.
acquisitive [ə'kwɪzɪtɪv] *a* gewinnsüchtig.
acquit [ə'kwɪt] *vt* (*free*) freisprechen; to ~ o.s. well sich bewähren; ~tal *n* Freispruch *m*.
acre ['eɪkə*] *n* Morgen *m*.
acrid ['ækrɪd] *a* (*smell, taste*) bitter; (*smoke*) beißend.
acrimonious [ækrɪ'məʊnɪəs] *a* bitter.
acrobat ['ækrəbæt] *n* Akrobat *m*.
across [ə'krɒs] *prep* über (+ *acc*); he lives ~ the river er wohnt auf der anderen Seite des Flusses // *ad* hinüber, herüber; ten metres ~ zehn Meter breit; he lives ~ from us er wohnt uns gegenüber.
act [ækt] *n* (*deed*) Tat *f*; (*JUR*) Gesetz *nt*; (*THEAT*) Akt *m*; (*THEAT: turn*) Nummer *f* // *vi* (*take action*) handeln; (*behave*) sich verhalten; (*pretend*) vorgeben; (*THEAT*) spielen // *vt* (*in play*) spielen; to ~ as fungieren als; ~ing *a* stellvertretend // *n* Schauspielkunst *f*; (*performance*) Aufführung *f*.
action ['ækʃən] *n* (*deed*) Tat *f*; Handlung *f*; (*motion*) Bewegung *f*; (*way of working*) Funktionieren *nt*; (*battle*) Einsatz *m*, Gefecht *nt*; (*lawsuit*) Klage *f*, Prozeß *m*; out of ~ (*person*) nicht einsatzfähig; (*thing*) außer Betrieb; to take ~ etwas unternehmen; ~ replay *n* (*TV*) wiederholung *f*.
active ['æktɪv] *a* (*brisk*) rege, tatkräftig; (*working*) aktiv; (*GRAM*) aktiv, Tätigkeits-; ~ly *ad* aktiv; (*dislike*) offen.
activity [æk'tɪvɪtɪ] *n* Aktivität *f*; (*doings*) Unternehmungen *pl*; (*occupation*) Tätigkeit *f*.
actor ['æktə*] *n* Schauspieler *m*.

actress ['æktrɪs] *n* Schauspielerin *f*.
actual ['æktjʊəl] *a* wirklich; ~ly *ad* tatsächlich; ~ly no eigentlich nicht.
acumen ['ækjʊmən] *n* Scharfsinn *m*.
acute [ə'kjuːt] *a* (*severe*) heftig, akut; (*keen*) scharfsinnig.
ad [æd] *n abbr of* **advertisement**.
A.D. *ad abbr* (= *Anno Domini*) *n. Chr.*
Adam ['ædəm] *n* Adam *m*; ~'s apple *n* Adamsapfel *m*.
adamant ['ædəmənt] *a* eisern; hartnäckig.
adapt [ə'dæpt] *vt* anpassen // *vi* sich anpassen (*to* an +*acc*); ~able *a* anpassungsfähig; ~ation [ædæp'teɪʃən] *n* (*THEAT etc*) Bearbeitung *f*; (*adjustment*) Anpassung *f*; ~er *or* ~or *n* (*ELEC*) Zwischenstecker *m*.
add [æd] *vt* (*join*) hinzufügen; (*numbers; also:* ~ up) addieren; ~ up *vi* (*make sense*) stimmen; ~ up to *vt* ausmachen.
adder ['ædə*] *n* Kreuzotter *f*, Natter *f*.
addict ['ædɪkt] *n* Süchtige(r) *mf*; ~ed [ə'dɪktɪd] *a*: ~ed to -süchtig; ~ion [ə'dɪkʃən] *n* Sucht *f*; ~ive *a*: to be ~ive süchtig machen.
addition [ə'dɪʃən] *n* Anhang *m*, Addition *f*; (*MATH*) Addition *f*, Zusammenzählen *nt*; in ~ zusätzlich, außerdem; ~al *a* zusätzlich, weiter.
additive ['ædɪtɪv] *n* Zusatz *m*.
address [ə'dres] *n* Adresse *f*; (*speech*) Ansprache *f* // *vt* (*letter*) adressieren; (*speak to*) ansprechen; (*make speech to*) eine Ansprache halten an (+*acc*).
adept ['ædept] *a* geschickt; to be ~ at gut sein in (+*dat*).
adequate ['ædɪkwɪt] *a* angemessen.
adhere [əd'hɪə*] *vi*: ~ to (*lit*) haften an (+*dat*); (*fig*) festhalten an (+*dat*).
adhesive [əd'hiːzɪv] *a* klebend; Kleb(e)- // *n* Klebstoff *m*; ~ tape *n* (*Brit*) Klebestreifen *m*; (*US*) Heftpflaster *nt*.
ad hoc [æd'hɒk] *a* (*decision, committee*) Ad-hoc- // *ad* (*decide, appoint*) ad hoc.
adjacent [ə'dʒeɪsənt] *a* benachbart; ~ to angrenzend an (+*acc*).
adjective ['ædʒəktɪv] *n* Adjektiv *nt*, Eigenschaftswort *nt*.
adjoining [ə'dʒɔɪnɪŋ] *a* benachbart, Neben-.
adjourn [ə'dʒɜːn] *vt* vertagen // *vi* abbrechen.
adjudicate [ə'dʒuːdɪkeɪt] *vi* entscheiden, ein Urteil fällen.
adjust [ə'dʒʌst] *vt* (*alter*) anpassen; (*put right*) regulieren, richtig stellen // *vi* sich anpassen (*to dat*); ~able *a* verstellbar.
ad-lib [æd'lɪb] *vti* improvisieren; ad lib *ad* aus dem Stegreif.
administer [æd'mɪnɪstə*] *vt* (*manage*) verwalten; (*dispense*) ausüben; (*justice*) sprechen; (*medicine*) geben.

administration [ədmɪnɪs'treɪʃən] n
Verwaltung f; (POL) Regierung f.
administrative [əd'mɪnɪstrətɪv] a
Verwaltungs-.
administrator [əd'mɪnɪstreɪtə*] n Verwaltungsbeamte(r) m.
admiral ['ædmərəl] n Admiral m.
Admiralty ['ædmərəltɪ] n (Brit)
Admiralität f.
admiration [ædmɪ'reɪʃən] n Bewunderung f.
admire [əd'maɪə*] vt (respect)
bewundern; (love) verehren; ~r n
Bewunderer m.
admission [əd'mɪʃən] n (entrance) Einlaß; (fee) Eintritt(spreis) m;
(confession) Geständnis nt.
admit [əd'mɪt] vt (let in) einlassen;
(confess) gestehen; (accept) anerkennen; ~tance n Zulassung f;
~tedly ad zugegebenermaßen.
admonish [əd'mɒnɪʃ] vt ermahnen.
ad nauseam [æd'nɔːsɪæm] ad (repeat,
talk) endlos.
ado [ə'duː] n: without more ~ ohne
weitere Umstände.
adolescence [ædə'lesns] n Jugendalter
nt.
adolescent [ædə'lesnt] a jugendlich // n
Jugendliche(r) mf.
adopt [ə'dɒpt] vt (child) adoptieren;
(idea) übernehmen; ~ion [ə'dɒpʃən] n
(of child) Adoption f; (of idea) Übernahme f.
adore [ə'dɔː*] vt anbeten; verehren.
adorn [ə'dɔːn] vt schmücken.
Adriatic [eɪdrɪ'ætɪk] n: the ~ (Sea) die
Adria.
adrift [ə'drɪft] ad Wind und Wellen
preisgegeben.
adult ['ædʌlt] n Erwachsene(r) mf.
adultery [ə'dʌltərɪ] n Ehebruch m.
advance [əd'vɑːns] n (progress) Vorrücken nt; (money) Vorschuß m // vt
(move forward) vorrücken; (money)
vorschießen; (argument) vorbringen // vi
vorwärtsgehen; in ~ im voraus; ~d a
(ahead) vorgerückt; (modern) fortgeschritten; (study) für Fortgeschrittene;
~ment n Förderung f; (promotion)
Beförderung f.
advantage [əd'vɑːntɪdʒ] n Vorteil m; to
have an ~ over sb jdm gegenüber im
Vorteil sein; to take ~ of (misuse) ausnutzen; (profit from) Nutzen ziehen aus;
~ous [ædvən'teɪdʒəs] a vorteilhaft.
advent ['ædvent] n Ankunft f; A~
Advent m.
adventure [əd'ventʃə*] n Abenteuer nt.
adventurous [əd'ventʃərəs] a
abenteuerlich, waghalsig.
adverb ['ædvɜːb] n Adverb nt, Umstandswort nt.
adversary ['ædvəsərɪ] n Gegner m.
adverse ['ædvɜːs] a widrig.

adversity [əd'vɜːsɪtɪ] n Widrigkeit f,
Mißgeschick nt.
advert ['ædvɜːt] n Anzeige f.
advertise ['ædvətaɪz] vt werben für // vi
annoncieren; to ~ for sth etw (per Anzeige) suchen.
advertisement [əd'vɜːtɪsmənt] n Anzeige f, Inserat nt.
advertiser ['ædvətaɪzə*] n (in newspaper etc) Inserent m.
advertising ['ædvətaɪzɪŋ] n Werbung f.
advice [əd'vaɪs] n Rat(schlag) m;
(notification) Benachrichtigung f.
advisable [əd'vaɪzəbl] a ratsam.
advise [əd'vaɪz] vt raten (+dat); ~r n
Berater m.
advisedly [əd'vaɪzədlɪ] ad (deliberately)
bewußt.
advisory [əd'vaɪzərɪ] a beratend,
Beratungs-.
advocate ['ædvəkeɪt] vt vertreten // n
['ædvəkət] Befürworter(in f) m.
Aegean [iː'dʒiːən] n: the ~ (Sea) die
Ägäis.
aerial ['ɛərɪəl] n Antenne f // a Luft-.
aerobics [ɛər'əʊbɪks] n Aerobic nt.
aerodrome ['ɛərədrəʊm] n (Brit) Flugplatz m.
aerodynamic [ɛərəʊdaɪ'næmɪks] a
aerodynamisch.
aeroplane ['ɛərəpleɪn] n Flugzeug nt.
aerosol ['ɛərəsɒl] n Aerosol nt;
Sprühdose f.
aesthetic [ɪs'θetɪk] a ästhetisch.
afar [ə'fɑː*] ad: from ~ aus der Ferne.
affable ['æfəbl] a umgänglich.
affair [ə'fɛə*] n (concern) Angelegenheit
f; (event) Ereignis nt; (love ~) Verhältnis nt.
affect [ə'fekt] vt (influence) (ein-)
wirken auf (+acc); (move deeply)
bewegen; this change doesn't ~ us diese
Änderung betrifft uns nicht; ~ed a
affektiert, gekünstelt.
affection [ə'fekʃən] n Zuneigung f;
~ate [ə'fekʃənɪt] a liebevoll.
affiliated [ə'fɪlɪeɪtɪd] a angeschlossen (to
dat).
affinity [ə'fɪnɪtɪ] n (attraction) gegenseitige Anziehung f; (relationship) Verwandtschaft f.
affirmation [æfə'meɪʃən] n Behauptung
f.
affirmative [ə'fɜːmətɪv] a bestätigend.
affix [ə'fɪks] vt aufkleben, anheften.
afflict [ə'flɪkt] vt quälen, heimsuchen.
affluence ['æfluəns] n (wealth) Wohlstand m.
affluent ['æfluənt] a wohlhabend,
Wohlstands-.
afford [ə'fɔːd] vt (sich) (dat) leisten;
(yield) bieten, einbringen.
affront [ə'frʌnt] n Beleidigung f.
Afghanistan [æf'gænɪstɑːn] n Afghanistan nt.

afield [ə'fi:ld] *ad*: far ~ weit fort.
afloat [ə'fləʊt] *a*: to be ~ schwimmen.
afoot [ə'fʊt] *ad* im Gang.
afraid [ə'freɪd] *a* ängstlich; **to be ~ of** Angst haben vor (+*dat*); **to be ~ to** sich scheuen; **I am ~ I have ...** ich habe leider ...; **I'm ~ so**/**not** leider/leider nicht; **I am ~ that ...** ich fürchte, (daß) ...
afresh [ə'freʃ] *ad* von neuem.
Africa ['æfrɪkə] *n* Afrika *nt*; **~n** *a* afrikanisch // *n* Afrikaner(in *f*) *m*.
aft [ɑ:ft] *ad* achtern.
after ['ɑ:ftə*] *prep* nach; (*following, seeking*) hinter ... her; (*in imitation*) nach, im Stil von // *ad*: **soon ~** bald danach // *cj* nachdem; **what are you ~?** was wollen Sie?; **~ he left** nachdem er gegangen war; **~ you!** nach Ihnen!; **~ all** letzten Endes; **~-effects** *npl* Nachwirkungen *pl*; **~life** *n* Leben *nt* nach dem Tode; **~math** *n* Auswirkungen *pl*; **~noon** *n* Nachmittag *m*; **good ~noon!** guten Tag!; **~s** *n* (*col: dessert*) Nachtisch *m*; **~-sales service** *n* (*Brit*) Kundendienst *m*; **~-shave (lotion)** *n* Rasierwasser *nt*; **~thought** *n* nachträgliche(r) Einfall *m*; **~wards** *ad* danach, nachher.
again [ə'gen] *ad* wieder, noch einmal; (*besides*) außerdem, ferner; **~ and ~** immer wieder.
against [ə'genst] *prep* gegen.
age [eɪdʒ] *n* (*of person*) Alter *nt*; (*in history*) Zeitalter *nt* // *vi* altern, alt werden // *vt* älter machen; **to come of ~** mündig werden; **20 years of ~** 20 Jahre alt; **it's been ~s since ...** es ist ewig her, seit ...; **~d** *a* ... Jahre alt, -jährig; ['eɪdʒɪd] (*elderly*) betagt; **the ~d** die Alten *pl*; **~ group** *n* Altersgruppe *f*; **~ limit** *n* Altersgrenze *f*.
agency ['eɪdʒənsɪ] *n* Agentur *f*; Vermittlung *f*; (*CHEM*) Wirkung *f*; **through** *or* **by the ~** of ... mit Hilfe von ...
agenda [ə'dʒendə] *n* Tagesordnung *f*.
agent ['eɪdʒənt] *n* (*COMM*) Vertreter *m*; (*spy*) Agent *m*.
aggravate ['ægrəveɪt] *vt* (*make worse*) verschlimmern; (*irritate*) reizen.
aggregate ['ægrɪgɪt] *n* Summe *f*.
aggression [ə'greʃən] *n* Aggression *f*.
aggressive *a* [ə'gresɪv] aggressiv.
aggrieved [ə'gri:vd] *a* bedrückt, verletzt.
aghast [ə'gɑ:st] *a* entsetzt.
agile ['ædʒaɪl] *a* flink; agil; (*mind*) rege.
agitate ['ædʒɪteɪt] *vt* rütteln; **to ~ for** sich starkmachen für.
ago [ə'gəʊ] *ad*: **two days ~** vor zwei Tagen; **not long ~** vor kurzem; **it's so long ~** es ist schon so lange her.
agog [ə'gɒg] *a* gespannt.
agonizing ['ægənaɪzɪŋ] *a* quälend.
agony ['ægənɪ] *n* Qual *f*; **to be in ~**

Qualen leiden.
agree [ə'gri:] *vt* (*date*) vereinbaren // *vi* (*have same opinion, correspond*) übereinstimmen (*with* mit); (*consent*) zustimmen; (*be in harmony*) sich vertragen; **to ~ to** sth einer Sache zustimmen; **to ~ that ...** (*admit*) zugeben; **daß ...; to ~ to do sth** sich bereit erklären, etw zu tun; **garlic doesn't ~ with me** Knoblauch vertrage ich nicht; **I ~** einverstanden, ich stimme zu; **to ~ on** sth sich auf etw (*acc*) einigen; **~able** *a* (*pleasing*) liebenswürdig; (*willing to consent*) einverstanden; **~d** *a* vereinbart; **~ment** *n* (*agreeing*) Übereinstimmung *f*; (*contract*) Vereinbarung *f*, Vertrag *m*; **to be in ~ment** übereinstimmen.
agricultural [ægrɪ'kʌltʃərəl] *a* landwirtschaftlich, Landwirtschafts-.
agriculture ['ægrɪkʌltʃə*] *n* Landwirtschaft *f*.
aground [ə'graʊnd] *ad*: **to run ~** auf Grund laufen.
ahead [ə'hed] *ad* vorwärts; **to be ~** voraus sein; **~ of time** der Zeit voraus; **go right** *or* **straight ~** gehen/fahren Sie geradeaus.
aid [eɪd] *n* (*assistance*) Hilfe *f*, Unterstützung *f*; (*person*) Hilfe *f*; (*thing*) Hilfsmittel *nt*; **in ~ of** zugunsten (+*gen*) // *vt* unterstützen, helfen (+*dat*); **~ and abet** *vti* Beihilfe leisten (*sb* jdm).
aide [eɪd] *n* (*person*) Gehilfe *m*; (*MIL*) Adjutant *m*.
AIDS [eɪdz] *n abbr* (= *acquired immune deficiency syndrome*) Aids *nt*.
ailing ['eɪlɪŋ] *a* kränkelnd.
ailment ['eɪlmənt] *n* Leiden *nt*.
aim [eɪm] *vt* (*gun, camera*) richten auf (+*acc*) // *vi* (*with gun*: *also*: **take ~**) zielen; (*intend*) beabsichtigen // *n* (*intention*) Absicht *f*, Ziel *nt*; (*pointing*) Zielen *nt*, Richten *nt*; **to ~ at** sth etw anstreben; **to ~ to do** vorhaben, etw zu tun; **~less** *a*, **~lessly** *ad* ziellos.
ain't [eɪnt] (*col*) = **am not; are not; is not; has not; have not.**
air [eə*] *n* Luft *f*; (*manner*) Miene *f*, Anschein *m*; (*MUS*) Melodie *f* // *vt* lüften; (*fig*) an die Öffentlichkeit bringen // *cpd* Luft-; **by ~** (*travel*) auf dem Luftweg; **to be on the ~** (*RADIO, TV*: *programme*) gesendet werden; **~bed** *n* (*Brit*) Luftmatratze *f*; **~-borne** *a* in der Luft; **~-conditioned** *a* mit Klimaanlage; **~-conditioning** *n* Klimaanlage *f*; **~craft** *n* Flugzeug *nt*, Maschine *f*; **~craft carrier** *n* Flugzeugträger *m*; **~field** *n* Flugplatz *m*; **~ force** *n* Luftwaffe *f*; **~ freshener** *n* Raumspray *nt*; **~gun** *n* Luftgewehr *nt*; **~ hostess** *n* (*Brit*) Stewardeß *f*; **~ letter** *n* (*Brit*) Luftpostbrief *m*; **~lift** *n* Luftbrücke *f*; **~line** *n* Luftverkehrsgesellschaft *f*; **~liner** *n*

Verkehrsflugzeug nt; ~lock n Luftblase f; ~mail n: by ~mail mit Luftpost; ~plane n (US) Flugzeug nt; ~port n Flughafen m, Flugplatz m; ~ raid n Luftangriff m; ~sick a luftkrank; ~strip n Landestreifen m; ~terminal n Terminal m; ~tight a luftdicht; ~ traffic controller n Fluglotse m; ~y a luftig; (manner) leichtfertig.

aisle [ail] n Gang m.

ajar [ə'dʒɑ:*] ad angelehnt; einen Spalt offen.

akin [ə'kın] a: ~ to ähnlich (+dat).

alacrity [ə'lækrıtı] n Bereitwilligkeit f.

alarm [ə'lɑ:m] n (warning) Alarm m; (bell etc) Alarmanlage f; (anxiety) Sorge f // vt erschrecken; ~ clock n Wecker m.

alas [ə'læs] interj ach.

Albania [æl'beınıə] n Albanien nt.

albeit [ɔːl'biːıt] cj obgleich.

album [ælbəm] n Album nt.

alcohol ['ælkəhɔl] n Alkohol m; ~ic [ælkə'hɔlık] a (drink) alkoholisch // n Alkoholiker(in f) m; ~ism n Alkoholismus m.

alderman ['ɔːldəmən] n, pl -men Stadtrat m.

ale [eıl] n Ale nt.

alert [ə'lɜːt] a wachsam // n Alarm m // vt alarmieren; to be on the ~ wachsam sein.

algebra ['ældʒıbrə] n Algebra f.

Algeria [æl'dʒıərıə] n Algerien nt.

alias ['eılıəs] ad alias // n Deckname m.

alibi ['ælıbaı] n Alibi nt.

alien ['eılıən] n Ausländer m // a (foreign) ausländisch; (strange) fremd; ~ to fremd (+dat); ~ate vt entfremden.

alight [ə'laıt] a brennend; (of building) in Flammen // vi (descend) aussteigen; (bird) sich setzen.

align [ə'laın] vt ausrichten.

alike [ə'laık] a gleich, ähnlich // ad gleich, ebenso; to look ~ sich (dat) ähnlich sehen.

alimony ['ælımənı] n Unterhalt m, Alimente pl.

alive [ə'laıv] a (living) lebend; (lively) lebendig, aufgeweckt; (full of) voll (with von), wimmelnd (with von).

all [ɔːl] a alle(r, s); ~ day/night den ganzen Tag/die ganze Nacht; ~ men are equal alle Menschen sind gleich; ~ five came alle fünf kamen; ~ the books/food die ganzen Bücher/das ganze Essen; ~ the time die ganze Zeit (über); ~ his life sein ganzes Leben (lang)

♦pron 1 alles; I ate it ~, I ate ~ of it ich habe alles gegessen; ~ of us/the boys went wir gingen alle/alle Jungen gingen; we ~ sat down wir setzten uns alle

2 (in phrases): above ~ vor allem; after ~ schließlich; at ~: not at ~ (in answer to question) überhaupt nicht; (in answer to thanks) gern geschehen; I'm not at ~ tired ich bin überhaupt nicht müde; anything at ~ will do es ist egal, welche(r, s); ~ in ~ alles in allem

♦ad ganz; ~ alone ganz allein; it's not as hard as ~ that so schwer ist es nun auch wieder nicht; ~ the more/the better um so mehr/besser; ~ but fast; the score is 2 ~ es steht 2 zu 2.

allay [ə'leı] vt (fears) beschwichtigen.

all clear ['ɔːl'klıə*] n Entwarnung f.

allegation [ælı'geıʃən] n Behauptung f.

allege [ə'ledʒ] vt (declare) behaupten; (falsely) vorgeben; ~dly [ə'ledʒıdlı] ad angeblich.

allegiance [ə'liːdʒəns] n Treue f.

allergic [ə'lɜːdʒık] a allergisch (to gegen).

allergy ['ælədʒı] n Allergie f.

alleviate [ə'liːvıeıt] vt lindern.

alley ['ælı] n Gasse f, Durchgang m.

alliance [ə'laıəns] n Bund m, Allianz f.

allied ['ælaıd] a vereinigt; (powers) alliiert; verwandt (to mit).

alligator ['ælıgeıtə*] n Alligator m.

all-in ['ɔːlın] a, ad (Brit: charge) alles inbegriffen, Gesamt-; ~ wrestling n Freistilringen nt.

all-night ['ɔːl'naıt] a (café, cinema) die ganze Nacht geöffnet, Nacht-.

allocate ['æləkeıt] vt zuteilen.

allot [ə'lɔt] vt zuteilen; ~ment n (share) Anteil m; (plot) Schrebergarten m.

all-out ['ɔːl'aut] a total; all out ad mit voller Kraft.

allow [ə'lau] vt (permit) erlauben, gestatten (sb jdm); (grant) bewilligen; (deduct) abziehen; (concede): to ~ that ... annehmen, daß ...; ~ for vt berücksichtigen, einplanen; ~ance n Beihilfe f; to make ~ances for berücksichtigen.

alloy ['ælɔı] n Metallegierung f.

all right ad (well) gut; (correct) richtig; (as answer) okay.

all-round ['ɔːl'raund] a (sportsman) allseitig, Allround-; (view) Rundum-.

all-time ['ɔːl'taım] a (record, high) ... aller Zeiten, Höchst-.

allude [ə'luːd] vi hinweisen, anspielen (to auf +acc).

alluring [ə'ljuərıŋ] a verlockend.

allusion [ə'luːʒən] n Anspielung f.

ally ['ælaı] n Verbündete(r) mf; (POL) Alliierte(r) m // vr [ə'laı]: to ~ o.s. with sich verbünden mit.

almighty [ɔːl'maıtı] a allmächtig.

almond ['ɑːmənd] n Mandel f.

almost ['ɔːlməust] ad fast, beinahe.

alms [ɑːmz] npl Almosen nt.

aloft [ə'lɔft] ad (be) in der Luft; (throw) in die Luft.

alone [ə'ləun] a, ad allein; to leave sth ~ etw sein lassen; let alone ... ge-

along [ə'lɒŋ] *prep* entlang, längs // *ad* (*onward*) vorwärts, weiter; ~ **with** zusammen mit; **he was limping** ~ er humpelte einher; **all** ~ (*all the time*) die ganze Zeit; ~**side** *ad* (*walk*) nebenher; (*come*) nebendran; (*be*) daneben // *prep* (*walk, compared with*) neben (+*dat*); (*come*) neben (+*acc*); (*be*) entlang, neben (+*dat*); (*of ship*) längsseits (+*gen*).

aloof [ə'lu:f] *a* zurückhaltend // *ad* fern; **to stand** ~ abseits stehen.

aloud [ə'laʊd] *ad* laut.

alphabet ['ælfəbet] *n* Alphabet *nt*; ~**ical** [ælfə'betɪkl] *a* alphabetisch.

alpine ['ælpaɪn] *a* alpin, Alpen-.

Alps [ælps] *npl*: **the** ~ die Alpen.

already [ɔ:l'redɪ] *ad* schon, bereits.

alright ['ɔ:l'raɪt] *ad* (*Brit*) = **all right.**

Alsatian [æl'seɪʃən] *n* (*dog*) Schäferhund *m*.

also ['ɔ:lsəʊ] *ad* auch, außerdem.

altar ['ɔ:ltə*] *n* Altar *m*.

alter ['ɔ:ltə*] *vt* ändern; (*dress*) umändern; ~**ation** [ɒltə'reɪʃən] *n* Änderung *f*; Umänderung *f*; (*to building*) Umbau *m*.

alternate [ɒl'tɜ:nɪt] *a* abwechselnd // *vi* ['ɒltɜ:neɪt] abwechseln (*with* mit); **on** ~ **days** jeden zweiten Tag.

alternating ['ɒltəneɪtɪŋ] *a*: ~ **current** Wechselstrom *m*.

alternative [ɒl'tɜ:nətɪv] *a* andere(r, s) // *n* Alternative *f*; ~**ly** *ad* im anderen Falle; ~**ly one could** ... oder man könnte ...

alternator ['ɒltɜ:neɪtə*] *n* (*AUT*) Lichtmaschine *f*.

although [ɔ:l'ðəʊ] *cj* obwohl.

altitude ['æltɪtju:d] *n* Höhe *f*.

alto ['æltəʊ] *n* Alt *m*.

altogether [ɔ:ltə'geðə*] *ad* (*on the whole*) im ganzen genommen; (*entirely*) ganz und gar.

aluminium [ælju'mɪnɪəm], (*US*) **aluminum** [ə'lu:mɪnəm] *n* Aluminium *nt*.

always ['ɔ:lweɪz] *ad* immer.

am [æm] *see* **be.**

a.m. *ad abbr* (= *ante meridiem*) vormittags.

amalgamate [ə'mælgəmeɪt] *vi* (*combine*) sich vereinigen // *vt* (*mix*) amalgamieren.

amass [ə'mæs] *vt* anhäufen.

amateur ['æmətɜ:*] *n* Amateur *m*; (*pej*) Amateur *m*, Stümper *m*; ~**ish** *a* (*pej*) dilettantisch, stümperhaft.

amaze [ə'meɪz] *vt* erstaunen; **to be** ~**d** (**at**) erstaunt sein (über); ~**ment** *n* höchste(s) Erstaunen *nt*.

amazing [ə'meɪzɪŋ] *a* höchst erstaunlich.

Amazon ['æməzən] *n* (*GEOG*) Amazonas *m*.

ambassador [æm'bæsədə*] *n* Botschafter *m*.

amber ['æmbə*] *n* Bernstein *m*; **at** ~ (*Brit AUT*) (auf) gelb.

ambiguous [æm'bɪgjʊəs] *a* zweideutig; (*not clear*) unklar.

ambition [æm'bɪʃən] *n* Ehrgeiz *m*.

ambitious [æm'bɪʃəs] *a* ehrgeizig.

ambivalent [æm'bɪvələnt] *n* (*attitude*) zwiespältig.

amble ['æmbl] *vi* (*usu*: ~ **along**) schlendern.

ambulance ['æmbjʊləns] *n* Krankenwagen *m*; ~**man** *n* Sanitäter *m*.

ambush ['æmbʊʃ] *n* Hinterhalt *m* // *vt* (aus dem Hinterhalt) überfallen.

amenable [ə'mi:nəbl] *a* gefügig; (*to reason*) zugänglich (*to dat*); (*to flattery*) empfänglich (*to* für); (*to law*) unterworfen (*to dat*).

amend [ə'mend] *vt* (*law etc*) abändern, ergänzen; **to make** ~**s** etw wiedergutmachen; ~**ment** *n* Abänderung *f*.

amenities [ə'mi:nɪtɪz] *npl* Einrichtungen *pl*.

America [ə'merɪkə] *n* Amerika *nt*; ~**n** *a* amerikanisch // *n* Amerikaner(in *f*) *m*.

amiable ['eɪmɪəbl] *a* liebenswürdig.

amicable ['æmɪkəbl] *a* freundschaftlich; (*settlement*) gütlich.

amid(st) [ə'mɪd(st)] *prep* mitten in *or* unter (+*dat*).

amiss [ə'mɪs] *ad*: **to take sth** ~ etw übelnehmen; **there's something** ~ **da stimmt irgend etwas nicht.

ammunition [æmjʊ'nɪʃən] *n* Munition *f*.

amnesia [æm'ni:zɪə] *n* Gedächtnisverlust *m*.

amnesty ['æmnɪstɪ] *n* Amnestie *f*.

among(st) [ə'mʌŋ(st)] *prep* unter.

amoral [æ'mɒrəl] *a* unmoralisch.

amorous ['æmərəs] *a* verliebt.

amount [ə'maʊnt] *n* (*of money*) Betrag *m*; (*of time, energy*) Aufwand *m* (*of an* +*dat*); (*of water, sand*) Menge *f* // *vi*: ~ **to** (*total*) sich belaufen auf (+*acc*); **this** ~**s to treachery** das kommt Verrat gleich; **it** ~**s to the same** es läuft aufs gleiche hinaus; **he won't** ~ **to much** aus ihm wird nie was.

amp(ère) ['æmp(eə*)] *n* Ampere *nt*.

amphibian [æm'fɪbɪən] *n* Amphibie *f*.

amphibious [æm'fɪbɪəs] *a* amphibisch, Amphibien-.

ample ['æmpl] *a* (*portion*) reichlich; (*dress*) weit, groß; ~ **time** genügend Zeit.

amplifier ['æmplɪfaɪə*] *n* Verstärker *m*.

amuse [ə'mju:z] *vt* (*entertain*) unterhalten; (*make smile*) belustigen; ~**ment** *n* (*feeling*) Unterhaltung *f*; (*recreation*) Zeitvertreib *m*; ~**ment arcade** *n* Spielhalle *f*.

an [æn, ən] *see* **a.**

anaemia [ə'ni:mɪə] *n* Anämie *f*.

anaemic [ə'niːmɪk] a blutarm.

anaesthetic [ænɪs'θetɪk] n Betäubungsmittel nt; **under ~** unter Narkose.

anaesthetist [æ'niːsθɪtɪst] n Anästhesist(in f) m.

analgesic [ænæl'dʒiːsɪk] n schmerzlindernde(s) Mittel nt.

analog(ue) ['ænəlɒg] a Analog-.

analogy [ə'nælədʒɪ] n Analogie f.

analyse ['ænəlaɪz] vt (Brit) analysieren.

analysis [ə'nælɪsɪs], pl **-ses** [-siːz] n Analyse f.

analyst ['ænəlɪst] n Analytiker(in f) m.

analytic(al) [ænə'lɪtɪk(əl)] a analytisch.

analyze ['ænəlaɪz] vt (US) = **analyse**.

anarchy ['ænəkɪ] n Anarchie f.

anathema [ə'næθɪmə] n (fig) Greuel nt.

anatomy [ə'nætəmɪ] n (structure) anatomische(r) Aufbau m; (study) Anatomie f.

ancestor ['ænsestə*] n Vorfahr m.

anchor ['æŋkə*] n Anker m // vi (also: **to drop ~**) ankern, vor Anker liegen // vt verankern; **to weigh ~** den Anker lichten; **~age** n Ankerplatz m.

anchovy ['æntʃəvɪ] n Sardelle f.

ancient ['eɪnʃənt] a alt; (car etc) uralt.

ancillary [æn'sɪlərɪ] a Hilfs-.

and [ænd] cj und; **~ so on** und so weiter; **try ~ come** versuche zu kommen; **better ~ better** immer besser.

Andes ['ændiːz] npl: **the ~** die Anden pl.

anemia [ə'niːmɪə] n (US) = **anaemia**.

anesthetic [ænɪs'θetɪk] n (US) = **anaesthetic**.

anew [ə'njuː] ad von neuem.

angel ['eɪndʒəl] n Engel m.

anger ['æŋgə*] n Zorn m // vt ärgern.

angle ['æŋgl] n Winkel m; (point of view) Standpunkt m; **~r** n Angler m.

Anglican ['æŋglɪkən] a anglikanisch // n Anglikaner(in f) m.

angling ['æŋglɪŋ] n Angeln nt.

Anglo- ['æŋgləʊ] pref Anglo-.

angrily ['æŋgrɪlɪ] ad ärgerlich, böse.

angry ['æŋgrɪ] a ärgerlich, ungehalten, böse; (wound) entzündet; **to be ~ with sb** auf jdn böse sein; **to be ~ at sth** über etw (acc) verärgert sein.

anguish ['æŋgwɪʃ] n Qual f.

angular ['æŋgjʊlə*] a eckig, winkelförmig; (face) kantig.

animal ['ænɪməl] n Tier nt; (living creature) Lèbewesen nt // a tierisch.

animate ['ænɪmeɪt] vt beleben // a ['ænɪmət] lebhaft; **~d** a lebendig; (film) Zeichentrick-.

animosity [ænɪ'mɒsɪtɪ] n Feindseligkeit f, Abneigung f.

aniseed ['ænɪsiːd] n Anis m.

ankle ['æŋkl] n (Fuß)knöchel m; **~ sock** n Söckchen nt.

annex ['æneks] n (also: Brit annexe) Anbau m // vt [ə'neks] anfügen; (POL) annektieren, angliedern.

annihilate [ə'naɪəleɪt] vt vernichten.

anniversary [ænɪ'vɜːsərɪ] n Jahrestag m.

annotate ['ænəteɪt] vt kommentieren.

announce [ə'naʊns] vt ankündigen, anzeigen; **~ment** n Ankündigung f; (official) Bekanntmachung f; **~r** n Ansager(in f) m.

annoy [ə'nɔɪ] vt ärgern; **don't get ~ed!** reg' dich nicht auf!; **~ance** n Ärgernis nt, Störung f; **~ing** a ärgerlich; (person) lästig.

annual ['ænjʊəl] a jährlich; (salary) Jahres- // n (plant) einjährige Pflanze f; (book) Jahrbuch nt; **~ly** ad jährlich.

annul [ə'nʌl] vt aufheben, annullieren; **~ment** n Aufhebung f, Annullierung f.

annum ['ænəm] n see **per**.

anomaly [ə'nɒməlɪ] n Abweichung f von der Regel.

anonymous [ə'nɒnɪməs] a anonym.

anorak ['ænəræk] n Anorak m, Windjacke f.

anorexia [ænə'reksɪə] n (MED) Magersucht f.

another [ə'nʌðə*] a, pron (different) ein(e) andere(r, s); (additional) noch eine(r, s); see also **one**.

answer ['ɑːnsə*] n Antwort f // vi antworten; (on phone) sich melden // vt (person) antworten (+dat); (letter, question) beantworten; (telephone) gehen an (+acc), abnehmen; (door) öffnen; **to ~ the phone** ans Telefon gehen; **in ~ to your letter** in Beantwortung Ihres Schreibens; **to ~ the bell** or **the door** aufmachen; **~ back** vi frech sein; **~ for** vt: **to ~ for sth** für etw verantwortlich sein; **~able** a: **to be ~ to sb for sth** jdm gegenüber für etw verantwortlich sein; **~ing machine** n Anrufbeantworter m.

ant [ænt] n Ameise f.

antagonism [æn'tægənɪzəm] n Antagonismus m.

antagonize [æn'tægənaɪz] vt reizen.

Antarctic [ænt'ɑːktɪk] a antarktisch // n: **the ~** die Antarktis.

antelope ['æntɪləʊp] n Antilope f.

antenatal [æntɪ'neɪtl] a vor der Geburt; **~ clinic** n Sprechstunde f für werdende Mütter.

antenna [æn'tenə], pl **~e** [-niː] n (BIOL) Fühler m; (RAD) Antenne f.

anthem ['ænθəm] n Hymne f; **national ~** Nationalhymne f.

anthology [æn'θɒlədʒɪ] n Gedichtsammlung f, Anthologie f.

anti- ['æntɪ] pref Gegen-, Anti-.

anti-aircraft ['æntɪ'eəkrɑːft] a Flugabwehr-.

antibiotic ['æntɪbaɪ'ɒtɪk] n Antibiotikum nt.

antibody ['æntɪbɒdɪ] n Antikörper m.

anticipate [æn'tɪsɪpeɪt] vt (expect: trouble, question) erwarten, rechnen mit;

(*look forward to*) sich freuen auf (+*acc*); (*do first*) vorwegnehmen; (*foresee*) ahnen, vorhersehen.

anticipation [æntɪsɪ'peɪʃən] *n* Erwartung *f*; (*foreshadowing*) Vorwegnahme *f*.

anticlimax ['æntɪ'klaɪmæks] *n* Ernüchterung *f*.

anticlockwise ['æntɪ'klɒkwaɪz] *ad* entgegen dem Uhrzeigersinn.

antics ['æntɪks] *npl* Possen *pl*.

anticyclone ['æntɪ'saɪkləʊn] *n* Hoch *nt*, Hochdruckgebiet *nt*.

antidote ['æntɪdəʊt] *n* Gegenmittel *nt*.

antifreeze ['æntɪfriːz] *n* Frostschutzmittel *nt*.

antihistamine [æntɪ'hɪstəmiːn] *n* Antihistamin *nt*.

antiquated ['æntɪkweɪtɪd] *a* antiquiert.

antique [æn'tiːk] *n* Antiquität *f* // *a* antik; (*old-fashioned*) altmodisch; ~ **shop** *n* Antiquitätenladen *m*.

antiquity [æn'tɪkwɪtɪ] *n* Altertum *nt*.

antiseptic [æntɪ'septɪk] *n* Antiseptikum *nt* // *a* antiseptisch.

antisocial [æntɪ'səʊʃl] *a* (*person*) ungesellig; (*law*) unsozial.

antlers ['æntləz] *npl* Geweih *nt*.

anus ['eɪnəs] *n* After *m*.

anvil ['ænvɪl] *n* Amboß *m*.

anxiety [æŋ'zaɪətɪ] *n* Angst *f*; (*worry*) Sorge *f*.

anxious ['æŋkʃəs] *a* ängstlich; (*worried*) besorgt; **to be** ~ **to do sth** etw unbedingt tun wollen.

any ['enɪ] ◆*a* 1 (*in questions etc*): **have you** ~ **butter?** haben Sie (etwas) Butter?; **have you** ~ **children?** haben Sie Kinder?; **if there are** ~ **tickets left** falls noch Karten da sind

2 (*with negative*): **I haven't** ~ **money/books** ich habe kein Geld/keine Bücher

3 (*no matter which*) jede(r, s) (beliebige); ~ **colour (at all)** jede beliebige Farbe; **choose** ~ **book you like** nehmen Sie ein beliebiges Buch

4 (*in phrases*): **in** ~ **case** in jedem Fall; ~ **day now** jeden Tag; **at** ~ **moment** jeden Moment; **at** ~ **rate** auf jeden Fall

◆*pron* 1 (*in questions etc*): **have you got** ~? haben Sie welche?; **can** ~ **of you sing?** kann (irgend)einer von euch singen?

2 (*with negative*): **I haven't** ~ (**of them**) ich habe keinen/keines (davon)

3 (*no matter which one(s)*): **take** ~ **of those books (you like)** nehmen Sie irgendeines dieser Bücher

◆*ad* 1 (*in questions etc*): **do you want** ~ **more soup/sandwiches?** möchten Sie noch Suppe/Brote?; **are you feeling** ~ **better?** fühlen Sie sich etwas besser?

2 (*with negative*): **I can't hear him** ~ **more** ich kann ihn nicht mehr hören.

anybody ['enɪbɒdɪ] *pron* (*no matter who*) jede(r); (*in questions etc*) (irgend)

jemand, (irgend) eine(r); (*with negative*): **I can't see** ~ ich kann niemanden sehen.

anyhow ['enɪhaʊ] *ad* (*at any rate*): **I shall go** ~ ich gehe sowieso; (*haphazard*): **do it** ~ **you like** machen Sie es, wie Sie wollen.

anyone ['enɪwʌn] *pron* = **anybody**.

anything ['enɪθɪŋ] *pron* 1 (*in questions etc*) (irgend) etwas; **can you see** ~? können Sie etwas sehen?

2 (*with negative*): **I can't see** ~ ich kann nichts sehen

3 (*no matter what*): **you can say** ~ **you like** Sie können sagen, was Sie wollen; ~ **will do** irgend etwas, irgendeine(r, s); **he'll eat** ~ er ißt alles.

anyway ['enɪweɪ] *ad* (*at any rate*) auf jeden Fall; (*besides*): ~, **I couldn't come even if I wanted to** jedenfalls könnte ich nicht kommen, selbst wenn ich wollte; **why are you phoning,** ~? warum rufst du überhaupt an?

anywhere ['enɪwɛə*] *ad* (*in questions etc*) irgendwo; (: *with direction*) irgendwohin; (*no matter where*) überall; (: *with direction*) überallhin; (*with negative*): **I can't see him** ~ ich kann ihn nirgendwo or nirgends sehen; **can you see him** ~? siehst du ihn irgendwo?; **put the books down** ~ leg die Bücher irgendwohin.

apart [ə'pɑːt] *ad* (*parted*) auseinander; (*away*) beiseite, abseits; **10 miles** ~ 10 Meilen auseinander; **to take** ~ auseinandernehmen; ~ **from** *prep* außer.

apartheid [ə'pɑːteɪt] *n* Apartheid *f*.

apartment [ə'pɑːtmənt] *n* (*US*) Wohnung *f*; ~ **building** *n* (*US*) Wohnhaus *nt*.

apathy ['æpəθɪ] *n* Teilnahmslosigkeit *f*, Apathie *f*.

ape [eɪp] *n* (Menschen)affe *m* // *vt* nachahmen.

aperture ['æpətjʊə*] *n* Öffnung *f*; (*PHOT*) Blende *f*.

apex ['eɪpeks] *n* Spitze *f*.

apiece [ə'piːs] *ad* pro Stück; (*per person*) pro Kopf.

apologetic [əpɒlə'dʒetɪk] *a* entschuldigend; **to be** ~ sich sehr entschuldigen.

apologize [ə'pɒlədʒaɪz] *vi* sich entschuldigen (*for sth to sb* für etw bei jdm).

apology [ə'pɒlədʒɪ] *n* Entschuldigung *f*.

apostle [ə'pɒsl] *n* Apostel *m*.

apostrophe [ə'pɒstrəfɪ] *n* Apostroph *m*.

appal [ə'pɔːl] *vt* erschrecken; ~**ling** *a* schrecklich.

apparatus [æpə'reɪtəs] *n* Gerät *nt*.

apparel [ə'pærəl] *n* (*US*) Kleidung *f*.

apparent [ə'pærənt] *a* offenbar; ~**ly** *ad* anscheinend.

apparition [æpə'rɪʃən] *n* (*ghost*) Erscheinung f, Geist m; (appearance) Erscheinen nt.

appeal [ə'pi:l] vi dringend ersuchen; dringend bitten (for um); sich wenden (to an +acc); (to public) appellieren (to an +acc); (JUR) Berufung einlegen // n Aufruf m; (JUR) Berufung f; it doesn't ~ to me es gefällt mir nicht; ~ing a ansprechend.

appear [ə'piə*] vi (come into sight) erscheinen; (be seen) auftauchen; (seem) scheinen; ~ance n (coming into sight) Erscheinen nt; (outward show) Äußere(s) nt; it would ~ that ... anscheinend ...

appease [ə'pi:z] vt beschwichtigen.

appendicitis [əpendı'saıtıs] n Blinddarmentzündung f.

appendix [ə'pendıks], pl -dices [-dısi:z] n (in book) Anhang m; (MED) Blinddarm m.

appetite ['æpıtaıt] n Appetit m; (fig) Lust f.

appetizer ['æpətaızə*] n Appetitanreger m.

appetizing ['æpıtaızıŋ] a appetitanregend.

applaud [ə'plɔ:d] vti Beifall klatschen (+dat), applaudieren.

applause [ə'plɔ:z] n Beifall m, Applaus m.

apple ['æpl] n Apfel m; ~ **tree** n Apfelbaum m.

appliance [ə'plaıəns] n Gerät nt.

applicable [ə'plıkəbl] a anwendbar; (in forms) zutreffend.

applicant ['æplıkənt] n Bewerber(in f) m.

application [æplı'keıʃən] n (request) Antrag m; (for job) Bewerbung f; (putting into practice) Anwendung f; (hard work) Fleiß m; ~ **form** n Bewerbungsformular nt.

applied [ə'plaıd] a angewandt.

apply [ə'plaı] vi (ask) sich wenden (to an +acc), sich melden; (be suitable) zutreffen // vt (place on) auflegen; (cream) auftragen; (put into practice) anwenden; to ~ for sth sich um etw bewerben; to ~ the brakes die Bremsen betätigen; to ~ o.s. to sth sich bei etw anstrengen.

appoint [ə'pɔınt] vt (to office) ernennen, berufen; (settle) festsetzen; ~ment n (meeting) Verabredung f; (at hairdresser etc) Bestellung f; (in business) Termin m; (choice for a position) Ernennung f; (UNIV) Berufung f.

appraisal [ə'preızl] n Beurteilung f.

appreciable [ə'pri:ʃəbl] a (perceptible) merklich; (able to be estimated) abschätzbar.

appreciate [ə'pri:ʃıeıt] vt (value) zu schätzen wissen; (understand) einsehen // vi (increase in value) im Wert steigen.

appreciation [əpri:ʃı'eıʃən] n Wert-

schätzung f; (COMM) Wertzuwachs m.

appreciative [ə'pri:ʃıətıv] a (showing thanks) dankbar; (showing liking) anerkennend.

apprehend [æprı'hend] vt (arrest) festnehmen; (understand) erfassen.

apprehension [æprı'henʃən] n Angst f.

apprehensive [æprı'hensıv] a furchtsam.

apprentice [ə'prentıs] n Lehrling m; ~ship n Lehrzeit f.

approach [ə'prəutʃ] vi sich nähern // vt herantreten an (+acc); (problem) herangehen an (+acc) // n Annäherung f; (to problem) Ansatz m; (path) Zugang m, Zufahrt f; ~able a zugänglich.

appropriate [ə'prəuprıət] a angemessen; (remark) angebracht // [ə'prəuprıeıt] vt (take for o.s.) sich aneignen; (set apart) bereitstellen.

approval [ə'pru:vəl] n (show of satisfaction) Beifall m; (permission) Billigung f; (COMM) on ~ bei Gefallen.

approve [ə'pru:v] vti billigen; I don't ~ of it/him ich halte nichts davon/von ihm; ~d **school** n (Brit) Erziehungsheim nt.

approximate [ə'prɒksımət] a annähernd, ungefähr // vt [ə'prɒksımeıt] nahekommen (+dat); ~ly ad rund, ungefähr.

apricot ['eıprıkɒt] n Aprikose f.

April ['eıprəl] n April m; ~ **Fools' Day** n der erste April.

apron ['eıprən] n Schürze f.

apt [æpt] a (suitable) passend; (able) begabt; (likely): to be ~ to do sth dazu neigen, etw zu tun.

aptitude ['æptıtju:d] n Begabung f.

aqualung ['ækwəlʌŋ] n Unterwasseratmungsgerät nt.

aquarium [ə'kwɛərıəm] n Aquarium nt.

Aquarius [ə'kwɛərıəs] n Wassermann m.

aquatic [ə'kwætık] a Wasser-.

Arab ['ærəb] n Araber(in f) m.

Arabia [ə'reıbıə] n Arabien nt.

Arabian [ə'reıbıən] a arabisch.

Arabic ['ærəbık] a arabisch // n Arabisch nt; ~ **numerals** arabische Ziffern.

arable ['ærəbl] a bebaubar, Kultur-.

arbitrary ['ɑ:bıtrərı] a willkürlich.

arbitration [ɑ:bı'treıʃən] n Schlichtung f.

arc [ɑ:k] n Bogen m.

arcade [ɑ:'keıd] n Säulengang m.

arch [ɑ:tʃ] n Bogen m // vt überwölben; (back) krumm machen.

archaeologist [ɑ:kı'ɒlədʒıst] n Archäologe m.

archaeology [ɑ:kı'ɒlədʒı] n Archäologie f.

archaic [ɑ:'keıık] a altertümlich.

archbishop ['ɑ:tʃ'bıʃəp] n Erzbischof m.

arch-enemy ['ɑ:tʃ'enəmı] n Erzfeind m.

archeology etc (US) = **archaeology** etc.

archer ['ɑːtʃə*] n Bogenschütze m; **~y** n Bogenschießen nt.

archipelago [ɑːkɪ'pelɪgəʊ] n Archipel m; (sea) Inselmeer nt.

architect ['ɑːkɪtekt] n Architekt(in f) m; **~ural** [ɑːkɪ'tektʃərəl] a architektonisch; **~ure** n Architektur f.

archives ['ɑːkaɪvz] npl Archiv nt.

archway ['ɑːtʃweɪ] n Bogen m.

Arctic ['ɑːktɪk] a arktisch // n: **the ~** die Arktis.

ardent ['ɑːdənt] a glühend.

arduous ['ɑːdjʊəs] a mühsam.

are [ɑː*] see **be**.

area ['ɛərɪə] n Fläche f; (of land) Gebiet nt; (part of sth) Teil m, Abschnitt m.

arena [ə'riːnə] n Arena f.

aren't [ɑːnt] = **are not**.

Argentina [ɑːdʒən'tiːnə] n Argentinien nt; **Argentinian** [ɑːdʒən'tɪnɪən] a argentinisch // n Argentinier(in f) m.

arguably ['ɑːgjʊəblɪ] ad wohl.

argue ['ɑːgjuː] vi diskutieren; (angrily) streiten.

argument ['ɑːgjʊmənt] n (theory) Argument m; (reasoning) Argumentation f; (row) Auseinandersetzung f, Streit m; **to have an ~** sich streiten; **~ative** [ɑːgjʊ'mentətɪv] a streitlustig.

aria ['ɑːrɪə] n Arie f.

arid ['ærɪd] a trocken.

Aries ['ɛəriːz] n Widder m.

arise, pt **arose**, pp **arisen** [ə'raɪz, ə'rəʊz, ə'rɪzn] vi aufsteigen; (get up) aufstehen; (difficulties etc) entstehen; (case) vorkommen; **to ~ from sth** herrühren von etw.

aristocracy [ærɪs'tɒkrəsɪ] n Adel m, Aristokratie f.

aristocrat ['ærɪstəkræt] n Adlige(r) mf, Aristokrat(in f) m.

arithmetic [ə'rɪθmətɪk] n Rechnen nt, Arithmetik f.

ark [ɑːk] n: **Noah's A~** die Arche Noah.

arm [ɑːm] n Arm m; (branch of military service) Zweig m // vt bewaffnen.

armaments ['ɑːməmənts] npl Ausrüstung f.

arm: ~chair n Lehnstuhl m; **~ed** a (forces) Streit-, bewaffnet; (robbery) bewaffnet.

armistice ['ɑːmɪstɪs] n Waffenstillstand m.

armour, (US) **armor** ['ɑːmə*] n (knight's) Rüstung f; (MIL) Panzerplatte f; **~ed car** n Panzerwagen m; **~y** n Waffenlager nt; (factory) Waffenfabrik f.

armpit ['ɑːmpɪt] n Achselhöhle f.

armrest ['ɑːmrest] n Armlehne f.

arms [ɑːmz] npl (weapons) Waffen pl; **~ race** n Wettrüsten nt.

army ['ɑːmɪ] n Armee f, Heer nt; (host) Heer nt.

aroma [ə'rəʊmə] n Duft m, Aroma nt; **~tic** [ærə'mætɪk] a aromatisch, würzig.

arose [ə'rəʊz] pt of **arise**.

around [ə'raʊnd] ad ringsherum; (almost) ungefähr // prep um ... herum; **is he ~?** ist er hier?

arouse [ə'raʊz] vt wecken.

arrange [ə'reɪndʒ] vt (time, meeting) festsetzen; (holidays) festlegen; (flowers, hair, objects) anordnen; **I ~d to meet him** ich habe mit ihm ausgemacht, ihn zu treffen; **it's all ~d** es ist alles arrangiert; **~ment** n (order) Reihenfolge f; (agreement) Vereinbarung f; **~ments** pl Pläne pl.

array [ə'reɪ] n (collection) Ansammlung f.

arrears [ə'rɪəz] npl (of debts) Rückstand m; (of work) Unerledigte(s) nt; **in ~** im Rückstand.

arrest [ə'rest] vt (person) verhaften; (stop) aufhalten // n Verhaftung f; **under ~** in Haft.

arrival [ə'raɪvəl] n Ankunft f.

arrive [ə'raɪv] vi ankommen (at in +dat, bei).

arrogance ['ærəgəns] n Überheblichkeit f, Arroganz f.

arrow ['ærəʊ] n Pfeil m.

arse [ɑːs] n (col!) Arsch m (!).

arsenal ['ɑːsɪnl] n Waffenlager nt, Zeughaus nt.

arsenic ['ɑːsnɪk] n Arsen nt.

arson ['ɑːsn] n Brandstiftung f.

art [ɑːt] n Kunst f; **A~s** pl Geisteswissenschaften pl.

artery ['ɑːtərɪ] n Schlagader f, Arterie f.

artful ['ɑːtfʊl] a verschlagen.

art gallery n Kunstgalerie f.

arthritis [ɑː'θraɪtɪs] n Arthritis f.

artichoke ['ɑːtɪtʃəʊk] n Artischocke f; **Jerusalem ~** Erdartischocke f.

article ['ɑːtɪkl] n (PRESS, GRAM) Artikel m; (thing) Gegenstand m, Artikel m; (clause) Abschnitt m, Paragraph m; **to do one's ~s** (JUR) seine Referendarzeit ableisten; **~ of clothing** Kleidungsstück nt.

articulate [ɑː'tɪkjʊlɪt] a (able to express o.s.) redegewandt; (speaking clearly) deutlich, verständlich; **to be ~** sich gut ausdrücken können // vt [ɑː'tɪkjʊleɪt] (connect) zusammenfügen, gliedern; **~d vehicle** n Sattelschlepper m.

artificial [ɑːtɪ'fɪʃəl] a künstlich, Kunst-; **~ respiration** n künstliche Atmung f.

artisan ['ɑːtɪzæn] n gelernte(r) Handwerker m.

artist ['ɑːtɪst] n Künstler(in f) m; **~ic** [ɑː'tɪstɪk] a künstlerisch; **~ry** n künstlerische(s) Können nt.

artless ['ɑːtlɪs] a ungekünstelt; (character) arglos.

art school n Kunsthochschule f.

as [æz] ◆cj **1** (referring to time) als; ~

the years went by mit den Jahren; he came in ~ I was leaving als er hereinkam, ging ich gerade; ~ **from** tomorrow ab morgen
2 (in comparisons): ~ **big** ~ so groß wie; **twice** ~ **big** ~ zweimal so groß wie; ~ **much/many** ~ soviel/so viele wie; ~ **soon** ~ sobald
3 (since, because) da; he left early ~ he had to be home by 10 er ging früher, da er um 10 zu Hause sein mußte
4 (referring to manner, way) wie; do ~ you wish mach was du willst; ~ she said wie sie sagte
5 (concerning): ~ **for** or **to** that was das betrifft or angeht
6: ~ **if** or **though** als ob.
♦prep as; he works ~ a driver er arbeitet als Fahrer; he gave it to me ~ a present er hat es mir als Geschenk gegeben; see also **long, such, well**.
a.s.a.p. abbr of **as soon as possible**.
ascend [ə'send] vi aufsteigen // vt besteigen; **~ancy** n Oberhand f.
ascent [ə'sent] n Aufstieg m; Besteigung f.
ascertain [æsə'teɪn] vt feststellen.
ascribe [əs'kraɪb] vt zuschreiben (to dat).
ash [æʃ] n Asche f; (tree) Esche f.
ashamed [ə'ʃeɪmd] a beschämt; to be ~ of sth sich für etw schämen.
ashen [æʃən] a (pale) aschfahl.
ashore [ə'ʃɔ:*] ad an Land.
ashtray ['æʃtreɪ] n Aschenbecher m.
Ash Wednesday n Aschermittwoch m.
Asia ['eɪʃə] n Asien nt; **~n, ~tic** [eɪsɪ'ætɪk] a asiatisch // n Asiat(in f) m.
aside [ə'saɪd] ad beiseite // n beiseite gesprochene Worte pl.
ask [ɑ:sk] vt fragen; (permission) bitten um; ~ him his name frage ihn nach seinem Namen; he ~ed to see you er wollte dich sehen; to ~ sb to do sth jdn bitten, etw zu tun; to ~ sb about sth jdn nach etw fragen; to ~ (sb) a question jdn etwas fragen; to ~ sb out to dinner jdn zum Essen einladen; to ~ after sb nach jdm fragen; (acc) bitten.
askance [əs'kɑ:ns] ad: to look ~ at sb jdn schief ansehen.
askew [əs'kju:] ad schief.
asking price ['ɑ:skɪŋ-] n Verkaufspreis m.
asleep [ə'sli:p] a: to be ~ schlafen; to fall ~ einschlafen.
asparagus [əs'pærəgəs] n Spargel m.
aspect ['æspekt] n Aspekt m.
aspersions [əs'pɜ:ʃənz] npl: to cast ~ on sb/sth sich abfällig über jdn/etw äußern.
asphyxiation [əsfɪksɪ'eɪʃən] n Erstickung f.
aspirations [æspə'reɪʃənz] npl: to have

~ **towards** sth etw anstreben.
aspire [əs'paɪə*] vi streben (to nach).
aspirin ['æsprɪn] n Aspirin nt.
ass [æs] n (lit, fig) Esel m; (US col!) Arsch m (!).
assailant [ə'seɪlənt] n Angreifer m.
assassin [ə'sæsɪn] n Attentäter(in f) m; **~ate** vt ermorden.
assault [ə'sɔ:lt] n Angriff m // vt überfallen; (woman) herfallen über (+acc).
assemble [ə'sembl] vt versammeln; (parts) zusammensetzen // vi sich versammeln.
assembly [ə'semblɪ] n (meeting) Versammlung f; (construction) Zusammensetzung f, Montage f; ~ **line** n Fließband nt.
assent [ə'sent] n Zustimmung f.
assert [ə'sɜ:t] vt erklären; **~ion** [ə'sɜ:ʃən] n Behauptung f.
assess [ə'ses] vt schätzen; **~ment** n Bewertung f, Einschätzung f; **~or** n Steuerberater m.
asset ['æset] n Vorteil m, Wert m; **~s** pl Vermögen nt; (estate) Nachlaß m.
assiduous [ə'sɪdjʊəs] a fleißig, aufmerksam.
assign [ə'saɪn] vt zuweisen.
assignment [ə'saɪnmənt] n Aufgabe f, Auftrag m.
assimilate [ə'sɪmɪleɪt] vt sich aneignen, aufnehmen.
assist [ə'sɪst] vt beistehen (+dat); **~ance** n Unterstützung f, Hilfe f; **~ant** n Assistent(in f) m, Mitarbeiter(in f) m; (Brit: also: **shop ~ant**) Verkäufer(in f) m.
assizes [ə'saɪzɪz] npl Landgericht nt.
associate [ə'səʊʃɪɪt] n (partner) Kollege m, Teilhaber m; (member) außerordentliche(s) Mitglied nt // vt [ə'səʊʃɪeɪt] verbinden (with mit) // vi [ə'səʊʃɪeɪt] (keep company) verkehren (with mit).
association [əsəʊsɪ'eɪʃən] n Verband m, Verein m; (PSYCH) Assoziation f; (link) Verbindung f.
assorted [ə'sɔ:tɪd] a gemischt.
assortment [ə'sɔ:tmənt] n Sammlung f; (COMM) Sortiment nt (of von), Auswahl f (of an +dat).
assume [ə'sju:m] vt (take for granted) annehmen; (put on) annehmen, sich geben; **~d name** n Deckname m.
assumption [ə'sʌmpʃən] n Annahme f.
assurance [ə'ʃʊərəns] n (firm statement) Versicherung f; (confidence) Selbstsicherheit f; (insurance) (Lebens)versicherung f.
assure [ə'ʃʊə*] vt (make sure) sicherstellen; (convince) versichern (+dat); (life) versichern.
asterisk ['æstərɪsk] n Sternchen nt.
astern [əs'tɜ:n] ad achtern.
asthma ['æsmə] n Asthma nt.

astonish [əs'tɒnɪʃ] *vt* erstaunen; ~ment *n* Erstaunen *nt*.

astound [əs'taʊnd] *vt* verblüffen.

astray [əs'treɪ] *ad* in die Irre; auf Abwege; **to go ~** *(go wrong)* sich vertun; **to lead ~** irreführen.

astride [əs'traɪd] *ad* rittlings // *prep* rittlings auf.

astrologer [əs'trɒlədʒə*] *n* Astrologe *m*, Astrologin *f*.

astrology [əs'trɒlədʒɪ] *n* Astrologie *f*.

astronaut ['æstrənɔ:t] *n* Astronaut(in *f*) *m*.

astronomer [əs'trɒnəmə*] *n* Astronom *m*.

astronomical [æstrə'nɒmɪkəl] *a* astronomisch; *(success)* riesig.

astronomy [əs'trɒnəmɪ] *n* Astronomie *f*.

astute [əs'tju:t] *a* scharfsinnig; schlau, gerissen.

asylum [ə'saɪləm] *n* *(home)* Heim *nt*; *(refuge)* Asyl *nt*.

at [æt, ət] *prep* **1** *(referring to position, direction)* an (+dat), bei (+dat); *(with place)* in (+dat); **~ the top** an der Spitze; **~ home/school** zu Hause/in der Schule; **~ the baker's** beim Bäcker; **to look ~ sth** auf etw *(acc)* blicken; **to throw sth ~ sb** etw nach jdm werfen **2** *(referring to time)*: **~ 4 o'clock** um 4 Uhr; **~ night** bei Nacht; **~ Christmas** zu Weihnachten; **~ times** manchmal **3** *(referring to rates, speed etc)*: **~ £1 a kilo** zu £1 pro Kilo; **two ~ a time** zwei auf einmal; **~ 50 km/h** mit 50 km/h **4** *(referring to manner)*: **~ a stroke** mit einem Schlag; **~ peace** in Frieden **5** *(referring to activity)*: **to be ~ work** bei der Arbeit sein; **to play ~ cowboys** Cowboy spielen; **to be good ~ sth** gut in etw *(dat)* sein **6** *(referring to cause)*: **shocked/surprised/annoyed ~ sth** schockiert/überrascht/verärgert über etw *(acc)*; **I went ~ his suggestion** ich ging auf seinen Vorschlag hin.

ate [et, eɪt] *pt of* **eat**.

atheist ['eɪθɪɪst] *n* Atheist(in *f*) *m*.

Athens ['æθɪnz] *n* Athen *nt*.

athlete ['æθli:t] *n* Athlet *m*, Sportler *m*.

athletic [æθ'letɪk] *a* sportlich, athletisch; **~s** *n* Leichtathletik *f*.

Atlantic [ət'læntɪk] *a* atlantisch // *n*: **the ~** *(Ocean)* der Atlantik.

atlas ['ætləs] *n* Atlas *m*.

atmosphere ['ætməsfɪə*] *n* Atmosphäre *f*.

atom ['ætəm] *n* Atom *nt*; *(fig)* bißchen *nt*; **~ic** [ə'tɒmɪk] *a* atomar, Atom-; **~(ic) bomb** *n* Atombombe *f*; **~izer** *n* Zerstäuber *m*.

atone [ə'təʊn] *vi* sühnen *(for acc)*.

atrocious [ə'trəʊʃəs] *a* gräßlich.

atrocity [ə'trɒsɪtɪ] *n* Scheußlichkeit *f*; *(deed)* Greueltat *f*.

attach [ə'tætʃ] *vt* *(fasten)* befestigen; *(importance etc)* legen *(to auf +acc)*; beimessen *(to dat)*; **to be ~ed to sb/sth** an jdm/etw hängen.

attaché [ə'tæʃeɪ] *n* Attaché *m*; **~ case** *n* Aktenkoffer *m*.

attachment [ə'tætʃmənt] *n* *(tool)* Zubehörteil *nt*; *(love)*: **~ (to sb)** Zuneigung *f* (zu jdm).

attack [ə'tæk] *vt* angreifen // *n* Angriff *m*; *(MED)* Anfall *m*; **~er** *n* Angreifer(in *f*) *m*.

attain [ə'teɪn] *vt* erreichen; **~ments** *npl* Kenntnisse *pl*.

attempt [ə'tempt] *n* Versuch *m* // *vt* versuchen; **~ed murder** Mordversuch *m*.

attend [ə'tend] *vt* *(go to)* teilnehmen (an +dat); *(lectures)* besuchen; **to ~ to** *(needs)* nachkommen (+dat); *(person)* sich kümmern um; **~ance** *n* *(presence)* Anwesenheit *f*; *(people present)* Besucherzahl *f*; **good ~ance** gute Teilnahme; **~ant** *n* *(companion)* Begleiter(in *f*) *m*; Gesellschafter(in *f*) *m*; *(in car park etc)* Wächter(in *f*) *m*; *(servant)* Bedienstete(r) *mf* // *a* begleitend; *(fig)* damit verbunden.

attention [ə'tenʃən] *n* Aufmerksamkeit *f*; *(care)* Fürsorge *f*; *(for machine etc)* Pflege *f* // *interj* *(MIL)* Achtung!; **for the ~ of ...** zu Händen (von) ...

attentive *a* [ə'tentɪv] aufmerksam.

attest [ə'test] *vi*: **to ~ to** sich verbürgen für.

attic ['ætɪk] *n* Dachstube *f*, Mansarde *f*.

attitude ['ætɪtju:d] *n* *(mental)* Einstellung *f*.

attorney [ə'tɜ:nɪ] *n* *(solicitor)* Rechtsanwalt *m*; **A~ General** *n* Justizminister *m*.

attract [ə'trækt] *vt* anziehen; *(attention)* erregen; **~ion** [ə'trækʃən] *n* Anziehungskraft *f*; *(thing)* Attraktion *f*; **~ive** *a* attraktiv.

attribute ['ætrɪbju:t] *n* Eigenschaft *f*, Attribut *nt* // *vt* [ə'trɪbju:t] zuschreiben *(to dat)*.

attrition [ə'trɪʃən] *n*: **war of ~** Zermürbungskrieg *m*.

aubergine ['əʊbəʒi:n] *n* Aubergine *f*.

auburn ['ɔ:bən] *a* kastanienbraun.

auction ['ɔ:kʃən] *n* *(also: sale by ~)* Versteigerung *f*, Auktion *f* // *vt* versteigern; **~eer** [ɔ:kʃə'nɪə*] *n* Versteigerer *m*.

audacity [ɔ:'dæsɪtɪ] *n* *(boldness)* Wagemut *m*; *(impudence)* Unverfrorenheit *f*.

audible ['ɔ:dɪbl] *a* hörbar.

audience ['ɔ:dɪəns] *n* Zuhörer *pl*, Zuschauer *pl*; *(with king etc)* Audienz *f*.

audio-typist ['ɔ:dɪəʊ'taɪpɪst] *n* Phonotypistin *f*.

audio-visual ['ɔ:dɪəʊ'vɪzjʊəl] *a* audiovisuell.

audit ['ɔːdɪt] vt prüfen.

audition [ɔː'dɪʃən] n Probe f.

auditorium [ɔːdɪ'tɔːrɪəm] n Zuschauerraum m.

augment [ɔːg'ment] vt vermehren.

augur ['ɔːgə*] vi bedeuten, voraussagen; this ~s well das ist ein gutes Omen.

August ['ɔːgəst] n August m.

aunt [aːnt] n Tante f; ~y, ~ie n Tantchen nt.

au pair ['əʊ'pɛə*] n (also: ~ girl) Aupair-Mädchen nt.

aura ['ɔːrə] n Nimbus m.

auspices ['ɔːspɪsɪz] npl: under the ~ of unter der Schirmherrschaft von.

auspicious [ɔːs'pɪʃəs] a günstig; verheißungsvoll.

austere [ɒs'tɪə*] a streng; (room) nüchtern.

austerity [ɒs'terɪtɪ] n Strenge f; (POL) wirtschaftliche Einschränkung f.

Australia [ɒs'treɪlɪə] n Australien nt; ~n a australisch; // n Australier(in f) m.

Austria ['ɒstrɪə] n Österreich nt; ~n a österreichisch // n Österreicher(in f) m.

authentic [ɔː'θentɪk] a echt, authentisch.

author ['ɔːθə*] n Autor m, Schriftsteller m; (beginner) Urheber m, Schöpfer m.

authoritarian [ɔːθɒrɪ'tɛərɪən] a autoritär.

authoritative [ɔː'θɒrɪtətɪv] a (account) maßgeblich; (manner) herrisch.

authority [ɔː'θɒrɪtɪ] n (power) Autorität f; (expert) Autorität f, Fachmann m; the authorities pl die Behörden pl.

authorize ['ɔːθəraɪz] vt bevollmächtigen; (permit) genehmigen.

auto ['ɔːtəʊ] n (US) Auto nt, Wagen m.

autobiography [ɔːtəʊbaɪ'ɒgrəfɪ] n Autobiographie f.

autograph ['ɔːtəgrɑːf] n (of celebrity) Autogramm nt // vt mit Autogramm versehen.

automatic [ɔːtə'mætɪk] a automatisch // n (gun) Selbstladepistole f; (car) Automatik m; ~ally ad automatisch.

automobile ['ɔːtəməbiːl] n (US) Auto(mobil) nt.

autonomous [ɔː'tɒnəməs] a autonom.

autumn ['ɔːtəm] n Herbst m.

auxiliary [ɔːg'zɪlɪərɪ] a Hilfs-.

Av. abbr of **avenue**.

avail [ə'veɪl] vt: ~ o.s. of sth sich einer Sache bedienen // n: to no ~ nutzlos.

availability [əveɪlə'bɪlɪtɪ] n Erhältlichkeit f, Vorhandensein nt.

available [ə'veɪləbl] a erhältlich; zur Verfügung stehend; (person) erreichbar, abkömmlich.

avalanche ['ævəlɑːnʃ] n Lawine f.

avarice ['ævərɪs] n Habsucht f, Geiz m.

Ave. abbr of **avenue**.

avenge [ə'vendʒ] vt rächen, sühnen.

avenue ['ævənjuː] n Allee f.

average ['ævərɪdʒ] n Durchschnitt m // a durchschnittlich, Durchschnitts- // vt (figures) den Durchschnitt nehmen von; (perform) durchschnittlich leisten; (in car etc) im Schnitt fahren; on ~ durchschnittlich, im Durchschnitt; ~ out vi: to ~ out at im Durchschnitt betragen.

averse [ə'vɜːs] a: to be ~ to doing sth eine Abneigung dagegen haben, etw zu tun.

avert [ə'vɜːt] vt (turn away) abkehren; (prevent) abwehren.

aviary ['eɪvɪərɪ] n Vogelhaus nt.

aviation [eɪvɪ'eɪʃən] n Luftfahrt f, Flugwesen nt.

avid ['ævɪd] a gierig (for auf +acc).

avocado [ævə'kɑːdəʊ] n (also: Brit: ~ pear) Avocado(birne) f.

avoid [ə'vɔɪd] vt vermeiden; ~ance n Vermeidung f.

await [ə'weɪt] vt erwarten, entgegensehen (+dat).

awake [ə'weɪk] a wach // (v: pt awoke, pp awoken or awaked) vt (auf)wecken // vi aufwachen; to be ~ wach sein; ~ning n Erwachen nt.

award [ə'wɔːd] n (prize) Preis m // vt zuerkennen.

aware [ə'wɛə*] a bewußt; to be ~ sich bewußt sein (of gen); ~ness n Bewußtsein nt.

awash [ə'wɒʃ] a überflutet.

away [ə'weɪ] ad weg, fort; two hours ~ by car zwei Autostunden entfernt; the holiday was two weeks ~ es war noch zwei Wochen bis zum Urlaub; ~ match n (SPORT) Auswärtsspiel nt.

awe [ɔː] n Ehrfurcht f; ~-inspiring, ~some a ehrfurchtgebietend.

awful ['ɔːfʊl] a (very bad) furchtbar; ~ly ad furchtbar, sehr.

awkward ['ɔːkwəd] a (clumsy) ungeschickt, linkisch; (embarrassing) peinlich.

awning ['ɔːnɪŋ] n Markise f.

awoke [ə'wəʊk], **awoken** [ə'wəʊkən] pt, pp of **awake**.

awry [ə'raɪ] ad schief; to go ~ (person) fehlgehen; (plans) schiefgehen.

axe, (US) **ax** [æks] n Axt f, Beil nt // vt (end suddenly) streichen.

axis, pl **axes** ['æksɪs, -siːz] n Achse f.

axle ['æksl] n Achse f.

ay(e) [aɪ] interj (yes) ja; the ayes pl die Jastimmen pl.

azalea [ə'zeɪlɪə] n Azalee f.

B

B [biː] n (MUS) H nt.

B.A. n abbr of **Bachelor of Arts**.

babble ['bæbl] vi schwätzen; (stream)

murmeln.

baby ['beɪbɪ] n Baby nt, Säugling m; ~ **carriage** n (US) Kinderwagen m; ~-**sit** vi Kinder hüten, babysitten; ~-**sitter** n Babysitter m.

bachelor ['bætʃələ*] n Junggeselle m; **B~** **of** **Arts/Science** (B.A./B.Sc.) Bakkalaureus m der philosophischen Fakultät/der Naturwissenschaften.

back [bæk] n (of person, horse) Rücken m; (of house) Rückseite f; (of train) Ende nt; (FOOTBALL) Verteidiger m // vt (support) unterstützen; (wager) wetten auf (+acc); (car) rückwärts fahren // vi (go backwards) rückwärts gehen or fahren // a hintere(r, s) // ad zurück; (to the rear) nach hinten; ~ **down** vi zurückstecken; ~ **out** vi sich zurückziehen; kneifen (col); ~ **up** vt (support) unterstützen; (car) zurücksetzen; (COMPUT) eine Sicherungskopie machen von; ~**bencher** n (Brit) Parlamentarier(in f) m; ~**bone** n Rückgrat nt; (support) Rückhalt m; ~**cloth** n Hintergrund m; ~**date** vt rückdatieren; ~**drop** n (THEAT) = ~**cloth**; (~ground) Hintergrund m; ~**fire** vi (plan) fehlschlagen; (TECH) fehlzünden; ~**ground** n Hintergrund m; (person's education) Vorbildung f; family ~**ground** Familienverhältnisse pl; ~**hand** n (TENNIS: also: ~**hand stroke**) Rückhand f; ~**handed** a (shot) Rückhand-; (compliment) zweifelhaft; ~**hander** n (Brit: bribe) Schmiergeld nt; ~**ing** n (support) Unterstützung f; ~**lash** n (fig) Gegenschlag m; ~**log** n (of work) Rückstand m; ~ **number** n (PRESS) alte Nummer f; ~**pack** n Rucksack m; ~ **pay** n (Gehalts- or Lohn)nachzahlung f; ~ **payments** pl Zahlungsrückstände pl; ~ **seat** n (AUT) Rücksitz m; ~**side** n (col) Hintern m; ~**stage** ad hinter den Kulissen; ~**stroke** n Rückenschwimmen nt; ~**up** a (train) Zusatz-; (plane) Sonder-; (COMPUT) Sicherungs- // n (see a) Zusatzzug m; Sondermaschine f; Sicherungskopie f; ~**ward** a (less developed) zurückgeblieben; (primitive) rückständig; ~**wards** ad rückwärts; ~**water** n (fig) Kaff nt; ~**yard** n Hinterhof m.

bacon ['beɪkən] n Schinkenspeck m.

bacteria [bæk'tɪərɪə] npl Bakterien pl.

bad [bæd] a schlecht, schlimm; to go ~ schlecht werden.

bade [bæd] pt of **bid**.

badge [bædʒ] n Abzeichen nt.

badger ['bædʒə*] n Dachs m.

badly ['bædlɪ] ad schlecht, schlimm; ~ wounded schwerverwundet; he needs it ~ er braucht es dringend; to be ~ off (for money) dringend Geld nötig haben.

badminton ['bædmɪntən] n Federball m, Badminton nt.

bad-tempered ['bæd'tempəd] a schlecht gelaunt.

baffle ['bæfl] vt (puzzle) verblüffen.

bag [bæg] n (sack) Beutel m; (paper) Tüte f; (hand~) Tasche f; (suitcase) Koffer m; (booty) Jagdbeute f; (col: old woman) alte Schachtel f // vt (put in sack) in einen Sack stecken; (hunting) erlegen; ~s of (col: lots of) eine Menge (+acc).

baggage ['bægɪdʒ] n Gepäck nt.

baggy ['bægɪ] a bauschig, sackartig.

bagpipes ['bægpaɪps] npl Dudelsack m.

Bahamas [bə'hɑːməz] npl: the ~ die Bahamas pl.

bail [beɪl] n (money) Kaution f // vt (prisoner: gen: grant ~ to) gegen Kaution freilassen; (boat: also: ~ out) ausschöpfen; on ~ (prisoner) gegen Kaution freigelassen; to ~ sb out die Kaution für jdn stellen; see also **bale**.

bailiff ['beɪlɪf] n Gerichtsvollzieher(in f) m.

bait [beɪt] n Köder m // vt mit einem Köder versehen; (fig) ködern.

bake [beɪk] vti backen; ~**d beans** gebackene Bohnen pl; ~**r** n Bäcker m; ~**ry** n Bäckerei f.

baking ['beɪkɪŋ] n Backen nt; ~ **powder** n Backpulver nt.

balance ['bæləns] n (scales) Waage f; (equilibrium) Gleichgewicht nt; (FIN: state of account) Saldo m; (difference) Bilanz f; (amount remaining) Restbetrag m // vt (weigh) wägen; (make equal) ausgleichen; ~ **of trade/payments** Handels-/Zahlungsbilanz f; ~**d** a ausgeglichen; ~ **sheet** n Bilanz f, Rechnungsabschluß m.

balcony ['bælkənɪ] n Balkon m.

bald [bɔːld] a kahl; (statement) knapp.

bale [beɪl] n Ballen m; to ~ or bail out (from a plane) abspringen.

baleful ['beɪlful] a (sad) unglückselig; (evil) böse.

ball [bɔːl] n Ball m; ~ **bearing** n Kugellager nt.

ballet ['bæleɪ] n Ballett nt; ~ **dancer** n Balletttänzer(in f) m.

balloon [bə'luːn] n (Luft)ballon m.

ballot ['bælət] n (geheime) Abstimmung f.

ball-point (pen) ['bɔːlpɔɪnt('pen)] n Kugelschreiber m.

ballroom ['bɔːlrum] n Tanzsaal m.

balm [bɑːm] n Balsam m.

Baltic ['bɔːltɪk] n: the ~ (Sea) die Ostsee.

balustrade [bæləs'treɪd] n Brüstung f.

bamboo [bæm'buː] n Bambus m.

ban [bæn] n Verbot nt // vt verbieten.

banana [bə'nɑːnə] n Banane f.

band [bænd] n Band nt; (group) Gruppe f; (of criminals) Bande f; (MUS) Kapelle f, Band f // vi (+ together) sich zusammentun.

bandage ['bændɪdʒ] n Verband m; (elastic) Bandage f // vt (cut) verbinden; (broken limb) bandagieren.

bandaid ['bændeɪd] n (US) Heftpflaster nt.

bandwagon ['bændwægən] n: to jump on the ~ (fig) auf den fahrenden Zug aufspringen.

bandy ['bændɪ] vt wechseln; ~(-legged) a o-beinig.

bang [bæŋ] n (explosion) Knall m; (blow) Hieb m // vti knallen.

bangle ['bæŋgl] n Armspange f.

bangs [bæŋz] npl (US: fringe) Pony m.

banish ['bænɪʃ] vt verbannen.

banister(s) ['bænɪstə*(z)] n (pl) (Treppen)geländer nt.

bank [bæŋk] n (raised ground) Erdwall m; (of lake etc) Ufer nt; (FIN) Bank f // vt (tilt: AVIAT) in die Kurve bringen; (money) einzahlen; to ~ on sth mit etw rechnen; ~ **account** n Bankkonto nt; ~ **card** n Scheckkarte f; ~**er** n Bankier m; ~**er's card** n (Brit) = ~ **card**; B~ **holiday** n (Brit) gesetzliche(r) Feiertag m; ~**ing** n Bankwesen nt; ~**note** n Banknote f; ~ **rate** n Banksatz m.

bankrupt ['bæŋkrʌpt] a: to be ~ bankrott sein; to go ~ Pleite machen; ~**cy** n Bankrott m.

bank statement n Kontoauszug m.

banner ['bænə*] n Banner nt.

banns [bænz] npl Aufgebot nt.

baptism ['bæptɪzəm] n Taufe f.

baptize [bæp'taɪz] vt taufen.

bar [bɑ:*] n (rod) Stange f; (obstacle) Hindernis nt; (of chocolate) Tafel f; (of soap) Stück nt; (for food, drink) Buffet nt, Bar f; (pub) Wirtschaft f; (MUS) Takt(strich) m // vt (fasten) verriegeln; (hinder) versperren; (exclude) ausschließen; **behind** ~s hinter Gittern; the B~: to be called to the B~ als Anwalt zugelassen werden; ~ **none** ohne Ausnahme.

barbaric [bɑ:'bærɪk] a primitiv, unkultiviert.

barbecue ['bɑ:bɪkju:] n Barbecue nt.

barbed wire ['bɑ:bd'waɪə*] n Stacheldraht m.

barber ['bɑ:bə*] n Herrenfriseur m.

bar code n (on goods) Registrierkode f.

bare [bɛə*] a nackt; (trees, country) kahl; (mere) bloß // vt entblößen; ~**back** ad ungesattelt; ~**faced** a unverfroren; ~**foot** a, ad barfuß; ~**ly** ad kaum, knapp.

bargain ['bɑ:gɪn] n (sth cheap) günstiger Kauf; (agreement: written) Kaufvertrag m; (: oral) Geschäft nt; into the ~ obendrein; ~ **for** vt: he got more than he ~ed for er erlebte sein blaues Wunder.

barge [bɑ:dʒ] n Lastkahn m; ~ **in** vi

hereinplatzen; ~ **into** vt rennen gegen.

bark [bɑ:k] n (of tree) Rinde f; (of dog) Bellen nt // vi (dog) bellen.

barley ['bɑ:lɪ] n Gerste f; ~ **sugar** n Malzbonbon nt.

barmaid ['bɑ:meɪd] n Bardame f.

barman ['bɑ:mən] n Barkellner m.

barn [bɑ:n] n Scheune f.

barometer [bə'rɒmɪtə*] n Barometer nt.

baron ['bærən] n Baron m; ~**ess** n Baronin f.

barracks ['bærəks] npl Kaserne f.

barrage ['bærɑ:ʒ] n (gunfire) Sperrfeuer nt; (dam) Staudamm m; Talsperre f.

barrel ['bærəl] n Faß nt; (of gun) Lauf m.

barren ['bærən] a unfruchtbar.

barricade [bærɪ'keɪd] n Barrikade f // vt verbarrikadieren.

barrier ['bærɪə*] n (obstruction) Hindernis nt; (fence) Schranke f.

barrister ['bærɪstə*] n (Brit) Rechtsanwalt m.

barrow ['bærəʊ] n (cart) Schubkarren m.

bartender ['bɑ:tendə*] n (US) Barmann or -kellner m.

barter ['bɑ:tə*] vt: to ~ sth for sth um etw handeln.

base [beɪs] n (bottom) Boden m, Basis f; (MIL) Stützpunkt m // vt gründen; (opinion, theory): to be ~d on basieren auf (+dat) // a (low) gemein; ~**ball** n Baseball m; ~**ment** n Kellergeschoß nt.

bases ['beɪsɪz] npl of **basis**; ['beɪsɪz] npl of **base**.

bash [bæʃ] vt (col) (heftig) schlagen.

bashful ['bæʃful] a schüchtern.

basic ['beɪsɪk] a grundlegend; ~**ally** ad im Grunde.

basil ['bæzl] n Basilikum nt.

basin ['beɪsn] n (dish) Schüssel f; (for washing, also valley) Becken nt; (dock) (Trocken)becken nt.

basis ['beɪsɪs], pl **-ses** [-si:z] n Basis f, Grundlage f.

bask [bɑ:sk] vi: to ~ in the sun sich sonnen.

basket ['bɑ:skɪt] n Korb m; ~**ball** n Basketball m.

bass [beɪs] n (MUS, also instrument) Baß m; (voice) Baßstimme f.

bassoon [bə'su:n] n Fagott nt.

bastard ['bɑ:stəd] n Bastard m; (col!) Arschloch nt (!).

bastion ['bæstɪən] n (lit, fig) Bollwerk nt.

bat [bæt] n (SPORT) Schlagholz nt; Schläger m; (ZOOL) Fledermaus f // vt: he didn't ~ an eyelid er hat nicht mit der Wimper gezuckt.

batch [bætʃ] n (of letters) Stoß m; (of samples) Satz m.

bated ['beɪtɪd] a: with ~ **breath** mit an-

gehaltenem Atem.
bath [bɑːθ] *n* Bad *nt*; (~ *tub*)
Badewanne *f*; *see also* **baths** // *vt*
baden; **to have a ~** baden.
bathe [beɪð] *vti* baden; **~r** *n*
Badende(r) *mf*.
bathing [ˈbeɪðɪŋ] *n* Baden *nt*; ~ **cap** *n*
Badekappe *f*; ~ **costume**, (*US*) ~ **suit**
n Badeanzug *m*; ~ **trunks** *npl* (*Brit*)
Badehose *f*.
bathrobe [ˈbɑːθrəʊb] *n* Bademantel *m*.
bathroom [ˈbɑːθrʊm] *n* Bad(ezimmer)
nt.
baths [bɑːðz] *npl* (Schwimm)bad *nt*.
bath towel *n* Badetuch *nt*.
batman [ˈbætmən] *n* (Offiziers)bursche
m.
baton [ˈbætən] *n* (*of police*)
Gummiknüppel *m*; (*MUS*) Taktstock *m*.
batter [ˈbætə*] *vt* verprügeln // *n*
Schlagteig *m*; (*for cake*) Biskuitteig *m*;
~ed *a* (*hat, pan*) verbeult.
battery [ˈbætərɪ] *n* (*ELEC*) Batterie *f*;
(*MIL*) Geschützbatterie *f*.
battle [ˈbætl] *n* Schlacht *f*; (*small*)
Gefecht *nt* // *vi* kämpfen; **~field** *n*
Schlachtfeld *nt*; **~ship** *n* Schlachtschiff
nt.
bawdy [ˈbɔːdɪ] *a* unflätig.
bawl [bɔːl] *vi* brüllen.
bay [beɪ] *n* (*of sea*) Bucht *f* // *vi* bellen;
to keep at a ~ unter Kontrolle halten.
bay window *n* Erkerfenster *nt*.
bazaar [bəˈzɑː*] *n* Basar *m*.
b. & b., B. & B. *abbr of* **bed and
breakfast**.
BBC *n abbr* (= *British Broadcasting
Corporation*) BBC.
B.C. *ad abbr* (= *before Christ*) v. Chr.
be, *pt* **was, were**, *pp* **been** [biː, wɒz,
wɜː*, biːn] ◆*aux v* **1** (*with present
participle: forming continuous tenses*):
what are you doing? was machst du
(gerade)?; **it is raining** es regnet; **I've
been waiting for you for hours** ich warte
schon seit Stunden auf dich
2 (*with pp: forming passives*): **to ~
killed** getötet werden; **the thief was nowhere to ~ seen** der Dieb war nirgendwo
zu sehen
3 (*in tag questions*): **it was fun, wasn't
it?** es hat Spaß gemacht, nicht wahr?
4 (+ *to* +*infinitive*): **the house is to ~
sold** das Haus soll verkauft werden; **he's
not to open it** er darf es nicht öffnen
◆*v* +*complement* **1** (*gen*) sein; **I'm tired**
ich bin müde; **I'm hot/cold** mir ist heiß/
kalt; **he's a doctor** er ist Arzt; **2 and 2
are 4** 2 und 2 ist *or* sind 4; **she's tall/
pretty** sie ist groß/hübsch; ~ **careful/
quiet** sei vorsichtig/ruhig
2 (*of health*): **how are you?** wie geht es
dir?; **he's very ill** er ist sehr krank; **I'm
better now** jetzt geht es mir besser
3 (*of age*): **how old are you?** wie alt bist

du? **I'm sixteen (years old)** ich bin
sechzehn (Jahre alt)
4 (*cost*): **how much was the meal?** was
or wieviel hat das Essen gekostet?;
that'll be £5.75, please das macht £5.75,
bitte
◆*vi* **1** (*exist, occur etc*) sein; **is there a
God?** gibt es einen Gott?; ~ **that as it
may** wie dem auch sei; **so ~ it** also gut
2 (*referring to place*) sein; **I won't ~
here tomorrow** ich werde morgen nicht
hier sein
3 (*referring to movement*): **where have
you been?** wo bist du gewesen?; **I've
been in the garden** ich war im Garten
◆*impers v* **1** (*referring to time, distance, weather*) sein; **it's 5 o'clock** es ist
5 Uhr; **it's 10 km to the village** es sind 10
km bis zum Dorf; **it's too hot/cold** es ist
zu heiß/kalt
2 (*emphatic*): **it's me** ich bin's; **it's the
postman** es ist der Briefträger.
beach [biːtʃ] *n* Strand *m* // *vt* (*ship*) auf
den Strand setzen.
beacon [ˈbiːkən] *n* (*signal*) Leuchtfeuer
nt; (*traffic ~*) Bake *f*.
bead [biːd] *n* Perle *f*; (*drop*) Tropfen *m*.
beak [biːk] *n* Schnabel *m*.
beaker [ˈbiːkə*] *n* Becher *m*.
beam [biːm] *n* (*of wood*) Balken *m*; (*of
light*) Strahl *m*; (*smile*) strahlende(s)
Lächeln *nt* // *vi* strahlen.
bean [biːn] *n* Bohne *f*; ~ **sprouts** *npl*
Sojasprossen *pl*.
bear [bɛə*] *n* Bär *m* // *v* (*pt* **bore**, *pp*
borne) *vt* (*weight, crops*) tragen;
(*tolerate*) ertragen; (*young*) gebären //
vi: **to ~ right/left** sich rechts/links
halten; ~ **out** *vt* (*suspicions etc*) bestätigen; ~ **up** *vi* sich halten.
beard [bɪəd] *n* Bart *m*; **~ed** *a* bärtig.
bearer [ˈbɛərə*] *n* Träger *m*.
bearing [ˈbɛərɪŋ] *n* (*posture*) Haltung *f*;
(*relevance*) Relevanz *f*; (*relation*)
Bedeutung *f*; (*TECH*) Kugellager *nt*; **~s**
pl (*direction*) Orientierung *f*; (**ball**) **~s**
pl (Kugel)lager *nt*.
beast [biːst] *n* Tier *nt*, Vieh *nt*; (*person*)
Bestie *f*; (*nasty person*) Biest *nt*; **~ly** *a*
viehisch; (*col*) scheußlich.
beat [biːt] *n* (*stroke*) Schlag *m*;
(*pulsation*) (Herz)schlag *m*; (*police
round*) Runde *f*, Revier *nt*; (*MUS*) Takt
m; Beat *m* // *vti*, *pt* **beat**, *pp* **beaten**
schlagen; **to ~ it** abhauen; ~ **off** *vt* abschlagen; ~ **up** *vt* zusammenschlagen;
~en *a*: **off the ~en track** abgelegen;
~ing *n* Prügel *pl*.
beautiful [ˈbjuːtɪfʊl] *a* schön; **~ly** *ad*
ausgezeichnet.
beauty [ˈbjuːtɪ] *n* Schönheit *f*; ~ **salon**
n Schönheitssalon *m*; ~ **spot** *n*
Schönheitsfleck *m*; (*Brit*: *TOURISM*)
(besonders) schöne(r) Ort *m*.
beaver [ˈbiːvə*] *n* Biber *m*.

became [bɪˈkeɪm] pt of **become**.

because [bɪˈkɒz] cj weil // prep: ~ **of** wegen (+gen or (col) dat).

beck [bek] n: to be at the ~ and call of sb nach jds Pfeife tanzen.

beckon ['bekən] vt (also: ~ to) ein Zeichen geben (sb jdm).

become [bɪˈkʌm] (irreg: like **come**) vt werden; (clothes) stehen (+dat) // vi werden.

becoming [bɪˈkʌmɪŋ] a (suitable) schicklich; (clothes) kleidsam.

bed [bed] n Bett nt; (of river) Flußbett nt; (foundation) Schicht f; (in garden) Beet nt; to go to ~ zu Bett gehen; **single/double** ~ Einzel/Doppelbett nt; ~ **and breakfast** n Übernachtung f mit Frühstück; ~**clothes** npl Bettwäsche f; ~**ding** n Bettzeug nt.

bedlam ['bedləm] n (uproar) tolle(s) Durcheinander nt.

bedraggled [bɪˈdrægld] a ramponiert.

bedridden ['bedrɪdn] a bettlägerig.

bedroom ['bedrum] n Schlafzimmer nt.

bedside ['bedsaɪd] n: at the ~ am Bett.

bed-sitter ['bed'sɪtə*] n (Brit) Einzimmerwohnung f, möblierte(s) Zimmer nt.

bedspread ['bedspred] n Tagesdecke f.

bedtime ['bedtaɪm] n Schlafenszeit f.

bee [biː] n Biene f.

beech [biːtʃ] n Buche f.

beef [biːf] n Rindfleisch nt; **roast** ~ Roastbeef nt; ~**burger** n Hamburger m.

beehive ['biːhaɪv] n Bienenstock m.

beeline ['biːlaɪn] n: to make a ~ for schnurstracks zugehen auf (+acc).

been [biːn] pp of **be**.

beer [bɪə*] n Bier nt.

beetle ['biːtl] n Käfer m.

beetroot ['biːtruːt] n (Brit) rote Bete f.

before [bɪˈfɔː*] prep vor // cj bevor // ad (of time) zuvor; früher; **the week** ~ die Woche zuvor or vorher; **I've done it** ~ das hab' ich schon mal getan; ~**hand** ad im voraus.

beg [beg] vti (implore) dringend bitten; (alms) betteln.

began [bɪˈgæn] pt of **begin**.

beggar ['begə*] n Bettler(in f) m.

begin [bɪˈgɪn], pt **began**, pp **begun** vti anfangen, beginnen; (found) gründen; to ~ **doing** or to do sth anfangen or beginnen, etw zu tun; to ~ **with** zunächst (einmal); ~**ner** n Anfänger m; ~**ning** n Anfang m.

begun [bɪˈgʌn] pp of **begin**.

behalf [bɪˈhɑːf] n: on ~ of im Namen (+gen); on my ~ für mich.

behave [bɪˈheɪv] vi sich benehmen.

behaviour, (US) **behavior** [bɪˈheɪvjə*] n Benehmen nt.

behead [bɪˈhed] vt enthaupten.

beheld [bɪˈheld] pt, pp of **behold**.

behind [bɪˈhaɪnd] prep hinter // ad (late) im Rückstand; (in the rear) hinten // n (col) Hinterteil nt; ~ **the scenes** (fig) hinter den Kulissen.

behold [bɪˈhəʊld] (irreg: like **hold**) vt (old) erblicken.

beige [beɪʒ] a beige.

being ['biːɪŋ] n (existence) (Da)sein nt; (person) Wesen nt; to come into ~ entstehen.

belated [bɪˈleɪtɪd] a verspätet.

belch [beltʃ] vi rülpsen // vt (smoke) ausspeien.

belfry ['belfrɪ] n Glockenturm m.

Belgian ['beldʒən] a belgisch // n Belgier(in f) m.

Belgium ['beldʒəm] n Belgien nt.

belie [bɪˈlaɪ] vt Lügen strafen (+acc).

belief [bɪˈliːf] n Glaube m (in an +acc); (conviction) Überzeugung f.

believe [bɪˈliːv] vt glauben (+dat); (think) glauben, meinen, denken // vi (have faith) glauben; to ~ **in** sth an etw (acc) glauben; ~**r** n Gläubige(r) mf.

belittle [bɪˈlɪtl] vt herabsetzen.

bell [bel] n Glocke f.

belligerent [bɪˈlɪdʒərənt] a (person) streitsüchtig; (country) kriegsführend.

bellow ['beləʊ] vti brüllen.

bellows ['beləʊz] npl (TECH) Gebläse nt; (for fire) Blasebalg m.

belly ['belɪ] n Bauch m.

belong [bɪˈlɒŋ] vi gehören (to sb jdm); (to club) angehören (+dat); it does not ~ **here** es gehört nicht hierher; ~**ings** npl Habe f.

beloved [bɪˈlʌvɪd] a innig geliebt // n Geliebte(r) mf.

below [bɪˈləʊ] prep unter // ad unten.

belt [belt] n (band) Riemen m; (round waist) Gürtel m // vt (fasten) mit Riemen befestigen; (col: beat) schlagen; ~**way** n (US AUT: ring road) Umgehungsstraße f.

bemused [bɪˈmjuːzd] a verwirrt.

bench [bentʃ] n (seat) Bank f; (workshop) Werkbank f; (judge's seat) Richterbank f; (judges) Richter pl.

bend [bend], pt, pp **bent** vt (curve) biegen; (stoop) beugen // vi sich biegen; sich beugen // n Biegung f; (Brit: in road) Kurve f; ~ **down** or **over** vi sich bücken.

beneath [bɪˈniːθ] prep unter // ad darunter.

benefactor ['benɪfæktə*] n Wohltäter(in f) m.

beneficial [benɪˈfɪʃl] a vorteilhaft; (to health) heilsam.

benefit ['benɪfɪt] n (advantage) Nutzen m // vt fördern // vi Nutzen ziehen (from aus).

Benelux ['benɪlʌks] n Beneluxstaaten pl.

benevolent [bɪˈnevələnt] a wohlwollend.

benign [bɪˈnaɪn] a (person) gütig; (climate) mild.

bent [bent] *pt, pp of* bend // *n* (*inclination*) Neigung *f* // *a* (*col: dishonest*) unehrlich; **to be ~ on** versessen sein auf (+acc).

bequest [bɪ'kwest] *n* Vermächtnis *nt*.

bereaved [bɪ'riːvd] *npl:* **the ~** die Hinterbliebenen *pl*.

bereft [bɪ'reft] *a:* **~ of** bar (+gen).

beret ['berɪ] *n* Baskenmütze *f*.

Berlin [bɜː'lɪn] *n* Berlin *nt*.

berm [bɜːm] *n* (*US AUT*) Seitenstreifen *m*.

Bermuda [bɜː'mjuːdə] *n* Bermuda *nt*.

berry ['berɪ] *n* Beere *f*.

berserk [bə'sɜːk] *a:* **to go ~** wild werden.

berth [bɜːθ] *n* (*for ship*) Ankerplatz *m*; (*in ship*) Koje *f*; (*in train*) Bett *nt* // *vt* am Kai festmachen // *vi* anlegen.

beseech [bɪ'siːtʃ], *pt, pp* besought [-sɔːt] *vt* anflehen.

beset [bɪ'set], *pt, pp* beset *vt* bedrängen.

beside [bɪ'saɪd] *prep* neben, bei; (*except*) außer; **to be ~ o.s.** außer sich sein (with vor +dat); **that's ~ the point** das tut nichts zur Sache.

besides [bɪ'saɪdz] *prep* außer, neben // *ad* außerdem.

besiege [bɪ'siːdʒ] *vt* (*MIL*) belagern; (*surround*) umlagern, bedrängen.

best [best] *a* beste(r, s) // *ad* am besten; **the ~ part** of (*quantity*) das meiste (+gen); **at ~** höchstens; **to make the ~ of it** das Beste daraus machen; **to do one's ~** sein Bestes tun; **to the ~ of my knowledge** meines Wissens; **to the ~ of my ability** so gut ich kann; **for the ~** zum Besten; **~ man** *n* Trauzeuge *m*.

bestow [bɪ'stəʊ] *vt* verleihen.

bet [bet] *n* Wette *f* // *vti, pt, pp* bet *or* betted wetten.

betray [bɪ'treɪ] *vt* verraten.

better ['betə*] *a, ad* besser // *vt* verbessern // *n:* **to get the ~ of sb** jdn überwinden; **he thought ~ of it** er hat sich eines Besseren besonnen; **you had ~ leave** Sie gehen jetzt wohl besser; **to get ~** (*MED*) gesund werden; **~ off** *a* (*richer*) wohlhabender.

betting ['betɪŋ] *n* Wetten *nt*; **~ shop** *n* (*Brit*) Wettbüro *nt*.

between [bɪ'twiːn] *prep* zwischen; (*among*) unter // *ad* dazwischen.

beverage ['bevərɪdʒ] *n* Getränk *nt*.

bevy ['bevɪ] *n* Schar *f*.

beware [bɪ'weə*] *vti* sich hüten vor (+dat); **'~ of the dog'** 'Vorsicht, bissiger Hund!'

bewildered [bɪ'wɪldəd] *a* verwirrt.

bewitching [bɪ'wɪtʃɪŋ] *a* bestrickend.

beyond [bɪ'jɒnd] *prep* (*place*) jenseits (+gen); (*time*) über ... hinaus; (*out of reach*) außerhalb (+gen); // *ad* darüber hinaus; **~ doubt** ohne Zweifel; **~ repair** nicht mehr zu reparieren.

bias ['baɪəs] *n* (*slant*) Neigung *f*; (*prejudice*) Vorurteil *nt*; **~(s)ed** *a* voreingenommen.

bib [bɪb] *n* Latz *m*.

Bible ['baɪbl] *n* Bibel *f*.

bicarbonate of soda [baɪ'kɑːbəneɪt-əv'səʊdə] *n* Natron *nt*.

bicker ['bɪkə*] *vi* zanken.

bicycle ['baɪsɪkl] *n* Fahrrad *nt*.

bid [bɪd] *n* (*offer*) Gebot *nt*; (*attempt*) Versuch *m* // *vti, pt* bade [bæd] *or* bid, *pp* bidden ['bɪdn] *or* bid (*offer*) bieten; **to ~ farewell** Lebewohl sagen; **~der** *n* (*person*) Steigerer *m*; **the highest ~der** der Meistbietende; **~ding** *n* (*command*) Geheiß *nt*.

bide [baɪd] *vt:* **~ one's time** abwarten.

bifocals [baɪ'əfəʊkəlz] *npl* Bifokalbrille *f*.

big [bɪg] *a* groß.

big dipper *n* Achterbahn *f*.

bigheaded ['bɪg'hedɪd] *a* eingebildet.

bigot ['bɪgət] *n* Frömmler *m*; **~ed** *a* bigott; **~ry** *n* Bigotterie *f*.

big top *n* Zirkuszelt *nt*.

bike [baɪk] *n* Rad *nt*.

bikini [bɪ'kiːnɪ] *n* Bikini *m*.

bile [baɪl] *n* (*BIOL*) Galle *f*.

bilingual [baɪ'lɪŋgwəl] *a* zweisprachig.

bill [bɪl] *n* (*account*) Rechnung *f*; (*POL*) Gesetzentwurf *m*; (*US FIN*) Geldschein *m*; **to fit** *or* **fill the ~** (*fig*) der/die/das richtige sein; **'post no ~s'** 'Plakate ankleben verboten'; **~board** *n* Reklameschild *nt*.

billet ['bɪlɪt] *n* Quartier *nt*.

billfold ['bɪlfəʊld] *n* (*US*) Geldscheintasche *f*.

billion ['bɪlɪən] *n* Billion *f*; (*US*) Milliarde *f*.

bin [bɪn] *n* Kasten *m*; (*dust~*) (Abfall)eimer *m*; **litter ~** *n* Abfalleimer *m*.

bind [baɪnd], *pt, pp* bound *vt* (*tie*) binden; (*tie together*) zusammenbinden; (*oblige*) verpflichten; **~ing** *n* (Buch)einband *m* // *a* verbindlich.

binge [bɪndʒ] *n* (*col*) Sauferei *f*.

bingo ['bɪngəʊ] *n* Bingo *nt*.

binoculars [bɪ'nɒkjʊləz] *npl* Fernglas *nt*.

biochemistry ['baɪəʊ'kemɪstrɪ] *n* Biochemie *f*.

biography [baɪ'ɒgrəfɪ] *n* Biographie *f*.

biological [baɪə'lɒdʒɪkəl] *a* biologisch.

biology [baɪ'ɒlədʒɪ] *n* Biologie *f*.

birch [bɜːtʃ] *n* Birke *f*.

bird [bɜːd] *n* Vogel *m*; (*Brit col: girl*) Mädchen *nt*; **~'s-eye view** *n* Vogelschau *f*; **~ watcher** *n* Vogelbeobachter(in *f*) *m*.

Biro ['baɪrəʊ] *n* ® Kugelschreiber *m*.

birth [bɜːθ] *n* Geburt *f*; **to give ~ to** zur Welt bringen; **~ certificate** *n*

Geburtsurkunde f; ~ **control** n
Geburtenkontrolle f; ~**day** n Geburtstag
m; ~**place** n Geburtsort m; ~ **rate** n
Geburtenrate f.
biscuit ['bɪskɪt] n Keks m.
bisect [baɪ'sekt] vt halbieren.
bishop ['bɪʃəp] n Bischof m.
bit [bɪt] pt of **bite** // n bißchen, Stückchen
nt; (horse's) Gebiß nt; (COMPUT) Bit
nt; a ~ tired etwas müde.
bitch [bɪtʃ] n (dog) Hündin f; (unpleasant woman) Weibsstück nt.
bite [baɪt], pt **bit**, pp **bitten** vti beißen //
n Biß m; (mouthful) Bissen m; let's
have a ~ to eat laß uns etwas essen; to
~ one's nails Nägel kauen.
biting ['baɪtɪŋ] a beißend.
bitten ['bɪtn] pp of **bite**.
bitter ['bɪtə*] a bitter; (memory etc)
schmerzlich; (person) verbittert // n
(Brit: beer) dunkles Bier; ~**ness** n
Bitterkeit f.
blab [blæb] vi klatschen // vt (also: ~
out) ausplaudern.
black [blæk] a schwarz; (night) finster //
vt schwärzen; (shoes) wichsen; (eye)
blau schlagen; (Brit INDUSTRY)
boykottieren; to give sb a ~ eye jdm ein
blaues Auge schlagen; in the ~ (bank
account) in den schwarzen Zahlen; ~
and blue a grün und blau; ~**berry** n
Brombeere f; ~**bird** n Amsel f; ~**board**
n (Wand)tafel f; ~**currant** n schwarze
Johannisbeere f; ~**en** vt schwärzen;
(fig) verunglimpfen; ~**ice** n Glatteis nt;
~**jack** n (US) Siebzehn und Vier; ~**leg**
n (Brit) Streikbrecher(in f) m; ~**list** n
schwarze Liste f; ~**mail** n Erpressung f
// vt erpressen; ~ **market** n
Schwarzmarkt m; ~**out** n Verdunklung
f; (MED): to have a ~**out** bewußtlos
werden; **the B~ Sea** n das Schwarze
Meer; ~ **sheep** n schwarze(s) Schaf nt;
~**smith** n Schmied m; ~ **spot** n (AUT)
Gefahrenstelle f; (for unemployment
etc) schwer betroffene(s) Gebiet nt.
bladder ['blædə*] n Blase f.
blade [bleɪd] n (of weapon) Klinge f; (of
grass) Halm m; (of oar) Ruderblatt nt.
blame [bleɪm] n Tadel m, Schuld f // vt
Vorwürfe machen (+dat); to ~ sb for
sth jdm die Schuld an etw (dat) geben;
he is to ~ er ist daran schuld.
bland [blænd] a mild.
blank [blæŋk] a leer, unbeschrieben;
(look) verdutzt; (verse) Blank- // n
(space) Lücke f; Zwischenraum m; (cartridge) Platzpatrone f; ~ **cheque** n
Blankoscheck m; (fig) Freibrief m.
blanket ['blæŋkɪt] n (Woll)decke f.
blare [blɛə*] vi (radio) plärren; (horn)
tuten; (MUS) schmettern.
blasé ['blɑːzeɪ] a blasiert.
blast [blɑːst] n Explosion f; (of wind)
Windstoß m // vt (blow up) sprengen; ~!

(col) verflixt!; ~-**off** n (SPACE)
(Raketen)abschuß m.
blatant ['bleɪtənt] a offenkundig.
blaze [bleɪz] n (fire) lodernde(s) Feuer
nt // vi lodern // vt: ~ **a trail** Bahn brechen.
blazer ['bleɪzə*] n Blazer m.
bleach [bliːtʃ] n (also: household ~)
Bleichmittel nt // vt bleichen.
bleachers ['bliːtʃəz] npl (US SPORT)
unüberdachte Tribüne.
bleak [bliːk] a kahl, rauh; (future)
trostlos.
bleary-eyed ['blɪəriaɪd] a triefäugig;
(on waking up) mit verschlafenen
Augen.
bleat [bliːt] vi blöken; (fig: complain)
meckern.
bleed [bliːd] v (pt, pp **bled** [bled]) vi
bluten // vt (draw blood) zur Ader
lassen; to ~ **to death** verbluten.
bleeper [bliːpə*] n (of doctor etc) Funk-
rufempfänger m.
blemish ['blemɪʃ] n Makel m // vt verun-
stalten.
blend [blend] n Mischung f // vt mischen
// vi sich mischen.
bless [bles], pt, pp **blessed** or **blest**
[blest] vt segnen; (give thanks) preisen;
(make happy) glücklich machen; ~ **you!**
Gesundheit!; ~**ing** n Segen m; (at table) Tischgebet nt; (happiness) Wohltat
f; Segen m; (good wish) Glück nt.
blew [bluː] pt of **blow**.
blight [blaɪt] vt zunichte machen.
blimey ['blaɪmɪ] interj (Brit col) verflucht.
blind [blaɪnd] a blind; (corner)
unübersichtlich // n (for window)
Rouleau nt // vt blenden; ~ **alley** n
Sackgasse f; ~**fold** n Augenbinde f // a,
ad mit verbundenen Augen // vt die
Augen verbinden (sb jdm); ~**ly** ad
blind; (fig) blindlings; ~**ness** n Blind-
heit f; ~ **spot** n (AUT) toter Winkel m;
(fig) schwache(r) Punkt m.
blink [blɪŋk] vi blinzeln; ~**ers** npl
Scheuklappen pl.
bliss [blɪs] n (Glück)seligkeit f.
blister ['blɪstə*] n Blase f // vi Blasen
werfen.
blithe [blaɪð] a munter.
blitz [blɪts] n Luftkrieg m.
blizzard ['blɪzəd] n Schneesturm m.
bloated ['bləʊtɪd] a aufgedunsen; (col:
full) nudelsatt.
blob [blɒb] n Klümpchen nt.
bloc [blɒk] n (POL) Block m.
block [blɒk] n (of wood) Block m, Klotz
m; (of houses) Häuserblock m // vt
hemmen; ~**ade** [blɒ'keɪd] n Blockade f
// vt blockieren; ~**age** n Verstopfung f;
~**buster** n Knüller m; ~ **of flats** n
(Brit) Häuserblock m; ~ **letters** n
Blockbuchstaben pl.

bloke [bləʊk] n (Brit col) Kerl m, Typ m.

blond(e) [blɒnd] a blond // n Blondine f.

blood [blʌd] n Blut nt; ~ **donor** n Blutspender m; ~ **group** n Blutgruppe f; ~ **pressure** n Blutdruck m; ~**shed** n Blutvergießen nt; ~**shot** a blutunterlaufen; ~**stained** a blutbefleckt; ~**stream** n Blut nt, Blutkreislauf m; ~ **test** n Blutprobe f; ~**thirsty** a blutrünstig; ~**y** a (Brit col!) verdammt; (lit) blutig; ~**y-minded** a (Brit col) stur.

bloom [bluːm] n Blüte f; (freshness) Glanz m // vi blühen.

blossom [ˈblɒsəm] n Blüte f // vi blühen.

blot [blɒt] n Klecks m // vt beklecksen; (ink) (ab)löschen; ~ **out** vt auslöschen.

blotchy [ˈblɒtʃɪ] a fleckig.

blotting paper [ˈblɒtɪŋpeɪpə*] n Löschpapier nt.

blouse [blaʊz] n Bluse f.

blow [bləʊ] n Schlag m // v (pt **blew**, pp **blown** [bləʊn]) vt blasen // vi (wind) wehen; to ~ one's nose sich (dat) die Nase putzen; ~ **away** vt wegblasen; ~ **down** vt unwehen; ~ **out** vi ausgehen; ~ **over** vi vorübergehen; ~ **up** vi explodieren // vt sprengen; ~**dry** n: to have a ~**dry** sich fönen lassen // vt fönen; ~**lamp** n (Brit) Lötlampe f; ~**out** n (AUT) geplatzte(r) Reifen m; ~**torch** n = ~**lamp**.

blue [bluː] a blau; (col: unhappy) niedergeschlagen; (obscene) pornographisch; (joke) anzüglich; out of the ~ (fig) aus heiterem Himmel; to have the ~s traurig sein; ~**bell** n Glockenblume f; ~**bottle** n Schmeißfliege f; ~ **film** n Pornofilm m; ~**print** n (fig) Entwurf m.

bluff [blʌf] vi bluffen, täuschen // n (deception) Bluff m; to **call** sb's ~ es darauf ankommen lassen.

blunder [ˈblʌndə*] n grobe(r) Fehler m, Schnitzer m // vi einen groben Fehler machen.

blunt [blʌnt] a (knife) stumpf; (talk) unverblümt // vt abstumpfen.

blur [blɜː*] n Fleck m // vt verschwommen machen.

blurb [blɜːb] n Waschzettel m.

blurt [blɜːt] vt: ~ **out** herausplatzen mit.

blush [blʌʃ] vi erröten // n (Scham)röte f.

blustery [ˈblʌstərɪ] a stürmisch.

boar [bɔː*] n Keiler m, Eber m.

board [bɔːd] n (of wood) Brett nt; (of card) Pappe f; (committee) Ausschuß m; (of firm) Aufsichtsrat m; (SCH) Direktorium nt; (NAUT, AVIAT): **on** ~ an Bord // vt (train) einsteigen in (+acc); (ship) an Bord gehen (+gen); ~ **and lodging** n Unterkunft f und Verpflegung; full/half ~ (Brit) Voll-/Halbpension f; to go by the ~ flachfallen, über Bord

gehen; ~ **up** vt mit Brettern vernageln; ~**er** n Kostgänger m; (SCH) Internatsschüler(in f) m; ~**ing card** n (AVIAT, NAUT) Bordkarte f; ~**ing house** n Pension f; ~**ing school** n Internat nt; ~ **room** n Sitzungszimmer nt.

boast [bəʊst] vi prahlen (about, of mit) // vt sich rühmen (+gen) // n Großtuerei f; Prahlerei f.

boat [bəʊt] n Boot nt; (ship) Schiff nt; ~**er** n (hat) Kreissäge f; ~**swain** [ˈbəʊsn] n = **bosun**.

bob [bɒb] vi sich auf und nieder bewegen; ~ **up** vi auftauchen // n (Brit col) = **shilling**.

bobbin [ˈbɒbɪn] n Spule f.

bobby [ˈbɒbɪ] n (Brit col) Bobby m.

bobsleigh [ˈbɒbsleɪ] n Bob m.

bode [bəʊd] vi: to ~ **well/ill** ein gutes/schlechtes Zeichen sein.

bodily [ˈbɒdɪlɪ] a, ad körperlich.

body [ˈbɒdɪ] n Körper m; (dead) Leiche f; (group) Mannschaft f; (AUT) Karosserie f; (trunk) Rumpf m; ~**guard** n Leibwache f; ~**work** n Karosserie f.

bog [bɒg] n Sumpf m // vt: to get ~ged down sich festfahren.

boggle [ˈbɒgl] vi stutzen; the mind ~s es ist kaum auszumalen.

bogus [ˈbəʊgəs] a unecht, Schein-.

boil [bɔɪl] vti kochen // n (MED) Geschwür nt; to come to the (Brit) or a (US) ~ zu kochen anfangen; to ~ **down to** (fig) hinauslaufen auf (+acc); ~ **over** vi überkochen; ~**ed potatoes** npl Salzkartoffeln pl; ~**er** n Boiler m; ~**er suit** n (Brit) Arbeitsanzug m; ~**ing point** n Siedepunkt m.

boisterous [ˈbɔɪstərəs] a ungestüm.

bold [bəʊld] a (fearless) unerschrocken; (handwriting) fest und klar.

bollard [ˈbɒləd] n (NAUT) Poller m; (Brit AUT) Pfosten m.

bolster [ˈbəʊlstə*] n Polster nt; ~ **up** vt unterstützen.

bolt [bəʊlt] n Bolzen m; (lock) Riegel m // ad: ~ **upright** kerzengerade // vt verriegeln; (swallow) verschlingen // vi (horse) durchgehen.

bomb [bɒm] n Bombe f // vt bombardieren; ~**ard** [bɒmˈbɑːd] vt bombardieren; ~**ardment** [bɒmˈbɑːdmənt] n Beschießung f; ~**shell** n (fig) Bombe f.

bona fide [ˈbəʊnəˈfaɪdɪ] a echt.

bond [bɒnd] n (link) Band nt; (FIN) Schuldverschreibung f.

bondage [ˈbɒndɪdʒ] n Sklaverei f.

bone [bəʊn] n Knochen m; (of fish) Gräte f; (piece of ~) Knochensplitter m // vt die Knochen herausnehmen (+dat); (fish) entgräten; ~ **idle** a stinkfaul.

bonfire [ˈbɒnfaɪə*] n Feuer nt im Freien.

bonnet ['bɒnɪt] *n* Haube *f*; (*for baby*) Häubchen *nt*; (*Brit AUT*) Motorhaube *f*.

bonus ['bəʊnəs] *n* Bonus *m*; (*annual ~*) Prämie *f*.

bony ['bəʊnɪ] *a* knochig, knochendürr.

boo [buː] *vt* auspfeifen.

booby trap ['buːbɪ-] *n* Falle *f*.

book [bʊk] *n* Buch *nt*; (*COMM*): ~s Bücher *pl* // *vt* (*ticket etc*) vorbestellen; (*person*) verwarnen; ~**case** *n* Bücherregal *nt*, Bücherschrank *m*; ~**ing office** *n* (*Brit RAIL*) Fahrkartenschalter *m*; (*Brit THEAT*) Vorverkaufsstelle *f*; ~**-keeping** *n* Buchhaltung *f*; ~**let** *n* Broschüre *f*; ~**maker** *n* Buchmacher *m*; ~**seller** *n* Buchhändler *m*; ~**shop**, ~ **store** *n* Buchhandlung *f*.

boom [buːm] *n* (*noise*) Dröhnen *nt*; (*busy period*) Hochkonjunktur *f* // *vi* dröhnen.

boon [buːn] *n* Wohltat *f*, Segen *m*.

boost [buːst] *n* Auftrieb *m*; (*fig*) Reklame *f* // *vt* Auftrieb geben; ~**er** *n* (*MED*) Wiederholungsimpfung *f*.

boot [buːt] *n* Stiefel *m*; (*Brit AUT*) Kofferraum *m* // *vt* (*kick*) einen Fußtritt geben; (*COMPUT*) laden; **to** ~ (*in addition*) obendrein.

booth [buːð] *n* (*at fair*) Bude *f*; (*telephone* ~) Zelle *f*; (*voting* ~) Kabine *f*.

booty ['buːtɪ] *n* Beute *f*.

booze [buːz] *n* (*col*) Alkohol *m*, Schnaps *m* // *vi* saufen.

border ['bɔːdə*] *n* Grenze *f*; (*edge*) Kante *f*; (*in garden*) (Blumen)rabatte *f* // *a* Grenz-; **the B~s** *Grenzregion f zwischen England und Schottland*; ~ **on** *vt* grenzen an (+*acc*); ~**line** *n* Grenze *f*.

bore [bɔː*] *pt* of **bear** // *vt* bohren; (*weary*) langweilen // *n* (*person*) langweilig(e*r*) Mensch *m*; (*thing*) langweilige Sache *f*; (*of gun*) Kaliber *nt*; **I am ~d** ich langweile mich; ~**dom** *n* Langeweile *f*.

boring ['bɔːrɪŋ] *a* langweilig.

born [bɔːn] *a*: **to be** ~ geboren werden.

borne [bɔːn] *pp* of **bear**.

borough ['bʌrə] *n* Stadt(gemeinde) *f*, Stadtbezirk *m*.

borrow ['bɒrəʊ] *vt* borgen.

bosom ['bʊzəm] *n* Busen *m*.

boss [bɒs] *n* Chef *m*, Boß *m* // *vt*: ~ **around** herumkommandieren; ~**y** *a* herrisch.

bosun ['bəʊsn] *n* Bootsmann *m*.

botany ['bɒtənɪ] *n* Botanik *f*.

botch [bɒtʃ] *vt* (*also*: ~ **up**) verpfuschen.

both [bəʊθ] *a* beide(s); ~ (**of**) **the books** beide Bücher // *pron* beide(s) // *ad*: ~ **X and Y** sowohl X wie *or* als auch Y.

bother ['bɒðə*] *vt* (*pester*) quälen // *vi* (*fuss*) sich aufregen // *n* Mühe *f*, Umstand *m*; **to** ~ **doing sth** sich (*dat*) die Mühe machen, etw zu tun; **what a** ~! wie ärgerlich!

bottle ['bɒtl] *n* Flasche *f* // *vt* (*in Flaschen*) abfüllen; ~ **up** *vt* aufstauen; ~**neck** *n* (*lit, fig*) Engpaß *m*; ~**-opener** *n* Flaschenöffner *m*.

bottom ['bɒtəm] *n* Boden *m*; (*of person*) Hintern *m*; (*riverbed*) Flußbett *nt* // *a* unterste(r, s).

bough [baʊ] *n* Zweig *m*, Ast *m*.

bought [bɔːt] *pt, pp* of **buy**.

boulder ['bəʊldə*] *n* Felsbrocken *m*.

bounce [baʊns] *vi* (*ball*) hochspringen; (*person*) herumhüpfen; (*cheque*) platzen // *vt* (*auf*)springen lassen // *n* (*rebound*) Aufprall *m*; ~**r** *n* Rausschmeißer *m*.

bound [baʊnd] *pt, pp* of **bind** // *n* Grenze *f*; (*leap*) Sprung *m* // *vi* (*spring, leap*) (auf)springen // *a* (*obliged*) gebunden, verpflichtet; **out of** ~**s** Zutritt verboten; **to be** ~ **to do sth** verpflichtet sein, etw zu tun, etw tun müssen; **it's** ~ **to happen** es muß so kommen; **to be** ~ **for ...** nach ... fahren.

boundary ['baʊndərɪ] *n* Grenze *f*.

bouquet [bʊ'keɪ] *n* Strauß *m*; (*of wine*) Blume *f*.

bourgeois ['bʊəʒwɑː] *a* kleinbürgerlich, bourgeois // *n* Spießbürger(in *f*) *m*.

bout [baʊt] *n* (*of illness*) Anfall *m*; (*of contest*) Kampf *m*.

bow *n* [bəʊ] (*ribbon*) Schleife *f*; (*weapon, MUS*) Bogen *m*; [baʊ] (*with head, body*) Verbeugung *f*; (*of ship*) Bug *m* // *vi* [baʊ] sich verbeugen; (*submit*) sich beugen (+*dat*).

bowels ['baʊəlz] *npl* Darm *m*; (*centre*) Innere *nt*.

bowl [bəʊl] *n* (*basin*) Schüssel *f*; (*of pipe*) (Pfeifen)kopf *m*; (*wooden ball*) (Holz)kugel *f* // *vti* (*die Kugel*) rollen; ~**s** *n* (*game*) Bowls-Spiel *nt*.

bow-legged ['bəʊlegɪd] *a* o-beinig.

bowler ['bəʊlə*] *n* Werfer *m*; (*Brit: also*: ~ **hat**) Melone *f*.

bowling ['bəʊlɪŋ] *n* Kegeln *nt*; ~ **alley** *n* Kegelbahn *f*; ~ **green** *n* Rasen *m* zum Bowling-Spiel.

bow tie ['bəʊ'taɪ] *n* Fliege *f*.

box [bɒks] *n* (*also*: **cardboard** ~) Schachtel *f*; (*bigger*) Kasten *m*; (*THEAT*) Loge *f* // *vt* einpacken // *vi* boxen; ~**er** *n* Boxer *m*; ~**ing** *n* (*SPORT*) Boxen *nt*; **B~ing Day** *n* (*Brit*) zweiter Weihnachtsfeiertag; ~**ing gloves** *npl* Boxhandschuhe *pl*; ~**ing ring** *n* Boxring *m*; ~ **office** *n* (Theater)kasse *f*; ~**room** *n* Rumpelkammer *f*.

boy [bɔɪ] *n* Junge *m*.

boycott ['bɔɪkɒt] *n* Boykott *m* // *vt* boykottieren.

boyfriend ['bɔɪfrend] *n* Freund *m*.

boyish ['bɔɪɪʃ] *a* jungenhaft.

B.R. *n abbr of* **British Rail**.

bra [brɑː] *n* BH *m*.

brace [breıs] *n* (*TECH*) Stütze *f*; (*MED*) Klammer *f* // *vt* stützen; **~s** *pl* (*Brit*) Hosenträger *pl*; **to ~ o.s. for sth** (*fig*) sich auf etw (*acc*) gefaßt machen.

bracelet ['breıslıt] *n* Armband *nt*.

bracing ['breısıŋ] *a* kräftigend.

bracken ['brækən] *n* Farnkraut *nt*.

bracket ['brækıt] *n* Halter *m*, Klammer *f*; (*in punctuation*) Klammer *f*; (*group*) Gruppe *f* // *vt* einklammern; (*fig*) in dieselbe Gruppe einordnen.

brag [bræg] *vi* sich rühmen.

braid [breıd] *n* (*hair*) Flechte *f*; (*trim*) Borte *f*.

Braille [breıl] *n* Blindenschrift *f*.

brain [breın] *n* (*ANAT*) Gehirn *nt*; (*intellect*) Intelligenz *f*, Verstand *m*; (*person*) kluge(r) Kopf *m*; **~s** *pl* Verstand *m*; **~child** *n* Erfindung *f*; **~wash** *vt* eine Gehirnwäsche vornehmen bei; **~wave** *n* Geistesblitz *m*; **~y** *a* gescheit.

braise [breız] *vt* schmoren.

brake [breık] *n* Bremse *f* // *vti* bremsen; **~ fluid** *n* Bremsflüssigkeit *f*; **~ light** *n* Bremslicht *nt*.

bramble ['bræmbl] *n* Brombeere *f*.

bran [bræn] *n* Kleie *f*; (*food*) Frühstückflocken *pl*.

branch [brɑːntʃ] *n* Ast *m*; (*division*) Zweig *m* // *vi* (*also:* **~ out**) (*road*) sich verzweigen.

brand [brænd] *n* (*COMM*) Marke *f*, Sorte *f*; (*on cattle*) Brandmal *nt* // *vt* brandmarken; (*COMM*) ein Warenzeichen geben (+*dat*).

brandish ['brændıʃ] *vt* (drohend) schwingen.

brand-new ['brænd'njuː] *a* funkelnagelneu.

brandy ['brændı] *n* Weinbrand *m*, Kognak *m*.

brash [bræʃ] *a* unverschämt.

brass [brɑːs] *n* Messing *nt*; **the ~** (*MUS*) das Blech; **~ band** *n* Blaskapelle *f*.

brassière ['bræsıə*] *n* Büstenhalter *m*.

brat [bræt] *n* ungezogene(s) Kind *nt*, Gör *nt*.

bravado [brə'vɑːdəu] *n* Tollkühnheit *f*.

brave [breıv] *a* tapfer // *n* indianische(r) Krieger *m* // *vt* die Stirn bieten (+*dat*).

bravery ['breıvərı] *n* Tapferkeit *f*.

brawl [brɔːl] *n* Rauferei *f*.

brawn [brɔːn] *n* (*ANAT*) Muskeln *pl*; (*strength*) Muskelkraft *f*.

bray [breı] *vi* schreien.

brazen ['breızn] *a* (*shameless*) unverschämt // *vt*: **~ it out** sich mit Lügen und Betrügen durchsetzen.

brazier ['breızıə*] *n* (*of workmen*) offene(r) Kohlenofen *m*.

Brazil [brə'zıl] *n* Brasilien *nt*; **~ian** *a* brasilianisch // *n* Brasilianer(in *f*) *m*.

breach [briːtʃ] *n* (*gap*) Lücke *f*; (*MIL*) Durchbruch *m*; (*of discipline*) Verstoß *m*

(gegen die Disziplin); (*of faith*) Vertrauensbruch *m* // *vt* durchbrechen; **~ of contract** Vertragsbruch *m*; **~ of the peace** öffentliche Ruhestörung *f*.

bread [bred] *n* Brot *nt*; **~ and butter** Butterbrot *nt*; **~bin**, (*US*) **~box** *n* Brotkasten *m*; **~crumbs** *npl* Brotkrumen *pl*; (*COOK*) Paniermehl *nt*; **~line** *n*: **to be on the ~line** sich gerade so durchschlagen.

breadth [bretθ] *n* Breite *f*.

breadwinner ['bredwınə*] *n* Ernährer *m*.

break [breık] *v* (*pt* **broke,** *pp* **broken**) *vt* (*destroy*) (ab- or zer)brechen; (*promise*) brechen, nicht einhalten // *vi* (*fall apart*) auseinanderbrechen; (*collapse*) zusammenbrechen; (*of dawn*) anbrechen // *n* (*gap*) Lücke *f*; (*chance*) Chance *f*, Gelegenheit *f*; (*fracture*) Bruch *m*; (*rest*) Pause *f*; **~ down** *vt* (*figures, data*) aufschlüsseln; (*undermine*) überwinden // *vi* (*car*) eine Panne haben; (*person*) zusammenbrechen; **~ even** *vi* die Kosten decken; **~ free** or **loose** *vi* sich losreißen; **~ in** *vt* (*animal*) abrichten; (*horse*) zureiten // *vi* (*burglar*) einbrechen; **~ into** *vt* (*house*) einbrechen in (+ *acc*); **~ off** *vi* abbrechen; **~ open** *vt* (*door etc*) aufbrechen; **~ out** *vi* ausbrechen; **to ~ out in spots** Pickel bekommen; **~ up** *vi* zerbrechen; (*fig*) sich zerstreuen; (*SCH*) in die Ferien gehen // *vt* brechen; **~age** *n* Bruch *m*, Beschädigung *f*; **~down** *n* (*TECH*) Panne *f*; (*MED: also:* **nervous ~down**) Zusammenbruch *m*; **~down van** *n* (*Brit*) Abschleppwagen *m*; **~er** *n* Brecher *m*.

breakfast ['brekfəst] *n* Frühstück *nt*.

break-in ['breıkın] *n* Einbruch *m*.

breaking ['breıkıŋ] *n*: **~ and entering** (*JUR*) Einbruch *m*.

breakthrough ['breıkθruː] *n* Durchbruch *m*.

breakwater ['breıkwɔːtə*] *n* Wellenbrecher *m*.

breast [brest] *n* Brust *f*; **~-feed** *vti* (*irreg: like* **feed**) stillen; **~-stroke** *n* Brustschwimmen *nt*.

breath [breθ] *n* Atem *m*; **out of ~** außer Atem; **under one's ~** flüsternd.

breathalyzer ['breθəlaızə*] *n* Röhrchen *nt*.

breathe [briːð] *vti* atmen; **~ in** *vti* einatmen; **~ out** *vti* ausatmen; **~r** *n* Verschnaufpause *f*.

breathing ['briːðıŋ] *n* Atmung *f*.

breathless ['breθlıs] *a* atemlos.

breath-taking ['breθteıkıŋ] *a* atemberaubend.

breed [briːd] *v* (*pt, pp* **bred** [bred]) *vi* sich vermehren // *vt* züchten // *n* (*race*) Rasse *f*, Zucht *f*; **~er** *n* (*person*) Züchter *m*; **~ing** *n* Züchtung *f*; (*up*-

bringing) Erziehung *f*; (*education*) Bildung *f*.

breeze [briːz] *n* Brise *f*.

breezy ['briːzi] *a* windig; (*manner*) munter.

brevity ['breviti] *n* Kürze *f*.

brew [bruː] *vt* brauen; (*plot*) anzetteln // *vi* (*storm*) sich zusammenziehen; **~ery** *n* Brauerei *f*.

bribe [braɪb] *n* Bestechungsgeld *nt* or -geschenk *nt* // *vt* bestechen; **~ry** ['braɪbəri] *n* Bestechung *f*.

bric-a-brac ['brɪkəbræk] *n* Nippes *pl*.

brick [brɪk] *n* Backstein *m*; **~layer** *n* Maurer *m*; **~works** *n* Ziegelei *f*.

bridal ['braɪdl] *a* Braut-.

bride [braɪd] *n* Braut *f*; **~groom** *n* Bräutigam *m*; **bridesmaid** *n* Brautjungfer *f*.

bridge [brɪdʒ] *n* Brücke *f*; (*NAUT*) Kommandobrücke *f*; (*CARDS*) Bridge *nt*; (*ANAT*) Nasenrücken *m* // *vt* eine Brücke schlagen über (+*acc*); (*fig*) überbrücken.

bridle ['braɪdl] *n* Zaum *m* // *vt* (*fig*) zügeln; (*horse*) aufzäumen; **~ path** *n* Reitweg *m*.

brief [briːf] *a* kurz // *n* (*JUR*) Akten *pl* // *vt* instruieren; **~s** *pl* Schlüpfer *m*, Slip *m*; **~case** *n* Aktentasche *f*; **~ing** *n* (genaue) Anweisung *f*; **~ly** *ad* kurz.

brigadier [brɪgə'dɪə*] *n* Brigadegeneral *m*.

bright [braɪt] *a* hell; (*cheerful*) heiter; (*idea*) klug; **~en (up)** *vt* aufhellen; (*person*) aufheitern // *vi* sich aufheitern.

brilliance ['brɪljəns] *n* Glanz *m*; (*of person*) Scharfsinn *m*.

brilliant ['brɪljənt] *a* glänzend.

brim [brɪm] *n* Rand *m*.

brine [braɪn] *n* Salzwasser *nt*.

bring [brɪŋ], *pt*, *pp* **brought** *vt* bringen; **~ about** *vt* zustande bringen; **~ back** *vt* zurückbringen; **~ down** *vt* (*price*) senken; **~ forward** *vt* (*meeting*) vorverlegen; (*COMM*) übertragen; **~ in** *vt* hereinbringen; (*harvest*) einbringen; **~ off** *vt* davontragen; (*success*) erzielen; **~ out** *vt* (*object*) herausbringen; **~ round** *or* **to** *vt* wieder zu sich bringen; **~ up** *vt* aufziehen; (*question*) zur Sprache bringen.

brink [brɪŋk] *n* Rand *m*.

brisk [brɪsk] *a* lebhaft.

brisket ['brɪskɪt] *n* Bruststück *nt*.

bristle ['brɪsl] *n* Borste *f* // *vi* sich sträuben; **bristling with** strotzend vor (+*dat*).

Britain ['brɪtən] *n* (*also:* **Great ~**) Großbritannien *nt*.

British ['brɪtɪʃ] *a* britisch; **the ~** *pl* die Briten *pl*; **the ~ Isles** *pl* die Britischen Inseln *pl*; **~ Rail** *n* die Britischen Eisenbahnen *pl*.

Briton ['brɪtən] *n* Brite *m*, Britin *f*.

brittle ['brɪtl] *a* spröde.

broach [brəʊtʃ] *vt* (*subject*) anschneiden.

broad [brɔːd] *a* breit; (*hint*) deutlich; (*daylight*) hellicht; (*general*) allgemein; (*accent*) stark; **in ~ daylight** am hellichten Tag; **~cast** *n* Rundfunkübertragung *f* // *vti*, *pt*, *pp* **~cast** übertragen, senden; **~en** *vt* erweitern // *vi* sich erweitern; **~ly** *ad* allgemein gesagt; **~-minded** *a* tolerant.

broccoli ['brɒkəlɪ] *n* Brokkoli *pl*.

brochure ['brəʊʃʊə*] *n* Broschüre *f*.

broil [brɔɪl] *vt* (*grill*) grillen.

broke [brəʊk] *pt* of **break** // *a* (*col*) pleite.

broken ['brəʊkən] *pp* of **break** // *a*: **~ leg** gebrochenes Bein; **in ~ English** in gebrochenen Englisch; **~-hearted** *a* untröstlich.

broker ['brəʊkə*] *n* Makler *m*.

brolly ['brɒlɪ] *n* (*Brit col*) Schirm *m*.

bronchitis [brɒŋ'kaɪtɪs] *n* Bronchitis *f*.

bronze [brɒnz] *n* Bronze *f*.

brooch [brəʊtʃ] *n* Brosche *f*.

brood [bruːd] *n* Brut *f* // *vi* brüten.

brook [brʊk] *n* Bach *m*.

broom [bruːm] *n* Besen *m*; **~stick** *n* Besenstiel *m*.

Bros. *abbr of* **Brothers.**

broth [brɒθ] *n* Suppe *f*, Fleischbrühe *f*.

brothel ['brɒθl] *n* Bordell *nt*.

brother ['brʌðə*] *n* Bruder *m*; **~-in-law** *n* Schwager *m*.

brought [brɔːt] *pt*, *pp* of **bring.**

brow [braʊ] *n* (*eyebrow*) (Augen)braue *f*; (*forehead*) Stirn *f*; (*of hill*) Bergkuppe *f*.

brown [braʊn] *a* braun // *n* Braun *nt* // *vt* bräunen; **~ bread** *n* Mischbrot *nt*; **~ie** *n* Wichtel *m*; **~ paper** *n* Packpapier *nt*; **~ sugar** *n* braune(r) Zucker *m*.

browse [braʊz] *vi* (*in books*) blättern; (*in shop*) schmökern, herumschauen.

bruise [bruːz] *n* Bluterguß *m*, blaue(r) Fleck *m* // *vt* einen blauen Fleck geben/ bekommen.

brunt [brʌnt] *n* volle Wucht *f*.

brush [brʌʃ] *n* Bürste *f*; (*for sweeping*) Handbesen *m*; (*for painting*) Pinsel *m*; (*fight*) kurze(r) Kampf *m*; (*MIL*) Scharmützel *nt*; (*fig*) Auseinandersetzung *f* // *vt* (*clean*) bürsten; (*sweep*) fegen; (*gen:* ~ **past**, ~ **against**) streifen; **~ aside** *vt* abtun; **~ up** *vt* (*knowledge*) auffrischen; **~wood** *n* Gestrüpp *nt*.

brusque [bruːsk] *a* schroff.

Brussels sprouts ['brʌslz'spraʊts] *npl* Rosenkohl *m*.

brutal ['bruːtl] *a* brutal.

brute [bruːt] *n* (*person*) Scheusal *nt* // *a*: **by ~ force** mit roher Kraft.

B.Sc. *n abbr of* **Bachelor of Science.**

bubble ['bʌbl] *n* (Luft)blase *f* // *vi* sprudeln; (*with joy*) übersprudeln; **~**

bath n Schaumbad nt; **~gum** n Kaugummi m or nt.

buck [bʌk] n Bock m; (US col) Dollar m // vi bocken; **to pass the ~** (to sb) die Verantwortung (auf jdn) abschieben; **~ up** vi (col) sich zusammenreißen.

bucket ['bʌkɪt] n Eimer m.

buckle ['bʌkl] n Schnalle f // vt (an- or zusammen)schnallen // vi (bend) sich verziehen.

bud [bʌd] n Knospe f // vi knospen, keimen.

Buddhism ['bʊdɪzəm] n Buddhismus m.

budding ['bʌdɪŋ] a angehend.

buddy ['bʌdɪ] n (col) Kumpel m.

budge [bʌdʒ] vti (sich) von der Stelle rühren.

budgerigar ['bʌdʒərɪgaː*] n Wellensittich m.

budget ['bʌdʒɪt] n Budget nt; (POL) Haushalt m // vi: **to ~ for sth** etw einplanen.

budgie ['bʌdʒɪ] n = budgerigar.

buff [bʌf] a (colour) lederfarben // n (enthusiast) Fan m.

buffalo ['bʌfələʊ], pl ~ or ~es n (Brit) Büffel m; (US: bison) Bison m.

buffer ['bʌfə*] n Puffer m; (COMPUT) Pufferspeicher m.

buffet ['bʌfɪt] n (blow) Schlag m; ['bʊfeɪ] (Brit: bar) Imbißraum m, Erfrischungsraum m; (food) (kaltes) Büffet nt // vt ['bʌfɪt] (herum)stoßen; **~ car** n (Brit) Speisewagen m.

bug [bʌg] n (lit, fig) Wanze f // vt verwanzen.

bugle ['bjuːgl] n Jagd- or Bügelhorn nt.

build [bɪld] vt, pt, pp **built** bauen // n Körperbau m; **~ up** vt aufbauen; **~er** n Bauunternehmer m; **~ing** n Gebäude nt; **~ing society** n (Brit) Bausparkasse f.

built [bɪlt] pt, pp of build // a: **~-in** a (cupboard) eingebaut; **~-up area** n Wohngebiet nt.

bulb [bʌlb] n (BOT) (Blumen)zwiebel f; (ELEC) Glühlampe f, Birne f.

Bulgaria [bʌl'gɛərɪə] n Bulgarien nt; **~n** a bulgarisch // n Bulgare m, Bulgarin f; (language) Bulgarisch nt.

bulge [bʌldʒ] n (Aus)bauchung f // vi sich (aus)bauchen.

bulk [bʌlk] n Größe f, Masse f; (greater part) Großteil m; **in ~** (COMM) en gros; **the ~ of** der größte Teil (+gen); **~head** n Schott nt; **~y** a (sehr) umfangreich; (goods) sperrig.

bull [bʊl] n (animal) Bulle m; (cattle) Stier m; (papal) Bulle f; **~dog** n Bulldogge f.

bulldozer ['bʊldəʊzə*] n Planierraupe f.

bullet ['bʊlɪt] n Kugel f.

bulletin ['bʊlɪtɪn] n Bulletin nt, Bekanntmachung f.

bulletproof ['bʊlɪtpruːf] a kugelsicher.

bullfight ['bʊlfaɪt] n Stierkampf m; **~er** n Stierkämpfer m; **~ing** n Stierkampf m.

bullion ['bʊlɪən] n Barren m.

bullock ['bʊlək] n Ochse m.

bullring ['bʊlrɪŋ] n Stierkampfarena f.

bull's-eye ['bʊlzaɪ] n Zentrum nt.

bully ['bʊlɪ] n Raufbold m // vt einschüchtern.

bum [bʌm] n (col: backside) Hintern m; (tramp) Landstreicher m; (nasty person) fieser Kerl m.

bumblebee ['bʌmblbiː] n Hummel f.

bump [bʌmp] n (blow) Stoß m; (swelling) Beule f // vti stoßen, prallen; **~ into** vt stoßen gegen; (person) treffen; **~er** n (AUT) Stoßstange f // a (edition) dick; (harvest) Rekord-; **~er cars** npl (US: dodgems) Autoskooter pl.

bumptious ['bʌmpʃəs] a aufgeblasen.

bumpy ['bʌmpɪ] a holprig.

bun [bʌn] n Korinthenbrötchen nt.

bunch [bʌntʃ] n (of flowers) Strauß m; (of keys) Bund m; (of people) Haufen m.

bundle ['bʌndl] n Bündel nt // vt (also: **~ up**) bündeln.

bungalow ['bʌŋgələʊ] n einstöckige(s) Haus nt, Bungalow m.

bungle ['bʌŋgl] vt verpfuschen.

bunion ['bʌnjən] n entzündete(r) Fußballen m.

bunk [bʌŋk] n Schlafkoje f; **~ beds** npl Etagenbett nt.

bunker ['bʌŋkə*] n (coal store) Kohlenbunker m; (golf) Sandloch nt.

bunny ['bʌnɪ] n (also: **~ rabbit**) Häschen nt.

bunting ['bʌntɪŋ] n Fahnentuch nt.

buoy [bɔɪ] n Boje f; (lifebuoy) Rettungsboje f; **~ up** vt Auftrieb geben (+dat); **~ant** a (floating) schwimmend; (fig) heiter.

burden ['bɜːdn] n (weight) Ladung f, Last f; (fig) Bürde f // vt belasten.

bureau ['bjʊərəʊ], pl **~x** [-z] n (Brit: writing desk) Sekretär m; (US: chest of drawers) Kommode f; (for information etc) Büro nt.

bureaucracy [bjʊ'rɒkrəsɪ] n Bürokratie f.

bureaucrat ['bjʊərəkræt] n Bürokrat(in f) m.

burglar ['bɜːglə*] n Einbrecher m; **~ alarm** n Einbruchssicherung f; **~y** n Einbruch m.

burial ['berɪəl] n Beerdigung f.

burly ['bɜːlɪ] a stämmig.

Burma ['bɜːmə] n Birma nt.

burn [bɜːn] vt (pt, pp **burned** or **burnt**) vt verbrennen // vi brennen // n Brandwunde f; **~ down** vti abbrennen; **~er** n Brenner m; **~ing** a brennend.

burrow ['bʌrəʊ] n (of fox) Bau m; (of rabbit) Höhle f // vt eingraben.

bursar ['bɜːsə*] n Kassenverwalter m, Quästor m; ~y n (Brit) Stipendium nt.

burst [bɜːst] v (pt, pp burst) vt zerbrechen // vi platzen; (into tears) ausbrechen // n Explosion f; (outbreak) Ausbruch m; (in pipe) Bruch(stelle f) m; to ~ into flames in Flammen aufgehen; to ~ into tears in Tränen ausbrechen; to ~ out laughing in Gelächter ausbrechen; ~ into vt (room etc) platzen in (+acc); ~ open vi aufbrechen.

bury ['berɪ] vt vergraben; (in grave) beerdigen.

bus [bʌs] n (Auto)bus m, Omnibus m.

bush [bʊʃ] n Busch m; to beat about the ~ wie die Katze um den heißen Brei herumgehen.

bushy ['bʊʃɪ] a buschig.

busily ['bɪzɪlɪ] ad geschäftig.

business ['bɪznɪs] n Geschäft nt; (concern) Angelegenheit f; it's none of your ~ es geht dich nichts an; to mean ~ es ernst meinen; to be away on ~ geschäftlich verreist sein; it's my ~ to ..., es ist meine Sache, zu ...; ~like a geschäftsmäßig; ~man n Geschäftsmann m; ~ trip n Geschäftsreise f; ~woman n Geschäftsfrau f.

busker ['bʌskə*] n (Brit) Straßenmusikant m.

bus-stop ['bʌsstɒp] n Bushaltestelle f.

bust [bʌst] n Büste f // a (broken) kaputt(gegangen); (business) pleite; to go ~ pleite machen.

bustle ['bʌsl] n Getriebe nt // vi hasten.

bustling ['bʌslɪŋ] a geschäftig.

busy ['bɪzɪ] a beschäftigt; (road) belebt // vi: to ~ o.s. sich beschäftigen; ~body n Übereifrige(r) mf; ~ signal n (US TEL) Besetztzeichen nt.

but [bʌt] ◆cj 1 (yet) aber; not X ~ Y nicht X sondern Y
2 (however): I'd love to come, ~ I'm busy ich würde gern kommen, bin aber beschäftigt
3 (showing disagreement, surprise etc): ~ that's fantastic! (aber) das ist ja fantastisch!
◆prep (apart from, except): nothing ~ trouble nichts als Ärger; no-one ~ him can do it niemand außer ihn kann es machen; ~ for you/your help ohne dich/deine Hilfe; anything ~ that alles, nur das nicht
◆ad (just, only): she's ~ a child sie ist noch ein Kind; had I ~ known wenn ich es nur gewußt hätte; I can ~ try ich kann es immerhin versuchen; all ~ finished so gut wie fertig.

butcher ['bʊtʃə*] n Metzger m; (murderer) Schlächter m // vt schlachten; (kill) abschlachten; ~'s (shop) n Metzgerei f.

butler ['bʌtlə*] n Butler m.

butt [bʌt] n (cask) große(s) Faß nt;

(Brit fig: target) Zielscheibe f; (thick end) dicke(s) Ende nt; (of gun) Kolben m; (of cigarette) Stummel m // vt (mit dem Kopf) stoßen; ~ in vi (interrupt) sich einmischen.

butter ['bʌtə*] n Butter f // vt buttern; ~ bean n Wachsbohne f; ~cup n Butterblume f.

butterfly ['bʌtəflaɪ] n Schmetterling m (SWIMMING: also: ~ stroke) Butterflystil m.

buttocks ['bʌtəks] npl Gesäß nt.

button ['bʌtn] n Knopf m // vti (also: ~ up) zuknöpfen.

buttress ['bʌtrɪs] n Strebepfeiler m; Stützbogen m.

buxom ['bʌksəm] a drall.

buy [baɪ], pt, pp bought vt kaufen // n Kauf m; to ~ sb a drink jdm einen Drink spendieren; ~er n Käufer(in f) m.

buzz [bʌz] n Summen nt // vi summen.

buzzer ['bʌzə*] n Summer m.

buzz word n Modewort nt.

by [baɪ] prep 1 (referring to cause, agent) von, durch; killed ~ lightning vom Blitz getötet; a painting ~ Picasso ein Gemälde von Picasso
2 (referring to method, manner, means): ~ bus/car/train mit dem Bus/Auto/Zug; to pay ~ cheque per Scheck bezahlen; ~ moonlight bei Mondschein; ~ saving hard, he ... indem er eisern sparte, ... er ...
3 (via, through) über (+acc); he came in ~ the back door er kam durch die Hintertür herein
4 (close to, past) bei, an (+dat); a holiday ~ the sea ein Urlaub am Meer; she rushed ~ me sie eilte an mir vorbei
5 (not later than): ~ 4 o'clock bis 4 Uhr; ~ this time tomorrow morgen um diese Zeit; ~ the time I got here it was too late als ich hier ankam, war es schon zu spät
6 (during): ~ day bei Tag
7 (amount): ~ the kilo/metre kiloweise/meterweise; paid ~ the hour stundenweise bezahlt
8 (MATH, measure): to divide ~ 3 durch 3 teilen; to multiply ~ 3 mit 3 malnehmen; a room 3 metres ~ 4 ein Zimmer 3 mal 4 Meter; it's broader ~ a metre es ist (um) einem Meter breiter
9 (according to) nach; it's all right ~ me von mir aus gern
10: (all) ~ oneself etc ganz allein
11: ~ the way übrigens
◆ad 1 see go, pass etc
2: ~ and ~ irgendwann; (with past tenses) nach einiger Zeit; ~ and large (on the whole) im großen und ganzen.

bye-(bye) ['baɪ('baɪ)] interj (auf) Wiedersehen.

by-election ['baɪɪ'lekʃən] n (Brit)

Nachwahl f.
bygone ['baɪɡɒn] a vergangen // n: let
~s be ~s laß(t) das Vergangene vergangen sein.
by(e)-law ['baɪlɔ:] n Verordnung f.
bypass ['baɪpɑ:s] n Umgehungsstraße f
// vt umgehen.
byproduct ['baɪprɒdʌkt] n Nebenprodukt nt.
bystander ['baɪstændə*] n Zuschauer m.
byte [baɪt] n (COMPUT) Byte nt.
byword ['baɪwɜ:d] n Inbegriff m.

C

C [si:] n (MUS): ~ **sharp/flat** Cis, cis nt/
Ces, ces nt.
C. abbr (= centigrade) C.
cab [kæb] n Taxi nt; (of train) Führer-
stand m; (of truck) Führersitz m.
cabaret ['kæbəreɪ] n Kabarett nt.
cabbage ['kæbɪdʒ] n Kohl(kopf) m.
cabin ['kæbɪn] n Hütte f; (NAUT) Kajüte
f; (AVIAT) Kabine f; ~ **cruiser** n
Motorjacht f.
cabinet ['kæbɪnɪt] n Schrank m; (for
china) Vitrine f; (POL) Kabinett nt; ~-
maker n Kunsttischler m.
cable ['keɪbl] n Drahtseil nt, Tau nt;
(TEL) (Leitungs)kabel nt; (telegram)
Kabel nt // vt kabeln, telegraphieren;
~-**car** n Seilbahn f; ~ **television** n
Kabelfernsehen nt.
cache [kæʃ] n geheime(s) (Waffen-/
Proviant)lager nt.
cackle ['kækl] vi gacken.
cactus ['kæktəs], pl **cacti** [-taɪ] n Kaktus
m, Kaktee f.
caddie, caddy ['kædɪ] n (GOLF)
Golfjunge m.
cadet [kə'det] n Kadett m.
cadge [kædʒ] vt schmarotzen.
Caesarean [si:'zɛərɪən] a: ~ (section)
n Kaiserschnitt m.
café ['kæfɪ] n Café nt, Restaurant nt.
cafeteria [kæfɪ'tɪərɪə] n Selbstbedie-
nungsrestaurant nt.
caffein(e) ['kæfi:n] n Koffein nt.
cage [keɪdʒ] n Käfig m // vt einsperren.
cagey ['keɪdʒɪ] a geheimnistuerisch,
zurückhaltend.
cagoule [kə'ɡu:l] n Windhemd nt.
cajole [kə'dʒəʊl] vt überreden.
cake [keɪk] n Kuchen m; (of soap) Stück
nt; ~d a verkrustet.
Cairo ['kaɪərəʊ] n Kairo nt.
calamity [kə'læmɪtɪ] n Unglück nt,
(Schicksals)schlag m.
calcium ['kælsɪəm] n Kalzium nt.
calculate ['kælkjʊleɪt] vt berechnen,
kalkulieren; **calculating** a berechnend;
calculation [-'leɪʃən] n Berechnung f;
calculator n Rechner m.
calculus ['kælkjʊləs] n Rechenart f.

calendar ['kælɪndə*] n Kalender m; ~
month n Kalendermonat m.
calf [kɑ:f], pl **calves** n Kalb nt; (also:
~skin) Kalbsleder nt; (ANAT) Wade f.
calibre, (US) caliber ['kælɪbə*] n
Kaliber nt.
call [kɔ:l] vt rufen; (name) nennen;
(meeting) einberufen; (awaken)
wecken; (TEL) anrufen // vi (shout)
rufen; (visit: also: ~ **in**, ~ **round**) vorbeikommen // n (shout) Ruf m; (TEL)
Anruf m; **to be** ~**ed** heißen; **on** ~ in
Bereitschaft; ~ **back** vi (return) wie-
derkommen; (TEL) zurückrufen; ~ **for**
vt (demand) erfordern, verlangen;
(fetch) abholen; ~ **off** vt (cancel)
absagen; ~ **on** vt (visit) besuchen;
(turn to) bitten; ~ **out** vi rufen; ~ **up**
vt (MIL) einberufen; ~**box** n (Brit)
Telefonzelle f; ~**er** n Besucher(in f) m;
(TEL) Anrufer m; ~ **girl** n Call-Girl nt;
~-**in** n (US: phone-in) Phone-in nt;
~**ing** n (vocation) Berufung f; ~**ing
card** n (US) Visitenkarte f.
callous a ['kæləs] herzlos.
calm [kɑ:m] n Ruhe f; (NAUT) Flaute f
// vt beruhigen // a ruhig; (person)
gelassen; ~ **down** vi sich beruhigen //
vt beruhigen.
Calor gas ['kælə'ɡæs] n ® Propangas
nt.
calorie ['kælərɪ] n Kalorie f.
calve [kɑ:v] vi kalben.
calves [kɑ:vz] pl of **calf**.
camber ['kæmbə*] n Wölbung f.
Cambodia [kæm'bəʊdjə] n Kambodscha
nt.
came [keɪm] pt of **come**.
camel ['kæməl] n Kamel nt.
cameo ['kæmɪəʊ] n Kamee f.
camera ['kæmərə] n Fotoapparat m;
(CINE, TV) Kamera f; **in** ~ unter Ausschluß der Öffentlichkeit; ~**man** n
Kameramann m.
camouflage ['kæməflɑ:ʒ] n Tarnung f //
vt tarnen.
camp [kæmp] n Lager nt // vi zelten,
campen // a affektiert.
campaign [kæm'peɪn] n Kampagne f;
(MIL) Feldzug m // vi (MIL) Krieg
führen; (fig) werben, Propaganda machen; (POL) den Wahlkampf führen.
campbed ['kæmp'bed] n (Brit)
Campingbett nt.
camper ['kæmpə*] n Camper(in f) m;
(vehicle) Camping-wagen m.
camping ['kæmpɪŋ] n: **to go** ~ zelten,
Camping machen.
campsite ['kæmpsaɪt] n Campingplatz
m.
campus ['kæmpəs] n Universitätsgelän-
de nt, Campus m.
can [kæn] n Büchse f, Dose f; (for
water) Kanne f // vt konservieren, in
Büchsen einmachen.

can [kæn] *aux v* (*negative* **cannot,** **can't**; *conditional and pt* **could**) **1** (*be able to, know how to*) können; I ~ see you tomorrow, if you like ich könnte Sie morgen sehen, wenn Sie wollen; I ~ swim ich kann schwimmen; ~ you speak German? sprechen Sie Deutsch? **2** (*may*) können, dürfen; could I have a word with you? könnte ich Sie kurz sprechen?

Canada ['kænədə] *n* Kanada *nt*; **Canadian** [kə'neidiən] *a* kanadisch // *n* Kanadier(in *f*) *m*.

canal [kə'næl] *n* Kanal *m*.

canary [kə'nɛəri] *n* Kanarienvogel *m*.

cancel ['kænsəl] *vt* absagen; (*delete*) durchstreichen; (*train*) streichen; ~**lation** [kænsə'leiʃən] *n* Absage *f*; Streichung *f*.

cancer ['kænsə*] *n* (*also ASTROL*: C~) Krebs *m*.

candid [kændid] *a* offen, ehrlich.

candidate ['kændideit] *n* Kandidat(in *f*) *m*.

candle ['kændl] *n* Kerze *f*; ~**light** *n* Kerzenlicht *nt*; ~**stick** *n* (*also*: ~ holder) Kerzenhalter *m*.

candour, (*US*) **candor** ['kændə*] *n* Offenheit *f*.

candy ['kændi] *n* Kandis(zucker) *m*; (*US*) Bonbons *pl*; ~-**floss** *n* (*Brit*) Zuckerwatte *f*.

cane [kein] *n* (*BOT*) Rohr *nt*; (*stick*) Stock *m* // *vt* (*Brit SCH*) schlagen.

canine ['kænain] *a* Hunde-.

canister ['kænistə*] *n* Blechdose *f*.

cannabis ['kænəbis] *n* Hanf *m*, Haschisch *nt*.

canned [kænd] *a* Büchsen-, eingemacht.

cannibal ['kænibəl] *n* Menschenfresser *m*.

cannon ['kænən] *pl* ~ *or* ~**s** *n* Kanone *f*.

cannot ['kænɒt] = **can not**.

canny ['kæni] *a* schlau.

canoe [kə'nu:] *n* Kanu *nt*.

canon ['kænən] *n* (*clergyman*) Domherr *m*; (*standard*) Grundsatz *m*.

canonize ['kænənaiz] *vt* heiligsprechen.

can opener *n* Büchsenöffner *m*.

canopy ['kænəpi] *n* Baldachin *m*.

can't [ka:nt] = **can not**.

cantankerous [kæn'tæŋkərəs] *a* zänkisch, mürrisch.

canteen [kæn'ti:n] *n* Kantine *f*; (*Brit: of cutlery*) Besteckkasten *m*; (*bottle*) Feldflasche *f*.

canter ['kæntə*] *n* Kanter *m* // *vi* in kurzem Galopp reiten.

canvas ['kænvəs] *n* Segeltuch *nt*; (*sail*) Segel *nt*; (*for painting*) Leinwand *f*; under ~ (*camping*) in Zelten.

canvass ['kænvəs] *vi* um Stimmen werben.

canyon ['kænjən] *n* Felsenschlucht *f*.

cap [kæp] *n* Mütze *f*; (*of pen*) Kappe *f*; (*of bottle*) Deckel *m* // *vt* (*surpass*) übertreffen; (*in sport*) aufstellen.

capability [keipə'biliti] *n* Fähigkeit *f*.

capable ['keipəbl] *a* fähig.

capacity [kə'pæsiti] *n* Fassungsvermögen *nt*; (*ability*) Fähigkeit *f*; (*position*) Eigenschaft *f*.

cape [keip] *n* (*garment*) Cape *nt*, Umhang *m*; (*GEOG*) Kap *nt*.

caper ['keipə*] *n* (*CULIN: gen*: ~s) Kaper *f*; (*prank*) Kapriole *f*.

capital ['kæpitl] *n* (~ *city*) Hauptstadt *f*; (*FIN*) Kapital *nt*; (~ *letter*) Großbuchstabe *m*; ~ **gains tax** *n* Kapitalertragssteuer *f*; ~**ism** *n* Kapitalismus *m*; ~**ist** *a* kapitalistisch // *n* Kapitalist(in *f*) *m*; **to** ~**ize on** *vt* Kapital schlagen aus; ~ **punishment** *n* Todesstrafe *f*.

capitulate [kə'pitjuleit] *vi* kapitulieren.

capricious [kə'priʃəs] *a* launisch.

Capricorn ['kæprikɔ:n] *n* Steinbock *m*.

capsize [kæp'saiz] *vti* kentern.

capsule ['kæpsju:l] *n* Kapsel *f*.

captain ['kæptin] *n* Kapitän *m*; (*MIL*) Hauptmann *m* // *vt* anführen.

caption ['kæpʃən] *n* (*heading*) Überschrift *f*; (*to picture*) Unterschrift *f*.

captivate ['kæptiveit] *vt* fesseln.

captive ['kæptiv] *n* Gefangene(r) *mf* // *a* gefangen(gehalten).

captivity [kæp'tiviti] *n* Gefangenschaft *f*.

capture ['kæptʃə*] *vt* gefangennehmen; (*place*) erobern; (*attention*) erregen // *n* Gefangennahme *f*; (*data* ~) Erfassung *f*.

car [ka:*] *n* Auto *nt*, Wagen *m*; (*RAIL*) Wagen *m*.

carafe [kə'ræf] *n* Karaffe *f*.

caramel ['kærəməl] *n* Karamelle *f*.

carat ['kærət] *n* Karat *nt*.

caravan ['kærəvæn] *n* (*Brit*) Wohnwagen *m*; (*in desert*) Karawane *f*; ~ **site** *n* (*Brit*) Campingplatz *m* für Wohnwagen.

carbohydrate [ka:bəu'haidreit] *n* Kohlenhydrat *nt*.

carbon ['ka:bən] *n* Kohlenstoff *m*; ~ **copy** *n* Durchschlag *m*; ~ **paper** *n* Kohlepapier *nt*.

carburettor, (*US*) **carburetor** ['ka:bjuretə*] *n* Vergaser *m*.

carcass ['ka:kəs] *n* Kadaver *m*.

card [ka:d] *n* Karte *f*; ~**board** *n* Pappe *f*; ~ **game** *n* Kartenspiel *nt*.

cardiac ['ka:diæk] *a* Herz-.

cardigan ['ka:digən] *n* Strickjacke *f*.

cardinal ['ka:dinl] *a*: ~ **number** *n* Kardinalzahl *f* // *n* (*REL*) Kardinal *m*.

card index *n* Kartei *f*; (*in library*) Katalog *m*.

care [kɛə*] *n* (*of teeth, car etc*) Pflege *f*; (*of children*) Fürsorge *f*; (*carefulness*) Sorgfalt *f*; (*worry*) Sorge *f* // *vi*: to ~ about sich kümmern um; ~ **of** (c/o) bei; in sb's ~ in jds Obhut; **I don't** ~ das ist mir egal; I couldn't ~ less es ist mir doch völlig egal; **to take ~** aufpassen; **to take ~ of** sorgen für; **to take ~ to do sth** sich bemühen, etw zu tun; ~ **for** vt sorgen für; (like) mögen.

career [kə'rıə*] n Karriere f, Laufbahn f // vi (also: ~ **along**) rasen.

carefree ['kɛəfriː] a sorgenfrei.

careful ['kɛəful] a sorgfältig; (be) ~! pass auf!

careless a ['kɛəlıs] nachlässig; ~**ness** n Nachlässigkeit f.

caress [kə'res] n Liebkosung f // vt liebkosen.

caretaker ['kɛəteıkə*] n Hausmeister m.

car-ferry ['kɑːferı] n Autofähre f.

cargo ['kɑːgəu], pl ~**es** n Schiffsladung f.

car hire n Autovermietung f.

Caribbean [kærı'biːən] n: **the ~** (Sea) die Karibik.

caricature ['kærıkətjuə*] n Karikatur f.

caring ['kɛərıŋ] a (society, organization) sozial eingestellt; (person) liebevoll.

carnage ['kɑːnıdʒ] n Blutbad nt.

carnal ['kɑːnl] a fleischlich.

carnation [kɑː'neıʃən] n Nelke f.

carnival ['kɑːnıvəl] n Karneval m, Fasching m; (US: fun fair) Kirmes f.

carnivorous [kɑː'nıvərəs] a fleischfressend.

carol ['kærl] n: (**Christmas**) ~ (Weihnachts)lied nt.

carp [kɑːp] n (fish) Karpfen m; ~ **at** vt herumnörgeln an (+dat).

car park n (Brit) Parkplatz m; (covered) Parkhaus nt.

carpenter ['kɑːpıntə*] n Zimmermann m.

carpentry ['kɑːpıntrı] n Zimmerei f.

carpet ['kɑːpıt] n Teppich m // vt mit einem Teppich auslegen; ~ **slippers** npl Pantoffeln pl; ~ **sweeper** n Teppichkehrer m.

carriage ['kærıdʒ] n Kutsche f; (RAIL, of typewriter) Wagen m; (of goods) Beförderung f; (bearing) Haltung f; ~ **return** n (on typewriter) Rücklauftaste f; ~**way** n (Brit: part of road) Fahrbahn f.

carrier ['kærıə*] n Träger(in f) m; (COMM) Spediteur m; ~ **bag** n (Brit) Tragetasche f.

carrot ['kærət] n Möhre f, Karotte f.

carry ['kærı] vti tragen; **to get carried away** (fig) sich nicht mehr bremsen können; ~ **on** vi (continue) weitermachen; (col: complain) Theater machen; ~ **out** vt (orders) ausführen; (investigation) durchführen; ~**cot** n (Brit) Babytragetasche f; ~**-on** n (col: fuss) Theater nt.

cart [kɑːt] n Wagen m, Karren m // vt schleppen.

cartilage ['kɑːtılıdʒ] n Knorpel m.

carton ['kɑːtən] n Karton m; (of milk) Tüte f.

cartoon [kɑː'tuːn] n (PRESS) Karikatur f; (comic strip) Comics pl; (CINE) (Zeichen)trickfilm m.

cartridge ['kɑːtrıdʒ] n Patrone f.

carve [kɑːv] vt (wood) schnitzen; (stone) meißeln; (meat) (vor)schneiden; ~ **up** vt aufschneiden.

carving ['kɑːvıŋ] n Schnitzerei f; ~ **knife** n Tranchiermesser nt.

car wash n Autowäsche f.

cascade [kæs'keıd] n Wasserfall m // vi kaskadenartig herabfallen.

case [keıs] n (box) Kasten m; (Brit: also: suit~) Koffer m; (JUR, matter) Fall m; **in ~ falls,** im Falle; **in any ~** jedenfalls, auf jeden Fall.

cash [kæʃ] n (Bar)geld nt // vt einlösen; ~ **on delivery** (C.O.D.) per Nachnahme; ~ **book** n Kassenbuch nt; ~ **card** n Scheckkarte f; ~ **desk** n (Brit) Kasse f; ~ **dispenser** n Geldautomat m.

cashew [kæ'ʃuː] n (also: ~ **nut**) Cashewnuß f.

cash flow n Cash-flow m.

cashier [kæ'ʃıə*] n Kassierer(in f) m.

cashmere ['kæʃmıə*] n Kaschmirwolle f.

cash register n Registrierkasse f.

casing ['keısıŋ] n Gehäuse nt.

casino [kə'siːnəu] n Kasino nt.

cask [kɑːsk] n Faß nt.

casket ['kɑːskıt] n Kästchen nt; (US: coffin) Sarg m.

casserole ['kæsərəul] n Kasserole f; (food) Auflauf m.

cassette [kæ'set] n Kassette f; ~ **player** n Kassettengerät nt.

cast [kɑːst], pt, pp **cast** vt werfen; (horns) verlieren; (metal) gießen; (THEAT) besetzen; (vote) abgeben // n (THEAT) Besetzung f; (also: **plaster** ~) Gipsverband m; ~ **off** vi (NAUT) losmachen.

castaway ['kɑːstəweı] n Schiffbrüchige(r) mf.

caste [kɑːst] n Kaste f.

casting vote ['kɑːstıŋ-] n (Brit) entscheidende Stimme f.

cast iron n Gußeisen nt.

castle ['kɑːsl] n Burg f; Schloß nt; (chess) Turm m.

castor ['kɑːstə*] n (wheel) Laufrolle f; ~ **oil** n Rizinusöl nt; ~ **sugar** n (Brit) Streuzucker m.

castrate [kæs'treıt] vt kastrieren.

casual ['kæʒjul] a (attitude) nachlässig; (dress) leger; (meeting) zufällig; (work) Gelegenheits-; ~**ly** ad (dress) zwanglos, leger; (remark) beiläufig.

casualty ['kæʒjultı] n Verletzte(r) mf; (dead) Tote(r) mf; (also: ~ **department**) Unfallstation f.

cat [kæt] n Katze f.

catalogue, *(US)* **catalog** ['kætəlɒg] *n*
Katalog *m* // *vt* katalogisieren.

catalyst ['kætəlɪst] *n* Katalysator *m*.

cataract ['kætərækt] *n* *(MED)* graue(r)
Star *m*.

catarrh [kə'tɑ:*] *n* Katarrh *m*.

catastrophe [kə'tæstrəfɪ] *n* Katastrophe
f.

catch [kætʃ] *v* *(pt, pp* **caught***)* *vt*
fangen; *(arrest)* fassen; *(train)* erreichen; *(person: by surprise)* ertappen;
(also: ~ **up***)* einholen // *vi (fire)* in Gang
kommen; *(in branches etc)* hängen-
bleiben // *n* *(fish etc)* Fang *m*; *(trick)*
Haken *m*; *(of lock)* Sperrhaken *m*; to ~
an illness sich *(dat)* eine Krankheit
holen; to ~ **fire** Feuer fangen; ~ **on** *vi*
(understand) begreifen; *(grow popular)*
ankommen; ~ **up** *vi* *(fig)* aufholen.

catching ['kætʃɪŋ] *a* ansteckend.

catchment area ['kætʃmənt-] *n* *(Brit)*
Einzugsgebiet *nt*.

catch phrase ['kætʃfreɪz] *n* Slogan *m*.

catchy ['kætʃɪ] *a* *(tune)* eingängig.

catechism ['kætɪkɪzəm] *n* Katechismus
m.

categoric(al)   *a*   [kætə'gɒrɪk(l)]
kategorisch.

category ['kætɪgərɪ] *n* Kategorie *f*.

cater ['keɪtə*] *vi* versorgen; ~ **for** *vt*
(Brit: party) ausrichten; *(: needs)* eingestellt sein auf *(+acc)*; ~**er** *n*
Lieferant(in *f*) *m* von Speisen und Ge-
tränken; ~**ing** *n* Gastronomie *f*.

caterpillar ['kætəpɪlə*] *n* Raupe *f*; ~
track *n* Gleiskette *f*.

cathedral [kə'θi:drəl] *n* Kathedrale *f*,
Dom *m*.

Catholic ['kæθəlɪk] *a* *(REL)* katholisch;
(tastes etc) **c~** vielseitig // *n* Katholik(in
f) *m*.

cat's-eye   ['kætsaɪ]   *n*   *(Brit AUT)*
Katzenauge *nt*.

cattle ['kætl] *npl* Vieh *nt*.

catty ['kætɪ] *a* gehässig.

caucus ['kɔ:kəs] *n* *(POL)* Gremium *nt*;
(US: meeting) Sitzung *f*.

caught [kɔ:t] *pt, pp of* **catch**.

cauliflower ['kɒlɪflaʊə*] *n* Blumenkohl
m.

cause [kɔ:z] *n* Ursache *f*; *(purpose)* Sache *f* // *vt* verursachen.

causeway ['kɔ:zweɪ] *n* Damm *m*.

caustic ['kɔ:stɪk] *a* ätzend; *(fig)* bissig.

caution ['kɔ:ʃən] *n* Vorsicht *f*; *(warning)* Verwarnung *f* // *vt* verwarnen.

cautious ['kɔ:ʃəs] *a* vorsichtig.

cavalier [kævə'lɪə*] *a* blasiert.

cavalry ['kævəlrɪ] *n* Kavallerie *f*.

cave [keɪv] *n* Höhle *f*; ~ **in** *vi* einstürzen; ~**man** *n* Höhlenmensch *m*.

cavern ['kævən] *n* Höhle *f*.

caviar(e) ['kævɪɑ:*] *n* Kaviar *m*.

cavity ['kævɪtɪ] *n* Loch *nt*.

cavort [kə'vɔ:t] *vi* umherspringen.

C.B. *n abbr* *(= Citizens' Band (Radio))*
CB.

C.B.I. *n abbr* *(= Confederation of British
Industry)* ≈ BDI *m*.

cc *n abbr* *(= cubic centimetres)* cc; *(=
carbon copy)* zk.

cease [si:s] *vi* aufhören // *vt* beenden;
~**fire** *n* Feuereinstellung *f*; ~**less** *a*
unaufhörlich.

cedar ['si:də*] *n* Zeder *f*.

cede [si:d] *vt* abtreten.

ceiling ['si:lɪŋ] *n* Decke *f*; *(fig)* Höchst-
grenze *f*.

celebrate ['selɪbreɪt] *vti* feiern; ~**d** *a*
gefeiert.

celebration [selɪ'breɪʃən] *n* Feier *f*.

celebrity   [sɪ'lebrɪtɪ]   *n*   gefeierte
Persönlichkeit *f*.

celery ['selərɪ] *n* Sellerie *m* or *f*.

celestial [sɪ'lestɪəl] *a* himmlisch.

celibacy ['selɪbəsɪ] *n* Zölibat *nt* or *m*.

cell [sel] *n* Zelle *f*; *(ELEC)* Element *nt*.

cellar ['selə*] *n* Keller *m*.

'cello ['tʃeləʊ] *n* Cello *nt*.

cellophane ['seləfeɪn] *n* ® Cellophan *nt*
®.

cellular ['seljʊlə*] *a* zellular.

cellulose ['seljʊləʊs] *n* Zellulose *f*.

Celt [kelt, selt] *n* Kelte *m*, Keltin *f*; ~**ic**
a keltisch.

cement [sɪ'ment] *n* Zement *m* // *vt*
zementieren; ~ **mixer** *n* Betonmischma-
schine *f*.

cemetery ['semɪtrɪ] *n* Friedhof *m*.

cenotaph ['senətɑ:f] *n* Ehrenmal *nt*.

censor ['sensə*] *n* Zensor *m* // *vt*
zensieren; ~**ship** *n* Zensur *f*.

censure ['senʃə*] *vt* rügen.

census ['sensəs] *n* Volkszählung *f*.

cent [sent] *n* *(US: coin)* Cent *m*; *see also*
per cent.

centenary [sen'ti:nərɪ] *n* Jahrhun-
dertfeier *f*.

center ['sentə*] *n* *(US)* = **centre**.

centi... ['sentɪ] *pref:* ~**grade** *a* Celsius;
~**metre,** *(US)* ~**meter** *n* Zentimeter
nt; ~**pede** *n* Tausendfüßler *m*.

central ['sentrəl] *a* zentral; **C~ America** *n* Mittelamerika *nt*; ~ **heating** *n*
Zentralheizung *f*; ~**ize** *vt* zentralisieren.

centre ['sentə*] *n* Zentrum *nt* // *vt* zen-
trieren; ~**-forward** *n* *(SPORT)* Mittel-
stürmer *m*; ~**-half** *n* *(SPORT)* Stopper
m.

century ['sentjʊrɪ] *n* Jahrhundert *nt*.

ceramic [sɪ'ræmɪk] *a* keramisch; ~**s** *npl*
Keramiken *pl*.

cereal ['sɪərɪəl] *n* *(grain)* Getreide *nt*;
(at breakfast) Getreideflocken *pl*.

cerebral ['serɪbrəl] *a* zerebral;
(intellectual) geistig.

ceremony ['serɪmənɪ] *n*; Zeremonie *f*;
to stand on ~ förmlich sein.

certain ['sɜ:tən] *a* sicher; *(particular)*
gewiß; **for** ~ ganz bestimmt; ~**ly** *ad* si-

cher, bestimmt; **~ty** n Gewißheit f.

certificate [sə'tıfıkıt] n Bescheinigung f; (SCH etc) Zeugnis nt.

certified ['sɜːtıfaıd] a: ~ **mail** n (US) Einschreiben nt; ~ **public accountant** n (US) geprüfter Buchhalter.

certify ['sɜːtıfaı] vt bescheinigen.

cervical ['sɜːvıkl] a (smear, cancer) Gebärmutterhals-.

cervix ['sɜːvıks] n Gebärmutterhals m.

cessation [se'seıʃən] n Einstellung f, Ende nt.

cesspit ['sespıt] n Senkgrube f.

c.f. abbr (= compare) vgl.

ch. abbr (= chapter) Kap.

chafe [tʃeıf] vt scheuern.

chaffinch ['tʃæfıntʃ] n Buchfink m.

chagrin ['ʃægrın] n Verdruß m.

chain [tʃeın] n Kette f // vt (also: ~ up) anketten; ~ **reaction** n Kettenreaktion f; ~**-smoke** vi kettenrauchen; ~ **store** n Kettenladen m.

chair [tʃɛə*] n Stuhl m; (arm~) Sessel m; (UNIV) Lehrstuhl m // vt (meeting) den Vorsitz führen bei; **~lift** n Sessellift m; **~man** n Vorsitzende(r) m.

chalet ['ʃæleı] n Chalet m.

chalice ['tʃælıs] n Kelch m.

chalk ['tʃɔːk] n Kreide f.

challenge ['tʃælındʒ] n Herausforderung f // vt herausfordern; (contest) bestreiten.

challenging ['tʃælındʒıŋ] a (tone) herausfordernd; (work) anspruchsvoll.

chamber ['tʃeımbə*] n Kammer f; ~ **of commerce** n Handelskammer f; **~maid** n Zimmermädchen nt; ~ **music** n Kammermusik f.

chamois ['ʃæmwɑː] n Gemse f.

champagne [ʃæm'peın] n Champagner m, Sekt m.

champion ['tʃæmpıən] n (SPORT) Meister(in f) m; (of cause) Verfechter(in f) m; **~ship** n Meisterschaft f.

chance [tʃɑːns] n (luck) Zufall m; (possibility) Möglichkeit f; (opportunity) Gelegenheit f, Chance f; (risk) Risiko nt // a zufällig // vt: to ~ it es darauf ankommen lassen; **by** ~ zufällig; **to take a** ~ ein Risiko eingehen.

chancellor ['tʃɑːnsələ*] n Kanzler m; **C~ of the Exchequer** n (Brit) Schatzkanzler m.

chandelier [ʃændı'lıə*] n Kronleuchter m.

change [tʃeındʒ] vt ändern; (replace, COMM: money) wechseln; (exchange) umtauschen; (transform) verwandeln // vi sich ändern; (~ trains) umsteigen; (~ clothes) sich umziehen; (be transformed): **to** ~ **into sth** sich in etw (acc) verwandeln // n Veränderung f; (money returned) Wechselgeld nt; (coins) Kleingeld nt; **to** ~ **one's mind** es sich (dat) anders überlegen; **for a** ~ zur

Abwechslung; **~able** a (weather) wechselhaft; ~ **machine** n Geldwechselautomat m; **~over** n Umstellung f.

changing ['tʃeındʒıŋ] a veränderlich; ~ **room** n (Brit) Umkleideraum m.

channel ['tʃænl] n (stream) Bachbett nt; (NAUT) Straße f; (TV) Kanal m; (fig) Weg m // vt (efforts) lenken; **the (English) C~** der Ärmelkanal; **the C~ Islands** npl die Kanalinseln pl.

chant [tʃɑːnt] n Gesang m; (of football fans etc) Sprechchor m // vt intonieren.

chaos ['keıɒs] n Chaos nt.

chap [tʃæp] n (col) Kerl m.

chapel ['tʃæpəl] n Kapelle f.

chaperon ['ʃæpərəʊn] n Anstandsdame f.

chaplain ['tʃæplın] n Kaplan m.

chapped ['tʃæpt] a (skin, lips) spröde.

chapter ['tʃæptə*] n Kapitel nt.

char [tʃɑː*] vt (burn) verkohlen // n (Brit) = **charlady**.

character ['kærıktə*] n Charakter m, Wesen nt; (in novel, film) Figur f; (in writing) Schriftzeichen nt; **~istic** [kærıktə'rıstık] a charakteristisch (of für) // n Kennzeichen nt; **~ize** vt charakterisieren, kennzeichnen.

charade [ʃə'rɑːd] n Scharade f.

charcoal ['tʃɑːkəʊl] n Holzkohle f.

charge [tʃɑːdʒ] n (cost) Preis m; (JUR) Anklage f; (explosive) Ladung f; (attack) Angriff m // vt (gun, battery) laden; (price) verlangen; (JUR) anklagen; (MIL) angreifen // vi (rush) (an)stürmen; **bank ~s** pl Bankgebühren pl; **free of** ~ kostenlos; **to reverse the ~s** (TEL) ein R-Gespräch führen; **to be in** ~ of verantwortlich sein für; **to take** ~ (die Verantwortung) übernehmen; **to** ~ **sth (up) to sb's account** jdm etw in Rechnung stellen; ~ **card** n Kundenkarte f.

charitable ['tʃærıtəbl] a wohltätig; (lenient) nachsichtig.

charity ['tʃærıtı] n (institution) Hilfswerk nt; (attitude) Nächstenliebe f.

charlady ['tʃɑːleıdı] n (Brit) Putzfrau f.

charlatan ['ʃɑːlətən] n Scharlatan m.

charm [tʃɑːm] n Charme m; (spell) Bann m; (object) Talisman m // vt bezaubern; **~ing** a reizend.

chart [tʃɑːt] n Tabelle f; (NAUT) Seekarte f // vt (course) abstecken.

charter ['tʃɑːtə*] vt chartern // n Schutzbrief m; **~ed accountant** n Wirtschaftsprüfer(in f) m; ~ **flight** n Charterflug m.

charwoman ['tʃɑːwʊmən] n = **charlady**.

chase [tʃeıs] vt jagen, verfolgen // n Jagd f.

chasm ['kæzəm] n Kluft f.

chassis ['ʃæsı] n Fahrgestell nt.

chastity ['tʃæstıtı] n Keuschheit f.

chat [tʃæt] *vi* (*also*: **have a ~**) plaudern // *n* Plauderei *f*; **~ show** *n* (*Brit*) Talkshow *f*.

chatter [ˈtʃætə*] *vi* schwatzen; (*teeth*) klappern // *n* Geschwätz *nt*; **~box** *n* Quasselstrippe *f*.

chatty [ˈtʃætɪ] *a* geschwätzig.

chauffeur [ˈʃəufə*] *n* Chauffeur *m*.

chauvinist [ˈʃəuvɪnɪst] *n* (*male ~*) Chauvi *m* (*col*); (*nationalist*) Chauvinist(in *f*) *m*.

cheap [tʃiːp] *a*, *ad* billig; **~ly** *ad* billig.

cheat [tʃiːt] *vti* betrügen; (*SCH*) mogeln // *n* Betrüger(in *f*) *m*.

check [tʃek] *vt* (*examine*) prüfen; (*make sure*) nachsehen; (*control*) kontrollieren; (*restrain*) zügeln; (*stop*) anhalten // *n* (*examination, restraint*) Kontrolle *f*; (*bill*) Rechnung *f*; (*pattern*) Karo(muster) *nt*; (*US*) = **cheque**; // *a* (*pattern, cloth*) kariert; **~ in** *vi* (*in hotel, airport*) einchecken // *vt* (*luggage*) abfertigen lassen; **~ out** *vi* (*of hotel*) abreisen; **~ up** *vi* nachschauen; **~ up on** *vt* kontrollieren; **~ered** *a* (*US*) = **chequered**; **~ers** *n* (*US*: *draughts*) Damespiel *nt*; **~-in** (**desk**) *n* Abfertigung *f*; **~ing account** *n* (*US*: *current account*) Girokonto *nt*; **~mate** *n* Schachmatt *nt*; **~out** *n* Kasse *f*; **~point** *n* Kontrollpunkt *m*; **~ room** *n* (*US*: *left-luggage office*) Gepäckaufbewahrung *f*; **~up** *n* (Nach)prüfung *f*; (*MED*) (ärztliche) Untersuchung *f*.

cheek [tʃiːk] *n* Backe *f*; (*fig*) Frechheit *f*; **~bone** *n* Backenknochen *m*; **~y** *a* frech.

cheep [tʃiːp] *vi* piepsen.

cheer [tʃɪə*] *n* Beifallsruf *m*; **~s** Hurrarufe *pl*; **~s!** Prost! // *vt* zujubeln; (*encourage*) aufmuntern // *vi* jauchzen; **~ up** *vi* bessere Laune bekommen // *vt* aufmuntern; **~ up!** nun lach doch mal!; **~ful** *a* fröhlich.

cheerio [ˈtʃɪərɪˈəu] *excl* (*Brit*) tschüs!

cheese [tʃiːz] *n* Käse *m*; **~board** *n* (gemischte) Käseplatte *f*.

cheetah [ˈtʃiːtə] *n* Gepard *m*.

chef [ʃef] *n* Küchenchef *m*.

chemical [ˈkemɪkəl] *a* chemisch // *n* Chemikalie *f*.

chemist [ˈkemɪst] *n* (*Brit*: *pharmacist*) Apotheker *m*, Drogist *m*; (*scientist*) Chemiker *m*; **~ry** *n* Chemie *f*; **~'s** (**shop**) *n* (*Brit*) Apotheke *f*, Drogerie *f*.

cheque [tʃek] *n* (*Brit*) Scheck *m*; **~book** *n* Scheckbuch *nt*; **~ card** *n* Scheckkarte *f*.

chequered [ˈtʃekəd] *a* (*fig*) bewegt.

cherish [ˈtʃerɪʃ] *vt* (*person*) lieben; (*hope*) hegen.

cherry [ˈtʃerɪ] *n* Kirsche *f*.

chess [tʃes] *n* Schach *nt*; **~board** *n* Schachbrett *nt*; **~man** *n* Schachfigur *f*.

chest [tʃest] *n* (*ANAT*) Brust *f*; (*box*) Ki- ste *f*; **~ of drawers** *n* Kommode *f*.

chestnut [ˈtʃesnʌt] *n* Kastanie *f*; **~ (tree)** *n* Kastanienbaum *m*.

chew [tʃuː] *vti* kauen; **~ing gum** *n* Kaugummi *m*.

chic [ʃiːk] *a* schick, elegant.

chick [tʃɪk] *n* Küken *nt*; (*US col*: *girl*) Biene *f*.

chicken [ˈtʃɪkɪn] *n* Huhn *nt*; (*food*) Hähnchen *nt* // **~ out** *vi* (*col*) kneifen (*col*).

chickenpox [ˈtʃɪkɪnpɒks] *n* Windpocken *pl*.

chicory [ˈtʃɪkərɪ] *n* (*in coffee*) Zichorie *f*; (*plant*) Chicorée *f*.

chief [tʃiːf] *n* (*of tribe*) Häuptling *m*; (*COMM*) Chef *m* // *a* Haupt-; **~ executive** *n* Geschäftsführer(in *f*) *m*; **~ly** *ad* hauptsächlich.

chiffon [ˈʃɪfɒn] *n* Chiffon *m*.

chilblain [ˈtʃɪlbleɪn] *n* Frostbeule *f*.

child [tʃaɪld], *pl* **~ren** [ˈtʃɪldrən] *n* Kind *nt*; **~birth** *n* Entbindung *f*; **~hood** *n* Kindheit *f*; **~ish** *a* kindisch; **~like** *a* kindlich; **~ minder** *n* (*Brit*) Tagesmutter *f*.

Chile [ˈtʃɪlɪ] *n* Chile *nt*; **~an** *a* chilenisch.

chill [tʃɪl] *n* Kühle *f*; (*MED*) Erkältung *f* // *vt* (*CULIN*) kühlen.

chilli [ˈtʃɪlɪ] *n* Peperoni *pl*; (*meal, spice*) Chili *m*.

chilly [ˈtʃɪlɪ] *a* kühl, frostig.

chime [tʃaɪm] *n* Geläut *nt* // *vi* ertönen.

chimney [ˈtʃɪmnɪ] *n* Schornstein *m*; **~ sweep** *n* Schornsteinfeger(in *f*) *m*.

chimpanzee [tʃɪmpænˈziː] *n* Schimpanse *m*.

chin [tʃɪn] *n* Kinn *nt*.

china [ˈtʃaɪnə] *n* Porzellan *nt*.

China [ˈtʃaɪnə] *n* China *nt*; **Chinese** [tʃaɪˈniːz] *a* chinesisch // *n*, *pl inv* Chinese *m*, Chinesin *f*; (*LING*) Chinesisch.

chink [tʃɪŋk] *n* (*opening*) Ritze *f*; (*noise*) Klirren *nt*.

chip [tʃɪp] *n* (*of wood etc*) Splitter *m*; (*gen pl*: *CULIN*) Pommes frites *pl*; (*in poker etc*; *US*: *crisp*) Chip *m* // *vt* absplittern; **~ in** *vi* Zwischenbemerkungen machen.

chiropodist [kɪˈrɒpədɪst] *n* (*Brit*) Fußpfleger(in *f*) *m*.

chirp [tʃɜːp] *vi* zwitschern.

chisel [ˈtʃɪzl] *n* Meißel *m*.

chit [tʃɪt] *n* Notiz *f*.

chitchat [ˈtʃɪttʃæt] *n* Plauderei *f*.

chivalrous [ˈʃɪvəlrəs] *a* ritterlich.

chivalry [ˈʃɪvəlrɪ] *n* Ritterlichkeit *f*.

chives [tʃaɪvz] *npl* Schnittlauch *m*.

chlorine [ˈklɔːriːn] *n* Chlor *nt*.

chock [tʃɒk] *n*: **~-a-block**, **~-full** *a* vollgepfropft.

chocolate [ˈtʃɒklɪt] *n* Schokolade *f*.

choice [tʃɔɪs] *n* Wahl *f*; (*of goods*) Aus-

wahl f // a Qualitäts-.
choir ['kwaɪə*] n Chor m; **~boy** n
Chorknabe m.
choke [tʃəʊk] vi ersticken // vt erdrosseln; (block) (ab)drosseln // n (AUT)
Starterklappe f.
cholera ['kɒlərə] n Cholera f.
cholesterol [kɒ'lestərəl] n Cholesterin
nt.
choose [tʃuːz], pt chose, pp chosen vt
wählen.
choosy ['tʃuːzi] a wählerisch.
chop [tʃɒp] vt (wood) spalten; (CULIN:
also: ~ up) (zer)hacken // n Hieb m;
(CULIN) Kotelett nt; **~s** pl (jaws)
Lefzen pl.
chopper ['tʃɒpə*] n (helicopter)
Hubschrauber m.
choppy ['tʃɒpi] a (sea) bewegt.
chopsticks ['tʃɒpstɪks] npl (Eß)stäb-
chen pl.
choral ['kɔːrəl] a Chor-.
chord [kɔːd] n Akkord m.
chore [tʃɔː*] n Pflicht f; **~s** pl
Hausarbeit f.
choreographer [kɒrɪ'ɒgrəfə*] n Choreo-
graph(in f) m.
chorister ['kɒrɪstə*] n Chorsänger(in f)
m.
chortle ['tʃɔːtl] vi glucksen.
chorus ['kɔːrəs] n Chor m; (in song) Refrain m.
chose [tʃəʊz], **chosen** ['tʃəʊzn] pt, pp
of **choose**.
Christ [kraɪst] n Christus m.
christen ['krɪsn] vt taufen.
Christian ['krɪstɪən] a christlich // n
Christ(in f) m; **~ity** [krɪstɪ'ænɪtɪ] n
Christentum nt; **~ name** n Vorname m.
Christmas ['krɪsməs] n Weihnachten pl;
~ card n Weihnachtskarte f; **~ Day** n
der erste Weihnachtstag; **~ Eve** n
Heiligabend m; **~ tree** n
Weihnachtsbaum m.
chrome [krəʊm] n = **chromium**
plating.
chromium ['krəʊmɪəm] n Chrom nt; **~
plating** n Verchromung f.
chronic ['krɒnɪk] a chronisch.
chronicle ['krɒnɪkl] n Chronik f.
chronological [krɒnə'lɒdʒɪkəl] a
chronologisch.
chubby ['tʃʌbɪ] a rundlich.
chuck [tʃʌk] vt werfen; **~ out** vt
(person) rauswerfen; (old clothes etc)
wegwerfen; **~ (up)** vt (Brit) hinwerfen.
chuckle ['tʃʌkl] vi in sich hineinlachen.
chug [tʃʌg] vi tuckern.
chum [tʃʌm] n Kumpel m.
chunk [tʃʌŋk] n Klumpen m; (of food)
Brocken m.
church [tʃɜːtʃ] n Kirche f; **~yard** n
Kirchhof m.
churlish ['tʃɜːlɪʃ] a grob.
churn [tʃɜːn] n (for butter) Butterfaß nt;

(for milk) Milchkanne f; **~ out** vt (col)
produzieren.
chute [ʃuːt] n Rutsche f; (rubbish ~)
Müllschlucker m.
CIA n abbr (US: = Central Intelligence
Agency) CIA m.
CID n abbr (Brit: = Criminal Investigation Department) Kripo f.
cider ['saɪdə*] n Apfelwein m.
cigar [sɪ'gɑː*] n Zigarre f.
cigarette [sɪgə'ret] n Zigarette f; **~
case** n Zigarettenetui nt; **~ end** n
Zigarettenstummel m; **~ holder** n
Zigarettenspitze f.
Cinderella [sɪndə'relə] n Aschenbrödel
nt.
cinders ['sɪndəz] npl Asche f.
cine ['sɪnɪ]: **~-camera** n (Brit)
Filmkamera f; **~-film** n (Brit)
Schmalfilm m.
cinema ['sɪnəmə] n Kino nt.
cinnamon ['sɪnəmən] n Zimt m.
cipher ['saɪfə*] n (code) Chiffre f.
circle ['sɜːkl] n Kreis m; (in cinema)
Rang m // vi kreisen // vt (surround) umgeben; (move round) kreisen um.
circuit ['sɜːkɪt] n (track) Rennbahn f;
(lap) Runde f; (ELEC) Stromkreis m;
~ous [sɜː'kjuːɪtəs] a weitschweifig.
circular ['sɜːkjʊlə*] a rund // n
Rundschreiben nt.
circulate ['sɜːkjʊleɪt] vi zirkulieren // vt
in Umlauf setzen; **circulation** [-'leɪʃən]
n (of blood) Kreislauf m; (of newspaper)
Auflage f; (of money) Umlauf m.
circumcise ['sɜːkəmsaɪz] vt be-
schneiden.
circumference [sə'kʌmfərəns] n
(Kreis)umfang m.
circumspect ['sɜːkəmspekt] a umsichtig.
circumstances ['sɜːkəmstənsəz] npl
Umstände pl; (financial condition) Verhältnisse pl.
circumvent [sɜːkəm'vent] vt umgehen.
circus ['sɜːkəs] n Zirkus m.
cistern ['sɪstən] n Zisterne f; (of W.C.)
Spülkasten m.
cite [saɪt] vt zitieren, anführen.
citizen ['sɪtɪzn] n Bürger(in f) m; **~ship**
n Staatsbürgerschaft f.
citrus ['sɪtrəs] a: **~ fruit** n Zitrusfrucht
f.
city ['sɪtɪ] n Großstadt f; **the C~** die City,
das Finanzzentrum Londons.
civic ['sɪvɪk] a (of town) städtisch; (of
citizen) Bürger-; **~ centre** n
Stadtverwaltung f.
civil ['sɪvɪl] a bürgerlich; (not military)
zivil; (polite) höflich; **~ engineer** n
Bauingenieur m; **~ian** [sɪ'vɪlɪən] n
Zivilperson f // a zivil, Zivil-.
civilization [sɪvɪlaɪ'zeɪʃən] n Zivilisation
f.
civilized a zivilisiert.

civil: ~ **law** n Zivilrecht nt; ~ **servant** n Staatsbeamte(r) m; **C~ Service** n Staatsdienst m; ~ **war** n Bürgerkrieg m.

clad [klæd] a: ~ **in** gehüllt in (+acc).

claim [kleɪm] vt beanspruchen; (have opinion) behaupten // vi (for insurance) Ansprüche geltend machen // n (demand) Forderung f; (right) Anspruch m; (pretension) Behauptung f; ~**ant** n Antragsteller(in f) m.

clairvoyant [klɛə'vɔɪənt] n Hellseher(in f) m.

clam [klæm] n Venusmuschel f.

clamber ['klæmbə*] vi kraxeln.

clammy ['klæmɪ] a klamm.

clamour ['klæmə*] vi: **to** ~ **for** nach etw verlangen.

clamp [klæmp] n Schraubzwinge f // vt einspannen; ~ **down on** vt Maßnahmen ergreifen gegen.

clan [klæn] n Clan m.

clandestine [klæn'destɪn] a geheim.

clang [klæŋ] vi scheppern.

clap [klæp] vi Klatschen // vt Beifall klatschen (+dat) // n (of hands) Klatschen nt; (of thunder) Donnerschlag m; ~**ping** n Klatschen nt.

claret ['klærɪt] n rote(r) Bordeaux(wein) m.

clarify ['klærɪfaɪ] vt klären, erklären.

clarinet [klærɪ'net] n Klarinette f.

clarity ['klærɪtɪ] n Klarheit f.

clash [klæʃ] n (fig) Konflikt m // vi zusammenprallen; (colours) sich beißen; (argue) sich streiten.

clasp [klɑːsp] n Griff m; (on jewels, bag) Verschluß m // vt umklammern.

class [klɑːs] n Klasse f // vt einordnen; ~-**conscious** a klassenbewußt.

classic ['klæsɪk] n Klassiker m // a klassisch; ~**al** a klassisch.

classified ['klæsɪfaɪd] a (information) Geheim-; ~ **advertisement** n Kleinanzeige f.

classify ['klæsɪfaɪ] vt klassifizieren.

class: ~**mate** n Klassenkamerad(in f) m; ~**room** n Klassenzimmer nt.

clatter ['klætə*] vi klappern; (feet) trappeln.

clause [klɔːz] n (JUR) Klausel f; (GRAM) Satz m.

claustrophobia [klɔːstrə'fəubɪə] n Platzangst f.

claw [klɔː] n Kralle f // vt (zer)kratzen.

clay [kleɪ] n Lehm m; (for pots) Ton m.

clean [kliːn] a sauber // vt reinigen; (clothes) reinigen; ~ **out** vt gründlich putzen; ~ **up** vt aufräumen; ~-**cut** a (person) adrett; (clear) klar; ~**er** n (person) Putzfrau f; ~**ing** n Putzen nt; (clothes) Reinigung f; ~**liness** ['klenlɪnɪs] n Reinlichkeit f.

cleanse [klenz] vt reinigen; ~**r** n (for face) Reinigungsmilch f.

clean-shaven ['kliːn'ʃeɪvn] a glattrasiert.

cleansing department ['klenzɪŋ-] n (Brit) Stadtreinigung f.

clear ['klɪə*] a klar; (road) frei // vt (road etc) freimachen; (obstacle) beseitigen; (JUR: suspect) freisprechen // vi klarwerden; (fog) sich lichten // ad: ~ **of** von ... entfernt; ~ **up** vt aufräumen; (solve) aufklären; ~**ance** ['klɪərns] n (removal) Räumung f; (free space) Lichtung f; (permission) Freigabe f; ~-**cut** a (case) eindeutig; ~**ing** n Lichtung f; ~**ing bank** n (Brit) Clearingbank f; ~**ly** ad klar; (obviously) eindeutig; ~**way** n (Brit) (Straße f mit) Halteverbot nt.

cleaver ['kliːvə*] n Hackbeil f.

clef [klef] n Notenschlüssel m.

cleft [kleft] n (in rock) Spalte f.

clemency ['klemənsɪ] n Milde f.

clench [klentʃ] vt (teeth) zusammenbeißen; (fist) ballen.

clergy ['klɜːdʒɪ] n Geistliche(n) pl; ~**man** n Geistliche(r) m.

clerical ['klerɪkəl] a (office) Schreib-, Büro-; (ECCL) geistlich.

clerk [klɑːk, (US) klɜːk] n (in office) Büroangestellte(r) mf; (US: sales person) Verkäufer(in f) m.

clever a ['klevə*] klug; (crafty) schlau.

cliché ['kliːʃeɪ] n Klischee nt.

click [klɪk] vt (heels) zusammenklappen; (tongue) schnalzen mit.

client ['klaɪənt] n Klient(in f) m; ~**ele** [kliːɑ̃'tel] n Kundschaft f.

cliff [klɪf] n Klippe f.

climate ['klaɪmɪt] n Klima nt.

climax ['klaɪmæks] n Höhepunkt m.

climb [klaɪm] vt besteigen // vi steigen, klettern // n Aufstieg m; ~-**down** n Abstieg m; ~**er** n Bergsteiger(in f) m; ~**ing** n Bergsteigen nt.

clinch [klɪntʃ] vt (decide) entscheiden; (deal) festmachen.

cling [klɪŋ], pt, pp **clung** [klʌŋ] vi (clothes) eng anliegen; **to** ~ **to** sich festklammern an (dat).

clinic ['klɪnɪk] n Klinik f; ~**al** a klinisch.

clink [klɪŋk] vi klimpern.

clip [klɪp] n Spange f; (also: **paper** ~) Klammer f // vt (papers) heften; (hair, hedge) stutzen; ~**pers** pl (for hedge) Heckenschere f; (for hair) Haarschneidemaschine f; ~**ping** n Ausschnitt m.

cloak [kləuk] n Umhang m // vt hüllen; ~**room** n (for coats) Garderobe f; (Brit: W.C.) Toilette f.

clock [klɒk] n Uhr f; ~ **in** or **on** vi stempeln; ~ **off** or **out** vi stempeln; ~**wise** ad im Uhrzeigersinn; ~**work** n Uhrwerk nt // a zum Aufziehen.

clog [klɒg] n Holzschuh m // vt verstopfen.

cloister ['klɔɪstə*] n Kreuzgang m.

clone [kləun] n Klon m.

close a, ad and derivatives [kləus] a (near) in der Nähe; (friend, connection, print) eng; (relative) nahe; (result) knapp; (examination) eingehend; (weather) schwül; (room) stickig // ad nahe, dicht; **to have a ~ shave** (fig) mit knapper Not davorkommen; **~ by, ~ at hand** a, ad in der Nähe // v and derivatives [kləuz] vt (shut) schließen; (end) beenden // vi (shop etc) schließen; (door etc) sich schließen // n Ende nt; **~ down** vi schließen; **~d** a (shop etc) geschlossen; **~d shop** n Gewerkschaftszwang m; **~-knit** a eng zusammengewachsen; **~ly** ad eng; (carefully) genau.

closet ['klɔzɪt] n Schrank m.

close-up ['kləusʌp] n Nahaufnahme f.

closure ['kləuʒə*] n Schließung f.

clot [klɒt] n (of blood) Blutgerinnsel nt; (fool) Blödmann m // vi gerinnen.

cloth [klɒθ] n (material) Tuch nt; (rag) Lappen m.

clothe [kləuð] vt kleiden; **~s** npl Kleider pl; **~s brush** n Kleiderbürste f; **~s line** n Wäscheleine f; **~s peg**, (US) **~s pin** n Wäscheklammer f.

clothing ['kləuðɪŋ] n Kleidung f.

cloud [klaud] n Wolke f; **~burst** n Wolkenbruch m; **~y** a bewölkt; (liquid) trüb.

clout [klaut] vt hauen.

clove [kləuv] n Gewürznelke f; **~ of garlic** n Knoblauchzehe f.

clover ['kləuvə*] n Klee m.

clown [klaun] n Clown m // vi (also: **~ about, ~ around**) kaspern.

cloying ['klɔɪɪŋ] a (taste, smell) übersüß.

club [klʌb] n (weapon) Knüppel m; (society) Klub m; (also: golf **~**) Golfschläger m // vt prügeln // vi: **to ~ together** zusammenlegen; **~s** npl (CARDS) Kreuz nt; **~ car** n (US RAIL) Speisewagen m; **~house** n Klubhaus nt.

cluck [klʌk] vi glucken.

clue [klu:] n Anhaltspunkt m; (in crosswords) Frage f; **I haven't a ~** (ich hab') keine Ahnung.

clump [klʌmp] n Gruppe f.

clumsy ['klʌmzɪ] a (person) unbeholfen; (shape) unförmig.

clung [klʌŋ] pt, pp of **cling**.

cluster ['klʌstə*] n (of trees etc) Gruppe f // vi sich drängen, sich scharen.

clutch [klʌtʃ] n Griff m; (AUT) Kupplung f // vt sich festklammern an (+dat).

clutter ['klʌtə*] vt vollpropfen; (desk) übersäen.

CM abbr (= centimetre) cm.

CND n abbr = Campaign for Nuclear Disarmament.

Co. abbr of **county; company**.

c/o abbr (= care of) c/o.

coach [kəutʃ] n (bus) Reisebus m; (old) Kutsche f; (RAIL) (Personen)wagen m; (trainer) Trainer m // vt (SCH) Nachhilfeunterricht geben (+dat); (SPORT) trainieren; **~ trip** n Busfahrt f.

coagulate [kəʊ'ægjuleɪt] vi gerinnen.

coal [kəul] n Kohle f; **~ face** n Streb m; **~ field** n Kohlengebiet nt.

coalition [kəuə'lɪʃən] n Koalition f.

coal: ~man, ~merchant n Kohlenhändler m; **~ mine** n Kohlenbergwerk nt.

coarse [kɔ:s] a (lit) grob; (fig) ordinär.

coast [kəust] n Küste f // vi dahinrollen; (AUT) im Leerlauf fahren; **~al** a Küsten-; **~guard** n Küstenwache f; **~line** n Küste (nlinie f.)

coat [kəut] n Mantel m; (on animals) Fell nt; (of paint) Schicht f // vt überstreichen; **~ of arms** n Wappen nt; **~hanger** n Kleiderbügel m; **~ing** n Überzug m; (of paint) Schicht f.

coax [kəuks] vt beschwatzen.

cob [kɒb] n see **corn**.

cobbler ['kɒblə*] n Schuster m.

cobbles ['kɒblz], **cobblestones** ['kɒblstəunz] npl Pflastersteine pl.

cobweb ['kɒbweb] n Spinnennetz nt.

cocaine [kə'keɪn] n Kokain n.

cock [kɒk] n Hahn m // vt (gun) entsichern; **~erel** n junge(r) Hahn m; **~eyed** a (fig) verrückt.

cockle ['kɒkl] n Herzmuschel f.

cockney ['kɒknɪ] n echte(r) Londoner m.

cockpit ['kɒkpɪt] n (AVIAT) Pilotenkanzel f.

cockroach ['kɒkrəutʃ] n Küchenschabe f.

cocktail ['kɒkteɪl] n Cocktail m; **~ cabinet** n Hausbar f; **~ party** n Cocktailparty f.

cocoa ['kəukəu] n Kakao m.

coconut ['kəukənʌt] n Kokosnuß f.

cocoon [kə'ku:n] n Kokon m.

cod [kɒd] n Kabeljau m.

C.O.D. abbr of **cash on delivery**.

code [kəud] n Kode m; (JUR) Kodex m.

cod-liver oil ['kɒdlɪvər-] n Lebertran m.

coercion [kəu'ɜ:ʃən] n Zwang m.

coffee ['kɒfɪ] n Kaffee m; **~ bar** n (Brit) Café nt; **~ bean** n Kaffeebohne f; **~ break** n Kaffeepause f; **~ grounds** npl Kaffeesatz m; **~pot** n Kaffeekanne f; **~ table** n Couchtisch m.

coffin ['kɒfɪn] n Sarg m.

cog [kɒg] n (Rad)zahn m.

cogent ['kəudʒənt] a triftig, überzeugend, zwingend.

cognac ['kɒnjæk] n Kognak m.

coherent [kəu'hɪərənt] a zusammenhängend; (person) verständlich.

cohesion [kəu'hi:ʒən] n Zusammenhang

m.

coil [kɔɪl] *n* Rolle *f*; (*ELEC*) Spule *f*; (*contraceptive*) Spirale *f* // *vt* aufwickeln.

coin [kɔɪn] *n* Münze *f* // *vt* prägen; **~age** *n* (*word*) Prägung *f*; **~-box** *n* (*Brit*) Münzfernsprecher *m*.

coincide [kəʊɪn'saɪd] *vi* (*happen together*) zusammenfallen; (*agree*) übereinstimmen; **~nce** [kəʊ'ɪnsɪdəns] *n* Zufall *m*.

coke [kəʊk] *n* Koks *m*.

Coke *n* ® (*drink*) Coca-Cola *f* ®.

colander ['kʌləndə*] *n* Durchschlag *m*.

cold [kəʊld] *a* kalt // *n* Kälte *f*; (*MED*) Erkältung *f*; I'm ~ mir ist kalt; **to catch** ~ sich erkälten; in ~ **blood** kaltblütig; **~ly** *ad* kalt; **~-shoulder** *vt* (jdm) die kalte Schulter zeigen; ~ **sore** *n* Erkältungsbläschen *nt*.

coleslaw ['kəʊlslɔ:] *n* Krautsalat *m*.

colic ['kɒlɪk] *n* Kolik *f*.

collaborate [kə'læbəreɪt] *vi* zusammenarbeiten.

collaboration [kəlæbə'reɪʃən] *n* Zusammenarbeit *f*; (*POL*) Kollaboration *f*.

collapse [kə'læps] *vi* (*people*) zusammenbrechen; (*things*) einstürzen // *n* Zusammenbruch *m*, Einsturz *m*.

collapsible [kə'læpsəbl] *a* zusammenklappbar, Klapp-.

collar ['kɒlə*] *n* Kragen *m*; **~bone** *n* Schlüsselbein *nt*.

collateral [kɒ'lætərəl] *n* (zusätzliche) Sicherheit.

colleague ['kɒli:g] *n* Kollege *m*, Kollegin *f*.

collect [kə'lekt] *vt* sammeln; (*Brit: call and pick up*) abholen // *vi* sich sammeln // *ad*: **to call ~** (*US TEL*) ein R-Gespräch führen; **~ion** [kə'lekʃən] *n* Sammlung *f*; (*ECCL*) Kollekte *f*; (*of post*) Leerung *f*.

collective [kə'lektɪv] *a* gemeinsam; (*POL*) kollektiv.

collector [kə'lektə*] *n* Sammler *m*; (*tax* ~) (Steuer)einnehmer *m*.

college ['kɒlɪdʒ] *n* (*UNIV*) College *nt*; (*TECH*) Fach-, Berufsschule *f*.

collide [kə'laɪd] *vi* zusammenstoßen.

colliery [kɒlɪərɪ] *n* (*Brit*) Zeche *f*.

collision [kə'lɪʒən] *n* Zusammenstoß *m*.

colloquial [kə'ləʊkwɪəl] *a* umgangssprachlich.

collusion [kə'lu:ʒən] *n* geheime(s) Einverständnis *nt*.

colon ['kəʊlən] *n* Doppelpunkt *m*; (*MED*) Dickdarm *m*.

colonel ['kɜ:nl] *n* Oberst *m*.

colonial [kə'ləʊnɪəl] *a* Kolonial-.

colonize ['kɒlənaɪz] *vt* kolonisieren.

colony ['kɒlənɪ] *n* Kolonie *f*.

colour, (*US*) **color** ['kʌlə*] *n* Farbe *f* // *vt* (*lit, fig*) färben // *vi* sich verfärben; **~s** *pl* (*of club*) Fahne *f*; ~ **bar** *n*

Rassenschranke *f*; **~-blind** *a* farbenblind; **~ed** *a* farbig; **~eds** *npl* Farbige *pl*; ~ **film** *n* Farbfilm *m*; **~ful** *a* bunt; (*personality*) schillernd; **~ing** *n* (*complexion*) Gesichtsfarbe *f*; (*substance*) Farbstoff *m*; ~ **scheme** *n* Farbgebung *f*; ~ **television** *n* Farbfernsehen *nt*.

colt [kəʊlt] *n* Fohlen *nt*.

column ['kɒləm] *n* Säule *f*; (*MIL*) Kolonne *f*; (*of print*) Spalte *f*; **~ist** ['kɒləmnɪst] *n* Kolumnist *m*.

coma ['kəʊmə] *n* Koma *nt*.

comb [kəʊm] *n* Kamm *m* // *vt* kämmen; (*search*) durchkämmen.

combat ['kɒmbæt] *n* Kampf *m* // *vt* bekämpfen.

combination [kɒmbɪ'neɪʃən] *n* Kombination *f*.

combine [kəm'baɪn] *vt* verbinden // *vi* sich vereinigen // *n* ['kɒmbaɪn] (*COMM*) Konzern *m*; ~ (**harvester**) *n* Mähdrescher *m*.

combustion [kəm'bʌstʃən] *n* Verbrennung *f*.

come [kʌm] *vi*, *pt* **came**, *pp* **come** kommen; **to ~ undone** aufgehen; ~ **about** *vi* geschehen; ~ **across** *vi* (*find*) stoßen auf (+*acc*); ~ **away** *vi* (*person*) weggehen; (*handle etc*) abgehen; ~ **back** *vi* zurückkommen; ~ **by** *vt* (*find*) zu etw kommen; ~ **down** *vi* (*price*) fallen; ~ **forward** *vi* (*volunteer*) sich melden; ~ **from** *vt* (*result*) kommen von; **where do you ~ from?** wo kommen Sie her?; **I ~ from London** ich komme aus London; ~ **in** *vi* hereinkommen; (*train*) einfahren; ~ **in for** *vt* abkriegen; ~ **into** *vt* (*inherit*) erben; ~ **off** *vi* (*handle*) abgehen; (*succeed*) klappen; ~ **on** *vi* (*progress*) vorankommen; ~ **on!** komm!; (*hurry*) beeil dich!; ~ **out** *vi* herauskommen; ~ **round** *vi* (*MED*) wieder zu sich kommen; ~ **to** *vi* (*MED*) wieder zu sich kommen; (*bill*) sich belaufen auf (+*acc*); ~ **up** *vi* hochkommen; (*sun*) aufgehen; (*problem*) auftauchen; ~ **up against** *vt* (*resistance, difficulties*) stoßen auf (+*acc*); ~ **upon** *vt* stoßen auf (+*acc*); ~ **up with** *vt* sich einfallen lassen.

comedian [kə'mi:dɪən] *n* Komiker *m*; **comedienne** [-'en] *n* Komikerin *f*.

comedown ['kʌmdaʊn] *n* Abstieg *m*.

comedy ['kɒmədɪ] *n* Komödie *f*.

comet ['kɒmɪt] *n* Komet *m*.

comeuppance [kʌm'ʌpəns] *n*: **to get one's ~** seine Quittung bekommen.

comfort ['kʌmfət] *n* Komfort *m*; (*consolation*) Trost *m* // *vt* trösten; **~able** *a* bequem; **~ably** *ad* (*sit etc*) bequem; (*live*) angenehm; ~ **station** *n* (*US*) öffentliche Toilette *f*.

comic ['kɒmɪk] *n* Comic(heft) *nt*; (*comedian*) Komiker *m* // *a* (also: **~al**) komisch.

coming ['kʌmɪŋ] n Kommen nt; ~(s) **and going(s)** n(pl) Kommen und Gehen nt.

comma ['kɒmə] n Komma nt.

command [kə'mɑ:nd] n Befehl m; (control) Führung f; (MIL) Kommando nt; (mastery) Beherrschung f // vt befehlen (+dat); (MIL) kommandieren; (be able to get) verfügen über (+acc); ~**eer** [kɒmən'dɪə*] vt requirieren; ~**er** n Kommandant m.

commandment [kə'mɑ:ndmənt] n (REL) Gebot nt.

commando [kə'mɑ:ndəʊ] n (Mitglied nt einer) Kommandotruppe f.

commemorate [kə'meməreɪt] vt gedenken (+gen).

commence [kə'mens] vti beginnen.

commend [kə'mend] vt (recommend) empfehlen; (praise) loben.

commensurate [kə'mensjʊrɪt] a entsprechend (with dat).

comment ['kɒment] n Bemerkung f // vi: to ~ (on) sich äußern (zu); ~**ary** ['kɒməntrɪ] n Kommentar m; ~**ator** ['kɒmənteɪtə*] n Kommentator m; (TV) Reporter(in f) m.

commerce ['kɒmɜ:s] n Handel m.

commercial [kə'mɜ:ʃəl] a kommerziell, geschäftlich; (training) kaufmännisch // n (TV) Fernsehwerbung f; ~ **break** n Werbespot m; ~**ize** vt kommerzialisieren.

commiserate [kə'mɪzəreɪt] vi: to ~ **with** Mitleid haben mit.

commission [kə'mɪʃən] n (act) Auftrag m; (fee) Provision f; (body) Kommission f // vt beauftragen; (MIL) zum Offizier ernennen; (work of art) in Auftrag geben; **out of** ~ außer Betrieb; ~**aire** [kəmɪʃə'neə*] n (Brit) Portier m; ~**er** n (POLICE) Polizeipräsident m.

commit [kə'mɪt] vt (crime) begehen; (entrust) anvertrauen; **to ~ o.s.** sich festlegen; ~**ment** n Verpflichtung f.

committee [kə'mɪtɪ] n Ausschuß m.

commodity [kə'mɒdɪtɪ] n Ware f.

common ['kɒmən] a (cause) gemeinsam; (pej) gewöhnlich; (widespread) üblich, häufig // n Gemeindeland nt; **the C~s** npl (Brit) das Unterhaus; ~**er** n Bürgerliche(r) mf; ~ **law** n Gewohnheitsrecht nt; ~**ly** ad gewöhnlich; **C~ Market** n Gemeinsame(r) Markt m; ~**place** a alltäglich; ~**room** n Gemeinschaftsraum m; ~ **sense** n gesunde(r) Menschenverstand m; **the C~wealth** n das Commonwealth.

commotion [kə'məʊʃən] n Aufsehen nt.

communal ['kɒmju:nl] a Gemeinde-; Gemeinschafts-.

commune ['kɒmju:n] n Kommune f // vi sich mitteilen (with dat).

communicate [kə'mju:nɪkeɪt] vt

(transmit) übertragen // vi (be in touch) in Verbindung stehen; (make self understood) sich verständigen.

communication [kəmju:nɪ'keɪʃən] n (message) Mitteilung f; (making understood) Kommunikation f; ~**s** pl (transport etc) Verkehrswege pl; ~ **cord** n (Brit) Notbremse f.

communion [kə'mju:nɪən] n (also: Holy C~) Abendmahl nt, Kommunion f.

communism ['kɒmjʊnɪzəm] n Kommunismus m.

communist ['kɒmjʊnɪst] n Kommunist(in f) m // a kommunistisch.

community [kə'mju:nɪtɪ] n Gemeinschaft f; ~ **centre** n Gemeinschaftszentrum nt; ~ **chest** n (US) Wohltätigkeitsfonds m.

commutation ticket [kɒmjʊ'teɪʃən-'tɪkɪt] n (US) Zeitkarte f.

commute [kə'mju:t] vi pendeln // vt umwandeln; ~**r** n Pendler m.

compact [kəm'pækt] a kompakt // n ['kɒmpækt] (for make-up) Puderdose f; ~ **disc** n Compact-disc f.

companion [kəm'pænɪən] n Begleiter(in f) m; ~**ship** n Gesellschaft f.

company ['kʌmpənɪ] n Gesellschaft f; (COMM also) Firma f; **to keep sb ~** jdm Gesellschaft leisten; ~ **secretary** n (Brit) ≈ Prokurist(in f) m.

comparable ['kɒmpərəbl] a vergleichbar.

comparative [kəm'pærətɪv] a (relative) relativ; ~**ly** ad verhältnismäßig.

compare [kəm'peə*] vt vergleichen // vi sich vergleichen lassen.

comparison [kəm'pærɪsn] n Vergleich m; **in ~ (with)** im Vergleich (mit or zu).

compartment [kəm'pɑ:tmənt] n (RAIL) Abteil nt; (in drawer etc) Fach nt.

compass ['kʌmpəs] n Kompaß m; ~**es** pl Zirkel m.

compassion [kəm'pæʃən] n Mitleid nt; ~**ate** a mitfühlend.

compatible [kəm'pætɪbl] a vereinbar; (COMPUT) kompatibel.

compel [kəm'pel] vt zwingen.

compendium [kəm'pendɪəm] n Kompendium nt.

compensate ['kɒmpenseɪt] vt entschädigen // vi: to ~ **for** Ersatz leisten für.

compensation [kɒmpen'seɪʃən] n Entschädigung f.

compère ['kɒmpeə*] n Conférencier m.

compete [kəm'pi:t] vi (take part) teilnehmen; (vie with) konkurrieren.

competence ['kɒmpɪtəns] n Fähigkeit f.

competent ['kɒmpɪtənt] a kompetent.

competition [kɒmpɪ'tɪʃən] n (contest) Wettbewerb m; (COMM, rivalry) Konkurrenz f.

competitive [kəm'petɪtɪv] *a* Konkurrenz-; (*COMM*) konkurrenzfähig.

competitor [kəm'petɪtə*] *n* (*COMM*) Konkurrent(in *f*) *m*; (*participant*) Teilnehmer(in *f*) *m*.

compile [kəm'paɪl] *vt* zusammenstellen.

complacency [kəm'pleɪsnsɪ] *n* Selbstzufriedenheit *f*.

complacent [kəm'pleɪsnt] *a* selbstzufrieden.

complain [kəm'pleɪn] *vi* sich beklagen; (*formally*) sich beschweren; ~**t** *n* Klage *f*; (*formal* ~) Beschwerde *f*; (*MED*) Leiden *nt*.

complement ['komplɪmənt] *n* Ergänzung *f*; (*ship's crew etc*) Bemannung *f* // *vt* ['komplɪment] ergänzen; ~**ary** [komplɪ'mentərɪ] *a* (sich) ergänzend.

complete [kəm'pliːt] *a* (*full*) vollkommen, ganz; (*finished*) fertig // *vt* vervollständigen; (*finish*) beenden; (*fill in: form*) ausfüllen; ~**ly** *ad* ganz.

completion [kəm'pliːʃən] *n* Fertigstellung *f*; (*of contract etc*) Abschluß *m*.

complex ['kompleks] *a* kompliziert.

complexion [kəm'plekʃən] *n* Gesichtsfarbe *f*; (*fig*) Aspekt *m*.

complexity [kəm'pleksɪtɪ] *n* Kompliziertheit *f*.

compliance [kəm'plaɪəns] *n* Fügsamkeit *f*, Einwilligung *f*; in ~ with sth etw (*dat*) gemäß.

complicate ['komplɪkeɪt] *vt* komplizieren; ~**d** *a* kompliziert.

complication [komplɪ'keɪʃən] *n* Komplikation *f*.

complicity [kəm'plɪsɪtɪ] *n* Mittäterschaft *f* (*in* bei).

compliment ['komplɪmənt] *n* Kompliment *nt* // *vt* ['komplɪment] ein Kompliment machen (*sb* jdm); ~**s** *pl* Grüße *pl*; to pay sb a ~ jdm ein Kompliment machen; ~**ary** [komplɪ'mentərɪ] *a* schmeichelhaft; (*free*) Frei-, Gratis-.

comply [kəm'plaɪ] *vi*: to ~ with erfüllen (+*acc*); entsprechen (+*dat*).

component [kəm'pəʊnənt] *a* Teil- *n* Bestandteil *m*.

compose [kəm'pəʊz] *vt* (*music*) komponieren; (*poetry*) verfassen; to ~ o.s. sich sammeln; ~**d** *a* gefaßt; ~**r** *n* Komponist(in *f*) *m*.

composite ['kompəzɪt] *a* zusammengesetzt.

composition [kompə'zɪʃən] *n* (*MUS*) Komposition *f*; (*SCH*) Aufsatz *m*; (*structure*) Zusammensetzung *f*, Aufbau *m*.

compost ['kompost] *n* Kompost *m*.

composure [kəm'pəʊʒə*] *n* Fassung *f*.

compound ['kompaʊnd] *n* (*CHEM*) Verbindung *f*; (*enclosure*) Lager *nt*; (*LING*) Kompositum *nt* // *a* zusammengesetzt; (*fracture*) kompliziert; ~ **interest** *n* Zinseszins *m*.

comprehend [komprɪ'hend] *vt* begreifen.

comprehension [komprɪ'henʃən] *n* Verständnis *nt*.

comprehensive [komprɪ'hensɪv] *a* umfassend; ~ **insurance** *n* Vollkasko *nt*; ~ (**school**) *n* (*Brit*) Gesamtschule *f*.

compress [kəm'pres] *vt* komprimieren // *n* ['kompres] (*MED*) Kompresse *f*.

comprise [kəm'praɪz] *vt* (*also*: be ~**d** of) umfassen, bestehen aus.

compromise ['komprəmaɪz] *n* Kompromiß *m* // *vt* kompromittieren // *vi* einen Kompromiß schließen.

compulsion [kəm'pʌlʃən] *n* Zwang *m*.

compulsive [kəm'pʌlsɪv] *a* zwanghaft.

compulsory [kəm'pʌlsərɪ] *a* obligatorisch.

computer [kəm'pjuːtə*] *n* Computer *m*, Rechner *m*; ~**ize** *vt* (*information*) computerisieren; (*company, accounts*) auf Computer umstellen; ~ **programmer** *n* Programmierer(in *f*) *m*; ~ **programming** *n* Programmieren *nt*; ~ **science** *n* Informatik *f*; **computing** *n* (*science*) Informatik *f*; (*work*) Computerei *f*.

comrade ['komrɪd] *n* Kamerad *m*; (*POL*) Genosse *m*; ~**ship** *n* Kameradschaft *f*.

con [kon] *vt* hereinlegen // *n* Schwindel *nt*.

concave ['kon'keɪv] *a* konkav.

conceal [kən'siːl] *vt* (*secret*) verschweigen; (*hide*) verbergen.

concede [kən'siːd] *vt* (*grant*) gewähren; (*point*) zugeben // *vi* (*admit*) zugeben.

conceit [kən'siːt] *n* Einbildung *f*; ~**ed** *a* eingebildet.

conceivable [kən'siːvəbl] *a* vorstellbar.

conceive [kən'siːv] *vt* (*idea*) ausdenken; (*imagine*) sich vorstellen // *vti* (*baby*) empfangen.

concentrate ['konsəntreɪt] *vi* sich konzentrieren (*on* auf +*acc*) // *vt* konzentrieren.

concentration [konsən'treɪʃən] *n* Konzentration *f*; ~ **camp** *n* Konzentrationslager *nt*, KZ *nt*.

concept ['konsept] *n* Begriff *m*.

conception [kən'sepʃən] *n* (*idea*) Vorstellung *f*; (*BIOL*) Empfängnis *f*.

concern [kən'sɜːn] *n* (*affair*) Angelegenheit *f*; (*COMM*) Unternehmen *nt*; (*worry*) Sorge *f* // *vt* (*interest*) angehen; (*be about*) handeln von; (*have connection with*) betreffen; to be ~**ed** (*about*) sich Sorgen machen (um); ~**ing** *prep* hinsichtlich (+*gen*).

concert ['konsət] *n* Konzert *nt*; ~**ed** [kən'sɜːtɪd] *a* gemeinsam; ~ **hall** *n* Konzerthalle *f*.

concertina [konsə'tiːnə] *n* Handharmonika *f*.

concerto [kən'tʃɜːtəʊ] *n* Konzert *nt*.

concession [kən'seʃən] n (yielding) Zugeständnis nt; tax ~ Steuer-Konzession f.
conciliation [kənsılı'eıʃən] n Versöhnung f; (official) Schlichtung f.
concise [kən'saıs] a präzis.
conclude [kən'kluːd] vt (end) beenden; (treaty) (ab)schließen; (decide) schließen, folgern.
conclusion [kən'kluːʒən] n (Ab)schluß m; (deduction) Schluß m.
conclusive [kən'kluːsıv] a schlüssig.
concoct [kən'kɒkt] vt zusammenbrauen; ~ion n Gebräu nt.
concourse [kɒŋkɔːs] n (Bahnhofs)halle f, Vorplatz m.
concrete [kɒŋkriːt] n Beton m // a konkret.
concur [kən'kɜː*] vi übereinstimmen.
concurrently [kən'kʌrəntlı] ad gleichzeitig.
concussion [kən'kʌʃən] n (Gehirn)erschütterung f.
condemn [kən'dem] vt (JUR) verurteilen; (building) abbruchreif erklären.
condensation [kɒnden'seıʃən] n Kondensation f.
condense [kən'dens] vi (CHEM) kondensieren // vt (fig) zusammendrängen; ~d milk n Kondensmilch f.
condescending [kɒndı'sendıŋ] a herablassend.
condition [kən'dıʃən] n (state) Zustand m; (presupposition) Bedingung f // vt (hair etc) behandeln; (accustom) gewöhnen; **on ~ that ...** unter der Bedingung, daß ...; ~al a bedingt; (GRAM) Bedingungs-; ~er n (for hair) Spülung f; (for fabrics) Weichspüler m; ~s pl (circumstances) Verhältnisse pl.
condolences [kən'dəʊlənsız] npl Beileid nt.
condom [kɒndəm] n Kondom nt or m.
condominium [kɒndə'mınıəm] n (US) Eigentumswohnung f; (block) Eigentumsblock m.
condone [kən'dəʊn] vt gutheißen.
conducive [kən'djuːsıv] a: ~ **to** dienlich (dat).
conduct [kɒndʌkt] n (behaviour) Verhalten nt; (management) Führung f // vt [kən'dʌkt] führen; (MUS) dirigieren; ~ed tour n Führung f; ~or [kən'dʌktə*] n (of orchestra) Dirigent m; (in bus, US: on train) Schaffner m; (ELEC) Leiter m; ~ress [kən'dʌktrıs] n (in bus) Schaffnerin f.
cone [kəʊn] n (MATH) Kegel m; (for ice cream) (Waffel)tüte f; (fir) Tannenzapfen m.
confectioner [kən'fekʃənə*] n Konditor m; ~'s (shop) n Konditorei f; ~y n Süßigkeiten pl.
confederation [kənfedə'reıʃən] n Bund m.

confer [kən'fɜː*] vt (degree) verleihen // vi (discuss) konferieren, verhandeln; ~ence [kɒnfərəns] n Konferenz f.
confess [kən'fes] vti gestehen; (ECCL) beichten; ~ion [kən'feʃən] n Geständnis nt; (ECCL) Beichte f; ~ional [kən'feʃənl] n Beichtstuhl m.
confetti [kən'fetı] n Konfetti nt.
confide [kən'faıd] vi: **to ~ in** (sich) anvertrauen (+dat).
confidence [kɒnfıdəns] n Vertrauen nt; (assurance) Selbstvertrauen nt; (secret) Geheimnis nt; **in ~** (speak, write) vertraulich; ~ **trick** n Schwindel m.
confident [kɒnfıdənt] a (sure) überzeugt; (self-assured) selbstsicher; ~ial [kɒnfı'denʃəl] a vertraulich.
confine [kən'faın] vt (limit) beschränken; (lock up) einsperren; ~s [kɒnfaınz] npl Grenzen pl; ~d a (space) eng; ~ment n (in prison) Haft f; (MED) Wochenbett nt.
confirm [kən'fɜːm] vt bestätigen; ~ation [kɒnfə'meıʃən] n Bestätigung f; (REL) Konfirmation f; ~ed a unverbesserlich; (bachelor) eingefleischt.
confiscate [kɒnfıskeıt] vt beschlagnahmen.
conflict [kɒnflıkt] n Konflikt m // vi [kən'flıkt] im Widerspruch stehen; ~ing [kən'flıktıŋ] a widersprüchlich.
conform [kən'fɔːm] vi (things) entsprechen (to dat); (people) sich anpassen (to dat); (to rules) sich richten (to nach); ~ist n Konformist(in f) m.
confound [kən'faʊnd] vt verblüffen; (throw into confusion) durcheinanderbringen.
confront [kən'frʌnt] vt (enemy) entgegentreten (+dat); (problems) sich stellen (+dat); **to ~ sb with sth** jdn mit etw konfrontieren; ~ation [kɒnfrən-'teıʃən] n Konfrontation f.
confuse [kən'fjuːz] vt verwirren; (sth with sth) verwechseln; ~d a verwirrt; **confusing** a verwirrend; **confusion** [kən'fjuːʒən] n (perplexity) Verwirrung f; (mixing up) Verwechslung f; (tumult) Aufruhr m.
congeal [kən'dʒiːl] vi (freeze) gefrieren; (clot) gerinnen.
congenial [kən'dʒiːnıəl] a angenehm.
congenital [kən'dʒenıtəl] a angeboren.
congested [kən'dʒestıd] a überfüllt.
congestion [kən'dʒestʃən] n Stau m.
conglomerate [kən'glɒmərət] n (COMM, GEOL) Konglomerat nt.
conglomeration [kənglɒmə'reıʃən] n Anhäufung f.
congratulate [kən'grætjʊleıt] vt beglückwünschen (on zu).
congratulations [kəngrætjʊ'leıʃənz] npl Glückwünsche pl; ~! gratuliere!,

herzlichen Glückwunsch!

congregate ['kɒŋgrɪgeɪt] *vi* sich versammeln.

congregation [kɒŋgrɪ'geɪʃən] *n* Gemeinde *f*.

congress ['kɒŋgres] *n* Kongreß *m*; **~man** *n* (US) Mitglied *nt* des amerikanischen Repräsentantenhauses.

conical ['kɒnɪkəl] *a* kegelförmig.

conifer ['kɒnɪfə*] *n* Nadelbaum *m*.

conjecture [kən'dʒektʃə*] *n* Vermutung *f*.

conjugal ['kɒndʒʊgəl] *a* ehelich.

conjugate ['kɒndʒʊgeɪt] *vt* konjugieren.

conjunction [kən'dʒʌŋkʃən] *n* Verbindung *f*; (GRAM) Konjunktion *f*.

conjunctivitis [kəndʒʌŋktɪ'vaɪtɪs] *n* Bindehautentzündung *f*.

conjure ['kʌndʒə*] *vi* zaubern; **~ up** *vi* heraufbeschwören; **~r** *n* Zauberkünstler(in *f*) *m*.

conk [kɒŋk]: **~ out** *vi* (col) den Geist aufgeben.

connect [kə'nekt] *vt* verbinden; (ELEC) anschließen; **to be ~ed with** ein Beziehung haben zu; (be related to) verwandt sein mit; **~ion** [kə'nekʃən] *n* Verbindung *f*; (relation) Zusammenhang *m*; (ELEC, TEL, RAIL) Anschluß *m*.

connive [kə'naɪv] *vi*: **to ~ at** stillschweigend dulden.

connoisseur [kɒnɪ'sɜ:*] *n* Kenner *m*.

conquer ['kɒŋkə*] *vt* (feelings) überwinden; (enemy) besiegen; (country) erobern; **~or** *n* Eroberer *m*.

conquest ['kɒŋkwest] *n* Eroberung *f*.

cons [kɒnz] *npl see* **convenience, pro.**

conscience ['kɒnʃəns] *n* Gewissen *nt*.

conscientious [kɒnʃɪ'enʃəs] *a* gewissenhaft.

conscious ['kɒnʃəs] *a* bewußt; (MED) bei Bewußtsein; **~ness** *n* Bewußtsein *nt*.

conscript ['kɒnskrɪpt] *n* Wehrpflichtige(r) *m*; **~ion** [kən'skrɪpʃən] *n* Wehrpflicht *f*.

consecrate ['kɒnsɪkreɪt] *vt* weihen.

consecutive [kən'sekjʊtɪv] *a* aufeinanderfolgend.

consensus [kən'sensəs] *n* allgemeine Übereinstimmung *f*.

consent [kən'sent] *n* Zustimmung *f* // *vi* zustimmen (to dat).

consequence ['kɒnsɪkwəns] *n* (importance) Bedeutung *f*; (effect) Folge *f*.

consequently ['kɒnsɪkwəntlɪ] *ad* folglich.

conservation [kɒnsə'veɪʃən] *n* Erhaltung *f*; (nature ~) Umweltschutz *m*.

conservative [kən'sɜ:vətɪv] *a* konservativ; **C~** *a* (Brit) konservativ // *n* Konservative(r) *mf*.

conservatory [kən'sɜ:vətrɪ] *n* (room) Wintergarten *m*.

conserve [kən'sɜ:v] *vt* erhalten.

consider [kən'sɪdə*] *vt* überlegen; (take into account) in Betracht ziehen; (regard as) halten für; **to ~ doing sth** denken daran, etw zu tun.

considerable [kən'sɪdərəbl] *a* beträchtlich.

considerably *ad* beträchtlich.

considerate [kən'sɪdərɪt] *a* rücksichtsvoll.

consideration [kənsɪdə'reɪʃən] *n* Rücksicht(nahme) *f*; (thought) Erwägung *f*; (reward) Entgelt *nt*.

considering [kən'sɪdərɪŋ] *prep* in Anbetracht (+gen).

consign [kən'saɪn] *vt* übergeben; **~ment** *n* Sendung *f*.

consist [kən'sɪst] *vi*: **to ~ of** bestehen aus.

consistency [kən'sɪstənsɪ] *n* (of material) Konsistenz *f*; (of argument, person) Konsequenz *f*.

consistent [kən'sɪstənt] *a* (person) konsequent; (argument) folgerichtig.

consolation [kɒnsə'leɪʃən] *n* Trost *m*.

console [kən'səʊl] *vt* trösten // *n* ['kɒnsəʊl] Kontroll(pult) *nt*.

consolidate [kən'sɒlɪdeɪt] *vt* festigen.

consommé [kən'sɒmeɪ] *n* Fleischbrühe *f*.

consonant ['kɒnsənənt] *n* Konsonant *m*.

conspicuous [kən'spɪkjʊəs] *a* (prominent) auffällig; (visible) deutlich sichtbar.

conspiracy [kən'spɪrəsɪ] *n* Verschwörung *f*.

conspire [kən'spaɪə*] *vi* sich verschwören.

constable ['kʌnstəbl] *n* (Brit) Polizist(in *f*) *m*; **chief ~** Polizeipräsident *m*.

constabulary [kən'stæbjʊlərɪ] *n* Polizei *f*.

constant ['kɒnstənt] *a* (continuous) ständig; (unchanging) konstant; **~ly** *ad* ständig.

constellation [kɒnstə'leɪʃən] *n* Sternbild *nt*.

consternation [kɒnstə'neɪʃən] *n* Bestürzung *f*.

constipated ['kɒnstɪpeɪtəd] *a* verstopft.

constipation [kɒnstɪ'peɪʃən] *n* Verstopfung *f*.

constituency [kən'stɪtjʊənsɪ] *n* Wahlkreis *m*.

constituent [kən'stɪtjʊənt] *n* (person) Wähler *m*; (part) Bestandteil *m*.

constitute ['kɒnstɪtjuːt] *vt* (make up) bilden; (amount to) darstellen.

constitution [kɒnstɪ'tjuːʃən] *n* Verfassung *f*; **~al** *a* Verfassungs-.

constraint [kən'streɪnt] *n* Zwang *m*; (shyness) Befangenheit *f*.

construct [kən'strʌkt] *vt* bauen; **~ion** [kən'strʌkʃən] *n* Konstruktion *f*; (building) Bau *m*; **~ive** *a* konstruktiv.

construe [kən'struː] *vt* deuten.

consul ['kɒnsl] *n* Konsul *m*; **~ate** ['kɒnsjulət] *n* Konsulat *nt*.

consult [kən'sʌlt] *vt* um Rat fragen; (*doctor*) konsultieren; (*book*) nachschlagen in (+*dat*); **~ant** *n* (*MED*) Facharzt *m*; (*other specialist*) Gutachter *m*; **~ation** [kɒnsəl'teiʃən] *n* Beratung *f*; (*MED*) Konsultation *f*; **~ing room** *n* Sprechzimmer *nt*.

consume [kən'sjuːm] *vt* verbrauchen; (*food*) konsumieren; **~r** *n* Verbraucher *m*; **~r goods** *npl* Konsumgüter *pl*; **consumerism** *n* Konsum *m*; **~r society** *n* Konsumgesellschaft *f*.

consummate ['kɒnsʌmeit] *vt* (*marriage*) vollziehen.

consumption [kən'sʌmpʃən] *n* Verbrauch *m*; (*of food*) Konsum *m*.

cont. *abbr* (= *continued*) Forts.

contact ['kɒntækt] *n* (*touch*) Berührung *f*; (*connection*) Verbindung *f*; (*person*) Kontakt *m* // *vt* sich in Verbindung setzen mit; **~ lenses** *npl* Kontaktlinsen *pl*.

contagious [kən'teidʒəs] *a* ansteckend.

contain [kən'tein] *vt* enthalten; **to ~ o.s.** sich zügeln; **~er** *n* Behälter *m*; (*transport*) Container *m*.

contamination [kəntæmi'neiʃən] *n* Verunreinigung *f*.

cont'd *abbr* (= *continued*) Forts.

contemplate ['kɒntəmpleit] *vt* (*look at*) (nachdenklich) betrachten; (*think about*) überdenken; (*plan*) vorhaben.

contemporary [kən'tempərəri] *a* zeitgenössisch // *n* Zeitgenosse *m*.

contempt [kən'tempt] *n* Verachtung *f*; **~ of court** (*JUR*) Mißachtung *f* des Gerichts; **~ible** *a* verachtenswert; **~uous** *a* verächtlich.

contend [kən'tend] *vt* (*argue*) behaupten // *vi* kämpfen; **~er** *n* (*for post*) Bewerber(in *f*) *m*; (*SPORT*) Wettkämpfer(in *f*) *m*.

content [kən'tent] *a* zufrieden // *vt* befriedigen // *n* ['kɒntent] (*also:* **~s**) Inhalt *m*; **~ed** *a* zufrieden.

contention [kən'tenʃən] *n* (*dispute*) Streit *m*; (*argument*) Behauptung *f*.

contentment [kən'tentmənt] *n* Zufriedenheit *f*.

contest ['kɒntest] *n* (Wett)kampf *m* // *vt* [kən'test] (*dispute*) bestreiten; (*JUR*) anfechten; (*POL*) kandidieren in (+*dat*); **~ant** [kən'testənt] *n* Bewerber(in *f*) *m*.

context ['kɒntekst] *n* Zusammenhang *m*.

continent ['kɒntinənt] *n* Kontinent *m*; **the C~** (*Brit*) das europäische Festland; **~al** [kɒnti'nentl] *a* kontinental; **~al quilt** *n* (*Brit*) Federbett *nt*.

contingency [kən'tindʒənsi] *n* Möglichkeit *f*.

contingent [kən'tindʒənt] *n* Kontingent *nt*.

continual [kən'tinjuəl] *a* (*endless*) fortwährend; (*repeated*) immer wiederkehrend; **~ly** *ad* immer wieder.

continuation [kəntinju'eiʃən] *n* Fortsetzung *f*.

continue [kən'tinjuː] *vi* (*person*) weitermachen; (*thing*) weitergehen // *vt* fortsetzen.

continuity [kɒnti'njuiti] *n* Kontinuität *f*.

continuous [kən'tinjuəs] *a* ununterbrochen; **~ stationery** *n* Endlospapier *nt*.

contort [kən'tɔːt] *vt* verdrehen; **~ion** [kən'tɔːʃən] *n* Verzerrung *f*.

contour ['kɒntuə*] *n* Umriß *m*; (*also:* **~ line**) Höhenlinie *f*.

contraband ['kɒntrəbænd] *n* Schmuggelware *f*.

contraception [kɒntrə'sepʃən] *n* Empfängnisverhütung *f*.

contraceptive [kɒntrə'septiv] *n* empfängnisverhütende(s) Mittel *nt* // *a* empfängnisverhütend.

contract ['kɒntrækt] *n* Vertrag *m* // (*vb*: [kən'trækt]) *vi* (*to do sth*) sich vertraglich verpflichten; (*muscle, metal*) sich zusammenziehen // *vt* zusammenziehen; **~ion** [kən'trækʃən] *n* (*shortening*) Verkürzung *f*; **~or** [kən'træktə*] *n* Unternehmer *m*.

contradict [kɒntrə'dikt] *vt* widersprechen (+*dat*); **~ion** [kɒntrə'dikʃən] *n* Widerspruch *m*; **~ory** *a* widersprüchlich.

contraption [kən'træpʃən] *n* (*col*) Apparat *m*.

contrary ['kɒntrəri] *a* (*opposite*) entgegengesetzt; [kən'treəri] (*obstinate*) widerspenstig // *n* Gegenteil *nt*; **on the ~** im Gegenteil.

contrast ['kɒntrɑːst] *n* Kontrast *m* // *vt* [kən'trɑːst] entgegensetzen; **~ing** [kən'trɑːstiŋ] *a* Kontrast-.

contravene [kɒntrə'viːn] *vt* verstoßen gegen.

contribute [kən'tribjuːt] *vti*: **to ~ to** beitragen zu.

contribution [kɒntri'bjuːʃən] *n* Beitrag *m*.

contributor [kən'tribjutə*] *n* Beitragende(r) *mf*.

contrive [kən'traiv] *vt* ersinnen // *vi*: **to ~ to do sth** es schaffen, etw zu tun.

control [kən'trəul] *vt* (*direct, test*) kontrollieren // *n* Kontrolle *f*; **~s** *pl* (*of vehicle*) Steuerung *f*; (*of engine*) Schalttafel *f*; **to be in ~ of** (*business, office*) leiten; (*group of children*) beaufsichtigen; **out of ~** außer Kontrolle; **under ~** unter Kontrolle; **~ panel** *n* Schalttafel *f*; **~ room** *n* Kontrollraum *m*; **~ tower** *n* (*AVIAT*) Kontrollturm *m*.

controversial [kɒntrə'vɜːʃəl] *a* umstritten.

controversy ['kɒntrəvɜːsi] *n* Kontroverse *f*.

conurbation [kɒnɜː'beɪʃən] n Ballungsgebiet nt.

convalesce [kɒnvə'les] vi genesen; **~nce** n Genesung f.

convector [kən'vektə*] n Heizlüfter m.

convene [kən'viːn] vt zusammenrufen // vi sich versammeln.

convenience [kən'viːnɪəns] n Annehmlichkeit f; all modern ~s, (Brit) all mod cons mit allem Komfort; at your ~ wann es Ihnen paßt.

convenient [kən'viːnɪənt] a günstig.

convent ['kɒnvənt] n Kloster nt.

convention [kən'venʃən] n Versammlung f; (custom) Konvention f; **~al** a konventionell.

converge [kən'vɜːdʒ] vi zusammenlaufen.

conversant [kən'vɜːsənt] a: to be ~ with bewandert sein in (+dat).

conversation [kɒnvə'seɪʃən] n Gespräch nt; **~al** a Unterhaltungs-.

converse [kən'vɜːs] vi sich unterhalten.

conversion [kən'vɜːʃən] n Umwandlung f; (esp REL) Bekehrung f.

convert [kən'vɜːt] vt (change) umwandeln; (REL) bekehren // n ['kɒnvɜːt] Bekehrte(r) mf; Konvertit(in f) m; **~ible** n (AUT) Kabriolett nt // a umwandelbar; (FIN) konvertierbar.

convex [kɒn'veks] a konvex.

convey [kən'veɪ] vt (carry) befördern; (feelings) vermitteln; **~or belt** n Fließband nt.

convict [kən'vɪkt] vt verurteilen // n ['kɒnvɪkt] Häftling m; **~ion** [kən'vɪkʃən] n (verdict) Verurteilung f; (belief) Überzeugung f.

convince [kən'vɪns] vt überzeugen; **~d** a: ~ that überzeugt davon, daß; **convincing** a überzeugend.

convoluted [kɒnvə'luːtɪd] a verwickelt; (style) gewunden.

convoy ['kɒnvɔɪ] n (of vehicles) Kolonne f; (protected) Konvoi m.

convulse [kən'vʌls] vt zusammenzucken lassen; to be ~d with laughter sich vor Lachen krümmen.

convulsion [kən'vʌlʃən] n (esp MED) Zuckung f, Krampf m.

coo [kuː] vi gurren.

cook [kʊk] vti kochen // n Koch m, Köchin f; ~ **book** n Kochbuch nt; **~er** n Herd m; **~ery** n Kochkunst f; **~ery book** (Brit) = ~ **book**; **~ie** n (US) Plätzchen nt; **~ing** n Kochen nt.

cool [kuːl] a kühl // vti (ab)kühlen; ~ **down** vti (fig) (sich) beruhigen; **~ness** n Kühle f; (of temperament) kühle(r) Kopf.

coop [kuːp] n Hühnerstall m // vt: ~ **up** (fig) einpferchen.

cooperate [kəʊ'ɒpəreɪt] vi zusammenarbeiten; **cooperation** [-'reɪʃən] n Zusammenarbeit f.

cooperative [kəʊ'ɒpərətɪv] a hilfsbereit; (COMM) genossenschaftlich // n (of farmers) Genossenschaft f; (~ store) Konsumladen m.

coordinate [kəʊ'ɔːdɪneɪt] vt koordinieren // n [kəʊ'ɔːdɪnət] (MATH) Koordinate f; **~s** pl (clothes) Kombinationen pl.

coordination [kəʊɔːdɪ'neɪʃən] n Koordination f.

cop [kɒp] n (col) Polyp m, Bulle m.

cope [kəʊp] vi: to ~ with fertig werden mit.

copious ['kəʊpɪəs] a reichhaltig.

copper ['kɒpə*] n (metal) Kupfer nt; (col: policeman) Polyp m, Bulle m; **~s** pl Kleingeld nt.

coppice ['kɒpɪs], **copse** [kɒps] n Unterholz nt.

copulate ['kɒpjʊleɪt] vi sich paaren.

copy ['kɒpɪ] n (imitation) Kopie f; (of book etc) Exemplar nt; (of newspaper) Nummer f // vt kopieren, abschreiben; **~right** n Copyright nt.

coral ['kɒrəl] n Koralle f; ~ **reef** n Korallenriff nt.

cord [kɔːd] n Schnur f; (ELEC) Kabel nt.

cordial ['kɔːdɪəl] a herzlich // n Fruchtsaft m.

cordon ['kɔːdn] n Absperrkette f; ~ **off** vt abriegeln.

corduroy ['kɔːdərɔɪ] n Kord(samt) m.

core [kɔː*] n Kern m // vt entkernen.

cork [kɔːk] n (bark) Korkrinde f; (stopper) Korken m; **~screw** n Korkenzieher m.

corn [kɔːn] n (Brit: wheat) Getreide nt, Korn nt; (US: maize) Mais m; (on foot) Hühnerauge nt; ~ **on the cob** Maiskolben m.

cornea ['kɔːnɪə] n Hornhaut f.

corned beef ['kɔːnd'biːf] n Corned Beef nt.

corner ['kɔːnə*] n Ecke f; (on road) Kurve f // vt in die Enge treiben; (market) monopolisieren // vi (AUT) in die Kurve gehen; **~stone** n Eckstein m.

cornet ['kɔːnɪt] n (MUS) Kornett nt; (Brit: of ice cream) Eistüte f.

cornflakes ['kɔːnfleɪks] npl Corn-flakes pl ®.

cornflour ['kɔːnflaʊə*] n (Brit), **cornstarch** ['kɔːnstɑːtʃ] n (US) Maizena nt ®.

Cornwall ['kɔːnwəl] n Cornwall nt.

corny ['kɔːnɪ] a (joke) blöd(e).

corollary [kə'rɒlərɪ] n Folgesatz m.

coronary ['kɒrənərɪ] n: ~ (**thrombosis**) n Herzinfarkt m.

coronation [kɒrə'neɪʃən] n Krönung f.

coroner ['kɒrənə*] n Untersuchungsrichter m.

coronet ['kɒrənɪt] n Adelskrone f.

corporal ['kɔːpərəl] n Obergefreite(r) m // a: ~ **punishment** Prügelstrafe f.

corporate ['kɔ:pərɪt] *a* gemeinschaft-lich, korporativ.

corporation [kɔ:pə'reɪʃən] *n (of town)* Gemeinde *f*; *(COMM)* Körperschaft *f*, Aktiengesellschaft *f*.

corps [kɔ:*], *pl* **corps** [kɔ:z] *n* (Armee)korps *nt*.

corpse [kɔ:ps] *n* Leiche *f*.

corpuscle ['kɔ:pʌsl] *n* Blutkörperchen *nt*.

corral [kə'rɑ:l] *n* Pferch *m*, Korral *m*.

correct [kə'rekt] *a (accurate)* richtig; *(proper)* korrekt // *vt* korrigieren; **~ion** [kə'rekʃən] *n* Berichtigung *f*.

correlation [kɔrɪ'leɪʃən] *n* Wechselbeziehung *f*.

correspond [kɔrɪs'pɔnd] *vi (agree)* übereinstimmen; *(exchange letters)* korrespondieren; **~ence** *n (similarity)* Entsprechung *f*; *(letters)* Briefwechsel *m*, Korrespondenz *f*; **~ence course** *n* Fernkurs *m*; **~ent** *n (PRESS)* Berichterstatter *m*.

corridor ['kɔrɪdɔ:*] *n* Gang *m*.

corroborate [kə'rɔbəreɪt] *vt* bestätigen.

corrode [kə'rəud] *vt* zerfressen // *vi* rosten; **corrosion** [kə'rəuʒən] *n* Korrosion *f*.

corrugated ['kɔrəgeɪtɪd] *a* gewellt; **~ iron** *n* Wellblech *nt*.

corrupt [kə'rʌpt] *a* korrupt // *vt* verderben; *(bribe)* bestechen; **~ion** [kə'rʌpʃən] *n (of society)* Verdorbenheit *f*; *(bribery)* Bestechung *f*.

corset ['kɔ:sɪt] *n* Korsett *nt*.

corsica ['kɔ:sɪkə] *n* Korsika *nt*.

cortège [kɔ:'teɪʒ] *n* Zug *m*; *(of funeral)* Leichenzug *m*.

cosh [kɔʃ] *n (Brit)* Totschläger *m*.

cosmetic [kɔz'metɪk] *n* Kosmetikum *nt*.

cosmic ['kɔzmɪk] *a* kosmisch.

cosmonaut ['kɔzmənɔ:t] *n* Kosmonaut(in *f*) *m*.

cosmopolitan [kɔzmə'pɔlɪtən] *a* international; *(city)* Welt-.

cosmos ['kɔzmɔs] *n* Kosmos *m*.

cosset ['kɔsɪt] *vt* verwöhnen.

cost [kɔst] *n* Kosten *pl*, Preis *m*; **~s** *pl* Kosten *pl* // *vti*, *pt*, *pp* **cost** kosten; how much does it ~? wieviel kostet das?; at all ~s um jeden Preis.

co-star ['kəustɑ:*] *n* eine(r) der Hauptdarsteller.

cost-effective ['kɔstɪ'fektɪv] *a* rentabel.

costly ['kɔstlɪ] *a* kostspielig.

cost-of-living ['kɔstəv'lɪvɪŋ] *a (allowance, index)* Lebenshaltungskosten.

cost price ['kɔst'praɪs] *n (Brit)* Selbstkostenpreis *m*.

costume ['kɔstju:m] *n* Kostüm *nt*; *(fancy dress)* Maskenkostüm *nt*; *(Brit: also:* swimming ~) Badeanzug *m*; **~ jewellery** *n* Modeschmuck *m*.

cosy ['kəuzɪ] *a (Brit)* behaglich; (: *atmosphere*) gemütlich.

cot [kɔt] *n (Brit: child's)* Kinderbett(chen) *nt*; *(US: campbed)* Feldbett *nt*.

cottage ['kɔtɪdʒ] *n* kleine(s) Haus *nt*; **~ cheese** *n* Hüttenkäse *m*; **~ industry** *n* Heimindustrie *f*; **~ pie** *n* Auflauf mit Hackfleisch und Kartoffelbrei.

cotton ['kɔtn] *n* Baumwolle *f*; *(thread)* Garn *nt*; **~ on to** *vt (col)* kapieren; **~ candy** *n (US)* Zuckerwatte *f*; **~ wool** *n (Brit)* Watte *f*.

couch [kautʃ] *n* Couch *f*.

couchette [ku:'ʃet] *n (on train, boat)* Liegewagen(platz) *m*.

cough [kɔf] *vi* husten // *n* Husten *m*; **~ drop** *n* Hustenbonbon *nt*.

could [kud] *pt of* can; **~n't** = **could not**.

council ['kaunsl] *n (of town)* Stadtrat *m*; **~ estate/house** *n (Brit)* Siedlung *f*/ Haus *nt* des sozialen Wohnungsbaus; **~lor** ['kaunsɪlə*] *n* Stadtrat *m*/-rätin *f*.

counsel ['kaunsl] *n (barrister)* Anwalt *m*; *(advice)* Rat(schlag) *m* // *vt* beraten; **~lor** *n* Berater *m*.

count [kaunt] *vti* zählen // *n (reckoning)* Abrechnung *f*; *(nobleman)* Graf *m*; **~ on** *vt* zählen auf (+*acc*); **~down** *n* Countdown *m*.

countenance ['kauntɪnəns] *n (old)* Antlitz *nt* // *vt (tolerate)* gutheißen.

counter ['kauntə*] *n (in shop)* Ladentisch *m*; *(in café)* Theke *f*; *(in bank, post office)* Schalter *m* // *vt* entgegnen; **~act** [kauntə'rækt] *vt* entgegenwirken (+*dat*); **~-espionage** *n* Spionageabwehr *f*.

counterfeit ['kauntəfi:t] *n* Fälschung *f* // *vt* fälschen // *a* gefälscht.

counterfoil ['kauntəfɔil] *n* (Kontroll)abschnitt *m*.

countermand ['kauntəmɑ:nd] *vt* rückgängig machen.

counterpart ['kauntəpɑ:t] *n (object)* Gegenstück *nt*; *(person)* Gegenüber *nt*.

counterproductive ['kauntəprə'dʌktɪv] *a* destruktiv.

countersign ['kauntəsain] *vt* gegenzeichnen.

countess ['kauntɪs] *n* Gräfin *f*.

countless ['kauntlɪs] *a* zahllos, unzählig.

country ['kʌntrɪ] *n* Land *nt*; **~ dancing** *n (Brit)* Volkstanz *m*; **~ house** *n* Landhaus *nt*; **~man** *n (national)* Landsmann *m*; *(rural)* Bauer *m*; **~side** *n* Landschaft *f*.

county ['kauntɪ] *n* Landkreis *m*; *(Brit)* Grafschaft *f*.

coup [ku:], *pl* **~s** [ku:z] *n* Coup *m*; (*also*: ~ **d'état**) *n* Staatsstreich *m*, Putsch *m*.

coupé [ku:'peɪ] *n (AUT)* Coupé *nt*.

couple ['kʌpl] *n* Paar *nt*; **a ~ of** ein paar // *vt* koppeln.

coupon ['ku:pɔn] *n* Gutschein *m*.

courage ['kʌrɪdʒ] n Mut m; **~ous** [kə'reɪdʒəs] a mutig.

courgette [kuə'ʒet] n (Brit) Zucchini f.

courier ['kurɪə*] n (for holiday) Reiseleiter m; (messenger) Kurier m.

course [kɔːs] n (race) Bahn f; (of stream) Lauf m; (golf ~) Platz m; (NAUT, SCH) Kurs m; (in meal) Gang m; **summer ~** n Sommerkurs m; **of ~** ad natürlich.

court [kɔːt] n (royal) Hof m; (JUR) Gericht nt // vt (woman) gehen mit; (danger) herausfordern; **to take to ~** vor Gericht bringen.

courteous ['kɜːtɪəs] a höflich.

courtesan [kɔːtɪ'zæn] n Kurtisane f.

courtesy ['kɜːtəsɪ] n Höflichkeit f.

court-house ['kɔːthaus] n (US) Gerichtsgebäude nt.

courtier ['kɔːtɪə*] n Höfling m.

court-martial ['kɔːt'mɑːʃəl], pl **courts-martial** ['kɔːts'mɑːʃəl] n Kriegsgericht nt // vt vor ein Kriegsgericht stellen.

courtroom ['kɔːtrum] n Gerichtssaal m.

courtyard ['kɔːtjɑːd] n Hof m.

cousin ['kʌzn] n Cousin m, Vetter m; Kusine f.

cove [kəuv] n kleine Bucht f.

covenant ['kʌvənənt] n (ECCL) Bund m; (JUR) Verpflichtung f.

cover ['kʌvə*] vt (spread over) bedecken; (shield) abschirmen; (include) sich erstrecken über (+acc); (protect) decken; (distance) zurücklegen; (report on) berichten über (+ acc) // n (lid) Deckel m; (for bed) Decke f; (MIL) Bedeckung f; (of book) Einband m; (of magazine) Umschlag; (insurance) Versicherung f; **to take ~** (from rain) sich unterstellen; (MIL) in Deckung gehen; **under ~** (indoors) drinnen; **under ~ of** im Schutze (+ gen); **under separate ~** (COMM) mit getrennter Post; **to ~ up for sb** jdn decken; **~age** ['kʌvrɪdʒ] n (PRESS: reports) Berichterstattung f; (distribution) Verbreitung f; **~ charge** n Bedienungsgeld nt; **~ing** n Bedeckung f; **~ing letter**, (US) **~ letter** n Begleitbrief m; **~ note** n (INSURANCE) vorläufige(r) Versicherungsschein m.

covert ['kʌvət] a geheim.

cover-up ['kʌvərʌp] n Vertuschung f.

covet ['kʌvɪt] vt begehren.

cow [kau] n Kuh f // vt einschüchtern.

coward ['kauəd] n Feigling m; **~ice** ['kauədɪs] n Feigheit f; **~ly** a feige.

cowboy ['kaubɔɪ] n Cowboy m.

cower ['kauə*] vi kauern.

coxswain ['kɒksn] n (abbr: cox) Steuermann m.

coy [kɔɪ] a schüchtern.

coyote [kɔɪ'əutɪ] n Präriewolf m.

cozy ['kəuzɪ] a (US) = **cosy.**

CPA (US) abbr of **certified public accountant.**

crab [kræb] n Krebs m; **~ apple** n Holzapfel m.

crack [kræk] n Riß m, Sprung m; (noise) Knall m // vt (break) springen lassen; (joke) reißen; (nut, safe) knacken; (whip) knallen lassen // a erstklassig; (troops) Elite-; **~ down** vi: **to ~ down (on)** hart durchgreifen (bei); **~ up** vi (fig) zusammenbrechen; **~er** n (firework) Knallkörper m, Kracher m; (biscuit) Keks m; (Christmas ~) Knallbonbon nt.

crackle ['krækl] vi knistern; (fire) prasseln.

cradle ['kreɪdl] n Wiege f.

craft [krɑːft] n (skill) (Hand- or Kunst)fertigkeit f; (trade) Handwerk nt; (NAUT) Schiff nt; **~sman** n Handwerker m; **~smanship** n (quality) handwerkliche Ausführung f; (ability) handwerkliche(s) Können nt; **~y** a schlau.

crag [kræg] n Klippe f.

cram [kræm] vt vollstopfen (with mit) // vi (learn) pauken; **to ~ sth into** etw in (+acc) stopfen.

cramp [kræmp] n Krampf m // vt (limit) einengen; (hinder) hemmen; **~ed** a (position) verkrampft; (space) eng.

crampon ['kræmpən] n Steigeisen nt.

cranberry ['krænbərɪ] n Preiselbeere f.

crane [kreɪn] n (machine) Kran m; (bird) Kranich m.

crank [kræŋk] n (lever) Kurbel f; (person) Spinner m; **~shaft** n Kurbelwelle f.

cranny ['krænɪ] n see **nook.**

crash [kræʃ] n (noise) Krachen nt; (with cars) Zusammenstoß m; (with plane) Absturz m; (COMM) Zusammenbruch m // vt (plane) abstürzen mit // vi (cars) zusammenstoßen; (plane) abstürzen; (economy) zusammenbrechen; (noise) knallen; **~ course** n Schnellkurs m; **~ helmet** n Sturzhelm m; **~ landing** n Bruchlandung f.

crass [kræs] a kraß.

crate [kreɪt] n (lit, fig) Kiste f.

crater ['kreɪtə*] n Krater m.

cravat(e) [krə'væt] n Halstuch nt.

crave [kreɪv] vt verlangen nach.

crawl [krɔːl] vi kriechen; (baby) krabbeln // n Kriechen nt; (swim) Kraul nt.

crayfish ['kreɪfɪʃ] n, pl inv (freshwater) Krebs m; (saltwater) Languste f.

crayon ['kreɪən] n Buntstift m.

craze [kreɪz] n Fimmel m.

crazy ['kreɪzɪ] a verrückt; **~ paving** n Mosaikpflaster nt.

creak [kriːk] vi knarren.

cream [kriːm] n (from milk) Rahm m, Sahne f; (polish, cosmetic) Creme f;

(fig: people) Elite *f* // a cremfarbig; ~
cake *n* Sahnetorte *f*; ~ **cheese** *n*
Rahmquark *m*; ~y *a* sahnig.
crease [kri:s] *n* Falte *f* // *vt* falten;
(untidy) zerknittern // *vi (wrinkle up)*
knittern.
create [kri'eit] *vt* erschaffen; *(cause)*
verursachen.
creation [kri'eiʃən] *n* Schöpfung *f*.
creative [kri'eitiv] *a* kreativ.
creator [kri'eitə*] *n* Schöpfer *m*.
creature ['kri:tʃə*] *n* Geschöpf *nt*.
crèche, creche [kreʃ] *n* Krippe *f*.
credence ['kri:dəns] *n*: to lend *or* give ~
to sth etw *(dat)* Glauben schenken.
credentials [kri'denʃəlz] *npl* Be-
glaubigungsschreiben *nt*.
credibility [kredi'biliti] *n* Glaubwürdig-
keit *f*.
credible ['kredibl] *a (person)*
glaubwürdig; *(story)* glaubhaft.
credit ['kredit] *n (COMM also)* Kredit *m*
// *vt* Glauben schenken (+*dat*); *(COMM)*
gutschreiben; ~s *pl (of film)* die Mit-
wirkenden; ~**able** *a* rühmlich; ~ **card**
n Kreditkarte *f*; ~**or** *n* Gläubiger *m*.
creed [kri:d] *n* Glaubensbekenntnis *nt*.
creek [kri:k] *n (inlet)* kleine Bucht *f*;
(US: river) kleine(r) Wasserlauf *m*.
creep [kri:p], *pt, pp* **crept** *vi* kriechen;
~**er** *n* Kletterpflanze *f*; ~**y** *a*
(frightening) gruselig.
cremation [kri'meiʃən] *n* Einäscherung
f.
crêpe [kreip] *n* Krepp *m*; ~ **bandage** *n*
(Brit) Elastikbinde *f*.
crept [krept] *pt, pp of* **creep**.
crescent ['kresnt] *n (of moon)*
Halbmond *m*.
cress [kres] *n* Kresse *f*.
crest [krest] *n (of cock)* Kamm *m*; *(of
wave)* Wellenkamm *m*; *(coat of arms)*
Wappen *nt*; ~**fallen** *a* niedergeschlagen.
Crete [kri:t] *n* Kreta *nt*.
crevasse [kri'væs] *n* Gletscherspalte *f*.
crevice ['krevis] *n* Riß *m*.
crew [kru:] *n* Besatzung *f*, Mannschaft *f*;
~**-cut** *n* Bürstenschnitt *m*; ~**-neck** *n*
runde(r) Ausschnitt *m*.
crib [krib] *n (bed)* Krippe *f* // *vt* spicken
(col).
crick [krik] *n* Muskelkrampf *m*.
cricket ['krikit] *n (insect)* Grille *f*;
(game) Kricket *nt*.
crime [kraim] *n* Verbrechen *nt*.
criminal ['kriminl] *n* Verbrecher *m* // *a*
kriminell; *(act)* strafbar.
crimson ['krimzn] *a* leuchtend rot.
cringe [krindʒ] *vi* sich ducken.
crinkle ['kriŋkl] *vt* zerknittern.
cripple ['kripl] *n* Krüppel *m* // *vt*
lahmlegen; *(MED)* verkrüppeln.
crisis ['kraisis], *pl* **-ses** ['kraisi:z] *n*
Krise *f*.
crisp [krisp] *a* knusprig; ~**s** *npl (Brit)*

Chips *pl*.
criss-cross ['kriskrɒs] *a* gekreuzt,
Kreuz-.
criterion [krai'tiəriən], *pl* **-ria**
[krai'tiəriə] *n* Kriterium *nt*.
critic ['kritik] *n* Kritiker(in *f*) *m*; ~**al** *a*
kritisch; ~**ally** *ad* kritisch; *(ill)* gefährlich; ~**ism** ['kritisizəm] *n* Kritik *f*;
~**ize** ['kritisaiz] *vt* kritisieren.
croak [krəuk] *vi* krächzen; *(frog)*
quaken.
crochet ['krəuʃei] *n* Häkelei *f*.
crockery ['krɒkəri] *n* Geschirr *nt*.
crocodile ['krɒkədail] *n* Krokodil *nt*.
crocus ['krəukəs] *n* Krokus *m*.
croft [krɒft] *n (Brit)* kleine(s) Pachtgut
nt.
crony ['krəuni] *n (col)* Kumpel *m*.
crook [kruk] *n (criminal)* Gauner *m*;
(stick) Hirtenstab *m*; ~**ed** ['krukid] *a*
krumm.
crop [krɒp] *n (harvest)* Ernte *f*; *(riding
~)* Reitpeitsche *f* // *vt* ernten; ~ **up** *vi*
passieren.
croquet ['krəukei] *n* Krocket *nt*.
croquette [krə'ket] *n* Krokette *f*.
cross [krɒs] *n* Kreuz *nt* // *vt (road)* überqueren; *(legs)* übereinander legen;
kreuzen // *a (annoyed)* böse; ~ **out** *vt*
streichen; ~ **over** *vi* hinübergehen;
~**bar** *n* Querstange *f*; ~**breed** *n* Kreuzung *f*; ~**country (race)** *n* Geländelauf
m; ~**-examine** *vt* ins Kreuzverhör
nehmen; ~**-eyed** *a*: to be ~**-eyed**
schielen; ~**fire** *n* Kreuzfeuer *nt*; ~**ing** *n*
(crossroads) (Straßen)kreuzung *f*; *(of
ship)* Überfahrt *f*; *(for pedestrians)*
Fußgängerüberweg *m*; ~**ing guard** *n*
(US) Schülerlotse *m*; ~ **purposes** *npl*:
to be at ~ purposes aneinander vor-
beireden; ~**-reference** *n* Querverweis
m; ~**roads** *n* Straßenkreuzung *f*; *(fig)*
Scheideweg *m*; ~ **section** *n* Querschnitt
m; ~**walk** *n (US)* Fußgängerüberweg
m; ~**wind** *n* Seitenwind *m*; ~**word
(puzzle)** *n* Kreuzworträtsel *nt*.
crotch [krɒtʃ] *n* Zwickel *m*; *(ANAT)*
Unterleib *nt*.
crotchet ['krɒtʃit] *n* Viertelnote *f*.
crotchety ['krɒtʃiti] *a* launenhaft.
crouch [krautʃ] *vi* hocken.
croupier ['kru:piei] *n* Croupier *m*.
crow [krəu] *n (bird)* Krähe *f*; *(of cock)*
Krähen *nt* // *vi* krähen.
crowbar ['krəubɑ:*] *n* Stemmeisen *nt*.
crowd [kraud] *n* Menge *f* // *vt (fill)* über-
füllen // *vi* drängen; ~**ed** *a* überfüllt.
crown [kraun] *n* Krone *f*; *(of head, hat)*
Kopf *m* // *vt* krönen; ~ **jewels** *pl*
Kronjuwelen *pl*; ~ **prince** *n* Kronprinz
m.
crow's-feet ['krəuzfi:t] *npl* Krähenfüße
pl.
crucial ['kru:ʃəl] *a* entscheidend.
crucifix ['kru:sifiks] *n* Kruzifix *nt*; ~**ion**

[kruːsɪ'fɪkʃən] n Kreuzigung f.
crucify ['kruːsɪfaɪ] vt kreuzigen.
crude [kruːd] a (raw) roh; (humour, behaviour) grob; (basic) primitiv; ~ **(oil)** n Rohöl nt.
cruel ['kruəl] a grausam; ~**ty** n Grausamkeit f.
cruet ['kruːɪt] n Gewürzständer m.
cruise [kruːz] n Kreuzfahrt f // vi kreuzen; ~**r** n (MIL) Kreuzer m.
crumb [krʌm] n Krume f.
crumble ['krʌmbl] vti zerbröckeln.
crumbly ['krʌmblɪ] a krümelig.
crumpet ['krʌmpɪt] n Tee(pfann)kuchen m.
crumple ['krʌmpl] vt zerknittern.
crunch [krʌntʃ] n: **the** ~ (fig) der Knackpunkt // vt knirschen; ~**y** a knusprig.
crusade [kruːˈseɪd] n Kreuzzug m.
crush [krʌʃ] n Gedränge nt; (drink): lemon ~ Zitronensaft m // vt zerdrücken; (rebellion) unterdrücken.
crust [krʌst] n Kruste f.
crutch [krʌtʃ] n Krücke f.
crux [krʌks] n der springende Punkt.
cry [kraɪ] vi (shout) schreien; (weep) weinen // n (call) Schrei m; ~ **off** vi (plötzlich) absagen.
crypt [krɪpt] n Krypta f.
cryptic ['krɪptɪk] a hintergründig.
crystal ['krɪstl] n Kristall m; (glass) Kristallglas nt; (mineral) Bergkristall m; ~-**clear** a kristallklar; ~**lize** vti (lit) kristallisieren; (fig) klären.
cub [kʌb] n Junge(s) nt; (also: ~ scout) Wölfling m.
Cuba ['kjuːbə] n Kuba nt; ~**n** a kubanisch // n Kubaner(in f) m.
cubbyhole ['kʌbɪhəʊl] n Eckchen nt.
cube [kjuːb] n Würfel m // vt (MATH) hoch drei nehmen; ~ **root** n Kubikwurzel f.
cubic ['kjuːbɪk] a würfelförmig; (centimetre etc) Kubik-; ~ **capacity** n Fassungsvermögen nt.
cubicle ['kjuːbɪkl] n Kabine f.
cuckoo ['kʊkuː] n Kuckuck m; ~ **clock** n Kuckucksuhr f.
cucumber ['kjuːkʌmbə*] n Gurke f.
cuddle ['kʌdl] vti herzen, drücken (col).
cue [kjuː] n (THEAT) Stichwort nt; (snooker ~) Billardstock m.
cuff [kʌf] n (Brit: of shirt, coat etc) Manschette f; Aufschlag m; (US) ~ **turn-up; off the** ~ ad aus dem Handgelenk; ~**link** n Manschettenknopf m.
cuisine [kwɪˈziːn] n Kochkunst f, Küche f.
cul-de-sac ['kʌldəsæk] n Sackgasse f.
culinary ['kʌlɪnərɪ] a Koch-.
cull [kʌl] vt (flowers) pflücken; (select) auswählen.
culminate ['kʌlmɪneɪt] vi gipfeln.

culmination [kʌlmɪˈneɪʃən] n Höhepunkt m.
culottes [kjuːˈlɒts] npl Hosenrock m.
culpable ['kʌlpəbl] a schuldig.
culprit ['kʌlprɪt] n Täter m.
cult [kʌlt] n Kult m.
cultivate ['kʌltɪveɪt] vt (AGR) bebauen; (mind) bilden.
cultivation [kʌltɪˈveɪʃən] n (AGR) Bebauung f; (of person) Bildung f.
cultural ['kʌltʃərəl] a kulturell, Kultur-.
culture ['kʌltʃə*] n Kultur f; ~**d** a gebildet.
cumbersome ['kʌmbəsəm] a (object) sperrig.
cummerbund ['kʌməbʌnd] n Kummerbund m.
cumulative ['kjuːmjʊlətɪv] a gehäuft.
cunning ['kʌnɪŋ] n Verschlagenheit f // a schlau.
cup [kʌp] n Tasse f; (prize) Pokal m.
cupboard ['kʌbəd] n Schrank m.
Cupid ['kjuːpɪd] n Amor m.
cup-tie ['kʌptaɪ] n (Brit) Pokalspiel nt.
curate ['kjʊərɪt] n (Catholic) Kurat m; (Protestant) Vikar m.
curator [kjʊˈreɪtə*] n Kustos m.
curb [kɜːb] vt zügeln // n (on spending etc) Einschränkung f; (US) Bordstein m.
curdle ['kɜːdl] vi gerinnen.
cure [kjʊə*] n Heilmittel nt; (process) Heilverfahren nt // vt heilen.
curfew ['kɜːfjuː] n Ausgangssperre f; Sperrstunde f.
curiosity [kjʊərɪˈɒsɪtɪ] n Neugier f.
curious ['kjʊərɪəs] a neugierig; (strange) seltsam.
curl [kɜːl] n Locke f // vt locken // vi sich locken; ~ **up** vi sich zusammenrollen; (person) sich anschmiegen; ~**er** n Lockenwickler m; ~**y** a lockig.
currant ['kʌrənt] n Korinthe f.
currency ['kʌrənsɪ] n Währung f; to gain ~ an Popularität gewinnen.
current ['kʌrənt] n Strömung f // a (expression) gängig, üblich; (issue) neueste; ~ **account** n (Brit) Girokonto nt; ~ **affairs** npl Zeitgeschehen nt; ~**ly** ad zur Zeit.
curriculum [kəˈrɪkjʊləm], pl ~**s** or **curricula** [kəˈrɪkjʊlə] n Lehrplan m; ~ **vitae (CV)** n Lebenslauf m.
curry ['kʌrɪ] n Currygericht nt // vt: **to** ~ favour with sich einschmeicheln bei; ~ **powder** n Curry(pulver) nt.
curse [kɜːs] vi (swear) fluchen (at auf +acc) // vt (insult) verwünschen // n Fluch m.
cursor ['kɜːsə*] n (COMPUT) Cursor m.
cursory ['kɜːsərɪ] a flüchtig.
curt [kɜːt] a schroff.
curtail [kɜːˈteɪl] vt abkürzen; (rights) einschränken.
curtain ['kɜːtn] n Vorhang m.
curtsey ['kɜːtsɪ] n Knicks m // vi

knicksen.

curve [kɜːv] n Kurve f; (of body, vase etc) Rundung f // vi sich biegen; (hips, breasts) sich runden; (road) einen Bogen machen.

cushion ['kʊʃən] n Kissen nt // vt dämpfen.

custard ['kʌstəd] n Vanillesoße f.

custodian [kʌs'təʊdɪən] n Kustos m, Verwalter(in f) m.

custody ['kʌstədɪ] n Aufsicht f; (police) Haft f; to take into ~ verhaften.

custom ['kʌstəm] n (tradition) Brauch m; (COMM) Kundschaft f; ~ary a üblich.

customer ['kʌstəmə*] n Kunde m, Kundin f.

customized ['kʌstəmaɪzd] a (car etc) mit Spezialausrüstung.

custom-made ['kʌstəm'meɪd] a speziell angefertigt.

customs ['kʌstəmz] npl Zoll m; ~ officer n Zollbeamte(r) mf.

cut [kʌt], pt, pp **cut** vt schneiden; (wages) kürzen; (prices) heruntersetzen; // vi schneiden; (intersect) sich schneiden // n Schnitt m; (wound) Schnittwunde f; (in book, income etc) Kürzung f; (share) Anteil m; to ~ a tooth zahnen; ~ **down** vt (tree) fällen; (reduce) einschränken; ~ **off** vt (lit, fig) abschneiden; (allowance) sperren; ~ **out** vt (shape) ausschneiden; (delete) streichen; ~ **up** vt (meat) aufschneiden; ~**back** n Kürzung; (CINE) Rückblende.

cute [kjuːt] a niedlich.

cuticle ['kjuːtɪkl] n Nagelhaut f.

cutlery ['kʌtlərɪ] n Besteck nt.

cutlet ['kʌtlɪt] n (pork) Kotelett nt; (veal) Schnitzel nt.

cutout ['kʌtaʊt] n (cardboard ~) Ausschneidemodell nt.

cut-price ['kʌtpraɪs], (US) **cut-rate** ['kʌtreɪt] a verbilligt.

cut throat ['kʌtθrəʊt] n Verbrechertyp m // a mörderisch.

cutting ['kʌtɪŋ] a schneidend // n (Brit: PRESS) Ausschnitt m; (: RAIL) Durchstich m.

CV n abbr of **curriculum vitae**.

cwt abbr of **hundredweight(s)**.

cyanide ['saɪənaɪd] n Zyankali nt.

cycle ['saɪkl] n Fahrrad nt; (series) Reihe f // vi radfahren; **cycling** ['saɪklɪŋ] n Radfahren nt; **cyclist** ['saɪklɪst] n Radfahrer(in f) m.

cyclone ['saɪkləʊn] n Zyklon m.

cygnet ['sɪgnɪt] n junge(r) Schwan m.

cylinder ['sɪlɪndə*] n Zylinder m; (TECH) Walze f; ~-**head gasket** n Zylinderkopfdichtung f.

cymbals ['sɪmbəlz] npl Becken nt.

cynic ['sɪnɪk] n Zyniker(in f) m; ~**al** a zynisch; ~**ism** ['sɪnɪsɪzəm] n Zynismus

m.

cypress ['saɪprɪs] n Zypresse f.

Cypriot ['sɪprɪət] a zypriotisch // n Zypriot(in f) m.

Cyprus ['saɪprəs] n Zypern nt.

cyst [sɪst] n Zyste f; ~**itis** n Blasenentzündung f.

czar [zɑː*] n Zar m.

Czech [tʃek] a tschechisch // n Tscheche m, Tschechin f.

Czechoslovakia [tʃekəslə'vækɪə] n die Tschechoslowakei; ~**n** a tschechoslowakisch // n Tschechoslowake m, Tchechoslowakin f.

D

D [diː] n (MUS): ~ **sharp/flat** Dis, dis nt/ Des, des nt.

dab [dæb] vt (wound, paint) betupfen // n (little bit) bißchen nt; (of paint) Tupfer m.

dabble ['dæbl] vi: to ~ **in** sth in etw (dat) machen.

dad [dæd], **daddy** ['dædɪ] n Papa m, Vati m; **daddy-long-legs** n Weberknecht m.

daffodil ['dæfədɪl] n Osterglocke f.

daft [dɑːft] a (col) blöd(e), doof.

dagger ['dægə*] n Dolch m.

daily ['deɪlɪ] a täglich // n (PRESS) Tageszeitung f; (woman) Haushaltshilfe f // ad täglich.

dainty ['deɪntɪ] a zierlich.

dairy ['dɛərɪ] n (Brit: shop) Milchgeschäft nt; (on farm) Molkerei f // a Milch-; ~ **farm** n Hof m mit Milchwirtschaft; ~ **produce** n Molkereiprodukte pl; ~ **store** n (US) Milchgeschäft nt.

dais ['deɪɪs] n Podium nt.

daisy ['deɪzɪ] n Gänseblümchen nt; ~ **wheel** n (on printer) Typenrad nt.

dale [deɪl] n Tal nt.

dam [dæm] n (Stau)damm m // vt stauen.

damage ['dæmɪdʒ] n Schaden m // vt beschädigen; ~**s** pl (JUR) Schaden(s)ersatz m.

damn [dæm] vt verdammen // n (col): I don't give a ~ das ist mir total egal // a (col: also: ~ed) verdammt; ~ **it!** verflucht!; ~**ing** a vernichtend.

damp [dæmp] a feucht // n Feuchtigkeit f // vt (also: ~**en**) befeuchten; (discourage) dämpfen.

damson ['dæmzən] n Damaszenerpflaume f.

dance [dɑːns] n Tanz m // vi tanzen; ~ **hall** n Tanzlokal nt; ~**r** n Tänzer m.

dancing ['dɑːnsɪŋ] n Tanzen nt.

dandelion ['dændɪlaɪən] n Löwenzahn m.

dandruff ['dændrəf] n (Kopf)schuppen pl.

Dane [dein] n Däne m, Dänin f.

danger ['deindʒə*] n Gefahr f; ~! (sign) Achtung!; **to be in ~ of doing sth** Gefahr laufen, etw zu tun; **~ous** a, **~ously** ad gefährlich.

dangle ['dæŋgl] vi baumeln // vt herabhängen lassen.

Danish ['deiniʃ] a dänisch // n Dänisch nt.

dapper ['dæpə*] a elegant.

dare [dɛə*] vt herausfordern // vi: **to ~ (to) do sth** es wagen, etw zu tun; **I ~ say** ich würde sagen; **~-devil** n Draufgänger(in f) m.

daring ['dɛəriŋ] a (audacious) verwegen; (bold) wagemutig; (dress) gewagt // n Mut m.

dark [dɑːk] a dunkel; (fig) düster, trübe; (deep colour) dunkel- // n Dunkelheit f; **to be left in the ~ about** im dunkeln sein über (+ acc); **after ~** nach Anbruch der Dunkelheit; **~en** vti verdunkeln; **~ glasses** npl Sonnenbrille f; **~ness** n Finsternis nt; **~room** n Dunkelkammer f.

darling ['dɑːliŋ] n Liebling m // a lieb.

darn [dɑːn] vt stopfen.

dart [dɑːt] n (weapon) Pfeil m; (in sewing) Abnäher m // vi sausen; **~s** npl (game) Pfeilwerfen nt; **~board** n Zielscheibe f.

dash [dæʃ] n Sprung m; (mark) (Gedanken)strich m; (small amount) bißchen m // vt (hopes) zunichte machen // vi stürzen; **~ away** or **off** vi davonstürzen.

dashboard ['dæʃbɔːd] n Armaturenbrett nt.

dashing ['dæʃiŋ] a schneidig.

data ['deitə] npl Einzelheiten pl, Daten pl; **~ base** n Datenbank f; **~ processing** n Datenverarbeitung f.

date [deit] n Datum nt; (for meeting etc) Termin m; (with person) Verabredung f; (fruit) Dattel f // vt (letter etc) datieren; (person) gehen mit; **~ of birth** Geburtsdatum nt; **to ~** ad bis heute; **out of ~** überholt; up to date; (clothes) modisch; (report) up-to-date; (with news) auf dem laufenden; **~d** a altmodisch.

daub [dɔːb] vt beschmieren; (paint) schmieren.

daughter ['dɔːtə*] n Tochter f; **~-in-law** n Schwiegertochter f.

daunting ['dɔːntiŋ] a entmutigend.

dawdle ['dɔːdl] vi trödeln.

dawn [dɔːn] n Morgendämmerung f // vi dämmern; (fig): **it ~ed on him that** ... es dämmerte ihm, daß ...

day [dei] n Tag m; **the ~ before/after** am Tag zuvor/danach; **the ~ after tomorrow** übermorgen; **the ~ before yesterday** vorgestern; **by ~** am Tage; **~break** n Tagesanbruch m; **~dream** vi mit

offenen Augen träumen; **~light** n Tageslicht nt; **~ return** n (Brit) Tagesrückfahrkarte f; **~time** n Tageszeit f; **~-to-~** a alltäglich.

daze [deiz] vt betäuben // n Betäubung f; **in a ~** benommen.

dazzle ['dæzl] vt blenden.

DC abbr (= direct current) Gleichstrom m.

D-day ['diːdei] n (HIST) Tag der Invasion durch die Alliierten (6.6.44); (fig) der Tag X.

deacon ['diːkən] n Diakon m.

dead [ded] a tot; (without feeling) gefühllos; // ad ganz; (exactly) genau; **to shoot sb ~** jdn erschießen; **~ tired** todmüde; **to stop ~** abrupt stehenbleiben; **the ~** pl die Toten pl; **~en** vt (pain) abtöten; (sound) ersticken; **~ end** n Sackgasse f; **~ heat** n tote(s) Rennen nt; **~line** n Stichtag m; **~lock** n Stillstand m; **~ly** a tödlich; **~pan** a undurchdringlich; **the D~ Sea** n das Tote Meer.

deaf [def] a taub; **~en** vt taub machen; **~ness** n Taubheit f; **~-mute** n Taubstumme(r) m.

deal [diːl] n Geschäft nt // vt, pt, pp **dealt** [delt] austeilen; (CARDS) geben; **a great ~ of** sehr viel; **~ in** vt handeln mit; **~ with** vt (person) behandeln; (subject) sich befassen mit; (problem) in Angriff nehmen; **~er** n (COMM) Händler m; (CARDS) Kartengeber m; **~ings** npl (FIN) Geschäfte pl; (relations) Beziehungen pl.

dean [diːn] n (Protestant) Superintendent m; (Catholic) Dechant m; (UNIV) Dekan m.

dear [diə*] a lieb; (expensive) teuer // n Liebling m // interj: **~ me!** du liebe Zeit!; **D~ Sir** Sehr geehrter Herr!; **D~ John** Lieber John!; **~ly** ad (love) herzlich; (pay) teuer.

death [deθ] n Tod m; (statistic) Todesfall m; (~ certificate) n Totenschein m; **~ duties** npl (Brit) Erbschaftssteuer f; **~ly** a totenähnlich, Toten-; **~ penalty** n Todesstrafe f; **~ rate** n Sterblichkeitsziffer f.

debar [dɪ'bɑː*] vt ausschließen.

debase [dɪ'beis] vt entwerten.

debatable [dɪ'beitəbl] a anfechtbar.

debate [dɪ'beit] n Debatte f // vt debattieren, diskutieren; (consider) überlegen.

debauchery [dɪ'bɔːtʃəri] n Ausschweifungen pl.

debilitating [dɪ'biliteitiŋ] a schwächend.

debit ['debit] n Schuldposten m // vt belasten.

debris ['debriː] n Trümmer pl.

debt [det] n Schuld f; **to be in ~** verschuldet sein; **~or** n Schuldner m.

debunk [di:'bʌŋk] vt entlarven.
decade ['dekeɪd] n Jahrzehnt nt.
decaffeinated [di:'kæfɪneɪtɪd] a koffein-frei.
decanter [dɪ'kæntə*] n Karaffe f.
decay [dɪ'keɪ] n Verfall m; (tooth ~) Karies m // vi verfallen; (teeth, meat etc) faulen; (leaves etc) verrotten.
deceased [dɪ'si:st] a verstorben.
deceit [dɪ'si:t] n Betrug m; ~ful a falsch.
deceive [dɪ'si:v] vt täuschen.
December [dɪ'sembə*] n Dezember m.
decency ['di:sənsɪ] n Anstand m.
decent [di:sənt] a (respectable) an-ständig; (pleasant) annehmbar.
deception [dɪ'sepʃən] n Betrug m.
deceptive [dɪ'septɪv] a irreführend.
decibel ['desɪbel] n Dezibel nt.
decide [dɪ'saɪd] vt entscheiden // vi sich entscheiden; **to ~ on sth** etw be-schließen; ~d a entschieden; ~dly [-dɪdlɪ] ad entschieden.
deciduous [dɪ'sɪdjuəs] a Laub-.
decimal ['desɪməl] a dezimal // n Dezimalzahl f; ~ **point** n Komma nt.
decimate ['desɪmeɪt] vt dezimieren.
decipher [dɪ'saɪfə*] vt entziffern.
decision [dɪ'sɪʒən] n Entscheidung f, Entschluß m.
decisive [dɪ'saɪsɪv] a entscheidend; (person) entschlossen.
deck [dek] n (NAUT) Deck nt; (of cards) Pack m; ~**chair** n Liegestuhl m.
declaration [deklə'reɪʃən] n Erklärung f.
declare [dɪ'kleə*] vt erklären; (CUS-TOMS) verzollen.
decline [dɪ'klaɪn] n (decay) Verfall m; (lessening) Rückgang m // vt (invitation) ablehnen // vi (of strength) nachlassen; (say no) ablehnen.
declutch ['di:'klʌtʃ] vi auskuppeln.
decode ['di:'kəud] vt entschlüsseln.
decompose [di:kəm'pəuz] vi (sich) zersetzen.
décor ['deɪkɔ:*] n Ausstattung f.
decorate ['dekəreɪt] vt (room: paper) tapezieren; (: paint) streichen; (adorn) (aus)schmücken; (cake) verzieren; (honour) auszeichnen.
decoration [dekə'reɪʃən] n (of house) (Wand)dekoration f; (medal) Orden m.
decorator ['dekəreɪtə*] n Maler m, An-streicher m.
decorum [dɪ'kɔ:rəm] n Anstand m.
decoy ['di:kɔɪ] n Lockvogel m.
decrease ['di:kri:s] n Abnahme f // v [di:'kri:s] vt vermindern // vi abnehmen.
decree [dɪ'kri:] n Erlaß m; ~ **nisi** n vorläufiges Scheidungsurteil nt.
decrepit [dɪ'krepɪt] a hinfällig.
dedicate ['dedɪkeɪt] vt widmen.
dedication [dedɪ'keɪʃən] n (devotion) Ergebenheit; (in book) Widmung f.

deduce [dɪ'dju:s] vt ableiten, schließen (from aus).
deduct [dɪ'dʌkt] vt abziehen; ~**ion** [dɪ'dʌkʃən] n (of money) Abzug m; (conclusion) (Schluß)folgerung f.
deed [di:d] n Tat f; (document) Urkunde f.
deem [di:m] vt: **to ~ sb/sth (to be)** sth jdn/etw für etw halten.
deep [di:p] a tief // ad: **the spectators stood 20 ~** die Zuschauer standen in 20 Reihen hintereinander; ~**en** vt vertiefen // vi (darkness) tiefer werden; ~**freeze** n Tiefkühlung f; ~**fry** vt fritieren; ~**ly** ad tief; ~**sea** diving n Tiefseetauchen nt; ~**seated** a tiefsitzend.
deer [dɪə*] n Reh nt; ~**skin** n Hirsch-/Rehleder nt.
deface [dɪ'feɪs] vt entstellen.
defamation [defə'meɪʃən] n Verleum-dung f.
default [dɪ'fɔ:lt] n Versäumnis nt // vi versäumen // n (COMPUT) Standardwert m; **by ~** durch Nichterscheinen nt.
defeat [dɪ'fi:t] n Niederlage f // vt schlagen; ~**ist** a defätistisch // n Defätist m.
defect ['di:fekt] n Fehler m // vi [dɪ'fekt] überlaufen; ~**ive** [dɪ'fektɪv] a fehlerhaft.
defence [dɪ'fens] n Verteidigung f; ~**less** a wehrlos.
defend [dɪ'fend] vt verteidigen; ~**ant** n Angeklagte(r) m; ~**er** n Verteidiger m.
defense [dɪ'fens] n (US) = **defence**.
defensive [dɪ'fensɪv] a defensiv // n: **on the ~** in der Defensive.
defer [dɪ'fɜ:*] vt verschieben.
deference ['defərəns] n Rücksichtnahme f.
defiance [dɪ'faɪəns] n Trotz m, Unnachgiebigkeit f; **in ~ of sth** etw (dat) zum Trotz.
defiant [dɪ'faɪənt] a trotzig, unnachgiebig.
deficiency [dɪ'fɪʃənsɪ] n (lack) Mangel m; (weakness) Schwäche f.
deficient [dɪ'fɪʃənt] a mangelhaft.
deficit ['defɪsɪt] n Defizit nt.
defile [dɪ'faɪl] vt beschmutzen.
define [dɪ'faɪn] vt bestimmen; (explain) definieren.
definite ['defɪnɪt] a (fixed) definitiv; (clear) eindeutig; ~**ly** ad bestimmt.
definition [defɪ'nɪʃən] n Definition f; (PHOT) Schärfe f.
deflate [dɪ'fleɪt] vt die Luft ablassen aus.
deflect [dɪ'flekt] vt ablenken.
deform [dɪ'fɔ:m] vt deformieren; ~**ity** n Mißbildung f.
defraud [dɪ'frɔ:d] vt betrügen.
defray [dɪ'freɪ] vt (costs) übernehmen.
defrost [di:'frɒst] vt (fridge) abtauen; (food) auftauen; ~**er** n (US: demister)

Gebläse *nt.*
deft [deft] *a* geschickt.
defunct [dı'fʌŋkt] *a* verstorben.
defuse [di:'fju:z] *vt* entschärfen.
defy [dı'faı] *vt* (*disobey*) sich widersetzen (+*dat*); (*orders, death*) trotzen (+*dat*); (*challenge*) herausfordern.
degenerate [dı'dʒenəreıt] *vi* degenerieren // *a* [dı'dʒenərıt] degeneriert.
degrading [dı'greıdıŋ] *a* erniedrigend.
degree [dı'gri:] *n* Grad *m*; (*UNIV*) Universitätsabschluß *m*; by ~s allmählich; to some ~ zu einem gewissen Grad.
dehydrated [di:haı'dreıtıd] *a* (*person*) ausgetrocknet; (*food*) Trocken-.
de-ice [di:'aıs] *vt* enteisen.
deign [deın] *vi* sich herablassen.
deity ['di:ıtı] *n* Gottheit *f.*
dejected [dı'dʒektıd] *a* niedergeschlagen.
delay [dı'leı] *vt* (*hold back*) aufschieben // *vi* (*linger*) sich aufhalten // *n* Aufschub *m*, Verzögerung *f*; (*of train etc*) Verspätung *f*; to be ~ed (*train*) Verspätung haben; without ~ unverzüglich.
delectable [dı'lektəbl] *a* köstlich; (*fig*) reizend.
delegate ['delıgıt] *n* Delegierte(r) *mf* // *vt* ['delıgeıt] delegieren.
delete [dı'li:t] *vt* (aus)streichen.
deliberate [dı'lıbərıt] *a* (*intentional*) absichtlich; (*slow*) bedächtig // *vi* [dı'lıbəreıt] (*consider*) überlegen; (*debate*) sich beraten; ~ly *ad* absichtlich.
delicacy ['delıkəsı] *n* Zartheit *f*; (*weakness*) Anfälligkeit *f*; (*food*) Delikatesse *f.*
delicate ['delıkıt] *a* (*fine*) fein; (*fragile*) zart; (*situation*) heikel; (*MED*) empfindlich.
delicatessen [delıkə'tesn] *n* Feinkostgeschäft *nt.*
delicious [dı'lıʃəs] *a* lecker.
delight [dı'laıt] *n* Wonne *f* // *vt* entzücken; to take ~ in sth Freude an etw (*dat*) haben; ~ed *a*: ~ed (at *or* with to do) entzückt (über +*acc*/etw zu tun); ~ful *a* entzückend, herrlich.
delinquency [dı'lıŋkwənsı] *n* Kriminalität *f.*
delinquent [dı'lıŋkwənt] *n* Straffällige(r) *mf* // *a* straffällig.
delirious [dı'lırıəs] *a* im Fieberwahn.
deliver [dı'lıvə*] *vt* (*goods*) (ab)liefern; (*letter*) zustellen; (*speech*) halten; ~y *n* (Ab)lieferung *f*; (*of letter*) Zustellung *f*; (*of speech*) Vortragsweise *f*; (*MED*) Entbindung *f*; to take ~y of in Empfang nehmen.
delude [dı'lu:d] *vt* täuschen.
deluge ['delju:dʒ] *n* Überschwemmung *f*; (*fig*) Flut *f* // *vt* (*fig*) überfluten.
delusion [dı'lu:ʒən] *n* (Selbst)täuschung

f.
de luxe [dı'lʌks] *a* Luxus-.
delve [delv] *vi*: to ~ into sich vertiefen in (+*acc*).
demand [dı'ma:nd] *vt* verlangen // *n* (*request*) Verlangen *nt*; (*COMM*) Nachfrage *f*; in ~ gefragt; on ~ auf Verlangen; ~ing *a* anspruchsvoll.
demarcation [di:ma:'keıʃən] *n* Abgrenzung *f.*
demean [dı'mi:n] *vt*: to ~ o.s. sich erniedrigen.
demeanour, (US) demeanor [dı'mi:nə*] *n* Benehmen *nt.*
demented [dı'mentıd] *a* wahnsinnig.
demise [dı'maız] *n* Ableben *nt.*
demister [di:'mıstə*] *n* (*AUT*) Gebläse *nt.*
demo ['deməu] *n abbr* (*col*: = *demonstration*) Demo *f.*
democracy [dı'mɒkrəsı] *n* Demokratie *f.*
democrat ['deməkræt] *n* Demokrat *m*; ~ic *a* [demə'krætık] demokratisch.
demolish [dı'mɒlıʃ] *vt* (*lit*) abreißen; (*fig*) vernichten.
demolition [demə'lıʃən] *n* Abbruch *m.*
demon ['di:mən] *n* Dämon *m.*
demonstrate ['demənstreıt] *vti* demonstrieren.
demonstration [demən'streıʃən] *n* Demonstration *f.*
demonstrator ['demənstreıtə*] *n* (*POL*) Demonstrant(in *f*) *m.*
demote [dı'məut] *vt* degradieren.
demure [dı'mjuə*] *a* ernst.
den [den] *n* (*of animal*) Höhle *f*; (*study*) Bude *f.*
denatured alcohol [di:'neıtʃəd-] *n* (*US*) ungenießbar gemachte(r) Alkohol *m.*
denial [dı'naıəl] *n* Leugnung *f*; official ~ Dementi *nt.*
denim ['denım] *a* Denim-; ~s *npl* Denim-Jeans *pl.*
Denmark ['denma:k] *n* Dänemark *nt.*
denomination [dınɒmı'neıʃən] *n* (*ECCL*) Bekenntnis *nt*; (*type*) Klasse *f*; (*FIN*) Wert *m.*
denominator [dı'nɒmıneıtə*] *n* Nenner *m.*
denote [dı'nəut] *vt* bedeuten.
denounce [dı'nauns] *vt* brandmarken.
dense [dens] *a* dicht; (*stupid*) schwer von Begriff; ~ly *ad* dicht.
density ['densıtı] *n* Dichte *f*; single-/double-~ disk *n* Diskette *f* mit einfacher/doppelter Dichte.
dent [dent] *n* Delle *f* // *vt* (*also*: make a ~ in) einbeulen.
dental ['dentl] *a* Zahn-; ~ surgeon *n* = dentist.
dentist ['dentıst] *n* Zahnarzt *m*/-ärztin *f*; ~ry *n* Zahnmedizin *f.*
dentures ['dentʃəz] *npl* Gebiß *nt.*

deny [dɪˈnaɪ] *vt* leugnen; *(officially)* dementieren; *(help)* abschlagen.

deodorant [diːˈəʊdərənt] *n* Deodorant *nt*.

depart [dɪˈpɑːt] *vi* abfahren; **to ~ from** *(fig: differ from)* abweichen von.

department [dɪˈpɑːtmənt] *n* *(COMM)* Abteilung *f*; *(UNIV)* Seminar *nt*; *(POL)* Ministerium *nt*; **~ store** *n* Warenhaus *nt*.

departure [dɪˈpɑːtʃə*] *n* *(of person)* Abreise *f*; *(of train)* Abfahrt *f*; *(of plane)* Abflug *m*; **new ~** Neuerung *f*; **~ lounge** *n* *(at airport)* Abflughalle *f*.

depend [dɪˈpend] *vi*: **to ~ on** abhängen von; *(rely on)* angewiesen sein auf *(+acc)*; **it ~s** es kommt darauf an; **~ing on the result** ... abhängend vom Resultat ...; **~able** *a* zuverlässig; **~ant** *n* Angehörige(r) *mf*; **~ence** *n* Abhängigkeit *f*; **~ent** *a* abhängig *(on* von*)* // *n* = **~ant**.

depict [dɪˈpɪkt] *vt* schildern.

depleted [dɪˈpliːtɪd] *a* aufgebraucht.

deplorable [dɪˈplɔːrəbl] *a* bedauerlich.

deplore [dɪˈplɔː*] *vt* mißbilligen.

deploy [dɪˈplɔɪ] *vt* einsetzen.

depopulation [ˈdiːpɒpjʊˈleɪʃən] *n* Entvölkerung *f*.

deport [dɪˈpɔːt] *vt* deportieren; **~ation** [diːpɔːˈteɪʃən] *n* Abschiebung *f*.

deportment [dɪˈpɔːtmənt] *n* Betragen *nt*.

depose [dɪˈpəʊz] *vt* absetzen.

deposit [dɪˈpɒzɪt] *n* *(in bank)* Guthaben *nt*; *(down payment)* Anzahlung *f*; *(security)* Kaution *f*; *(CHEM)* Niederschlag *m* // *vt* *(in bank)* deponieren; *(put down)* niederlegen; **~ account** *n* Sparkonto *nt*.

depot [ˈdepəʊ] *n* Depot *nt*.

depraved [dɪˈpreɪvd] *a* verkommen.

depreciate [dɪˈpriːʃɪeɪt] *vi* im Wert sinken; **depreciation** [-ˈeɪʃən] *n* Wertminderung *f*.

depress [dɪˈpres] *vt* *(press down)* niederdrücken; *(in mood)* deprimieren; **~ed** *a* deprimiert; **~ing** *a* deprimierend; **~ion** [dɪˈpreʃən] *n* *(in mood)* Depression *f*; *(in trade)* Wirtschaftskrise *f*; *(hollow)* Vertiefung *f*; *(MET)* Tief *(druckgebiet) nt*.

deprivation [deprɪˈveɪʃən] *n* Not *f*.

deprive [dɪˈpraɪv] *vt*: **to ~ sb of sth** jdn etw *(gen)* berauben; **~d** *a* *(child)* sozial benachteiligt; *(area)* unterentwickelt.

depth [depθ] *n* Tiefe *f*; **in the ~s of** despair in tiefster Verzweiflung.

deputation [depjʊˈteɪʃən] *n* Abordnung *f*.

deputize [ˈdepjʊtaɪz] *vi* vertreten *(for acc)*.

deputy [ˈdepjʊtɪ] *a* stellvertretend // *n* (Stell) vertreter *m*.

derail [dɪˈreɪl] *vt*: **to be ~ed** entgleisen;

~ment *n* Entgleisung *f*.

deranged [dɪˈreɪndʒd] *a* verrückt.

derby [ˈdɑːbɪ] *n* *(US: bowler hat)* Melone *f*.

derelict [ˈderɪlɪkt] *a* verlassen.

deride [dɪˈraɪd] *vt* auslachen.

derisory [dɪˈraɪsərɪ] *a* spöttisch.

derivative [dɪˈrɪvətɪv] *n* Derivat *nt* // *a* abgeleitet.

derive [dɪˈraɪv] *vt* *(get)* gewinnen; *(deduce)* ableiten // *vi* *(come from)* abstammen.

dermatitis [dɜːməˈtaɪtɪs] *n* Hautentzündung *f*.

derogatory [dɪˈrɒgətərɪ] *a* geringschätzig.

derrick [ˈderɪk] *n* Drehkran *m*.

derv [dɜːv] *n* *(Brit)* Dieselkraftstoff *m*.

descend [dɪˈsend] *vti* hinuntersteigen; **to ~ from** abstammen von; **~ant** *n* Nachkomme *m*.

descent [dɪˈsent] *n* *(coming down)* Abstieg *m*; *(origin)* Abstammung *f*.

describe [dɪsˈkraɪb] *vt* beschreiben.

description [dɪsˈkrɪpʃən] *n* Beschreibung *f*; *(sort)* Art *f*.

descriptive [dɪsˈkrɪptɪv] *a* beschreibend; *(word)* anschaulich.

desecrate [ˈdesɪkreɪt] *vt* schänden.

desert [ˈdezət] *n* Wüste *f* // *v* [dɪˈzɜːt] *vt* verlassen; *(temporarily)* im Stich lassen // *vi* *(MIL)* desertieren; **~er** *n* Deserteur *m*; **~ion** [dɪˈzɜːʃən] *n* *(of wife)* Verlassen *nt*; *(MIL)* Fahnenflucht *f*; **~ island** *n* einsame Insel *f*; **~s** [dɪˈzɜːts] *pl*: **to get one's just ~s** seinen gerechten Lohn bekommen.

deserve [dɪˈzɜːv] *vt* verdienen.

deserving [dɪˈzɜːvɪŋ] *a* verdienstvoll.

design [dɪˈzaɪn] *n* *(plan)* Entwurf; *(planning)* Design *nt* // *vt* entwerfen.

designate [ˈdezɪgneɪt] *vt* bestimmen // *a* [ˈdezɪgnɪt] designiert.

designer [dɪˈzaɪnə*] *n* Designer(in *f*) *m*; *(TECH)* Konstrukteur(in *f*) *m*; *(fashion ~)* Modeschöpfer(in *f*) *m*.

desirable [dɪˈzaɪərəbl] *n* wünschenswert.

desire [dɪˈzaɪə*] *n* Wunsch *m*, Verlangen *nt* // *vt* *(lust)* begehren; *(ask for)* wollen.

desk [desk] *n* Schreibtisch *m*; *(Brit: in shop, restaurant)* Kasse *f*.

desolate [ˈdesəlɪt] *a* öde; *(sad)* trostlos.

desolation [desəˈleɪʃən] *n* Trostlosigkeit *f*.

despair [dɪsˈpeə*] *n* Verzweiflung *f* // *vi* verzweifeln *(of* an *+dat)*.

despatch [dɪsˈpætʃ] *n, vt* = **dispatch**.

desperate *a*, **~ly** *ad* [ˈdespərɪt, -ɪtlɪ] verzweifelt.

desperation [despəˈreɪʃən] *n* Verzweiflung *f*.

despicable [dɪsˈpɪkəbl] *a* abscheulich.

despise [dɪsˈpaɪz] *vt* verachten.

despite [dɪsˈpaɪt] *prep* trotz *(+gen)*.

despondent [dɪsˈpɒndənt] *a* mutlos.

dessert [dɪ'zɜːt] n Nachtisch m;
~**spoon** n Dessertlöffel m.

destination [destɪ'neɪʃən] n (of person)
(Reise)ziel nt; (of goods) Bestimmungs-
ort m.

destine ['destɪn] vt (set apart) bestimmen.

destiny ['destɪnɪ] n Schicksal nt.

destitute ['destɪtjuːt] a notleidend.

destroy [dɪs'trɔɪ] vt zerstören; ~**er** n
(NAUT) Zerstörer m.

destruction [dɪs'trʌkʃən] n Zerstörung
f.

destructive [dɪs'trʌktɪv] a zerstörend.

detach [dɪ'tætʃ] vt loslösen; ~**able** a
abtrennbar; ~**ed** a (attitude) distanziert; (house) Einzel-; ~**ment** n
(MIL) Sonderkommando nt; (fig) Abstand m.

detail ['diːteɪl] n Einzelheit f, Detail nt //
vt (relate) ausführlich berichten;
(appoint) abkommandieren; **in** ~ **im**
Detail; ~**ed** a detailliert.

detain [dɪ'teɪn] vt aufhalten; (imprison)
in Haft halten.

detect [dɪ'tekt] vt entdecken; ~**ion**
[dɪ'tekʃən] n Aufdeckung f; ~**ive** n
Detektiv m; ~**ive story** n
Krimi(nalgeschichte f) m; ~**or** n
Detektor m.

détente ['deɪtɑ̃ːnt] n Entspannung f.

detention [dɪ'tenʃən] n Haft f; (SCH)
Nachsitzen nt.

deter [dɪ'tɜː*] vt abschrecken.

detergent [dɪ'tɜːdʒənt] n Waschmittel
nt.

deteriorate [dɪ'tɪərɪəreɪt] vi sich verschlechtern; **deterioration** [-'reɪʃən] n
Verschlechterung f.

determination [dɪtɜːmɪ'neɪʃən] n Entschlossenheit f.

determine [dɪ'tɜːmɪn] vt bestimmen;
~**d** a entschlossen.

deterrent [dɪ'terənt] n Abschreckungs-
mittel nt.

detest [dɪ'test] vt verabscheuen.

detonate ['detəneɪt] vt explodieren
lassen // vi detonieren.

detour ['diːtuə*] n Umweg m; (US AUT:
diversion) Umleitung f // vt (US: traffic)
umleiten.

detract [dɪ'trækt] vi schmälern (from
acc).

detriment ['detrɪmənt] n: **to the** ~ **of**
zum Schaden (+gen); ~**al** [detrɪ'mentl]
a schädlich.

devaluation [dɪvæljʊ'eɪʃən] n Abwer-
tung f.

devalue ['diː'væljuː] vt abwerten.

devastate ['devəsteɪt] vt verwüsten.

devastating ['devəsteɪtɪŋ] a verheerend.

develop [dɪ'veləp] vt entwickeln;
(resources) erschließen // vi sich entwickeln; ~**ing country** n Entwick-

lungsland nt; ~**ment** n Entwicklung f.

deviate ['diːvɪeɪt] vi abweichen; **devia-
tion** [-'eɪʃən] n Abweichung f.

device [dɪ'vaɪs] n Gerät nt.

devil ['devl] n Teufel m; ~**ish** a
teuflisch.

devious ['diːvɪəs] a (means) krumm;
(person) verschlagen.

devise [dɪ'vaɪz] vt entwickeln.

devoid [dɪ'vɔɪd] a: ~ **of** ohne.

devolution [diːvə'luːʃən] n (POL)
Dezentralisierung f.

devote [dɪ'vəʊt] vt widmen (to dat); ~**d**
a ergeben; **devotee** [devəʊ'tiː] n An-
hänger(in f) m, Verehrer(in f) m.

devotion [dɪ'vəʊʃən] n (piety) Andacht
f; (loyalty) Ergebenheit f, Hingabe f.

devour [dɪ'vaʊə*] vt verschlingen.

devout [dɪ'vaʊt] a andächtig.

dew [djuː] n Tau m.

dexterity [deks'terɪtɪ] n Geschicklichkeit
f.

DHSS n abbr (Brit) = Department of
Health and Society Security.

diabetes [daɪə'biːtiːz] n Zuckerkrankheit
f.

diabetic [daɪə'betɪk] a zuckerkrank;
(food) Diabetiker- // n Diabetiker m.

diabolical [daɪə'bɒlɪkl] a (col: weather,
behaviour) saumäßig.

diagnose ['daɪəgnəʊz] vt diagno-
stizieren.

diagnosis [daɪəg'nəʊsɪs], pl -**ses**
[-'nəʊsiːz] n Diagnose f.

diagonal [daɪ'ægənl] a diagonal // n
Diagonale f.

diagram ['daɪəgræm] n Diagramm nt,
Schaubild nt.

dial ['daɪəl] n (TEL) Wählscheibe f; (of
clock) Zifferblatt nt // vt wählen; ~
code n (US) = **dialling code**; ~ **tone**
n (US) = **dialling tone**.

dialect ['daɪəlekt] n Dialekt m.

dialling ['daɪəlɪŋ]: ~ **code** n Vorwahl f;
~ **tone** n Amtszeichen nt.

dialogue ['daɪəlɒg] n Dialog m.

diameter [daɪ'æmɪtə*] n Durchmesser
m.

diamond ['daɪəmənd] n Diamant m; ~**s**
pl (CARDS) Karo nt.

diaper ['daɪəpə*] n (US) Windel f.

diaphragm ['daɪəfræm] n Zwerchfell nt.

diarrhoea, (US) **diarrhea** [daɪə'riːə] n
Durchfall m.

diary ['daɪərɪ] n Taschenkalender m;
(account) Tagebuch nt.

dice [daɪs] n Würfel pl // vt in Würfel
schneiden.

dichotomy [daɪ'kɒtəmɪ] n Kluft f.

dictate ['dɪkteɪt] vt diktieren; ~**s**
['dɪkteɪts] pl Gebote pl.

dictation [dɪk'teɪʃən] n Diktat nt.

dictator [dɪk'teɪtə*] n Diktator m.

dictatorship [dɪk'teɪtəʃɪp] n Diktatur f.

diction ['dɪkʃən] n Ausdrucksweise f.

dictionary ['dɪkʃənrɪ] n Wörterbuch nt.
did [dɪd] pt of **do.**
didn't ['dɪdənt] = **did not.**
die [daɪ] vi sterben; **to be dying for sth/to do sth** etw unbedingt haben wollen/ darauf brennen, etw zu tun; ~ **away** vi schwächer werden; ~ **down** vi nachlassen; ~ **out** vi aussterben.
diehard ['daɪhɑːd] n Dickkopf m; (POL) Reaktionär m.
diesel ['diːzəl]: ~ **engine** n Dieselmotor m; ~ **(oil)** n Diesel(kraftstoff) m.
diet ['daɪət] n Nahrung f; (special food) Diät f; (slimming) Abmagerungskur f // vi (also: **be on a** ~) eine Abmagerungskur machen.
differ ['dɪfə*] vi sich unterscheiden; (disagree) anderer Meinung sein; ~**ence** n Unterschied m; ~**ent** a anders; (two things) verschieden; ~**ential** [dɪfə'renʃəl] n (in wages) Lohnstufe f; ~**entiate** [dɪfə'renʃɪeɪt] vti unterscheiden; ~**ently** ad anders; (from one another) unterschiedlich.
difficult ['dɪfɪkəlt] a schwierig; ~**y** n Schwierigkeit f.
diffident ['dɪfɪdənt] a schüchtern.
diffuse [dɪ'fjuːs] a langatmig // vt [dɪ'fjuːz] vt verbreiten.
dig [dɪg] v (pt, pp **dug**) vt graben // n (prod) Stoß m; (remark) Spitze f; (archaeological) Ausgrabung f; ~ **in** vi (MIL) sich eingraben; ~ **into** vt (sb's past) wühlen in (+dat); (savings) angreifen; ~ **up** vt ausgraben; (fig) aufgabeln.
digest [daɪ'dʒest] vt verdauen // n ['daɪdʒest] Auslese f; ~**ion** n Verdauung f; ~**ive** a (juices, system) Verdauungs-.
digit ['dɪdʒɪt] n Ziffer f; (ANAT) Finger m; ~**al** a digital, Digital-.
dignified ['dɪgnɪfaɪd] a würdevoll.
dignity ['dɪgnɪtɪ] n Würde f.
digress [daɪ'gres] vi abschweifen.
digs [dɪgz] npl (Brit col) Bude f.
dilapidated [dɪ'læpɪdeɪtɪd] a baufällig.
dilate [daɪ'leɪt] vti (sich) weiten.
dilemma [daɪ'lemə] n Dilemma nt.
diligent ['dɪlɪdʒənt] a fleißig.
dilute [daɪ'luːt] vt verdünnen.
dim [dɪm] a trübe; (stupid) schwer von Begriff // vt verdunkeln; **to** ~ **one's headlights** (esp US) abblenden.
dime [daɪm] n (US) Zehncentstück nt.
dimension [dɪ'menʃən] n Dimension f.
diminish [dɪ'mɪnɪʃ] vti verringern.
diminutive [dɪ'mɪnjʊtɪv] a winzig // n Verkleinerungsform f.
dimmer ['dɪmə*] n (US AUT) Abblendschalter m.
dimple ['dɪmpl] n Grübchen nt.
din [dɪn] n Getöse nt.
dine [daɪn] vi speisen; ~**r** n Tischgast m; (RAIL) Speisewagen m.

dinghy ['dɪŋgɪ] n Dinghy nt; **rubber** ~ Schlauchboot nt.
dingy ['dɪndʒɪ] a armselig.
dining car ['daɪnɪŋkɑː*] n (Brit) Speisewagen m.
dining room ['daɪnɪŋrʊm] n Eßzimmer nt; (in hotel) Speisezimmer nt.
dinner ['dɪnə*] n (lunch) Mittagessen nt; (evening) Abendessen nt; (public) Festessen nt; ~ **jacket** n Smoking m; ~ **party** n Tischgesellschaft f; ~ **time** n Tischzeit f.
dinosaur ['daɪnəsɔː*] n Dinosaurier m.
dint [dɪnt] n: **by** ~ **of** durch.
diocese ['daɪəsɪs] n Diözese f.
dip [dɪp] n (hollow) Senkung f; (bathe) kurze(s) Bad(en) nt // vt eintauchen; (Brit AUT: lights) abblenden // vi (slope) sich senken, abfallen.
diploma [dɪ'pləʊmə] n Diplom nt.
diplomacy [dɪ'pləʊməsɪ] n Diplomatie f.
diplomat ['dɪpləmæt] n Diplomat(in f) m; ~**ic** [dɪplə'mætɪk] a diplomatisch.
dipstick ['dɪpstɪk] n Ölmeßstab m.
dipswitch ['dɪpswɪtʃ] n (Brit AUT) Ablendschalter n.
dire [daɪə*] a schrecklich.
direct [daɪ'rekt] a direkt // vt leiten; (film) die Regie führen (+gen); (aim) richten; (order) anweisen; **can you** ~ **me to ...?** können Sie mir sagen, wie ich zu ... komme?
direction [dɪ'rekʃən] n Richtung f; (CINE) Regie f; Leitung f; ~**s** (for use) Gebrauchsanleitung f; (orders) Anweisungen pl; **sense of** ~ Orientierungssinn m.
directly [dɪ'rektlɪ] ad direkt; (at once) sofort.
director [dɪ'rektə*] n Direktor m; (of film) Regisseur m.
directory [dɪ'rektərɪ] n (TEL) Telefonbuch nt.
dirt [dɜːt] n Schmutz m, Dreck m; ~-**cheap** a spottbillig; ~**y** a schmutzig // vt beschmutzen; ~**y trick** n gemeiner Trick.
disability [dɪsə'bɪlɪtɪ] n Körperbehinderung f.
disabled [dɪs'eɪbld] a körperbehindert.
disadvantage [dɪsəd'vɑːntɪdʒ] n Nachteil m.
disaffection [dɪsə'fekʃən] n Entfremdung f.
disagree [dɪsə'griː] vi nicht übereinstimmen; (quarrel) (sich) streiten; (food) nicht bekommen (with dat); ~**able** a unangenehm; ~**ment** n (between persons) Streit m; (between things) Widerspruch m.
disallow [dɪsə'laʊ] vt nicht zulassen.
disappear [dɪsə'pɪə*] vi verschwinden; ~**ance** n Verschwinden nt.
disappoint [dɪsə'pɔɪnt] vt enttäuschen; ~**ed** a enttäuscht; ~**ing** a enttäu-

schend; **~ment** *n* Enttäuschung *f.*

disapproval [dɪsə'pruːvəl] *n* Mißbilligung *f.*

disapprove [dɪsə'pruːv] *vi* mißbilligen (*of acc*).

disarm [dɪs'ɑːm] *vt* entwaffnen; (*POL*) abrüsten; **~ament** *n* Abrüstung *f.*

disarray ['dɪsə'reɪ] *n*: to be in ~ (*army*) in Auflösung (begriffen) sein; (*clothes*) in unordentlichen Zustand sein.

disaster [dɪ'zɑːstə*] *n* Katastrophe *f.*

disastrous [dɪ'zɑːstrəs] *a* verhängnisvoll.

disband [dɪs'bænd] *vt* auflösen // *vi* auseinandergehen.

disbelief ['dɪsbə'liːf] *n* Ungläubigkeit *f.*

disc [dɪsk] *n* Scheibe *f*; (*record*) (Schall)platte *f*; (*COMPUT*) = **disk.**

discard ['dɪskɑːd] *vt* ablegen.

discern [dɪ'sɜːn] *vt* erkennen; **~ing** *a* scharfsinnig.

discharge [dɪs'tʃɑːdʒ] *vt* (*ship*) entladen; (*duties*) nachkommen (+*dat*); (*dismiss*) entlassen; (*gun*) abschießen; (*JUR*) freisprechen // *n* ['dɪstʃɑːdʒ] (*of ship, ELEC*) Entladung *f*; (*dismissal*) Entlassung *f*; (*MED*) Ausfluß *m.*

disciple [dɪ'saɪpl] *n* Jünger *m.*

discipline ['dɪsɪplɪn] *n* Disziplin *f* // *vt* (*train*) schulen; (*punish*) bestrafen.

disc jockey ['dɪskdʒɔkɪ] *n* Diskjockey *m.*

disclaim [dɪs'kleɪm] *vt* nicht anerkennen.

disclose [dɪs'kləʊz] *vt* enthüllen.

disclosure [dɪs'kləʊʒə*] *n* Enthüllung *f.*

disco ['dɪskəʊ] *n abbr of* **discothèque.**

discoloured, (*US*) **discolored** [dɪs'kʌləd] *a* verfärbt.

discomfort [dɪs'kʌmfət] *n* Unbehagen *nt.*

disconcert [dɪskən'sɜːt] *vt* aus der Fassung bringen.

disconnect ['dɪskə'nekt] *vt* abtrennen.

discontent ['dɪskən'tent] *n* Unzufriedenheit *f*; **~ed** *a* unzufrieden.

discontinue ['dɪskən'tɪnjuː] *vt* einstellen.

discord ['dɪskɔːd] *n* Zwietracht *f*; (*noise*) Dissonanz *f*; **~ant** [dɪs'kɔːdənt] *a* uneinig.

discothèque ['dɪskəʊtek] *n* Diskothek *f.*

discount ['dɪskaʊnt] *n* Rabatt *m* // *vt* [dɪs'kaʊnt] außer acht lassen.

discourage [dɪs'kʌrɪdʒ] *vt* entmutigen; (*prevent*) abraten.

discouraging [dɪs'kʌrɪdʒɪŋ] *a* entmutigend.

discourteous [dɪs'kɜːtɪəs] *a* unhöflich.

discover [dɪs'kʌvə*] *vt* entdecken; **~y** *n* Entdeckung *f.*

discredit [dɪs'kredɪt] *vt* in Verruf bringen.

discreet *a* [dɪs'kriːt] diskret.

discrepancy [dɪs'krepənsɪ] *n* Diskrepanz *f.*

discriminate [dɪs'krɪmɪneɪt] *vi* unterscheiden; to ~ against diskriminieren.

discriminating [dɪs'krɪmɪneɪtɪŋ] *a* anspruchsvoll.

discrimination [dɪskrɪmɪ'neɪʃən] *n* Urteilsvermögen *nt*; (*pej*) Diskriminierung *f.*

discuss [dɪs'kʌs] *vt* diskutieren, besprechen; **~ion** [dɪs'kʌʃən] *n* Diskussion *f*, Besprechung *f.*

disdain [dɪs'deɪn] *vt* verachten // *n* Verachtung *f.*

disease [dɪ'ziːz] *n* Krankheit *f.*

disembark [dɪsɪm'bɑːk] *vt* aussteigen lassen // *vi* von Bord gehen.

disenchanted ['dɪsɪn'tʃɑːntɪd] *a* desillusioniert.

disengage [dɪsɪn'geɪdʒ] *vt* (*AUT*) auskuppeln.

disentangle ['dɪsɪn'tæŋgl] *vt* entwirren.

disfigure [dɪs'fɪgə*] *vt* entstellen.

disgrace [dɪs'greɪs] *n* Schande *f* // *vt* Schande bringen über (+*acc*); **~ful** *a* unerhört.

disgruntled [dɪs'grʌntld] *a* verärgert.

disguise [dɪs'gaɪz] *vt* verkleiden; (*feelings*) verhehlen // *n* Verkleidung *f*; in ~ verkleidet, maskiert.

disgust [dɪs'gʌst] *n* Abscheu *f* // *vt* anwidern; **~ing** *a* widerlich.

dish [dɪʃ] *n* Schüssel *f*; (*food*) Gericht *nt*; to do *or* wash the ~es abwaschen; ~ up *vt* auftischen; ~ **cloth** *n* Spüllappen *m.*

dishearten [dɪs'hɑːtn] *vt* entmutigen.

dishevelled [dɪ'ʃevəld] *a* (*hair*) zerzaust; (*clothing*) ungepflegt.

dishonest [dɪs'ɔnɪst] *a* unehrlich; **~y** *n* Unehrlichkeit *f.*

dishonour, (*US*) dishonor [dɪs'ɔnə*] *n* Unehre *f*; **~able** *a* unehrenhaft.

dish towel *n* (*US: tea towel*) Geschirrtuch *nt.*

dishwasher ['dɪʃwɒʃə*] *n* Geschirrspülmaschine *f.*

disillusion [dɪsɪ'luːʒən] *vt* enttäuschen, desillusionieren.

disincentive ['dɪsɪn'sentɪv] *n* Entmutigung *f.*

disinfect [dɪsɪn'fekt] *vt* desinfizieren; **~ant** *n* Desinfektionsmittel *nt.*

disintegrate [dɪs'ɪntɪgreɪt] *vi* sich auflösen.

disinterested [dɪs'ɪntrɪstɪd] *a* uneigennützig; (*col*) uninteressiert.

disjointed [dɪs'dʒɔɪntɪd] *a* unzusammenhängend.

disk [dɪsk] *n* (*COMPUT*) Diskette *f*; **single-/double-sided** ~ einseitige/beidseitige Diskette; ~ **drive** *n* Diskettenlaufwerk *nt*; **~ette** *n* (*US*) = **disk.**

dislike [dɪs'laɪk] *n* Abneigung *f* // *vt* nicht leiden können.

dislocate ['dısləʊkeıt] vt auskugeln.

dislodge [dıs'lɒdʒ] vt verschieben; (MIL) aus der Stellung werfen.

disloyal ['dıs'lɔıəl] a treulos.

dismal ['dızməl] a trostlos, trübe.

dismantle [dıs'mæntl] vt demontieren.

dismay [dıs'meı] n Bestürzung f // vt bestürzen.

dismiss [dıs'mıs] vt (employee) entlassen; (idea) von sich weisen; (send away) wegschicken; (JUR) abweisen; ~al n Entlassung f.

dismount [dıs'maunt] vi absteigen.

disobedience [dısə'bi:dıəns] n Ungehorsam m.

disobedient [dısə'bi:dıənt] a ungehorsam.

disobey ['dısə'beı] vt nicht gehorchen (+dat).

disorder [dıs'ɔ:də*] n (confusion) Verwirrung f; (commotion) Aufruhr m; (MED) Erkrankung f.

disorderly [dıs'ɔ:dəlı] a (untidy) unordentlich; (unruly) ordnungswidrig.

disorganized [dıs'ɔ:gənaızd] a unordentlich.

disown [dıs'əʊn] vt (son) verstoßen.

disparaging [dıs'pærıdʒıŋ] a geringschätzig.

disparity [dıs'pærıtı] n Verschiedenheit f.

dispassionate [dıs'pæʃnıt] a objektiv.

dispatch [dıs'pætʃ] vt (goods) abschicken, abfertigen // n Absendung f; (esp MIL) Meldung f.

dispel [dıs'pel] vt zerstreuen.

dispensary [dıs'pensərı] n Apotheke f.

dispense [dıs'pens]: ~ with vt verzichten auf (+acc); ~r n (container) Spender m.

dispensing [dıs'pensıŋ] a: ~ chemist (Brit) Apotheker m.

dispersal [dıs'pə:səl] n Zerstreuung f.

disperse [dıs'pə:s] vt zerstreuen // vi sich verteilen.

dispirited [dıs'pırıtıd] a niedergeschlagen.

displace [dıs'pleıs] vt verschieben; ~d person n Verschleppte(r) mf.

display [dıs'pleı] n (of goods) Auslage f; (of feeling) Zurschaustellung f // vt zeigen; (ostentatiously) vorführen; (goods) ausstellen.

displease [dıs'pli:z] vt mißfallen (+dat).

displeasure [dıs'pleʒə*] n Mißfallen nt.

disposable [dıs'pəʊzəbl] a Wegwerf-; ~ nappy n Papierwindel f.

disposal [dıs'pəʊzəl] n (of property) Verkauf m; (throwing away) Beseitigung f; to be at one's ~ einem zur Verfügung stehen.

dispose [dıs'pəʊz]: ~ of vt loswerden.

disposed [dıs'pəʊzd] a geneigt.

disposition [dıspə'zıʃən] n Wesen nt.

disproportionate [dısprə'pɔ:ʃnıt] a unverhältnismäßig.

disprove [dıs'pru:v] vt widerlegen.

dispute [dıs'pju:t] n Streit m; (also: industrial ~) Arbeitskampf m // vt bestreiten.

disqualify [dıs'kwɒlıfaı] vt disqualifizieren.

disquiet [dıs'kwaıət] n Unruhe f.

disregard [dısrı'ga:d] vt nicht (be)achten.

disrepair ['dısrı'peə*] n: to fall into ~ verfallen.

disreputable [dıs'repjʊtəbl] a verrufen.

disrespectful [dısrıs'pektfʊl] a respektlos.

disrupt [dıs'rʌpt] vt stören; (service) unterbrechen; ~ion [dıs'rʌpʃən] n Störung f, Unterbrechung f.

dissatisfaction ['dıssætıs'fækʃən] n Unzufriedenheit f.

dissatisfied ['dıs'sætısfaıd] a unzufrieden.

dissect [dı'sekt] vt zerlegen, sezieren.

disseminate [dı'semıneıt] vt verbreiten.

dissent [dı'sent] n abweichende Meinung f.

dissertation [dısə'teıʃən] n wissenschaftliche Arbeit f; (PhD) Doktorarbeit f.

disservice [dıs'sɜ:vıs] n: to do sb a ~ jdm einen schlechten Dienst erweisen.

dissident ['dısıdənt] a andersdenkend // n Dissident m.

dissimilar [dı'sımılə*] a unähnlich (to dat).

dissipate [dı'sıpeıt] vt (waste) verschwenden; (scatter) zerstreuen.

dissociate [dı'səʊʃıeıt] vt trennen.

dissolute ['dısəlu:t] a liederlich.

dissolution [dısə'lu:ʃən] n Auflösung f.

dissolve [dı'zɒlv] vt auflösen // vi sich auflösen.

dissuade [dı'sweıd] vt: to ~ sb from doing sth jdn davon abbringen, etw zu tun.

distance ['dıstəns] n Entfernung f; in the ~ in der Ferne.

distant ['dıstənt] a entfernt, fern; (with time) fern; (formal) distanziert.

distaste [dıs'teıst] n Abneigung f; ~ful a widerlich.

distended [dıs'tendıd] a (stomach) aufgebläht.

distil [dıs'tıl] vt destillieren; ~lery n Brennerei f.

distinct [dıs'tıŋkt] a (separate) getrennt; (clear) klar, deutlich; as ~ from im Unterschied zu; ~ion [dıs'tıŋkʃən] n Unterscheidung f; (eminence) Auszeichnung f; ~ive a bezeichnend.

distinguish [dıs'tıŋgwıʃ] vt unterscheiden; ~ed a (eminent) berühmt; ~ing a bezeichnend.

distort [dıs'tɔ:t] vt verdrehen; (mis-

represent) entstellen; **~ion** [dɪs'tɔ:ʃən]
n Verzerrung *f*.

distract [dɪs'trækt] *vt* ablenken; **~ing** *a*
verwirrend; **~ion** [dɪs'trækʃən] *n*
(*distress*) Raserei *f*; (*diversion*) Zerstreuung *f*.

distraught [dɪs'trɔ:t] *a* bestürzt.

distress [dɪs'tres] *n* Not *f*; (*suffering*)
Qual *f* // *vt* quälen; **~ing** *a* er-
schütternd; **~ signal** *n* Notsignal *nt*.

distribute [dɪs'trɪbju:t] *vt* verteilen.

distribution [dɪstrɪ'bju:ʃən] *n* Verteilung *f*.

distributor [dɪs'trɪbjutə*] *n* Verteiler *m*.

district [ˈdɪstrɪkt] *n* (*of country*) Kreis
m; (*of town*) Bezirk *m*; **~ attorney** *n*
(*US*) Oberstaatsanwalt *m*; **~ nurse** *n*
(*Brit*) Kreiskrankenschwester *f*.

distrust [dɪs'trʌst] *n* Mißtrauen *nt* // *vt*
mißtrauen (+*dat*).

disturb [dɪs'tɜ:b] *vt* stören; (*agitate*)
erregen; **~ance** *n* Störung *f*; **~ed** *a*
beunruhigt; **emotionally ~ed** emotional
gestört; **~ing** *a* beunruhigend.

disuse ['dɪs'ju:s] *n*: **to fall into ~** außer
Gebrauch kommen.

disused ['dɪs'ju:zd] *a* außer Gebrauch.

ditch [dɪtʃ] *n* Graben *m* // *vt* (*person*)
loswerden; (*plan*) fallenlassen.

dither ['dɪðə*] *vi* verdattert sein.

ditto ['dɪtəu] *ad* dito, ebenfalls.

divan [dɪ'væn] *n* Liegesofa *nt*.

dive [daɪv] *n* (*into water*) Kopfsprung *m*;
(*AVIAT*) Sturzflug *m* // *vi* tauchen; **~r** *n*
Taucher *m*.

diverge [daɪ'vɜ:dʒ] *vi* auseinandergehen.

diverse [daɪ'vɜ:s] *a* verschieden.

diversion [daɪ'vɜ:ʃən] *n* Ablenkung *f*;
(*Brit AUT*) Umleitung *f*.

diversity [daɪ'vɜ:sɪtɪ] *n* Vielfalt *f*.

divert [daɪ'vɜ:t] *vt* ablenken; (*traffic*)
umleiten.

divide [dɪ'vaɪd] *vt* teilen // *vi* sich teilen;
~d highway *n* (*US*) Schnellstraße *f*.

dividend ['dɪvɪdend] *n* Dividende *f*.

divine [dɪ'vaɪn] *a* göttlich.

diving ['daɪvɪŋ] *n* (*SPORT*) Turm-
springen *nt*; (*underwater ~*) Tauchen
nt; **~ board** *n* Sprungbrett *nt*.

divinity [dɪ'vɪnɪtɪ] *n* Gottheit *f*; (*subject*)
Religion *f*.

division [dɪ'vɪʒən] *n* Teilung *f*; (*MIL*)
Division *f*; (*part*) Abteilung *f*; (*in
opinion*) Uneinigkeit *f*; (*Brit POL*) Abstimmung *f* durch Hammelsprung.

divorce [dɪ'vɔ:s] *n* (*Ehe*)scheidung *f* // *vt*
scheiden; **~d** *a* geschieden; **~e**
[dɪvɔ:'si:] *n* Geschiedene(r) *mf*.

divulge [daɪ'vʌldʒ] *vt* preisgeben.

D.I.Y. *n abbr* (*Brit*) *of* **do-it-yourself.**

dizzy ['dɪzɪ] *a* schwindlig.

DJ *n abbr of* **disc jockey.**

do [du:] ♦ *n* (*col: party etc*) Fete *f*
♦ *v* (*pt* did, *pp* done) *aux v* **1** (*in negative constructions and questions*): **I don't**

understand ich verstehe nicht; **didn't you
know?** wußtest du das nicht?; **what ~
you think?** was meinen Sie?

2 (*for emphasis, in polite expressions*):
she does seem rather tired sie scheint
wirklich sehr müde zu sein; **~ sit down/
help yourself** setzen Sie sich doch hin/
greifen Sie doch zu

3 (*used to avoid repeating v*): **she
swims better than I ~** sie schwimmt
besser als ich; **she lives in Glasgow — so
~ I** sie wohnt in Glasgow — ich auch

4 (*in question tags*): **you like him, don't
you?** du magst ihn doch, oder?

♦*vt* **1** (*carry out, perform etc*) tun, machen; **what are you ~ing tonight?** was
machst du heute abend?; **I've got nothing to ~** ich habe nichts zu tun; **to ~
one's hair/nails** sich die Haare/Nägel machen

2 (*AUT etc*) fahren

♦*vi* **1** (*act, behave*): **~ as I ~** mach es
wie ich

2 (*get on, fare*): **he's ~ing well/badly at
school** er ist gut/schlecht in der Schule;
how ~ you ~? guten Tag

3 (*be suitable*) gehen; (*be sufficient*)
reichen; **to make ~ (with)** auskommen
mit

do away with *vt* (*kill*) umbringen;
(*abolish: law etc*) abschaffen

do up *vt* (*laces, dress, buttons*) zumachen; (*renovate: room, house*)
renovieren

do with *vt* (*need*) brauchen; (*be
connected*) zu tun haben mit

do without *vti* auskommen ohne.

docile ['dəusaɪl] *a* gefügig.

dock [dɒk] *n* Dock *nt*; (*JUR*) An-
klagebank *f* // *vi* ins Dock gehen; **~s** *pl*
Hafen *m*; **~er** *n* Hafenarbeiter *m*;
~yard *n* Werft *f*.

doctor ['dɒktə*] *n* Arzt *m*, Arztin *f*;
(*UNIV*) Doktor *m* // *vt* (*fig*) fälschen;
(*drink etc*) etw beimischen (+*dat*); **D~
of Philosophy (Ph. D.)** *n* Doktor *m* der
Philosophie (Dr. Phil.).

doctrine ['dɒktrɪn] *n* Doktrin *f*.

document ['dɒkjumənt] *n* Dokument *nt*;
~ary [dɒkju'mentərɪ] *n* Dokumentarbe-
richt *m*; (*film*) Dokumentarfilm *m* // *a*
dokumentarisch; **~ation** [dɒkjumen'teɪ-
ʃən] *n* dokumentarische(r) Nachweis
m.

dodge [dɒdʒ] *n* Kniff *m* // *vt* ausweichen
(+*dat*); **~ms** *npl* (*Brit*) Autoskooter *m*.

doe [dəu] *n* (*roe deer*) Ricke *f*; (*red
deer*) Hirschkuh *f*; (*rabbit*) Weibchen *nt*.

does [dʌz] *v see* **do**; **~n't** = **~ not.**

dog [dɒg] *n* Hund *m*; **~ collar** *n*
Hundehalsband *nt*; (*ECCL*) Kragen *m*
des Geistlichen; **~-eared** *a* mit
Eselsohren.

dogged ['dɒgɪd] *a* hartnäckig.

dogsbody ['dɒgzbɒdɪ] *n* Mädchen *nt* für

alles.

doings ['duːɪŋz] npl (activities) Treiben nt.

do-it-yourself ['duːɪtjə'self] n Do-it-yourself nt.

doldrums ['dɔldrəmz] npl: to be in the ~ (business) Flaute haben; (person) deprimiert sein.

dole [dəʊl] n (Brit) Stempelgeld nt; to be on the ~ stempeln gehen; ~ out vt ausgeben, austeilen.

doleful ['dəʊlfʊl] a traurig.

doll [dɔl] n Puppe f // vt: ~ o.s. up sich aufdonnern.

dollar ['dɔlə*] n Dollar m.

dolphin ['dɔlfɪn] n Delphin m.

domain [dəʊ'meɪn] n Domäne f.

dome [dəʊm] n Kuppel f.

domestic [də'mestɪk] a häuslich; (within country) Innen-, Binnen-; (animal) Haus-; ~ated a (person) häuslich; (animal) zahm.

dominant ['dɔmɪnənt] a vorherrschend.

dominate ['dɔmɪneɪt] vt beherrschen.

domineering [dɔmɪ'nɪərɪŋ] a herrisch.

dominion [də'mɪnɪən] n (rule) Regierungsgewalt f; (land) Staatsgebiet nt mit Selbstverwaltung.

domino ['dɔmɪnəʊ] n, pl ~es Dominostein m; ~es n (game) Domino(spiel) nt.

don [dɔn] n (Brit) akademische(r) Lehrer m.

donate [dəʊ'neɪt] vt (blood, little money) spenden; (lot of money) stiften.

donation [dəʊ'neɪʃən] n Spende f.

done [dʌn] pp of do.

donkey ['dɔŋkɪ] n Esel m.

donor ['dəʊnə*] n Spender m.

don't [dəʊnt] = do not.

doodle ['duːdl] vi kritzeln.

doom [duːm] n böse(s) Geschick nt; (downfall) Verderben nt // vt: to be ~ed zum Untergang verurteilt sein; ~sday n der Jüngste Tag.

door [dɔː*] n Tür f; ~bell n Türklingel f; ~-handle n Türklinke f; ~man n Türsteher m; ~mat n Fußmatte f; ~step n Türstufe f; ~way n Türöffnung f.

dope [dəʊp] n (drug) Aufputschmittel nt // vt (horse etc) dopen.

dopey ['dəʊpɪ] a (col) bekloppt.

dormant ['dɔːmənt] a latent.

dormitory ['dɔːmɪtrɪ] n Schlafsaal m.

dormouse ['dɔːmaʊs] pl -mice [-maɪs] n Haselmaus f.

DOS [dɔs] n abbr (= disk operating system) DOS nt.

dosage ['dəʊsɪdʒ] n Dosierung f.

dose [dəʊs] n Dosis f.

doss house ['dɔs-] n (Brit) Bleibe f.

dot [dɔt] n Punkt m; ~ted vt with übersät mit; on the ~ pünktlich.

dote [dəʊt]: ~ on vt vernarrt sein in

(+acc).

dot-matrix printer [dɔt'meɪtrɪks-] n Matrixdrucker m.

double ['dʌbl] a, ad doppelt // n Doppelgänger m // vt verdoppeln // vi sich verdoppeln; on the ~, at the ~ (Brit) im Laufschritt; ~s n (TENNIS) Doppel nt; ~ bass n Kontrabaß m; ~ bed n Doppelbett nt; ~ bend n (Brit) S-Kurve f; ~-breasted a zweireihig; ~cross vt hintergehen; ~decker n Doppeldecker m; ~ glazing n (Brit) Doppelverglasung f; ~ room n Doppelzimmer nt.

doubly ['dʌblɪ] ad doppelt.

doubt [daʊt] n Zweifel m // vt bezweifeln; ~ful a zweifelhaft; ~less ad ohne Zweifel.

dough [dəʊ] n Teig m; ~nut n Berliner m.

douse [daʊz] vt (drench) mit Wasser begießen, durchtränken; (extinguish) ausmachen.

dove [dʌv] n Taube f; ~tail vi (plans) übereinstimmen.

dowdy ['daʊdɪ] a unmodern.

down [daʊn] n (fluff) Flaum m; (hill) Hügel m // ad unten; (motion) herunter; hinunter // prep: to go ~ the street die Straße hinuntergehen // vt niederschlagen; ~ with X! nieder mit X!; ~ under (Brit col) Australien nt; ~-and-out n Tramp m; ~-at-heel a schäbig; ~cast a niedergeschlagen; ~fall n Sturz m; ~hearted a niedergeschlagen; ~hill ad bergab; ~ payment n Anzahlung f; ~pour n Platzregen m; ~right a ausgesprochen; ~stairs ad unten; (motion) nach unten; ~stream ad flußabwärts; ~-to-earth a praktisch; ~town ad in die/der Innenstadt; ~ward a, ad, ~wards ad abwärts, nach unten.

dowry ['daʊrɪ] n Mitgift f.

doz. abbr (= dozen) Dtzd.

doze [dəʊz] vi dösen; ~ off vi einnicken.

dozen ['dʌzn] n Dutzend nt.

Dr. abbr of doctor; drive.

drab [dræb] a düster, eintönig.

draft [drɑːft] n Entwurf m; (FIN) Wechsel m; (US MIL) Einberufung f // vt skizzieren.

draftsman ['drɑːftsmən] n (US) = draughtsman.

drag [dræg] vt schleppen; (river) mit einem Schleppnetz absuchen // vi sich (dahin)schleppen // n (bore) etwas Blödes; in ~ als Tunte; ~ on vi sich in die Länge ziehen.

dragon ['drægən] n Drache m; ~fly n Libelle f.

drain [dreɪn] n (lit) Abfluß m; (fig: burden) Belastung f // vt ableiten; (exhaust) erschöpfen // vi (of water) abfließen; ~**age** n Kanalisation f; ~**ing board**, (US) ~**board** n Ablaufbrett nt; ~**pipe** n Abflußrohr nt.

drama ['drɑːmə] n Drama nt; ~**tic** [drə'mætɪk] a dramatisch; ~**tist** n Dramatiker m; ~**tize** vt (events) dramatisieren; (adapt: for TV, cinema) bearbeiten.

drank [dræŋk] pt of **drink**.

drape [dreɪp] vt drapieren // npl: ~**s** (US) Vorhänge pl; ~**r** n (Brit) Tuchhändler m.

drastic ['dræstɪk] a drastisch.

draught, (US) **draft** [drɑːft] n Zug m; (NAUT) Tiefgang m; ~**s** n (Brit) Damespiel nt; (also): on ~ vom Faß; ~**board** n (Brit) Zeichenbrett n.

draughtsman ['drɑːftsmən] n technische(r) Zeichner m.

draw [drɔː], pt **drew**, pp **drawn** vt ziehen; (crowd) anlocken; (picture) zeichnen; (money) abheben; (water) schöpfen // vi (SPORT) unentschieden spielen // n (SPORT) Unentschieden nt; (lottery) Ziehung f; ~ **near** vi näherrücken; ~ **out** vi (train) ausfahren; (lengthen) sich hinziehen; ~ **up** vi (stop) halten // vt (document) aufsetzen; ~**back** n Nachteil m; ~**bridge** n Zugbrücke f.

drawer [drɔːʳ] n Schublade f.

drawing ['drɔːɪŋ] n Zeichnung f; Zeichnen nt; ~ **board** n Reißbrett nt; ~ **pin** n (Brit) Reißzwecke f; ~ **room** n Salon m.

drawl [drɔːl] n schleppende Sprechweise f.

drawn [drɔːn] pp of **draw**.

dread [dred] n Furcht f // vt fürchten; ~**ful** a furchtbar.

dream [driːm] n Traum m // vti, pt, pp **dreamed** or **dreamt** [dremt] träumen (about von); ~**er** n Träumer m; ~**y** a verträumt.

dreary ['drɪərɪ] a trostlos, öde.

dredge [dredʒ] vt ausbaggern.

dregs [dregz] npl Bodensatz m; (fig) Abschaum m.

drench [drentʃ] vt durchnässen.

dress [dres] n Kleidung f; (garment) Kleid nt // vt anziehen; (MED) verbinden; to get ~**ed** sich anziehen; ~ **up** vi sich fein machen; ~ **circle** n (Brit) erste(r) Rang m; ~**er** n (furniture) Anrichte f; ~**ing** n (MED) Verband m; (COOK) Soße f; ~**ing gown** n (Brit) Morgenrock m; ~**ing room** n (THEAT) Garderobe f; (SPORT) Umkleideraum m; ~**ing table** n Toilettentisch m; ~**maker** n Schneiderin f; ~**making** n Schneidern nt; ~ **rehearsal** n Generalprobe f; ~ **shirt** n Frackhemd nt; ~**y** a (col) schick.

dribble ['drɪbl] vi sabbern // vt (ball) dribbeln.

drew [druː] pt of **draw**.

dried [draɪd] a getrocknet; (fruit also) Dörr-; ~ **milk** n Milchpulver nt.

drier ['draɪəʳ] n = **dryer**.

drift [drɪft] n Strömung f; (snow~) Schneewehe f; (fig) Richtung f // vi sich treiben lassen; ~**wood** n Treibholz nt.

drill [drɪl] n Bohrer m; (MIL) Drill m // vt bohren; (MIL) ausbilden // vi bohren (for nach).

drink [drɪŋk] n Getränk nt; (spirits) Drink m // vti, pt **drank**, pp **drunk** trinken; ~**er** n Trinker m; ~**ing water** n Trinkwasser nt.

drip [drɪp] n Tropfen m // vi tropfen; ~**dry** a bügelfrei; ~**ping** n Bratenfett nt.

drive [draɪv] n Fahrt f; (road) Einfahrt f; (campaign) Aktion f; (energy) Schwung m; (SPORT) Schlag m; (also: **disk** ~) Diskettenlaufwerk nt // v (pt **drove**, pp **driven** ['drɪvn]) vt (car) fahren; (animals) treiben; (power) antreiben; (force) treiben // vi fahren; **to** ~ **sb mad** jdn verrückt machen; **left-/right-hand** ~ Links-/Rechtssteuerung f.

drivel ['drɪvl] n Faselei f.

driver ['draɪvəʳ] n Fahrer m; ~'**s license** n (US) Führerschein m.

driveway ['draɪvweɪ] n Auffahrt f; (longer) Zufahrtsstraße f.

driving ['draɪvɪŋ] a (rain) stürmisch; ~ **instructor** n Fahrlehrer m; ~ **lesson** n Fahrstunde f; ~ **licence** n (Brit) Führerschein m; ~ **mirror** n Rückspiegel m; ~ **school** n Fahrschule f; ~ **test** n Fahrprüfung f.

drizzle ['drɪzl] n Nieselregen m // vi nieseln.

drone [drəun] n (sound) Brummen nt; (bee) Drohne f.

drool [druːl] vi sabbern.

droop [druːp] vi (schlaff) herabhängen.

drop [drɔp] n (of liquid) Tropfen m; (fall) Fall m // vt fallen lassen; (lower) senken; (abandon) fallenlassen // vi (fall) herunterfallen; ~**s** pl (MED) Tropfen pl; ~ **off** vi (sleep) einschlafen // vt (passenger) absetzen; ~ **out** vi (withdraw) ausscheiden; ~**out** n Aussteiger m; ~**per** n Pipette f; ~**pings** npl Kot m.

drought [draut] n Dürre f.

drove [drəuv] pt of **drive**.

drown [draun] vt ertränken; (sound) übertönen // vi ertrinken.

drowsy ['drauzɪ] a schläfrig.

drudgery ['drʌdʒərɪ] n Plackerei f.

drug [drʌg] n (MED) Arznei f; (narcotic) Rauschgift nt // vt betäuben; ~ **addict** n Rauschgiftsüchtige(r) mf; ~**gist** n (US) Drogist(in f) m; ~**store** n (US) Drogerie f.

drum [drʌm] n Trommel f // vi trommeln; ~**s** pl Schlagzeug nt; ~**mer** n Trommler m.

drunk [drʌŋk] *pp of* **drink** // *a* betrunken // *n* (*also*: **~ard**) Trinker(in *f*) *m*; **~en** *a* betrunken.

dry [draɪ] *a* trocken // *vt* (ab)trocknen // *vi* trocknen; ~ **up** *vi* austrocknen // *vt* (*dishes*) abtrocknen; **~-cleaning** *n* chemische Reinigung *f*; **~er** *n* Trockner *m*; (*US: spin-drier*) (Wäsche)schleuder *f*; ~ **goods store** *n* (*US*) Kurzwarengeschäft *nt*; **~ness** *n* Trockenheit *f*; ~ **rot** *n* Hausschwamm *m*.

dual ['djʊəl] *a* doppelt; ~ **carriageway** *n* (*Brit*) zweispurige Fahrbahn *f*; **~-control** *a* mit Doppelsteuerung; ~ **nationality** *n* doppelte Staatsangehörigkeit *f*; **~-purpose** *a* Mehrzweck-.

dubbed [dʌbd] *a* (*film*) synchronisiert.

dubious ['djuːbɪəs] *a* zweifelhaft.

duchess ['dʌtʃɪs] *n* Herzogin *f*.

duck [dʌk] *n* Ente *f* // *vi* sich ducken; **~ling** *n* Entchen *nt*.

duct [dʌkt] *n* Röhre *f*.

dud [dʌd] *n* Niete *f* // *a* (*cheque*) ungedeckt.

due [djuː] *a* fällig; (*fitting*) angemessen // *n* Gebühr *f*; (*right*) Recht *nt* // *ad* (*south etc*) genau; **~s** *pl* (*for club, union*) Beitrag *m*; (*in harbour*) Gebühren *pl*; ~ **to** wegen (+*gen*).

duel ['djʊəl] *n* Duell *nt*.

duet [djuː'et] *n* Duett *nt*.

duffel ['dʌfl] *a*: ~ **bag** *n* Matchbeutel *m*, Matchsack *m*; ~ **coat** *n* Dufflecoat *m*.

dug [dʌg] *pt, pp of* **dig**.

duke [djuːk] *n* Herzog *m*.

dull [dʌl] *a* (*colour, weather*) trübe; (*stupid*) schwer von Begriff; (*boring*) langweilig // *vt* abstumpfen.

duly ['djuːlɪ] *ad* ordnungsgemäß.

dumb [dʌm] *a* (*lit*) stumm; (*col: stupid*) doof, blöde; **~founded** [dʌm'faundɪd] *a* verblüfft.

dummy ['dʌmɪ] *n* Schneiderpuppe *f*; (*substitute*) Attrappe *f*; (*Brit: for baby*) Schnuller *m* // *a* Schein-.

dump [dʌmp] *n* Abfallhaufen *m*; (*MIL*) Stapelplatz *m*; (*col: place*) Nest *nt* // *vt* abladen, auskippen; **~ing** *n* (*COMM*) Schleuderexport *m*; (*of rubbish*) Schuttabladen *nt*.

dumpling ['dʌmplɪŋ] *n* Kloß *m*, Knödel *m*.

dumpy ['dʌmpɪ] *a* pummelig.

dunce [dʌns] *n* Dummkopf *m*.

dune [djuːn] *n* Düne *f*.

dung [dʌŋ] *n* Dünger *m*.

dungarees [dʌŋgə'riːz] *npl* Latzhose *f*.

dungeon ['dʌndʒən] *n* Kerker *m*.

dupe [djuːp] *n* Gefoppte(r) *m* // *vt* hintergehen, anführen.

duplex ['djuːpleks] *n* (*US*) zweistöckige Wohnung *f*.

duplicate ['djuːplɪkɪt] *n* Duplikat *nt* // *vt* ['djuːplɪkeɪt] verdoppeln; (*make copies*)

kopieren; **in** ~ in doppelter Ausführung.

duplicity [djuː'plɪsɪtɪ] *n* Doppelspiel *nt*.

durable ['djʊərəbl] *a* haltbar.

duration [djʊə'reɪʃən] *n* Dauer *f*.

duress [djʊə'res] *n*: **under** ~ unter Zwang.

during ['djʊərɪŋ] *prep* während (+*gen*).

dusk [dʌsk] *n* Abenddämmerung *f*.

dust [dʌst] *n* Staub *m* // *vt* abstauben; (*sprinkle*) bestäuben; **~bin** *n* (*Brit*) Mülleimer *m*; **~er** *n* Staubtuch *nt*; ~ **jacket** *n* Schutzumschlag *m*; **~man** *n* (*Brit*) Müllmann *m*; **~y** *a* staubig.

Dutch [dʌtʃ] *a* holländisch, niederländisch // *n* (*LING*) Holländisch *nt*, Niederländisch *nt*; **the** ~ *pl* die Holländer, die Niederländer; **to go** ~ getrennte Kasse machen; **~man/woman** *n* Holländer *m*, Niederländer *m*/Holländerin *f*, Niederländerin *f*.

dutiful ['djuːtɪful] *a* pflichtbewußt.

duty ['djuːtɪ] *n* Pflicht *f*; (*job*) Aufgabe *f*; (*tax*) Einfuhrzoll *m*; **on** ~ im Dienst; **~-free** *a* zollfrei.

duvet ['duːveɪ] *n* (*Brit*) Daunendecke *nt*.

dwarf [dwɔːf], *pl* **dwarves** [dwɔːvz] *n* Zwerg *m* // *vt* überragen.

dwell [dwel], *pt, pp* **dwelt** [dwelt] *vi* wohnen; ~ **on** *vt* verweilen bei; **~ing** *n* Wohnung *f*.

dwindle ['dwɪndl] *vi* schwinden.

dye [daɪ] *n* Farbstoff *m* // *vt* färben.

dying ['daɪɪŋ] *a* (*person*) sterbend; (*moments*) letzt.

dyke [daɪk] *n* (*Brit: channel*) Kanal *m*; (: *barrier*) Deich *m*, Damm *m*.

dynamic [daɪ'næmɪk] *a* dynamisch.

dynamite ['daɪnəmaɪt] *n* Dynamit *nt*.

dynamo ['daɪnəməu] *n* Dynamo *m*.

E

E [iː] *n* (*MUS*) E *nt*.

each [iːtʃ] *a* jeder/jede/jedes // *pron* (ein) jeder/(eine) jede/(ein) jedes; ~ **other** einander, sich.

eager *a* ['iːgə*] eifrig.

eagle ['iːgl] *n* Adler *m*.

ear [ɪə*] *n* Ohr *nt*; (*of corn*) Ähre *f*; **~ache** *n* Ohrenschmerzen *pl*; **~drum** *n* Trommelfell *nt*.

earl [ɜːl] *n* Graf *m*.

early ['ɜːlɪ] *a, ad* früh; ~ **retirement** *n* vorzeitige Pensionierung.

earmark ['ɪəmɑːk] *vt* vorsehen.

earn [ɜːn] *vt* verdienen.

earnest ['ɜːnɪst] *a* ernst; **in** ~ *ad* im Ernst.

earnings ['ɜːnɪŋz] *npl* Verdienst *m*.

earphones ['ɪəfəunz] *npl* Kopfhörer *pl*.

earring ['ɪərɪŋ] *n* Ohrring *m*.

earshot ['ɪəʃɒt] *n* Hörweite *f*.

earth [ɜːθ] *n* Erde *f*; (*Brit ELEC*) Erdung *f* // *vt* erden; **~enware** *n* Steingut *nt;* ~**quake** *n* Erdbeben *nt.*

earthy ['ɜːθɪ] *a* roh; *(sensual)* sinnlich.

earwig ['ɪəwɪg] *n* Ohrwurm *m.*

ease [iːz] *n (simplicity)* Leichtigkeit *f; (social)* Ungezwungenheit *f // vt (pain)* lindern; *(burden)* erleichtern; **at ~** ungezwungen; *(MIL)* rührt euch!; **~ off** *or* **up** *vi* nachlassen.

easel ['iːzl] *n* Staffelei *f.*

easily ['iːzɪlɪ] *ad* leicht.

east [iːst] *n* Osten *m // a* östlich *// ad* nach Osten.

Easter ['iːstə*] *n* Ostern *nt;* **~ egg** *n* Osterei *nt.*

easterly ['iːstəlɪ] *a* östlich, Ost-.

eastern ['iːstən] *a* östlich.

East Germany *n* die DDR.

eastward(s) ['iːstwəd(z)] *ad* ostwärts.

easy ['iːzɪ] *a (task)* einfach; *(life)* bequem; *(manner)* ungezwungen, natürlich *// ad* leicht; **~ chair** *n* Sessel *m;* **~-going** *a* gelassen; *(lax)* lässig.

eat [iːt], *pt* **ate,** *pp* **eaten** ['iːtn] *vt* essen; *(animals)* fressen; *(destroy)* (zer)fressen; **~ into, ~ away** *vt* zerfressen.

eau de Cologne [əʊdəkə'ləʊn] *n* Kölnisch Wasser *nt.*

eaves [iːvz] *npl* Dachrand *m.*

eavesdrop ['iːvzdrɒp] *vi* lauschen; **to ~ on sb** jdn belauschen.

ebb [eb] *n* Ebbe *f // vi (fig: also:* **~ away)** (ab)ebben; **~ tide** *n* Ebbe *f.*

ebony ['ebənɪ] *n* Ebenholz *nt.*

ebullient [ɪ'bʌlɪənt] *a* sprudelnd, temperamentvoll.

eccentric [ɪk'sentrɪk] *a* exzentrisch *// n* Exzentriker(in *f) m.*

ecclesiastical [ɪkliːzɪ'æstɪkəl] *a* kirchlich.

echo ['ekəʊ], *pl* **~es** *n* Echo *nt // vt* zurückwerfen; *(fig)* nachbeten *// vi* widerhallen.

eclipse [ɪ'klɪps] *n* Finsternis *f // vt* verfinstern.

ecology [ɪ'kɒlədʒɪ] *n* Ökologie *f.*

economic [iːkə'nɒmɪk] *a* wirtschaftlich; **~al** *a* wirtschaftlich; *(person)* sparsam; **~s** *n* Volkswirtschaft *f.*

economist [ɪ'kɒnəmɪst] *n* Volkswirt(schaftler) *m.*

economize [ɪ'kɒnəmaɪz] *vi* sparen.

economy [ɪ'kɒnəmɪ] *n (thrift)* Sparsamkeit *f; (of country)* Wirtschaft *f.*

ecstasy ['ekstəsɪ] *n* Ekstase *f.*

ecstatic [eks'tætɪk] *a* hingerissen.

ecumenical [iːkjʊ'menɪkəl] *a* ökumenisch.

eczema ['eksɪmə] *n* Ekzem *nt.*

edge [edʒ] *n* Rand *m; (of knife)* Schneide *f // vt (SEWING)* einfassen; **on ~** *(fig)* = edgy; **to ~ away from** langsam abrücken von; **~ways** *ad:* **he couldn't get a word in** ~ways er kam überhaupt nicht zu Wort.

edgy ['edʒɪ] *a* nervös.

edible ['edɪbl] *a* eßbar.

edict ['iːdɪkt] *n* Erlaß *m.*

edifice ['edɪfɪs] *n* Gebäude *nt.*

edit ['edɪt] *vt* redigieren; **~ion** [ɪ'dɪʃən] *n* Ausgabe *f;* **~or** *n (of newspaper)* Redakteur *m; (of book)* Lektor *m;* **~orial** [edɪ'tɔːrɪəl] *a* Redaktions- *// n* Leitartikel *m.*

educate ['edjukeɪt] *vt* erziehen, (aus)bilden.

education [edju'keɪʃən] *n (teaching)* Unterricht *m; (system)* Schulwesen *nt; (schooling)* Erziehung *f;* Bildung *f;* **~al** *a* pädagogisch.

EEC *n abbr* (= *European Economic Community)* EG *f.*

eel [iːl] *n* Aal *m.*

eerie ['ɪərɪ] *a* unheimlich.

effect [ɪ'fekt] *n* Wirkung *f // vt* bewirken; **~s** *pl (sound, visual)* Effekte *pl;* **in ~** in der Tat; **to take ~** *(law)* in Kraft treten; *(drug)* wirken; **~ive** *a,* **~ly** *ad* wirksam, effektiv.

effeminate [ɪ'femɪnɪt] *a* weibisch.

effervescent [efə'vesnt] *a (lit, fig)* sprudelnd.

efficacy ['efɪkəsɪ] *n* Wirksamkeit *f.*

efficiency [ɪ'fɪʃənsɪ] *n* Leistungsfähigkeit *f.*

efficient [ɪ'fɪʃənt] *a* tüchtig; *(TECH)* leistungsfähig; *(method)* wirksam.

effigy ['efɪdʒɪ] *n* Abbild *nt.*

effort ['efət] *n* Anstrengung *f;* **~less** *a* mühelos.

effrontery [ɪ'frʌntərɪ] *n* Unverfrorenheit *f.*

effusive [ɪ'fjuːsɪv] *a* überschwenglich.

e.g. *ad abbr* (= *exempli gratia)* z.B.

egalitarian [ɪgælɪ'tɛərɪən] *a* Gleichheits-, egalitär.

egg [eg] *n* Ei *nt;* **~ on** *vt* anstacheln; **~cup** *n* Eierbecher *m;* **~plant** *n (esp US)* Aubergine *f;* **~shell** *n* Eierschale *f.*

ego ['iːgəʊ] *n* Ich *nt,* Selbst *nt.*

egotism ['egəʊtɪzəm] *n* Ichbezogenheit *f.*

egotist ['egəʊtɪst] *n* Egozentriker *m.*

Egypt ['iːdʒɪpt] *n* Ägypten *nt;* **~ian** [ɪ'dʒɪpʃən] *a* ägyptisch *// n* Ägypter(in *f) m.*

eiderdown ['aɪdədaʊn] *n* Daunendecke *f.*

eight [eɪt] *num* acht; **~een** *num* achtzehn; **eighth** [eɪtθ] *a* achte(r, s) *// n* Achtel *nt;* **~y** *num* achtzig.

Eire ['ɛərə] *n* Irland *nt.*

either ['aɪðə*] *cj:* **~ ... or** entweder ... oder *// pron:* **~ of the two** eine(r, s) von beiden; **I don't want ~** ich will keins von beiden *// a:* **on ~ side** auf beiden Seiten *// ad:* **I don't ~** ich auch nicht.

eject [ɪ'dʒekt] *vt* ausstoßen, vertreiben.

eke [iːk]: **~ out** *vt* strecken.

elaborate [ɪ'læbərɪt] *a* sorgfältig ausgearbeitet, ausführlich // v [ɪˈlæbəreɪt] vt sorgfältig ausarbeiten // vi ausführlich darstellen; **~ly** ad genau, ausführlich.

elapse [ɪˈlæps] vi vergehen.

elastic [ɪˈlæstɪk] n Gummiband nt // a elastisch; **~ band** n (Brit) Gummiband nt.

elated [ɪˈleɪtɪd] a froh.

elation [ɪˈleɪʃən] n gehobene Stimmung f.

elbow [ˈelbəʊ] n Ellbogen m.

elder [ˈeldə*] a älter // n Ältere(r) mf; **~ly** a ältere(r, s) // n: the ~ly die Älteren.

eldest [ˈeldɪst] a älteste(r, s) // n Älteste(r) mf.

elect [ɪˈlekt] vt wählen // a zukünftig; **~ion** n Wahl f; **~ioneering** [ɪlekʃəˈnɪərɪŋ] n Wahlpropaganda f; **~or** n Wähler m; **~oral** a Wahl-; **~orate** n Wähler pl, Wählerschaft f.

electric [ɪˈlektrɪk] a elektrisch, Elektro-; **~al** a elektrisch; **~ blanket** n Heizdecke f; **~ chair** n elektrische(r) Stuhl m; **~ fire** n elektrische(r) Heizofen m.

electrician [ɪlekˈtrɪʃən] n Elektriker m.

electricity [ɪlekˈtrɪsɪtɪ] n Elektrizität f.

electrify [ɪˈlektrɪfaɪ] vt elektrifizieren; (fig) elektrisieren.

electrocute [ɪˈlektrəʊkjuːt] vt durch elektrischen Strom töten.

electronic [ɪlekˈtrɒnɪk] a elektronisch, Elektronen-; **~ mail** n elektronische(r) Briefkasten m; **~s** n Elektronik f.

elegance [ˈelɪɡəns] n Eleganz f.

elegant [ˈelɪɡənt] a elegant.

element [ˈelɪmənt] n Element nt; **~ary** [elɪˈmentərɪ] a einfach; (primary) Grund-.

elephant [ˈelɪfənt] n Elefant m.

elevate [ˈelɪveɪt] vt emporheben.

elevation [elɪˈveɪʃən] n (height) Erhebung f; (ARCHIT) (Quer)schnitt m.

elevator [ˈelɪveɪtə*] n (US) Fahrstuhl m, Aufzug m.

eleven [ɪˈlevn] num elf; **~ses** npl (Brit) zweite(s) Frühstück nt; **~th** a elfte(r, s).

elf [elf], pl **elves** [elvz] n Elfe f.

elicit [ɪˈlɪsɪt] vt herausbekommen.

eligible [ˈelɪdʒəbl] a wählbar; to be ~ for a pension pensionsberechtigt sein.

eliminate [ɪˈlɪmɪneɪt] vt ausschalten.

elimination [ɪlɪmɪˈneɪʃən] n Ausschaltung f.

elite [erˈliːt] n Elite f.

elm [elm] n Ulme f.

elocution [eləˈkjuːʃən] n Sprecherziehung f.

elongated [ˈiːlɒŋɡeɪtɪd] a verlängert.

elope [ɪˈləʊp] vi entlaufen; **~ment** n Entlaufen m.

eloquence [ˈeləkwəns] n Beredsamkeit f.

eloquent [ˈeləkwənt] a redegewandt.

else [els] ad sonst; **who ~**? wer sonst?; sb ~ jd anders; **or ~** sonst; **~where** ad anderswo, woanders.

elucidate [ɪˈluːsɪdeɪt] vt erläutern.

elude [ɪˈluːd] vt entgehen (+dat).

elusive [ɪˈluːsɪv] a schwer faßbar.

elves [elvz] npl of **elf**.

emaciated [ɪˈmeɪsɪeɪtɪd] a abgezehrt.

emanate [ˈeməneɪt] vi ausströmen (from aus).

emancipate [ɪˈmænsɪpeɪt] vt emanzipieren; (slave) freilassen.

emancipation [ɪmænsɪˈpeɪʃən] n Emanzipation f; Freilassung f.

embankment [ɪmˈbæŋkmənt] n (of river) Uferböschung f; (of road) Straßendamm m.

embargo [ɪmˈbɑːɡəʊ], pl **~es** n Embargo nt.

embark [ɪmˈbɑːk] vi sich einschiffen; **~ on** vt unternehmen; **~ation** [embɑːˈkeɪʃən] n Einschiffung f.

embarrass [ɪmˈbærəs] vt in Verlegenheit bringen; **~ed** a verlegen; **~ing** a peinlich; **~ment** n Verlegenheit f.

embassy [ˈembəsɪ] n Botschaft f.

embed [ɪmˈbed] vt einbetten.

embellish [ɪmˈbelɪʃ] vt verschönern.

embers [ˈembəz] npl Glut(asche) f.

embezzle [ɪmˈbezl] vt unterschlagen; **~ment** n Unterschlagung f.

embitter [ɪmˈbɪtə*] vt verbittern.

embody [ɪmˈbɒdɪ] vt (ideas) verkörpern; (new features) (in sich) vereinigen.

embossed [ɪmˈbɒst] a geprägt.

embrace [ɪmˈbreɪs] vt umarmen; (include) einschließen // vi sich umarmen // n Umarmung f.

embroider [ɪmˈbrɔɪdə*] vt (be)sticken; (story) ausschmücken; **~y** n Stickerei f.

emerald [ˈemərəld] n Smaragd m.

emerge [ɪˈmɜːdʒ] vi auftauchen; (truth) herauskommen.

emergence [ɪˈmɜːdʒəns] n Erscheinen nt.

emergency [ɪˈmɜːdʒənsɪ] n Notfall m; **~ cord** n (US) Notbremse f; **~ exit** n Notausgang m; **~ landing** n Notlandung f; the **~ services** npl die Notdienste pl.

emery board [ˈemərɪ-] n Papiernagelfeile f.

emetic [ɪˈmetɪk] n Brechmittel nt.

emigrant [ˈemɪɡrənt] n Auswanderer m.

emigrate [ˈemɪɡreɪt] vi auswandern.

emigration [emɪˈɡreɪʃən] n Auswanderung f.

eminence [ˈemɪnəns] n hohe(r) Rang m.

eminent [ˈemɪnənt] a bedeutend.

emission [ɪˈmɪʃən] n Ausströmen nt.

emit [ɪˈmɪt] vt von sich (dat) geben.

emotion [ɪˈməʊʃən] n Emotion f, Gefühl nt; **~al** a (person) emotional; (scene) ergreifend.

emotive [ɪˈməʊtɪv] a gefühlsbetont.

emperor [ˈempərə*] n Kaiser m.

emphasis [ˈemfəsɪs], pl **-ses** [-siːz] n (LING) Betonung f; (fig) Nachdruck m.

emphasize [ˈemfəsaɪz] vt betonen.

emphatic a, **~ally** ad [ɪmˈfætɪk, -əlɪ] nachdrücklich.

empire [ˈempaɪə*] n Reich nt.

empirical [emˈpɪrɪkəl] a empirisch.

employ [ɪmˈplɔɪ] vt (hire) anstellen; (use) verwenden; **~ee** [emplɔɪˈiː] n Angestellte(r) mf; **~er** n Arbeitgeber(in f) m; **~ment** n Beschäftigung f; **~ment agency** n Stellenvermittlung f.

empower [ɪmˈpaʊə*] vt: to ~ sb to do sth jdn ermächtigen, etw zu tun.

empress [ˈemprɪs] n Kaiserin f.

emptiness [ˈemptɪnɪs] n Leere f.

empty [ˈemptɪ] a leer // n (bottle) Leergut nt // vt (contents) leeren; (container) ausleeren // vi (water) abfließen; (river) münden; (house) sich leeren; **~-handed** a mit leeren Händen.

emulate [ˈemjʊleɪt] vt nacheifern (+dat).

emulsion [ɪˈmʌlʃən] n Emulsion f.

enable [ɪˈneɪbl] vt: to ~ sb to do sth es jdm ermöglichen, etw zu tun.

enamel [ɪˈnæməl] n Email nt; (of teeth) (Zahn)schmelz m.

enact [ɪnˈækt] vt (law) erlassen; (play) aufführen; (role) spielen.

encased [ɪnˈkeɪst] a: ~ in (enclosed) eingeschlossen in (+dat); (covered) verkleidet mit.

enchant [ɪnˈtʃɑːnt] vt bezaubern; **~ing** a entzückend.

encircle [ɪnˈsɜːkl] vt umringen.

encl. abbr (= enclosed) Anl.

enclose [ɪnˈkləʊz] vt einschließen; (in letter) beilegen (in, with dat); **~d** (in letter) beigelegt, anbei.

enclosure [ɪnˈkləʊʒə*] n Einfriedung f; (in letter) Anlage f.

encompass [ɪnˈkʌmpəs] vt (include) umfassen.

encore [ˈɒŋkɔː*] n Zugabe f.

encounter [ɪnˈkaʊntə*] n Begegnung f; (MIL) Zusammenstoß m // vt treffen; (resistance) stoßen auf (+acc).

encourage [ɪnˈkʌrɪdʒ] vt ermutigen; **~ment** n Ermutigung f, Förderung f.

encouraging   [ɪnˈkʌrɪdʒɪŋ]   a ermutigend, vielversprechend.

encroach [ɪnˈkrəʊtʃ] vi: to ~ (up)on eindringen in (+acc); (time) in Anspruch nehmen.

encrusted [ɪnˈkrʌstəd] a: ~ with besetzt mit.

encumber [ɪnˈkʌmbə*] vt: to be **~ed** with (parcels) beladen sein mit; (debts) belastet sein mit.

encyclop(a)edia [ensaɪkləʊˈpiːdɪə] n Konversationslexikon nt.

end [end] n Ende nt, Schluß m; (purpose) Zweck m // vt (also: **bring to an ~**, **put an ~ to**) beenden // vi zu Ende gehen; **in the ~** zum Schluß; **on ~** (object) hochkant; **to stand on ~** (hair) zu Berge stehen; **for hours on ~** stundenlang; **~ up** vi landen.

endanger [ɪnˈdeɪndʒə*] vt gefährden.

endearing [ɪnˈdɪərɪŋ] a gewinnend.

endeavour, (US) **endeavor** [ɪnˈdevə*] n Bestrebung f // vi sich bemühen.

ending [ˈendɪŋ] n Ende nt.

endless [ˈendlɪs] a endlos.

endorse [ɪnˈdɔːs] vt unterzeichnen; (approve) unterstützen; **~ment** n (on licence) Eintrag m.

endow [ɪnˈdaʊ] vt: ~ sb with sth jdm etw verleihen; (with money) jdm etw stiften.

endurance [ɪnˈdjʊərəns] n Ausdauer f.

endure [ɪnˈdjʊə*] vt ertragen // vi (last) (fort)dauern.

enemy [ˈenɪmɪ] n Feind m // a feindlich.

energetic [enəˈdʒetɪk] a tatkräftig.

energy [ˈenədʒɪ] n Energie f.

enforce [ɪnˈfɔːs] vt durchsetzen.

engage [ɪnˈgeɪdʒ] vt (employ) einstellen; (in conversation) verwickeln; (TECH) einschalten // vi (TECH) ineinandergreifen; (clutch) fassen; **to ~ in** sich beteiligen an (+dat); **~d** a verlobt; (Brit: TEL, toilet) besetzt; (: busy) beschäftigt; **to get ~d** sich verloben; **~d tone** n (Brit TEL) Besetztzeichen nt; **~ment** n (appointment) Verabredung f; (to marry) Verlobung f; (MIL) Gefecht nt; **~ment ring** n Verlobungsring m.

engaging [ɪnˈgeɪdʒɪŋ] a gewinnend.

engender [ɪnˈdʒendə*] vt hervorrufen.

engine [ˈendʒɪn] n (AUT) Motor m; (RAIL) Lokomotive f; ~ **driver** n Lokführer(in f) m.

engineer [endʒɪˈnɪə*] n Ingenieur m; (US RAIL) Lokomotivführer m.

engineering [endʒɪˈnɪərɪŋ] n Technik f.

England [ˈɪŋglənd] n England nt.

English [ˈɪŋglɪʃ] a englisch // n (LING) Englisch nt; **the ~** pl die Engländer; **the ~ Channel** n der Ärmelkanal m; **~man/woman** n Engländer m/ Engländerin f.

engraving [ɪnˈgreɪvɪŋ] n Stich m.

engrossed [ɪnˈgrəʊst] a vertieft.

engulf [ɪnˈgʌlf] vt verschlingen.

enhance [ɪnˈhɑːns] vt steigern, heben.

enigma [ɪˈnɪgmə] n Rätsel nt; **~tic** [enɪgˈmætɪk] a rätselhaft.

enjoy [ɪnˈdʒɔɪ] vt genießen; (privilege) besitzen; **to ~ o.s.** sich amüsieren; **~able** a erfreulich; **~ment** n Genuß m, Freude f.

enlarge [ɪnˈlɑːdʒ] vt erweitern; (PHOT) vergrößern // vi: **to ~ on** sich etw weiter ausführen; **~ment** n Vergrößerung f.

enlighten [ɪnˈlaɪtn] vt aufklären; **the**

E~ment n (HIST) die Aufklärung.

enlist [ɪn'lɪst] vt gewinnen // vi (MIL) sich melden.

enmity ['enmɪtɪ] n Feindschaft f.

enormity [ɪ'nɔːmɪtɪ] n Ungeheuerlichkeit f.

enormous [ɪ'nɔːməs] a ungeheuer.

enough [ɪ'nʌf] a, ad genug; funnily ~ komischerweise.

enquire [ɪn'kwaɪə*] vti = inquire.

enrage [ɪn'reɪdʒ] vt wütend machen.

enrich [ɪn'rɪtʃ] vt bereichern.

enrol [ɪn'rəʊl] vt einschreiben // vi (register) sich anmelden; ~ment n (for course) Anmeldung f.

en route [ɑːn'ruːt] ad unterwegs.

ensign ['ensaɪn] n (NAUT) Flagge f; (MIL) Fähnrich m.

enslave [ɪn'sleɪv] vt versklaven.

ensue [ɪn'sjuː] vi folgen, sich ergeben.

ensure [ɪn'ʃʊə*] vt garantieren.

entail [ɪn'teɪl] vt mit sich bringen.

entangle [ɪn'tæŋgl] vt verwirren, verstricken.

enter ['entə*] vt eintreten in (+dat), betreten; (club) beitreten (+dat); (in book) eintragen // vi hereinkommen, hineingehen; ~ **for** vt sich beteiligen an (+dat); ~ **into** vt (agreement) eingehen; (plans) eine Rolle spielen bei; ~ (**up)on** vt beginnen.

enteritis [entə'raɪtɪs] n Dünndarmentzündung f.

enterprise ['entəpraɪz] n (in person) Initiative f; (COMM) Unternehmen nt.

enterprising ['entəpraɪzɪŋ] a unternehmungslustig.

entertain [entə'teɪn] vt (guest) bewirten; (amuse) unterhalten; ~**er** n Unterhaltungskünstler(in f) m; ~**ing** a unterhaltsam; ~**ment** n Unterhaltung f.

enthralled [ɪn'θrɔːld] a gefesselt.

enthusiasm [ɪn'θuːzɪæzəm] n Begeisterung f.

enthusiast [ɪn'θuːzɪæst] n Enthusiast m; ~**ic** [ɪnθuːzɪ'æstɪk] a begeistert.

entice [ɪn'taɪs] vt verleiten, locken.

entire [ɪn'taɪə*] a ganz; ~**ly** ad ganz, völlig; ~**ty** [ɪn'taɪərətɪ] n: in its ~ty in seiner Gesamtheit.

entitle [ɪn'taɪtl] vt (allow) berechtigen; (name) betiteln; ~**ed** a (book) mit dem Titel.

entity ['entɪtɪ] n Ding nt, Wesen nt.

entourage [ɒntu'rɑːʒ] n Gefolge nt.

entrails ['entreɪlz] npl Eingeweide pl.

entrance ['entrəns] n Eingang m; (entering) Eintritt m // vt [ɪn'trɑːns] hinreißen; ~ **examination** n Aufnahmeprüfung f; ~ **fee** n Eintrittsgeld nt; ~ **ramp** n (US AUT) Einfahrt f.

entrant ['entrənt] n (for exam) Kandidat m; (in race) Teilnehmer m.

entreat [ɪn'triːt] vt anflehen.

entrenched [ɪn'trentʃt] a (fig) verwurzelt.

entrepreneur [ɒntrəprə'nɜː*] n Unternehmer(in f) m.

entrust [ɪn'trʌst] vt anvertrauen (sb with sth jdm etw).

entry ['entrɪ] n Eingang m; (THEAT) Auftritt m; (in account) Eintragung f; (in dictionary) Eintrag m; 'no ~' 'Eintritt verboten'; (for cars) 'Einfahrt verboten'; ~ **form** n Anmeldeformular nt; ~ **phone** n Sprechanlage f.

enumerate [ɪ'njuːməreɪt] vt aufzählen.

enunciate [ɪ'nʌnsɪeɪt] vt aussprechen.

envelop [ɪn'veləp] vt einhüllen.

envelope ['envələʊp] n Umschlag m.

enviable ['envɪəbl] a beneidenswert.

envious ['envɪəs] a neidisch.

environment [ɪn'vaɪərənmənt] n Umgebung f; (ecology) Umwelt f; ~**al** [ɪnvaɪərən'mentl] a Umwelt-.

envisage [ɪn'vɪzɪdʒ] vt sich (dat) vorstellen.

envoy ['envɔɪ] n Gesandte(r) mf.

envy ['envɪ] n Neid m // vt: to ~ sb sth jdn um etw beneiden.

enzyme ['enzaɪm] n Enzym nt.

ephemeral [ɪ'femərəl] a flüchtig.

epic ['epɪk] n Epos nt // a episch.

epidemic [epɪ'demɪk] n Epidemie f.

epilepsy ['epɪlepsɪ] n Epilepsie f.

epileptic [epɪ'leptɪk] a epileptisch // n Epileptiker(in f) m.

episode ['epɪsəʊd] n (incident) Vorfall m; (story) Episode f.

epistle [ɪ'pɪsl] n Brief m.

epitaph ['epɪtɑːf] n Grab(in)schrift f.

epithet ['epɪθət] n Beiname m.

epitome [ɪ'pɪtəmɪ] n Inbegriff m.

epitomize [ɪ'pɪtəmaɪz] vt verkörpern.

equable ['ekwəbl] a ausgeglichen.

equal ['iːkwl] a gleich // n Gleichgestellte(r) mf // vt gleichkommen (+dat); ~ **to the task** der Aufgabe gewachsen; ~**ity** [ɪ'kwolɪtɪ] n Gleichheit f; (equal rights) Gleichberechtigung f; ~**ize** vt gleichmachen // vi (SPORT) ausgleichen; ~**izer** n (SPORT) Ausgleich(streffer) m; ~**ly** ad gleich.

equanimity [ekwə'nɪmɪtɪ] n Gleichmut m.

equate [ɪ'kweɪt] vt gleichsetzen.

equation [ɪ'kweɪʒən] n Gleichung f.

equator [ɪ'kweɪtə*] n Äquator m.

equestrian [ɪ'kwestrɪən] a Reit-.

equilibrium [iːkwɪ'lɪbrɪəm] n Gleichgewicht nt.

equinox ['iːkwɪnɒks] n Tag- und Nachtgleiche f.

equip [ɪ'kwɪp] vt ausrüsten; ~**ment** n Ausrüstung f; (TECH) Gerät nt.

equitable ['ekwɪtəbl] a gerecht, billig.

equities ['ekwɪtɪz] npl (Brit COMM) Stammaktien pl.

equivalent [ɪ'kwɪvələnt] a gleichwertig (to dat), entsprechend (to dat) // n

Äquivalent *nt*; (*in money*) Gegenwert *m*.

equivocal [ɪ'kwɪvəkəl] *a* zweideutig.

era ['ɪərə] *n* Epoche *f*, Ära *f*.

eradicate [ɪ'rædɪkeɪt] *vt* ausrotten.

erase [ɪ'reɪz] *vt* ausradieren; (*tape*) löschen; ~ *n* Radiergummi *m*.

erect [ɪ'rekt] *a* aufrecht // *vt* errichten.

erection [ɪ'rekʃən] *n* Errichtung *f*; (ANAT) Erektion *f*.

ermine ['ɜːmɪn] *n* Hermelin(pelz) *m*.

erode [ɪ'rəud] *vt* zerfressen; (*land*) auswaschen.

erotic [ɪ'rɒtɪk] *a* erotisch; ~**ism** [ɪ'rɒtɪsɪzəm] *n* Erotik *f*.

err [ɜː*] *vi* sich irren.

errand ['erənd] *n* Besorgung *f*; ~ **boy** *n* Laufbursche *m*.

erratic [ɪ'rætɪk] *a* unberechenbar.

erroneous [ɪ'rəunɪəs] *a* irrig.

error ['erə*] *n* Fehler *m*.

erudite ['erʊdaɪt] *a* gelehrt.

erupt [ɪ'rʌpt] *vi* ausbrechen; ~**ion** *n* Ausbruch *m*.

escalate ['eskəleɪt] *vi* sich steigern.

escalator ['eskəleɪtə*] *n* Rolltreppe *f*.

escape [ɪs'keɪp] *n* Flucht *f*; (*of gas*) Entweichen *nt* // *vti* entkommen (+*dat*); (*prisoners*) fliehen; (*leak*) entweichen.

escapism [ɪs'keɪpɪzəm] *n* Flucht *f* (vor der Wirklichkeit).

escort ['eskɔːt] *n* (*person accompanying*) Begleiter *m*; (*guard*) Eskorte *f* // *vt* [ɪs'kɔːt] (*lady*) begleiten; (MIL) eskortieren.

Eskimo ['eskɪməu] *n* Eskimo *m*.

especially [ɪs'peʃəlɪ] *ad* besonders.

espionage ['espɪənɑːʒ] *n* Spionage *f*.

esplanade ['espləneɪd] *n* Promenade *f*.

espouse [ɪ'spauz] *vt* Partei ergreifen für.

Esquire [ɪs'kwaɪə*] *n* (*abbr* Esq.) J. Brown ~ Herrn J. Brown.

essay ['eseɪ] *n* Aufsatz *m*; (LITER) Essay *m*.

essence ['esəns] *n* (*quality*) Wesen *nt*; (*extract*) Essenz *f*.

essential [ɪ'senʃəl] *a* (*necessary*) unentbehrlich; (*basic*) wesentlich // *n* Allernötigste(s) *nt*; ~**ly** *ad* eigentlich.

establish [ɪs'tæblɪʃ] *vt* (*set up*) gründen; (*prove*) nachweisen; ~**ed** *a* anerkannt; (*belief, laws etc*) herrschend; ~**ment** *n* (*setting up*) Einrichtung *f*; the E~ment das Establishment.

estate [ɪs'teɪt] *n* Gut *nt*; (*Brit: housing* ~) Siedlung *f*; (*will*) Nachlaß *m*; ~ **agent** *n* (*Brit*) Grundstücksmakler *m*; ~ **car** *n* (*Brit*) Kombiwagen *m*.

esteem [ɪs'tiːm] *n* Wertschätzung *f*.

esthetic [es'θetɪk] *a* (US) = **aesthetic**.

estimate ['estɪmət] *n* Schätzung *f*; (*of price*) (Kosten)voranschlag *m* // *vt* ['estɪmeɪt] schätzen.

estimation [estɪ'meɪʃən] *n* Einschätzung *f*; (*esteem*) Achtung *f*.

estranged [ɪ'streɪndʒd] *a* entfremdet.

estuary ['estjuərɪ] *n* Mündung *f*.

etc *abbr* (= *et cetera*) etc.

etching ['etʃɪŋ] *n* Kupferstich *m*.

eternal [ɪ'tɜːnl] *a* ewig.

eternity [ɪ'tɜːnɪtɪ] *n* Ewigkeit *f*.

ether ['iːθə*] *n* (MED) Äther *m*.

ethical ['eθɪkəl] *a* ethisch.

ethics ['eθɪks] *n* Ethik *f* // *npl* Moral *f*.

Ethiopia [iːθɪ'əupɪə] *n* Äthiopien *nt*.

ethnic ['eθnɪk] *a* Volks-, ethnisch.

etiquette ['etɪket] *n* Etikette *f*.

euphemism ['juːfɪmɪzəm] *n* Euphemismus *m*.

Eurocheque ['juərəu'tʃek] *n* Euroscheck *m*.

Europe ['juərəp] *n* Europa *nt*; ~**an** [-'piːən] *a* europäisch // *n* Europäer(in *f*) *m*.

evacuate [ɪ'vækjueɪt] *vt* (*place*) räumen; (*people*) evakuieren.

evacuation [ɪvækju'eɪʃən] *n* Räumung *f*; Evakuierung *f*.

evade [ɪ'veɪd] *vt* (*escape*) entkommen (+*dat*); (*avoid*) meiden; (*duty*) sich entziehen (+*dat*).

evaluate [ɪ'væljueɪt] *vt* bewerten; (*information*) auswerten.

evaporate [ɪ'væpəreɪt] *vi* verdampfen // *vt* verdampfen lassen; ~**d milk** *n* Kondensmilch *f*.

evasion [ɪ'veɪʒən] *n* Umgehung *f*.

evasive [ɪ'veɪzɪv] *a* ausweichend.

eve [iːv] *n*: on the ~ of am Vorabend (+*gen*).

even ['iːvən] *a* eben; gleichmäßig; (*score etc*) unentschieden; (*number*) gerade // *ad*: ~ **you** sogar du; ~ **if** selbst wenn; ~ **so** dennoch; **to get** ~ **with sb** jdm heimzahlen; ~ **out** *vi* sich ausgleichen.

evening ['iːvnɪŋ] *n* Abend *m*; **in the** ~ abends, am Abend; ~ **class** *n* Abendschule *f*; ~ **dress** *n* (*man's*) Gesellschaftsanzug *m*; (*woman's*) Abendkleid *nt*.

event [ɪ'vent] *n* (*happening*) Ereignis *nt*; (SPORT) Disziplin *f*; **in the** ~ **of** im Falle (+*gen*); ~**ful** *a* ereignisreich.

eventual [ɪ'ventʃuəl] *a* (*final*) schließlich; ~**ity** [ventʃu'ælɪtɪ] *n* Möglichkeit *f*; ~**ly** *ad* (*at last*) am Ende; (*given time*) schließlich.

ever ['evə*] *ad* (*always*) immer; (*at any time*) je(mals); ~ **since** *ad* seitdem // *cj* seit; ~**green** *n* Immergrün *nt*; ~**lasting** *a* immerwährend.

every ['evrɪ] *a* jede(r, s); ~ **other/third day** jeden zweiten/dritten Tag; ~ **one of** them alle; **I have** ~ **confidence in him** ich habe uneingeschränktes Vertrauen in ihn; **we wish you** ~ **success** wir wünschen Ihnen viel Erfolg; **he's** ~ **as clever as his brother** er ist genauso klug wie sein Bruder; ~ **now and then** ab und zu; ~**body** *pron* = ~**one**; ~**day** *a* (*daily*) täglich; (*commonplace*) alltäglich, Alltags-; ~**one** *pron* jeder, alle *pl*; ~**thing** *pron* alles; ~**where** *ad* überall(hin); (*wherever*) wohin; ~**where you** go wohin du auch gehst.

evict [ɪ'vɪkt] *vt* ausweisen; ~**ion** *n* Ausweisung *f*.

evidence ['evɪdəns] *n* (*sign*) Spur *f*; (*proof*) Beweis *m*; (*testimony*) Aussage *f*.

evident ['evɪdənt] *a* augenscheinlich; ~**ly** *ad* offensichtlich.

evil ['iːvl] *a* böse // *n* Böse *nt*.

evocative [ɪ'vɒkətɪv] *a*: to be ~ of sth an etw (*acc*) erinnern.

evoke [ɪ'vəʊk] *vt* hervorrufen.

evolution [iːvə'luːʃən] *n* Entwicklung *f*; (*of life*) Evolution *f*.

evolve [ɪ'vɒlv] *vt* entwickeln // *vi* sich entwickeln.

ewe [juː] *n* Mutterschaf *nt*.

ex- [eks] *pref* Ex-, Alt-, ehemalig.

exacerbate [ek'sæsəbeɪt] *vt* verschlimmern.

exact [ɪg'zækt] *a* genau // *vt* (*demand*) verlangen; ~**ing** *a* anspruchsvoll; ~**itude** *n* Genauigkeit *f*.

exaggerate [ɪg'zædʒəreɪt] *vti* übertreiben.

exaggeration [ɪgzædʒə'reɪʃən] *n* Übertreibung *f*.

exalted [ɪg'zɔːltɪd] *a* (*position, style*) hoch; (*person*) exaltiert.

exam [ɪg'zæm] *n abbr of* **examination**.

examination [ɪgzæmɪ'neɪʃən] *n* Untersuchung *f*; (*SCH*) Prüfung *f*, Examen *nt*; (*customs*) Kontrolle *f*.

examine [ɪg'zæmɪn] *vt* untersuchen; (*SCH*) prüfen; (*consider*) erwägen; ~**r** *n* Prüfer *m*.

example [ɪg'zɑːmpl] *n* Beispiel *nt*; for ~ zum Beispiel.

exasperate [ɪg'zɑːspəreɪt] *vt* zum Verzweifeln bringen.

exasperating [ɪg'zɑːspəreɪtɪŋ] *a* ärgerlich, zum Verzweifeln bringend.

exasperation [ɪgzɑːspə'reɪʃən] *n* Verzweiflung *f*.

excavate ['ekskəveɪt] *vt* ausgraben.

excavation [ekskə'veɪʃən] *n* Ausgrabung *f*.

exceed [ɪk'siːd] *vt* überschreiten; (*hopes*) übertreffen.

excel [ɪk'sel] *vi* sich auszeichnen.

excellence ['eksələns] *n* Vortrefflichkeit *f*.

excellency ['eksələnsɪ] *n*: His E~ Seine Exzellenz *f*.

excellent ['eksələnt] *a* ausgezeichnet.

except [ɪk'sept] *prep* (*also*: ~ for, ~ing) außer (+*dat*) // *vt* ausnehmen; ~**ion** [ɪk'sepʃən] *n* Ausnahme *f*; to take ~ion to Anstoß nehmen an (+*dat*); ~**ional** [ɪk'sepʃənl] *a* außergewöhnlich.

excerpt ['eksɜːpt] *n* Auszug *m*.

excess [ek'ses] *n* Übermaß *nt* (*of* an +*dat*); Exzeß *m*; ~ **baggage** *n* Mehrgepäck *nt*; ~ **fare** *n* Nachlösegebühr *f*; ~**ive** *a* übermäßig.

exchange [ɪks'tʃeɪndʒ] *n* Austausch *m*; (*also*: telephone ~) Zentrale *f* // *vt* (*goods*) tauschen; (*greetings*) austauschen; (*money, blows*) wechseln; ~ **rate** *n* Wechselkurs *m*.

Exchequer [ɪks'tʃekə*] *n*: the ~ (*Brit*) das Schatzamt.

excise ['eksaɪz] *n* Verbrauchssteuer *f* // *vt* [ek'saɪz] (*MED*) herausschneiden.

excite [ɪk'saɪt] *vt* erregen; to get ~d sich aufregen; ~**ment** *n* Aufregung *f*.

exciting [ɪk'saɪtɪŋ] *a* spannend.

exclaim [ɪks'kleɪm] *vi* ausrufen.

exclamation [eksklə'meɪʃən] *n* Ausruf *m*; ~ **mark** *n* Ausrufezeichen *nt*.

exclude [ɪks'kluːd] *vt* ausschließen.

exclusion [ɪks'kluːʒən] *n* Ausschluß *m*.

exclusive [ɪks'kluːsɪv] *a* (*select*) exklusiv; (*sole*) ausschließlich, Allein-; ~ of exklusive (+*gen*); ~**ly** *ad* nur, ausschließlich.

excommunicate [ekskə'mjuːnɪkeɪt] *vt* exkommunizieren.

excrement ['ekskrɪmənt] *n* Kot *m*.

excruciating [ɪks'kruːʃieɪtɪŋ] *a* qualvoll.

excursion [ɪks'kɜːʃən] *n* Ausflug *m*.

excusable [ɪks'kjuːzəbl] *a* entschuldbar.

excuse [ɪks'kjuːs] *n* Entschuldigung *f* // *vt* [ɪks'kjuːz] entschuldigen; ~ me! entschuldigen Sie!

ex-directory ['eksdaɪ'rektərɪ] *a* (*Brit*): to be ~ nicht im Telefonbuch stehen.

execute ['eksɪkjuːt] *vt* (*carry out*) ausführen; (*kill*) hinrichten.

execution [eksɪ'kjuːʃən] *n* Ausführung *f*; (*killing*) Hinrichtung *f*; ~**er** *n* Scharfrichter *m*.

executive [ɪg'zekjutɪv] *n* (*COMM*) Geschäftsführer *m*; (*POL*) Exekutive *f* // *a* Exekutiv-, ausführend.

executor [ɪg'zekjutə*] *n* Testamentsvollstrecker *m*.

exemplary [ɪg'zemplərɪ] *a* musterhaft.

exemplify [ɪg'zemplɪfaɪ] *vt* veranschaulichen.

exempt [ɪg'zempt] *a* befreit // *vt* befreien; ~**ion** [ɪg'zempʃən] *n* Befreiung *f*.

exercise ['eksəsaɪz] *n* Übung *f* // *vt* (*power*) ausüben; (*muscle, patience*) üben; (*dog*) ausführen // *vi* Sport treiben; ~ **book** *n* (Schul)heft *nt*.

exert [ɪg'zɜːt] *vt* (*influence*) ausüben; ~ o.s. sich anstrengen; ~**ion** [-ʃən] *n* Anstrengung *f*.

exhale [eks'heɪl] *vti* ausatmen.

exhaust [ɪg'zɔːst] *n* (*fumes*) Abgase *pl*; (*pipe*) Auspuffrohr *nt* // *vt* erschöpfen; ~**ed** *a* erschöpft; ~**ion** *n* Erschöpfung *f*; ~**ive** *a* erschöpfend.

exhibit [ɪg'zɪbɪt] n (ART) Ausstellungsstück nt; (JUR) Beweisstück nt // vt ausstellen; **~ion** [eksɪ'bɪʃən] n (ART) Ausstellung f; (of temper etc) Zurschaustellung f; **~ionist** [eksɪ'bɪʃənɪst] n Exhibitionist m.

exhilarating [ɪg'zɪləreɪtɪŋ] a erhebend.

exhort [ɪg'zɔːt] vt ermahnen.

exile ['eksaɪl] n Exil nt; (person) Verbannte(r) mf // vt verbannen.

exist [ɪg'zɪst] vi existieren; **~ence** n Existenz f; **~ing** a bestehend.

exit ['eksɪt] n Ausgang m; (THEAT) Abgang m // vi (THEAT) abtreten; (COMPUT) aus einem Programm herausgehen; **~ ramp** n (US AUT) Ausfahrt f.

exonerate [ɪg'zɒnəreɪt] vt entlasten.

exorbitant [ɪg'zɔːbɪtənt] a übermäßig; (price) Phantasie.

exotic [ɪg'zɒtɪk] a exotisch.

expand [ɪks'pænd] vt ausdehnen // vi sich ausdehnen.

expanse [ɪks'pæns] n Fläche f.

expansion [ɪks'pænʃən] n Erweiterung f.

expatriate [eks'pætrɪɪt] n Ausländer(in f) m.

expect [ɪks'pekt] vt erwarten; (suppose) annehmen // vi: to be **~ing** ein Kind erwarten; **~ancy** n Erwartung f; **~ant mother** n werdende Mutter f; **~ation** [ekspek'teɪʃən] n Hoffnung f.

expedience [ɪks'piːdɪəns], **expediency** [ɪks'piːdɪənsɪ] n Zweckdienlichkeit f.

expedient [ɪks'piːdɪənt] a zweckdienlich // n (Hilfs)mittel nt.

expedition [ekspɪ'dɪʃən] n Expedition f.

expel [ɪks'pel] vt ausweisen; (student) (ver)weisen.

expend [ɪks'pend] vt (effort) aufwenden; **~iture** n Ausgaben pl.

expense [ɪks'pens] n Kosten pl; **~s** pl Spesen pl; at the **~** of auf Kosten von; **~ account** n Spesenkonto nt.

expensive [ɪks'pensɪv] a teuer.

experience [ɪks'pɪərɪəns] n (incident) Erlebnis nt; (practice) Erfahrung f // vt erleben; **~d** a erfahren.

experiment [ɪks'perɪmənt] n Versuch m, Experiment nt // vi [ɪks'perɪment] experimentieren; **~al** [ɪksperɪ'mentl] a experimentell.

expert ['ekspɜːt] n Fachmann m; (official) Sachverständige(r) m // a erfahren; **~ise** [ekspə'tiːz] n Sachkenntnis f.

expire [ɪks'paɪə*] vi (end) ablaufen; (die) sterben; (ticket) verfallen.

expiry [ɪks'paɪərɪ] n Ablauf m.

explain [ɪks'pleɪn] vt erklären.

explanation [eksplə'neɪʃən] n Erklärung f.

explanatory [ɪks'plænətərɪ] a erklärend.

explicit [ɪks'plɪsɪt] a ausdrücklich.

explode [ɪks'pləud] vi explodieren // (bomb) sprengen; (theory) platzen lassen.

exploit ['eksplɔɪt] n (Helden)tat f // vt [ɪks'plɔɪt], ausbeuten; **~ation** [eksplɔɪ'teɪʃən] n Ausbeutung f.

exploration [eksplɔ:'reɪʃən] n Erforschung f.

exploratory [ɪks'plɔrətərɪ] a Probe.

explore [ɪks'plɔː*] vt (travel) erforschen; (search) untersuchen; **~r** n Erforscher(in f) m.

explosion [ɪks'pləuʒən] n (lit) Explosion f; (fig) Ausbruch m.

explosive [ɪks'pləuzɪv] a explosiv, Spreng // n Sprengstoff m.

exponent [eks'pəunənt] n Exponent m.

export [eks'pɔːt] vt exportieren // n ['ekspɔːt] Export m // cpd (trade) Export; **~er** n Exporteur m.

expose [ɪks'pəuz] vt (to danger etc) aussetzen (to dat); (imposter) entlarven.

exposed [ɪks'pəuzd] a (position) exponiert.

exposure [ɪks'pəuʒə*] n (MED) Unterkühlung f; (PHOT) Belichtung f; **~ meter** n Belichtungsmesser m.

expound [ɪks'paund] vt entwickeln.

express [ɪks'pres] a ausdrücklich; (speedy) Expreß, Eil // n (RAIL) Zug m // ad (send) per Expreß // vt ausdrücken; to **~** o.s. sich ausdrücken; **~ion** [ɪks'preʃən] n Ausdruck m; **~ive** a ausdrucksvoll; **~ly** ad ausdrücklich; **~way** n (US: urban motorway) Schnellstraße f.

expulsion [ɪks'pʌlʃən] n Ausweisung f.

expurgate ['ekspɜːgeɪt] vt zensieren.

exquisite [eks'kwɪzɪt] a erlesen.

extend [ɪks'tend] vt (visit etc) verlängern; (building) ausbauen; (hand) ausstrecken; (welcome) bieten // vi (land) sich erstrecken.

extension [ɪks'tenʃən] n Erweiterung f; (of building) Anbau m; (TEL) Apparat m.

extensive [ɪks'tensɪv] a (knowledge) umfassend; (use) weitgehend.

extent [ɪks'tent] n Ausdehnung f; (fig) Ausmaß nt; to a certain **~** bis zu einem gewissen Grade; to such an **~** that ... dermaßen, daß ...; to what **~**? inwieweit?

extenuating [eks'tenjueɪtɪŋ] a mildernd.

exterior [eks'tɪərɪə*] a äußere(r, s), Außen // n Äußere(s) nt.

exterminate [eks'tɜːmɪneɪt] vt ausrotten.

extermination [ekstɜːmɪ'neɪʃən] n Ausrottung f.

external [eks'tɜːnl] a äußere(r, s), Außen.

extinct [ɪks'tɪŋkt] a ausgestorben; **~ion** [ɪks'tɪŋkʃən] n Aussterben nt.

extinguish [ɪks'tɪŋgwɪʃ] vt

(aus)löschen; **~er** n Löschgerät nt.

extort [ıks'tɔːt] vt erpressen (sth from sb jdn um etw); **~ion** [ıks'tɔːʃən] n Erpressung f; **~ionate** [ıks'tɔːʃənıt] a überhöht, erpresserisch.

extra ['ekstrə] a zusätzlich // ad besonders // n (for car etc) Extra nt; (charge) Zuschlag m; (THEAT) Statist m.

extra... [ekstrə] pref außer...

extract [ıks'trækt] vt (heraus)ziehen // n ['ekstrækt] (from book etc) Auszug m; (COOK) Extrakt m.

extracurricular ['ekstrəkə'rıkjulə*] a außerhalb des Stundenplans.

extradite ['ekstrədaıt] vt ausliefern.

extramarital [ekstrə'mærıtl] a außerehelich.

extramural [ekstrə'mjuərl] a (course) Volkshochschul-.

extraordinary [ıks'trɔːdnrı] a außerordentlich; (amazing) erstaunlich.

extravagance [ıks'trævəgəns] n Verschwendung f; (lack of restraint) Zügellosigkeit f; (an ~) Extravaganz f.

extravagant [ıks'trævəgənt] a extravagant.

extreme [ıks'triːm] a (edge) äußerste(r, s), hinterste(r, s); (cold) äußerste(r, s); (behaviour) außergewöhnlich, übertrieben // n Extrem nt; **~ly** ad äußerst, höchst.

extremity [ıks'tremıtı] n (end) Spitze f, äußerste(s) Ende nt; (hardship) bitterste Not f; (ANAT) Hand f; Fuß m.

extricate ['ekstrıkeıt] vt losmachen, befreien.

extrovert ['ekstrəuvəːt] n extrovertierte(r) Mensch m.

exuberant [ıg'zuːbərənt] a ausgelassen.

exude [ıg'zjuːd] vt absondern.

exult [ıg'zʌlt] vi frohlocken.

eye [aı] n Auge nt; (of needle) Öhr nt // vt betrachten; (up and down) mustern; **to keep an ~ on** aufpassen auf (+acc); **~ball** n Augapfel m; **~bath** n Augenbad nt; **~brow** n Augenbraue f; **~brow pencil** n Augenbrauenstift m; **~drops** npl Augentropfen pl; **~lash** n Augenwimper f; **~lid** n Augenlid nt; **~liner** n Eyeliner nt; **~opener** n: that was an **~opener** das hat mir die Augen geöffnet; **~shadow** n Lidschatten m; **~sight** n Sehkraft f; **~sore** n Schandfleck m; **~ witness** n Augenzeuge m.

F

F [ef] n (MUS) F nt.

F. abbr (= Fahrenheit) F.

fable ['feıbl] n Fabel f.

fabric ['fæbrık] n Stoff m; (fig) Gefüge nt.

fabrication [fæbrı'keıʃən] n Erfindung f.

fabulous ['fæbjuləs] a sagenhaft.

face [feıs] n Gesicht nt; (surface) Oberfläche f; (of clock) Zifferblatt nt // vt (point towards) liegen nach; (situation, difficulty) sich stellen (+dat); **~ down** (person) mit dem Gesicht nach unten; (card) mit der Vorderseite nach unten; **to make** or **pull a ~** das Gesicht verziehen; **in the ~ of** angesichts (+gen); **on the ~ of it** so, wie es aussieht; **~ to ~** Auge in Auge; **to ~ up to sth** einer Sache ins Auge sehen; **~ cloth** n (Brit) Waschlappen m; **~ cream** n Gesichtscreme f; **~ lift** n Facelifting nt; **~ powder** n (Gesichts)puder m.

facet ['fæsıt] n Aspekt m; (of gem) Facette f.

facetious [fə'siːʃəs] a witzig.

face value n Nennwert m; (fig) **to take sth at its ~** etw für bare Münze nehmen.

facial ['feıʃəl] a Gesichts-.

facile ['fæsaıl] a oberflächlich; (US: easy) leicht.

facilitate [fə'sılıteıt] vt erleichtern.

facilities [fə'sılıtız] npl Einrichtungen pl; **credit ~** Kreditmöglichkeiten pl.

facing ['feısıŋ] a zugekehrt // prep gegenüber.

fact [fækt] n Tatsache f; **in ~** in der Tat.

faction ['fækʃən] n Splittergruppe f.

factor ['fæktə*] n Faktor m.

factory ['fæktərı] n Fabrik f.

factual ['fæktjuəl] a sachlich.

faculty ['fækəltı] n Fähigkeit f; (UNIV) Fakultät f; (US: teaching staff) Lehrpersonal m.

fad [fæd] n Tick m; (fashion) Masche f.

fade [feıd] vi (lose colour) verblassen; (grow dim) nachlassen; (sound, memory) schwächer werden; (wither) verwelken.

fag [fæg] n (col: cigarette) Kippe f.

fail [feıl] vt (exam) nicht bestehen; (student) durchfallen lassen; (courage) verlassen; (memory) im Stich lassen // vi (supplies) zu Ende gehen; (student) durchfallen; (eyesight) nachlassen; (light) schwächer werden; (crop) fehlschlagen; (remedy) nicht wirken; **~ to do sth** (neglect) es unterlassen, etw zu tun; (be unable) es nicht schaffen, etw zu tun; **without ~** unbedingt; **~ing** n Schwäche f // prep mangels (+gen); **~ure** n (person) Versager m; (act) Versagen nt; (TECH) Defekt m.

faint [feınt] a schwach // n Ohnmacht f // vi ohnmächtig werden.

fair [feə*] a schön; (hair) blond; (skin) hell; (just) gerecht, fair; (not very good) mittelmäßig; (sizeable) ansehnlich // ad (play) fair // n (COMM) Messe f; (Brit: fun~) Jahrmarkt m; **~ly** ad (honestly) gerecht, fair; (rather) ziemlich; **~ness** n Fairneß f.

fairy ['fɛərɪ] n Fee f; ~ **tale** n Märchen nt.

faith [feɪθ] n Glaube m; (trust) Vertrauen nt; (sect) Bekenntnis nt; ~**ful** a, ~**fully** ad treu; yours ~**fully** (Brit) hochachtungsvoll.

fake [feɪk] n (thing) Fälschung f; (person) Schwindler m // a vorgetäuscht // vt fälschen.

falcon ['fɔːlkən] n Falke m.

fall [fɔːl] n Fall m, Sturz m; (decrease) Fallen nt; (of snow) (Schnee)fall m; (US: autumn) Herbst m // vi, pt **fell**, pp **fallen** ['fɔːlən] (lit, fig) fallen; (night) hereinbrechen; ~**s** pl (waterfall) Fälle pl; ~ **back** vi zurückweichen; ~ **back on** vt zurückgreifen auf (+ acc); ~ **behind** vi zurückbleiben; ~ **down** vi (person) hinfallen; (building) einstürzen; ~ **flat** vi (lit) platt hinfallen; (joke) nicht ankommen; ~ **for** vt (trick) hereinfallen auf (+acc); (person) sich verknallen in (+acc); ~ **in** vi (roof) einstürzen; ~ **off** vi herunterfallen (von); (diminish) sich vermindern; ~ **out** vi sich streiten; (MIL) wegtreten; ~ **through** vi (plan) ins Wasser fallen.

fallacy ['fæləsɪ] n Trugschluß m.

fallen ['fɔːlən] pp of **fall**.

fallible ['fæləbl] a fehlbar.

fallout ['fɔːlaʊt] n radioaktive(r) Niederschlag m; ~ **shelter** n Atombunker m.

fallow ['fæləʊ] a brach(liegend).

false [fɔːls] a falsch; (artificial) künstlich; under ~ pretences unter Vorspiegelung falscher Tatsachen; ~ **alarm** n Fehlalarm m; ~ **teeth** npl (Brit) Gebiß nt.

falter ['fɔːltə*] vi schwanken; (in speech) stocken.

fame [feɪm] n Ruhm m.

familiar [fə'mɪlɪə*] a bekannt; (intimate) familiär; to be ~ with vertraut sein mit; ~**ize** vt vertraut machen.

family ['fæmɪlɪ] n Familie f; (relations) Verwandtschaft f; ~ **business** n Familienunternehmen nt; ~ **doctor** n Hausarzt m.

famine ['fæmɪn] n Hungersnot f.

famished ['fæmɪʃt] a ausgehungert.

famous ['feɪməs] a berühmt; ~**ly** ad (get on) prächtig.

fan [fæn] n (folding) Fächer m; (ELEC) Ventilator m; (admirer) Fan m // vt fächeln; ~ **out** vi sich (fächerförmig) ausbreiten.

fanatic [fə'nætɪk] n Fanatiker(in f) m.

fan belt n Keilriemen m.

fanciful ['fænsɪful] a (odd) seltsam; (imaginative) phantasievoll.

fancy ['fænsɪ] n (liking) Neigung f; (imagination) Einbildung f // a schick // vt (like) gern haben; wollen; (imagine) sich einbilden; he fancies her er mag

sie; ~ **dress** n Maskenkostüm nt; ~-**dress ball** n Maskenball m.

fang [fæŋ] n Fangzahn m; (snake's) Giftzahn m.

fantastic [fæn'tæstɪk] a phantastisch.

fantasy ['fæntəzɪ] n Phantasie f.

far [fɑː*] a weit // ad weit entfernt; (very much) weitaus, by ~ bei weitem; so ~ soweit; bis jetzt; go as ~ as the farm gehen Sie bis zum Bauernhof; as ~ as I know soweit or soviel ich weiß; ~**away** a weit entfernt.

farce [fɑːs] n Farce f.

farcical ['fɑːsɪkəl] a lächerlich.

fare [fɛə*] n Fahrpreis m; Fahrgeld nt; (food) Kost f.

Far East n: the ~ der Ferne Osten.

farewell [fɛə'wel] n Abschied(sgruß m) m // interj lebe wohl!

farm [fɑːm] n Bauernhof m, Farm f // vt bewirtschaften; ~**er** n Bauer m, Landwirt m; ~**hand** n Landarbeiter m; ~**house** n Bauernhaus nt; ~**ing** n Landwirtschaft f; ~**land** n Ackerland nt; ~**yard** n Hof m.

fart [fɑːt] (col!) n Furz m // vi furzen.

farther ['fɑːðə*] ad weiter.

farthest ['fɑːðɪst] a fernste(r, s) // ad am weitesten.

fascinate ['fæsɪneɪt] vt faszinieren.

fascination [fæsɪ'neɪʃən] n Faszination f.

fascist ['fæʃɪst] n Faschist m // a faschistisch.

fashion ['fæʃən] n (of clothes) Mode f; (manner) Art f (und Weise f) // vt machen; in ~ in Mode; out of ~ unmodisch; ~**able** a (clothes) modisch; (place) elegant; ~ **show** n Mode(n)schau f.

fast [fɑːst] a schnell; (firm) fest // ad schnell; (firmly) fest // n Fasten nt // vi fasten; to be ~ (clock) vorgehen.

fasten ['fɑːsn] vt (attach) befestigen; (seat belt) festmachen; (with rope) zuschnüren // vi sich schließen lassen; ~**er**, ~**ing** n Verschluß m.

fastidious [fæs'tɪdɪəs] a wählerisch.

fat [fæt] a dick // n Fett nt.

fatal ['feɪtl] a tödlich; (disastrous) verhängnisvoll; ~**ity** [fə'tælɪtɪ] n (road death etc) Todesopfer nt; ~**ly** ad tödlich.

fate [feɪt] n Schicksal nt; ~**ful** a (prophetic) schicksalsschwer; (important) schicksalhaft.

father ['fɑːðə*] n Vater m; (REL) Pater m; ~-**in-law** n Schwiegervater m; ~**ly** a väterlich.

fathom ['fæðəm] n Klafter m // vt ausloten; (fig) ergründen.

fatigue [fə'tiːg] n Ermüdung f.

fatten ['fætn] vt dick machen; (animals) mästen // vi dick werden.

fatty ['fætɪ] a fettig // n (col) Dickerchen nt.

fatuous ['fætjʊəs] a albern, affig.

faucet ['fɔːsɪt] n (US) Wasserhahn m.

fault [fɔːlt] n (defect) Defekt m; (ELEC) Störung f; (blame) Schuld f; (GEOG) Verwerfung f; it's your ~ du bist daran schuld; at ~ im Unrecht // vt: to ~ sth etwas an etw (dat) auszusetzen haben; ~less a tadellos; ~y a fehlerhaft, defekt.

favour, (US) **favor** ['feɪvə*] n (approval) Wohlwollen nt; (kindness) Gefallen m // vt (prefer) vorziehen; in ~ of für; zugunsten (+gen); to find ~ with sb bei jdm Anklang finden; ~able a günstig; ~ite ['feɪvərɪt] a Lieblings- // n (child) Liebling m; (SPORT) Favorit m; ~itism n (SCH) Bevorzugung f.

fawn [fɔːn] a rehbraun // n (colour) Rehbraun nt; (animal) (Reh)kitz nt // vi: to ~ (up)on (fig) katzbuckeln vor (+dat).

fax [fæks] n (document) Fax nt; (machine) Telefax nt // vt per Fax schicken.

FBI ['efbiː'aɪ] n abbr (US: = Federal Bureau of Investigation) FBI nt.

fear [fɪə*] n Furcht f // vt fürchten; ~ful a (timid) furchtsam; (terrible) fürchterlich; ~less a furchtlos.

feasible ['fiːzəbl] a durchführbar.

feast [fiːst] n Festmahl nt; (REL: also: ~ day) Feiertag m // vi sich gütlich tun (on an +dat).

feat [fiːt] n Leistung f.

feather ['feðə*] n Feder f.

feature ['fiːtʃə*] n (Gesichts)zug m; (important part) Grundzug m; (CINE, PRESS) Feature nt // vt darstellen; (advertising etc) groß herausbringen // vi vorkommen; featuring X mit X; ~ film n Spielfilm m.

February ['februərɪ] n Februar m.

fed [fed] pt, pp of **feed**.

federal ['fedərəl] a Bundes-.

federation [fedə'reɪʃən] n (society) Verband m; (of states) Staatenbund m.

fed-up [fed'ʌp] a: to be ~ with sth etw satt haben; I'm ~ ich habe die Nase voll.

fee [fiː] n Gebühr f.

feeble ['fiːbl] a (person) schwach; (excuse) lahm.

feed [fiːd] n (for baby) Essen nt; (for animals) Futter nt // vt, pt, pp, fed füttern; (support) ernähren; (data) eingeben; to ~ on fressen; ~back n (information) Feedback nt; ~ing bottle n (Brit) Flasche f.

feel [fiːl] n: it has a soft ~ es fühlt sich weich an; to get the ~ of sth sich an etw (acc) gewöhnen // v (pt, pp felt) vt (sense) fühlen; (touch) anfassen; (think) meinen // vi (person) sich fühlen; (thing) sich anfühlen; I ~ cold mir ist kalt; I ~ like a cup of tea ich habe Lust auf eine Tasse Tee; ~ about or around vi herumsuchen; ~er n Fühler m; ~ing n

Gefühl nt; (opinion) Meinung f.

feet [fiːt] pl of **foot**.

feign [feɪn] vt vortäuschen.

feline ['fiːlaɪn] a katzenartig.

fell [fel] pt of **fall** // vt (tree) fällen.

fellow ['feləʊ] n (man) Kerl m; ~ citizen n Mitbürger(in f) m; ~ countryman n Landsmann m; ~ men npl Mitmenschen pl; ~ship n (group) Körperschaft f; (friendliness) Kameradschaft f; (scholarship) Forschungsstipendium nt; ~ **student** n Kommilitone m, Kommilitonin f.

felony ['felənɪ] n schwere(s) Verbrechen nt.

felt [felt] pt, pp of **feel** // n Filz m; ~-**tip pen** n Filzstift m.

female ['fiːmeɪl] n (of animals) Weibchen nt // a weiblich.

feminine ['femɪnɪn] a (GRAM) weiblich; (qualities) fraulich.

feminist ['femɪnɪst] n Feminist(in f) m.

fence [fens] n Zaun m // vt (also: ~ in) einzäunen // vi fechten.

fencing ['fensɪŋ] n Zaun m; (SPORT) Fechten nt.

fend [fend] vi: ~ for o.s. sich (allein) durchschlagen; ~ off vt abwehren.

fender ['fendə*] n Kaminvorsetzer m; (US AUT) Kotflügel m.

ferment [fə'ment] vi (CHEM) gären // ['fɜːment] n (excitement) Unruhe f.

fern [fɜːn] n Farn m.

ferocious [fə'rəʊʃəs] a wild, grausam.

ferret ['ferɪt] n Frettchen nt // vt: to ~ out aufspüren.

ferry ['ferɪ] n Fähre f // vt übersetzen.

fertile ['fɜːtaɪl] a fruchtbar.

fertilize ['fɜːtɪlaɪz] vt (AGR) düngen; (BIOL) befruchten; ~r n (Kunst)dünger m.

fervent ['fɜːvənt] a (admirer) glühend; (hope) innig.

fervour, (US) **fervor** ['fɜːvə*] n Leidenschaft f.

fester ['festə*] vi eitern.

festival ['festɪvəl] n (REL etc) Fest nt; (ART, MUS) Festspiele pl.

festive ['festɪv] a festlich; the ~ season (Christmas) die Festzeit f.

festivity [fes'tɪvɪtɪ] n Festlichkeit f.

festoon [fes'tuːn] vt: to ~ with schmücken mit.

fetch [fetʃ] vt holen; (in sale) einbringen.

fetching ['fetʃɪŋ] a reizend.

fête [feɪt] n Fest nt.

fetus ['fiːtəs] n (US) = **foetus**.

feud [fjuːd] n Fehde f; ~al a Feudal-.

fever ['fiːvə*] n Fieber nt; ~ish a (MED) fiebrig; (fig) fieberhaft.

few [fjuː] a wenig; **a** ~ a, pron einige; ~er a weniger; ~est a wenigste(r, s).

fiancé [fɪ'ɑːnseɪ] n Verlobte(r) m; ~e n Verlobte f.

fib [fɪb] n Flunkerei f // vi flunkern.

fibre, (US) **fiber** ['faɪbə*] n Faser f; **~glass** n Glaswolle f.

fickle ['fɪkl] a unbeständig.

fiction ['fɪkʃən] n (novels) Romanliteratur f; (story) Erdichtung f; **~al** a erfunden.

fictitious [fɪk'tɪʃəs] a erfunden, fingiert.

fiddle ['fɪdl] n Geige f; (trick) Schwindelei f // vt (Brit: accounts) frisieren; ~ **with** vi herumfummeln an (+dat).

fidelity [fɪ'delɪtɪ] n Treue f.

fidget ['fɪdʒɪt] vi zappeln.

field [fiːld] n Feld nt; (range) Gebiet nt; ~ **marshal** n Feldmarschall m; **~work** n (UNIV) Feldforschung f.

fiend [fiːnd] n Teufel m; **~ish** a teuflisch.

fierce [fɪəs] a wild.

fiery ['faɪərɪ] a (hot-tempered) hitzig.

fifteen [fɪf'tiːn] num fünfzehn.

fifth [fɪfθ] a fünfte(r, s) // n Fünftel nt.

fifty ['fɪftɪ] num fünfzig; **~-~** a halbe halbe, fifty fifty (col).

fig [fɪg] n Feige f.

fight [faɪt] n Kampf m; (brawl) Schlägerei f; (argument) Streit m // v (pt, pp **fought**) vt kämpfen gegen; sich schlagen mit; (fig) bekämpfen // vi kämpfen; sich schlagen; streiten; **~er** n Kämpfer(in f) m; (plane) Jagdflugzeug nt; **~ing** n Kämpfen nt; (war) Kampfhandlungen pl.

figment ['fɪgmənt] n: ~ **of the imagination** reine Einbildung f.

figurative ['fɪgərətɪv] a bildlich.

figure ['fɪgə*] n (of person) Figur f; (person) Gestalt f; (number) Ziffer f // vt (US: imagine) glauben // vi (appear) erscheinen; ~ **out** vt herausbekommen; **~head** n (NAUT, fig) Galionsfigur f; ~ **of speech** n Redensart f.

filament ['fɪləmənt] n Faden m; (ELEC) Glühfaden m.

filch [fɪltʃ] vt (col) filzen.

file [faɪl] n (tool) Feile f; (dossier) Akte f; (folder) Aktenordner m; (COMPUT) Datei f; (row) Reihe f // vt (metal, nails) feilen; (papers) abheften; (claim) einreichen // vi: to ~ **in/out** hintereinander hereinkommen/hinausgehen; **to ~ past** vorbeimarschieren.

filing ['faɪlɪŋ] n Ablage f; ~ **cabinet** n Aktenschrank m.

fill [fɪl] vt füllen; (occupy) ausfüllen; (satisfy) sättigen // n: **to eat one's ~** sich richtig satt essen; ~ **in** vt (hole) (auf)füllen; (form) ausfüllen; ~ **up** vt (container) auffüllen; (form) ausfüllen // vi (AUT) tanken.

fillet ['fɪlɪt] n Filet nt; ~ **steak** n Filetsteak nt.

filling ['fɪlɪŋ] n (COOK) Füllung f; (for tooth) (Zahn)plombe f; ~ **station** n

Tankstelle f.

film [fɪlm] n Film m // vt (scene) filmen; ~ **star** n Filmstar m; **~strip** n Filmstreifen m.

filter ['fɪltə*] n Filter m // vt filtern; ~ **lane** n (Brit) Abbiegespur f; **~-tipped** a Filter-.

filth [fɪlθ] n Dreck m; **~y** a dreckig; (weather) scheußlich.

fin [fɪn] n Flosse f.

final ['faɪnl] a letzte(r, s); End-; (conclusive) endgültig // n (FOOTBALL etc) Endspiel nt; (SPORT) Schlußrunde f; **~e** [fɪ'nɑːlɪ] n (MUS) Finale nt; **~ist** n (SPORT) Schlußrundenteilnehmer m; **~ize** vt endgültige Form geben (+dat); abschließen; **~ly** ad (lastly) zuletzt; (eventually) endlich; (irrevocably) endgültig.

finance [faɪ'næns] n Finanzwesen nt; **~s** pl Finanzen pl // vt finanzieren.

financial [faɪ'nænʃəl] a Finanz-; finanziell.

find [faɪnd] pt, pp **found** vt finden // n Fund m; **to ~ sb guilty** jdn für schuldig erklären; ~ **out** vt herausfinden; **~ings** npl (JUR) Ermittlungsergebnis nt (of report) Befund m.

fine [faɪn] a fein; (good) gut; (weather) schön // ad (well) gut; (small) klein // n (JUR) Geldstrafe f // vt (JUR) mit einer Geldstrafe belegen; ~ **arts** npl die schönen Künste pl.

finery ['faɪnərɪ] n Putz m.

finger ['fɪŋgə*] n Finger m // vt befühlen; **~nail** n Fingernagel m; **~print** n Fingerabdruck m; **~tip** n Fingerspitze f.

finicky ['fɪnɪkɪ] a pingelig.

finish ['fɪnɪʃ] n Ende nt; (SPORT) Ziel nt; (of object) Verarbeitung f; (of paint) Oberflächenwirkung f // vt beenden; (book) zu Ende lesen // vi aufhören; (SPORT) ans Ziel kommen; **to be ~ed with sth** fertig sein mit etw; **~ing line** n Ziellinie f; **~ing school** n Mädchenpensionat nt.

finite ['faɪnaɪt] a endlich, begrenzt.

Finland ['fɪnlənd] n Finnland nt.

Finn [fɪn] n Finne m, Finnin f; **~ish** a finnisch // n (LING) Finnisch nt.

fir [fɜː*] n Tanne f.

fire [faɪə*] n Feuer nt; (in house etc) Brand m // vt (gun) abfeuern; (imagination) entzünden; (dismiss) hinauswerfen // vi (AUT) zünden; **to be on ~** brennen; ~ **alarm** n Feueralarm m; **~arm** n Schußwaffe f; ~ **brigade** (Brit), ~ **department** (US) n Feuerwehr f; ~ **engine** n Feuerwehrauto nt; ~ **escape** n Feuerleiter f; ~ **extinguisher** n Löschgerät nt; **~man** n Feuerwehrmann m; **~place** n Kamin *m*; **~side** *n* Kamin *m*; **~station** *n* Feuerwehrwache *f*; **~works** *npl* Feuerwerk *nt.*

firing ['faɪərɪŋ] *n* Schießen *nt*; ~ **squad** *n* Exekutionskommando *nt.*

firm [fɜːm] *a* fest // *n* Firma *f.*

first [fɜːst] *a* erste(r, s) // *ad* zuerst; (*arrive*) als erste(r); (*happen*) zum erstenmal // *n* (*person: in race*) Erste(r) *mf*; (*UNIV*) Eins *f*; (*AUT*) erste(r) Gang *m*; **at** ~ zuerst; ~ **of all** zu allererst; ~ **aid** *n* Erste Hilfe *f*; **~-aid kit** *n* Verbandskasten *m*; **~-class** *a* erstklassig; (*travel*) erster Klasse; **~-hand** *a* aus erster Hand; **~ly** *ad* erstens; ~ **name** *n* Vorname *m*; **~-rate** *a* erstklassig.

fiscal ['fɪskəl] *a* Finanz-.

fish [fɪʃ] *n, pl inv* Fisch *m* // *vi* fischen; angeln; **to go ~ing** angeln gehen; (*in sea*) fischen gehen; **~erman** *n* Fischer *m*; ~ **farm** *n* Fischzucht *f*; ~ **fingers** *npl* (*Brit*) Fischstäbchen; **~ing boat** *n* Fischerboot *nt*; **~ing line** *n* Angelschnur *f*; **~ing rod** *n* Angel(rute) *f*; **~monger's (shop)** *n* Fischhändler *m*; ~ **slice** *n* Fischvorleger *m*; **~ sticks** *npl* (*US*) ~ **fingers**; **~y** *a* (*col: suspicious*) faul.

fission ['fɪʃən] *n* Spaltung *f.*

fissure ['fɪʃə*] *n* Riß *m.*

fist [fɪst] *n* Faust *f.*

fit [fɪt] *a* (*MED*) gesund; (*SPORT*) in Form, fit; (*suitable*) geeignet // *vt* passen (+*dat*); (*insert, attach*) einsetzen // *vi* (*correspond*) passen (zu); (*clothes*) passen; (*in space, gap*) hineinpassen // *n* (*of clothes*) Sitz *m*; (*MED, of anger*) Anfall *m*; (*of laughter*) Krampf *m*; **by ~s and starts** (*move*) ruckweise; (*work*) unregelmäßig; ~ **in** *vi* hineinpassen; (*fig: person*) passen; ~ **out** *vt* (*also:* ~ **up**) ausstatten; **~ful** *a* (*sleep*) unruhig; **~ment** *n* Einrichtungsgegenstand *m*; **~ness** *n* (*suitability*) Eignung *f*; (*MED*) Gesundheit *f*; (*SPORT*) Fitneß *f*; **~ted carpet** *n* Teppichboden *m*; **~ted kitchen** *n* Einbauküche *f*; **~ter** *n* (*TECH*) Monteur *m*; **~ting** *a* passend // *n* (*of dress*) Anprobe *f*; (*piece of equipment*) (Ersatz)teil *nt*; **~ting room** *n* Anproberaum *m*; **~tings** *npl* Zubehör *nt.*

five [faɪv] *num* fünf; **~r** *n* (*col: Brit*) Fünf-Pfund-Note *f*; (: *US*) Fünf-Dollar-Note *f.*

fix [fɪks] *vt* befestigen; (*settle*) festsetzen; (*repair*) reparieren // *n*: **in a** ~ in der Klemme; ~ **up** *vt* (*meeting*) arrangieren; **to** ~ **sb up with sth** jdm etw (*acc*) verschaffen; **~ation** *n* Fixierung *f*; **~ed** *a* fest; **~ture** ['fɪkstʃə*] *n* Installationsteil *nt*; (*SPORT*) Spiel *nt.*

fizz [fɪz] *vi* sprudeln.

fizzle ['fɪzl] *vi*: **to ~ out** verpuffen.

fizzy ['fɪzɪ] *a* Sprudel-, sprudelnd.

flabbergasted ['flæbəgɑːstɪd] *a* (*col*) platt.

flabby ['flæbɪ] *a* wabbelig.

flag [flæg] *n* Fahne *f* // *vi* (*strength*) nachlassen; (*spirit*) erlahmen; ~ **down** *vt* anhalten.

flagpole ['flægpəʊl] *n* Fahnenstange *f.*

flagrant ['fleɪgrənt] *a* kraß.

flair [flɛə*] *n* Talent *nt.*

flak [flæk] *n* Flakfeuer *nt.*

flake [fleɪk] *n* (*of snow*) Flocke *f*; (*of rust*) Schuppe *f* // *vi* (*also:* ~ **off**) abblättern.

flamboyant [flæm'bɔɪənt] *a* extravagant.

flame [fleɪm] *n* Flamme *f.*

flamingo [flə'mɪŋgəʊ] *n* Flamingo *m.*

flammable ['flæməbl] *a* brennbar.

flan [flæn] *n* (*Brit*) Obsttorte *f.*

flank [flæŋk] *n* Flanke *f* // *vt* flankieren.

flannel ['flænl] *n* Flanell *m*; (*Brit: also:* **face ~**) Waschlappen *m*; (*Brit col*) Geschwafel *nt*; **~s** *pl* Flanellhose *f.*

flap [flæp] *n* Klappe *f*; (*col: crisis*) (helle) Aufregung *f* // *vt* (*wings*) schlagen mit // *vi* flattern.

flare [flɛə*] *n* (*signal*) Leuchtsignal *nt*; (*in skirt etc*) Weite *f*; ~ **up** *vi* aufflammen; (*fig*) aufbrausen; (*revolt*) (plötzlich) ausbrechen.

flash [flæʃ] *n* Blitz *m*; (*also:* **news ~**) Kurzmeldung *f*; (*PHOT*) Blitzlicht *nt* // *vt* aufleuchten lassen // *vi* aufleuchten; **in a** ~ im Nu; ~ **by** *or* **past** *vi* vorbeirasen; **~back** *n* Rückblende *f*; **~bulb** *n* Blitzlichtbirne *f*; ~ **cube** *n* Blitzwürfel *m*; **~light** *n* Blitzlicht *nt.*

flashy ['flæʃɪ] *a* (*pej*) knallig.

flask [flɑːsk] *n* (*CHEM*) Kolben *m*; (*also:* **vacuum ~**) Thermosflasche *f.*

flat [flæt] *a* flach; (*dull*) matt; (*MUS*) erniedrigt; (*beer*) schal; (*tyre*) platt // *n* (*Brit: rooms*) Wohnung *f*; (*MUS*) b *nt*; (*AUT*) Platte(r) *m*; **to work** ~ **out** auf Hochtouren arbeiten; **~ly** *ad* glatt; **~ten** *vt* (*also:* **~ten out**) ebnen.

flatter ['flætə*] *vt* schmeicheln (+*dat*); **~ing** *a* schmeichelhaft; **~y** *n* Schmeichelei *f.*

flatulence ['flætjʊləns] *n* Blähungen *pl.*

flaunt [flɔːnt] *vt* prunken mit.

flavour, (*US*) **flavor** ['fleɪvə*] *n* Geschmack *m* // *vt* würzen; **strawberry-~ed** *a* mit Erdbeergeschmack; **~ing** *n* Würze *f.*

flaw [flɔː] *n* Fehler *m*; **~less** *a* einwandfrei.

flax [flæks] *n* Flachs *m*; **~en** *a* flachsfarben.

flea [fliː] *n* Floh *m.*

fleck [flek] *n* (*mark*) Fleck *m*; (*pattern*) Tupfen *m.*

flee [fliː] *pt, pp* **fled** [fled] *vi* fliehen // *vt* fliehen vor (+*dat*); (*country*) fliehen aus.

fleece [fliːs] *n* Vlies *nt* // *vt* (*col*)

schröpfen.

fleet [fliːt] n Flotte f.

fleeting ['fliːtɪŋ] a flüchtig.

Flemish ['flemɪʃ] a flämisch.

flesh [fleʃ] n Fleisch nt; ~ **wound** n Fleischwunde f.

flew [fluː] pt of **fly**.

flex [fleks] n Kabel nt // vt beugen; ~**ibility** [fleksɪ'bɪlɪtɪ] n Biegsamkeit f; (fig) Flexibilität f; ~**ible** a biegsam; (plans) flexibel.

flick [flɪk] n leichte(r) Schlag m // vt leicht schlagen; ~ **through** vt durchblättern.

flicker ['flɪkə*] n Flackern nt // vi flackern.

flier ['flaɪə*] n Flieger m.

flight [flaɪt] n Flug m; (fleeing) Flucht f; (also: ~ of steps) Treppe f; to take ~ die Flucht ergreifen; to put to ~ in die Flucht schlagen; ~ **attendant** n (US) Steward(eß f) m; ~ **deck** n Flugdeck nt.

flimsy ['flɪmzɪ] a (thin) hauchdünn; (excuse) fadenscheinig.

flinch [flɪntʃ] vi zurückschrecken (away from vor +dat).

fling [flɪŋ], pt, pp **flung** vt schleudern.

flint [flɪnt] n Feuerstein m.

flip [flɪp] vt werfen.

flippant ['flɪpənt] a schnippisch.

flipper ['flɪpə*] n Flosse f.

flirt [flɜːt] vi flirten // n: he/she is a ~ er/sie flirtet gern; ~**ation** [flɜː'teɪʃən] n Flirt m.

flit [flɪt] vi flitzen.

float [fləʊt] n (FISHING) Schwimmer m; (esp in procession) Plattformwagen m // vi schwimmen; (in air) schweben // vt (COMM) gründen; (currency) floaten.

flock [flɒk] n (of sheep, REL) Herde f; (of birds) Schwarm m; (of people) Schar f.

flog [flɒg] vt prügeln; (col: sell) verkaufen.

flood [flʌd] n Überschwemmung f; (fig) Flut f // vt überschwemmen; ~**ing** n Überschwemmung f; ~**light** n Flutlicht nt.

floor [flɔː*] n (Fuß)boden m; (storey) Stock m // vt (person) zu Boden schlagen; **ground** ~ (Brit), **first** ~ (US) n Erdgeschoß nt; **first** ~ (Brit), **second** ~ (US) n erste(r) Stock m; ~**board** n Diele f; ~ **show** n Kabarettvorstellung f.

flop [flɒp] n Plumps m; (failure) Reinfall m // vi (fail) durchfallen.

floppy ['flɒpɪ] a hängend; ~ (**disk**) n (COMPUT) Diskette f.

flora ['flɔːrə] n Flora f; ~**l** a Blumen-.

florid ['flɒrɪd] a (style) blumig.

florist ['flɒrɪst] n Blumenhändler(in f) m; ~**'s** (**shop**) n Blumengeschäft nt.

flounce [flaʊns] vi: to ~ **out** hinaus-

stürmen.

flounder ['flaʊndə*] vi (fig) ins Schleudern kommen // n (ZOOL) Flunder f.

flour ['flaʊə*] n Mehl nt.

flourish ['flʌrɪʃ] vi blühen; gedeihen // n (waving) Schwingen nt; (of trumpets) Tusch m, Fanfare f; ~**ing** a blühend.

flout [flaʊt] vt mißachten.

flow [fləʊ] n Fließen nt; (of sea) Flut f // vi fließen; ~ **chart** n Flußdiagramm nt.

flower ['flaʊə*] n Blume f // vi blühen; ~ **bed** n Blumenbeet nt; ~**pot** n Blumentopf m; ~**y** a (style) blumenreich.

flown [fləʊn] pp of **fly**.

flu [fluː] n Grippe f.

fluctuate ['flʌktjʊeɪt] vi schwanken.

fluctuation [flʌktjʊ'eɪʃən] n Schwankung f.

fluent a, ~**ly** ad ['fluːənt, -lɪ] fließend.

fluff [flʌf] n Fussel f; ~**y** a flaumig.

fluid ['fluːɪd] n Flüssigkeit f // a (lit) flüssig; (fig: plans) veränderbar.

fluke [fluːk] n (col) Dusel m.

flung [flʌŋ] pt, pp of **fling**.

fluoride ['flʊəraɪd] n Fluorid nt.

flurry ['flʌrɪ] n (of activity) Aufregung f; (of snow) Gestöber nt.

flush [flʌʃ] n Erröten nt; (of excitement) Glühen nt // vt (aus)spülen // vi erröten // a glatt; ~ **out** vt aufstöbern; ~**ed** a rot.

flustered ['flʌstəd] a verwirrt.

flute [fluːt] n Querflöte f.

flutter ['flʌtə*] n Flattern nt // vi flattern.

flux [flʌks] n: in a state of ~ im Fluß.

fly [flaɪ] n (insect) Fliege f; (on trousers: also: **flies**) (Hosen)schlitz m // v (pt **flew**, pp **flown**) vt fliegen // vi fliegen; (flee) fliehen; (flag) wehen; ~ **away** or **off** vi (bird, insect) wegfliegen; ~**ing** n Fliegen nt // a: with ~**ing colours** mit fliegenden Fahnen; ~**ing start** gute(r) Start m; ~**ing visit** Stippvisite f; ~**ing saucer** n fliegende Untertasse f; ~**over** n (Brit) Überführung f; ~**past** n Luftparade f; ~**sheet** n (for tent) Regendach nt.

foal [fəʊl] n Fohlen nt.

foam [fəʊm] n Schaum m // vi schäumen ~ **rubber** n Schaumgummi m.

fob [fɒb] vt: to ~ **off** andrehen (sb with sth jdm etw); (with promise) abspeisen.

focal ['fəʊkəl] a Brenn-.

focus ['fəʊkəs] n, pl ~**es** Brennpunkt m // vt (attention) konzentrieren; (camera) scharf einstellen // vi sich konzentrieren (on auf +acc); **in** ~ scharf eingestellt; **out of** ~ unscharf.

fodder ['fɒdə*] n Futter nt.

foe [fəʊ] n (liter) Feind m.

foetus ['fiːtəs] n Fötus m.

fog [fɒg] n Nebel m; ~ **lamp** n (AUT)

Nebellampe f; **~gy** a neblig.

foil [fɔɪl] vt vereiteln // n (metal, also fig) Folie f; (fencing) Florett nt.

fold [fəʊld] n (bend, crease) Falte f; (AGR) Pferch m // vt falten; **~ up** vt (map etc) zusammenfalten // vi (business) eingehen; **~er** n Schnellhefter m; **~ing** a (chair etc) Klapp-.

foliage ['fəʊlɪɪdʒ] n Laubwerk nt.

folk [fəʊk] npl Volk nt // a Volks-; **~s** pl Leute pl; **~lore** ['fəʊklɔː*] n (study) Volkskunde f; (tradition) Folklore f; **~ song** n Volkslied nt; (modern) Folksong m.

follow ['fɒləʊ] vt folgen (+dat); (fashion) mitmachen // vi folgen; **~ up** vt verfolgen; **~er** n Anhänger(in f) m; **~ing** a folgend // n (people) Gefolgschaft f.

folly ['fɒlɪ] n Torheit f.

fond [fɒnd] a: to be **~ of** gern haben.

fondle ['fɒndl] vt streicheln.

font [fɒnt] n Taufbecken nt.

food [fuːd] n Essen nt; (for animals) Futter nt; **~ mixer** n Küchenmixer m; **~ poisoning** n Lebensmittelvergiftung f; **~ processor** n Küchenmaschine f; **~stuffs** npl Lebensmittel pl.

fool [fuːl] n Narr m, Närrin f // vt (deceive) hereinlegen // vi (also: **~ around**) (herum)albern; **~hardy** a tollkühn; **~ish** a albern; **~proof** a idiotensicher.

foot [fʊt] n, pl feet Fuß m // vt (bill) bezahlen; on **~** zu Fuß; **~age** n (CINE) Filmmaterial nt; **~ball** n Fußball m; (game: Brit) Fußball m; (: US) Football m; **~ball player** n (Brit: also: **~baller**) Fußball(spiel)er m; (US) Footballer m; **~brake** n Fußbremse f; **~bridge** n Fußgängerbrücke f; **~hills** npl Ausläufer pl; **~hold** n Halt m; **~ing** n (lit) Halt m; (fig) Verhältnis nt; **~lights** npl Rampenlicht nt; **~man** n Bedienstete(r) m; **~note** n Fußnote f; **~path** n Fußweg m; **~print** n Fußabdruck m; **~sore** a fußkrank; **~step** n Schritt m; **~wear** n Schuhzeug nt.

for [fɔː*] ♦prep 1 für; is this **~** me? ist das für mich?; the train **~** London der Zug nach London; he went **~** the paper er ging die Zeitung holen; give it to me — what **~**? gib es mir — warum?

2 (because of) wegen; **~** this reason aus diesem Grunde

3 (referring to distance): there are roadworks **~** 5 km die Baustelle ist 5 km lang; we walked **~** miles wir sind meilenweit gegangen

4 (referring to time) seit; (: with future sense) für; he was away **~** 2 years er war zwei Jahre lang weg

5 (with infinitive clauses): it is not **~** me to decide das kann ich nicht ent-

scheiden; **~** this to be possible ... damit dies möglich wird/wurde ...

6 (in spite of) trotz (+gen or (col) +dat); **~** all his complaints obwohl er sich ständig beschwert

♦cj denn.

forage ['fɒrɪdʒ] n (Vieh)futter nt.

foray ['fɒreɪ] n Raubzug m.

forbid [fə'bɪd], pt **forbad(e)** [fə'bæd], pp **forbidden** [fə'bɪdn] vt verbieten; **~ding** a einschüchternd.

force [fɔːs] n Kraft f; (compulsion) Zwang m // vt zwingen; (lock) aufbrechen; in **~** (rule) gültig; (group) in großer Stärke; the **F~s** pl (Brit) die Streitkräfte; **~d** [fɔːst] a (smile) gezwungen; (landing) Not-; **~-feed** vt zwangsernähren; **~ful** a (speech) kraftvoll; (personality) resolut.

forceps ['fɔːseps] npl Zange f.

forcibly ['fɔːsəblɪ] ad zwangsweise.

ford [fɔːd] n Furt f // vt durchwaten.

fore [fɔː*] n: to the **~** in den Vordergrund.

forearm ['fɔːrɑːm] n Unterarm m.

foreboding [fɔː'bəʊdɪŋ] n Vorahnung f.

forecast ['fɔːkɑːst] n Vorhersage f // vt (irreg: like cast) voraussagen.

forecourt ['fɔːkɔːt] n (of garage) Vorplatz m.

forefathers ['fɔːfɑːðəz] npl Vorfahren pl.

forefinger ['fɔːfɪŋgə*] n Zeigefinger m.

forefront ['fɔːfrʌnt] n Spitze f.

forego [fɔː'gəʊ] (irreg: like go) vt verzichten auf (+acc).

foreground ['fɔːgraʊnd] n Vordergrund m.

forehead ['fɒrɪd] n Stirn f.

foreign ['fɒrɪn] a Auslands-; (accent) ausländisch; (trade) Außen-; (body) Fremd-; **~er** n Ausländer(in f) m; **~ exchange** n Devisen pl; **F~ Minister** n (Brit) Außenminister m; **F~ Office** n Außenministerium nt.

foreleg ['fɔːleg] n Vorderbein nt.

foreman ['fɔːmən] n Vorarbeiter m.

foremost ['fɔːməʊst] a erste(r, s) // ad: first and **~** vor allem.

forensic [fə'rensɪk] a gerichtsmedizinisch.

forerunner ['fɔːrʌnə*] n Vorläufer m.

foresee [fɔː'siː] (irreg: like see) vt vorhersehen; **~able** a absehbar.

foreshadow [fɔː'ʃædəʊ] vt andeuten.

foresight ['fɔːsaɪt] n Voraussicht f.

forest ['fɒrɪst] n Wald m.

forestall [fɔː'stɔːl] vt zuvorkommen (+dat).

forestry ['fɒrɪstrɪ] n Forstwirtschaft f.

foretaste ['fɔːteɪst] n Vorgeschmack m.

foretell [fɔː'tel] (irreg: like tell) vt vorhersagen.

forever [fə'revə*] ad für immer.

foreword ['fɔːwɜːd] n Vorwort nt.

forfeit ['fɔːfɪt] n Einbuße f // vt verwirken.

forgave [fə'geɪv] pt of **forgive**.

forge [fɔːdʒ] n Schmiede f // vt fälschen; (iron) schmieden; ~ **ahead** vi Fortschritte machen; ~**r** n Fälscher m; ~**ry** n Fälschung f.

forget [fə'get], pt **forgot**, pp **forgotten** vti vergessen; ~**ful** a vergeßlich; ~**me-not** n Vergißmeinnicht nt.

forgive [fə'gɪv], pt **forgave**, pp **forgiven** vt verzeihen (sb for sth jdm etw).

forgiveness [fə'gɪvnəs] n Verzeihung f.

forgo [fɔː'gəu] see **forego**.

forgot [fə'gɒt] pt of **forget**.

forgotten [fə'gɒtn] pp of **forget**.

fork [fɔːk] n Gabel f; (in road) Gabelung f // vi (road) sich gabeln; ~ **out** vt (col: pay) blechen; ~**-lift truck** n Gabelstapler m.

forlorn [fə'lɔːn] a (person) verlassen; (hope) vergeblich.

form [fɔːm] n Form f; (type) Art f; (figure) Gestalt f; (SCH) Klasse f; (bench) (Schul)bank f; (document) Formular nt // vt formen; (be part of) bilden.

formal ['fɔːməl] a formell; (occasion) offiziell; ~**ity** [fɔː'mælɪtɪ] n Förmlichkeit f; ~**ities** pl Formalitäten pl; ~**ly** ad (ceremoniously) formell; (officially) offiziell.

format ['fɔːmæt] n Format nt // vt (COMPUT) formatieren.

formation [fɔː'meɪʃən] n Bildung f; (AVIAT) Formation f.

formative ['fɔːmətɪv] a (years) formend.

former ['fɔːmə*] a früher; (opposite of latter) erstere(r, s); ~**ly** ad früher.

formidable ['fɔːmɪdəbl] a furchtbar.

formula ['fɔːmjulə] n Formel f; ~**te** ['fɔːmjuleɪt] vt formulieren.

forsake [fə'seɪk], pt **forsook** [fə'suk], pp **forsaken** [fə'seɪkən] vt verlassen.

fort [fɔːt] n Feste f, Fort nt.

forte ['fɔːtɪ] n Stärke f, starke Seite f.

forth [fɔːθ] ad: **and so** ~ und so weiter; ~**coming** a kommend; (character) entgegenkommend; ~**right** a offen; ~**with** ad umgehend.

fortification [fɔːtɪfɪ'keɪʃən] n Befestigung f.

fortify ['fɔːtɪfaɪ] vt (ver)stärken; (protect) befestigen.

fortitude ['fɔːtɪtjuːd] n Seelenstärke f.

fortnight ['fɔːtnaɪt] n vierzehn Tage pl; ~**ly** a zweiwöchentlich // ad alle vierzehn Tage.

fortress ['fɔːtrɪs] n Festung f.

fortuitous [fɔː'tjuːɪtəs] a zufällig.

fortunate ['fɔːtʃənɪt] a glücklich; ~**ly** ad glücklicherweise, zum Glück.

fortune ['fɔːtʃən] n Glück nt; (money) Vermögen nt; ~**-teller** n Wahrsager(in

f) m.

forty ['fɔːtɪ] num vierzig.

forum ['fɔːrəm] n Forum nt.

forward ['fɔːwəd] a vordere(r, s); (movement) vorwärts; (person) vorlaut; (planning) Voraus- // ad vorwärts // n (SPORT) Stürmer m // vt (send) schicken; (help) fördern; ~**(s)** ad vorwärts.

forwent [fɔː'went] pt of **forgo**.

fossil ['fɒsl] n Fossil nt, Versteinerung f.

foster ['fɒstə*] vt (talent) fördern; ~ **child** n Pflegekind nt; ~ **mother** n Pflegemutter f.

fought [fɔːt] pt, pp of **fight**.

foul [faul] a schmutzig; (language) gemein; (weather) schlecht // n (SPORT) Foul nt // vt (mechanism) blockieren; (SPORT) foulen; ~ **play** n (SPORT) Foulspiel nt; (LAW) Verbrechen nt.

found [faund] pt, pp of **find** // vt gründen; ~**ation** [faun'deɪʃən] n (act) Gründung f; (fig) Fundament nt; (also: ~**ation cream**) Grundierungscreme f; ~**ations** pl Fundament nt.

founder ['faundə*] n Gründer(in f) m // vi sinken.

foundry ['faundrɪ] n Gießerei f.

fountain ['fauntɪn] n (Spring)brunnen m; ~ **pen** n Füllfederhalter m.

four [fɔː*] num vier; **on all** ~**s** auf allen vieren; ~**-poster** n Himmelbett nt; ~**some** n Quartett nt; ~**teen** num vierzehn; ~**teenth** a vierzehnte(r, s) ~**th** a vierte(r, s).

fowl [faul] n Huhn nt; (food) Geflügel nt.

fox [fɒks] n Fuchs m // vt täuschen; ~**trot** n Foxtrott m.

foyer ['fɔɪeɪ] n Foyer nt, Vorhalle f.

fraction ['frækʃən] n (MATH) Bruch m; (part) Bruchteil m.

fracture ['fræktʃə*] n (MED) Bruch m // vt brechen.

fragile ['frædʒaɪl] a zerbrechlich.

fragment ['frægmənt] n Bruchstück nt; (small part) Splitter m.

fragrance ['freɪgrəns] n Duft m.

fragrant ['freɪgrənt] a duftend.

frail [freɪl] a schwach, gebrechlich.

frame [freɪm] n Rahmen m; (of spectacles: also: ~**s**) Gestell nt; (body) Gestalt f // vt einrahmen; (col: incriminate): **to** ~ **sb** jdm etw anhängen; ~ **of mind** n Verfassung f; ~**work** n Rahmen m; (of society) Gefüge nt.

France [frɑːns] n Frankreich nt.

franchise ['fræntʃaɪz] n (POL) (aktives) Wahlrecht nt; (COMM) Lizenz f.

frank [fræŋk] a offen // vt (letter) frankieren; ~**ly** ad offen gesagt; ~**ness** n Offenheit f.

frantic ['fræntɪk] a verzweifelt.

fraternal [frə'tɜːnl] a brüderlich.

fraternity [frə'tɜːnɪtɪ] n (club) Vereinigung f; (spirit) Brüderlichkeit f; (US SCH) Studentenverbindung f.

fraternize ['frætənaɪz] vi fraternisieren.

fraud [frɔːd] n (trickery) Betrug m; (person) Schwindler(in f) m.

fraudulent ['frɔːdjʊlənt] a betrügerisch.

fraught [frɔːt] a voller (with gen).

fray [freɪ] n Rauferei f // vti ausfransen; tempers were ~ed die Gemüter waren erhitzt.

freak [friːk] n Monstrosität f; (storm etc) Ausnahmeerscheinung f.

freckle ['frekl] n Sommersprosse f.

free [friː] a frei; (loose) lose; (liberal) freigebig // vt (set free) befreien; (unblock) freimachen; ~ (of charge), for ~ ad gratis, umsonst; ~dom n Freiheit f; ~-for-all n (fight) allgemeine(s) Handgemenge nt; ~ gift n Geschenk nt; ~hold property n (freie(r)) Grundbesitz m; ~ kick n Freistoß m; ~lance a frei; (artist) freischaffend; ~ly ad frei; (admit) offen; ~mason n Freimaurer m; ~post n ≈ Gebühr zahlt Empfänger; ~-range a (hen) Farmhof-; (eggs) Land-; ~ trade n Freihandel m; ~way n (US) Autobahn f; ~wheel vi im Freilauf fahren; ~ will n: of one's own ~ will aus freien Stücken.

freeze [friːz] v (pt froze, pp frozen) vi gefrieren; (feel cold) frieren // vt (lit, fig) einfrieren // n (fig, FIN) Stopp m; ~r n Tiefkühltruhe f; (in fridge) Gefrierfach nt.

freezing ['friːzɪŋ] a eisig; (~ cold) eiskalt; ~ point n Gefrierpunkt m.

freight [freɪt] n Fracht f; ~ train n Güterzug m.

French [frentʃ] a französisch // n (LING) Französisch nt; the ~ pl die Franzosen; ~ bean n grüne Bohne f; ~ fried (potatoes) (Brit), ~ fries (US) npl Pommes frites pl; ~man/woman n Franzose m/Französin f; ~ window n Verandatür f.

frenzy ['frenzɪ] n Raserei f.

frequency ['friːkwənsɪ] n Häufigkeit f; (PHYS) Frequenz f.

frequent ['friːkwənt] a häufig // [friˈkwent] vt (regelmäßig) besuchen.

fresco ['freskəʊ] n Fresko nt.

fresh [freʃ] a frisch; ~en vi (also: ~en up) (sich) auffrischen; (person) sich frisch machen; ~er n (Brit UNIV: col) Erstsemester nt; ~ly ad gerade; ~man n (US) = ~er; ~ness n Frische f; ~water a (fish) Süßwasser-.

fret [fret] vi sich (dat) Sorgen machen.

friar ['fraɪə*] n Klosterbruder m.

friction ['frɪkʃən] n (lit, fig) Reibung f.

Friday ['fraɪdeɪ] n Freitag m.

fridge [frɪdʒ] n (Brit) Kühlschrank m.

fried [fraɪd] a gebraten.

friend [frend] n Freund(in f) m; ~liness n Freundlichkeit f; ~ly a

freundlich; (relations) freundschaftlich; ~ship n Freundschaft f.

frieze [friːz] n Fries m.

frigate ['frɪgɪt] n Fregatte f.

fright [fraɪt] n Schrecken m; to take ~ es mit der Angst zu tun bekommen; ~en vt erschrecken; to be ~ened Angst haben; ~ening a schrecklich; ~ful a, ~fully ad (col) furchtbar.

frigid ['frɪdʒɪd] a (woman) frigide.

frill [frɪl] n Rüsche f.

fringe [frɪndʒ] n Besatz m; (Brit: of hair) Pony m; (fig) Peripherie f; ~ benefits npl zusätzliche Leistungen pl.

frisk [frɪsk] vt durchsuchen.

frisky ['frɪskɪ] a lebendig, ausgelassen.

fritter ['frɪtə*] vt: to ~ away vergeuden.

frivolous ['frɪvələs] a frivol.

frizzy ['frɪzɪ] a kraus.

fro [frəʊ] see to.

frock [frɒk] n Kleid nt.

frog [frɒg] n Frosch m; ~man n Froschmann m.

frolic ['frɒlɪk] vi ausgelassen sein.

from [frɒm] prep 1 (indicating starting place) von; (indicating origin etc) aus (+dat); a letter/telephone call ~ my sister ein Brief/Anruf von meiner Schwester; where do you come ~? woher kommen Sie?; to drink ~ the bottle aus der Flasche trinken

2 (indicating time) von ... an; (: past) seit; ~ one o'clock to or until or till two von ein Uhr bis zwei; ~ January (on) ab Januar

3 (indicating distance) von ... (entfernt)

4 (indicating price, number etc) ab (+dat); ~ £10 ab £10; there were ~ 20 to 30 people there es waren zwischen 20 und 30 Leute da

5 (indicating difference): he can't tell red ~ green er kann nicht zwischen rot und grün unterscheiden; to be different ~ sb/sth anders sein als jd/etw

6 (because of, on the basis of): ~ what he says aus dem, was er sagt; weak ~ hunger schwach vor Hunger.

front [frʌnt] n Vorderseite f; (of house) Fassade f; (promenade: also: sea ~) Strandpromenade f; (MIL, POL, MET) Front f; (fig: appearances) Fassade f // a (forward) vordere(r, s), Vorder-; (first) vorderste(r, s); in ~ ad vorne; in ~ of vor; ~age n Vorderfront f; ~al a frontal, Vorder-; ~ier ['frʌntɪə*] n Grenze f; ~ door n Haustür f; ~ page n Titelseite f; ~ room n (Brit) Wohnzimmer nt; ~-wheel drive n Vorderradantrieb m.

frost [frɒst] n Frost m; ~bite n Erfrierung f; ~ed a (glass) Milch-; ~y a frostig.

froth [frɒθ] n Schaum m.

frown [fraʊn] n Stirnrunzeln nt // vi die Stirn runzeln.

froze [frəʊz] *pt of* **freeze.**

frozen [frəʊzn] *pp of* **freeze.**

frugal ['fru:gəl] *a* sparsam, bescheiden.

fruit [fru:t] *n, pl inv* (*as collective*) Obst *nt;* (*particular*) Frucht *f;* ~**erer** *n* Obsthändler *m;* ~**erer's** (**shop**) *n* Obsthandlung *f;* ~**ful** *a* fruchtbar; ~**ion** [fru:'ɪʃən] *n:* to come to ~**ion** in Erfüllung gehen; ~ **juice** *n* Fruchtsaft *m;* ~ **machine** *n* (*Brit*) Spielautomat *m;* ~ **salad** *n* Obstsalat *m.*

frustrate [frʌs'treɪt] *vt* vereiteln; ~**d** *a* gehemmt; (*PSYCH*) frustriert.

fry [fraɪ], *pt, pp* **fried** *vt* braten; small ~ *pl* kleine Fische *pl;* ~**ing pan** *n* Bratpfanne *f.*

ft. *abbr of* **foot, feet.**

fuddy-duddy ['fʌdɪdʌdɪ] *n* altmodische(r) Kauz *m.*

fudge [fʌdʒ] *n* Karamellen *pl.*

fuel [fjʊəl] *n* Treibstoff *m;* (*for heating*) Brennstoff *m;* (*for lighter*) Benzin *nt;* ~ **oil** *n* (*diesel fuel*) Heizöl *nt;* ~ **tank** *n* Tank *m.*

fugitive ['fju:dʒɪtɪv] *n* Flüchtling *m.*

fulfil [fʊl'fɪl] *vt* (*duty*) erfüllen; (*promise*) einhalten; ~**ment** *n* Erfüllung *f.*

full [fʊl] *a* (*box, bottle, price*) voll; (*person: satisfied*) satt; (*member, power, employment, moon*) Voll-; (*complete*) vollständig, voll; (*speed*) höchste(r, s); (*skirt*) weit // *ad*: ~ **well** sehr wohl; **in** ~ vollständig; ~**length** *a* (*portrait*) lebensgroß; ~ **moon** *n* Vollmond *m;* ~**scale** *a* (*attack*) General-; (*drawing*) in Originalgröße; ~ **stop** *n* Punkt *m;* ~**time** *a* (*job*) Ganztags- // *ad* (*work*) ganztags // *n* (*SPORT*) Spielschluß *nt;* ~**y** *ad* völlig; ~**y-fledged** *a* (*lit, fig*) flügge.

fulsome ['fʊlsəm] *a* übertrieben.

fumble ['fʌmbl] *vi* herumfummeln (*with* an +*dat*).

fume [fju:m] *vi* qualmen; (*fig*) kochen (*col*); ~**s** *pl* Abgase *pl.*

fumigate ['fju:mɪgeɪt] *vt* ausräuchern.

fun [fʌn] *n* Spaß *m;* to make ~ of sich lustig machen über (+*acc*).

function ['fʌŋkʃən] *n* Funktion *f;* (*occasion*) Veranstaltung *f* // *vi* funktionieren; ~**al** *a* funktionell.

fund [fʌnd] *n* (*money*) Geldmittel *pl,* Fonds *m;* (*store*) Vorrat *m;* ~**s** *pl* Mittel *pl.*

fundamental [fʌndə'mentl] *a* fundamental, grundlegend.

funeral ['fju:nərəl] *n* Beerdigung *f;* ~ **parlour** *n* Leichenhalle *f;* ~ **service** *n* Trauergottesdienst *m.*

funfair ['fʌnfeə*] *n* (*Brit*) Jahrmarkt *m.*

fungus ['fʌŋgəs], *pl* -**gi** ['fʌŋgaɪ] *n* Pilz *m.*

funnel ['fʌnl] *n* Trichter *m;* (*NAUT*) Schornstein *m.*

funny ['fʌnɪ] *a* komisch.

fur [fɜ:*] *n* Pelz *m;* ~ **coat** *n* Pelzmantel *m.*

furious ['fjʊərɪəs] *a* wütend; (*attempt*) heftig.

furlong ['fɜ:lɒŋ] *n* = 220 yards.

furlough ['fɜ:ləʊ] *n* (*US MIL*) Urlaub *m.*

furnace ['fɜ:nɪs] *n* (Brenn)ofen *m.*

furnish ['fɜ:nɪʃ] *vt* einrichten; (*supply*) versehen; ~**ings** *npl* Einrichtung *f.*

furniture ['fɜ:nɪtʃə*] *n* Möbel *pl;* piece of ~ Möbelstück *nt.*

furrow ['fʌrəʊ] *n* Furche *f.*

furry ['fɜ:rɪ] *a* (*tongue*) pelzig; (*animal*) Pelz-.

further ['fɜ:ðə*] *a* weitere(r, s) // *ad* weiter // *vt* fördern; ~ **education** *n* Weiterbildung *f;* Erwachsenenbildung *f;* ~**more** *ad* ferner.

furthest ['fɜ:ðɪst] *superl of* **far.**

furtive ['fɜ:tɪv] *a* verstohlen.

fury ['fjʊərɪ] *n* Wut *f,* Zorn *m.*

fuse [fju:z] *n* (*ELEC*) Sicherung *f;* (*of bomb*) Zünder *m* // *vt* verschmelzen // *vi* (*Brit ELEC*) durchbrennen; ~ **box** *n* Sicherungskasten *m.*

fuselage ['fju:zəlɑ:ʒ] *n* Flugzeugrumpf *m.*

fusion ['fju:ʒən] *n* Verschmelzung *f.*

fuss [fʌs] *n* Theater *nt;* ~**y** *a* kleinlich.

futile ['fju:taɪl] *a* zwecklos, sinnlos.

futility [fju:'tɪlɪtɪ] *n* Zwecklosigkeit *f.*

future ['fju:tʃə*] *a* zukünftig // *n* Zukunft *f;* in (the) ~ in Zukunft.

fuze [fju:z] (*US*) = **fuse.**

fuzzy ['fʌzɪ] *a* (*indistinct*) verschwommen; (*hair*) kraus.

G

G [dʒi:] *n* (*MUS*) G *nt.*

gabble ['gæbl] *vi* plappern.

gable ['geɪbl] *n* Giebel *m.*

gadget ['gædʒɪt] *n* Vorrichtung *f.*

Gaelic ['geɪlɪk] *a* gälisch // *n* (*LING*) Gälisch *nt.*

gaffe [gæf] *n* Fauxpas *m.*

gag [gæg] *n* Knebel *m;* (*THEAT*) Gag *m* // *vt* knebeln.

gaily ['geɪlɪ] *ad* lustig, fröhlich.

gain [geɪn] *vt* (*obtain*) erhalten; (*win*) gewinnen // *vi* (*improve*) gewinnen (*in* an +*dat*); (*clock*) vorgehen // *n* Gewinn *m;* to ~ on sb jdn einholen.

gait [geɪt] *n* Gang *m.*

gal. *abbr of* **gallon.**

gala ['gɑ:lə] *n* Fest *nt.*

galaxy ['gæləksɪ] *n* Sternsystem *nt.*

gale [geɪl] *n* Sturm *m.*

gallant ['gælənt] *a* tapfer; (*polite*) galant; ~**ry** *n* Tapferkeit *f;* Galanterie *f.*

gallbladder ['gɔ:lblædə*] *n* Gallenblase *f.*

gallery ['gælərɪ] *n* (*also:* **art** ~) Galerie

f.

galley ['gælɪ] n (ship's kitchen) Kombüse f; (ship) Galeere f.

gallon ['gælən] n Gallone f.

gallop ['gæləp] n Galopp m // vi galoppieren.

gallows ['gæləʊz] n Galgen m.

gallstone ['gɔ:lstəʊn] n Gallenstein m.

galore [gə'lɔ:*] ad in Hülle und Fülle.

galvanize ['gælvənaɪz] vt (metal) galvanisieren; (fig) elektrisieren.

gamble ['gæmbl] vi (um Geld) spielen // vt (risk) aufs Spiel setzen // n Risiko nt; ~r n Spieler(in f) m.

gambling ['gæmblɪŋ] n Glücksspiel nt.

game [geɪm] n Spiel nt; (hunting) Wild nt // a bereit (for zu); ~keeper n Wildhüter m.

gammon ['gæmən] n geräucherte(r) Schinken m.

gamut ['gæmət] n Tonskala f.

gang [gæŋ] n (of criminals, youths) Bande f; (of workmen) Kolonne f // vi: to ~ up on sb sich gegen jdn verschwören.

gangrene ['gæŋgri:n] n Brand m.

gangster ['gæŋstə*] n Gangster m.

gangway ['gæŋweɪ] n (NAUT) Laufplanke f; (aisle) Gang m.

gaol [dʒeɪl] (Brit) = **jail**.

gap [gæp] n Lücke f.

gape [geɪp] vi glotzen.

gaping ['geɪpɪŋ] a (wound) klaffend; (hole) gähnend.

garage ['gærɑ:ʒ] n Garage f; (for repair) (Auto)reparaturwerkstatt f; (for petrol) Tankstelle f.

garbage ['gɑ:bɪdʒ] n Abfall m; ~ can n (US) Mülltonne f.

garbled ['gɑ:bld] a (story) verdreht.

garden ['gɑ:dn] n Garten m; ~er n Gärtner(in f) m; ~ing n Gärtnern nt.

gargle ['gɑ:gl] vi gurgeln.

gargoyle ['gɑ:gɔɪl] n Wasserspeier m.

garish ['gɛərɪʃ] a grell.

garland ['gɑ:lənd] n Girlande f.

garlic ['gɑ:lɪk] n Knoblauch m.

garment ['gɑ:mənt] n Kleidungsstück nt.

garnish ['gɑ:nɪʃ] vt (food) garnieren.

garrison ['gærɪsən] n Garnison f.

garrulous ['gærʊləs] a geschwätzig.

garter ['gɑ:tə*] n (US) Strumpfband nt.

gas [gæs] n Gas nt; (esp US: petrol) Benzin nt // vt vergasen; ~ cooker n (Brit) Gasherd m; ~ cylinder n Gasflasche f; ~ fire n Gasofen m.

gash [gæʃ] n klaffende Wunde f // vt tief verwunden.

gasket ['gæskɪt] n Dichtungsring m.

gas: ~mask n Gasmaske f; ~ **meter** n Gaszähler m.

gasoline ['gæsəli:n] n (US) Benzin nt.

gasp [gɑ:sp] vi keuchen; (in astonishment) tief Luft holen // n Keu-

chen nt.

gas: ~ ring n Gasring m; **~sy** a (drink) sprudelnd; ~ **tap** n Gashahn m.

gastric ['gæstrɪk] a Magen-.

gate [geɪt] n Tor nt; (barrier) Schranke f; ~**crash** vt (Brit: party) platzen in (+acc); ~**way** n Toreingang m.

gather ['gæðə*] vt (people) versammeln; (things) sammeln // vi (understand) annehmen; (deduce) schließen (from aus); (assemble) sich versammeln; to ~ speed schneller werden; ~ing n Versammlung f.

gauche [gəʊʃ] a linkisch.

gaudy ['gɔ:dɪ] a schreiend.

gauge [geɪdʒ] n (instrument) Meßgerät nt; (RAIL) Spurweite f; (dial) Anzeiger m; (measure) Maß nt // vt (lit) (ab)messen; (fig) abschätzen.

gaunt [gɔ:nt] a hager.

gauntlet ['gɔ:ntlɪt] n (knight's) (Fehde)handschuh m.

gauze [gɔ:z] n Gaze f.

gave [geɪv] pt of **give**.

gay [geɪ] a (homosexual) schwul; (lively) lustig.

gaze [geɪz] n Blick m // vi (an)blicken (at acc).

gazelle [gə'zel] n Gazelle f.

gazetteer [gæzɪ'tɪə*] n geographische(s) Lexikon nt.

gazumping [gə'zʌmpɪŋ] n (Brit) Verkauf eines Hauses an einen zweiten Bieter trotz Zusage an den ersten.

GB n abbr (= Great Britain) GB.

GCE n abbr (Brit) of **General Certificate of Education.**

GCSE n abbr (Brit: = General Certificate of Secondary Education) ≃ Hauptschulabschluß m.

gear [gɪə*] n Getriebe nt; (equipment) Ausrüstung f; (AUT) Gang m // vt (fig: adapt): to be ~ed ausgerichtet sein (to auf +acc); top or (US) **high/low** ~ höchste(r)/niedrige(r) Gang m; **in** ~ eingekuppelt; ~ **box** n Getriebe(gehäuse) nt; ~ **lever**, ~ **shift** (US) n Schalthebel m.

geese [gi:s] npl of **goose**.

gel [dʒel] n Gel nt.

gelatin(e) ['dʒelətɪn] n Gelatine f.

gelignite ['dʒelɪgnaɪt] n Plastiksprengstoff m.

gem [dʒem] n Edelstein m; (fig) Juwel nt.

Gemini ['dʒemɪni:] n Zwillinge pl.

gender ['dʒendə*] n (GRAM) Geschlecht nt.

gene [dʒi:n] n Gen nt.

general ['dʒenərəl] n General m // a allgemein; ~ **delivery** n (US) Ausgabe(schalter m) f postlagernder Sendungen; ~ **election** n allgemeine Wahlen pl; ~**ization** [-aɪ'zeɪʃən] n Verallgemeinerung f; ~**ize** vi verallgemeinern; **~ly** *ad* allgemein, im allgemeinen; **~ practitioner (G.P.)** *n* praktische(r) Arzt *m*, praktische Ärztin *f*.

generate ['dʒenəreɪt] *vt* erzeugen.

generation [dʒenə'reɪʃən] *n* Generation *f*; (*act*) Erzeugung *f*.

generator ['dʒenəreɪtə*] *n* Generator *m*.

generosity [dʒenə'rɒsɪtɪ] *n* Großzügigkeit *f*.

generous ['dʒenərəs] *a* großzügig.

genetics [dʒɪ'netɪks] *n* Genetik *f*.

Geneva [dʒɪ'niːvə] *n* Genf *nt*.

genial ['dʒiːnɪəl] *a* freundlich, jovial.

genitals ['dʒenɪtlz] *npl* Genitalien *pl*.

genius ['dʒiːnɪəs] *n* Genie *nt*.

genocide ['dʒenəʊsaɪd] *n* Völkermord *m*.

gent [dʒent] *n abbr of* **gentleman**.

genteel [dʒen'tiːl] *a* (*polite*) wohlanständig; (*affected*) affektiert.

gentle ['dʒentl] *a* sanft, zart.

gentleman ['dʒentlmən] *n* Herr *m*; (*polite*) Gentleman *m*.

gentleness ['dʒentlnɪs] *n* Zartheit *f*, Milde *f*.

gently ['dʒentlɪ] *ad* zart, sanft.

gentry ['dʒentrɪ] *n* Landadel *m*.

gents [dʒents] *n*: G~ (*lavatory*) Herren.

genuine ['dʒenjʊɪn] *a* echt.

geographic(al) [dʒɪə'græfɪk(əl)] *a* geographisch.

geography [dʒɪ'ɒgrəfɪ] *n* Geographie *f*.

geological [dʒɪəʊ'lɒdʒɪkəl] *a* geologisch.

geologist [dʒɪ'ɒlədʒɪst] *n* Geologe *m*, Geologin *f*.

geology [dʒɪ'ɒlədʒɪ] *n* Geologie *f*.

geometry [dʒɪ'ɒmɪtrɪ] *n* Geometrie *f*.

geranium [dʒɪ'reɪnɪəm] *n* Geranie *f*.

geriatric [dʒerɪ'ætrɪk] *a* Alten- // *n* Greis(in *f*) *m*.

germ [dʒɜːm] *n* Keim *m*; (*MED*) Bazillus *m*.

German ['dʒɜːmən] *a* deutsch // *n* Deutsche(r) *mf*; (*LING*) Deutsch *nt*; **~ measles** *n* Röteln *pl*.

Germany ['dʒɜːmənɪ] *n* Deutschland *nt*.

germination [dʒɜːmɪ'neɪʃən] *n* Keimen *nt*.

gesticulate [dʒes'tɪkjʊleɪt] *vi* gestikulieren.

gesture ['dʒestʃə*] *n* Geste *f*.

get [get], *pt, pp* **got**, *pp* **gotten** (*US*) ◆*vi* 1 (*become, be*) werden; **to ~ old/ tired** alt/müde werden; **to ~ married** heiraten

2 (*go*) (an)kommen, gehen

3 (*begin*): **to ~ to know sb** jdn kennenlernen; **let's ~ going** *or* **started** fangen wir an!

4 (*modal aux v*): **you've got to do it** du mußt es tun

◆*vt* 1: **to ~ sth done** (*do*) etw machen;

(*have done*) etw machen lassen; **to ~ sth going** *or* **to go** etw in Gang bringen *or* bekommen; **to ~ sb to do sth** jdn dazu bringen, etw zu tun

2 (*obtain: money, permission, results*) erhalten; (*find: job, flat*) finden; (*fetch: person, doctor, object*) holen; **to ~ sth for sb** jdm etw besorgen; **~ me Mr Jones, please** (*TEL*) verbinden Sie mich bitte mit Mr Jones

3 (*receive: present, letter*) bekommen, kriegen; (*acquire: reputation etc*) erwerben

4 (*catch*) bekommen, kriegen; (*hit: target etc*) treffen, erwischen; **~ him!** (*to dog*) faß!

5 (*take, move*) bringen; **to ~ sth to sb** jdm etw bringen

6 (*understand*) verstehen; (*hear*) mitbekommen; **I've got it!** ich hab's!

7 (*have, possess*): **to have got etw** haben.

get about *vi* herumkommen; (*news*) sich verbreiten

get along *vi* (*people*) (gut) zurechtkommen; (*depart*) sich (*acc*) auf den Weg machen

get at *vt* (*facts*) herausbekommen; **to ~ at sb** (*nag*) an jdm herumnörgeln

get away *vi* (*leave*) sich (*acc*) davonmachen; (*escape*) entkommen (*from dat*); **to ~ away with sth** mit etw davon kommen

get back *vi* (*return*) zurückkommen // *vt* zurückbekommen

get by *vi* (*pass*) vorbeikommen; (*manage*) zurechtkommen

get down *vi* (her)untergehen // *vt* (*depress*) fertigmachen; **to ~ down to** in Angriff nehmen; (*find time to do*) kommen zu

get in *vi* (*train*) ankommen; (*arrive home*) heimkommen

get into *vt* (*enter*) hinein-/ hereinkommen in (+*acc*); (: *car train etc*) einsteigen in (+*acc*); (*clothes*) anziehen

get off *vi* (*from train etc*) aussteigen; (*from horse*) absteigen // *vt* aussteigen aus; absteigen von

get on *vi* (*progress*) vorankommen; (*be friends*) auskommen; (*age*) alt werden; (*onto train etc*) einsteigen; (*onto horse*) aufsteigen // *vt* einsteigen in (+*acc*); aufsteigen auf (+*acc*)

get out *vi* (*of house*) herauskommen; (*of vehicle*) aussteigen // *vt* (*take out*) herausholen

get out of *vt* (*duty etc*) herumkommen um

get over *vt* (*illness*) sich (*acc*) erholen von; (*surprise*) verkraften; (*news*) fassen; (*loss*) sich abfinden mit

get round *vt* herumkommen; (*fig: person*) herumkriegen

get through to vt (TEL) durchkommen zu

get together vi zusammenkommen

get up vi aufstehen // vt hinaufbringen;
(go up) hinaufgehen; (organize) auf die
Beine stellen

get up to vt (reach) erreichen; (prank
etc) anstellen.

getaway ['getǝweɪ] n Flucht f.

geyser ['giːzǝ*] n Geiser m; (heater)
Durchlauferhitzer m.

ghastly ['gɑːstlɪ] a (horrible) gräßlich.

gherkin ['gɜːkɪn] n Gewürzgurke f.

ghetto ['getǝʊ] n G(h)etto nt.

ghost [gǝʊst] n Gespenst nt; ~ly a
gespenstisch.

giant ['dʒaɪǝnt] n Riese m // a riesig,
Riesen-.

gibberish ['dʒɪbǝrɪʃ] n dumme(s) Geschwätz nt.

gibe [dʒaɪb] n spöttische Bemerkung f.

giblets ['dʒɪblɪts] npl Geflügelinnereien
pl.

giddiness ['gɪdɪnǝs] n Schwindelgefühl
nt.

giddy ['gɪdɪ] a schwindlig.

gift [gɪft] n Geschenk nt; (ability) Begabung f; ~ed a begabt; ~ token or
voucher n Geschenkgutschein m.

gigantic [dʒaɪˈgæntɪk] a riesenhaft.

giggle ['gɪgl] vi kichern // n Gekicher nt.

gild [gɪld] vt vergolden.

gill [dʒɪl] n (1/4 pint) Viertelpinte f // n
[gɪl] (of fish) Kieme f.

gilt [gɪlt] n Vergoldung f // a vergoldet;
~-edged a mündelsicher.

gimmick ['gɪmɪk] n Gag m.

gin [dʒɪn] n Gin m.

ginger ['dʒɪndʒǝ*] n Ingwer m; ~ ale
n, ~ beer n Ingwerbier nt; ~bread n
Pfefferkuchen m; ~-haired a rothaarig.

gingerly ['dʒɪndʒǝlɪ] ad behutsam.

gipsy ['dʒɪpsɪ] n Zigeuner(in f) m.

giraffe [dʒɪˈrɑːf] n Giraffe f.

girder ['gɜːdǝ*] n Eisenträger m.

girdle ['gɜːdl] n Hüftgürtel m.

girl [gɜːl] n Mädchen nt; ~friend n
Freundin f; ~ish a mädchenhaft.

giro ['dʒaɪrǝʊ] n (bank ~) Giro nt; (post
office ~) Postscheckverkehr m.

girth [gɜːθ] n (measure) Umfang m;
(strap) Sattelgurt m.

gist [dʒɪst] n Wesentliche(s) nt.

give [gɪv], pt gave, pp given vt geben //
vi (break) nachgeben; ~ away vt (give
free) verschenken; (betray) verraten; ~
back vt zurückgeben; ~ in vi
nachgeben // vt (hand in) abgeben; ~
off vt abgeben; ~ out vt verteilen; (announce) bekanntgeben; ~ up vti aufgeben; to ~ o.s. up sich stellen; (after
siege) sich ergeben; ~ way vi (Brit:
traffic) Vorfahrt lassen; (to feelings)
nachgeben (+dat).

glacier ['glæsɪǝ*] n Gletscher m.

glad [glæd] a froh.

gladioli [glædɪˈǝʊlaɪ] npl Gladiolen pl.

gladly ['glædlɪ] ad gern(e).

glamorous ['glæmǝrǝs] a reizvoll.

glamour ['glæmǝ*] n Glanz m.

glance [glɑːns] n Blick m // vi
(hin)blicken (at auf +acc); ~ off vi (fly
off) abprallen von.

glancing ['glɑːnsɪŋ] a (blow) Streif-.

gland [glænd] n Drüse f.

glare [glɛǝ*] n (light) grelle(s) Licht nt;
(stare) wilde(r) Blick m // vi grell
scheinen; (angrily) böse ansehen (at
acc).

glaring ['glɛǝrɪŋ] a (injustice)
schreiend; (mistake) kraß.

glass [glɑːs] n Glas nt; (mirror: also:
looking ~) Spiegel m; ~es pl Brille f;
~house n Gewächshaus nt; ~ware n
Glaswaren pl; ~y a glasig.

glaze [gleɪz] vt verglasen; (finish with a
~) glasieren // n Glasur f; ~d a (eye)
glasig; (pottery) glasiert.

glazier ['gleɪzɪǝ*] n Glaser m.

gleam [gliːm] n Schimmer m // vi
schimmern; ~ing a schimmernd.

glean [gliːn] vt (fig) ausfindig machen.

glee [gliː] n Frohsinn m.

glen [glen] n Bergtal nt.

glib [glɪb] a oberflächlich.

glide [glaɪd] vi gleiten; ~r n (AVIAT)
Segelflugzeug nt.

gliding ['glaɪdɪŋ] n Segelfliegen nt.

glimmer ['glɪmǝ*] n Schimmer m.

glimpse [glɪmps] n flüchtige(r) Blick m
// vt flüchtig erblicken.

glint [glɪnt] n Glitzern nt // vi glitzern.

glisten ['glɪsn] vi glänzen.

glitter ['glɪtǝ*] vi funkeln // n Funkeln nt.

gloat [glǝʊt] vi: to ~ over sich weiden
an (+dat).

global ['glǝʊbl] a global.

globe [glǝʊb] n Erdball m; (sphere)
Globus m.

gloom [gluːm] n (darkness) Dunkel nt;
(depression) düstere Stimmung f; ~y a
düster.

glorify ['glɔːrɪfaɪ] vt verherrlichen.

glorious ['glɔːrɪǝs] a glorreich.

glory ['glɔːrɪ] n Ruhm m.

gloss [glɒs] n (shine) Glanz m; ~ over
vt übertünchen.

glossary ['glɒsǝrɪ] n Glossar nt.

glossy ['glɒsɪ] a (surface) glänzend.

glove [glʌv] n Handschuh m; ~ compartment n (AUT) Handschuhfach nt.

glow [glǝʊ] vi glühen // n Glühen nt.

glower ['glaʊǝ*] vi: to ~ at finster an-
blicken.

glucose ['gluːkǝʊs] n Traubenzucker m.

glue [gluː] n Klebstoff m // vt kleben.

glum [glʌm] a bedrückt.

glut [glʌt] n Überfluß m.

glutton ['glʌtn] n Vielfraß m; a ~ for
work ein Arbeitstier n; ~y n Völlerei f.

glycerin(e) ['glisəri:n] n Glyzerin nt.
gnarled [nɑ:ld] a knorrig.
gnat [næt] n Stechmücke f.
gnaw [nɔ:] vt nagen an (+dat).
gnome [nəum] n Gnom m.
go [gəu], pt **went**, pp **gone** vi gehen;
(travel) reisen, fahren; (depart: train)
(ab)fahren; (be sold) verkauft werden;
(work) gehen, funktionieren; (fit, suit)
passen (with zu); (become) werden;
(break etc) nachgeben // n (pl ~es)
(energy) Schwung m; (attempt) Versuch
m; he's going to do it er wird es tun; to
~ for a walk spazieren gehen; to ~ dancing tanzen gehen; how did it ~? wie
war's?; to have a ~ at sth etw versuchen; to be on the ~ auf Trab sein;
whose ~ is it? wer ist dran?; ~ **about**
vi (rumour) umgehen // vt: how do I ~
about this? wie packe ich das an?; ~
ahead vi (proceed) weitergehen; ~
along vi dahingehen, dahinfahren // vt
entlanggehen, entlangfahren; to ~ **along**
with (agree to support) zustimmen
(+dat); ~ **away** vi (depart) weggehen;
~ **back** vi (return) zurückgehen; ~
back on vt (promise) nicht halten; ~
by vi (years, time) vergehen // vt sich
richten nach; ~ **down** vi (sun) untergehen // vt hinuntergehen, hin-
unterfahren; ~ **for** vt (fetch) holen
(gehen); (like) mögen; (attack) sich
stürzen auf (+acc); ~ **in** vi hineingehen; ~ **in for** vt (competition)
teilnehmen an; ~ **into** vt (enter) hineingehen in (+acc); (study) sich
befassen mit; ~ **off** vi (depart)
weggehen; (lights) ausgehen; (milk etc)
sauer werden; (explode) losgehen // vt
(dislike) nicht mehr mögen; ~ **on** vi
(continue) weitergehen; (col: complain)
meckern; (lights) angehen; to ~ **on** with
sth mit etw weitermachen; ~ **out** vi
(fire, light) ausgehen; (of house) hinaus-
gehen; ~ **over** vi (ship) kentern // vt
(examine, check) durchgehen; ~
through vt (town etc) durchgehen,
durchfahren; ~ **up** vi (price) steigen;
~ **without** vt sich behelfen ohne; (food)
entbehren.
goad [gəud] vt anstacheln.
go-ahead ['gəuəhed] a zielstrebig; (progressive) fortschrittlich // n grüne(s)
Licht nt.
goal [gəul] n Ziel nt; (SPORT) Tor nt;
~**keeper** n Torwart m; ~-**post** n
Torpfosten m.
goat [gəut] n Ziege f.
gobble ['gɔbl] vt (also: ~ **down**, ~ **up**)
hinunterschlingen.
go-between ['gəubitwi:n] n Mit-
telsmann n.
goblet ['gɔblit] n Kelch(glas nt) m.
god [gɔd] n Gott m; G~ n Gott m;
~**child** n Patenkind nt; ~**daughter** n

Patentochter f; ~**dess** n Göttin f;
~**father** n Pate m; ~-**forsaken** a
gottverlassen; ~**mother** n Patin f;
~**send** n Geschenk nt des Himmels;
~**son** n Patensohn m.
goggles ['gɔglz] npl Schutzbrille f.
going ['gəuiŋ] n (horse-racing) Bahn f //
a (rate) gängig; (concern) gutgehend;
it's hard ~ es ist schwierig.
gold [gəuld] n Gold nt // a golden; ~**en**
a golden, Gold-; ~**fish** n Goldfisch m; ~
mine n Goldgrube f; ~-**plated** a ~-
goldet; ~**smith** n Goldschmied(in f) m.
golf [gɔlf] n Golf nt; ~**ball** n (also on
typewriter) Golfball m; ~ **club** n
(society) Golfklub m; (stick) Golfschläger m; ~ **course** n Golfplatz m;
~**er** n Golfspieler(in f) m.
gondola ['gɔndələ] n Gondel f.
gone [gɔn] pp of **go**.
gong [gɔŋ] n Gong m.
good [gud] n (benefit) Wohl nt; (moral
excellence) Güte f // a gut; ~**s** pl Waren
pl, Güter pl; a ~ deal (of) ziemlich viel;
a ~ many ziemlich viele; ~**bye!** interj
auf Wiedersehen!; G~ **Friday** n Karfreitag m; ~-**looking** a gutaussehend;
~ **morning!** interj guten Morgen!; ~-
natured a gutmütig; (dog) harmlos;
~**ness** n Güte f; (virtue) Tugend f; ~**s**
train n (Brit) Güterzug; ~**will** n
(favour) Wohlwollen nt; (COMM)
Firmenansehen nt.
goose [gu:s], pl **geese** n Gans f.
gooseberry ['guzbəri] n Stachelbeere f.
gooseflesh ['gu:sfleʃ] n, **goose pim-**
ples npl Gänsehaut f.
gore [gɔ:*] vt aufspießen // n Blut nt.
gorge [gɔ:dʒ] n Schlucht f // vr: to ~ o.s.
(sich voll) fressen.
gorgeous ['gɔ:dʒəs] a prächtig.
gorilla [gə'rilə] n Gorilla m.
gorse [gɔ:s] n Stechginster m.
gory ['gɔ:ri] a blutig.
go-slow ['gəu'sləu] n (Brit) Bummel-
streik m.
gospel ['gɔspəl] n Evangelium nt.
gossip ['gɔsip] n Klatsch m; (person)
Klatschbase f // vi klatschen.
got [gɔt] pt, pp of **get**; ~**ten** (US) pp of
get.
gout [gaut] n Gicht f.
govern ['gʌvən] vt regieren; verwalten.
governess ['gʌvənis] n Gouvernante f.
government ['gʌvnmənt] n Regierung
f.
governor ['gʌvənə*] n Gouverneur m.
gown [gaun] n Gewand nt; (UNIV) Robe
f.
G.P. n abbr of **general practitioner**.
grab [græb] vt packen.
grace [greis] n Anmut f; (blessing)
Gnade f; (prayer) Tischgebet nt // vt
(adorn) zieren; (honour) auszeichnen; 5
days' ~ 5 Tage Aufschub m; ~**ful** a an-

mutig.
gracious ['greɪʃəs] a gnädig; (kind) freundlich.
grade [greɪd] n Grad m; (slope) Gefälle nt // vt (classify) einstufen; ~ **crossing** n (US) Bahnübergang m; ~ **school** n (US) Grundschule f.
gradient ['greɪdɪənt] n Steigung f; Gefälle nt.
gradual ['grædjʊəl] a allmählich.
graduate ['grædjʊɪt] n: to be a ~ das Staatsexamen haben // vi ['grædjʊeɪt] das Staatsexamen machen.
graduation [grædjʊ'eɪʃən] n Erlangung f eines akademischen Grades.
graffiti [grə'fi:tɪ] npl Graffiti pl.
graft [grɑ:ft] n (hard work) Schufterei f; (MED) Verpflanzung f // vt propfen; (fig) aufpropfen; (MED) verpflanzen.
grain [greɪn] n Korn nt; (in wood) Maserung f.
gram [græm] n Gramm nt.
grammar ['græmə*] n Grammatik f; ~ **school** n (Brit) Gymnasium nt.
gramme [græm] = **gram**.
granary ['grænərɪ] n Kornspeicher m.
grand [grænd] a großartig; ~**children** npl Enkel pl; ~**dad** n Opa m; ~**daughter** n Enkelin f; ~**eur** ['grændjə*] n Erhabenheit f; ~**father** n Großvater m; ~**iose** ['grændɪəʊs] a (imposing) großartig; (pompous) schwülstig; ~**ma** n Oma f; ~**mother** n Großmutter f; ~**pa** n = ~**dad**; ~**parents** npl Großeltern pl; ~ **piano** n Flügel m; ~**son** n Enkel m; ~**stand** n Haupttribüne f.
granite ['grænɪt] n Granit m.
granny ['grænɪ] n Oma f.
grant [grɑ:nt] vt gewähren // n Unterstützung f; (UNIV) Stipendium nt; to take sth for ~ed etw als selbstverständlich (an)nehmen.
granulated sugar ['grænjʊleɪtɪd-] n Zuckerraffinade f.
granule ['grænju:l] n Körnchen nt.
grape [greɪp] n (Wein)traube f.
grapefruit ['greɪpfru:t] n Pampelmuse f, Grapefruit f.
graph [grɑ:f] n Schaubild nt; ~**ic** ['græfɪk] a (descriptive) anschaulich; (drawing) graphisch; ~**ics** ['græfɪks] npl Grafik f.
grapple ['græpl] vi: to ~ **with** kämpfen mit.
grasp [grɑ:sp] vt ergreifen; (understand) begreifen // n Griff m; (of subject) Beherrschung f; ~**ing** a habgierig.
grass [grɑ:s] n Gras nt; ~**hopper** n Heuschrecke f; ~**land** n Weideland nt; ~**-roots** a an der Basis; ~ **snake** n Ringelnatter f.
grate [greɪt] n Kamin m // vi (sound) knirschen; (on nerves) zerren (on an +dat) // vt (cheese) reiben.

grateful ['greɪtfʊl] a dankbar.
grater ['greɪtə*] n Reibe f.
gratify ['grætɪfaɪ] vt befriedigen.
gratifying ['grætɪfaɪɪŋ] a erfreulich.
grating ['greɪtɪŋ] n (iron bars) Gitter nt // a (noise) knirschend.
gratitude ['grætɪtju:d] n Dankbarkeit f.
gratuity [grə'tju:ɪtɪ] n Gratifikation f.
grave [greɪv] n Grab nt // a (serious) ernst.
gravel ['grævəl] n Kies m.
grave: ~ **stone** n Grabstein m; ~**yard** n Friedhof m.
gravity ['grævɪtɪ] n Schwerkraft f; (seriousness) Schwere f.
gravy ['greɪvɪ] n (Braten)soße f.
gray [greɪ] a = **grey**.
graze [greɪz] vi grasen // vt (touch) streifen; (MED) abschürfen // n (MED) Abschürfung f.
grease [gri:s] n (fat) Fett nt; (lubricant) Schmiere f // vt (ab)schmieren; ~**proof** a (Brit: paper) Butterbrot-.
greasy ['gri:sɪ] a fettig.
great [greɪt] a groß; (col: good) prima; ~**-grandfather/mother** n Urgroßvater m/mutter f; ~**ly** ad sehr; ~**ness** n Größe f.
Greece [gri:s] n Griechenland nt.
greed [gri:d] n (also: ~**iness**) Gier f (for nach); (meanness) Geiz m; ~**y** a gierig.
Greek [gri:k] a griechisch // n Grieche m, Griechin f; (LING) Griechisch nt.
green [gri:n] a grün // n (village ~) Dorfwiese f; ~ **belt** n Grüngürtel m; ~ **card** n (AUT) grüne Versicherungskarte f; ~**ery** n Grün nt; grüne(s) Laub nt; ~**gage** n Reineclaude f; ~**grocer** n (Brit) Obst- und Gemüsehändler m; ~**house** n Gewächshaus nt; ~**ish** a grünlich.
Greenland ['gri:nlənd] n Grönland nt.
greet [gri:t] vt grüßen; ~**ing** n Gruß m; ~**ing(s) card** n Glückwunschkarte f.
gregarious [grɪ'gɛərɪəs] a gesellig.
grenade [grɪ'neɪd] n Granate f.
grew [gru:] pt of **grow**.
grey [greɪ] a grau; ~**-haired** a grauhaarig; ~**hound** n Windhund m; ~**ish** a gräulich.
grid [grɪd] n Gitter nt; (ELEC) Leitungsnetz nt; (on map) Gitternetz nt.
grief [gri:f] n Gram m, Kummer m.
grievance ['gri:vəns] n Beschwerde f.
grieve [gri:v] vi sich grämen // vt betrüben.
grievous ['gri:vəs] a: ~ **bodily harm** (JUR) schwere Körperverletzung f.
grill [grɪl] n Grill m // vt (Brit) grillen; (question) in die Mangel nehmen.
grille [grɪl] n (on car etc) (Kühler)gitter nt.
grim [grɪm] a grimmig; (situation) düster.
grimace [grɪ'meɪs] n Grimasse f // vi

Grimassen schneiden.
grime [graɪm] *n* Schmutz *m*.
grimy ['graɪmɪ] *a* schmutzig.
grin [grɪn] *n* Grinsen *nt* // *vi* grinsen.
grind [graɪnd] *vt*, *pt*, *pp* **ground** mahlen; (*US: meat*) durch den Fleischwolf drehen; (*sharpen*) schleifen; (*teeth*) knirschen mit // *n* (*bore*) Plackerei *f*.
grip [grɪp] *n* Griff *m*; (*suitcase*) Handkoffer *m* // *vt* packen; **~ping** *a* (*exciting*) spannend.
grisly ['grɪzlɪ] *a* gräßlich.
gristle ['grɪsl] *n* Knorpel *m*.
grit [grɪt] *n* Splitt *m*; (*courage*) Mut *m* // *vt* (*teeth*) knirschen mit; (*road*) (mit Splitt (be)streuen.
groan [grəʊn] *n* Stöhnen *nt* // *vi* stöhnen.
grocer ['grəʊsə*] *n* Lebensmittelhändler *m*; **~ies** *pl* Lebensmittel *pl*; **~'s (shop)** *n* Lebensmittelgeschäft *nt*.
groggy ['grɒgɪ] *a* benommen.
groin [grɔɪn] *n* Leistengegend *f*.
groom [gru:m] *n* (*also*: **bride~**) Bräutigam *m*; (*for horses*) Pferdeknecht *m* // *vt* (*horse*) striegeln; (**well-**)**~ed** gepflegt.
groove [gru:v] *n* Rille *f*, Furche *f*.
grope [grəʊp] *vi* tasten; **~ for** *vt* suchen nach.
gross [grəʊs] *a* (*coarse*) dick, plump; (*bad*) grob, schwer; (*COMM*) brutto; **~ly** *ad* höchst.
grotesque [grəʊ'tɛsk] *a* grotesk.
grotto ['grɒtəʊ] *n* Grotte *f*.
ground [graʊnd] *pt*, *pp* of **grind** // *n* Boden *m*; (*land*) Grundbesitz *m*; (*reason*) Grund *m*; (*US: also:* **~ wire**) Endleitung *f*; **~s** *pl* (*dregs*) Bodensatz *m*; (*around house*) (Garten)anlagen *pl* // *vi* (*run ashore*) stranden, auflaufen; **on the ~** am Boden; **to the ~** zu Boden; **to gain/lose ~** Boden gewinnen/verlieren; **~ cloth** *n* (*US*) = **~ sheet**; **~ing** *n* (*instruction*) Anfangsunterricht *m*; **~less** *a* grundlos; **~sheet** *n* (*Brit*) Zeltboden *m*; **~ staff** *n* Bodenpersonal *nt*; **~ swell** *n* (*of sea*) Dünung; (*fig*) Zurnahme *f*; **~work** *n* Grundlage *f*.
group [gru:p] *n* Gruppe *f* // *vti* (*also:* **~ together**) (sich) gruppieren.
grouse [graʊs] *n*, *pl inv* (*bird*) schottische(s) Moorhuhn *nt* // *vi* (*complain*) meckern.
grove [grəʊv] *n* Gehölz *nt*, Hain *m*.
grovel ['grɒvl] *vi* (*fig*) kriechen.
grow [grəʊ], *pt* **grew**, *pp* **grown** *vi* wachsen; (*become*) werden // *vt* (*raise*) anbauen; **~ up** *vi* aufwachsen; **~er** *n* Züchter *m*; **~ing** *a* zunehmend.
growl [graʊl] *vi* knurren.
grown [grəʊn] *pp* of **grow**; **~-up** *n* Erwachsene(r) *mf*.
growth [grəʊθ] *n* Wachstum *nt*; (*increase*) Zunahme *f*; (*of beard etc*)

Wuchs *m*.
grub [grʌb] *n* Made *f*, Larve *f*; (*col: food*) Futter *nt*; **~by** *a* schmutzig.
grudge [grʌdʒ] *n* Groll *m* // *vt* misgönnen (*sb sth* jdm etw); **to bear sb a ~** einen Groll gegen jdn hegen.
gruelling ['grʊəlɪŋ] *a* (*climb, race*) mörderisch.
gruesome ['gru:səm] *a* grauenhaft.
gruff [grʌf] *a* barsch.
grumble ['grʌmbl] *vi* murren.
grumpy ['grʌmpɪ] *a* verdrießlich.
grunt [grʌnt] *vi* grunzen // *n* Grunzen *nt*.
G-string ['dʒi:-] *n* Minislip *m*.
guarantee [gærən'ti:] *n* Garantie *f* // *vt* garantieren.
guard [gɑ:d] *n* (*sentry*) Wache *f*; (*Brit: RAIL*) Zugbegleiter *m* // *vt* bewachen; **~ed** *a* vorsichtig; **~ian** *n* Vormund *m*; (*keeper*) Hüter *m*; **~'s van** *n* (*Brit RAIL*) Dienstwagen *m*.
guerrilla [gə'rɪlə] *n* Guerilla(kämpfer) *m*; **~ warfare** *n* Guerillakrieg *m*.
guess [gɛs] *vt* (er)raten, schätzen // *n* Vermutung *f*; **~work** *n* Raterei *f*.
guest [gɛst] *n* Gast *m*; **~-house** *n* Pension *f*; **~ room** *n* Gastzimmer *nt*.
guffaw [gʌ'fɔ:] *vi* schallend lachen.
guidance ['gaɪdəns] *n* (*control*) Leitung *f*; (*advice*) Beratung *f*.
guide [gaɪd] *n* Führer *m* // *vt* führen; (**girl**) **~** *n* Pfadfinderin *f*; **~book** *n* Reiseführer *m*; **~ dog** *n* Blindenhund *m*; **~lines** *npl* Richtlinien *pl*.
guild [gɪld] *n* (*HIST*) Gilde *f*; **~hall** *n* (*Brit*) Stadthalle *f*.
guile [gaɪl] *n* Arglist *f*.
guillotine [gɪlə'ti:n] *n* Guillotine *f*.
guilt [gɪlt] *n* Schuld *f*; **~y** *a* schuldig.
guinea pig ['gɪnɪ-] *n* Meerschweinchen *nt*; (*fig*) Versuchskaninchen *n*.
guise [gaɪz] *n*: **in the ~ of** in der Form (+*gen*).
guitar [gɪ'tɑ:*] *n* Gitarre *f*.
gulf [gʌlf] *n* Golf *m*; (*fig*) Abgrund *m*.
gull [gʌl] *n* Möwe *f*.
gullet ['gʌlɪt] *n* Schlund *m*.
gullible ['gʌlɪbl] *a* leichtgläubig.
gully ['gʌlɪ] *n* (Wasser)rinne *f*.
gulp [gʌlp] *vt* (*also:* **~ down**) hinunterschlucken // *vi* (*gasp*) schlucken.
gum [gʌm] *n* (*around teeth*) Zahnfleisch *nt*; (*glue*) Klebstoff *m*; (*also:* **chewing-~**) Kaugummi *m* // *vt* gummieren; **~boots** *npl* (*Brit*) Gummistiefel *pl*.
gumption ['gʌmpʃən] *n* (*col*) Mumm *m*.
gun [gʌn] *n* Schußwaffe *f*; **~boat** *n* Kanonenboot *nt*; **~fire** *n* Geschützfeuer *nt*; **~man** *n* bewaffnete(r) Verbrecher *m*; **~ner** *n* Kanonier *m*, Artillerist *m*; **~point** *n*: **at ~point** mit Waffengewalt; **~powder** *n* Schießpulver *nt*; **~shot** *n* Schuß *m*; **~smith** *n* Büchsenmacher(in *f*) *m*.
gurgle ['gɜ:gl] *vi* gluckern.

guru ['guru:] n Guru m.

gush [gʌʃ] vi (rush out) hervorströmen; (fig) schwärmen.

gusset ['gʌsɪt] n Keil m, Zwickel m.

gust [gʌst] n Windstoß m, Bö f.

gusto ['gʌstəu] n Genuß m, Lust f.

gut [gʌt] n (ANAT) Gedärme pl; (string) Darm m; ~s pl (fig) Schneid m.

gutter ['gʌtə*] n Dachrinne f; (in street) Gosse f.

guttural ['gʌtərəl] a guttural, Kehl-.

guy [gaɪ] n (also: ~rope) Halteseil nt; (man) Typ m, Kerl m.

guzzle ['gʌzl] vti (drink) saufen; (eat) fressen.

gym [dʒɪm] n (also: gymnasium) Turnhalle f; (also: gymnastics) Turnen nt; ~nast ['dʒɪmnæst] n Turner(in f) m; ~nastics [dʒɪm'næstɪks] n Turnen nt, Gymnastik f; ~ shoes npl Turnschuhe pl; ~ slip n (Brit) Schulträgerrock.

gynaecologist, (US) **gynecologist** [gaɪnɪ'kɒlədʒɪst] n Frauenarzt m/-ärztin f.

gynaecology, (US) **gynecology** [gaɪnɪ'kɒlədʒɪ] n Gynäkologie f, Frauenheilkunde f.

gypsy ['dʒɪpsɪ] n = **gipsy**.

gyrate [dʒaɪ'reɪt] vi kreisen.

H

haberdashery [hæbə'dæʃərɪ] n (Brit) Kurzwaren pl.

habit ['hæbɪt] n (An)gewohnheit f; (monk's) Habit nt or m.

habitable ['hæbɪtəbl] a bewohnbar.

habitat ['hæbɪtæt] n Lebensraum m.

habitual [hə'bɪtjuəl] a gewohnheitsmäßig; ~ly ad gewöhnlich.

hack [hæk] vt hacken // n Hieb m; (writer) Schreiberling m.

hackneyed ['hæknɪd] a abgedroschen.

had [hæd] pt, pp of **have**.

haddock ['hædək], pl ~ or ~s n Schellfisch m.

hadn't ['hædnt] = **had not**.

haemorrhage, (US) **hemorrhage** ['hemərɪdʒ] n Blutung f.

haemorrhoids, (US) **hemorrhoids** ['hemərɔɪdz] npl Hämorrhoiden pl.

haggard ['hægəd] a abgekämpft.

haggle ['hægl] vi feilschen.

Hague [heɪg] n: The ~ Den Haag nt.

hail [heɪl] n Hagel m // vt umjubeln // vi hageln; ~stone n Hagelkorn nt.

hair [heə*] n Haar nt, Haare pl; (one ~) Haar nt; ~brush n Haarbürste f; ~cut n Haarschnitt m; to get a ~cut sich (dat) die Haare schneiden lassen; ~do n Frisur f; ~dresser n Friseur m, Friseuse f; ~dresser's n Friseursalon m; ~ dryer n Trockenhaube f; (hand)

Fön m; ~grip n Klemme f; ~net n Haarnetz nt; ~pin n Haarnadel f; ~pin bend, (US) ~pin curve n Haarnadelkurve f; ~raising a haarsträubend; ~ remover n Enthaarungsmittel nt; ~ spray n Haarspray nt; ~style n Frisur f; ~y a haarig.

hake [heɪk] n Seehecht m.

half [hɑːf], pl **halves** n Hälfte f // a halb // ad halb, zur Hälfte; ~-an-hour eine halbe Stunde; two and a ~ zweieinhalb; to cut sth in ~ etw halbieren; ~-back n Läufer m; ~-breed n, ~-caste n Mischling m; ~-hearted a lustlos; ~-hour n halbe Stunde f; ~penny ['heɪpnɪ] n (Brit) halbe(r) Penny m; (at) ~-price zum halben Preis; ~ term n (Brit SCH) Ferien pl in der Mitte des Trimesters; ~-time n Halbzeit f; ~way ad halbwegs, auf halbem Wege.

hall [hɔːl] n Saal m; (entrance ~) Hausflur m; (building) Halle f; ~ of residence n (Brit) Studentenwohnheim nt.

hallmark ['hɔːlmɑːk] n Stempel m.

hallo [hʌ'ləu] see **hello**.

Hallowe'en ['hæləu'iːn] n Tag m vor Allerheiligen.

hallucination [həluːsɪ'neɪʃən] n Halluzination f.

hallway ['hɔːlweɪ] n Korridor m.

halo ['heɪləu] n Heiligenschein m.

halt [hɔːlt] n Halt m // vti anhalten.

halve [hɑːv] vt halbieren.

halves [hɑːvz] pl of **half**.

ham [hæm] n Schinken m.

hamburger ['hæmbɜːgə*] n Hamburger m.

hamlet ['hæmlɪt] n Weiler m.

hammer ['hæmə*] n Hammer m // vt hämmern.

hammock ['hæmək] n Hängematte f.

hamper ['hæmpə*] vt (be)hindern // n Picknickkorb m.

hamster ['hæmstə*] n Hamster m.

hand [hænd] n Hand f; (of clock) (Uhr)zeiger m; (worker) Arbeiter m // vt (pass) geben; to give sb a ~ jdm helfen; at ~ nahe; to ~ zur Hand; in ~ (under control) unter Kontrolle; (being done) im Gange; (extra) übrig; on ~ zur Verfügung; on the one ~ ..., on the other ~ ... einerseits ..., andererseits ...; ~ in vt abgeben; (forms) einreichen; ~ out vt austeilen; ~ over vt (deliver) übergeben; (surrender) abgeben; (: prisoner) ausliefern; ~bag n Handtasche f; ~book n Handbuch nt; ~brake n Handbremse f; ~cuffs npl Handschellen pl; ~ful n Handvoll f; (col: person) Plage f.

handicap ['hændɪkæp] n Handikap nt // vt benachteiligen; **mentally/physically** ~ped geistig/körperlich behindert.

handicraft ['hændɪkrɑːft] n Kunsthandwerk *nt*.

handiwork ['hændiwɜ:k] *n* Arbeit *f*; *(fig)* Werk *nt*.

handkerchief ['hæŋkətʃif] *n* Taschentuch *nt*.

handle ['hændl] *n* (*of door etc*) Klinke *f*; (*of cup etc*) Henkel *m*; (*for winding*) Kurbel *f* // *vt* (*touch*) anfassen; (*deal with: things*) sich befassen mit; (: *people*) umgehen mit; **~bar(s)** *n(pl)* Lenkstange *f*.

hand: ~ luggage *n* Handgepäck *nt*; **~made** *a* handgefertigt; **~out** *n* (*distribution*) Verteilung *f*; (*charity*) Geldzuwendung *f*; (*leaflet*) Flugblatt *nt*; **~rail** *n* Geländer *nt*; (*on ship*) Reling *f*; **~shake** *n* Händedruck *f*.

handsome ['hænsəm] *a* gutaussehend.

handwriting ['hændraitiŋ] *n* Handschrift *f*.

handy ['hændi] *a* praktisch; (*shops*) leicht erreichbar.

handyman ['hændimən] *n* Bastler *m*.

hang [hæŋ] *v* (*pt, pp* **hung**) *vt* aufhängen; (*criminal: pt, pp* **hanged**) hängen // *vi* hängen // *n*: **to get the ~ of sth** (*col*) den richtigen Dreh bei etw herauskriegen; **~ about** *vi* sich herumtreiben; **~ on** *vi* (*wait*) warten; **~ up** *vi* (*TEL*) auflegen.

hanger ['hæŋə*] *n* Kleiderbügel *m*.

hanger-on ['hæŋər'ɒn] *n* Anhänger (in *f*) *m*.

hang-gliding ['hæŋglaidiŋ] *n* Drachenfliegen *nt*.

hangover ['hæŋəuvə*] *n* Kater *m*.

hang-up ['hæŋʌp] *n* Komplex *m*.

hanker ['hæŋkə*] *vi* sich sehnen (*for, after* nach).

hankie, hanky ['hæŋki] *n abbr of* **handkerchief**.

haphazard ['hæp'hæzəd] *a* zufällig.

happen ['hæpən] *vi* sich ereignen, passieren; **as it ~s** I'm going there today zufällig(erweise) gehe ich heute (dort) hin; **~ing** *n* Ereignis *nt*.

happily ['hæpili] *ad* glücklich; (*fortunately*) glücklicherweise.

happiness ['hæpinəs] *n* Glück *nt*.

happy ['hæpi] *a* glücklich; **~ birthday!** alles Gute zum Geburtstag!; **~-go-lucky** *a* sorglos.

harass ['hærəs] *vt* plagen; **~ment** *n* Belästigung *f*.

harbour, (*US*) **harbor** ['hɑ:bə*] *n* Hafen *m* // *vt* (*hope etc*) hegen; (*criminal etc*) Unterschlupf gewähren.

hard [hɑ:d] *a* (*firm*) hart; (*difficult*) schwer; (*harsh*) hart(herzig) // *ad* (*work*) hart; (*try*) sehr; (*push, hit*) fest; **no ~ feelings!** ich nehme es dir nicht übel; **~ of hearing** schwerhörig; **to be ~ done by** übel dran sein; **~back** *n* kartonierte Ausgabe *f*; **~ cash** *n* Bargeld *nt*; **~ disk** *n* (*COMPUT*) Fest-

platte *f*; **~en** *vt* erhärten; (*fig*) verhärten // *vi* hart werden; (*fig*) sich verhärten; **~-headed** *a* nüchtern; **~ labour** *n* Zwangsarbeit *f*.

hardly ['hɑ:dli] *ad* kaum.

hard: ~ness *n* Härte *f*; (*difficulty*) Schwierigkeit *f*; **~ship** *n* Not *f*; **~-up** *a* knapp bei Kasse; **~ware** *n* Eisenwaren *pl*; (*COMPUT*) Hardware *f*; **~ware shop** *n* Eisenwarenhandlung *f*; **~-wearing** *a* strapazierfähig; **~-working** *a* fleißig.

hardy ['hɑ:di] *a* widerstandsfähig.

hare [heə*] *n* Hase *m*; **~-brained** *a* schwachsinnig.

harm [hɑ:m] *n* Schaden *m* // *vt* schaden (+*dat*); **out of ~'s way** in Sicherheit; **~ful** *a* schädlich; **~less** *a* harmlos.

harmonica [hɑ:'mɒnikə] *n* Mundharmonika *f*.

harmonious [hɑ:'məuniəs] *a* harmonisch.

harmonize ['hɑ:mənaiz] *vt* abstimmen // *vi* harmonieren.

harmony ['hɑ:məni] *n* Harmonie *f*.

harness ['hɑ:nis] *n* Geschirr *nt* // *vt* (*horse*) anschirren; (*fig*) nutzbar machen.

harp [hɑ:p] *n* Harfe *f* // *vi*: **to ~ on about sth** auf etw (*dat*) herumreiten.

harpoon [hɑ:'pu:n] *n* Harpune *f*.

harrowing ['hærəuiŋ] *a* nervenaufreibend.

harsh [hɑ:ʃ] *a* (*rough*) rauh; (*severe*) streng; **~ness** *n* Härte *f*.

harvest ['hɑ:vist] *n* Ernte *f* // *vti* ernten.

harvester ['hɑ:vistə*] *n* Mähbinder *m*.

has [hæz] *v see* **have**.

hash [hæʃ] *vt* kleinhacken // *n* (*mess*) Kuddelmuddel *m*; (*meat*) Haschee *nt*.

hashish ['hæʃiʃ] *n* Haschisch *nt*.

hasn't ['hæznt] = **has not**.

hassle ['hæsl] *n* (*col*) Theater *nt*.

haste [heist] *n* Eile *f*; **~n** ['heisn] *vt* beschleunigen // *vi* eilen.

hasty ['heisti] *a* hastig; (*rash*) vorschnell.

hat [hæt] *n* Hut *m*.

hatch [hætʃ] *n* (*NAUT: also:* **~-way**) Luke *f*; (*in house*) Durchreiche *f* // *vi* (*young*) ausschlüpfen // *vt* (*brood*) ausbrüten; (*plot*) aushecken.

hatchback ['hætʃbæk] *n* (*AUT*) (Auto *m* mit) Heckklappe *f*.

hatchet ['hætʃit] *n* Beil *nt*.

hate [heit] *vt* hassen // *n* Haß *m*; **~ful** *a* verhaßt.

hatred ['heitrid] *n* Haß *m*.

haughty ['hɔ:ti] *a* hochnäsig, überheblich.

haul [hɔ:l] *vt* ziehen // *n* (*catch*) Fang *m*; **~age** *n* Spedition *f*; **~ier**, (*US*) **~er** *n* Spediteur *m*.

haunch [hɔ:ntʃ] *n* Lende *f*.

haunt [hɔ:nt] *vt* (*ghost*) spuken in

(+*dat*); (*memory*) verfolgen; (*pub*) häufig besuchen ; **the castle is ~ed** in dem Schloß spukt es.

have, *pt, pp* **had** [hæv, hæd] ◆*aux v* **1** haben; (*esp with vs of motion*) sein; **to ~ arrived/slept** angekommen sein/ geschlafen haben; **to ~ been** gewesen sein; **having eaten** *or* **when he had eaten,** he left nachdem er gegessen hatte, ging er

2 (*in tag questions*): **you've done it, ~n't you?** du hast es doch gemacht, oder nicht?

3 (*in short answers and questions*): **you've made a mistake — no I ~n't/so I ~** du hast einen Fehler gemacht — nein(, hab ich nicht)/ja, stimmt; **we ~n't paid — yes we ~!** wir haben nicht bezahlt — doch; **I've been there before, ~ you?** ich war schon einmal da, du auch?

◆*modal aux v* (*be obliged*): **to ~ (got) to** do sth etw tun müssen; **you ~n't to** tell her du darfst es ihr nicht erzählen

◆*vt* **1** (*possess*) haben; **he has (got) blue eyes** er hat blaue Augen; **I ~ (got) an idea** ich habe eine Idee

2 (*referring to meals etc*): **to ~ breakfast/a cigarette** frühstücken/eine Zigarette rauchen

3 (*receive, obtain etc*) haben; **may I ~ your address?** kann ich Ihre Adresse haben?; **to ~ a baby** ein Kind bekommen

4 (*maintain, allow*): **he will ~ it that he is right** er besteht darauf, daß er recht hat; **I won't ~ it** das lasse ich mir nicht bieten

5: **to ~ sth done** etw machen lassen; **to ~ sb do sth** jdn etw machen lassen; **he soon had them all laughing** er brachte sie alle zum Lachen

6 (*experience, suffer*): **she had her bag stolen** man hat ihr die Tasche gestohlen; **he had his arm broken** er hat sich den Arm gebrochen

7 (+ *noun: take, hold etc*): **to ~ a walk/ rest** spazierengehen/sich ausruhen; **to ~ a meeting/party** eine Besprechung/Party haben

have out *vt*: **to ~ it out with sb** (*settle a problem etc*) etw mit jdm bereden.

haven ['heɪvn] *n* Zufluchtsort *m*.

haven't ['hævnt] = **have not.**

haversack ['hævəsæk] *n* Rucksack *m*.

havoc ['hævək] *n* Verwüstung *f*.

Hawaii [hə'waɪiː] *n* Hawaii *nt*.

hawk [hɔːk] *n* Habicht *m*.

hay [heɪ] *n* Heu *nt*; **~ fever** *n* Heuschnupfen *m*; **~stack** *n* Heuschober *m*.

haywire ['heɪwaɪə*] *a* (*col*) durcheinander.

hazard ['hæzəd] *n* Risiko *nt* // *vt* aufs Spiel setzen; **~ous** *a* gefährlich; **~ (warning) lights** *npl* (*AUT*) Warnblinklicht *nt*.

haze [heɪz] *n* Dunst *m*.

hazelnut ['heɪzlnʌt] *n* Haselnuß *f*.

hazy ['heɪzɪ] *a* (*misty*) dunstig; (*vague*) verschwommen.

he [hiː] *pron* er.

head [hed] *n* Kopf *m*; (*leader*) Leiter *m* // *vt* (an)führen, leiten; (*ball*) köpfen; **~s (or tails)** kopf (oder Zahl); **~ first** mit dem Kopf nach unten; **~ over heels** kopfüber; **~ for** *vt* zugehen auf (+*acc*); **~ache** *n* Kopfschmerzen *pl*; **~dress** *n* Kopfschmuck *m*; **~ing** *n* Überschrift *f*; **~lamp** *n* (*Brit*) Scheinwerfer *m*; **~land** *n* Landspitze *f*; **~light** *n* = **~lamp**; **~line** *n* Schlagzeile *f*; **~long** *ad* kopfüber; **~master** *n* (*of primary school*) Rektor *m*; (*of secondary school*) Direktor *m*; **~mistress** *n* Rektorin *f*; Direktorin *f*; **~ office** *n* Zentrale *f*; **~on** *a* Frontal-; **~phones** *npl* Kopfhörer *pl*; **~quarters (HQ)** *npl* Zentrale *f*; (*MIL*) Hauptquartier *nt*; **~rest** *n* Kopfstütze *f*; **~room** *n* (*of bridges etc*) lichte Höhe *f*; **~scarf** *n* Kopftuch *nt*; **~strong** *a* eigenwillig; **~ waiter** *n* Oberkellner *m*; **~way** *n* Fortschritte *pl*; **~wind** *n* Gegenwind *m*; **~y** *a* berauschend.

heal [hiːl] *vt* heilen // *vi* verheilen.

health [helθ] *n* Gesundheit *f*; **your ~!** prost!; **~ food** *n* Reformkost *f*; **the H~ Service** *n* (*Brit*) das Gesundheitswesen *nt*; **~y** *a* gesund.

heap [hiːp] *n* Haufen *m* // *vt* häufen.

hear [hɪə*] *v* (*pt, pp* **heard** [hɜːd]) *vt* hören; (*listen to*) anhören // *vi* hören; **~ing** *n* Gehör *nt*; (*JUR*) Verhandlung *f*; **~ing aid** *n* Hörapparat *m*; **~say** *n* Hörensagen *nt*.

hearse [hɜːs] *n* Leichenwagen *m*.

heart [hɑːt] *n* Herz *nt*; **~s** *pl* (*CARDS*) Herz *nt*; **by ~** auswendig; **~ attack** *n* Herzanfall *m*; **~beat** *n* Herzschlag *m*; **~breaking** *a* herzzerbrechend; **~broken** *a* (ganz)gebrochen; **~burn** *n* Sodbrennen *nt*; **~ failure** *n* Herzschlag *m*; **~felt** *a* aufrichtig.

hearth [hɑːθ] *n* Herd *m*.

heartily ['hɑːtɪlɪ] *ad* herzlich; (*eat*) herzhaft.

heartless ['hɑːtlɪs] *a* herzlos.

hearty ['hɑːtɪ] *a* kräftig; (*friendly*) freundlich.

heat [hiːt] *n* Hitze *f*; (*of food, water etc*) Wärme *f*; (*SPORT: also:* **qualifying ~**) Ausscheidungsrunde *f* // *vt* (*house*) heizen; (*substance*) heiß machen, erhitzen; **~ up** *vi* warm werden // *vt* aufwärmen; **~ed** *a* erhitzt; (*fig*) hitzig; **~er** *n* (Heiz)ofen *m*.

heath [hiːθ] *n* (*Brit*) Heide *f*.

heathen ['hiːðən] *n* Heide *m* // *a* heidnisch, Heiden-.

heather ['heðə*] *n* Heidekraut *nt*.

heating ['hiːtɪŋ] *n* Heizung *f*.

heatstroke ['hi:tstrəʊk] n Hitzschlag m.
heatwave ['hi:tweɪv] n Hitzewelle f.
heave [hi:v] vt hochheben; (sigh) ausstoßen // vi wogen; (breast) sich heben // n Heben nt.
heaven ['hevn] n Himmel m; ~ly a himmlisch.
heavily ['hevɪlɪ] ad schwer.
heavy ['hevɪ] a schwer; ~ **goods vehicle (HGV)** n Lastkraftwagen (LKW) m; ~**weight** n (SPORT) Schwergewicht nt.
Hebrew ['hi:bru:] a hebräisch // n (LING) Hebräisch nt.
heckle ['hekl] vt unterbrechen.
hectic ['hektɪk] a hektisch.
he'd [hi:d] = **he had; he would**.
hedge [hedʒ] n Hecke f // vt einzäunen // vi (fig) ausweichen; **to ~ one's bets** sich absichern.
hedgehog ['hedʒhɒg] n Igel m.
heed [hi:d] vt (also: **take ~ of**) beachten // n Beachtung f; ~**less** a achtlos.
heel [hi:l] n Ferse f; (of shoe) Absatz m // vt (shoes) mit Absätzen versehen.
hefty ['heftɪ] a (person) stämmig; (portion) reichlich.
heifer ['hefə*] n Färse f.
height [haɪt] n (of person) Größe f; (of object) Höhe f; ~**en** vt erhöhen.
heir [ɛə*] n Erbe m; ~**ess** ['ɛərɪs] n Erbin f; ~**loom** n Erbstück nt.
helicopter ['helɪkɒptə*] n Hubschrauber m.
heliport ['helɪpɔ:t] n Hubschrauberlandeplatz m.
hell [hel] n Hölle f // interj verdammt!
he'll [hi:l] = **he will, he shall**.
hellish ['helɪʃ] a höllisch, verteufelt.
hello [hʌ'ləʊ] interj Hallo.
helm [helm] n Ruder nt, Steuer nt.
helmet ['helmɪt] n Helm m.
helmsman ['helmzmən] n Steuermann m.
help [help] n Hilfe f // vt helfen (+dat); I can't ~ it ich kann nichts dafür; ~ yourself bedienen Sie sich; ~**er** n Helfer m; ~**ful** a hilfreich; ~**ing** n Portion f; ~**less** a hilflos.
hem [hem] n Saum m // vt säumen; ~ **in** vt einengen.
he-man ['hi:mæn] n (col) Macho m.
hemorrhage ['hemərɪdʒ] n (US) = **haemorrhage**.
hemorrhoids ['hemərɔɪdz] npl (US) = **haemorrhoids**.
hen [hen] n Henne f.
hence [hens] ad von jetzt an; (therefore) daher; ~**forth** ad von nun an; (from then on) von da an.
henchman ['hentʃmən] n Gefolgsmann m.
henpecked ['henpekt] a: **to be ~** unter dem Pantoffel stehen; ~ **husband** n Pantoffelheld m.
her [hɜ:*] pron (acc) sie; (dat) ihr //

poss a ihr; see also **me, my**.
herald ['herəld] n (Vor)bote m // vt verkünden.
heraldry ['herəldrɪ] n Wappenkunde f.
herb [hɜ:b] n Kraut nt.
herd [hɜ:d] n Herde f.
here [hɪə*] ad hier; (to this place) hierher; ~**after** ad hernach, künftig // n Jenseits nt; ~**by** ad hiermit.
hereditary [hɪ'redɪtərɪ] a erblich.
heredity [hɪ'redɪtɪ] n Vererbung f.
heresy ['herəsɪ] n Ketzerei f.
heretic ['herətɪk] n Ketzer m.
heritage ['herɪtɪdʒ] n Erbe nt.
hermetically [hɜ:'metɪkəlɪ] ad: ~ **sealed** hermetisch verschlossen.
hermit ['hɜ:mɪt] n Einsiedler m.
hernia ['hɜ:nɪə] n Bruch m.
hero ['hɪərəʊ], pl ~**es** n Held m; ~**ic** [hɪ'rəʊɪk] a heroisch.
heroin ['herəʊɪn] n Heroin nt.
heroine ['herəʊɪn] n Heldin f.
heroism ['herəʊɪzəm] n Heldentum nt.
heron ['herən] n Reiher m.
herring ['herɪŋ] n Hering m.
hers [hɜ:z] pron ihre(r, s); see also **mine**.
herself [hɜ:'self] pron sich (selbst); (emphatic) selbst; see also **oneself**.
he's [hi:z] = **he is, he has**.
hesitant ['hezɪtənt] a zögernd.
hesitate ['hezɪteɪt] vi zögern.
hesitation [hezɪ'teɪʃən] n Zögern nt.
hew [hju:], pt **hewed**, pp **hewn** vt hauen, hacken.
hexagon ['heksəgən] n Sechseck nt; ~**al** [hek'sægənəl] a sechseckig.
heyday ['heɪdeɪ] n Blüte f, Höhepunkt m.
HGV n abbr of **heavy goods vehicle**.
hi [haɪ] interj he, hallo.
hiatus [haɪ'eɪtəs] n (gap) Lücke f.
hibernation [haɪbə'neɪʃən] n Winterschlaf m.
hiccough, hiccup ['hɪkʌp] vi den Schluckauf haben; ~**s** pl Schluckauf m.
hide [haɪd] n (skin) Haut f, Fell nt // v (pt, hid [hɪd], pp hidden ['hɪdn]) vt verstecken // vi sich verstecken; ~**-and-seek** n Versteckspiel nt; ~**away** n Versteck nt.
hideous ['hɪdɪəs] a abscheulich.
hiding ['haɪdɪŋ] n (beating) Tracht f Prügel; **to be in ~** (concealed) sich versteckt halten; ~ **place** n Versteck nt.
hi-fi ['haɪfaɪ] n Hi-Fi nt // a Hi-Fi-.
high [haɪ] a hoch; (wind) stark // ad hoch; ~**boy** a (US: tallboy) hochbeinige Kommode f; ~**brow** a (betont) intellektuell; ~**chair** n Hochstuhl m; ~**er education** n Hochschulbildung f; ~**-handed** a eigenmächtig; ~**-heeled** a hochhackig; ~**jack** vt = **hijack**; ~ **jump** n (SPORT) Hochsprung m; **the H~lands** npl das schottische Hochland;

~light n (fig) Höhepunkt m // vt hervorheben; **~ly** ad höchst; **~ly strung** a überempfindlich; **~ness** n Höhe f; **H~ness** n Hoheit f; **~-pitched** a hoch; **~-rise block** n Hochhaus nt; **~ school** n (US) Oberschule f; **~ season** n (Brit) Hochsaison f; **~ street** n (Brit) Hauptstraße f.

highway ['haɪweɪ] n Landstraße f; **H~ Code** n (Brit) Straßenverkehrsordnung f.

hijack ['haɪdʒæk] vt entführen; **~er** n Entführer(in f) m.

hike [haɪk] vi wandern // n Wanderung f; **~r** n Wanderer m.

hilarious [hɪ'lɛərɪəs] a lustig.

hill [hɪl] n Berg m; **~side** n (Berg)hang m; **~y** a hügelig.

hilt [hɪlt] n Heft nt; **up to the ~** ganz und gar.

him [hɪm] pron (acc) ihn; (dat) ihm; see also **me**.

himself [hɪm'self] pron sich (selbst); (emphatic) selbst; see also **oneself**.

hind [haɪnd] a hinter, Hinter-.

hinder ['hɪndə*] vt (stop) hindern; (delay) behindern.

hindrance ['hɪndrəns] n (delay) Behinderung f; (obstacle) Hindernis nt.

hindsight ['haɪndsaɪt] n: **with ~** im nachhinein.

Hindu ['hɪnduː] n Hindu m.

hinge [hɪndʒ] n Scharnier nt; (on door) Türangel f // vi (fig) abhängen (on von).

hint [hɪnt] n Tip m; (trace) Anflug m // vt: **to ~ that** andeuten, daß // vi andeuten (at acc).

hip [hɪp] n Hüfte f.

hippopotamus [hɪpə'pɒtəməs], pl **~es** or **-mi** [-maɪ] n Nilpferd nt.

hire ['haɪə*] vt (worker) anstellen; (Brit: car) mieten // n Miete f; **for ~** (taxi) frei; **~ purchase (H.P.)** n (Brit) Teilzahlungskauf m.

his [hɪz] poss a sein // poss pron seine(r, s); see also **my, mine**.

hiss [hɪs] vi zischen // n Zischen nt.

historian [hɪs'tɔːrɪən] n Historiker m.

historic [hɪs'tɒrɪk] a historisch.

historical [hɪs'tɒrɪkəl] a historisch, geschichtlich.

history ['hɪstərɪ] n Geschichte f.

hit [hɪt] vt, pt, pp **hit** schlagen; (injure) treffen // n (blow) Schlag m; (success) Erfolg m (MUS) Hit m; **to ~ it off with sb** prima mit jdm auskommen; **~-and-run driver** n jd, der Fahrerflucht begeht.

hitch [hɪtʃ] vt festbinden; (also: **~ up**) hochziehen // n (difficulty) Haken m; **to ~ a lift** trampen.

hitch-hike ['hɪtʃhaɪk] vi trampen, **~r** n Tramper m.

hitherto ['hɪðə'tuː] ad bislang.

hive [haɪv] n Bienenkorb m // vt: **to ~ off**

ausgliedern.

HMS abbr = His(Her) Majesty's Ship.

hoard [hɔːd] n Schatz m // vt horten, hamstern.

hoarding ['hɔːdɪŋ] n Bretterzaun m; (Brit: for advertising) Reklamewand f.

hoarfrost ['hɔː'frɒst] n (Rauh)reif m.

hoarse [hɔːs] a heiser, rauh.

hoax [həʊks] n Streich m.

hob [hɒb] n Kochmulde f.

hobble ['hɒbl] vi humpeln.

hobby ['hɒbɪ] n Hobby nt; **~-horse** n (fig) Steckenpferd nt.

hobo ['həʊbəʊ] n (US) Tippelbruder m.

hock [hɒk] n (wine) weiße(r) Rheinwein m.

hockey ['hɒkɪ] n Hockey nt.

hoe [həʊ] n Hacke f // vt hacken.

hog [hɒg] n Schlachtschwein nt // vt mit Beschlag belegen; **to go the whole ~** aufs Ganze gehen.

hoist [hɔɪst] n Winde f // vt hochziehen.

hold [həʊld] v (pt, pp **held**) vt halten; (contain) enthalten; (be able to contain) fassen; (breath) anhalten; (meeting) abhalten // vi (withstand pressure) aushalten // n (grasp) Halt m; (NAUT) Schiffsraum m; **~ the line!** (TEL) bleiben Sie am Apparat!; **to ~ one's own** sich behaupten; **~ back** vt zurückhalten; **~ down** vt niederhalten; (job) behalten; **~ off** vt (enemy) abwehren; **~ on** vi sich festhalten; (resist) durchhalten; (wait) warten; **~ on to** vt an etw (dat) festhalten; (keep) behalten; **~ out** vt hinhalten // vi aushalten; **~ up** vt (delay) aufhalten; (rob) überfallen; **~all** n (Brit) Reisetasche f; **~er** n Behälter m; **~ing** n (share) (Aktien)anteil m; **~up** n (Brit: in traffic) Stockung f; (robbery) Überfall m.

hole [həʊl] n Loch nt // vt durchlöchern.

holiday ['hɒlədɪ] n (day) Feiertag m; freie(r) Tag m; (vacation) Urlaub m; (SCH) Ferien pl; **~ camp** n Ferienlager nt; **~-maker** n (Brit) Urlauber(in f) m; **~ resort** n Ferienort m.

holiness ['həʊlɪnɪs] n Heiligkeit f.

Holland ['hɒlənd] n Holland nt.

hollow ['hɒləʊ] a hohl; (fig) leer // n Vertiefung f; **~ out** vt aushöhlen.

holly ['hɒlɪ] n Stechpalme f.

holocaust ['hɒləkɔːst] n Inferno nt.

holster ['həʊlstə*] n Pistolenhalfter m.

holy ['həʊlɪ] a heilig; **the H~ Ghost** or **Spirit** n der Heilige Geist.

homage ['hɒmɪdʒ] n Huldigung f; **to pay ~ to** huldigen (+dat).

home [həʊm] n Zuhause nt; (institution) Heim nt, Anstalt f // a einheimisch; (POL) inner // ad heim, nach Hause; **at ~** zu Hause; **~ address** n Heimatadresse f; **~coming** n Heimkehr f; **~ computer** n Heimcomputer m; **~land**

n Heimat (land *nt*) *f*; **~less** *a* obdachlos; **~ly** *a* häuslich; (*US: ugly*) unscheinbar; **~-made** *a* selbstgemacht; **H~ Office** *n* (*Brit*) Innenministerium *nt*; **~ rule** *n* Selbstverwaltung *f*; **H~ Secretary** *n* (*Brit*) Innenminister (in *f*) *m*; **~sick** *a*: **to be ~sick** Heimweh haben; **~ town** *n* Heimatstadt *f*; **~ward** *a* heimwärts; **~work** *n* Hausaufgaben *pl*.

homicide ['hɒmɪsaɪd] *n* (*US*) Totschlag *m*.

homoeopathy [həʊmɪ'ɒpəθɪ] *n* Homöopathie *f*.

homogeneous [hɒmə'dʒiːnɪəs] *a* homogen.

homosexual ['hɒməʊ'seksjʊəl] *a* homosexuell // *n* Homosexuelle(r) *mf*.

honest ['ɒnɪst] *a* ehrlich; **~ly** *ad* ehrlich; **~y** *n* Ehrlichkeit *f*.

honey ['hʌnɪ] *n* Honig *m*; **~comb** *n* Honigwabe *f*; **~moon** *n* Flitterwochen *pl*, Hochzeitsreise *f*; **~suckle** *n* Geißblatt *nt*.

honk [hɒŋk] *vi* hupen.

honorary ['ɒnərərɪ] *a* Ehren-.

honour, (*US*) **honor** ['ɒnə*] *vt* ehren; (*cheque*) einlösen // *n* Ehre *f*; **~able** *a* ehrenwert; (*intention*) ehrenhaft; **~s degree** *n* (*SCH*) akademischer Grad mit Prüfung im Spezialfach.

hood [hʊd] *n* Kapuze *f*; (*Brit AUT*) Verdeck *nt*; (*US AUT*) Kühlerhaube *f*.

hoodlum ['huːdləm] *n* Rowdy *m*; (*member of gang*) Gangster *m*.

hoodwink ['hʊdwɪŋk] *vt* reinlegen.

hoof [huːf], *pl* **hooves** *n* Huf *m*.

hook [hʊk] *n* Haken *m* // *vt* einhaken.

hooligan ['huːlɪgən] *n* Rowdy *m*.

hoop [huːp] *n* Reifen *m*.

hoot [huːt] *vi* (*AUT*) hupen; **~er** *n* (*NAUT*) Dampfpfeife *f*; (*Brit AUT*) (Auto) hupe *f*.

hoover ['huːvə*] ® (*Brit*) *n* Staubsauger *m* // *vt* staubsaugen.

hooves [huːvz] *pl* of **hoof**.

hop [hɒp] *vi* hüpfen, hopsen // *n* (*jump*) Hopser *m*.

hope [həʊp] *vti* hoffen // *n* Hoffnung *f*; **I hope so/not** hoffentlich/hoffentlich nicht; **~ful** *a* hoffnungsvoll; (*promising*) vielversprechend; **~fully** *ad* hoffentlich; **~less** *a* hoffnungslos.

hops [hɒps] *npl* Hopfen *m*.

horizon [hə'raɪzn] *n* Horizont *m*; **~tal** [hɒrɪ'zɒntl] *a* horizontal.

hormone ['hɔːməʊn] *n* Hormon *nt*.

horn [hɔːn] *n* Horn *nt*; (*AUT*) Hupe *f*.

hornet ['hɔːnɪt] *n* Hornisse *f*.

horny ['hɔːnɪ] *a* schwielig; (*US col*) scharf.

horoscope ['hɒrəskəʊp] *n* Horoskop *nt*.

horrible ['hɒrɪbl] *a* fürchterlich.

horrid ['hɒrɪd] *a* scheußlich.

horrify ['hɒrɪfaɪ] *vt* entsetzen.

horror ['hɒrə*] *n* Schrecken *m*; **~ film**

n Horrorfilm *m*.

hors d'oeuvre [ɔː'dɜːvr] *n* Vorspeise *f*.

horse [hɔːs] *n* Pferd *nt*; **on ~back** beritten; **~ chestnut** *n* Roßkastanie *f*; **~man/woman** *n* Reiter *m*/Reiterin *f*; **~power (h.p.)** *n* Pferdestärke *f*, PS *nt*; **~-racing** *n* Pferderennen *nt*; **~radish** *n* Meerrettich *m*; **~shoe** *n* Hufeisen *nt*.

horticulture ['hɔːtɪkʌltʃə*] *n* Gartenbau *m*.

hose(pipe) ['həʊz(paɪp)] *n* Schlauch *m*.

hosiery ['həʊzɪərɪ] *n* Strumpfwaren *pl*.

hospitable [hɒs'pɪtəbl] *a* gastfreundlich.

hospital ['hɒspɪtl] *n* Krankenhaus *nt*.

hospitality [hɒspɪ'tælɪtɪ] *n* Gastfreundschaft *f*.

host [həʊst] *n* Gastgeber *m*; (*innkeeper*) (Gast) wirt *m*; (*large number*) Heerschar *f*; (*ECCL*) Hostie *f*.

hostage ['hɒstɪdʒ] *n* Geisel *f*.

hostel ['hɒstəl] *n* Herberge *f*; (*youth*) **~** *n* Jugendherberge *f*.

hostess ['həʊstes] *n* Gastgeberin *f*.

hostile ['hɒstaɪl] *a* feindlich.

hostility [hɒs'tɪlɪtɪ] *n* Feindschaft *f*; **hostilities** *pl* Feindseligkeiten *pl*.

hot [hɒt] *a* heiß; (*drink, food, water*) warm; (*spiced*) scharf; **I'm ~** mir ist heiß; **~bed** *n* (*fig*) Nährboden *m*; **~ dog** *n* heiße(s) Würstchen *nt*.

hotel [həʊ'tel] *n* Hotel *nt*; **~ier** *n* Hotelier *m*.

hot: **~headed** *a* hitzig; **~house** *n* Treibhaus *nt*; **~ line** *n* (*POL*) heiße(r) Draht *m*; **~ly** *ad* (*argue*) hitzig; **~plate** *n* Kochplatte *f*; **~-water bottle** *n* Wärmflasche *f*.

hound [haʊnd] *n* Jagdhund *m* // *vt* hetzen.

hour ['aʊə*] *n* Stunde *f*; (*time of day*) (Tages) zeit *f*; **~ly** *a, ad* stündlich.

house [haʊs] *n* Haus *nt* // *vt* [haʊz] unterbringen; **on the ~** auf Kosten des Hauses; **~boat** *n* Hausboot *nt*; **~breaking** *n* Einbruch *m*; **~coat** *n* Morgenmantel *m*; **~hold** *n* Haushalt *m*; **~keeper** *n* Haushälterin *f*; **~keeping** *n* Haushaltung *f*; **~warming party** *n* Einweihungsparty *f*; **~wife** *n* Hausfrau *f*; **~work** *n* Hausarbeit *f*.

housing ['haʊzɪŋ] *n* (*act*) Unterbringung *f*; (*houses*) Wohnungen *pl*; (*POL*) Wohnungsbau *m*; (*covering*) Gehäuse *nt*; **~ development,** (*Brit*) **~ estate** *n* (Wohn) siedlung *f*.

hovel ['hɒvəl] *n* elende Hütte *f*.

hover ['hɒvə*] *vi* (*bird*) schweben; (*person*) herumstehen; **~craft** *n* Luftkissenfahrzeug *nt*.

how [haʊ] *ad* wie; **~ are you?** wie geht es Ihnen?; **~ much milk?** wieviel Milch?; **~ many people?** wie viele Leute?

however [haʊ'evə*] *ad* (*but*) (je) doch, aber; **~ you phrase it** wie Sie es auch ausdrücken.

howl [haʊl] n Heulen nt // vi heulen.

h.p., H.P. abbr of **hire purchase; horse power.**

H.Q. abbr of **headquarters.**

hub [hʌb] n Radnabe f.

hubbub ['hʌbʌb] n Tumult m.

hubcap ['hʌbkæp] n Radkappe f.

huddle ['hʌdl] vi: to ~ **together** sich zusammendrängen.

hue [hju:] n Färbung f; ~ **and cry** n Zetergeschrei m.

huff [hʌf] n: to go into a ~ einschnappen.

hug [hʌg] vt umarmen // n Umarmung f.

huge [hju:dʒ] a groß, riesig.

hulk [hʌlk] n (ship) abgetakelte(s) Schiff nt; (person) Koloß m.

hull [hʌl] n Schiffsrumpf m.

hullo [hʌ'ləʊ] see **hello.**

hum [hʌm] vti summen.

human ['hju:mən] a menschlich // n (also: ~ **being**) Mensch m.

humane [hju:'meɪn] a human.

humanity [hju:'mænɪtɪ] n Menschheit f; (kindliness) Menschlichkeit f.

humble ['hʌmbl] a demütig; (modest) bescheiden // vt demütigen.

humbug ['hʌmbʌg] n Humbug m; (Brit: sweet) Pfefferminzbonbon m.

humdrum ['hʌmdrʌm] a stumpfsinnig.

humid ['hju:mɪd] a feucht; ~**ity** [hju:'mɪdɪtɪ] n Feuchtigkeit f.

humiliate [hju:'mɪlɪeɪt] vt demütigen.

humiliation [hju:mɪlɪ'eɪʃən] n Demütigung f.

humility [hju:'mɪlɪtɪ] n Demut f.

humorous ['hju:mərəs] a humorvoll.

humour, (US) humor ['hju:mə*] n (fun) Humor m; (mood) Stimmung f // vt bei Stimmung halten.

hump [hʌmp] n Buckel m.

hunch [hʌntʃ] n (Vor)ahnung f; ~**back** n Bucklige(r) mf; ~**ed** a gekrümmt.

hundred ['hʌndrɪd] num hundert; ~**weight** n Zentner m (Brit) = 50.8 kg; (US) = 45.3 kg.

hung [hʌŋ] pt, pp of **hang.**

Hungarian [hʌŋ'gɛərɪən] a ungarisch // n Ungar(in f) m; (LING) Ungarisch nt.

Hungary ['hʌŋgərɪ] n Ungarn nt.

hunger ['hʌŋgə*] n Hunger m // vi hungern; ~ **strike** n Hungerstreik m.

hungry ['hʌŋgrɪ] a hungrig; **to be** ~ Hunger haben.

hunk [hʌŋk] n (of bread) Stück nt.

hunt [hʌnt] vt jagen; (search) suchen (for acc) // vi jagen // n Jagd f; ~**er** n Jäger m; ~**ing** n Jagd f.

hurdle ['hɜ:dl] n (lit, fig) Hürde f.

hurl [hɜ:l] vt schleudern.

hurrah [hʊ'rɑ:], **hurray** [hʊ'reɪ] n Hurra nt.

hurricane ['hʌrɪkən] n Orkan m.

hurried ['hʌrɪd] a eilig; (hasty) übereilt; ~**ly** ad übereilt, hastig.

hurry ['hʌrɪ] n Eile f // vi sich beeilen // vt (an)treiben; (job) übereilen; **to be in** a ~ es eilig haben; ~ **up** vi sich beeilen // vt (person) zur Eile antreiben; (work) vorantreiben.

hurt [hɜ:t], pt, pp **hurt** vt weh tun (+dat); (injure, fig) verletzen // vi weh tun; ~**ful** a schädlich; (remark) verletzend.

hurtle ['hɜ:tl] vi sausen.

husband ['hʌzbənd] n (Ehe)mann m.

hush [hʌʃ] n Stille f // vt zur Ruhe bringen // interj pst, still.

husk [hʌsk] n Spelze f.

husky ['hʌskɪ] a (voice) rauh; (figure) stämmig // n Eskimohund m.

hustle ['hʌsl] vt (push) stoßen; (hurry) antreiben // n: ~ **and bustle** Geschäftigkeit f.

hut [hʌt] n Hütte f.

hutch [hʌtʃ] n (Kaninchen)stall m.

hyacinth ['haɪəsɪnθ] n Hyazinthe f.

hybrid ['haɪbrɪd] n Kreuzung f // a Misch-.

hydrant ['haɪdrənt] n (also: **fire** ~) Hydrant m.

hydraulic [haɪ'drɒlɪk] a hydraulisch.

hydrofoil ['haɪdrəʊfɔɪl] n Tragflügelboot nt.

hydrogen ['haɪdrɪdʒən] n Wasserstoff m.

hygiene ['haɪdʒi:n] n Hygiene f.

hygienic [haɪ'dʒi:nɪk] a hygienisch.

hymn [hɪm] n Kirchenlied nt.

hype [haɪp] n (col) Publicity f.

hypermarket ['haɪpə'mɑ:kɪt] n (Brit) Hypermarket m.

hyphen ['haɪfən] n Bindestrich m.

hypnosis [hɪp'nəʊsɪs] n Hypnose f.

hypnotic [hɪp'nɒtɪk] a hypnotisierend.

hypnotize ['hɪpnətaɪz] vt hypnotisieren.

hypocrisy [hɪ'pɒkrɪsɪ] n Heuchelei f.

hypocrite ['hɪpəkrɪt] n Heuchler m.

hypocritical [hɪpə'krɪtɪkəl] a scheinheilig, heuchlerisch.

hypothermia ['haɪpəʊ'θɜ:mɪə] n Unterkühlung f.

hypothetic(al) [haɪpəʊ'θetɪk(əl)] a hypothetisch.

hysterical [hɪs'terɪkəl] a hysterisch.

hysterics [hɪs'terɪks] npl hysterische(r) Anfall m.

I

I [aɪ] pron ich.

ice [aɪs] n Eis nt // vt (COOK) mit Zuckerguß überziehen // vi (also: ~ **up**) vereisen; ~ **axe** n Eispickel m; ~**berg** n Eisberg m; ~**box** n (US) Kühlschrank m; ~ **cream** n Eis nt; ~ **cube** n Eiswürfel m; ~ **hockey** n Eishockey nt.

Iceland ['aɪslənd] n Island nt.

ice: ~ **lolly** n (Brit) Eis nt am Stiel; ~

rink n (Kunst)eisbahn f; ~ **skating** n Schlittschuhlaufen nt.

icicle ['aɪsɪkl] n Eiszapfen m.

icing ['aɪsɪŋ] n (on cake) Zuckerguß m; (on window) Vereisung f; ~ **sugar** n (Brit) Puderzucker m.

icon ['aɪkɒn] n Ikone f.

icy ['aɪsɪ] a (slippery) vereist; (cold) eisig.

I'd [aɪd] = I would; I had.

idea [aɪ'dɪə] n Idee f.

ideal [aɪ'dɪəl] n Ideal nt // a ideal; ~**ist** n Idealist m.

identical [aɪ'dentɪkəl] a identisch; (twins) eineiig.

identification [aɪdentɪfɪ'keɪʃən] n Identifizierung f; **means of** ~ Ausweispapiere pl.

identify [aɪ'dentɪfaɪ] vt identifizieren; (regard as the same) gleichsetzen.

identikit picture [aɪ'dentɪkɪt-] n Phantombild nt.

identity [aɪ'dentɪtɪ] n Identität f; ~ **card** n Personalausweis m.

ideology [aɪdɪ'ɒlədʒɪ] n Ideologie f.

idiom ['ɪdɪəm] n (expression) Redewendung f; (dialect) Idiom nt; ~**atic** [-'mætɪk] a idiomatisch.

idiosyncrasy [ɪdɪə'sɪŋkrəsɪ] n Eigenart f.

idiot ['ɪdɪət] n Idiot(in f) m; ~**ic** [ɪdɪ'ɒtɪk] a idiotisch.

idle ['aɪdl] a (doing nothing) untätig; (lazy) faul; (useless) nutzlos; (machine) still(stehend); (threat, talk) leer // vi (machine) leerlaufen // vt: **to** ~ **away the time** die Zeit vertrödeln; ~**ness** n Müßiggang m; Faulheit f.

idol ['aɪdl] n Idol nt; ~**ize** vt vergöttern.

i.e. abbr (= that is) d.h.

if [ɪf] cj **1** wenn; (in case also) falls; ~ **I were you** wenn ich Sie wäre
2 (although): (even) ~ (selbst or auch) wenn
3 (whether) ob
4: ~ **so/not** wenn ja/nicht; ~ **only** ... wenn ... doch nur ...; ~ **only I could** wenn ich doch nur könnte; see also **as**.

ignite [ɪg'naɪt] vt (an)zünden // vi sich entzünden.

ignition [ɪg'nɪʃən] n Zündung f; **to switch on/off the** ~ den Motor anlassen/abstellen; ~ **key** n (AUT) Zündschlüssel m.

ignorance ['ɪgnərəns] n Unwissenheit f.

ignorant ['ɪgnərənt] a unwissend; **to be** ~ **of** nicht wissen.

ignore [ɪg'nɔː*] vt ignorieren.

I'll [aɪl] = I will, I shall.

ill [ɪl] a krank // n Übel nt // ad schlecht; **to take** or **be taken** ~ krank werden; ~-**advised** a unklug; ~-**at-ease** a unbehaglich.

illegal a [ɪ'liːgəl] illegal.

illegible [ɪ'ledʒəbl] a unleserlich.

illegitimate [ɪlɪ'dʒɪtɪmət] a unehelich.

ill: ~-**fated** a unselig; ~ **feeling** n Verstimmung f.

illicit [ɪ'lɪsɪt] a verboten.

illiterate [ɪ'lɪtərət] a ungebildet.

ill-mannered ['ɪl'mænəd] a ungehobelt.

illness ['ɪlnəs] n Krankheit f.

illogical [ɪ'lɒdʒɪkəl] a unlogisch.

ill-treat ['ɪl'triːt] vt mißhandeln.

illuminate [ɪ'luːmɪneɪt] vt beleuchten.

illumination [ɪluːmɪ'neɪʃən] n Beleuchtung f; ~**s** pl festliche Beleuchtung f.

illusion [ɪ'luːʒən] n Illusion f; **to be under the** ~ **that** ... sich (dat) einbilden, daß ...

illusory [ɪ'luːsərɪ] a trügerisch.

illustrate ['ɪləstreɪt] vt (book) illustrieren; (explain) veranschaulichen.

illustration [ɪləs'treɪʃən] n Illustration f; (explanation) Veranschaulichung f.

illustrious [ɪ'lʌstrɪəs] a berühmt.

ill will ['ɪl'wɪl] n Groll m.

I'm [aɪm] = I am.

image ['ɪmɪdʒ] n Bild nt; (public ~) Image nt; ~**ry** n Symbolik f.

imaginary [ɪ'mædʒɪnərɪ] a eingebildet; (world) Phantasie-.

imagination [ɪmædʒɪ'neɪʃən] n Einbildung f; (creative) Phantasie f.

imaginative [ɪ'mædʒɪnətɪv] a phantasiereich, einfallsreich.

imagine [ɪ'mædʒɪn] vt sich vorstellen; (wrongly) sich einbilden.

imbalance [ɪm'bæləns] n Unausgeglichenheit f.

imbecile ['ɪmbəsiːl] n Schwachsinnige(r) mf.

imbue [ɪm'bjuː] vt: **to** ~ **sth with etw** erfüllen mit.

imitate ['ɪmɪteɪt] vt imitieren.

imitation [ɪmɪ'teɪʃən] n Imitation f.

immaculate [ɪ'mækjʊlɪt] a makellos; (dress) tadellos; (ECCL) unbefleckt.

immaterial [ɪmə'tɪərɪəl] a unwesentlich; **it is** ~ **whether** ... es ist unwichtig, ob ...

immature [ɪmə'tjʊə*] a unreif.

immediate [ɪ'miːdɪət] a (instant) sofortig; (near) unmittelbar; (relatives) nächste(r, s); (needs) dringlich; ~**ly** ad sofort; ~**ly next to** direkt neben.

immense [ɪ'mens] a unermeßlich.

immerse [ɪ'mɜːs] vt eintauchen; **to be** ~**d in** (fig) vertieft sein in (+acc).

immersion heater [ɪ'mɜːʃənhiːtə*] n (Brit) Boiler m.

immigrant ['ɪmɪgrənt] n Einwanderer m.

immigrate ['ɪmɪgreɪt] vi einwandern.

immigration [ɪmɪ'greɪʃən] n Einwanderung f.

imminent ['ɪmɪnənt] a bevorstehend.

immobile [ɪ'məʊbaɪl] a unbeweglich.

immobilize [ɪ'məʊbɪlaɪz] vt lähmen.

immoral [ɪ'mɒrəl] a unmoralisch; ~**ity** [ɪmə'rælɪtɪ] n Unsittlichkeit f.

immortal [ɪ'mɔ:tl] a unsterblich; ~ize vt unsterblich machen.

immune [ɪ'mju:n] a (secure) sicher (from vor +dat); (MED) immun.

immunity [ɪ'mju:nɪtɪ] n (MED, JUR) Immunität f; (fig) Freiheit f.

immunize ['ɪmjʊnaɪz] vt immunisieren.

imp [ɪmp] n Kobold m.

impact ['ɪmpækt] n (lit) Aufprall m; (fig) Wirkung f.

impair [ɪm'pɛə*] vt beeinträchtigen.

impale [ɪm'peɪl] vt aufspießen.

impart [ɪm'pɑ:t] vt mitteilen; (knowledge) vermitteln; (exude) abgeben.

impartial [ɪm'pɑ:ʃəl] a unparteiisch.

impassable [ɪm'pɑ:səbl] a unpassierbar.

impasse [æm'pɑ:s] n Sackgasse f.

impassive [ɪm'pæsɪv] a gelassen.

impatience [ɪm'peɪʃəns] n Ungeduld f.

impatient a [ɪm'peɪʃənt] ungeduldig.

impeccable [ɪm'pekəbl] a tadellos.

impede [ɪm'pi:d] vt (be)hindern.

impediment [ɪm'pedɪmənt] n Hindernis nt; (in speech) Sprachfehler m.

impending [ɪm'pendɪŋ] a bevorstehend.

impenetrable [ɪm'penɪtrəbl] a (lit, fig) undurchdringlich.

imperative [ɪm'perətɪv] a (necessary) unbedingt erforderlich // n (GRAM) Imperativ m, Befehlsform f.

imperceptible [ɪmpə'septəbl] a nicht wahrnehmbar.

imperfect [ɪm'pɔ:fɪkt] a (faulty) fehlerhaft; ~ion [-'fekʃən] n Unvollkommenheit f; (fault) Fehler m.

imperial [ɪm'pɪərɪəl] a kaiserlich; ~ism n Imperialismus m.

impersonal [ɪm'pɔ:snl] a unpersönlich.

impersonate [ɪm'pɔ:səneɪt] vt sich ausgeben als; (for amusement) imitieren.

impertinent [ɪm'pɔ:tɪnənt] a unverschämt, frech.

impervious [ɪm'pɔ:vɪəs] a (fig) unempfänglich (to für).

impetuous [ɪm'petjʊəs] a ungestüm.

impetus ['ɪmpɪtəs] n Triebkraft f; (fig) Auftrieb m.

impinge [ɪm'pɪndʒ]: ~ on vt beeinträchtigen.

implacable [ɪm'plækəbl] a unerbittlich.

implement ['ɪmplɪmənt] n Werkzeug nt // ['ɪmplɪment] vt ausführen.

implicate ['ɪmplɪkeɪt] vt verwickeln.

implication [ɪmplɪ'keɪʃən] n (effect) Auswirkung f; (in crime) Verwicklung f.

implicit [ɪm'plɪsɪt] a (suggested) unausgesprochen; (utter) vorbehaltlos.

implore [ɪm'plɔ:*] vt anflehen.

imply [ɪm'plaɪ] vt (hint) andeuten; (be evidence for) schließen lassen auf (+acc).

impolite [ɪmpə'laɪt] a unhöflich.

import [ɪm'pɔ:t] vt einführen // n

['ɪmpɔ:t] Einfuhr f; (meaning) Bedeutung f.

importance [ɪm'pɔ:təns] n Bedeutung f.

important [ɪm'pɔ:tənt] a wichtig; it's not ~ es ist unwichtig.

importer [ɪm'pɔ:tə*] n Importeur m.

impose [ɪm'pəuz] vti auferlegen (on dat); (penalty, sanctions) verhängen (on gegen); to ~ (o.s.) on sb sich jdm aufdrängen.

imposing [ɪm'pəuzɪŋ] a eindrucksvoll.

imposition [ɪmpə'zɪʃən] n (of burden, fine) Auferlegung f; (SCH) Strafarbeit f; to be an ~ (on person) eine Zumutung sein.

impossible a [ɪm'pɒsəbl] unmöglich.

impostor [ɪm'pɒstə*] n Hochstapler m.

impotence ['ɪmpətəns] Impotenz f.

impotent ['ɪmpətənt] a machtlos; (sexually) impotent.

impound [ɪm'paund] vt beschlagnahmen.

impoverished [ɪm'pɒvərɪʃt] a verarmt.

impracticable [ɪm'præktɪkəbl] a undurchführbar.

impractical [ɪm'præktɪkəl] a unpraktisch.

imprecise [ɪmprə'saɪs] a ungenau.

impregnable [ɪm'pregnəbl] a (castle) uneinnehmbar.

impregnate ['ɪmpregneɪt] vt (saturate) sättigen; (fertilize) befruchten.

impress [ɪm'pres] vt (influence) beeindrucken; (imprint) (auf)drücken; to ~ sth on sb jdm etw einschärfen.

impression [ɪm'preʃən] n Eindruck m; (on wax, footprint) Abdruck m; (of book) Auflage f; (take-off) Nachahmung f; I was under the ~ ich hatte den Eindruck; ~able a leicht zu beeindrucken; ~ist n Impressionist m.

impressive [ɪm'presɪv] a eindrucksvoll.

imprint ['ɪmprɪnt] n Abdruck m.

imprison [ɪm'prɪzn] vt ins Gefängnis schicken; ~ment n Inhaftierung f.

improbable [ɪm'prɒbəbl] a unwahrscheinlich.

impromptu [ɪm'prɒmptju:] a, ad aus dem Stegreif, improvisiert.

improper [ɪm'prɒpə*] a (indecent) unanständig; (unsuitable) unpassend.

improve [ɪm'pru:v] vt verbessern // vi besser werden; ~ment n (Ver)besserung f.

improvise ['ɪmprəvaɪz] vti improvisieren.

imprudent [ɪm'pru:dənt] a unklug.

impudent ['ɪmpjʊdənt] a unverschämt.

impulse ['ɪmpʌls] n Impuls m; to act on ~ spontan handeln.

impulsive [ɪm'pʌlsɪv] a impulsiv.

impunity [ɪm'pju:nɪtɪ] n Straflosigkeit f.

impure [ɪm'pjʊə*] a (dirty) verunreinigt; (bad) unsauber.

impurity [ɪm'pjʊərɪtɪ] n Unreinheit f;

(TECH) Verunreinigung *f*.

in [ɪn] ◆*prep* **1** *(indicating place, position)* in (+ *dat*); *(with motion)* in (+ *acc*); ~ **here/there** hier/dort; ~ **London** in London; ~ **the United States** in den Vereinigten Staaten

2 *(indicating time: during)* in (+ *dat*); ~ **summer** im Sommer; ~ **1988** im Jahre) 1988; ~ **the afternoon** nachmittags, am Nachmittag

3 *(indicating time: in the space of)* innerhalb von; **I'll see you** ~ **2 weeks** *or* ~ **2 weeks' time** ich sehe Sie in zwei Wochen

4 *(indicating manner, circumstances, state etc)* in (+ *dat*); ~ **the sun/rain** in der Sonne/im Regen; ~ **English/French** auf Englisch/Französisch; ~ **a loud/soft voice** mit lauter/leiser Stimme

5 *(with ratios, numbers)*: **1** ~ **10** jeder zehnte; **20 pence** ~ **the pound** 20 Pence pro Pfund; **they lined up** ~ **twos** sie stellten sich in Zweierreihe auf

6 *(referring to people, works)*: **the disease is common** ~ **children** die Krankheit ist bei Kindern häufig; ~ **Dickens** bei Dickens; **we have a loyal friend** ~ **him** er ist uns ein treuer Freund

7 *(indicating profession etc)*: **to be** ~ **teaching/the army** Lehrer(in)/beim Militär sein; **to be** ~ **publishing** im Verlagswesen arbeiten

8 *(with present participle)*: ~ **saying this, I ...** wenn ich das sage, ... ich; ~ **accepting this view, he ...** weil er diese Meinung akzeptierte, ... er

◆*ad*: **to be** ~ *(person: at home, work)* dasein; *(train, ship, plane)* angekommen sein; *(in fashion)* in sein; **to ask sb** ~ jdn hereinbitten; **to run/limp** *etc* ~ hereingerannt/-gehumpelt *etc* kommen

◆*n*: **the** ~**s and outs** *(of proposal, situation etc)* die Feinheiten.

in., ins *abbr of* **inch(es).**

inability [ɪnə'bɪlɪtɪ] *n* Unfähigkeit *f*.

inaccessible [ɪnæk'sesəbl] *a* unzugänglich.

inaccurate [ɪn'ækjʊrɪt] *a* ungenau; *(wrong)* unrichtig.

inactivity [ɪnæk'tɪvɪtɪ] *n* Untätigkeit *f*.

inadequate [ɪn'ædɪkwət] *a* unzulänglich.

inadvertently [ɪnəd'vɜːtəntlɪ] *ad* unabsichtlich.

inadvisable [ɪnəd'vaɪzəbl] *a* nicht ratsam.

inane [ɪ'neɪn] *a* dumm, albern.

inanimate [ɪn'ænɪmət] *a* leblos.

inappropriate [ɪnə'prəʊprɪət] *a (clothing)* ungeeignet; *(remark)* unangebracht.

inarticulate [ɪnɑː'tɪkjʊlət] *a* unklar.

inasmuch as [ɪnəz'mʌtʃəz] *ad* da; *(in so far as)* soweit.

inaudible [ɪn'ɔːdəbl] *a* unhörbar.

inaugural [ɪ'nɔːgjʊrəl] *a* Eröffnungs-.

inaugurate [ɪ'nɔːgjʊreɪt] *vt (open)* einweihen; *(admit to office)* (feierlich) einführen.

inauguration [ɪnɔːgjʊ'reɪʃən] *n* Eröffnung *f*; (feierliche) Amtseinführung *f*.

in-between [ɪnbɪ'twiːn] *a* Zwischen-.

inborn ['ɪn'bɔːn] *a* angeboren.

inbred ['ɪn'bred] *a* angeboren.

Inc. *abbr (US) of* **incorporated.**

incalculable [ɪn'kælkjʊləbl] *a (consequences)* unabsehbar.

incapable [ɪn'keɪpəbl] *a* unfähig *(of doing sth* etw zu tun).

incapacitate [ɪnkə'pæsɪteɪt] *vt* untauglich machen.

incapacity [ɪnkə'pæsɪtɪ] *n* Unfähigkeit *f*.

incarcerate [ɪn'kɑːsəreɪt] *vt* einkerkern.

incarnation [ɪnkɑː'neɪʃən] *n (ECCL)* Menschwerdung *f*; *(fig)* Inbegriff *m*.

incendiary [ɪn'sendɪərɪ] *a* Brand- .

incense ['ɪnsens] *n* Weihrauch *m* // *vt* [ɪn'sens] erzürnen.

incentive [ɪn'sentɪv] *n* Anreiz *m*.

incessant *a*, ~**ly** *ad* [ɪn'sesnt, -lɪ] unaufhörlich.

incest ['ɪnsest] *n* Inzest *m*.

inch [ɪntʃ] *n* Zoll *m*; **to be within an** ~ **of** kurz davor sein; **he didn't give an** ~ er gab keinen Zentimeter nach; **to** ~ **forward** *vi* sich Stückchen für Stückchen vorwärts bewegen.

incidence ['ɪnsɪdəns] *n* Auftreten *nt*; *(of crime)* Quote *f*.

incident ['ɪnsɪdənt] *n* Vorfall *m*; *(disturbance)* Zwischenfall *m*.

incidental [ɪnsɪ'dentl] *a (music)* Begleit-; *(unimportant)* nebensächlich; *(remark)* beiläufig; ~**ly** [-'dentəlɪ] *ad* übrigens.

incinerator [ɪn'sɪnəreɪtə*] *n* Verbrennungsofen *m*.

incipient [ɪn'sɪpɪənt] *a* beginnend.

incision [ɪn'sɪʒən] *n* Einschnitt *m*.

incisive [ɪn'saɪsɪv] *a (style)* treffend; *(person)* scharfsinnig.

incite [ɪn'saɪt] *vt* anstacheln.

inclination [ɪnklɪ'neɪʃən] *n* Neigung *f*.

incline ['ɪnklaɪn] *n* Abhang *m* // [ɪn'klaɪn] *vt* neigen; *(fig)* veranlassen // *vi* sich neigen; **to be** ~**d to do sth** dazu neigen, etw zu tun.

include [ɪn'kluːd] *vt* einschließen; *(on list, in group)* aufnehmen.

including [ɪn'kluːdɪŋ] *prep*: ~ **X X** inbegriffen.

inclusion [ɪn'kluːʒən] *n* Aufnahme *f*.

inclusive [ɪn'kluːsɪv] *a* inklusive; *(COMM)* inklusive; ~ **of** einschließlich (+ *gen*).

incoherent [ɪnkəʊ'hɪərənt] *a* zusammenhanglos.

income [ɪn'kʌm] *n* Einkommen *nt*; *(from business)* Einkünfte *pl*; ~ **tax** Lohnsteuer *f*; *(of self-employed)* Einkommenssteuer f.

incoming ['ınkʌmıŋ] a: ~ **flight** eintreffende Maschine f.

incomparable [ın'kɒmpərəbl] a unvergleichlich.

incompatible [ınkəm'pætəbl] a unvereinbar; (people) unverträglich.

incompetence [ın'kɒmpıtəns] n Unfähigkeit f.

incompetent [ın'kɒmpıtənt] a unfähig.

incomplete [ınkəm'pli:t] a unvollständig.

incomprehensible [ınkɒmprı'hensəbl] a unverständlich.

inconceivable [ınkən'si:vəbl] a unvorstellbar.

incongruous [ın'kɒŋgruəs] a seltsam; (remark) unangebracht.

inconsiderate [ınkən'sıdərət] a rücksichtslos.

inconsistency [ınkən'sıstənsı] n Widersprüchlichkeit f; (state) Unbeständigkeit f.

inconsistent [ınkən'sıstənt] a (action, speech) widersprüchlich; (person, work) unbeständig; ~ **with** nicht übereinstimmend mit.

inconspicuous [ınkən'spıkjuəs] a unauffällig.

incontinent [ın'kɒntınənt] a (MED) nicht fähig, Stuhl und Harn zurückzuhalten.

inconvenience [ınkən'vi:nıəns] n Unbequemlichkeit f; (trouble to others) Unannehmlichkeiten pl.

inconvenient [ınkən'vi:nıənt] a ungelegen; (journey) unbequem.

incorporate [ın'kɔ:pəreıt] vt (include) aufnehmen; (contain) enthalten.

incorporated [ın'kɔ:pəreıtıd] a: ~**d company** (US: abbr Inc.) eingetragene Aktiengesellschaft f.

incorrect [ınkə'rekt] a unrichtig.

incorrigible [ın'kɒrıdʒəbl] a unverbesserlich.

incorruptible [ınkə'rʌptəbl] a unzerstörbar; (person) unbestechlich.

increase ['ınkri:s] n Zunahme f; (pay ~) Gehaltserhöhung f; (in size) Vergrößerung f // vt [ın'kri:s] erhöhen; (wealth, rage) vermehren; (business) erweitern // vi zunehmen; (prices) steigen; (in size) größer werden; (in number) sich vermehren.

increasing [ın'kri:sıŋ] a (number) steigend.

increasingly [ın'kri:sıŋlı] ad zunehmend.

incredible [ın'kredəbl] a unglaublich.

incredulous [ın'kredjuləs] a ungläubig.

increment ['ınkrımənt] n Zulage f.

incriminate [ın'krımıneıt] vt belasten.

incubation [ınkju'beıʃən] n Ausbrüten nt.

incubator ['ınkjubeıtə*] n Brutkasten

m.

incumbent [ın'kʌmbənt] n Amtsinhaber(in f) m // a: **it is** ~ **on him to ...** es obliegt ihm, ...

incur [ın'kɜ:*] vt sich zuziehen; (debts) machen.

incurable [ın'kjuərəbl] a unheilbar; (fig) unverbesserlich.

incursion [ın'kɜ:ʃən] n Einfall m.

indebted [ın'detıd] a (obliged) verpflichtet (to sb jdm).

indecent [ın'di:snt] a unanständig; ~ **assault** n (Brit) Notzucht f; ~ **exposure** n Exhibitionismus m.

indecisive [ındı'saısıv] a (battle) nicht entscheidend; (person) unentschlossen.

indeed [ın'di:d] ad tatsächlich, in der Tat; yes ~! Allerdings!

indefinite [ın'defınıt] a unbestimmt; ~**ly** ad auf unbestimmte Zeit; (wait) unbegrenzt lange.

indelible [ın'deləbl] a unauslöschlich.

indemnify [ın'demnıfaı] vt entschädigen; (safeguard) versichern.

indemnity [ın'demnıtı] n (insurance) Versicherung f; (compensation) Schadenersatz m.

independence [ındı'pendəns] n Unabhängigkeit f.

independent [ındı'pendənt] a unabhängig.

indestructible [ˌındıs'trʌktəbl] a unzerstörbar.

indeterminate [ˌındı'tɜ:mınıt] a unbestimmt.

index ['ındeks] n Index m; ~ **card** n Karteikarte f; ~ **finger** n Zeigefinger m; ~**-linked**, (US) ~**ed** a (salaries) der Inflationsrate (dat) angeglichen; (pensions) dynamisch.

India ['ındıə] n Indien nt; ~**n** a indisch // n Inder(in f) m; **Red** ~**n** Indianer(in f) m; **the** ~**n Ocean** n der Indische Ozean.

indicate ['ındıkeıt] vt anzeigen; (hint) andeuten.

indication [ındı'keıʃən] n Anzeichen nt; (information) Angabe f.

indicative [ın'dıkətıv] a: ~ **of** bezeichnend für // n (GRAM) Indikativ m.

indicator ['ındıkeıtə*] n (sign) (An)zeichen nt; (AUT) Richtungsanzeiger m.

indices ['ındısi:z] pl of **index**.

indict [ın'daıt] vt anklagen; ~**ment** n Anklage f.

indifference [ın'dıfrəns] n Gleichgültigkeit f; Unwichtigkeit f.

indifferent [ın'dıfrənt] a gleichgültig; (mediocre) mäßig.

indigenous [ın'dıdʒınəs] a einheimisch.

indigestion [ındı'dʒestʃən] n Verdauungsstörung f.

indignant [ın'dıgnənt] a: **to be** ~ **about**

sth über etw (acc) empört sein.

indignation [ɪndɪg'neɪʃən] n Entrüstung f.

indignity [ɪn'dɪgnɪtɪ] n Demütigung f.

indirect a, ~ly ad [ɪndɪ'rekt, -lɪ] indirekt.

indiscreet [ɪndɪs'kriːt] a (insensitive) taktlos; (telling secrets) indiskret.

indiscretion [ɪndɪs'kreʃən] n Taktlosigkeit f; Indiskretion f.

indiscriminate [ɪndɪs'krɪmɪnət] a wahllos; kritiklos.

indispensable [ɪndɪs'pensəbl] a unentbehrlich.

indisposed [ɪndɪs'pəuzd] a unpäßlich.

indisputable [ɪndɪs'pjuːtəbl] a unbestreitbar; (evidence) unanfechtbar.

indistinct [ɪndɪs'tɪŋkt] a undeutlich.

individual [ɪndɪ'vɪdjuəl] n Individuum nt // a individuell; (case) Einzel-; (of, for one person) eigen, individuell; (characteristic) eigentümlich; ~ly ad einzeln, individuell.

indivisible [ɪndɪ'vɪzəbl] a unteilbar.

indoctrinate [ɪn'dɒktrɪneɪt] vt indoktrinieren.

Indonesia [ɪndəu'niːzɪə] n Indonesien nt.

indoor ['ɪndɔː*] a Haus-; Zimmer-; Innen-; (SPORT) Hallen-; ~s [ɪn'dɔːz] ad drinnen, im Haus.

induce [ɪn'djuːs] vt dazu bewegen; (reaction) herbeiführen; ~ment n Veranlassung f; (incentive) Anreiz m.

induction [ɪn'dʌkʃən] n (MED: of birth) Einleitung f; ~ course n (Brit) Einführungskurs m.

indulge [ɪn'dʌldʒ] vt (give way) nachgeben (+dat); (gratify) frönen (+dat) // vi frönen (in dat); ~nce n Nachsicht f; (enjoyment) Genuß m; ~nt a nachsichtig; (pej) nachgiebig.

industrial [ɪn'dʌstrɪəl] a Industrie-, industriell; (dispute, injury) Arbeits-; ~ action n Arbeitskampfmaßnahmen pl; ~ estate n (Brit) Industriegebiet nt; ~ist n Industrielle(r) mf; ~ize vt industrialisieren; ~ park n (US) = ~ estate.

industrious [ɪn'dʌstrɪəs] a fleißig.

industry ['ɪndəstrɪ] n Industrie f; (diligence) Fleiß m.

inebriated [ɪ'niːbrɪeɪtɪd] a betrunken.

inedible [ɪn'edɪbl] a ungenießbar.

ineffective [ɪnɪ'fektɪv], **ineffectual** [ɪnɪ'fektjuəl] a unwirksam; (person) untauglich.

inefficiency [ɪnɪ'fɪʃənsɪ] n Ineffizienz f.

inefficient [ɪnɪ'fɪʃənt] a ineffizient; (ineffective) unwirksam.

inept [ɪ'nept] a (remark) unpassend; (person) ungeeignet.

inequality [ɪnɪ'kwɒlɪtɪ] n Ungleichheit f.

inert [ɪ'nɜːt] a träge; (CHEM) inaktiv; (motionless) unbeweglich.

inertia [ɪ'nɜːʃə] n Trägheit f.

inescapable [ɪnɪs'keɪpəbl] a unvermeidbar.

inevitable [ɪn'evɪtəbl] a unvermeidlich.

inexcusable [ɪnɪks'kjuːzəbl] a unverzeihlich.

inexhaustible [ɪnɪg'zɔːstəbl] a unerschöpflich.

inexorable [ɪn'eksərəbl] a unerbittlich.

inexpensive [ɪnɪks'pensɪv] a preiswert.

inexperience [ɪnɪks'pɪərɪəns] n Unerfahrenheit f; ~d a unerfahren.

inexplicable [ɪnɪks'plɪkəbl] a unerklärlich.

inextricably [ɪnɪks'trɪkəblɪ] ad untrennbar.

infallible [ɪn'fæləbl] a unfehlbar.

infamous ['ɪnfəməs] a (place) verrufen; (deed) schändlich; (person) niederträchtig.

infamy ['ɪnfəmɪ] n Verrufenheit f; Niedertracht f; (disgrace) Schande f.

infancy ['ɪnfənsɪ] n frühe Kindheit f; (fig) Anfangsstadium nt.

infant ['ɪnfənt] n kleine(s) Kind nt, Säugling m; ~ile a kindisch, infantil; ~ school n (Brit) Grundschule f (für die ersten beiden Jahrgänge).

infantry ['ɪnfəntrɪ] n Infanterie f.

infatuated [ɪn'fætjueɪtɪd] a vernarrt; to become ~ with sich vernarren in (+acc).

infatuation [ɪnfætjʊ'eɪʃən] n Vernarrtheit f (with in +acc).

infect [ɪn'fekt] vt anstecken (also fig); ~ed with (illness) infiziert mit; ~ion n Infektion f; ~ious [ɪn'fekʃəs] a ansteckend.

infer [ɪn'fɜː*] vt schließen; ~ence ['ɪnfərəns] n Schlußfolgerung f.

inferior [ɪn'fɪərɪə*] a (rank) untergeordnet; (quality) minderwertig // n Untergebene(r) m; ~ity [ɪnfɪərɪ'ɒrɪtɪ] n Minderwertigkeit f; (in rank) untergeordnete Stellung f; ~ity complex n Minderwertigkeitskomplex m.

infernal [ɪn'fɜːnl] a höllisch.

infertile [ɪn'fɜːtaɪl] a unfruchtbar.

infertility [ɪnfɜː'tɪlɪtɪ] n Unfruchtbarkeit f.

infested [ɪn'festɪd] a: to be ~ with wimmeln von.

infidelity [ɪnfɪ'delɪtɪ] n Untreue f.

in-fighting ['ɪnfaɪtɪŋ] n Nahkampf m.

infiltrate ['ɪnfɪltreɪt] vt infiltrieren; (spies) einschleusen // vi (MIL, liquid) einsickern; (POL) unterwandern (into acc).

infinite ['ɪnfɪnɪt] a unendlich.

infinitive [ɪn'fɪnɪtɪv] n Infinitiv m.

infinity [ɪn'fɪnɪtɪ] n Unendlichkeit f.

infirm [ɪn'fɜːm] a gebrechlich.

infirmary [ɪn'fɜːmərɪ] n Krankenhaus nt.

infirmity [ɪn'fɜːmɪtɪ] n Schwäche f, Gebrechlichkeit f.

inflamed [ɪn'fleɪmd] a entzündet.

inflammable [ɪnˈflæməbl] a (Brit) feuergefährlich.

inflammation [ɪnfləˈmeɪʃən] n Entzündung f.

inflatable [ɪnˈfleɪtəbl] a aufblasbar.

inflate [ɪnˈfleɪt] vt aufblasen; (tyre) aufpumpen; (prices) hochtreiben.

inflation [ɪnˈfleɪʃən] n Inflation f; ~ary a (increase) inflationistisch; (situation) inflationär.

inflexible [ɪnˈfleksəbl] a (person) nicht flexibel; (opinion) starr; (thing) unbiegsam.

inflict [ɪnˈflɪkt] vt zufügen (sth on sb jdm etw); (wound) beibringen (on dat).

influence [ˈɪnfluəns] n Einfluß m // vt beeinflussen.

influential [ɪnfluˈenʃəl] a einflußreich.

influenza [ɪnfluˈenzə] n Grippe f.

influx [ˈɪnflʌks] n (of people) Zustrom m; (of ideas) Eindringen nt.

inform [ɪnˈfɔːm] vt informieren; to keep sb ~ed jdn auf dem laufenden halten // vi: to ~ on sb jdn denunzieren.

informal [ɪnˈfɔːməl] a zwanglos; ~ity [ɪnfɔːˈmælɪti] n Ungezwungenheit f.

informant [ɪnˈfɔːmənt] n Informant(in f) m.

information [ɪnfəˈmeɪʃən] n Auskunft f, Information f; **a piece of** ~ eine Auskunft, eine Information; ~ **office** n Informationsbüro nt.

informative [ɪnˈfɔːmətɪv] a informativ; (person) mitteilsam.

informer [ɪnˈfɔːmə*] n Denunziant(in f) m.

infra-red [ˈɪnfrəˈred] a infrarot.

infrequent [ɪnˈfriːkwənt] a selten.

infringe [ɪnˈfrɪndʒ] vt (law) verstoßen gegen; ~ **upon** vt verletzen; ~**ment** n Verstoß m, Verletzung f.

infuriating [ɪnˈfjuərɪeɪtɪŋ] a ärgerlich.

infusion [ɪnˈfjuːʒən] n (tea etc) Aufguß m.

ingenious [ɪnˈdʒiːnɪəs] a genial.

ingenuity [ɪndʒɪˈnjuːɪti] n Genialität f.

ingenuous [ɪnˈdʒenjuəs] a aufrichtig; (naive) naiv.

ingot [ˈɪŋgət] n Barren m.

ingrained [ɪnˈgreɪnd] a tiefsitzend (attr).

ingratiate [ɪnˈgreɪʃɪeɪt] vt einschmeicheln (o.s. with sb sich bei jdm).

ingratitude [ɪnˈgrætɪtjuːd] n Undankbarkeit f.

ingredient [ɪnˈgriːdɪənt] n Bestandteil m; (COOK) Zutat f.

inhabit [ɪnˈhæbɪt] vt bewohnen; ~**ant** n Bewohner(in f) m; (of island, town) Einwohner(in f) m.

inhale [ɪnˈheɪl] vt einatmen; (MED, cigarettes) inhalieren.

inherent [ɪnˈhɪərənt] a innewohnend (in dat).

inherit [ɪnˈherɪt] vt erben; ~**ance** n Erbe nt, Erbschaft f.

inhibit [ɪnˈhɪbɪt] vt hemmen; **to** ~ **sb from doing sth** jdn daran hindern, etw zu tun; ~**ion** [ɪnhɪˈbɪʃən] n Hemmung f.

inhospitable [ɪnhɒsˈpɪtəbl] a (person) ungastlich; (country) unwirtlich.

inhuman [ɪnˈhjuːmən] a unmenschlich.

inimitable [ɪˈnɪmɪtəbl] a unnachahmlich.

iniquity [ɪˈnɪkwɪti] n Ungerechtigkeit f.

initial [ɪˈnɪʃəl] a anfänglich, Anfangs- // n Initiale f // vt abzeichnen; (POL) paraphieren; ~**s** pl Initialen pl; ~**ly** ad anfangs.

initiate [ɪˈnɪʃɪeɪt] vt einführen; (negotiations) einleiten; **to** ~ **sb into a secret** jdn in ein Geheimnis einweihen; **to** ~ **proceedings against sb** (JUR) gerichtliche Schritte gegen jdn einleiten.

initiation [ɪnɪʃɪˈeɪʃən] n Einführung f; Einleitung f.

initiative [ɪˈnɪʃətɪv] n Initiative f.

inject [ɪnˈdʒekt] vt einspritzen; (fig) einflößen; ~**ion** n Spritze f.

injunction [ɪnˈdʒʌŋkʃən] n Verfügung f.

injure [ˈɪndʒə*] vt verletzen; ~**d** a (person, arm) verletzt.

injury [ˈɪndʒərɪ] n Verletzung f; **to play** ~ **time** (SPORT) nachspielen.

injustice [ɪnˈdʒʌstɪs] n Ungerechtigkeit f.

ink [ɪŋk] n Tinte f.

inkling [ˈɪŋklɪŋ] n (dunkle) Ahnung f.

inlaid [ˈɪnˈleɪd] a eingelegt, Einlege-.

inland [ˈɪnlænd] a Binnen-; (domestic) Inlands- // ad landeinwärts; ~ **revenue** n (Brit) Fiskus m.

in-laws [ˈɪnlɔːz] npl (parents-in-law) Schwiegereltern pl; (others) angeheiratete Verwandte pl.

inlet [ˈɪnlet] n Einlaß m; (bay) kleine Bucht f.

inmate [ˈɪnmeɪt] n Insasse m.

inn [ɪn] n Gasthaus nt, Wirtshaus nt.

innate [ɪˈneɪt] a angeboren.

inner [ˈɪnə*] a inner, Innen-; (fig) verborgen; ~ **city** n Innenstadt f; ~ **tube** n (of tyre) Schlauch m.

innings [ˈɪnɪŋz] n (CRICKET) Innenrunde f.

innocence [ˈɪnəsns] n Unschuld f; (ignorance) Unkenntnis f.

innocent [ˈɪnəsnt] a unschuldig.

innocuous [ɪˈnɒkjuəs] a harmlos.

innovation [ɪnəuˈveɪʃən] n Neuerung f.

innuendo [ɪnjuˈendəu] n (versteckte) Anspielung f.

innumerable [ɪˈnjuːmərəbl] a unzählig.

inoculation [ɪnɒkjuˈleɪʃən] n Impfung f.

inopportune [ɪnˈɒpətjuːn] a (remark) unangebracht; (visit) ungelegen.

inordinately [ɪˈnɔːdɪnɪtlɪ] ad unmäßig.

in-patient [ˈɪnpeɪʃənt] n stationäre(r) Patient(in f) m.

input [ˈɪnput] n (COMPUT) Eingabe f;

(*power* ~) Energiezufuhr *f*; (*of energy, work*) Aufwand *m*.

inquest ['ɪnkwest] *n* gerichtliche Untersuchung *f*.

inquire [ɪn'kwaɪə*] *vi* sich erkundigen // *vt* (*price*) sich erkundigen nach; ~ **into** *vt* untersuchen.

inquiry [ɪn'kwaɪərɪ] *n* (*question*) Erkundigung *f*; (*investigation*) Untersuchung *f*; ~ **office** *n* (*Brit*) Auskunft(sbüro *nt*) *f*.

inquisitive [ɪn'kwɪzɪtɪv] *a* neugierig.

inroad ['ɪnrəud] *n* (*MIL*) Einfall *m*; (*fig*) Eingriff *m*.

insane [ɪn'seɪn] *a* wahnsinnig; (*MED*) geisteskrank.

insanity [ɪn'sænɪtɪ] *n* Wahnsinn *m*.

insatiable [ɪn'seɪʃəbl] *a* unersättlich.

inscribe [ɪn'skraɪb] *vt* eingravieren; (*book etc*): **to** ~ (**to sb**) (jdm) widmen.

inscription [ɪn'skrɪpʃən] *n* (*on stone*) Inschrift *f*; (*in book*) Widmung *f*.

inscrutable [ɪn'skru:təbl] *a* unergründlich.

insect ['ɪnsekt] *n* Insekt *nt*; ~**icide** [ɪn'sektɪsaɪd] *n* Insektenvertilgungsmittel *nt*.

insecure [ɪnsɪ'kjuə*] *a* (*person*) unsicher; (*thing*) nicht fest *or* sicher.

insecurity [ɪnsɪ'kjuərɪtɪ] *n* Unsicherheit *f*.

insemination [ɪnsemɪ'neɪʃən] *n*: **artificial** ~ künstliche Befruchtung *f*.

insensible [ɪn'sensɪbl] *a* (*unconscious*) bewußtlos.

insensitive [ɪn'sensɪtɪv] *a* (*to pain*) unempfindlich; (*without feelings*) gefühllos.

inseparable [ɪn'sepərəbl] *a* (*people*) unzertrennlich; (*word*) untrennbar.

insert [ɪn'sɜ:t] *vt* einfügen; (*coin*) einwerfen; (*stick into*) hineinstecken; (*advert*) aufgeben // *n* ['ɪnsɜ:t] (*in book*) Einlage *f*; (*in magazine*) Beilage *f*; ~**ion** *n* Einfügung *f*; (*PRESS*) Inserat *nt*.

in-service ['ɪn'sɜ:vɪs] *a* (*training*) berufsbegleitend.

inshore ['ɪn'ʃɔ:*] *a* Küsten- // *ad* ['ɪn'ʃɔ:*] an der Küste.

inside ['ɪn'saɪd] *n* Innenseite *f*, Innere(s) *nt* // *a* innere(r, s), Innen- // *ad* (*place*) innen; (*direction*) nach innen, hinein // *prep* (*place*) in (+*dat*); (*direction*) in (+*acc*) ... hinein; (*time*) innerhalb (+*gen*); ~ **10 minutes** unter 10 Minuten; ~**s** *pl* (*col*) Eingeweide *nt*; ~ **forward** *n* (*SPORT*) Halbstürmer *m*; ~ **lane** *n* (*AUT: in Britain*) linke Spur; ~ **out** *ad* linksherum; (*know*) in- und auswendig.

insidious [ɪn'sɪdɪəs] *a* heimtückisch.

insight ['ɪnsaɪt] *n* Einsicht *f*; Einblick *m* (*into* in +*acc*).

insignificant [ɪnsɪg'nɪfɪkənt] *a* unbedeutend.

insincere [ɪnsɪn'sɪə*] *a* unaufrichtig.

insinuate [ɪn'sɪnjueɪt] *vt* (*hint*) andeuten.

insipid [ɪn'sɪpɪd] *a* fad(e).

insist [ɪn'sɪst] *vi* bestehen (*on* auf +*acc*); ~**ence** *n* Bestehen *nt*; ~**ent** *a* hartnäckig; (*urgent*) dringend.

insole ['ɪnsəul] *n* Einlegesohle *f*.

insolence ['ɪnsələns] *n* Frechheit *f*.

insolent ['ɪnsələnt] *a* frech.

insoluble [ɪn'sɒljubl] *a* unlösbar; (*CHEM*) unlöslich.

insolvent [ɪn'sɒlvənt] *a* zahlungsunfähig.

insomnia [ɪn'sɒmnɪə] *n* Schlaflosigkeit *f*.

inspect [ɪn'spekt] *vt* prüfen; (*officially*) inspizieren; ~**ion** *n* Inspektion *f*; ~**or** *n* (*official*) Inspektor *m*; (*police*) Polizeikommissar *m*; (*Brit: on buses, trains*) Kontrolleur *m*.

inspiration [ɪnspɪ'reɪʃən] *n* Inspiration *f*.

inspire [ɪn'spaɪə*] *vt* (*respect*) einflößen (*in dat*); (*hope*) wecken (*in* in +*dat*); (*person*) inspirieren.

instability [ɪnstə'bɪlɪtɪ] *n* Unbeständigkeit *f*, Labilität *f*.

install [ɪn'stɔ:l] *vt* (*put in*) installieren; (*telephone*) anschließen; (*establish*) einsetzen; ~**ation** [ɪnstə'leɪʃən] *n* (*of person*) (Amts)einsetzung *f*; (*of machinery*) Installierung *f*; (*machines etc*) Anlage *f*.

instalment, (*US*) **installment** [ɪn'stɔ:lmənt] *n* Rate *f*; (*of story*) Fortsetzung *f*; **to pay in** ~**s** auf Raten zahlen.

instance ['ɪnstəns] *n* Fall *m*; (*example*) Beispiel *nt*; **for** ~ zum Beispiel; **in the first** ~ zunächst.

instant ['ɪnstənt] *n* Augenblick *m* // *a* augenblicklich, sofortig; ~ **coffee** *n* Pulverkaffee *m*.

instantaneous [ɪnstən'teɪnɪəs] *a* unmittelbar.

instantly ['ɪnstəntlɪ] *ad* sofort.

instead [ɪn'sted] *ad* statt dessen; ~ **of** *prep* anstatt (+*gen*).

instep ['ɪnstep] *n* Spann *m*; (*of shoe*) Blatt *nt*.

instigation [ɪnstɪ'geɪʃən] *n* Veranlassung *f*; (*of crime etc*) Anstiftung *f*.

instil [ɪn'stɪl] *vt* (*fig*) beibringen (*in sb* jdm).

instinct ['ɪnstɪŋkt] *n* Instinkt *m*; ~**ive** [ɪn'stɪŋktɪv] *a* instinktiv.

institute ['ɪnstɪtju:t] *n* Institut *nt* // *vt* einführen; (*search*) einleiten.

institution [ɪnstɪ'tju:ʃən] *n* Institution *f*; (*home*) Anstalt *f*.

instruct [ɪn'strʌkt] *vt* anweisen; (*officially*) instruieren; ~**ion** [ɪn'strʌkʃən] *n* Unterricht *m*; ~**ions** *pl* Anweisungen *pl*; (*for use*) Gebrauchsanweisung *f*; ~**ive** *a* lehrreich; ~**or** *n* Lehrer *m*; (*MIL*) Ausbilder *m*.

instrument ['ɪnstrʊmənt] n Instrument nt; **~al** [ɪnstru'mentl] a (MUS) Instrumental-; (helpful) behilflich (in bei); **~ panel** n Armaturenbrett nt.

insubordinate [ɪnsə'bɔːdənət] a aufsässig, widersetzlich.

insubordination ['ɪnsəbɔːdɪ'neɪʃən] n Gehorsamsverweigerung f.

insufferable [ɪn'sʌfərəbl] a unerträglich.

insufficient [ɪnsə'fɪʃnt] a ungenügend.

insular ['ɪnsjələ*] a (fig) engstirnig.

insulate ['ɪnsjʊleɪt] vt (ELEC) isolieren; (fig) abschirmen (from vor +dat).

insulating tape n Isolierband nt.

insulation [ɪnsjʊ'leɪʃən] n Isolierung f.

insulin ['ɪnsjʊlɪn] n Insulin nt.

insult ['ɪnsʌlt] n Beleidigung f // [ɪn'sʌlt] vt beleidigen; **~ing** [ɪn'sʌltɪŋ] a beleidigend.

insuperable [ɪn'suːpərəbl] a unüberwindlich.

insurance [ɪn'ʃʊərəns] n Versicherung f; **fire/life ~** Feuer-/Lebensversicherung; **~ agent** n Versicherungsvertreter m; **~ policy** n Versicherungspolice f.

insure [ɪn'ʃʊə*] vt versichern.

insurrection [ɪnsə'rekʃən] n Aufstand m.

intact [ɪn'tækt] a unversehrt.

intake ['ɪnteɪk] n (place) Einlaßöffnung f; (act) Aufnahme f; (Brit SCH): **an ~ of 200 a year** ein Neuzugang von 200 im Jahr.

intangible [ɪn'tændʒəbl] a nicht greifbar.

integral ['ɪntɪgrəl] a (essential) wesentlich; (complete) vollständig; (MATH) Integral-.

integrate ['ɪntɪgreɪt] vt integrieren // vi sich integrieren.

integrity [ɪn'tegrɪtɪ] n (honesty) Redlichkeit f, Integrität f.

intellect ['ɪntɪlekt] n Intellekt m; **~ual** [ɪntɪ'lektjʊəl] a geistig, intellektuell // n Intellektuelle(r) mf.

intelligence [ɪn'telɪdʒəns] n (understanding) Intelligenz f; (news) Information f; (MIL) Geheimdienst m.

intelligent [ɪn'telɪdʒənt] a intelligent; **~ly** ad klug; (write, speak) verständlich.

intelligentsia [ɪntelɪ'dʒentsɪə] n Intelligenz f.

intelligible [ɪn'telɪdʒəbl] a verständlich.

intend [ɪn'tend] vt beabsichtigen; **that was ~ed for you** das war für dich gedacht.

intense [ɪn'tens] a stark, intensiv; (person) ernsthaft; **~ly** ad äußerst; (study) intensiv.

intensify [ɪn'tensɪfaɪ] vt verstärken, intensivieren.

intensity [ɪn'tensɪtɪ] n Intensität f.

intensive [ɪn'tensɪv] a intensiv; **~ care**

unit n Intensivstation f.

intent [ɪn'tent] n Absicht f; **to all ~s and purposes** praktisch; **to be ~ on doing sth** fest entschlossen sein, etw zu tun.

intention [ɪn'tenʃən] n Absicht f.

intentional a, **~ly** ad [ɪn'tenʃənl, -nəlɪ] absichtlich.

intently [ɪn'tentlɪ] ad konzentriert.

inter [ɪn'tɜː*] vt beerdigen.

interact [ɪntər'ækt] vi aufeinander einwirken; **~ion** n Wechselwirkung f.

intercede [ɪntə'siːd] vi sich verwenden.

intercept [ɪntə'sept] vt abfangen.

interchange ['ɪntə'tʃeɪndʒ] n (exchange) Austausch m; (on roads) Verkehrskreuz nt // [ɪntə'tʃeɪndʒ] vt austauschen; **~able** [ɪntə'tʃeɪndʒəbl] a austauschbar.

intercom ['ɪntəkɒm] n (Gegen-)sprechanlage f.

intercourse ['ɪntəkɔːs] n (exchange) Beziehungen pl; (sexual) Geschlechtsverkehr m.

interest ['ɪntrest] n Interesse nt; (FIN) Zinsen pl; (COMM: share) Anteil m; (group) Interessengruppe f // vt interessieren; **~ed** a (having claims) beteiligt; (attentive) interessiert; **to be ~ed in** sich interessieren für; **~ing** a interessant; **~ rate** n Zinssatz m.

interface ['ɪntəfeɪs] n (COMPUT) Schnittstelle f, Interface nt.

interfere [ɪntə'fɪə*] vi (meddle) sich einmischen (with in +acc); (disrupt) stören (with acc).

interference [ɪntə'fɪərəns] n Einmischung f; (TV) Störung f.

interim ['ɪntərɪm] n: **in the ~** inzwischen.

interior [ɪn'tɪərɪə*] n Innere(s) nt // a innere(r, s), Innen-; **~ designer** n Innenarchitekt(in f) m.

interjection [ɪntə'dʒekʃən] n Ausruf m.

interlock [ɪntə'lɒk] vi ineinandergreifen.

interloper ['ɪntələʊpə*] n Eindringling m.

interlude ['ɪntəluːd] n Pause f.

intermarry [ɪntə'mærɪ] vi untereinander heiraten.

intermediary [ɪntə'miːdɪərɪ] n Vermittler m.

intermediate [ɪntə'miːdɪət] a Zwischen-, Mittel-.

interminable [ɪn'tɜːmɪnəbl] a endlos.

intermission [ɪntə'mɪʃən] n Pause f.

intermittent [ɪntə'mɪtənt] a periodisch, stoßweise.

intern [ɪn'tɜːn] vt internieren // ['ɪntɜːn] n (US) Assistenzarzt m/ -ärztin f.

internal [ɪn'tɜːnl] a (inside) innere(r, s); (domestic) Inlands-; **~ly** ad innen; (MED) innerlich; **'not to be taken ~ly'** 'nur zur äußerlichen Anwendung'; **I~ Revenue Service (IRS)** n (US) Finanzamt nt.

international [ɪntəˈnæʃnəl] a international // n (SPORT) Nationalspieler(in f) m; (: match) internationale(s) Spiel nt.

interplay ['ɪntəpleɪ] n Wechselspiel nt.

interpret [ɪnˈtɜːprɪt] vt (explain) auslegen, interpretieren; (translate) dolmetschen; ~ation ['teɪʃən] n Interpretation f; ~er n Dolmetscher(in f) m.

interrelated [ɪntərɪˈleɪtɪd] a untereinander zusammenhängend.

interrogate [ɪnˈterəgeɪt] vt verhören.

interrogation [ɪntərəˈgeɪʃən] n Verhör nt.

interrogative [ɪntəˈrɒgətɪv] a Frage-.

interrupt [ɪntəˈrʌpt] vt unterbrechen; ~ion n Unterbrechung f.

intersect [ɪntəˈsekt] vt (durch)schneiden // vi sich schneiden; ~ion n (of roads) Kreuzung f; (of lines) Schnittpunkt m.

intersperse [ɪntəˈspɜːs] vt: to ~ sth with sth etw mit etw durchsetzen.

intertwine [ɪntəˈtwaɪn] vti (sich) verflechten.

interval ['ɪntəvəl] n Abstand m; (Brit: SCH, THEAT, SPORT) Pause f; at ~s in Abständen.

intervene [ɪntəˈviːn] vi dazwischenliegen; (act) einschreiten (in gegen).

intervention [ɪntəˈvenʃən] n Eingreifen nt, Intervention f.

interview ['ɪntəvjuː] n (PRESS etc) Interview nt; (for job) Vorstellungsgespräch nt // vt interviewen; ~er n Interviewer m.

intestine [ɪnˈtestɪn] n: large/small ~ Dick-/Dünndarm m.

intimacy ['ɪntɪməsɪ] n Intimität f.

intimate ['ɪntɪmət] a (inmost) innerste(r, s); (knowledge) eingehend; (familiar) vertraut; (friends) eng // ['ɪntɪmeɪt] vt andeuten.

intimidate [ɪnˈtɪmɪdeɪt] vt einschüchtern.

intimidation [ɪntɪmɪˈdeɪʃən] n Einschüchterung f.

into ['ɪntu] prep (motion) in (+acc) ... hinein; 5 ~ 25 25 durch 5.

intolerable [ɪnˈtɒlərəbl] a unerträglich.

intolerant [ɪnˈtɒlərənt] a: ~ of unduldsam gegen(über).

intoxicate [ɪnˈtɒksɪkeɪt] vt berauschen; ~d a betrunken.

intoxication [ɪntɒksɪˈkeɪʃən] n Rausch m.

intractable [ɪnˈtræktəbl] a schwer zu handhaben; (problem) schwer lösbar.

intransigent [ɪnˈtrænsɪdʒənt] a unnachgiebig.

intravenous [ɪntrəˈviːnəs] a intravenös.

in-tray ['ɪntreɪ] n Eingangskorb m.

intrepid [ɪnˈtrepɪd] a unerschrocken.

intricate ['ɪntrɪkət] a kompliziert.

intrigue [ɪnˈtriːg] n Intrige f // vt faszinieren // vi intrigieren.

intriguing [ɪnˈtriːgɪŋ] a faszinierend.

intrinsic [ɪnˈtrɪnsɪk] a innere(r, s); (difference) wesentlich.

introduce [ɪntrəˈdjuːs] vt (person) vorstellen (to sb jdm); (sth new) einführen; (subject) anschneiden; to ~ sb to sth jdn in etw (acc) einführen.

introduction [ɪntrəˈdʌkʃən] n Einführung f; (to book) Einleitung f.

introductory [ɪntrəˈdʌktərɪ] a Einführungs-, Vor-.

introspective [ɪntrəuˈspektɪv] a nach innen gekehrt.

introvert ['ɪntrəuvɜːt] n Introvertierte(r) mf // a introvertiert.

intrude [ɪnˈtruːd] vi stören (on acc); ~r n Eindringling m.

intrusion [ɪnˈtruːʒən] n Störung f.

intrusive [ɪnˈtruːsɪv] a aufdringlich.

intuition [ɪntjuːˈɪʃən] n Intuition f.

inundate ['ɪnʌndeɪt] vt (lit, fig) überschwemmen.

invade [ɪnˈveɪd] vt einfallen in (+acc); ~r n Eindringling m.

invalid ['ɪnvəlɪd] n (disabled) Invalide m // a (ill) krank; (disabled) invalide; [ɪnˈvælɪd] (not valid) ungültig.

invaluable [ɪnˈvæljuəbl] a unschätzbar.

invariable [ɪnˈvɛərɪəbl] a unveränderlich.

invariably [ɪnˈvɛərɪəblɪ] ad ausnahmslos.

invasion [ɪnˈveɪʒən] n Invasion f.

invent [ɪnˈvent] vt erfinden; ~ion [ɪnˈvenʃən] n Erfindung f; ~ive a erfinderisch; ~or n Erfinder m.

inventory ['ɪnvəntrɪ] n Inventar nt.

inverse ['ɪnvɜːs] n Umkehrung f // a umgekehrt.

invert [ɪnˈvɜːt] vt umdrehen; ~ed commas npl (Brit) Anführungsstriche pl.

invertebrate [ɪnˈvɜːtɪbrət] n wirbellose(s) Tier nt.

invest [ɪnˈvest] vt investieren.

investigate [ɪnˈvestɪgeɪt] vt untersuchen.

investigation [ɪnvestɪˈgeɪʃən] n Untersuchung f.

investigator [ɪnˈvestɪgeɪtə*] n Untersuchungsbeamte(r) m.

investiture [ɪnˈvestɪtʃə*] n Amtseinsetzung f.

investment [ɪnˈvestmənt] n Investition f.

investor [ɪnˈvestə*] n (Geld)anleger m.

inveterate [ɪnˈvetərət] a unverbesserlich.

invidious [ɪnˈvɪdɪəs] a unangenehm; (distinctions, remark) ungerecht.

invigilate [ɪnˈvɪdʒɪleɪt] vti (in exam) Aufsicht führen (über).

invigorating [ɪnˈvɪgəreɪtɪŋ] a stärkend.

invincible [ɪnˈvɪnsəbl] a unbesiegbar.

inviolate [ɪn'vaɪələt] a unverletzt.
invisible [ɪn'vɪzəbl] a unsichtbar; ~ **ink**
n Geheimtinte f.
invitation [ɪnvɪ'teɪʃən] n Einladung f.
invite [ɪn'vaɪt] vt einladen.
inviting [ɪn'vaɪtɪŋ] a einladend.
invoice ['ɪnvɔɪs] n Rechnung f // vt
(goods) in Rechnung stellen (sth for sb
jdm etw acc).
invoke [ɪn'vəuk] vt anrufen.
involuntary [ɪn'vɒləntərɪ] a unabsichtlich.
involve [ɪn'vɒlv] vt (entangle) verwickeln; (entail) mit sich bringen; ~d a
verwickelt; ~ment n Verwicklung f.
inward ['ɪnwəd] a innere(r, s); (curve)
Innen-; ~(s) ad nach innen; ~ly ad im
Innern.
I/O abbr (= input/output) I/O.
iodine ['aɪədiːn] n Jod nt.
iota [aɪ'əutə] n (fig) bißchen nt.
IOU n abbr of **I owe you.**
IQ n abbr (= intelligence quotient) IQ m.
IRA n abbr (= Irish Republican Army)
IRA f.
Iran [ɪ'rɑːn] n Iran nt; ~**ian** [ɪ'reɪnɪən] a
iranisch // n Iraner(in f) m; (LING)
Iranisch nt.
Iraq [ɪ'rɑːk] n Irak; ~**i** a irakisch // n
Iraker(in f) m; (LING) Irakisch nt.
irascible [ɪ'ræsɪbl] a reizbar.
irate [aɪ'reɪt] a zornig.
Ireland ['aɪələnd] n Irland nt.
irksome ['ɜːksəm] a lästig.
iron ['aɪən] n Eisen nt; (for ironing)
Bügeleisen nt // a eisern // vt bügeln; ~
out vt (lit, fig) ausbügeln; **I~ Curtain** n
Eiserne(r) Vorhang m.
ironic(al) [aɪ'rɒnɪk(əl)] a ironisch; (coincidence etc) witzig.
ironing ['aɪənɪŋ] n Bügeln nt; (laundry)
Bügelwäsche f; ~ **board** n Bügelbrett
nt.
ironmonger ['aɪənmʌŋgə*] n (Brit)
Eisenwarenhändler m; ~'s (shop) n
Eisenwarenhandlung f.
iron ore ['aɪənɔː*] n Eisenerz nt.
irony ['aɪərənɪ] n Ironie f.
irrational [ɪ'ræʃənl] a irrational.
irreconcilable [ɪrekən'saɪləbl] a
unvereinbar.
irrefutable [ɪrɪ'fjuːtəbl] a unwiderleg-
bar.
irregular [ɪ'regjulə*] a unregelmäßig;
(shape) ungleich(mäßig); (fig) unüblich;
(behaviour) ungehörig; ~**ity**
[ɪregju'lærɪtɪ] n Unregelmäßigkeit f; Un-
gleichmäßigkeit f; (fig) Vergehen nt.
irrelevant [ɪ'reləvənt] a belanglos,
irrelevant.
irreparable [ɪ'repərəbl] a nicht wieder-
gutzumachen.
irreplaceable [ɪrɪ'pleɪsəbl] a unersetz-
lich.
irrepressible [ɪrɪ'presəbl] a nicht zu

unterdrücken; (joy) unbändig.
irresistible [ɪrɪ'zɪstəbl] a unwidersteh-
lich.
irresolute [ɪ'rezəluːt] a unentschlossen.
irrespective [ɪrɪ'spektɪv]: ~ **of** prep ungeachtet (+gen).
irresponsible [ɪrɪ'spɒnsəbl] a ver-
antwortungslos.
irreverent [ɪ'revərənt] a respektlos.
irrevocable [ɪ'revəkəbl] a unwiderruf-
bar.
irrigate ['ɪrɪgeɪt] vt bewässern.
irrigation [ɪrɪ'geɪʃən] n Bewässerung f.
irritable ['ɪrɪtəbl] a reizbar.
irritate ['ɪrɪteɪt] vt irritieren, reizen (also
MED).
irritation [ɪrɪ'teɪʃən] n (anger) Ärger
m; (MED) Reizung f.
IRS n abbr of **Internal Revenue Service.**
is [ɪz] v see **be.**
Islam ['ɪzlɑːm] n Islam m.
island ['aɪlənd] n Insel f; ~**er** n
Inselbewohner(in f) m.
isle [aɪl] n (kleine) Insel f.
isn't ['ɪznt] = **is not.**
isolate ['aɪsəuleɪt] vt isolieren; ~**d** a
isoliert; (case) Einzel-.
isolation [aɪsəu'leɪʃən] n Isolierung f.
Israel ['ɪzreɪəl] n Israel nt; ~**i** [ɪz'reɪlɪ] a
israelisch // n Israeli mf.
issue ['ɪʃuː] n (matter) Frage f;
(outcome) Ausgang m; (of newspaper,
shares) Ausgabe f; (offspring)
Nachkommenschaft f // vt ausgeben;
(warrant) erlassen; (documents) ausstellen; (orders) erteilen; (books) herausgeben; (verdict) aussprechen; **to be
at ~** zur Debatte stehen; **to take ~ with
sb over sth** jdm in etw (dat) widersprechen.
isthmus ['ɪsməs] n Landenge f.
it [ɪt] pron **1** (specific: subject) er/sie/es;
(: direct object) ihn/sie/es; (: indirect
object) ihm/ihr/ihm; **about/from/in/of** ~
darüber/davon/darin/davon
2 (impersonal) es; ~'s **raining** es regnet; **it's Friday tomorrow** morgen ist
Freitag; **who is** ~? — ~'s **me** wer ist
da? — ich (bin's).
Italian [ɪ'tæljən] a italienisch // n
Italiener(in f) m; (LING) Italienisch nt.
italic [ɪ'tælɪk] a kursiv; ~**s** npl
Kursivschrift f.
Italy ['ɪtəlɪ] n Italien nt.
itch [ɪtʃ] n Juckreiz m; (fig) Lust f // vi
jucken; **to be** ~**ing to do sth** darauf
brennen, etw zu tun; ~**y** a juckend.
it'd ['ɪtd] = **it would; it had.**
item ['aɪtəm] n Gegenstand m; (on list)
Posten m; (in programme) Nummer f;
(in agenda) (Programm)punkt m; (in
newspaper) (Zeitungs)notiz f; ~**ize** vt
verzeichnen.
itinerant [ɪ'tɪnərənt] a (person) um-

herreisend.

itinerary [aɪ'tɪnərərɪ] n Reiseroute f.

it'll ['ɪtl] = it will, it shall.

its [ɪts] poss a (masculine, neuter) sein; (feminine) ihr.

it's [ɪts] = it is; it has.

itself [ɪt'self] pron sich (selbst); (emphatic) selbst.

ITV n abbr (Brit) of **Independent Television**.

I.U.D. n abbr (= intra-uterine device) Pessar nt.

I've [aɪv] = I have.

ivory ['aɪvərɪ] n Elfenbein nt; ~ **tower** n (fig) Elfenbeinturm m.

ivy ['aɪvɪ] n Efeu nt.

J

jab [dʒæb] vti (hinein)stechen // n Stich m, Stoß m; (col) Spritze f.

jabber ['dʒæbə*] vi plappern.

jack [dʒæk] n (AUT) (Wagen)heber m; (CARDS) Bube m; ~ **up** vt aufbocken.

jackal ['dʒækəl] n (ZOOL) Schakal m.

jackdaw ['dʒækdɔː] n Dohle f.

jacket ['dʒækɪt] n Jacke f; (of book) Schutzumschlag m; (TECH) Ummantelung f.

jack-knife ['dʒæknaɪf] vi (truck) sich zusammenschieben.

jack plug n (ELEC) Buchsenstecker m.

jackpot ['dʒækpɒt] n Haupttreffer m.

jade [dʒeɪd] n (stone) Jade m.

jaded ['dʒeɪdɪd] a ermattet.

jagged ['dʒægɪd] a zackig.

jail [dʒeɪl] n Gefängnis nt // vt einsperren; ~**er** n Gefängniswärter m.

jam [dʒæm] n Marmelade f; (also: traffic ~) (Verkehrs)stau m; (col: trouble) Klemme f // vt (wedge) einklemmen; (cram) hineinzwängen; (obstruct) blockieren // vi sich verklemmen; to ~ sth into sth etw in etw (acc) hineinstopfen.

Jamaica [dʒə'meɪkə] n Jamaika nt.

jangle ['dʒæŋgl] vti klimpern.

janitor ['dʒænɪtə*] n Hausmeister m.

January ['dʒænjuərɪ] n Januar m.

Japan [dʒə'pæn] n Japan nt; ~**ese** [dʒæpə'niːz] a japanisch // n, pl inv Japaner(in f) m; (LING) Japanisch nt.

jar [dʒɑː*] n Glas nt // vi kreischen; (colours etc) nicht harmonieren.

jargon ['dʒɑːgən] n Fachsprache f, Jargon m.

jaundice ['dʒɔːndɪs] n Gelbsucht f; ~**d** a (fig) mißgünstig.

jaunt [dʒɔːnt] n Spritztour f; ~**y** a (lively) munter; (brisk) flott.

javelin ['dʒævlɪn] n Speer m.

jaw [dʒɔː] n Kiefer m.

jay [dʒeɪ] n (ZOOL) Eichelhäher m.

jaywalker ['dʒeɪwɔːkə*] n unvorsicht-

ige(r) Fußgänger m.

jazz [dʒæz] n Jazz m; ~ **up** vt (MUS) verjazzen; (enliven) aufpolieren; ~**y** a (colour) schreiend, auffallend.

jealous ['dʒeləs] a (envious) mißgünstig; (husband) eifersüchtig; ~**y** n Mißgunst f; Eifersucht f.

jeans [dʒiːnz] npl Jeans pl.

jeep [dʒiːp] n Jeep m.

jeer [dʒɪə*] vi höhnisch lachen (at über +acc), verspotten (at sb jdn).

jelly ['dʒelɪ] n Gelee nt; (dessert) Grütze f; ~**fish** n Qualle f.

jeopardize ['dʒepədaɪz] vt gefährden.

jeopardy ['dʒepədɪ] n: to be in ~ in Gefahr sein.

jerk [dʒɜːk] n Ruck m; (col: idiot) Trottel m // vi ruckartig bewegen // vi sich ruckartig bewegen.

jerkin ['dʒɜːkɪn] n Wams nt.

jerky ['dʒɜːkɪ] a (movement) ruckartig; (ride) rüttelnd.

jersey ['dʒɜːzɪ] n Pullover m.

jest [dʒest] n Scherz m; in ~ im Spaß // vi spaßen.

Jesus ['dʒiːzəs] n Jesus m.

jet [dʒet] n (stream: of water etc) Strahl m; (spout) Düse f; (AVIAT) Düsenflugzeug nt; ~**black** a rabenschwarz; ~ **engine** n Düsenmotor m; ~**lag** n Jet-lag m.

jettison ['dʒetɪsn] vt über Bord werfen.

jetty ['dʒetɪ] n Landesteg m, Mole f.

Jew [dʒuː] n Jude m.

jewel ['dʒuːəl] n (lit, fig) Juwel nt; ~**(l)er** n Juwelier m; ~**(l)er's (shop)** n Juwelier m; ~**(le)ry** n Schmuck m.

Jewess ['dʒuːɪs] n Jüdin f.

Jewish ['dʒuːɪʃ] a jüdisch.

jibe [dʒaɪb] n spöttische Bemerkung f.

jiffy ['dʒɪfɪ] n (col): in a ~ sofort.

jigsaw (puzzle) ['dʒɪgsɔː(pʌzl)] n Puzzle(spiel) nt.

jilt [dʒɪlt] vt den Laufpaß geben (+dat).

jingle ['dʒɪŋgl] n (advertisement) Werbesong m // vti klimpern; (bells) bimmeln.

jinx [dʒɪŋks] n: there's a ~ on it es ist verhext.

jitters ['dʒɪtəz] npl (col): to get the ~ einen Bammel kriegen.

job [dʒɒb] n (piece of work) Arbeit f; (position) Stellung f; (duty) Aufgabe f; (difficulty) Mühe f; it's a good ~ he ... es ist ein Glück, daß er ...; just the ~ genau das Richtige; ~**centre** n (Brit) Arbeitsamt nt; ~**less** a arbeitslos.

jockey ['dʒɒkɪ] n Jockei m // vi: to ~ for position sich in eine gute Position drängeln.

jocular ['dʒɒkjulə*] a scherzhaft.

jog [dʒɒg] vt (an)stoßen // vi (run) joggen; to ~ along vor sich (acc) hinwursteln; (work) seinen Gang gehen; ~**ging** n Jogging nt.

join [dʒɔɪn] vt (put together) verbinden (to mit); (club) beitreten (+dat); (person) sich anschließen (+dat) // vi (unite) sich vereinigen // n Verbindungsstelle f, Naht f; ~ **in** vti mitmachen (sth bei etw); ~ **up** vi (MIL) zur Armee gehen.

joiner ['dʒɔɪnə*] n Schreiner m; ~y n Schreinerei f.

joint [dʒɔɪnt] n (TECH) Fuge f; (of bones) Gelenk nt; (of meat) Braten m; (col: place) Lokal nt // a gemeinsam; ~ **account** n (with bank etc) gemeinsame(s) Konto nt; ~**ly** ad gemeinsam.

joist [dʒɔɪst] n Träger m.

joke [dʒəʊk] n Witz m // vi Witze machen; **to play a ~ on sb** jdm einen Streich spielen; ~**r** n Witzbold m; (CARDS) Joker m.

jolly ['dʒɒlɪ] a lustig // ad (col) ganz schön.

jolt [dʒəʊlt] n (shock) Schock m; (jerk) Stoß m // vt (push) stoßen; (shake) durchschütteln; (fig) aufrütteln // vi holpern.

Jordan ['dʒɔːdən] n Jordanien nt; (river) Jordan m.

jostle ['dʒɒsl] vt anrempeln.

jot [dʒɒt] n: **not one ~** kein Jota nt; ~ **down** vt notieren; ~**ter** n (Brit) Notizblock m.

journal ['dʒɜːnl] n (diary) Tagebuch nt; (magazine) Zeitschrift f; ~**ese** ['dʒɜːnə'liːz] n Zeitungsstil m; ~**ism** n Journalismus m; ~**ist** n Journalist(in f) m.

journey ['dʒɜːnɪ] n Reise f.

jovial ['dʒəʊvɪəl] a jovial.

joy [dʒɔɪ] n Freude f; ~**ful**, ~**ous** a freudig; ~ **ride** n Schwarzfahrt f; ~**stick** n Steuerknüppel m; (COMPUT) Joystick m.

J.P. n abbr of **Justice of the Peace.**

Jr abbr of **junior.**

jubilant ['dʒuːbɪlənt] a triumphierend.

jubilee ['dʒuːbɪliː] n Jubiläum nt.

judge [dʒʌdʒ] n Richter m; (fig) Kenner m // vt (JUR: person) die Verhandlung führen über (+acc); (case) verhandeln; (assess) beurteilen; (estimate) einschätzen; ~**ment** n (JUR) Urteil nt; (ECCL) Gericht nt; (ability) Urteilsvermögen nt.

judicial [dʒuːˈdɪʃəl] a gerichtlich, Justiz-.

judiciary [dʒuːˈdɪʃɪərɪ] n Gerichtsbehörden pl; (judges) Richterstand m.

judicious [dʒuːˈdɪʃəs] a weis(e).

judo ['dʒuːdəʊ] n Judo nt.

jug [dʒʌg] n Krug m.

juggernaut ['dʒʌgənɔːt] n (Brit: huge truck) Schwertransporter m.

juggle ['dʒʌgl] vti jonglieren; ~**r** n Jongleur m.

Jugoslav ['juːgəʊˈslɑːv] etc = **Yugoslav** etc.

juice [dʒuːs] n Saft m.

juicy ['dʒuːsɪ] a (lit, fig) saftig.

jukebox ['dʒuːkbɒks] n Musikautomat m.

July [dʒuːˈlaɪ] n Juli m.

jumble ['dʒʌmbl] n Durcheinander nt // vt (also: ~ up) durcheinanderwerfen; (facts) durcheinanderbringen; ~ **sale** n (Brit) Basar m, Flohmarkt m.

jumbo (jet) ['dʒʌmbəʊ-] n Jumbo(-Jet) m.

jump [dʒʌmp] vi springen; (nervously) zusammenzucken // vt überspringen // n Sprung m; **to ~ the queue** (Brit) sich vordrängeln.

jumper ['dʒʌmpə*] n (Brit: pullover) Pullover m; (US: dress) Trägerkleid nt; ~ **cables** npl (US) = **jump leads.**

jump leads npl (Brit) Überbrückungskabel nt.

jumpy ['dʒʌmpɪ] a nervös.

Jun abbr of **junior.**

junction ['dʒʌŋkʃən] n (Brit: of roads) (Straßen)kreuzung f; (RAIL) Knotenpunkt m.

juncture ['dʒʌŋktʃə*] n: **at this ~** in diesem Augenblick.

June [dʒuːn] n Juni m.

jungle ['dʒʌŋgl] n Dschungel m.

junior ['dʒuːnɪə*] a (younger) jünger; (after name) junior; (SPORT) Junioren-; (lower position) untergeordnet; (for young people) Junioren- // n Jüngere(r) mf; ~ **school** n (Brit) Grundschule f.

junk [dʒʌŋk] n (rubbish) Plunder m; (ship) Dschunke f; ~ **food** n Plastikessen nt; ~**shop** n Ramschladen m.

Junr abbr of **junior.**

jurisdiction [dʒʊərɪsˈdɪkʃən] n Gerichtsbarkeit f; (range of authority) Zuständigkeit(sbereich m) f.

juror ['dʒʊərə*] n Geschworene(r) mf; (in competition) Preisrichter m.

jury ['dʒʊərɪ] n (court) Geschworene pl; (in competition) Jury f.

just [dʒʌst] a gerecht // ad (recently, now) gerade, eben; (barely) gerade noch; (exactly) genau, gerade; (only) nur, bloß; (a small distance) gleich; (absolutely) einfach; ~ **as I arrived** gerade als ich ankam; ~ **as nice** genauso nett; ~ **as well** um so besser; ~ **now** soeben, gerade; ~ **try** versuch es mal.

justice ['dʒʌstɪs] n (fairness) Gerechtigkeit f; ~ **of the peace** n Friedensrichter m.

justifiable ['dʒʌstɪfaɪəbl] a berechtigt.

justification [dʒʌstɪfɪˈkeɪʃən] n Rechtfertigung f.

justify ['dʒʌstɪfaɪ] vt rechtfertigen; (text) justieren.

justly ['dʒʌstlɪ] ad (say) mit Recht;

(*condemn*) gerecht.

jut [dʒʌt] *vi* (*also:* ~ **out**) herausragen, vorstehen.

juvenile ['dʒuːvənaɪl] *a* (*young*) jugendlich; (*for the young*) Jugend- // *n* Jugendliche(r) *mf*.

juxtapose ['dʒʌkstəpəʊz] *vt* nebeneinanderstellen.

K

K *abbr* (= *one thousand*) Tsd.; (= *Kilobyte*) K.

kangaroo [kæŋgə'ruː] *n* Känguruh *nt*.

karate [kə'rɑːtɪ] *n* Karate *nt*.

kebab [kə'bæb] *n* Kebab *m*.

keel [kiːl] *n* Kiel *m*; **on an even ~** (*fig*) im Lot.

keen [kiːn] *a* begeistert; (*intelligence, wind, blade*) scharf; (*sight, hearing*) gut; **to be ~ to do** *or* **on doing sth** etw unbedingt tun wollen; **to be ~ on sth/sb** scharf auf etw/jdn sein.

keep [kiːp], *pt, pp* **kept** *vt* (*retain*) behalten; (*have*) haben; (*animals, one's word*) halten; (*support*) versorgen; (*maintain in state*) halten; (*preserve*) aufbewahren; (*restrain*) abhalten // *vi* (*continue in direction*) sich halten; (*food*) sich halten; (*remain: quiet etc*) bleiben // *n* Unterhalt *m*; (*tower*) Burgfried *m*; (*col*): **for ~s** für immer; **to ~ sth to o.s.** etw für sich behalten; **it ~s happening** es passiert immer wieder; ~ **back** *vt* fernhalten; (*secret*) verschweigen; ~ **on** *vi*: ~ **on doing sth** etw immer weiter tun; ~ **out** *vt* nicht hereinlassen; '~ **out**' 'Eintritt verboten!'; ~ **up** *vi* Schritt halten // *vt* aufrechterhalten; (*continue*) weitermachen; **to ~ up with** Schritt halten mit; ~**er** *n* Wärter(in *f*) *m*; (*goal*~) Torhüter(in *f*) *m*; ~-**fit** *n* keep-fit *nt*; ~**ing** *n* (*care*) Obhut *f*; **in ~ing with** in Übereinstimmung mit; ~**sake** *n* Andenken *nt*.

keg [keg] *n* Faß *nt*.

kennel ['kenl] *n* Hundehütte *f*; ~**s** *pl*: **to put a dog in ~s** einen Hund in Pflege geben.

Kenya ['kenjə] *n* Kenia *nt*; ~**n** *a* kenianisch // *n* Kenianer(in *f*) *m*.

kept [kept] *pt, pp of* **keep**.

kerb ['kɜːb] *n* (*Brit*) Bordstein *m*.

kernel ['kɜːnl] *n* Kern *m*.

kerosene ['kerəsiːn] *n* Kerosin *nt*.

ketchup ['ketʃəp] *n* Ketchup *nt or m*.

kettle ['ketl] *n* Kessel *m*; ~**drum** *n* Pauke *f*.

key [kiː] *n* Schlüssel *m*; (*of piano, typewriter*) Taste *f*; (*MUS*) Tonart *f* // *vt* (*also:* ~ **in**) eingeben; ~**board** *n* Tastatur *f*; ~**ed up** *a* (*person*) überdreht; ~**hole** *n* Schlüsselloch *nt*; ~**note** *n* Grundton *m*; ~ **ring** *n* Schlüsselring *m*.

khaki ['kɑːkɪ] *n* K(h)aki *nt* // *a* k(h)aki(farben).

kibbutz [kɪ'bʊts] *n* Kibbutz *m*.

kick [kɪk] *vt* einen Fußtritt geben (+*dat*), treten // *vi* treten; (*baby*) strampeln; (*horse*) ausschlagen // *n* (Fuß)tritt *m*; (*thrill*) Spaß *m*; **he does it for ~s** er macht das aus Jux; ~ **off** *vi* (*SPORT*) anstoßen; ~-**off** *n* (*SPORT*) Anstoß *m*.

kid [kɪd] *n* (*col: child*) Kind *nt*; (*goat*) Zicklein *nt*; (*leather*) Glacéleder *nt* // *vi* (*col*) Witze machen.

kidnap ['kɪdnæp] *vt* entführen; ~**per** *n* Entführer *m*; ~**ping** *n* Entführung *f*.

kidney ['kɪdnɪ] *n* Niere *f*.

kill [kɪl] *vt* töten, umbringen // *vi* töten // *n* Tötung *f*; (*hunting*) (Jagd)beute *f*; ~**er** *n* Mörder(in *f*) *m*; ~**ing** *n* Mord *m*; ~**joy** *n* Spaßverderber(in *f*) *m*.

kiln [kɪln] *n* Brennofen *m*.

kilo ['kiːləʊ] *n* Kilo *nt*; ~**byte** *n* (*COMPUT*) Kilobyte *nt*; ~**gram(me)** *n* Kilogramm *nt*; ~**metre**, (*US*) ~**meter** *n* Kilometer *m*; ~**watt** *n* Kilowatt *nt*.

kilt [kɪlt] *n* Schottenrock *m*.

kin [kɪn] *n* Verwandtschaft *f*.

kind [kaɪnd] *a* freundlich // *n* Art *f*; **a ~ of** eine Art von; (**two**) **of a ~** (zwei) von der gleichen Art; **in ~** auf dieselbe Art; (*in goods*) in Naturalien.

kindergarten ['kɪndəgɑːtn] *n* Kindergarten *m*.

kind-hearted ['kaɪnd'hɑːtɪd] *a* gutherzig.

kindle ['kɪndl] *vt* (*set on fire*) anzünden; (*rouse*) reizen, (er)wecken.

kindly ['kaɪndlɪ] *a* freundlich // *ad* liebenswürdig(erweise); **would you ~ ...?** wären Sie so freundlich und ...?

kindness ['kaɪndnəs] *n* Freundlichkeit *f*.

kindred ['kɪndrəd] *n* Verwandtschaft *f* // *a*: ~ **spirit** *n* Gleichgesinnte(r) *mf*.

king [kɪŋ] *n* König *m*; ~**dom** *n* Königreich *nt*; ~**fisher** *n* Eisvogel *m*; ~-**size** *a* (*cigarette*) Kingsize.

kinky ['kɪŋkɪ] *a* (*col*) (*person, ideas*) verrückt; (*sexual*) abartig.

kiosk ['kiːɒsk] *n* (*Brit TEL*) Telefonhäuschen *nt*.

kipper ['kɪpə*] *n* Räucherhering *m*.

kiss [kɪs] *n* Kuß *m* // *vt* küssen // *vi*: **they ~ed** sie küßten sich.

kit [kɪt] *n* Ausrüstung *f*; (*tools*) Werkzeug *nt*.

kitchen ['kɪtʃɪn] *n* Küche *f*; ~ **sink** *n* Spülbecken *nt*.

kite [kaɪt] *n* Drachen *m*.

kith [kɪθ] *n*: ~ **and kin** Blutsverwandte *pl*.

kitten ['kɪtn] *n* Kätzchen *nt*.

kitty ['kɪtɪ] *n* (*money*) Kasse *f*.

km *abbr* (= *kilometre*) km.

knack [næk] *n* Dreh *m*, Trick *m*.

knapsack ['næpsæk] *n* Rucksack *m*; (*MIL*) Tornister *m*.

knead [ni:d] *vt* kneten.
knee [ni:] *n* Knie *nt*; **~cap** *n* Kniescheibe *f*.
kneel [ni:l], *pt, pp* **knelt** *vi* (also: ~ **down**) knien.
knell [nel] *n* Grabgeläute *nt*.
knelt [nelt] *pt, pp* of **kneel**.
knew [nju:] *pt* of **know**.
knickers ['nɪkəz] *npl* (Brit) Schlüpfer *m*.
knife [naɪf], *pl* **knives** *n* Messer *nt* // *vt* erstechen.
knight [naɪt] *n* Ritter *m*; (chess) Springer *m*; **~hood** *n* (title): **to get a ~hood** zum Ritter geschlagen werden.
knit [nɪt] *vti* stricken // *vi* (bones) zusammenwachsen; **~ting** *n* (occupation) Stricken *nt*; (work) Strickzeug *nt*; **~ting machine** *n* Strickmaschine *f*; **~ting needle** *n* Stricknadel *f*; **~wear** *n* Strickwaren *pl*.
knives [naɪvz] *pl* of **knife**.
knob [nɒb] *n* Knauf *m*; (on instrument) Knopf *m*; (Brit: of butter etc) kleine(s) Stück *nt*.
knock [nɒk] *vt* schlagen; (criticize) heruntermachen // *n* Schlag *m*; (on door) Klopfen *nt*; **to ~ at** or **on the door** an die Tür klopfen; **~ down** *vt* umwerfen; (with car) anfahren; **~ off** *vi* (do quickly) hinhauen; (col: steal) klauen // *vi* (finish) Feierabend machen; **~ out** *vt* ausschlagen; (BOXING) k.o. schlagen; **~ over** *vt* (person, object) umwerfen; (with car) anfahren; **~er** *n* (on door) Türklopfer *m*; **~-kneed** *a* x-beinig; **~out** *n* (lit) K.o.-Schlag *m*; (fig) Sensation *f*.
knot [nɒt] *n* Knoten *m* // *vt* (ver)knoten.
knotty ['nɒtɪ] *a* (fig) kompliziert.
know [nəʊ], *pt* **knew** *pp* **known** *vt* wissen; (be able to) können; (be acquainted with) kennen; (recognize) erkennen; **to ~ how to do sth** wissen, wie man etw macht, etw tun können; **to ~ about** or **of sth/sb** etw/jdn kennen; **~-all** *n* Alleswisser *m*; **~-how** *n* Kenntnis *f*, Know-how *nt*; **~ing** *a* (look, smile) wissend; **~ingly** *ad* wissend; (intentionally) wissentlich.
knowledge ['nɒlɪdʒ] *n* Wissen *nt*, Kenntnis *f*; **~able** *a* informiert.
known [nəʊn] *pp* of **know**.
knuckle ['nʌkl] *n* Fingerknöchel *m*.
K.O. *n* abbr of **Knockout**.
Korea [kə'rɪə] *n* Korea *nt*.
kosher ['kəʊʃə*] *a* koscher.

L

l. abbr of **litre**.
lab [læb] *n* (col) Labor *nt*.
label ['leɪbl] *n* Etikett *nt* // *vt* etikettieren.
laboratory [lə'bɒrətərɪ] *n* Laboratorium

nt.
laborious [lə'bɔːrɪəs] *a* mühsam.
labour, (US) labor ['leɪbə*] *n* Arbeit *f*; (workmen) Arbeitskräfte *pl*; (MED) Wehen *pl* // *vi*: **to ~ (at)** sich abmühen (mit) // *vt* breittreten (col); **in ~** (MED) in den Wehen; **L~, the L~ party** (Brit) die Labour Party; **hard ~** Zwangsarbeit *f*; **~ed** *a* (movement) gequält; (style) schwerfällig; **~er** *n* Arbeiter *m*.
lace [leɪs] *n* (fabric) Spitze *f*; (of shoe) Schnürsenkel *m*; (braid) Litze *f* // *vt* (also ~ **up**) (zu)schnüren.
lack [læk] *n* Mangel *m* // *vt* nicht haben; **sb ~s sth** jdm fehlt etw (nom); **to be ~ing** fehlen; **sb is ~ing in sth** es fehlt jdm an etw (dat); **through** or **for ~ of** aus Mangel an (+dat).
lackadaisical [lækə'deɪzɪkəl] *a* lasch.
lacquer ['lækə*] *n* Lack *m*.
lad [læd] *n* Junge *m*.
ladder ['lædə*] *n* Leiter *f*; (Brit: in tights) Laufmasche *f* // *vt* (Brit: tights) Laufmaschen bekommen in (+dat).
laden ['leɪdn] *a* beladen, voll.
ladle ['leɪdl] *n* Schöpfkelle *f*.
lady ['leɪdɪ] *n* Dame *f*; (title) Lady *f*; **young ~** junge Dame; **the ladies' (room)** die Damentoilette; **~bird**, (US) **~bug** *n* Marienkäfer *m*; **~-in-waiting** *n* Hofdame *f*; **~like** *a* damenhaft, vornehm; **~ship** *n*: **your ~ship** Ihre Ladyschaft.
lag [læg] *vi* (also: ~ **behind**) zurückbleiben // *vt* (pipes) verkleiden.
lager ['lɑːgə*] *n* helle(s) Bier *nt*.
lagging ['lægɪŋ] *n* Isolierung *f*.
laid [leɪd] *pt, pp* of **lay**; **~ back** *a* (col) cool.
lain [leɪn] *pp* of **lie**.
lair [lɛə*] *n* Lager *nt*.
laity ['leɪtɪ] *n* Laien *pl*.
lake [leɪk] *n* See *m*.
lamb [læm] *n* Lamm *nt*; (meat) Lammfleisch *nt*; **~ chop** *n* Lammkotelett *nt*; **lambswool** *n* Lammwolle *f*.
lame [leɪm] *a* lahm; (excuse) faul.
lament [lə'ment] *n* Klage *f* // *vt* beklagen.
laminated ['læmɪneɪtɪd] *a* beschichtet.
lamp [læmp] *n* Lampe *f*; (in street) Straßenlaterne *f*.
lampoon [læm'puːn] *vt* verspotten.
lamp: ~post *n* (Brit) Laternenpfahl *m*; **~shade** *n* Lampenschirm *m*.
lance [lɑːns] *n* Lanze *f* // *vt* (MED) aufschneiden; **~ corporal** *n* (Brit) Obergefreite(r) *m*.
land [lænd] *n* Land *nt* // *vi* (from ship) an Land gehen; (AVIAT, end up) landen // *vt* (obtain) kriegen; (passengers) absetzen; (goods) abladen; (troops, space probe) landen; **~ing** *n* Landung *f*; (on stairs) (Treppen)absatz *m*; **~ing**

gear n Fahrgestell nt; **~ing stage** n (Brit) Landesteg m; **~ing strip** n Landebahn f; **~lady** n (Haus)wirtin f; **~locked** a landumschlossen, Binnen-; **~lord** n (of house) Hauswirt m, Besitzer m; (of pub) Gastwirt m; (of land) Grundbesitzer m; **~mark** n Wahrzeichen nt; (fig) Meilenstein m; **~owner** n Grundbesitzer m.

landscape ['lændskeip] n Landschaft f.

landslide ['lændslaid] n (GEOG) Erdrutsch m; (POL) überwältigende(r) Sieg m.

lane [lein] n (in town) Gasse f; (in country) Weg m; (of motorway) Fahrbahn f, Spur f; (SPORT) Bahn f.

language ['længwidʒ] n Sprache f; bad ~ unanständige Ausdrücke; ~ **laboratory** n Sprachlabor nt.

languid ['længwid] a schlaff, matt.

languish ['længwiʃ] vi schmachten.

lank [læŋk] a dürr.

lanky ['læŋki] a schlaksig.

lantern ['læntən] n Laterne f.

lap [læp] n Schoß m; (SPORT) Runde f // vt (also: ~ **up**) auflecken // vi (water) plätschern.

lapel [lə'pel] n Revers nt or m.

lapse [læps] n (moral) Fehltritt m // vi (decline) nachlassen; (expire) ablaufen; (claims) erlöschen; **to ~ into bad habits** sich schlechte Gewohnheiten angewöhnen.

larceny ['lɑːsəni] n Diebstahl m.

lard [lɑːd] n Schweineschmalz m.

larder ['lɑːdə*] n Speisekammer f.

large [lɑːdʒ] a groß; **at ~** auf freiem Fuß; **~ly** ad zum größten Teil; **~-scale** a groß angelegt, Groß-.

largesse [lɑː'ʒes] n Freigebigkeit f.

lark [lɑːk] n (bird) Lerche f; (joke) Jux m; ~ **about** vi (col) herumalbern.

laryngitis [lærin'dʒaitis] n Kehlkopfentzündung f.

larynx ['læriŋks] n Kehlkopf m.

lascivious [lə'siviəs] a wollüstig.

laser ['leizə*] n Laser m; ~ **printer** n Laserdrucker m.

lash [læʃ] n Peitschenhieb m; (eye~) Wimper f // vt (rain) schlagen gegen; (whip) peitschen; (bind) festbinden; ~ **out** vi (with fists) um sich schlagen; (spend money) sich in Unkosten stürzen // vt (money etc) springen lassen.

lass [læs] n Mädchen nt.

lasso [læ'suː] n Lasso nt.

last [lɑːst] a letzte(r, s) // ad zuletzt; (last time) das letztemal // vi (continue) dauern; (remain good) sich halten; (money) ausreichen; **at ~** endlich; ~ **night** gestern abend; ~ **week** letzte Woche; ~ **but one** vorletzte(r, s); **~-ditch** a (attempt) in letzter Minute; **~ing** a dauerhaft; (shame etc) andauernd; **~ly** ad schließlich; **~-minute** a in letzter

Minute.

latch [lætʃ] n Riegel m.

late [leit] a spät; (dead) verstorben // ad spät; (after proper time) zu spät; **to be ~** zu spät kommen; **of ~** in letzter Zeit; **in ~ May** Ende Mai; **~comer** n Nachzügler(in f) m; **~ly** ad in letzter Zeit.

lateness ['leitnəs] n (of person) Zuspätkommen nt; (of train) Verspätung f; ~ **of the hour** die vorgerückte Stunde.

later ['leitə*] a (date etc) später; (version etc) neuer // ad später.

lateral ['lætərəl] a seitlich.

latest ['leitist] a (fashion) neueste(r, s) // n (news) Neu(e)ste(s) nt; **at the ~** spätestens.

lathe [leið] n Drehbank f.

lather ['lɑːðə*] n (Seifen)schaum m; vt einschäumen // vi schäumen.

Latin ['lætin] n Latein nt // a lateinisch; (Roman) römisch; ~ **America** n Lateinamerika nt; **~-American** a lateinamerikanisch.

latitude ['lætitjuːd] n (GEOG) Breite f; (freedom) Spielraum m.

latter ['lætə*] a (second of two) letztere; (coming at end) letzte(r, s), später // n: **the ~** der/die/das letztere, die letzteren; **~ly** ad in letzter Zeit.

lattice ['lætis] n Gitter nt.

laudable ['lɔːdəbl] a löblich.

laugh [lɑːf] n Lachen nt // vi lachen; ~ **at** vt lachen über (+acc); ~ **off** vt lachend abtun; **~able** a lachhaft; **~ing stock** n Zielscheibe f des Spottes; **~ter** n Gelächter nt.

launch [lɔːntʃ] n (of ship) Stapellauf m; (of rocket) Abschuß m; (boat) Barkasse f; (of product) Einführung f // vt (set afloat) vom Stapel lassen; (rocket) (ab)schießen; (product) auf den Markt bringen; **~ing** n Stapellauf m; **~(ing) pad** n Abschußrampe f.

launder ['lɔːndə*] vt waschen.

launderette [lɔːn'dret], (US) **laundromat** ['lɔːndrəmæt] n Waschsalon m.

laundry ['lɔːndri] n (place) Wäscherei f; (clothes) Wäsche f; **to do the ~** waschen.

laureate ['lɔːriət] a see **poet**.

laurel ['lɔrəl] n Lorbeer m.

lavatory ['lævətri] n Toilette f.

lavender ['lævində*] n Lavendel m.

lavish ['læviʃ] a (extravagant) verschwenderisch; (generous) großzügig // vt (money) verschwenden (on auf +acc); (attentions, gifts) überschütten mit (on sb jdn).

law [lɔː] n Gesetz nt; (system) Recht nt; (as studies) Jura no art; **~-abiding** a gesetzestreu; ~ **and order** n Recht und Ordnung f; ~ **court** n Gerichtshof m; **~ful** a gesetzlich; **~less** a gesetzlos.

lawn [lɔːn] n Rasen m; **~mower** n Rasenmäher m; ~ **tennis** n

Rasentennis *m*.

law school *n* Rechtsakademie *f*.

lawsuit ['lɔːsuːt] *n* Prozeß *m*.

lawyer ['lɔːjə*] *n* Rechtsanwalt *m*, Rechtsanwältin *f*.

laxative ['læksətɪv] *n* Abführmittel *nt*.

laxity ['læksɪtɪ] *n* Laxheit *f*.

lay [leɪ] *pt of* **lie** // *a* Laien- // *vt, pt, pp* **laid** (*place*) legen; (*table*) dekken; (*egg*) legen; (*trap*) stellen; (*money*) wetten; ~ **aside** *vt* zurücklegen; ~ **by** *vt* (*set aside*) beiseite legen; ~ **down** *vt* hinlegen; (*rules*) vorschreiben; (*arms*) strecken; **to** ~ **down the law** Vorschriften machen; ~ **off** *vt* (*workers*) (vorübergehend) entlassen; ~ **on** *vt* (*water, gas*) anschließen; (*concert etc*) veranstalten; ~ **out** *vt* (*her*)auslegen; (*money*) ausgeben; (*corpse*) aufbahren; ~ **up** *vt* (*subj: illness*) ans Bett fesseln; (*supplies*) anlegen; ~**about** *n* Faulenzer *m*; ~**-by** *n* (*Brit*) Parkbucht *f*; (*bigger*) Rastplatz *m*.

layer ['leɪə*] *n* Schicht *f*.

layette [leɪ'et] *n* Babyausstattung *f*.

layman ['leɪmən] *n* Laie *m*.

layout ['leɪaʊt] *n* Anlage *f*; (*ART*) Layout *nt*.

laze [leɪz] *vi* faulenzen.

laziness ['leɪzɪnəs] *n* Faulheit *f*.

lazy ['leɪzɪ] *a* faul; (*slow-moving*) träge.

lb. *abbr of* **pound** (*weight*).

lead [liːd] *n* (*front position*) Führung *f*; (*distance, time ahead*) Vorsprung *f*; (*example*) Vorbild *nt*; (*clue*) Tip *m*; (*of police*) Spur *f*; (*THEAT*) Hauptrolle *f*; (*dog's*) Leine *f*; [led] (*chemical*) Blei *nt*; (*of pencil*) (Bleistift)mine *f* // *a* [led] bleiern, Blei- // *v* [liːd] (*pt, pp* **led**) *vt* (*guide*) führen; (*group etc*) leiten // *vi* (*be first*) führen; **in the** ~ (*SPORT, fig*) in Führung; ~ **astray** *vt* irreführen; ~ **away** *vt* wegführen; (*prisoner*) abführen; ~ **back** *vi* zurückführen; ~ **on** *vt* anführen; ~ **on to** *vt* (*induce*) dazu bringen; ~ **to** *vt* (*street*) (hin)führen nach; (*result in*) führen zu; ~ **up to** *vt* (*drive*) führen zu; (*speaker etc*) hinführen auf (+*acc*).

leaden ['ledn] *a* (*sky, sea*) bleiern; (*heavy: footsteps*) bleischwer.

leader ['liːdə*] *n* Führer *m*, Leiter *m*; (*of party*) Vorsitzende(r) *m*; (*PRESS*) Leitartikel *m*; ~**ship** *n* (*office*) Leitung *f*; (*quality*) Führerschaft *f*.

leading ['liːdɪŋ] *a* führend; ~ **lady** *n* (*THEAT*) Hauptdarstellerin *f*; ~ **light** *n* (*person*) führende(r) Geist *m*.

leaf [liːf] *pl* **leaves** *n* Blatt *nt* // *vi*: **to** ~ **through** durchblättern; **to turn over a new** ~ einen neuen Anfang nachen.

leaflet ['liːflɪt] *n* (*advertisement*) Prospekt *m*; (*pamphlet*) Flugblatt *nt*; (*for information*) Merkblatt *nt*.

league [liːg] *n* (*union*) Bund *m*; (*SPORT*)

Liga *f*; **to be in** ~ **with** unter einer Decke stecken mit.

leak [liːk] *n* undichte Stelle *f*; (*in ship*) Leck *nt* // *vt* (*liquid etc*) durchlassen // *vi* (*pipe etc*) undicht sein; (*liquid etc*) auslaufen; **the information was** ~**ed to the enemy** die Information wurde dem Feind zugespielt; ~ **out** *vi* (*liquid etc*) auslaufen; (*information*) durchsickern.

leaky ['liːkɪ] *a* undicht.

lean [liːn] *a* mager // (*v: pt, pp* **leaned** *or* **leant** [lent]) *vi* sich neigen // *vt* (an)lehnen; **to** ~ **against sth an etw** (*dat*) angelehnt sein; **sich an etw** (*acc*) anlehnen; ~ **back** *vi* sich zurücklehnen; ~ **forward** *vi* sich vorbeugen; ~ **on** *vi* sich stützen auf (+*acc*); ~ **out** *vi* sich hinauslehnen; ~ **over** *vi* sich hinüberbeugen; ~**ing** *n* Neigung *f* // *a* schief; ~**-to** *n* Anbau *m*.

leap [liːp] *n* Sprung *m* // *vi, pt, pp* **leaped** *or* **leapt** [lept] springen; ~**frog** *n* Bockspringen *nt*; ~ **year** *n* Schaltjahr *nt*.

learn [lɜːn], *pt, pp* **learned** *or* **learnt** [lɜːnt] *vti* lernen; (*find out*) erfahren; **to** ~ **how to do sth etw** (er)lernen; ~**ed** ['lɜːnɪd] *a* gelehrt; ~**er** *n* Anfänger(in *f*) *m*; (*AUT*) (*Brit: also* ~ **driver**) Fahrschüler(in *f*) *m*; ~**ing** *n* Gelehrsamkeit *f*.

lease [liːs] *n* (*of property*) Mietvertrag *m* // *vt* pachten.

leash [liːʃ] *n* Leine *f*.

least [liːst] *a* geringste(r, s) // *ad* am wenigsten // *n* Mindeste(s) *nt*; **the** ~ **possible effort** möglichst geringer Aufwand; **at** ~ zumindest; **not in the** ~! durchaus nicht!

leather ['leðə*] *n* Leder *nt*.

leave [liːv], *pt, pp* **left** *vt* verlassen; (~ *behind*) zurücklassen; (*forget*) vergessen; (*allow to remain*) lassen; (*after death*) hinterlassen; (*entrust*) überlassen (*to sb* jdm) // *vi* weggehen, wegfahren; (*for journey*) abreisen; (*bus, train*) abfahren // *n* Erlaubnis *f*; (*MIL*) Urlaub *m*; **to be left** (*remain*) übrigbleiben; **there's some milk left over** es ist noch etwas Milch übrig; **on** ~ auf Urlaub; ~ **behind** *vt* (*person, object*) dalassen; (*forget*) liegenlassen, stehenlassen; ~ **out** *vt* auslassen; ~ **of absence** *n* Urlaub.

leaves [liːvz] *pl of* **leaf**.

Lebanon ['lebənən] *n* Libanon *m*.

lecherous ['letʃərəs] *a* lüstern.

lecture ['lektʃə*] *n* Vortrag *m*; (*UNIV*) Vorlesung *f* // *vi* einen Vortrag halten; (*UNIV*) lesen // *vt* (*scold*) abkanzeln; **to give a** ~ **on sth** einen Vortrag über etwas halten; ~**r** *n* Vortragende(r) *mf*; (*Brit: UNIV*) Dozent(in *f*) *m*.

led [led] *pt, pp of* **lead**.

ledge [ledʒ] *n* Leiste *f*; (*window* ~) Sims *m or nt*; (*of mountain*) (Fels)vorsprung *m.*

ledger ['ledʒə*] *n* Hauptbuch *nt.*

lee [li:] *n* Windschatten *m*; (*NAUT*) Lee *f.*

leech [li:tʃ] *n* Blutegel *m.*

leek [li:k] *n* Lauch *m.*

leer [lɪə*] *vi* schielen (*at* nach).

leeway ['li:weɪ] *n* (*fig*): to have some ~ etwas Spielraum haben.

left [left] *pt, pp of* **leave** // *a* linke(r, s) // *n* (*side*) linke Seite *f* // *ad* links; **on** the ~ links; **to the** ~ nach links; **the** L~ (*POL*) die Linke *f*; **~-handed** *a* linkshändig; **~-hand side** *n* linke Seite *f*; **~-luggage (office)** *n* (*Brit*) Gepäckaufbewahrung *f*; **~-overs** *pl* Reste *pl*; **~-wing** *a* linke(r, s).

leg [leg] *n* Bein *nt*; (*of meat*) Keule *f*; (*stage*) Etappe *f*; **1st/2nd** ~ (*SPORT*) 1./2. Etappe.

legacy ['legəsɪ] *n* Erbe *nt*, Erbschaft *f.*

legal ['li:gəl] *a* gesetzlich; (*allowed*) legal; ~ **holiday** *n* (*US*) gesetzlicher Feiertag; **~ize** *vt* legalisieren; **~ly** *ad* gesetzlich; legal; ~ **tender** *n* gesetzliche(s) Zahlungsmittel *nt.*

legend ['ledʒənd] *n* Legende *f*; **~ary** *a* legendär.

legible ['ledʒəbl] *a* leserlich.

legislation [ledʒɪs'leɪʃən] *n* Gesetzgebung *f.*

legislative ['ledʒɪslətɪv] *a* gesetzgebend.

legislature ['ledʒɪslətʃə*] *n* Legislative *f.*

legitimate [lɪ'dʒɪtɪmət] *a* rechtmäßig, legitim; (*child*) ehelich.

legroom ['legrʊm] *n* Platz *m* für die Beine.

leisure ['leʒə*] *n* Freizeit *f*; **to be at** ~ Zeit haben; **~ly** *a* gemächlich.

lemon ['lemən] *n* Zitrone *f*; (*colour*) Zitronengelb *nt*; **~ade** [lemə'neɪd] *n* Limonade *f.*

lend [lend], *pt, pp* **lent** *vt* leihen; **to** ~ **sb sth** jdm etw leihen; **~ing library** *n* Leihbibliothek *f.*

length [leŋθ] *n* Länge *f*; (*section of road, pipe etc*) Strecke *f*; (*of material*) Stück *nt*; **at** ~ (*lengthily*) ausführlich; (*at last*) schließlich; **~en** *vt* verlängern // *vi* länger werden; **~ways** *ad* längs; **~y** *a* sehr lang, langatmig.

lenient ['li:nɪənt] *a* nachsichtig.

lens [lenz] *n* Linse *f*; (*PHOT*) Objektiv *nt.*

lent [lent] *pt, pp of* **lend.**

Lent [lent] *n* Fastenzeit *f.*

lentil ['lentl] *n* Linse *f.*

Leo ['li:əʊ] *n* Löwe *m.*

leotard ['li:ətɑ:d] *n* Trikot *nt*, Gymnastikanzug *m.*

leper ['lepə*] *n* Leprakranke(r) *mf.*

leprosy ['leprəsɪ] *n* Lepra *f.*

lesbian ['lezbɪən] *a* lesbisch // *n* Lesbierin *f.*

less [les] *a, ad, pron* weniger; ~ **than** half weniger als die Hälfte; ~ **than ever** weniger denn je; ~ **and** ~ immer weniger; **the** ~ **he works** je weniger er arbeitet.

lessen ['lesn] *vi* abnehmen // *vt* verringern, verkleinern.

lesser ['lesə*] *a* kleiner, geringer; **to a** ~ **extent** in geringerem Maße.

lesson ['lesn] *n* (*SCH*) Stunde *f*; (*unit of study*) Lektion *f*; (*fig*) Lehre *f*; (*ECCL*) Lesung *f*; **a maths** ~ eine Mathestunde.

lest [lest] *cj*: ~ **it happen** damit es nicht passiert.

let [let] *vt, pt, pp* **let** lassen; (*Brit: lease*) vermieten; **to** ~ **sb do sth** jdn etw tun lassen; **to** ~ **sb know sth** jdn etw wissen lassen; **~'s go!** gehen wir!; ~ **him come** soll er doch kommen; ~ **down** *vt* hinunterlassen; (*disappoint*) enttäuschen; ~ **go** *vi* loslassen // *vt* (*things*) loslassen; (*person*) gehen lassen; ~ **in** *vt* hereinlassen; (*water*) durchlassen; ~ **off** *vt* (*gun*) abfeuern; (*steam*) ablassen; (*forgive*) laufen lassen; ~ **on** *vi* durchblicken lassen; (*pretend*) vorgeben; ~ **out** *vt* herauslassen; (*scream*) fahren lassen; ~ **up** *vi* nachlassen; (*stop*) aufhören.

lethal ['li:θəl] *a* tödlich.

letter ['letə*] *n* (*of alphabet*) Buchstabe *m*; (*message*) Brief *m*; ~ **bomb** *n* Briefbombe *f*; **~box** *n* (*Brit*) Briefkasten *m*; ~ **of credit** *n* Akkreditiv *m*; **~ing** *n* Beschriftung *f.*

lettuce ['letɪs] *n* (Kopf)salat *m.*

let-up ['letʌp] *n* (*col*) Nachlassen *nt.*

leukaemia, (*US*) **leukemia** [lu:'ki:mɪə] *n* Leukämie *f.*

level ['levl] *a* (*ground*) eben; (*at same height*) auf gleicher Höhe; (*equal*) gleich gut; (*head*) kühl // *ad* auf gleicher Höhe // *n* (*instrument*) Wasserwaage *f*; (*altitude*) Höhe *f*; (*flat place*) ebene Fläche *f*; (*position on scale*) Niveau *nt*; (*amount, degree*) Grad *m*; // *vt* (*ground*) einebnen; (*blow*) versetzen (*at sb* jdm); (*remark*) richten (*at* gegen); **to draw** ~ **with** gleichziehen mit; **to be** ~ **with** auf einer Höhe sein mit; **'A'** ~**s** *npl* (*Brit*) ≈ Abitur *nt*; **'O'** ~**s** *npl* (*Brit*) ≈ mittlere Reife; **on the** ~ (*fig: honest*) ehrlich; ~ **off** *or* **out** *vi* flach or eben werden; (*fig*) sich ausgleichen; (*plane*) horizontal fliegen // *vt* (*ground*) planieren; (*differences*) ausgleichen; ~ **crossing** *n* (*Brit*) Bahnübergang *m*; **~-headed** *a* vernünftig.

lever ['li:və*] *n* Hebel *m*; (*fig*) Druckmittel *nt* // *vt* (hoch)stemmen; **~age** *n* Hebelkraft *f*; (*fig*) Einfluß *m.*

levity ['levɪtɪ] *n* Leichtfertigkeit *f.*

levy ['levɪ] *n* (*of taxes*) Erhebung *f*; (*tax*) Abgaben *pl*; (*MIL*) Aushebung *f* // *vt* erheben; (*MIL*) ausheben.

lewd [lu:d] *a* unzüchtig, unanständig.

liability [laɪə'bɪlɪtɪ] *n* (*burden*) Belastung *f*; (*duty*) Pflicht *f*; (*debt*) Verpflichtung *f*; (*proneness*) Anfälligkeit *f*; (*responsibility*) Haftung *f*.

liable ['laɪəbl] *a* (*responsible*) haftbar; (*prone*) anfällig; **to be ~ for** etw (*dat*) unterliegen; **it's ~ to happen** es kann leicht vorkommen.

liaise [lɪ'eɪz] *vi* zusammenarbeiten (*with* mit).

liaison [lɪ'eɪzɒn] *n* Verbindung *f*.

liar ['laɪə*] *n* Lügner *m*.

libel ['laɪbəl] *n* Verleumdung *f* // *vt* verleumden.

liberal ['lɪbərəl] *a* (*generous*) großzügig; (*open-minded*) aufgeschlossen; (*POL*) liberal.

liberate ['lɪbəreɪt] *vt* befreien.

liberation [lɪbə'reɪʃən] *n* Befreiung *f*.

liberty ['lɪbətɪ] *n* Freiheit *f*; (*permission*) Erlaubnis *f*; **to be at ~ to do sth** etw tun dürfen; **to take the ~ of doing sth** sich (*dat*) erlauben, etw zu tun.

Libra ['li:brə] *n* Waage *f*.

librarian [laɪbreərɪən] *n* Bibliothekar(in *f*) *m*.

library ['laɪbrərɪ] *n* Bibliothek *f*; (*lending ~*) Bücherei *f*.

Libya ['lɪbɪə] *n* Libyen *nt*; **~n** *a* libysch // *n* Libyer(in *f*) *m*.

lice [laɪs] *npl* of **louse**.

licence, (*US*) **license** ['laɪsəns] *n* (*permit*) Erlaubnis *f*; (*also: driving ~*, (*US*) *driver's ~*) Führerschein *m*; (*excess*) Zügellosigkeit *f*; **~ number** *n* (Kraftfahrzeug)kennzeichen *nt*; **~ plate** *n* (*US AUT*) Nummernschild *nt*.

license ['laɪsəns] *n* (*US*) = **licence** // *vt* genehmigen, konzessionieren; **~d** *a* (*for alcohol*) konzessioniert (*für den Ausschank von Alkohol*).

licentious [laɪ'senʃəs] *a* ausschweifend.

lichen ['laɪkən] *n* Flechte *f*.

lick [lɪk] *vt* lecken // *n* Lecken *nt*; **a ~ of paint** ein bißchen Farbe.

licorice ['lɪkərɪs] *n* = **liquorice**.

lid [lɪd] *n* Deckel *m*; (*eye~*) Lid *nt*.

lido ['li:dəʊ] *n* (*Brit*) Freibad *nt*.

lie [laɪ] *n* Lüge *f* // *vi* lügen // *vi*, *pt* **lay**, *pp* **lain** (*rest, be situated*) liegen; (*put o.s. in position*) sich legen; **to ~ low** (*fig*) untertauchen; **~ about** *vi* (*things*) herumliegen; (*people*) faulenzen; **~-down** *n*: **to have a ~-down** (*Brit*) ein Nickerchen machen; **~-in** *n*: **to have a ~-in** (*Brit*) sich ausschlafen.

lieu [lu:] *n*: **in ~ of** anstatt (*+gen*).

lieutenant [lef'tenənt] *n* Leutnant *m*.

life [laɪf], *pl* **lives** *n* Leben *nt*; **~ assurance** (*Brit*) *n* Lebensversicherung *f*; **~belt** (*Brit*) *n* Rettungsring *m*; **~boat** *n* Rettungsboot *nt*; **~guard** *n* Rettungsschwimmer *m*; **~ insurance** *n* = **~ assurance**; **~ jacket** *n* Schwimmweste *f*; **~less** *a* (*dead*) leblos; (*dull*) langweilig; **~like** *a* lebenswahr, naturgetreu; **~line** *n* (*lit*) Rettungsleine *f*; (*fig*) Rettungsanker *m*; **~long** *a* lebenslang; **~ preserver** *n* (*US*) = **~belt**; **~-saver** *n* Lebensretter(in *f*) *m*; **~ sentence** *n* lebenslängliche Freiheitsstrafe; **~-sized** *a* in Lebensgröße; **~ span** *n* Lebensspanne *f*; **~style** *n* Lebensstil *m*; **~ support system** *n* (*MED*) Lebenserhaltungssystem *nt*; **~time** *n*: **in his ~time** während er lebte; **once in a ~time** einmal im Leben.

lift [lɪft] *vt* hochheben // *vi* sich heben // *n* (*Brit: elevator*) Aufzug *m*, Lift *m*; **to give sb a ~** (*Brit*) jdn mitnehmen; **~-off** *n* Abheben *nt* (vom Boden).

ligament ['lɪgəmənt] *n* Band *nt*.

light [laɪt] *n* Licht *nt*; (*for cigarette etc*): **have you got a ~?** haben Sie Feuer?; **~s** *pl* (*AUT*) Beleuchtung *f* // *vt*, *pt*, *pp* **lighted** *or* **lit** beleuchten; (*lamp*) anmachen; (*fire, cigarette*) anzünden // *a* (*bright*) hell; (*pale*) hell-; (*not heavy, easy*) leicht; (*punishment*) milde; (*touch*) leicht; **~ up** *vi* (*lamp*) aufgehen; (*face*) aufleuchten // *vt* (*illuminate*) beleuchten; (*lights*) anmachen; **~ bulb** *n* Glühbirne *f*; **~en** *vi* (*brighten*) hell werden; (*lightning*) blitzen // *vt* (*give light to*) erhellen; (*hair*) aufhellen; (*gloom*) aufheitern; (*make less heavy*) leichter machen; (*fig*) erleichtern; **~er** *n* Feuerzeug *nt*; **~-headed** *a* (*thoughtless*) leichtsinnig; (*giddy*) schwindlig; **~-hearted** *a* leichtherzig, fröhlich; **~house** *n* Leuchtturm *m*; **~ing** *n* Beleuchtung *f*; **~ly** *ad* leicht; (*irresponsibly*) leichtfertig; **to get off ~ly** mit einem blauen Auge davonkommen; **~ness** *n* (*of weight*) Leichtigkeit *f*; (*of colour*) Helle *f*.

lightning ['laɪtnɪŋ] *n* Blitz *m*; **~ conductor**, (*US*) **~ rod** *n* Blitzableiter *m*.

light: ~ pen *n* Lichtstift *m*; **~weight** *a* (*suit*) leicht; **~weight boxer** *n* Leichtgewichtler *m*; **~ year** *n* Lichtjahr *nt*.

like [laɪk] *vt* mögen, gernhaben // *prep* wie // *a* (*similar*) ähnlich; (*equal*) gleich // *n*: **the ~** dergleichen; **his ~s and dislikes** was er mag und was er nicht mag; **I would ~**, **I'd ~** ich möchte gern; **would you ~ a coffee?** möchten Sie einen Kaffee?; **to be** *or* **look ~ sb/sth** jdm/etw ähneln; **that's just ~ him** das ist typisch für ihn; **do it ~ this** mach es so; **it is nothing ~ ...** es ist nicht zu vergleichen mit ...; **~able** *a* sympathisch.

likelihood ['laɪklɪhʊd] *n* Wahrscheinlichkeit *f*.

likely ['laɪklɪ] *a* wahrscheinlich; **he's ~ to leave** er geht möglicherweise; **not ~!**

wohl kaum.

likeness ['laıknıs] n Ähnlichkeit f; (portrait) Bild nt.

likewise ['laıkwaız] ad ebenso.

liking ['laıkıŋ] n Zuneigung f; (taste for) Vorliebe f.

lilac ['laılək] n Flieder m // a (colour) fliederfarben.

lily ['lılı] n Lilie f; ~ **of the valley** n Maiglöckchen nt.

limb [lım] n Glied nt.

limber ['lımbə*]: ~ **up** vi sich auflockern; (fig) sich vorbereiten.

limbo ['lımbəu] n: **to be in** ~ (fig) in der Schwebe sein.

lime [laım] n (tree) Linde f; (fruit) Limone f; (substance) Kalk m.

limelight ['laımlaıt] n: **to be in the** ~ (fig) im Rampenlicht stehen.

limestone ['laımstəun] n Kalkstein m.

limit ['lımıt] n Grenze f; (col) Höhe f // vt begrenzen, einschränken; ~**ation** n Einschränkung f; ~**ed** a beschränkt; **to be** ~**ed to** sich beschränken auf (acc); ~**ed (liability) company (Ltd)** n (Brit) Gesellschaft f mit beschränkter Haftung, GmbH f.

limp [lımp] n Hinken nt // vi hinken // a schlaff.

limpet ['lımpıt] n (fig) Klette f.

limpid ['lımpıd] a klar.

line [laın] n Linie f; (rope) Leine f; (on face) Falte f; (row) Reihe f; (of hills) Kette f; (US: queue) Schlange f; (company) Linie f, Gesellschaft f; (RAIL) Strecke f; (pl) Geleise pl; (TEL) Leitung f; (written) Zeile f; (direction) Richtung f; (fig: business) Branche f; (range of items) Kollektion f // vt (coat) füttern; (border) säumen; **in** ~ **with** in Übereinstimmung mit; ~ **up** vi sich aufstellen // vt aufstellen; (prepare) sorgen für; (support) mobilisieren; (surprise) planen.

linear ['lınıə*] a gerade; (measure) Längen-.

lined [laınd] a (face) faltig; (paper) liniert.

linen ['lının] n Leinen nt; (sheets etc) Wäsche f.

liner ['laınə*] n Überseedampfer m.

linesman ['laınzmən] n (SPORT) Linienrichter m.

line-up ['laınʌp] n Aufstellung f.

linger ['lıŋgə*] vi (remain long) verweilen; (taste) (zurück)bleiben; (delay) zögern, verharren.

lingerie ['lænʒəri:] n Damenunterwäsche f.

lingering ['lıŋgərıŋ] a (doubt) zurückbleibend; (disease) langwierig; (taste) nachhaltend; (look) lang.

lingo ['lıŋgəu], pl ~**es** n (col) Sprache f.

linguist ['lıŋgwıst] n Sprachkundige(r) mf; (UNIV) Sprachwissenschaftler(in f)

m.

linguistic [lıŋ'gwıstık] a sprachlich; sprachwissenschaftlich; ~**s** n Sprachwissenschaft f, Linguistik f.

lining ['laınıŋ] n (of clothes) Futter nt.

link [lıŋk] n Glied nt; (connection) Verbindung f; ~**s** pl (GOLF) Golfplatz m // vt verbinden; ~ **up** vt verbinden // vi zusammenkommen; (companies) sich zusammenschließen; ~-**up** n (TEL) Verbindung f; (of spaceships) Kopplung f.

lino ['laınəu] n, **linoleum** [lı'nəulıəm] n Linoleum nt.

linseed oil ['lınsi:d'ɔıl] n Leinöl nt.

lion ['laıən] n Löwe m; ~**ess** n Löwin f.

lip [lıp] n Lippe f; (of jug) Schnabel m; ~**read** vi irreg von den Lippen ablesen; ~ **salve** n Lippenbalsam m; **to pay** ~ **service (to)** ein Lippenbekenntnis ablegen (zu); ~**stick** n Lippenstift m.

liqueur [lı'kjuə*] n Likör m.

liquid ['lıkwıd] n Flüssigkeit f // a flüssig.

liquidate ['lıkwıdeıt] vt liquidieren.

liquidation [lıkwı'deıʃən] n Liquidation f.

liquidize ['lıkwıdaız] vt (CULIN) (im Mixer) pürieren.

liquidizer ['lıkwıdaızə*] n Mixgerät nt.

liquor ['lıkə*] n Alkohol m.

liquorice ['lıkərıs] n Lakritze f.

liquor store n (US) Spirituosengeschäft nt.

Lisbon ['lızbən] n Lissabon f.

lisp [lısp] n Lispeln nt // vti lispeln.

list [lıst] n Liste f, Verzeichnis nt; (of ship) Schlagseite f // vt (write down) eine Liste machen von; (verbally) aufzählen // vi (ship) Schlagseite haben.

listen ['lısn] vi hören; ~ **to** vt zuhören (+dat); ~**er** n (Zu)hörer(in f) m.

listless ['lıstləs] a lustlos.

lit [lıt] pt, pp of **light**.

literacy ['lıtərəsı] n Fähigkeit f zu lesen und zu schreiben.

literal ['lıtərəl] a buchstäblich; (translation) wortwörtlich; ~**ly** ad wörtlich; buchstäblich.

literary ['lıtərərı] a literarisch.

literate ['lıtərət] a des Lesens und Schreibens kundig.

literature ['lıtrətʃə*] n Literatur f.

lithe [laıð] a geschmeidig.

litigation [lıtı'geıʃən] n Prozeß m.

litre, (US) **liter** ['li:tə*] n Liter m.

litter ['lıtə*] n (rubbish) Abfall m; (of animals) Wurf m // vt in Unordnung bringen; **to be** ~**ed with** übersät sein mit; ~ **bin** n (Brit) Abfalleimer m.

little ['lıtl] a klein // ad, n wenig; **a** ~ ein bißchen; ~ **by** ~ nach und nach.

live [lıv] vi leben; (dwell) wohnen // vt (life) führen // a [laıv] lebendig; (MIL) scharf; (ELEC) geladen; (broadcast) live; ~ **down** vt: I'll never ~ it down das wird man mir nie vergessen; ~ **on**

vi weiterleben; **to ~ on** sth von etw leben; **to ~ together** *vi* zusammenleben; *(share a flat)* zusammenwohnen; **~ up to** *vt (standards)* gerecht werden (+*dat*); *(principles)* anstreben; *(hopes)* entsprechen (+*dat*).

livelihood ['laɪvlɪhʊd] *n* Lebensunterhalt *m*.

lively ['laɪvlɪ] *a* lebhaft, lebendig.

liven up ['laɪvn-] *vt* beleben.

liver ['lɪvə*] *n* (ANAT) Leber *f*.

livery ['lɪvərɪ] *n* Livree *f*.

lives [laɪvz] *pl of* **life**.

livestock ['laɪvstɒk] *n* Vieh *nt*.

livid ['lɪvɪd] *a* (*lit*) bläulich; *(furious)* fuchsteufelswild.

living ['lɪvɪŋ] *n* (Lebens)unterhalt *m* // *a* lebendig; *(language etc)* lebend; **to earn** *or* **make a ~** sich *(dat)* seinen Lebensunterhalt verdienen; **~ conditions** *npl* Wohnverhältnisse *pl*; **~ room** *n* Wohnzimmer *nt*; **~ standards** *npl* Lebensstandard *m*; **~ wage** *n* ausreichender Lohn *m*.

lizard ['lɪzəd] *n* Eidechse *f*.

load [ləʊd] *n* *(burden)* Last *f*; *(amount)* Ladung *f* // *vt (also: ~ up)*: **~ (with)** (be)laden (mit); (COMPUT) laden; *(camera)* Film einlegen in (+*acc*); *(gun)* laden; **a ~ of, ~s of** *(fig)* jede Menge; **~ed** *a* beladen; *(dice)* präpariert; *(question)* Fang-; *(col: rich)* steinreich; **~ing bay** *n* Ladeplatz *m*.

loaf [ləʊf] *n* Brot *nt* // *vi (also: ~ about, ~ around)* herumlungern, faulenzen.

loan [ləʊn] *n* Leihgabe *f*; (FIN) Darlehen *nt* // *vt* leihen; **on ~** geliehen.

loath [ləʊθ] *a*: **to be ~ to do sth** etw ungern tun.

loathe [ləʊð] *vt* verabscheuen.

loathing ['ləʊðɪŋ] *n* Abscheu *f*.

loaves [ləʊvz] *pl of* **loaf**.

lobby ['lɒbɪ] *n* Vorhalle *f*; (POL) Lobby *f* // *vt* politisch beeinflussen (wollen).

lobe [ləʊb] *n* Ohrläppchen *nt*.

lobster ['lɒbstə*] *n* Hummer *m*.

local ['ləʊkəl] *a* ortsansässig, Orts- // *n* *(pub)* Stammwirtschaft *f*; **the ~s** *pl* die Ortsansässigen *pl*; **~ anaesthetic** *n* (MED) örtliche Betäubung *f*; **~ authority** *n* städtische Behörden *pl*; **~ call** *n* (TEL) Ortsgespräch *nt*; **~ government** *n* Gemeinde-/Kreisverwaltung *f*; **~ity** [ləʊ'kælɪtɪ] *n* Ort *m*; **~ly** *ad* örtlich, am Ort.

locate [ləʊ'keɪt] *vt* ausfindig machen; *(establish)* errichten.

location [ləʊ'keɪʃən] *n* Platz *m*, Lage *f*; **on ~** (CINE) auf Außenaufnahme.

loch [lɒx] *n* (Scot) See *m*.

lock [lɒk] *n* Schloß *nt*; (NAUT) Schleuse *f*; *(of hair)* Locke *f* // *vt (fasten)* (ver)schließen // *vi (door etc)* sich schließen (lassen); *(wheels)* blockieren.

locker ['lɒkə*] *n* Spind *m*.

locket ['lɒkɪt] *n* Medaillon *nt*.

lockout ['lɒkaʊt] *n* Aussperrung *f*.

locksmith ['lɒksmɪθ] *n* Schlosser(in *f*) *m*.

lock-up ['lɒkʌp] *n* Gefängnis *nt*.

locum ['ləʊkəm] *n* (MED) Vertreter(in *f*) *m*.

locust ['ləʊkəst] *n* Heuschrecke *f*.

lodge [lɒdʒ] *n* *(gatehouse)* Pförtnerhaus *nt*; *(freemasons')* Loge *f* // *vi* (in Untermiete) wohnen *(with* bei); *(get stuck)* stecken(bleiben) // *vt (protest)* einreichen; **~r** *n* (Unter)mieter *m*.

lodgings ['lɒdʒɪŋz] *n* (Miet)wohnung *f*.

loft [lɒft] *n* (Dach)boden *m*.

lofty ['lɒftɪ] *a* hoch(ragend); *(proud)* hochmütig.

log [lɒg] *n* Klotz *m*; *(book)* = **logbook**.

logbook ['lɒgbʊk] *n* Bordbuch *nt*; *(for lorry)* Fahrtenschreiber *m*; (AUT) Kraftfahrzeugbrief *m*.

loggerheads ['lɒgəhedz] *npl*: **to be at ~** sich in den Haaren liegen.

logic ['lɒdʒɪk] *n* Logik *f*; **~al** *a* logisch.

logistics [lɒ'dʒɪstɪks] *npl* Logistik *f*.

logo ['ləʊgəʊ] *n* Firmenzeichen *nt*.

loin [lɔɪn] *n* Lende *f*.

loiter ['lɔɪtə*] *vi* herumstehen.

loll [lɒl] *vi (also: ~ about)* sich rekeln.

lollipop ['lɒlɪpɒp] *n* (Dauer)lutscher *m*; **~ man/lady** *n* (Brit) ≈ Schülerlotse *m*.

London ['lʌndən] *n* London *nt*; **~er** *n* Londoner(in *f*) *m*.

lone [ləʊn] *a* einsam.

loneliness ['ləʊnlɪnəs] *n* Einsamkeit *f*.

lonely ['ləʊnlɪ] *a* einsam.

loner ['ləʊnə*] *n* Einzelgänger(in *f*) *m*.

long [lɒŋ] *a* lang; *(distance)* weit // *ad* lange // *vi* sich sehnen *(for* nach); **before ~** bald; **as ~ as** solange; **in the ~ run** auf die Dauer; **don't be ~!** beeil dich!; **how ~ is the street?** wie lang ist die Straße?; **how ~ is the lesson?** wie lange dauert die Stunde; **6 metres ~** 6 Meter lang; **6 months ~** 6 Monate lang; **all night ~** die ganze Nacht; **he no ~er comes** er kommt nicht mehr; **~ ago** vor langer zeit; **~ before** lange vorher; **at ~ last** endlich; **~-distance** *a* Fern-.

longevity [lɒn'dʒevɪtɪ] *n* Langlebigkeit *f*.

long: **~-haired** *a* langhaarig; **~hand** *n* Langschrift *f*; **~ing** *n* Sehnsucht *f* // *a* sehnsüchtig.

longitude ['lɒŋgɪtjuːd] *n* Längengrad *m*.

long: **~ jump** *n* Weitsprung *m*; **~-lost** *a* längst verloren geglaubt; **~-playing record** *n* Langspielplatte *f*; **~-range** *a* Langstrecken-, Fern-; **~-sighted** *a* weitsichtig; **~-standing** *a* alt, seit langer Zeit bestehend; **~-suffering** *a* schwer geprüft; **~-term** *a* langfristig; **~ wave** *n* Langwelle *f*; **~-winded** *a* langatmig.

loo [lu:] n (Brit col) Klo nt.

look [lʊk] vi schauen; (seem) aussehen; (building etc): to ~ on to the sea aufs Meer gehen; // n Blick m; ~s pl Aussehen nt; ~ after vt (care for) sorgen für; (watch) aufpassen auf (+acc); ~ at vt ansehen; (consider) sich überlegen; ~ back vi sich umsehen; (fig) zurückblicken; ~ down on vt (fig) herabsehen auf (+acc); ~ for vt (seek) suchen; ~ forward to vt sich freuen auf (+acc); (in letters): we ~ forward to hearing from you wir hoffen, bald von Ihnen zu hören; ~ into vt untersuchen; ~ on vi zusehen; ~ out vi hinaussehen; (take care) aufpassen; ~ out for vt Ausschau halten nach; (be careful) achtgeben auf (+acc); ~ round vi sich umsehen; ~ to vt (take care of) achtgeben auf (+acc); (rely on) sich verlassen auf (+acc); ~ up vi aufblicken; (improve) sich bessern // vt (word) nachschlagen; (person) besuchen; ~ up to vt aufsehen zu; ~-out n (watch) Ausschau f; (person) Wachposten m; (place) Ausguck m; (prospect) Aussichten pl; to be on the ~-out for sth nach etw Ausschau halten.

loom [lu:m] n Webstuhl m // vi sich abzeichnen.

loony [ˈluːnɪ] n (col) Verrückte(r) mf.

loop [lu:p] n Schlaufe f; ~hole n (fig) Hintertürchen nt.

loose [lu:s] a lose, locker; (free) frei; (inexact) unpräzise // vt lösen, losbinden; ~ change n Kleingeld nt; ~ chippings npl (on road) Rollsplit m; ~ end n: to be at a ~ end (Brit) or at ~ ends (US) nicht wissen, was man tun soll; ~ly ad locker, lose; ~n vt lockern, losmachen.

loot [lu:t] n Beute f // vt plündern; ~ing n Plünderung f.

lop [lɒp]: ~ off vt abhacken.

lop-sided [ˈlɒpˈsaɪdɪd] a schief.

lord [lɔːd] n (ruler) Herr m; (Brit, title) Lord m; the L~ (Gott) der Herr m; the (House of) L~s das Oberhaus; ~ship n: your L~ship Eure Lordschaft.

lore [lɔː*] n Überlieferung f.

lorry [ˈlɒrɪ] n (Brit) Lastwagen m; ~ driver n (Brit) Lastwagenfahrer(in f) m.

lose [lu:z], pt, pp lost vt verlieren; (chance) verpassen // vi verlieren; to ~ (time) (clock) nachgehen; ~r n Verlierer m.

loss [lɒs] n Verlust m; at a ~ (COMM) mit Verlust; (unable) außerstande.

lost [lɒst] pt, pp of **lose** // a verloren; ~ property, (US) ~ and found n Fundsachen pl.

lot [lɒt] n (quantity) Menge f; (fate, at auction) Los nt; (col: people, things) Haufen m; the ~ alles; (people) alle; a ~ of sing viel // pl viele; ~s of massenhaft, viel(e); I read a ~ ich lese viel; to draw ~s for sth etw verlosen.

lotion [ˈləʊʃən] n Lotion f.

lottery [ˈlɒtərɪ] n Lotterie f.

loud [laʊd] a laut; (showy) schreiend // ad laut; (Brit) Megaphon nt; ~ly ad laut; ~speaker n Lautsprecher m.

lounge [laʊndʒ] n (in hotel) Gesellschaftsraum m; (in house) Wohnzimmer nt // vi sich herumlümmeln; ~ suit n (Brit) Straßenanzug m.

louse [laʊs], pl **lice** n Laus f.

lousy [ˈlaʊzɪ] a (fig) miserabel.

lout [laʊt] n Lümmel m.

louvre, (US) **louver** [ˈluːvə*] a (door, window) Jalousie-.

lovable [ˈlʌvəbl] a liebenswert.

love [lʌv] n Liebe f; (person) Liebling m; (SPORT) null // vt (person) lieben; (activity) gerne mögen; to ~ to do sth etw (sehr) gerne tun; to be in ~ with sb in jdn verliebt sein; to make ~ sich lieben; for the ~ of aus Liebe zu; '15 ~' (TENNIS) 15 null; ~ affair n (Liebes)verhältnis nt; ~ letter n Liebesbrief m; ~ life n Liebesleben nt.

lovely [ˈlʌvlɪ] a schön.

lover [ˈlʌvə*] n Liebhaber(in f) m.

loving [ˈlʌvɪŋ] a liebend, liebevoll.

low [ləʊ] a niedrig; (rank) niedere(r, s); (level, note, neckline) tief; (intelligence, density) gering; (vulgar) ordinär; (not loud) leise; (depressed) gedrückt // ad (not high) niedrig; (not loudly) leise // n (low point) Tiefstand m; (MET) Tief nt; to feel ~ sich mies fühlen; turn (down) ~ vt leiser stellen; ~-cut a (dress) tiefausgeschnitten.

low: ~-fat a fettarm, Mager-; ~ lands npl (GEO) Flachland nt; ~ly a bescheiden; ~-lying a tiefgelegen.

loyal [ˈlɔɪəl] a treu; ~ty n Treue f.

lozenge [ˈlɒzɪndʒ] n Pastille f.

L.P. n abbr of **long-playing record**.

L-plates [ˈelpleɪts] npl (Brit) L-Schild nt (für Fahrschüler).

Ltd abbr of **limited company**.

lubricant [ˈluːbrɪkənt] n Schmiermittel nt.

lubricate [ˈluːbrɪkeɪt] vt schmieren.

lucid [ˈluːsɪd] a klar; (sane) bei klarem Verstand; (moment) licht.

luck [lʌk] n Glück nt; **bad** ~ n Pech nt; **good** ~! viel Glück!; ~ily ad glücklicherweise, zum Glück; ~y a Glücks-; to be ~y Glück haben.

lucrative [ˈluːkrətɪv] a einträglich.

ludicrous [ˈluːdɪkrəs] a grotesk.

lug [lʌg] vt schleppen.

luggage ['lʌgɪdʒ] n Gepäck nt; ~ **rack** n Gepäcknetz nt.
lugubrious [luː'guːbrɪəs] a traurig.
lukewarm ['luːkwɔːm] a lauwarm; (indifferent) lau.
lull [lʌl] n Flaute f // vt einlullen; (calm) beruhigen.
lullaby ['lʌləbaɪ] n Schlaflied nt.
lumbago [lʌm'beɪgəʊ] n Hexenschuß m.
lumber ['lʌmbə*] n Plunder m; (wood) Holz nt; ~**jack** n Holzfäller m.
luminous ['luːmɪnəs] a Leucht-.
lump [lʌmp] n Klumpen m; (MED) Schwellung f; (in breast) Knoten m; (of sugar) Stück nt // vt (also: ~ **together**) zusammentun; (judge together) in einen Topf werfen; ~ **sum** n Pauschalsumme f; ~**y** a klumpig.
lunacy ['luːnəsɪ] n Irrsinn m.
lunar ['luːnə*] a Mond-.
lunatic ['luːnətɪk] n Wahnsinnige(r) mf // a wahnsinnig, irr; ~ **asylum** n Irrenanstalt f.
lunch [lʌntʃ] n (also ~**eon** [-ən]) Mittagessen nt; ~**time** n Mittagszeit f; ~**eon meat** n Frühstücksfleisch nt; ~**eon voucher** n Essensmarke f.
lung [lʌŋ] n Lunge f.
lunge [lʌndʒ] vi (also: ~ **forward**) (los)stürzen; **to** ~ **at** sich stürzen auf (+acc).
lurch [lɜːtʃ] vi taumeln; (NAUT) schlingern // n Ruck m; (NAUT) Schlingern nt; **to leave sb in the** ~ jdn im Stich lassen.
lure [ljʊə*] n Köder m; (fig) Lockung f // vt (ver)locken.
lurid ['ljʊərɪd] a (shocking) grausig, widerlich; (colour) grell.
lurk [lɜːk] vi lauern.
luscious ['lʌʃəs] a köstlich.
lush [lʌʃ] a satt; (vegetation) üppig.
lust [lʌst] n (sensation) Wollust f; (greed) Gier f // vi gieren (after nach).
lustre, (US) **luster** ['lʌstə*] n Glanz m.
lusty ['lʌstɪ] a gesund und munter.
Luxembourg ['lʌksəmbɜːg] n Luxemburg nt.
luxuriant [lʌg'zjʊərɪənt] a üppig.
luxurious [lʌg'zjʊərɪəs] a luxuriös, Luxus-.
luxury ['lʌkʃərɪ] n Luxus m // cpd Luxus-.
lying ['laɪɪŋ] n Lügen nt // a verlogen.
lynx [lɪŋks] n Luchs m.
lyric ['lɪrɪk] n Lyrik f; (pl: words for song) (Lied)text m // a lyrisch; ~**al** a lyrisch, gefühlvoll.

M

M. abbr of **metre; mile; million.**
M.A. abbr of **Master of Arts.**

mac [mæk] n (Brit col) Regenmantel m.
macaroni [mækə'rəʊnɪ] n Makkaroni pl.
mace [meɪs] n Amtsstab m; (spice) Muskat m.
machine [mə'ʃiːn] n Maschine f // vt (dress etc) mit der Maschine nähen; ~ **gun** n Maschinengewehr nt; ~ **language** n (COMPUT) Maschinensprache f; ~**ry** [mə'ʃiːnərɪ] n Maschinerie f.
macho ['mætʃəʊ] a macho.
mackerel ['mækrəl] n Makrele f.
mackintosh ['mækɪntɒʃ] n (Brit) Regenmantel m.
mad [mæd] a verrückt; (dog) tollwütig; (angry) wütend; ~ **about** (fond of) verrückt nach, versessen auf (+acc).
madam ['mædəm] n gnädige Frau f.
madden ['mædn] vt verrückt machen; (make angry) ärgern.
made [meɪd] pt, pp of **make.**
Madeira [mə'dɪərə] n (GEOG) Madeira nt; (wine) Madeira m.
made-to-measure ['meɪdtə'meʒə*] a (Brit) Maß-.
madly ['mædlɪ] ad wahnsinnig.
madman ['mædmən] n Verrückte(r) m, Irre(r) m.
madness ['mædnəs] n Wahnsinn m.
Madrid [mə'drɪd] n Madrid nt.
Mafia ['mæfɪə] n Mafia f.
magazine ['mægəziːn] n Zeitschrift f; (in gun) Magazin nt.
maggot ['mægət] n Made f.
magic ['mædʒɪk] n Zauberei f, Magie f; (fig) Zauber m // a magisch, Zauber-; ~**al** a magisch; ~**ian** [mə'dʒɪʃən] n Zauberer m.
magistrate ['mædʒɪstreɪt] n (Friedens)richter m.
magnanimous [mæg'nænɪməs] a großmütig.
magnesium [mæg'niːzɪəm] n Magnesium nt.
magnet ['mægnɪt] n Magnet m; ~**ic** [mæg'netɪk] a magnetisch; ~**ic tape** n Magnetband nt; ~**ism** n Magnetismus m; (fig) Ausstrahlungskraft f.
magnificence [mæg'nɪfɪsəns] n Großartigkeit f.
magnificent [mæg'nɪfɪsənt] a großartig.
magnify ['mægnɪfaɪ] vt vergrößern; ~**ing glass** n Lupe f.
magnitude ['mægnɪtjuːd] n (size) Größe f; (importance) Ausmaß nt.
magpie ['mægpaɪ] n Elster f.
mahogany [mə'hɒgənɪ] n Mahagoni nt // cpd Mahagoni-.
maid [meɪd] n Dienstmädchen nt; **old** ~ n alte Jungfer f.
maiden ['meɪdn] n (liter) Maid f // a (flight, speech) Jungfern-; ~ **name** n Mädchenname m.
mail [meɪl] n Post f // vt aufgeben; ~ **box** n (US) Briefkasten m; ~**ing list** n Anschreibeliste f; ~ **order** n Bestellung

f durch die Post; ~ **order firm** *n* Versandhaus *nt*.

maim [meim] *vt* verstümmeln.

main [mein] *a* hauptsächlich, Haupt // *n* (*pipe*) Hauptleitung *f*; **the ~s** (*ELEC*) das Stromnetz *nt*; **in the ~** im großen und ganzen; **~frame** *a* (*COMPUT*) Großrechner *m*; **~land** *n* Festland *nt*; **~ road** *n* Hauptstraße *f*; **~stay** *n* (*fig*) Hauptstütze *f*; **~stream** *n* Hauptrichtung *f*.

maintain [mein'tein] *vt* (*machine, roads*) instand halten; (*support*) unterhalten; (*keep up*) aufrechterhalten; (*claim*) behaupten; (*innocence*) beteuern.

maintenance ['meintənəns] *n* (*TECH*) Wartung *f*; (*of family*) Unterhalt *m*.

maize [meiz] *n* Mais *m*.

majestic [mə'dʒestik] *a* majestätisch.

majesty ['mædʒisti] *n* Majestät *f*.

major ['meidʒə*] *n* Major *m* // *a* (*MUS*) Dur; (*more important*) Haupt-; (*bigger*) größer.

Majorca [mə'jɔːkə] *n* Mallorca *nt*.

majority [mə'dʒɔriti] *n* Mehrheit *f*; (*JUR*) Volljährigkeit *f*.

make [meik] *vt, pt, pp* **made** machen; (*appoint*) ernennen (zu); (*cause to do sth*) veranlassen; (*reach*) erreichen; (*in time*) schaffen; (*earn*) verdienen // *n* Marke *f*; **to ~ sth happen** etw geschehen lassen; **to ~ it** es schaffen; **what time do you ~ it?** wie spät hast du es? **to ~ do with** auskommen mit; **~ for** *vi* gehen/ fahren nach; **~ out** *vt* (*write out*) ausstellen; (*understand*) verstehen; (*write: cheque*) ausstellen; **~ up** *vt* (*make*) machen; (*face*) schminken; (*quarrel*) beilegen; (*story etc*) erfinden // *vi* sich versöhnen; **~ up for** *vt* wiedergutmachen; (*COMM*) vergüten; **~-believe** *n* Phantasie *f*; **~r** *n* (*COMM*) Hersteller *m*; **~shift** *a* behelfsmäßig, Not-; **~-up** *n* Schminke *f*, Make-up *nt*; **~-up remover** *n* Make-up-Entferner *m*.

making ['meikiŋ] *n*: **in the ~** im Entstehen; **to have the ~s of** das Zeug haben zu.

malaise [mæ'leiz] *n* Unbehagen *nt*.

Malaya [mə'leiə] *n* Malaya *nt*.

Malaysia [mə'leiziə] *n* Malaysia *nt*.

male [meil] *n* Mann *m*; (*animal*) Männchen *nt* // *a* männlich.

malevolent [mə'levələnt] *a* übelwollend.

malfunction [mæl'fʌŋkʃən] *n* (*MED*) Funktionsstörung *f*; (*of machine*) Defekt *m*.

malice ['mælis] *n* Bosheit *f*.

malicious [mə'liʃəs] *a* böswillig, gehässig.

malign [mə'lain] *vt* verleumden // *a* böse.

malignant [mə'lignənt] *a* bösartig.

mall [mɔːl] *n* (*also*: **shopping ~**) Einkaufszentrum *nt*.

malleable ['mæliəbl] *a* formbar.

mallet ['mælit] *n* Holzhammer *m*.

malnutrition ['mælnjuː'triʃən] *n* Unterernährung *f*.

malpractice ['mæl'præktis] *n* Amtsvergehen *nt*.

malt [mɔːlt] *n* Malz *nt*.

Malta ['mɔːltə] *n* Malta *nt*; **Maltese** [-'tiːz] *a* maltesisch // *n, pl inv* Malteser(in *f*) *m*.

maltreat [mæl'triːt] *vt* mißhandeln.

mammal ['mæməl] *n* Säugetier *nt*.

mammoth ['mæməθ] *n* Mammut *nt* // *a* Mammut-.

man [mæn], *pl* **men** *n* Mann *m*; (*human race*) der Mensch, die Menschen *pl* // *vt* bemannen.

manage ['mænidʒ] *vi* zurechtkommen // *vt* (*control*) führen, leiten; (*cope with*) fertigwerden mit; **~able** *a* (*person, animal*) fügsam; (*object*) handlich; **~ment** *n* (*control*) Führung *f*, Leitung *f*; (*directors*) Management *nt*; **~r** *n* Geschäftsführer *m*; **~ress** ['mænidʒə'res] *n* Geschäftsführerin *f*; **~rial** [mænə'dʒiəriəl] *a* (*post*) leitend; (*problem etc*) Management-.

managing ['mænidʒiŋ] *a*: **~ director** *n* Betriebsleiter *m*.

mandarin ['mændərin] *n* (*fruit*) Mandarine *f*.

mandatory ['mændətəri] *a* obligatorisch.

mane [mein] *n* Mähne *f*.

maneuver [mə'nuːvə*] (*US*) = **manoeuvre**.

manfully ['mænfuli] *ad* mannhaft.

mangle ['mæŋgl] *vt* verstümmeln // *n* Mangel *f*.

mango ['mæŋgəu], *pl* **~es** *n* Mango(pflaume) *f*.

mangy ['meindʒi] *a* (*dog*) räudig.

manhandle ['mænhændl] *vt* grob behandeln.

manhole ['mænhəul] *n* (Straßen)schacht *m*.

manhood ['mænhud] *n* Mannesalter *nt*; (*manliness*) Männlichkeit *f*.

man-hour ['mæn'auə*] *n* Arbeitsstunde *f*.

manhunt ['mænhʌnt] *n* Fahndung *f*.

mania ['meiniə] *n* Manie *f*; **~c** ['meiniæk] *n* Wahnsinnige(r) *mf*.

manic ['mænik] *a* (*behaviour, activity*) hektisch; **~-depressive** *n* Manisch-Depressive(r) *mf*.

manicure ['mænikjuə*] *n* Maniküre *f*; **~ set** *n* Necessaire *nt*.

manifest ['mænifest] *vt* offenbaren // *a* offenkundig; **~ation** *n* (*sign*) Anzeichen *nt*.

manifesto [mæni'festəu] *n* Manifest *nt*.

manipulate [mə'nipjuleit] *vt* handhaben; (*fig*) manipulieren.

mankind [mæn'kaɪnd] n Menschheit f.

manly ['mænlɪ] a männlich; mannhaft.

man-made ['mæn'meɪd] a (fibre) künstlich.

manner ['mænə*] n Art f, Weise f; in a ~ of speaking sozusagen; ~s pl Manieren pl; ~ism n (of person) Angewohnheit f; (of style) Maniertheit f.

manoeuvre, (US) **maneuver** [mə'nuːvə*] vti manövrieren // n (MIL) Feldzug m; (general) Manöver nt, Schachzug m.

manor ['mænə*] n Landgut nt; ~ house n Herrenhaus nt.

manpower ['mænpauə*] n Arbeitskräfte pl.

mansion ['mænʃən] n Villa f.

manslaughter ['mænslɔːtə*] n Totschlag m.

mantelpiece ['mæntlpiːs] n Kaminsims m.

mantle ['mæntl] n (cloak) lange(r) Umhang m.

manual ['mænjʊəl] a manuell, Hand- // n Handbuch nt.

manufacture [mænju'fæktʃə*] vt herstellen // n Herstellung f; ~r n Hersteller m.

manure [mə'njʊə*] n Dünger m.

manuscript ['mænjuskrɪpt] n Manuskript nt.

Manx [mæŋks] a der Insel Man.

many ['menɪ] a, pron viele; a great ~ sehr viele; ~ a time oft.

map [mæp] n (Land)karte f; (of town) Stadtplan m // vt eine Karte machen von; ~ out vt (fig) ausarbeiten.

maple ['meɪpl] n Ahorn m.

mar [mɑː*] vt verderben.

marathon ['mærəθən] n (SPORT) Marathonlauf m; (fig) Marathon m.

marauder [mə'rɔːdə*] n Plünderer m.

marble ['mɑːbl] n Marmor m; (for game) Murmel f.

March [mɑːtʃ] n März m.

march [mɑːtʃ] vi marschieren // n Marsch m; ~past n Vorbeimarsch m.

mare [mɛə*] n Stute f.

margarine [mɑːdʒə'riːn] n Margarine f.

margin ['mɑːdʒɪn] n Rand m; (extra amount) Spielraum m; (COMM) Spanne f; ~al a (note) Rand-; (difference etc) geringfügig; ~ al (seat) n (POL) Wahlkreis, der nur mit knapper Mehrheit gehalten wird.

marigold ['mærɪgəʊld] n Ringelblume f.

marina [mə'riːnə] n Yachthafen m.

marinate ['mærɪneɪt] vt marinieren.

marine [mə'riːn] a Meeres-, See- // n (MIL) Marineinfanterist m.

marital ['mærɪtl] a ehelich, Ehe-; ~ status n Familienstand m.

maritime ['mærɪtaɪm] a See-.

mark [mɑːk] n (coin) Mark f; (spot) Fleck m; (scar) Kratzer m; (sign) Zeichen nt; (target) Ziel nt; (SCH) Note f // vt (make mark) Flecken/Kratzer machen auf (+acc); (indicate) markieren; (exam) korrigieren; to ~ time (lit, fig) auf der Stelle treten; ~ out vt bestimmen; (area) abstecken; ~ed a deutlich; ~er n (in book) (Lese)zeichen nt; (on road) Schild nt.

market ['mɑːkɪt] n Markt m; (stock ~) Börse f // vt (COMM: new product) auf den Markt bringen; (sell) vertreiben; ~ garden n (Brit) Handelsgärtnerei f; ~ing n Marketing nt; ~ place n Marktplatz m ~ research n Marktforschung f; ~ value n Marktwert m.

marksman ['mɑːksmən] n Scharfschütze m.

marmalade ['mɑːməleɪd] n Orangenmarmelade f.

maroon [mə'ruːn] vt aussetzen // a (colour) kastanienbraun.

marquee [mɑː'kiː] n große(s) Zelt nt.

marriage ['mærɪdʒ] n Ehe f; (wedding) Heirat f; ~ bureau n Heiratsinstitut nt; ~ certificate n Heiratsurkunde f.

married ['mærɪd] a (person) verheiratet; (couple, life) Ehe-.

marrow ['mærəʊ] n (Knochen)mark nt; (vegetable) Kürbis m.

marry ['mærɪ] vt (join) trauen; (take as husband, wife) heiraten // vi (also: get married) heiraten.

Mars [mɑːz] n (planet) Mars m.

marsh [mɑːʃ] n Sumpf m.

marshal ['mɑːʃəl] n (US) Bezirkspolizeichef m // vt (an)ordnen, arrangieren.

marshy ['mɑːʃɪ] a sumpfig.

martial ['mɑːʃəl] a kriegerisch; ~ law n Kriegsrecht m.

martyr ['mɑːtə*] n (lit, fig) Märtyrer(in f) m // vt zum Märtyrer machen; ~dom n Martyrium nt.

marvel ['mɑːvəl] n Wunder nt // vi sich wundern (at über +acc); ~lous, (US) ~ous a wunderbar.

Marxist ['mɑːksɪst] n Marxist(in f) m.

marzipan [mɑːzɪ'pæn] n Marzipan nt.

mascara [mæs'kɑːrə] n Wimperntusche f.

mascot ['mæskət] n Maskottchen nt.

masculine ['mæskjʊlɪn] a männlich.

mash [mæʃ] n Brei m; ~ed potatoes npl Kartoffelbrei m or -püree nt.

mask [mɑːsk] n (lit, fig) Maske f // vt maskieren, verdecken.

mason ['meɪsn] n (stone~) Steinmetz m; (free~) Freimaurer m; ~ic [mə'sɒnɪk] a Freimaurer-; ~ry n Mauerwerk nt.

masquerade [mæskə'reɪd] n Maskerade f // vi: to ~ as sich ausgeben als.

mass [mæs] n Masse f; (greater part) Mehrheit f; (REL) Messe f // vi sich sammeln; the ~es npl die Masse(n) f(pl).

massacre ['mæsəkə*] n Blutbad nt // vt niedermetzeln, massakrieren.

massage ['mæsɑːʒ] n Massage f // vt massieren.

massive ['mæsɪv] a gewaltig, massiv.

mass media ['mæs'miːdɪə] npl Massenmedien pl.

mass production n Massenproduktion f.

mast [mɑːst] n Mast m.

master ['mɑːstə*] n Herr m; (NAUT) Kapitän m; (teacher) Lehrer m; (artist) Meister m // vt meistern; (language etc) beherrschen; **M~ of Arts/Science (M.A./M.Sc.)** n Magister m der philosophischen/naturwissenschaftlichen Fakultät; ~ **key** n Hauptschlüssel m; ~**ly** a meisterhaft; ~**mind** n Kapazität f // vt geschickt lenken; ~**piece** n Meisterwerk nt; ~ **plan** n kluge(r) Plan m; ~**y** n Können nt.

masturbate ['mæstəbeɪt] vi masturbieren, onanieren.

mat [mæt] n Matte f; (for table) Untersetzer m // a = **mat(t)**.

match [mætʃ] n Streichholz nt; (sth corresponding) Pendant nt; (SPORT) Wettkampf m; (ball games) Spiel nt // vt (be alike, suit) passen zu; (equal) gleichkommen (+dat) // vi zusammenpassen; it's a good ~ es paßt gut (for zu); ~**box** n Streichholzschachtel f; ~**ing** a passend.

mate [meɪt] n (companion) Kamerad m; (spouse) Lebensgefährte m; (of animal) Weibchen nt/Männchen nt; (NAUT) Schiffsoffizier m // vi (animals) sich paaren // vt (animals) paaren.

material [mə'tɪərɪəl] n Material nt; (for book, cloth) Stoff m // a (important) wesentlich; (damage) Sach-; (comforts etc) materiell; ~**s** pl Materialien pl; ~**istic** a materialistisch; ~**ize** vi sich verwirklichen, zustande kommen.

maternal [mə'tɜːnl] a mütterlich, Mutter-.

maternity [mə'tɜːnɪtɪ] a (dress) Umstands-; (benefit) Wochen-; ~ **hospital** n Entbindungsheim nt.

math [mæθ] n (US) = **maths**.

mathematics [mæθə'mætɪks] n Mathematik f.

maths [mæθs], (US) **math** [mæθ] n Mathe f.

matinée ['mætɪneɪ] n Matinee f.

mating ['meɪtɪŋ] n Paarung f; ~ **call** n Lockruf m.

matrices ['meɪtrɪsiːz] pl of **matrix**.

matriculation [mətrɪkjuˈleɪʃən] n Immatrikulation f.

matrimonial [mætrɪˈməʊnɪəl] a ehelich, Ehe-.

matrimony ['mætrɪmənɪ] n Ehestand m.

matrix ['meɪtrɪks], pl **matrices** n Matrize f; (GEOL etc) Matrix f.

matron ['meɪtrən] n (MED) Oberin f; (SCH) Hausmutter f; ~**ly** a matronenhaft.

mat(t) [mæt] a (paint) matt.

matted ['mætɪd] a verfilzt.

matter ['mætə*] n (substance) Materie f; (affair) Angelegenheit f // vi darauf ankommen; it **doesn't** ~ es macht nichts; **no** ~ how/what egal wie/was; what is the ~? was ist los?; as a ~ of course selbstverständlich; as a ~ of fact eigentlich; ~**-of-fact** a sachlich, nüchtern.

mattress ['mætrəs] n Matratze f.

mature [mə'tjʊə*] a reif // vi reif werden.

maturity [mə'tjʊərɪtɪ] n Reife f.

maudlin ['mɔːdlɪn] a gefühlsduselig.

maul [mɔːl] vt übel zurichten.

mauve [məʊv] a mauve.

maximum ['mæksɪməm] a Höchst-, Maximal- // n, pl **maxima** ['mæksɪmə] Maximum nt.

May [meɪ] n Mai m.

may [meɪ] vi (be possible) können; (have permission) dürfen; **he** ~ **come** er kommt vielleicht.

maybe ['meɪbiː] ad vielleicht.

Mayday ['meɪdeɪ] n (message) SOS nt.

mayhem ['meɪhem] n Chaos nt; (US) Körperverletzung f.

mayonnaise [meɪəˈneɪz] n Mayonnaise f.

mayor [mɛə*] n Bürgermeister m; ~**ess** (wife) (die) Frau f Bürgermeister; (lady ~) Bürgermeisterin f.

maypole ['meɪpəʊl] n Maibaum m.

maze [meɪz] n (lit) Irrgarten m; (fig) Wirrwarr nt.

M.D. abbr of **Doctor of Medicine**.

me [miː] pron **1** (direct) mich; it's ~ ich bin's

2 (indirect) mir; **give them to** ~ gib sie mir

3 (after prep: +acc) mich; (: +dat) mir; **with/without** ~ mit mir/ohne mich.

meadow ['medəʊ] n Wiese f.

meagre, (US) **meager** ['miːgə*] a dürftig, spärlich.

meal [miːl] n Essen nt, Mahlzeit f; (grain) Schrotmehl nt; **to have a** ~ essen (gehen); ~**time** n Essenszeit f.

mean [miːn] a (stingy) geizig; (spiteful) gemein; (average) durchschnittlich, Durchschnitts- // vt, pt, pp **meant** (signify) bedeuten; (intend) vorhaben, beabsichtigen // n (average) Durchschnitt m; ~**s** pl Mittel pl; (wealth) Vermögen nt; **by** ~**s of** durch; **by all** ~**s** selbstverständlich; **by no** ~**s** keineswegs; **do you** ~ **me?** meinst du mich?; **do you** ~ **it?** meinst du das ernst?; **what do you** ~? was willst du damit sagen?; **to be meant for sb/sth** für jdn/etw bestimmt sein.

meander [mɪˈændə*] vi sich schlängeln.
meaning [ˈmiːnɪŋ] n Bedeutung f; (of life) Sinn m; ~**ful** a bedeutungsvoll; (life) sinnvoll; ~**less** a sinnlos.
meanness [ˈmiːnnəs] n (stinginess) Geiz m; (spitefulness) Gemeinheit f.
meant [ment] pt, pp of **mean**.
meantime [ˈmiːntaɪm], **meanwhile** [ˈmiːnwaɪl] ad inzwischen.
measles [ˈmiːzlz] n Masern pl.
measly [ˈmiːzlɪ] a (col) poplig.
measure [ˈmeʒə*] vti messen // n Maß nt; (step) Maßnahme f; ~**d** a (slow) gemessen; ~**ments** npl Maße pl.
meat [miːt] n Fleisch nt; **cold** ~ n Aufschnitt m; ~ **ball** n Fleischkloß m; ~ **pie** n Fleischpastete f; ~**y** a (lit) fleischig; (fig) gehaltvoll.
Mecca [ˈmekə] n Mekka nt (also fig).
mechanic [mɪˈkænɪk] n Mechaniker m; ~**s** n Mechanik f // npl Technik f; ~**al** a mechanisch.
mechanism [ˈmekənɪzəm] n Mechanismus m.
mechanize [ˈmekənaɪz] vt mechanisieren.
medal [ˈmedl] n Medaille f; (decoration) Orden m; ~**list**, (US) ~**ist** n Medaillengewinner(in f) m.
meddle [ˈmedl] vi sich einmischen (in in +acc); to ~ **with** sth sich an etw (dat) zu schaffen machen.
media [ˈmiːdɪə] npl Medien pl.
mediaeval [medɪˈiːvəl] a = **medieval**.
median [ˈmiːdɪən] n (US: also: ~ **strip**) Mittelstreifen m.
mediate [ˈmiːdɪeɪt] vi vermitteln.
mediation [miːdɪˈeɪʃən] n Vermittlung f.
mediator [ˈmiːdɪeɪtə*] n Vermittler m.
Medicaid [ˈmedɪkeɪd] n (US) medizinisches Versorgungsprogramm für Sozialschwache.
medical [ˈmedɪkəl] a medizinisch; Medizin-; ärztlich // n (ärztliche) Untersuchung f.
Medicare [ˈmedɪkeə*] n (US) staatliche Krankenversicherung besonders für Ältere.
medicated [ˈmedɪkeɪtɪd] a medizinisch.
medication [medɪˈkeɪʃən] n (drugs etc) Medikamente pl.
medicinal [meˈdɪsɪnl] a medizinisch, Heil-.
medicine [ˈmedsɪn] n Medizin f; (drugs) Arznei f.
medieval [medɪˈiːvəl] a mittelalterlich.
mediocre [miːdɪˈəʊkə*] a mittelmäßig.
mediocrity [miːdɪˈɒkrɪtɪ] n Mittelmäßigkeit f.
meditate [ˈmedɪteɪt] vi nachdenken (on über +acc); meditieren.
meditation [medɪˈteɪʃən] n Nachsinnen nt; Meditation f.
Mediterranean [medɪtəˈreɪnɪən] a

Mittelmeer-; (person) südländisch; the ~ (Sea) das Mittelmeer.
medium [ˈmiːdɪəm] a mittlere(r, s), Mittel-, mittel- // n Mitte f; (means) Mittel nt; (person) Medium nt; **happy** ~ goldener Mittelweg; ~ **wave** n Mittelwelle f.
medley [ˈmedlɪ] n Gemisch nt.
meek [miːk] a sanft(mütig); (pej) duckmäuserisch.
meet [miːt], pt, pp **met** vt (encounter) treffen, begegnen (+dat); (by arrangement) sich treffen mit; (difficulties) stoßen auf (+acc); (become acquainted with) kennenlernen; (fetch) abholen; (join) zusammentreffen mit; (satisfy) entsprechen (+dat) // vi sich treffen; (become acquainted) sich kennenlernen; ~ **with** vt (problems) stoßen auf (+acc); (US: people) zusammentreffen mit; ~**ing** n Treffen nt; (business ~) Besprechung f; (of committee) Sitzung f; (assembly) Versammlung f.
megabyte [ˈmegəbaɪt] n (COMPUT) Megabyte nt.
melancholy [ˈmelənkəlɪ] a (person) melancholisch; (sight, event) traurig.
mellow [ˈmeləʊ] a mild, weich; (fruit) reif; (fig) gesetzt // vi reif werden.
melodious [mɪˈləʊdɪəs] a wohlklingend.
melody [ˈmelədɪ] n Melodie f.
melon [ˈmelən] n Melone f.
melt [melt] vi schmelzen; (anger) verfliegen // vt schmelzen; ~ **away** vi dahinschmelzen; ~ **down** vt einschmelzen; ~**down** n (in nuclear reactor) Kernschmelze f; ~**ing point** n Schmelzpunkt m; ~**ing pot** n (fig) Schmelztiegel m.
member [ˈmembə*] n Mitglied nt; (of tribe, species) Angehörige(r) m; (ANAT) Glied nt; **M~ of Parliament (MP)** n (Brit) Parlamentsmitglied nt; **M~ of the European Parliament (MEP)** n (Brit) Mitglied nt des Europäischen Parlaments; ~**ship** n Mitgliedschaft f; to seek ~**ship of** einen Antrag auf Mitgliedschaft stellen; ~**ship card** n Mitgliedskarte f.
memento [məˈmentəʊ] n Andenken nt.
memo [ˈmeməʊ] n Mitteilung f.
memoirs [ˈmemwɑːz] npl Memoiren pl.
memorable [ˈmemərəbl] a denkwürdig.
memorandum [meməˈrændəm], pl **-da** [-də] n Mitteilung f.
memorial [mɪˈmɔːrɪəl] n Denkmal nt // a Gedenk-.
memorize [ˈmeməraɪz] vt sich einprägen.
memory [ˈmemərɪ] n Gedächtnis nt; (of computer) Speicher m; (sth recalled) Erinnerung f.
men [men] pl of **man**.
menace [ˈmenɪs] n Drohung f; Gefahr f

// vt bedrohen.
menacing ['menɪsɪŋ] a drohend.
menagerie [mɪ'nædʒərɪ] n Tierschau f.
mend [mend] vt reparieren, flicken // vi
(ver)heilen // n ausgebesserte Stelle f; on
the ~ auf dem Wege der Besserung;
~ing n (articles) Flickarbeit f.
menial ['miːnɪəl] a niedrig.
meningitis [menɪn'dʒaɪtɪs] n
Hirnhautentzündung f, Meningitis f.
menopause ['menəʊpɔːz] n
Wechseljahre pl, Menopause f.
menstruation [menstrʊ'eɪʃən] n Menstruation f.
mental ['mentl] a geistig, Geistes-;
(arithmetic) Kopf-; (hospital) Nerven-;
(cruelty) seelisch; (col: abnormal) verrückt; ~ity [men'tælɪtɪ] n Mentalität f.
menthol ['menθəl] n Menthol nt.
mention ['menʃən] n Erwähnung f // vt
erwähnen; don't ~ it! bitte (sehr), gern
geschehen.
mentor ['mentɔː*] n Mentor m.
menu ['menjuː] n Speisekarte f.
MEP n abbr of **Member of the European Parliament.**
mercenary ['mɜːsɪnərɪ] a (person)
geldgierig; (MIL) Söldner- // n Söldner
m.
merchandise ['mɜːtʃəndaɪz] n
(Handels)ware f.
merchant ['mɜːtʃənt] n Kaufmann m;
~ **navy**, (US) ~ **marine** n
Handelsmarine f.
merciful ['mɜːsɪful] a gnädig.
merciless ['mɜːsɪləs] a erbarmungslos.
mercury ['mɜːkjʊrɪ] n Quecksilber nt.
mercy ['mɜːsɪ] n Erbarmen nt; Gnade f;
at the ~ of ausgeliefert (+dat).
mere a, ~ly ad [mɪə*, 'mɪəlɪ] bloß.
merge [mɜːdʒ] vt verbinden; (COMM)
fusionieren // vi verschmelzen; (roads)
zusammenlaufen; (COMM) fusionieren;
~r n (COMM) Fusion f.
meringue [mə'ræŋ] n Baiser nt.
merit ['merɪt] n Verdienst nt;
(advantage) Vorzug m // vt verdienen.
mermaid ['mɜːmeɪd] n Wassernixe f.
merry ['merɪ] a fröhlich; ~-go-round n
Karussell nt.
mesh [meʃ] n Masche f // vi (gears)
ineinandergreifen.
mesmerize ['mezməraɪz] vt hypnotisieren; (fig) faszinieren.
mess [mes] n Unordnung f; (dirt)
Schmutz m; (trouble) Schwierigkeiten
pl; (MIL) Messe f; ~ **about** or **around**
vi (tinker with) herummurksen (with an
+dat); (play the fool) herumalbern; (do
nothing in particular) herumgammeln;
~ **up** vt verpfuschen; (make untidy) in
Unordnung bringen.
message ['mesɪdʒ] n Mitteilung f; to get
the ~ kapieren.
messenger ['mesɪndʒə*] n Bote m.

Messrs ['mesəz] abbr (on letters) die
Herren.
messy ['mesɪ] a schmutzig; (untidy)
unordentlich.
met [met] pt, pp of **meet.**
metabolism [me'tæbəlɪzəm] n
Stoffwechsel m.
metal ['metl] n Metall nt.
metaphor ['metəfɔː*] n Metapher f.
mete [miːt]: **to ~ out** vt austeilen.
meteorology [miːtɪə'rɒlədʒɪ] n
Meteorologie f.
meter ['miːtə*] n Zähler m; (US) =
metre.
method ['meθəd] n Methode f; ~ical
[mɪ'θɒdɪkəl] a methodisch; **M~ist**
['meθədɪst] a methodistisch // n Metho-
dist(in f) m; ~ology [meθə'dɒlədʒɪ] n
Methodik f.
meths [meθs], **methylated spirit**
['meθɪleɪtɪd'spɪrɪt] n (Brit) (Brenn)-
spiritus m.
meticulous [mɪ'tɪkjʊləs] a (über)genau.
metre, (US) **meter** ['miːtə*] n Meter m
or nt.
metric ['metrɪk] a (also: ~al) metrisch.
metropolitan [metrə'pɒlɪtən] a der
Großstadt; **the M~ Police** n (Brit) die
Londoner Polizei.
mettle ['metl] n Mut m.
mew [mjuː] vi (cat) miauen.
mews [mjuːz] n: ~ **cottage** n (Brit)
ehemaliges Kutscherhäuschen.
Mexican ['meksɪkən] a mexikanisch // n
Mexikaner(in f) m.
Mexico ['meksɪkəʊ] n Mexiko nt; ~
City n Mexiko City f.
miaow [miː'aʊ] vi miauen.
mice [maɪs] pl of **mouse.**
microchip ['maɪkrəʊtʃɪp] n Mikrochip
m.
micro(computer)
['maɪkrəʊ(kəm'pjuːtə*)] n Mikro-
computer m.
microcosm ['maɪkrəʊkɒzəm] n Mikro-
kosmos m.
microfilm ['maɪkrəʊfɪlm] n Mikrofilm m
// vt auf Mikrofilm aufnehmen.
microphone ['maɪkrəfəʊn] n Mikrophon
nt.
microprocessor ['maɪkrəʊ'prəʊsesə*] n
Mikroprozessor m.
microscope ['maɪkrəskəʊp] n Mikro-
skop nt.
microwave ['maɪkrəʊweɪv] n (also: ~
oven) Mikrowelle(nherd nt) f.
mid [mɪd] a: in ~ **afternoon** am
Nachmittag; in ~ **air** in der Luft; in ~
May Mitte Mai.
midday ['mɪd'deɪ] n Mittag m.
middle ['mɪdl] n Mitte f; (waist) Taille f
// a mittlere(r, s), Mittel-; in the ~ of
mitten in (+dat); ~-aged a mittleren
Alters; **the M~ Ages** npl das Mit-
telalter; ~-class a Mittelstands-; the

M~ East n der Nahe Osten; **~man** n (COMM) Zwischenhändler m; **~ name** n zweiter Vorname m; **~ weight** n (BOXING) Mittelgewicht nt.

middling ['mɪdlɪŋ] a mittelmäßig.

midge [mɪdʒ] n Mücke f.

midget ['mɪdʒɪt] n Liliputaner(in f) m.

Midlands ['mɪdləndz] npl die Midlands pl.

midnight ['mɪdnaɪt] n Mitternacht f.

midriff ['mɪdrɪf] n Taille f.

midst [mɪdst] n: **in the ~ of** (persons) mitten unter (+dat); (things) mitten in (+dat).

midsummer ['mɪd'sʌmə*] n Hochsommer m.

midway ['mɪd'weɪ] ad auf halbem Wege // a Mittel-.

midweek ['mɪd'wi:k] ad in der Mitte der Woche.

midwife ['mɪdwaɪf], pl **-wives** [-waɪvz] n Hebamme f; **~ry** ['mɪdwɪfərɪ] n Geburtshilfe f.

midwinter ['mɪd'wɪntə*] n tiefste(r) Winter m.

might [maɪt] v pt of **may** // n Macht f, Kraft f; **I ~ come** ich komme vielleicht; **I ~ as well** go ich könnte genauso gut gehen; **you ~ like to try** du könntest vielleicht versuchen; **~y** a, ad mächtig.

migraine ['mi:greɪn] n Migräne f.

migrant ['maɪgrənt] a Wander-; (bird) Zug-.

migrate [maɪ'greɪt] vi (ab)wandern; (birds) (fort)ziehen.

migration [maɪ'greɪʃən] n Wanderung f, Zug m.

mike [maɪk] n = **microphone.**

Milan [mɪ'læn] n Mailand nt.

mild [maɪld] a mild; (medicine, interest) leicht; (person) sanft.

mildew ['mɪldju:] n (on plants) Mehltau m; (on food) Schimmel m.

mildly ['maɪldlɪ] ad leicht; **to put it ~** gelinde gesagt.

mile [maɪl] n Meile f; **~age** n Meilenzahl f; **~stone** n (lit, fig) Meilenstein m.

military ['mɪlɪtərɪ] a militärisch, Militär-, Wehr-.

militate ['mɪlɪteɪt] vi entgegenwirken (against dat).

militia [mɪ'lɪʃə] n Miliz f.

milk [mɪlk] n Milch f // vt (lit, fig) melken; **~ chocolate** n Milchschokolade f; **~man** n Milchmann m; **~ shake** n Milchmixgetränk nt; **~y** a milchig; **M~y Way** n Milchstraße f.

mill [mɪl] n Mühle f; (factory) Fabrik f // vt mahlen // vi (move around) umherlaufen.

millennium [mɪ'lenɪəm], pl **~s** or **-ia** [-nɪə] n Jahrtausend nt.

miller ['mɪlə*] n Müller m.

millet ['mɪlɪt] n Hirse f.

milligram(me) ['mɪlɪgræm] n Milligramm nt.

millimetre, (US) **millimeter** ['mɪlimi:tə*] n Millimeter m.

milliner ['mɪlɪnə*] n Hutmacher(in f) m; **~y** n (hats) Hüte pl.

million ['mɪljən] n Million f; **a ~ times** tausendmal; **~aire** [mɪljə'nɛə*] n Millionär(in f) m.

millstone ['mɪlstəʊn] n Mühlstein m.

milometer [maɪ'lɒmɪtə*] n Kilometerzähler m.

mime [maɪm] n Pantomime f // vti mimen.

mimic ['mɪmɪk] n Mimiker m // vti nachahmen; **~ry** ['mɪmɪkrɪ] n Nachahmung f; (BIOL) Mimikry f.

min. abbr (= minute(s); minimum) min.

minaret [mɪnə'ret] n Minarett nt.

mince [mɪns] vt (zer)hacken // vi (walk) trippeln // n (meat) Hackfleisch nt; **~meat** n süße Pastetenfüllung f; **~ pie** n gefüllte (süße) Pastete f; **mincer** n Fleischwolf m.

mind [maɪnd] n Verstand m, Geist m; (opinion) Meinung f // vt aufpassen auf (+acc); (object to) etwas haben gegen; **on my ~** auf dem Herzen; **to my ~** meiner Meinung nach; **to be out of one's ~** wahnsinnig sein; **to bear** or **keep in ~** bedenken; **to change one's ~** es sich (dat) anders überlegen; **to make up one's ~** sich entschließen; **I don't ~** das macht mir nichts aus; **~ you, ...** allerdings ...; **never ~!** macht nichts!; **'~ the step'** 'Vorsicht Stufe'; **~ your own business** kümmern Sie sich um Ihre eigenen Angelegenheiten; **minder** n Aufpasser(in f) m; **~ful** a achtsam (of auf +acc); **~less** a sinnlos.

mine [maɪn] n (coal~) Bergwerk nt; (MIL) Mine f // vt abbauen; (MIL) verminen.

mine [maɪn] pron meine(r, s); **that book is ~** das Buch gehört mir; **a friend of ~** ein Freund von mir.

minefield ['maɪnfi:ld] n Minenfeld nt.

miner ['maɪnə*] n Bergarbeiter m.

mineral ['mɪnərəl] a mineralisch, Mineral- // n Mineral nt; **~s** pl (Brit: soft drinks) alkoholfreie Getränke pl; **~ water** n Mineralwasser nt.

minesweeper ['maɪnswi:pə*] n Minensuchboot m.

mingle ['mɪŋgl] vi sich mischen (with unter +acc).

miniature ['mɪnɪtʃə*] a Miniatur- // n Miniatur f.

minibus ['mɪnɪbʌs] n Kleinbus m.

minim ['mɪnɪm] n halbe Note f.

minimal ['mɪnɪml] a minimal.

minimize ['mɪnɪmaɪz] vt auf das Mindestmaß beschränken.

minimum ['mɪnɪməm] n, pl **minima**

['mɪnɪmə] Minimum *nt* // *a* Mindest-.

mining ['maɪnɪŋ] *n* Bergbau *m* // *a* Bergbau-, Berg-.

miniskirt ['mɪnɪskɜːt] *n* Minirock *m*.

minister ['mɪnɪstə*] *n* (*Brit POL*) Minister *m*; (*ECCL*) Pfarrer *m* // *vi*: to ~ to sb sich um jdn kümmern; **~ial** [mɪnɪs'tɪərɪəl] *a* ministeriell, Minister-.

ministry ['mɪnɪstrɪ] *n* (*Brit POL*) Ministerium *nt*; (*ECCL*: *office*) geistliche(s) Amt *nt*.

mink [mɪŋk] *n* Nerz *m*; ~ **coat** *n* Nerzmantel *m*.

minnow ['mɪnəʊ] *n* Elritze *f*.

minor ['maɪnə*] *a* kleiner; (*operation*) leicht; (*problem, poet*) unbedeutend; (*MUS*) Moll // *n* (*Brit: under 18*) Minderjährige(r) *mf*.

minority [maɪ'nɒrɪtɪ] *n* Minderheit *f*.

mint [mɪnt] *n* Minze *f*; (*sweet*) Pfefferminzbonbon *nt* // *vt* (*coins*) prägen; **the (Royal) M~**, (*US*) **the (US) M~** die Münzanstalt; **in ~ condition** in tadellosem Zustand.

minus ['maɪnəs] *n* Minuszeichen *nt*; (*amount*) Minusbetrag *m* // *prep* minus, weniger.

minuscule ['mɪnəskjuːl] *a* winzig.

minute [maɪ'njuːt] *a* winzig; (*detailed*) minuziös // *n* ['mɪnɪt] Minute *f*; (*moment*) Augenblick *m*; **~s** *pl* Protokoll *nt*.

miracle ['mɪrəkl] *n* Wunder *nt*.

miraculous [mɪ'rækjʊləs] *a* wunderbar.

mirage ['mɪrɑːʒ] *n* Fata Morgana *f*.

mire ['maɪə*] *n* Morast *m*.

mirror ['mɪrə*] *n* Spiegel *m* // *vt* (*wider*)spiegeln.

mirth [mɜːθ] *n* Heiterkeit *f*.

misadventure [mɪsəd'ventʃə*] *n* Mißgeschick *nt*, Unfall *m*.

misanthropist [mɪ'zænθrəpɪst] *n* Menschenfeind *m*.

misapprehension ['mɪsæprɪ'henʃən] *n* Mißverständnis *nt*.

misbehave ['mɪsbɪ'heɪv] *vi* sich schlecht benehmen.

miscalculate ['mɪs'kælkjʊleɪt] *vt* falsch berechnen.

miscarriage ['mɪskærɪdʒ] *n* (*MED*) Fehlgeburt *f*; ~ **of justice** *n* Fehlurteil *nt*.

miscellaneous [mɪsɪ'leɪnɪəs] *a* verschieden.

mischance [mɪs'tʃɑːns] *n* Mißgeschick *nt*.

mischief ['mɪstʃɪf] *n* Unfug *m*.

mischievous ['mɪstʃɪvəs] *a* (*person*) durchtrieben; (*glance*) verschmitzt; (*rumour*) bösartig.

misconception ['mɪskən'sepʃən] *n* fälschliche Annahme *f*.

misconduct [mɪs'kɒndʌkt] *n* Vergehen *nt*; **professional ~** Berufsvergehen *nt*.

misconstrue ['mɪskən'struː] *vt* mißver-

stehen.

misdeed [mɪs'diːd] *n* Untat *f*.

misdemeanour, (*US*) **misdemeanor** [mɪsdɪ'miːnə*] *n* Vergehen *nt*.

miser ['maɪzə*] *n* Geizhals *m*.

miserable ['mɪzərəbl] *a* (*unhappy*) unglücklich; (*headache, weather*) fürchterlich; (*poor*) elend; (*contemptible*) erbärmlich.

miserly ['maɪzəlɪ] *a* geizig.

misery ['mɪzərɪ] *n* Elend *nt*, Qual *f*.

misfire ['mɪs'faɪə*] *vi* (*gun*) versagen; (*engine*) fehlzünden; (*plan*) fehlgehen.

misfit ['mɪsfɪt] *n* Außenseiter *m*.

misfortune [mɪs'fɔːtʃən] *n* Unglück *nt*.

misgiving(s) [mɪs'gɪvɪŋ(z)] *n(pl)* Bedenken *pl*.

misguided ['mɪs'gaɪdɪd] *a* fehlgeleitet; (*opinions*) irrig.

mishandle ['mɪs'hændl] *vt* falsch handhaben.

mishap ['mɪshæp] *n* Mißgeschick *nt*.

misinform ['mɪsɪn'fɔːm] *vt* falsch unterrichten.

misinterpret ['mɪsɪn'tɜːprɪt] *vt* falsch auffassen.

misjudge ['mɪs'dʒʌdʒ] *vt* falsch beurteilen.

mislay [mɪs'leɪ] (*irreg: like* lay) *vt* verlegen.

mislead [mɪs'liːd] (*irreg: like* lead) *vt* (*deceive*) irreführen; **~ing** *a* irreführend.

mismanage ['mɪs'mænɪdʒ] *vt* schlecht verwalten.

misnomer ['mɪs'nəʊmə*] *n* falsche Bezeichnung *f*.

misogynist [mɪ'sɒdʒɪnɪst] *n* Weiberfeind *m*.

misplace ['mɪs'pleɪs] *vt* verlegen.

misprint ['mɪsprɪnt] *n* Druckfehler *m*.

Miss [mɪs] *n* Fräulein *nt*.

miss [mɪs] *vt* (*fail to hit, catch*) verfehlen; (*not notice*) verpassen; (*be too late*) versäumen, verpassen; (*omit*) auslassen; (*regret the absence of*) vermissen // *vi* fehlen // *n* (*shot*) Fehlschuß *m*; (*failure*) Fehlschlag *m*; **that was a near ~** das war sehr knapp; **I ~ you** du fehlst mir; ~ **out** *vt* auslassen.

missal ['mɪsəl] *n* Meßbuch *nt*.

misshapen ['mɪs'ʃeɪpən] *a* mißgestaltet.

missile ['mɪsaɪl] *n* Rakete *f*.

missing ['mɪsɪŋ] *a* (*person*) vermißt; (*thing*) fehlend; **to be ~** fehlen.

mission ['mɪʃən] *n* (*work*) Auftrag *m*; (*people*) Delegation *f*; (*REL*) Mission *f*; **~ary** *n* Missionar(in *f*) *m*.

misspell ['mɪs'spel] (*irreg: like* spell) *vt* falsch schreiben.

misspent ['mɪs'spent] *a* (*youth*) vergeudet.

mist [mɪst] *n* Dunst *m*, Nebel *m* // *vi* (*also*: ~ **over**, ~ **up**) sich trüben; (: *Brit: windows*) sich beschlagen.

mistake [mɪs'teɪk] n Fehler m // vt
(irreg: like take) (misunderstand)
mißverstehen; (mix up) verwechseln
(for mit); to make a ~ einen Fehler machen; by ~ aus Versehen; to ~ A for B
A mit B verwechseln; ~n a (idea)
falsch; to be ~n sich irren.

mister ['mɪstə*] n (col) Herr m; see **Mr.**

mistletoe ['mɪsltəʊ] n Mistel f.

mistook [mɪs'tʊk] pt of **mistake.**

mistress ['mɪstrɪs] n (teacher) Lehrerin
f; (in house) Herrin f; (lover) Geliebte
f; see **Mrs.**

mistrust ['mɪs'trʌst] vt mißtrauen
(+dat).

misty ['mɪstɪ] a neblig.

misunderstand ['mɪsʌndə'stænd]
(irreg: like **understand**) vti mißverstehen, falsch verstehen; ~ing n
Mißverständnis nt; (disagreement)
Meinungsverschiedenheit f.

misuse ['mɪs'juːs] n falsche(r) Gebrauch
m // ['mɪs'juːz] vt falsch gebrauchen.

mitigate ['mɪtɪgeɪt] vt mildern.

mitt(en) ['mɪt(n)] n Fausthandschuh m.

mix [mɪks] vt (blend) (ver)mischen // vi
(liquids) sich (ver)mischen lassen; (people: get on) sich vertragen; (: associate)
Kontakt haben // n (mixture) Mischung
f; ~ up vt (mix) zusammenmischen;
(confuse) verwechseln; ~ed a
gemischt; ~ed-up a durcheinander;
~er n (for food) Mixer m; ~ture n
Mischung f; ~-up n Durcheinander nt

mm abbr (= millimetre) mm.

moan [məʊn] n Stöhnen nt; (complaint)
Klage f // vi stöhnen: (complain)
maulen.

moat [məʊt] n (Burg)graben m.

mob [mɒb] n Mob m; (the masses)
Pöbel m // vt (star) herfallen über
(+acc).

mobile ['məʊbaɪl] a beweglich; (library
etc) fahrbar // n (decoration) Mobile nt;
~ home n Wohnwagen m.

mobility [məʊ'bɪlɪtɪ] n Beweglichkeit f.

mobilize ['məʊbɪlaɪz] vt mobilisieren.

moccasin ['mɒkəsɪn] n Mokassin m.

mock [mɒk] vt verspotten; (defy)
trotzen (+dat) // a Schein-; ~ery n
Spott m; (person) Gespött nt.

mod [mɒd] a see **convenience.**

mode [məʊd] n (Art f und) Weise f.

model ['mɒdl] n Modell nt; (example)
Vorbild nt; (in fashion) Mannequin nt //
a (railway) Modell-; (perfect) Muster-;
vorbildlich // vt (make) bilden; (clothes)
vorführen // vi als Mannequin arbeiten.

modem ['məʊdem] n Modem nt.

moderate ['mɒdərət] a gemäßigt // n
(POL) Gemäßigte(r) mf // ['mɒdəreɪt] vi
sich mäßigen // vt mäßigen.

moderation [mɒdə'reɪʃən] n Mäßigung
f; in ~ mit Maßen.

modern ['mɒdən] a modern; (history,

languages) neuere(r, s); (Greek etc)
Neu-; ~ize vt modernisieren.

modest ['mɒdɪst] a bescheiden; ~y n
Bescheidenheit f.

modicum ['mɒdɪkəm] n bißchen nt.

modification [mɒdɪfɪ'keɪʃən] n
(Ab)änderung f.

modify ['mɒdɪfaɪ] vt abändern.

module ['mɒdjʊl] n (component)
(Bau)element nt; (SPACE) (Raum)-
kapsel f.

mogul ['məʊgəl] n (fig) Mogul m.

mohair ['məʊhɛə*] n Mohair m.

moist [mɔɪst] a feucht; ~en ['mɔɪsn] vt
befeuchten; ~ure n Feuchtigkeit f;
~urizer n Feuchtigkeitscreme f.

molar ['məʊlə*] n Backenzahn m.

molasses [mə'læsɪz] npl Melasse f.

mold [məʊld], n, vt (US) = **mould.**

mole [məʊl] n (spot) Leberfleck m; (animal) Maulwurf m; (pier) Mole f.

molest [məʊ'lest] vt belästigen.

mollycoddle ['mɒlɪkɒdl] vt verhätscheln.

molt [məʊlt] vi (US) = **moult.**

molten ['məʊltən] a geschmolzen.

mom [mɒm] n (US) = **mum.**

moment ['məʊmənt] n Moment m,
Augenblick m; (importance) Tragweite
f; at the ~ im Augenblick; ~ary a kurz;
~ous [məʊ'mentəs] a folgenschwer.

momentum [məʊ'mentəm] n Schwung
m; to gather ~ in Fahrt kommen.

mommy ['mɒmɪ] n (US) = **mummy.**

Monaco ['mɒnəkəʊ] n Monaco nt.

monarch ['mɒnək] n Herrscher(in f) m;
~y n Monarchie f.

monastery ['mɒnəstrɪ] n Kloster nt.

monastic [mə'næstɪk] a klösterlich,
Kloster-.

Monday ['mʌndeɪ] n Montag m.

monetary ['mʌnɪtərɪ] a Geld-; (of
currency) Währungs-.

money ['mʌnɪ] n Geld nt; to make ~
Geld verdienen; ~lender n
Geldverleiher m; ~ order n Postanweisung f; ~-spinner n (col) Verkaufs-
schlager m (col).

mongol ['mɒŋgəl] n (MED)
mongoloide(s) Kind nt // a mongolisch;
(MED) mongoloid.

mongrel ['mʌŋgrəl] n Promenaden-
mischung f.

monitor ['mɒnɪtə*] n (SCH)
Klassenordner m; (television ~) Monitor
m // vt (broadcasts) abhören; (control)
überwachen.

monk [mʌŋk] n Mönch m.

monkey ['mʌŋkɪ] n Affe m; ~ nut n
(Brit) Erdnuß f; ~ wrench n (TECH)
Engländer m, Franzose m.

mono- ['mɒnəʊ] pref Mono-.

monochrome ['mɒnəkrəʊm] a
schwarz-weiß.

monopolize [mə'nɒpəlaɪz] vt beherr-

schen.
monopoly [mə'nɒpəlɪ] n Monopol nt.
monosyllable ['mɒnəsɪləbl] n einsilbige(s) Wort nt.
monotone ['mɒnətəʊn] n gleichbleibende(r) Ton(fall) m; **to speak in a** ~ monoton sprechen.
monotonous [mə'nɒtənəs] a eintönig.
monotony [mə'nɒtənɪ] n Eintönigkeit f, Monotonie f.
monster ['mɒnstə*] n Ungeheuer nt; (person) Scheusal nt.
monstrosity [mɒns'trɒsɪtɪ] n Ungeheuerlichkeit f; (thing) Monstrosität f.
monstrous ['mɒnstrəs] a (shocking) gräßlich, ungeheuerlich; (huge) riesig.
month [mʌnθ] n Monat m; **~ly** a monatlich, Monats- // ad einmal im Monat // n (magazine) Monatsschrift f.
monument ['mɒnjʊmənt] n Denkmal nt; **~al** [mɒnjʊ'mentl] a (huge) gewaltig; (ignorance) ungeheuer.
moo [muː] vi muhen.
mood [muːd] n Stimmung f, Laune f; **to be in a good/bad** ~ gute/schlechte Laune haben; **~y** a launisch.
moon [muːn] n Mond m; **~light** n Mondlicht nt; **~lighting** n Schwarzarbeit f; **~lit** a mondhell.
moor [mʊə*] n Heide f, Hochmoor nt // vt (ship) festmachen, verankern // vi anlegen; **~ings** npl Liegeplatz m.
moorland ['mʊələnd] n Heidemoor nt.
moose [muːs] n Elch m.
mop [mɒp] n Mop m // vt (auf)wischen; ~ **up** vt aufwischen.
mope [məʊp] vi Trübsal blasen.
moped ['məʊped] n Moped nt.
moral ['mɒrəl] a moralisch; (values) sittlich; (virtuous) tugendhaft // n Moral f; **~s** pl Moral f; **~e** [mɒ'rɑːl] n Moral f; **~ity** [mə'rælɪtɪ] n Sittlichkeit f.
morass [mə'ræs] n Sumpf m.
morbid ['mɔːbɪd] a krankhaft; (jokes) makaber.
more [mɔː*] ◆ a (greater in number etc) mehr; (additional) noch mehr; **do you want (some)** ~ **tea?** möchten Sie noch etwas Tee?; **I have no** or **I don't have any** ~ **money** ich habe kein Geld mehr ◆ pron (greater amount) mehr; (further or additional amount) noch mehr; **is there any** ~? gibt es noch mehr?; (left over) ist noch etwas da?; **there's no** ~ es ist nichts mehr da ◆ ad mehr; ~ **dangerous/easily** etc (than) gefährlicher/einfacher etc (als); ~ **and** ~ immer mehr; ~ **and more excited** immer aufgeregter; ~ **or less** mehr oder weniger; ~ **than ever** mehr denn je; ~ **beautiful than ever** schöner denn je.
moreover [mɔː'rəʊvə*] ad überdies.
morgue [mɔːg] n Leichenschauhaus nt.
moribund ['mɒrɪbʌnd] a aussterbend.

Mormon ['mɔːmən] n Mormone m, Mormonin f.
morning ['mɔːnɪŋ] n Morgen; m **in the** ~ am Morgen; **7 o'clock in the** ~ 7 Uhr morgens.
Morocco [mə'rɒkəʊ] n Marokko nt.
moron ['mɔːrɒn] n Schwachsinnige(r) mf.
morose [mə'rəʊs] a mürrisch.
morphine ['mɔːfiːn] n Morphium nt.
Morse [mɔːs] n (also: ~ **code**) Morsealphabet nt.
morsel ['mɔːsl] n Bissen m.
mortal ['mɔːtl] a sterblich; (deadly) tödlich; (very great) Todes- // n (human being) Sterbliche(r) mf; **~ity** [mɔː'tælɪtɪ] n Sterblichkeit f; (death rate) Sterblichkeitsziffer f.
mortar ['mɔːtə*] n (for building) Mörtel m; (bowl) Mörser m; (MIL) Granatwerfer m.
mortgage ['mɔːgɪdʒ] n Hypothek f // vt eine Hypothek aufnehmen (+acc); ~ **company** n (US) ≈ Bausparkasse f.
mortify ['mɔːtɪfaɪ] vt beschämen.
mortuary ['mɔːtjʊərɪ] n Leichenhalle f.
Moscow ['mɒskəʊ] n Moskau nt.
Moslem ['mɒzləm] a, n = **Muslim.**
mosque [mɒsk] n Moschee f.
mosquito [mɒs'kiːtəʊ], pl **~es** n Moskito m.
moss [mɒs] n Moos nt.
most [məʊst] a meiste(r, s) // ad am meisten; (very) höchst // n das meiste, der größte Teil; (people) die meisten; ~ **men** die meisten Männer; **at the (very)** ~ allerhöchstens; **to make the** ~ **of** das Beste machen aus; **a** ~ **interesting book** ein höchst interessantes Buch; **~ly** ad größtenteils.
MOT n abbr (Brit) (= Ministry of Transport): **the** ~ (test) ≈ der TÜV.
motel [məʊ'tel] n Motel nt.
moth [mɒθ] n Nachtfalter m; (wooleating) Motte f; **~ball** n Mottenkugel f.
mother ['mʌðə*] n Mutter f // vt bemuttern; **~hood** n Mutterschaft f; **~-in-law** n Schwiegermutter f; **~ly** a mütterlich; **~-to-be** a werdende Mutter f; ~ **tongue** n Muttersprache f.
motif [məʊ'tiːf] n Motiv nt.
motion ['məʊʃən] n Bewegung f; (in meeting) Antrag m // vti winken (+dat), zu verstehen geben (+dat); **~less** a regungslos; ~ **picture** n Film m.
motivated ['məʊtɪveɪtɪd] a motiviert.
motivation [məʊtɪ'veɪʃən] n Motivierung f.
motive ['məʊtɪv] n Motiv nt, Beweggrund m // a treibend.
motley ['mɒtlɪ] a bunt.
motor ['məʊtə*] n Motor m; (Brit col: vehicle) Auto nt // a Motor-; **~bike** n Motorrad nt; **~boat** n Motorboot nt; **~car** n (Brit) Auto nt; **~cycle** n

Motorrad nt; **~cycle racing** n Motorradrennen nt; **~cyclist** n Motorradfahrer(in f) m; **~ing** n (Brit) Autofahren nt // a Auto-; **~ist** ['məutərist] n Autofahrer(in f) m; **~ racing** n (Brit) Autorennen nt; **~ scooter** n Motorroller m; **~ vehicle** n Kraftfahrzeug nt; **~way** n (Brit) Autobahn f.

mottled ['mɒtld] a gesprenkelt.

motto ['mɒtəu], pl **~es** n Motto nt.

mould, (US) **mold** [məuld] n Form f; (mildew) Schimmel m // vt (lit, fig) formen; **~er** vi (decay) vermodern; **~y** a schimmelig.

moult, (US) **molt** [məult] vi sich mausern.

mound [maund] n (Erd)hügel m.

mount [maunt] n (liter: hill) Berg m; (horse) Pferd nt; (for jewel etc) Fassung f // vt (horse) steigen auf (+acc); (put in setting) fassen; (exhibition) veranstalten; (attack) unternehmen // vi (also: **~ up**) sich häufen; (on horse) aufsitzen.

mountain ['mauntin] n Berg m // cpd Berg-; **~eer** [mauntɪ'nɪə*] n Bergsteiger(in f) m; **~eering** n Bergsteigen nt; **~ous** a bergig; **~ rescue team** n Bergwacht f; **~side** n Berg(ab)hang m.

mourn [mɔ:n] vt betrauen, beklagen // vi trauern (for um); **~er** n Trauernde(r) mf; **~ful** a traurig; **~ing** n (grief) Trauer f // cpd (dress) Trauer-; in **~ing** (period etc) in Trauer; (dress) in Trauerkleidung f.

mouse [maus], pl **mice** n Maus f; **~trap** n Mausefalle f.

mousse [mu:s] n (CULIN) Creme f; (cosmetic) Schaumfestiger m.

moustache [məs'ta:ʃ] n Schnurrbart m.

mousy ['mausi] a (colour) mausgrau; (person) schüchtern.

mouth [mauθ], pl **~s** [mauðz] n Mund m; (general) Öffnung f; (of river) Mündung f; **~ful** n Mundvoll m; **~ organ** n Mundharmonika f; **~piece** n (lit) Mundstück nt; (fig) Sprachrohr nt; **~wash** n Mundwasser nt; **~watering** a lecker, appetitlich.

movable ['mu:vəbl] a beweglich.

move [mu:v] n (movement) Bewegung f; (in game) Zug m; (step) Schritt m; (of house) Umzug m // vt bewegen; (people) transportieren; (in job) versetzen; (emotionally) bewegen // vi sich bewegen; (vehicle, ship) fahren; (go to another house) umziehen; **to ~ sb to do sth** jdn veranlassen, etw zu tun; **to get a ~ on** sich beeilen; **~ about or around** vi sich hin- und herbewegen; (travel) unterwegs sein; **~ along** vi weitergehen; (cars) weiterfahren; **~ away** vi weggehen; **~ back** vi zurückgehen; (to the rear) zurückwei-

chen; **~ forward** vi vorwärtsgehen, sich vorwärtsbewegen // vt vorschieben; (time) vorverlegen; **~ in** vi (to house) einziehen; (troops) einrücken; **~ on** vi weitergehen // vt weitergehen lassen; **~ out** vi (of house) ausziehen; (troops) abziehen; **~ over** vi zur Seite rücken; **~ up** vi aufsteigen; (in job) befördert werden // vt nach oben bewegen; (in job) befördern; **~ment** n Bewegung f.

movie ['mu:vɪ] n Film m; **to go to the ~s** ins Kino gehen; **~ camera** n Filmkamera f.

moving ['mu:vɪŋ] a beweglich; (touching) ergreifend.

mow [məu], pt **mowed**, pp **mowed** or **mown** vt mähen; **~ down** vt (fig) niedermähen; **~er** n (machine) Mähmaschine f; (lawn~) Rasenmäher m.

MP n abbr of **Member of Parliament**.

m.p.h. abbr of **miles per hour**.

Mr, Mr. [mɪstə*] Herr m.

Mrs, Mrs. ['mɪsɪz] Frau f.

Ms, Ms. [mɪz] n (= Miss or Mrs) Frau f.

M.Sc. abbr of **Master of Science**.

much [mʌtʃ] a viel // ad sehr; viel // n viel, eine Menge f; **how ~ is it?** wieviel kostet das?; **too ~** zuviel; **it's not ~** es ist nicht viel; **as ~ as** sosehr, soviel; **however ~ he tries** sosehr er es auch versucht.

muck [mʌk] n (lit) Mist m; (fig) Schmutz m; **~ about or around** vi (col) herumalbern (with an +dat); **~ up** vt (col: ruin) vermasseln; (dirty) dreckig machen; **~y** a (dirty) dreckig.

mucus ['mju:kəs] n Schleim m.

mud [mʌd] n Schlamm m.

muddle ['mʌdl] n Durcheinander nt // (also: **~ up**) durcheinanderbringen; **~ through** vi sich durchwursteln.

muddy ['mʌdɪ] a schlammig.

mudguard ['mʌdgɑːd] n Schutzblech nt.

mud-slinging ['mʌdslɪŋɪŋ] n (col) Verleumdung f.

muff [mʌf] n Muff m // vt (chance) verpassen; (lines) verpatzen (col).

muffin ['mʌfɪn] n süße(s) Teilchen nt.

muffle ['mʌfl] vt (sound) dämpfen; (wrap up) einhüllen; **~d** a gedämpft.

muffler ['mʌflə*] n (US AUT) Schalldämpfer m.

mug [mʌg] n (cup) Becher m; (col: face) Visage f; (col: fool) Trottel m // vt überfallen und ausrauben; **~ging** n Überfall m.

muggy ['mʌgɪ] a (weather) schwül.

mule [mju:l] n Maulesel m.

mull [mʌl]: **~ over** vt nachdenken über (+acc).

mulled [mʌld] a (wine) Glüh-.

multi- ['mʌltɪ] pref Multi-, multi-.

multicoloured, (US) **multicolored**

['mʌltɪ'kʌləd] a mehrfarbig.
multifarious [mʌltɪ'fɛərɪəs] a mannigfaltig.
multi-level ['mʌltɪlevl] a (US) = **multi-storey**.
multiple ['mʌltɪpl] n Vielfache(s) nt // a mehrfach; (many) mehrere; ~ **sclerosis** n multiple Sklerose f.
multiply ['mʌltɪplaɪ] vt multiplizieren (by mit) // vi (BIOL) sich vermehren.
multistorey ['mʌltɪ'stɔːrɪ] a (Brit: building, car park) mehrstöckig.
multitude ['mʌltɪtjuːd] n Menge f.
mum [mʌm] a: to keep ~ den Mund halten (about über +acc) // n (Brit col) Mutti f.
mumble ['mʌmbl] vti murmeln // n Gemurmel nt.
mummy ['mʌmɪ] n (dead body) Mumie f; (Brit col) Mami f.
mumps [mʌmps] n Mumps m.
munch [mʌntʃ] vti mampfen.
mundane ['mʌn'deɪn] a banal.
municipal [mjuː'nɪsɪpəl] a städtisch, Stadt-; ~**ity** [mjuːnɪsɪ'pælɪtɪ] n Stadt f mit Selbstverwaltung.
mural ['mjʊərəl] n Wandgemälde nt.
murder ['mɜːdə*] n Mord m // vt ermorden; ~**er** n Mörder m; ~**ous** a Mord-; (fig) mörderisch.
murky ['mɜːkɪ] a finster.
murmur ['mɜːmə*] n Murmeln nt; (of water, wind) Rauschen nt // vti murmeln.
muscle ['mʌsl] n Muskel m; ~ **in** vi mitmischen.
muscular ['mʌskjʊlə*] a Muskel-; (strong) muskulös.
muse [mjuːz] vi (nach)sinnen.
museum [mjuː'zɪəm] n Museum nt.
mushroom ['mʌʃruːm] n Champignon m; Pilz m // vi (fig) emporschießen.
music ['mjuːzɪk] n Musik f; (printed) Noten pl; ~**al** a (sound) melodisch; (person) musikalisch // n (show) Musical nt; ~**al instrument** n Musikinstrument nt; ~ **hall** n (Brit) Varieté nt; ~**ian** [mjuː'zɪʃən] n Musiker(in f) m.
musk [mʌsk] n Moschus m.
Muslim ['mʌzlɪm] a moslemisch // n Moslem m.
muslin ['mʌzlɪn] n Musselin m.
mussel ['mʌsl] n Miesmuschel f.
must [mʌst] v aux müssen; (in negation) dürfen // n Muß nt; the film is a ~ den Film muß man einfach gesehen haben.
mustard ['mʌstəd] n Senf m.
muster ['mʌstə*] vt (MIL) antreten lassen; (courage) zusammennehmen.
mustn't ['mʌsnt] = **must not**.
musty ['mʌstɪ] a muffig.
mute [mjuːt] a stumm // n (person) Stumme(r) mf; (MUS) Dämpfer m.
muted ['mjuːtɪd] a gedämpft.
mutilate ['mjuːtɪleɪt] vt verstümmeln.

mutilation [mjuːtɪ'leɪʃən] n Verstümmelung f.
mutiny ['mjuːtɪnɪ] n Meuterei f // vi meutern.
mutter ['mʌtə*] vti murmeln.
mutton ['mʌtn] n Hammelfleisch nt.
mutual ['mjuːtjʊəl] a gegenseitig; beiderseitig; ~**ly** ad gegenseitig; für beide Seiten.
muzzle ['mʌzl] n (of animal) Schnauze f; (for animal) Maulkorb m; (of gun) Mündung f // vt einen Maulkorb anlegen (+dat).
my [maɪ] a mein; this is ~ car das ist mein Auto; I've washed ~ hair ich habe mir die Haare gewaschen.
myopic [maɪ'ɒpɪk] a kurzsichtig.
myriad ['mɪrɪəd] n: a ~ of (people, things) unzählige.
myself [maɪ'self] pron mich (acc); mir (dat); (emphatic) selbst; see also **oneself**.
mysterious [mɪs'tɪərɪəs] a geheimnisvoll.
mystery ['mɪstərɪ] n (secret) Geheimnis nt; (sth difficult) Rätsel nt.
mystify ['mɪstɪfaɪ] vt ein Rätsel sein (+dat); verblüffen.
mystique [mɪs'tiːk] n geheimnisvolle Natur f.
myth [mɪθ] n Mythos m; (fig) Erfindung f; ~**ology** [mɪ'θɒlədʒɪ] n Mythologie f.

N

n/a abbr (= not applicable) nicht zutreffend.
nab [næb] vt (col) schnappen.
nag [næg] n (horse) Gaul m; (person) Nörgler(in f) m // vti herumnörgeln (sb an jdm); ~**ging** a (doubt) nagend // n Nörgelei f.
nail [neɪl] n Nagel m // vt nageln; to ~ sb down to doing sth jdn darauf festnageln, etw zu tun; ~**brush** n Nagelbürste f; ~**file** n Nagelfeile f; ~ **polish** n Nagellack m; ~ **polish remover** n Nagellackentferner m; ~ **scissors** npl Nagelschere f; ~ **varnish** n (Brit) = ~ **polish**.
naive [naɪ'iːv] a naiv.
naked ['neɪkɪd] a nackt.
name [neɪm] n Name m; (reputation) Ruf m // vt nennen; (sth new) benennen; (appoint) ernennen; by ~ mit Namen; I know him only by ~ ich kenne ihn nur dem Namen nach; **maiden** ~ Mädchenname m; what's your ~? wie heißen Sie?; **in the** ~ **of** im Namen (+gen); (for the sake of) um (+gen) willen; ~**less** a namenlos; ~**ly** ad nämlich; ~**sake** n Namensvetter m.
nanny ['nænɪ] n Kindermädchen nt.
nap [næp] n (sleep) Nickerchen nt; (on

cloth) Strich *m*; **to be caught ~ping** (*fig*) überrumpelt werden.

nape [neɪp] *n* Nacken *m*.

napkin ['næpkɪn] *n* (*at table*) Serviette *f*; (*Brit: for baby*) Windel *f*.

nappy ['næpɪ] *n* (*Brit: for baby*) Windel *f*; **~ liner** *n* Windeleinlage *f*; **~ rash** *n* wunde Stellen *pl*.

narcissus [nɑːˈsɪsəs], *pl* **-si** [-saɪ] *n* (*BOT*) Narzisse *f*.

narcotic [nɑːˈkɒtɪk] *a* betäubend // *n* Betäubungsmittel *nt*.

narrative ['nærətɪv] *n* Erzählung *f* // *a* erzählend.

narrator [nəˈreɪtə*] *n* Erzähler(in *f*) *m*.

narrow ['nærəʊ] *a* eng, schmal; (*limited*) beschränkt // *vi* sich verengen; **to have a ~ escape** mit knapper Not davonkommen; **to ~ sth down to sth** etw auf etw (*acc*) einschränken; **~ly** *ad* (*miss*) knapp; (*escape*) mit knapper Not; **~-minded** *a* engstirnig.

nasty ['nɑːstɪ] *a* ekelhaft, fies; (*business, wound*) schlimm.

nation ['neɪʃən] *n* Nation *f*, Volk *nt*; **~al** ['næʃənl] *a* national, National-, Landes- // *n* Staatsangehörige(r) *mf*; **~al dress** *n* Tracht *f*; **N~al Health Service (NHS)** *n* (*Brit*) Staatliche(r) Gesundheitsdienst *m*; **N~al Insurance** *n* (*Brit*) Sozialversicherung *f*; **~alism** ['næʃnəlɪzəm] *n* Nationalismus *m*; **~alist** ['næʃnəlɪst] *n* Nationalist(in *f*) *m* // *a* nationalistisch; **~ality** [næʃəˈnælɪtɪ] *n* Staatsangehörigkeit *f*; **~alize** ['næʃnəlaɪz] *vt* verstaatlichen; **~ally** ['næʃnəlɪ] *ad* national, auf Staatsebene; **~-wide** *a*, *ad* allgemein, landesweit.

native ['neɪtɪv] *n* (*born in*) Einheimische(r) *mf*; (*original inhabitant*) Eingeborene(r) *mf* // *a* (*coming from a certain place*) einheimisch; (*of the original inhabitants*) Eingeborenen-; (*belonging by birth*) heimatlich, Heimat-; (*inborn*) angeboren, natürlich; **a ~ of Germany** ein gebürtiger Deutscher; **a ~ speaker of French** ein französischer Muttersprachler; **~ language** *n* Muttersprache *f*.

Nativity [nəˈtɪvɪtɪ] *n*: **the ~** Christi Geburt *no art*.

NATO ['neɪtəʊ] *n abbr* (= *North Atlantic Treaty Organization*) NATO *f*.

natter ['nætə*] (*Brit col*) *vi* quatschen // *n* Gequatsche *nt*.

natural ['nætʃrəl] *a* natürlich; Natur-; (*inborn*) (an)geboren; **~ gas** *n* Erdgas *nt*; **~ist** *n* Naturkundler(in *f*) *m*; **~ize** *vt* (*foreigner*) einbürgern; (*plant etc*) einführen; **~ly** *ad* natürlich.

nature ['neɪtʃə*] *n* Natur *f*; **by ~** von Natur (aus).

naught [nɔːt] *n* = **nought**.

naughty ['nɔːtɪ] *a* (*child*) unartig, ungezogen; (*action*) ungehörig.

nausea ['nɔːsɪə] *n* (*sickness*) Übelkeit *f*; (*disgust*) Ekel *m*; **~te** ['nɔːsɪeɪt] *vt* anekeln.

nautical ['nɔːtɪkəl] *a* nautisch; See-; (*expression*) seemännisch.

naval ['neɪvəl] *a* Marine-, Flotten-; **~ officer** *n* Marineoffizier *m*.

nave [neɪv] *n* Kirchen(haupt)schiff *nt*.

navel ['neɪvəl] *n* Nabel *m*.

navigate ['nævɪgeɪt] *vi* navigieren.

navigator ['nævɪgeɪtə*] *n* Steuermann *m*; (*AVIAT*) Navigator *m*; (*AUT*) Beifahrer(in *f*) *m*.

navvy ['nævɪ] *n* (*Brit*) Straßenarbeiter *m*.

navy ['neɪvɪ] *n* (Kriegs)marine *f*; **~(-blue)** *n* Marineblau *nt* // *a* marineblau.

NB *abbr* (= *nota bene*) NB.

near [nɪə*] *a* nah; **~** *ad* in der Nähe // *prep* (*also*: **~ to**: *space*) in der Nähe (+*gen*); (: *time*) um (+*acc*) ... herum // *vt* sich nähern (+*dat*); **a ~ miss** knapp daneben; **~by** *a* nahe (gelegen) // *ad* in der Nähe; **~ly** *ad* fast; **I ~ly fell** ich wäre fast gefallen; **~side** *n* (*AUT*) Beifahrerseite *f* // *a* auf der Beifahrerseite.

neat *a*, **~ly** *ad* ['niːt, -lɪ] (*tidy*) ordentlich; (*solution*) sauber; (*pure*) pur.

nebulous ['nebjʊləs] *a* nebulös.

necessarily ['nesɪsərɪlɪ] *ad* unbedingt.

necessary ['nesɪsərɪ] *a* notwendig, nötig; **he did all that was ~** er erledigte alles, was nötig war.

necessitate [nɪˈsesɪteɪt] *vt* erforderlich machen.

necessity [nɪˈsesɪtɪ] *n* (*need*) Not *f*; (*compulsion*) Notwendigkeit *f*; **necessities** *pl* das Notwendigste.

neck [nek] *n* Hals *m* // *vi* (*col*) knutschen; **~ and ~** Kopf an Kopf.

necklace ['neklɪs] *n* Halskette *f*.

neckline ['neklaɪn] *n* Ausschnitt *m*.

necktie ['nektaɪ] *n* (*US*) Krawatte *f*.

née [neɪ] *a* geborene.

need [niːd] *n* Bedürfnis *nt* (*for* für); (*lack*) Mangel *m*; (*necessity*) Notwendigkeit *f*; (*poverty*) Not *f* // *vt* brauchen; **I ~ to do it** ich muß es tun; **you don't ~ to go** du brauchst nicht zu gehen.

needle ['niːdl] *n* Nadel *f* // *vt* (*fig: col*) ärgern.

needless ['niːdlɪs] *a* unnötig; **~ to say** natürlich.

needlework ['niːdlwɜːk] *n* Handarbeit *f*.

needn't ['niːdnt] = **need not**.

needy ['niːdɪ] *a* bedürftig.

negation [nɪˈgeɪʃən] *n* Verneinung *f*.

negative ['negətɪv] *n* (*PHOT*) Negativ *nt* // *a* negativ; (*answer*) abschlägig.

neglect [nɪˈglekt] *vt* vernachlässigen // *n* Vernachlässigung *f*.

negligence ['neglɪdʒəns] *n* Nachlässigkeit *f*.

negligible ['neglɪdʒəbl] a unbedeutend, geringfügig.

negotiable [nɪ'gəʊʃɪəbl] a (cheque) übertragbar, einlösbar.

negotiate [nɪ'gəʊʃɪeɪt] vi verhandeln // vt (treaty) abschließen; (difficulty) überwinden; (corner) nehmen; **negotiation** [-'eɪʃən] n Verhandlung f; **negotiator** n Unterhändler m.

Negress ['niːgres] n Negerin f.

Negro ['niːgrəʊ] n Neger m // a Neger-.

neigh [neɪ] vi wiehern.

neighbour, (US) **neighbor** ['neɪbə*] n Nachbar(in f) m; **~hood** n Nachbarschaft f; Umgebung f; **~ing** a benachbart, angrenzend.

neither ['naɪðə*] a, pron keine(r, s) (von beiden) // cj: **he can't do it, and ~ can I** er kann es nicht und ich auch nicht // ad: **~ good nor bad** weder gut noch schlecht.

nephew ['nefjuː] n Neffe m.

nerve [nɜːv] n Nerv m; (courage) Mut m; (impudence) Frechheit f; **to have a fit of ~s** in Panik geraten; **~-racking** a nervenaufreibend.

nervous ['nɜːvəs] a (of the nerves) Nerven-; (timid) nervös, ängstlich; **~ breakdown** n Nervenzusammenbruch m; **~ness** n Nervosität f.

nest [nest] n Nest nt // vi nisten; **~ egg** n (fig) Notgroschen m.

nestle ['nesl] vi sich kuscheln.

net [net] n Netz nt // a netto, Netto- // vt netto einnehmen; **~ball** n Netzball m; **~ curtain** n Store m.

Netherlands ['neðələndz] npl: **the ~** die Niederlande pl.

nett [net] a = **net**.

netting ['netɪŋ] n Netz(werk) nt.

nettle ['netl] n Nessel f.

network ['netwɜːk] n Netz nt.

neuter ['njuːtə*] a (BIOL) geschlechtslos; (GRAM) sächlich // vt kastrieren.

neutral ['njuːtrəl] a neutral // n (AUT) Leerlauf m; **~ity** [njuː'trælɪtɪ] n Neutralität f; **~ize** vt (fig) ausgleichen.

never ['nevə*] ad nie(mals); **I ~ went** ich bin gar nicht gegangen; **~ in my life** nie im Leben; **~-ending** a endlos; **~theless** [nevəðə'les] ad trotzdem, dennoch.

new [njuː] a neu; a neugeboren; **~comer** n Neuankömmling m; **~-fangled** a (pej) neumodisch; **~-found** a neuentdeckt; **~ly** ad frisch, neu; **~lyweds** npl Frischvermählte pl; **~ moon** n Neumond m.

news [njuːz] n Nachricht f; (RAD, TV) Nachrichten pl; **a piece of ~** eine Nachricht; **~ agency** n Nachrichtenagentur f; **~agent** n (Brit) Zeitungshändler m; **~caster** n Nachrichtensprecher(in f) m; **~ dealer** n

(US) = **~agent**; **~ flash** n Kurzmeldung f; **~letter** n Rundschreiben nt; **~paper** n Zeitung f; **~print** n Zeitungspapier nt; **~reader** n = **~caster**; **~reel** n Wochenschau f; **~stand** n Zeitungsstand m.

newt [njuːt] n Wassermolch m.

New Year n Neujahr nt; **~'s Day** n Neujahrstag m; **~'s Eve** n Silvester(abend m) nt.

New York [-'jɔːk] n New York nt.

New Zealand [-'ziːlənd] n Neuseeland nt; **~er** n Neuseeländer(in f) m.

next [nekst] a nächste(r, s) // ad (after) dann, darauf; (next time) das nächstemal; **the ~ day** am nächsten or folgenden Tag; **~ time** das nächste Mal; **~ year** nächstes Jahr; **~ door** ad nebenan // a (neighbour, flat) von nebenan; **~ of kin** n Familienangehörige(r) mf; **~ to** prep neben; **~ to nothing** so gut wie nichts.

NHS n abbr of **National Health Service.**

nib [nɪb] n Spitze f.

nibble ['nɪbl] vt knabbern an (+dat).

nice [naɪs] a (person) nett; (thing) schön; (subtle) fein; **~-looking** a gutaussehend; **~ly** ad gut, nett; **niceties** ['naɪsɪtɪz] npl Feinheiten pl.

nick [nɪk] n Einkerbung f // vt (col: steal) klauen; **in the ~ of time** gerade rechtzeitig.

nickel ['nɪkl] n Nickel nt; (US) Nickel m (5 cents).

nickname ['nɪkneɪm] n Spitzname m // vt taufen.

Nigeria [naɪ'dʒɪərɪə] n Nigeria nt.

niece [niːs] n Nichte f.

niggardly ['nɪgədlɪ] a geizig.

niggling ['nɪglɪŋ] a pedantisch; (doubt, worry) quälend; (detail) kleinlich.

night [naɪt] n Nacht f; (evening) Abend m; **the ~ before last** vorletzte Nacht; **at or by ~** (after midnight) nachts; (before midnight) abends; **~cap** n (drink) Schlummertrunk m; **~club** n Nachtlokal nt; **~dress** n Nachthemd nt; **~fall** n Einbruch m der Nacht; **~ gown** n = **~dress**; **~ie** n (col) Nachthemd nt.

nightingale ['naɪtɪŋgeɪl] n Nachtigall f.

nightly ['naɪtlɪ] a, ad jeden Abend; jede Nacht.

nightmare ['naɪtmeə*] n Alptraum m.

night: ~ porter n Nachtportier m; **~ school** n Abendschule f; **~ shift** n Nachtschicht f; **~time** n Nacht f.

nil [nɪl] n Null f.

Nile [naɪl] n: **the ~** der Nil.

nimble ['nɪmbl] a beweglich.

nine [naɪn] num neun; **~teen** num neunzehn; **~ty** num neunzig.

ninth [naɪnθ] a neunte(r, s).

nip [nɪp] vt kneifen // n Kneifen nt.

nipple ['nɪpl] n Brustwarze f.

nippy ['nɪpɪ] *a* (*col: person*) flink; (*Brit col: car*) flott; (: *cold*) frisch.

nitrogen ['naɪtrədʒən] *n* Stickstoff *m*.

no [nəu] ◆ *ad* (*opposite of 'yes'*) nein; to answer ~ (*to question*) mit Nein antworten; (*to request*) nein sagen; ~ thank you nein, danke
◆ *a* (*not any*) kein(e); I have ~ money/time ich habe kein Geld/keine Zeit; '~ smoking' 'Rauchen verboten'
◆ *n, pl* ~es Nein *nt*; (~ *vote*) Neinstimme *f*.

nobility [nəu'bɪlɪtɪ] *n* Adel *m*.

noble ['nəubl] *a* (*rank*) adlig; (*splendid*) nobel, edel.

nobody ['nəubədɪ] *pron* niemand, keiner.

nocturnal [nɒk'tɜ:nl] *a* (*tour, visit*) nächtlich; (*animal*) Nacht-.

nod [nɒd] *vi* nicken // *vt* nicken mit // *n* Nicken *nt*; ~ off *vi* einnicken.

noise [nɔɪz] *n* (*sound*) Geräusch *nt*; (*unpleasant, loud*) Lärm *m*.

noisy ['nɔɪzɪ] *a* laut; (*crowd*) lärmend.

nominal ['nɒmɪnl] *a* nominell.

nominate ['nɒmɪneɪt] *vt* (*suggest*) vorschlagen; (*in election*) aufstellen; (*appoint*) ernennen.

nomination [nɒmɪ'neɪʃən] *n* (*election*) Nominierung *f*; (*appointment*) Ernennung *f*.

nominee [nɒmɪ'ni:] *n* Kandidat(in *f*) *m*.

non- [nɒn] *pref* Nicht-, un-; ●-**alcoholic** *a* alkoholfrei; ~-**aligned** *a* bündnisfrei.

nonchalant ['nɒnʃələnt] *a* lässig.

non-committal ['nɒnkə'mɪtl] *a* (*reserved*) zurückhaltend; (*uncommitted*) unverbindlich.

nondescript ['nɒndɪskrɪpt] *a* mittelmäßig.

none [nʌn] *a, pron* kein(e, er, es) // *ad*: ~ of you keiner von euch; I've ~ left ich habe keine(n) mehr; he's ~ the worse for it es hat ihm nicht geschadet.

nonentity [nɒ'nentɪtɪ] *n* Null *f* (*col*).

nonetheless ['nʌnðə'les] *ad* nichtsdestoweniger.

non: ~-**existent** *a* nicht vorhanden; ~-**fiction** *n* Sachbücher *pl*.

nonplussed [nɒn'plʌst] *a* verdutzt.

nonsense ['nɒnsəns] *n* Unsinn *m*.

non: ~-**smoker** *n* Nichtraucher(in *f*) *m*; ~-**stick** *a* (*pan, surface*) Teflon- ®; ~-**stop** *a* Nonstop-.

noodles ['nu:dlz] *npl* Nudeln *pl*.

nook [nuk] *n* Winkel *m*; ~s and crannies Ecken und Winkel.

noon [nu:n] *n* (12 Uhr) Mittag *m*.

no one ['nəuwʌn] *pron* = **nobody**.

noose [nu:s] *n* Schlinge *f*.

nor [nɔ:*] *cj* = **neither** // *ad see* **neither**.

normal ['nɔ:məl] *a* normal; ~**ly** *ad* normal; (*usually*) normalerweise.

north [nɔ:θ] *n* Norden *m* // *a* nördlich, Nord- // *ad* nördlich, nach *or* im Norden;

~-**east** *n* Nordosten *m*; ~**erly** ['nɔ:ðəlɪ] *a* nördlich; ~**ern** ['nɔ:ðən] *a* nördlich, Nord-; **N~ern Ireland** *n* Nordirland *nt*; **N~ Pole** *n* Nordpole *m*; **N~ Sea** *n* Nordsee *f*; ~**ward(s)** *ad* nach Norden; ~-**west** *n* Nordwesten *m*.

Norway ['nɔ:weɪ] *n* Norwegen *nt*; **Norwegian** [-'wi:dʒən] *a* norwegisch // *n* Norweger(in *f*) *m*; (*LING*) Norwegisch *nt*.

nose [nəuz] *n* Nase *f* // *vi*: to ~ about herumschnüffeln; ~**bleed** *n* Nasenbluten *nt*; ~-**dive** *n* Sturzflug *m*; ~**y** *a* = **nosy**.

nostril ['nɒstrɪl] *n* Nasenloch *nt*.

nosy ['nəuzɪ] *a* (*col*) neugierig.

not [nɒt] *ad* nicht; he is ~ *or* isn't here er ist nicht hier; it's too late, isn't it? es ist zu spät, oder *or* nicht wahr?; ~ yet/now noch nicht/nicht jetzt; *see also* **all, only.**

notably ['nəutəblɪ] *ad* (*especially*) besonders; (*noticeably*) bemerkenswert.

notary ['nəutərɪ] *n* Notar(in *f*) *m*.

notch [nɒtʃ] *n* Kerbe *f*, Einschnitt *m*.

note [nəut] *n* (*MUS*) Note *f*, Ton *m*; (*short letter*) Nachricht *f*; (*POL*) Note *f*; (*comment, attention*) Notiz *f*; (*of lecture etc*) Aufzeichnung *f*; (*bank~*) Schein *m*; (*fame*) Ruf *m* // *vt* (*observe*) bemerken; (*write down*) notieren; ~**book** *n* Notizbuch *nt*; ~**d** *a* bekannt; ~**pad** *n* Notizblock *m*; ~**paper** *n* Briefpapier *nt*.

nothing ['nʌθɪŋ] *n* nichts; ~ **new/much** nichts Neues/nicht viel; **for** ~ umsonst.

notice ['nəutɪs] *n* (*announcement*) Bekanntmachung *f*; (*warning*) Ankündigung *f*; (*dismissal*) Kündigung *f* // *vt* bemerken; **to take** ~ **of** beachten; **at short** ~ kurzfristig; **until further** ~ bis auf weiteres; **to hand in one's** ~ kündigen; ~**able** *a* merklich; ~ **board** *n* Anschlagtafel *f*.

notify ['nəutɪfaɪ] *vt* benachrichtigen.

notion ['nəuʃən] *n* Idee *f*.

notorious [nəu'tɔ:rɪəs] *a* berüchtigt.

notwithstanding [nɒtwɪθ'stændɪŋ] *ad* trotzdem; ~ **this** ungeachtet dessen.

nought [nɔ:t] *n* Null *f*.

noun [naun] *n* Substantiv *nt*.

nourish ['nʌrɪʃ] *vt* nähren; ~**ing** *a* nahrhaft; ~**ment** *n* Nahrung *f*.

novel ['nɒvl] *n* Roman *m* // *a* neu(artig); ~**ist** *n* Schriftsteller(in *f*) *m*; ~**ty** *n* Neuheit *f*.

November [nəu'vembə*] *n* November *m*.

novice ['nɒvɪs] *n* Neuling *m*; (*ECCL*) Novize *m*.

now [nau] *ad* jetzt; **right** ~ jetzt, gerade; **by** ~ imzwischen; **just** ~ gerade; ~ **and then**, ~ **and again** ab und zu, manchmal; **from** ~ **on** von jetzt an; ~**adays** *ad* heutzutage.

nowhere ['nəuwɛə*] *ad* nirgends.

nozzle ['nɒzl] n Düse f.

nubile ['njuːbaɪl] a (woman) gut entwickelt.

nuclear ['njuːklɪə*] a (energy etc) Atom-, Kern-.

nucleus ['njuːklɪəs], pl ~lei [-lɪaɪ] n Kern m.

nude [njuːd] a nackt // n (ART) Akt m; in the ~ nackt.

nudge [nʌdʒ] vt leicht anstoßen.

nudist ['njuːdɪst] n Nudist(in f) m.

nudity ['njuːdɪtɪ] n Nacktheit f.

nuisance ['njuːsns] n Ärgernis nt; what a ~! wie ärgerlich!

nuke [njuːk] (col) n Kernkraftwerk nt // vt atomar vernichten.

null [nʌl] a: ~ and void null und nichtig.

numb [nʌm] a taub, gefühllos // vt betäuben.

number ['nʌmbə*] n Nummer f; (numeral also) Zahl f; (quantity) (An)zahl f // vt (give a number to) numerieren; (amount to) sein; to be ~ed among gezählt werden zu; a ~ of (several) einige; they were ten in ~ sie waren zehn an der Zahl; ~ plate n (Brit AUT) Nummernschild nt.

numeral ['njuːmərəl] n Ziffer f.

numerate ['njuːmərɪt] a rechenkundig.

numerical [njuː'merɪkəl] a (order) zahlenmäßig.

numerous ['njuːmərəs] a zahlreich.

nun [nʌn] n Nonne f.

nurse [nɜːs] n Krankenschwester f; (for children) Kindermädchen nt // vt (patient) pflegen; (doubt etc) hegen.

nursery ['nɜːsərɪ] n (for children) Kinderzimmer nt; (for plants) Gärtnerei f; (for trees) Baumschule f; ~ **rhyme** n Kinderreim m; ~ **school** n Kindergarten m; ~ **slope** n (Brit SKI) Idiotenhügel m (col), Anfängerhügel m.

nursing ['nɜːsɪŋ] n (profession) Krankenpflege f; ~ **home** n Privatklinik f.

nurture ['nɜːtʃə*] vt aufziehen.

nut [nʌt] n Nuß f; (screw) Schraubenmutter f; (col) Verrückte(r) mf; ~s a (col: crazy) verrückt.

nutcrackers ['nʌtkrækəz] npl Nußknacker m.

nutmeg ['nʌtmeg] n Muskat(nuß f) m.

nutrient ['njuːtrɪənt] n Nährstoff m.

nutrition [njuː'trɪʃən] n Nahrung f.

nutritious [njuː'trɪʃəs] a nahrhaft.

nutshell ['nʌtʃel] n: in a ~ in aller Kürze.

nylon ['naɪlɒn] n Nylon nt // a Nylon-.

O

oak [əʊk] n Eiche f // a Eichen(holz)-.

O.A.P. abbr of **old-age pensioner**.

oar [ɔː*] n Ruder nt.

oath [əʊθ] n (statement) Eid m, Schwur m; (swearword) Fluch m; on (Brit) or under ~ unter Eid.

oatmeal ['əʊtmiːl] n Haferschrot m.

oats [əʊts] npl Hafer m.

obedience [ə'biːdɪəns] n Gehorsam m.

obedient [ə'biːdɪənt] a gehorsam.

obesity [əʊ'biːsɪtɪ] n Fettleibigkeit f.

obey [ə'beɪ] vti gehorchen (+dat).

obituary [ə'bɪtjuərɪ] n Nachruf m.

object ['ɒbdʒɪkt] n (thing) Gegenstand m, Objekt nt; (purpose) Ziel nt // [əb'dʒekt] vi dagegen sein, Einwände haben (to gegen); (morally) Anstoß nehmen (to an +acc); expense is no ~ Ausgaben spielen keine Rolle; I ~! ich protestiere!; to ~ that einwenden, daß; ~ion [əb'dʒekʃən] n (reason against) Einwand m, Einspruch m; (dislike) Abneigung f; I have no ~ion to ... ich habe nichts gegen ... einzuwenden; ~ionable [əb'dʒekʃnəbl] a nicht einwandfrei; (language) anstößig; ~ive [əb'dʒektɪv] n Ziel nt // a objektiv.

obligation [ɒblɪ'geɪʃən] n Verpflichtung f; **without** ~ unverbindlich.

obligatory [ɒ'blɪgətərɪ] a obligatorisch.

oblige [ə'blaɪdʒ] vt (compel) zwingen; (do a favour) einen Gefallen tun (+dat); to be ~ed to sb for sth jdm für etw verbunden sein.

obliging [ə'blaɪdʒɪŋ] a entgegenkommend.

oblique [ə'bliːk] a schräg, schief // n Schrägstrich m.

obliterate [ə'blɪtəreɪt] vt auslöschen.

oblivion [ə'blɪvɪən] n Vergessenheit f.

oblivious [ə'blɪvɪəs] a nicht bewußt (of gen).

oblong ['ɒblɒŋ] n Rechteck nt // a länglich.

obnoxious [əb'nɒkʃəs] a widerlich.

obscene [əb'siːn] a obszön.

obscenity [əb'senɪtɪ] n Obszönität f; ob**scenities** pl Zoten pl.

obscure [əb'skjuə*] a unklar; (indistinct) undeutlich; (unknown) unbekannt, obskur; (dark) düster // vt verdunkeln; (view) verbergen; (confuse) verwirren.

obscurity [əb'skjuərɪtɪ] n Unklarheit f; (darkness) Dunkelheit f.

obsequious [əb'siːkwɪəs] a servil.

observance [əb'zɜːvəns] n Befolgung f.

observant [əb'zɜːvənt] a aufmerksam.

observation [ɒbzə'veɪʃən] n (noticing) Beobachtung f; (surveillance) Überwachung f; (remark) Bemerkung f.

observatory [əb'zɜːvətrɪ] n Sternwarte f, Observatorium nt.

observe [əb'zɜːv] vt (notice) bemerken; (watch) beobachten; (customs) einhalten; ~r n Beobachter(in f) m.

obsess [əb'ses] vt verfolgen, quälen; ~ion [əb'seʃən] n Besessenheit f, Wahn m; ~ive a krankhaft.

obsolescence [ɒbsə'lesns] n Veralten nt.

obsolete ['ɒbsəliːt] a überholt, veraltet.

obstacle ['ɒbstəkl] n Hindernis nt; ~ **race** n Hindernisrennen nt.

obstetrics [ɒb'stetrɪks] n Geburtshilfe f.

obstinate a, ~**ly** ad ['ɒbstɪnət, -lɪ] hartnäckig, stur.

obstruct [əb'strʌkt] vt versperren; (pipe) verstopfen; (hinder) hemmen; ~**ion** [əb'strʌkʃən] n Versperrung f; Verstopfung f; (obstacle) Hindernis nt.

obtain [əb'teɪn] vt erhalten, bekommen; (result) erzielen.

obtrusive [əb'truːsɪv] a aufdringlich.

obvious ['ɒbvɪəs] a offenbar, offensichtlich; ~**ly** ad offensichtlich.

occasion [ə'keɪʒən] n Gelegenheit f; (special event) Ereignis nt; (reason) Anlaß m // vt veranlassen; ~**al** a, ~**ally** ad gelegentlich.

occupant ['ɒkjupənt] n Inhaber(in f) m; (of house etc) Bewohner(in f) m.

occupation [ɒkju'peɪʃən] n (employment) Tätigkeit f, Beruf m; (pastime) Beschäftigung f; (of country) Besetzung f, Okkupation f; ~**al hazard** n Berufsrisiko nt.

occupier ['ɒkjupaɪə*] n Bewohner(in f) m.

occupy ['ɒkjupaɪ] vt (take possession of) besetzen; (seat) belegen; (live in) bewohnen; (position, office) bekleiden; (position in sb's life) einnehmen; (time) beanspruchen; to ~ o.s. with or by doing sich mit etw beschäftigen.

occur [ə'kɜː*] vi vorkommen; to ~ to sb jdm einfallen; ~**rence** n (event) Ereignis nt; (appearing) Auftreten nt.

ocean ['əuʃən] n Ozean m, Meer nt; ~-**going** a Hochsee-.

o'clock [ə'klɒk] ad: it is 5 ~ es ist 5 Uhr.

OCR n abbr of **optical character reader**.

octagonal [ɒk'tægənl] a achteckig.

October [ɒk'təubə*] n Oktober m.

octopus ['ɒktəpəs] n Krake f; (small) Tintenfisch m.

odd [ɒd] a (strange) sonderbar; (not even) ungerade; (the other part missing) einzeln; (surplus) übrig; 60~ so um die 60; at ~ times ab und zu; to be the ~ one out (person) das fünfte Rad am Wagen sein; (thing) nicht dazugehören; ~**s and ends** npl Krimskrams m; ~**ity** n (strangeness) Merkwürdigkeit f; (queer person) seltsame(r) Kauz m; (thing) Kuriosität f; ~-**job man** n Mädchen nt für alles; ~ **jobs** npl gelegentlich anfallende Arbeiten; ~**ly** ad seltsam; ~**ment** npl Reste pl; ~**s** pl Chancen pl; (betting) Gewinnchancen pl; it makes no ~s es spielt keine Rolle; at ~s uneinig.

odious ['əudɪəs] a verhaßt; (action) abscheulich.

odometer [əu'dɒmətə*] n (esp US) Tacho(meter) m.

odour, (US) **odor** ['əudə*] n Geruch m.

of [ɒv, əv] prep 1 von (+dat), use of gen: the history ~ Germany die Geschichte Deutschlands; a friend ~ ours ein Freund von uns; a boy ~ 10 ein 10-jähriger Junge; that was kind ~ you das war sehr freundlich von Ihnen
2 (expressing quantity, amount, dates etc): a kilo ~ flour ein Kilo Mehl; how much ~ this do you need? wieviel brauchen Sie (davon)?; there were 3 ~ them (people) sie waren zu dritt; (objects) es gab 3 (davon); a cup ~ tea/vase ~ flowers eine Tasse Tee/Vase mit Blumen; the 5th ~ July der 5. Juli
3 (from, out of) aus; a bridge made ~ wood eine Holzbrücke, eine Brücke aus Holz.

off [ɒf] ad (absent) weg, fort; (switch) aus(geschaltet), ab(geschaltet); (Brit: food: bad) schlecht; to be ~ (to leave) gehen; to be ~ sick krank sein; a day ~ ein freier Tag; to have an ~ day einen schlechten Tag haben; he had his coat ~ er hatte seinen Mantel aus; 10% ~ (COMM) 10% Rabatt; 5 km ~ (the road) 5 km (von der Straße) entfernt; ~ the coast vor der Küste; I'm ~ meat (no longer eat it) ich esse kein Fleisch mehr; (no longer like it) ich mag kein Fleisch mehr; on the ~ chance auf gut Glück.

offal ['ɒfəl] n Innereien pl.

off-colour ['ɒf'kʌlə*] a nicht wohl.

offence, (US) **offense** [ə'fens] n (crime) Vergehen nt, Straftat f; (insult) Beleidigung f; to take ~ at gekränkt sein wegen.

offend [ə'fend] vt beleidigen; ~**er** n Gesetzesübertreter m.

offensive [ə'fensɪv] a (unpleasant) übel, abstoßend; (weapon) Kampf-; (remark) verletzend // n Angriff m.

offer ['ɒfə*] n Angebot f; on ~ zum Verkauf angeboten // vt anbieten; (opinion) äußern; (resistance) leisten; ~**ing** n Gabe f.

offhand ['ɒf'hænd] a lässig // ad ohne weiteres.

office ['ɒfɪs] n Büro nt; (position) Amt nt; doctor's ~ (US) Praxis f; to take ~ sein Amt antreten; (POL) die Regierung übernehmen; ~ **automation** n Büroautomatisierung f; ~ **block**, (US) ~ **building** n Büro(hoch)haus nt; ~ **hours** npl Dienstzeit f; (US MED) Sprechstunde f.

officer ['ɒfɪsə*] n (MIL) Offizier m; (public ~) Beamte(r) m.

official [ə'fɪʃəl] a offiziell, amtlich // n Beamte(r) m; ~**dom** n Beamtentum nt.

officiate [əˈfɪʃɪeɪt] vi amtieren.
officious [əˈfɪʃəs] a aufdringlich.
offing [ˈɒfɪŋ] n: in the ~ in (Aus)sicht.
off-licence [ˈɒflaɪsəns] n (Brit: shop) Wein- und Spirituosenhandlung f.
off-peak [ˈɒfpiːk] a (charges) verbilligt.
off-season [ˈɒfsiːzn] a außer Saison.
offset [ˈɒfset] vt (irreg: like set) ausgleichen // n (also: ~ printing) Offset(druck) m.
offshoot [ˈɒfʃuːt] n (fig) (of organization) Zweig m; (of discussion etc) Randergebnis nt.
offshore [ˈɒfˈʃɔː*] ad in einiger Entfernung von der Küste // a küstennah, Küsten-.
offside [ˈɒfˈsaɪd] a (SPORT) im Abseits // ad abseits // n (AUT) Fahrerseite f.
offspring [ˈɒfsprɪŋ] n Nachkommenschaft f; (one) Sprößling m.
offstage [ˈɒfˈsteɪdʒ] ad hinter den Kulissen.
off: ~-**the-cuff** ad unvorbereitet, aus dem Stegreif; ~-**the-peg**, (US) ~-**the-rack** ad von der Stange; ~-**white** a naturweiß.
often [ˈɒfən] ad oft.
ogle [ˈəʊgl] vt liebäugeln mit.
oh [əʊ] interj oh, ach.
oil [ɔɪl] n Öl nt // vt ölen; ~**can** n Ölkännchen nt; ~**field** n Ölfeld nt; ~ **filter** n (AUT) Ölfilter m; ~**fired** a Öl-; ~ **painting** n Ölgemälde nt; ~**rig** n Ölplattform f; ~**skins** npl Ölzeug nt; ~ **tanker** n (Öl)tanker m; ~ **well** n Ölquelle f; ~**y** a ölig; (dirty) ölbeschmiert.
ointment [ˈɔɪntmənt] n Salbe f.
O.K., okay [ˈəʊˈkeɪ] interj in Ordnung, O.K. // a in Ordnung // vt genehmigen.
old [əʊld] a alt; how ~ are you? wie alt bist du?; he's 10 years old er ist 10 Jahre alt; ~ **age** n Alter nt; ~**age pensioner** (O.A.P.) n (Brit) Rentner(in f) m; ~**fashioned** a altmodisch.
olive [ˈɒlɪv] n (fruit) Olive f; (colour) Olive nt // a Oliven-; (coloured) olivenfarbig; ~ **oil** n Olivenöl nt.
Olympic [əʊˈlɪmpɪk] a olympisch; ~ **Games**, ~**s** pl Olympische Spiele pl.
omelet(te) [ˈɒmlət] n Omelett nt.
ominous [ˈɒmɪnəs] a bedrohlich.
omission [əʊˈmɪʃən] n Auslassung f; (neglect) Versäumnis nt.
omit [əʊˈmɪt] vt auslassen; (fail to do) versäumen.
on [ɒn] ◆prep 1 (indicating position) auf (+dat); (with v of motion) auf(+acc); (on vertical surface, part of body) an (+dat/acc); it's ~ the table es ist auf dem Tisch; she put the book ~ the table sie legte das Buch auf den Tisch; ~ the left links
2 (indicating means, method, condition etc): ~ foot (go, be) zu Fuß; ~ the

train/plane (go) mit dem Zug/Flugzeug; (be) im Zug/Flugzeug; ~ the telephone/ television am Telefon/im Fernsehen; to be ~ drugs Drogen nehmen; to be ~ holiday/business im Urlaub/auf Geschäftsreise sein
3 (referring to time): ~ Friday (am) Freitag; ~ Fridays freitags; ~ June 20th am 20. Juni; a week ~ Friday Freitag in einer Woche; ~ arrival he ... als er ankam, ... er ...
4 (about, concerning) über (+acc)
◆ad see also v + on 1 (referring to dress) an; she put her boots/hat ~ sie zog ihre Stiefel an/setzte ihren Hut auf
2 (further, continuously) weiter; to walk ~ weitergehen
◆a 1 (functioning, in operation: machine, TV, light) an; (: tap) aufgedreht; (: brakes) angezogen; is the meeting still ~? findet die Versammlung noch statt?; there's a good film ~ es läuft ein guter Film
2: that's not ~! (col: of behaviour) das liegt nicht drin!
once [wʌns] ◆ad einmal // cj wenn ... einmal; ~ he had left/it was done nachdem er gegangen war/es fertig war; at ~ sofort; (at the same time) gleichzeitig; ~ a week einmal in der Woche; ~ more noch einmal; ~ and for all ein für allemal; ~ upon a time es war einmal.
oncoming [ˈɒnkʌmɪŋ] a (traffic) Gegen-, entgegenkommend.
one [wʌn] ◆num eins; (with noun, referring back to noun) ein/eine/ein; it is ~ (o'clock) es ist eins, es ist ein Uhr; ~ hundred and fifty einhundertfünfzig
◆a 1 (sole) einzige(r, s); the ~ book which das einzige Buch, welches
2 (same) derselbe/dieselbe/dasselbe; they came in the ~ car sie kamen alle in dem einen Auto
3 (indefinite): ~ day I discovered ... eines Tages bemerkte ich ...
◆pron 1 eine(r, s); do you have a red ~? haben Sie einen roten/eine rote/ein rotes?; this ~ diese(r, s); that ~ der/ die/das; which ~? welche(r, s)?; ~ by ~ einzeln
2: ~ another einander; do you two ever see ~ another? seht ihr beide euch manchmal?
3 (impersonal) man; ~ never knows man kann nie wissen; to cut ~'s finger sich in den Finger schneiden.
one: ~-**armed bandit** n einarmiger Bandit m; ~-**day excursion** n (US: day return) Tagesrückfahrkarte f; ~-**man** a Einmann-; ~-**man band** n Einmannkapelle f; (fig) Einmannbetrieb m; ~-**off** n (Brit col) Einzelfall m.
oneself [wʌnˈself] pron (reflexive: after prep) sich; (~ personally) sich selbst or selber; (emphatic) (sich) selbst; to hurt

~ sich verletzen.
one: **~-sided** *a* (*argument*) einseitig; **~-to-~** *a* (*relationship*) eins-zu-eins; **~-upmanship** *n* die Kunst, anderen um eine Nasenlänge voraus zu sein; **~-way** *a* (*street*) Einbahn-.

ongoing ['ɒngəʊɪŋ] *a* momentan; (*progressing*) sich entwickelnd.

onion ['ʌnjən] *n* Zwiebel *f*.

onlooker ['ɒnlʊkə*] *n* Zuschauer(in *f*) *m*.

only ['əʊnlɪ] *ad* nur, bloß // *a* einzige(r, s) // *cj* nur, bloß; **an ~ child** ein Einzelkind; **not ~ ... but also ...** nicht nur ... sondern auch ...

onset ['ɒnset] *n* (*beginning*) Beginn *m*.

onslaught ['ɒnslɔːt] *n* Angriff *m*.

onto ['ɒntu] *prep* = **on to**.

onus ['əʊnəs] *n* Last *f*, Pflicht *f*.

onwards ['ɒnwədz] *ad* (*place*) voran, vorwärts; **from that day ~** von dem Tag an; **from today ~** ab heute.

ooze [uːz] *vi* sickern.

opaque [əʊ'peɪk] *a* undurchsichtig.

OPEC *n abbr* (= *Organization of Petroleum-Exporting Countries*) OPEC *f*.

open ['əʊpən] *a* offen; (*public*) öffentlich; (*mind*) aufgeschlossen // *vt* öffnen, aufmachen; (*trial, motorway, account*) eröffnen // *vi* (*begin*) anfangen; (*shop*) aufmachen; (*door, flower*) aufgehen; (*play*) Premiere haben; **in the ~** (*air*) im Freien; **~ on to** *vi* sich öffnen auf (+ *acc*); **~ up** *vt* (*route*) erschließen; (*shop, prospects*) eröffnen // *vi* öffnen; **~ing** *n* (*hole*) Öffnung *f*; (*beginning*) Anfang *m*; (*good chance*) Gelegenheit *f*; **~ly** *ad* offen; (*publicly*) öffentlich; **~-minded** *a* aufgeschlossen; **~-necked** *a* offen; **~-plan** *a* (*office*) Großraum-; (*flat etc*) offen angelegt.

opera ['ɒpərə] *n* Oper *f*; **~ house** *n* Opernhaus *nt*.

operate ['ɒpəreɪt] *vt* (*machine*) bedienen; (*brakes, light*) betätigen // *vi* (*machine*) laufen, in Betrieb sein; (*person*) arbeiten; (*MED*): **to ~ on** operieren.

operatic [ɒpə'rætɪk] *a* Opern-.

operating ['ɒpəreɪtɪŋ]: **~ table** *n* Operationstisch *m*; **~ theatre** *n* Operationssaal *m*.

operation [ɒpə'reɪʃən] *n* (*working*) Betrieb *m*; (*MED*) Operation *f*; (*undertaking*) Unternehmen *nt*; (*MIL*) Einsatz *m*; **to be in ~** (*JUR*) in Kraft sein; (*machine*) in Betrieb sein; **to have an ~** (*MED*) operiert werden; **~al** *a* einsatzbereit.

operative ['ɒpərətɪv] *a* wirksam; (*MED*) operativ.

operator ['ɒpəreɪtə*] *n* (*of machine*) Arbeiter *m*; (*TEL*) Telefonist(in *f*) *m*.

ophthalmic [ɒf'θælmɪk] *a* Augen-.

opinion [ə'pɪnjən] *n* Meinung *f*; **in my ~**

meiner Meinung nach; **~ated** *a* starrsinnig; **~ poll** *n* Meinungsumfrage *f*.

opponent [ə'pəʊnənt] *n* Gegner *m*.

opportunity [ɒpə'tjuːnɪtɪ] *n* Gelegenheit *f*, Möglichkeit *f*; **to take the ~ of doing** die Gelegenheit ergreifen, etw zu tun.

oppose [ə'pəʊz] *vt* entgegentreten (+*dat*); (*argument, idea*) ablehnen; (*plan*) bekämpfen; **to be ~d to sth** gegen etw sein; **as ~d to** im Gegensatz zu.

opposing [ə'pəʊzɪŋ] *a* gegnerisch; (*points of view*) entgegengesetzt.

opposite ['ɒpəzɪt] *a* (*house*) gegenüberliegend; (*direction*) entgegengesetzt // *ad* gegenüber // *prep* gegenüber // *n* Gegenteil *nt*.

opposition [ɒpə'zɪʃən] *n* (*resistance*) Widerstand *m*; (*POL*) Opposition *f*; (*contrast*) Gegensatz *m*.

oppress [ə'pres] *vt* unterdrücken; (*heat etc*) bedrücken; **~ion** [ə'preʃən] *n* Unterdrückung *f*; **~ive** *a* (*authority, law*) repressiv; (*burden, thought*) bedrückend; (*heat*) drückend.

opt [ɒpt] *vi*: **to ~ for** sich entscheiden für; **to ~ to do sth** sich entscheiden, etw zu tun; **~ out of** *vi* sich drücken vor (+*dat*); (*of society*) ausflippen aus (+*dat*).

optical ['ɒptɪkəl] *a* optisch; **~ character reader (OCR)** *n* optische(s) Lesegerät *nt* (OCR *nt*).

optician [ɒp'tɪʃən] *n* Optiker *m*.

optimist ['ɒptɪmɪst] *n* Optimist *m*; **~ic** ['ɒptɪ'mɪstɪk] *a* optimistisch.

optimum ['ɒptɪməm] *a* optimal.

option ['ɒpʃən] *n* Wahl *f*; (*COMM*) Option *f*; **to keep one's ~s open** sich alle Möglichkeiten offenhalten; **~al** *a* freiwillig; (*subject*) wahlfrei; **~al extras** *n* Extras auf Wunsch.

opulent ['ɒpjʊlənt] *a* sehr reich.

or [ɔː*] *cj* oder; **he could not read ~ write** er konnte weder lesen noch schreiben; **~ else** sonst.

oral ['ɔːrəl] *a* mündlich // *n* (*exam*) mündliche Prüfung *f*.

orange ['ɒrɪndʒ] *n* (*fruit*) Apfelsine *f*, Orange *f*; (*colour*) Orange *nt* // *a* orange.

orator ['ɒrətə*] *n* Redner(in *f*) *m*.

orbit ['ɔːbɪt] *n* Umlaufbahn *f*.

orchard ['ɔːtʃəd] *n* Obstgarten *m*.

orchestra ['ɔːkɪstrə] *n* Orchester *nt*; (*US: seating*) Parkett *nt*.

orchid ['ɔːkɪd] *n* Orchidee *f*.

ordain [ɔː'deɪn] *vt* (*ECCL*) weihen; (*decide*) verfügen.

ordeal [ɔː'diːl] *n* Qual *f*.

order ['ɔːdə*] *n* (*sequence*) Reihenfolge *f*; (*good arrangement*) Ordnung *f*; (*command*) Befehl *m*; (*JUR*) Anordnung *f*; (*peace*) Ordnung *f*; (*condition*) Zustand *m*; (*rank*) Klasse *f*; (*COMM*) Bestellung *f*; (*ECCL, honour*) Orden *m* // *vt* (*also:* put in ~) ordnen; (*command*) befehlen (*sth etw acc, sb* jdm); (*COMM*) bestellen; **in** ~ in der Reihenfolge; **in** (**working**) ~ in gutem Zustand; **in** ~ **to** do sth um etw zu tun; **on** ~ (*COMM*) auf Bestellung; **to** ~ **sb** **to** **do** **sth** jdm befehlen, etw zu tun; ~ **form** *n* Bestellschein *m*; ~**ly** *n* (*MIL*) Sanitäter *m*; (*MED*) Pfleger *m* // *a* (*tidy*) ordentlich; (*well-behaved*) ruhig.

ordinary ['ɔːdnrɪ] *a* gewöhnlich; **out of the** ~ außergewöhnlich.

ordnance ['ɔːdnəns] *n* Artillerie *f*; **O~ Survey** *n* (*Brit*) amtlicher Kartographiedienst.

ore [ɔː*] *n* Erz *nt*.

organ ['ɔːgən] *n* (*MUS*) Orgel *f*; (*BIOL, fig*) Organ *nt*.

organization [ɔːgənaɪ'zeɪʃən] *n* Organisation *f*; (*make-up*) Struktur *f*.

organize ['ɔːgənaɪz] *vt* organisieren; ~**r** *n* Organisator *m*, Veranstalter *m*.

oriental [ɔːrɪ'entəl] *a* orientalisch.

origin ['ɒrɪdʒɪn] *n* Ursprung *m*; (*of the world*) Anfang *m*, Entstehung *f*.

original [ə'rɪdʒɪnl] *a* (*first*) ursprünglich; (*painting*) original; (*idea*) originell // *n* Original *nt*; ~**ly** *ad* ursprünglich; originell.

originate [ə'rɪdʒɪneɪt] *vi* entstehen // *vt* ins Leben rufen; **to** ~ **from** stammen aus.

ornament ['ɔːnəmənt] *n* Schmuck *m*; (*on mantelpiece*) Nippesfigur *f*; ~**al** [ɔːnə'mentl] *a* Zier-.

ornate [ɔː'neɪt] *a* reich verziert.

orphan ['ɔːfən] *n* Waise *f*, Waisenkind *nt* // *vt*: **to be** ~**ed** Waise werden; ~**age** *n* Waisenhaus *nt*.

orthodox ['ɔːθədɒks] *a* orthodox; ~**y** *n* Orthodoxie *f*; (*fig*) Konventionalität *f*.

orthopaedic [ɔːθəʊ'piːdɪk], (*US*) **orthopedic** *a* orthopädisch.

ostensibly [ɒs'tensəblɪ] *ad* vorgeblich, angeblich.

ostentatious [ɒsten'teɪʃəs] *a* großtuerisch, protzig.

ostracize ['ɒstrəsaɪz] *vt* ausstoßen.

ostrich ['ɒstrɪtʃ] *n* Strauß *m*.

other ['ʌðə*] *a* andere(r, s) // *pron* andere(r, s) // *ad*: ~ **than** anders als; **the** ~ (one) der, die, das andere; **the** ~ **day** neulich; ~**s** (~ *people*) andere; ~**wise** *ad* (*in a different way*) anders; (*or else*) sonst.

ouch [aʊtʃ] *interj* aua.

ought [ɔːt] *v aux* sollen; **I** ~ **to** do it ich sollte es tun; **this** ~ **to have been corrected** das hätte korrigiert werden sollen.

ounce [aʊns] *n* Unze *f*.

our [aʊə*] *poss a* unser; *see also* **my**; ~**s** *poss pron* unsere(r, s); *see also* **mine**; ~**selves** *pron* uns (selbst); (*emphatic*) (wir) selbst; *see also* **oneself**.

oust [aʊst] *vt* verdrängen.

out [aʊt] *ad* hinaus/heraus; (*not indoors*) draußen; (*not alight*) aus; (*unconscious*) bewußtlos; (*results*) bekanntgegeben; **to eat/go** ~ auswärts essen/ausgehen; ~ **there** da draußen; **he is** ~ (*absent*) er ist nicht da; **he was** ~ **in his calculations** seine Berechnungen waren nicht richtig; ~ **loud** *ad* laut; ~ **of** *prep* aus; (*away from*) außerhalb (+*gen*); **to be** ~ **of milk** *etc* keine Milch *etc* mehr haben; ~ **of order** außer Betrieb; ~-**and-** ~ *a* (*liar, theft etc*) ausgemacht.

outback ['aʊtbæk] *n* Hinterland *nt*.

outboard (motor) ['aʊtbɔːd ('məʊtə*)] *n* Außenbordmotor *m*.

outbreak ['aʊtbreɪk] *n* Ausbruch *m*.

outburst ['aʊtbɜːst] *n* Ausbruch *m*.

outcast ['aʊtkɑːst] *n* Ausgestoßene(r) *mf*.

outcome ['aʊtkʌm] *n* Ergebnis *nt*.

outcrop ['aʊtkrɒp] *n* (*of rock*) Felsnase *f*.

outcry ['aʊtkraɪ] *n* Protest *m*.

outdated ['aʊt'deɪtɪd] *a* überholt.

outdo [aʊt'duː] *vt* (*irreg: like* do) übertrumpfen.

outdoor ['aʊtdɔː*] *a* Außen-; (*SPORT*) im Freien; ~**s** *ad* im Freien.

outer ['aʊtə*] *a* äußere(r, s); ~ **space** *n* Weltraum *m*.

outfit ['aʊtfɪt] *n* Kleidung *f*; ~**ters** *n* (*Brit: for men's clothes*) Herrenausstatter *m*.

outgoing ['aʊtgəʊɪŋ] *a* (*character*) aufgeschlossen; ~**s** *npl* (*Brit*) Ausgaben *pl*.

outgrow [aʊt'grəʊ] *vt* (*irreg: like* grow) (*clothes*) herauswachsen aus; (*habit*) ablegen.

outhouse ['aʊthaʊs] *n* Nebengebäude *nt*.

outing ['aʊtɪŋ] *n* Ausflug *m*.

outlandish [aʊt'lændɪʃ] *a* eigenartig.

outlaw ['aʊtlɔː] *n* Geächtete(r) *m* // *vt* ächten; (*thing*) verbieten.

outlay ['aʊtleɪ] *n* Auslage *f*.

outlet ['aʊtlet] *n* Auslaß *m*, Abfluß *m*; (*also:* retail ~) Absatzmarkt *m*; (*US ELEC*) Steckdose *f*; (*for emotions*) Ventil *nt*.

outline ['aʊtlaɪn] *n* Umriß *m*.

outlive [aʊt'lɪv] *vt* überleben.

outlook ['aʊtlʊk] *n* (*lit, fig*) Aussicht *f*; (*attitude*) Einstellung *f*.

outlying ['aʊtlaɪɪŋ] *a* entlegen; (*district*) Außen-.

outmoded [aʊt'məʊdɪd] *a* veraltet.

outnumber [aʊt'nʌmbə*] *vt* zahlenmäßig überlegen sein (+*dat*).

out: ~-**of-date** *a* (*passport*) abgelaufen; (*clothes etc*) altmodisch; (*ideas etc*) überholt; ~-**of-the-way** *a* abgelegen.

outpatient ['aʊtpeɪʃənt] *n* ambulante(r) Patient(in *f*) *m*.

outpost ['aʊtpəʊst] *n* (*MIL, fig*) Vorposten *m*.

output ['aʊtpʊt] *n* Leistung *f*, Produktion *f*; (COMPUT) Ausgabe *f*.

outrage ['aʊtreɪdʒ] *n* (cruel deed) Ausschreitung *f*; (indecency) Skandal *m* // *vt* (morals) verstoßen gegen; (person) empören; **~ous** [aʊt'reɪdʒəs] *a* unerhört.

outright ['aʊtraɪt] *ad* (at once) sofort; (openly) ohne Umschweife // *a* (denial) völlig; (sale) Total-; (winner) unbestritten.

outset ['aʊtset] *n* Beginn *m*.

outside ['aʊt'saɪd] *n* Außenseite *f* // *a* äußere(r, s), Außen-; (chance) gering // *ad* außen // *prep* außerhalb (+gen); at the ~ (fig) maximal; (time) spätestens; to go ~ nach draußen gehen; ~ **lane** *n* (AUT) äußere Spur *f*; **~-left** *n* (FOOTBALL) Linksaußen *m*; ~ **line** *n* (TEL) Amtsanschluß *m*; **~r** *n* Außenseiter(in *f*) *m*.

outsize ['aʊtsaɪz] *a* übergroß.

outskirts ['aʊtskɜːts] *npl* Stadtrand *m*.

outspoken [aʊt'spəʊkən] *a* freimütig.

outstanding [aʊt'stændɪŋ] *a* hervorragend; (debts etc) ausstehend.

outstay [aʊt'steɪ] *vt*: to ~ one's welcome länger bleiben als erwünscht.

outstretched ['aʊtstretʃt] *a* ausgestreckt.

outstrip [aʊt'strɪp] *vt* übertreffen.

out-tray ['aʊttreɪ] *n* Ausgangskorb *m*.

outward ['aʊtwəd] *a* äußere(r, s); (journey) Hin-; (freight) ausgehend // *ad* nach außen; **~ly** *ad* äußerlich.

outweigh [aʊt'weɪ] *vt* (fig) überwiegen.

outwit [aʊt'wɪt] *vt* überlisten.

oval ['əʊvəl] *a* oval // *n* Oval *nt*.

ovary ['əʊvərɪ] *n* Eierstock *m*.

ovation [əʊ'veɪʃən] *n* Beifallssturm *m*.

oven ['ʌvn] *n* Backofen *m*; **~proof** *a* feuerfest.

over ['əʊvə*] *ad* (across) hinüber/ herüber; (finished) vorbei; (left) übrig; (again) wieder, noch einmal // *prep* über; // *pref* (excessively) übermäßig; ~ here hier(hin); ~ there dort(hin); all ~ (everywhere) überall; (finished) vorbei; ~ and ~ immer wieder; ~ and above darüber hinaus; to ask sb ~ jdn einladen; to bend ~ sich bücken.

overall ['əʊvərɔːl] *n* (Brit) Kittel *m* // *a* (situation) allgemein; (length) Gesamt- // *ad* insgesamt; **~s** *pl* Overall *m*.

overawe [əʊvə'ɔː] *vt* (frighten) einschüchtern; (make impression) überwältigen.

overbalance [əʊvə'bæləns] *vi* Übergewicht bekommen.

overbearing [əʊvə'bɛərɪŋ] *a* aufdringlich.

overboard ['əʊvəbɔːd] *ad* über Bord.

overbook [əʊvə'bʊk] *vi* überbuchen.

overcast ['əʊvəkɑːst] *a* bedeckt.

overcharge [əʊvə'tʃɑːdʒ] *vt*: to ~ sb von jdm zuviel verlangen.

overcoat ['əʊvəkəʊt] *n* Mantel *m*.

overcome [əʊvə'kʌm] *vt* (irreg: like come) überwinden.

overcrowded [əʊvə'kraʊdɪd] *a* überfüllt.

overcrowding [əʊvə'kraʊdɪŋ] *n* Überfüllung *f*.

overdo [əʊvə'duː] *vt* (irreg: like do) (cook too much) verkochen; (exaggerate) übertreiben.

overdose ['əʊvədəʊs] *n* Überdosis *f*.

overdraft ['əʊvədrɑːft] *n* (Konto)überziehung *f*.

overdrawn [əʊvə'drɔːn] *a* (account) überzogen.

overdue ['əʊvə'djuː] *a* überfällig.

overestimate ['əʊvər'estɪmeɪt] *vt* überschätzen.

overexcited ['əʊvərɪk'saɪtɪd] *a* überreizt; (children) aufgeregt.

overflow [əʊvə'fləʊ] *vi* überfließen // *n* ['əʊvəfləʊ] (excess) Überschuß *m*; (also: ~ pipe) Überlaufrohr *nt*.

overgrown ['əʊvə'grəʊn] *a* (garden) verwildert.

overhaul [əʊvə'hɔːl] *vt* (car) überholen; (plans) überprüfen // *n* ['əʊvəhɔːl] Überholung *f*.

overhead ['əʊvəhed] *a* Hoch-; (wire) oberirdisch; (lighting) Decken- // *ad* ['əʊvə'hed] oben; **~s** *pl*, (US) ~ *n* allgemeine Unkosten *pl*.

overhear [əʊvə'hɪə*] *vt* (irreg: like hear) (mit an)hören.

overheat [əʊvə'hiːt] *vi* (engine) heiß laufen.

overjoyed [əʊvə'dʒɔɪd] *a* überglücklich.

overkill ['əʊvəkɪl] *n* (fig) Rundumschlag *m*.

overland ['əʊvəlænd] *a* Überland- // *ad* [əʊvə'lænd] (travel) über Land.

overlap [əʊvə'læp] *vi* sich überschneiden; (objects) sich teilweise decken // *n* ['əʊvəlæp] Überschneidung *f*.

overleaf [əʊvə'liːf] *ad* umseitig.

overload ['əʊvə'ləʊd] *vt* überladen.

overlook [əʊvə'lʊk] *vt* (view from above) überblicken; (not notice) übersehen; (pardon) hinwegsehen über (+acc).

overnight ['əʊvə'naɪt] *a* (journey) Nacht- // *ad* über Nacht; ~ **stay** *n* Übernachtung *f*.

overpass ['əʊvəpɑːs] *n* Überführung *f*.

overpower [əʊvə'paʊə*] *vt* überwältigen; **~ing** *a* überwältigend.

overrate ['əʊvə'reɪt] *vt* überschätzen.

override [əʊvə'raɪd] *vt* (irreg: like ride) (order, decision) aufheben; (objection) übergehen.

overriding [əʊvə'raɪdɪŋ] *a* vorherrschend.

overrule [əʊvə'ruːl] *vt* verwerfen.

overrun [ˌəʊvəˈrʌn] *vt* (*irreg: like* **run**) (*country*) einfallen in; (*time limit*) überziehen.

overseas [ˈəʊvəˈsiːz] *ad* nach/in Übersee // *a* überseeisch, Übersee-.

overseer [ˈəʊvəsɪə*] *n* Aufseher *m*.

overshadow [əʊvəˈʃædəʊ] *vt* überschatten.

overshoot [ˈəʊvəˈʃuːt] *vt* (*irreg: like* **shoot**) (*runway*) hinausschießen über (+*acc*).

oversight [ˈəʊvəsaɪt] *n* (*mistake*) Versehen *nt*.

oversleep [ˈəʊvəˈsliːp] *vi* (*irreg: like* **sleep**) verschlafen.

overspill [ˈəʊvəspɪl] *n* (Bevölkerungs)-überschuß *m*.

overstate [ˈəʊvəˈsteɪt] *vt* übertreiben.

overstep [əʊvəˈstep] *vt*: **to ~ the mark** zu weit gehen.

overt [əʊˈvɜːt] *a* offen(kundig).

overtake [əʊvəˈteɪk] *vti* (*irreg: like* **take**) überholen.

overthrow [əʊvəˈθrəʊ] *vt* (*irreg: like* **throw**) (*POL*) stürzen.

overtime [ˈəʊvətaɪm] *n* Überstunden *pl*.

overtone [ˈəʊvətəʊn] *n* (*fig*) Note *f*.

overturn [əʊvəˈtɜːn] *vti* umkippen.

overweight [ˈəʊvəˈweɪt] *a* zu dick.

overwhelm [əʊvəˈwelm] *vt* überwältigen; **~ing** *a* überwältigend.

overwork [əʊvəˈwɜːk] *n* Überarbeitung *f* // *vt* überlasten // *vi* sich überarbeiten.

overwrought [əʊvəˈrɔːt] *a* überreizt.

owe [əʊ] *vt* schulden; **to ~ sth to sb** (*money*) jdm etw schulden; (*favour etc*) jdm etw verdanken; **owing to** *prep* wegen (+*gen*).

owl [aʊl] *n* Eule *f*.

own [əʊn] *vt* besitzen // *a* eigen; **a room of my ~** mein eigenes Zimmer; **to get one's ~ back** sich rächen; **on one's ~** allein; **~ up** *vi* zugeben (*to sth* etw *acc*); **~er** *n* Besitzer(in *f*) *m*; **~ership** *n* Besitz *m*.

ox [ɒks], *pl* **~en** [ˈɒksn] *n* Ochse *m*.

oxtail [ˈɒksteɪl] *n*: **~ soup** *n* Ochsenschwanzsuppe *f*.

oxygen [ˈɒksɪdʒən] *n* Sauerstoff *m*; **~ mask** *n* Sauerstoffmaske *f*; **~ tent** *n* Sauerstoffzelt *nt*.

oyster [ˈɔɪstə*] *n* Auster *f*.

oz. *abbr of* **ounce(s)**.

P

p [piː] *abbr of* **penny, pence**.

P.A. *n abbr of* **personal assistant; public address system**.

p.a. *abbr of* **per annum**.

pa [pɑː] *n* (*col*) Papa *m*.

pace [peɪs] *n* Schritt *m*; (*speed*) Tempo *nt* // *vi* schreiten; **to keep ~ with** Schritt halten mit; **~-maker** *n* Schrittmacher

m.

pacific [pəˈsɪfɪk] *a* pazifisch; // *n*: **the P~ (Ocean)** der Pazifik.

pacifist [ˈpæsɪfɪst] *n* Pazifist *m*.

pacify [ˈpæsɪfaɪ] *vt* befrieden; (*calm*) beruhigen.

pack [pæk] *n* (*of goods*) Packung *f*; (*of hounds*) Meute *f*; (*of cards*) Spiel *nt*; (*gang*) Bande *f* // *vti* (*case*) packen; (*clothes*) einpacken; **to ~ sb off to** jdn nach ... schicken; **~ it in!** laß es gut sein!

package [ˈpækɪdʒ] *n* Paket *nt*; **~ tour** *n* Pauschalreise.

packed lunch [ˈpækt-] *n* Lunchpaket *nt*.

packet [ˈpækɪt] *n* Päckchen *nt*.

packing [ˈpækɪŋ] *n* (*action*) Packen *nt*; (*material*) Verpackung *f*; **~ case** *n* (Pack)kiste *f*.

pact [pækt] *n* Pakt *m*, Vertrag *m*.

pad [pæd] *n* (*of paper*) (Schreib)block *m*; (*padding*) Polster *nt* // *vt* polstern; **~ding** *n* Polsterung *f*.

paddle [ˈpædl] *n* Paddel *nt*; (*US: for table tennis*) Schläger *m* // *vt* (*boat*) paddeln // *vi* (*in sea*) planschen; **~ steamer** *n* Raddampfer *m*.

paddling pool [ˈpædlɪŋ-] *n* (*Brit*) Planschbecken *nt*.

paddock [ˈpædək] *n* Koppel *f*.

paddy field [ˈpædɪ-] *n* Reisfeld *nt*.

padlock [ˈpædlɒk] *n* Vorhängeschloß *nt* // *vt* verschließen.

paediatrics,   (*US*)   **pediatrics** [piːdɪˈætrɪks] *n* Kinderheilkunde *f*.

pagan [ˈpeɪgən] *a* heidnisch // *n* Heide *m*, Heidin *f*.

page [peɪdʒ] *n* Seite *f*; (*person*) Page *m* // *vt* (*in hotel etc*) ausrufen lassen.

pageant [ˈpædʒənt] *n* Festzug *m*; **~ry** *n* Gepränge *nt*.

paid [peɪd] *pt*, *pp of* **pay** // *a* bezahlt; **to put ~ to** (*Brit*) zunichte machen.

pail [peɪl] *n* Eimer *m*.

pain [peɪn] *n* Schmerz *m*; **to be in ~** Schmerzen haben; **on ~ of death** bei Todesstrafe; **to take ~s to do sth** sich (*dat*) Mühe geben, etw zu tun; **~ed** *a* (*expression*) gequält; **~ful** *a* (*physically*) schmerzhaft; (*embarrassing*) peinlich; (*difficult*) mühsam; **~fully** *ad* (*fig: very*) schrecklich; **~killer** *n* Schmerzmittel *nt*; **~less** *a* schmerzlos; **~staking** *a* gewissenhaft.

paint [peɪnt] *n* Farbe *f* // *vt* anstreichen; (*picture*) malen; **to ~ the door blue** die Tür blau streichen; **~brush** *n* Pinsel *m*; **~er** *n* Maler *m*; **~ing** *n* Malerei *f*; (*picture*) Gemälde *nt*; **~work** *n* Anstrich *m*; (*of car*) Lack *m*.

pair [peə*] *n* Paar *nt*; **~ of scissors** *n* Schere *f*; **~ of trousers** *n* Hose *f*.

pajamas [pəˈdʒɑːməz] *npl* (*US*) Schlafanzug *m*.

Pakistan [pɑːkɪˈstɑːn] *n* Pakistan *nt*; **~i**

a pakistanisch // *n* Pakistani *mf*.
pal [pæl] *n* (*col*) Kumpel *m*.
palace ['pæləs] *n* Palast *m*, Schloß *nt*.
palatable ['pælətəbl] *a* schmackhaft.
palate ['pælɪt] *n* Gaumen *m*.
palatial [pə'leɪʃəl] *a* palastartig.
palaver [pə'lɑːvə*] *n* (*col*) Theater *nt*.
pale [peɪl] *a* blaß, bleich; **to be beyond
the ~** die Grenzen überschreiten.
Palestine ['pælɪstaɪn] *n* Palästina *nt*;
Palestinian [-'tɪnɪən] *a* palästinensisch //
n Palästinenser(in *f*) *m*.
paling ['peɪlɪŋ] *n* (*stake*) Zaunpfahl *m*;
(*fence*) Lattenzaum *m*.
pall [pɔːl] *n* (*of smoke*) (Rauch)wolke *f* //
vi jeden Reiz verlieren, verblassen;
~bearer *n* Sargträger *m*.
pallet ['pælɪt] *n* (*for goods*) Palette *f*.
pallid ['pælɪd] *a* blaß, bleich.
pallor ['pælə*] *n* Blässe *f*.
palm [pɑːm] *n* (*of hand*) Handfläche *f*;
(*also*: **~ tree**) Palme *f* // *vt*: **to ~ sth off
on sb** jdm etw andrehen; **P~ Sunday** *n*
Palmsonntag *m*.
palpable ['pælpəbl] *a* (*lit, fig*) greifbar.
palpitation [pælpɪ'teɪʃən] *n* Herzklopfen
nt.
paltry ['pɔːltrɪ] *a* armselig.
pamper ['pæmpə*] *vt* verhätscheln.
pamphlet ['pæmflət] *n* Broschüre *f*.
pan [pæn] *n* Pfanne *f* // *vi* (*CINE*)
schwenken.
panacea [pænə'sɪə] *n* (*fig*) Allheilmittel
nt.
panache [pə'næʃ] *n* Schwung *m*.
pancake ['pænkeɪk] *n* Pfannkuchen *m*.
pancreas ['pæŋkrɪəs] *n* Bauchspeichel-
drüse *f*.
panda ['pændə] *n* Panda *m*; **~ car** *n*
(*Brit*) (Funk)streifenwagen *m*.
pandemonium [pændɪ'məʊnɪəm] *n*
Hölle *f*; (*noise*) Höllenlärm *m*.
pander ['pændə*] *vi* sich richten (*to*
nach).
pane [peɪn] *n* (Fenster)scheibe *f*.
panel ['pænl] *n* (*of wood*) Tafel *f*; (*TV*)
Diskussionsrunde *f*; **~ling**, (*US*) **~ing** *n*
Täfelung *f*.
pang [pæŋ] *n*: **~s of hunger** quälende(r)
Hunger *m*; **~s of conscience**
Gewissensbisse *pl*.
panic ['pænɪk] *n* Panik *f* // *vi* in Panik
geraten; **don't ~** (nur) keine Panik!;
~ky *a* (*person*) überängstlich; **~-
stricken** *a* von panischem Schrecken
erfaßt; (*look*) panisch.
pansy ['pænzɪ] *n* (*flower*) Stiefmütter-
chen *nt*; (*col*) Schwule(r) *m*.
pant [pænt] *vi* keuchen; (*dog*) hecheln.
panties ['pæntɪz] *npl* (Damen)slip *m*.
pantihose ['pæntɪhəʊz] *n* (*US*)
Strumpfhose *f*.
pantomime ['pæntəmaɪm] *n* (*Brit*)
Märchenkomödie *f* um Weihnachten.
pantry ['pæntrɪ] *n* Vorratskammer *f*.

pants [pænts] *npl* (*Brit*: *woman's*)
Schlüpfer *m*; (: *man's*) Unterhose *f*;
(*US*: *trousers*) Hose *f*.
papal ['peɪpəl] *a* päpstlich.
paper ['peɪpə*] *n* Papier *nt*;
(*newspaper*) Zeitung *f*; (*essay*) Referat
nt // *a* Papier-, aus Papier // *vt* (*wall*)
tapezieren; **~s** *pl* (*identity*) Aus-
weis(papiere *pl*) *m*; **~back** *n* Taschenbuch *nt*; **~ bag** *n* Tüte *f*; **~ clip** *n*
Büroklammer *f*; **~ hankie** *n* Tempota-
schentuch ® *nt*; **~weight** *n* Briefbe-
schwerer *m*; **~work** *n* Schreibarbeit *f*.
par [pɑː*] *n* (*COMM*) Nennwert *m*;
(*GOLF*) Par *nt*; **on a ~ with** ebenbürtig
(+*dat*).
parable ['pærəbl] *n* (*REL*) Gleichnis *nt*.
parachute ['pærəʃuːt] *n* Fallschirm *m* //
vi (mit dem Fallschirm) abspringen.
parade [pə'reɪd] *n* Parade *f* // *vt* aufmar-
schieren lassen // *vi* paradieren, vorbeimarschieren.
paradise ['pærədaɪs] *n* Paradies *nt*.
paradox ['pærədɒks] *n* Paradox *nt*;
~ically [pærə'dɒksɪkəlɪ] *ad* paradoxer-
weise.
paraffin ['pærəfɪn] *n* (*Brit*) Paraffin *nt*.
paragon ['pærəgən] *n* Muster *m*.
paragraph ['pærəgrɑːf] *n* Absatz *m*.
parallel ['pærəlel] *a* parallel // *n*
Parallele *f*.
paralysis [pə'rælɪsɪs] *n* Lähmung *f*.
paralyze ['pærəlaɪz] *vt* lähmen.
parameter [pə'ræmɪtə*] *n* Parameter
m; **~s** *pl* Rahmen *m*.
paramount ['pærəmaʊnt] *a* höchste(r,
s), oberste(r, s).
parapet ['pærəpɪt] *n* Brüstung *f*.
paraphernalia [pærəfə'neɪlɪə] *n*
Zubehör *nt*, Utensilien *pl*.
paraphrase ['pærəfreɪz] *vt* umschreiben.
paraplegic [pærə'pliːdʒɪk] *n* Quer-
schnittsgelähmte(r) *mf*.
parasite ['pærəsaɪt] *n* (*lit, fig*)
Schmarotzer *m*, Parasit *m*.
parasol ['pærəsɒl] *n* Sonnenschirm *m*.
paratrooper ['pærətruːpə*] *n* Fall-
schirmjäger *m*.
parcel ['pɑːsl] *n* Paket *nt* // *vt* (*also*: **~
up**) einpacken.
parch [pɑːtʃ] *vt* (aus)dörren; **~ed** *a*
ausgetrocknet; (*person*) am Verdursten.
parchment ['pɑːtʃmənt] *n* Pergament
nt.
pardon ['pɑːdn] *n* Verzeihung *f* // *vt*
(*JUR*) begnadigen; **~ me!, I beg your ~!**
verzeihen Sie bitte!; **~ me?** (*US*), (**I beg
your**) **~?** wie bitte?
parent ['peərənt] *n* Elternteil *m*; **~s** *pl*
Eltern *pl*; **~al** [pə'rentl] *a* elterlich,
Eltern-.
parenthesis [pə'renθɪsɪs], *pl* **-theses**
[-θɪsiːz] *n* Klammer *f*; (*sentence*) Paren-
these *f*.
Paris ['pærɪs] *n* Paris *nt*.

parish ['pærɪʃ] n Gemeinde f.

parity ['pærɪtɪ] n (FIN) Umrechnungskurs m, Parität f.

park [pɑːk] n Park m // vti parken.

parking ['pɑːkɪŋ] n Parken nt; 'no ~' 'Parken verboten'; ~ **lot** n (US) Parkplatz m; ~ **meter** n Parkuhr f; ~ **ticket** n Strafzettel m.

parlance ['pɑːləns] n Sprachgebrauch m.

parliament ['pɑːləmənt] n Parlament nt; ~**ary** [pɑːlə'mentərɪ] a parlamentarisch, Parlaments-.

parlour, (US) **parlor** ['pɑːlə*] n Salon m, Wohnzimmer nt.

parochial [pə'rəʊkɪəl] a Gemeinde-; (narrow-minded) eng(stirnig).

parole [pə'rəʊl] n: on ~ (prisoner) auf Bewährung.

paroxysm ['pærəksɪzəm] n Anfall m.

parrot ['pærət] n Papagei m.

parry ['pærɪ] vt parieren, abwehren.

parsimonious [pɑːsɪ'məʊnɪəs] a knauserig.

parsley ['pɑːslɪ] n Petersilie m.

parsnip ['pɑːsnɪp] n Pastinake f.

parson ['pɑːsn] n Pfarrer m.

part [pɑːt] n (piece) Teil m; (THEAT) Rolle f; (of machine) Teil nt // ad = **partly** // vt trennen; (hair) scheiteln // vi (people) sich trennen; **to take ~ in** teilnehmen an (+dat); **to take sth in good ~** etw nicht übelnehmen; **to take sb's ~** sich auf jds Seite stellen; **for my ~** ich für meinen Teil; **for the most ~** meistens, größtenteils; **in ~ exchange** (Brit) in Zahlung; ~ **with** vt hergeben; (renounce) aufgeben; ~**ial** ['pɑːʃəl] a (incomplete) teilweise; (biased) parteiisch; **to be ~ial to** eine (besondere) Vorliebe haben für.

participant [pɑː'tɪsɪpənt] n Teilnehmer(in f) m.

participate [pɑː'tɪsɪpeɪt] vi teilnehmen (in an +dat).

participation [pɑːtɪsɪ'peɪʃən] n Teilnahme f; (sharing) Beteiligung f.

participle ['pɑːtɪsɪpl] n Partizip nt.

particle ['pɑːtɪkl] n Teilchen nt; (GRAM) Partikel m.

particular [pə'tɪkjələ*] a bestimmt; (exact) genau; (fussy) eigen; ~**s** pl (details) Einzelheiten pl; Personalien pl; **in ~** ad, ~**ly** ad besonders.

parting ['pɑːtɪŋ] n (separation) Abschied m; (Brit: of hair) Scheitel m // a Abschieds-.

partition [pɑː'tɪʃən] n (wall) Trennwand f; (division) Teilung f // vt aufteilen.

partly ['pɑːtlɪ] ad zum Teil, teilweise.

partner ['pɑːtnə*] n Partner m // vt der Partner sein von; ~**ship** n Partnerschaft f; (COMM) Teilhaberschaft f.

partridge ['pɑːtrɪdʒ] n Rebhuhn nt.

part-time ['pɑːt'taɪm] a Teilzeit- // ad stundenweise.

party ['pɑːtɪ] n (POL, JUR) Partei f; (group) Gesellschaft f; (celebration) Party f // a (dress) Party-; (politics) Partei-; ~ **line** n (TEL) Gemeinschaftsanschluß m.

pass [pɑːs] vt (on foot) vorbeigehen an (+dat); (driving) vorbeifahren an (+dat); (surpass) übersteigen; (hand on) weitergeben; (approve) genehmigen; (time) verbringen; (exam) bestehen // vi (go by) vorbeigehen; vorbeifahren; (years) vergehen; (be successful) bestehen // n (in mountains) Paß m; (permission) Passierschein m; (SPORT) Paß m; (in exam): **to get a ~** bestehen; **to ~ sth through sth** etw durch etw führen; **to make a ~ at sb** (col) bei jdm Annäherungsversuche machen; ~ **away** vi (euph) verscheiden; ~ **by** vi vorbeigehen; vorbeifahren; (years) vergehen; ~ **for** vi gehalten werden für; ~ **on** vt weitergeben; ~ **out** vi (faint) ohnmächtig werden; ~ **up** vt vorbeigehen lassen; ~**able** a (road) passierbar; (fairly good) passabel.

passage ['pæsɪdʒ] n (corridor) Gang m; (in book) (Text)stelle f; (voyage) Überfahrt f; ~**way** n Durchgang m.

passbook ['pɑːsbʊk] n Sparbuch nt.

passenger ['pæsɪndʒə*] n Passagier m; (on bus) Fahrgast m.

passer-by ['pɑːsə'baɪ] n Passant(in f) m.

passing ['pɑːsɪŋ] a (car) vorbeifahrend; (thought, affair) momentan; **in ~** en passant; ~ **place** n (AUT) Ausweichstelle f.

passion ['pæʃən] n Leidenschaft f; ~**ate** a leidenschaftlich.

Passover ['pɑːsəʊvə*] n Passahfest nt.

passport ['pɑːspɔːt] n (Reise)paß m; ~ **control** n Paßkontrolle f.

password ['pɑːswɜːd] n Parole f, Kennwort nt, Losung f.

past [pɑːst] prep (motion) an (+dat) .... vorbei; (position) hinter (+dat); (later than) nach // a (years) vergangen; (president etc) ehemalig // n Vergangenheit f; **he's ~ forty** er ist über vierzig; **for the ~ few/3 days** in den letzten paar/3 Tagen; **to run ~** vorbeilaufen.

pasta ['pæstə] n Teigwaren pl.

paste [peɪst] n (fish ~ etc) Paste f; (glue) Kleister m // vt kleben; (put ~ on) mit Kleister bestreichen.

pasteurized ['pæstəraɪzd] a pasteurisiert.

pastime ['pɑːstaɪm] n Zeitvertreib m.

pastor ['pɑːstə*] n Pfarrer m.

pastry ['peɪstrɪ] n Blätterteig m; (tarts etc) Stückchen pl.

pasture ['pɑːstʃə*] n Weide f.

pasty ['pæstɪ] n (Fleisch)pastete f // ['peɪstɪ] a bläßlich, käsig.

pat [pæt] n leichte(r) Schlag m, Klaps m

// vt tätscheln.

patch [pætʃ] n Fleck m // vt flicken; (to go through) a bad ~ eine Pechsträhne (haben); ~ **up** vt flicken; (quarrel) beilegen; ~**y** a (irregular) ungleichmäßig.

pâté ['pæteɪ] n Pastete f.

patent ['peɪtənt] n Patent nt // vt patentieren lassen; (by authorities) patentieren // a offenkundig; ~ **leather** n Lackleder nt.

paternal [pə'tɜ:nl] a väterlich.

paternity [pə'tɜ:nɪtɪ] n Vaterschaft f.

path [pɑ:θ] n Pfad m; Weg m; (of the sun) Bahn f.

pathetic [pə'θetɪk] a (very bad) kläglich.

pathology [pə'θɒlədʒɪ] n Pathologie f.

pathos ['peɪθɒs] n Rührseligkeit f.

pathway ['pɑ:θweɪ] n Weg m.

patience ['peɪʃəns] n Geduld f; (Brit: CARDS) Patience f.

patient ['peɪʃənt] n Patient(in f) m, Kranke(r) mf // a geduldig.

patio ['pætɪəʊ] n Innenhof m; (outside) Terrasse f.

patriotic [pætrɪ'ɒtɪk] a patriotisch.

patrol [pə'trəʊl] n Patrouille f; (police) Streife f // vt patrouillieren in (+dat) // vi (police) die Runde machen; (MIL) patrouillieren; ~ **car** n Streifenwagen m; ~**man** n (US) (Streifen)polizist m.

patron ['peɪtrən] n (in shop) (Stamm)kunde m; (in hotel) (Stamm)gast m; (supporter) Förderer m; ~ **of the arts** Mäzen m; ~**age** ['pætrənɪdʒ] n Schirmherrschaft f; ~**ize** ['pætrənaɪz] vt (support) unterstützen; (shop) besuchen; (treat condescendingly) von oben herab behandeln; ~ **saint** n Schutzpatron(in f) m.

patter ['pætə*] n (sound: of feet) Trappeln nt; (: of rain) Prasseln nt; (sales talk) Gerede nt // vi (feet) trappeln; (rain) prasseln.

pattern ['pætən] n Muster nt; (sewing) Schnittmuster nt; (knitting) Strickanleitung f.

paunch [pɔ:ntʃ] n Wanst m.

pauper ['pɔ:pə*] n Arme(r) mf.

pause [pɔ:z] n Pause f // vi innehalten.

pave [peɪv] vt pflastern; to ~ the way for den Weg bahnen für.

pavement ['peɪvmənt] n (Brit) Bürgersteig m.

pavilion [pə'vɪlɪən] n Pavillon m; (SPORT) Klubhaus nt.

paving ['peɪvɪŋ] n Straßenpflaster nt; ~ **stone** n Pflasterstein m.

paw [pɔ:] n Pfote f; (of big cats) Tatze f, Pranke f // vt (scrape) scharren; (handle) betatschen.

pawn [pɔ:n] n; (chess) Bauer m // vt verpfänden; ~**broker** n Pfandleiher m; ~**shop** n Pfandhaus nt.

pay [peɪ] n Bezahlung f, Lohn m // v (pt, pp **paid**) vt bezahlen // vi zahlen; (be profitable) sich bezahlt machen; to ~ attention achtgeben (to auf +acc); ~ **back** vt zurückzahlen; ~ **for** vt bezahlen; ~ **in** vt einzahlen; ~ **off** vt abzahlen // vi (scheme, decision) sich bezahlt machen; ~ **up** vi bezahlen; ~**able** a zahlbar, fällig; ~**ee** [peɪ'i:] n Zahlungsempfänger m; ~ **envelope** n (US) = ~ **packet**; ~**ment** n Bezahlung f; **advance** ~**ment** Vorauszahlung f; **monthly** ~**ment** monatliche Rate f; ~ **packet** n (Brit) Lohntüte f; ~ **phone** n Münzfernsprecher m; ~**roll** n Lohnliste f; ~ **slip** n Lohn-/Gehaltsstreifen m.

PC n abbr of **personal computer**.

p.c. abbr of **per cent**.

pea [pi:] n Erbse f.

peace [pi:s] n Friede(n) m; ~**able** a friedlich; ~**ful** a friedlich, ruhig; ~**keeping** a Friedens-.

peach [pi:tʃ] n Pfirsich m.

peacock ['pi:kɒk] n Pfau m.

peak [pi:k] n Spitze f; (of mountain) Gipfel m; (fig) Höhepunkt m; (of cap) (Mützen)schirm m; ~ **period** n Stoßzeit f, Hauptzeit f.

peal [pi:l] n (Glocken)läuten nt; ~**s of laughter** schallende(s) Gelächter nt.

peanut ['pi:nʌt] n Erdnuß f; ~ **butter** n Erdnußbutter f.

pear [peə*] n Birne f.

pearl [pɜ:l] n Perle f.

peasant ['pezənt] n Bauer m.

peat [pi:t] n Torf m.

pebble ['pebl] n Kiesel m.

peck [pek] vti picken // n (with beak) Schnabelhieb m; (kiss) flüchtige(r) Kuß m; ~**ing order** n Hackordnung f; ~**ish** a (Brit col) ein bißchen hungrig.

peculiar [pɪ'kju:lɪə*] a (odd) seltsam; ~ **to** charakteristisch für; ~**ity** [pɪkju:lɪ'ærɪtɪ] n (singular quality) Besonderheit f; (strangeness) Eigenartigkeit f.

pedal ['pedl] n Pedal nt // vti (cycle) fahren, radfahren.

peddler ['pedlə*] n Hausierer(in f) m; (of drugs) Drogenhändler(in f) m.

pedestal ['pedɪstl] n Sockel m.

pedestrian [pɪ'destrɪən] n Fußgänger m // a Fußgänger-; (humdrum) langweilig; ~ **crossing** n (Brit) Fußgängerüberweg m.

pediatrics [pi:dɪ'ætrɪks] n (US) = **paediatrics**.

pedigree ['pedɪgri:] n Stammbaum m // cpd (animal) reinrassig, Zucht-.

pedlar ['pedlə*] n = **peddler**.

pee [pi:] vi (col) pissen, pinkeln.

peek [pi:k] vi gucken.

peel [pi:l] n Schale f // vt schälen // vi (paint etc) abblättern; (skin) sich schälen.

peep [pi:p] n (Brit: look) neugierige(r) Blick m; (sound) Piepsen nt // vi (Brit: look) gucken; ~ **out** vi herausgucken; ~**hole** n Guckloch nt.

peer [pɪə*] vi starren; (peep) gucken // n (nobleman) Peer m; (equal) Ebenbürtige(r) m; ~**age** n Peerswürde f.

peeved [pi:vd] a ärgerlich; (person) sauer.

peevish ['pi:vɪʃ] a verdrießlich.

peg [peg] n (stake) Pflock m; **clothes ~** n (Brit) Wäscheklammer f.

pelican ['pelɪkən] n Pelikan m; ~ **crossing** n (Brit AUT) Ampelüberweg m.

pellet ['pelɪt] n Kügelchen nt.

pelmet ['pelmɪt] n Blende f.

pelt [pelt] vt bewerfen // vi (rain) schütten // n Pelz m, Fell nt.

pelvis ['pelvɪs] n Becken nt.

pen [pen] n (fountain ~) Federhalter m; (ball-point ~) Kuli m; (for sheep) Pferch m.

penal ['pi:nl] a Straf-; ~**ize** vt (punish) bestrafen; (disadvantage) benachteiligen; ~**ty** ['penəltɪ] n Strafe f; (FOOTBALL) Elfmeter m; ~**ty (kick)** n Elfmeter m.

penance ['penəns] n Buße f.

pence [pens] (Brit) pl of penny.

pencil ['pensl] n Bleistift m; ~ **case** n Federmäppchen nt; ~ **sharpener** n Bleistiftspitzer m.

pendant ['pendənt] n Anhänger m.

pending ['pendɪŋ] prep bis (zu) // a unentschieden, noch offen.

pendulum ['pendjuləm] n Pendel nt.

penetrate ['penɪtreɪt] vt durchdringen; (enter into) eindringen in (+acc).

penetration [penɪ'treɪʃən] n Durchdringen nt; Eindringen nt.

penfriend ['penfrend] n (Brit) Brieffreund(in f) m.

penguin ['peŋgwɪn] n Pinguin m.

penicillin [penɪ'sɪlɪn] n Penizillin nt.

peninsula [pɪ'nɪnsjələ] n Halbinsel f.

penis ['pi:nɪs] n Penis m.

penitence ['penɪtəns] n Reue f.

penitent ['penɪtənt] a reuig.

penitentiary [penɪ'tenʃərɪ] n (US) Zuchthaus nt.

penknife ['pennaɪf] n Federmesser nt.

pen name n Pseudonym nt.

penniless ['penɪləs] a mittellos.

penny ['penɪ] n, pl **pennies** ['penɪz] or (Brit) **pence** [pens] Penny m; (US) Centstück nt.

penpal ['penpæl] n Brieffreund(in f) m.

pension ['penʃən] n Rente f; ~**er** n (Brit) Rentner(in f) m; ~ **fund** n Rentenfonds m.

pensive ['pensɪv] a nachdenklich.

Pentecost ['pentɪkɒst] n Pfingsten pl or nt.

penthouse ['penthaʊs] n Dachterrassenwohnung f.

pent-up ['pentʌp] a (feelings) angestaut.

penultimate [pɪ'nʌltɪmət] a vorletzte(r, s).

people ['pi:pl] n (nation) Volk nt // npl (persons) Leute pl; (inhabitants) Bevölkerung f // vt besiedeln; **several ~** came mehrere Leute kamen; ~ **say that** ... man sagt, daß ...

pep [pep] n (col) Schwung m, Schmiß m; ~ **up** vt aufmöbeln.

pepper ['pepə*] n Pfeffer m; (vegetable) Paprika m // vt (pelt) bombardieren; ~**mint** n (plant) Pfefferminze f; (sweet) Pfefferminz nt.

peptalk ['peptɔ:k] n (col) Anstachelung f.

per [pɜ:*] prep pro; ~ **day/person** pro Tag/Person; ~ **annum** ad pro Jahr; ~ **capita** a (income) Pro-Kopf- // ad pro Kopf.

perceive [pə'si:v] vt (realize) wahrnehmen; (understand) verstehen.

per cent [pə'sent] n Prozent nt.

percentage [pə'sentɪdʒ] n Prozentsatz m.

perception [pə'sepʃən] n Wahrnehmung f; (insight) Einsicht f.

perceptive [pə'septɪv] a (person) aufmerksam; (analysis) tiefgehend.

perch [pɜ:tʃ] n Stange f; (fish) Flußbarsch m // vi sitzen, hocken.

percolator ['pɜ:kəleɪtə*] n Kaffeemaschine f.

percussion [pɜ:'kʌʃən] n (MUS) Schlagzeug nt.

peremptory [pə'remptərɪ] a schroff.

perennial [pə'renɪəl] a wiederkehrend; (everlasting) unvergänglich.

perfect ['pɜ:fɪkt] a vollkommen; (crime, solution) perfekt // n (GRAM) Perfekt nt // [pə'fekt] vt vervollkommnen; ~**ion** [pə'fekʃən] n Vollkommenheit f; ~**ionist** [pə'fekʃənɪst] n Perfektionist m; ~**ly** ad vollkommen, perfekt; (quite) ganz, einfach.

perforate ['pɜ:fəreɪt] vt durchlöchern.

perform [pə'fɔ:m] vt (carry out) durchor ausführen; (task) verrichten; (THEAT) spielen, geben // vi (THEAT) auftreten; ~**ance** n Durchführung f; (efficiency) Leistung f; (show) Vorstellung f; ~**er** n Künstler(in f) m; ~**ing** a (animal) dressiert.

perfume ['pɜ:fju:m] n Duft m; (lady's) Parfüm nt.

perfunctory [pə'fʌŋktərɪ] a oberflächlich, mechanisch.

perhaps [pə'hæps] ad vielleicht.

peril ['perɪl] n Gefahr f.

perimeter [pə'rɪmɪtə*] n Peripherie f; (of circle etc) Umfang m.

period ['pɪərɪəd] n Periode f; (GRAM)

Punkt m; (MED) Periode f // a (costume) historisch; **~ic** [-'ɒdɪk] a periodisch; **~ical** [-'ɒdɪkəl] n Zeitschrift f; **~ically** [-'ɒdɪkəlɪ] ad periodisch.

peripheral [pə'rɪfərəl] a Rand-, peripher // n (COMPUT) Peripheriegerät nt.

perish ['perɪʃ] vi umkommen; (fruit) verderben; **~able** a (fruit) leicht verderblich.

perjury ['pɜːdʒərɪ] n Meineid m.

perk [pɜːk] n (col: fringe benefit) Vergünstigung f; **~ up** vi munter werden; **~y** a (cheerful) keck.

perm [pɜːm] n Dauerwelle f.

permanent ['pɜːmənənt] a dauernd, ständig.

permeate ['pɜːmɪeɪt] vti durchdringen.

permissible [pə'mɪsəbl] a zulässig.

permission [pə'mɪʃən] n Erlaubnis f.

permit ['pɜːmɪt] n Zulassung f // [pə'mɪt] vt erlauben, zulassen.

pernicious [pɜː'nɪʃəs] a schädlich.

perpendicular [pɜːpən'dɪkjʊlə*] a senkrecht.

perpetrate ['pɜːpɪtreɪt] vt begehen.

perpetual [pə'petjʊəl] a dauernd, ständig.

perpetuate [pə'petjʊeɪt] vt verewigen, bewahren.

perplex [pə'pleks] vt verblüffen.

persecute ['pɜːsɪkjuːt] vt verfolgen.

persecution [pɜːsɪ'kjuːʃən] n Verfolgung f.

perseverance [pɜːsɪ'vɪərəns] n Ausdauer f.

persevere [pɜːsɪ'vɪə*] vi durchhalten.

Persian ['pɜːʃən] a persisch // n Perser(in f) m; **the (~) Gulf** der Persische Golf.

persist [pə'sɪst] vi (in belief etc) bleiben (in bei); (rain, smell) andauern; (continue) nicht aufhören; **~ence** n Beharrlichkeit f; **~ent** a beharrlich; (unending) ständig.

person ['pɜːsn] n Person f; **in ~** persönlich; **~able** a gut aussehend; **~al** a persönlich; (private) privat; (of body) körperlich, Körper-; **~al assistant (P.A.)** n Assistent(in f) m; **~al computer (PC)** n Personalcomputer m; **~ality** [pɜːsə'nælɪtɪ] n Persönlichkeit f; **~ally** ad persönlich; **~ify** [pɜː'sɒnɪfaɪ] vt verkörpern.

personnel [pɜːsə'nel] n Personal nt.

Perspex ['pɜːspeks] n ® Plexiglas nt ®.

perspiration [pɜːspə'reɪʃən] n Transpiration f.

perspire [pəs'paɪə*] vi transpirieren.

persuade [pə'sweɪd] vt überreden; (convince) überzeugen.

persuasion [pə'sweɪʒən] n Überredung f; Überzeugung f.

persuasive [pə'sweɪsɪv] a überzeugend.

pert [pɜːt] a keck.

pertaining [pɜː'teɪnɪŋ]: **~ to** a betreffend (+acc).

pertinent ['pɜːtɪnənt] a relevant.

perturb [pə'tɜːb] vt beunruhigen.

peruse [pə'ruːz] vt lesen.

pervade [pɜː'veɪd] vt erfüllen.

perverse [pə'vɜːs] a pervers; (obstinate) eigensinnig.

pervert ['pɜːvɜːt] n perverse(r) Mensch m // [pə'vɜːt] vt verdrehen; (morally) verderben.

pessimist ['pesɪmɪst] n Pessimist m; **~ic** [pesɪ'mɪstɪk] a pessimistisch.

pest [pest] n (insect) Schädling m; (fig: person) Nervensäge f; (: thing) Plage f.

pester ['pestə*] vt plagen.

pesticide ['pestɪsaɪd] n Insektenvertilgungsmittel nt.

pet [pet] n (animal) Haustier nt // vt liebkosen, streicheln // vi (col) Petting machen.

petal ['petl] n Blütenblatt nt.

peter out ['piːtə-] vi allmählich zu Ende gehen.

petite [pə'tiːt] a zierlich.

petition [pə'tɪʃən] n Bittschrift f.

petrified ['petrɪfaɪd] a versteinert; (person) starr (vor Schreck).

petrify ['petrɪfaɪ] vt versteinern; (person) erstarren lassen.

petrol ['petrəl] (Brit) n Benzin nt, Kraftstoff m; **two-/four-star ~** ≃ Normal-/Superbenzin nt; **~ can** n Benzinkanister m.

petroleum [pɪ'trəʊlɪəm] n Petroleum nt.

petrol: ~pump n (Brit: in car) Benzinpumpe f; (: at garage) Zapfsäule f; **~ station** n (Brit) Tankstelle f; **~ tank** n (Brit) Benzintank m.

petty ['petɪ] a (unimportant) unbedeutend; (mean) kleinlich; **~ cash** n Portokasse f; **~ officer** n Maat m.

petulant ['petjʊlənt] a leicht reizbar.

pew [pjuː] n Kirchenbank f.

pewter ['pjuːtə*] n Zinn nt.

pharmacist ['fɑːməsɪst] n Pharmazeut m; (druggist) Apotheker m.

pharmacy ['fɑːməsɪ] n Pharmazie f; (shop) Apotheke f.

phase [feɪz] n Phase f; **~ out** vt langsam abbauen; (model) auslaufen lassen; (person) absetzen.

Ph.D. abbr of **Doctor of Philosophy.**

pheasant ['feznt] n Fasan m.

phenomenon [fɪ'nɒmɪnən], pl **-mena** [-mɪnə] n Phänomen nt.

philanthropist [fɪ'lænθrəpɪst] n Philanthrop m, Menschenfreund m.

Philippines ['fɪlɪpiːnz] npl: **the ~** die Philippinen pl.

philosopher [fɪ'lɒsəfə*] n Philosoph m.

philosophy [fɪ'lɒsəfɪ] n Philosophie f.

phlegm [flem] n (MED) Schleim m; (calmness) Gelassenheit f; **~atic** [fleg'mætɪk] a gelassen.

phone [fəʊn] n Telefon nt // vti telefonieren, anrufen; **to be on the ~** telephonieren; **~ back** vti zurückrufen; **~ up** vti anrufen; **~ book** n Telefonbuch nt; **~ box** or **booth** n Telefonzelle f; **~ call** n Telefonanruf m; **~-in** n (RADIO, TV) Phone-in nt.

phoney ['fəʊnɪ] a (col) unecht // n (person) Schwindler m; (thing) Fälschung; (pound note) Blüte f.

phonograph ['fəʊnəgrɑːf] n (US) Grammophon nt.

photo ['fəʊtəʊ] n Foto nt.

photocopier ['fəʊtəʊkɒpɪə*] n Kopiergerät nt.

photocopy ['fəʊtəʊkɒpɪ] n Fotokopie f // vt fotokopieren.

photogenic [fəʊtəʊ'dʒenɪk] a fotogen.

photograph ['fəʊtəgrɑːf] n Fotografie f, Aufnahme f // vt fotografieren; **~er** [fə'tɒgrəfə*] n Fotograf m; **~ic** ['fəʊtə'græfɪk] a fotografisch; **~y** [fə'tɒgrəfɪ] n Fotografie f.

phrase [freɪz] n Satz m; (expression) Ausdruck m // vt ausdrücken, formulieren; **~ book** n Sprachführer m.

physical ['fɪzɪkəl] a physikalisch; (bodily) körperlich, physisch; **~ education** n Turnen nt; **~ly** ad physikalisch.

physician [fɪ'zɪʃən] n Arzt m.

physics ['fɪzɪks] n Physik f.

physiotherapy [fɪzɪə'θerəpɪ] n Heilgymnastik f, Physiotherapie f.

physique [fɪ'ziːk] n Körperbau m.

pianist ['pɪənɪst] n Pianist(in f) m.

piano ['pjɑːnəʊ] n Klavier nt.

pick [pɪk] n (tool) Pickel m; (choice) Auswahl f // vt (fruit) pflücken; (choose) aussuchen; **take your ~** such dir etwas aus; **to ~ sb's pocket** jdn bestehlen; **~ off** vt (kill) abschießen; **~ on** vt (person) herumhacken auf (+dat); **~ out** vt auswählen; **~ up** vi (improve) sich erholen // vt (lift up) aufheben; (learn) (schnell) mitbekommen; (collect) abholen; (girl) (sich dat) anlachen; (AUT: passenger) mitnehmen; (speed) gewinnen an (+dat); **to ~ o.s. up** aufstehen.

picket ['pɪkɪt] n (striker) Streikposten m // vt (factory) (Streik)posten aufstellen vor (+dat) // vi (Streik)posten stehen.

pickle ['pɪkl] n (salty mixture) Pökel m; (col) Klemme f // vt (in Essig) einlegen; einpökeln.

pickpocket ['pɪkpɒkɪt] n Taschendieb m.

pickup ['pɪkʌp] n (Brit: on record player) Tonabnehmer m; (small truck) Lieferwagen m.

picnic ['pɪknɪk] n Picknick nt // vi picknicken.

pictorial [pɪk'tɔːrɪəl] a in Bildern.

picture ['pɪktʃə*] n Bild nt // vt (visualize) sich (dat) vorstellen; **in the ~** (fig) im Bild; **the ~s** pl (Brit) das Kino; **~ book** n Bilderbuch nt.

picturesque [pɪktʃə'resk] a malerisch.

pie [paɪ] n (meat) Pastete f; (fruit) Torte f.

piece [piːs] n Stück nt // vt: **to ~ together** zusammenstückeln; (fig) sich (dat) zusammenreimen; **to take to ~s** in Einzelteile zerlegen; **~meal** ad stückweise, Stück für Stück; **~work** n Akkordarbeit f.

pie chart n Kreisdiagramm nt.

pier [pɪə*] n Pier m, Mole f.

pierce [pɪəs] vt durchstechen, durchbohren (also look); durchdringen (also fig).

piercing ['pɪəsɪŋ] a durchdringend.

piety ['paɪətɪ] n Frömmigkeit f.

pig [pɪg] n Schwein nt.

pigeon ['pɪdʒən] n Taube f; **~hole** n (compartment) Ablegefach nt.

piggy bank ['pɪgɪbæŋk] n Sparschwein nt.

pigheaded ['pɪg'hedɪd] a dickköpfig.

piglet ['pɪglət] n Ferkel nt.

pigskin ['pɪgskɪn] n Schweinsleder nt.

pigsty ['pɪgstaɪ] n (lit, fig) Schweinestall m.

pigtail ['pɪgteɪl] n Zopf m.

pike [paɪk] n Pike f; (fish) Hecht m.

pilchard ['pɪltʃəd] n Sardine f.

pile [paɪl] n Haufen m; (of books, wood) Stapel m; (in ground) Pfahl m; (on carpet) Flausch m // vti (also: ~ up) sich anhäufen.

piles [paɪlz] n Hämorrhoiden pl.

pile-up ['paɪlʌp] n (AUT) Massenzusammenstoß m.

pilfering ['pɪlfərɪŋ] n Diebstahl m.

pilgrim ['pɪlgrɪm] n Pilger(in f) m; **~age** n Wallfahrt f.

pill [pɪl] n Tablette f, Pille f; **the ~** die (Antibaby)pille.

pillage ['pɪlɪdʒ] vt plündern.

pillar ['pɪlə*] n Pfeiler m, Säule f (also fig); **~ box** n (Brit) Briefkasten m.

pillion ['pɪljən] n Soziussitz m.

pillory ['pɪlərɪ] vt (fig) anprangern.

pillow ['pɪləʊ] n Kissen nt; **~case** n Kissenbezug m.

pilot ['paɪlət] n Pilot m; (NAUT) Lotse m // a (scheme etc) Versuchs- // vt führen; (ship) lotsen; **~ light** n Zündflamme f.

pimp [pɪmp] n Zuhälter m.

pimple ['pɪmpl] n Pickel m.

pimply ['pɪmplɪ] a pick(e)lig.

pin [pɪn] n Nadel f; (for sewing) Stecknadel f; (TECH) Stift m, Bolzen m // vt stecken, heften (to an +acc); (keep in one position) pressen, drücken; **to ~ sth on sb** (fig) jdm etw anhängen; **~s and needles** n Kribbeln nt; **~ down** vt (fig: person) festnageln (to auf +acc).

pinafore ['pınəfɔ:*] n Schürze f; ~ **dress** n Kleiderrock m.

pinball ['pınbɔ:l] n Flipper m.

pincers ['pınsəz] npl Kneif- or Beißzange f; (MED) Pinzette f.

pinch [pıntʃ] n Zwicken, Kneifen nt; (of salt) Prise f // vti zwicken, kneifen; (shoe) drücken // vt (col: steal) klauen; (arrest) schnappen; **at a** ~ notfalls, zur Not.

pincushion ['pınkuʃən] n Nadelkissen nt.

pine [paın] n (also: ~ **tree**) Kiefer f // vi: ~ **for** sich sehnen nach; ~ **away** vi sich zu Tode sehnen.

pineapple ['paınæpl] n Ananas f.

ping [pıŋ] n Klingeln nt; ~-**pong** n Pingpong nt.

pink [pıŋk] a rosa inv // n Rosa nt; (BOT) Nelke f.

pinnacle ['pınəkl] n Spitze f.

pinpoint ['pınpɔınt] vt festlegen.

pinstripe ['pınstraıp] n Nadelstreifen m.

pint [paınt] n Pint nt; (Brit col: of beer) große(s) Bier nt.

pious ['paıəs] a fromm.

pip [pıp] n Kern m; (Brit: time signal on radio) Zeitzeichen nt.

pipe [paıp] n (smoking) Pfeife f; (tube) Rohr nt; (in house) (Rohr)leitung f // vti (durch Rohre) leiten; (MUS) blasen; ~**s** pl (also: **bag**~**s**) Dudelsack m; ~ **down** vi (be quiet) die Luft anhalten; ~ **cleaner** n Pfeifenreiniger m; ~-**dream** n Luftschloß nt; ~**line** n (for oil) Pipeline f; ~**r** n Pfeifer m; (bagpipes) Dudelsackbläser m.

piping ['paıpıŋ] ad: ~ **hot** siedend heiß.

piquant ['pi:kənt] a pikant.

pique [pi:k] n gekränkte(r) Stolz m.

pirate ['paıərıt] n Pirat m, Seeräuber m; ~ **radio** n (Brit) Piratensender m.

Pisces ['paısi:z] n Fische pl.

piss [pıs] vi (col) pissen; ~**ed** a (col: drunk) voll.

pistol ['pıstl] n Pistole f.

piston ['pıstən] n Kolben m.

pit [pıt] n Grube f; (THEAT) Parterre nt; (orchestra ~) Orchestergraben m // vt (mark with scars) zerfressen; (compare: o.s.) messen (against mit); (: sb/sth) messen (against an +dat); the ~**s** pl (motor racing) die Boxen.

pitch [pıtʃ] n Wurf m; (of trader) Stand m; (SPORT) (Spiel)feld nt; (MUS) Tonlage f; (substance) Pech nt // vt werfen; (set up) aufschlagen // vi (NAUT) rollen; **to** ~ **a tent** ein Zelt aufbauen; ~-**black** a pechschwarz; ~**ed battle** n offene Schlacht f.

pitcher ['pıtʃə*] n Krug m.

pitchfork ['pıtʃfɔ:k] n Heugabel f.

piteous ['pıtıəs] a kläglich, erbärmlich.

pitfall ['pıtfɔ:l] n (fig) Falle f.

pith [pıθ] n Mark nt.

pithy ['pıθı] a prägnant.

pitiful ['pıtıful] a (deserving pity) bedauernswert; (contemptible) jämmerlich.

pitiless ['pıtıləs] a erbarmungslos.

pittance ['pıtəns] n Hungerlohn m.

pity ['pıtı] n (sympathy) Mitleid nt // vt Mitleid haben mit; **what a** ~! wie schade!

pivot ['pıvət] n Drehpunkt m // vi sich drehen (on um).

pixie ['pıksı] n Elf(e f) m.

pizza ['pi:tsə] n Pizza f.

placard ['plækɑ:d] n Plakat nt, Anschlag m.

placate [plə'keıt] vt beschwichtigen.

place [pleıs] n Platz m; (spot) Stelle f; (town etc) Ort m // vt setzen, stellen, legen; (order) aufgeben; (SPORT) plazieren; (identify) unterbringen; **to take** ~ stattfinden; **to be** ~**d third** (in race, exam) auf dem dritten Platz liegen; **out of** ~ nicht am rechten Platz; (fig: remark) unangebracht; **in the first** ~ erstens; **to change** ~**s with sb** mit jdm den Platz tauschen.

placid ['plæsıd] a gelassen, ruhig.

plagiarism ['pleıdʒıərızəm] n Plagiat nt.

plague [pleıg] n Pest f; (fig) Plage f // vt plagen.

plaice [pleıs] n Scholle f.

plain [pleın] a (clear) klar, deutlich; (simple) einfach, schlicht; (not beautiful) alltäglich // n Ebene f; **in** ~ **clothes** (police) in Zivil(kleidung); ~ **chocolate** n Bitterschokolade f.

plaintiff ['pleıntıf] n Kläger m.

plaintive ['pleıntıv] a wehleidig.

plait [plæt] n Zopf m // vt flechten.

plan [plæn] n Plan m // vt planen; **according to** ~ planmäßig; **to** ~ **to do sth** vorhaben, etw zu tun.

plane [pleın] n Ebene f; (AVIAT) Flugzeug nt; (tool) Hobel m; (tree) Platane f.

planet ['plænıt] n Planet m.

plank [plæŋk] n Brett nt.

planning ['plænıŋ] n Planung f; **family** ~ Familienplanung f; ~ **permission** n Baugenehmigung f.

plant [plɑ:nt] n Pflanze f; (TECH) (Maschinen)anlage f; (factory) Fabrik f, Werk nt // vt pflanzen; (set firmly) stellen.

plantation [plæn'teıʃən] n Plantage f.

plaque [plæk] n Gedenktafel f; (on teeth) (Zahn)belag m.

plaster ['plɑ:stə*] n Gips m; (in house) Verputz m; (Brit: also: sticking ~) Pflaster nt; (for fracture: also: ~ **of Paris**) Gipsverband m // vt gipsen; (hole) zugipsen; (ceiling) verputzen; (fig: with pictures etc) be- or verkleben; ~**ed** a (col) besoffen; ~**er** n Gipser m.

plastic ['plæstɪk] n Plastik nt or f // a (made of plastic) Plastik-; (ART) plastisch, bildend; ~ **bag** n Plastiktüte f.

plasticine ['plæstɪsi:n] n Plastilin nt.

plastic surgery n plastische Chirurgie f.

plate [pleɪt] n Teller m; (gold/silver) vergoldete(s)/versilberte(s) Tafelgeschirr nt; (flat sheet) Platte f; (in book) (Bild)tafel f.

plate glass n Tafelglas nt.

platform ['plætfɔ:m] n (at meeting) Plattform f, Podium nt; (RAIL) Bahnsteig m; (POL) Parteiprogramm nt; ~ **ticket** n Bahnsteigkarte f.

platinum ['plætɪnəm] n Platin nt.

platoon [plə'tu:n] n (MIL) Zug m.

platter ['plætə*] n Platte f.

play [pleɪ] n Spiel nt (also TECH); (THEAT) (Theater)stück nt // vti spielen; (another team) spielen gegen; to ~ **safe** auf Nummer sicher gehen; ~ **down** vt herunterspielen; ~ **up** vi (cause trouble) frech werden; (bad leg etc) weh tun // vt (person) plagen; to ~ **up to sb** jdm flattieren; ~-**acting** n Schauspielerei f; ~**boy** n Playboy m; ~**er** n Spieler(in f) m; ~**ful** a spielerisch; ~**ground** n Spielplatz m; ~**group** n Kindergarten m; ~**ing card** n Spielkarte f; ~**ing field** n Sportplatz m; ~**mate** n Spielkamerad m; ~-**off** n (SPORT) Entscheidungsspiel nt; ~**pen** n Laufstall m; ~**school** n = ~**group**; ~**thing** n Spielzeug nt; ~**wright** n Theaterschriftsteller m.

plc abbr (= public limited company) AG.

plea [pli:] n Bitte f; (general appeal) Appell m; (JUR) Plädoyer nt.

plead [pli:d] vt (poverty) zur Entschuldigung anführen; (JUR: sb's case) vertreten // vi (beg) dringend bitten (with sb jdn); (JUR) plädieren.

pleasant ['pleznt] a angenehm; ~**ness** n Angenehme(s) nt; (of person) Freundlichkeit f; ~**ries** npl (polite remarks) Nettigkeiten pl.

please [pli:z] vti (be agreeable to) gefallen (+dat); ~! bitte!; ~ **yourself!** wie du willst!; ~**d** a zufrieden (glad) erfreut (with über +acc); ~**d to meet you** angenehm.

pleasing ['pli:zɪŋ] a erfreulich.

pleasure ['pleʒə*] n Freude f; (old: will) Wünsche pl // cpd Vergnügungs-; 'it's a ~' 'gern geschehen'.

pleat [pli:t] n Falte f.

plectrum ['plektrəm] n Plektron nt.

pledge [pledʒ] n Pfand nt; (promise) Versprechen nt // vt verpfänden; (promise) geloben, versprechen.

plentiful ['plentɪful] a reichlich.

plenty ['plentɪ] n Fülle f, Überfluß m; ~ **of** eine Menge, viel.

pleurisy ['pluərɪsɪ] n Rippenfellentzündung f.

pliable ['plaɪəbl] a biegsam; (person) beeinflußbar.

pliers ['plaɪəz] npl (Kneif)zange f.

plight [plaɪt] n (Not)lage f.

plimsolls ['plɪmsɒlz] npl (Brit) Turnschuhe pl.

plod [plɒd] vi (work) sich abplagen; (walk) trotten; ~**der** n Arbeitstier nt.

plonk [plɒŋk] n (Brit col: wine) billige(r) Wein m // vt: to ~ **sth down** etw hinknallen.

plot [plɒt] n Komplott nt; (story) Handlung f; (of land) Grundstück nt // vt markieren; (curve) zeichnen; (movements) nachzeichnen // vi (plan secretly) sich verschwören; ~**ter** n (instrument) Plotter m.

plough, (US) **plow** [plaʊ] n Pflug m // vt pflügen; ~ **back** vt (COMM) wieder in das Geschäft stecken; ~ **through** vt (water) durchpflügen; (book) sich kämpfen durch.

ploy [plɔɪ] n Masche f.

pluck [plʌk] vt (fruit) pflücken; (guitar) zupfen; (goose) rupfen // n Mut m; to ~ **up courage** all seinen Mut zusammennehmen; ~**y** a beherzt.

plug [plʌg] n Stöpsel m; (ELEC) Stecker m; (col: publicity) Schleichwerbung f; (AUT) Zündkerze f // vt (zu)stopfen; (col: advertise) Reklame machen für; ~ **in** vt (ELEC) anschließen.

plum [plʌm] n Pflaume f, Zwetschge f // a (job etc) Bomben-.

plumage ['plu:mɪdʒ] n Gefieder nt.

plumb [plʌm] a senkrecht // n Lot nt // ad (exactly) genau // vt ausloten; (fig) sondieren.

plumber ['plʌmə*] n Klempner m, Installateur m.

plumbing ['plʌmɪŋ] n (craft) Installieren nt; (fittings) Leitungen pl.

plume [plu:m] n Feder f; (of smoke etc) Fahne f.

plummet ['plʌmɪt] vi (ab)stürzen.

plump [plʌmp] a rundlich, füllig // vt plumpsen lassen; to ~ **for** (col: choose) sich entscheiden für.

plunder ['plʌndə*] n Plünderung f; (loot) Beute f // vt plündern.

plunge [plʌndʒ] n Sturz m // vt stoßen // vi (sich) stürzen; to **take the** ~ den Sprung wagen.

plunging ['plʌndʒɪŋ] a (neckline) offenherzig.

pluperfect ['plu:'pɜ:fɪkt] n Plusquamperfekt nt.

plural ['pluərəl] n Plural m, Mehrzahl f.

plus [plʌs] n (also: ~ **sign**) Plus(zeichen) nt // prep plus, und; **ten/ twenty** ~ mehr als zehn/zwanzig.

plush [plʌʃ] a (also ~**y**: col: luxurious) feudal.

ply [plaɪ] vt (trade) (be)treiben; (with questions) zusetzen (+dat); (ship, taxi) befahren // vi (ship, taxi) verkehren; **three-~** (wool) Dreifach-; **to ~ sb with drink** jdn zum Trinken animieren; **~wood** n Sperrholz nt.

P.M. abbr of **Prime Minister**.

p.m. ad abbr (= post meridiem) p.m.

pneumatic [njuː'mætɪk] a pneumatisch; (TECH) Luft-; **~ drill** n Preßlufthammer m.

pneumonia [njuː'məʊnɪə] n Lungenentzündung f.

poach [pəʊtʃ] vt (COOK) pochieren; (game) stehlen // vi (steal) wildern (for nach); **~ed** a (egg) verloren; **~er** n Wilddieb m; **~ing** n Wildern nt.

P.O. Box n abbr of **Post Office Box**.

pocket ['pɒkɪt] n Tasche f; (of resistance) (Widerstands)nest nt // vt einstecken; **to be out of ~** (Brit) kein Geld haben; **~book** n Taschenbuch nt; **~ knife** n Taschenmesser nt; **~ money** n Taschengeld nt.

pod [pɒd] n Hülse f; (of peas also) Schote f.

podgy ['pɒdʒɪ] a pummelig.

podiatrist [pɒ'diːətrɪst] n (US) Fußpfleger(in f) m.

poem ['pəʊəm] n Gedicht nt.

poet ['pəʊɪt] n Dichter m, Poet m; **~ic** [pəʊ'etɪk] a poetisch, dichterisch; **~ laureate** n Hofdichter m; **~ry** n Poesie f; (poems) Gedichte pl.

poignant ['pɔɪnjənt] a (touching) ergreifend.

point [pɔɪnt] n Punkt m (also in discussion, scoring); (spot also) Stelle f; (sharpened tip) Spitze f; (moment) (Zeit)punkt m; (purpose) Zweck m; (idea) Argument nt; (decimal) Dezimalstelle f; (personal characteristic) Seite f // vt zeigen mit; (gun) richten // vi zeigen; **~s** pl (RAIL) Weichen pl; **to be on the ~ of doing sth** drauf und dran sein, etw zu tun; **to make a ~ of** Wert darauf legen; **to get the ~** verstehen, worum es geht; **to come to the ~** zur Sache kommen; **there's no ~ (in doing)** es hat keinen Sinn (etw zu tun); **~ out** vt hinweisen auf (+acc); **~ to** vt zeigen auf (+acc); **~-blank** ad (at close range) aus nächster Entfernung; (bluntly) unverblümt; **~ed** a, **~edly** ad spitz, scharf; (fig) gezielt; **~er** n Zeigestock m; (on dial) Zeiger m; **~less** a sinnlos; **~ of view** n Stand- or Gesichtspunkt m.

poise [pɔɪz] n Haltung f; (fig) Gelassenheit f.

poison ['pɔɪzn] n (lit, fig) Gift nt // vt vergiften; **~ing** n Vergiftung f; **~ous** a giftig, Gift-.

poke [pəʊk] vt stoßen; (put) stecken; (fire) schüren; (hole) bohren; **~ about**

vi herumstochern; (nose around) herumwühlen.

poker ['pəʊkə*] n Schürhaken m; (CARDS) Poker nt; **~-faced** a undurchdringlich.

poky ['pəʊkɪ] a eng.

Poland ['pəʊlənd] n Polen nt.

polar ['pəʊlə*] a Polar-, polar; **~ bear** n Eisbär m; **~ize** vt polarisieren.

Pole [pəʊl] n Pole m, Polin f.

pole [pəʊl] n Stange f, Pfosten m; (flag~, telegraph ~ also) Mast m; (ELEC, GEOG) Pol m; (SPORT) (vaulting ~) Stab m; (ski ~) Stock m; **~ bean** n (US: runner bean) Stangenbohne f; **~ vault** n Stabhochsprung m.

police [pə'liːs] n Polizei f // vt kontrollieren; **~ car** n Polizeiwagen m; **~man** n Polizist m; **~ state** n Polizeistaat m; **~ station** n (Polizei)revier nt, Wache f; **~woman** n Polizistin f.

policy ['pɒlɪsɪ] n Politik f; (insurance) (Versicherungs)police f.

polio ['pəʊlɪəʊ] n (spinale) Kinderlähmung f, Polio f.

Polish ['pəʊlɪʃ] a polnisch // n Polnisch nt.

polish ['pɒlɪʃ] n Politur f; (for floor) Wachs nt; (for shoes) Creme f; (nail ~) Lack m; (shine) Glanz m; (of furniture) Politur f; (fig) Schliff m // vt polieren; (shoes) putzen; (fig) den letzten Schliff geben (+dat); **~ off** vt (col: work) erledigen; (food) wegputzen; (drink) hinunterschütten; **~ed** a glänzend (also fig); (manners) verfeinert.

polite [pə'laɪt] a höflich; **~ness** n Höflichkeit f.

politic ['pɒlɪtɪk] a (prudent) diplomatisch; **~al** a, **~ally** ad [pə'lɪtɪkəl, -ɪ] politisch; **~ian** [pɒlɪ'tɪʃən] n Politiker m; **~s** pl Politik f.

polka ['pɒlkə] n Polka f; **~ dot** n Tupfen m.

poll [pəʊl] n Abstimmung f; (in election) Wahl f; (votes cast) Wahlbeteiligung f; (opinion ~) Umfrage f // vt (votes) erhalten.

pollination [pɒlɪ'neɪʃən] n Befruchtung f.

polling ['pəʊlɪŋ]: **~ booth** n (Brit) Wahlkabine f; **~ day** n (Brit) Wahltag m; **~ station** n (Brit) Wahllokal nt.

pollute [pə'luːt] vt verschmutzen, verunreinigen; **pollution** [pə'luːʃən] n Verschmutzung f.

polo ['pəʊləʊ] n Polo nt; **~-neck** n Rollkragen(pullover) m.

polystyrene [pɒlɪ'staɪriːn] n Styropor nt.

polytechnic [pɒlɪ'teknɪk] n technische Hochschule f.

polythene ['pɒlɪθiːn] n Plastik nt.

pomegranate ['pɒməgrænɪt] n Granatapfel m.

pommel ['pʌml] *vt* mit den Fäusten bearbeiten // *n* Sattelknopf *m*.

pompom ['pɒmpɒm] *n*, **pompon** ['pɒmpɒn] *n* Troddel *f*; Pompon *m*.

pompous ['pɒmpəs] *a* aufgeblasen; (*language*) geschwollen.

pond [pɒnd] *n* Teich *m*, Weiher *m*.

ponder ['pɒndə*] *vt* nachdenken über (+*acc*); ~**ous** *a* schwerfällig.

pong [pɒŋ] *n* (*Brit col*) Mief *m*.

pontiff ['pɒntɪf] *n* Pontifex *m*.

pontificate [pɒn'tɪfɪkeɪt] *vi* (*fig*) geschwollen reden.

pontoon [pɒn'tu:n] *n* Ponton *m*; (*CARDS*) 17-und-4 *nt*.

pony ['pəʊnɪ] *n* Pony *nt*; ~**tail** *n* Pferdeschwanz *m*; ~ **trekking** *n* (*Brit*) Ponyreiten *nt*.

poodle ['pu:dl] *n* Pudel *m*.

pool [pu:l] *n* (*swimming* ~) Schwimmbad *nt*; (*private*) Swimming pool *m*; (*of spilt liquid, blood*) Lache *f*; (*fund*) (gemeinsame) Kasse *f*; (*billiards*) Poolspiel *nt* // *vt* (*money etc*) zusammenlegen; **typing** ~ Schreibzentrale *f*; (**football**) ~**s** Toto *nt*.

poor [pʊə*] *a* arm; (*not good*) schlecht; **the** ~ *pl* die Armen *pl*; ~**ly** *ad* schlecht; (*dressed*) ärmlich // *a* schlecht.

pop [pɒp] *n* Knall *m*; (*music*) Popmusik *f*; (*drink*) Limo(nade) *f*; (*US col*) Pa *m* // *vt* (*put*) stecken; (*balloon*) platzen lassen // *vi* knallen; ~ **in** *vi* kurz vorbeigehen; ~ **out** *vi* (*person*) kurz rausgehen; (*thing*) herausspringen; ~ **up** *vi* auftauchen; ~ **concert** *n* Popkonzert *nt*; ~**corn** *n* Puffmais *m*.

pope [pəʊp] *n* Papst *m*.

poplar ['pɒplə*] *n* Pappel *f*.

poppy ['pɒpɪ] *n* Mohn *m*.

Popsicle ['pɒpsɪkl] *n* ® (*US: ice lolly*) Eis *nt* am Stiel.

populace ['pɒpjuləs] *n* Volk *nt*.

popular ['pɒpjulə*] *a* beliebt, populär; (*of the people*) volkstümlich; (*widespread*) allgemein; ~**ity** [pɒpju'lærɪtɪ] *n* Beliebtheit *f*, Popularität *f*; ~**ize** *vt* popularisieren; ~**ly** *ad* allgemein, überall.

population [pɒpju'leɪʃən] *n* Bevölkerung *f*; (*of town*) Einwohner *pl*.

populous ['pɒpjuləs] *a* dicht besiedelt.

porcelain ['pɔ:slɪn] *n* Porzellan *nt*.

porch [pɔ:tʃ] *n* Vorbau *m*, Veranda *f*.

porcupine ['pɔ:kjupaɪn] *n* Stachelschwein *nt*.

pore [pɔ:*] *n* Pore *f*; ~ **over** *vt* brüten über (+*dat*).

pork [pɔ:k] *n* Schweinefleisch *nt*.

pornography [pɔ:'nɒgrəfɪ] *n* Pornographie *f*.

porous ['pɔ:rəs] *a* porös; (*skin*) porig.

porpoise ['pɔ:pəs] *n* Tümmler *m*.

porridge ['pɒrɪdʒ] *n* Haferbrei *m*.

port [pɔ:t] *n* Hafen *m*; (*town*) Hafenstadt *f*; (*NAUT: left side*) Backbord *nt*; (*wine*) Portwein *m*; ~ **of call** Anlaufhafen *m*.

portable ['pɔ:təbl] *a* tragbar.

portent ['pɔ:tent] *n* schlimme(s) Vorzeichen *nt*.

porter ['pɔ:tə*] *n* Pförtner(in *f*) *m*; (*for luggage*) (Gepäck)träger *m*.

portfolio [pɔ:t'fəʊlɪəʊ] *n* (*case*) Mappe *f*; (*POL*) Geschäftsbereich *m*; (*FIN*) Portefeuille *nt*; (*of artist*) Kollektion *f*.

porthole ['pɔ:thəʊl] *n* Bullauge *nt*.

portion ['pɔ:ʃən] *n* Teil *m*, Stück *nt*; (*of food*) Portion *f*.

portly ['pɔ:tlɪ] *a* korpulent, beleibt.

portrait ['pɔ:trɪt] *n* Porträt *nt*.

portray [pɔ:'treɪ] *vt* darstellen; ~**al** *n* Darstellung *f*.

Portugal ['pɔ:tjʊgəl] *n* Portugal *nt*.

Portuguese [pɔ:tjʊ'gi:z] *a* portugiesisch // *n*, *pl inv* Portugiese *m*, Portugiesin *f*; (*LING*) Portugiesisch *nt*.

pose [pəʊz] *n* Stellung *f*, Pose *f* (*also affectation*) // *vi* posieren // *vt* stellen.

posh [pɒʃ] *a* (*col*) (piek)fein.

position [pə'zɪʃən] *n* Stellung *f*; (*place*) Lage *f*; (*job*) Stelle *f*; (*attitude*) Standpunkt *m* // *vt* aufstellen.

positive ['pɒzɪtɪv] *a* positiv; (*convinced*) sicher; (*definite*) eindeutig.

posse ['pɒsɪ] *n* (*US*) Aufgebot *nt*.

possess [pə'zes] *vt* besitzen; ~**ion** [pə'zeʃən] *n* Besitz *m*; ~**ive** *a* besitzergreifend, eigensüchtig.

possibility [pɒsə'bɪlɪtɪ] *n* Möglichkeit *f*.

possible ['pɒsəbl] *a* möglich; **as big as** ~ so groß wie möglich, möglichst groß.

possibly ['pɒsəblɪ] *ad* möglicherweise, vielleicht; **I cannot** ~ **come** ich kann unmöglich kommen.

post [pəʊst] *n* (*Brit: letters, delivery*) Post *f*; (*pole*) Pfosten *m*, Pfahl *m*; (*place of duty*) Posten *m*; (*job*) Stelle *f* // *vt* (*notice*) anschlagen; (*Brit: letters*) aufgeben; (*Brit: appoint*) versetzen; (*soldiers*) aufstellen; ~**age** *n* Postgebühr *f*, Porto *nt*; ~**al** *a* Post-; ~**al order** *n* Postanweisung *f*; ~**box** *n* (*Brit*) Briefkasten *m*; ~**card** *n* Postkarte *f*; ~**code** *n* (*Brit*) Postleitzahl *f*.

postdate [pəʊst'deɪt] *vt* (*cheque*) nachdatieren.

poster ['pəʊstə*] *n* Plakat *nt*, Poster *nt*.

poste restante ['pəʊst'restã:nt] *n* Aufbewahrungsstelle *f* für postlagernde Sendungen.

posterior [pɒs'tɪərɪə*] *n* (*col*) Hintern *m*.

posterity [pɒs'terɪtɪ] *n* Nachwelt *f*.

postgraduate ['pəʊst'grædjuɪt] *n* Weiterstudierende(r) *mf*.

postman ['pəʊstmən] *n* Briefträger *m*.

postmark ['pəʊstma:k] *n* Poststempel *m*.

postmaster ['pəʊstma:stə*] *n* Postmeister m.

post-mortem ['pəust'mɔːtəm] n Autopsie f.

post office ['pəustɒfɪs] n Postamt nt, Post f (also organization); **Post Office Box (P.O. Box)** n Postfach nt (Postf.).

postpone [pə'spəun] vt verschieben; ~ment n Verschiebung f.

postscript ['pəusskrɪpt] n Postskript nt; (to affair) Nachspiel nt.

postulate ['pɒstjuleɪt] vt voraussetzen; (maintain) behaupten.

posture ['pɒstʃə*] n Haltung f // vi posieren.

postwar ['pəust'wɔː*] a Nachkriegs-.

posy ['pəuzɪ] n Blumenstrauß m.

pot [pɒt] n Topf m; (tea~) Kanne f; (col: marijuana) Hasch m // vt (plant) eintopfen; **to go to** ~ (col: work, performance) auf den Hund kommen.

potato [pə'teɪtəu] pl ~es n Kartoffel f; ~ **peeler** n Kartoffelschäler m.

potent ['pəutənt] a stark; (argument) zwingend.

potential ['pəu'tenʃəl] a potentiell // n Potential nt; ~ly ad potentiell.

pothole ['pɒthəul] n (Brit: underground) Höhle f; (in road) Schlagloch nt.

potholing ['pɒthəulɪŋ] n (Brit): to go ~ Höhlen erforschen.

potion ['pəuʃən] n Trank m.

potluck ['pɒt'lʌk] n: to take ~ with sth etw auf gut Glück nehmen.

potshot ['pɒtʃɒt] n: to take a ~ at sth auf etw (acc) ballern.

potted ['pɒtɪd] a (food) eingelegt, eingemacht; (plant) Topf-; (fig: book, version) konzentriert.

potter ['pɒtə*] n Töpfer m // vi herumhantieren; ~y n Töpferwaren pl; (place) Töpferei f.

potty ['pɒtɪ] a (col) verrückt // n Töpfchen nt.

pouch [pautʃ] n Beutel m.

pouf(fe) [puːf] n Sitzkissen nt.

poultry ['pəultrɪ] n Geflügel nt.

pounce [pauns] vi sich stürzen (on auf +acc) // n Sprung m, Satz m.

pound [paund] n (FIN, weight) Pfund nt; (for cars, animals) Auslösestelle f; (for stray animals) (Tier)asyl nt // vt (zer)stampfen // vi klopfen, hämmern; ~ **sterling** n Pfund Sterling nt.

pour [pɔː*] vt gießen, schütten // vi gießen; (crowds etc) strömen; ~ **away** or **off** vt abgießen; ~ **in** vi (people) hereinströmen; ~ **out** vi (people) herausströmen // vt (drink) einschenken; ~ing a: ~ing rain strömende(r) Regen m.

pout [paut] vi schmollen.

poverty ['pɒvətɪ] n Armut f; ~-stricken a verarmt, sehr arm.

powder ['paudə*] n Pulver nt; (cosmetic) Puder m // vt pulverisieren; **to** ~ **one's nose** sich (dat) die Nase

pudern; ~ **compact** n Puderdose f; ~ed **milk** n Milchpulver nt; ~ **room** n Damentoilette f; ~y a pulverig.

power [pauə*] n Macht f (also POL); (ability) Fähigkeit f; (strength) Stärke f; (MATH) Potenz f; (ELEC) Strom m // vt betreiben, antreiben; **to be in** ~ (POL etc) an der Macht sein; ~ **cut**, (US) ~ **failure** n Stromausfall m; ~ed a: ~ed by betrieben mit; ~ful a (person) mächtig; (engine, government) stark; ~less a machtlos; ~ **point** n (Brit) elektrische(r) Anschluß m; ~ **station** n Elektrizitätswerk nt.

p.p. abbr (= per procurationem): ~ J. Smith i.A. J. Smith.

PR abbr of **public relations.**

practicable ['præktɪkəbl] a durchführbar.

practical a, ~ly ad ['præktɪkəl, -ɪ] praktisch; ~ity [-'kælɪtɪ] n (of person) praktische Veranlagung f; (of situation etc) Durchführbarkeit f; ~ **joke** n Streich m.

practice ['præktɪs] n Übung f; (reality) Praxis f; (custom) Brauch m; (in business) Usus m; (doctor's, lawyer's) Praxis f // vti (US) = **practise; in** ~ (in reality) in der Praxis; **out of** ~ außer Übung.

practise, (US) **practice** ['præktɪs] vt üben; (profession) ausüben // vi (sich) üben; (doctor, lawyer) praktizieren.

practising, (US) **practicing** ['præktɪsɪŋ] a praktizierend; (Christian etc) aktiv.

practitioner [præk'tɪʃənə*] n praktische(r) Arzt m.

pragmatic [præg'mætɪk] a pragmatisch.

prairie ['prɛərɪ] n Prärie f, Steppe f.

praise [preɪz] n Lob nt // vt loben; ~worthy a lobenswert.

pram [præm] n (Brit) Kinderwagen m.

prance [prɑːns] vi (horse) tänzeln; (person) stolzieren; (gaily) herumhüpfen.

prank [præŋk] n Streich m.

prattle ['prætl] vi schwatzen, plappern.

prawn [prɔːn] n Garnele f; Krabbe f.

pray [preɪ] vi beten; ~er [prɛə*] n Gebet nt.

preach [priːtʃ] vi predigen; ~er n Prediger m.

preamble [priː'æmbl] n Einleitung f.

precarious [prɪ'kɛərɪəs] a prekär, unsicher.

precaution [prɪ'kɔːʃən] n (Vorsichts)maßnahme f.

precede [prɪ'siːd] vti vorausgehen (+dat); ~nce ['presɪdəns] n Vorrang m; ~nt ['presɪdənt] n Präzedenzfall m.

preceding [prɪ'siːdɪŋ] a vorhergehend.

precept ['priːsept] n Gebot nt, Regel f.

precinct ['priːsɪŋkt] n (US: district) Bezirk m; (round building): ~s Gelände nt; (area, environs): ~s Umgebung f;

pedestrian ~ Fußgängerzone *f*; **shopping** ~ Geschäftsviertel *nt*.

precious ['preʃəs] *a* kostbar, wertvoll; (*affected*) preziös, geziert.

precipice ['presipis] *n* Abgrund *m*.

precipitate [prɪ'sɪpɪtɪt] *a* überstürzt, übereilt // *vt* [prɪ'sɪpɪteɪt] hinunterstürzen; (*events*) heraufbeschwören.

precise *a*, ~**ly** *ad* [prɪ'saɪs, -lɪ] genau, präzis; **precision** [-'sɪʒən] *n* Präzision *f*.

preclude [prɪ'kluːd] *vt* ausschließen.

precocious [prɪ'kəʊʃəs] *a* frühreif.

preconceived ['priːkən'siːvd] *a* (*idea*) vorgefaßt.

precondition ['priːkən'dɪʃən] *n* Vorbedingung *f*, Voraussetzung *f*.

precursor [prɪ'kɜːsə*] *n* Vorläufer *m*.

predator ['predətə*] *n* Raubtier *nt*.

predecessor ['priːdɪsesə*] *n* Vorgänger *m*.

predestination [priːdestɪ'neɪʃən] *n* Vorherbestimmung *f*.

predicament [prɪ'dɪkəmənt] *n* mißliche Lage *f*.

predict [prɪ'dɪkt] *vt* voraussagen; ~**able** *a* vorhersagbar; ~**ion** [prɪ'dɪkʃən] *n* Voraussage *f*.

predominantly [prɪ'dɒmɪnəntlɪ] *ad* überwiegend, hauptsächlich.

predominate [prɪ'dɒmɪneɪt] *vi* vorherrschen; (*fig also*) überwiegen.

pre-eminent [priː'emɪnənt] *a* hervorragend, herausragend.

pre-empt [priː'empt] *vt* (*action, decision*) vorwegnehmen.

preen [priːn] *vt* putzen; **to** ~ **o.s.** (*person*) sich herausputzen.

prefab ['priːfæb] *n* Fertighaus *nt*.

prefabricated ['priːfæbrɪkeɪtɪd] *a* vorgefertigt, Fertig-.

preface ['prefɪs] *n* Vorwort *nt*.

prefect ['priːfekt] *n* Präfekt *m*; (*SCH*) Aufsichtsschüler(in *f*) *m*.

prefer [prɪ'fɜː*] *vt* vorziehen, lieber mögen; **to** ~ **to do sth etw lieber tun**; ~**able** ['prefərəbl] *a* vorzuziehen(d) (*to dat*); ~**ably** ['prefərəblɪ] *ad* vorzugsweise, am liebsten; ~**ence** ['prefərəns] *n* Präferenz *f*, Vorzug *m*; ~**ential** [prefə'renʃəl] *a* bevorzugt, Vorzugs-.

prefix ['priːfɪks] *n* Vorsilbe *f*, Präfix *nt*.

pregnancy ['pregnənsɪ] *n* Schwangerschaft *f*.

pregnant ['pregnənt] *a* schwanger.

prejudice ['predʒʊdɪs] *n* (*opinion*) Vorurteil *nt*; (*bias*) Voreingenommenheit *f*; (*harm*) Schaden *m* // *vt* beeinträchtigen; ~**d** *a* (*person*) voreingenommen.

preliminary [prɪ'lɪmɪnərɪ] *a* einleitend, Vor-.

prelude ['preljuːd] *n* Vorspiel *nt*; (*fig also*) Auftakt *m*.

premarital ['priː'mærɪtl] *a* vorehelich.

premature ['premətʃʊə*] *a* vorzeitig, verfrüht; (*birth*) Früh-.

premeditated [priː'medɪteɪtɪd] *a* geplant; (*murder*) vorsätzlich.

premier ['premɪə*] *a* erste(r, s) // *n* Premier *m*.

première [premɪ'ɛə*] *n* Premiere *f*; Uraufführung *f*.

premise ['premɪs] *n* Voraussetzung *f*, Prämisse *f*; ~**s** *pl* Räumlichkeiten *pl*; (*grounds*) Gelände *nt*; **on the** ~**s** im Hause.

premium ['priːmɪəm] *n* Prämie *f*; **to be at a** ~ über pari stehen; ~ **bond** *n* (*Brit*) Prämienanleihe *f*.

premonition [premə'nɪʃən] *n* Vorahnung *f*.

preoccupation [priːɒkjʊ'peɪʃən] *n* Sorge *f*.

preoccupied [priː'ɒkjʊpaɪd] *a* (*look*) geistesabwesend.

prep [prep] *n* (*SCH: study*) Hausaufgabe *f*; ~ **school** *n* = **preparatory school**.

prepaid ['priːˈpeɪd] *a* vorausbezahlt; (*letter*) frankiert.

preparation ['prepə'reɪʃən] *n* Vorbereitung *f*.

preparatory [prɪ'pærətərɪ] *a* Vor(bereitungs)-; ~ **school** *n* private Vorbereitungsschule für die Public School in Großbritannien oder die Hochschule in den USA.

prepare [prɪ'pɛə*] *vt* vorbereiten (*for* auf +*acc*) // *vi* sich vorbereiten; **to be** ~**d to ... bereit sein zu ...**

preponderance [prɪ'pɒndərəns] *n* Übergewicht *nt*.

preposition [prepə'zɪʃən] *n* Präposition *f*, Verhältniswort *nt*.

preposterous [prɪ'pɒstərəs] *a* absurd.

prerequisite ['priːˈrekwɪzɪt] *n* (unerläßliche) Voraussetzung *f*.

prerogative [prɪ'rɒgətɪv] *n* Vorrecht *nt*.

Presbyterian [prezbɪ'tɪərɪən] *a* presbyterianisch // *n* Presbyterier(in *f*) *m*.

preschool ['priːskuːl] *a* Vorschul-.

prescribe [prɪs'kraɪb] *vt* vorschreiben; (*MED*) verschreiben.

prescription [prɪs'krɪpʃən] *n* (*MED*) Rezept *nt*.

presence ['prezns] *n* Gegenwart *f*; ~ **of mind** *n* Geistesgegenwart *f*.

present ['preznt] *a* (*here*) anwesend; (*current*) gegenwärtig // *n* Gegenwart *f*; (*gift*) Geschenk *nt* // *vt* [prɪ'zent] vorlegen; (*introduce*) vorstellen; (*show*) zeigen; (*give*): **to** ~ **sb with sth jdm etw** überreichen; **at** ~ im Augenblick; ~**able** [prɪ'zentəbl] *a* präsentabel; ~**ation** *n* Überreichung *f*; ~-**day** *a* heutig; ~**er** *n* (*RADIO, TV*) Moderator(in *f*) *m*; ~**ly** *ad* bald; (*at present*) im Augenblick.

preservation [prezə'veɪʃən] *n* Erhaltung *f*.

preservative [prɪˈzɜːvətɪv] n Konservierungsmittel nt.
preserve [prɪˈzɜːv] vt erhalten; (food) einmachen // n (jam) Eingemachte(s) nt; (hunting) Schutzgebiet nt.
preside [prɪˈzaɪd] vi den Vorsitz haben.
presidency [ˈprezɪdənsɪ] n (POL) Präsidentschaft f.
president [ˈprezɪdənt] n Präsident m; ~ial [prezɪˈdenʃəl] a Präsidenten-; (election) Präsidentschafts-; (system) Präsidial-.
press [pres] n Presse f; (printing house) Druckerei f // vt drücken; (iron) bügeln; (urge) (be)drängen // vi (push) drücken; to be ~ed for time unter Zeitdruck stehen; to ~ for sth drängen auf etw (acc); ~ on vi vorwärtsdrängen; ~ agency n Presseagentur f; ~ conference n Pressekonferenz f; ~ing a dringend; ~-stud n (Brit) Druckknopf m; ~-up n (Brit) Liegestütz m.
pressure [ˈpreʃə*] n Druck m; ~ cooker n Schnellkochtopf m; ~ gauge n Druckmesser m.
pressurized [ˈpreʃəraɪzd] a Druck-.
prestigious [presˈtɪdʒəs] a Prestige-.
presumably [prɪˈzjuːməblɪ] ad vermutlich.
presume [prɪˈzjuːm] vti annehmen; to ~ to do sth sich erlauben, etw zu tun.
presumption [prɪˈzʌmpʃən] n Annahme f.
presumptuous [prɪˈzʌmptjuəs] a anmaßend.
presuppose [priːsəˈpəuz] vt voraussetzen.
pretence, (US) pretense [prɪˈtens] n Vorgabe f, Vortäuschung f; (false claim) Vorwand m.
pretend [prɪˈtend] vt vorgeben, so tun als ob ... // vi so tun; to ~ to sth Anspruch erheben auf etw (acc).
pretense [prɪˈtens] n (US) = pretence.
pretension [prɪˈtenʃən] n Anspruch m; (impudent claim) Anmaßung f.
pretentious [prɪˈtenʃəs] a angeberisch.
pretext [ˈpriːtekst] n Vorwand m.
pretty [ˈprɪtɪ] a hübsch // ad (col) ganz schön.
prevail [prɪˈveɪl] vi siegen (against, over über +acc); (custom) vorherrschen; to ~ (up)on sb to do sth jdn dazu bewegen, etw zu tun; ~ing a vorherrschend.
prevalent [ˈprevələnt] a vorherrschend.
prevent [prɪˈvent] vt (stop) verhindern, verhüten; to ~ sb from doing sth jdn (daran) hindern, etw zu tun; ~ative n Vorbeugungsmittel nt; ~ion [prɪˈvenʃən] n Verhütung f, Schutz m (of gegen); ~ive a vorbeugend, Schutz-.
preview [ˈpriːvjuː] n private Voraufführung f; (trailer) Vorschau f.
previous [ˈpriːvɪəs] a früher, vorherig;

~ly ad früher.
prewar [ˈpriːˈwɔː*] a Vorkriegs-.
prey [preɪ] n Beute f; ~ on vt Jagd machen auf (+acc); it was ~ing on his mind es quälte sein Gewissen.
price [praɪs] n Preis m; (value) Wert m // vt (label) auszeichnen; ~less a (lit, fig) unbezahlbar; ~ list n Preisliste f.
prick [prɪk] n Stich m // vti stechen; to ~ up one's ears die Ohren spitzen.
prickle [ˈprɪkl] n Stachel m, Dorn m.
prickly [ˈprɪklɪ] a stachelig; (fig: person) reizbar; ~ heat n Hitzebläschen pl.
pride [praɪd] n Stolz m; (arrogance) Hochmut m // vt: to ~ o.s. on sth auf etw (acc) stolz sein.
priest [priːst] n Priester m; ~ess n Priesterin f; ~hood n Priesteramt nt.
prig [prɪg] n Selbstgefällige(r) mf.
prim [prɪm] a prüde.
primarily [ˈpraɪmərɪlɪ] ad vorwiegend.
primary [ˈpraɪmərɪ] a (main) Haupt-; (SCH) Grund-; ~ school n (Brit) Grundschule f.
prime [praɪm] a erste(r, s); (excellent) erstklassig // vt vorbereiten; (gun) laden; in the ~ of life in der Blüte der Jahre; P~ Minister (P.M.) n Premierminister m, Ministerpräsident m; ~r n Fibel f.
primeval [praɪˈmiːvəl] a vorzeitlich; (forests) Ur-.
primitive [ˈprɪmɪtɪv] a primitiv.
primrose [ˈprɪmrəuz] n (gelbe) Primel f.
primus (stove) [ˈpraɪməs (stəuv)] n ® (Brit) Primuskocher m.
prince [prɪns] n Prinz m; (ruler) Fürst m; **princess** [prɪnˈses] n Prinzessin f; Fürstin f.
principal [ˈprɪnsɪpəl] a Haupt- // n (SCH) (Schul)direktor m, Rektor m; (money) (Grund)kapital nt; ~ity [prɪnsɪˈpælɪtɪ] n Fürstentum nt.
principle [ˈprɪnsəpl] n Grundsatz m, Prinzip nt; in ~ im Prinzip; on ~ aus Prinzip, prinzipiell.
print [prɪnt] n Druck m; (made by feet, fingers) Abdruck m; (PHOT) Abzug m // vt drucken; (name) in Druckbuchstaben schreiben; (Photo) abziehen; out of ~ vergriffen; ~ed matter n Drucksache f; ~er n Drucker m; ~ing n Drucken nt; (of photos) Abziehen nt; ~out n (COMPUT) Ausdruck m.
prior [ˈpraɪə*] a früher // n Prior m; ~ to sth vor etw (dat); ~ to going abroad, she had ... bevor sie ins Ausland ging, hatte sie ...
priority [praɪˈɒrɪtɪ] n Vorrang m; Priorität f.
prise [praɪz] vt: to ~ open aufbrechen.
prison [ˈprɪzn] n Gefängnis nt // a Gefängnis-; (system etc) Strafvollzugs-; ~er n Gefangene(r) mf.

pristine ['prɪstiːn] a makellos.

privacy ['prɪvəsɪ] n Ungestörtheit f, Ruhe f; Privatleben nt.

private ['praɪvɪt] a privat, Privat-; (secret) vertraulich, geheim // n einfache(r) Soldat m; '~' (on envelope) persönlich; in ~ privat, unter vier Augen; ~ **enterprise** n Privatunternehmen nt; ~ **eye** n Privatdetektiv m; ~**ly** ad privat; vertraulich, geheim; ~ **property** n Privatbesitz m; ~ **school** n Privatschule f; **privatize** vt privatisieren.

privet ['prɪvɪt] n Liguster m.

privilege ['prɪvɪlɪdʒ] n Privileg nt; ~**d** a bevorzugt, privilegiert.

privy ['prɪvɪ] a geheim, privat; **P~ Council** n Geheime(r) Staatsrat m.

prize [praɪz] n Preis m // a (example) erstklassig; (idiot) Voll- // vt (hoch)schätzen; ~ **giving** n Preisverteilung f; ~**winner** n Preisträger(in f) m.

pro [prəʊ] n (professional) Profi m; the ~s and cons pl das Für und Wider.

probability [prɒbə'bɪlɪtɪ] n Wahrscheinlichkeit f.

probable a, **probably** ad ['prɒbəbl, -blɪ] wahrscheinlich.

probation [prə'beɪʃən] n Probe(zeit) f; (JUR) Bewährung f; on ~ auf Probe; auf Bewährung.

probe [prəʊb] n Sonde f; (enquiry) Untersuchung f // vti erforschen.

problem ['prɒbləm] n Problem nt; ~**atic** [prɒblɪ'mætɪk] a problematisch.

procedure [prə'siːdʒə*] n Verfahren nt.

proceed [prə'siːd] vi (advance) vorrücken; (start) anfangen; (carry on) fortfahren; (set about) vorgehen; ~**ings** pl Verfahren nt; ~**s** ['prəʊsiːdz] pl Erlös m.

process ['prəʊses] n Prozeß m; (method) Verfahren nt // vt bearbeiten; (food) verarbeiten; (film) entwickeln; ~**ing** n (PHOT) Entwickeln nt.

procession [prə'seʃən] n Prozession f, Umzug m; funeral ~ Trauerprozession f.

proclaim [prə'kleɪm] vt verkünden.

proclamation [prɒklə'meɪʃən] n Verkündung f.

procrastinate [prəʊ'kræstɪneɪt] vi zaudern.

procreation [prəʊkrɪ'eɪʃən] n (Er)zeugung f.

procure [prə'kjʊə*] vt beschaffen.

prod [prɒd] vt stoßen // n Stoß m.

prodigal ['prɒdɪgəl] a verschwenderisch (of mit).

prodigious [prə'dɪdʒəs] a gewaltig; (wonderful) wunderbar.

prodigy ['prɒdɪdʒɪ] n Wunder nt.

produce n ['prɒdjuːs] (AGR) (Boden)produkte pl, (Natur)erzeugnis nt // vt [prə'djuːs] herstellen, produzieren; (cause) hervorrufen; (farmer) erzeugen;

(yield) liefern, bringen; (play) inszenieren; ~**r** n Erzeuger m, Hersteller m, Produzent m (also CINE).

product ['prɒdʌkt] n Produkt nt, Erzeugnis nt.

production [prə'dʌkʃən] n Produktion f, Herstellung f; (thing) Erzeugnis nt, Produkt nt; (THEAT) Inszenierung f; ~ **line** n Fließband nt.

productive [prə'dʌktɪv] a produktiv; (fertile) ertragreich, fruchtbar.

productivity [prɒdʌk'tɪvɪtɪ] n Produktivität f.

profess [prə'fes] vt bekennen; (show) zeigen; (claim to be) vorgeben.

profession [prə'feʃən] n Beruf m; (declaration) Bekenntnis nt; ~**al** [prə'feʃənl] n Fachmann m; (SPORT) Berufsspieler(in f) m // a Berufs-; (expert) fachlich; (player) professionell.

professor [prə'fesə*] n Professor m.

proficiency [prə'fɪʃənsɪ] n Können nt.

proficient [prə'fɪʃənt] a fähig.

profile ['prəʊfaɪl] n Profil nt; (fig: report) Kurzbiographie f.

profit ['prɒfɪt] n Gewinn m // vi profitieren (by, from von); ~**ability** [prɒfɪtə'bɪlɪtɪ] n Rentabilität f; ~**able** a einträglich, rentabel.

profiteering [prɒfɪ'tɪərɪŋ] n Profitmacherei f.

profound [prə'faʊnd] a tief.

profuse [prə'fjuːs] a überreich; ~**ly** ad überschwenglich; (sweat) reichlich.

profusion [prə'fjuːʒən] n Überfülle f, Überfluß m (of an +dat).

progeny ['prɒdʒɪnɪ] n Nachkommenschaft f.

programme, (US) **program** ['prəʊgræm] n Programm nt // vt planen; (computer) programmieren.

programmer ['prəʊgræmə*] n Programmierer(in f) m.

programming, (US) **programing** ['prəʊgræmɪŋ] n Programmieren nt.

progress ['prəʊgres] n Fortschritt m // vi [prə'gres] fortschreiten, weitergehen; in ~ im Gang; ~**ion** [prə'greʃən] n Folge f; ~**ive** [prə'gresɪv] a fortschrittlich, progressiv.

prohibit [prə'hɪbɪt] vt verbieten; to ~ sb from doing sth jdm untersagen, etw zu tun; ~**ion** [prəʊɪ'bɪʃən] n Verbot nt; (US) Alkoholverbot nt, Prohibition f; ~**ive** a (price etc) unerschwinglich.

project n ['prɒdʒekt] n Projekt nt // v [prə'dʒekt] vt vorausplanen; (film etc) projizieren; (personality, voice) zum Tragen bringen // vi (stick out) hervorragen, (her)vorstehen.

projectile [prə'dʒektaɪl] n Geschoß nt.

projection [prə'dʒekʃən] n Projektion f; (sth prominent) Vorsprung m.

projector [prə'dʒektə*] n Projektor m.

proletariat [prəʊlə'tɛərɪət] n Proletariat

nt.

proliferate [prə'lıfəreıt] *vi* sich vermehren.

prolific [prə'lıfık] *a* fruchtbar; *(author etc)* produktiv.

prologue ['prəʊlɒg] *n* Prolog *m*; *(event)* Vorspiel *nt.*

prolong [prə'lɒŋ] *vt* verlängern.

prom [prɒm] *n abbr of* **promenade** *and* **promenade concert** // *n (US: college ball)* Studentenball *m.*

promenade [prɒmı'nɑːd] *n* Promenade *f*; ~ **concert** *n* Promenadenkonzert *nt.*

prominence ['prɒmınəns] *n* (große) Bedeutung *f.*

prominent ['prɒmınənt] *a* bedeutend; *(politician)* prominent; *(easily seen)* herausragend, auffallend.

promiscuous [prə'mıskjʊəs] *a* lose.

promise ['prɒmıs] *n* Versprechen *nt*; *(hope)* Aussicht *f (of* auf + *acc)* // *vti* versprechen.

promising ['prɒmısıŋ] *a* vielversprechend.

promontory ['prɒməntrı] *n* Vorsprung *m.*

promote [prə'məʊt] *vt* befördern; *(help on)* fördern, unterstützen; ~**r** *n (in sport, entertainment)* Veranstalter *m*; *(for charity etc)* Organisator *m.*

promotion [prə'məʊʃən] *n (in rank)* Beförderung *f*; *(furtherance)* Förderung *f*; *(COMM)* Werbung *f (of* für).

prompt [prɒmpt] *a* prompt, schnell // *ad (punctually)* genau // *n (COMPUT)* Meldung *f* // *vt* veranlassen; *(THEAT)* soufflieren (+ *dat)*; **to ~ sb to do sth** jdn dazu veranlassen, etw zu tun; ~**ly** *ad* sofort.

prone [prəʊn] *a* hingestreckt; **to be ~ to** sth zu etw neigen.

prong [prɒŋ] *n* Zinke *f.*

pronoun ['prəʊnaʊn] *n* Fürwort *nt.*

pronounce [prə'naʊns] *vt* aussprechen; *(JUR)* verkünden // *vi (give an opinion)* sich äußern (*on* zu); ~**d** *a* ausgesprochen; ~**ment** *n* Erklärung *f.*

pronunciation [prənʌnsı'eıʃən] *n* Aussprache *f.*

proof [pruːf] *n* Beweis *m*; *(PRINT)* Korrekturfahne *f*; *(of alcohol)* Alkoholgehalt *m* // *a* sicher.

prop [prɒp] *n* Stütze *f (also fig)*; *(THEAT)* Requisit *nt* // *vt (also:* ~ *up)* (ab)stützen.

propaganda [prɒpə'gændə] *n* Propaganda *f.*

propagate ['prɒpəgeıt] *vt* fortpflanzen; *(news)* propagieren, verbreiten.

propel [prə'pel] *v* (an)treiben; ~**ler** *n* Propeller *m*; ~**ling pencil** *n* Drehbleistift *m.*

propensity [prə'pensıtı] *n* Tendenz *f.*

proper ['prɒpə*] *a* richtig; *(seemly)* schicklich; ~**ly** *ad* richtig; ~ **noun** *n*

Eigenname *m.*

property ['prɒpətı] *n* Eigentum *nt*; *(quality)* Eigenschaft *f*; *(land)* Grundbesitz *m*; ~ **owner** *n* Grundbesitzer *m.*

prophecy ['prɒfısı] *n* Prophezeiung *f.*

prophesy ['prɒfısaı] *vt* prophezeien.

prophet ['prɒfıt] *n* Prophet *m.*

proportion [prə'pɔːʃən] *n* Verhältnis *nt*; *(share)* Teil *m* // *vt* abstimmen (*to* auf +*acc)*; ~**al** *a* proportional; ~**ate** *a* verhältnismäßig.

proposal [prə'pəʊzl] *n* Vorschlag *m*; *(of marriage)* Heiratsantrag *m.*

propose [prə'pəʊz] *vt* vorschlagen; *(toast)* ausbringen // *vi (offer marriage)* einen Heiratsantrag machen; **to ~ to do** sth beabsichtigen, etw zu tun.

proposition [prɒpə'zıʃən] *n* Angebot *nt*; *(statement)* Satz *m.*

proprietor [prə'praıətə*] *n* Besitzer *m*, Eigentümer *m.*

propriety [prə'praıətı] *n* Anstand *m.*

pro rata [prəʊ'rɑːtə] *ad* anteilmäßig.

prose [prəʊz] *n* Prosa *f.*

prosecute ['prɒsıkjuːt] *vt* (strafrechtlich) verfolgen.

prosecution [prɒsı'kjuːʃən] *n (JUR)* strafrechtliche Verfolgung *f*; *(party)* Anklage *f.*

prosecutor ['prɒsıkjuːtə*] *n* Vertreter *m* der Anklage; **Public P~** *n* Staatsanwalt *m.*

prospect ['prɒspekt] *n* Aussicht *f* // *v* [prəs'pekt] *vt* auf Bodenschätze hin untersuchen // *vi* suchen *(for* nach); ~**ing** [prəs'pektıŋ] *n (for minerals)* Suche *f*; ~**ive** [prəs'pektıv] *a* möglich; ~**or** [prəs'pektə*] *n* (Gold)sucher *m*; ~**us** [prəs'pektəs] *n* (Werbe)prospekt *m.*

prosper ['prɒspə*] *vi* blühen, gedeihen; *(person)* erfolgreich sein; ~**ity** [prɒs'perıtı] *n* Wohlstand *m*; ~**ous** *a* wohlhabend, reich.

prostitute ['prɒstıtjuːt] *n* Prostituierte *f.*

prostrate ['prɒstreıt] *a* ausgestreckt (liegend); ~ **with grief/exhaustion** von Schmerz/Erschöpfung übermannt.

protagonist [prəʊ'tægənıst] *n* Hauptperson *f*, Held *m.*

protect [prə'tekt] *vt* (be)schützen; ~**ion** [prə'tekʃən] *n* Schutz *m*; ~**ive** *a* Schutz-, (be)schützend.

protégé ['prɒteʒeı] *n* Schützling *m.*

protein ['prəʊtiːn] *n* Protein *nt*, Eiweiß *nt.*

protest ['prəʊtest] *n* Protest *m* // *v* [prə'test] *vi* protestieren *(against* gegen) // *vt (affirm)* beteuern.

Protestant ['prɒtıstənt] *a* protestantisch // *n* Protestant(in *f*) *m.*

protracted [prə'træktıd] *a* sich hinziehend.

protrude [prə'truːd] *vi* (her)vorstehen.

proud [praʊd] *a* stolz *(of* auf +*acc).*

prove [pruːv] vt beweisen // vi: to ~ (to be) correct sich als richtig erweisen; to ~ o.s. sich bewähren.

proverb ['prɒvɜːb] n Sprichwort nt; ~ial [prə'vɜːbɪəl] a sprichwörtlich.

provide [prə'vaɪd] vt versehen; (supply) besorgen; to ~ sb with sth jdn mit etw versorgen; ~ for vt sorgen für; (emergency) Vorkehrungen treffen für; ~d (that) cj vorausgesetzt (, daß); **Providence** ['prɒvɪdəns] n die Vorsehung.

providing [prə'vaɪdɪŋ] cj vorausgesetzt (, daß).

province ['prɒvɪns] n Provinz f; (division of work) Bereich m.

provincial [prə'vɪnʃəl] a provinziell, Provinz-.

provision [prə'vɪʒən] n Vorkehrung f; (condition) Bestimmung f; ~s pl (food) Vorräte pl, Proviant m; ~al a provisorisch.

proviso [prə'vaɪzəʊ] n Bedingung f.

provoke [prə'vəʊk] vt provozieren; (cause) hervorrufen.

prow [praʊ] n Bug m.

prowess ['praʊes] n überragende(s) Können nt.

prowl [praʊl] vi herumstreichen; (animal) schleichen // n: on the ~ umherstreifend; ~er n Eindringling m.

proximity [prɒk'sɪmɪtɪ] n Nähe f.

proxy ['prɒksɪ] n (Stell)vertreter m; (document) Vollmacht f; by ~ durch einen Stellvertreter.

prudence ['pruːdəns] n Umsicht f.

prudent ['pruːdənt] a klug, umsichtig.

prudish ['pruːdɪʃ] a prüde.

prune [pruːn] n Backpflaume f // vt ausputzen; (fig) zurechtstutzen.

pry [praɪ] vi seine Nase stecken (into in +acc).

PS abbr (= postscript) PS.

pseudo- ['sjuːdəʊ] pref Pseudo-; **pseudonym** ['sjuːdənɪm] n Pseudonym nt, Deckname m.

psychiatrist [saɪ'kaɪətrɪst] n Psychiater m.

psychic ['saɪkɪk] a (also: ~al) übersinnlich; (person) paranormal begabt.

psychoanalyse, (US) **psychoanalyze** [saɪkəʊ'ænəlaɪz] vt psychoanalytisch behandeln.

psychoanalyst [saɪkəʊ'ænəlɪst] n Psychoanalytiker(in f) m.

psychological [saɪkə'lɒdʒɪkəl] a psychologisch.

psychologist [saɪ'kɒlədʒɪst] n Psychologe m, Psychologin f.

psychology [saɪ'kɒlədʒɪ] n Psychologie f.

PTO abbr (= please turn over).

pub [pʌb] n abbr (= public house) Kneipe f.

pubic ['pjuːbɪk] a Scham-.

public ['pʌblɪk] a öffentlich // n (also:

general ~) Öffentlichkeit f; in ~ in der Öffentlichkeit; ~ address system **(P.A.)** n Lautsprecheranlage f; ~ly ad öffentlich.

publican ['pʌblɪkən] n Wirt m.

publication [pʌblɪ'keɪʃən] n Veröffentlichung f.

public: ~ company n Aktiengesellschaft f; ~ convenience n (Brit) öffentliche Toiletten pl; ~ holiday n gesetzliche(r) Feiertag m; ~ house n (Brit) Lokal nt, Kneipe f.

publicity [pʌb'lɪsɪtɪ] n Publicity f, Werbung f.

publicize ['pʌblɪsaɪz] vt bekannt machen; (advertise) Publicity machen für.

public: ~ opinion n öffentliche Meinung f; ~ relations (PR) pl Public Relations pl; ~ school n (Brit) Privatschule f; (US) staatliche Schule f; ~ spirited a mit Gemeinschaftssinn; ~ transport n öffentliche Verkehrsmittel pl.

publish ['pʌblɪʃ] vt veröffentlichen; (event) bekanntgeben; ~er n Verleger m; ~ing n (business) Verlagswesen nt.

puce [pjuːs] a violettbraun.

pucker ['pʌkə*] vt (face) verziehen; (lips) kräuseln.

pudding ['pʊdɪŋ] n (Brit: course) Nachtisch m; Pudding m; black ~ ≈ Blutwurst f.

puddle ['pʌdl] n Pfütze f.

puff [pʌf] n (of wind etc) Stoß m; (cosmetic) Puderquaste f // vt blasen, pusten; (pipe) paffen // vi keuchen, schnaufen; (smoke) paffen; to ~ out smoke Rauch ausstoßen; ~ed a (col: out of breath) außer Puste.

puff pastry, (US) **puff paste** ['pʌf'peɪstrɪ, 'pʌf'peɪst] n Blätterteig m.

puffy ['pʌfɪ] a aufgedunsen.

pull [pʊl] n Ruck m; (influence) Beziehung f // vt ziehen; (trigger) abdrücken // vi ziehen; to ~ sb's leg jdn auf den Arm nehmen; to ~ to pieces (lit) in Stücke reißen; (fig) verreißen; to ~ one's punches sich zurückhalten; to ~ one's weight sich in die Riemen legen; to ~ o.s. together sich zusammenreißen; ~ apart vt (break) zerreißen; (dismantle) auseinandernehmen; (fighters) trennen; ~ down vt (house) abreißen; ~ in vi hineinfahren; (stop) anhalten; (RAIL) einfahren; ~ off vt (deal etc) abschließen; ~ out vi (car) herausfahren; (fig: partner) aussteigen // vt herausziehen; ~ over vi (AUT) an die Seite fahren; ~ round, ~ through vi durchkommen; ~ up vi anhalten // vt (uproot) herausreißen; (stop) anhalten.

pulley ['pʊlɪ] n Rolle f, Flaschenzug m.

pullover ['pʊləʊvə*] n Pullover m.

pulp [pʌlp] n Brei m; (of fruit) Fruchtfleisch nt.

pulpit ['pʊlpɪt] n Kanzel f.
pulsate [pʌl'seɪt] vi pulsieren.
pulse [pʌls] n Puls m.
pummel ['pʌml] vt mit den Fäusten bearbeiten.
pump [pʌmp] n Pumpe f; (shoe) leichter (Tanz)schuh m // vt pumpen; ~ up vt (tyre) aufpumpen.
pumpkin ['pʌmpkɪn] n Kürbis m.
pun [pʌn] n Wortspiel nt.
punch [pʌntʃ] n (tool) Locher m; (blow) (Faust)schlag m; (drink) Punsch m, Bowle f // vt lochen; (strike) schlagen, boxen; ~line n Pointe f; ~-up n (Brit col) Keilerei f.
punctual ['pʌŋktjʊəl] a pünktlich.
punctuate ['pʌŋktjʊeɪt] vt mit Satzzeichen versehen; (fig) unterbrechen.
punctuation [pʌŋktju'eɪʃən] n Zeichensetzung f, Interpunktion f.
puncture ['pʌŋktʃə*] n Loch nt; (AUT) Reifenpanne f // vt durchbohren.
pundit ['pʌndɪt] n Gelehrte(r) m.
pungent ['pʌndʒənt] a scharf.
punish ['pʌnɪʃ] vt bestrafen; (in boxing etc) übel zurichten; ~ment n Strafe f; (action) Bestrafung f.
punk [pʌŋk] n (also: ~ rocker) Punker(in f) m; (also: ~ rock) Punk m; (US col: hoodlum) Ganove m.
punt [pʌnt] n Stechkahn m.
punter ['pʌntə*] n (Brit: better) Wetter m.
puny ['pjuːnɪ] a kümmerlich.
pup [pʌp] n = **puppy**.
pupil ['pjuːpl] n Schüler(in f) m; (in eye) Pupille f.
puppet ['pʌpɪt] n Puppe f; Marionette f.
puppy ['pʌpɪ] n junge(r) Hund m.
purchase ['pɜːtʃɪs] n Kauf m; (grip) Halt m // vt kaufen, erwerben; ~r n Käufer(in f) m.
pure [pjʊə*] a rein (also fig); ~ly ['pjʊəlɪ] ad rein.
purgatory ['pɜːgətərɪ] n Fegefeuer nt.
purge [pɜːdʒ] n Säuberung f (also POL); (medicine) Abführmittel nt // vt reinigen; (body) entschlacken.
purify ['pjʊərɪfaɪ] vt reinigen.
purity ['pjʊərɪtɪ] n Reinheit f.
purl [pɜːl] n linke Masche f.
purple ['pɜːpl] a violett; (face) dunkelrot.
purport [pɜː'pɔːt] vi vorgeben.
purpose ['pɜːpəs] n Zweck m, Ziel nt; (of person) Absicht f; on ~ absichtlich; ~ful a zielbewußt, entschlossen.
purr [pɜː*] n Schnurren nt // vi schnurren.
purse [pɜːs] n Portemonnaie nt, Geldbeutel m // vt (lips) zusammenpressen, schürzen.
purser ['pɜːsə*] n Zahlmeister m.
pursue [pə'sjuː] vt verfolgen; (study) nachgehen (+dat); ~r n Verfolger m.

pursuit [pə'sjuːt] n Verfolgung f; (occupation) Beschäftigung f.
purveyor [pɜː'veɪə*] n Lieferant m.
pus [pʌs] n Eiter m.
push [pʊʃ] n Stoß m, Schub m; (MIL) Vorstoß m // vt stoßen, schieben; (button) drücken; (idea) durchsetzen // vi stoßen, schieben; ~ aside vt beiseiteschieben; ~ off vi (col) abschieben; ~ on vi weitermachen; ~ through vt durchdrücken; (policy) durchsetzen; ~ up vt (total) erhöhen; (prices) hochtreiben; ~chair n (Brit) (Kinder)sportwagen m; ~over n (col) Kinderspiel nt; ~-up n (US: press-up) Liegestütz m; ~y a (col) aufdringlich.
puss [pʊs], **pussy(-cat)** ['pʊsɪ(kæt)] n Mieze(katze) f.
put [pʊt], pt, pp put vt setzen, stellen, legen; (express) ausdrücken, sagen; (write) schreiben; ~ about vi (turn back) wenden // vt (spread) verbreiten; ~ across vt (explain) erklären; ~ away vt weglegen; (store) beiseitelegen; ~ back vt zurückstellen or -legen; ~ by vt zurücklegen, sparen; ~ down vt hinstellen or -legen; (rebellion) niederschlagen; (animal) einschläfern; (in writing) niederschreiben; ~ forward vt (idea) vorbringen; (clock) vorstellen; ~ in vt (application, complaint) einreichen; ~ off vt verschieben; (discourage) abbringen von; ~ on vt (clothes etc) anziehen; (light etc) anschalten, anmachen; (play etc) aufführen; (brake) anziehen; ~ out vt (hand etc) (her)ausstrecken; (news, rumour) verbreiten; (light etc) ausschalten, ausmachen; ~ up vt (tent) aufstellen; (building) errichten; (price) erhöhen; (person) unterbringen; to ~ up with sich abfinden mit.
putrid ['pjuːtrɪd] a faul.
putt [pʌt] n (golf) putten // n (golf) Putten nt; ~ing green n Rasenfläche f zum Putten.
putty ['pʌtɪ] n Kitt m; (fig) Wachs nt.
put-up ['pʊtʌp] a: ~ job abgekartete(s) Spiel nt.
puzzle ['pʌzl] n Rätsel nt; (toy) Geduldspiel nt // vt verwirren // vi sich den Kopf zerbrechen.
puzzling ['pʌzlɪŋ] a rätselhaft, verwirrend.
pyjamas [pɪ'dʒɑːməz] npl (Brit) Schlafanzug m, Pyjama m.
pylon ['paɪlən] n Mast m.

Q

quack [kwæk] n Quaken nt; (doctor) Quacksalber m // vi quaken.
quad [kwɒd] abbr of **quadrangle**, **quadruplet**.

quadrangle ['kwɒdræŋgl] n (court) Hof m; (MATH) Viereck nt.

quadruple ['kwɒ'dru:pl] a vierfach // vi sich vervierfachen // vt vervierfachen.

quadruplets [kwɒ'dru:pləts] npl Vierlinge pl.

quagmire ['kwægmaɪə*] n Morast m.

quail [kweɪl] n (bird) Wachtel f // vi (vor Angst) zittern.

quaint [kweɪnt] a kurios; malerisch.

quake [kweɪk] vi beben, zittern // n abbr of **earthquake**.

Quaker ['kweɪkə*] n Quäker(in f) m.

qualification [kwɒlɪfɪ'keɪʃən] n Qualifikation f; (sth which limits) Einschränkung f.

qualified ['kwɒlɪfaɪd] a (competent) qualifiziert; (limited) bedingt.

qualify ['kwɒlɪfaɪ] vt (prepare) befähigen; (limit) einschränken // vi sich qualifizieren (for für); to ~ as a doctor/lawyer sein juristisches/medizinisches Staatsexamen machen.

quality ['kwɒlɪtɪ] n Qualität f; (characteristic) Eigenschaft f.

qualm [kwɑ:m] n Bedenken nt.

quandary ['kwɒndərɪ] n: to be in a ~ in Verlegenheit sein.

quantity ['kwɒntɪtɪ] n Menge f; ~ surveyor n Baukostenkalkulator m.

quarantine ['kwɒrənti:n] n Quarantäne f.

quarrel ['kwɒrəl] n Streit m // vi sich streiten; ~some a streitsüchtig.

quarry ['kwɒrɪ] n Steinbruch m; (animal) Wild nt; (fig) Opfer nt.

quart [kwɔ:t] n Quart nt.

quarter ['kwɔ:tə*] n Viertel nt; (of year) Quartal nt // vt (divide) vierteln; (MIL) einquartieren; ~s pl (esp MIL) Quartier nt; ~ of an hour n Viertelstunde f; ~ final n Viertelfinale nt; ~ly a vierteljährlich; ~master n Quartiermeister m.

quash [kwɒʃ] vt (verdict) aufheben.

quasi- ['kwɑ:zɪ] pref Quasi-.

quaver ['kweɪvə*] n (Brit MUS) Achtelnote f // vi (tremble) zittern.

quay [ki:] n Kai m.

queasy ['kwi:zɪ] a übel.

queen [kwi:n] n Königin f; ~ mother n Königinmutter f.

queer [kwɪə*] a seltsam // n (col: homosexual) Schwule(r) m.

quell [kwel] vt unterdrücken.

quench [kwentʃ] vt (thirst) löschen.

querulous ['kwerʊləs] a nörglerisch.

query ['kwɪərɪ] n (question) (An)frage f; (question mark) Fragezeichen nt // vt in Zweifel ziehen, in Frage stellen.

quest [kwest] n Suche f.

question ['kwestʃən] n Frage f // vt (ask) (be)fragen; (suspect) verhören; (doubt) in Frage stellen, bezweifeln; beyond ~ ohne Frage; out of the ~ ausge-

schlossen; ~able a zweifelhaft; ~ mark n Fragezeichen nt.

questionnaire [kwestʃə'nɛə*] n Fragebogen m.

queue [kju:] n (Brit) n Schlange f // vi (also: ~ up) Schlange stehen.

quibble ['kwɪbl] vi kleinlich sein.

quick [kwɪk] a schnell // n (of nail) Nagelhaut f; cut to the ~ (fig) tief getroffen; be ~! mach schnell!; ~en vt (hasten) beschleunigen // vi sich beschleunigen; ~ly a schnell; ~sand n Treibsand m; ~-witted a schlagfertig.

quid [kwɪd] n (Brit col: £1) Pfund nt.

quiet ['kwaɪət] a (without noise) leise; (peaceful, calm) still, ruhig // n Stille f, Ruhe f // vt, vi (US) = ~en; keep ~! sei still!; ~en (also: ~en down) vi ruhig werden // vt beruhigen; ~ly ad leise, ruhig; ~ness n Ruhe f, Stille f.

quilt [kwɪlt] n (continental ~) Steppdecke f.

quin [kwɪn] abbr of **quintuplet**.

quinine [kwɪ'ni:n] n Chinin nt.

quintuplets [kwɪn'tju:pləts] npl Fünflinge pl.

quip [kwɪp] n witzige Bemerkung f.

quirk [kwɜ:k] n (oddity) Eigenart f.

quit [kwɪt], pt, pp quit or quitted vt verlassen // vi aufhören.

quite [kwaɪt] ad (completely) ganz, völlig; (fairly) ziemlich; ~ a few of them ziemlich viele von ihnen; ~ (so)! richtig!

quits [kwɪts] a quitt; let's call it ~ lassen wir's gut sein.

quiver ['kwɪvə*] vi zittern // n (for arrows) Köcher m.

quiz [kwɪz] n (competition) Quiz nt // vt prüfen; ~zical a fragend.

quorum ['kwɔ:rəm] n beschlußfähige Anzahl f.

quota ['kwəʊtə] n Anteil m; (COMM) Quote f.

quotation [kwəʊ'teɪʃən] n Zitat nt; (price) Kostenvoranschlag m; ~ marks pl Anführungszeichen pl.

quote [kwəʊt] n see quotation // vi (from book) zitieren // vt (from book) zitieren; (price) angeben.

R

rabbi ['ræbaɪ] n Rabbiner m; (title) Rabbi m.

rabbit ['ræbɪt] n Kaninchen nt; ~ hole n Kaninchenbau m; ~ hutch n Kaninchenstall m.

rabble ['ræbl] n Pöbel m.

rabies ['reɪbi:z] n Tollwut f.

RAC n abbr (Brit) of Royal Automobile Club.

raccoon [rə'ku:n] n Waschbär m.

race [reɪs] n (species) Rasse f;

(*competition*) Rennen *nt*; (*on foot also*) Wettlauf *m*; (*rush*) Hetze *f* // *vt* um die Wette laufen mit; (*horses*) laufen lassen // *vi* (*run*) rennen; (*in contest*) am Rennen teilnehmen; ~ **car** *n* (*US*) = **racing car**; ~ **car driver** *n* (*US*) = **racing driver**; ~**course** *n* (*for horses*) Rennbahn *f*; ~**horse** *n* Rennpferd *nt*; ~**track** *n* (*for cars etc*) Rennstrecke *f*.

racial ['reɪʃəl] *a* Rassen-; ~**ist** *a* rassistisch // *n* Rassist *m*.

racing ['reɪsɪŋ] *n* Rennen *nt*; ~ **car** *n* (*Brit*) Rennwagen *m*; ~ **driver** *n* (*Brit*) Rennfahrer *m*.

racism ['reɪsɪzəm] *n* Rassismus *m*.

racist ['reɪsɪst] *n* Rassist *m* // *a* rassistisch.

rack [ræk] *n* Ständer *m*, Gestell *nt* // *vt* plagen; **to go to** ~ **and ruin** verfallen; **to** ~ **one's brains** sich (*dat*) den Kopf zerbrechen.

racket ['rækɪt] *n* (*din*) Krach *m*; (*scheme*) (Schwindel)geschäft *nt*; (*TENNIS*) (Tennis)schläger *m*.

racoon [rə'kuːn] *n* = **raccoon**.

racquet ['rækɪt] *n* = **racket** (*TENNIS*).

racy ['reɪsɪ] *a* gewagt; (*style*) spritzig.

radar ['reɪdɑː*] *n* Radar *nt or m*.

radial ['reɪdɪəl] *a* (*also*: *US*: ~-**ply**) radial.

radiance ['reɪdɪəns] *n* strahlende(r) Glanz *m*.

radiant ['reɪdɪənt] *a* strahlend; (*giving out rays*) Strahlungs-.

radiate ['reɪdɪeɪt] *vti* ausstrahlen; (*roads, lines*) strahlenförmig wegführen.

radiation [reɪdɪ'eɪʃən] *n* (Aus)strahlung *f*.

radiator ['reɪdɪeɪtə*] *n* (*for heating*) Heizkörper *m*; (*AUT*) Kühler *m*.

radical *a*, ~**ly** *ad* ['rædɪkəl, -ɪ] radikal.

radii ['reɪdɪaɪ] *npl of* **radius**.

radio ['reɪdɪəu] *n* Rundfunk *m*, Radio *nt*; (*set*) Radio *nt*, Radioapparat *m*; **on the** ~ im Radio.

radio... ['reɪdɪəu] *pref* Radio-; ~**active** *a* radioaktiv; ~**logy** [reɪdɪ'ɒlədʒɪ] *n* Strahlenkunde *f*.

radio station *n* Rundfunkstation *f*.

radiotherapy ['reɪdɪəu'θerəpɪ] *n* Röntgentherapie *f*.

radish ['rædɪʃ] *n* (*big*) Rettich *m*; (*small*) Radieschen *nt*.

radius ['reɪdɪəs], *pl* **radii** [-ɪaɪ] *n* Radius *m*; (*area*) Umkreis *m*.

RAF *n abbr of* **Royal Air Force**.

raffle ['ræfl] *n* Verlosung *f*, Tombola *f* // *vt* verlosen.

raft [rɑːft] *n* Floß *nt*.

rafter ['rɑːftə*] *n* Dachsparren *m*.

rag [ræg] *n* (*cloth*) Lumpen *m*, Lappen *m*; (*col*: *newspaper*) Käseblatt *nt*; (*Univ*: *for charity*) studentische Sammelaktion *f* // *vt* (*Brit*) auf den Arm nehmen; ~**s** *pl* Lumpen *pl*; ~**-and-**

bone man *n* (*Brit*) = ~**man**; ~ **doll** *n* Flickenpuppe *f*.

rage [reɪdʒ] *n* Wut *f*; (*fashion*) große Mode *f* // *vi* wüten, toben.

ragged ['rægɪd] *a* (*edge*) gezackt; (*clothes*) zerlumpt.

ragman ['rægmæn] *n* Lumpensammler *m*.

raid [reɪd] *n* Überfall *m*; (*MIL*) Angriff *m*; (*by police*) Razzia *f* // *vt* überfallen; ~**er** *n* (*person*) (Bank)räuber *m*.

rail [reɪl] *n* Schiene *f* (*on stair*) Geländer *nt*; (*of ship*) Reling *f*; (*RAIL*) Schiene *f*; ~**s** *pl* Geleise *pl*; **by** ~ per Bahn; ~**ing(s)** *n(pl)* Geländer *nt*; ~**road** *n* (*US*), ~**way** *n* (*Brit*) Eisenbahn *f*; ~**way line** *n* (*Brit*) (Eisen)bahnlinie *f*; (: *track*) Gleis *nt*; ~**wayman** *n* (*Brit*) Eisenbahner *m*; ~**way station** *n* (*Brit*) Bahnhof *m*.

rain [reɪn] *n* Regen *m* // *vti* regnen; **in the** ~ im Regen; **it's** ~**ing** es regnet; ~**bow** *n* Regenbogen *m*; ~**coat** *n* Regenmantel *m*; ~**drop** *n* Regentropfen *m*; ~**fall** *n* Niederschlag *m*; ~**y** *a* (*region, season*) Regen-; (*day*) regnerisch, verregnet.

raise [reɪz] *n* (*esp US*: *increase*) (Gehalts)erhöhung *f* // *vt* (*lift*) (hoch)heben; (*increase*) erhöhen; (*question*) aufwerfen; (*doubts*) äußern; (*funds*) beschaffen; (*family*) großziehen, (*livestock*) züchten; **to** ~ **one's voice** die Stimme erheben.

raisin ['reɪzən] *n* Rosine *f*.

rake [reɪk] *n* Rechen *m*, Harke *f*; (*person*) Wüstling *m* // *vt* rechen, harken; (*with gun*) (mit Feuer) bestreichen; (*search*) (durch)suchen.

rakish ['reɪkɪʃ] *a* verwegen.

rally ['rælɪ] *n* (*POL etc*) Kundgebung *f*; (*AUT*) Rallye *f* // *vt* (*MIL*) sammeln // *vi* Kräfte sammeln; ~ **round** *vti* (sich) scharen um; (*help*) zu Hilfe kommen (+*dat*).

RAM *n abbr* (= *random access memory*) RAM *m*.

ram [ræm] *n* Widder *m*; (*instrument*) Ramme *f* // *vt* (*strike*) rammen; (*stuff*) (hinein)stopfen.

ramble ['ræmbl] *n* Wanderung *f* // *vi* (*talk*) schwafeln; ~**r** *n* Wanderer *m*.

rambling ['ræmblɪŋ] *a* (*speech*) weitschweifig; (*town*) ausgedehnt.

ramp [ræmp] *n* Rampe *f*; **on/off** ~ (*US AUT*) Ein-/Ausfahrt *f*.

rampage [ræm'peɪdʒ] *n*: **to be on the** ~ (*also* ~ *vi*) randalieren.

rampant ['ræmpənt] *a* wild wuchernd.

rampart ['ræmpɑːt] *n* (*Schutz*)wall *m*.

ramshackle ['ræmʃækl] *a* baufällig.

ran [ræn] *pt of* **run**.

ranch [rɑːntʃ] *n* Ranch *f*.

rancid ['rænsɪd] *a* ranzig.

rancour, (*US*) **rancor** ['ræŋkə*] *n* Verbitterung f, Groll m.

random ['rændəm] a ziellos, wahllos // n: at ~ aufs Geratewohl; ~ **access** n (COMPUT) wahlfreie(r) Zugriff m.

randy ['rændɪ] a (Brit col) geil, scharf.

rang [ræŋ] pt of **ring**.

range [reɪndʒ] n Reihe f; (of mountains) Kette f; (COMM) Sortiment nt; (selection) (große) Auswahl f (of an +dat); (reach) (Reich)weite f; (of gun) Schußweite f; (for shooting practice) Schießplatz m; (stove) (großer) Herd m // vt (set in row) anordnen, aufstellen; (roam) durchstreifen // vi: to ~ over (wander) umherstreifen in (+dat); (extend) sich erstrecken auf (+acc); prices ranging from £5 to £10 Preise, die sich zwischen £5 und £10 bewegen; ~r n Förster m.

rank [ræŋk] n (row) Reihe f; (Brit: also: taxi ~) (Taxi)stand m; (MIL) Rang m; (social position) Stand m // vi (have ~) gehören (among zu) // a (strong-smelling) stinkend; (extreme) krass; the ~ and file (fig) die breite Masse.

rankle ['ræŋkl] vi nagen.

ransack ['rænsæk] vt (plunder) plündern; (search) durchwühlen.

ransom ['rænsəm] n Lösegeld nt; to hold sb to ~ jdn gegen Lösegeld festhalten.

rant [rænt] vi hochtrabend reden.

rap [ræp] n Schlag m // vt klopfen.

rape [reɪp] n Vergewaltigung f; (BOT) Raps m // vt vergewaltigen; ~ (seed) oil n Rapsöl nt.

rapid ['ræpɪd] a rasch, schnell; ~s npl Stromschnellen pl; ~ity [rə'pɪdɪtɪ] n Schnelligkeit f; ~ly ad schnell.

rapist ['reɪpɪst] n Vergewaltiger m.

rapport [ræ'pɔː*] n gute(s) Verhältnis nt.

rapture ['ræptʃə*] n Entzücken nt.

rapturous ['ræptʃərəs] a (applause) stürmisch; (expression) verzückt.

rare [rɛə*] a selten, rar; (underdone) nicht durchgebraten.

rarely ['rɛəlɪ] ad selten.

raring ['rɛərɪŋ] a: to be ~ to go (col) es kaum erwarten können, bis es losgeht.

rarity ['rɛərɪtɪ] n Seltenheit f.

rascal ['rɑːskəl] n Schuft m.

rash [ræʃ] a übereilt; (reckless) unbesonnen // n (Haut)ausschlag m.

rasher ['ræʃə*] n Speckscheibe f.

raspberry ['rɑːzbərɪ] n Himbeere f.

rasping ['rɑːspɪŋ] a (noise) kratzend; (voice) krächzend.

rat [ræt] n (animal) Ratte f; (person) Halunke m.

rate [reɪt] n (proportion) Rate f; (price) Tarif m; (speed) Tempo nt // vt (ein)schätzen; ~s pl (Brit) Grundsteuer f; to ~ as für etw halten; ~able value n (Brit) Einheitswert m (als Bemessungsgrundlage); ~payer n (Brit) Steuerzahler(in f) m.

rather ['rɑːðə*] ad (in preference) lieber, eher; (to some extent) ziemlich; I would or I'd ~ go ich würde lieber gehen.

ratify ['rætɪfaɪ] vt bestätigen; (POL) ratifizieren.

rating ['reɪtɪŋ] n Klasse f; (Brit: sailor) Matrose m.

ratio ['reɪʃɪəʊ] n Verhältnis nt; in the ~ of 100 to 1 im Verhältnis 100 zu 1.

ration ['ræʃən] n (usually pl) Ration f // vt rationieren.

rational a, ~ly ad ['ræʃənl, -nəlɪ] rational; ~e [ræʃə'nɑːl] n Grundprinzip nt; ~ize ['ræʃnəlaɪz] vt rationalisieren.

rat race ['rætreɪs] n Konkurrenzkampf m.

rattle ['rætl] n (sound) Rasseln nt; (toy) Rassel f // vi rattern, klappern // vt rasseln mit; ~snake n Klapperschlange f.

raucous ['rɔːkəs] a heiser, rauh.

ravage ['rævɪdʒ] vt verheeren; ~s pl verheerende Wirkungen pl.

rave [reɪv] vi (talk wildly) phantasieren; (rage) toben.

raven ['reɪvn] n Rabe m.

ravenous ['rævənəs] a heißhungrig.

ravine [rə'viːn] n Schlucht f.

raving ['reɪvɪŋ] a: ~ lunatic völlig Wahnsinnige(r) mf.

ravishing ['rævɪʃɪŋ] a atemberaubend.

raw [rɔː] a roh; (tender) wund (gerieben); (inexperienced) unerfahren; to get a ~ deal (col) schlecht wegkommen; ~ material n Rohmaterial nt.

ray [reɪ] n (of light) Strahl m; ~ of hope Hoffnungsschimmer m.

raze [reɪz] vt dem Erdboden gleichmachen.

razor ['reɪzə*] n Rasierapparat m; ~ blade n Rasierklinge f.

Rd abbr of **road**.

re [riː] prep (COMM) betreffs (+ gen).

reach [riːtʃ] n Reichweite f; (of river) Strecke f // vt (arrive at) erreichen; (give) reichen // vi (try to get) langen (for nach); (stretch) sich erstrecken; within ~ (shops etc) in erreichbarer Weite or Entfernung; out of ~ außer Reichweite; ~ out vi die Hand ausstrecken; to ~ out for sth nach etw greifen.

react [riː'ækt] vi reagieren; ~ion [riː'ækʃən] n Reaktion f.

read [riːd] pt, pp read [red] vti lesen; (aloud) vorlesen; ~ out vt vorlesen; ~able a leserlich; (worth ~ing) lesenswert; ~er n (person) Leser(in f) m; (book) Lesebuch nt; ~ership n Leserschaft f.

readily ['redɪlɪ] ad (willingly) bereitwillig; (easily) prompt.

readiness ['redınəs] n (willingness) Bereitwilligkeit f; (being ready) Bereitschaft f; in ~ (prepared) bereit.

reading ['ri:dıŋ] n Lesen nt.

readjust ['ri:ə'dʒʌst] vt neu einstellen // vi (person): to ~ to sich wieder anpassen an (+acc).

ready ['redı] a (prepared, willing) bereit; // ad: ~-cooked vorgekocht // n: at the ~ bereit; ~-made a gebrauchsfertig, Fertig-; (clothes) Konfektions-; ~ money n Bargeld nt; ~ reckoner n Rechentabelle f; ~-to-wear a Konfektions-.

real [rıəl] a wirklich; (actual) eigentlich; (not fake) echt; in ~ terms effektiv; ~ estate n Grundbesitz m; ~istic a, ~istically ad realistisch.

reality [ri:'ælıtı] n Wirklichkeit f, Realität f; in ~ in Wirklichkeit.

realization [rıəlaı'zeıʃən] n (understanding) Erkenntnis f; (fulfilment) Verwirklichung f.

realize ['rıəlaız] vt (understand) begreifen; (make real) verwirklichen; (money) einbringen; I didn't ~ ... ich wußte nicht, ...

really ['rıəlı] ad wirklich.

realm [relm] n Reich nt.

realtor ['rıəltɔː*] n (US) Grundstücksmakler(in f) m.

reap [ri:p] vt ernten.

reappear ['ri:ə'pıə*] vi wieder erscheinen.

rear [rıə*] a hintere(r, s), Rück- // n Rückseite f; (last part) Schluß m // vt (bring up) aufziehen // vi (horse) sich aufbäumen; ~guard n Nachhut f.

rearmament ['ri:'ɑːməmənt] n Wiederaufrüstung f.

rearrange ['ri:ə'reındʒ] vt umordnen.

rear-view mirror ['rıəvjuː-] n Rückspiegel m.

reason ['ri:zn] n (cause) Grund m; (ability to think) Verstand m; (sensible thoughts) Vernunft f // vi (think) denken; (use arguments) argumentieren; to ~ with sb mit jdm diskutieren; it stands to ~ that es ist logisch, daß; ~able a vernünftig; (fairly) ziemlich; ~ed a (argument) durchdacht; ~ing n Urteilen nt; (argumentation) Beweisführung f.

reassurance ['ri:ə'ʃuərəns] n Beruhigung f; (confirmation) Bestätigung f.

reassure ['ri:ə'ʃuə*] vt beruhigen; to ~ sb of sth jdm etw versichern.

reassuring ['ri:ə'ʃuərıŋ] a beruhigend.

rebate ['ri:beıt] n Rückzahlung f.

rebel ['rebl] n Rebell m; ~lion [rı'belıən] n Rebellion f, Aufstand m.

rebirth ['ri:'bɜːθ] n Wiedergeburt f.

rebound [rı'baund] vi zurückprallen // ['ri:baund] n Rückprall m.

rebuff [rı'bʌf] n Abfuhr f // vt abblitzen

lassen.

rebuild ['ri:'bıld] vt irreg wiederaufbauen; (fig) wiederherstellen.

rebuke [rı'bjuːk] n Tadel m // vt tadeln, rügen.

rebut [rı'bʌt] vt widerlegen.

recalcitrant [rı'kælsıtrənt] a widerspenstig.

recall [rı'kɔːl] vt (call back) zurückrufen; (remember) sich erinnern an (+acc) // n Rückruf m.

recant [rı'kænt] vi widerrufen.

recap ['ri:kæp] vti wiederholen.

recapitulate [,ri:kə'pıtjuleıt] vti = recap.

rec'd abbr (= received) Eing.

recede [rı'si:d] vi zurückweichen.

receding [rı'si:dıŋ] a: ~ hair Stirnglatze f.

receipt [rı'si:t] n (document) Quittung f; (receiving) Empfang m; ~s pl Einnahmen pl.

receive [rı'si:v] vt erhalten; (visitors etc) empfangen; ~r n (TEL) Hörer m.

recent ['ri:snt] a vor kurzem (geschehen), neuerlich; (modern) neu; ~ly ad kürzlich, neulich.

receptacle [rı'septəkl] n Behälter m.

reception [rı'sepʃən] n Empfang m; ~ desk n Empfang m; (in hotel) Rezeption f; ~ist n (in hotel) Empfangschef m/-dame f; (MED) Sprechstundenhilfe f.

receptive [rı'septıv] a aufnahmebereit.

recess [rı'ses] n (break) Ferien pl; (hollow) Nische f; ~ion [rı'seʃən] n Rezession f.

recharge ['ri:'tʃɑːdʒ] vt (battery) aufladen.

recipe ['resıpı] n Rezept nt.

recipient [rı'sıpıənt] n Empfänger m.

reciprocal [rı'sıprəkəl] a gegenseitig; (mutual) wechselseitig.

recital [rı'saıtl] n Vortrag m.

recite [rı'saıt] vt vortragen, aufsagen.

reckless ['rekləs] a leichtsinnig; (driving) fahrlässig.

reckon ['rekən] vt (count) (be- or er)rechnen; (estimate) schätzen; (think): I ~ that ... ich nehme an, daß ...; ~ on vt rechnen mit; ~ing n (calculation) Rechnen nt.

reclaim [rı'kleım] vt (land) abgewinnen (from dat); (expenses) zurückverlangen.

reclamation [reklə'meıʃən] n (of land) Gewinnung f.

recline [rı'klaın] vi sich zurücklehnen.

reclining [rı'klaınıŋ] a Liege-.

recluse [rı'kluːs] n Einsiedler m.

recognition [rekəg'nıʃən] n (recognizing) Erkennen nt; (acknowledgement) Anerkennung f; **transformed beyond ~** völlig verändert.

recognizable ['rekəgńaızəbl] a erkennbar.

recognize ['rekəgnaɪz] vt erkennen; (POL, approve) anerkennen; to ~ as anerkennen als; to ~ by erkennen an (+dat).

recoil [rɪ'kɔɪl] vi (in horror) zurückschrecken; (rebound) zurückprallen; (person): to ~ from doing sth davor zurückschrecken, etw zu tun.

recollect [rekə'lekt] vt sich erinnern an (+acc); ~ion n Erinnerung f.

recommend [rekə'mend] vt empfehlen; ~ation n Empfehlung f.

recompense ['rekəmpens] n (compensation) Entschädigung f; (reward) Belohnung f // vt entschädigen; belohnen.

reconcile ['rekənsaɪl] vt (facts) vereinbaren; (people) versöhnen; to ~ o.s. to sth sich mit etw abfinden.

reconciliation [rekənsɪlɪ'eɪʃən] n Versöhnung f.

recondition ['ri:kən'dɪʃən] vt (machine) generalüberholen.

reconnaissance [rɪ'kɒnɪsəns] n Aufklärung f.

reconnoitre, (US) **reconnoiter** [rekə'nɔɪtə*] vt erkunden // vi aufklären.

reconsider ['ri:kən'sɪdə*] vti von neuem erwägen, (es) überdenken.

reconstruct ['ri:kən'strʌkt] vt wiederaufbauen; (crime) rekonstruieren; ~ion ['ri:kən'strʌkʃən] n Rekonstruktion f.

record ['rekɔːd] n Aufzeichnung f; (MUS) Schallplatte f; (best performance) Rekord m // a (time) Rekord- // vt [rɪ'kɔːd] aufzeichnen; (music etc) aufnehmen; in ~ time in Rekordzeit; **off the ~** a vertraulich // ad im Vertrauen; ~ **card** n (in file) Karteikarte f; ~**ed delivery** [rɪ'kɔːdɪd-] n (Brit POST) Einschreiben nt; ~**er** [rɪ'kɔːdə*] n (TECH) Registriergerät nt; (MUS) Blockflöte f; ~ **holder** n (SPORT) Rekordinhaber m; ~**ing** [rɪ'kɔːdɪŋ] n (MUS) Aufnahme f; ~ **player** n Plattenspieler m.

recount ['ri:kaʊnt] n Nachzählung f // vt (count again) nachzählen; [rɪ'kaʊnt] (tell) berichten.

recoup [rɪ'ku:p] vt: to ~ one's losses seinen Verlust wiedergutmachen.

recourse [rɪ'kɔːs] n: to have ~ to Zuflucht nehmen zu or bei.

recover [rɪ'kʌvə*] vt (get back) zurückerhalten; ['ri:'kʌvə*] (quilt etc) neu überziehen // vi sich erholen; ~**y** n Wiedererlangung f; (of health) Erholung f.

recreate ['ri:krɪ'eɪt] vt wiederherstellen.

recreation [rekrɪ'eɪʃən] n Erholung f; ~**al** a Erholungs-.

recrimination [rɪkrɪmɪ'neɪʃən] n Gegenbeschuldigung f.

recruit [rɪ'kruːt] n Rekrut m // vt rekrutieren; ~**ment** n Rekrutierung f.

rectangle ['rektæŋgl] n Rechteck nt.

rectangular [rek'tæŋgjʊlə*] a rechteckig, rechtwinklig.

rectify ['rektɪfaɪ] vt berichtigen.

rector ['rektə*] n (REL) Pfarrer m; (SCH) Direktor(in f) m.

rectory ['rektərɪ] n Pfarrhaus nt.

recuperate [rɪ'ku:pəreɪt] vi sich erholen.

recur [rɪ'kɜː*] vi sich wiederholen; ~**rence** n Wiederholung f; ~**rent** a wiederkehrend.

red [red] n Rot nt; (POL) Rote(r) m // a rot; **in the ~** in den roten Zahlen; ~ **carpet treatment** n Sonderbehandlung f, große(r) Bahnhof m; **R~ Cross** n Rote(s) Kreuz nt; ~**currant** n rote Johannisbeere f; ~**den** vti (sich) röten; (blush) erröten; ~**dish** a rötlich.

redeem [rɪ'diːm] vt (COMM) einlösen; (save) retten.

redeeming [rɪ'diːmɪŋ] a: ~ **feature** versöhnende(s) Moment nt.

redeploy ['ri:dɪ'plɔɪ] vt (resources) umverteilen.

red-haired ['red'heəd] a rothaarig.

red-handed ['red'hændɪd] ad: to be caught ~ auf frischer Tat ertappt werden.

redhead ['redhed] n Rothaarige(r) mf.

red herring ['red'herɪŋ] n Ablenkungsmanöver nt.

red-hot ['red'hɒt] a rotglühend.

redirect ['ri:daɪ'rekt] vt umleiten.

red light ['red'laɪt] n: to go through a ~ (AUT) bei Rot über die Ampel fahren; **red-light district** n Strichviertel nt.

redo ['ri:'du:] vt (irreg: like do) nochmals machen.

redolent ['redəʊlənt] a: ~ **of** riechend nach; (fig) erinnernd an (+acc).

redouble [ri:'dʌbl] vt: to ~ one's efforts seine Anstrengungen verdoppeln.

redress [rɪ'dres] n Entschädigung f // vt wiedergutmachen.

Red Sea n: the ~ das Rote Meer.

redskin ['redskɪn] n Rothaut f.

red tape n Bürokratismus m.

reduce [rɪ'dju:s] vt (price) herabsetzen (to auf +acc); (speed, temperature) vermindern; (photo) verkleinern; '~ speed now' (AUT) ≈ 'langsam'; **at a ~d price** zum ermäßigten Preis.

reduction [rɪ'dʌkʃən] n Herabsetzung f; Verminderung f; Verkleinerung f; (amount of money) Nachlaß m.

redundancy [rɪ'dʌndənsɪ] n Überflüssigkeit f; (of workers) Entlassung f.

redundant [rɪ'dʌndənt] a überflüssig; (workers) ohne Arbeitsplatz; to be made ~ arbeitslos werden.

reed [ri:d] n Schilf nt; (MUS) Rohrblatt nt.

reef [ri:f] n Riff nt.

reek [ri:k] vi stinken (of nach).

reel [ri:l] n Spule f, Rolle f // vt (also: ~ in) wickeln, spulen // vi (stagger) taumeln.

ref [ref] n abbr (col: = referee) Schiri m.

refectory [rɪ'fektərɪ] n (UNIV) Mensa f; (SCH) Speisesaal m; (ECCL) Refektorium nt.

refer [rɪ'fɜ:*] vt: to ~ sb to sb/sth jdn an jdn/etw verweisen // vi: to ~ to (to book) nachschlagen in (+dat); (mention) sich beziehen auf (+acc).

referee [refə'ri:] n Schiedsrichter m; (Brit: for job) Referenz f // vt schiedsrichtern.

reference ['refrəns] n (allusion) Anspielung f (to auf +acc); (for job) Referenz f; (in book) Verweis m; (number, code) Aktenzeichen nt; with ~ to in bezug auf (+acc); ~ book n Nachschlagewerk nt; ~ number n Aktenzeichen nt.

referendum [refə'rendəm], pl -da [-də] n Volksabstimmung f.

refill ['ri:'fɪl] vt nachfüllen // n ['ri:fɪl] (for pen) Ersatzmine f.

refine [rɪ'faɪn] vt (purify) raffinieren; ~d a kultiviert; ~ment n Kultiviertheit f.

reflect [rɪ'flekt] vt (light) reflektieren; (fig) (wider)spiegeln // vi (meditate) nachdenken (on über +acc); it ~s badly/well on him das stellt ihn in ein schlechtes/gutes Licht; ~ion n Reflexion f; (image) Spiegelbild nt; (thought) Überlegung f; on ~ion wenn man sich (dat) das recht überlegt.

reform [rɪ'fɔ:m] n Reform f // vt (person) bessern; ~atory n (US) Besserungsanstalt f.

refrain [rɪ'freɪn] vi unterlassen (from acc) // n Refrain m.

refresh [rɪ'freʃ] vt erfrischen; ~er course n (Brit) Wiederholungskurs m; ~ing a erfrischend; ~ments pl Erfrischungen pl.

refrigeration [rɪfrɪdʒə'reɪʃən] n Kühlung f.

refrigerator [rɪ'frɪdʒəreɪtə*] n Kühlschrank m.

refuel ['ri:'fjʊəl] vti auftanken.

refuge ['refju:dʒ] n Zuflucht f; to take ~ in sich flüchten in (+acc).

refugee [refju'dʒi:] n Flüchtling m.

refund ['ri:fʌnd] n Rückvergütung f // vt [rɪ'fʌnd] zurückerstatten.

refurbish ['ri:'fɜ:bɪʃ] vt aufpolieren.

refusal [rɪ'fju:zəl] n (Ver)weigerung f; first ~ n Vorkaufsrecht nt.

refuse ['refju:s] n Abfall m, Müll m // v [rɪ'fju:z] vt abschlagen // vi sich weigern; ~ collection n Müllabfuhr f.

refute [rɪ'fju:t] vt widerlegen.

regain [rɪ'geɪn] vt wiedergewinnen; (consciousness) wiedererlangen.

regal ['ri:gəl] a königlich.

regalia [rɪ'geɪlɪə] npl Insignien pl.

regard [rɪ'gɑ:d] n Achtung f // vt ansehen; to send one's ~s to sb jdn grüßen lassen; 'with kindest ~s' mit freundlichen Grüßen; ~ing, as ~s, with ~ to bezüglich (+gen), in bezug auf (+acc); ~less a ohne Rücksicht (of auf +acc) // ad trotzdem.

regenerate [rɪ'dʒenəreɪt] vt erneuern.

régime [reɪ'ʒi:m] n Regime nt.

regiment ['redʒɪmənt] n Regiment nt // vt (fig) reglementieren; ~al [redʒɪ'mentl] a Regiments-.

region ['ri:dʒən] n Region f; in the ~ of (fig) so um; ~al a örtlich, regional.

register ['redʒɪstə*] n Register nt // vt (list) registrieren; (emotion) zeigen; (write down) eintragen // vi (at hotel) sich eintragen; (with police) sich melden (with bei); (make impression) wirken, ankommen; ~ed a (Brit: letter) Einschreibe-, eingeschrieben; ~ed trademark n eingetragene(s) Warenzeichen nt.

registrar [redʒɪs'trɑ:*] n Standesbeamte(r) m.

registration [redʒɪs'treɪʃən] n (act) Registrierung f; (number) polizeiliche(s) Kennzeichen nt.

registry office ['redʒɪstrɪ'ɒfɪs] n (Brit) Standesamt nt; to get married in a ~ standesamtlich heiraten.

regret [rɪ'gret] n Bedauern nt // vt bedauern; ~fully ad mit Bedauern, ungern; ~table a bedauerlich.

regroup ['ri:gru:p] vt umgruppieren // vi sich umgruppieren.

regular ['regjulə*] a regelmäßig; (usual) üblich; (col) regelrecht // n (client etc) Stammkunde m; ~ity [regju'lærɪt] n Regelmäßigkeit f; ~ly ad regelmäßig.

regulate ['regjuleɪt] vt regeln, regulieren.

regulation [regju'leɪʃən] n (rule) Vorschrift f; (control) Regulierung f.

rehabilitation ['ri:həbɪlɪ'teɪʃən] n (of criminal) Resozialisierung f.

rehearsal [rɪ'hɜ:səl] n Probe f.

rehearse [rɪ'hɜ:s] vt proben.

reign [reɪn] n Herrschaft f // vi herrschen.

reimburse [ri:ɪm'bɜ:s] vt entschädigen, zurückzahlen (sb for sth jdm etw).

rein [reɪn] n Zügel m.

reincarnation ['ri:ɪnkɑ:'neɪʃən] n Wiedergeburt f.

reindeer ['reɪndɪə*] n Ren nt.

reinforce [ri:ɪn'fɔ:s] vt verstärken; ~d concrete n Stahlbeton m; ~ment n Verstärkung f; ~ments pl (MIL) Verstärkungstruppen pl.

reinstate ['ri:ɪn'steɪt] vt wiedereinsetzen.

reissue ['ri:'ɪʃu:] vt neu herausgeben.

reiterate [ri:'ɪtəreɪt] vt wiederholen.

reject ['ri:dʒekt] n (COMM) Aus-

schuß(artikel) *m* // [rɪˈdʒekt] *vt*
ablehnen; **~ion** [rɪˈdʒekʃən] *n*
Zurückweisung *f*.

rejoice [rɪˈdʒɔɪs] *vi*: to ~ at *or* over sich
freuen über.

rejuvenate [rɪˈdʒuːvɪneɪt] *vt* verjüngen.

rekindle [ˈriːˈkɪndl] *vt* wieder anfachen.

relapse [rɪˈlæps] *n* Rückfall *m*.

relate [rɪˈleɪt] *vt* (*tell*) erzählen;
(*connect*) verbinden // *vi* zusammenhän-
gen (to mit); (*form relationship*) eine
Beziehung aufbauen (to zu); **~d** a verwandt (to mit).

relating [rɪˈleɪtɪŋ] *prep*: ~ to bezüglich
(+*gen*).

relation [rɪˈleɪʃən] *n* Verwandte(r) *mf*;
(*connection*) Beziehung *f*; **~ship** *n* Verhältnis *nt*, Beziehung *f*.

relative [ˈrelətɪv] *n* Verwandte(r) *mf* // *a*
relativ; **~ly** *ad* verhältnismäßig.

relax [rɪˈlæks] *vi* (*slacken*) sich lockern;
(*muscles, person*) sich entspannen // *vt*
(*ease*) lockern, entspannen; **~ation**
[riːlækˈseɪʃən] *n* Entspannung *f*; **~ed** *a*
entspannt, locker; **~ing** *a* entspannend.

relay [ˈriːleɪ] *n* (*SPORT*) Staffel *f* // *vt*
(*message*) weiterleiten; (*RAD, TV*) übertragen.

release [rɪˈliːs] *n* (*freedom*) Entlassung
f; (*TECH*) Auslöser *m* // *vt* befreien;
(*prisoner*) entlassen; (*report, news*) ver-
lautbaren, bekanntgeben.

relegate [ˈreləgeɪt] *vt* (*SPORT*): to be
~d absteigen.

relent [rɪˈlent] *vi* nachgeben; **~less** *a*,
~lessly *ad* unnachgiebig.

relevant [ˈreləvənt] *a* wichtig, relevant;
~ to relevant für.

reliability [rɪlaɪəˈbɪlɪtɪ] *n* Zuverlässigkeit
f.

reliable *a*, **reliably** *ad* [rɪˈlaɪəbl, -blɪ]
zuverlässig; to be reliably informed that
... aus zuverlässiger Quelle wissen, daß
...

reliance [rɪˈlaɪəns] *n* Abhängigkeit *f* (on
von).

relic [ˈrelɪk] *n* (*from past*) Überbleibsel
nt; (*REL*) Reliquie *f*.

relief [rɪˈliːf] *n* Erleichterung *f*; (*help*)
Hilfe *f*; (*person*) Ablösung *f*.

relieve [rɪˈliːv] *vt* (*ease*) erleichtern;
(*bring help*) entlasten; (*person*) ablösen;
to ~ sb of sth jdm etw abnehmen; to ~
o.s. (*euph*) sich erleichtern (*euph*).

religion [rɪˈlɪdʒən] *n* Religion *f*.

religious [rɪˈlɪdʒəs] *a* religiös; **~ly** *ad*
religiös; (*conscientiously*) gewissenhaft.

relinquish [rɪˈlɪŋkwɪʃ] *vt* aufgeben.

relish [ˈrelɪʃ] *n* Würze *f* // *vt* genießen; to
~ doing etw gern tun.

relocate [ˈriːləʊˈkeɪt] *vt* verlegen // *vi*
umziehen.

reluctance [rɪˈlʌktəns] *n* Widerstreben
nt, Abneigung *f*.

reluctant [rɪˈlʌktənt] *a* widerwillig; **~ly**

ad ungern.

rely [rɪˈlaɪ]: ~ on *vt* sich verlassen auf
(+*acc*).

remain [rɪˈmeɪn] *vi* (*be left*) übrigbleiben; (*stay*) bleiben; **~der** *n* Rest
m; **~ing** *a* übrig(geblieben); **~s** *npl*
Überreste *pl*.

remand [rɪˈmɑːnd] *n*: on ~ in Untersu-
chungshaft // *vt*: to ~ in custody in
Untersuchungshaft schicken; ~ home *n*
(*Brit*) Untersuchungsgefängnis *nt* für
Jugendliche.

remark [rɪˈmɑːk] *n* Bemerkung *f* // *vt*
bemerken; **~able** *a*, **~ably** *ad*
bemerkenswert.

remarry [ˈriːˈmærɪ] *vi* sich wieder ver-
heiraten.

remedial [rɪˈmiːdɪəl] *a* Heil-; (*teaching*)
Hilfsschul-.

remedy [ˈremədɪ] *n* Mittel *nt* // *vt* (*pain*)
abhelfen (+*dat*); (*trouble*) in Ordnung
bringen.

remember [rɪˈmembə*] *vt* sich erinnern
an (+*acc*).

remembrance [rɪˈmembrəns] *n* Erinnerung *f*; (*official*) Gedenken *nt*.

remind [rɪˈmaɪnd] *vt*: to ~ sb to do sth
jdn daran erinnern, etw zu tun; to ~ sb
of sth jdn an etw (*acc*) erinnern; she ~s
me of her mother sie erinnert mich an
ihre Mutter; **~er** *n* Mahnung *f*.

reminisce [remɪˈnɪs] *vi* in Erinnerungen
schwelgen.

reminiscent [remɪˈnɪsnt] *a*: be ~ of sth
an etw (*acc*) erinnern.

remiss [rɪˈmɪs] *a* nachlässig.

remission [rɪˈmɪʃən] *n* Nachlaß *m*; (*of
debt, sentence*) Erlaß *m*.

remit [rɪˈmɪt] *vt* (*money*) überweisen (*to
an* +*acc*); **~tance** *n* Geldanweisung *f*.

remnant [ˈremnənt] *n* Rest *m*; **~s** *pl*
(*COMM*) Einzelstücke *pl*.

remorse [rɪˈmɔːs] *n* Gewissensbisse *pl*;
~ful *a* reumütig; **~less** *a*, **~lessly** *ad*
unbarmherzig.

remote [rɪˈməʊt] *a* abgelegen; (*slight*)
gering; ~ **control** *n* Fernsteuerung *f*;
~ly *ad* entfernt.

remould [ˈriːməʊld] *n* (*Brit*)
runderneuerte(r) Reifen *m*.

removable [rɪˈmuːvəbl] *a* entfernbar.

removal [rɪˈmuːvəl] *n* Beseitigung *f*; (*of
furniture*) Umzug *m*; (*from office*) Entlassung *f*; ~ **van** *n* (*Brit*) Möbelwagen
m.

remove [rɪˈmuːv] *vt* beseitigen, entfernen; **~rs** *npl* Möbelspedition *f*.

remuneration [rɪmjuːnəˈreɪʃən] *n* Vergütung *f*, Honorar *nt*.

render [ˈrendə*] *vt* machen; (*translate*)
übersetzen; **~ing** *n* (*MUS*) Wiedergabe
f.

renew [rɪˈnjuː] *vt* erneuern; (*contract,
licence*) verlängern; (*replace*) ersetzen;
~al *n* Erneuerung *f*; Verlängerung *f*.

renounce [rɪ'naʊns] vt (give up) verzichten auf (+acc); (disown) verstoßen.

renovate ['renəveɪt] vt renovieren; (building) restaurieren.

renown [rɪ'naʊn] n Ruf m; **~ed** a namhaft.

rent [rent] n Miete f; (for land) Pacht f // vt (hold as tenant) mieten; pachten; (let) vermieten; verpachten; (car etc) mieten; (firm) vermieten; **~al** n Miete f.

renunciation [rɪnʌnsɪ'eɪʃən] n Verzicht m (of auf +acc).

reorganize ['riː'ɔːgənaɪz] vt umgestalten, reorganisieren.

rep [rep] n abbr of **representative; repertory.**

repair [rɪ'pɛə*] n Reparatur f // vt reparieren; (damage) wiedergutmachen; **in good/bad ~** in gutem/schlechtem Zustand; **~ kit** n Werkzeugkasten m.

repartee [repɑː'tiː] n Witzeleien pl.

repatriate [riː'pætrɪeɪt] vt in die Heimat zurückschicken.

repay [riː'peɪ] vt (irreg: like pay) zurückzahlen; (reward) vergelten; **~ment** n Rückzahlung f; (fig) Vergeltung f.

repeal [rɪ'piːl] n Aufhebung f // vt aufheben.

repeat [rɪ'piːt] n (RAD, TV) Wiederholung(ssendung) f // vt wiederholen; **~edly** ad wiederholt.

repel [rɪ'pel] vt (drive back) zurückschlagen; (disgust) abstoßen; **~lent** a abstoßend // n: **insect ~lent** Insektenmittel nt.

repent [rɪ'pent] vti: **to ~ (of)** bereuen; **~ance** n Reue f.

repercussion [riːpə'kʌʃən] n Auswirkung f; **to have ~s** ein Nachspiel haben.

repertory ['repətərɪ] n Repertoire nt.

repetition [repə'tɪʃən] n Wiederholung f.

repetitive [rɪ'petɪtɪv] a sich wiederholend.

replace [rɪ'pleɪs] vt ersetzen; (put back) zurückstellen; **~ment** n Ersatz m.

replay ['riːpleɪ] n (of match) Wiederholungsspiel nt; (of tape, film) Wiederholung f.

replenish [rɪ'plenɪʃ] vt ergänzen.

replete [rɪ'pliːt] a (zum Platzen) voll.

replica ['replɪkə] n Kopie f.

reply [rɪ'plaɪ] n Antwort f // vi antworten; **~ coupon** n Antwortschein m.

report [rɪ'pɔːt] n Bericht m; (Brit SCH) Zeugnis nt // vt (tell) berichten; (give information against) melden; (to police) anzeigen // vi (make report) Bericht erstatten; (present o.s.): **to ~ (to sb)** sich (bei jdm) melden; **~ card** n (US, Scot) Zeugnis nt; **~edly** ad wie verlautet; **~er** n Reporter m.

repose [rɪ'pəʊz] n: **in ~** (face, mouth) gelassen.

reprehensible [reprɪ'hensɪbl] a tadelnswert.

represent [reprɪ'zent] vt darstellen; (speak for) vertreten; **~ation** [-'teɪʃən] n Darstellung f; (being represented) Vertretung f; **~ations** pl (protest) Vorhaltungen pl; **~ative** n (person) Vertreter m; (US POL) Abgeordnete(r) mf // a repräsentativ.

repress [rɪ'pres] vt unterdrücken; **~ion** [rɪ'preʃən] n Unterdrückung f.

reprieve [rɪ'priːv] n (cancellation) Begnadigung f; (fig) Gnadenfrist f // vt (JUR) begnadigen.

reprimand ['reprɪmɑːnd] n Verweis m // vt einen Verweis erteilen (+dat).

reprint ['riːprɪnt] n Neudruck m // ['riː'prɪnt] vt wieder abdrucken.

reprisal [rɪ'praɪzəl] n Vergeltung f.

reproach [rɪ'prəʊtʃ] n Vorwurf m // vt Vorwürfe machen (+dat); **to ~ sb with sth** jdm etw vorwerfen; **~ful** a vorwurfsvoll.

reproduce [riːprə'djuːs] vt reproduzieren // vi (have offspring) sich vermehren.

reproduction [riːprə'dʌkʃən] n (ART, PHOT) Reproduktion f; (breeding) Fortpflanzung f.

reproductive [riːprə'dʌktɪv] a reproduktiv; (breeding) Fortpflanzungs-.

reprove [rɪ'pruːv] vt: **to ~ sb for sth** jdn für etw tadeln.

republic [rɪ'pʌblɪk] n Republik f.

repudiate [rɪ'pjuːdɪeɪt] vt zurückweisen.

repugnant [rɪ'pʌgnənt] a widerlich.

repulse [rɪ'pʌls] vt (drive back) zurückschlagen; (reject) abweisen.

repulsive [rɪ'pʌlsɪv] a abstoßend.

reputable ['repjʊtəbl] a angesehen.

reputation [repjʊ'teɪʃən] n Ruf m.

repute [rɪ'pjuːt] n hohe(s) Ansehen nt; **~d** a, **~dly** ad angeblich.

request [rɪ'kwest] n Bitte f // vt (thing) erbitten; **to ~ sth of or from sb** jdn um etw bitten; (formally) jdn um etw ersuchen; **~ stop** n (Brit) Bedarfshaltestelle f.

require [rɪ'kwaɪə*] vt (need) brauchen; (demand) erfordern; **~ment** n (condition) Anforderung f; (need) Bedarf m.

requisite ['rekwɪzɪt] n Erfordernis nt // a erforderlich; **toilet ~s** (Brit) Toilettenartikel pl.

requisition [rekwɪ'zɪʃən] n Anforderung f // vt beschlagnahmen; **to ~ (for sth)** (etw) anfordern.

resale ['riːseɪl] n Weiterverkauf m.

rescind [rɪ'sɪnd] vt aufheben.

rescue ['reskjuː] n Rettung f // vt retten; **~ from** vt befreien aus; **~ party** n Rettungsmannschaft f; **~r** n Retter m.

research [rɪ'sɜːtʃ] n Forschung f // vi forschen // vt erforschen; **~er** n Forscher m.

resemblance [rɪ'zemblǝns] n Ähnlichkeit f.

resemble [rɪ'zembl] vt ähneln (+dat).

resent [rɪ'zent] vt übelnehmen; **~ful** a nachtragend, empfindlich; **~ment** n Verstimmung f, Unwille m.

reservation [rezǝ'veɪʃǝn] n (of seat) Reservierung f; (THEAT) Vorbestellung f; (doubt) Vorbehalt m; (land) Reservat nt.

reserve [rɪ'zɜːv] n (store) Vorrat m, Reserve f; (manner) Zurückhaltung f; (game ~) Naturschutzgebiet nt; (SPORT) Ersatzspieler(in f) m // vt reservieren; (judgement) sich (dat) vorbehalten; **~s** pl (MIL) Reserve f; in ~ in Reserve; **~d** a reserviert.

reshape [riː'ʃeɪp] vt umformen.

reshuffle [riː'ʃʌfl] n: cabinet ~ (POL) Kabinettsumbildung f // vt (POL) umbilden.

reside [rɪ'zaɪd] vi wohnen, ansässig sein.

residence ['rezɪdǝns] n (house) Wohnsitz m; (living) Aufenthalt m.

resident ['rezɪdǝnt] n (in house) Bewohner m; (in area) Einwohner m // a wohnhaft, ansässig; **~ial** [-'denʃǝl] a Wohn-.

residue ['rezɪdjuː] n Rest m; (CHEM) Rückstand m; (fig) Bodensatz m.

resign [rɪ'zaɪn] vt (office) aufgeben, zurücktreten von // vi (from office) zurücktreten; (employee) kündigen; to be **~ed** to sth, to ~ o.s. to sth sich mit etw abfinden; **~ation** [rezɪg'neɪʃǝn] n (from job) Kündigung f; (POL) Rücktritt m; (submission) Resignation f; **~ed** a resigniert.

resilience [rɪ'zɪlɪǝns] n Spannkraft f; (of person) Unverwüstlichkeit f.

resilient [rɪ'zɪlɪǝnt] a unverwüstlich.

resin ['rezɪn] n Harz nt.

resist [rɪ'zɪst] vt widerstehen (+dat); **~ance** n Widerstand m.

resolute a, **~ly** ad ['rezǝluːt, -lɪ] entschlossen, resolut.

resolution [rezǝ'luːʃǝn] n (firmness) Entschlossenheit f; (intention) Vorsatz m; (decision) Beschluß m.

resolve [rɪ'zɒlv] n Entschlossenheit f // vt (decide) beschließen // vi sich lösen; **~d** a (fest) entschlossen.

resonant ['rezǝnǝnt] a voll.

resort [rɪ'zɔːt] n (holiday place) Erholungsort m; (help) Zuflucht f // vi Zuflucht nehmen (to zu); as a last ~ als letzter Ausweg.

resound [rɪ'zaʊnd] vi: to ~ (with) widerhallen von; **~ing** a nachhallend; (success) groß.

resource [rɪ'sɔːs] n Findigkeit f; **~s** pl (financial) Geldmittel pl; (natural) Bodenschätze pl; **~ful** a findig.

respect [rɪs'pekt] n Respekt m // vt achten, respektieren; **~s** npl Grüße pl; with ~ to in bezug auf (+acc), hinsichtlich (+gen); in this ~ in dieser Hinsicht; **~ability** [rɪspektǝ'bɪlɪtɪ] n Anständigkeit f; **~able** a (decent) anständig; (fairly good) leidlich; **~ful** a höflich.

respective [rɪs'pektɪv] a jeweilig; **~ly** ad beziehungsweise.

respiration [respɪ'reɪʃǝn] n Atmung f.

respite ['respaɪt] n Ruhepause f.

resplendent [rɪs'plendǝnt] a strahlend.

respond [rɪs'pɒnd] vi antworten; (react) reagieren (to auf +acc).

response [rɪs'pɒns] n Antwort f; Reaktion f; (to advert etc) Resonanz f.

responsibility [rɪspɒnsǝ'bɪlɪtɪ] n Verantwortung f.

responsible [rɪs'pɒnsǝbl] a (reliable) verantwortungsvoll; verantwortlich (for für).

responsive [rɪs'pɒnsɪv] a empfänglich.

rest [rest] n Ruhe f; (break) Pause f; (remainder) Rest m // vi sich ausruhen; (be supported) (auf)liegen // vt (lean): to ~ sth on/against sth etw gegen etw (acc) lehnen; the ~ of them die übrigen; it ~s with him to ... es liegt bei ihm, zu ....

restaurant ['restǝrɔ̃ːŋ] n Restaurant nt; ~ car n (Brit) Speisewagen m.

restful ['restful] a erholsam, ruhig.

rest home ['resthǝʊm] n Erholungsheim nt.

restitution [restɪ'tjuːʃǝn] n Rückgabe f; to make ~ to sb for sth jdn für etw entschädigen.

restive ['restɪv] a unruhig.

restless ['restlǝs] a unruhig.

restore [rɪs'tɔː*] vt (order) wiederherstellen; (customs) wieder einführen; (person to position) wiedereinsetzen; (give back) zurückgeben; (paintings) restaurieren.

restrain [rɪs'treɪn] vt zurückhalten; (curiosity etc) beherrschen; (person): to ~ sb from doing sth jdn davon abhalten, etw zu tun; **~ed** a (style etc) gedämpft, verhalten; **~t** n (self-control) Zurückhaltung f.

restrict [rɪs'trɪkt] vt einschränken; **~ion** [rɪs'trɪkʃǝn] n Einschränkung f; **~ive** a einschränkend.

rest room ['restrʊm] n (US) Toilette f.

restructure ['riː'strʌktʃǝ*] vt umstrukturieren.

result [rɪ'zʌlt] n Resultat nt, Folge f; (of exam, game) Ergebnis nt // vi zur Folge haben (in acc); as a ~ of als Folge (+gen).

resume [rɪ'zjuːm] vt fortsetzen; (occupy again) wieder einnehmen // vi (work etc) wieder beginnen.

résumé ['reɪzjuːmeɪ] n Zusammenfassung f.

resumption [rɪ'zʌmpʃǝn] n Wiederaufnahme f.

resurgence [rɪ'sɜːdʒəns] n Wiedererwachen nt.

resurrection [rezə'rekʃən] n Auferstehung f.

resuscitate [rɪ'sʌsɪteɪt] vt wiederbeleben.

resuscitation [rɪsʌsɪ'teɪʃən] n Wiederbelebung f.

retail ['riːteɪl] n Einzelhandel m // a Einzelhandels- // v ['riː'teɪl] vt im kleinen verkaufen // vi im Einzelhandel kosten; ~**er** ['riːteɪlə*] n Einzelhändler m, Kleinhändler m; ~ **price** n Ladenpreis m.

retain [rɪ'teɪn] vt (keep) (zurück)-behalten; ~**er** n (servant) Gefolgsmann m; (fee) (Honorar)vorschuß m.

retaliate [rɪ'tælɪeɪt] vi: to ~ (against) zum Vergeltungsschlag (gegen +acc) ausholen.

retaliation [rɪtælɪ'eɪʃən] n Vergeltung f.

retarded [rɪ'tɑːdɪd] a zurückgeblieben.

retch [retʃ] vi würgen.

retentive [rɪ'tentɪv] a (memory) gut.

reticent ['retɪsənt] a schweigsam.

retina ['retɪnə] n Netzhaut f.

retinue ['retɪnjuː] n Gefolge nt.

retire [rɪ'taɪə*] vi (from work) in den Ruhestand treten; (withdraw) sich zurückziehen; (go to bed) schlafen gehen; ~**d** a (person) pensioniert, im Ruhestand; ~**ment** n Ruhestand m.

retiring [rɪ'taɪərɪŋ] a zurückhaltend.

retort [rɪ'tɔːt] n (reply) Erwiderung f; (SCI) Retorte f // vi (scharf) erwidern.

retrace [rɪ'treɪs] vt zurückverfolgen; to ~ one's steps denselben Weg zurückgehen.

retract [rɪ'trækt] vt (statement) zurücknehmen; (claws) einziehen // vi einen Rückzieher machen; ~**able** a (aerial) ausziehbar.

retrain [rɪː'treɪn] vt umschulen; ~**ing** n Umschulung f.

retread ['riːtred] n (tyre) Reifen m mit erneuerter Lauffläche.

retreat [rɪ'triːt] n Rückzug m; (place) Zufluchtsort m // vi sich zurückziehen.

retribution [retrɪ'bjuːʃən] n Strafe f.

retrieval [rɪ'triːvəl] n Wiedergewinnung f.

retrieve [rɪ'triːv] vt wiederbekommen; (rescue) retten; ~**r** n Apportierhund m.

retrograde ['retrəʊɡreɪd] a (step) Rück-; (policy) rückschrittlich.

retrospect ['retrəʊspekt] n: in ~ im Rückblick, rückblickend; ~**ive** [retrəʊ'spektɪv] a (action) rückwirkend; (look) rückblickend.

return [rɪ'tɜːn] n Rückkehr f; (profits) Ertrag m (Brit: rail ticket etc) Rückfahrkarte f; (: plane) Rückflugkarte f // a (journey, match) Rück- // vi zurückkehren or -kommen //

vt zurückgeben, zurücksenden; (pay back) zurückzahlen; (elect) wählen; (verdict) aussprechen; ~**s** npl (COMM) Gewinn m; (receipts) Einkünfte; in ~ dafür; by ~ of post postwendend; many happy ~**s** (of the day)! herzlichen Glückwunsch zum Geburtstag.

reunion [riː'juːnjən] n Wiedervereinigung f; (SCH etc) Treffen nt.

reunite [rɪːjuː'naɪt] vt wiedervereinigen.

rev [rev] n abbr (= revolution: AUT) Drehzahl f // vti (also: ~ up) (den Motor) auf Touren bringen.

revamp ['riː'væmp] vt aufpolieren.

reveal [rɪ'viːl] vt enthüllen; ~**ing** a aufschlußreich.

reveille [rɪ'vælɪ] n Wecken nt.

revel ['revl] vi: to ~ in sth/in doing sth seine Freude an etw (dat) haben/daran haben, etw zu tun.

revelation [revə'leɪʃən] n Offenbarung f.

revelry ['revlrɪ] n Rummel m.

revenge [rɪ'vendʒ] n Rache f; to take ~ on sich rächen an (+dat).

revenue ['revənjuː] n Einnahmen pl.

reverberate [rɪ'vɜːbəreɪt] vi widerhallen.

revere [rɪ'vɪə*] vt (ver)ehren; **reverence** ['revərəns] n Ehrfurcht f.

Reverend ['revərənd] a: the ~ Robert Martin ≈ Pfarrer Robert Martin.

reverent ['revərənt] a ehrfurchtsvoll.

reverie ['revərɪ] n Träumerei f.

reversal [rɪ'vɜːsəl] n Umkehrung f.

reverse [rɪ'vɜːs] n Rückseite f; (AUT: gear) Rückwärtsgang m // a (order, direction) entgegengesetzt // vt umkehren // vi (Brit AUT) rückwärts fahren; ~-**charge call** n (Brit) R-Gespräch nt; **reversing lights** npl (AUT) Rückfahrscheinwerfer pl.

revert [rɪ'vɜːt] vi zurückkehren; to ~ to (to bad state) zurückfallen in (+acc).

review [rɪ'vjuː] n (MIL) Truppenschau f; (of book) Rezension f; (magazine) Zeitschrift f // vt Rückschau halten auf (+acc); (MIL) mustern; (book) rezensieren; (reexamine) von neuem untersuchen; ~**er** n (critic) Rezensent m.

revile [rɪ'vaɪl] vt verunglimpfen.

revise [rɪ'vaɪz] vt (book) überarbeiten; (reconsider) ändern, revidieren.

revision [rɪvɪʒən] n Prüfung f; (COMM) Revision f; (SCH) Wiederholung f.

revitalize ['riː'vaɪtəlaɪz] vt neu beleben.

revival [rɪ'vaɪvəl] n Wiederbelebung f; (REL) Erweckung f; (THEAT) Wiederaufnahme f.

revive [rɪ'vaɪv] vt wiederbeleben; (fig) wieder auffrischen // vi wiedererwachen; (fig) wieder aufleben.

revoke [rɪ'vəʊk] vt aufheben.

revolt [rɪ'vəʊlt] n Aufstand m, Revolte f // vi sich auflehnen // vt entsetzen; ~**ing**

a widerlich.

revolution [revə'luːʃən] *n* (*turn*) Umdrehung *f*; (*POL*) Revolution *f*; ~**ary** *a* revolutionär // *n* Revolutionär *m*; ~**ize** *vt* revolutionieren.

revolve [rɪ'vɒlv] *vi* kreisen; (*on own axis*) sich drehen.

revulsion [rɪ'vʌlʃən] *n* Ekel *m*.

reward [rɪ'wɔːd] *n* Belohnung *f* // *vt* belohnen; ~**ing** *a* lohnend.

rewire ['riː'waɪə*] *vt* (*house*) neu verkabeln.

reword ['riː'wɜːd] *vt* anders formulieren.

rewrite ['riː'raɪt] (*irreg: like* write) *vt* umarbeiten, neu schreiben.

rheumatism ['ruːmətɪzəm] *n* Rheumatismus *m*, Rheuma *nt*.

Rhine [raɪn] *n*: the ~ der Rhein.

Rhone [rəʊn] *n*: the ~ die Rhone.

rhubarb ['ruːbɑːb] *n* Rhabarber *m*.

rhyme [raɪm] *n* Reim *m*.

rhythm ['rɪðəm] *n* Rhythmus *m*.

rib [rɪb] *n* Rippe *f* // *vt* (*mock*) hänseln, aufziehen.

ribald ['rɪbəld] *a* saftig.

ribbon ['rɪbən] *n* Band *nt*; in ~s (*torn*) in Fetzen.

rice [raɪs] *n* Reis *m*; ~ **pudding** *n* Milchreis *m*.

rich [rɪtʃ] *a* reich; (*food*) reichhaltig; the ~ die Reichen *pl*; ~**es** *npl* Reichtum *m*; ~**ly** *ad* reich; (*deserve*) völlig; ~**ness** *n* Reichtum *m*; (*of food*) Reichhaltigkeit *f*.

rickets ['rɪkɪts] *n* Rachitis *f*.

rickety ['rɪkɪtɪ] *a* wack(e)lig.

ricochet ['rɪkəʃeɪ] *n* Abprallen *nt*; (*shot*) Querschläger *m* // *vi* abprallen.

rid [rɪd], *pt, pp* rid *vt* befreien (*of* von); to get ~ of loswerden.

ridden ['rɪdn] *pp of* ride.

riddle ['rɪdl] *n* Rätsel *nt* // *vt*: to be ~d with völlig durchlöchert sein von.

ride [raɪd] *n* (*in vehicle*) Fahrt *f*; (*on horse*) Ritt *m* // (*v: pt* rode, *pp* ridden) *vt* (*horse*) reiten; (*bicycle*) fahren // *vi* fahren, reiten; to take sb for a ~ mit jdm eine Fahrt *etc* machen; (*fig*) jdn aufs Glatteis führen; to ~ at anchor (*NAUT*) vor Anker liegen; ~**r** *n* Reiter *m*; (*addition*) Zusatz *m*.

ridge [rɪdʒ] *n* Kamm *m*; (*of roof*) First *m*.

ridicule ['rɪdɪkjuːl] *n* Spott *m* // *vt* lächerlich machen.

ridiculous *a*, ~**ly** *ad* [rɪ'dɪkjʊləs, -lɪ] lächerlich.

riding ['raɪdɪŋ] *n* Reiten *nt*; ~ **school** *n* Reitschule *f*.

rife [raɪf] *a* weit verbreitet; to be ~ grassieren; to be ~ with voll sein von.

riffraff ['rɪfræf] *n* Pöbel *m*.

rifle ['raɪfl] *n* Gewehr *nt* // *vt* berauben; ~ **range** *n* Schießstand *m*.

rift [rɪft] *n* Spalte *f*; (*fig*) Bruch *m*.

rig [rɪg] *n* (*outfit*) Takelung *f*; (*fig*) Aufmachung *f*; (*oil* ~) Bohrinsel *f* // *vt* (*election etc*) manipulieren; ~ **out** *vt* (*Brit*) ausstatten; ~ **up** *vt* zusammenbasteln; ~**ging** *n* Takelage *f*.

right [raɪt] *a* (*correct, just*) richtig, recht; (*right side*) rechte(r, s) // *n* Recht *nt*; (*not left, POL*) Rechte *f* // *ad* (*on the right*) rechts; (*to the right*) nach rechts; (*look, work*) richtig, recht; (*directly*) gerade; (*exactly*) genau // *vt* in Ordnung bringen, korrigieren // *interj* gut; ~ away sofort; to be ~ recht haben; ~ now in diesem Augenblick, eben; ~ in the middle genau in der Mitte; by ~s von Rechts wegen; on the ~ rechts; to be in the ~ im Recht sein; ~ **angle** *n* rechte(r) Winkel *m*; ~**eous** ['raɪtʃəs] *a* rechtschaffen; ~**ful** *a* rechtmäßig; ~**handed** *a* rechtshändig; ~**hand man** *n* rechte Hand *f*; ~**hand side** *n* rechte Seite *f*; ~**ly** *ad* mit Recht; ~ **of way** *n* Vorfahrt *f*; ~**wing** *n* rechte(r) Flügel *m*.

rigid ['rɪdʒɪd] *a* (*stiff*) starr, steif; (*strict*) streng; ~**ity** [rɪ'dʒɪdɪtɪ] *n* Starrheit *f*; Strenge *f*.

rigmarole ['rɪgmərəʊl] *n* Gewäsch *nt*.

rigorous ['rɪgərəs] *a* streng.

rigour, (*US*) **rigor** ['rɪgə*] *n* Strenge *f*, Härte *f*.

rile [raɪl] *vt* ärgern.

rim [rɪm] *n* (*edge*) Rand *m*; (*of wheel*) Felge *f*.

rind [raɪnd] *n* Rinde *f*.

ring [rɪŋ] *n* Ring *m*; (*of people*) Kreis *m*; (*arena*) Manege *f*; (*of telephone*) Klingeln *nt* // *vti* (*pt* rang, *pp* rung) (*bell*) läuten; (*Brit: also:* ~ up) anrufen; ~ **back** *vti* zurückrufen; ~ **off** *vi* (*Brit*) aufhängen; ~**ing** *n* Klingeln *nt*; (*of large bell*) Läuten *nt*; (*in ears*) Klingen *nt*; ~**ing tone** *n* (*TEL*) Rufzeichen *nt*.

ringleader ['rɪŋliːdə*] *n* Anführer *m*, Rädelsführer *m*.

ringlets ['rɪŋlɪts] *npl* Ringellocken *pl*.

ring road ['rɪŋ'rəʊd] *n* (*Brit*) Umgehungsstraße *f*.

rink [rɪŋk] *n* (*ice* ~) Eisbahn *f*.

rinse [rɪns] *n* Spülen *nt* // *vt* spülen.

riot ['raɪət] *n* Aufruhr *m* // *vi* randalieren; to run ~ (*people*) randalieren; (*vegetation*) wuchern; ~**er** *n* Aufrührer *m*; ~**ous** *a*, ~**ously** *ad* aufrührerisch; (*noisy*) lärmend.

rip [rɪp] *n* Schlitz *m*, Riß *m* // *vti* (zer)reißen.

ripcord ['rɪpkɔːd] *n* Reißleine *f*.

ripe [raɪp] *a* reif; ~**n** *vti* reifen (lassen).

rip-off ['rɪpɒf] *n* (*col*): it's a ~! das ist Wucher!

ripple ['rɪpl] *n* kleine Welle *f* // *vt* kräuseln // *vi* sich kräuseln.

rise [raɪz] *n* (*slope*) Steigung *f*; (*esp in*

wages: Brit) Erhöhung *f*; (*growth*) Aufstieg *m // vi* (*pt* **rose**, *pp* **risen** ['rɪzn]) aufstehen; (*sun*) aufgehen; (*smoke*) aufsteigen; (*mountain*) sich erheben; (*ground*) ansteigen; (*prices*) steigen; (*in revolt*) sich erheben; **to give ~ to** Anlaß geben zu; **to ~ to the occasion** sich der Lage gewachsen zeigen; **rising** *a* (*increasing: tide, numbers, prices*) steigend; (*sun, moon*) aufgehend *//* *a* (*uprising*) Aufstand *m*.

risk [rɪsk] *n* Gefahr *f*, Risiko *nt // vt* (*venture*) wagen; (*chance loss of*) riskieren, aufs Spiel setzen; **to take** *or* **run the ~ of doing** das Risiko eingehen, zu tun; **at ~** in Gefahr; **at one's own ~** auf eigene Gefahr; **~y** *a* riskant.

risqué ['rɪskeɪ] *a* gewagt.

rissole ['rɪsəʊl] *n* Fleischklößchen *nt*.

rite [raɪt] *n* Ritus *m*; **last ~s** *pl* Letzte Ölung *f*.

ritual ['rɪtjʊəl] *n* Ritual *nt // a* ritual, Ritual-; (*fig*) rituell.

rival ['raɪvəl] *n* Rivale *m*, Konkurrent *m // a* rivalisierend *// vt* rivalisieren mit; (*COMM*) konkurrieren mit; **~ry** *n* Rivalität *f*; Konkurrenz *f*.

river ['rɪvə*] *n* Fluß *m*, Strom *m // cpd* (*port, traffic*) Fluß-; **up/down ~** flußaufwärts/-abwärts; **~bank** *n* Flußufer *nt*; **~bed** *n* Flußbett *nt*.

rivet ['rɪvɪt] *n* Niete *f // vt* (*fasten*) (ver)nieten.

Riviera [rɪvɪ'ɛərə] *n*: **the ~** die Riviera.

road [rəʊd] *n* Straße *f // cpd* Straßen-; **major/minor ~** Haupt-/Nebenstraße *f*; **~block** *n* Straßensperre *f*; **~hog** *n* Verkehrsrowdy *m*; **~map** *n* Straßenkarte *f*; **~ safety** *n* Verkehrssicherheit *f*; **~side** *n* Straßenrand *m // a* an der Landstraße (gelegen); **~ sign** *n* Straßenschild *nt*; **~ user** *n* Verkehrsteilnehmer *m*; **~way** *n* Fahrbahn *f*; **~ works** *pl* Straßenbauarbeiten *pl*; **~worthy** *a* verkehrssicher.

roam [rəʊm] *vi* (umher)streifen *// vt* durchstreifen.

roar [rɔː*] *n* Brüllen *nt*, Gebrüll *nt // vi* brüllen; **to ~ with laughter** brüllen vor Lachen; **to do a ~ing trade** ein Riesengeschäft machen.

roast [rəʊst] *n* Braten *m // vt* braten, schmoren; **~ beef** *n* Roastbeef *nt*.

rob [rɒb] *vt* bestehlen, berauben; (*bank*) ausrauben; **to ~ sb of sth** jdm etw rauben; **~ber** *n* Räuber *m*; **~bery** *n* Raub *m*.

robe [rəʊb] *n* (*dress*) Gewand *nt*; (*US*) Hauskleid *nt*; (*judge's*) Robe *f*.

robin ['rɒbɪn] *n* Rotkehlchen *nt*.

robot ['rəʊbɒt] *n* Roboter *m*.

rock [rɒk] *n* Felsen *m*; (*Brit: sweet*) Zuckerstange *f // vti* wiegen, schaukeln; **on the ~s** (*drink*) mit Eis(würfeln); (*marriage*) gescheitert; (*ship*) auf-

gelaufen; **~ and roll** *n* Rock and Roll *m*; **~-bottom** *n* (*fig*) Tiefpunkt *m*; **~ery** *n* Steingarten *m*.

rocket ['rɒkɪt] *n* Rakete *f*.

rocking: **~chair** *n* Schaukelstuhl *m*; **~ horse** *n* Schaukelpferd *nt*.

rocky ['rɒkɪ] *a* felsig.

rod [rɒd] *n* (*bar*) Stange *f*; (*stick*) Rute *f*.

rode [rəʊd] *pt of* **ride**.

rodent ['rəʊdənt] *n* Nagetier *nt*.

roe [rəʊ] *n* (*deer*) Reh *nt*; (*of fish*) Rogen *m*; **hard/soft ~** Rogen *m*/Milch *f*.

rogue [rəʊg] *n* Schurke *m*.

role [rəʊl] *n* Rolle *f*.

roll [rəʊl] *n* Rolle *f*; (*bread*) Brötchen *nt*; (*list*) (Namens)liste *f*; (*of drum*) Wirbel *m // vt* (*turn*) rollen, (herum)wälzen; (*grass etc*) walzen *// vi* (*swing*) schlingern; (*sound*) (g)rollen; **~ about** *or* **around** *vi* herumkugeln; (*ship*) schlingern; (*dog etc*) sich wälzen; **~ by** *vi* (*time*) verfließen; **~ in** *vi* (*mail*) hereinkommen; **~ over** *vi* sich (herum)drehen; **~ up** *vi* (*arrive*) kommen, auftauchen *// vt* (*carpet*) aufrollen; **~ call** *n* Namensaufruf *m*; **~er** *n* Rolle *f*, Walze *f*; (*road ~er*) Straßenwalze *f*; **~er coaster** *n* Achterbahn *f*; **~er skates** *pl* Rollschuhe *pl*.

rolling ['rəʊlɪŋ] *a* (*landscape*) wellig; **~ pin** *n* Nudel- or Wellholz *nt*; **~ stock** *n* Wagenmaterial *nt*.

ROM *n* *abbr* (= *read only memory*) ROM *m*.

Roman [rəʊmən] *a* römisch *// n* Römer(in *f*) *m*; **~ Catholic** *a* römisch-katholisch *// n* Katholik(in *f*) *m*.

romance [rəʊ'mæns] *n* Romanze *f*; (*story*) (Liebes)roman *m*.

Romania [rəʊ'meɪnɪə] *n* = **Rumania**.

Roman numeral *n* römische Ziffer.

romantic [rəʊ'mæntɪk] *a* romantisch; **~ism** [rəʊ'mæntɪsɪzəm] *n* Romantik *f*.

Rome [rəʊm] *n* Rom *nt*.

romp [rɒmp] *n* Tollen *nt // vi* (*also: ~ about*) herumtollen.

rompers ['rɒmpəz] *npl* Spielanzug *m*.

roof [ruːf], *pl* **~s** *n* Dach *nt*; (*of mouth*) Gaumen *m // vt* überdachen, überdecken; **~ing** *n* Deckmaterial *nt*; **~ rack** *n* (*AUT*) Dachgepäckträger *m*.

rook [rʊk] *n* (*bird*) Saatkrähe *f*; (*chess*) Turm *m*.

room [rʊm] *n* Zimmer *nt*, Raum *m*; (*space*) Platz *m*; (*fig*) Spielraum *m*; **~s** *pl* Wohnung *f*; **'~s to let'**, (*US*) **'~s for rent'** 'Zimmer zu vermieten'; **single/double ~** Einzel-/Doppelzimmer *nt*; **~ing house** *n* (*US*) Mietshaus *nt* (*mit möblierten Wohnungen*); **~-mate** *n* Mitbewohner(in *f*) *m*; **~ service** *n* Zimmerbedienung *f*; **~y** *a* geräumig.

roost [ruːst] *n* Hühnerstange *f // vi* auf der Stange hocken.

rooster ['ru:stə*] n Hahn m.
root [ru:t] n (lit, fig) Wurzel f // vi wurzeln; ~ **about** vi (fig) herumwühlen; ~ **for** vt Stimmung machen für; ~ **out** vt ausjäten; (fig) ausrotten.
rope [rəup] n Seil nt // vt (tie) festschnüren; **to know the** ~s sich auskennen; **to** ~ **sb in** jdn gewinnen; ~ **off** vt absperren; ~ **ladder** n Strickleiter f.
rosary ['rəuzəri] n Rosenkranz m.
rose [rəuz] pt of **rise** // n Rose f // a Rosen-, rosenrot.
rosé ['rəuzei] n Rosé m.
rosebud ['rəuzbʌd] n Rosenknospe f.
rosebush ['rəuzbuʃ] n Rosenstock m.
rosemary ['rəuzməri] n Rosmarin m.
rosette [rəu'zet] n Rosette f.
roster ['rɒstə*] n Dienstplan m.
rostrum ['rɒstrəm] n Rednerbühne f.
rosy ['rəuzi] a rosig.
rot [rɒt] n Fäulnis f; (nonsense) Quatsch m // vti verfaulen (lassen).
rota ['rəutə] n Dienstliste f.
rotary ['rəutəri] a rotierend.
rotate [rəu'teit] vt rotieren lassen; (two or more things in order) turnusmäßig wechseln // vi rotieren.
rotating [rəu'teitiŋ] a rotierend.
rotation [rəu'teiʃən] n Umdrehung f.
rote [rəut] n: **by** ~ auswendig.
rotten ['rɒtn] a faul; (fig) schlecht, gemein; **to feel** ~ (ill) sich elend fühlen.
rotund [rəu'tʌnd] a rundlich.
rouble, (US) **ruble** ['ru:bl] n Rubel m.
rough [rʌf] a (not smooth) rauh; (path) uneben; (violent) roh, grob; (crossing) stürmisch; (without comforts) hart, unbequem; (unfinished, makeshift) grob; (approximate) ungefähr // n (Brit: person) Rowdy m, Rohling m; (GOLF): **in the** ~ im Rauh // vt: **to** ~ **it** primitiv leben; **to sleep** ~ im Freien schlafen; ~**age** n Ballaststoffe pl; ~**-and-ready** a provisorisch; (work) zusammengehauen; ~**cast** n Rauhputz nt; ~ **copy** n, ~ **draft** n Entwurf m; ~**en** vt aufrauhen; ~**ly** ad grob; (about) ungefähr; ~**ness** n Rauheit f; (of manner) Ungeschliffenheit f.
Roumania [ru:'meintə] n = **Rumania**.
round [raund] a rund; (figures) aufgerundet // ad (in a circle) rundherum // prep um ... herum // n Runde f; (of ammunition) Magazin nt // vt (corner) biegen um; **all** ~ überall; **the way** ~ der Umweg; **all the year** ~ das ganze Jahr über; **it's just** ~ **the corner** (fig) es ist gerade um die Ecke; ~ **the clock** ad rund um die Uhr; **to go** ~ **to sb's (house)** jdn besuchen; **to go** ~ **the back** durch den Hintereingang gehen; **to go** ~ **a house** um ein Haus herumgehen; **enough to go** ~ genug für alle; **to go the** ~s (story) die Runde machen; **a** ~ **of applause** ein Beifall m; **a** ~ **of drinks/** sandwiches eine Runde Drinks/ Sandwiches; ~ **off** vt abrunden; ~ **up** vt (end) abschließen; (figures) aufrunden; ~**about** n (Brit: traffic) Kreisverkehr m; (: merry-go-round) Karussell nt // a auf Umwegen; ~**ers** npl (game) ≃ Schlagball m; ~**ly** ad (fig) gründlich; ~**-shouldered** a mit abfallenden Schultern; ~ **trip** n Rundreise f; ~**up** n Zusammentreiben nt, Sammeln nt.
rouse [rauz] vt (waken) (auf)wecken; (stir up) erregen.
rousing ['rauziŋ] a (welcome) stürmisch; (speech) zündend.
route [ru:t] n Weg m, Route f; ~ **map** n (Brit: for journey) Streckenkarte f.
routine [ru:'ti:n] n Routine f // a Routine-.
roving ['rəuviŋ] a (reporter) im Außendienst.
row [rəu] n (line) Reihe f // vti (boat) rudern; **in a** ~ (fig) hintereinander.
row [rau] n (noise) Lärm m; (dispute) Streit m // vi sich streiten.
rowboat ['rəubəut] n (US) Ruderboot nt.
rowdy ['raudi] a rüpelhaft // n (person) Rowdy m.
rowing ['rəuiŋ] n Rudern nt; (SPORT) Rudersport m; ~ **boat** n (Brit) Ruderboot nt.
royal ['rɔiəl] a königlich, Königs-; ~ **Air Force (RAF)** n Königliche Luftwaffe f.
royalty ['rɔiəlti] n (family) königliche Familie f; (for book) Tantieme f.
rpm abbr (= revs per minute) U/min.
R.S.V.P. abbr (= répondez s'il vous plaît) u.A.w.g.
Rt Hon. abbr (Brit: = Right Honourable) Abgeordnete(r) mf.
rub [rʌb] n (problem) Haken m // vt reiben; **to** ~ **sb up** or (US) ~ **sb the wrong way** jdn aufreizen; ~ **off** vi (lit, fig) abfärben (on auf +acc); ~ **out** vt herausreiben; (with eraser) ausradieren.
rubber ['rʌbə*] n Gummi m; (Brit) Radiergummi m; ~ **band** n Gummiband nt; ~ **plant** n Gummibaum m; ~**y** a gummiartig.
rubbish ['rʌbiʃ] n (waste) Abfall m; (nonsense) Blödsinn m, Quatsch m; ~ **bin** n (Brit) Mülleimer m; ~ **dump** n Müllabladeplatz m.
rubble ['rʌbl] n (Stein)schutt m.
ruby ['ru:bi] n Rubin m // a rubinrot.
rucksack ['rʌksæk] n Rucksack m.
ructions ['rʌkʃənz] npl Krach m.
rudder ['rʌdə*] n Steuerruder nt.
ruddy ['rʌdi] a (colour) rötlich; (col: bloody) verdammt.
rude [ru:d] a unverschämt; (shock) hart; (awakening) unsanft; (unrefined, rough) grob; ~**ness** n Unverschämtheit f; Grobheit f.

rudiment ['ru:dımənt] n Grundlage f.
rueful ['ru:fʊl] a reuevoll; (situation) beklagenswert.
ruffian ['rʌfɪən] n Rohling m.
ruffle ['rʌfl] vt kräuseln.
rug [rʌg] n Brücke f; (in bedroom) Bettvorleger m; (Brit: for knees) (Reise)decke f.
rugby ['rʌgbɪ] n (also: ~ football) Rugby nt.
rugged ['rʌgɪd] a (coastline) zerklüftet; (features) markig.
rugger ['rʌgə*] n (Brit col) Rugby nt.
ruin ['ru:ɪn] n Ruine f; (downfall) Ruin m // vt ruinieren; ~s pl Trümmer pl; ~ous a ruinierend.
rule [ru:l] n Regel f; (government) Regierung f; (for measuring) Lineal nt // vti (govern) herrschen über (+acc), regieren; (decide) anordnen, entscheiden; (make lines) linieren; as a ~ in der Regel; ~ out vt ausschließen; ~d a (paper) liniert; ~r n Lineal nt; Herrscher m.
ruling ['ru:lɪŋ] a (party) Regierungs-; (class) herrschend // n (JUR) Entscheid m.
rum [rʌm] n Rum m.
Rumania [ru:'meɪnɪə] n Rumänien nt; ~n a rumänisch // n Rumäne m, Rumänin f; (LING) Rumänisch nt.
rumble ['rʌmbl] n Rumpeln nt; (of thunder) Rollen nt // vi rumpeln; grollen.
rummage ['rʌmɪdʒ] vi durchstöbern.
rumour, (US) **rumor** ['ru:mə*] n Gerücht nt // vt: it is ~ed that man sagt or man munkelt, daß.
rump [rʌmp] n Hinterteil nt; ~ steak n Rumpsteak nt.
rumpus [rʌmpəs] n Spektakel m.
run [rʌn] n Lauf m; (in car) (Spazier)fahrt f; (series) Serie f, Reihe f; (ski ~) (Ski)abfahrt f; (in stocking) Laufmasche f // v (pt ran, pp run) vt (cause to run) laufen lassen; (car, train, bus) fahren; (race, distance) laufen, rennen; (manage) leiten; (COMPUT) laufen lassen; (pass: hand, eye) gleiten lassen // vi laufen; (move quickly also) rennen; (bus, train) fahren; (flow) fließen, laufen; (colours) (ab)färben; there was a ~ on (meat, tickets) es gab einen Ansturm auf (+acc); on the ~ auf der Flucht; in the long ~ auf die Dauer; I'll ~ you to the station ich fahre dich zum Bahnhof; to ~ a risk ein Risiko eingehen; ~ about or around vi (children) umherspringen; ~ across vt (find) stoßen auf (+acc); ~ away vi weglaufen; ~ down vi (clock) ablaufen // vt (production, factory) allmählich auflösen; (with car) überfahren; (talk against) heruntermachen; to be ~ down erschöpft or abgespannt sein; ~ in vt (Brit: car) einfahren; ~ into vt (meet:

person) zufällig treffen; (: trouble) bekommen; (collide with) rennen/fahren gegen; ~ off vi fortlaufen; ~ out vi (person) hinausrennen; (liquid) auslaufen; (lease) ablaufen; (money) ausgehen; he ran out of money/petrol ihm ging das Geld/Benzin aus; ~ over vt (in accident) überfahren; ~ through vt (instructions) durchgehen; ~ up vt (debt, bill) machen; ~ up against vt (difficulties) stoßen auf (+acc); ~away a (horse) ausgebrochen; (person) flüchtig.
rung [rʌŋ] pp of ring // n Sprosse f.
runner ['rʌnə*] n Läufer(in f) m; (for sleigh) Kufe f; ~ bean n (Brit) Stangenbohne f; ~-up n Zweite(r) mf.
running ['rʌnɪŋ] n (of business) Leitung f; (of machine) Betrieb m // a (water) fließend; (commentary) laufend; to be in/out of the ~ for sth im/aus dem Rennen für etw sein; 3 days ~ 3 Tage lang or hintereinander.
runny ['rʌnɪ] a dünn.
run-of-the-mill ['rʌnəvðə'mɪl] a gewöhnlich, alltäglich.
run-up ['rʌnʌp] n: ~ to (election etc) Endphase vor (+dat).
runway ['rʌnweɪ] n Startbahn f.
rupee [ru:'pi:] n Rupie f.
rupture ['rʌptʃə*] n (MED) Bruch m // vt: to ~ o.s. sich (dat) einen Bruch zuziehen.
rural ['rʊərəl] a ländlich, Land-.
ruse [ru:z] n Kniff m, List f.
rush [rʌʃ] n Eile f, Hetze f; (FIN) starke Nachfrage f // vt (carry along) auf dem schnellsten Wege schaffen or transportieren; (attack) losstürmen auf (+acc); don't ~ me dräng mich nicht // vi (hurry) eilen, stürzen; ~ hour n Hauptverkehrszeit f.
rusk [rʌsk] n Zwieback m.
Russia ['rʌʃə] n Rußland nt; ~n a russisch // n Russe m, Russin f; (LING) Russisch nt.
rust [rʌst] n Rost m // vi rosten.
rustic ['rʌstɪk] a bäuerlich, ländlich.
rustle ['rʌsl] vi rauschen, rascheln // vt rascheln lassen; (cattle) stehlen.
rustproof ['rʌstpru:f] a rostfrei.
rusty ['rʌstɪ] a rostig.
rut [rʌt] n (in track) Radspur f; to be in a ~ im Trott stecken.
ruthless ['ru:θlɪs] a rücksichtslos.
rye [raɪ] n Roggen m; ~ bread n Roggenbrot nt.

S

sabbatical [sə'bætɪkəl] a: ~ year n Beurlaubungs- or Forschungsjahr nt.
sabotage ['sæbətɑ:ʒ] n Sabotage f // vt sabotieren.

saccharin(e) ['sækərɪn] n Saccharin nt.
sachet ['sæʃeɪ] n (of shampoo) Briefchen nt, Kissen nt.
sack [sæk] n Sack m // vt (col) hinauswerfen; (pillage) plündern; **to get the ~** rausfliegen; **~ing** n (material) Sackleinen nt; (col) Rausschmiß m.
sacred ['seɪkrɪd] a heilig.
sacrifice ['sækrɪfaɪs] n Opfer nt // vt (lit, fig) opfern.
sacrilege ['sækrɪlɪdʒ] n Schändung f.
sad [sæd] a traurig; **~den** vt traurig machen, betrüben.
saddle ['sædl] n Sattel m // vt (burden) aufhalsen (sb with sth jdm etw); **~bag** n Satteltasche f.
sadly ['sædlɪ] ad traurig; (unfortunately) leider; she is ~ lacking (in) ... ihr fehlt es leider ...
sadness ['sædnəs] n Traurigkeit f.
sae abbr (= stamped addressed envelope) adressierte(r) Rückumschlag m.
safe [seɪf] a (free from danger) sicher; (careful) vorsichtig // n Safe m; **~ and sound** gesund und wohl; (just) to be on the ~ side um ganz sicher zu gehen; **~conduct** n freie(s) Geleit nt; **~deposit** n (vault) Tresorraum m; (box) Banksafe m; **~guard** n Sicherung f // vt sichern, schützen; **~keeping** n sichere Verwahrung f; **~ly** ad sicher; (arrive) wohlbehalten.
safety ['seɪftɪ] n Sicherheit f; ~ **belt** n Sicherheitsgurt m; ~ **pin** n Sicherheitsnadel f; ~ **valve** n Sicherheitsventil nt.
sag [sæg] vi (durch)sacken.
sage [seɪdʒ] n (herb) Salbei m; (man) Weise(r) m.
Sagittarius [sædʒɪ'tɛərɪəs] n Schütze m.
Sahara [sə'hɑːrə] n: the ~ (Desert) die (Wüste) Sahara.
said [sed] pt, pp of **say**.
sail [seɪl] n Segel nt; (trip) Fahrt f // vt segeln // vi segeln; (begin voyage: person) abfahren; (: ship) auslaufen; (fig: cloud etc) dahinsegeln; **to go for a ~** segeln gehen; **they ~ed into Copenhagen** sie liefen in Kopenhagen ein; **to ~ through** vti (fig) spielend schaffen; **~boat** n (US) Segelboot nt; **~ing** n Segeln nt; **~ing ship** n Segelschiff nt; **~or** n Matrose m, Seemann m.
saint [seɪnt] n Heilige(r) mf; **~ly** a heilig, fromm.
sake [seɪk] n: for the ~ of um (+gen) willen.
salad ['sæləd] n Salat m; ~ **bowl** n Salatschüssel f; ~ **cream** n (Brit) gewürzte Mayonnaise f; ~ **dressing** n Salatsoße f.
salami [sə'lɑːmɪ] n Salami f.
salary ['sælərɪ] n Gehalt nt.
sale [seɪl] n Verkauf m; (reduced prices)

Schlußverkauf m; 'for ~' zu verkaufen; on ~ zu verkaufen; **~room** n Verkaufsraum m; **~s assistant**, (US) **~s clerk** n Verkäufer(in f) m; **salesman** n Verkäufer m; (representative) Vertreter m; **saleswoman** n Verkäuferin f.
salient ['seɪlɪənt] a bemerkenswert.
saliva [sə'laɪvə] n Speichel m.
sallow ['sæləʊ] a fahl; (face) bleich.
salmon ['sæmən] n Lachs m.
saloon [sə'luːn] n (Brit AUT) Limousine f; (ship's lounge) Salon m.
salt [sɔːlt] n Salz nt // vt (cure) einsalzen; (flavour) salzen; ~ **away** vt (col: money) auf die hohe Kante legen; **~cellar** n Salzfaß nt; ~ **water** a Salzwasser-; **~y** a salzig.
salutary ['sæljʊtərɪ] a nützlich.
salute [sə'luːt] n (MIL) Gruß m; (with guns) Salutschüsse pl // vt (MIL) salutieren.
salvage ['sælvɪdʒ] n (from ship) Bergung f; (property) Rettung f // vt bergen; retten.
salvation [sæl'veɪʃən] n Rettung f; **S~ Army** n Heilsarmee f.
same [seɪm] a, pron (similar) gleiche(r, s); (identical) derselbe/dieselbe/ dasselbe; **the ~ book as** das gleiche Buch wie; **at the ~ time** zur gleichen Zeit, gleichzeitig; (however) zugleich, andererseits; **all or just the ~** trotzdem; **the ~ to you!** gleichfalls.
sample ['sɑːmpl] n Probe f // vt probieren.
sanctify ['sæŋktɪfaɪ] vt weihen.
sanctimonious [sæŋktɪ'məʊnɪəs] a scheinheilig.
sanctity ['sæŋktɪtɪ] n Heiligkeit f; (fig) Unverletzlichkeit f.
sanctuary ['sæŋktjʊərɪ] n (for fugitive) Asyl nt; (refuge) Zufluchtsort m; (for animals) Schutzgebiet nt.
sand [sænd] n Sand m // vt (furniture) schmirgeln; **~s** pl Sand m.
sandal ['sændl] n Sandale f.
sand: **~box** n (US) = **~pit**; **~castle** n Sandburg f; ~ **dune** n (Sand)düne f; **~paper** n Sandpapier nt; **~pit** n Sandkasten m; **~stone** n Sandstein m.
sandwich ['sænwɪdʒ] n Sandwich m or nt // vt (also: ~ **in**) einklemmen; **~ed between** eingeklemmt zwischen; **cheese/ham ~** Käse-/Schinkenbrot; ~ **board** n Reklametafel f; ~ **course** n (Brit) Ausbildungsgang m mit abwechselnden Theorie- und Praxisteilen.
sandy ['sændɪ] a sandig; (hair) rotblond.
sane [seɪn] a geistig gesund or normal; (sensible) vernünftig, gescheit.
sang [sæŋ] pt of **sing**.
sanitary ['sænɪtərɪ] a hygienisch; ~ **towel**, (US) ~ **napkin** n (Monats)binde f.
sanitation [sænɪ'teɪʃən] n sanitäre Ein-

richtungen *pl;* ~ **department** *n* (US) Stadtreinigung *f.*

sanity ['sænɪtɪ] *n* geistige Gesundheit *f;* (*good sense*) Vernunft *f.*

sank [sæŋk] *pt of* **sink.**

Santa Claus [sæntə'klɔ:z] *n* Nikolaus *m,* Weihnachtsmann *m.*

sap [sæp] *n* (*of plants*) Saft *m* // *vt* (*strength*) schwächen.

sapling ['sæplɪŋ] *n* junge(r) Baum *m.*

sapphire ['sæfaɪə*] *n* Saphir *m.*

sarcastic [sɑː'kæstɪk] *a* sarkastisch.

sardine [sɑː'diːn] *n* Sardine *f.*

Sardinia [sɑː'dɪnɪə] *n* Sardinien *nt.*

sardonic [sɑː'dɒnɪk] *a* zynisch.

sash [sæʃ] *n* Schärpe *f.*

sat [sæt] *pt, pp of* **sit.**

Satan ['seɪtn] *n* Satan *m.*

satchel ['sætʃəl] *n* (SCH) Schulmappe *f.*

sated ['seɪtɪd] *a* (*appetite, person*) gesättigt.

satin ['sætɪn] *n* Satin *m* // *a* Satin-.

satisfaction [sætɪs'fækʃən] *n* Befriedigung *f,* Genugtuung *f.*

satisfactory [sætɪs'fæktərɪ] *a* zufriedenstellend, befriedigend.

satisfy ['sætɪsfaɪ] *vt* befriedigen, zufriedenstellen; (*convince*) überzeugen; (*conditions*) erfüllen; ~**ing** *a* befriedigend; (*meal*) sättigend.

saturate ['sætʃəreɪt] *vt* (durch)tränken.

saturation [sætʃə'reɪʃən] *n* Durchtränkung *f;* (CHEM, fig) Sättigung *f.*

Saturday ['sætədeɪ] *n* Samstag *m,* Sonnabend *m.*

sauce [sɔ:s] *n* Soße *f,* Sauce *f;* ~**pan** *n* Kasserolle *f.*

saucer ['sɔ:sə*] *n* Untertasse *f.*

saucy ['sɔ:sɪ] *a* frech, keck.

Saudi ['saʊdɪ]: ~ **Arabia** *n* Saudi-Arabien *nt;* ~ (**Arabian**) *a* saudiarabisch // *n* Saudiaraber(in *f*) *m.*

sauna ['sɔ:nə] *n* Sauna *f.*

saunter ['sɔ:ntə*] *vi* schlendern.

sausage ['sɒsɪdʒ] *n* Wurst *f;* ~ **roll** *n* Wurst *f* im Schlafrock, Wurstpastete *f.*

sauté ['səʊteɪ] *a* Röst-.

savage ['sævɪdʒ] *a* wild // *n* Wilde(r) *mf* // *vt* (*animals*) zerfleischen; ~**ry** *n* Roheit *f,* Grausamkeit *f.*

save [seɪv] *vt* retten; (*money, electricity etc*) sparen; (*strength etc*) aufsparen; (COMPUT) speichern // *vi* (*also:* ~ up) sparen // *n* (SPORT) (Ball)abwehr *f* // *prep, cj* außer, ausgenommen.

saving ['seɪvɪŋ] *a:* the ~ **grace** of das Versöhnende an (+ *dat*) // *n* Sparen *nt,* Ersparnis *f;* ~**s** *pl* Ersparnisse *pl;* ~**s bank** *n* Sparkasse *f;* ~**s account** *n* Sparkonto *nt.*

saviour, (US) **savior** ['seɪvjə*] *n* (ECCL) Erlöser *m.*

savour, (US) **savor** ['seɪvə*] *vt* (*taste*) schmecken; (*fig*) genießen; ~**y** *a* pikant, würzig.

saw [sɔ:] *pt of* **see** // *n* (*tool*) Säge *f* // *vti, pt* **sawed,** *pp* **sawed** *or* **sawn** sägen; ~**dust** *n* Sägemehl *nt;* ~**mill** *n* Sägewerk *nt;* ~**n-off shotgun** *n* Gewehr *nt* mit abgesägtem Lauf.

say [seɪ] *n:* to have no/a ~ in sth (kein) Mitspracherecht bei etw haben; let him have his ~ laß ihn doch reden // *vti, pt, pp* **said** sagen; to ~ yes/no ja/nein sagen; that goes without ~ing das versteht sich von selbst; that is to ~ das heißt; ~**ing** *n* Sprichwort *nt.*

scab [skæb] *n* Schorf *m;* (*pej*) Streikbrecher *m.*

scaffold ['skæfəʊld] *n* (*for execution*) Schafott *nt;* ~**ing** *n* (Bau)gerüst *nt.*

scald [skɔ:ld] *n* Verbrühung *f* // *vt* (*burn*) verbrühen; (*clean*) auskochen.

scale [skeɪl] *n* (*of fish*) Schuppe *f;* (MUS) Tonleiter *f;* (*on map, size*) Maßstab *m;* (*gradation*) Skala *f* // *vt* (*climb*) erklimmen; ~**s** *pl* (*balance*) Waage *f;* on a large ~ (*fig*) im großen, in großem Umfang; ~ of charges Gebührenordnung *f;* ~ **down** *vt* verkleinern; ~ **model** *n* maßstabgetreue(s) Modell *nt.*

scallop ['skɒləp] *n* Kammuschel *f.*

scalp [skælp] *n* Kopfhaut *f.*

scamper ['skæmpə*] *vi:* ~ **away,** ~ **off** verschwinden.

scampi ['skæmpɪ] *npl* Scampi *pl.*

scan [skæn] *vt* (*examine*) genau prüfen; (*quickly*) überfliegen; (*horizon*) absuchen; (*poetry*) skandieren.

Scandinavia [skændɪ'neɪvɪə] *n* Skandinavien *nt;* ~**n** *a* skandinavisch // *n* Skandinavier(in *f*) *m.*

scant [skænt] *a* knapp; ~**ily** *ad* knapp, dürftig; ~**iness** *n* Knappheit *f;* ~**y** *a* knapp, unzureichend.

scapegoat ['skeɪpgəʊt] *n* Sündenbock *m.*

scar [skɑ:*] *n* Narbe *f* // *vt* durch Narben entstellen.

scarce ['skeəs] *a* selten, rar; (*goods*) knapp; ~**ly** *ad* kaum.

scarcity ['skeəsɪtɪ] *n* Mangel *m.*

scare ['skeə*] *n* Schrecken *m* // *vt* erschrecken; to ~ sb stiff jdn zu Tode erschrecken; to be ~d Angst haben; bomb ~ Bombendrohung *f;* ~**crow** *n* Vogelscheuche *f.*

scarf [skɑ:f], *pl* **scarves** *n* Schal *m;* (*head*~) Kopftuch *nt.*

scarlet ['skɑ:lət] *a* scharlachrot // *n* Scharlachrot *nt;* ~ **fever** *n* Scharlach *m.*

scarves [skɑ:vz] *pl of* **scarf.**

scary ['skeərɪ] *a* (col) schaurig.

scathing ['skeɪðɪŋ] *a* scharf, vernichtend.

scatter ['skætə*] *vt* (*sprinkle*) (ver)streuen; (*disperse*) zerstreuen // *vi* sich zerstreuen; ~**brained** *a* flatterhaft, schusselig.

scavenger ['skævɪndʒə*] n (animal) Aasfresser m.

scenario [sɪ'nɑːrɪəʊ] n (THEAT. CINE) Szenarium nt; (fig) Szenario nt.

scene [siːn] n (of happening) Ort m; (of play, incident) Szene f; (view) Anblick m; (argument) Szene f, Auftritt m; ~ry ['siːnərɪ] n (THEAT) Bühnenbild nt; (landscape) Landschaft f.

scenic ['siːnɪk] a landschaftlich.

scent [sent] n Parfüm nt; (smell) Duft m // vt parfümieren.

schedule ['ʃedjuːl] n (list) Liste f; (plan) Programm nt; (of work) Zeitplan m // vt planen; on ~ pünktlich; to be ahead of/behind ~ dem Zeitplan voraus/ im Rückstand sein; ~d flight n (not charter) Linienflug m.

scheme [skiːm] n Schema nt; (dishonest) Intrige f; (plan of action) Plan m // vi intrigieren // vt planen.

scheming ['skiːmɪŋ] a intrigierend.

scholar ['skɒlə*] n Gelehrte(r) m; (holding scholarship) Stipendiat m; ~ly a gelehrt; ~ship n Gelehrsamkeit f; (grant) Stipendium nt.

school [skuːl] n Schule f; (UNIV) Fakultät f // vt schulen; (dog) trainieren; ~ age n schulpflichtige(s) Alter nt; ~book n Schulbuch nt; ~boy n Schüler m; ~ children npl Schüler pl, Schulkinder pl; ~days pl (alte) Schulzeit f; ~girl n Schülerin f; ~ing n Schulung f, Ausbildung f; ~master n Lehrer m; ~mistress n Lehrerin f; ~teacher n Lehrer(in f) m.

sciatica [saɪ'ætɪkə] n Ischias m or nt.

science ['saɪəns] n Wissenschaft f; (natural ~) Naturwissenschaft f.

scientific [saɪən'tɪfɪk] a wissenschaftlich; (natural sciences) naturwissenschaftlich.

scientist ['saɪəntɪst] n Wissenschaftler(in f) m.

scintillating ['sɪntɪleɪtɪŋ] a sprühend.

scissors ['sɪzəz] npl Schere f; a pair of ~ eine Schere.

scoff [skɒf] vt (Brit col: eat) fressen // vi (mock) spotten (at über +acc).

scold [skəʊld] vt schimpfen.

scone [skɒn] n weiche(s) Teegebäck nt.

scoop [skuːp] n Schaufel f; (news) sensationelle Erstmeldung f // vt (also: ~ out or up) schaufeln.

scooter ['skuːtə*] n Motorroller m; (child's) Roller m.

scope [skəʊp] n Ausmaß nt; (opportunity) (Spiel)raum m.

scorch [skɔːtʃ] n Brandstelle f // vt versengen; ~ing a brennend.

score [skɔː*] n (in game) Punktzahl f; (final ~) (Spiel)ergebnis nt; (MUS) Partitur f; (line) Kratzer m; (twenty) 20, 20 Stück // vt (goal) schießen; (points) machen; (mark) einritzen // vi

(keep record) Punkte zählen; on that ~ in dieser Hinsicht; what's the ~? wie steht's? ~ out vt ausstreichen; ~board n Anschreibetafel f; ~r n Torschütze m; (recorder) (Auf)schreiber m.

scorn ['skɔːn] n Verachtung f // vt verhöhnen; ~ful a verächtlich.

Scorpio ['skɔːpɪəʊ] n Skorpion m.

Scot [skɒt] n Schotte m, Schottin f.

scotch [skɒtʃ] vt (end) unterbinden; S~ n Scotch m.

scot-free ['skɒt'friː] ad: to get off ~ (unpunished) ungeschoren davonkommen.

Scotland ['skɒtlənd] n Schottland nt.

Scots [skɒts] a schottisch; ~man/ -woman n Schotte m/Schottin f.

Scottish ['skɒtɪʃ] a schottisch.

scoundrel ['skaʊndrəl] n Schuft m.

scour ['skaʊə*] vt (search) absuchen; (clean) schrubben.

scourge [skɜːdʒ] n (whip) Geißel f; (plague) Qual f.

scout [skaʊt] n (MIL) Späher m; (also: boy ~) Pfadfinder m // vi: ~ around vi sich umsehen (for nach).

scowl [skaʊl] n finstere(r) Blick m // vi finster blicken.

scrabble ['skræbl] vi (claw) kratzen (at an + dat); (also: ~ around: search) (herum)tasten // n: S~ ® Scrabble nt ®.

scraggy ['skrægɪ] a dürr, hager.

scram [skræm] vi (col) abhauen.

scramble ['skræmbl] n (climb) Kletterei f; (struggle) Kampf m // vi klettern; (fight) sich schlagen; to ~ out/through krabbeln ausdurch; to ~ for sth sich um etw raufen; ~d eggs npl Rührei nt.

scrap [skræp] n (bit) Stückchen nt; (fight) Keilerei f; (also: ~ iron) Schrott // vt verwerfen // vi (fight) streiten, sich prügeln; ~book n Einklebealbum nt; ~ dealer n Schrotthändler(in f) m; ~s pl Reste pl; (waste) Abfall m.

scrape [skreɪp] n Kratzen nt; (trouble) Klemme f // vt kratzen; (car) zerkratzen; (clean) abkratzen // vi (make harsh noise) kratzen; to ~ through gerade noch durchkommen; ~r n Kratzer m.

scrap heap ['skræphiːp] n Schrotthaufen m; on the ~ (fig) beim alten Eisen.

scrap merchant ['skræpmɜːtʃənt] n (Brit) Altwarenhändler(in f) m.

scrappy ['skræpɪ] a zusammengestoppelt.

scratch [skrætʃ] n (wound) Kratzer m, Schramme f // a: ~ team zusammengewürfelte Mannschaft // vt kratzen; (car) zerkratzen // vi (sich) kratzen; to start from ~ ganz von vorne anfangen; to be up to ~ den Anforderungen entsprechen.

scrawl [skrɔːl] n Gekritzel nt // vti kritzeln.

scrawny ['skrɔːnɪ] a (person, neck) dürr.

scream [skriːm] n Schrei m // vi schreien.

scree [skriː] n Geröll(halde f) nt.

screech [skriːtʃ] n Schrei m // vi kreischen.

screen [skriːn] n (protective) Schutzschirm m; (film) Leinwand f; (TV) Bildschirm m // vt (shelter) (be)schirmen; (film) zeigen, vorführen; ~ing n (MED) Untersuchung f; ~play n Drehbuch nt.

screw [skruː] n Schraube f // vt (fasten) schrauben; (vulgar) bumsen; ~ up vt (paper etc) zerknüllen; (col: ruin) vermasseln (col); ~driver n Schraubenzieher m.

scribble ['skrɪbl] n Gekritzel nt // vt kritzeln.

script [skrɪpt] n (handwriting) Handschrift f; (for film) Drehbuch nt; (THEAT) Manuskript nt, Text m.

Scripture ['skrɪptʃə*] n Heilige Schrift f.

scroll [skrəʊl] n Schriftrolle f.

scrounge [skraʊndʒ] vt (col): to ~ sth off or from sb etw bei jdm abstauben // n: on the ~ beim Schnorren.

scrub [skrʌb] n (clean) Schrubben nt; (in countryside) Gestrüpp nt // vt (clean) schrubben; (reject) fallenlassen.

scruff [skrʌf] n: by the ~ of the neck am Genick.

scruffy ['skrʌfɪ] a unordentlich, vergammelt.

scrum(mage) ['skrʌm(ɪdʒ)] n Getümmel nt.

scruple ['skruːpl] n Skrupel m, Bedenken nt.

scrupulous ['skruːpjʊləs] a peinlich genau, gewissenhaft.

scrutinize ['skruːtɪnaɪz] vt genau prüfen.

scrutiny ['skruːtɪnɪ] n genaue Untersuchung f.

scuff [skʌf] vt (shoes) abstoßen.

scuffle ['skʌfl] n Handgemenge nt.

scullery ['skʌlərɪ] n Spülküche f.

sculptor ['skʌlptə*] n Bildhauer(in f) m.

sculpture ['skʌlptʃə*] n (ART) Bildhauerei f; (statue) Skulptur f.

scum [skʌm] n (lit, fig) Abschaum m.

scupper ['skʌpə*] vt (NAUT) versenken; (fig) zerstören.

scurrilous ['skʌrɪləs] a unflätig.

scurry ['skʌrɪ] vi huschen.

scuttle ['skʌtl] n (also: coal ~) Kohleneimer m // vt (ship) versenken // vi (scamper): to ~ away or off sich davonmachen.

scythe [saɪð] n Sense f.

SDP n abbr (Brit: = Social Democratic Party) Sozialdemokratische Partei f.

sea [siː] n Meer nt (also fig), See f // a Meeres-, See-; by ~ (travel) auf dem Seeweg; on the ~ (boat) auf dem Meer;

(town) am Meer; to be all at ~ (fig) nicht durchblicken; out to or at ~ aufs Meer (hinaus); ~board n Küste f; ~ breeze n Seewind m; ~food n Meeresfrüchte pl; ~ front n Strandpromenade f; ~going a seetüchtig, Hochsee-; ~gull n Möwe f.

seal [siːl] n (animal) Robbe f, Seehund m; (stamp, impression) Siegel nt // vt versiegeln.

sea level ['siːlevl] n Meeresspiegel m.

sea lion ['siːlaɪən] n Seelöwe m.

seam [siːm] n Saum m; (edges joining) Naht f; (of coal) Flöz nt.

seaman ['siːmən] n Seemann m.

seamy ['siːmɪ] a (people, café) zwielichtig; (life) anrüchig.

seaplane ['siːpleɪn] n Wasserflugzeug nt.

seaport ['siːpɔːt] n Seehafen m.

search [sɜːtʃ] n Suche f (for nach) // vi suchen // vt (examine) durchsuchen; in ~ of auf der Suche nach; ~ for vt suchen nach; ~ through vt durchsuchen; ~ing a (look) forschend; ~light n Scheinwerfer m; ~ party n Suchmannschaft f; ~ warrant n Durchsuchungsbefehl m.

seashore ['siːʃɔː*] n Meeresküste f.

seasick ['siːsɪk] a seekrank; ~ness n Seekrankheit f.

seaside ['siːsaɪd] n Küste f; ~ resort n Badeort m.

season ['siːzn] n Jahreszeit f; (e.g. Christmas) Zeit f, Saison f // vt (flavour) würzen; ~al a Saison-; ~ed a (fig) erfahren; ~ing n Gewürz nt, Würze f; ~ ticket n (RAIL) Zeitkarte f; (THEAT) Abonnement nt.

seat [siːt] n Sitz m, Platz m; (in Parliament) Sitz m; (part of body) Gesäß nt; (part of garment) Hosenboden m // vt (place) setzen; (have space for) Sitzplätze bieten für; to be ~ed sitzen; ~ belt n Sicherheitsgurt m.

sea water ['siːwɔːtə*] n Meerwasser nt.

seaweed ['siːwiːd] n (See)tang m.

seaworthy ['siːwɜːðɪ] a seetüchtig.

sec. abbr (= second(s)) Sek.

secluded [sɪ'kluːdɪd] a abgelegen.

seclusion [sɪ'kluːʒən] n Zurückgezogenheit f.

second ['sekənd] a zweite(r, s) // ad (in ~ position) an zweiter Stelle // n Sekunde f; (person) Zweite(r) m; (COMM: imperfect) zweite Wahl f; (SPORT) Sekundant m (AUT: also: ~ gear) zweiter Gang; (Brit SCOL: degree) mittlere Note bei Prüfungen // vt (support) unterstützen; ~ary a zweitrangig; ~ary school n höhere Schule f, Mittelschule f; ~-class a zweiter Klasse; ~-hand a aus zweiter Hand; (car etc) gebraucht; ~ hand n (on clock) Sekundenzeiger m; ~ly ad zweitens; ~ment [sɪ'kɒndmənt] n (Brit) Abordnung f; ~-

rate *a* mittelmäßig; **~ thoughts** *npl*: **to have ~ thoughts** es sich (*dat*) anders überlegen; **on ~ thoughts** *or* (*US*) **thought** oder lieber (nicht).

secrecy ['siːkrəsɪ] *n* Geheimhaltung *f*.

secret ['siːkrət] *n* Geheimnis *nt* // *a* geheim, Geheim-; **in ~, ~ly** *ad* geheim.

secretarial [sekrə'tɛərɪəl] *a* Sekretärinnen-.

secretary ['sekrətrɪ] *n* Sekretär(in *f*) *m*; (*government*) Minister *m*.

secretion [sɪ'kriːʃən] *n* Absonderung *f*.

secretive ['siːkrətɪv] *a* geheimtuerisch.

section ['sekʃən] *n* Teil *m*; (*department*) Abteilung *f*; (*of document*) Abschnitt *m*.

sector ['sektə*] *n* Sektor *m*.

secular ['sekjulə*] *a* weltlich, profan.

secure [sɪ'kjuə*] *a* (*safe*) sicher; (*firmly fixed*) fest // *vt* (*make firm*) befestigen, sichern; (*obtain*) sichern.

security [sɪ'kjuərɪtɪ] *n* Sicherheit *f*; (*pledge*) Pfand *nt*; (*document*) Wertpapier *nt*; (*national ~*) Staatssicherheit *f*.

sedan [sɪ'dæn] *n* (*US AUT*) Limousine *f*.

sedate [sɪ'deɪt] *a* gesetzt // *vt* (*MED*) ein Beruhigungsmittel geben (+*dat*).

sedation [sɪ'deɪʃən] *n* (*MED*) Einfluß *m* von Beruhigungsmitteln.

sedative ['sedətɪv] *n* Beruhigungsmittel *nt* // *a* beruhigend, einschläfernd.

sedentary ['sedntrɪ] *a* (*job*) sitzend.

sediment ['sedɪmənt] *n* (Boden)satz *m*.

sedition [sə'dɪʃən] *n* Aufwiegelung *f*.

seduce [sɪ'djuːs] *vt* verführen.

seduction [sɪ'dʌkʃən] *n* Verführung *f*.

seductive [sɪ'dʌktɪv] *a* verführerisch.

see [siː] *v* (*pt* **saw**, *pp* **seen**) *vt* sehen; (*understand*) (ein)sehen, erkennen; (*visit*) besuchen // *vi* (*be aware*) sehen; (*find out*) nachsehen // *n* (*ECCL: R.C.*) Bistum *m*; (: *Protestant*) Kirchenkreis *m*; **to ~ sb to the door** jdn hinausgleiten; **to ~ that** (*ensure*) dafür sorgen, daß; **to ~ about** sich kümmern um; **~ you soon!** bis bald!; **to ~ sth through** etw durchfechten; **to ~ through sb/sth** jdn/etw durchschauen; **to ~ to it** dafür sorgen; **to ~ sb off** jdn zum Zug etc begleiten.

seed [siːd] *n* Samen *m* // *vt* (*Tennis*) plazieren; **to go to ~** (*plant*) schießen; (*fig*) herunterkommen; **~ling** *n* Setzling *m*; **~y** *a* (*café*) übel; (*person*) zweifelhaft.

seeing ['siːɪŋ] *cj*: **~ (that)** da.

seek [siːk] *vt*, *pt*, *pp* **sought** *vt* suchen.

seem [siːm] *vi* scheinen; **there ~s to be ... es** scheint, ...; **~ingly** *ad* anscheinend.

seen [siːn] *pp of* **see**.

seep [siːp] *vi* sickern.

seesaw ['siːsɔː] *n* Wippe *f*.

seethe [siːð] *vi*: **to ~ with anger** vor Wut kochen.

see-through ['siːθruː] *a* (*dress*) durchsichtig.

segment ['segmənt] *n* Teil *m*; (*of circle*) Ausschnitt *m*.

segregate ['segrɪgeɪt] *vt* trennen.

seize [siːz] *vt* (*grasp*) (er)greifen, packen; (*power*) ergreifen; (*take legally*) beschlagnahmen; **~ (up)on** *vt* sich stürzen auf (+*acc*); **~ up** *vi* (*TECH*) sich festfressen.

seizure ['siːʒə*] *n* (*illness*) Anfall *m*.

seldom ['seldəm] *ad* selten.

select [sɪ'lekt] *a* ausgewählt // *vt* auswählen; **~ion** [sɪ'lekʃən] *n* Auswahl *f*; **~ive** *a* (*person*) wählerisch.

self [self] *pron* selbst // *n*, *pl* **selves** Selbst *nt*, Ich *nt*; **the ~** das Ich; **~-assured** *a* selbstbewußt; **~-catering** *a* (*Brit*) für Selbstversorger; **~-centred**, (*US*) **~-centered** *a* egozentrisch; **~-confidence** *n* Selbstvertrauen *nt*, Selbstbewußtsein *nt*; **~-conscious** *a* gehemmt, befangen; **~-contained** *a* (*complete*) (in sich) geschlossen; (*person*) verschlossen; (*Brit: flat*) separat; **~-control** *n* Selbstbeherrschung *f*; **~-defence**, (*US*) **~-defense** *n* Selbstverteidigung *f*; **~-discipline** *n* Selbstdisziplin *f*; **~-employed** *a* frei(schaffend); **~-evident** *a* offensichtlich; **~-governing** *a* selbstverwaltet; **~-indulgent** *a* zügellos; **~-interest** *n* Eigennutz *m*; **~-ish** *a* egoistisch, selbstsüchtig; **~-ishness** *n* Egoismus *m*, Selbstsucht *f*; **~-lessly** *ad* selbstlos; **~-pity** *n* Selbstmitleid *nt*; **~-portrait** *n* Selbstbildnis *nt*; **~-possessed** *a* selbstbeherrscht; **~-preservation** *n* Selbsterhaltung *f*; **~-reliant** *a* unabhängig; **~-respect** *n* Selbstachtung *f*; **~-righteous** *a* selbstgerecht; **~-sacrifice** *n* Selbstaufopferung *f*; **~-satisfied** *a* selbstzufrieden; **~-service** *a* Selbstbedienungs-; **~-sufficient** *a* selbstgenügsam; **~-taught** *a* selbsterlernt; **a ~-taught person** ein Autodidakt.

sell [sel] *v* (*pt*, *pp* **sold**) *vt* verkaufen // *vi* verkaufen; (*goods*) sich verkaufen; **to ~ at** *or* **for £10** für £10 verkaufen; **~ off** *vt* verkaufen; **~ out** *vi* alles verkaufen; **~-by date** *n* Verfalldatum *nt*; **~er** *n* Verkäufer *m*; **~ing price** *n* Verkaufspreis *m*.

Sellotape ['seləuteɪp] *n* ® (*Brit*) Tesafilm *m* ®.

sellout ['selaut] *n* (*of tickets*): **it was a ~** es war ausverkauft.

selves [selvz] *pl of* **self**.

semaphore ['seməfɔː*] *n* Winkzeichen *pl*.

semblance ['sembləns] *n* Anschein *m*.

semen ['siːmən] *n* Sperma *nt*.

semester [sɪ'mestə*] *n* (*US*) Semester

nt.

semi ['semɪ] *n* = ~**detached house**; ~**circle** *n* Halbkreis *m*; ~**colon** *n* Semikolon *nt*; ~**conductor** *n* Halbleiter *m*; ~**detached house** *n* (*Brit*) Doppelhaus *nt*; ~**final** *n* Halbfinale *nt.*

seminary ['semɪnərɪ] *n* (*REL*) Priesterseminar *nt.*

semiskilled ['semɪ'skɪld] *a* angelernt.

send [send] *v* (*pt*, *pp* **sent**) *vt* senden, schicken; (*col: inspire*) hinreißen; ~ **away** *vt* wegschicken; ~ **away for** *vt* anfordern; ~ **back** *vt* zurückschicken; ~ **for** *vt* holen lassen; ~ **off** *vt* (*goods*) abschicken; (*Brit SPORT: player*) vom Feld schicken; ~ **out** *vt* (*invitation*) aussenden; ~ **up** *vt* hinaufsenden; (*Brit: parody*) verulken; ~**er** *n* Absender *m*; ~-**off** *n*: a good ~-off eine Abschiedsparty.

senior ['siːnɪə*] *a* (*older*) älter; (*higher rank*) Ober- // *n* (*older person*) Ältere(r) *m*; (*higher ranking*) Rangälteste(r) *m*; ~ **citizen** *n* ältere(r) Mitbürger(in *f*) *m*; ~**ity** [siːnɪ'ɒrɪtɪ] *n* (*of age*) höhere(s) Alter *nt*; (*in rank*) höhere(r) Dienstgrad *m.*

sensation [sen'seɪʃən] *n* Gefühl *nt*; (*excitement*) Sensation *f*, Aufsehen *nt.*

sense [sens] *n* Sinn *m*; (*understanding*) Verstand *m*, Vernunft *f*; (*feeling*) Gefühl *nt* // *vt* fühlen, spüren; ~ **of humour** Humor *m*; **to make** ~ Sinn ergeben; ~**less** *a* sinnlos; (*unconscious*) besinnungslos.

sensibility [sensɪ'bɪlɪtɪ] *n* Empfindsamkeit *f*; (*feeling hurt*) Empfindlichkeit *f*; **sensibilities** *npl* Zartgefühl *nt.*

sensible ['sensəbl] *a* vernünftig.

sensitive ['sensɪtɪv] *a* empfindlich (*to gegen*).

sensitivity [sensɪ'tɪvɪtɪ] *n* Empfindlichkeit *f*; (*artistic*) Feingefühl *nt*; (*tact*) Feinfühligkeit *f.*

sensual ['sensjʊəl] *a* sinnlich.

sensuous ['sensjʊəs] *a* sinnlich.

sent [sent] *pt*, *pp* of **send.**

sentence ['sentəns] *n* Satz *m*; (*JUR*) Strafe *f*; Urteil *nt* // *vt*: ~ **to** ~ **sb to death/** to 5 years jdn zum Tode/zu 5 Jahren verurteilen.

sentiment ['sentɪmənt] *n* Gefühl *nt*; (*thought*) Gedanke *m*; ~**al** [sentɪ'mentl] *a* sentimental; (*of feelings rather than reason*) gefühlsmäßig.

sentry ['sentrɪ] *n* (Schild)wache *f.*

separate ['sepərət] *a* getrennt, separat // ['sepəreɪt] *vt* trennen // *vi* sich trennen; ~**ly** *ad* getrennt; ~**s** *npl* (*clothes*) Röcke, Pullover *etc.*

separation [sepə'reɪʃən] *n* Trennung *f.*

September [sep'tembə*] *n* September *m.*

septic ['septɪk] *a* vereitert, septisch; ~ **tank** *n* Klärbehälter *m.*

sequel ['siːkwəl] *n* Folge *f.*

sequence ['siːkwəns] *n* (Reihen)folge *f.*

sequin ['siːkwɪn] *n* Paillette *f.*

serene [sə'riːn] *a* heiter.

serenity [sɪ'renɪtɪ] *n* Heiterkeit *f.*

sergeant ['saːdʒənt] *n* Feldwebel *m*; (*police*) (Polizei)wachtmeister *m.*

serial ['sɪərɪəl] *n* Fortsetzungsroman *m*; (*TV*) Fernsehserie *f* // *a* (*number*) (fort)laufend; ~**ize** *vt* in Fortsetzungen veröffentlichen/senden.

series ['sɪərɪz] *n*, *pl inv* Serie *f*, Reihe *f.*

serious ['sɪərɪəs] *a* ernst; (*injury*) schwer; ~**ly** *ad* ernst(haft); (*hurt*) schwer; ~**ness** *n* Ernst *m*, Ernsthaftigkeit *f.*

sermon ['sɜːmən] *n* Predigt *f.*

serrated [se'reɪtɪd] *a* gezackt.

servant ['sɜːvənt] *n* Diener(in *f*) *m.*

serve [sɜːv] *vt* dienen (+*dat*); (*guest, customer*) bedienen; (*food*) servieren; (*writ*) zustellen (*on sb* jdm) // *vi* dienen, nützen; (*at table*) servieren; (*TENNIS*) geben, aufschlagen; **it** ~**s him right** das geschieht ihm recht; **that'll** ~ **as a table** das geht als Tisch; ~ **out** *or* **up** *vt* (*food*) auftragen, servieren.

service ['sɜːvɪs] *n* (*help*) Dienst *m*; (*trains etc*) Verbindung *f*; (*hotel*) Service *m*, Bedienung *f*; (*set of dishes*) Service *nt*; (*REL*) Gottesdienst *m*; (*car*) Inspektion *f*; (*for TVs etc*) Kundendienst *m*; (*TENNIS*) Aufschlag *m* // *vt* (*AUT, TECH*) warten, überholen; **the S**~**s** *pl* (*armed forces*) die Streitkräfte *pl*; **to be of** ~ **to sb** jdm einen großen Dienst erweisen; ~**able** *a* brauchbar; ~ **area** *n* (*on motorway*) Raststätte *f*; ~ **charge** *n* (*Brit*) Bedienung *f*; ~**man** *n* (*soldier etc*) Soldat *m*; ~ **station** *n* (Groß)tankstelle *f.*

serviette [sɜːvɪ'et] *n* Serviette *f.*

servile ['sɜːvaɪl] *a* unterwürfig.

session ['seʃən] *n* Sitzung *f*; (*POL*) Sitzungsperiode *f*; **to be in** ~ tagen.

set [set] *n* (*collection of things*) Satz *m*, Set *nt*; (*RAD, TV*) Apparat *m*; (*TENNIS*) Satz *m*; (*group of people*) Kreis *m*; (*CINE*) Szene *f*; (*THEAT*) Bühnenbild *nt* // *a* festgelegt; (*ready*) bereit // *v* (*pt*, *pp* **set**) *vt* (*place*) setzen, stellen, legen; (*arrange*) (an)ordnen; (*table*) decken; (*time, price*) festsetzen; (*alarm, watch*) stellen; (*jewels*) (ein)fassen; (*task*) stellen; (*exam*) ausarbeiten // *vi* (*sun*) untergehen; (*become hard*) fest werden; (*bone*) zusammenwachsen; **to be** ~ **on doing sth** etw unbedingt tun wollen; **to** ~ **to music** vertonen; **to** ~ **on fire** anstecken; **to** ~ **free** freilassen; **to** ~ **sth going** etw in Gang bringen; **to** ~ **sail** losfahren; ~ **about** *vt* (*task*) anpacken; ~ **aside** *vt* beiseitelegen; ~ **back** *vt* zurückwerfen; (*in time*): **to** ~ **back (by)** zurückwerfen (um); ~ **off** *vi* aufbrechen

// vt (explode) sprengen; (alarm) losgehen lassen; (show up well) hervorheben; ~ **out** vi: to ~ out to do sth vorhaben, etw zu tun // vt (arrange) anlegen, arrangieren; (state) darlegen; ~ **up** vt (organization) aufziehen; (record) aufstellen; (monument) erstellen; ~**back** n Rückschlag m; ~ **menu** n Tageskarte f.

settee [se'ti:] n Sofa nt.

setting ['setɪŋ] n Hintergrund m.

settle ['setl] vt beruhigen; (pay) begleichen, bezahlen; (agree) regeln // vi (also: ~ **down**) sich einleben; (come to rest) sich niederlassen; (sink) sich setzen; (calm down) sich beruhigen; to ~ **for** sth sich mit etw zufriedengeben; ~ **in** vi sich eingewöhnen; to ~ **on** sth sich für etw entscheiden; to ~ **up** with sb mit jdm abrechnen; ~**ment** n Regelung f; (payment) Begleichung f; (colony) Siedlung f; ~**r** n Siedler m.

setup ['setʌp] n (situation) Lage f.

seven ['sevn] num sieben; ~**teen** num siebzehn; ~**th** a siebte(r, s) // n Siebtel nt; ~**ty** num siebzig.

sever ['sevə*] vt abtrennen.

several ['sevrəl] a mehrere, verschiedene // pron mehrere; ~ **of us** einige von uns.

severance ['sevərəns] n: ~ **pay** Abfindung f.

severe [sɪ'vɪə*] a (strict) streng; (serious) schwer; (climate) rauh.

severity [sɪ'verɪtɪ] n Strenge f; Schwere f; Ernst m.

sew [səʊ], pt sewed, pp sewn vti nähen; ~ **up** vt zunähen.

sewage ['sju:ɪdʒ] n Abwässer pl.

sewer ['sjuə*] n (Abwasser)kanal m.

sewing ['səʊɪŋ] n Näharbeit f; ~ **machine** n Nähmaschine f.

sewn [səʊn] pp of **sew**.

sex [seks] n Sex m; (gender) Geschlecht nt; to have ~ **with** sb mit jdm Geschlechtsverkehr haben; ~**ist** a sexistisch // n Sexist(in) f) m.

sexual ['seksjʊəl] a sexuell, geschlechtlich, Geschlechts-.

sexy ['seksɪ] a sexy.

shabby ['ʃæbɪ] a (lit, fig) schäbig.

shack [ʃæk] n Hütte f.

shackles ['ʃæklz] npl (lit, fig) Fesseln pl, Ketten pl.

shade [ʃeɪd] n Schatten m; (for lamp) Lampenschirm m; (colour) Farbton m // vt abschirmen; in the ~ im Schatten; a ~ **smaller** ein bißchen kleiner.

shadow ['ʃædəʊ] n Schatten m // vt (follow) beschatten // a: ~ **cabinet** n (Brit POL) Schattenkabinett nt; ~**y** a schattig.

shady ['ʃeɪdɪ] a schattig; (fig) zwielichtig.

shaft [ʃɑːft] n (of spear etc) Schaft m;

(in mine) Schacht m; (TECH) Welle f; (of light) Strahl m.

shaggy ['ʃægɪ] a struppig.

shake [ʃeɪk] v (pt shook, pp shaken) vt schütteln, rütteln; (shock) erschüttern // vi (move) schwanken; (tremble) zittern, beben // n (jerk) Schütteln nt, Rütteln nt; to ~ **hands** die Hand geben (with dat); to ~ **one's head** den Kopf schütteln; ~ **off** vt abschütteln; ~ **up** vt (lit) aufschütteln; (fig) aufrütteln.

shaky ['ʃeɪkɪ] a zittrig; (weak) unsicher.

shall [ʃæl] v aux: **I** ~ **go** ich werde gehen.

shallow ['ʃæləʊ] a seicht.

sham [ʃæm] n Schein m // a unecht, falsch.

shambles ['ʃæmblz] n sing Durcheinander nt.

shame [ʃeɪm] n Scham f; (disgrace, pity) Schande f // vt beschämen; it is a ~ **that** es ist schade, daß; it is a ~ **to do** ... es ist eine Schande, ... zu tun; **what a** ~! wie schade!; ~**faced** a beschämt; ~**ful** a schändlich; ~**less** a schamlos.

shampoo [ʃæm'pu:] n Shampoo(n) nt // vt (hair) waschen; ~ **and set** n Waschen nt und Legen.

shamrock ['ʃæmrɒk] n Kleeblatt nt.

shandy ['ʃændɪ] n Bier nt mit Limonade.

shan't [ʃɑːnt] = **shall not**.

shanty town ['ʃæntɪ-] n Elendsviertel nt.

shape [ʃeɪp] n Form f // vt formen, gestalten // vi (also: ~ **up**) sich entwickeln; to take ~ Gestalt annehmen; -**shaped** suff: **heart-shaped** herzförmig; ~**less** a formlos; ~**ly** a wohlproportioniert.

share [ʃeə*] n (An)teil m; (FIN) Aktie f // vt teilen; to ~ **out** (among or between) verteilen (unter or zwischen); ~**holder** n Aktionär(in f) m.

shark [ʃɑːk] n Hai(fisch) m; (swindler) Gauner m.

sharp [ʃɑːp] a scharf; (pin) spitz; (person) clever; (MUS) erhöht // n (MUS) Kreuz nt // ad (MUS) zu hoch; **nine o'clock** ~ Punkt neun; ~**en** vt schärfen; (pencil) spitzen; ~**ener** n (also: **pencil** ~**ener**) Anspitzer m; ~**eyed** a scharfsichtig; ~**ly** ad (turn, stop) plötzlich; (stand out, contrast) deutlich; (criticize, retort) scharf.

shatter ['ʃætə*] vt zerschmettern; (fig) zerstören // vi zerspringen.

shave [ʃeɪv] n Rasur f // vt rasieren // vi sich rasieren; to have a ~ sich rasieren (lassen); ~**r** n (also: **electric shaver**) Rasierapparat m.

shaving ['ʃeɪvɪŋ] n (action) Rasieren nt; ~**s** pl (of wood etc) Späne pl; ~ **brush** n Rasierpinsel m; ~ **cream** n Rasierkrem f.

shawl [ʃɔːl] n Schal m, Umhang m.

she [ʃiː] pron sie // a weiblich; ~-**bear** n

Bärenweibchen *nt.*

sheaf [ʃiːf], *pl* **sheaves** *n* Garbe *f.*

shear [ʃɪə*], *pt* **sheared**, *pp* **sheared** or **shorn** *vt* scheren; ~ **off** *vi* abbrechen; ~**s** *pl* Heckenschere *f.*

sheath [ʃiːθ] *n* Scheide *f*; (*condom*) Kondom *m* or *nt.*

sheaves [ʃiːvz] *pl of* **sheaf.**

shed [ʃed] *n* Schuppen *m*; (*for animals*) Stall *m* // *vt, pt, pp* **shed** (*leaves etc*) verlieren; (*tears*) vergießen.

she'd [ʃiːd] = **she had; she would.**

sheen [ʃiːn] *n* Glanz *m.*

sheep [ʃiːp] *n* Schaf *nt*; ~**dog** *n* Schäferhund *m*; ~**ish** *a* verlegen; ~**skin** *n* Schaffell *nt.*

sheer [ʃɪə*] *a* bloß, rein; (*steep*) steil; (*transparent*) (hauch)dünn // *ad* (*directly*) direkt.

sheet [ʃiːt] *n* Bettuch *nt*, Bettlaken *nt*; (*of paper*) Blatt *nt*; (*of metal etc*) Platte *f*; (*of ice*) Fläche *f.*

shelf [ʃelf], *pl* **shelves** *n* Bord *nt*, Regal *nt.*

she'll [ʃiːl] = **she will; she shall.**

shell [ʃel] *n* Schale *f*; (*sea*~) Muschel *f*; (*explosive*) Granate *f* // *vt* (*peas*) schälen; (*fire on*) beschießen.

shellfish [ʃelfɪʃ] *n* Schalentier *nt*; (*as food*) Meeresfrüchte *pl.*

shelter [ʃeltə*] *n* Schutz *m*; (*air-raid* ~) Bunker *m* // *vt* schützen, bedecken; (*refugees*) aufnehmen // *vi* sich unterstellen; ~**ed** *a* (*life*) behütet; (*spot*) geschützt.

shelve [ʃelv] *vt* aufschieben // *vi* abfallen.

shelves [ʃelvz] *pl of* **shelf.**

shepherd [ʃepəd] *n* Schäfer *m* // *vt* treiben, führen; ~**'s pie** *n* Auflauf *m* aus Hackfleisch und Kartoffelbrei.

sherry [ʃerɪ] *n* Sherry *m.*

she's [ʃiːz] = **she is; she has.**

Shetland [ʃetlənd] *n* (*also:* the ~**s**, the ~ **Isles**) die Shetlandinseln *pl.*

shield [ʃiːld] *n* Schild *m*; (*fig*) Schirm *m* // *vt* (be)schirmen; (*TECH*) abschirmen.

shift [ʃɪft] *n* Verschiebung *f*; (*work*) Schicht *f* // *vt* (ver)rücken, verschieben; (*arm*) wegnehmen // *vi* sich verschieben; ~**less** *a* (*person*) träge; ~ **work** *n* Schichtarbeit *f*; ~**y** *a* verschlagen.

shilly-shally [ʃɪlɪʃælɪ] *vi* zögern.

shin [ʃɪn] *n* Schienbein *nt.*

shine [ʃaɪn] *n* Glanz *m*, Schein *m* // *v* (*pt, pp* **shone**) *vt* polieren // *vi* scheinen; (*fig*) glänzen; **to** ~ **a torch on sb** jdn (mit einer Lampe) anleuchten.

shingle [ʃɪŋgl] *n* Strandkies *m*; ~**s** *pl* (*MED*) Gürtelrose *f.*

shiny [ʃaɪnɪ] *a* glänzend.

ship [ʃɪp] *n* Schiff *nt* // *vt* verschiffen; ~**building** *n* Schiffbau *m*; ~**ment** *n* Schiffsladung *f*; ~**per** *n* Verschiffer *m*; ~**ping** *n* (*act*) Verschiffung *f*; (*ships*)

Schiffahrt *f*; ~**shape** *a* in Ordnung; ~**wreck** *n* Schiffbruch *m*; (*destroyed ship*) Wrack *nt* // *vt*: **to be** ~**wrecked** Schiffbruch erleiden; ~**yard** *n* Werft *f.*

shire [ʃaɪə*] *n* (*Brit*) Grafschaft *f.*

shirk [ʃɜːk] *vt* ausweichen (+*dat*).

shirt [ʃɜːt] *n* (Ober)hemd *nt*; **in** ~ **sleeves** in Hemdsärmeln; ~**y** *a* (*col*) mürrisch.

shit [ʃɪt] *interj* (*col!*) Scheiße *f* (!).

shiver [ʃɪvə*] *n* Schauer *m* // *vi* frösteln, zittern.

shoal [ʃəʊl] *n* (Fisch)schwarm *m.*

shock [ʃɔk] *n* Erschütterung *f*; (*mental*) Schock *m*; (*ELEC*) Schlag *m* // *vt* erschüttern; (*offend*) schockieren; ~ **absorber** *n* Stoßdämpfer *m*; ~**ing** *a* unerhört.

shod [ʃɒd] *pt, pp of* **shoe** // *a* beschuht.

shoddy [ʃɒdɪ] *a* schäbig.

shoe [ʃuː] *n* Schuh *m*; (*of horse*) Hufeisen *nt* // *vt, pt, pp* **shod** (*horse*) beschlagen; ~**brush** *n* Schuhbürste *f*; ~**horn** *n* Schuhlöffel *m*; ~**lace** *n* Schnürsenkel *m*; ~ **polish** *n* Schuhcreme *f*; ~ **shop** *n* Schuhgeschäft *nt*; ~**string** *n* (*fig*): **on a** ~**string** mit sehr wenig Geld.

shone [ʃɒn] *pt, pp of* **shine.**

shoo [ʃuː] *interj* sch!; (*to dog etc*) pfui!

shook [ʃʊk] *pt of* **shake.**

shoot [ʃuːt] *n* (*branch*) Schößling *m* // *v* (*pt, pp* **shot**) *vt* (*gun*) abfeuern; (*goal, arrow*) schießen; (*kill*) erschießen; (*film*) drehen // *vi* (*gun, move quickly*) schießen; ~ (**at**) schießen (auf) (+*acc*); ~ **down** *vt* abschießen; ~ **in/out** *vi* hinein-/hinausschießen; ~ **up** *vi* (*fig*) aus dem Boden schießen; ~**ing** *n* Schießerei *f*; ~**ing star** *n* Sternschnuppe *f.*

shop [ʃɒp] *n* (*esp Brit*) Geschäft *nt*, Laden *m*; (*workshop*) Werkstatt *f* // *vi* (*also:* go ~**ping**) einkaufen gehen; ~ **assistant** *n* (*Brit*) Verkäufer(in *f*) *m*; ~ **floor** *n* (*Brit*) Werkstatt *f*; ~**keeper** *n* Geschäftsinhaber *m*; ~**lifting** *n* Ladendiebstahl *m*; ~**per** *n* Käufer(in *f*) *m*; ~**ping** *n* Einkaufen *nt*, Einkauf *m*; ~**ping bag** *n* Einkaufstasche *f*; ~**ping centre**, (*US*) ~**ping center** *n* Einkaufszentrum *nt*; ~**-soiled** *a* angeschmutzt; ~ **steward** *n* (*Brit INDUSTRY*) Betriebsrat *m*; ~ **window** *n* Schaufenster *nt.*

shore [ʃɔː*] *n* Ufer *nt*; (*of sea*) Strand *m* // *vt*: ~ **up** abstützen.

shorn [ʃɔːn] *pp of* **shear.**

short [ʃɔːt] *a* kurz; (*person*) klein; (*curt*) kurz angebunden; (*measure*) zu knapp // *a* (*also:* ~ **film**) Kurzfilm *m* // *ad* (*suddenly*) plötzlich // *vi* (*ELEC*) einen Kurzschluß haben; **to be** ~ **of sth** nicht genug von etw haben; **in** ~ kurz gesagt; ~ **of doing sth** ohne so weit zu gehen, etw zu tun; **everything ~ of ...** alles außer ...; **it is ~ for** das ist die Kurzform von; **to cut ~** abkürzen; **to fall ~ of sth** etw nicht erreichen; **to stop ~** plötzlich anhalten; **to stop ~ of** haltmachen vor; **~age** n Knappheit f, Mangel m; **~bread** n Mürbegebäck nt; **~change** vt: **to ~change sb** jdm zuwenig herausgeben; **~circuit** n Kurzschluß m // vi einen Kurzschluß haben // vt kurzschließen; **~coming** n Mangel m; **~(crust) pastry** n (Brit) Mürbeteig m; **~ cut** n Abkürzung f; **~en** vt (ab)kürzen; (clothes) kürzer machen; **~fall** n Defizit nt; **~hand** n (Brit) Stenographie f; **~hand typist** n (Brit) Stenotypistin f; **~list** n (Brit: for job) engere Wahl f; **~lived** a kurzlebig; **~ly** ad bald; **~ness** n Kürze f; **~s** npl Shorts pl; **~-sighted** a (Brit: lit, fig) kurzsichtig; **~-staffed** a: **to be ~-staffed** zu wenig Personal haben; **~ story** n Kurzgeschichte f; **~-tempered** a leicht aufbrausend; **~-term** a (effect) kurzfristig; **~ wave** n (RAD) Kurzwelle f.

shot [ʃɒt] pt, pp of **shoot** // n (from gun) Schuß m; (person) Schütze m; (try) Versuch m; (injection) Spritze f; (PHOT) Aufnahme f; **like a ~** wie der Blitz; **~gun** n Schrotflinte f.

should [ʃud] v aux: **I ~ go now** ich sollte jetzt gehen; **he ~ be there now** er sollte eigentlich schon hier sein; **I ~ go if I were you** ich würde gehen, wenn ich du wäre; **I ~ like to** ich möchte gerne.

shoulder ['ʃəuldə*] n Schulter f; (Brit: of road): **hard ~** Seitenstreifen m // vt (rifle) schultern; (fig) auf sich nehmen; **~ blade** n Schulterblatt nt; **~ bag** n Umhängetasche f; **~ strap** n (MIL) Schulterklappe; (of dress etc) Träger m.

shouldn't ['ʃudnt] = **should not**.

shout [ʃaut] n Schrei m; (call) Ruf m // vt rufen // vi schreien; **~ down** vt niederbrüllen; **~ing** n Geschrei nt.

shove [ʃʌv] n Schubs m, Stoß m // vt schieben, stoßen, schubsen; (col: put): **to ~ sth in(to) sth** etw in etw (acc) hineinschieben; **~ off** vi (NAUT) abstoßen; (fig col) abhauen.

shovel ['ʃʌvl] n Schaufel f // vt schaufeln.

show [ʃəu] n (display) Schau f; (exhibition) Ausstellung f; (CINE, THEAT) Vorstellung f, Show f // v (pt **showed**, pp **shown**) vt zeigen; (kindness) erweisen // vi zu sehen sein: **to be on ~** (exhibits etc) ausgestellt sein; **to ~ sb in** jdn hereinführen; **to ~ sb out** jdn hinausbegleiten; **~ off** vi (pej) angeben // vt (display) ausstellen; **~ up** vi (stand out) sich abheben; (arrive) erscheinen // vt aufzeigen; (unmask) bloßstellen; **~ business** n

Showbusineß nt; **~down** n Kraftprobe f.

shower ['ʃauə*] n Schauer m; (of stones) (Stein)hagel m; (~ bath) Dusche f // vi duschen // vt: **to ~ sb with sth** jdn mit etw überschütten; **~proof** a wasserabstoßend.

showing ['ʃəuiŋ] n Vorführung f.

show jumping ['ʃəudʒʌmpiŋ] n Turnierreiten nt.

shown [ʃəun] pp of **show**.

show-off ['ʃəuɒf] n Angeber(in f) m.

showpiece ['ʃəupi:s] n Paradestück nt.

showroom ['ʃəurum] n Ausstellungsraum m.

shrank [ʃræŋk] pt of **shrink**.

shred [ʃred] n Fetzen m // vt zerfetzen; (COOK) raspeln; **~der** n (vegetable ~) Gemüseschneider m; (document) Reißwolf m.

shrewd [ʃru:d] a clever.

shriek [ʃri:k] n Schrei m // vti kreischen, schreien.

shrimp [ʃrimp] n Krabbe f, Garnele f.

shrink [ʃriŋk] v (pt **shrank**, pp **shrunk**) vi schrumpfen, eingehen // vt einschrumpfen lassen; **to ~ from doing sth** davor zurückschrecken, etw zu tun; **~age** n Schrumpfung f; **~-wrap** vt einschweißen.

shrivel ['ʃrivl] vti (also: **~ up**) schrumpfen, schrumpeln.

shroud [ʃraud] n Leichentuch nt // vt: **~ed in mystery** mit einem Geheimnis umgeben.

Shrove Tuesday ['ʃrəuv'tju:zdei] n Fastnachtsdienstag m.

shrub [ʃrʌb] n Busch m, Strauch m; **~bery** n Gebüsch nt.

shrug [ʃrʌg] n Achselzucken nt // vi: **to ~ (one's shoulders)** die Achseln zucken; **~ off** vt auf die leichte Schulter nehmen.

shrunk [ʃrʌŋk] pp of **shrink**.

shudder ['ʃʌdə*] n Schauder m // vi schaudern.

shuffle ['ʃʌfl] n (CARDS) (Karten)-mischen; // vt (cards) mischen; **to ~ (one's feet)** schlurfen.

shun [ʃʌn] vt scheuen, (ver)meiden.

shunt [ʃʌnt] vt rangieren.

shut [ʃʌt] v (pt, pp **shut**) vt schließen, zumachen // vi sich schließen (lassen); **~ down** vti schließen; **~ off** vt (supply) abdrehen; **~ up** vi (keep quiet) den Mund halten // vt (close) zuschließen; **~ter** n Fensterladen m; (PHOT) Verschluß m.

shuttle ['ʃʌtl] n (plane, train etc) Pendelflugzeug nt/-zug m etc; (space ~) Raumtransporter m; (also: **~ service**) Pendelverkehr m.

shuttlecock ['ʃʌtlkɒk] n Federball m.

shy [ʃai] a schüchtern; **~ness** n Schüchternheit f.

Siamese [saiə'mi:z] a: **~ cat** n

Siamkatze *f*.

Siberia [saɪ'bɪərɪə] *n* Sibirien *nt*.

sibling ['sɪblɪŋ] *n* Geschwister *nt*.

Sicily ['sɪsɪlɪ] *n* Sizilien *nt*.

sick [sɪk] *a* krank; (*joke*) makaber; I feel ~ mir ist schlecht; I was ~ ich habe gebrochen; to be ~ of sb/sth jdn/etw satt haben; ~ **bay** *n* (Schiffs)lazarett *nt*; **~en** *vt* (*disgust*) krankmachen // *vi* krank werden; **~ening** *a* (*sight*) widerlich; (*annoying*) zum Weinen.

sickle ['sɪkl] *n* Sichel *f*.

sick leave ['sɪkliːv] *n*: to be on ~ krank geschrieben sein.

sickly ['sɪklɪ] *a* kränklich, blaß; (*causing nausea*) widerlich.

sickness ['sɪknəs] *n* Krankheit *f*; (*vomiting*) Übelkeit *f*, Erbrechen *nt*.

sick pay ['sɪkpeɪ] *n* Krankengeld *nt*.

side [saɪd] *n* Seite *f* // *a* (*door, entrance*) Seiten-, Neben- // *vi*: to ~ with sb jds Partei ergreifen; by the ~ of neben; ~ by ~ nebeneinander; on all ~s von allen Seiten; to take ~s (with) Partei nehmen (für); **~boards** (*Brit*), **~burns** *pl* Koteletten *pl*; **~car** *n* Beiwagen *m*; **~ drum** *n* (MUS) kleine Trommel; **~ effect** *n* Nebenwirkung *f*; **~light** *n* (AUT) Parkleuchte *f*; **~line** *n* (SPORT) Seitenlinie *f*; (*fig: hobby*) Nebenbeschäftigung *f*; **~long** *a* Seiten-; **~saddle** *ad* im Damensattel; ~ **show** *n* Nebenausstellung *f*; **~step** *vt* (*fig*) ausweichen; ~ **street** *n* Seitenstraße *f*; **~track** *vt* (*fig*) ablenken; **~walk** *n* (US) Bürgersteig *m*; **~ways** *ad* seitwärts.

siding ['saɪdɪŋ] *n* Nebengleis *nt*.

sidle ['saɪdl] *vi*: to ~ up sich heranmachen (to an +acc).

siege [siːdʒ] *n* Belagerung *f*.

sieve [sɪv] *n* Sieb *nt* // *vt* sieben.

sift [sɪft] *vt* sieben; (*fig*) sichten.

sigh [saɪ] *n* Seufzer *m* // *vi* seufzen.

sight [saɪt] *n* (*power of seeing*) Sehvermögen *nt*; (*look*) Blick *m*; (*fact of seeing*) Anblick *m*; (*of gun*) Visier *nt* // *vt* sichten; in ~ in Sicht; out of ~ außer Sicht; **~seeing** *n* Besuch *m* von Sehenswürdigkeiten; to go **~seeing** Sehenswürdigkeiten besichtigen.

sign [saɪn] *n* Zeichen *nt*; (*notice, road ~ etc*) Schild *nt* // *vt* unterschreiben; to ~ sth over to sb jdm etw überschreiben; ~ **on** *vi* (MIL) sich verpflichten; (*as unemployed*) sich (arbeitslos) melden // *vt* (MIL) verpflichten; (*employee*) anstellen; ~ **up** *vi* (MIL) sich verpflichten // *vt* verpflichten.

signal ['sɪgnl] *n* Signal *nt* // *vt* ein Zeichen geben (+dat); **~man** *n* (RAIL) Stellwerkswärter(in *f*) *m*.

signature ['sɪgnətʃə*] *n* Unterschrift *f*; ~ **tune** *n* Erkennungsmelodie *f*.

signet ring ['sɪgnətrɪŋ] *n* Siegelring *m*.

significance [sɪg'nɪfɪkəns] *n* Bedeutung *f*.

significant [sɪg'nɪfɪkənt] *a* (*meaning sth*) bedeutsam; (*important*) bedeutend.

signify ['sɪgnɪfaɪ] *vt* bedeuten; (*show*) andeuten, zu verstehen geben.

sign language ['saɪnlæŋgwɪdʒ] *n* Zeichensprache *f*, Fingersprache *f*.

signpost ['saɪnpəʊst] *n* Wegweiser *m*.

silence ['saɪləns] *n* Stille *f*; (*of person*) Schweigen *nt* // *vt* zum Schweigen bringen; **~r** *n* (*on gun*) Schalldämpfer *m*; (*Brit AUT*) Auspufftopf *m*.

silent ['saɪlənt] *a* still; (*person*) schweigsam; to remain ~ schweigen; ~ **partner** *n* (COMM) stille(r) Teilhaber *m*.

silk [sɪlk] *n* Seide *f* // *a* seiden, Seiden-; **~y** *a* seidig.

silly ['sɪlɪ] *a* dumm, albern.

silt [sɪlt] *n* Schlamm *m*, Schlick *m*.

silver ['sɪlvə*] *n* Silber *nt* // *a* silbern, Silber-; ~ **paper** *n* (*Brit*) Silberpapier *nt*; **~-plated** *a* versilbert; **~smith** *n* Silberschmied *m*; **~ware** *n* Silber *nt*; **~y** *a* silbern.

similar ['sɪmɪlə*] *a* ähnlich (to dat); **~ity** [sɪmɪ'lærɪtɪ] *n* Ähnlichkeit *f*; **~ly** *ad* in ähnlicher Weise.

simile ['sɪmɪlɪ] *n* Vergleich *m*.

simmer ['sɪmə*] *vti* sieden (lassen).

simpering ['sɪmpərɪŋ] *a* albern.

simple ['sɪmpl] *a* einfach; **~(-minded)** *a* einfältig; **~ton** *n* Einfaltspinsel *m*.

simplicity [sɪm'plɪsɪtɪ] *n* Einfachheit *f*; (*of person*) Einfältigkeit *f*.

simplify ['sɪmplɪfaɪ] *vt* vereinfachen.

simply ['sɪmplɪ] *ad* einfach.

simulate ['sɪmjʊleɪt] *vt* simulieren.

simultaneous [sɪməl'teɪnɪəs] *a* gleichzeitig.

sin [sɪn] *n* Sünde *f* // *vi* sündigen.

since [sɪns] *ad* seither // *prep* seit, seitdem // *cj* (*time*) seit; (*because*) da, weil; ~ then seitdem.

sincere [sɪn'sɪə*] *a* aufrichtig; yours **~ly** mit freundlichen Grüßen.

sincerity [sɪn'serɪtɪ] *n* Aufrichtigkeit *f*.

sinew ['sɪnjuː] *n* Sehne *f*.

sinful ['sɪnful] *a* sündig, sündhaft.

sing [sɪŋ], *pt* sang, *pp* sung *vti* singen.

Singapore [sɪŋgə'pɔː*] *n* Singapur *nt*.

singe [sɪndʒ] *vt* versengen.

singer ['sɪŋə*] *n* Sänger(in *f*) *m*.

single ['sɪŋgl] *a* (*one only*) einzig; (*bed, room*) Einzel-, einzeln; (*unmarried*) ledig; (*Brit: ticket*) einfach; (*having one part only*) einzeln // *n* (*Brit: also*: ~ ticket) einfache Fahrkarte *f*; **~s** *n* (TENNIS) Einzel *nt*; ~ **out** *vt* aussuchen, auswählen; ~ **bed** *n* Einzelbett *nt*; **~-breasted** *a* einreihig; in ~ file hintereinander; **~-handed** *a* allein; **~-minded** *a* zielstrebig; ~ **room** *n* Einzelzimmer *nt*.

singlet ['sɪŋglət] n Unterhemd nt.

singly ['sɪŋglɪ] ad einzeln, allein.

singular ['sɪŋgjulə*] a (GRAM) Singular-; (odd) merkwürdig, seltsam // n (GRAM) Einzahl f, Singular m.

sinister ['sɪnɪstə*] a (evil) böse; (ghostly) unheimlich.

sink [sɪŋk] n Spülbecken nt // v (pt sank, pp sunk) vt (ship) versenken // vi sinken; to ~ sth into (teeth, claws) etw schlagen in (+acc); ~ in vi (news etc) eingehen (+dat).

sinner ['sɪnə*] n Sünder(in f) m.

sip [sɪp] n Schlückchen nt // vt nippen an (+dat).

siphon ['saɪfən] n Siphon(flasche f) m; ~ off vt absaugen; (fig) abschöpfen.

sir [sɜ:*] n (respect) Herr m; (knight) Sir m; S~ John Smith Sir John Smith; yes ~ ja(wohl, mein Herr).

siren ['saɪərən] n Sirene f.

sirloin ['sɜ:lɔɪn] n Lendenstück nt.

sissy ['sɪsɪ] n (col) Waschlappen m.

sister ['sɪstə*] n Schwester f; (Brit: nurse) Oberschwester f; (nun) Ordensschwester f; ~-in-law n Schwägerin f.

sit [sɪt] v (pt, pp sat) vi sitzen; (hold session) tagen // vt (exam) machen; ~ down vi sich hinsetzen; ~ in on vt dabeisein bei; ~ up vi (after lying) sich aufsetzen; (straight) sich gerade setzen; (at night) aufbleiben.

sitcom ['sɪtkɔm] n abbr (= situation comedy) Situationskomödie f.

site [saɪt] n Platz m; (also: building ~) Baustelle f // vt legen.

sitting ['sɪtɪŋ] n (meeting) Sitzung f; ~ room n Wohnzimmer nt.

situated ['sɪtjueɪtɪd] a: to be ~ liegen.

situation [sɪtju'eɪʃən] n Situation f, Lage f; (place) Lage f; (employment) Stelle f; ~s vacant (Brit) Stellenangebote pl.

six [sɪks] num sechs; ~teen num sechzehn; ~th a sechste(r, s) // n Sechstel nt; ~ty num sechzig.

size [saɪz] n Größe f; (of project) Umfang m; ~ up vt (assess) abschätzen, einschätzen; ~able a ziemlich groß, ansehnlich.

sizzle ['sɪzl] vi zischen; (COOK) brutzeln.

skate [skeɪt] n Schlittschuh m; (fish: pl inv) Rochen m // vi Schlittschuh laufen; ~r n Schlittschuhläufer(in f) m.

skating ['skeɪtɪŋ] n Eislauf m; to go ~ Eislaufen gehen; ~ rink n Eisbahn f.

skeleton ['skelɪtn] n Skelett nt; (fig) Gerüst m; ~ key n Dietrich m; ~ staff n Notbesetzung f.

sketch [sketʃ] n Skizze f; (THEAT) Sketch m // vt skizzieren; ~book n Skizzenbuch nt; ~y a skizzenhaft.

skewer ['skjuə*] n Fleischspieß m.

ski [ski:] n Ski m, Schi m // vi Ski or Schi laufen; ~ boot n Skistiefel m.

skid [skɪd] n (AUT) Schleudern nt // vi rutschen; (AUT) schleudern.

skier ['ski:ə*] n Skiläufer(in f) m.

skiing ['ski:ɪŋ] n: to go ~ Skilaufen gehen.

ski-jump ['ski:dʒʌmp] n Sprungschanze f // vi Ski springen.

skilful ['skɪlful] a geschickt.

ski-lift ['ski:lɪft] n Skilift m.

skill [skɪl] n Können nt; ~ed a geschickt; (worker) Fach-, gelernt.

skim [skɪm] vt (liquid) abschöpfen; (glide over) gleiten über (+acc) // vi: ~ through (book) überfliegen; ~med milk n Magermilch f

skimp [skɪmp] vt (do carelessly) oberflächlich tun; ~y a (work) schlecht gemacht; (dress) knapp.

skin [skɪn] n Haut f; (peel) Schale f // vt abhäuten; schälen; ~-deep a oberflächlich; ~ diving n Schwimmtauchen nt; ~ny a dünn; ~tight a (dress etc) hauteng.

skip [skɪp] n Sprung m // vi hüpfen; (with rope) Seil springen // vt (pass over) übergehen.

ski: ~ pants npl Skihosen pl; ~ pole n Skistock m.

skipper ['skɪpə*] n Kapitän m // vt führen.

skipping rope ['skɪpɪŋrəup] n (Brit) Hüpfseil nt.

skirmish ['skɜ:mɪʃ] n Scharmützel nt.

skirt [skɜ:t] n Rock m // vt herumgehen um; (fig) umgehen; ~ing board n (Brit) Fußleiste f.

ski suit n Skianzug m.

skit [skɪt] n Parodie f.

skittle ['skɪtl] n Kegel m; ~s n (game) Kegeln nt.

skive [skaɪv] vi (Brit col) schwänzen.

skulk [skʌlk] vi sich herumdrücken.

skull [skʌl] n Schädel m.

skunk [skʌŋk] n Stinktier nt.

sky [skaɪ] n Himmel m; ~light n Oberlicht nt; ~scraper n Wolkenkratzer m.

slab [slæb] n (of stone) Platte f.

slack [slæk] a (loose) locker; (business) flau; (careless) nachlässig, lasch // vi nachlässig sein // n: to take up the ~ straffziehen; ~s pl Hose(n pl) f; ~en (also: ~en off) vi locker werden; (become slower) nachlassen, stocken // vt (loosen) lockern.

slag [slæg] n Schlacke f; ~ heap n Halde f.

slain [sleɪn] pp of slay.

slam [slæm] n Knall m // vt (door) zuschlagen; (throw down) knallen // vi zuschlagen.

slander ['slɑ:ndə*] n Verleumdung f // vt verleumden.

slant [slɑ:nt] n (lit) Schräge f; (fig) Tendenz f // vt schräg legen // vi schräg liegen; ~ed, ~ing a schräg.

slap [slæp] n Klaps m // vt einen Klaps geben (+dat) // ad (directly) geradewegs; ~dash a salopp; ~stick (comedy) Klamauk m; ~-up a (Brit: meal) erstklassig, prima.

slash [slæʃ] n Schnittwunde f // vt (auf)schlitzen; (expenditure) radikal kürzen.

slat [slæt] n (of wood, plastic) Leiste f.

slate [sleɪt] n (stone) Schiefer m; (roofing) Dachziegel m // vt (criticize) verreißen.

slaughter ['slɔ:tə*] n (of animals) Schlachten nt; (of people) Gemetzel nt // vt schlachten; (people) niedermetzeln; ~house n Schlachthof m.

Slav [slɑ:v] a slawisch.

slave [sleɪv] n Sklave m, Sklavin f // vi schuften, sich schinden; ~ry n Sklaverei f; (work) Schinderei f.

slay [sleɪ], pt slew, pp slain vt ermorden.

sleazy ['sli:zɪ] a (place) schmierig.

sledge [sledʒ] n Schlitten m; ~hammer n Schmiedehammer m.

sleek [sli:k] a glatt; (shape) rassig.

sleep [sli:p] n Schlaf m // vi, pt, pp slept schlafen; to go to ~ einschlafen; ~ in vi ausschlafen; (oversleep) verschlafen; ~er n (person) Schläfer m; (Brit RAIL) Schlafwagen m; (beam) Schwelle f; ~ing bag n Schlafsack m; ~ing car n Schlafwagen m; ~ing pill n Schlaftablette f; ~less a (night) schlaflos; ~walker n Schlafwandler(in f) m; ~y a schläfrig.

sleet [sli:t] n Schneeregen m.

sleeve [sli:v] n Ärmel m; (of record) Umschlag m; ~less a ärmellos.

sleigh [sleɪ] n Pferdeschlitten m.

sleight [slaɪt] n: ~ of hand Fingerfertigkeit f.

slender ['slendə*] a schlank; (fig) gering.

slept [slept] pt, pp of sleep.

slew [slu:] vi (veer) (herum)schwenken // pt of slay.

slice [slaɪs] n Scheibe f // vt in Scheiben schneiden.

slick [slɪk] a (clever) raffiniert, aalglatt // n Ölteppich m.

slide [slaɪd] n Rutschbahn f; (PHOT) Dia(positiv) nt; (Brit: for hair) (Haar)spange f // v (pt, pp slid) vt schieben // vi (slip) gleiten, rutschen; ~ rule n Rechenschieber m.

sliding ['slaɪdɪŋ] a (door) Schiebe-; ~ scale n gleitende Skala f.

slight [slaɪt] a zierlich; (trivial) geringfügig; (small) gering // n Kränkung f // vt (offend) kränken; not in the ~est nicht im geringsten; ~ly ad etwas, ein bißchen.

slim [slɪm] a schlank; (book) dünn;

(chance) gering // vi eine Schlankheitskur machen.

slime [slaɪm] n Schleim m.

slimming ['slɪmɪŋ] n Schlankheitskur f.

slimy ['slaɪmɪ] a glitschig; (dirty) schlammig; (person) schmierig.

sling [slɪŋ] n Schlinge f; (weapon) Schleuder f // vt, pt, pp slung schleudern.

slip [slɪp] n (mistake) Flüchtigkeitsfehler m; (petticoat) Unterrock m; (of paper) Zettel m // vt (put) stecken, schieben // vi (lose balance) ausrutschen; (move) gleiten, rutschen; (decline) nachlassen; (move smoothly) ~ into/out of (room etc) hinein-/hinausschlüpfen; to give sb the ~ jdm entwischen; ~ of the tongue Versprecher m; it ~ped my mind das ist mir entfallen; to ~ sth on/off etw über-/abstreifen; ~ away vi sich wegstehlen; ~ by vi (time) verstreichen; ~ in vt hineingleiten lassen // vi (errors) sich einschleichen; ~ped disc n Bandscheibenschaden m.

slipper ['slɪpə*] n Hausschuh m.

slippery ['slɪpərɪ] a glatt.

slip: ~-road n (Brit) Auffahrt f/Ausfahrt f; ~shod a schlampig; ~-up n Panne f; ~way n Auslaufbahn f.

slit [slɪt] n Schlitz m // vt, pt, pp slit aufschlitzen.

slither ['slɪðə*] vi schlittern; (snake) sich schlängeln.

sliver ['slɪvə*] n (of glass, wood) Splitter m; (of cheese etc) Scheibchen nt.

slob [slɒb] n (col) Klotz m.

slog [slɒg] vi (work hard) schuften // n: it was a ~ es war eine Plackerei.

slogan ['sləʊgən] n Schlagwort nt; (COMM) Werbespruch m.

slop [slɒp] vi (also: ~ over) überschwappen // vt verschütten.

slope [sləʊp] n Neigung f; (of mountains) (Ab)hang m // vi: ~ down sich senken; ~ up ansteigen.

sloping ['sləʊpɪŋ] a schräg.

sloppy ['slɒpɪ] a schlampig.

slot [slɒt] n Schlitz m // vt: to ~ sth in etw einlegen; ~ machine n (Brit: vending machine) Automat m; (for gambling) Spielautomat m.

sloth [sləʊθ] n (laziness) Faulheit.

slouch [slaʊtʃ] vi: to ~ about (laze) herumhängen (col).

slovenly ['slʌvnlɪ] a schlampig; (speech) salopp.

slow [sləʊ] a langsam; to be ~ (clock) nachgehen; (stupid) begriffsstutzig sein // ad langsam; ~ down vi langsamer werden // vt verlangsamen; ~ up vi sich verlangsamen, sich verzögern // vt aufhalten, langsamer machen; '~' (road sign) 'Langsam'; ~ly ad langsam; in ~ motion in Zeitlupe.

sludge [slʌdʒ] n Schlamm m.

slug [slʌg] *n* Nacktschnecke *f*; (*col: bullet*) Kugel *f*; **~gish** *a* träge; (*COMM*) schleppend.

sluice [sluːs] *n* Schleuse *f*.

slumber ['slʌmbə*] *n* Schlummer *m*.

slump [slʌmp] *n* Rückgang *m* // *vi* fallen, stürzen.

slung [slʌŋ] *pt, pp of* **sling**.

slur [slɜː*] *n* Undeutlichkeit *f*; (*insult*) Verleumdung *f* // *vt* (*words*) verschlucken **~red** [slɜːd] *a* (*pronunciation*) undeutlich.

slush [slʌʃ] *n* (*snow*) Schneematsch *m*; **~ fund** *n* Schmiergeldfonds *m*.

slut [slʌt] *n* Schlampe *f*.

sly [slaɪ] *a* schlau.

smack [smæk] *n* Klaps *m* // *vt* einen Klaps geben (+*dat*); **to ~ one's lips** schmatzen, sich (*dat*) die Lippen lecken; **~ of** *vi* riechen nach.

small [smɔːl] *a* klein; **~ ads** *npl* (*Brit*) Kleinanzeigen *pl*; **in the ~ hours** in den frühen Morgenstunden; **~ change** *n* Kleingeld *nt*; **~ holder** *n* (*Brit*) Kleinbauer *m*; **~pox** *n* Pocken *pl*; **~ talk** *n* Geplauder *nt*.

smart [smɑːt] *a* (*fashionable*) elegant, schick; (*neat*) adrett; (*clever*) clever; (*quick*) scharf // *vi* brennen, schmerzen; **~en up** *vi* sich in Schale werfen // *vt* herausputzen.

smash [smæʃ] *n* Zusammenstoß *m*; (*TENNIS*) Schmetterball *m* // *vt* (*break*) zerschmettern; (*destroy*) vernichten // *vi* (*break*) zersplittern, zerspringen; **~ing** *a* (*col*) toll.

smattering ['smætərɪŋ] *n* oberflächliche Kenntnis *f*.

smear [smɪə*] *n* Fleck *m* // *vt* beschmieren.

smell [smel] *n* Geruch *m*; (*sense*) Geruchssinn *m* // *vti, pt, pp* **smelt** or **smelled** riechen (*of* nach); **~y** *a* übelriechend.

smelt [smelt] *vt* (*ore*) schmelzen.

smile [smaɪl] *n* Lächeln *nt* // *vi* lächeln; **smiling** *a* lächelnd.

smirk [smɜːk] *n* blöde(s) Grinsen *nt*.

smith [smɪθ] *n* Schmied *m*; **~y** ['smɪðɪ] *n* Schmiede *f*.

smock [smɒk] *n* Kittel *m*.

smoke [sməʊk] *n* Rauch *m* // *vt* rauchen; (*food*) räuchern // *vi* rauchen; **~d** *a* (*bacon*) geräuchert; (*glass*) Rauch-; **~r** *n* Raucher(in *f*) *m*; (*RAIL*) Raucherabteil *nt*; **~ screen** *n* Rauchwand *f*.

smoking ['sməʊkɪŋ] *n*: 'no ~' 'Rauchen verboten'.

smoky ['sməʊkɪ] *a* rauchig; (*room*) verraucht; (*taste*) geräuchert.

smolder ['sməʊldə*] *vi* (*US*) = **smoulder**.

smooth [smuːð] *a* glatt // *vt* (*also: ~ out*) glätten, glattstreichen.

smother ['smʌðə*] *vt* ersticken.

smoulder, (*US*) **smolder** ['sməʊldə*] *vi* schwelen.

smudge [smʌdʒ] *n* Schmutzfleck *m* // *vt* beschmieren.

smug [smʌg] *a* selbstgefällig.

smuggle ['smʌgl] *vt* schmuggeln; **~r** *n* Schmuggler *m*.

smuggling ['smʌglɪŋ] *n* Schmuggel *m*.

smutty ['smʌtɪ] *a* schmutzig.

snack [snæk] *n* Imbiß *m*; **~ bar** *n* Imbißstube *f*.

snag [snæg] *n* Haken *m*.

snail [sneɪl] *n* Schnecke *f*.

snake [sneɪk] *n* Schlange *f*.

snap [snæp] *n* Schnappen *nt*; (*photograph*) Schnappschuß *m* // *a* (*decision*) schnell // *vt* (*break*) zerbrechen; (*PHOT*) knipsen // *vi* (*break*) brechen; (*speak*) anfauchen; **to ~ shut** zuschnappen; **~ at** *vt* schnappen nach; **~ off** *vt* (*break*) abbrechen; **~ up** *vt* aufschnappen; **~py** *a* flott; **~shot** *n* Schnappschuß *m*.

snare [snɛə*] *n* Schlinge *f* // *vt* mit einer Schlinge fangen.

snarl [snɑːl] *n* Zähnefletschen *nt* // *vi* (*dog*) knurren.

snatch [snætʃ] *n* (*small amount*) Bruchteil *m* // *vt* schnappen, packen.

sneak [sniːk] *vi* schleichen // *n* (*col*) Petze(r) *mf*.

sneakers ['sniːkəz] *npl* (*US*) Freizeitschuhe *pl*.

sneaky ['sniːkɪ] *a* raffiniert.

sneer [snɪə*] *n* Hohnlächeln *nt* // *vi* spötteln.

sneeze [sniːz] *n* Niesen *nt* // *vi* niesen.

sniff [snɪf] *n* Schnüffeln *nt* // *vi* schnieben; (*smell*) schnüffeln // *vt* schnuppern.

snigger ['snɪgə*] *n* Kichern *nt* // *vi* hämisch kichern.

snip [snɪp] *n* Schnippel *m*, Schnipsel *m* // *vt* schnippeln.

sniper ['snaɪpə*] *n* Heckenschütze *m*.

snippet ['snɪpɪt] *n* Schnipsel *m*; (*of conversation*) Fetzen *m*.

snivelling ['snɪvlɪŋ] *a* weinerlich.

snooker ['snuːkə*] *n* Snooker *nt*.

snoop [snuːp] *vi*: **to ~ about** herumschnüffeln.

snooty ['snuːtɪ] *a* (*col*) hochnäsig.

snooze [snuːz] *n* Nickerchen *nt* // *vi* ein Nickerchen machen, dösen.

snore [snɔː*] *vi* schnarchen // *n* Schnarchen *nt*.

snorkel ['snɔːkl] *n* Schnorchel *m*.

snort [snɔːt] *n* Schnauben *nt* // *vi* schnauben.

snout [snaʊt] *n* Schnauze *f*.

snow [snəʊ] *n* Schnee *m* // *vi* schneien; **~ball** *n* Schneeball *m* // *vi* eskalieren; **~bound** *a* eingeschneit; **~drift** *n* Schneewehe *f*; **~drop** *n* Schneeglöckchen *nt*; **~fall** *n* Schneefall *m*; **~flake** *n* Schneeflocke *f*; **~man** *n* Schneemann

m; **~plough**, *(US)* **~plow** *n*
Schneepflug *m*; **~ shoe** *n* Schneeschuh
m; **~storm** *n* Schneesturm *m*.

snub [snʌb] *vt* schroff abfertigen // *n*
Verweis *m*; **~-nosed** *a* stupsnasig.

snuff [snʌf] *n* Schnupftabak *m*.

snug [snʌg] *a* gemütlich, behaglich.

snuggle ['snʌgl] *vi*: to ~ up to sb sich
an jdn kuscheln.

so [səʊ] ◆ *ad* **1** *(thus)* so; *(likewise)*
auch; ~ **saying he walked away** indem
er das sagte, ging er; **if** ~ wenn ja; **I
didn't do it — you did** ~! ich hab das
nicht gemacht — hast du wohl! ~ **do I**,
~ **am I** *etc* ich auch; ~ **it is!** tatsächlich!; **I hope/think** ~ hoffentlich/ich
glaube schon; ~ **far** bis jetzt
2 *(in comparisons etc: to such a degree)*
so; ~ **quickly/big** *(that)* so schnell/groß,
daß; **I'm** ~ **glad to see you** ich freue
mich so, dich zu sehen
3: ~ **much** *a* so viel // *ad* so sehr; ~
many *a* so viele
4 *(phrases)*: **10 or** ~ etwa 10; ~ **long!**
(col: goodbye) tschüs!
◆ *conj* **1** *(expressing purpose)*: ~ **as to**
um nicht; ~ **(that)** damit
2 *(expressing result)* also; ~ **I was right
after all** ich hatte also doch recht; ~ **you
see ...** wie du siehst ...

soak [səʊk] *vt* durchnässen; *(leave in
liquid)* einweichen // *vi* (ein)weichen; ~
in *vi* einsickern; ~ **up** *vt* aufsaugen.

so-and-so ['səʊənsəʊ] *n (somebody)*
soundso *m*.

soap [səʊp] *n* Seife *f*; **~flakes** *pl*
Seifenflocken *pl*; ~ **opera** *n*
Familienserie *f (im Fernsehen, Radio)*;
~ **powder** *n* Waschpulver *nt*; **~y** *a*
seifig, Seifen-.

soar [sɔ:*] *vi* aufsteigen; *(prices)* in die
Höhe schnellen.

sob [sɒb] *n* Schluchzen *nt* // *vi*
schluchzen.

sober ['səʊbə*] *a (lit, fig)* nüchtern; ~
up *vi* nüchtern werden.

so-called ['səʊ'kɔ:ld] *a* sogenannt.

soccer ['sɒkə*] *n* Fußball *m*.

sociable ['səʊʃəbl] *a* gesellig.

social ['səʊʃəl] *a* sozial; *(friendly, living
with others)* gesellig // *n* gesellige(r)
Abend *m*; ~ **club** *n* Verein *m (für
Freizeitgestaltung)*; **~ism** *n* Sozialismus
m; **~ist** *n* Sozialist(in *f*) *m* // *a* sozial-
istisch; **~ize** *vi*: to ~ (with) gesellschaft-
lich verkehren (mit); **~ly** *ad* gesell-
schaftlich, privat; ~ **security** *n*
Sozialversicherung *f*; ~ **work** *n*
Sozialarbeit *f*; ~ **worker** *n*
Sozialarbeiter(in *f*) *m*.

society [sə'saɪətɪ] *n* Gesellschaft *f*;
(fashionable world) die große Welt.

sock [sɒk] *n* Socke *f*.

socket ['sɒkɪt] *n (ELEC)* Steckdose *f*;
(of eye) Augenhöhle *f*; *(TECH)*

Rohransatz *m*.

sod [sɒd] *n* Rasenstück *nt*; *(col!)*
Saukerl *m* (!).

soda ['səʊdə] *n* Soda *f*; *(also:* ~ **water)**
Soda(wasser) *nt*; *(US: also:* ~ **pop)**
Limonade *f*.

sodden ['sɒdn] *a* durchweicht.

sodium ['səʊdɪəm] *n* Natrium *nt*.

sofa ['səʊfə] *n* Sofa *nt*.

soft [sɒft] *a* weich; *(not loud)* leise;
(weak) nachgiebig; ~ **drink** alkohol-
freie(s) Getränk *nt*; **~en** ['sɒfn] *vt*
weich machen; *(blow)* abschwächen,
mildern // *vi* weich werden; **~ly** *ad*
sanft; leise; **~ness** *n* Weichheit *f*; *(fig)*
Sanftheit *f*.

software ['sɒftwɛə*] *n (COMPUT)*
Software *f*.

soggy ['sɒgɪ] *a (ground)* sumpfig;
(bread) aufgeweicht.

soil [sɔɪl] *n* Erde *f* // *vt* beschmutzen;
~ed *a* beschmutzt.

solace ['sɒləs] *n* Trost *m*.

solar ['səʊlə*] *a* Sonnen-.

sold [səʊld] *pt, pp of* **sell**; ~ **out** *a*
(COMM) ausverkauft.

solder ['səʊldə*] *vt* löten // *n* Lötmetall
nt.

soldier ['səʊldʒə*] *n* Soldat *m*.

sole [səʊl] *n* Sohle *f*; *(fish)* Seezunge *f* //
a alleinig, Allein-; **~ly** *ad* ausschließlich; ~ **trader** *n (COMM)* Ein-
zelunternehmen *nt*.

solemn ['sɒləm] *a* feierlich.

solicit [sə'lɪsɪt] *vt (request)* bitten um //
vi (prostitute) Kunden anwerben.

solicitor [sə'lɪsɪtə*] *n* Rechtsanwalt *m*/
-anwältin *f*.

solid ['sɒlɪd] *a (hard)* fest; *(of same
material)* massiv; *(not hollow)* voll, ganz;
(without break) voll, ganz; *(reliable,
sensible)* solide // *n* Feste(s) *nt*.

solidarity [sɒlɪ'dærɪtɪ] *n* Solidarität *f*.

solidify [sə'lɪdɪfaɪ] *vi* fest werden.

solitary ['sɒlɪtərɪ] *a* einsam, einzeln; ~
confinement *n* Einzelhaft *f*.

solitude ['sɒlɪtjuːd] *n* Einsamkeit *f*.

soluble ['sɒljʊbl] *a (substance)* löslich;
(problem) (auf)lösbar.

solution [sə'luːʃən] *n (lit, fig)* Lösung *f*;
(of mystery) Erklärung *f*.

solve [sɒlv] *vt* (auf)lösen.

solvent ['sɒlvənt] *a (FIN)* zahlungsfähig
// *n (CHEM)* Lösungsmittel *nt*.

sombre, *(US)* **somber** ['sɒmbə*] *a* düster.

some [sʌm] ◆ *a* **1** *(a certain amount or
number of)* einige; *(a few)* ein paar;
(with singular nouns) etwas; ~ **tea/
biscuits** etwas Tee/ein paar Plätzchen;
I've got ~ **money, but not much** ich habe
ein bißchen Geld, aber nicht viel
2 *(certain: in contrasts)* manche(r, s);
~ **people say that ...** manche Leute
sagen, daß ...

3 (*unspecified*) irgendein(e); ~ **woman was asking for you** da hat eine Frau nach Ihnen gefragt; ~ **day** eines Tages; ~ **day next week** irgendwann nächste Woche
◆*pron* **1** (*a certain number*) einige; **have you got ~?** Haben Sie welche?
2 (*a certain amount*) etwas; **I've read ~ of the book** ich habe das Buch teilweise gelesen
◆*ad*: ~ **10 people** etwa 10 Leute.

somebody ['sʌmbədi] *pron*, **someone** ['sʌmwʌn] *pron* jemand; (*direct obj*) jemand(en); (*indirect obj*) jemandem.

somersault ['sʌməsɔ:lt] *n* Salto *m* // *vi* einen Salto machen.

something ['sʌmθiŋ] *pron* etwas.

sometime ['sʌmtaim] *ad* (irgend) einmal.

sometimes ['sʌmtaimz] *ad* manchmal.

somewhat ['sʌmwɒt] *ad* etwas.

somewhere ['sʌmwɛə*] *ad* irgendwo; (*to a place*) irgendwohin; ~ **else** irgendwo anders.

son [sʌn] *n* Sohn *m*.

sonar ['səunɑ:*] *n* Echolot *nt*.

song [sɒŋ] *n* Lied *nt*.

sonic ['sɒnik] *a* Schall-; ~ **boom** *n* Überschallknall *m*.

son-in-law ['sʌninlɔ:] *n* Schwiegersohn *m*.

sonny ['sʌni] *n* (*col*) Kleine(r) *m*.

soon [su:n] *ad* bald; ~ **afterwards** kurz danach; ~**er** *ad* (*time*) früher; (*for preference*) lieber; ~**er or later** früher oder später.

soot [sut] *n* Ruß *m*.

soothe [su:ð] *vt* (*person*) beruhigen; (*pain*) lindern.

sophisticated [sə'fistikeitid] *a* (*person*) kultiviert; (*machinery*) hochentwickelt.

sophomore ['sɒfəmɔ:*] *n* (*US*) College-Student *m* im 2. Jahr.

soporific [sɒpə'rifik] *a* einschläfernd.

sopping ['sɒpiŋ] *a* patschnaß.

soppy ['sɒpi] *a* (*col*) schmalzig.

sorcerer ['sɔ:sərə*] *n* Hexenmeister *m*.

sordid ['sɔ:did] *a* erbärmlich.

sore [sɔ:*] *a* schmerzend; (*point*) wund // *n* Wunde *f*; ~**ly** *ad* (*tempted f*) stark, sehr.

sorrow ['sɒrəu] *n* Kummer *m*, Leid *nt*; ~**ful** *a* sorgenvoll.

sorry ['sɒri] *a* traurig, erbärmlich; ~**!** Entschuldigung!; **to feel ~ for sb** jdn bemitleiden; **I feel ~ for him** er tut mir leid.

sort [sɔ:t] *n* Art *f*, Sorte *f* // *vt* (*also*: ~ **out**) (*papers*) sortieren, sichten; (*problems*) in Ordnung bringen; ~**ing office** *n* Sortierstelle *f*.

SOS *n* SOS *nt*.

so-so ['səu'səu] *ad* so(-so) la-la.

sought [sɔ:t] *pt, pp of* **seek**.

soul [səul] *n* Seele *f*; (*music*) Soul *m*;

~**-destroying** *a* trostlos; ~**ful** *a* seelenvoll.

sound [saund] *a* (*healthy*) gesund; (*safe*) sicher; (*sensible*) vernünftig; (*theory*) stichhaltig; (*thorough*) tüchtig, gehörig // *ad*: **to be ~ asleep** fest schlafen // *n* (*noise*) Geräusch *nt*, Laut *m*; (*GEOG*) Sund *m* // *vt* erschallen lassen; (*alarm*) (Alarm) schlagen; (*MED*) abhorchen // *vi* (*make a sound*) schallen, tönen; (*seem*) klingen; **to ~ like** sich anhören wie; ~ **out** *vt* (*opinion*) erforschen; (*person*) auf den Zahn fühlen (+*dat*); ~ **barrier** *n* Schallmauer *f*; ~ **effects** *npl* Toneffekte *pl*; ~**ing** *n* (*NAUT etc*) Lotung *f*; ~**ly** *ad* (*sleep*) fest; (*beat*) tüchtig; ~**proof** *a* (*room*) schalldicht; ~**-track** *n* Tonstreifen *m*; (*music*) Filmmusik *f*.

soup [su:p] *n* Suppe *f*; **in the ~** (*col*) in der Tinte; ~ **plate** *n* Suppenteller *m*; ~**spoon** *n* Suppenlöffel *m*.

sour ['sauə*] *a* (*lit, fig*) sauer; **it's ~ grapes** (*fig*) die Trauben hängen zu hoch.

source [sɔ:s] *n* (*lit, fig*) Quelle *f*.

south [sauθ] *n* Süden *m* // *a* Süd-, südlich // *ad* nach Süden, südwärts; **S~ Africa** *n* Südafrika *nt*; **S~ African** *a* südafrikanisch // *n* Südafrikaner(in *f*) *m*; **S~ America** *n* Südamerika *nt*; **S~ American** *a* südamerikanisch // *n* Südamerikaner(in *f*) *m*; ~**-east** *n* Südosten *m*; ~**erly** ['sʌðəli] *a* südlich; ~**ern** ['sʌðən] *a* südlich, Süd-; **S~ Pole** *n* Südpol *m*; ~**ward(s)** *ad* südwärts, nach Süden; ~**-west** *n* Südwesten *m*.

souvenir [su:və'niə*] *n* Souvenir *nt*.

sovereign ['sɒvrin] *n* (*ruler*) Herrscher(in *f*) *m* // *a* (*independent*) souverän.

soviet ['səuviət] *a* sowjetisch; **the S~ Union** die Sowjetunion.

sow [sau] *n* Sau *f* // *vt* [səu], *pt* **sowed**, *pp* **sown** [səun] (*lit, fig*) säen.

soy [sɔi] *n*: ~ **sauce** Sojasauce *f*.

soya bean ['sɔiə'bi:n] *n* Sojabohne *f*.

spa [spa:] *n* (*place*) Kurort *m*.

space [speis] *n* Platz *m*, Raum *m*; (*universe*) Weltraum *m*, All *nt*; (*length of time*) Abstand *m* // *vt* (*also*: ~ **out**) verteilen; ~**craft**, ~ **ship** *n* Raumschiff *nt*; ~**man** *n* Raumfahrer *m*; **spacing** *n* Abstand *m*; (*also*: **spacing out**) Verteilung *f*.

spacious ['speiʃəs] *a* geräumig, weit.

spade [speid] *n* Spaten *m*; ~**s** *n* (*CARDS*) Pik *nt*.

Spain [spein] *n* Spanien *nt*.

span [spæn] *n* Spanne *f*; (*of bridge etc*) Spannweite *f* // *vt* überspannen.

Spaniard ['spænjəd] *n* Spanier(in *f*) *m*.

Spanish ['spæniʃ] *a* spanisch // *n* (*LING*) Spanisch *nt*; **the ~** *npl* die Spanier.

spank [spæŋk] *vt* verhauen, versohlen.

spanner ['spænə*] *n* (*Brit*) Schrauben-

schlüssel *m.*
spar [spɑ:*] *n* (*NAUT*) Sparren *m* // *vi* (*BOXING*) einen Sparring machen.
spare [spɛə*] *a* Ersatz- // *n* = ~ **part** // *vt* (*lives, feelings*) verschonen; (*trouble*) ersparen; **to** ~ (*surplus*) übrig; ~ **part** *n* Ersatzteil *nt;* ~ **time** *n* Freizeit *f;* ~ **wheel** *n* (*AUT*) Reservereifen *m.*
sparing ['spɛərɪŋ] *a:* **to be** ~ **with** geizen mit; ~**ly** *ad* sparsam; (*eat, spend etc*) in Maßen.
spark [spɑ:k] *n* Funken *m;* ~**(ing) plug** *n* Zündkerze *f.*
sparkle ['spɑ:kl] *n* Funkeln *nt;* (*gaiety*) Schwung *m* // *vi* funkeln.
sparkling ['spɑ:klɪŋ] *a* funkelnd; (*wine*) Schaum-; (*conversation*) spritzig, geistreich.
sparrow ['spærəu] *n* Spatz *m.*
sparse [spɑ:s] *a* spärlich.
spasm ['spæzəm] *n* (*MED*) Krampf *m;* (*fig*) Anfall *m;* ~**odic** [spæz'mɒdɪk] *a* (*fig*) sprunghaft.
spat [spæt] *pt, pp of* **spit.**
spate [speɪt] *n* (*fig*) Flut *f,* Schwall *m;* **in** ~ (*river*) angeschwollen.
spatter ['spætə*] *vt* bespritzen, verspritzen.
spatula ['spætjulə] *n* Spatel *m.*
spawn [spɔ:n] *vi* laichen // *n* Laich *m.*
speak [spi:k] *v* (*pt* **spoke**, *pp* **spoken**) *vt* sprechen, reden; (*truth*) sagen; (*language*) sprechen // *vi* sprechen (*to* mit *or* zu); ~ **to sb of** *or* **about sth** mit jdm über etw (*acc*) sprechen; ~ **up!** sprich lauter!; ~**er** *n* Sprecher(in *f*) *m,* Redner(in *f*) *m;* (*loud~er*) Lautsprecher *m;* (*POL*): **the S~er der** Vorsitzende (*Brit*) des Parlaments *or* (*US*) des Kongresses.
spear [spɪə*] *n* Speer *m* // *vt* aufspießen; ~**head** *vt* (*attack etc*) anführen.
spec [spek] *n* (*col*): **on** ~ auf gut Glück.
special ['speʃəl] *a* besondere(r, s); ~**ist** *n* (*TECH*) Fachmann *m;* (*MED*) Facharzt *m,* Fachärztin *f;* ~**ity** [speʃɪ'ælɪtɪ] *n* Spezialität *f;* (*study*) Spezialgebiet *nt;* ~**ize** *vi* sich spezialisieren (**in** *auf* +*acc*); ~**ly** *ad* besonders; (*explicitly*) extra.
species ['spi:ʃiːz] *n* Art *f.*
specific [spə'sɪfɪk] *a* spezifisch; ~**ally** *ad* spezifisch.
specification [spesɪfɪ'keɪʃən] *n* Angabe *f;* (*stipulation*) Bedingung; ~**s** *pl* (*TECH*) technische Daten *pl.*
specify ['spesɪfaɪ] *vt* genau angeben.
specimen ['spesɪmɪn] *n* Probe *f.*
speck [spek] *n* Fleckchen *nt.*
speckled ['spekld] *a* gesprenkelt.
specs [speks] *npl* (*col*) Brille *f.*
spectacle ['spektəkl] *n* Schauspiel *nt;* ~**s** *pl* Brille *f.*
spectator [spek'teɪtə*] *n* Zuschauer(in *f*) *m.*

spectre, (*US*) **specter** ['spektə*] *n* Geist *m,* Gespenst *nt.*
speculate ['spekjuleɪt] *vi* spekulieren.
speech [spi:tʃ] *n* Sprache *f;* (*address*) Rede *f;* (*manner of speaking*) Sprechweise *f;* ~**less** *a* sprachlos.
speed [spi:d] *n* Geschwindigkeit *f;* (*gear*) Gang *m* // *vi* (*JUR*) (zu) schnell fahren; **at full** *or* **top** ~ mit Höchstgeschwindigkeit; ~ **up** *vt* beschleunigen // *vi* schneller werden/fahren; ~**boat** *n* Schnellboot *nt;* ~**ily** *ad* schleunigst; ~**ing** *n* zu schnelles Fahren; ~ **limit** *n* Geschwindigkeitsbegrenzung *f;* ~**ometer** [spɪ'dɒmɪtə*] *n* Tachometer *m;* ~**way** *n* (*bike racing*) Motorradrennstrecke *f;* ~**y** *a* schnell.
spell [spel] *n* (*magic*) Bann *m;* (*period of time*) Zeitlang *f* // *vt, pt, pp* **spelt** (*Brit*) *or* **spelled** buchstabieren; (*imply*) bedeuten; **to cast a** ~ **on sb** jdn verzaubern; ~**bound** *a* (wie) gebannt; ~**ing** *n* Rechtschreibung *f.*
spend [spend], *pt, pp* **spent** [spent] *vt* (*money*) ausgeben; (*time*) verbringen; ~**thrift** *n* Verschwender(in *f*) *m.*
sperm [spɜ:m] *n* (*BIOL*) Samenflüssigkeit *f.*
spew [spju:] *vt* (er)brechen.
sphere [sfɪə*] *n* (*globe*) Kugel *f;* (*fig*) Sphäre *f,* Gebiet *nt.*
spherical ['sferɪkəl] *a* kugelförmig.
spice [spaɪs] *n* Gewürz *nt* // *vt* würzen.
spick-and-span ['spɪkən'spæn] *a* blitzblank.
spider ['spaɪdə*] *n* Spinne *f.*
spike [spaɪk] *n* Dorn *m,* Spitze *f.*
spill [spɪl] *v* (*pt, pp* **spilt** [spɪlt] *or* **spilled**) *vt* verschütten // *vi* sich ergießen; ~ **over** *vi* überlaufen; (*fig*) sich ausbreiten.
spin [spɪn] *n* (*trip in car*) Spazierfahrt *f;* (*AVIAT*) (Ab)trudeln *nt;* (*on ball*) Drall *m* // *v* (*pt, pp* **spun**) *vt* (*thread*) spinnen; (*like top*) (herum)wirbeln // *vi* sich drehen; ~ **out** *vt* in die Länge ziehen.
spinach ['spɪnɪtʃ] *n* Spinat *m.*
spinal ['spaɪnl] *a* Rückgrat-; ~ **cord** *n* Rückenmark *nt.*
spindly ['spɪndlɪ] *a* spindeldürr.
spin-dryer ['spɪn'draɪə*] *n* (*Brit*) Wäscheschleuder *f.*
spine [spaɪn] *n* Rückgrat *nt;* (*thorn*) Stachel *m;* ~**less** *a* (*lit, fig*) rückgratlos.
spinning ['spɪnɪŋ] *n* Spinnen *nt;* ~ **top** *n* Kreisel *m;* ~ **wheel** *n* Spinnrad *nt.*
spin-off ['spɪnɒf] *n* Nebenprodukt *nt.*
spinster ['spɪnstə*] *n* unverheiratete Frau *f;* (*old*) alte Jungfer *f.*
spire [spaɪə*] *n* Turm *m.*
spirit ['spɪrɪt] *n* Geist *m;* (*humour, mood*) Stimmung *f;* (*courage*) Mut *m;* (*verve*) Elan *m;* (*alcohol*) Alkohol *m;* ~**s** *pl* Spirituosen *pl;* **in good** ~**s** gut auf-

gelegt; ~ed *a* beherzt; ~ **level** *n* Wasserwaage *f*.

spiritual ['spɪrɪtjʊəl] *a* geistig, seelisch; (*REL*) geistlich // *n* Spiritual *nt*.

spit [spɪt] *n* (*for roasting*) (Brat)spieß *m*; (*saliva*) Spucke *f* // *vi*, *pt*, *pp* **spat** spucken; (*rain*) sprühen; (*make a sound*) zischen; (*cat*) fauchen.

spite [spaɪt] *n* Gehässigkeit *f* // *vt* kränken; in ~ of trotz (+*gen or dat*); ~ful *a* gehässig.

spittle ['spɪtl] *n* Speichel *m*, Spucke *f*.

splash [splæʃ] *n* Spritzer *m*; (*of colour*) (Farb)fleck *m* // *vt* bespritzen // *vi* spritzen.

spleen [spliːn] *n* (*ANAT*) Milz *f*.

splendid ['splendɪd] *a* glänzend.

splendour, (*US*) **splendor** ['splendə*] *n* Pracht *f*.

splint [splɪnt] *n* Schiene *f*.

splinter ['splɪntə*] *n* Splitter *m* // *vi* (zer)splittern.

split [splɪt] *n* Spalte *f*; (*fig*) Spaltung *f*; (*division*) Trennung *f* // *v* (*pt*, *pp* **split**) *vt* spalten // *vi* (*divide*) reißen; ~ **up** *vi* sich trennen.

splutter ['splʌtə*] *vi* stottern.

spoil [spɔɪl], *pt*, *pp* **spoilt** or **spoiled** *vt* (*ruin*) verderben; (*child*) verwöhnen; ~**s** *npl* Beute *f*; ~**sport** *n* Spielverderber *m*.

spoke [spəʊk] *pt of* **speak** // *n* Speiche *f*.

spoken ['spəʊkn] *pp of* **speak**.

spokesman ['spəʊksmən] *n* Sprecher *m*.

spokeswoman ['spəʊkswʊmən] *n* Sprecherin *f*.

sponge [spʌndʒ] *n* Schwamm *m* // *vt* abwaschen // *vi* auf Kosten leben (*on gen*); ~ **bag** *n* (*Brit*) Kulturbeutel *m*; ~ **cake** *n* Rührkuchen *m*.

sponsor ['spɒnsə*] *n* Sponsor *m* // *vt* fördern; ~**ship** *n* Finanzierung *f*; (*public*) Schirmherrschaft *f*.

spontaneous [spɒn'teɪnɪəs] *a* spontan.

spooky ['spuːkɪ] *a* (*col*) gespenstisch.

spool [spuːl] *n* Spule *f*, Rolle *f*.

spoon [spuːn] *n* Löffel *m*; ~**-feed** *vt* *irreg* (*lit*) mit dem Löffel füttern; (*fig*) hochpäppeln; ~**ful** *n* Löffel(voll) *m*.

sport [spɔːt] *n* Sport *m*; (*person*) feine(r) Kerl *m*; ~**ing** *a* (*fair*) sportlich, fair; to give sb a ~**ing** chance jdm eine faire Chance geben; ~**s car** *n* Sportwagen *m*; ~**s jacket**, (*US*) ~ **jacket** Sportjackett *nt*; **sportsman** *n* Sportler *m*; **sportsmanship** *n* Sportlichkeit *f*; **sportswear** *n* Sportkleidung *f*; **sportswoman** *n* Sportlerin *f*; ~**y** *a* sportlich.

spot [spɒt] *n* Punkt *m*; (*dirty*) Fleck(en) *m*; (*place*) Stelle *f*; (*MED*) Pickel *m* // *vt* erspähen; (*mistake*) bemerken; on the ~ an Ort und Stelle; (*at once*) auf der Stelle; ~ **check** *n* Stichprobe *f*;

~**less** *a* fleckenlos; ~**light** *n* Scheinwerferlicht *nt*; (*lamp*) Scheinwerfer *m*; ~**ted** *a* gefleckt; ~**ty** *a* (*face*) pickelig.

spouse [spaʊz] *n* Gatte *m*/Gattin *f*.

spout [spaʊt] *n* (*of pot*) Tülle *f*; (*jet*) Wasserstrahl *m* // *vi* speien.

sprain [spreɪn] *n* Verrenkung *f* // *vt* verrenken.

sprang [spræŋ] *pt of* **spring**.

sprawl [sprɔːl] *vi* sich strecken.

spray [spreɪ] *n* Spray *nt*; (*off sea*) Gischt *f*; (*of flowers*) Zweig *m* // *vt* besprühen, sprayen.

spread [spred] *n* (*extent*) Verbreitung *f*; (*col: meal*) Schmaus *m*; (*for bread*) Aufstrich *m* // *v* (*pt*, *pp* **spread**) *vt* ausbreiten; (*scatter*) verbreiten; (*butter*) streichen // *vi* sich ausbreiten; ~**-eagled** *a*: to be ~**-eagled** alle viere von sich strecken.

spree [spriː] *n* (*shopping*) Einkaufsbummel *m*; to go on a ~ einen draufmachen.

sprightly ['spraɪtlɪ] *a* munter, lebhaft.

spring [sprɪŋ] *n* (*leap*) Sprung *m*; (*metal*) Feder *f*; (*season*) Frühling *m*; (*water*) Quelle *f* // *vi*, *pt* **sprang**, *pp* **sprung** (*leap*) springen; ~ **up** *vi* (*problem*) auftauchen; ~**board** *n* Sprungbrett *nt*; ~**-clean** *n* (*also*: ~**-cleaning**) *n* Frühjahrsputz *m*; ~**time** *n* Frühling *m*; ~**y** *a* federnd, elastisch.

sprinkle ['sprɪŋkl] *vt* (*salt*) streuen; (*liquid*) sprenkeln; to ~ water on, ~ with water mit Wasser besprengen.

sprinkler ['sprɪŋklə*] *n* (*for lawn*) Sprenger *m*; (*for fire fighting*) Sprinkler *m*.

sprite [spraɪt] *n* Elfe *f*; Kobold *m*.

sprout [spraʊt] *vi* sprießen; **(Brussels)** ~**s** *npl* Rosenkohl *m*.

spruce [spruːs] *n* Fichte *f* // *a* schmuck, adrett.

sprung [sprʌŋ] *pp of* **spring**.

spry [spraɪ] *a* flink, rege.

spun [spʌn] *pt*, *pp of* **spin**.

spur [spɜː*] *n* Sporn *m*; (*fig*) Ansporn *m* // *vt* (*also*: ~ **on**) (*fig*) anspornen; on the ~ of the moment spontan.

spurious ['spjʊərɪəs] *a* falsch.

spurn [spɜːn] *vt* verschmähen.

spurt [spɜːt] *n* (*jet*) Strahl *m*; (*acceleration*) Spurt *m* // *vi* (*liquid*) schießen.

spy [spaɪ] *n* Spion(in *f*) *m* // *vi* spionieren // *vt* erspähen; ~**ing** *n* Spionage *f*.

sq. *abbr of* **square**.

squabble ['skwɒbl] *n* Zank *m* // *vi* sich zanken.

squad [skwɒd] *n* (*MIL*) Abteilung *f*; (*police*) Kommando *nt*.

squadron ['skwɒdrən] *n* (*cavalry*) Schwadron *f*; (*NAUT*) Geschwader *nt*; (*air force*) Staffel *f*.

squalid ['skwɒlɪd] a verkommen.
squall [skwɔːl] n Bö f, Windstoß m.
squalor ['skwɒlə*] n Verwahrlosung f.
squander ['skwɒndə*] vt verschwenden.
square [skwɛə*] n Quadrat nt; (open space) Platz m; (instrument) Winkel m; (col: person) Spießer m // a viereckig; (col: ideas, tastes) spießig // vt (arrange) ausmachen; (MATH) ins Quadrat erheben // vi (agree) übereinstimmen; all ~ quitt; a ~ meal eine ordentliche Mahlzeit; 2 metres ~ 2 Meter im Quadrat; 1 ~ metre 1 Quadratmeter; ~ly ad fest, gerade.
squash [skwɒʃ] n (Brit: drink) Saft m // vt zerquetschen.
squat [skwɒt] a untersetzt // vi hocken; ~ter n Hausbesetzer m.
squawk [skwɔːk] vi kreischen.
squeak [skwiːk] vi quiek(s)en; (spring, door etc) quietschen.
squeal [skwiːl] vi schrill schreien.
squeamish ['skwiːmɪʃ] a empfindlich.
squeeze [skwiːz] n (POL) Geldknappheit f // vt pressen, drücken; (orange) auspressen; ~ out vt ausquetschen.
squelch [skwɛltʃ] vi platschen.
squid [skwɪd] n Tintenfisch m.
squiggle ['skwɪgl] n Schnörkel m.
squint [skwɪnt] vi schielen (at nach) // n: to have a ~ schielen.
squire ['skwaɪə*] n (Brit) Gutsherr m.
squirm [skwɜːm] vi sich winden.
squirrel ['skwɪrəl] n Eichhörnchen nt.
squirt [skwɜːt] vti spritzen.
Sr abbr (= senior) sen.
St abbr (= saint) hl., St.; (= street) Str.
stab [stæb] n (blow) Stich m; (col: try) Versuch m // vt erstechen.
stabilize ['steɪbɪlaɪz] vt stabilisieren // vi sich stabilisieren.
stable ['steɪbl] a stabil // n Stall m.
stack [stæk] n Stapel m // vt stapeln.
stadium ['steɪdɪəm] n Stadion nt.
staff [stɑːf] n (stick, MIL) Stab m; (personnel) Personal nt; (Brit SCH) Lehrkräfte pl // vt (with people) besetzen.
stag [stæg] n Hirsch m.
stage [steɪdʒ] n Bühne f; (of journey) Etappe f; (degree) Stufe f; (point) Stadium nt // vt (put on) aufführen; (simulate) inszenieren; (demonstration) veranstalten; in ~s etappenweise; ~coach n Postkutsche f; ~ door n Bühneneingang m; ~ manager n Intendant m.
stagger ['stægə*] vi wanken, taumeln // vt (amaze) verblüffen; (hours) staffeln; ~ing a unglaublich.
stagnant ['stægnənt] a stagnierend; (water) stehend.
stagnate [stæg'neɪt] vi stagnieren.
stag party n Männerabend m (vom

Bräutigam vor der Hochzeit gegeben).
staid [steɪd] a gesetzt.
stain [steɪn] n Fleck m // vt beflecken; ~ed glass window buntes Glasfenster nt; ~less a (steel) rostfrei; ~ remover n Fleckentferner m.
stair [stɛə*] n (Treppen)stufe f; ~case n Treppenhaus nt, Treppe f; ~s pl Treppe f; ~way n Treppenaufgang m.
stake [steɪk] n (post) Pfahl m; (money) Einsatz m // vt (bet money) setzen; to be at ~ auf dem Spiel stehen.
stale [steɪl] a alt; (bread) altbacken.
stalemate ['steɪlmeɪt] n (CHESS) Patt nt; (fig) Stillstand m.
stalk [stɔːk] n Stengel m, Stiel m // vt (game) jagen; ~ off vi abstolzieren.
stall [stɔːl] n (in stable) Stand m, Box f; (in market) (Verkaufs)stand m // vt (AUT) (den Motor) abwürgen // vi (AUT) stehenbleiben; (avoid) Ausflüchte machen; ~s npl (Brit THEAT) Parkett nt.
stallion ['stæliən] n Zuchthengst m.
stalwart ['stɔːlwət] n treue(r) Anhänger m.
stamina ['stæmɪnə] n Durchhaltevermögen nt, Zähigkeit f.
stammer ['stæmə*] n Stottern nt // vti stottern, stammeln.
stamp [stæmp] n Briefmarke f; (for document) Stempel m // vi stampfen // vt (mark) stempeln; (mail) frankieren; (foot) stampfen mit; ~ album n Briefmarkenalbum nt; ~ collecting n Briefmarkensammeln nt.
stampede [stæm'piːd] n panische Flucht f.
stance [stæns] n Haltung f.
stand [stænd] n (for objects) Gestell nt; (seats) Tribüne f // v (pt, pp stood) vi stehen; (rise) aufstehen; (decision) feststehen // vt setzen, stellen; (endure) aushalten; (person) ausstehen; (nonsense) dulden; to make a ~ Widerstand leisten; to ~ for parliament (Brit) für das Parlament kandidieren; ~ by vi (be ready) bereitstehen // vt (opinion) treu bleiben (+dat); ~ down vi (withdraw) zurücktreten; ~ for vt (signify) stehen für; (permit, tolerate) hinnehmen; ~ in for vt einspringen für; ~ out vi (be prominent) hervorstechen; ~ up vi (rise) aufstehen; ~ up for vt sich einsetzen für; ~ up to vt: ~ up to sth/sb vt einer Sache gewachsen sein/sich jdm gegenüber behaupten.
standard ['stændəd] n (measure) Norm f; (flag) Fahne f // a (size etc) Normal-; ~s npl (morals) Maßstäbe pl; ~ize vt vereinheitlichen; ~ lamp n (Brit) Stehlampe f; ~ of living n Lebensstandard m.
stand-by ['stændbaɪ] n Reserve f; to be on ~ in Bereitschaft sein; ~ ticket n (AVIAT) Standby-Ticket nt.

stand-in ['stændɪn] n Ersatz m.

standing ['stændɪŋ] a (erect) stehend; (permanent) ständig; (invitation) offen // n (duration) Dauer f; (reputation) Ansehen nt; of many years' ~ langjährig; ~ **order** n (Brit: at bank) Dauerauftrag m; ~ **orders** pl (MIL) Vorschrift; ~ **room** n Stehplatz m.

stand-offish ['stænd'ɒfɪʃ] a zurückhaltend, sehr reserviert.

standpoint ['stændpɔɪnt] n Standpunkt m.

standstill ['stændstɪl] n: to be at a ~ stillstehen; to come to a ~ zum Stillstand kommen.

stank [stæŋk] pt of **stink**.

staple ['steɪpl] n (in paper) Heftklammer f; (article) Haupterzeugnis nt // a Grund-, Haupt- // vt (fest)klammern; ~**r** n Heftmaschine f.

star [stɑː*] n Stern m; (person) Star m // vi die Hauptrolle spielen.

starboard ['stɑːbəd] n Steuerbord nt.

starch [stɑːtʃ] n Stärke f.

stardom ['stɑːdəm] n Berühmtheit f.

stare [stɛə*] n starre(r) Blick m // vi starren (at auf +acc); ~ **at** vt anstarren.

starfish ['stɑːfɪʃ] n Seestern m.

stark [stɑːk] a öde // ad: ~ **naked** splitternackt.

starling ['stɑːlɪŋ] n Star m.

starry ['stɑːrɪ] a Sternen-; ~**-eyed** a (innocent) blauäugig.

start [stɑːt] n Anfang m; (SPORT) Start m; (lead) Vorsprung m // vt in Gang setzen; (car) anlassen // vi anfangen; (car) anspringen; (on journey) aufbrechen; (SPORT) starten; (with fright) zusammenfahren; to ~ **doing** or to do sth anfangen, etw zu tun; ~ **off** vi anfangen; (begin moving) losgehen/-fahren; ~ **up** vi anfangen; (startled) auffahren // vt beginnen; (car) anlassen; (engine) starten; ~**er** n (AUT) Anlasser m; (for race) Starter m; (Brit COOK) Vorspeise f; ~**ing point** n Ausgangspunkt m.

startle ['stɑːtl] vt erschrecken.

startling ['stɑːtlɪŋ] a erschreckend.

starvation [stɑːˈveɪʃən] n Verhungern nt.

starve [stɑːv] vi verhungern // vt verhungern lassen; I'm starving ich sterbe vor Hunger.

state [steɪt] n (condition) Zustand m; (POL) Staat m // vt erklären; (facts) angeben; the S~s die Staaten; to be in a ~ durchdrehen; ~**ly** a würdevoll; ~**ment** n Aussage f; (POL) Erklärung f; **statesman** n Staatsmann m.

static ['stætɪk] n: ~ **electricity** n Reibungselektrizität f.

station ['steɪʃən] n (RAIL etc) Bahnhof m; (police etc) Wache f; (in society) Stand m // vt stationieren.

stationary ['steɪʃənərɪ] a stillstehend; (car) parkend.

stationer ['steɪʃənə*] n Schreibwarenhändler m; ~**'s** n (shop) Schreibwarengeschäft nt; ~**y** n Schreibwaren pl.

station master ['steɪʃənmɑːstə*] n Bahnhofsvorsteher m.

station wagon ['steɪʃənwægən] n Kombiwagen m.

statistics [stəˈtɪstɪks] n Statistik f.

statue ['stætjuː] n Statue f.

stature ['stætʃə*] n Größe f.

status ['steɪtəs] n Status m.

statute ['stætjuːt] n Gesetz nt.

statutory ['stætjʊtərɪ] a gesetzlich.

staunch [stɔːntʃ] a standhaft.

stave [steɪv]: ~ **off** vt (attack) abwehren; (threat) abwenden.

stay [steɪ] n Aufenthalt m // vi bleiben; (reside) wohnen; to ~ **put** an einem Ort und Stelle bleiben; to ~ **the night** übernachten; ~ **behind** vi zurückbleiben; ~ **in** vi (at home) zu Hause bleiben; ~ **on** vi (continue) länger bleiben; ~ **out** vi (of house) wegbleiben; ~ **up** vi (at night) aufbleiben; ~**ing power** n Durchhaltevermögen nt.

stead [sted] n: **in sb's** ~ an jds Stelle; to **stand sb in good** ~ jdm zugute kommen.

steadfast ['stedfəst] a standhaft, treu.

steadily ['stedɪlɪ] ad stetig, regelmäßig.

steady ['stedɪ] a (firm) fest, stabil; (regular) gleichmäßig; (reliable) beständig; (hand) ruhig; (job, boyfriend) fest // vt festigen; to ~ **o.s. on** or **against** sth sich stützen auf or gegen etw (acc).

steak [steɪk] n Steak nt; (fish) Filet nt.

steal [stiːl] v (pt **stole**, pp **stolen**) vti stehlen // vi sich stehlen.

stealth [stelθ] n Heimlichkeit f; ~**y** ['stelθɪ] a verstohlen, heimlich.

steam [stiːm] n Dampf m // vt (COOK) im Dampfbad erhitzen // vi dampfen; ~ **engine** n Dampfmaschine f; ~**er** n Dampfer m; ~**roller** n Dampfwalze f; ~**ship** n = ~**er**; ~**y** a dampfig.

steel [stiːl] n Stahl m // a Stahl-; (fig) stählern; ~**works** n Stahlwerke pl.

steep [stiːp] a steil; (price) gepfeffert // vt einweichen.

steeple ['stiːpl] n Kirchturm m; ~**chase** n Hindernisrennen nt.

steer [stɪə*] vti steuern; (car etc) lenken; ~**ing** n (AUT) Steuerung f; ~**ing wheel** n Steuer- or Lenkrad nt.

stellar ['stelə*] a Stern(en)-.

stem [stem] n Stiel m // vt aufhalten; ~ **from** vt abstammen von.

stench [stentʃ] n Gestank m.

stencil ['stensl] n Schablone f // vt (auf)drucken.

stenographer [steˈnɒgrəfə*] n (US) Stenograph(in f) m.

step [step] *n* Schritt *m*; (*stair*) Stufe *f* //
vi treten, schreiten; **to take** ~**s** Schritte
unternehmen; ~**s** *pl* = ~**ladder**; **in/out
of** ~ (**with**) im/nicht im Gleichklang
(mit); ~**-daughter** *n* Stieftochter *f*; ~
down *vi* (*fig*) abtreten; ~ **off** *vt* aussteigen aus (+*dat*); ~ **up** *vt* steigern;
~**brother** *n* Stiefbruder *m*; ~**father** *n*
Stiefvater *m*; ~**ladder** *n* Trittleiter *f*;
~**mother** *n* Stiefmutter *f*; ~**ping stone**
n Stein *m*; (*fig*) Sprungbrett *nt*;
~**sister** *n* Stiefschwester *f*; ~**son** *n*
Stiefsohn *m*.

stereo ['steriəu] *n* Stereoanlage *f* // *a*
(*also:* ~**phonic**) *a* stereophonisch.

stereotype ['stiəriətaip] *n* Prototyp *m*;
(*fig*) Klischee *nt* // *vt* stereotypieren;
(*fig*) stereotyp machen.

sterile ['sterail] *a* steril; (*person*) unfruchtbar.

sterling ['stɜːlɪŋ] *a* (*FIN*) Sterling-;
(*character*) gediegen // *n* (*ECON*) Pfund
Sterling; **a pound** ~ ein Pfund Sterling.

stern [stɜːn] *a* streng // *n* Heck *nt*,
Achterschiff *nt*.

stew [stjuː] *n* Eintopf *m* // *vti* schmoren.

steward ['stjuːəd] *n* Steward *m*; ~**ess** *n*
Stewardess *f*.

stick [stik] *n* Stock *m*; (*of chalk etc*)
Stück *nt* // *v* (*pt, pp* **stuck**) *vt* (*stab*) stechen; (*fix*) stecken; (*put*) stellen; (*gum*)
(an)kleben; (*col: tolerate*) vertragen //
vi (*stop*) steckenbleiben; (*get stuck*)
klemmen; (*hold fast*) kleben, haften; ~
out *vi* (*project*) hervorstehen aus; ~ **up**
vi (*project*) in die Höhe stehen; ~ **up
for** *vt* (*defend*) eintreten für; ~**er** *n* Aufkleber *m*; ~**ing plaster** *n* Heftpflaster
nt.

stickler ['stiklə*] *n* Pedant *m* (*for* in
+*acc*).

stick-up ['stikʌp] *n* (*col*) (Raub)überfall
m.

sticky ['stiki] *a* klebrig; (*atmosphere*)
stickig.

stiff [stif] *a* steif; (*difficult*) hart; (*paste*)
dick; (*drink*) stark; ~**en** *vt* versteifen,
(ver)stärken // *vi* sich versteifen; ~**ness**
n Steifheit *f*.

stifle ['staifl] *vt* unterdrücken.

stifling ['staiflɪŋ] *a* drückend.

stigma ['stigmə], *pl* (*BOT, MED, REL*)
~**ta** [-tə], (*fig*) ~**s** *n* Stigma *nt*.

stile [stail] *n* Steige *f*.

stiletto [sti'letəu] *n* (*Brit: also:* ~ **heel**)
Pfennigabsatz *m*.

still [stil] *a* still // *ad* (*immer*) noch;
(*anyhow*) immerhin; ~**born** *a* tot-
geboren; ~ **life** *n* Stilleben *nt*.

stilt [stilt] *n* Stelze *f*.

stilted ['stiltid] *a* gestelzt.

stimulate ['stimjuleit] *vt* anregen,
stimulieren.

stimulus ['stimjuləs], *pl* **-li** [-lai] *n* Anregung *f*, Reiz *m*.

sting [stiŋ] *n* Stich *m*; (*organ*) Stachel *m*
// *vti, pt, pp* **stung** stechen; (*on skin*)
brennen.

stingy ['stindʒi] *a* geizig, knauserig.

stink [stiŋk] *n* Gestank *m* // *vi, pt* **stank**,
pp **stunk** stinken; ~**ing** *a* (*fig*) widerlich.

stint [stint] *n* Pensum *nt*; (*period*)
Betätigung *f* // *vi* knausern; **to do one's**
~ seine Arbeit tun; (*share*) seinen Teil
beitragen.

stipulate ['stipjuleit] *vt* festsetzen.

stir [stɜː*] *n* Bewegung *f*; (*COOK*)
Rühren *nt*; (*sensation*) Aufsehen *nt* // *vt*
(um)rühren // *vi* sich rühren; ~ **up** *vt*
mob aufhetzen; (*mixture*) umrühren;
(*dust*) aufwirbeln.

stirrup ['stirəp] *n* Steigbügel *m*.

stitch [stitʃ] *n* (*with needle*) Stich *m*;
(*MED*) Faden *m*; (*of knitting*) Masche *f*;
(*pain*) Stich *m* // *vt* nähen.

stoat [stəut] *n* Wiesel *nt*.

stock [stɔk] *n* Vorrat *m*; (*COMM*) (Waren)lager *nt*; (*live*~) Vieh *nt*; (*COOK*)
Brühe *f*; (*FIN*) Grundkapital *nt* // *a* stets
vorrätig; (*standard*) Normal- // *vt* (*in
shop*) führen; **in/out of** ~ vorrätig/nicht
vorrätig; **to take** ~ **of** Inventur machen
von; (*fig*) Bilanz ziehen aus; ~**s** *npl*
Aktien *pl*; ~**s and shares** Effekten *pl*; ~
up with Reserven anlegen von.

stockbroker ['stɔkbrəukə*] *n*
Börsenmakler *m*.

stock cube *n* Brühwürfel *m*.

stock exchange *n* Börse *f*.

stocking ['stɔkiŋ] *n* Strumpf *m*.

stockist ['stɔkist] *n* Händler *m*.

stock market ['stɔkmɑːkit] *n* Börse *f*.

stock phrase *n* Standardsatz *m*.

stockpile ['stɔkpail] *n* Vorrat *m* // *vt*
aufstapeln.

stocktaking ['stɔkteikiŋ] *n* (*Brit
COMM*) Inventur *f*, Bestandsaufnahme *f*.

stocky ['stɔki] *a* untersetzt.

stodgy ['stɔdʒi] *a* pampig; (*fig*) trocken.

stoke [stəuk] *vt* schüren.

stole [stəul] *pt of* **steal** // *n* Stola *f*.

stolen ['stəulən] *pp of* **steal**.

stolid ['stɔlid] *a* stur.

stomach ['stʌmək] *n* Bauch *m*, Magen
m // *vt* vertragen; ~**-ache** *n* Magen- *or*
Bauchschmerzen *pl*.

stone [stəun] *n* Stein *m*; (*Brit: weight*)
Gewichtseinheit *f* = 6.35 *kg* // *vt* (*olive*)
entkernen; (*kill*) steinigen; ~**-cold** *a*
eiskalt; ~**-deaf** *a* stocktaub; ~**work** *n*
Mauerwerk *nt*.

stony ['stəuni] *a* steinig.

stood [stud] *pt, pp of* **stand**.

stool [stuːl] *n* Hocker *m*.

stoop [stuːp] *vi* sich bücken.

stop [stɔp] *n* Halt *m*; (*bus*~) Haltestelle
f; (*punctuation*) Punkt *m* // *vt* anhalten;
(*bring to end*) aufhören (mit), sein
lassen // *vi* aufhören; (*clock*) stehen-

bleiben; (remain) bleiben; to ~ **doing**
sth aufhören, etw zu tun; ~ **dead** vi
innehalten; ~ **off** vi kurz haltmachen;
~ **up** vt (hole) zustopfen, verstopfen;
~gap n Notlösung f; **~lights** npl
(AUT) Bremslichter pl; **~over** n (on
journey) Zwischenaufenthalt m.

stoppage ['stɒpɪdʒ] n (An)halten nt;
(traffic) Verkehrsstockung f; (strike)
Arbeitseinstellung f.

stopper ['stɒpə*] n Propfen m, Stöpsel
m.

stop press n letzte Meldung f.

stopwatch ['stɒpwɒtʃ] n Stoppuhr f.

storage ['stɔːrɪdʒ] n Lagerung f; ~
heater n (Nachtstrom)speicherofen m.

store [stɔː*] n Vorrat m; (place) Lager
nt, Warenhaus nt; (Brit: large shop)
Kaufhaus nt; (US) Laden m; **~s** pl Vorräte pl // vt lagern; ~ **up** vt sich eindecken mit; **~room** n Lagerraum m,
Vorratsraum m.

storey, (US) **story** ['stɔːrɪ] n Stock m.

stork [stɔːk] n Storch m.

storm [stɔːm] n (lit, fig) Sturm m // vti
stürmen; **~y** a stürmisch.

story ['stɔːrɪ] n Geschichte f; (lie) Märchen nt; (US) = **storey**; **~book** n Ge-
schichtenbuch nt; **~teller** n Ge-
schichtenerzähler m.

stout [staut] a (bold) tapfer; (too fat)
beleibt // n Starkbier nt; (also: sweet ~)
≈ Malzbier nt.

stove [stəuv] n (Koch)herd m; (for
heating) Ofen m.

stow [stəu] vt verstauen; **~away** n
blinde(r) Passagier m.

straddle ['strædl] vt (horse, fence)
rittlings sitzen auf (+dat); (fig) überbrücken.

straggle ['strægl] vi (branches etc) wuchern; (people) nachhinken; **~r** n
Nachzügler m; **straggling, straggly** a
(hair) zottig.

straight [streɪt] a gerade; (honest)
offen, ehrlich; (drink) pur // ad (direct)
direkt, geradewegs; to put or get sth ~
etw in Ordnung bringen; **~away** ad
sofort; ~ **off** ad sofort; **~en** vt (also:
~en out) (lit) gerade machen; (fig)
klarstellen; **~-faced** ad ohne die Miene
zu verziehen // a: to be **~-faced** keine
Miene verziehen; **~forward** a einfach,
unkompliziert.

strain [streɪn] n Belastung f; (streak,
trace) Zug m; (of music) Fetzen m // vt
überanstrengen; (stretch) anspannen;
(muscle) zerren; (filter) (durch)seihen //
vi sich anstrengen; **~ed** a (laugh)
gezwungen; (relations) gespannt; **~er** n
Sieb nt.

strait [streɪt] n Straße f, Meerenge f; **~-
jacket** n Zwangsjacke f; **~-laced** a
engherzig, streng.

strand [strænd] n (lit, fig) Faden m; (of

hair) Strähne f; **~ed** (lit, fig) ge-
strandet.

strange [streɪndʒ] a fremd; (unusual)
seltsam; **~r** n Fremde(r) mf.

strangle ['stræŋgl] vt erwürgen; **~hold**
n (fig) Umklammerung f.

strap [stræp] n Riemen m; (on clothes)
Träger m // (car) festschnallen.

strapping ['stræpɪŋ] a stramm.

strata ['strɑːtə] pl of **stratum**.

stratagem ['strætədʒəm] n (Kriegs)list
f.

strategic [strə'tiːdʒɪk] a strategisch.

strategy ['strætədʒɪ] n (fig) Strategie f.

stratum ['strɑːtəm], pl **-ta** n Schicht f.

straw [strɔː] n Stroh nt; (single stalk,
drinking ~) Strohhalm m; that's the last
~! das ist der Gipfel!

strawberry ['strɔːbərɪ] n Erdbeere f.

stray [streɪ] a (animal) verirrt;
(thought) zufällig // vi herumstreunen.

streak [striːk] n Streifen m; (in
character) Einschlag m; (in hair)
Strähne f // vt streifen // vi zucken;
(move quickly) flitzen; ~ of bad luck
Pechsträhne f; **~y** a gestreift; (bacon)
durchwachsen.

stream [striːm] n (brook) Bach m; (fig)
Strom m // vt (SCH) in (Lei-
stungs)gruppen einteilen // vi strömen;
to ~ **in/out** (people) hinein-/
hinausströmen.

streamer ['striːmə*] n (pennon) Wimpel
m; (of paper) Luftschlange f.

streamlined ['striːmlaɪnd] a
stromlinienförmig; (effective) rationell.

street [striːt] n Straße f // a Straßen-;
~car n (US) Straßenbahn f; ~ **lamp** n
Straßenlaterne f; ~ **plan** n Stadtplan
m; **~wise** a (col): to be **~wise** wissen,
wo es lang geht.

strength [streŋθ] n Stärke f (also fig);
Kraft f; **~en** vt (ver)stärken.

strenuous ['strenjuəs] a anstrengend.

stress [stres] n Druck m; (mental) Streß
m; (GRAM) Betonung f // vt betonen.

stretch [stretʃ] n Strecke f // vt ausdehnen, strecken // vi sich erstrecken;
(person) sich strecken; ~ **out** vi sich
ausstrecken // vt ausstrecken.

stretcher ['stretʃə*] n Tragbahre f.

strewn [struːn] a: ~ **with** übersät mit.

stricken ['strɪkən] a (person) ergriffen;
(city, country) heimgesucht; ~ **with** (arthritis, disease) leidend unter.

strict [strɪkt] a (exact) genau; (severe)
streng; **~ly** ad streng, genau.

stride [straɪd] n lange(r) Schritt m // vi,
pt **strode**, pp **stridden** ['strɪdn]
schreiten.

strident ['straɪdənt] a schneidend,
durchdringend.

strife [straɪf] n Streit m.

strike [straɪk] n Streik m; (attack)
Schlag m // v (pt, pp **struck**) vt (hit)

schlagen; (*collide*) stoßen gegen; (*come to mind*) einfallen (+*dat*); (*stand out*) auffallen (+*dat*); (*find*) finden // vi (*stop work*) streiken; (*attack*) zuschlagen; (*clock*) schlagen; **on ~** (*workers*) im Streik; **to ~ a match** ein Streichholz anzünden; **~ down** vt (*lay low*) niederschlagen; **~ out** vt (*cross out*) ausstreichen; **~ up** vt (*music*) anstimmen; (*friendship*) schließen; **~r** n Streikende(r) mf.

striking ['straikiŋ] a auffallend.

string [striŋ] n Schnur f; (*row*) Reihe f; (*MUS*) Saite f // v (*pt, pp* strung) vt: **to ~ together** aneinanderreihen // vi: **to ~ out** (sich) verteilen; **the ~s** pl (*MUS*) die Streichinstrumente pl; **to pull ~s** (*fig*) Föden ziehen; **~ bean** n grüne Bohne f; **~(ed) instrument** n (*MUS*) Saiteninstrument nt.

stringent ['strindʒənt] a streng.

strip [strip] n Streifen m // vt (*uncover*) abstreifen, abziehen; (*clothes*) ausziehen; (*TECH*) auseinandernehmen // vi (*undress*) sich ausziehen; **~ cartoon** n Bildserie f.

stripe [straip] n Streifen m; **~d** a gestreift.

strip lighting n Neonlicht nt.

stripper ['stripə*] n Stripteasetänzerin f.

strive [straiv] vi, pt **strove**, pp **striven** ['strivn] streben (*for* nach).

strode [strəud] pt of stride.

stroke [strəuk] n Schlag m; (*swim, row*) Stoß m; (*TECH*) Hub m; (*MED*) Schlaganfall m; (*caress*) Streicheln nt // vt streicheln; **at a ~** mit einem Schlag.

stroll [strəul] n Spaziergang m // vi schlendern; **~er** n (*US: pushchair*) Sportwagen m.

strong [stroŋ] a stark; (*firm*) fest; **they are 50 ~** sie sind 50 Mann stark; **~box** n Kassette f; **~hold** n Hochburg f; **~ly** ad stark; **~room** n Tresor m.

strove [strəuv] pt of strive.

struck [strʌk] pt, pp of strike.

structure ['strʌktʃə*] n Struktur f, Aufbau m; (*building*) Bau m.

struggle ['strʌgl] n Kampf m // vi (*fight*) kämpfen.

strum [strʌm] vt (*guitar*) klimpern auf (+*dat*).

strung [strʌŋ] pt, pp of string.

strut [strʌt] n Strebe f, Stütze f // vi stolzieren.

stub [stʌb] n Stummel m; (*of cigarette*) Kippe f // vt: **to ~ one's toe** sich (*dat*) den Zeh anstoßen; **~ out** vt ausdrücken.

stubble ['stʌbl] n Stoppel f.

stubborn ['stʌbən] a hartnäckig.

stuck [stʌk] pt, pp of **stick** // a (*jammed*) klemmend; **~-up** a hochnäsig.

stud [stʌd] n (*button*) Kragenknopf m; (*place*) Gestüt nt // vt (*fig*): **~ded with**

übersät mit.

student ['stju:dənt] n Student(in f) m; (*US also*) Schüler(in f) m // a Studenten-; **~ driver** n (*US*) Fahrschüler(in f) m.

studio ['stju:diəu] n Studio nt; (*for artist*) Atelier nt; **~ flat**, (*US*) **~ apartment** n Appartement nt.

studious ['stju:diəs] a lernbegierig.

study ['stʌdi] n Studium nt; (*investigation also*) Untersuchung f; (*room*) Arbeitszimmer nt; (*essay etc*) Studie f // vt studieren; (*face*) erforschen; (*evidence*) prüfen // vi studieren.

stuff [stʌf] n Stoff m; (*col*) Zeug nt // vt stopfen, füllen; (*animal*) ausstopfen; **~ing** n Füllung f; **~y** a (*room*) schwül; (*person*) spießig.

stumble ['stʌmbl] vi stolpern; **to ~ across** (*fig*) zufällig stoßen auf (+*acc*).

stumbling block ['stʌmbliŋblɔk] n Hindernis nt.

stump [stʌmp] n Stumpf m // vt umwerfen.

stun [stʌn] vt betäuben; (*shock*) niederschmettern.

stung [stʌŋ] pt, pp of sting.

stunk [stʌŋk] pp of stink.

stunning ['stʌniŋ] a betäubend; (*news*) überwältigend, umwerfend.

stunt [stʌnt] n Kunststück nt, Trick m; **~ed** a verkümmert; **~man** n Stuntman m.

stupefy ['stju:pifai] vt betäuben; (*by news*) bestürzen.

stupendous [stju'pendəs] a erstaunlich, enorm.

stupid ['stju:pid] a dumm; **~ity** [stju'piditi] n Dummheit f.

stupor ['stju:pə*] n Betäubung f.

sturdy ['stɜ:di] a kräftig, robust.

stutter ['stʌtə*] n Stottern nt // vi stottern.

sty [stai] n Schweinestall m.

stye [stai] n Gerstenkorn nt.

style [stail] n Stil m; (*fashion*) Mode f.

stylish ['stailiʃ] a modisch.

stylist ['stailist] n (*hair ~*) Friseur m, Friseuse f.

stylus ['stailəs] n (Grammophon)nadel f.

suave [swɑ:v] a zuvorkommend.

sub- [sʌb] pref Unter-.

subconscious ['sʌb'kɔnʃəs] a unterbewußt // n: **the ~** das Unterbewußte.

subcontract ['sʌbkən'trækt] vt (*vertraglich*) untervermitteln.

subdivide ['sʌbdi'vaid] vt unterteilen.

subdue [səb'dju:] vt unterwerfen; **~d** a (*lighting*) gedämpft; (*person*) still.

subject ['sʌbdʒikt] n (*of kingdom*) Untertan m; (*citizen*) Staatsangehörige(r) mf; (*topic*) Thema nt; (*SCH*) Fach nt; (*GRAM*) Subjekt nt // vt [səb'dʒekt] (*subdue*) unterwerfen; (*expose*) aussetzen // a ['sʌbdʒikt]: **to be**

~ **to** unterworfen sein (+*dat*); (*exposed*) ausgesetzt sein (+*dat*); **~ive** [səb'dʒɛktɪv] *a* subjektiv; ~ **matter** *n* Thema *nt*.

subjugate ['sʌbdʒugeɪt] *vt* unterjochen.

subjunctive [səb'dʒʌŋktɪv] *a* Konjunktiv- // *n* Konjunktiv *m*.

sublet ['sʌb'let] (*irreg*: *like* let) *vt* untervermieten.

sublime [sə'blaɪm] *a* erhaben.

submachine gun ['sʌbmə'ʃiːn-] *n* Maschinenpistole *f*.

submarine [sʌbmə'riːn] *n* Unterseeboot *nt*, U-Boot *nt*.

submerge [səb'mɜːdʒ] *vt* untertauchen; (*flood*) überschwemmen // *vi* untertauchen.

submission [səb'mɪʃən] *n* (*obedience*) Gehorsam *m*; (*claim*) Behauptung *f*; (*of plan*) Unterbreitung *f*.

submissive [səb'mɪsɪv] *a* demütig, unterwürfig (*pej*).

submit [səb'mɪt] *vt* behaupten; (*plan*) unterbreiten // *vi* (*give in*) sich ergeben.

subnormal ['sʌb'nɔːməl] *a* minderbegabt.

subordinate [sə'bɔːdɪnət] *a* untergeordnet // *n* Untergebene(r) *mf*.

subpoena [sə'piːnə] *n* Vorladung *f* // *vt* vorladen.

subscribe [səb'skraɪb] *vi* (*to view etc*) unterstützen; (*to newspaper*) abonnieren (*to acc*); **~r** *n* (*to periodical*) Abonnent *m*; (*TEL*) Telefonteilnehmer *m*.

subscription [səb'skrɪpʃən] *n* Abonnement *nt*; (*money subscribed*) (Mitglieds)beitrag *m*.

subsequent ['sʌbsɪkwənt] *a* folgend, später; **~ly** *ad* später.

subside [səb'saɪd] *vi* sich senken; **subsidence** [sʌb'saɪdəns] *n* Senkung *f*.

subsidiary [səb'sɪdɪərɪ] *a* Neben- // *n* (*company*) Tochtergesellschaft *f*.

subsidize ['sʌbsɪdaɪz] *vt* subventionieren.

subsidy ['sʌbsɪdɪ] *n* Subvention *f*.

subsistence [səb'sɪstəns] *n* Unterhalt *m*.

substance ['sʌbstəns] *n* Substanz *f*.

substantial [səb'stænʃəl] *a* (*strong*) fest, kräftig; (*important*) wesentlich; **~ly** *ad* erheblich.

substantiate [səb'stænʃɪeɪt] *vt* begründen, belegen.

substitute ['sʌbstɪtjuːt] *n* Ersatz *m* // *vt* ersetzen.

substitution [sʌbstɪ'tjuːʃən] *n* Ersetzung *f*.

subterfuge ['sʌbtəfjuːdʒ] *n* Vorwand *m*; (*trick*) Trick *m*.

subterranean [sʌbtə'reɪnɪən] *a* unterirdisch.

subtitle ['sʌbtaɪtl] *n* Untertitel *m*.

subtle ['sʌtl] *a* fein; **~ty** *n* Feinheit *f*.

subtotal [sʌb'təʊtl] *n* Zwischensumme *f*.

subtract [səb'trækt] *vt* abziehen; **~ion** [səb'trækʃən] *n* Abziehen *nt*, Subtraktion *f*.

suburb ['sʌbɜːb] *n* Vorort *m*; the ~s die Außenbezirke; **~an** [sə'bɜːbən] *a* Vorort(s)-, Stadtrand-; **~ia** [sə'bɜːbɪə] *n* Vorstadt *f*.

subversive [səb'vɜːsɪv] *a* subversiv.

subway ['sʌbweɪ] *n* (*US*) U-Bahn *f*; (*Brit*) Unterführung *f*.

succeed [sək'siːd] *vi* gelingen (+*dat*), Erfolg haben // *vt* (nach)folgen (+*dat*); he ~ed in doing it es gelang ihm, es zu tun; **~ing** *a* (nach)folgend.

success [sək'ses] *n* Erfolg *m*; **~ful** *a*, **~fully** *ad* erfolgreich; to be **~ful** (in doing sth) Erfolg haben (bei etw).

succession [sək'seʃən] *n* (Aufeinander)folge *f*; (*to throne*) Nachfolge *f*.

successive *a* [sək'sesɪv] aufeinanderfolgend.

successor [sək'sesə*] *n* Nachfolger(in *f*) *m*.

succinct [sək'sɪŋkt] *a* knapp.

succulent ['sʌkjulənt] *a* saftig.

succumb [sə'kʌm] *vi* erliegen (*to dat*); (*yield*) nachgeben.

such [sʌtʃ] *a* solche(r, s); ~ **a book** so ein Buch; **~ books** solche Bücher; ~ **courage** so ein Mut; ~ **a long trip** so eine lange Reise; ~ **a lot of** so viel(e); ~ **as** wie; **a noise** ~ **as** to ein derartiger Lärm, daß; **as** ~ an sich; **~-and-~** a time/town die und die Zeit/Stadt.

suck [sʌk] *vt* saugen; (*ice cream etc*) lutschen; **~er** *n* (*col*) Idiot *m*.

suction ['sʌkʃən] *n* Saugkraft *f*.

sudden ['sʌdn] *a* plötzlich; **all of a** ~ auf einmal; **~ly** *ad* plötzlich.

suds [sʌdz] *npl* Seifenlauge *f*; (*lather*) Seifenschaum *m*.

sue [suː] *vt* verklagen.

suede [sweɪd] *n* Wildleder *nt*.

suet ['suɪt] *n* Nierenfett *nt*.

Suez ['suːɪz] *n*: the ~ **Canal** der Suezkanal *m*.

suffer ['sʌfə*] *vt* (er)leiden // *vi* leiden; **~er** *n* Leidende(r) *mf*; **~ing** *n* Leiden *nt*.

suffice [sə'faɪs] *vi* genügen.

sufficient *a*, **~ly** *ad* [sə'fɪʃənt, -lɪ] ausreichend.

suffix ['sʌfɪks] *n* Nachsilbe *f*.

suffocate ['sʌfəkeɪt] *vti* ersticken.

suffocation [sʌfə'keɪʃən] *n* Ersticken *nt*.

suffrage ['sʌfrɪdʒ] *n* Wahlrecht *nt*.

sugar ['ʃugə*] *n* Zucker *m* // *vt* zuckern; ~ **beet** *n* Zuckerrübe *f*; ~ **cane** *n* Zuckerrohr *nt*; **~y** *a* süß.

suggest [sə'dʒest] *vt* vorschlagen; (*show*) schließen lassen auf (+*acc*); **~ion** [sə'dʒestʃən] *n* Vorschlag *m*; **~ive** *a* anregend; (*indecent*) zweideutig.

suicide ['suɪsaɪd] *n* Selbstmord *m*; to

commit ~ Selbstmord begehen.

suit [suːt] n Anzug m; (CARDS) Farbe f // vt passen (+dat); (clothes) stehen (+dat); well ~ed (well matched: couple) gut zusammenpassend; ~able a geeignet, passend; ~ably ad passend, angemessen.

suitcase ['suːtkeɪs] n (Hand)koffer m.

suite [swiːt] n (of rooms) Zimmerflucht f; (of furniture) Einrichtung f; (MUS) Suite f.

suitor ['suːtə*] n (JUR) Kläger(in f) m.

sulfur ['sʌlfə*] n (US) = **sulphur**.

sulk [sʌlk] vi schmollen; ~y a schmollend.

sullen ['sʌlən] a mürrisch.

sulphur, (US) **sulfur** ['sʌlfə*] n Schwefel m.

sultry ['sʌltrɪ] a schwül.

sum [sʌm] n Summe f; (money also) Betrag m; (arithmetic) Rechenaufgabe f; ~ up vti zusammenfassen.

summarize ['sʌməraɪz] vt kurz zusammenfassen.

summary ['sʌmərɪ] n Zusammenfassung f // a (justice) kurzerhand erteilt.

summer ['sʌmə*] n Sommer m // a Sommer-; ~house n (in garden) Gartenhaus nt; ~time n Sommerzeit f.

summit ['sʌmɪt] n Gipfel m; ~ (conference) n Gipfelkonferenz f.

summon ['sʌmən] vt herbeirufen; (JUR) vorladen; (gather up) aufbringen; ~s n (JUR) Vorladung f // vt vorladen.

sump [sʌmp] n (Brit AUT) Ölwanne f.

sumptuous ['sʌmptjuəs] a prächtig.

sun [sʌn] n Sonne f; ~bathe vi sich sonnen; ~burn n Sonnenbrand m.

Sunday ['sʌndeɪ] n Sonntag m; ~ school n Sonntagsschule f.

sundial ['sʌndaɪəl] n Sonnenuhr f.

sundown ['sʌndaʊn] n Sonnenuntergang m.

sundry ['sʌndrɪ] a verschieden; all and ~ alle; **sundries** npl Verschiedene(s) nt.

sunflower ['sʌnflaʊə*] n Sonnenblume f.

sung [sʌŋ] pp of **sing**.

sunglasses ['sʌnɡlɑːsɪz] npl Sonnenbrille f.

sunk [sʌŋk] pp of **sink**.

sunlight ['sʌnlaɪt] n Sonnenlicht nt.

sunlit ['sʌnlɪt] a sonnenbeschienen.

sunny ['sʌnɪ] a sonnig.

sunrise ['sʌnraɪz] n Sonnenaufgang m.

sunset ['sʌnset] n Sonnenuntergang m.

sunshade ['sʌnʃeɪd] n Sonnenschirm m.

sunshine ['sʌnʃaɪn] n Sonnenschein m.

sunstroke ['sʌnstrəʊk] n Hitzschlag m.

suntan ['sʌntæn] n (Sonnen)bräune f; ~ oil n Sonnenöl nt.

super ['suːpə*] a (col) prima, klasse; Super-, Über-.

superannuation ['suːpərænjʊ'eɪʃən] n Pension f.

superb [suː'pɜːb] a ausgezeichnet, her-

vorragend.

supercilious [suːpə'sɪlɪəs] a herablassend.

superficial [suːpə'fɪʃəl] a oberflächlich.

superfluous [su'pɜːfluəs] a überflüssig.

superhuman [suːpə'hjuːmən] a (effort) übermenschlich.

superimpose ['suːpərɪm'pəʊz] vt übereinanderlegen.

superintendent [suːpərɪn'tendənt] n Polizeichef m.

superior [su'pɪərɪə*] a überlegen; (better) besser // n Vorgesetzte(r) mf; ~ity [supɪərɪ'ɒrɪtɪ] n Überlegenheit f.

superlative [su'pɜːlətɪv] a überragend.

superman ['suːpəmæn] n Übermensch m.

supermarket ['suːpəmɑːkɪt] n Supermarkt m.

supernatural [suːpə'nætʃərəl] a übernatürlich.

superpower ['suːpəpaʊə*] n Weltmacht f.

supersede [suːpə'siːd] vt ersetzen.

supersonic ['suːpə'sɒnɪk] n Überschall-.

superstition [suːpə'stɪʃən] n Aberglaube m.

superstitious [suːpə'stɪʃəs] a abergläubisch.

supervise ['suːpəvaɪz] vt beaufsichtigen, kontrollieren.

supervision [suːpə'vɪʒən] n Aufsicht f.

supervisor ['suːpəvaɪzə*] n Aufsichtsperson f; ~y a Aufsichts-.

supine ['suːpaɪn] a auf dem Rücken liegend.

supper ['sʌpə*] n Abendessen nt.

supplant [sə'plɑːnt] vt (person, thing) ersetzen.

supple ['sʌpl] a geschmeidig.

supplement ['sʌplɪmənt] n Ergänzung f; (in book) Nachtrag m // vt [sʌplɪ'ment] ergänzen; ~ary [sʌplɪ'mentərɪ] a ergänzend.

supplier [sə'plaɪə*] n Lieferant m.

supply [sə'plaɪ] vt liefern // n Vorrat m; (supplying) Lieferung f // a (teacher etc) Aushilfs-; **supplies** npl (food) Vorräte pl; (MIL) Nachschub m.

support [sə'pɔːt] n Unterstützung f; (TECH) Stütze f // vt (hold up) stützen, tragen; (provide for) ernähren; (be in favour of) unterstützen; ~er n Anhänger(in f) m.

suppose [sə'pəʊz] vti annehmen; to be ~d to do sth etw tun sollen; ~dly [sə'pəʊzɪdlɪ] ad angeblich.

supposing [sə'pəʊzɪŋ] cj angenommen.

supposition [sʌpə'zɪʃən] n Voraussetzung f.

suppress [sə'pres] vt unterdrücken; ~ion [sə'preʃən] n Unterdrückung f.

supremacy [su'preməsɪ] n Vorherrschaft f, Oberhoheit f.

supreme [su'priːm] a oberste(r, s),

höchste(r, s).

surcharge ['sɜːʃɑːdʒ] n Zuschlag m.

sure [ʃʊə*] a sicher, gewiß; ~! (of course) klar!; **to make ~ of sth/that** sich einer Sache vergewissern/vergewissern, daß; ~ **enough** (with past) tatsächlich; (with future) ganz bestimmt; ~**footed** a sicher (auf den Füßen); ~**ly** ad (certainly) sicherlich, gewiß; ~**ly it's wrong** das ist doch wohl falsch.

surety ['ʃʊərəti] n Sicherheit f; (person) Bürge m.

surf [sɜːf] n Brandung f.

surface ['sɜːfis] n Oberfläche f // vt (roadway) teeren // vi auftauchen; ~ **mail** n gewöhnliche Post f.

surfboard ['sɜːfbɔːd] n Wellenreiterbrett nt.

surfeit ['sɜːfit] n Übermaß nt.

surfing ['sɜːfiŋ] n Wellenreiten nt.

surge [sɜːdʒ] n Woge f // vi wogen.

surgeon ['sɜːdʒən] n Chirurg(in f) m.

surgery ['sɜːdʒəri] n (Brit: place) Praxis f; (time) Sprechstunde f; (treatment) Operation f; **to undergo ~** operiert werden; ~ **hours** npl (Brit) Sprechstunden pl.

surgical ['sɜːdʒikəl] a chirurgisch; ~ **spirit** n (Brit) Wundbenzin nt.

surly ['sɜːli] a verdrießlich, grob.

surmount [sɜːˈmaʊnt] vt überwinden.

surname ['sɜːneim] n Zuname m.

surpass [sɜːˈpɑːs] vt übertreffen.

surplus ['sɜːpləs] n Überschuß m // a überschüssig, Über(schuß)-.

surprise [səˈpraiz] n Überraschung f // vt überraschen.

surprising [səˈpraiziŋ] a überraschend; ~**ly** ad überraschend(erweise).

surrender [səˈrendə*] n Kapitulation f // vi sich ergeben.

surreptitious [sʌrəpˈtiʃəs] a verstohlen.

surrogate ['sʌrəgit] n Ersatz m; ~ **mother** n Leihmutter f.

surround [səˈraʊnd] vt umgeben; ~**ing** a (countryside) umliegend // n: ~**ings** pl Umgebung f; (environment) Umwelt f.

surveillance [sɜːˈveiləns] n Überwachung f.

survey ['sɜːvei] n Übersicht f // [sɜːˈvei] vt überblicken; (land) vermessen; ~**or** [səˈveiə*] n Land(ver)messer(in f) m.

survival [səˈvaivəl] n Überleben nt.

survive [səˈvaiv] vti überleben.

survivor [səˈvaivə*] n Überlebende(r) mf.

susceptible [səˈseptəbl] a empfindlich (to gegen); (to charms etc) empfänglich (to für).

suspect ['sʌspekt] n Verdächtige(r) mf // a verdächtig // [səˈspekt] vt verdächtigen; (think) vermuten.

suspend [səsˈpend] vt verschieben; (from work) suspendieren; (hang up) aufhängen; (SPORT) sperren; ~**ed sen-**

tence n (LAW) zur Bewährung ausgesetzte Strafe; ~**er belt** n Strumpf(halter)gürtel m; ~**ers** npl (Brit) Strumpfhalter m; (men's) Sokkenhalter m; (US) Hosenträger m.

suspense [səsˈpens] n Spannung f.

suspension [səsˈpenʃən] n (from work) Suspendierung f; (SPORT) Sperrung f; (AUT) Federung f; ~ **bridge** n Hängebrücke f.

suspicion [səsˈpiʃən] n Mißtrauen nt; Verdacht m.

suspicious [səsˈpiʃəs] a mißtrauisch; (causing suspicion) verdächtig.

sustain [səsˈtein] vt (maintain) aufrechterhalten; (confirm) bestätigen; (JUR) anerkennen; (injury) davontragen; ~**ed** a (effort) anhaltend.

sustenance ['sʌstinəns] n Nahrung f.

swab [swɒb] n (MED) Tupfer m.

swagger ['swægə*] vi stolzieren.

swallow ['swɒləʊ] n (bird) Schwalbe f; (of food etc) Schluck m // vt (ver)schlucken; ~ **up** vt verschlingen.

swam [swæm] pt of **swim**.

swamp [swɒmp] n Sumpf m // vt überschwemmen.

swan [swɒn] n Schwan m.

swap [swɒp] n Tausch m // vt (ein)tauschen (for gegen).

swarm [swɔːm] n Schwarm m // vi wimmeln (with von).

swarthy ['swɔːði] a dunkel, braun.

swat [swɒt] vt totschlagen.

sway [swei] vi schwanken; (branches) schaukeln, sich wiegen // vt schwenken; (influence) beeinflussen.

swear [sweə*] vi, pt **swore**, pp **sworn** vi (promise) schwören; (curse) fluchen; **to ~ to sth** schwören auf etw (acc); ~**word** n Fluch m.

sweat [swet] n Schweiß m // vi schwitzen.

sweater ['swetə*] n Pullover.

sweatshirt ['swetʃɜːt] n Sweatshirt nt.

sweaty ['sweti] a verschwitzt.

swede [swiːd] n (Brit) Steckrübe f.

Swede [swiːd] n Schwede m, Schwedin f.

Sweden ['swiːdn] n Schweden nt.

Swedish ['swiːdiʃ] a schwedisch // n (LING) Schwedisch nt.

sweep [swiːp] n (chimney ~) Schornsteinfeger m // v (pt, pp **swept**) vt fegen, kehren // vi (go quickly) rauschen; ~ **away** vt wegfegen; ~ **past** vi vorbeisausen; ~ **up** vt zusammenkehren; ~**ing** a (gesture) schwungvoll; (statement) verallgemeinernd.

sweet [swiːt] n (course) Nachtisch m; (candy) Bonbon nt // a süß; ~**corn** n Zuckermais m; ~**en** vt süßen; (fig) versüßen; ~**heart** n Liebste(r) mf; ~**ness** n Süße f; ~ **pea** n Gartenwicke f.

swell [swel] n Seegang m // a (col) todschick // v (pt **swelled**, pp **swollen** or **swelled**) vt (numbers) vermehren // vi (also: ~ up) (an)schwellen; **~ing** n Schwellung f.

sweltering ['sweltərɪŋ] a drückend.

swept [swept] pt, pp of **sweep**.

swerve [swɜːv] vi ausscheren.

swift [swɪft] n Mauersegler m // a, **~ly** ad geschwind, schnell, rasch.

swig [swɪg] n Zug m.

swill [swɪl] n (for pigs) Schweinefutter nt // vt spülen.

swim [swɪm] n: to go for a ~ schwimmen gehen // v (pt **swam**, pp **swum**) vi schwimmen // vt (cross) (durch)schwimmen; **~mer** n Schwimmer(in f) m; **~ming** n Schwimmen nt; **~ming cap** n Badehaube f, Badekappe f; **~ming costume** n (Brit) Badeanzug m; **~ming pool** n Schwimmbecken nt; (private) Swimming-Pool m; **~suit** n Badeanzug m.

swindle ['swɪndl] n Schwindel m, Betrug m // vt betrügen.

swine [swaɪn] n (lit, fig) Schwein nt.

swing [swɪŋ] n (child's) Schaukel f; (swinging) Schwung m; (MUS) Swing m // v (pt, pp **swung**) vt schwingen // vi schwingen, schaukeln; (turn quickly) schwenken; **in full ~** in vollem Gange; **~ bridge** n Drehbrücke f; **~ door**, (US) **~ing door** n Schwingtür f.

swingeing ['swɪndʒɪŋ] a (Brit) hart; (taxation, cuts) extrem.

swipe [swaɪp] n Hieb m // vt (col) (hit) hart schlagen; (steal) klauen.

swirl [swɜːl] vi wirbeln.

swish [swɪʃ] a (col: smart) schick // vi zischen; (grass, skirts) rascheln.

Swiss [swɪs] a Schweizer, schweizerisch // n Schweizer(in f) m; **the ~** die Schweizer pl.

switch [swɪtʃ] n (ELEC) Schalter m; (change) Wechsel m // vti (ELEC) schalten; (change) wechseln; **~ off** vt ab- or ausschalten; **~ on** vt an- or einschalten; **~board** n Zentrale f; (board) Schaltbrett nt.

Switzerland ['swɪtsələnd] n die Schweiz f.

swivel ['swɪvl] vti (also: ~ round) (sich) drehen.

swollen ['swəʊlən] pp of **swell**.

swoon [swuːn] vi (old) in Ohnmacht fallen.

swoop [swuːp] n Sturzflug m; (esp by police) Razzia f // vi (also: ~ down) stürzen.

swop [swɒp] = **swap**.

sword [sɔːd] n Schwert nt; **~fish** n Schwertfisch m.

swore [swɔː*] pt of **swear**.

sworn [swɔːn] pp of **swear**.

swot [swɒt] vti pauken.

swum [swʌm] pp of **swim**.

swung [swʌŋ] pt, pp of **swing**.

sycamore ['sɪkəmɔː*] n (US) Platane f; (Brit) Bergahorn m.

syllable ['sɪləbl] n Silbe f.

syllabus ['sɪləbəs] n Lehrplan m.

symbol ['sɪmbəl] n Symbol nt; **~ic(al)** [sɪm'bɒlɪk(əl)] a symbolisch.

symmetry ['sɪmɪtrɪ] n Symmetrie f.

sympathetic [sɪmpə'θetɪk] a mitfühlend.

sympathize ['sɪmpəθaɪz] vi mitfühlen; **~r** n Mitfühlende(r) mf; (POL) Sympathisant(in f) m.

sympathy ['sɪmpəθɪ] n Mitleid nt, Mitgefühl nt; (condolence) Beileid nt; **with our deepest ~** mit tiefempfundenem Beileid.

symphony ['sɪmfənɪ] n Sinfonie f.

symposium [sɪm'pəʊzɪəm] n Tagung f.

symptom ['sɪmptəm] n Symptom nt; **~atic** [sɪmptə'mætɪk] a (fig) bezeichnend (of für).

synagogue ['sɪnəgɒg] n Synagoge f.

synchronize ['sɪŋkrənaɪz] vt synchronisieren // vi gleichzeitig sein or ablaufen.

syncopated ['sɪŋkəpeɪtɪd] a synkopiert.

syndicate ['sɪndɪkət] n Konsortium nt.

synonym ['sɪnənɪm] n Synonym nt.

synonymous [sɪ'nɒnɪməs] a: ~ (with) gleichbedeutend (mit).

synopsis [sɪ'nɒpsɪs] n Zusammenfassung f.

syphon ['saɪfən] = **siphon**.

Syria ['sɪrɪə] n Syrien nt.

syringe [sɪ'rɪndʒ] n Spritze f.

syrup ['sɪrəp] n Sirup m; (of sugar) Melasse f.

system ['sɪstəm] n System nt; **~atic** [sɪstə'mætɪk] a systematisch; **~ disk** n (COMPUT) Systemdiskette f; **~s analyst** n Systemanalytiker(in f) m.

T

ta [tɑː] interj (Brit col) danke.

tab [tæb] n Aufhänger m; (name ~) Schild nt; **to keep ~s on** (fig) genau im Auge behalten.

table ['teɪbl] n Tisch m; (list) Tabelle f // vt (Parl: propose) vorlegen, einbringen; **to lay** or **set the ~** den Tisch decken; **~ of contents** n Inhaltsverzeichnis nt; **~ lamp** n Tischlampe f.

tablecloth ['teɪblklɒθ] n Tischtuch nt.

table d'hôte ['tɑːbl'dəʊt] n Tagesmenü nt.

tablemat ['teɪblmæt] n Untersatz m.

tablespoon ['teɪblspuːn] n Eßlöffel m; **~ful** n Eßlöffel(voll) m.

tablet ['tæblət] n (MED) Tablette f; (for writing) Täfelchen nt.

table tennis ['teɪbltenɪs] n Tischtennis

nt.

table wine ['teɪblwaɪn] n Tafelwein m.

tabloid ['tæblɔɪd] n Zeitung f in kleinem
Format; (pej) Boulevardzeitung.

tabulate ['tæbjʊleɪt] vt tabellarisch
ordnen.

tacit a, **~ly** ad ['tæsɪt, -lɪ] stillschweigend.

taciturn ['tæsɪtɜːn] a wortkarg.

tack [tæk] n (small nail) Stift m; (US:
thumb~) Reißzwecke f; (stitch) Heft-
stich m; (NAUT) Lavieren nt; (course)
Kurs m // vt (nail) nageln; (stitch)
heften // vi aufkreuzen.

tackle ['tækl] n (for lifting) Flaschenzug
m; (NAUT) Takelage f; (SPORT)
Tackling nt // vt (deal with) anpacken,
in Angriff nehmen; (person) festhalten;
(player) angehen.

tacky ['tækɪ] a klebrig.

tact [tækt] n Takt m; **~ful** a, **~fully** ad
taktvoll.

tactical ['tæktɪkəl] a taktisch.

tactics ['tæktɪks] npl Taktik f.

tactless a, **~ly** ad ['tæktləs, -lɪ] taktlos.

tadpole ['tædpəʊl] n Kaulquappe f.

taffy ['tæfɪ] n (US) Sahnebonbon nt.

tag [tæg] n (label) Schild nt, Anhänger
m; (maker's name) Etikett nt; (phrase)
Floskel f; **~ along** vi mitkommen.

tail [teɪl] n Schwanz m; (of list) Schluß
m // vt folgen (+dat); **~ away**, **~ off**
vi abfallen, schwinden; **~back** n (Brit
AUT) (Rück)stau m; **~ coat** n Frack
m; **~ end** n Schluß m, Ende nt; **~gate**
n (AUT) Heckklappe f.

tailor ['teɪlə*] n Schneider m; **~ing** n
Schneidern nt; **~-made** a (lit) maßge-
schneidert; (fig) wie auf den Leib geschnitten (for sb jdm).

tailwind ['teɪlwɪnd] n Rückenwind m.

tainted ['teɪntɪd] a verdorben.

take [teɪk], pt **took**, pp **taken** vt
nehmen; (trip, exam) machen;
(capture: person) fassen; (: town) einnehmen; (carry to a place) bringen;
(MATH: subtract) abziehen (from von);
(extract, quotation) entnehmen (from
dat); (get for o.s.) sich (dat) nehmen;
(gain, obtain) bekommen; (FIN, COMM)
einnehmen; (PHOT) machen; (put up
with) hinnehmen; (respond to) aufnehmen; (interpret) auffassen;
(assume) annehmen; (contain) Platz
haben für; (GRAM) stehen mit; to **~ sth
from sb** jdm etw wegnehmen; **~ after**
vt ähnlich sein (+dat); **~ apart** vt auseinandernehmen; **~ away** vt (remove)
wegnehmen; (carry off) wegbringen; **~
back** vt (return) zurückbringen; (retract) zurücknehmen; **~ down** vt (pull
down) abreißen; (write down) aufschreiben; **~ in** vt (deceive) hereinlegen; (understand) begreifen;
(include) einschließen; **~ off** vi (plane)

starten // vt (remove) wegnehmen;
(clothing) ausziehen; (imitate) nachmachen; **~ on** vt (undertake) übernehmen; (engage) einstellen; (opponent)
antreten gegen; **~ out** vt (girl, dog)
ausführen; (extract) herausnehmen;
(insurance) abschließen; (licence) sich
(dat) geben lassen; (book) ausleihen;
(remove) entfernen; to **~ sth out of sth**
(drawer, pocket etc) etw aus etw herausnehmen; **~ over** vt übernehmen // vi
ablösen (from acc); **~ to** vt (like)
mögen; (adopt as practice) sich (dat)
angewöhnen; **~ up** vt (raise) aufnehmen; (hem) kürzer machen;
(occupy) in Anspruch nehmen; (engage
in) sich befassen mit; **~away**, (US)
~out a zum Mitnehmen; **~-home pay**
n Nettolohn m; **~off** n (AVIAT) Start
m; (imitation) Nachahmung f; **~over** n
(COMM) Übernahme f.

takings ['teɪkɪŋz] npl (COMM) Einnahmen pl.

talc [tælk] n (also: **~um powder**)
Talkumpuder m.

tale [teɪl] n Geschichte f, Erzählung f; to
tell **~s** (fig: lie) Geschichten erfinden.

talent ['tælənt] n Talent nt; **~ed** a
begabt.

talk [tɔːk] n (conversation) Gespräch nt;
(rumour) Gerede nt; (speech) Vortrag
m // vi sprechen, reden; **~s** pl (POL etc)
Gespräche pl; to **~ sb into doing sth** jdn
überreden, etw zu tun; to **~ sb out of
doing sth** jdm ausreden, etw zu tun; to **~
shop** fachsimpeln; **~ about** vi sprechen
von (+dat) or über (+acc); **~ over** vt
besprechen; **~ative** a gesprächig.

tall [tɔːl] a groß; (building) hoch; **to be 1
m 80 ~** 1,80 m groß sein; **~boy** n (Brit)
Kommode f; **~ story** n übertriebene
Geschichte f.

tally ['tælɪ] n Abrechnung f // vi übereinstimmen (with mit).

talon ['tælən] n Kralle f.

tame [teɪm] a zahm; (fig) fade.

tamper ['tæmpə*]: **~ with** vt herumpfuschen an (+dat).

tampon ['tæmpɔn] n Tampon m.

tan [tæn] n (on skin) (Sonnen)bräune f;
(colour) Gelbbraun nt // a (colour)
(gelb)braun // vt bräunen; (skins)
gerben // vi braun werden.

tang [tæŋ] n Schärfe f.

tangent ['tændʒənt] n Tangente f; to go
off at a **~** (fig) vom Thema abkommen.

tangerine [tændʒə'riːn] n Mandarine f.

tangible ['tændʒəbl] a greifbar.

tangle ['tæŋgl] n Durcheinander nt;
(trouble) Schwierigkeiten pl; to get
in(to) a **~** sich verheddern.

tank [tæŋk] n (container) Tank m,
Behälter m; (MIL) Panzer m.

tanker ['tæŋkə*] n (ship) Tanker m;
(vehicle) Tankwagen m.

tanned [tænd] a (skin) gebräunt.
tantalizing ['tæntəlaızıŋ] a verlockend; (annoying) quälend.
tantamount ['tæntəmaunt] a gleichbedeutend (to mit).
tantrum ['tæntrəm] n Wutanfall m.
tap [tæp] n Hahn m; (gentle blow) Klopfen nt // vt (strike) klopfen; (supply) anzapfen; (telephone) abhören; **on** ~ (fig: resources) zur Hand.
tap-dancing ['tæpdɑːnsıŋ] n Steppen nt.
tape [teıp] n Band nt; (magnetic) (Ton)band nt; (adhesive) Klebstreifen m // vt (record) aufnehmen; ~ **measure** n Maßband nt.
taper ['teıpə*] n (dünne) Wachskerze f // vi spitz zulaufen.
tape recorder n Tonbandgerät nt.
tapestry ['tæpıstrı] n Wandteppich m.
tar [tɑː*] n Teer m.
target ['tɑːgıt] n Ziel nt; (board) Zielscheibe f; ~ **practice** n Zielschießen nt.
tariff ['tærıf] n (duty paid) Zoll m; (list) Tarif m.
tarmac ['tɑːmæk] n (AVIAT) Rollfeld nt.
tarnish ['tɑːnıʃ] vt (lit) matt machen; (fig) beflecken.
tarpaulin [tɑːˈpɔːlın] n Plane f.
tarragon ['tærəgən] n Estragon m.
tart [tɑːt] n (Obst)torte f; (col) Nutte f // a scharf; ~ **up** vt (col) aufmachen (col); (person) auftakeln (col).
tartan ['tɑːtən] n Schottenkaro nt // a mit Schottenkaro.
tartar ['tɑːtə*] n Zahnstein m; ~(**e**) **sauce** n Remouladensoße f.
task [tɑːsk] n Aufgabe f; **to take sb to** ~ sich (dat) jdn vornehmen; ~ **force** n Sondertrupp m.
tassel ['tæsəl] n Quaste f.
taste [teıst] n Geschmack m; (sense) Geschmackssinn m; (small quantity) Kostprobe f; (liking) Vorliebe f // vt schmecken; (try) probieren // vi schmecken (of nach); **you can** ~ **the garlic** (in it) man kann den Knoblauch herausschmecken; **can I have a** ~ **of this wine?** kann ich diesen Wein probieren?; **to have a** ~ **for sth** etw mögen; **in good/bad** ~ geschmackvoll/geschmacklos; ~**ful** a, ~**fully** ad geschmackvoll; ~**less** a (insipid) fade; (in bad taste) geschmacklos; ~**lessly** ad geschmacklos.
tasty ['teıstı] a schmackhaft.
tatters ['tætəz] npl: **in** ~ in Fetzen.
tattoo [tə'tuː] n (MIL) Zapfenstreich m; (on skin) Tätowierung f // vt tätowieren.
tatty ['tætı] a (Brit col) schäbig.
taught [tɔːt] pt, pp of **teach**.
taunt [tɔːnt] n höhnische Bemerkung f // vt verhöhnen.
Taurus ['tɔːrəs] n Stier m.
taut [tɔːt] a straff.
tawdry ['tɔːdrı] a (bunt und) billig.

tawny ['tɔːnı] a gelbbraun.
tax [tæks] n Steuer f // vt besteuern; (strain) strapazieren; (strength) angreifen; ~**able** a (income) steuerpflichtig; ~**ation** [tæk'seıʃən] n Besteuerung f; ~ **avoidance** n Steuerumgehung f; ~ **collector** n Steuereinnehmer m; ~ **disc** n (Brit AUT) Kraftfahrzeugsteuerplakette f (, die an der Windschutzscheibe angebracht wird); ~ **evasion** n Steuerhinterziehung f; ~**-free** a steuerfrei.
taxi ['tæksı] n Taxi nt // vi (plane) rollen; ~ **driver** n Taxifahrer m; ~ **rank** (Brit), ~ **stand** n Taxistand m.
taxpayer ['tækspeıə*] n Steuerzahler m.
tax relief n Steuerermäßigung f.
tax return n Steuererklärung f.
TB abbr (= tuberculosis) Tb f, Tbc f.
tea [tiː] n Tee m; (meal) (frühes) Abendessen nt; **high** ~ n (Brit) Abendessen nt; ~ **bag** n Teebeutel m; ~ **break** n (Brit) Teepause f.
teach [tiːtʃ] pt, pp **taught** vti lehren; (SCH also) unterrichten; (show) beibringen (sb sth jdm etw); ~**er** n Lehrer(in f) m; ~**ing** n (teacher's work) Unterricht m; (doctrine) Lehre f.
tea cosy n Teewärmer m.
teacup ['tiːkʌp] n Teetasse f.
tea leaves ['tiːliːvz] npl Teeblätter pl.
team [tiːm] n (workers) Team nt; (SPORT) Mannschaft f; (animals) Gespann nt.
teapot ['tiːpɒt] n Teekanne f.
tear [teə*] n Riß m; [tıə*] Träne f // v [teə*] (pt **tore**, pp **torn**) vt zerreißen; (muscle) zerren // vi (zer)reißen; (rush) rasen; ~ **along** vi (rush) entlangrasen; ~ **up** vt (sheet of paper etc) zerreißen; ~**ful** ['tıəful] a weinend; (voice) weinerlich; ~ **gas** ['tıəgæs] n Tränengas nt.
tearoom ['tiːrʊm] n Teestube f.
tease [tiːz] n Hänsler m // vt necken.
tea set n Teeservice nt.
teaspoon ['tiːspuːn] n Teelöffel m.
teat [tiːt] n (of woman) Brustwarze f; (of animal) Zitze f; (of bottle) Sauger m.
tea time n (in the afternoon) Teestunde f; (mealtime) Abendessen nt.
tea towel n Küchenhandtuch nt.
technical ['teknıkəl] a technisch; (knowledge, terms) Fach-; ~**ity** [teknı'kælıtı] n technische Einzelheit f; (JUR) Formsache f; ~**ly** ad technisch; (speak) spezialisiert; (fig) genau genommen.
technician [tek'nıʃən] n Techniker m.
technique [tek'niːk] n Technik f.
technological [teknə'lɒdʒıkəl] a technologisch.
technology [tek'nɒlədʒı] n Technologie f.
teddy (bear) ['tedı(beə*)] n Teddybär m.
tedious a, ~**ly** ad ['tiːdıəs, -lı] lang-

weilig, ermüdend.

tee [ti:] n (GOLF) Abschlagstelle f; (object) Tee m.

teem [ti:m] vi (swarm) wimmeln (with von); it is ~ing (with rain) es gießt in Strömen.

teenage ['ti:neɪdʒ] a (fashions etc) Teenager-, jugendlich; ~r n Teenager m, Jugendliche(r) mf.

teens [ti:nz] npl Teenageralter nt; to be in one's ~ im Teenageralter sein.

tee-shirt ['ti:ʃɜːt] n T-Shirt nt.

teeter ['ti:tə*] vi schwanken.

teeth [ti:θ] npl of tooth.

teethe [ti:ð] vi zahnen.

teething ['ti:ðɪŋ]: ~ ring n Beißring m; ~ troubles npl (fig) Kinderkrankheiten pl.

teetotal ['ti:'təʊtl] a abstinent.

telecommunications ['telɪkəmju:nɪ-'keɪʃənz] npl Fernmeldewesen nt.

telegram ['telɪgræm] n Telegramm nt.

telephone ['telɪfəʊn] n Telefon nt, Fernsprecher m // vt anrufen; (message) telefonisch mitteilen; ~ booth, (Brit) ~ box n Telefonzelle f; ~ call n Telefongespräch nt, Anruf m; ~ directory n Telefonbuch nt; ~ number n Telefonnummer f.

telephoto lens ['telɪfəʊtəʊ'lenz] n Teleobjektiv nt.

telescope ['telɪskəʊp] n Teleskop nt, Fernrohr nt // vt ineinanderschieben.

televise ['telɪvaɪz] vt durch das Fernsehen übertragen.

television ['telɪvɪʒən] n Fernsehen nt; ~ (set) n Fernsehapparat m, Fernseher m.

telex ['teleks] n Telex nt // vt per Telex schicken.

tell [tel], pt, pp told vt (story) erzählen; (secret) ausplaudern; (say, make known) sagen (sth to sb jdm etw); (distinguish) erkennen (sb by sth jdn an etw dat); (be sure) wissen // vi (talk) sprechen (of von); (be sure) wissen; (divulge) es verraten; (have effect) sich auswirken; (distinguish): to ~ sth from etw unterscheiden von; to ~ sb to do sth jdm sagen, daß er etw tun soll; to ~ sb off jdn ausschimpfen; ~er n Kassenbeamte(r) mf; ~ing a verräterisch; (blow) hart; ~tale a verräterisch.

telly ['telɪ] n (Brit col) abbr of television.

temerity [tɪ'merɪtɪ] n (Toll)kühnheit f.

temp [temp] n abbr (= temporary) f // vi Aushilfskraft f // vi als Aushilfskraft arbeiten.

temper ['tempə*] n (disposition) Temperament nt; (anger) Zorn m // vt (tone down) mildern; (metal) härten; to be in a (bad) ~ wütend sein; to lose one's ~ die Beherrschung verlieren.

temperament ['temprəmənt] n Temperament nt; ~al [tempərə'mentl] a (moody) launisch.

temperance ['tempərəns] n Mäßigung f; (abstinence) Enthaltsamkeit f.

temperate ['tempərət] a gemäßigt.

temperature ['temprɪtʃə*] n Temperatur f; (Med: high ~) Fieber nt; to have or run a ~ Fieber haben.

tempest ['tempɪst] n (wilder) Sturm m.

tempi ['tempi] npl of tempo.

template ['templət] n Schablone f.

temple ['templ] n Tempel m; (ANAT) Schläfe f.

temporal ['tempərəl] a (of time) zeitlich; (worldly) irdisch, weltlich.

temporarily ['tempərərɪlɪ] ad zeitweilig, vorübergehend.

temporary ['tempərərɪ] a vorläufig; (road, building) provisorisch.

tempt [tempt] vt (persuade) verleiten; (attract) reizen, (ver)locken; to ~ sb into doing sth jdn dazu verleiten, etw zu tun; ~ation [temp'teɪʃən] n Versuchung f; ~ing a (person) verführerisch; (object, situation) verlockend.

ten [ten] num zehn.

tenable ['tenəbl] a haltbar.

tenacious a, ~ly ad [tə'neɪʃəs, -lɪ] zäh, hartnäckig.

tenacity [tə'næsɪtɪ] n Zähigkeit f, Hartnäckigkeit f.

tenancy ['tenənsɪ] n Mietverhältnis nt.

tenant ['tenənt] n Mieter m; (of larger property) Pächter m.

tend [tend] vt (look after) sich kümmern um // vi neigen (to zu); to ~ to do sth (things) etw gewöhnlich tun.

tendency ['tendənsɪ] n Tendenz f; (of person also) Neigung f.

tender ['tendə*] a zart; (loving) zärtlich // n (COMM: offer) Kostenanschlag m // vt (an)bieten; (resignation) einreichen; (money): legal ~ n gesetzliche(s) Zahlungsmittel nt; ~ness n Zartheit f; (being loving) Zärtlichkeit f.

tendon ['tendən] n Sehne f.

tenement ['tenəmənt] n Mietshaus nt.

tenet ['tenət] n Lehre f.

tennis ['tenɪs] n Tennis nt; ~ ball n Tennisball m; ~ court n Tennisplatz m; ~ player n Tennisspieler(in f) m; ~ racket n Tennisschläger m; ~ shoes npl Tennisschuhe pl.

tenpin bowling ['tenpɪn-] n Bowling nt.

tense [tens] a angespannt // n Zeitform f.

tension ['tenʃən] n Spannung f.

tent [tent] n Zelt nt.

tentacle ['tentəkl] n Fühler m; (of sea animals) Fangarm m.

tentative ['tentətɪv] a (movement) unsicher; (offer) Probe-; (arrangement) vorläufig; (suggestion) unverbindlich; ~ly ad versuchsweise; (try, move) vorsichtig.

tenterhooks ['tentəhʊks] npl: to be on ~ auf die Folter gespannt sein.

tenth [tenθ] a zehnte(r, s).

tent peg n Hering m.

tent pole n Zeltstange f.

tenuous ['tenjʊəs] a schwach.

tenure ['tenjʊə*] n (of land) Besitz m; (of office) Amtszeit f.

tepid ['tepɪd] a lauwarm.

term [tɜːm] n (period of time) Zeit(raum m) f; (limit) Frist f; (SCH) Quartal nt; (UNIV) Trimester nt; (expression) Ausdruck m // vt (be)nennen; ~s pl (conditions) Bedingungen pl; in the short/long ~ auf kurze/lange Sicht; to be on good ~s with sb gut mit jdm auskommen; to come to ~s with (person) sich einigen mit; (problem) sich abfinden mit.

terminal ['tɜːmɪnl] n (Brit: also: coach ~) Endstation f; (AVIAT) Terminal m; (COMPUT) Terminal nt or m // a Schluß-; (MED) unheilbar.

terminate ['tɜːmɪneɪt] vt beenden // vi enden, aufhören (in auf +dat).

terminus ['tɜːmɪnəs], pl -mini [-mɪnaɪ] n Endstation f.

terrace ['terəs] n (Brit: row of houses) Häuserreihe f; (in garden etc) Terrasse f; the ~s (Brit SPORT) die Ränge; ~d a (garden) terrassenförmig angelegt; (house) Reihen-.

terrible ['terəbl] a schrecklich, entsetzlich, fürchterlich.

terribly ['terəblɪ] ad fürchterlich.

terrific [tə'rɪfɪk] a unwahrscheinlich; ~! klasse!

terrify ['terɪfaɪ] vt erschrecken.

territorial [terɪ'tɔːrɪəl] a Gebiets-, territorial.

territory ['terɪtərɪ] n Gebiet nt.

terror ['terə*] n Schrecken m; (POL) Terror m; ~ist n Terrorist(in f) m; ~ize vt terrorisieren.

terse [tɜːs] a knapp, kurz, bündig.

test [test] n Probe f; (examination) Prüfung f; (PSYCH, TECH) Test m // vt prüfen; (PSYCH) testen.

testicle ['testɪkl] n Hoden m.

testify ['testɪfaɪ] vi aussagen; bezeugen (to acc); to ~ to sth etw bezeugen.

testimony ['testɪmənɪ] n (JUR) Zeugenaussage f; (fig) Zeugnis nt.

test match n (SPORT) Länderkampf m.

test tube n Reagenzglas nt.

testy ['testɪ] a gereizt; reizbar.

tetanus ['tetənəs] n Wundstarrkrampf m, Tetanus m.

tetchy ['tetʃɪ] a empfindlich.

tether ['teðə*] vt anbinden // n: at the end of one's ~ völlig am Ende.

text [tekst] n Text m; (of document) Wortlaut m; ~book n Lehrbuch nt.

textiles ['tekstaɪlz] npl Textilien pl.

texture ['tekstʃə*] n Beschaffenheit f.

Thai [taɪ] a thailändisch // n Thailänder(in f) m; (LING) Thailändisch nt; ~land n Thailand nt.

Thames [temz] n: the ~ die Themse.

than [ðæn] prep (in comparisons) als.

thank [θæŋk] vt danken (+dat); you've him to ~ for your success Sie haben Ihren Erfolg ihm zu verdanken; ~ful a dankbar; ~less a undankbar; ~s npl Dank m // interj danke; ~s to dank (+gen); ~ you (very much) danke (vielmals), danke schön; **T~sgiving (Day)** n (US) Thanksgiving Day m.

that [ðæt] ♦ a (demonstrative: pl those) der/die/das, jene(r, s); ~ one das da
♦pron 1 (demonstrative: pl those) das; who's/what's ~? wer ist da/was ist das?; is ~ you? bist du das?; ~'s what he said genau das hat er gesagt; what happened after ~? was passierte danach?; ~ is das heißt
2 (relative: subject) der/die/das, die; (: direct obj) den/die/das, die; (: indirect obj) dem/der/dem, denen; all (~) I have alles, was ich habe
3 (relative: of time): the day (~) an dem Tag, als; the winter (~) he came in dem Winter, in dem er kam
♦cj daß; he thought ~ I was ill er dachte, daß ich krank sei or er dachte, ich sei krank
♦ad (demonstrative) so; I can't work ~ much ich kann nicht soviel arbeiten

thatched [θætʃt] a strohgedeckt; (cottage) mit Strohdach.

thaw [θɔː] n Tauwetter nt // vi tauen; (frozen foods, fig: people) auftauen // vt (auf)tauen lassen.

the [ðiː, ðə] definite art 1 der/die/das; to play ~ piano/violin Klavier/Geige spielen; I'm going to ~ butcher's/~ cinema ich gehe zum Fleischer/ins Kino; Elizabeth ~ First Elisabeth die Erste
2 (+ adjective to form noun) das, die; ~ rich and ~ poor die Reichen und die Armen
3 (in comparisons): ~ more he works ~ more he earns je mehr er arbeitet, desto mehr verdient er.

theatre, (US) **theater** ['θɪətə*] n Theater nt; (for lectures etc) Saal m; (MED) Operationssaal m; ~goer n Theaterbesucher(in f) m.

theatrical [θɪ'ætrɪkəl] a Theater-; (career) Schauspieler-; (showy) theatralisch.

theft [θeft] n Diebstahl m.

their [ðeə*] poss a ihr; ~s poss pron ihre(r, s); see also **my, mine.**

them [ðem, ðəm] pron (acc) sie; (dat) ihnen; see also **me.**

theme [θiːm] n Thema nt; (MUS) Motiv nt; ~ song n Titelmusik f.

themselves [ðəm'selvz] pl pron

(reflexive) sich (selbst); *(emphatic)* selbst; *see also* **oneself.**

then [ðen] *ad (at that time)* damals; *(next)* dann // *cj* also, folglich; *(furthermore)* ferner // *a* damalig; **the ~** president der damalige Präsident; **from ~ on** von da an; **by ~** bis dahin.

theology [θɪ'nlədʒɪ] *n* Theologie *f.*

theoretical *a,* **~ly** *ad* [θɪə'retɪkəl, -ɪ] theoretisch.

theory ['θɪərɪ] *n* Theorie *f.*

therapist ['θerəpɪst] *a* Therapeut(in *f*) *m.*

therapy ['θerəpɪ] *n* Therapie *f.*

there [ðeə*] *ad* **1: ~** is, **~** are es *or* da ist/sind; *(~ exists/exist also)* es gibt; **~ are 3 of them** *(people, things)* es gibt drei davon; **~ has been an accident** da war ein Unfall

2 *(referring to place)* da, dort; *(with v of movement)* dahin, dorthin; **put it in/on ~** leg es dahinein/dorthinauf

3: ~, ~ *(spoken to child)* na, na.

thermometer [θə'mɒmɪtə*] *n* Thermometer *nt.*

Thermos ['θɜːməs] *n* ® Thermosflasche *f.*

thesaurus [θɪ'sɔːrəs] *n* Synonymwörterbuch *nt.*

these [ðiːz] *pl pron, a* diese.

thesis ['θiːsɪs] *n (for discussion)* These *f;* *(UNIV)* Dissertation *f,* Doktorarbeit *f.*

they [ðeɪ] *pl pron* sie; *(people in general)* man; **~ say that ...** *(it is said that)* es wird gesagt, daß ...; **~'d = they had; they would; ~'ll = they shall, they will; ~'re = they are; ~'ve = they have.**

thick [θɪk] *a* dick; *(forest)* dicht; *(liquid)* dickflüssig; *(slow, stupid)* dumm, schwer von Begriff // *n:* **in the ~ of** mitten in *(+dat)*; **it's 20 cm ~** es ist 20 cm dick *or* stark; **~en** *vi (fog)* dichter werden // *vt (sauce etc)* verdicken; **~ness** *n (of object)* Dicke *f;* Dichte *f;* Dickflüssigkeit *f;* **~set** *a* untersetzt; **~skinned** *a* dickhäutig.

thief [θiːf], *pl* **thieves** [θiːvz] *n* Dieb(in *f*) *m.*

thieving ['θiːvɪŋ] *n* Stehlen *nt* // *a* diebisch.

thigh [θaɪ] *n* Oberschenkel *m.*

thimble ['θɪmbl] *n* Fingerhut *m.*

thin [θɪn] *a* dünn; *(person also)* mager; *(excuse)* schwach // *vt:* **to ~ (down)** *(sauce, paint)* verdünnen.

thing [θɪŋ] *n* Ding *nt;* *(affair)* Sache *f;* **my ~s** meine Sachen *pl;* **the best ~ would be to ...** das beste wäre, ...; **how are ~s?** wie geht's?

think [θɪŋk], *pt, pp* **thought** *vti* denken; **what did you ~ of them?** was halten Sie von ihnen?; **to ~ about** sth/sb nachdenken über etw/jdn; **I'll ~ about it** ich überlege es mir; **to ~ of doing sth**

vorhaben *or* beabsichtigen, etw zu tun; **I ~ so/not** ich glaube (schon)/glaube nicht; **to ~ well of sb** viel von jdm halten; **~ over** *vt* überdenken; **~ up** *vt* sich *(dat)* ausdenken; **~ tank** *n* Experten-gruppe *f.*

thinly ['θɪnlɪ] *ad* dünn; *(disguised)* kaum.

third [θɜːd] *a* dritte(r, s) // *n (person)* Dritte(r) *mf;* *(part)* Drittel *nt;* **~ly** *ad* drittens; **~ party insurance** *n (Brit)* Haftpflichtversicherung *f;* **~-rate** *a* minderwertig; **the T~ World** *n* die Dritte Welt *f.*

thirst [θɜːst] *n (lit, fig)* Durst *m;* **~y** *a (person)* durstig; *(work)* durstig machend; **to be ~y** Durst haben.

thirteen [θɜː'tiːn] *num* dreizehn.

thirty ['θɜːtɪ] *num* dreißig.

this [ðɪs] ♦*a (demonstrative: pl* **these***)* diese(r, s); **~ evening** heute abend; **~ one** diese(r, s) (da)

♦*pronoun (demonstrative: pl* **these***)* dies, das; **who/what is ~?** wer/was ist das?; **~ is where I live** hier wohne ich; **~ is what he said** das hat er gesagt; **~ is Mr Brown** *(in introductions/photo)* dies ist Mr Brown; *(on telephone)* hier ist Mr Brown

♦*ad (demonstrative)*: **~ high/long** *etc* so groß/lang *etc.*

thistle ['θɪsl] *n* Distel *f.*

thong [θɒŋ] *n* (Leder)riemen *m.*

thorn [θɔːn] *n* Dorn *m;* **~y** *a* dornig; *(problem)* schwierig.

thorough ['θʌrə] *a* gründlich; **~bred** *n* Vollblut *nt* // *a* reinrassig, Vollblut-; **~fare** *n* Straße *f;* **'no ~fare'** 'Durchfahrt verboten'; **~ly** *ad* gründlich; *(extremely)* äußerst.

those [ðəʊz] *pl pron* die (da), jene // *a* die, jene.

though [ðəʊ] *cj* obwohl // *ad* trotzdem.

thought [θɔːt] *pt, pp of* **think** // *n (idea)* Gedanke *m;* *(thinking)* Denken *nt,* Denkvermögen *nt;* **~ful** *a (thinking)* gedankenvoll, nachdenklich; *(kind)* rücksichtsvoll, aufmerksam; **~less** *a* gedankenlos, unbesonnen; *(unkind)* rücksichtslos.

thousand ['θaʊzənd] *num* tausend; **two ~** zweitausend; **~s of** Tausende (von); **~th** *a* tausendste(r, s).

thrash [θræʃ] *vt (lit)* verdreschen; *(fig)* (vernichtend) schlagen; **~ about** *vi* um sich schlagen; **~ out** *vt* ausdiskutieren.

thread [θred] *n* Faden *m,* Garn *nt;* *(on screw)* Gewinde *nt;* *(in story)* Faden *m* // *vt (needle)* einfädeln; **~bare** *a (lit, fig)* fadenscheinig.

threat [θret] *n* Drohung *f;* *(danger)* Gefahr *f;* **~en** *vt* bedrohen // *vi* drohen; **to ~en sb with sth** jdm etw androhen.

three [θriː] *num* drei; **~-dimensional** *a* dreidimensional; **~-piece suit** *n* dreiteilige(r) Anzug m; **~-piece suite** n dreiteilige Polstergarnitur f; **~-ply** a (wool) dreifach; (wood) dreischichtig; **~-wheeler** n Dreiradwagen m.

thresh [θreʃ] vti dreschen.

threshold ['θreʃhəʊld] n Schwelle f.

threw [θruː] pt of **throw**.

thrift [θrɪft] n Sparsamkeit f; **~y** a sparsam.

thrill [θrɪl] n Reiz m, Erregung f // vt begeistern, packen; to be ~ed (with gift etc) sich unheimlich freuen über (+acc); **~er** n Krimi m; **~ing** a spannend; (news) aufregend.

thrive [θraɪv], pt **throve** [θrəʊv], pp **thrived** or **thriven** ['θrɪvn] vi gedeihen (on bei).

thriving ['θraɪvɪŋ] a blühend.

throat [θrəʊt] n Hals m, Kehle f; to have a sore ~ Halsschmerzen haben.

throb [θrɒb] n Pochen nt // vi klopfen, pochen.

throes [θrəʊz] npl: in the ~ of mitten in (+dat).

throng [θrɒŋ] n (Menschen)schar f // vt sich drängen in (+dat).

throttle ['θrɒtl] n Gashebel m // vt erdrosseln.

through [θruː] prep durch; (time) während (+gen); (because of) aus, durch // ad durch // a (ticket, train) durchgehend; (finished) fertig; to put sb ~ (TEL) jdn verbinden (to mit) to be ~ (TEL) eine Verbindung haben; (have finished) fertig sein; 'no ~ way' (Brit) Sackgasse f; **~out** [θruː'aʊt] prep (place) überall in (+dat); (time) während (+gen) // ad überall; die ganze Zeit.

throve [θrəʊv] pt of **thrive**.

throw [θrəʊ] n Wurf m // vt, pt **threw**, pp **thrown** werfen; to ~ a party eine Party geben; ~ **away** vt wegwerfen; (waste) verschenken; (money) verschwenden; ~ **off** vt abwerfen; (pursuer) abschütteln; ~ **out** vt hinauswerfen; (rubbish) wegwerfen; (plan) verwerfen; ~ **up** vti (vomit) speien; **~away** a Wegwerf-; **~-in** n Einwurf m.

thru [θruː] (US) = **through**.

thrush [θrʌʃ] n Drossel f.

thrust [θrʌst] n (TECH) Schubkraft f // vti, pt, pp **thrust** (push) stoßen.

thud [θʌd] n dumpfe(r) (Auf)schlag m.

thug [θʌg] n Schlägertyp m.

thumb [θʌm] n Daumen m // vt (book) durchblättern; to ~ a lift per Anhalter fahren (wollen); **~tack** n (US) Reißzwecke f.

thump [θʌmp] n (blow) Schlag m; (noise) Bums m // vi hämmern, pochen // vt schlagen auf (+acc).

thunder ['θʌndə*] n Donner m // vi donnern; (train etc) to ~ past vorbeidonnern // vt brüllen; **~bolt** n Blitz

nt; **~clap** n Donnerschlag m; **~storm** n Gewitter nt, Unwetter nt; **~y** a gewitterschwül.

Thursday ['θɜːzdeɪ] n Donnerstag m.

thus [ðʌs] ad (in this way) so; (therefore) somit, also, folglich.

thwart [θwɔːt] vt vereiteln, durchkreuzen; (person) hindern.

thyme [taɪm] n Thymian m.

thyroid ['θaɪrɔɪd] n Schilddrüse f.

tic [tɪk] n Tick m.

tick [tɪk] n (sound) Ticken nt; (mark) Häkchen nt // vi ticken // vt abhaken; in a ~ (Brit col) sofort; ~ **off** vt abhaken; (person) ausschimpfen; ~ **over** vi (engine) im Leerlauf laufen; (fig) auf Sparflamme laufen.

ticket ['tɪkɪt] n (for travel) Fahrkarte f, (for entrance) (Eintritts)karte f; (price ~) Preisschild nt; (luggage ~) (Gepäck)schein m; (raffle ~) Los nt; (parking ~) Strafzettel m; (permission) Parkschein m; ~ **collector** n Fahrkartenkontrolleur m; ~ **office** n (RAIL etc) Fahrkartenschalter m; (THEAT etc) Kasse f.

tickle ['tɪkl] n Kitzeln nt // vt kitzeln; (amuse) amüsieren.

ticklish ['tɪklɪʃ] a (lit, fig) kitzlig.

tidal ['taɪdl] a Flut-, Tide-; ~ **wave** n Flutwelle f.

tidbit ['tɪdbɪt] n (US) Leckerbissen m.

tiddlywinks ['tɪdlɪwɪŋks] n Floh(hüpf)spiel nt.

tide [taɪd] n Gezeiten pl; high/low ~ Flut f/Ebbe f.

tidy ['taɪdɪ] a ordentlich // vt aufräumen, in Ordnung bringen.

tie [taɪ] n (Brit: necktie) Kravatte f, Schlips m; (sth connecting) Band nt; (SPORT) Unentschieden nt // vt (fasten, restrict) binden // vi (SPORT) unentschieden spielen; (in competition) gleich sein; to ~ in a bow zur Schleife binden; to ~ a knot in sth einen Knoten in etw (acc) machen; ~ **down** vt (lit) festbinden; to ~ sb down to jdn binden an (+acc); ~ **up** vt (dog) anbinden; (parcel) verschnüren; (boat) festmachen; (person) fesseln; to be ~d up (busy) beschäftigt sein.

tier [tɪə*] n Rang m; (of cake) Etage f.

tight [taɪt] a (close) eng, knapp; (schedule) gedrängt; (firm) fest; (control) streng; (stretched) stramm, (an)gespannt; (col) blau, stramm // ad (squeeze) fest; **~s** pl (Brit) Strumpfhose f; **~en** vt anziehen, anspannen; (restrictions) verschärfen // vi sich spannen; **~-fisted** a knauserig; **~ly** ad eng; fest; (stretched) straff; **~-rope** n Seil nt.

tile [taɪl] n (in roof) Dachziegel m; (on wall or floor) Fliese f; **~d** a (roof) gedeckt, Ziegel-; (floor, wall) mit Fliesen belegt.

till [tɪl] n Kasse f // vt bestellen // prep, cj = **until**.

tiller ['tɪlə*] n Ruderpinne f.

tilt [tɪlt] vt kippen, neigen // vi sich neigen.

timber ['tɪmbə*] n Holz nt; (trees) Baumbestand m.

time [taɪm] n Zeit f; (occasion) Mal nt; (rhythm) Takt m // vt zur rechten Zeit tun, zeitlich einrichten; (SPORT) stoppen; **in 2 weeks' ~** in 2 Wochen; a **long ~** lange; **for the ~ being** vorläufig; **4 at a ~** zu jeweils 4; **from ~ to ~** gelegentlich; **to have a good ~** sich amüsieren; **in ~** (soon enough) rechtzeitig; (after some time) mit der Zeit; (MUS) im Takt; **in no ~** im Handumdrehen; **any ~** jederzeit; on **~** pünktlich, rechtzeitig; **five ~s** 5 fünfmal 5; **what ~ is it?** wieviel Uhr ist es?, wie spät ist es?; **~ bomb** n Zeitbombe f; **~lag** n (in travel) Verzögerung f; (difference) Zeitunterschied m; **~less** a (beauty) zeitlos; **~ limit** n Frist f; **~ly** a rechtzeitig; günstig; **~ off** n freie Zeit f; **timer** n (~ switch: in kitchen) Schaltuhr f; **~ scale** n Zeitspanne f; **~ switch** n (Brit) Zeitschalter m; **~table** n Fahrplan m; (SCH) Stundenplan m; **~ zone** n Zeitzone f.

timid ['tɪmɪd] a ängstlich, schüchtern.

timing ['taɪmɪŋ] n Wahl f des richtigen Zeitpunkts, Timing nt; (AUT) Einstellung f.

timpani ['tɪmpənɪ] npl Kesselpauken pl.

tin [tɪn] n (metal) Blech nt; (container) Büchse f, Dose f; **~foil** n Staniolpapier nt.

tinge [tɪndʒ] n (colour) Färbung f; (fig) Anflug m // vt färben; **~d with** mit einer Spur von.

tingle ['tɪŋgl] n Prickeln nt // vi prickeln.

tinker ['tɪŋkə*] n Kesselflicker m; **~ with** vt herumpfuschen an (+dat).

tinkle ['tɪŋkl] vi klingeln.

tinned [tɪnd] a (Brit: food) Dosen-, Büchsen-.

tin opener ['tɪnəupnə*] n (Brit) Dosen- or Büchsenöffner m.

tinsel ['tɪnsəl] n Rauschgold nt.

tint [tɪnt] n Farbton m; (slight colour) Anflug m; (hair) Tönung f; **~ed** a getönt.

tiny ['taɪnɪ] a winzig.

tip [tɪp] n (pointed end) Spitze f; (money) Trinkgeld nt; (hint) Wink m, Tip m // vt (slant) kippen; (hat) antippen; (~ over) umkippen; (waiter) ein Trinkgeld geben (+dat); **~-off** n Hinweis m, Tip m; **~ped** a (Brit: cigarette) Filter-.

tipsy ['tɪpsɪ] a beschwipst.

tiptoe ['tɪptəu] n: **on ~** auf Zehenspitzen.

tiptop ['tɪp'tɒp] a: **in ~ condition** tipptopp, erstklassig.

tire ['taɪə*] n (US) = **tyre** // vti ermüden, müde machen/werden; **~d** a müde; **to be ~d of sth** etw satt haben; **~less** a, **~lessly** ad unermüdlich; **~some** a lästig.

tiring ['taɪərɪŋ] a ermüdend.

tissue ['tɪʃuː] n Gewebe nt; (paper handkerchief) Papiertaschentuch nt; **~ paper** n Seidenpapier nt.

tit [tɪt] n (bird) Meise f; **~s** pl (col: breasts) Busen m; **~ for tat** wie du mir, so ich dir.

titbit ['tɪtbɪt], (US) **tidbit** ['tɪdbɪt] n Leckerbissen m.

titillate ['tɪtɪleɪt] vt kitzeln.

titivate ['tɪtɪveɪt] vt schniegeln.

title ['taɪtl] n Titel m; **~ deed** n Eigentumsurkunde f; **~ role** n Hauptrolle f.

titter ['tɪtə*] vi kichern.

TM abbr (= trademark) Wz.

to [tuː, tə] ◆prep 1 (direction) zu, nach; **to go ~ France/school** nach Frankreich/zur Schule gehen; **~ the left** nach links
2 (as far as) bis
3 (with expressions of time) vor; **a quarter ~ 5** Viertel vor 5
4 (for, of) für; **secretary ~ the director** Sekretärin des Direktors
5 (expressing indirect object): **to give sth ~ sb** jdm etw geben; **to talk ~ sb** mit jdm sprechen; **I sold it ~ a friend** ich habe es einem Freund verkauft
6 (in relation to) zu; **30 miles ~ the gallon** 30 Meilen pro Gallone
7 (purpose, result) zu; **~ my surprise** zu meiner Überraschung
◆with v 1 (infinitive): **~ go/eat** trinken/essen; **to want ~ do sth** etw tun wollen; **try/start ~ do sth** versuchen/anfangen, etw zu tun; **he has a lot ~ lose** er hat viel zu verlieren
2 (with v omitted): **I don't want ~** ich will (es) nicht
3 (purpose, result) um; **I did it ~ help you** ich tat es, um dir zu helfen
4 (after adjective etc): **ready ~ use** gebrauchsfertig; **too old/young ~ ...** zu alt/jung, um ...
◆ad: **push/pull the door ~** die Tür zuschieben/zuziehen.

toad [təud] n Kröte f; **~stool** n Giftpilz m.

toast [təust] n (bread) Toast m; (drinking) Trinkspruch m // vt trinken auf (+acc); (bread) toasten; (warm) wärmen; **~er** n Toaster m.

tobacco [tə'bækəu] n Tabak m; **~nist** [tə'bækənɪst] n Tabakhändler m; **~nist's (shop)** n Tabakladen m.

toboggan [tə'bɒgən] n (Rodel)schlitten m.

today [tə'deɪ] ad heute; (at the present time) heutzutage.

toddler ['tɒdlə*] n Kleinkind nt.

toddy ['tɒdɪ] n (Whisky) grog m.

to-do [tə'du:] n Theater nt.

toe [təʊ] n Zehe f; (of sock, shoe) Spitze f // vt: to ~ the line (fig) sich einfügen; **~nail** n Zehennagel m.

toffee ['tɒfɪ] n Sahnebonbon nt; ~ **apple** n (Brit) kandierte(r) Apfel m.

together [tə'geðə*] ad zusammen; (at the same time) gleichzeitig; ~ **with** prep zusammen/gleichzeitig mit; **~ness** n (company) Beisammensein nt.

toil [tɔɪl] n harte Arbeit f, Plackerei f // vi sich abmühen, sich plagen.

toilet ['tɔɪlət] n Toilette f // cpd Toiletten-; ~ **bag** n Waschbeutel m; ~ **paper** n Toilettenpapier nt; **~ries** ['tɔɪlətrɪz] npl Toilettenartikel pl; ~ **roll** n Rolle f Toilettenpapier; ~ **water** n Toilettenwasser nt.

token ['təʊkən] n Zeichen nt; (gift ~) Gutschein m; **book/record** ~ (Brit) Bücher-/Plattengutschein m.

Tokyo ['təʊkjəʊ] n Tokio nt.

told [təʊld] pt, pp of **tell**.

tolerable ['tɒlərəbl] a (bearable) erträglich; (fairly good) passabel.

tolerate ['tɒləreɪt] vt dulden; (noise) ertragen.

toll [təʊl] n Gebühr f // vi (bell) läuten.

tomato [tə'mɑːtəʊ] n, pl ~es Tomate f.

tomb [tuːm] n Grab(mal) nt.

tomboy ['tɒmbɔɪ] n Wildfang m.

tombstone ['tuːmstəʊn] n Grabstein m.

tomcat ['tɒmkæt] n Kater m.

tomorrow [tə'mɒrəʊ] n Morgen nt // ad morgen; **the day after** ~ übermorgen; ~ **morning** morgen früh; **a week** ~ morgen in einer Woche.

ton [tʌn] n (Brit) Tonne f; (US: also: short ~) 907,18 kg; (metric ~) Tonne f; **~s of** (col) eine Unmenge von.

tone [təʊn] n Ton m; ~ **down** vt (criticism, demands) mäßigen; (colours) abtonen; ~ **up** vt in Form bringen; **~-deaf** a ohne musikalisches Gehör.

tongs [tɒŋz] npl Zange f; (curling ~) Lockenstab m.

tongue [tʌŋ] n Zunge f; (language) Sprache f; **with** ~ **in cheek** scherzhaft; **~-tied** a stumm, sprachlos; **~-twister** n Zungenbrecher m.

tonic ['tɒnɪk] n (MED) Stärkungsmittel nt; (drink) Tonic nt.

tonight [tə'naɪt] ad heute abend.

tonsil ['tɒnsl] n Mandel f; **~litis** [tɒnsɪ'laɪtɪs] n Mandelentzündung f.

too [tuː] ad zu; (also) auch; ~ **bad!** Pech!

took [tʊk] pt of **take**.

tool [tuːl] n (lit, fig) Werkzeug nt; **~box** n Werkzeugkasten m.

toot [tuːt] n Hupen nt // vi tuten; (AUT) hupen.

tooth [tuːθ] n, pl **teeth** Zahn m; **~ache**

n Zahnschmerzen pl, Zahnweh nt; **~brush** n Zahnbürste f; **~paste** n Zahnpasta f; **~pick** n Zahnstocher m.

top [tɒp] n Spitze f; (of mountain) Gipfel m; (of tree) Wipfel m; (toy) Kreisel m; (~ gear) vierte(r) Gang m // a oberste(r, s) // vt (list) an erster Stelle stehen auf (+dat); **on** ~ **of** oben auf (+dat); **from** ~ **to bottom** von oben bis unten; ~ **up**, (US) ~ **off** vt auffüllen; ~ **floor** n oberste Stockwerk nt; ~ **hat** n Zylinder m; **~-heavy** a kopflastig.

topic ['tɒpɪk] n Thema nt, Gesprächsgegenstand m; **~al** a aktuell.

topless ['tɒpləs] a (dress) oben ohne.

top-level ['tɒplevl] a auf höchster Ebene.

topmost ['tɒpməʊst] a oberste(r, s).

topple ['tɒpl] vti stürzen, kippen.

top-secret ['tɒp'siːkrət] a streng geheim.

topsy-turvy ['tɒpsɪ'tɜːvɪ] ad durcheinander // a auf den Kopf gestellt.

torch [tɔːtʃ] n (Brit ELEC) Taschenlampe f; (with flame) Fackel f.

tore [tɔː*] pt of **tear**.

torment ['tɔːment] n Qual f // [tɔː'ment] vt (distress) quälen.

torn [tɔːn] pp of **tear** // a hin- und hergerissen.

torrent ['tɒrənt] n Sturzbach m; **~ial** [tə'renʃəl] a wolkenbruchartig.

torrid ['tɒrɪd] a heiß.

tortoise ['tɔːtəs] n Schildkröte f; **~shell** ['tɔːtəʃel] n Schildpatt m.

tortuous ['tɔːtjʊəs] a gewunden.

torture ['tɔːtʃə*] n Folter f // vt foltern.

Tory ['tɔːrɪ] n (Brit POL) Tory m // a Tory-, konservativ.

toss [tɒs] vt schleudern; **to** ~ **a coin, to** ~ **up for sth** etw mit einer Münze entscheiden; **to** ~ **and turn** (in bed) sich hin und her werfen.

tot [tɒt] n (small quantity) bißchen nt; (small child) Knirps m.

total ['təʊtl] n Gesamtheit f; (money) Endsumme f // a Gesamt-, total // vt (add up) zusammenzählen; (amount to) sich belaufen auf.

totalitarian [təʊtælɪ'teərɪən] a totalitär.

totally ['təʊtəlɪ] ad total.

totter ['tɒtə*] vi wanken, schwanken.

touch [tʌtʃ] n Berührung f; (sense of feeling) Tastsinn m // vt (feel) berühren; (come against) leicht anstoßen; (emotionally) rühren; **a** ~ **of** (fig) eine Spur von; **to get in** ~ **with sb** sich mit jdm in Verbindung setzen; **to lose** ~ (friends) Kontakt verlieren; ~ **on** vt (topic) berühren, erwähnen; ~ **up** vt (paint) auffrischen; **~-and-go** a riskant, knapp; **~down** n Landen nt, Niedergehen nt; **~ing** a rührend; **~line** n Seitenlinie f; **~y** a empfindlich, reizbar.

tough [tʌf] a zäh; (difficult) schwierig // n Schläger(typ) m; **~en** vt zäh machen; (make strong) abhärten.

toupée ['tu:peɪ] n Toupet nt.

tour [tuə*] n Tour f // vi umherreisen; (THEAT) auf Tour sein/gehen; **~ing** n Umherreisen nt; (THEAT) Tournee f.

tourism ['tuərɪzm] n Fremdenverkehr m, Tourismus m.

tourist ['tuərɪst] n Tourist(in f) // cpd (class) Touristen-; **~ office** n Verkehrsamt nt.

tournament ['tuənəmənt] n Tournier nt.

tousled ['tauzld] a zerzaust.

tout [taut] vi: to ~ for auf Kundenfang gehen für // n: ticket ~ Kundenschlepper(in f) m.

tow [təu] vt (ab)schleppen; on or (US) in ~ (AUT) im Schlepp.

toward(s) [tə'wɔːd(z)] prep (with time) gegen; (in direction of) nach.

towel ['tauəl] n Handtuch nt; **~ling** n (fabric) Frottee nt or m; ~ **rail**, (US) ~ **rack** n Handtuchstange f.

tower ['tauə*] n Turm m; ~ **block** n (Brit) Hochhaus nt; **~ing** a hochragend.

town [taun] n Stadt f; to go to ~ (fig) sich ins Zeug legen; ~ **centre** n Stadtzentrum nt; ~ **clerk** n Stadtdirektor m; ~ **council** n Stadtrat m; ~ **hall** n Rathaus nt ~ **plan** n Stadtplan m; ~ **planning** n Stadtplanung f.

towrope ['təurəup] n Abschlepptau nt.

tow truck n (US: breakdown lorry) Abschleppwagen m.

toxic ['tɒksɪk] a giftig, Gift-.

toy [tɔɪ] n Spielzeug nt; ~ **with** vt spielen mit; **~shop** n Spielwarengeschäft nt.

trace [treɪs] n Spur f // vt (follow a course) nachspüren (+dat); (find out) aufspüren; (copy) durchpausen; **tracing paper** n Pauspapier nt.

track [træk] n (mark) Spur f; (path) Weg m; (race-~) Rennbahn f; (RAIL) Gleis nt // vt verfolgen; to keep ~ of sb jdn im Auge behalten; ~ **down** vt aufspüren; ~ **suit** n Trainingsanzug m.

tract [trækt] n (of land) Gebiet nt; (booklet) Traktat nt.

traction ['trækʃən] n (power) Zugkraft f; (AUT: grip) Bodenhaftung f; (MED): in ~ im Streckverband.

trade [treɪd] n (commerce) Handel m; (business) Geschäft nt, Gewerbe nt; (people) Geschäftsleute pl; (skilled manual work) Handwerk nt // vt handeln (in mit) // vt tauschen; ~ **in** vt in Zahlung geben; ~ **fair** n Messe f; **~-in price** n Preis m, zu dem etw in Zahlung genommen wird; **~mark** n Warenzeichen nt; ~ **name** n Handelsbezeichnung f; **~r** n Händler m; **tradesman** n (shopkeeper) Geschäftsmann m; (work-

man) Handwerker m; (delivery man) Lieferant m; ~ **union** n Gewerkschaft f; ~ **unionist** n Gewerkschaftler(in f) m.

trading ['treɪdɪŋ] n Handel m; ~ **estate** n (Brit) Industriegelände nt.

tradition [trə'dɪʃən] n Tradition f; **~al** a traditionell, herkömmlich.

traffic ['træfɪk] n Verkehr m; (esp in drugs) Handel m (in mit) // vi: to ~ in (esp drugs) handeln mit; ~ **circle** n (US) Kreisverkehr m; ~ **jam** n Verkehrsstauung f; ~ **lights** npl Verkehrsampeln pl; ~ **warden** n = Verkehrspolizist m, Politesse f (ohne amtliche Befugnisse).

tragedy ['trædʒədɪ] n Tragödie f.

tragic ['trædʒɪk] a tragisch.

trail [treɪl] n (track) Spur f; (of smoke) Rauchfahne f; (of dust) Staubwolke f; (road) Pfad m, Weg m // vt (animal) verfolgen; (person) folgen (+dat); (drag) schleppen // vi (hang loosely) schleifen; (plants) sich ranken; (be behind) hinterherhinken; (SPORT) weit zurückliegen; (walk) zuckeln; ~ **behind** vi zurückbleiben; **~er** n Anhänger m; (US: caravan) Wohnwagen m; (for film) Vorschau f; ~ **truck** n (US) Sattelschlepper m.

train [treɪn] n Zug m; (of dress) Schleppe f; (series) Folge f // vt (teach: person) ausbilden; (: animal) abrichten; (: mind) schulen; (SPORT) trainieren; (aim) richten (on auf +acc) // vi (exercise) trainieren; (study) ausgebildet werden; ~ **of thought** Gedankengang m; **~ed** a (eye) geschult; (person, voice) ausgebildet; **~ee** n Lehrling m; Praktikant(in f) m; **~er** n (SPORT) Trainer m; Ausbilder m; **~ing** n (for occupation) Ausbildung f; (SPORT) Training nt; in **~ing** im Training; **~ing college** n Pädagogische Hochschule f, Lehrerseminar nt; **~ing shoes** npl Turnschuhe pl.

traipse [treɪps] vi latschen.

trait [treɪ(t)] n Zug m, Merkmal nt.

traitor ['treɪtə*] n Verräter m.

trajectory [trə'dʒektərɪ] n Flugbahn f.

tram(car) ['træm(kɑ:*)] n Straßenbahn f.

tramp [træmp] n Landstreicher m // vi (walk heavily) stampfen, stapfen; (travel on foot) wandern.

trample ['træmpl] vt (nieder)trampeln // vi (herum)trampeln; to ~ (underfoot) herumtrampeln auf (+dat).

tranquil ['træŋkwɪl] a ruhig, friedlich; **~ity** [træŋ'kwɪlɪtɪ] n Ruhe f; **~izer** n Beruhigungsmittel nt.

transact [træn'zækt] vt abwickeln; **~ion** n Abwicklung f; (piece of business) Geschäft nt, Transaktion f.

transcend [træn'send] vt übersteigen.

transcript ['trænskript] n Abschrift f, Kopie f; (JUR) Protokoll nt; ~ion [træn'skrɪpʃən] n Transkription f; (product) Abschrift f.

transfer ['trænsfə*] n (transferring) Übertragung f; (of business) Umzug m; (being transferred) Versetzung f; (design) Abziehbild nt; (SPORT) Transfer m // [træns'fɜ:*] vt (business) verlegen; (person) versetzen; (prisoner) überführen; (drawing) übertragen; (money) überweisen; to ~ the charges (Brit TEL) ein R-Gespräch führen.

transform [træns'fɔ:m] vt umwandeln; ~ation [trænsfə'meɪʃən] n Umwandlung f, Verwandlung f; ~er n (ELEC) Transformator m.

transfusion [træns'fju:ʒən] n Blutübertragung f, Transfusion f.

transient ['trænzɪənt] a kurz(lebig).

transistor [træn'zɪstə*] n (ELEC) Transistor m; (radio) Transistorradio nt.

transit ['trænzɪt] n: in ~ unterwegs.

transition [træn'zɪʃən] n Übergang m; ~al a Übergangs-.

transitory ['trænzɪtərɪ] a vorübergehend.

translate [trænz'leɪt] vti übersetzen.

translation [trænz'leɪʃən] n Übersetzung f.

translator [trænz'leɪtə*] n Übersetzer(in f) m.

transmission [trænz'mɪʃən] n (of information) Übermittlung f; (ELEC, MED, TV) Übertragung f; (AUT) Getriebe nt.

transmit [trænz'mɪt] vt (message) übermitteln; (ELEC, MED, TV) übertragen; ~ter n Sender m.

transparency [træns'pɛərənsɪ] n Durchsichtigkeit f; (Brit PHOT) Dia(positiv) nt.

transparent [træns'pærənt] a (lit) durchsichtig; (fig) offenkundig.

transpire [træns'paɪə*] vi (turn out) sich herausstellen; (happen) passieren.

transplant [træns'plɑ:nt] vt umpflanzen; (MED) verpflanzen; (fig: person) verpflanzen // ['trænsplɑ:nt] n (MED) Transplantation f; (organ) Transplantat nt.

transport ['trænspɔ:t] n Transport m, Beförderung f // vt [træns'pɔ:t] befördern; transportieren; means of ~ Transportmittel nt; ~ation [trænspɔ::'teɪʃən] n Transport m, Beförderung f; (means) Beförderungsmittel nt; (cost) Transportkosten pl; ~ café n (Brit) Fernfahrerlokal nt.

transverse ['trænzvɜ:s] a Quer-; (position) horizontal; (engine) querliegend.

trap [træp] n Falle f; (carriage) zweirädrige(r) Einspänner m; (col: mouth) Klappe f // vt fangen; (person) in eine Falle locken; ~door n Falltür f.

trappings ['træpɪŋz] npl Aufmachung f.

trash [træʃ] n (rubbish) Plunder m; (nonsense) Mist m; ~ can n (US) Mülleimer m.

travel ['trævl] n Reisen nt // vi reisen // vt (distance) zurücklegen; (country) bereisen; ~ agency n Reisebüro nt; ~ agent n Reisebürokaufmann m; Reisebürokauffrau f; (on tyre) Profil nt // ~ler, (US) ~er n Reisende(r) mf; (salesman) Handlungsreisende(r) m; ~ler's cheque, (US) ~er's check n Reisescheck m; ~ling, (US) ~ing n Reisen nt; ~ sickness n Reisekrankheit f.

tray [treɪ] n (tea ~) Tablett nt; (receptacle) Schale f; (for mail) Ablage f.

treacherous ['tretʃərəs] a verräterisch; (road) tückisch.

treachery ['tretʃərɪ] n Verrat m.

treacle ['tri:kl] n Sirup m, Melasse f.

tread [tred] n Schritt m, Tritt m; (of stair) Stufe f; (on tyre) Profil nt // vi, pt trod, pp trodden treten; ~ on vt treten auf (+acc).

treason ['tri:zn] n Verrat m.

treasure ['treʒə*] n Schatz m // vt schätzen.

treasurer ['treʒərə*] n Kassenverwalter m, Schatzmeister m.

treasury ['treʒərɪ] n (POL) Finanzministerium nt.

treat [tri:t] n besondere Freude f // vt (deal with) behandeln; to ~ sb to sth jdn zu etw einladen.

treatise ['tri:tɪz] n Abhandlung f.

treatment ['tri:tmənt] n Behandlung f.

treaty ['tri:tɪ] n Vertrag m.

treble ['trebl] a dreifach // vt verdreifachen; ~ clef n Violinschlüssel m.

tree [tri:] n Baum m; ~ trunk n Baumstamm m.

trellis ['trelɪs] n Gitter nt; (for gardening) Spalier nt.

tremble ['trembl] vi zittern; (ground) beben.

trembling ['tremblɪŋ] n Zittern nt // a zitternd.

tremendous [trə'mendəs] a gewaltig, kolossal; (col: very good) prima.

tremor ['tremə*] n Zittern nt; (of earth) Beben nt.

trench [trentʃ] n Graben m; (MIL) Schützengraben m.

trend [trend] n Tendenz f; ~y a (col) modisch.

trepidation [trepɪ'deɪʃən] n Beklommenheit f.

trespass ['trespəs] vi widerrechtlich betreten (on acc); 'no ~ing' 'Betreten verboten.'

tress [tres] n Locke f.

trestle ['tresl] n Bock m; ~ table n Klapptisch m.

trial ['traɪəl] n (JUR) Prozeß m; (test)

Versuch m, Probe f; (hardship) Prüfung f; by ~ and error durch Ausprobieren.

triangle ['traɪæŋgl] n Dreieck nt; (MUS) Triangel f.

triangular [traɪ'æŋgjʊlə*] a dreieckig.

tribal ['traɪbəl] a Stammes-.

tribe [traɪb] n Stamm m; **tribesman** n Stammesangehörige(r) m.

tribulation [trɪbjʊ'leɪʃən] n Not f, Mühsal f.

tribunal [traɪ'bjuːnl] n Gericht nt; (inquiry) Untersuchungsausschuß m.

tributary ['trɪbjʊtərɪ] n Nebenfluß m.

tribute ['trɪbjuːt] n (admiration) Zeichen nt der Hochachtung; **to pay ~** to jdm/ einer Sache Tribut zollen.

trice [traɪs] n: **in a ~** im Nu.

trick [trɪk] n Trick m; (CARDS) Stich m // vt überlisten, beschwindeln; **to play a ~ on sb** jdm einen Streich spielen; **that should do the ~** das müßte eigentlich klappen; **~ery** n Tricks pl.

trickle ['trɪkl] n Tröpfeln nt; (small river) Rinnsal nt // vi tröpfeln; (seep) sickern.

tricky ['trɪkɪ] a (problem) schwierig; (situation) kitzlig.

tricycle ['traɪsɪkl] n Dreirad nt.

trifle ['traɪfl] n Kleinigkeit f; (COOK) Trifle m // ad: **a ~** ein bißchen.

trifling ['traɪflɪŋ] a geringfügig.

trigger ['trɪgə*] n Drücker m; **~ off** vt auslösen.

trim [trɪm] a gepflegt; (figure) schlank // n (gute) Verfassung f; (embellishment, on car) Verzierung f // vt (clip) schneiden; (trees) stutzen; (decorate) besetzen; (sails) trimmen; **~mings** npl (decorations) Verzierung(en pl) f; (extras) Zubehör nt.

Trinity ['trɪnɪtɪ] n: **the ~** die Dreieinigkeit.

trinket ['trɪŋkɪt] n kleine(s) Schmuckstück nt.

trip [trɪp] n (kurze) Reise f; (outing) Ausflug m; (stumble) Stolpern nt // vi (walk quickly) trippeln; (stumble) stolpern; **on a ~** auf Reisen; **~ up** vi stolpern; (fig also) einen Fehler machen // vt zu Fall bringen; (fig) hereinlegen.

tripe [traɪp] n (food) Kutteln pl; (rubbish) Mist m.

triple ['trɪpl] a dreifach.

triplets ['trɪplɪts] npl Drillinge pl.

triplicate ['trɪplɪkət] n: **in ~** in dreifacher Ausfertigung.

tripod ['traɪpɒd] n (PHOT) Stativ nt.

trite [traɪt] a banal.

triumph ['traɪʌmf] n Triumph m // vi triumphieren; **to ~ (over)** triumphieren (über (+acc)) **~ant** [traɪ'ʌmfənt] a triumphierend.

trivia ['trɪvɪə] npl Trivialitäten pl.

trivial ['trɪvɪəl] a gering(fügig), trivial.

trod [trɒd], **trodden** ['trɒdn] pt, pp of

tread.

trolley ['trɒlɪ] n Handwagen m; (in shop) Einkaufswagen; (for luggage) Kofferkuli m; (table) Teewagen m; **~ bus** n O(berleitungs)bus m.

troop [truːp] n Schar f; (MIL) Trupp m; **~s** pl Truppen pl; **~ in/out** vi hinein-/ hinausströmen; **~er** n Kavallerist m; **~ing the colour** n (ceremony) Fahnenparade f.

tropic ['trɒpɪk] n Wendekreis m; **~al** a tropisch.

trot [trɒt] n Trott m // vi trotten; **on the ~** (Brit fig: col) in einer Tour.

trouble ['trʌbl] n (problems) Ärger m; (worry) Sorge f, (in country, industry) Unruhen pl; (effort) Mühe f; (MED): **stomach ~** Magenbeschwerden pl; // vt (disturb) stören; **to ~ to do sth** sich bemühen, etw zu tun; **to be in ~** Probleme or Ärger haben; **~s** pl (POL etc) Unruhen pl; **to go to the ~ of doing sth** sich die Mühe machen, etw zu tun; **what's the ~?** was ist los?; (to sick person) wo fehlt's?; **~d** a (person) beunruhigt; (country) geplagt; **~free** a sorglos; **~maker** n Unruhestifter m; **~shooter** n Vermittler m; **~some** a lästig, unangenehm; (child) schwierig.

trough [trɒf] n (vessel) Trog m; (channel) Rinne f, Kanal m; (MET) Tief nt.

trounce [traʊns] vt (esp SPORT) vernichtend schlagen.

trousers ['traʊzəz] npl Hose f.

trousseau ['truːsəʊ], pl **~x** or **~s** [-z] n Aussteuer f.

trout [traʊt] n Forelle f.

trowel ['traʊəl] n Kelle f.

truant ['trʊənt] n: **to play ~** (Brit) (die Schule) schwänzen.

truce [truːs] n Waffenstillstand m.

truck [trʌk] n Lastwagen m; (RAIL) offene(r) Güterwagen m; **~ driver** n Lastwagenfahrer m; **~ farm** n (US) Gemüsegärtnerei f.

truculent ['trʌkjʊlənt] a trotzig.

trudge [trʌdʒ] vi (mühselig) dahinschleppen.

true [truː] a (exact) wahr; (genuine) echt; (friend) treu.

truly ['truːlɪ] ad wirklich; **yours ~** Ihr sehr ergebener.

trump [trʌmp] n (CARDS) Trumpf m; **~ed-up** a erfunden.

trumpet ['trʌmpɪt] n Trompete f.

truncheon ['trʌntʃən] n Gummiknüppel m.

trundle ['trʌndl] vt schieben // vi: **~ along** entlangrollen.

trunk [trʌŋk] n (of tree) (Baum)stamm m; (ANAT) Rumpf m; (box) Truhe f, Überseekoffer m; (of elephant) Rüssel m; (US AUT) Kofferraum; **~s** pl Badehose f; **~ (up)** vt fesseln.

truss [trʌs] n (MED) Bruchband nt.

trust [trʌst] n (confidence) Vertrauen nt; (for property etc) Treuhandvermögen nt // vt (rely on) vertrauen (+dat), sich verlassen auf (+acc); (hope) hoffen; (entrust); to ~ sth to sb jdm etw anvertrauen; ~ed a treu; ~ee [trʌs'tiː] n Vermögensverwalter m; ~ful a, ~ing a vertrauensvoll; ~worthy a vertrauenswürdig; (account) glaubwürdig; ~y a treu, zuverlässig.

truth [truːθ] pl ~s [truːðz] n Wahrheit f; ~ful a ehrlich.

try [traɪ] n Versuch m; to have a ~ es versuchen // vt (attempt) versuchen; (test) (aus)probieren; (JUR: person) unter Anklage stellen; (: case) verhandeln; (courage, patience) auf die Probe stellen // vi (make effort) versuchen, sich bemühen; to ~ to do sth versuchen, etw zu tun; ~ on vt (dress) anprobieren; (hat) aufprobieren; ~ out vt ausprobieren; ~ing a schwierig.

T-shirt [ˈtiːʃɜːt] n T-shirt nt.

T-square [ˈtiːskweə*] n Reißschiene f.

tub [tʌb] n Wanne f, Kübel m; (for margarine etc) Becher m.

tubby [ˈtʌbɪ] a rundlich.

tube [tjuːb] n (pipe) Röhre f, Rohr nt; (for toothpaste etc) Tube f; (in London) U-Bahn f; (AUT: for tyre) Schlauch m.

tube station [ˈtjuːbsteɪʃən] n (Brit) U-Bahnstation f.

tubing [ˈtjuːbɪŋ] n Schlauch m; a piece of ~ ein (Stück) Schlauch.

tubular [ˈtjuːbjʊlə*] a röhrenförmig.

TUC n abbr (Brit) of **Trades Union Congress.**

tuck [tʌk] n (fold) Falte f, Einschlag m // vt (put) stecken; (gather) fälteln, einschlagen; ~ away vt wegstecken; ~ in vt hineinstecken; (blanket etc) feststecken; (person) zudecken // vi (eat) hineinhauen, zulangen; ~ up vt (child) warm zudecken; ~ shop n Süßwarenladen m.

Tuesday [ˈtjuːzdeɪ] n Dienstag m.

tuft [tʌft] n Büschel m.

tug [tʌg] n (jerk) Zerren nt, Ruck m; (NAUT) Schleppdampfer m // vti zerren, ziehen; (boat) schleppen; ~-of-war n Tauziehen nt.

tuition [tjuːˈɪʃən] n (Brit) Unterricht m; (: private ~) Privatunterricht m; (US: school fees) Schulgeld nt.

tulip [ˈtjuːlɪp] n Tulpe f.

tumble [ˈtʌmbl] n (fall) Sturz m // vi (fall) fallen, stürzen; ~ to vt kapieren; ~down a baufällig; ~ dryer n (Brit) Trockner m; **tumbler** n (glass) Trinkglas nt.

tummy [ˈtʌmɪ] n (col) Bauch m.

tuna [ˈtjuːnə] n Thunfisch m.

tune [tjuːn] n Melodie f // vt (put in tune) stimmen; (AUT) richtig einstellen; to

sing in ~/out of ~ richtig/falsch singen; to be out of ~ with nicht harmonieren mit; ~ in vi einstellen (to acc); ~ up vi (MUS) stimmen; **tuner** n (person) (Instrumenten)stimmer m; (part) Tuner m; **piano tuner** n Klavierstimmer(in f) m; ~ful a melodisch.

tunic [ˈtjuːnɪk] n Waffenrock m; (loose garment) lange Bluse f.

tuning [ˈtjuːnɪŋ] n (RAD, AUT) Einstellen nt; (MUS) Stimmen nt; ~ fork n Stimmgabel f.

Tunisia [tjuːˈnɪzɪə] n Tunesien nt.

tunnel [ˈtʌnl] n Tunnel m, Unterführung f // vi einen Tunnel anlegen.

turbulent [ˈtɜːbjʊlənt] a stürmisch.

tureen [tjʊˈriːn] n Terrine f.

turf [tɜːf] n Rasen m; (piece) Sode f // vt mit Grassoden belegen; ~ out vt (col) rauswerfen.

turgid [ˈtɜːdʒɪd] a geschwollen.

Turk [tɜːk] n Türke m, Türkin f.

turkey [ˈtɜːkɪ] n Puter m, Truthahn m.

Turkey [ˈtɜːkɪ] n Türkei f; **Turkish** a türkisch // n (LING) Türkisch nt.

turmoil [ˈtɜːmɔɪl] n Aufruhr m, Tumult m.

turn [tɜːn] n (rotation) (Um)drehung f; (performance) (Programm)nummer f; (MED) Schock m // vt (rotate) drehen; (change position of) umdrehen, wenden; (page) umblättern; (transform): to ~ sth into sth etw in etw (acc) verwandeln; (direct) zuwenden // vi (rotate) sich drehen; (change direction: in car) abbiegen; (: wind) drehen; (~ round) umdrehen, wenden; (become) werden; (leaves) sich verfärben; (milk) sauer werden; (weather) umschlagen; to do sb a good ~ jdm etw Gutes tun; it's your ~ du bist dran or an der Reihe; in ~, by ~s abwechseln; to take ~s sich abwechseln; it gave me quite a ~ das hat mich schön erschreckt; 'no left ~' (AUT) 'Linksabbiegen verboten'; ~ away vi sich abwenden; ~ back vt umdrehen; (person) zurückschicken; (clock) zurückstellen // vi umkehren; ~ down vt (refuse) ablehnen; (fold down) umschlagen; ~ in vi (go to bed) ins Bett gehen // vt (fold inwards) einwärts biegen; ~ off vi abbiegen // vt ausschalten; (tap) zudrehen; (machine, electricity) abstellen; ~ on vt (light) anschalten, einschalten; (tap) aufdrehen; (machine) anstellen; ~ out vi (prove to be) sich erweisen; (people) sich entwickeln; how did the cake ~ out? wie ist der Kuchen geworden? // vt (light) ausschalten; (gas) abstellen; (produce) produzieren; ~ round vi (person, vehicle) sich herumdrehen; (rotate) sich drehen; ~ up vi auftauchen; (happen) passieren, sich ereignen // vt (collar) hochklappen, hochstellen;

(*nose*) rümpfen; (*increase: radio*) lauter stellen; (: *heat*) höher drehen; **~ing** *n* (*in road*) Abzweigung *f*; **~ing point** *n* Wendepunkt *m*.

turnip ['tɜːnɪp] *n* Steckrübe *f*.

turnout ['tɜːnəut] *n* (Besucher)zahl *f*; (COMM) Produktion *f*.

turnover ['tɜːnəuvə*] *n* Umsatz *m*;_ (*of staff*) Wechsel *m*.

turnpike ['tɜːnpaɪk]   *n*   (US) gebührenpflichtige Straße *f*.

turnstile ['tɜːnstaɪl] *n* Drehkreuz *nt*.

turntable ['tɜːnteɪbl] *n* (*of record-player*) Plattenteller *m*; (RAIL) Drehscheibe *f*.

turn-up ['tɜːnʌp] *n* (*Brit: on trousers*) Aufschlag *m*.

turpentine ['tɜːpəntaɪn] *n* Terpentin *nt*.

turquoise ['tɜːkwɔɪz] *n* (*gem*) Türkis *m*; (*colour*) Türkis *nt* // *a* türkisfarben.

turret ['tʌrɪt] *n* Turm *m*.

turtle ['tɜːtl] *n* Schildkröte *f*; **~ neck (sweater)** *n* (Pullover *m* mit) Schildkrötkragen *m*.

tusk [tʌsk] *n* Stoßzahn *m*.

tussle ['tʌsl] *n* Balgerei *f*.

tutor ['tjuːtə*] *n* (*teacher*) Privatlehrer *m*; (*college instructor*) Tutor *m*; **~ial** [tjuːˈtɔːrɪəl] *n* (UNIV) Kolloquium *nt*, Seminarübung *f*.

tuxedo [tʌkˈsiːdəu] *n* (US) Smoking *m*.

TV ['tiːˈviː] *n abbr* (= *television*) TV *nt*.

twang [twæŋ] *n* scharfe(r) Ton *m*; (*of voice*) Näseln *nt*.

tweezers ['twiːzəz] *npl* Pinzette *f*.

twelfth [twelfθ] *a* zwölfte(r, s).

twelve [twelv] *num a* zwölf; **at ~ o'clock** (*midday*) um 12 Uhr; (*midnight*) um Null Uhr.

twentieth ['twentɪθ] *a* zwanzigste(r, s).

twenty ['twentɪ] *num a* zwanzig.

twice [twaɪs] *ad* zweimal; **~ as much** doppelt soviel.

twiddle ['twɪdl] *vti*: **to ~ (with) sth** an etw (*dat*) herumdrehen; **to ~ one's thumbs** (*fig*) Däumchen drehen.

twig [twɪg] *n* dünne(r) Zweig *m* // *vt* (*col*) kapieren, merken.

twilight ['twaɪlaɪt] *n* Zwielicht *nt*.

twin [twɪn] *n* Zwilling *m* // *a* Zwillings-; (*very similar*) Doppel- // *vt* (*towns*) zu Partnerstädten machen; **~-bedded room** *n* Zimmer *nt* mit zwei Einzelbetten.

twine [twaɪn] *n* Bindfaden *m* // *vi* binden.

twinge [twɪndʒ] *n* stechende(r) Schmerz *m*, Stechen *nt*.

twinkle ['twɪŋkl] *n* Funkeln *nt*, Blitzen *nt* // *vi* funkeln.

twirl [twɜːl] *n* Wirbel *m* // *vti* (herum)wirbeln.

twist [twɪst] *n* (*twisting*), Drehung *f*; (*bend*) Kurve *f* // *vt* (*turn*) drehen; (*make crooked*) verbiegen; (*distort*) ver-

drehen // *vi* (*wind*) sich drehen; (*curve*) sich winden.

twit [twɪt] *n* (*col*) Idiot *m*.

twitch [twɪtʃ] *n* Zucken *nt* // *vi* zucken.

two [tuː] *num* zwei; **to put ~ and ~ together** seine Schlüsse ziehen; **~-door** *a* zweitürig; **~-faced** *a* falsch; **~-fold** *a*, *ad* zweifach, doppelt; **to increase ~fold** verdoppeln; **~-piece** *a* zweiteilig; **~-piece (suit)** *n* Zweiteiler *m*; **~-piece (swimsuit)** *n* zweiteilige(r) Badeanzug *m*; **~-seater** *n* (*plane, car*) Zweisitzer *m*; **~-some** *n* Paar *nt*; **~-way** *a* (*traffic*) Gegen-.

tycoon [taɪˈkuːn] *n*: (**business**) **~** (Industrie)magnat *m*.

type [taɪp] *n* Typ *m*, Art *f*; (PRINT) Type *f* // *vti* maschineschreiben, tippen; **~-cast** *a* (THEAT, TV) auf eine Rolle festgelegt; **~face** *n* Schrift *f*; **~script** *n* maschinegeschriebene(r) Text *m*; **~writer** *n* Schreibmaschine *f*; **~written** *a* maschinegeschrieben.

typhoid ['taɪfɔɪd] *n* Typhus *m*.

typical *a*, **~ly** *ad* ['tɪpɪkəl, -klɪ] typisch (*of* für).

typify ['tɪpɪfaɪ] *vt* typisch sein für.

typing ['taɪpɪŋ] *n* Maschineschreiben *nt*.

typist ['taɪpɪst] *n* Maschinenschreiber(in *f*) *m*, Tippse *f* (*col*).

tyre, (US) **tire** [taɪə*] *n* Reifen *m*; **~ pressure** *n* Reifendruck *m*.

U

U-bend ['juːbend] *n* (*in pipe*) U-Bogen *m*.

ubiquitous [juːˈbɪkwɪtəs] *adj* überall zu findend; allgegenwärtig.

udder ['ʌdə*] *n* Euter *nt*.

UFO ['juːfəu] *n abbr* (= *unidentified flying object*) UFO *nt*.

ugh [ɜːh] *interj* hu.

ugliness ['ʌglɪnəs] *n* Häßlichkeit *f*.

ugly ['ʌglɪ] *a* häßlich; (*bad*) böse, schlimm.

U.K. *n abbr of* **United Kingdom.**

ulcer ['ʌlsə*] *n* Geschwür *nt*.

Ulster ['ʌlstə*] *n* Ulster *nt*.

ulterior [ʌlˈtɪərɪə*] *a*: **~ motive** *n* Hintergedanke *m*.

ultimate ['ʌltɪmət] *a* äußerste(r, s), allerletzte(r, s); **~ly** *ad* schließlich, letzten Endes.

ultrasound ['ʌltrəˈsaund] *n* (MED) Ultraschall *m*.

umbilical cord [ʌmˈbɪlɪkl kɔːd] *n* Nabelschnur *f*.

umbrella [ʌmˈbrelə] *n* Schirm *m*.

umpire ['ʌmpaɪə*] *n* Schiedsrichter *m* // *vti* schiedsrichtern.

umpteen [ʌmpˈtiːn] *num* (*col*) zig; **for the ~th time** zum X-ten Mal.

UN, UNO *n abbr* (= *United Nations*

(Organization)) UN *f*, UNO *f*.

unable ['ʌn'eɪbl] *a*: to be ~ to do sth etw nicht tun können.

unaccompanied ['ʌnə'kʌmpənɪd] *a* ohne Begleitung.

unaccountably ['ʌnə'kaʊntəblɪ] *ad* unerklärlich.

unaccustomed ['ʌnə'kʌstəmd] *a* nicht gewöhnt (*to* an +*acc*); (*unusual*) ungewohnt.

unanimous *a*, ~**ly** *ad* [ju:'næniməs, -lɪ] einmütig; (*vote*) einstimmig.

unarmed [ʌn'ɑːmd] *a* unbewaffnet.

unashamed ['ʌnə'ʃeɪmd] *a* schamlos.

unassuming [ʌnə'sju:mɪŋ] *a* bescheiden.

unattached ['ʌnə'tætʃt] *a* ungebunden.

unattended ['ʌnə'tendɪd] *a* (*person*) unbeaufsichtigt; (*thing*) unbewacht.

unauthorized ['ʌn'ɔːθəraɪzd] *a* unbefugt.

unavoidable [ʌnə'vɔɪdəbl] *a* unvermeidlich.

unaware ['ʌnə'weə*] *a*: to be ~ of sth sich (*dat*) einer Sache nicht bewußt sein; ~**s** *ad* unversehens.

unbalanced ['ʌn'bælənst] *a* unausgeglichen; (*mentally*) gestört.

unbearable [ʌn'beərəbl] *a* unerträglich.

unbeatable ['ʌn'biːtəbl] *a* unschlagbar.

unbeknown(st) ['ʌnbɪ'nəʊn(st)] *ad*: ~ to me ohne mein Wissen.

unbelievable [ʌnbɪ'liːvəbl] *a* unglaublich.

unbend ['ʌn'bend] (*irreg: like* **bend**) *vt* geradebiegen // *vi* aus sich herausgehen.

unbiased ['ʌn'baɪəst] *a* unparteiisch.

unbreakable ['ʌn'breɪkəbl] *a* unzerbrechlich.

unbridled [ʌn'braɪdld] *a* ungezügelt.

unbroken ['ʌn'brəʊkən] *a* (*period*) ununterbrochen; (*spirit*) ungebrochen; (*record*) unübertroffen.

unburden ['ʌn'bɜːdn] *vt*: ~ o.s. (jdm) sein Herz ausschütten.

unbutton ['ʌn'bʌtn] *vt* aufknöpfen.

uncalled-for [ʌn'kɔːldfɔː*] *a* unnötig.

uncanny [ʌn'kænɪ] *a* unheimlich.

unceasing [ʌn'siːsɪŋ] *a* unaufhörlich.

unceremonious ['ʌnserɪ'məʊnɪəs] *a* (*abrupt, rude*) brüsk; (*exit, departure*) überstürzt.

uncertain [ʌn'sɜːtn] *a* unsicher; (*doubtful*) ungewiß; (*unreliable*) unbeständig; (*vague*) undeutlich, vage; ~**ty** *n* Ungewißheit *f*.

unchanged ['ʌn'tʃeɪndʒd] *a* unverändert.

unchecked ['ʌn'tʃekt] *a* ungeprüft; (*not stopped: advance*) ungehindert.

uncivilized ['ʌn'sɪvɪlaɪzd] *a* unzivilisiert.

uncle ['ʌŋkl] *n* Onkel *m*.

uncomfortable [ʌn'kʌmfətəbl] *a* unbequem, ungemütlich.

uncommon [ʌn'kɔmən] *a* ungewöhnlich; (*outstanding*) außergewöhnlich.

uncompromising [ʌn'kɔmprəmaɪzɪŋ] *a* kompromißlos, unnachgiebig.

unconcerned [ʌnkən'sɜːnd] *a* unbekümmert; (*indifferent*) gleichgültig.

unconditional ['ʌnkən'dɪʃənl] *a* bedingungslos.

uncongenial ['ʌnkən'dʒiːnɪəl] *a* unangenehm.

unconscious [ʌn'kɔnʃəs] *a* (MED) bewußtlos; (*not meant*) unbeabsichtigt; the ~ das Unbewußte; ~**ly** *ad* unbewußt.

uncontrollable ['ʌnkən'trəʊləbl] *a* unkontrollierbar, unbändig.

unconventional [ʌnkən'venʃənl] *a* unkonventionell.

uncouth [ʌn'kuːθ] *a* grob.

uncover [ʌn'kʌvə*] *vt* aufdecken.

undecided ['ʌndɪ'saɪdɪd] *a* unschlüssig.

undeniable [ʌndɪ'naɪəbl] *a* unleugbar.

under ['ʌndə*] *prep* unter // *ad* darunter; ~ there da drunter; ~ **repair** in Reparatur; ~-**age** *a* minderjährig.

undercarriage ['ʌndəkærɪdʒ] *n* (Brit AVIAT) Fahrgestell *nt*.

undercharge [ʌndə'tʃɑːdz] *vt* jdm zu wenig berechnen.

underclothes ['ʌndəkləʊðz] *npl* Unterwäsche *f*.

undercoat ['ʌndəkəʊt] *n* (paint) Grundierung *f*.

undercover ['ʌndəkʌvə*] *a* Geheim-.

undercurrent ['ʌndəkʌrənt] *n* Unterströmung *f*.

undercut ['ʌndəkʌt] *vt* (*irreg: like* **cut**) unterbieten.

underdeveloped ['ʌndədɪ'veləpt] *a* Entwicklungs-, unterentwickelt.

underdog ['ʌndədɔg] *n* Unterlegene(r) *mf*.

underdone ['ʌndə'dʌn] *a* (COOK) nicht gar, nicht durchgebraten.

underestimate ['ʌndər'estɪmeɪt] *vt* unterschätzen.

underexposed ['ʌndərɪks'pəʊzd] *a* unterbelichtet.

underfed ['ʌndə'fed] *a* unterernährt.

underfoot ['ʌndə'fʊt] *ad* am Boden.

undergo ['ʌndə'gəʊ] *vt* (*irreg: like* **go**) (*experience*) durchmachen; (*operation, test*) sich unterziehen (+*dat*).

undergraduate ['ʌndə'grædjʊət] *n* Student (in *f*) *m*.

underground ['ʌndəgraʊnd] *n* U-Bahn *f* // *a* Untergrund-.

undergrowth ['ʌndəgrəʊθ] *n* Gestrüpp *nt*, Unterholz *nt*.

underhand(ed) ['ʌndə'hænd(ɪd)] *a* hinterhältig.

underlie [ʌndə'laɪ] *vt* (*irreg: like* **lie**) (*form the basis of*) zugrundeliegen (+*dat*).

underline [ʌndə'laɪn] *vt* unterstreichen; (*emphasize*) betonen.

underling ['ʌndəlɪŋ] *n* Handlanger *m*.

undermine [ʌndə'maɪn] vt untergraben.

underneath [ʌndə'niːθ] ad darunter // prep unter.

underpaid ['ʌndə'peɪd] a unterbezahlt.

underpants ['ʌndəpænts] npl Unterhose f.

underpass ['ʌndəpɑːs] n (Brit) Unterführung f.

underprivileged ['ʌndə'prɪvɪlɪdʒd] a benachteiligt, unterprivilegiert.

underrate [ʌndə'reɪt] vt unterschätzen.

undershirt ['ʌndəʃɜːt] n (US) Unterhemd nt.

undershorts ['ʌndəʃɔːts] npl (US) Unterhose f.

underside ['ʌndəsaɪd] n Unterseite f.

underskirt ['ʌndəskɜːt] n (Brit) Unterrock m.

understand [ʌndə'stænd] vti (irreg: like stand) verstehen; I ~ that ... ich habe gehört, daß ...; am I to ~ that ...? soll das (etwa) heißen, daß ...?; what do you ~ by that? was verstehen Sie darunter?; it is understood that ... es wurde vereinbart, daß ...; to make o.s. understood sich verständlich machen; is that understood? ist das klar?; ~able a verständlich; ~ing n Verständnis nt // a verständnisvoll.

understood [ʌndə'stʊd] pt, pp of understand // a klar; (implied) angenommen.

understudy ['ʌndəstʌdɪ] n Ersatz-(schau)spieler(in f) m.

undertake [ʌndə'teɪk] (irreg: like take) vt unternehmen // vi : to ~ to do sth sich verpflichten, etw zu tun.

undertaker ['ʌndəteɪkə*] n Leichenbestatter m.

undertaking [ʌndə'teɪkɪŋ] n (enterprise) Unternehmen nt; (promise) Verpflichtung f.

undertone ['ʌndətəʊn] n: in an ~ mit gedämpfter Stimme.

underwater ['ʌndə'wɔːtə*] ad unter Wasser // a Unterwasser-.

underwear ['ʌndəwɛə*] n Unterwäsche f.

underworld ['ʌndəwɜːld] n (of crime) Unterwelt f.

underwriter ['ʌndəraɪtə*] n Assekurant m.

undesirable [ʌndɪ'zaɪərəbl] a unerwünscht.

undies ['ʌndɪz] npl (col) (Damen)-unterwäsche f.

undisputed ['ʌndɪs'pjuːtɪd] a unbestritten.

undo ['ʌn'duː] vt (irreg: like do) (unfasten) öffnen, aufmachen; (work) zunichte machen; ~ing n Verderben nt.

undoubted [ʌn'daʊtɪd] a unbezweifelt; ~ly ad zweifellos, ohne Zweifel.

undress ['ʌn'dres] vti (sich) ausziehen.

undue ['ʌndjuː] a übermäßig.

undulating ['ʌndjʊleɪtɪŋ] a wellenförmig; (country) wellig.

unduly ['ʌn'djuːlɪ] ad übermäßig.

unearth ['ʌn'ɜːθ] vt (dig up) ausgraben; (discover) ans Licht bringen.

unearthly [ʌn'ɜːθlɪ] a (hour) nachtschlafen.

uneasy [ʌn'iːzɪ] a (worried) unruhig; (feeling) ungut.

uneconomic(al) ['ʌniːkə'nɒmɪk(əl)] a unwirtschaftlich.

uneducated ['ʌn'edjʊkeɪtɪd] a ungebildet.

unemployed ['ʌnɪm'plɔɪd] a arbeitslos; the ~ die Arbeitslosen pl.

unemployment ['ʌnɪm'plɔɪmənt] n Arbeitslosigkeit f.

unending [ʌn'endɪŋ] a endlos.

unerring ['ʌn'ɜːrɪŋ] a unfehlbar.

uneven ['ʌn'iːvən] a (surface) uneben; (quality) ungleichmäßig.

unexpected a, ~ly ad [ʌnɪk'spektɪd,-lɪ] unerwartet.

unfailing [ʌn'feɪlɪŋ] a nie versagend.

unfair ['ʌn'feə*] a ungerecht, unfair.

unfaithful ['ʌn'feɪθfʊl] a untreu.

unfamiliar [ʌnfə'mɪlɪə*] a ungewohnt; (person, subject) unbekannt.

unfashionable [ʌn'fæʃnəbl] a unmodern; (area, hotel etc) nicht in Mode.

unfasten ['ʌn'fɑːsn] vt öffnen, aufmachen.

unfavourable, (US) **unfavorable** ['ʌn'feɪvərəbl] a ungünstig.

unfeeling [ʌn'fiːlɪŋ] a gefühllos, kalt.

unfinished ['ʌn'fɪnɪʃt] a unvollendet.

unfit ['ʌn'fɪt] a ungeeignet (for zu, für); (in bad health) nicht fit.

unfold [ʌn'fəʊld] vt entfalten; (paper) auseinanderfalten // vi (develop) sich entfalten.

unforeseen ['ʌnfɔː'siːn] a unvorhergesehen.

unforgettable [ʌnfə'getəbl] a unvergeßlich.

unforgivable ['ʌnfə'gɪvəbl] a unverzeihlich.

unfortunate [ʌn'fɔːtʃnət] a unglücklich, bedauerlich; ~ly ad leider.

unfounded ['ʌn'faʊndɪd] a unbegründet.

unfriendly ['ʌn'frendlɪ] a unfreundlich.

ungainly [ʌn'geɪnlɪ] a linkisch.

ungodly [ʌn'gɒdlɪ] a (hour) nachtschlafend; (row) heillos.

ungrateful [ʌn'greɪtfʊl] a undankbar.

unhappiness [ʌn'hæpɪnəs] n Unglück nt, Unglückseligkeit f.

unhappy [ʌn'hæpɪ] a unglücklich; ~ with (arrangements etc) unzufrieden mit.

unharmed ['ʌn'hɑːmd] a wohlbehalten, unversehrt.

unhealthy [ʌn'helθɪ] a ungesund.

unheard-of [ʌn'hɜːdɒv] a unerhört.

unhook [ʌn'huk] vt (from wall) vom Haken nehmen; (dress) loshaken.

unhurt [ʌn'hɜːt] a unverletzt.

unidentified [ʌnaɪ'dentɪfaɪd] a unbekannt, nicht identifiziert.

uniform ['juːnɪfɔːm] n Uniform f // a einheitlich; **~ity** [juːnɪ'fɔːmɪtɪ] n Einheitlichkeit f.

unify ['juːnɪfaɪ] vt vereinigen.

unilateral ['juːnɪ'lætərəl] a einseitig.

uninhabited [ʌnɪn'hæbɪtɪd] a unbewohnt.

unintentional ['ʌnɪn'tenʃənl] a unabsichtlich.

union ['juːnjən] n (uniting) Vereinigung f; (alliance) Bund m, Union f; (trade ~) Gewerkschaft f; **U~ Jack** n Union Jack m.

unique [juː'niːk] a einzig(artig).

unison ['juːnɪzn] n Einstimmigkeit f; in ~ einstimmig.

unit ['juːnɪt] n Einheit f; **kitchen ~** Küchenelement nt.

unite [juː'naɪt] vt vereinigen // vi sich vereinigen; **~d** a vereinigt; (together) vereint; **U~d Kingdom (U.K.)** n Vereinigtes Königreich; **U~d Nations (Organization) (UN, UNO)** n Vereinte Nationen pl; **U~d States (of America) (US, USA)** n Vereinigte Staaten pl (von Amerika) (US, USA f).

unit trust ['juːnɪt'trʌst] n (Brit) Treuhandgesellschaft f.

unity ['juːnɪtɪ] n Einheit f; (agreement) Einigkeit f.

universal [juːnɪ'vɜːsəl] a allgemein.

universe ['juːnɪvɜːs] n (Welt) all nt.

university [juːnɪ'vɜːsɪtɪ] n Universität f.

unjust ['ʌn'dʒʌst] a ungerecht.

unkempt ['ʌn'kempt] a ungepflegt.

unkind [ʌn'kaɪnd] a unfreundlich.

unknown ['ʌn'nəun] a unbekannt (to dat).

unlawful [ʌn'lɔːful] a illegal.

unleash ['ʌn'liːʃ] vt entfesseln.

unless [ən'les] cj wenn nicht, es sei denn ...; ~ **he comes** es sei denn, er kommt; ~ **otherwise stated** sofern nicht anders angegeben.

unlike ['ʌn'laɪk] a unähnlich // prep im Gegensatz zu.

unlimited [ʌn'lɪmɪtɪd] a unbegrenzt.

unlisted [ʌn'lɪstɪd] a (US) nicht im Telefonbuch stehend.

unload ['ʌn'ləud] vt entladen.

unlock ['ʌn'lɒk] vt aufschließen.

unlucky [ʌn'lʌkɪ] a unglücklich; (person) unglückselig; **to be ~** Pech haben.

unmarried ['ʌn'mærɪd] a unverheiratet, ledig.

unmask ['ʌn'mɑːsk] vt entlarven.

unmistakable ['ʌnmɪs'teɪkəbl] a unverkennbar.

unmitigated [ʌn'mɪtɪgeɪtɪd] a ungemildert, ganz.

unnatural [ʌn'nætʃrəl] a unnatürlich.

unnecessary ['ʌn'nesəsərɪ] a unnötig.

unnoticed [ʌn'nəutɪst] a: **to go ~** unbemerkt bleiben.

UNO ['juːnəu] n abbr of **United Nations Organization**.

unobtainable ['ʌnəb'teɪnəbl] a: **this number is ~** kein Anschluß unter dieser Nummer.

unobtrusive [ʌnəb'truːsɪv] a unauffällig.

unofficial [ʌnə'fɪʃl] a inoffiziell.

unpack ['ʌn'pæk] vti auspacken.

unpalatable [ʌn'pælətəbl] a (truth) bitter.

unparalleled [ʌn'pærəleld] a beispiellos.

unpleasant [ʌn'pleznt] a unangenehm.

unplug ['ʌn'plʌg] vt den Stecker herausziehen von.

unprecedented [ʌn'presɪdəntɪd] a beispiellos.

unpredictable [ʌnprɪ'dɪktəbl] a unvorhersehbar; (weather, person) unberechenbar.

unprofessional [ʌnprə'feʃənl] a unprofessionell.

unqualified ['ʌn'kwɒlɪfaɪd] a (success) uneingeschränkt, voll; (person) unqualifiziert.

unquestionably [ʌn'kwestʃənəblɪ] ad fraglos.

unravel [ʌn'rævəl] vt (disentangle) auffasern, entwirren; (solve) lösen.

unreal ['ʌn'rɪəl] a unwirklich.

unrealistic [ʌnrɪə'lɪstɪk] a unrealistisch.

unreasonable [ʌn'riːznəbl] a unvernünftig; (demand) übertrieben.

unrelated [ʌnrɪ'leɪtɪd] a ohne Beziehung; (family) nicht verwandt.

unrelenting ['ʌnrɪ'lentɪŋ] a unerbittlich.

unreliable [ʌnrɪ'laɪəbl] a unzuverlässig.

unremitting [ʌnrɪ'mɪtɪŋ] a (efforts, attempts) unermüdlich.

unreservedly [ʌnrɪzɜː'vɪdlɪ] ad offen; (believe, trust) uneingeschränkt; (cry) rückhaltlos.

unrest [ʌn'rest] n (discontent) Unruhe f; (fighting) Unruhen pl.

unroll ['ʌn'rəul] vt aufrollen.

unruly [ʌn'ruːlɪ] a (child) undiszipliniert; schwer lenkbar.

unsafe [ʌn'seɪf] a nicht sicher.

unsaid ['ʌn'sed] a: **to leave sth ~** etw ungesagt sein lassen.

unsatisfactory ['ʌnsætɪs'fæktərɪ] a unbefriedigend; unzulänglich.

unsavoury, (US) **unsavory** ['ʌn'seɪvərɪ] a (fig) widerwärtig.

unscathed [ʌn'skeɪðd] a unversehrt.

unscrew ['ʌn'skruː] vt aufschrauben.

unscrupulous [ʌn'skruːpjuləs] a skrupellos.

unsettled ['ʌn'setld] a (person) rastlos;

(weather) wechselhaft.

unshaven [ʌn'ʃeɪvn] *a* unrasiert.

unsightly [ʌn'saɪtlɪ] *a* unansehnlich.

unskilled [ʌn'skɪld] *a* ungelernt.

unspeakable [ʌn'spi:kəbl] *a (joy)* unsagbar; *(crime)* scheußlich.

unstable [ʌn'steɪbl] *a* instabil; *(mentally)* labil.

unsteady [ʌn'stedɪ] *a* unsicher; *(growth)* unregelmäßig.

unstuck [ʌn'stʌk] *a*: to come ~ *(lit)* sich lösen; *(fig)* ins Wasser fallen.

unsuccessful [ʌnsək'sesful] *a* erfolglos.

unsuitable [ʌn'su:təbl] *a* unpassend.

unsuspecting ['ʌnsəs'pektɪŋ] *a* nichtsahnend.

unsympathetic ['ʌnsɪmpə'θetɪk] *a* gefühllos; *(response)* abweisend; *(unlikeable)* unsympathisch.

untapped ['ʌn'tæpt] *a (resources)* ungenützt.

unthinkable [ʌn'θɪŋkəbl] *a* unvorstellbar.

untidy [ʌn'taɪdɪ] *a* unordentlich.

untie ['ʌn'taɪ] *vt* aufschnüren.

until [ən'tɪl] *prep, cj* bis; ~ he comes bis er kommt; ~ then bis dann.

untimely [ʌn'taɪmlɪ] *a (death)* vorzeitig.

untold ['ʌn'təʊld] *a* unermeßlich.

untoward [ʌntə'wɔːd] *a* widrig.

unused ['ʌn'ju:zd] *a* unbenutzt.

unusual [ʌn'ju:ʒʊəl] *a* ungewöhnlich.

unveil [ʌn'veɪl] *vt* enthüllen.

unwavering [ʌn'weɪvərɪŋ] *a* standhaft, unerschütterlich.

unwelcome [ʌn'welkəm] *a (at a bad time)* unwillkommen; *(unpleasant)* unerfreulich.

unwell ['ʌn'wel] *a*: to feel *or* be ~ sich nicht wohl fühlen.

unwieldy [ʌn'wi:ldɪ] *a* sperrig.

unwilling ['ʌn'wɪlɪŋ] *a*: to be ~ to do sth nicht bereit sein, etw zu tun; ~ly *ad* widerwillig.

unwind ['ʌn'waɪnd] *(irreg: like wind) vt (lit)* abwickeln // *vi (relax)* sich entspannen.

unwise [ʌn'waɪz] *a* unklug.

unwitting [ʌn'wɪtɪŋ] *a* unwissentlich.

unworkable [ʌn'wɜ:kəbl] *a (plan)* undurchführbar.

unworthy [ʌn'wɜ:ðɪ] *a (person)* nicht wert *(of gen)*.

unwrap ['ʌn'ræp] *vt* auspacken.

unwritten ['ʌn'rɪtn] *a* ungeschrieben.

up [ʌp] ◆ *prep*: to be ~ sth oben auf etw *(dat)* sein; to go ~ sth (auf) etw *(acc)* hinauf gehen; to go ~ that road gehen Sie die Straße hinauf

◆ *ad* **1** *(upwards, higher)* oben; put it a bit higher ~ stell es etwas weiter nach oben; ~ there da oben, dort oben; ~ above hoch oben

2: to be ~ *(out of bed)* auf; *(prices, level)* gestiegen; *(building, tent)* stehen

3: ~ to *(as far as)* bis; ~ to now bis jetzt

4: to be ~ to *(depending on)*: it's ~ to you das hängt von dir ab; it's not ~ to me to decide die Entscheidung liegt nicht bei mir; *(equal to)*: he's not ~ to it *(job, task etc)* er ist dem nicht gewachsen; his work is not ~ to the required standard seine Arbeit entspricht nicht dem geforderten Niveau; *(col: be doing)*: what is he ~ to? *(showing disapproval, suspicion)* was führt er im Schilde?

◆ **~s and downs** *npl (in life, career)* Höhen und Tiefen *pl*.

upbringing ['ʌpbrɪŋɪŋ] *n* Erziehung *f*.

update [ʌp'deɪt] *vt* auf den neuesten Stand bringen.

upgrade [ʌp'greɪd] *vt* höher einstufen.

upheaval [ʌp'hi:vəl] *n* Umbruch *m*.

uphill ['ʌp'hɪl] *a* ansteigend; *(fig)* mühsam // *ad*: to go ~ bergauf gehen/fahren.

uphold [ʌp'həʊld] *vt (irreg: like hold)* unterstützen.

upholstery [ʌp'həʊlstərɪ] *n* Polster *nt*; Polsterung *f*.

upkeep ['ʌpki:p] *n* Instandhaltung *f*.

upon [ə'pɒn] *prep* auf.

upper ['ʌpə*] *n (on shoe)* Oberleder *nt* // *a* obere(r, s), höhere(r, s); to have the ~ hand die Oberhand haben; ~-**class** *a* vornehm; ~**most** *a* oberste(r, s), höchste(r, s); what was ~most in my mind was mich in erster Linie beschäftigte.

upright ['ʌpraɪt] *a* aufrecht.

uprising ['ʌpraɪzɪŋ] *n* Aufstand *m*.

uproar ['ʌprɔː*] *n* Aufruhr *m*.

uproot [ʌp'ru:t] *vt* ausreißen.

upset ['ʌpset] *n* Aufregung *f* // *vt* [ʌp'set] *(irreg: like set) (overturn)* umwerfen; *(disturb)* aufregen, bestürzen; *(plans)* durcheinanderbringen // *a* [ʌp'set] *(person)* aufgeregt; *(stomach)* verdorben.

upshot ['ʌpʃɒt] *n* (End)ergebnis *nt*.

upside-down ['ʌpsaɪd'daʊn] *ad* verkehrt herum; *(fig)* drunter und drüber.

upstairs [ʌp'stɛəz] *ad* oben; *(go)* nach oben // *a (room)* obere(r, s), Ober- // *n* obere(s) Stockwerk *nt*.

upstart ['ʌpstɑ:t] *n* Emporkömmling *m*.

upstream ['ʌp'stri:m] *ad* stromaufwärts.

uptake ['ʌpteɪk] *n*: to be quick on the ~ schnell begreifen; to be slow on the ~ schwer von Begriff sein.

uptight ['ʌp'taɪt] *a (col: nervous)* nervös; *(: inhibited)* verklemmt.

up-to-date ['ʌptə'deɪt] *a (clothes)* modisch, modern; *(information)* neueste(r, s); to bring sth up to date etw auf den neuesten Stand bringen.

upturn ['ʌptɜ:n] *n* Aufschwung *m*.

upward ['ʌpwəd] *a* nach oben gerichtet; ~**(s)** *ad* aufwärts.

uranium [juə'reɪnɪəm] *n* Uran *nt*.

urban ['ɜːbən] a städtisch, Stadt-.
urbane [ɜː'beɪn] a höflich.
urchin ['ɜːtʃɪn] n (boy) Schlingel m; (sea ~) Seeigel m.
urge [ɜːdʒ] n Drang m // vt: to ~ sb to do sth jdn (dazu) drängen, etw zu tun.
urgency ['ɜːdʒənsɪ] n Dringlichkeit f.
urgent ['ɜːdʒənt] a dringend.
urinal ['juərɪnl] n (MED) Urinflasche f; (public) Pissoir nt.
urinate ['juərɪneɪt] vi urinieren.
urine ['juərɪn] n Urin m, Harn m.
urn [ɜːn] n Urne f; (tea ~) Teemaschine f.
us [ʌs] pron uns; see also **me.**
US, USA n abbr of **United States (of America)**.
usage ['juːzɪdʒ] n Gebrauch m; (esp LING) Sprachgebrauch m.
use [juːs] n (employment) Gebrauch m; (point) Zweck m // vt [juːz] gebrauchen; in ~ in Gebrauch; out of ~ außer Gebrauch; to be of ~ nützlich sein; it's no ~ es hat keinen Zweck; what's the ~? was soll's?; ~d to [juːst] gewöhnt an (+acc); she ~d to live here sie hat früher mal hier gewohnt; ~ up [juːz] vt aufbrauchen, verbrauchen; ~d [juːzd] a (car) Gebraucht-; ~ful a nützlich; ~fulness n Nützlichkeit f; ~less a nutzlos, unnütz; ~r ['juːzə*] n Benutzer m; ~r-friendly a (computer) benutzerfreundlich.
usher ['ʌʃə*] n Platzanweiser m; ~ette [ʌʃə'ret] n Platzanweiserin f.
USSR n: the ~ die UdSSR.
usual ['juːʒuəl] a gewöhnlich, üblich; as ~ wie üblich; ~ly ad gewöhnlich.
usurp [juː'zɜːp] vt an sich reißen.
utensil [juː'tensl] n Gerät nt; kitchen ~s Küchengeräte pl.
utilitarian [juːtɪlɪ'teərɪən] a Nützlichkeits-.
utility [juː'tɪlɪtɪ] n (usefulness) Nützlichkeit f; (also public ~) öffentliche(r) Versorgungsbetrieb m; ~ room n Hauswirtschaftsraum m.
utilize ['juːtɪlaɪz] vt benützen.
utmost ['ʌtməust] a äußerste(r, s) // n: to do one's ~ sein möglichstes tun.
utter ['ʌtə*] a äußerste(r, s) höchste(r, s), völlig // vt äußern, aussprechen; ~ance n Äußerung f; ~ly ad äußerst, absolut, völlig.
U-turn ['juː'tɜːn] n (AUT) Kehrtwendung f.

V

v. abbr of **verse; versus; volt; vide**.
vacancy ['veɪkənsɪ] n (Brit: job) offene Stelle f; (room) freies Zimmer nt.
vacant ['veɪkənt] a leer; (unoccupied) frei; (house) leerstehend, unbewohnt;

(stupid) (gedanken)leer; ~ lot n (US) unbebaute(s) Grundstück nt.
vacate [və'keɪt] vt (seat) frei machen; (room) räumen.
vacation [və'keɪʃən] n Ferien pl, Urlaub m; ~ist n (US) Ferienreisende(r) mf.
vaccinate ['væksɪneɪt] vt impfen.
vaccine ['væksiːn] n Impfstoff m.
vacuum ['vækjum] n Vakuum nt; ~ bottle (US), ~ flask (Brit) n Thermosflasche f; ~ cleaner n Staubsauger m; ~-packed a vakuumversiegelt.
vagina [və'dʒaɪnə] n Scheide f.
vagrant ['veɪɡrənt] n Landstreicher m.
vague [veɪɡ] a vage; (absent-minded) geistesabwesend; ~ly ad unbestimmt, vage.
vain [veɪn] a eitel; (attempt) vergeblich; in ~ vergebens, umsonst.
valentine ['væləntaɪn] n (also: ~ card) Valentinsgruß m.
valet ['væleɪ] n Kammerdiener m.
valiant a, ~ly ad ['væliənt, -lɪ] tapfer.
valid ['vælɪd] a gültig; (argument) stichhaltig; (objection) berechtigt; ~ity [və'lɪdɪtɪ] n Gültigkeit f.
valley ['vælɪ] n Tal nt.
valour, (US) valor ['vælə*] n Tapferkeit f.
valuable ['væljuəbl] a wertvoll; (time) kostbar; ~s npl Wertsachen pl.
valuation [vælju'eɪʃən] n (FIN) Schätzung f; Beurteilung f.
value ['væljuː] n Wert m; (usefulness) Nutzen m // vt (prize) (hoch)schätzen, werthalten; (estimate) schätzen; ~ added tax (VAT) n (Brit) Mehrwertsteuer f (MwSt); ~d a (hoch)geschätzt.
valve [vælv] n Ventil nt; (BIOL) Klappe f; (RAD) Röhre f.
van [væn] n Lieferwagen m (Brit: RAIL) Waggon m.
vandalize ['vændəlaɪz] vt mutwillig beschädigen.
vanguard ['vænɡɑːd] n (fig) Spitze f.
vanilla [və'nɪlə] n Vanille f.
vanish ['vænɪʃ] vi verschwinden.
vanity ['vænɪtɪ] n Eitelkeit f; ~ case n Schminkkoffer m.
vantage ['vɑːntɪdʒ] n: ~ point gute(r) Aussichtspunkt m.
vapour, (US) vapor ['veɪpə*] n (mist) Dunst m; (gas) Dampf m.
variable ['veərɪəbl] a wechselhaft, veränderlich; (speed, height) regulierbar.
variance ['veərɪəns] n: to be at ~ (with) nicht übereinstimmen (mit).
variation [veərɪ'eɪʃən] n Variation f; (of temperature, prices) Schwankung f.
varicose ['værɪkəus] a: ~ veins npl Krampfadern pl.
varied ['veərɪd] a unterschiedlich; (life) abwechslungsreich.
variety [və'raɪətɪ] n (difference)

Abwechslung f; (varied collection) Vielfalt f; (COMM) Auswahl f; (sort) Sorte f, Art f; ~ **show** n Varieté nt.
various ['vɛərɪəs] a verschieden; (several) mehrere.
varnish ['vɑːnɪʃ] n Lack m; (on pottery) Glasur f // vt lackieren.
vary ['vɛərɪ] vt (alter) verändern; (give variety to) abwechslungsreicher gestalten // vi sich (ver)ändern; (prices) schwanken; (weather) unterschiedlich sein.
vase [vɑːz] n Vase f.
Vaseline ['væsɪliːn] n ® Vaseline f.
vast [vɑːst] a weit, groß, riesig.
VAT [væt] n abbr of **Value Added Tax**.
vat [væt] n große(s) Faß nt.
vault [vɔːlt] n (of roof) Gewölbe nt; (tomb) Gruft f; (in bank) Tresorraum m; (leap) Sprung m // vt (also: ~ over) überspringen.
vaunted ['vɔːntɪd] a: much-~ vielgerühmt.
VCR n abbr of **video cassette recorder**.
VD n abbr of **venereal disease**.
VDU n abbr of **visual display unit**.
veal [viːl] n Kalbfleisch nt.
veer [vɪə*] vi sich drehen; (of car) ausscheren.
vegetable ['vedʒətəbl] n Gemüse nt // a Gemüse-; ~s pl Gemüse nt.
vegetarian [vedʒɪ'tɛərɪən] n Vegetarier(in f) m // a vegetarisch.
vegetate ['vedʒɪteɪt] vi (dahin)vegetieren.
vehemence ['viːɪməns] n Heftigkeit f.
vehement ['viːɪmənt] a heftig.
vehicle ['viːɪkl] n Fahrzeug nt; (fig) Mittel nt.
veil [veɪl] n (lit, fig) Schleier m // vt verschleiern.
vein [veɪn] n Ader f; (mood) Stimmung f.
velocity [vɪ'lɒsɪtɪ] n Geschwindigkeit f.
velvet ['velvɪt] n Samt m // a Samt-.
vendetta [ven'detə] n Fehde f; (in family) Blutrache f.
vending machine ['vendɪŋməʃiːn] n Automat m.
vendor ['vendɔː*] n Verkäufer m.
veneer [və'nɪə*] n (lit) Furnier(holz) nt; (fig) äußere(r) Anstrich m.
venereal [vɪ'nɪərɪəl] a: ~ **disease** (VD) Geschlechtskrankheit f.
Venetian blind [vɪ'niːʃən-] n Jalousie f.
vengeance ['vendʒəns] n Rache f; with a ~ gewaltig.
venison ['venɪsn] n Reh(fleisch) nt.
venom ['venəm] n Gift nt.
vent [vent] n Öffnung f; (in coat) Schlitz m; (fig) Ventil nt // vt (emotion) abreagieren.
ventilate ['ventɪleɪt] vt belüften.
ventilator ['ventɪleɪtə*] n Ventilator m.

ventriloquist [ven'trɪləkwɪst] n Bauchredner m.
venture ['ventʃə*] n Unternehmung f, Projekt nt // vt wagen; (life) aufs Spiel setzen // vi sich wagen.
venue ['venjuː] n Schauplatz m.
verb [vɜːb] n Zeitwort nt, Verb nt; ~**al** a (spoken) mündlich; (translation) wörtlich; (of a verb) verbal, Verbal-; ~**ally** ad mündlich; (as a verb) verbal.
verbatim [vɜː'beɪtɪm] ad Wort für Wort // a wortwörtlich.
verbose [vɜː'bəus] a wortreich.
verdict ['vɜːdɪkt] n Urteil nt.
verge [vɜːdʒ] n (Brit) Rand m; 'soft ~s' (Brit AUT) 'Seitenstreifen nicht befahrbar'; on the ~ of doing sth im Begriff, etw zu tun // vi: ~ on grenzen an (+acc).
verify ['verɪfaɪ] vt (über)prüfen; (confirm) bestätigen; (theory) beweisen.
veritable ['verɪtəbl] a wirklich, echt.
vermin ['vɜːmɪn] npl Ungeziefer nt.
vermouth ['vɜːməθ] n Wermut m.
vernacular [və'nækjulə*] n Landessprache f.
versatile ['vɜːsətaɪl] a vielseitig.
versatility [vɜːsə'tɪlɪtɪ] n Vielseitigkeit f.
verse [vɜːs] n (poetry) Poesie f; (stanza) Strophe f; (of Bible) Vers m; in ~ in Versform.
versed [vɜːst] a: (well-)~ in bewandert in (+dat), beschlagen in (+dat).
version ['vɜːʃən] n Version f; (of car) Modell nt.
versus ['vɜːsəs] prep gegen.
vertebra ['vɜːtɪbrə] n, pl ~**e** [-briː] (Rücken)wirbel m.
vertebrate ['vɜːtɪbrət] a (animal) Wirbel-.
vertical ['vɜːtɪkəl] a senkrecht.
vertigo ['vɜːtɪgəu] n Schwindel m.
verve [vɜːv] n Schwung m.
very ['verɪ] ad sehr // a (extreme) äußerste(r, s); **the ~ book which** genau das Buch, welches; **the ~ last** der/die/das allerletzte; **at the ~ least** allerwenigstens; ~ **much** sehr.
vessel ['vesl] n (ship) Schiff nt; (container) Gefäß nt.
vest [vest] n (Brit) Unterhemd nt; (US: waistcoat) Weste f; ~**ed interests** npl finanzielle Beteiligung f; (people) finanziell Beteiligte pl; (fig) persönliche(s) Interesse nt.
vestige ['vestɪdʒ] n Spur f.
vestry ['vestrɪ] n Sakristei f.
vet [vet] n abbr (= veterinary surgeon) Tierarzt m/-ärztin f // vt genau prüfen.
veterinary ['vetɪnərɪ] a Veterinär-; ~ **surgeon**, (US) **veterinarian** n Tierarzt m/-ärztin f.
veto ['viːtəu] n, pl ~**es** Veto nt // vt sein Veto einlegen gegen.
vex [veks] vt ärgern; ~**ed** a verärgert;

~ed question umstrittene Frage f.

VHF abbr (= very high frequency) UKW f.

via ['vaɪə] prep über (+acc).

viable ['vaɪəbl] a (plan) durchführbar; (company) rentabel.

vibrant ['vaɪbrənt] a (lively) lebhaft; (bright) leuchtend; (full of emotion: voice) bebend.

vibrate [vaɪ'breɪt] vi zittern, beben; (machine, string) vibrieren.

vibration [vaɪ'breɪʃən] n Schwingung f; (of machine) Vibrieren nt.

vicar ['vɪkə*] n Pfarrer m; ~age n Pfarrhaus nt.

vicarious [vɪ'keərɪəs] a nachempfunden.

vice [vaɪs] n (evil) Laster nt; (TECH) Schraubstock m // pref: ~-**chairman** n stellvertretende(r) Vorsitzende(r) m; ~-**president** n Vizepräsident m.

vice squad n ≈ Sittenpolizei f.

vice versa ['vaɪsɪ'vɜːsə] ad umgekehrt.

vicinity [vɪ'sɪnɪtɪ] n Umgebung f; (closeness) Nähe f.

vicious ['vɪʃəs] a gemein, böse; ~ **circle** n Teufelskreis m.

victim ['vɪktɪm] n Opfer nt; ~ize vt benachteiligen.

victor ['vɪktə*] n Sieger m.

Victorian [vɪk'tɔːrɪən] a viktorianisch; (fig) (sitten)streng.

victorious [vɪk'tɔːrɪəs] a siegreich.

victory ['vɪktərɪ] n Sieg m.

video ['vɪdɪəʊ] a Fernseh-, Bild- // n (~ film) Video nt; (also: ~ cassette) Videocasette f; (also: ~ cassette recorder) Videorekorder m; ~ tape n Videoband nt.

vie [vaɪ] vi wetteifern.

Vienna [vɪ'enə] n Wien nt.

view [vjuː] n (sight) Sicht f, Blick m; (scene) Aussicht f; (opinion) Ansicht f; (intention) Absicht f // vt (situation) betrachten; (house) besichtigen; to have sth in ~ etw beabsichtigen; on ~ ausgestellt; in ~ of wegen (+gen), angesichts (+gen); ~er n (viewfinder) Sucher m; (Phot: small projector) Gucki m; (TV) Fernsehzuschauer(in f) m; ~finder n Sucher m; ~point n Standpunkt m.

vigil ['vɪdʒɪl] n (Nacht)wache f; ~ance n Wachsamkeit f; ~ant a wachsam.

vigorous a, ~ly ad ['vɪgərəs, -lɪ] kräftig; (protest) energisch, heftig.

vigour, (US) **vigor** ['vɪgə*] n Vitalität f; (of protest) Heftigkeit f.

vile [vaɪl] a (mean) gemein; (foul) abscheulich.

vilify ['vɪlɪfaɪ] vt verleumden.

villa ['vɪlə] n Villa f.

village ['vɪlɪdʒ] n Dorf nt; ~r n Dorfbewohner(in f) m.

villain ['vɪlən] n Schurke m.

vindicate ['vɪndɪkeɪt] vt rechtfertigen.

vindictive [vɪn'dɪktɪv] a nachtragend, rachsüchtig.

vine [vaɪn] n Rebstock m, Rebe f.

vinegar ['vɪnɪgə*] n Essig m.

vineyard ['vɪnjəd] n Weinberg m.

vintage ['vɪntɪdʒ] n (of wine) Jahrgang m; ~ **wine** n edle(r) Wein m.

viola [vɪ'əʊlə] n Bratsche f.

violate ['vaɪəleɪt] vt (law) übertreten; (rights, rule, neutrality) verletzen; (sanctity, woman) schänden.

violation [vaɪə'leɪʃən] n Verletzung f; Übertretung f.

violence ['vaɪələns] n (force) Heftigkeit f; (brutality) Gewalttätigkeit f.

violent a, ~ly ad ['vaɪələnt, -lɪ] (strong) heftig; (brutal) gewalttätig, brutal; (contrast) kraß; (death) gewaltsam.

violet ['vaɪələt] n Veilchen nt // a veilchenblau, violett.

violin [vaɪə'lɪn] n Geige f, Violine f; ~ist n Geiger(in f) m.

VIP n abbr (= very important person) VIP m.

virgin ['vɜːdʒɪn] n Jungfrau f // a jungfräulich, unberührt; **the Blessed V~** die heilige Jungfrau Maria; ~ity [vɜː'dʒɪnɪtɪ] n Unschuld f.

Virgo ['vɜːgəʊ] n Jungfrau f.

virile ['vɪraɪl] a männlich.

virility [vɪ'rɪlɪtɪ] n Männlichkeit f.

virtually ['vɜːtjʊəlɪ] ad praktisch, fast.

virtue ['vɜːtjuː] n (moral goodness) Tugend f; (good quality) Vorteil m, Vorzug m; **by ~ of** aufgrund (+gen).

virtuous ['vɜːtjʊəs] a tugendhaft.

virulent ['vɪrjʊlənt] a (poisonous) bösartig; (bitter) scharf, geharnischt.

virus ['vaɪərəs] n Virus m.

visa ['viːzə] n Visum nt.

vis-à-vis ['viːzəviː] prep gegenüber.

viscous ['vɪskəs] a zähflüssig.

visibility [vɪzɪ'bɪlɪtɪ] n (MET) Sicht(weite) f.

visible ['vɪzəbl] a sichtbar.

visibly ['vɪzəblɪ] ad sichtlich.

vision ['vɪʒən] n (ability) Sehvermögen nt; (foresight) Weitblick m; (in dream, image) Vision f.

visit ['vɪzɪt] n Besuch m // vt besuchen; (town, country) fahren nach; ~ing a (professor) Gast-; ~ing **card** n Visitenkarte f; ~ing **hours** npl (in hospital etc) Besuchszeiten pl; ~or n (in house) Besucher(in f) m; (in hotel) Gast m; ~or's **book** n Gästebuch m.

visor ['vaɪzə*] n Visier nt; (on cap) Schirm m; (AUT) Blende f.

vista ['vɪstə] n Aussicht f.

visual ['vɪzjʊəl] a Seh-, visuell; ~ **aid** n Anschauungsmaterial nt; ~ **display unit** (VDU) n Bildschirm(gerät nt) m; ~ize vt sich (dat) vorstellen.

vital ['vaɪtl] a (important) unerläßlich; (necessary for life) Lebens-, lebenswichtig; (lively) vital; ~ity [vaɪ'tælɪtɪ] n Vitalität f; **~ly** ad: **~ly important** aüßerst wichtig; **~ statistics** npl (fig) Maße pl.

vitamin ['vɪtəmɪn] n Vitamin nt.

vivacious [vɪ'veɪʃəs] a lebhaft.

vivid a, **~ly** ad ['vɪvɪd, -lɪ] (graphic) lebendig; (memory) lebhaft; (bright) leuchtend.

V-neck ['viː'nek] n V-Ausschnitt m.

vocabulary [vəʊ'kæbjʊlərɪ] n Wortschatz m, Vokabular nt.

vocal ['vəʊkəl] a Vokal-, Gesang-; (fig) lautstark; **~ cords** npl Stimmbänder pl.

vocation [vəʊ'keɪʃən] n (calling) Berufung f; **~al** a Berufs-.

vociferous a, **~ly** ad [vəʊ'sɪfərəs, -lɪ] lautstark.

vodka ['vɒdkə] n Wodka m.

vogue [vəʊg] n Mode f.

voice [vɔɪs] n (lit) Stimme f; (fig) Mitspracherecht nt // vt äußern.

void [vɔɪd] n Leere f // a (invalid) nichtig, ungültig; (empty): **~ of** ohne, bar (+ gen); see **null**.

volatile ['vɒlətaɪl] a (gas) flüchtig; (person) impulsiv; (situation) brisant.

volcano [vɒl'keɪnəʊ] n Vulkan m.

volition [və'lɪʃən] n Wille m; of one's own **~** aus freiem Willen.

volley ['vɒlɪ] n (of guns) Salve f; (of stones) Hagel m; (of words) Schwall m; (tennis) Flugball m; **~ball** n Volleyball m.

volt [vəʊlt] n Volt nt; **~age** n (Volt)spannung f.

voluble ['vɒljʊbl] a redselig.

volume ['vɒljuːm] n (book) Band m; (size) Umfang m; (space) Rauminhalt m; (of sound) Lautstärke f.

voluminous [və'luːmɪnəs] a üppig; (clothes) wallend; (correspondence, notes) umfangreich.

voluntary a, **voluntarily** ad ['vɒləntərɪ, -lɪ] freiwillig.

volunteer [vɒlən'tɪə*] n Freiwillige(r) mf // vi sich freiwillig melden; **to ~ to do** sth sich anbieten, etw zu tun.

voluptuous [və'lʌptjʊəs] a sinnlich.

vomit ['vɒmɪt] n Erbrochene(s) nt // vt spucken // vi sich übergeben.

vote [vəʊt] n Stimme f; (ballot) Abstimmung f; (result) Abstimmungsergebnis nt; (right to vote) Wahlrecht nt // vti wählen; **~ of thanks** n Dankesworte pl; **~r** n Wähler(in f) m.

voting ['vəʊtɪŋ] n Wahl f.

vouch [vaʊtʃ]: **~ for** vt bürgen für.

voucher ['vaʊtʃə*] n Gutschein m.

vow [vaʊ] n Versprechen nt; (REL) Gelübde nt // vt geloben.

vowel ['vaʊəl] n Vokal m.

voyage ['vɔɪɪdʒ] n Reise f.

vulgar ['vʌlgə*] a (rude) vulgär; (of common people) allgemein, Volks-; **~ity** [vʌl'gærɪtɪ] n Vulgarität f.

vulnerable ['vʌlnərəbl] a (easily injured) verwundbar; (sensitive) verletzlich.

vulture ['vʌltʃə*] n Geier m.

W

wad [wɒd] n (bundle) Bündel nt; (of paper) Stoß m; (of money) Packen m.

waddle ['wɒdl] vi watscheln.

wade [weɪd] vi: **to ~ through** waten durch.

wafer ['weɪfə*] n Waffel f; (ECCL) Hostie f; (COMPUT) Scheibe f.

waffle ['wɒfl] n Waffel f; (col: empty talk) Geschwafel nt // vi (col) schwafeln.

waft [wɑːft] vti wehen.

wag [wæg] vt (tail) wedeln mit // vi (tail) wedeln.

wage [weɪdʒ] n (also: **~s**) (Arbeits)lohn m // vt: **to ~ war** Krieg führen; **~ earner** n Lohnempfänger(in f) m; **~ packet** n Lohntüte f.

wager ['weɪdʒə*] n Wette f // vti wetten.

waggle ['wægl] vt (tail) wedeln mit // vi wedeln.

wag(g)on ['wægən] n (horse-drawn) Fuhrwerk nt; (US AUT) Wagen m; (Brit RAIL) Waggon m.

wail [weɪl] n Wehgeschrei nt // vi wehklagen, jammern.

waist [weɪst] n Taille f; **~coat** n (Brit) Weste f; **~line** n Taille f.

wait [weɪt] n Wartezeit f // vi warten; lie in **~ for** sb jdm auflauern; **I can't ~ to** see him ich kann's kaum erwarten, ihn zu sehen; **no ~ing** (Brit AUT) Halteverbot nt; **~ behind** vi zurückbleiben; **~ for** vt warten auf (+acc); **~ on** vt bedienen; **~er** n Kellner m; (as address) Herr Ober m; **~ing list** n Warteliste f; **~ing room** n (MED) Wartezimmer nt; (RAIL) Wartesaal m; **~ress** n Kellnerin f; (as address) Fräulein nt.

waive [weɪv] vt verzichten auf (+acc).

wake [weɪk] v (pt **woke** or **waked**, pp **woken** or **waked**) vt wecken // vi (also: **~ up**) aufwachen; **to ~ up to** (fig) sich bewußt werden // n (NAUT) Kielwasser nt; (for dead) Totenwache f.

waken ['weɪkən] vt aufwecken.

Wales [weɪlz] n Wales nt.

walk [wɔːk] n Spaziergang m; (way of walking) Gang m; (route) Weg m // vi gehen; (stroll) spazierengehen; (longer) wandern; **~s of life** Sphären pl; a 10-minute **~** 10 Minuten zu Fuß; **to ~ out on** sb (col) jdn sitzenlassen; **~er** n Spaziergänger m; (hiker) Wanderer m; **~ie-talkie** n tragbare(s) Sprechfunkgerät nt; **~ing** n Gehen nt; (hiking) Wandern nt // a Wander-; **~ing shoes** npl Wanderschuhe pl; **~ing stick** n

Spazierstock *m*; **~out** *n* Streik *m*;
~over *n* (col) leichte(r) Sieg *m*; **~
way** *n* Fußweg *m*.
wall [wɔːl] *n* (inside) Wand *f*; (outside)
Mauer *f*; **~ed** *a* von Mauern umgeben.
wallet ['wɒlɪt] *n* Brieftasche *f*.
wallflower ['wɔːlflauə*] *n* Goldlack *m*;
to be a ~ (fig) ein Mauerblümchen sein.
wallop ['wɒləp] *vt* (col) schlagen, verprügeln.
wallow ['wɒləu] *vi* sich wälzen.
wallpaper ['wɔːlpeɪpə*] *n* Tapete *f*.
wally ['wɒlɪ] *n* (col) Idiot *m*.
walnut ['wɔːlnʌt] *n* Walnuß *f*.
waltz [wɔːlts] *n* Walzer *m* // *vi* Walzer
tanzen.
wan [wɒn] *a* bleich.
wand [wɒnd] *n* (also: **magic ~**) Zauber-
stab *m*.
wander ['wɒndə*] *vi* (roam) (herum)wandern; (fig) abschweifen.
wane [weɪn] *vi* abnehmen; (fig)
schwinden.
wangle ['wæŋgl] *vt* (Brit col): to ~ sth
etw richtig hindrehen.
want [wɒnt] *n* (lack) Mangel *m* (of an
+dat); for ~ of aus Mangel an (+dat);
mangels (+gen); **~s** *pl* (needs)
Bedürfnisse *pl* // *vt* (need) brauchen;
(desire) wollen; (lack) nicht haben; to ~
to do sth etw tun wollen; to ~ sb to do
sth wollen, daß jd etw tut; **~ing** *a*: to be
found **~ing** sich als unzulänglich
erweisen.
wanton ['wɒntən] *a* mutwillig, zügellos.
war [wɔː*] *n* Krieg *m*; to make ~ Krieg
führen.
ward [wɔːd] *n* (in hospital) Station *f*;
(child) Mündel *nt*; (of city) Bezirk *m*; **~
off** *vt* abwenden, abwehren.
warden ['wɔːdən] *n* (guard) Wächter *m*,
Aufseher *m*; (Brit: in youth hostel) Herbergsvater *m*; (UNIV) Heimleiter *m*;
(Brit: also: **traffic ~**) ≈ Verkehrspolizist
m, Politesse *f*.
warder ['wɔːdə*] *n* (Brit) Gefängniswärter *m*.
wardrobe ['wɔːdrəub] *n* Kleiderschrank
m; (clothes) Garderobe *f*.
warehouse ['wɛəhaus] *n* Lagerhaus *nt*.
wares [wɛəz] *npl* Ware *f*.
warfare ['wɔːfɛə*] *n* Krieg *m*;
Kriegsführung *f*.
warhead ['wɔːhed] *n* Sprengkopf *m*.
warily ['wɛərɪlɪ] *ad* vorsichtig.
warlike ['wɔːlaɪk] *a* kriegerisch.
warm [wɔːm] *a* warm; (welcome) herzlich; I'm ~ mir ist warm // *vti* wärmen;
~ up *vt* aufwärmen // *vi* warm werden;
~hearted *a* warmherzig; **~ly** *ad*
warm; herzlich; **warmth** *n* Wärme *f*;
Herzlichkeit *f*.
warn [wɔːn] *vt* warnen (of, against vor
+dat); **~ing** *n* Warnung *f*; without **~ing**
unerwartet; **~ing light** *n* Warnlicht *nt*;

~ing triangle *n* (AUT) Warndreieck *nt*.
warp [wɔːp] *vt* verziehen; **~ed** *a* (lit)
wellig; (fig) pervers.
warrant ['wɒrənt] *n* Haftbefehl *m*.
warranty ['wɒrəntɪ] *n* Garantie *f*.
warren ['wɒrən] *n* Labyrinth *nt*.
warrior ['wɒrɪə*] *n* Krieger *m*.
Warsaw ['wɔːsɔː] *n* Warschau *nt*.
warship ['wɔːʃɪp] *n* Kriegsschiff *nt*.
wart [wɔːt] *n* Warze *f*.
wartime ['wɔːtaɪm] *n* Krieg *m*.
wary ['wɛərɪ] *a* mißtrauisch.
was [wɒz, wəz] *pt of* **be**.
wash [wɒʃ] *n* Wäsche *f* // *vt* waschen;
(dishes) abwaschen // *vi* sich waschen;
(do washing) waschen; to have a ~ sich
waschen; ~ **away** *vt* abwaschen,
wegspülen; ~ **off** *vt* abwaschen; ~ **up**
vi (Brit) spülen; (US) sich waschen;
~able *a* waschbar; **~basin, (US) ~
bowl** *n* Waschbecken *nt*; ~ **cloth** *n*
(US: face cloth) Waschlappen *m*; **~er** *n*
(TECH) Dichtungsring *m*; (machine)
Waschmaschine *f*; **~ing** *n* Wäsche *f*;
~ing machine *n* Waschmaschine *f*;
~ing powder *n* (Brit) Waschpulver *nt*;
~ing-up *n* Abwasch *m*; **~ing-up liquid**
n Spülmittel *nt*; **~-out** *n* (col: event)
Reinfall *m*; (: person) Niete *f*; **~room**
n Waschraum *m*.
wasn't ['wɒznt] = **was not**.
wasp [wɒsp] *n* Wespe *f*.
wastage ['weɪstɪdʒ] *n* Verlust *m*; natural ~ Verschleiß *m*.
waste [weɪst] *n* (wasting) Verschwendung *f*; (what is wasted) Abfall *m*; **~s** *pl*
Einöde *f* // *a* (useless) überschüssig,
Abfall- // *vt* (object) verschwenden;
(time, life) vergeuden // *vi*: ~ **away** verfallen; to lay ~ verwüsten; ~ **disposal
unit** *n* (Brit) Müllschlucker *m*; **~ful** *a*
verschwenderisch; (process) aufwendig;
~ **ground** *n* (Brit) unbebautes Grundstück *nt*; **~land** *n* Ödland *nt*; **~paper
basket** *n* Papierkorb *m*; ~ **pipe** *n*
Abflußrohr *nt*.
watch [wɒtʃ] *n* Wache *f*; (for time) Uhr
f // *vt* ansehen; (observe) beobachten;
(be careful of) aufpassen auf (+acc);
(guard) bewachen // *vi* zusehen; to be on
the ~ (for sth) (auf etw acc) aufpassen; to
~ TV fernsehen; to ~ sb doing sth
jdm bei etw zuschauen; ~ **out** *vi* Ausschau halten; (be careful) aufpassen; ~
out! paß auf!; **~dog** *n* (lit) Wachthund
m; (fig) Wächter *m*; **~ful** *a* wachsam;
~maker *n* Uhrmacher *m*; **~man** *n* (also:
night ~man) (Nacht)wächter *m*; ~
strap *n* Uhrarmband *nt*.
water ['wɔːtə*] *n* Wasser *nt*; **~s** *pl*
Gewässer *nt* // *vt* (be)gießen; (river)
bewässern; (horses) tränken // *vi* (eye)
tränen; ~ **down** *vt* verwässern; ~
closet *n* (Brit) (Wasser)klosett *nt*;
~colour, (US) ~color *n* (painting)

Aquarell nt; (paint) Wasserfarbe f; ~cress n (Brunnen)kresse f; ~fall n Wasserfall m; ~ heater n Heißwassergerät nt; ~ing can n Gießkanne f; ~ level n Wasserstand m; ~lily n Seerose f; ~line n Wasserlinie f; ~logged a (ground) voll Wasser; (wood) mit Wasser vollgesogen; ~ main n Haupt(wasser)leitung f; ~mark n Wasserzeichen nt; (on wall) Wasserstandsmarke f; ~melon n Wassermelone f; ~ polo n Wasserball(spiel) nt; ~proof a wasserdicht; ~shed n Wasserscheide f; ~-skiing n Wasserschilaufen nt; ~ tank n Wassertank m; ~tight a wasserdicht; ~ way n Wasserweg m; ~works npl Wasserwerk nt; ~y a wäss(e)rig.

wave [weɪv] n Welle f; (with hand) Winken nt // vt (move to and fro) schwenken; (hand, flag) winken mit; (hair) wellen // vi (person) winken; (flag) wehen; ~length n (lit, fig) Wellenlänge f.

waver ['weɪvə*] vi schwanken.

wavy ['weɪvɪ] a wellig.

wax [wæks] n Wachs nt; (sealing ~) Siegellack m; (in ear) Ohrenschmalz nt // vt (floor) (ein)wachsen // vi (moon) zunehmen; ~works npl Wachsfigurenkabinett nt.

way [weɪ] n Weg m; (method) Art und Weise f; (direction) Richtung f; (habit) Gewohnheit f; (distance) Entfernung f; (condition) Zustand m; which ~? — this ~ welche Richtung? — hier entlang; on the ~ (en route) unterwegs; to be in the ~ im Weg sein; to go out of one's ~ to do sth sich besonders anstrengen, um etw zu tun; to lose one's ~ sich verirren; give ~ (Brit AUT) Vorfahrt achten!; in a ~ in gewisser Weise; by the ~ übrigens; in some ~s in gewisser Hinsicht; '~ in' (Brit) 'Eingang'; '~ out' (Brit) 'Ausgang'.

waylay [weɪˈleɪ] vt (irreg: like lay) auflauern (+dat).

wayward ['weɪwəd] a eigensinnig.

W.C. ['dʌblju:'siː] n (Brit) WC nt.

we [wiː] pl pron wir.

weak [wiːk] a schwach; ~en vt schwächen // vi schwächer werden; ~ling n Schwächling m; ~ly a schwach; ~ness n Schwäche f.

wealth [welθ] n Reichtum m; (abundance) Fülle f; ~y a reich.

wean [wiːn] vt entwöhnen.

weapon ['wepən] n Waffe f.

wear [wɛə*] n (clothing): sports/baby ~ Sport-/Babykleidung f; (use) Verschleiß m // v (pt wore, pp worn) vt (have on) tragen; (smile etc) haben; (use) abnutzen // vi (last) halten; (become old) (sich) verschleißen; evening ~ Abendkleidung f; ~ and tear Verschleiß

m; ~ away vt verbrauchen // vi schwinden; ~ down vt (people) zermürben; ~ off vi sich verlieren; ~ out vt verschleißen; (person) erschöpfen.

weary ['wɪərɪ] a müde // vt ermüden // vi überdrüssig werden (of gen).

weather ['weðə*] n Wetter nt // vt verwittern lassen; (resist) überstehen; under the ~ (fig: ill) angeschlagen (col); ~-beaten a verwittert; ~cock n Wetterhahn m; ~ forecast n Wettervorhersage f; ~ vane m Wetterfahne f.

weave [wiːv], pt wove, pp woven vt weben; ~r n Weber(in f) m; **weaving** n (craft) Webkunst f.

web [web] n Netz nt; (membrane) Schwimmhaut f.

wed [wed], pt, pp wedded vt heiraten // n: the newly-~s die Frischvermählten.

we'd [wiːd] = we had; we would.

wedding ['wedɪŋ] n Hochzeit f; silver/golden ~ (Brit) silver/golden ~ anniversary Silberhochzeit f/Goldene Hochzeit; ~ day n Hochzeitstag m; ~ dress n Hochzeitskleid nt; ~ present n Hochzeitsgeschenk nt; ~ ring n Trau- or Ehering m.

wedge [wedʒ] n Keil m; (of cheese etc) Stück nt // vt (fasten) festklemmen; (pack tightly) einkeilen.

wedlock ['wedlɒk] n Ehe f.

Wednesday ['wenzdeɪ] n Mittwoch m.

wee [wiː] a (esp Scot) klein, winzig.

weed [wiːd] n Unkraut nt // vt jäten; ~killer n Unkrautvertilgungsmittel nt; ~y a (person) schmächtig.

week [wiːk] n Woche f; a ~ today/on Friday heute/Freitag in einer Woche; ~day n Wochentag m; ~end n Wochenende nt; ~ly a, ad wöchentlich; (wages, magazine) Wochen-.

weep [wiːp], pt, pp wept vi weinen; ~ing willow n Trauerweide f.

weigh [weɪ] vti wiegen; to ~ anchor den Anker lichten; ~ down vt niederdrücken; ~ up vt abschätzen.

weight [weɪt] n Gewicht nt; to lose/put on ~ abnehmen/zunehmen; ~ing n (allowance) Zulage f; ~-lifter n Gewichtheber m; ~y a (heavy) gewichtig; (important) schwerwiegend.

weir [wɪə*] n (Stau)wehr nt.

weird [wɪəd] a seltsam.

welcome ['welkəm] n Willkommen nt, Empfang m // vt begrüßen; thank you — you're ~! danke — nichts zu danken.

weld [weld] n Schweißnaht f // vt schweißen; ~ing n Schweißen nt.

welfare ['welfeə*] n Wohl nt; (social) Fürsorge f; ~ state n Wohlfahrtsstaat m; ~ work n Fürsorge f.

well [wel] n Brunnen m; (oil ~) Quelle f // a (in good health) gesund // ad gut //

interj nun, na schön; **I'm ~** es geht mir gut; **as ~ auch; as ~ as** sowohl als auch; **~ done!** gut gemacht!; **get ~ soon!** gute Besserung; **to do ~** (*person*) gut zurechtkommen; (*business*) gut gehen; **~ up** *vi* emporsteigen; (*fig*) aufsteigen.

we'll [wi:l] = **we will, we shall**.

well-behaved ['welbɪ'heɪvd] *a* wohlerzogen.

well-being ['welbi:ɪŋ] *n* Wohl *nt*.

well-built ['wel'bɪlt] *a* kräftig gebaut.

well-deserved ['weldɪ'zɜ:vd] *a* wohlverdient.

well-dressed ['wel'drest] *a* gut gekleidet.

well-heeled ['wel'hi:ld] *a* (col: *wealthy*) gut gepolstert.

wellingtons ['welɪŋtənz] *npl* (also: **wellington boots**) Gummistiefel *pl*.

well-known ['wel'nəʊn] *a* bekannt.

well-mannered ['wel'mænəd] *a* wohlerzogen.

well-meaning ['wel'mi:nɪŋ] *a* (*person*) wohlmeinend; (*action*) gutgemeint.

well-off ['wel'ɒf] *a* gut situiert.

well-read ['wel'red] *a* (*sehr*) belesen.

well-to-do ['weltə'du:] *a* wohlhabend.

well-wisher ['welwɪʃə*] *n* Gönner *m*.

Welsh [welʃ] *a* walisisch; **the ~** *npl* die Waliser; **~man/woman** *n* Waliser *m*/ Waliserin *f*; **~ rarebit** *n* überbackene Käseschnitte *pl*.

went [went] *pt of* **go**.

wept [wept] *pt, pp of* **weep**.

were [wɜ:*] *pt pl of* **be**.

we're [wɪə*] = **we are**.

weren't [wɜ:nt] = **were not**.

west [west] *n* Westen *m* // *a* West-, westlich // *ad* westwärts, nach Westen; **the W~** *n* der Westen; **the W~ Country** *n* (*Brit*) der Südwesten Englands; **~erly** *a* westlich; **~ern** *a* westlich, West- // *n* (CINE) Western *m*; **W~ Germany** *n* Westdeutschland *nt*, Bundesrepublik Deutschland *f*; **W~ Indian** *a* westindisch // *a* West-indier(in *f*) *m*; **W~ Indies** *npl* Westindische Inseln *pl*; **~ward(s)** *ad* westwärts.

wet [wet] *a* naß; **to get ~** naß werden; '**~ paint**' 'frisch gestrichen'; **~ blanket** *n* (*fig*) Triefel *m*; **~ suit** *n* Taucheranzug *m*.

we've [wi:v] = **we have**.

whack [wæk] *n* Schlag *m* // *vt* schlagen.

whale [weɪl] *n* Wal *m*.

wharf [wɔ:f] *n* Kai *m*.

what [wɒt] ◆*a* **1** (*in direct/indirect questions*) welche(r, s), was für ein(e); **~ size is it?** welche Größe ist das? **2** (*in exclamations*) was für ein(e); **~ a mess!** was für ein Durcheinander!

◆ *pron* (*interrogative/relative*) was; **~ are you doing?** was machst du gerade?; **~ are you talking about?** wovon reden

Sie?; **~ is it called?** wie heißt das?; **~ about ...?** wie wär's mit ...?; **I saw ~** you did ich habe gesehen, was du gemacht hast

◆*interj* (*disbelieving*) wie, was; **~, no coffee!** wie, kein Kaffee?; **I've crashed the car — ~!** ich hatte einen Autounfall — was!

wheat [wi:t] *n* Weizen *m*; **~ germ** *n* Weizenkeim *m*.

wheedle ['wi:dl] *vt:* **to ~ sb into doing sth** jdn dazu überreden, etw zu tun; **to ~ sth out of sb** jdm etw abluchsen.

wheel [wi:l] *n* Rad *nt*; (*steering* **~**) Lenkrad *nt*; (*disc*) Scheibe *f* // *vt* schieben; **~barrow** *n* Schubkarren *m*; **~chair** *n* Rollstuhl *m*; **~ clamp** *n* (AUT) Radblockierung *f* (*von der Polizei an falschparkenden Autos angebracht*).

wheeze [wi:z] *vi* keuchen.

when [wen] ◆*ad* wenn

◆*cj* **1** (*at, during, after the time that*) wenn; (*with past reference*) als; **she was reading ~ I came in** sie las, als ich hereinkam; **be careful ~ you cross the road** seien Sie vorsichtig, wenn Sie über die Straße gehen

2 (*on, at which*) als; **on the day ~ I met him** an dem Tag, an dem ich ihn traf.

3 (*whereas*) wo ... doch.

where [wɛə*] *ad* (*place*) wo; (*direction*) wohin; **~ from** woher; **~abouts** ['wɛərə'baʊts] *ad* wo // *n* Aufenthaltsort *m*; **nobody knows his ~abouts** niemand weiß, wo er ist; **~as** [wɛər'æz] *cj* während, wo ... doch; **whereby** *pron* woran, wodurch, womit, wovon; **whereupon** *cj* worauf, wonach; (*at beginning of sentence*) daraufhin.

wherever [wɛər'evə*] *ad* wo (immer).

wherewithal ['wɛəwɪðɔ:l] *n* nötige (Geld)mittel *pl*.

whet [wet] *vt* (*appetite*) anregen.

whether ['weðə*] *cj* ob; **I don't know ~ to accept or not** ich weiß nicht, ob ich es annehmen soll oder nicht; **~ you go or not** ob du gehst oder nicht.

which [wɪtʃ] ◆*a* **1** (*interrogative: direct, indirect*) welche(r, s); **~ one?** welche(r, s)?

2: **in ~ case** in diesem Fall; **by ~ time** zu dieser Zeit

◆*pron* **1** (*interrogative*) welche(r, s); (*of people also*) wer

2 (*relative*) der/die/das; (*referring to clause*) was; **the apple ~ you ate/~ is on the table** der Apfel, den du gegessen hast/der auf dem Tisch liegt; **he said he saw her, ~ is true** er sagte, er habe sie gesehen, was auch stimmt.

whiff [wɪf] *n* Hauch *m*.

while [waɪl] *n* Weile *f* // *cj* während; **for a ~** eine Zeitlang; **~ away** *vt* (*time*) sich (*dat*) vertreiben.

whim [wɪm] *n* Laune *f*.

whimper ['wɪmpə*] n Wimmern nt // vi wimmern.

whimsical ['wɪmzɪkəl] a launisch.

whine [waɪn] n Gewinsel nt, Gejammer nt // vi heulen, winseln.

whip [wɪp] n Peitsche f; (POL) Fraktionsführer m // vt (beat) peitschen; (snatch) reißen; n ~**ped cream** n Schlagsahne; ~**round** n (Brit col) Geldsammlung f.

whirl [wɜːl] n Wirbel m // vti (herum)wirbeln; ~**pool** n Wirbel m; ~**wind** n Wirbelwind m.

whirr [wɜː*] vi schwirren, surren.

whisk [wɪsk] n Schneebesen m // vt (cream etc) schlagen; **to** ~ **sb away or off** mit jdm davon sausen.

whisker ['wɪskə*] n (of animal) Barthaare pl; ~**s** pl (of man) Backenbart m.

whisky, (US, Ireland) whiskey ['wɪskɪ] n Whisky m.

whisper ['wɪspə*] n Flüstern nt // vti flüstern.

whistle ['wɪsl] n Pfiff m; (instrument) Pfeife f // vti pfeifen.

white [waɪt] n Weiß nt; (of egg) Eiweiß nt // a weiß; ~ **coffee** n (Brit) Kaffee m mit Milch; ~-**collar worker** n Angestellte(r) m; ~ **elephant** n (fig) Fehlinvestition f; ~ **lie** n Notlüge f; ~**ness** n Weiß nt; ~ **paper** n (POL) Weißbuch nt; ~**wash** n (paint) Tünche f; (fig) Ehrenrettung f // vt weißen, tünchen; (fig) reinwaschen.

whiting ['waɪtɪŋ] n Weißfisch m.

Whitsun ['wɪtsn] n Pfingsten nt.

whittle ['wɪtl] vt: **to** ~ **away or down** stutzen, verringern.

whizz [wɪz] vi: **to** ~ **past or by** vorbeizischen, vorbeischwirren; ~ **kid** n (col) Kanone f.

who [huː] pron 1 (interrogative) wer; (acc) wen; (dat) wem; ~ **is it?**, ~'s **there?** wer ist da?
2 (relative) der/die/das; **the man/woman** ~ **spoke to me** der Mann/die Frau, der/die mit mir sprach.

whole [həʊl] a ganz // n Ganze(s) nt; **the** ~ **of the town** die ganze Stadt; **on the** ~, **as a** ~ im großen und ganzen; ~**hearted** a rückhaltlos; ~**heartedly** ad von ganzem Herzen; ~**meal** a (bread, flour) Vollkorn-; ~**sale** n Großhandel m // a (trade) Großhandels-; (destruction) Massen-; ~**saler** n Großhändler m; ~**some** a bekömmlich, gesund; ~**wheat** a = ~**meal**.

wholly ['həʊlɪ] ad ganz, völlig.

whom [huːm] pron 1 (interrogative: acc) wen; (: dat) wem; ~ **did you see?** wen haben Sie gesehen?; **to** ~ **did you give it?** wem haben Sie es gegeben?
2 (relative: acc) den/die/das; (: dat) dem/der/dem; **the man** ~ **I saw/to** ~ **I** spoke der Mann, den ich sah/mit dem ich sprach.

whooping cough ['huːpɪŋkɒf] n Keuchhusten m.

whore [hɔː*] n Hure f.

whose [huːz] a (poss: interrog) wessen; ~ **book is this?**, ~ **is this book?** wessen Buch ist das?; (: rel) dessen; (after f and pl) deren // pron wessen; ~ **is this?** wem gehört das?

why [waɪ] ◆ ad warum, weshalb
◆ cj warum, weshalb; **that's not** ~ **I'm here** ich bin nicht deswegen hier; **that's the reason** ~ deshalb
◆ interj (expressing surprise, shock, annoyance) na so was; (explaining) also dann; ~, **it's you!** na so was, du bist es!

wick [wɪk] n Docht m.

wicked ['wɪkɪd] a böse.

wicker ['wɪkə*] n (also: ~**work**) Korbgeflecht nt.

wicket ['wɪkɪt] n Tor nt, Dreistab m.

wide [waɪd] a breit; (plain) weit; (in firing) daneben // ad: **open** ~ weit offen; **to shoot** ~ daneben schießen; ~-**angle lens** n Weitwinkelobjektiv nt; ~-**awake** a hellwach; ~**ly** ad weit; (known) allgemein; ~**n** vt erweitern; ~-**open** a weit geöffnet; ~**spread** a weitverbreitet.

widow ['wɪdəʊ] n Witwe f; ~**ed** a verwitwet; ~**er** n Witwer m.

width [wɪdθ] n Breite f, Weite f.

wield [wiːld] vt schwingen, handhaben.

wife [waɪf] n (Ehe)frau f, Gattin f.

wig [wɪg] n Perücke f.

wiggle ['wɪgl] n Wackeln nt // vt wackeln mit // vi wackeln.

wild [waɪld] a wild; (violent) heftig; (plan, idea) verrückt; **the** ~**s** die Wildnis; ~**erness** ['wɪldənəs] n Wildnis f, Wüste f; ~-**goose chase** n (fig) fruchtlose(s) Unternehmen nt; ~**life** n Tierwelt f; ~**ly** ad wild, ungestüm; (exaggerated) irrsinnig.

wilful ['wɪlfʊl] a (intended) vorsätzlich; (obstinate) eigensinnig.

will [wɪl] ◆ v aux 1 (forming future tense) werden; **I** ~ **finish it tomorrow** ich mache es morgen zu Ende
2 (in conjectures, predictions): **he** ~ **or he'll be there by now** er dürfte jetzt da sein; **that** ~ **be the postman** das wird der Postbote sein
3 (in commands, requests, offers): ~ **you be quiet!** sei endlich still!; ~ **you help me?** hilfst du mir?; ~ **you have a cup of tea?** Trinken Sie eine Tasse Tee?; **I won't put up with it!** das lasse ich mir nicht gefallen!
◆ vt wollen; ~**ing** a gewillt, bereit; ~**ingly** ad bereitwillig, gern; ~**ingness** n (Bereit)willigkeit f.

willow ['wɪləʊ] n Weide f.

willpower ['wɪl'paʊə*] n Willenskraft f.

willy-nilly ['wɪlɪ'nɪlɪ] *ad* einfach so.
wilt [wɪlt] *vi* (ver)welken.
wily ['waɪlɪ] *a* gerissen.
win [wɪn] *n* Sieg *m* // *vti, pt, pp* **won**
gewinnen; **to** ~ **sb over** *or* (*Brit*) **round**
jdn gewinnen, jdn dazu bringen.
wince [wɪns] *n* Zusammenzucken *nt* // *vi*
zusammenzucken.
winch [wɪntʃ] *n* Winde *f*.
wind [waɪnd] *v* (*pt, pp* **wound**) *vt*
(*rope*) winden; (*bandage*) wickeln // *vi*
(*turn*) sich winden; ~ **up** *vt* (*clock*) aufziehen; (*debate*) (ab)schließen.
wind [wɪnd] *n* Wind *m*; (*MED*)
Blähungen *pl*; ~**fall** *n* unverhoffte(r)
Glücksfall *m*.
winding ['waɪndɪŋ] *a* (*road*) gewunden.
wind instrument ['wɪndɪnstrʊmənt] *n*
Blasinstrument *nt*.
windmill ['wɪndmɪl] *n* Windmühle *f*.
window ['wɪndəʊ] *n* Fenster *nt*; ~ **box**
n Blumenkasten *m*; ~ **cleaner** *n* Fen-
sterputzer *m*; ~ **envelope** *n* Fenster-
briefumschlag *m*; ~ **ledge** *n* Fen-
stersims *m*; ~ **pane** *n* Fensterscheibe *f*;
~**sill** *n* Fensterbank *f*.
windpipe ['wɪndpaɪp] *n* Luftröhre *f*.
windscreen ['wɪndskriːn], (*US*) **windshield** ['wɪndʃiːld] *n* Windschutzscheibe
f; ~ **washer** *n* Scheibenwaschanlage *f*;
~ **wiper** *n* Scheibenwischer *m*.
windswept ['wɪndswept] *a* vom Wind
gepeitscht; (*person*) zerzaust.
windy ['wɪndɪ] *a* windig.
wine [waɪn] *n* Wein *m*; ~ **cellar** *n*
Weinkeller *m*; ~**glass** *n* Weinglas *nt*;
~ **list** *n* Weinkarte *f*; ~ **merchant** *n*
Weinhändler *m*; ~ **tasting** *n* Weinprobe
f; ~ **waiter** *n* Weinkellner *m*.
wing [wɪŋ] *n* Flügel *m*; (*MIL*) Gruppe *f*;
~**s** *pl* (*THEAT*) Seitenkulisse *f*; ~**er** *n*
(*SPORT*) Flügelstürmer *m*.
wink [wɪŋk] *n* Zwinkern *nt* // *vi*
zwinkern, blinzeln.
winner ['wɪnə*] *n* Gewinner *m*;
(*SPORT*) Sieger *m*.
winning ['wɪnɪŋ] *a* (*team*) siegreich,
Sieger-; (*goal*) entscheidend // *n*: ~**s** *pl*
Gewinn *m*; ~ **post** *n* Ziel *nt*.
winter ['wɪntə*] *n* Winter *m* // *a*
(*clothes*) Winter- // *vi* überwintern;
~ **sports** *npl* Wintersport *m*.
wintry ['wɪntrɪ] *a* Winter-, winterlich.
wipe [waɪp] *n*: to give sth a ~ etw
(ab)wischen; ~ **off** *vt* abwischen; ~
out *vt* (*debt*) löschen; (*destroy*) auslöschen; ~ **up** *vt* aufwischen.
wire ['waɪə*] *n* Draht *m*; (*telegram*)
Telegramm *nt* // *vt* telegrafieren (*sb*
jdm, *sth* etw).
wireless ['waɪəlɪs] *n* (*Brit*)
Radio(apparat *m*) *nt*.
wiring ['waɪərɪŋ] *n* elektrische Leitungen
pl.
wiry ['waɪərɪ] *a* drahtig.

wisdom ['wɪzdəm] *n* Weisheit *f*; (*of
decision*) Klugheit *f*; ~ **tooth** *n*
Weisheitszahn *m*.
wise [waɪz] *a* klug, weise.
...wise [waɪz] *suff*: time~ zeitlich
gesehen.
wisecrack ['waɪzkræk] *n* Witzelei *f*.
wish [wɪʃ] *n* Wunsch *m* // *vt* wünschen;
best ~es (*on birthday etc*) alles Gute;
with best ~es herzliche Grüße; **to** ~ **sb
goodbye** jdn verabschieden; **he** ~**ed me
well** er wünschte mir Glück; **to** ~ **to do
sth** etw tun wollen; ~ **for** *vt* sich (*dat*)
wünschen; ~**ful thinking** *n*
Wunschdenken *nt*.
wishy-washy ['wɪʃɪ'wɒʃɪ] *a* (*col:
colour*) verwaschen; (: *ideas, argument*)
verschwommen.
wisp [wɪsp] *n* (Haar)strähne *f*; (*of
smoke*) Wölkchen *nt*.
wistful ['wɪstfʊl] *a* sehnsüchtig.
wit [wɪt] *n* (*also:* ~s) Verstand *m no pl*;
(*amusing ideas*) Witz *m*; (*person*)
Witzbold *m*.
witch [wɪtʃ] *n* Hexe *f*; ~**craft** *n* Hexerei
f.
with [wɪð, wɪθ] *prep* **1** (*accompanying,
in the company of*) mit; **we stayed** ~
friends wir übernachteten bei Freunden;
I'll be ~ **you in a minute** einen Augenblick, ich bin sofort da; **I'm not** ~ **you** (*I
don't understand*) das verstehe ich nicht;
to be ~ **it** (*col: up-to-date*) auf dem
laufenden sein; (: *alert*) (voll) da sein
(*col*)
2 (*descriptive, indicating manner etc*)
mit; **the man** ~ **the grey hat** der Mann
mit dem grauen Hut; **red** ~ **anger** rot
vor Wut.
withdraw [wɪθ'drɔː] (*irreg: like draw*)
vt zurückziehen; (*money*) abheben;
(*remark*) zurücknehmen // *vi* sich
zurückziehen; ~**al** *n* Zurückziehung *f*;
Abheben *nt*; Zurücknahme *f*; ~**n** *a*
(*person*) verschlossen.
wither ['wɪðə*] *vi* (ver)welken.
withhold [wɪθ'həʊld] *vt* (*irreg: like
hold*) vorenthalten (*from sb* jdm).
within [wɪð'ɪn] *prep* innerhalb (+*gen*) //
ad: ~ **reach** in Reichweite; ~ **sight of** in
Sichtweite von; ~ **the week** innerhalb
dieser Woche.
without [wɪð'aʊt] *prep* ohne.
withstand [wɪθ'stænd] *vt* (*irreg: like
stand*) widerstehen (+*dat*).
witness ['wɪtnəs] *n* Zeuge *m*, Zeugin *f* //
vt (*see*) sehen, miterleben; (*sign
document*) beglaubigen; ~ **box**, (*US*) ~
stand *n* Zeugenstand *m*.
witticism ['wɪtɪsɪzəm] *n* witzige
Bemerkung *f*.
witty ['wɪtɪ] *a* witzig, geistreich.
wives [waɪvz] *pl of* **wife**.
wizard ['wɪzəd] *n* Zauberer *m*.
wk *abbr of* **week**.

wobble ['wɒbl] *vi* wackeln.

woe [wəʊ] *n* Kummer *m*.

woke [wəʊk], **woken** ['wəʊkən] *pt, pp* of **wake**.

woman ['wʊmən] *n, pl* **women** Frau *f*; ~ **doctor** *n* Ärztin *f*; **women's lib** *n* (col) Frauenrechtsbewegung *f*; ~**ly** *a* weiblich.

womb [wu:m] *n* Gebärmutter *f*.

women ['wɪmɪn] *pl* of **woman**.

wonder ['wʌndə*] *n* (marvel) Wunder *nt*; (surprise) Staunen *nt*, Verwunderung *f* // *vi* sich wundern // *vt*: I ~ whether ... ich frage mich, ob ...; it's no ~ that es ist kein Wunder, daß; to ~ at sich wundern über (+acc); to ~ about sich Gedanken machen über (+acc); ~**ful** *a* wunderbar, herrlich; ~**fully** *ad* wunderbar.

won't [wəʊnt] = **will not**.

wood [wʊd] *n* Holz *nt*; (forest) Wald *m*; ~ **carving** *n* Holzschnitzerei *f*; ~**ed** *a* bewaldet; ~**en** *a* (lit, fig) hölzern; ~**pecker** *n* Specht *m*; ~**wind** *n* Blasinstrumente *pl*; ~**work** *n* Holzwerk *nt*; (craft) Holzarbeiten *pl*; ~**worm** *n* Holzwurm *m*.

wool [wʊl] *n* Wolle *f*; to pull the ~ over sb's eyes (fig) jdm Sand in die Augen streuen; ~**len**, (US) ~**en** *a* Woll-; ~**lens** *npl* Wollsachen *pl*; ~**ly**, (US) ~**y** *a* wollig; (fig) schwammig.

word [wɜ:d] *n* Wort *nt*; (news) Bescheid *m* // *vt* formulieren; in other ~s anders gesagt; to break/keep one's ~ sein Wort brechen/halten; ~ **processing** *n* Textverarbeitung *f*; ~ **processor** *n* Textverarbeitungsgerät *nt*; ~**ing** *n* Wortlaut *m*.

work [wɜ:k] *n* Arbeit *f*; (ART, LITER) Werk *nt* // *vi* arbeiten; (machine) funktionieren; (medicine) wirken; (succeed) klappen; to be out of ~ arbeitslos sein; ~**s** *n sing* (Brit: factory) Fabrik *f*, Werk *nt*; *pl* (of watch) Werk *nt*; ~ **loose** *vi* sich lockern; ~ **on** *vi* weiterarbeiten // *vt* (be engaged in) arbeiten an (+dat); (influence) bearbeiten; ~ **out** *vi* (sum) aufgehen; (plan) klappen // *vt* (problem) lösen; (plan) ausarbeiten; it ~s out at £100; or macht £100; ~ **up** *vt*: to get ~ed up sich aufregen; ~**able** *a* (soil) bearbeitbar; (plan) ausführbar; **workaholic** *n* Arbeitssüchtige(r) *mf*; ~**er** *n* Arbeiter(in *f*) *m*; ~**force** *n* Arbeiterschaft *f*; ~**ing class** *n* Arbeiterklasse *f*; ~**ing-class** *a* Arbeiter-; in ~**ing order** *n* betriebsfähigem Zustand; ~**man** *n* Arbeiter *m*; ~**manship** *n* Arbeit *f*, Ausführung *f*; ~**sheet** *n* Arbeitsblatt *nt*; ~**shop** *n* Werkstatt *f*; ~ **station** *n* Arbeitsplatz *m*; ~**-to-rule** *n* (Brit) Dienst *m* nach Vorschrift.

world [wɜ:ld] *n* Welt *f*; to think the ~ of sb große Stücke auf jdn halten; ~**ly** *a* weltlich, irdisch; ~**-wide** *a* weltweit.

worm [wɜ:m] *n* Wurm *m*.

worn [wɔ:n] *pp* of **wear** // *a* (clothes) abgetragen; ~**-out** *a* (object) abgenutzt; (person) völlig erschöpft.

worried ['wʌrɪd] *a* besorgt, beunruhigt.

worry ['wʌrɪ] *n* Sorge *f* // *vt* beunruhigen // *vi* (feel uneasy) sich sorgen, sich (dat) Gedanken machen; ~**ing** *a* beunruhigend.

worse [wɜ:s] *a comp of* **bad** schlechter, schlimmer // *ad comp of* **badly** schlimmer, ärger // *n* Schlimmere(s) *nt*, Schlechtere(s) *nt*; a change for the ~ eine Verschlechterung; ~**n** *vt* verschlimmern // *vi* sich verschlechtern; ~ **off** *a* (fig) schlechter dran.

worship ['wɜ:ʃɪp] *n* Verehrung *f* // *vt* anbeten; Your W~ (Brit: to mayor) Herr/ Frau Bürgermeister; (: to judge) Euer Ehren.

worst [wɜ:st] *a superl of* **bad** schlimmste(r, s), schlechteste(r, s) // *ad superl of* **badly** am schlimmsten, am ärgsten // *n* Schlimmste(s) *nt*, Ärgste(s) *nt*; at ~ schlimmstenfalls.

worsted ['wʊstɪd] *n* Kammgarn *nt*.

worth [wɜ:θ] *n* Wert *m* // *a* wert; it's ~ it es lohnt sich; to be ~ one's while (to do) die Mühe wert sein (, etw zu tun); ~**less** *a* wertlos; (person) nichtsnutzig; ~**while** *a* lohnend, der Mühe wert.

worthy [wɜ:ðɪ] *a* wert (of gen), würdig (of gen).

would [wʊd] *v aux* **1** (conditional tense): if you asked him he ~ do it wenn du ihn fragtest, würde er es tun; if you had asked him he ~ have done it wenn du ihn gefragt hättest, hätte er es getan **2** (in offers, invitations, requests): ~ you like a biscuit? möchten Sie ein Plätzchen?; ~ you ask him to come in? würden Sie ihn bitte hereinbitten? **3** (in indirect speech): I said I ~ do it ich sagte, ich würde es tun **4** (emphatic): it WOULD have to snow today! es mußte ja ausgerechnet heute schneien! **5** (insistence): she ~n't behave sie wollte sich partout nicht anständig benehmen **6** (conjecture): it ~ have been midnight es ungefähr Mitternacht gewesen sein; it ~ seem so es sieht wohl so aus **7** (indicating habit): he ~ go there on Mondays er ging jeden Montag dorthin.

wouldn't ['wʊdnt] = **would not**.

wound [waʊnd] *pt, pp* of **wind** // *n* [wu:nd] (lit, fig) Wunde *f* // *vt* [wu:nd] verwunden, verletzen (also fig).

wove [wəʊv], **woven** ['wəʊvən] *pt, pp* of **weave**.

wrangle ['ræŋgl] *n* Streit *m* // *vi* sich zanken.

wrap [ræp] n (stole) Schal m // vt (also: ~ up) einwickeln; ~ up vt (deal) abschließen; ~per n Umschlag m, Schutzhülle f; ~ping paper n Einwickelpapier nt.
wrath [rɒθ] n Zorn m.
wreak [ri:k] vt (havoc) anrichten; (vengeance) üben.
wreath [ri:θ] n Kranz m.
wreck [rek] n (ship) Wrack nt; (sth ruined) Ruine f // vt zerstören; ~age n Trümmer pl.
wren [ren] n Zaunkönig m.
wrench [rentʃ] n (spanner) Schraubenschlüssel m; (twist) Ruck m // vt reißen, zerren; to ~ sth from sb jdm etw entreißen or entwinden.
wrestle ['resl] vi: to ~ (with sb) mit jdm ringen; **wrestler** n Ringer(in f) m; **wrestling** n Ringen nt.
wretched ['retʃɪd] a (hovel) elend; (col) verflixt; I feel ~ mir ist elend.
wriggle ['rɪgl] n Schlängeln nt // vi sich winden.
wring [rɪŋ], pt, pp **wrung** vt wringen.
wrinkle ['rɪŋkl] n Falte f, Runzel f // vt runzeln // vi sich runzeln; (material) knittern.
wrist [rɪst] n Handgelenk nt; ~watch n Armbanduhr f.
writ [rɪt] n gerichtliche(r) Befehl m.
write [raɪt], pt **wrote**, pp **written** vti schreiben; ~ down vt aufschreiben; ~ off vt (dismiss) abschreiben; ~ out (essay) abschreiben; (cheque) ausstellen; ~ up vt schreiben; ~-off n: it is a ~-off das kann man abschreiben; ~r n Schriftsteller m.
writhe [raɪð] vi sich winden.
writing ['raɪtɪŋ] n (act) Schreiben nt; (hand~) (Hand)schrift f; in ~ schriftlich; ~ paper n Schreibpapier nt.
written ['rɪtn] pp of **write**.
wrong [rɒŋ] a (incorrect) falsch; (morally) unrecht; he was ~ in doing that es war nicht recht von ihm, das zu tun; you are ~ about that, you've got it ~ da hast du unrecht; be in the ~ im Unrecht sein; what's ~ with your leg? was ist mit deinem Bein los?; to go ~ (plan) schiefgehen; (person) einen Fehler machen // n Unrecht nt // vt Unrecht tun (+dat); ~ful a unrechtmäßig; ~ly ad falsch; (accuse) zu Unrecht.
wrote [rəut] pt of **write**.
wrought [rɔːt] a: ~ **iron** n Schmiedeeisen nt.
wrung [rʌŋ] pt, pp of **wring**.
wry [raɪ] a ironisch.
wt. abbr of **weight**.

X

Xmas ['eksməs] n abbr of **Christmas**.
X-ray ['eks'reɪ] n Röntgenaufnahme f // vt röntgen; ~s npl Rontgenstrahlen pl.

Y

yacht [jɒt] n Jacht f; ~ing n (Sport)segeln nt; ~sman n Sportsegler m.
Yank [jæŋk], **Yankee** ['jæŋkɪ] n (col) Ami m.
yap [jæp] vi (dog) kläffen.
yard [jɑːd] n Hof m; (measure) (englische) Elle f, Yard nt, 0,91 m; ~stick n (fig) Maßstab m.
yarn [jɑːn] n (thread) Garn nt; (story) (Seemanns)garn nt.
yawn [jɔːn] n Gähnen nt // vi gähnen; ~ing a (gap) gähnend.
yd. abbr of **yard(s)**.
yeah [jɛə] ad (col) ja.
year [jɪə*] n Jahr nt; be 8 ~s old acht Jahre alt sein; an eight-~-old child ein achtjähriges Kind; ~ly a, ad jährlich.
yearn [jɜːn] vi sich sehnen (for nach); ~ing n Verlangen nt, Sehnsucht f.
yeast [ji:st] n Hefe f.
yell [jel] n gellende(r) Schrei m // vi laut schreien.
yellow ['jeləu] a gelb // n Gelb nt.
yelp [jelp] n Gekläff nt // vi kläffen.
yeoman ['jəumən] n: Y~ of the Guard Leibgardist m.
yes [jes] ad ja // n Ja nt, Jawort nt; to say/answer ~ ja sagen/mit Ja antworten.
yesterday ['jestədeɪ] ad gestern // n Gestern nt; ~ morning/evening gestern morgen/abend; all day ~ gestern den ganzen Tag; the day before ~ vorgestern.
yet [jet] ad noch; (in question) schon; (up to now) bis jetzt; it is not finished ~ es ist noch nicht fertig; the best ~ das bisher beste; as ~ bis jetzt; (in past) bis dahin // cj doch, dennoch.
yew [ju:] n Eibe f.
yield [ji:ld] n Ertrag m // vt (result, crop) hervorbringen; (interest, profit) abwerfen; (concede) abtreten // vi nachgeben; (MIL) sich ergeben, '~' (US AUT) 'Vorfahrt gewähren'.
YMCA n abbr (= Young Men's Christian Association) CVJM m.
yoga ['jəugə] n Joga m.
yog(h)ourt, **yog(h)urt** ['jɒgət] n Joghurt m.
yoke [jəuk] n (lit, fig) Joch nt.
yolk [jəuk] n Eidotter m, Eigelb nt.
yonder ['jɒndə*] ad dort drüben, da drüben // a jene(r, s) dort.

you [ju:] *pron* **1** (*subject, in comparisons: German familiar form: sing*) du; (: *pl*) ihr; (*in letters also*) Du, Ihr; (: *German polite form*) Sie; ~ Germans ihr Deutschen; she's younger than ~ sie ist jünger als du/Sie
2 (*direct object, after prep + acc: German familiar form: sing*) dich; (: *pl*) euch; (*in letters also*) Dich, Euch; (: *German polite form*) Sie; I know ~ ich kenne dich/euch/Sie.
3 (*indirect object, after prep + dat: German familiar form: sing*) dir; (: *pl*) euch (*in letters also*) Dir, Euch; (: *German polite form*) Ihnen; I gave it to ~ ich gab es dir/euch/Ihnen
4 (*impersonal: one: subject*) man; (: *direct object*) einen; (: *indirect object*) einem; fresh air does ~ good frische Luft tut gut.

you'd [ju:d] = **you had; you would.**
you'll [ju:l] = **you will, you shall.**
young [jʌŋ] *a* jung // *npl* die Jungen; **~ish** *a* ziemlich jung; **~ster** *n* Junge *m*, junge(r) Bursche *m*/junge(s) Mädchen *nt*.
your [jɔ:*] *poss a* (*familiar: sing*) dein; (: *pl*) euer, eure *pl*; (*polite*) Ihr; *see also* **my.**
you're [ˈjuə*] = **you are.**
yours [jɔ:z] *poss pron* (*familiar: sing*) deine(r, s); (: *pl*) eure(r, s); (*polite*) Ihre(r, s); ~ **sincerely/faithfully** mit freundlichen Grüßen; *see also* **mine.**
yourself [jɔ:ˈself] *pron* (*emphatic*) selbst; (*familiar: sing*) (*acc*) dich (selbst); (*dat*) dir (selbst); (: *pl*) euch (selbst); (*polite*) sich (selbst); *see also* **oneself.**
youth [ju:θ] *n* Jugend *f*; (*young man*) junge(r) Mann *m*; **~s** *pl* Jugendliche *pl*;

~ **club** *n* Jugendzentrum *nt*; **~ful** *a* jugendlich; ~ **hostel** *n* Jugendherberge *f*.
you've [ju:v] = **you have.**
YTS *n abbr* (*Brit*: = *Youth Training Scheme*) staatliches Förderprogramm für arbeitslose Jugendliche.
Yugoslav [ˈju:gəʊˈslɑ:v] *a* jugoslawisch // *n* Jugoslawe *m*, Jugoslawin *f*.
Yugoslavia [ˈju:gəʊˈslɑ:vɪə] *n* Jugoslawien *nt*.
YWCA *n abbr* (= *Young Women's Christian Association*) CVJF *m*.

Z

zap [zæp] *vt* (*COMPUT*) löschen.
zeal [zi:l] *n* Eifer *m*; **~ous** [ˈzeləs] *a* eifrig.
zebra [ˈzi:brə] *n* Zebra *nt*; ~ **crossing** [ˈzi:brəˈkrɒsɪŋ] *n* (*Brit*) Zebrastreifen *m*.
zero [ˈzɪərəʊ] *n* Null *f*; (*on scale*) Nullpunkt *m*.
zest [zest] *n* Begeisterung *f*.
zigzag [ˈzɪgzæg] *n* Zickzack *m*.
zip [zɪp] *n* (*also*: ~ **fastener**, (*US*) **~per**) Reißverschluß *m* // *vt* (*also*: ~ **up**) den Reißverschluß zumachen (+*gen*); ~ **code** *n* (*US*) Postleitzahl *f*.
zodiac [ˈzəʊdɪæk] *n* Tierkreis *m*.
zombie [ˈzɒmbɪ] *n*: like a ~ (*fig*) wie im Tran.
zoo [zu:] *n* Zoo *m*.
zoology [zəʊˈɒlədʒɪ] *n* Zoologie *f*.
zoom [zu:m] *vi*: to ~ **past** vorbeisausen; ~ **lens** *n* Zoomobjektiv *nt*.
zucchini [zu:ˈki:nɪ] *npl* (*US: courgettes*) Zucchini *f*.

GERMAN IRREGULAR VERBS
*with 'sein'

infinitive	present indicative (2nd, 3rd sing.)	preterite	past participle
aufschrecken*	schrickst auf, schrickt auf	schrak or schreckte auf	aufgeschreckt
ausbedingen	bedingst aus, bedingt aus	bedang or bedingte aus	ausbedungen
backen	bäckst, bäckt	backte or buk	gebacken
befehlen	befiehlst, befiehlt	befahl	befohlen
beginnen	beginnst, beginnt	. begann	begonnen
beißen	beißt, beißt	biß	gebissen
bergen	birgst, birgt	barg	geborgen
bersten*	birst, birst	barst	geborsten
bescheißen*	bescheißt, bescheißt	beschiß	beschissen
bewegen	bewegst, bewegt	bewog	bewogen
biegen	biegst, biegt	bog	gebogen
bieten	bietest, bietet	bot	geboten
binden	bindest, bindet	band	gebunden
bitten	bittest, bittet	bat	gebeten
blasen	bläst, bläst	blies	geblasen
bleiben*	bleibst, bleibt	blieb	geblieben
braten	brätst, brät	briet	gebraten
brechen*	brichst, bricht	brach	gebrochen
brennen	brennst, brennt	brannte	gebrannt
bringen	bringst, bringt	brachte	gebracht
denken	denkst, denkt	dachte	gedacht
dreschen	drisch(e)st, drischt	drasch	gedroschen
dringen*	dringst, dringt	drang	gedrungen
dürfen	darfst, darf	durfte	gedurft
empfehlen	empfiehlst, empfiehlt	empfahl	empfohlen
erbleichen*	erbleichst, erbleicht	erbleichte	erblichen
erlöschen*	erlischt, erlischt	erlosch	erloschen
erschrecken*	erschrickst, erschrickt	erschrak	erschrocken
essen	ißt, ißt	aß	gegessen
fahren*	fährst, fährt	fuhr	gefahren
fallen*	fällst, fällt	fiel	gefallen
fangen	fängst, fängt	fing	gefangen
fechten	fichtst, ficht	focht	gefochten
finden	findest, findet	fand	gefunden
flechten	flichtst, flicht	flocht	geflochten
fliegen*	fliegst, fliegt	flog	geflogen
fliehen*	fliehst, flieht	floh	geflohen
fließen*	fließt, fließt	floß	geflossen
fressen	frißt, frißt	fraß	gefressen
frieren	frierst, friert	fror	gefroren
gären*	gärst, gärt	gor	gegoren
gebären	gebierst, gebiert	gebar	geboren
geben	gibst, gibt	gab	gegeben
gedeihen*	gedeihst, gedeiht	gedieh	gediehen
gehen*	gehst, geht	ging	gegangen
gelingen*	——, gelingt	gelang	gelungen
gelten	giltst, gilt	galt	gegolten
genesen*	gene(se)st, genest	genas	genesen
genießen	genießt, genießt	genoß	genossen
geraten*	gerätst, gerät	geriet	geraten
geschehen*	——, geschieht	geschah	geschehen

infinitive	present indicative (2nd, 3rd sing.)	preterite	past participle
gewinnen	gewinnst, gewinnt	gewann	gewonnen
gießen	gießt, gießt	goß	gegossen
gleichen	gleichst, gleicht	glich	geglichen
gleiten*	gleitest, gleitet	glitt	geglitten
glimmen	glimmst, glimmt	glomm	geglommen
graben	gräbst, gräbt	grub	gegraben
greifen	greifst, greift	griff	gegriffen
haben	hast, hat	hatte	gehabt
halten	hältst, hält	hielt	gehalten
hängen	hängst, hängt	hing	gehangen
hauen	haust, haut	haute	gehauen
heben	hebst, hebt	hob	gehoben
heißen	heißt, heißt	hieß	geheißen
helfen	hilfst, hilft	half	geholfen
kennen	kennst, kennt	kannte	gekannt
klimmen*	klimmst, klimmt	klomm	geklommen
klingen	klingst, klingt	klang	geklungen
kneifen	kneifst, kneift	kniff	gekniffen
kommen*	kommst, kommt	kam	gekommen
können	kannst, kann	konnte	gekonnt
kriechen*	kriechst, kriecht	kroch	gekrochen
laden	lädst, lädt	lud	geladen
lassen	läßt, läßt	ließ	gelassen
laufen*	läufst, läuft	lief	gelaufen
leiden	leidest, leidet	litt	gelitten
leihen	leihst, leiht	lieh	geliehen
lesen	liest, liest	las	gelesen
liegen*	liegst, liegt	lag	gelegen
lügen	lügst, lügt	log	gelogen
mahlen	mahlst, mahlt	mahlte	gemahlen
meiden	meidest, meidet	mied	gemieden
melken	melkst, melkt	melkte	gemolken
messen	mißt, mißt	maß	gemessen
mißlingen*	——, mißlingt	mißlang	mißlungen
mögen	magst, mag	mochte	gemocht
müssen	mußt, muß	mußte	gemußt
nehmen	nimmst, nimmt	nahm	genommen
nennen	nennst, nennt	nannte	genannt
pfeifen	pfeifst, pfeift	pfiff	gepfiffen
preisen	preist, preist	pries	gepriesen
quellen*	quillst, quillt	quoll	gequollen
raten	rätst, rät	riet	geraten
reiben	reibst, reibt	rieb	gerieben
reißen*	reißt, reißt	riß	gerissen
reiten*	reitest, reitet	ritt	geritten
rennen*	rennst, rennt	rannte	gerannt
riechen	riechst, riecht	roch	gerochen
ringen	ringst, ringt	rang	gerungen
rinnen*	rinnst, rinnt	rann	geronnen
rufen	rufst, ruft	rief	gerufen
salzen	salzt, salzt	salzte	gesalzen
saufen	säufst, säuft	soff	gesoffen
saugen	saugst, saugt	sog	gesogen
schaffen	schaffst, schafft	schuf	geschaffen
scheiden	scheidest, scheidet	schied	geschieden
scheinen	scheinst, scheint	schien	geschienen
schelten	schiltst, schilt	schalt	gescholten

infinitive	present indicative (2nd, 3rd sing.)	preterite	past participle
scheren	scherst, schert	schor	geschoren
schieben	schiebst, schiebt	schob	geschoben
schießen	schießt, schießt	schoß	geschossen
schinden	schindest, schindet	schindete	geschunden
schlafen	schläfst, schläft	schlief	geschlafen
schlagen	schlägst, schlägt	schlug	geschlagen
schleichen*	schleichst, schleicht	schlich	geschlichen
schleifen	schleifst, schleift	schliff	geschliffen
schließen	schließt, schließt	schloß	geschlossen
schlingen	schlingst, schlingt	schlang	geschlungen
schmeißen	schmeißt, schmeißt	schmiß	geschmissen
schmelzen*	schmilzt, schmilzt	schmolz	geschmolzen
schneiden	schneidest, schneidet	schnitt	geschnitten
schreiben	schreibst, schreibt	schrieb	geschrieben
schreien	schreist, schreit	schrie	geschrie(e)n
schreiten	schreitest, schreitet	schritt	geschritten
schweigen	schweigst, schweigt	schwieg	geschwiegen
schwellen*	schwillst, schwillt	schwoll	geschwollen
schwimmen*	schwimmst, schwimmt	schwamm	geschwommen
schwinden*	schwindest, schwindet	schwand	geschwunden
schwingen	schwingst, schwingt	schwang	geschwungen
schwören	schwörst, schwört	schwor	geschworen
sehen	siehst, sieht	sah	gesehen
sein*	bist, ist	war	gewesen
senden	sendest, sendet	sandte	gesandt
singen	singst, singt	sang	gesungen
sinken*	sinkst, sinkt	sank	gesunken
sinnen	sinnst, sinnt	sann	gesonnen
sitzen*	sitzt, sitzt	saß	gesessen
sollen	sollst, soll	sollte	gesollt
speien	speist, speit	spie	gespie(e)n
spinnen	spinnst, spinnt	spann	gesponnen
sprechen	sprichst, spricht	sprach	gesprochen
sprießen*	sprießt, sprießt	sproß	gesprossen
springen*	springst, springt	sprang	gesprungen
stechen	stichst, sticht	stach	gestochen
stecken	steckst, steckt	steckte or stak	gesteckt
stehen	stehst, steht	stand	gestanden
stehlen	stiehlst, stiehlt	stahl	gestohlen
steigen*	steigst, steigt	stieg	gestiegen
sterben*	stirbst, stirbt	starb	gestorben
stinken*	stinkst, stinkt	stank	gestunken
stoßen	stößt, stößt	stieß	gestoßen
streichen	streichst, streicht	strich	gestrichen
streiten*	streitest, streitet	stritt	gestritten
tragen	trägst, trägt	trug	getragen
treffen	triffst, trifft	traf	getroffen
treiben*	treibst, treibt	trieb	getrieben
treten*	trittst, tritt	trat	getreten
trinken	trinkst, trinkt	trank	getrunken
trügen	trügst, trügt	trog	getrogen
tun	tust, tut	tat	getan
verderben	verdirbst, verdirbt	verdarb	verdorben
verdrießen	verdrießt, verdrießt	verdroß	verdrossen
vergessen	vergißt, vergißt	vergaß	vergessen
verlieren	verlierst, verliert	verlor	verloren

infinitive	present indicative (2nd, 3rd sing.)	preterite	past participle
verschleißen	verschleißt, verschleißt	verschliß	verschlissen
wachsen*	wächst, wächst	wuchs	gewachsen
wägen	wägst, wägt	wog	gewogen
waschen	wäschst, wäscht	wusch	gewaschen
weben	webst, webt	webte or wob	gewoben
weichen*	weichst, weicht	wich	gewichen
weisen	weist, weist	wies	gewiesen
wenden	wendest, wendet	wandte	gewandt
werben	wirbst, wirbt	warb	geworben
werden*	wirst, wird	wurde	geworden
werfen	wirfst, wirft	warf	geworfen
wiegen	wiegst, wiegt	wog	gewogen
winden	windest, windet	wand	gewunden
wissen	weißt, weiß	wußte	gewußt
wollen	willst, will	wollte	gewollt
wringen	wringst, wringt	wrang	gewrungen
zeihen	zeihst, zeiht	zieh	geziehen
ziehen*	ziehst, zieht	zog	gezogen
zwingen	zwingst, zwingt	zwang	gezwungen

UNREGELMÄSSIGE ENGLISCHE VERBEN

present	pt	pp	present	pt	pp
arise	arose	arisen	fling	flung	flung
awake	awoke	awaked	fly (flies)	flew	flown
be (am, is, are; being)	was, were	been	forbid	forbade	forbidden
			forecast	forecast	forecast
bear	bore	born(e)	forego	forewent	foregone
beat	beat	beaten	foresee	foresaw	foreseen
become	became	become	foretell	foretold	foretold
begin	began	begun	forget	forgot	forgotten
behold	beheld	beheld	forgive	forgave	forgiven
bend	bent	bent	forsake	forsook	forsaken
beseech	besought	besought	freeze	froze	frozen
beset	beset	beset	get	got	got, (US) gotten
bet	bet, betted	bet, betted	give	gave	given
bid	bid, bade	bid, bidden	go (goes)	went	gone
bind	bound	bound	grind	ground	ground
bite	bit	bitten	grow	grew	grown
bleed	bled	bled	hang	hung, hanged	hung, hanged
blow	blew	blown			
break	broke	broken	have (has; having)	had	had
breed	bred	bred			
bring	brought	brought	hear	heard	heard
build	built	built	hide	hid	hidden
burn	burnt, burned	burnt, burned	hit	hit	hit
			hold	held	held
burst	burst	burst	hurt	hurt	hurt
buy	bought	bought	keep	kept	kept
can	could	(been able)	kneel	knelt, kneeled	knelt, kneeled
cast	cast	cast			
catch	caught	caught	know	knew	known
choose	chose	chosen	lay	laid	laid
cling	clung	clung	lead	led	led
come	came	come	lean	leant, leaned	leant, leaned
cost	cost	cost			
creep	crept	crept	leap	leapt, leaped	leapt, leaped
cut	cut	cut			
deal	dealt	dealt	learn	learnt, learned	learnt, learned
dig	dug	dug			
do (3rd person: he/she/it does)	did	done	leave	left	left
			lend	lent	lent
			let	let	let
			lie (lying)	lay	lain
draw	drew	drawn	light	lit, lighted	lit, lighted
dream	dreamed, dreamt	dreamed, dreamt	lose	lost	lost
			make	made	made
drink	drank	drunk	may	might	—
drive	drove	driven	mean	meant	meant
dwell	dwelt	dwelt	meet	met	met
eat	ate	eaten	mistake	mistook	mistaken
fall	fell	fallen	mow	mowed	mown, mowed
feed	fed	fed	must	(had to)	(had to)
feel	felt	felt	pay	paid	paid
fight	fought	fought	put	put	put
find	found	found	quit	quit, quitted	quit, quitted
flee	fled	fled	read	read	read

223

present	pt	pp	present	pt	pp
rid	rid	rid	split	split	split
ride	rode	ridden	spoil	spoiled, spoilt	spoiled, spoilt
ring	rang	rung	spread	spread	spread
rise	rose	risen	spring	sprang	sprung
run	ran	run	stand	stood	stood
saw	sawed	sawn	steal	stole	stolen
say	said	said	stick	stuck	stuck
see	saw	seen	sting	stung	stung
seek	sought	sought	stink	stank	stunk
sell	sold	sold	stride	strode	stridden
send	sent	sent	strike	struck	struck, stricken
set	set	set	strive	strove	striven
shake	shook	shaken	swear	swore	sworn
shall	should	—	sweep	swept	swept
shear	sheared	shorn, sheared	swell	swelled	swollen, swelled
shed	shed	shed	swim	swam	swum
shine	shone	shone	swing	swung	swung
shoot	shot	shot	take	took	taken
show	showed	shown	teach	taught	taught
shrink	shrank	shrunk	tear	tore	torn
shut	shut	shut	tell	told	told
sing	sang	sung	think	thought	thought
sink	sank	sunk	throw	threw	thrown
sit	sat	sat	thrust	thrust	thrust
slay	slew	slain	tread	trod	trodden
sleep	slept	slept	wake	woke, waked	woken, waked
slide	slid	slid			
sling	slung	slung	waylay	waylaid	waylaid
slit	slit	slit	wear	wore	worn
smell	smelt, smelled	smelt, smelled	weave	wove, weaved	woven, weaved
sow	sowed	sown, sowed	wed	wedded, wed	wedded, wed
speak	spoke	spoken			
speed	sped, speeded	sped, speeded	weep	wept	wept
spell	spelt, spelled	spelt, spelled	win	won	won
			wind	wound	wound
spend	spent	spent	withdraw	withdrew	withdrawn
spill	spilt, spilled	spilt, spilled	withhold	withheld	withheld
			withstand	withstood	withstood
spin	spun	spun	wring	wrung	wrung
spit	spat	spat	write	wrote	written

NUMMER

NUMBERS

ein(s)	1	one
zwei	2	two
drei	3	three
vier	4	four
fünf	5	five
sechs	6	six
sieben	7	seven
acht	8	eight
neun	9	nine
zehn	10	ten
elf	11	eleven
zwölf	12	twelve
dreizehn	13	thirteen
vierzehn	14	fourteen
fünfzehn	15	fifteen
sechzehn	16	sixteen
siebzehn	17	seventeen
achtzehn	18	eighteen
neunzehn	19	nineteen
zwanzig	20	twenty
einundzwanzig	21	twenty-one
zweiundzwanzig	22	twenty-two
dreißig	30	thirty
vierzig	40	forty
fünfzig	50	fifty
sechzig	60	sixty
siebzig	70	seventy
achtzig	80	eighty
neunzig	90	ninety
hundert	100	a hundred
hunderteins	101	a hundred and one
zweihundert	200	two hundred
zweihunderteins	201	two hundred and one
dreihundert	300	three hundred
dreihunderteins	301	three hundred and one
tausend	1000	a thousand
tausend(und)eins	1001	a thousand and one
fünftausend	5000	five thousand
eine Million	1000000	a million

erste(r,s)	1.	first	1st
zweite(r,s)	2.	second	2nd
dritte(r,s)	3.	third	3rd
vierte(r,s)	4.	fourth	4th
fünfte(r,s)	5.	fifth	5th
sechste(r,s)	6.	sixth	6th
siebte(r,s)	7.	seventh	7th
achte(r,s)	8.	eighth	8th
neunte(r,s)	9.	ninth	9th
zehnte(r,s)	10.	tenth	10th

elfte (r,s)	11.	eleventh		11th
zwölfte (r,s)	12.	twelfth		12th
dreizehnte (r,s)	13.	thirteenth		13th
vierzehnte (r,s)	14.	fourteenth		14th
fünfzehnte (r,s)	15.	fifteenth		15th
sechzehnte (r,s)	16.	sixteenth		16th
siebzehnte (r,s)	17.	seventeenth		17th
achtzehnte (r,s)	18.	eighteenth		18th
neunzehnte (r,s)	19.	nineteenth		19th
zwanzigste (r,s)	20.	twentieth		20th
einundzwanzigste (r,s)	21.	twenty-first		21st
dreißigste (r,s)	30.	thirtieth		30th
hundertste (r,s)	100.	hundredth		100th
hunderterste (r,s)	101.	hundred-and-first		101st
tausendste (r,s)	1000.	thousandth		1000th

Bruche usw.

Fractions etc.

ein Halb	½	a half	
ein Drittel	⅓	a third	
ein Viertel	¼	a quarter	
ein Fünftel	⅕	a fifth	
null Komma fünf	0,5	(nought) point five	0.5
drei Komma vier	3,4	three point four	3.4
sechs Komma acht neun	6,89	six point eight nine	6.89
zehn Prozent	10%	ten per cent	
hundert Prozent	100%	a hundred per cent	

Beispiele

Examples

er wohnt in Nummer 10
es steht in Kapitel 7
auf Seite 7
er wohnt im 7. Stock
er wurde 7.
im Maßstab eins zu
   zwanzigtausend

he lives at number 10
it's in chapter 7
on page 7
he lives on the 7th floor
he came in 7th
scale one to twenty thousand

UHRZEIT

THE TIME

wieviel Uhr ist es?, wie spät ist es?
es ist ...

what time is it?
it's ...

Mitternacht, zwölf Uhr nachts	midnight, twelve p.m.
ein Uhr (morgens *or* früh)	one o'clock (in the morning), one (a.m.)
fünf nach eins, ein Uhr fünf	five past one
zehn nach eins, ein Uhr zehn	ten past one
viertel nach eins, ein Uhr fünfzehn	a quarter past one, one fifteen
fünf vor halb zwei, ein Uhr fünfundzwanzig	twenty-five past one, one twenty-five
halb zwei, ein Uhr dreißig	half past one, one thirty
fünf nach halb zwei, ein Uhr fünfunddreißig	twenty-five to two, one thirty-five
zwanzig vor zwei, ein Uhr vierzig	twenty to two, one forty
viertel vor zwei, ein Uhr fünfundvierzig	a quarter to two, one forty-five
zehn vor zwei, ein Uhr fünfzig	ten to two, one fifty
zwölf Uhr (mittags), Mittag	twelve o'clock, midday, noon
halb eins (mittags *or* nachmittags), zwölf Uhr dreißig	half past twelve, twelve thirty (p.m.)
zwei Uhr (nachmittags)	two o'clock (in the afternoon), two (p.m.)
halb acht (abends)	half past seven (in the evening), seven thirty (p.m.)

um wieviel Uhr?
um Mitternacht
um sieben Uhr

at what time?
at midnight
at seven o'clock

in zwanzig Minuten
vor fünfzehn Minuten

in twenty minutes
fifteen minutes ago